INTENT OF ŚRĪMAD BHAGAVAD GĪTĀ

INTENT OF ŚRĪMAD BHAGAVAD GĪTĀ

PATH TO SELF-REALIZATION

BHARAT C. PATEL

White Falcon Publishing
www.whitefalconpublishing.com

Intent of Śrīmad Bhagavad Gītā
Bharat C. Patel

www.whitefalconpublishing.com

First Edition, 2022

Cover design by White Falcon Publishing, 2022

ISBN - 978-1-63640-703-6

DEDICATION

ॐ श्री परमात्मने नमः

Oṃ! May my obeisance be to the supreme imperishable Reality

Hey Bhagavāna Vāsudeva Śrī Kṛṣṇa! The supreme imperishable Reality! The Brahman! The Parabrahma! By Your grace, Your undivided devotee has made this humble effort to cognize Your divine words. Forgive me for any error in my vision of Your intent.

For Tejas and Shailen...my future.
For Taru, Ratna, Hershil, and Ashish...my present.
For Surbhiben and Chhotabhai...my past.
I dedicate this work to you, my family, whose presence in this mortal world has been an infinite source of inspiration and wisdom.

TABLE OF CONTENTS

Page

Dedication v

Foreword xi

Preface xv

Introduction 1

What is the Object of Human Pursuit? 7

What are Dharma, Artha, Kāma, and Mokṣa? 7

Dharma (धर्म) 7

Artha (अर्थ) 7

Kāma (काम) 7

Mokṣa (मोक्ष) 8

What is Pratyakṣa-Jñāna, Parokṣa-Jñāna and Aparokṣa-Jñāna? 9

Pratyakṣa (प्रत्यक्ष) 9

Parokṣa (परोक्ष) 10

Aparokṣa (अपरोक्ष) 10

What does Bhagavāna mean? 11

What is Bondage? What is Liberation? 13

What are the types of Liberation? 15

What are the means for Liberation? 16

What is Prāṇa? 19

How can Knowledge deplete Karma? 21

What is the root of Karma? 27

What is the root of Doership? ... 31

What is the cause of Discriminating-Vision? ... 31

What is the reality of Discrimination and Limitation? ... 32

Depletion of Karma is possible through Knowledge ... 37

Sāṅkhya and Yoga ... 42

Refutation of deeming Sāṅkhya and Yoga as Independent Paths ... 48

Karma-Saṃnyāsa, as depicted by some, is Injudicious ... 50

Variant-Yoga, as depicted by some, is Injudicious and Discordant ... 50

Mutual Discordance in the Variant-Yoga Components ... 52

Can Variant-Yoga, as depicted by some, provide Liberation? ... 53

Are Desireless-Actions of Variant-Yoga useful? ... 57

Liberation and Public Well-being through the oneness of Sāṅkhya and Yoga ... 59

Nature of Karma ... 62

Cause and Effect in the activity of Karma ... 65

Major Levels of Vacillations and Distinctions of Doers ... 68

Critique ... 74

The Sāṅkhya Yoga - Chapter 2 ... 74

What are the characteristics of a Sage of Stable Wisdom (Sthitaprajña)? ... 82

The Karma Yoga - Chapter 3 ... 85

The Jñāna Karma Saṃnyāsa Yoga - Chapter 4 ... 99

The Yoga of Renunciation - Chapter 5 ... 104

The Yoga of Meditation - Chapter 6 ... 110

The Yoga of Knowledge and Realization - Chapter 7 ... 117

The Yoga of the Supreme Imperishable Reality - Chapter 8 ... 118

The Yoga of the Royal Knowledge of Royal Profundity - Chapter 9 ... 120

The Yoga of the Divine Manifestations - Chapter 10 ... 122

The Yoga of the Vision of the Cosmic-Form - Chapter 11 ... 123

The Yoga of Devotion - Chapter 12 ... 124

The Yoga of the Field and the Knower of the Field - Chapter 13 ... 126

The Yoga of the Threefold Constituents - Chapter 14 ... 130

The Yoga of the Supreme Personality - Chapter 15 ... 131

The Yoga of the Attributes - Divine and Demonic - Chapter 16 ... *133*

The Yoga of the Threefold Faith - Chapter 17 ... *134*

The Yoga of Liberation and Renunciation - Chapter 18 ... *135*

Epilogue ... 140

Establishing oneness in the Ātmā through concentration of the Mind ... 144

Universal Prayer ... *146*

Prayer to relinquish Gratification of the Sense-Objects ... *147*

Prayer to relinquish Attachment ... *147*

Prayer to be Desireless ... *148*

Prayer to remove Vacillations ... *149*

Prayer to remove Grief ... *149*

Prayer to control Anger ... *150*

Prayer for Total Renunciation ... *151*

Prayer for restraining Ego ... *151*

Prayer to strengthen Mental Power ... *152*

Chapter 1 - The Despondency of Arjuna ... 155

Clarification ... *164*

Chapter 2 - The Sāṅkhya Yoga ... 168

Clarification ... *215*

Chapter 3 - The Karma Yoga ... 218

Clarification ... *236*

Chapter 4 - The Jñāna Karma Saṃnyāsa Yoga ... 238

Clarification ... *254*

Chapter 5 - The Yoga of Renunciation ... 256

Clarification ... *268*

Chapter 6 - The Yoga of Meditation ... 271

Clarification ... *286*

Chapter 7 - The Yoga of Knowledge and Realization ... 289

Clarification ... *300*

Chapter 8 - The Yoga of the Supreme Imperishable Reality ... 302

Clarification ... *314*

Chapter 9 - The Yoga of the Royal Knowledge of Royal Profundity **316**

Clarification *329*

Chapter 10 - The Yoga of the Divine Manifestations **331**

Clarification *343*

Chapter 11 - The Yoga of the Vision of the Cosmic-Form **347**

Clarification *362*

Chapter 12 - The Yoga of Devotion **365**

Clarification *374*

Chapter 13 - The Yoga of the Field and the Knower of the Field **376**

Clarification *395*

Chapter 14 - The Yoga of the Threefold Constituents **398**

Clarification *407*

Chapter 15 - The Yoga of the Supreme Personality **410**

Clarification *421*

Chapter 16 - The Yoga of the Attributes - Divine and Demonic **424**

Clarification *432*

Chapter 17 - The Yoga of the Threefold Faith **433**

Clarification *441*

Chapter 18 - The Yoga of Liberation and Renunciation **443**

Clarification *469*

Śrīmad Bhagavad Gītā Dhyāna **473**

Antecedent **475**

Glossary **485**

Pronunciation Guide **567**

FOREWORD

Dr. Bharat C. Patel, a graduate of St. Xavier's High School, Ahmedabad, secured first place in the Gujarat SSC examination in 1963 and Gujarat University B.E. Electrical Engineering in 1968. As a technocrat, he has served with distinction in various executive positions in the New Jersey state government for four decades. In his childhood, having learned Sanskrit from the father of Late K. K. Shastri, the *Bhīṣma Pitā* of the Sanskrit world of Gujarat in the last century, he developed a deep love and admiration for *Upaniṣads* and *Gītā*. Shri Bharatbhai's firm beliefs about Indian religion, philosophy, and culture were inherited from his grandfather and father. He has devoted his life to studying *Bhagavad Gītā* for six decades, and today we see "Intent of Śrīmad Bhagavad Gītā" as the ripened fruit of his tree of labor in the form of penance (तपः परिश्रमपादयस्य पक्कम् फलम्।). Congratulations!

According to *Śrīmad Bhagavad Gītā,* this is not only the outcome of this birth only, but it is deeply rooted in his previous birth also. See : पूर्वाभ्यासेन तेनैव ह्रियते ह्यवशोऽपि सः | जिज्ञासुरपि योगस्य शब्दब्रह्मातिवर्तते || - B.G. VI-44. "Due to former practice, he is carried away in a manner beyond his control. Even he who desires the knowledge of Yoga goes beyond *Śabda-Brahman.*" According to my humble opinion, Shri Bharatbhai has gone beyond the *Śabda-Brahman*. Congratulations!

Shri Bharatbhai's intention is evident. He has refuted the views of some modern scholars governed by their limitations in understanding the real intent of *Bhagavad Gītā*. The book provides considerable material to avoid misgivings about *Gītā*'s real intent. It is noteworthy that Shri Bharatbhai has successfully pointed out that only the fire of knowledge can burn the deeply rooted *ahaṃkāra*, the root cause of bondage, which is the outcome of nescience. "ऋते ज्ञानान्न मुक्तिः - There is no liberation without knowledge" is our ancient dictum which is made here clearly understandable for future generations, especially the youngsters. Congratulations!

Shri Bharatbhai hopes that "all those who are *Gitā* lovers will find this work helpful" (page xvii). I have the same feeling that the labor put in by Shri Bharatbhai, the *Tapasyā* – penance of 60 years which he observed, would never go in vain. He deserves our congratulation, especially since he is a man destined to be a technocrat but has successfully maintained his family tradition of three generations while maintaining a love for nation, religion, and culture and spent unimaginable time studying *Gītā* and tracing the intent of *Śrīmad Bhagavad Gītā*. Congratulations!

So as far as his interpretations are concerned, I would like to point out here that liberty in thought, in other words, democracy in thinking, is provided to a person right from the Vedic Age in India. Rigveda – "एकं सद् विप्रा बहुधा वदन्ति - RV. I-165-46. The wise talk about one truth in many ways." Lord *Śrī Kṛṣṇa* Himself has said - मम देहे गुडाकेश यच्चान्यद्द्रष्टुमिच्छसि || - B.G. 11-7. "O Arjuna! you may see in My body whatever you desire to see." While after providing the most thought-provoking dialogue, which is capable of leading to liberation, Lord *Śrī Kṛṣṇa* gave complete freedom to Arjuna to act as per his desire. यथेच्छसि तथा कुरु - B.G. XVIII-63. "Act as your Sweet-will." Such liberty to his followers is the unique feature of *Hindu Sanātana Dharma* because no other religion in the world has given its followers such liberty of thought and action. "The Intent of Śrīmad Bhagavad Gītā" is the outcome of such liberty of thought provided by Indian religious tradition. Shri Bharatbhai has studied almost all his predecessors, including *Ācāryas* like *Śaṅkarācārya*, *Rāmānujācārya* and modern scholars like Swami Atmanandji, Swami Vivekananda, Swami Chinmayananda, B. G. Tilak, Dr. Radhakrishnan and so on. Congratulations!

The author has successfully refuted the interpretation of some modern commentators that *Karma-Yoga* and *Sāṅkhya-Yoga* are separate. He has achieved this by properly understanding the words of Lord *Śrī Kṛṣṇa* – साङ्ख्ययोगौ पृथग्बाला: प्रवदन्ति न पण्डिता: | - B.G. V-4. "Only the dull-witted ones call *Sāṅkhya* and *Yoga* are separate, not the persons of wisdom." The planning of the book deserves special note. The elaborate introduction deals with various subjects like *Dharma*, *Artha*, *Kāma*, *Mokṣa*, *Pratyakṣa* and *Parokṣa Jñāna*, Liberation, *Karma*, Doership, *Sāṅkhya-Yoga,* and Nature of *Karma*. The various *Yogas* of all the eighteen chapters of *Śrīmad Bhagavad Gītā*, the oneness of *Atmā*, and multiple topics such as relinquishing attachment, desire-less-ness, removal of grief, restraining ego, total renunciation, strengthening mental power, and so on. Here, the last portion of prayers is the author's original contribution, which distinguishes this book from others. Congratulations!

The complete text of *Śrīmad Bhagavad Gītā,* along with *Dhyāna Mantras,* is given with word-to-word meaning and translation, which enables the reader to reach the original intent of *Śrīmad Bhagavad Gītā*. The glossary prepared with great labor and care is a remarkable feature that adds a feather to the book's cap. The pronunciation guide will provide proper guidance to the readers. Congratulations!

I am taken aback by how the amazingly modern method of presenting his thoughts is. To quote an example, "When the taste of peace is acquired, naturally, the fountainhead of devotion becomes potent, then whether it is a duty or whether it is *karma* all of them are let go by him, just as a glass drops on its own from the hands of an intoxicated person." The expression is modern and yet conveys the real depth of the statement. Such instances are many. He has a tendency and capacity to examine concepts in great detail so readers may benefit without effort. *Bhagavad Gītā* explains Sat-सत् and Asat-असत् in II-16, and one would find its detailed clarification given (pages 178 to 180) by Shri Bharatbhai is eye-opening and pleasing too. Congratulations!

Shri Bharatbhai's study, understanding, and presentation deserve special mention. Verse no. 12 of the XIIth chapter of *Śrīmad Bhagavad Gītā* is marked as *Kūṭa-Śloka* (कूट-श्लोक) in tradition, and many scholars of the past and present have tried their best to reach to the root of its meaning. I am pleased to note that Shri Bharatbhai has explained it following the spirit of *Bhagavad Gītā* (page 371). For its detailed clarification, we must carefully read pages 124 - 126, where the concept is vividly discussed and clarified. Congratulations!

Shri Bharatbhai has an independent opinion of his own for the intent of *Śrīmad Bhagavad Gītā,* and he has put forth well-studied and convincing arguments for it, which according to my humble opinion, deserves our Congratulations!

When we read such a book by an independent and bold thinker, we must be free from pre-conceived thoughts and be ready to accept what is shedding new light on the subject. Here I am reminded a line by Mahakavi Kalidasa – हंसो हि क्षीरमादत्ते तन्मिश्रा वर्जयत्यपः- A.S. VI-29. "*Haṃsa* accepts the milk and leaves the water mixed with it aside."

Shri Bharatbhai had a *manthana* – churning of the ocean-like subject and provided us the nectar in the form of "Intent of Śrīmad Bhagavad Gītā." Congratulations!

Shri Bharatbhai is fortunate to have a devoted wife like Taruben and all other family members who have constantly supported him. I congratulate all of them.

I am sure that the "Intent of Śrīmad Bhagavad Gītā" will prove a beacon of light for the lovers of *Śrīmad Bhagavad Gītā*. I heartily congratulate Shri Dr. Bharat C. Patel for his contribution and wish him success.

Readers of this book, which is both *Brahma-Vidyā* (philosophy) and *Yoga- Śāstra* (ethics), would find solace in life and would receive a joy that could be termed "word-less wonder, (शब्दातीत-अद्भुत)."

In the end, I am reminded of a statement of Dr. S. Radhakrishnan, the learned President of India, that "Whatever way you adopt to reach the top, the view from the top is the same."

Veda-Ratna
Mahāmahopādhyāya
Gautam Patel
Honored by the President of India

***

Greetings. It gave me great joy and thrill to go through, with great interest and intensity, Dr. Bharatbhai Patel's incredible, inspired, and inspiring spiritual, literary contribution "Intent of Śrīmad Bhagavad Gītā." His dedication to the work of knowledge to present and future young generations makes it of long-lasting value and worth. This detailed divine writing will guide them neither to become "*Naṣṭa*"- lost nor "*Bhraṣṭa*" -fallen, but become Stable and Able - *Sthitaprajña* - for gaining *(Lābha)* and rising *(Utkṛṣṭa)* and then becoming noble and superior (*Śreṣṭha*). All generations can get inspired by this work. Clear exposition, with solid reasoning and logic, given at the beginning in the preface about the Intent of Śrīmad Bhagavad Gītā sets the direction for the book and life in the right way. While *Niṣkāma-Karma* and *Upāsanā* are required and well covered in the book, they are not the ultimate destination. The destination of humanity is *Naiṣkarmya-Siddhi* - Liberation, *Mokṣa*- the realization that the self is *Brahman* - the Ultimate Spirit and Consciousness - *Caitanya* and *Paramānanda*. This is well detailed and covered in all chapters, especially chapter 2 (*Sthitaprajña*), chapter 6 (*Yoga*), chapter 9 (*Rāja-Yoga*), chapter 13 (*Akṣara Parabrahma*), and chapter 18 (*Naiṣkarmya-Siddhi*). While the whole work is worthy, in chapter 9, the explanation on page 121 reveals the entire work is exemplary. The intent of this exposition of *Bhagavad Gītā* is brought out excellently -"Even though desireless duty-bound intellect can remove the root of desire-ridden duty, undivided devotion, and knowledge of being *Ātmā* of all, renunciation of desireless duty-bound intellect is also required." Such statements exemplify the intent of *Bhagavad Gitā* throughout this book. Further, the explanation on page 138, covering 18.50 to 18.53 about *Naiṣkarmya-Siddhi, Brahmabhūta- Prasannātmā*, and transcendence, is most valuable.

Namaste to all - narayana

narayana.guruji@gmail.com

GURUJI SRI G. NARAYANA, the Chairman Emeritus of Excel Industries Limited, former Chairman and Director of many companies, is a mentor, contributor, educator, and trainer in the spirit of leadership and management, leading a missionary life of contributing and assisting individuals in experiencing their inner light and potential and promoting peace and harmony. He has authored more than 600 books and articles on 108 Upanishads, Brahma Sutras, Bhagavad-Gita, Tao, Zen, Holy Bible, Holy Quran, Dhammapada, Yoga Sutras, Bhakti Sutras, Management, Education, Leadership, and Life and Spirituality.

PREFACE

Is it not axiomatic that when one wants to go to a distant place, before leaving one's house, the path to the destination is first ascertained, and once the path is decided, only one departs? When this order for physical travel to a distant place is irrefutable, then for the attainment of subtler than subtle supreme-bliss (परमानन्द, Paramānanda), query for the path is necessary, why would one be surprised?

It is a definite tenet of Vedānta (वेदान्त)[1]that, though own true nature of a Jīva (जीव),[2]is Asti-Bhāti-Priya (अस्ति-भाति-प्रिय),[3]and it is always attained, yet due to impurity (मल, Mala),[4] vacillations (विक्षेप, Vikṣepa)[5]and shrouding (आवरण, Āvaraṇa)[6]- the three faults (दोष, Doṣa) residing in the conscience, Jīva has a perception of non-attainment and separateness. The only aim of the Vedas is to sequentially remove these faults and make the heart of Jīva realize supreme bliss. Thus, was the origination of the Trikāṇḍātmaka Veda (त्रिकाण्डात्मक वेद) - consists of three components divided as follows: 1) Karmakāṇḍa (कर्मकाण्ड), 2) Upāsanākāṇḍa (उपासनाकाण्ड) and 3) Jñānakāṇḍa (ज्ञानकाण्ड). The three components in sequential order are there only to remove faults residing in the heart. Among them, first, malevolence, malicious impressions, or evil inclinations (दुर्वासना, Durvāsanā) is named Mala-Doṣa, the fault of impurity. It can only be removed by Karma Kāṇḍa, that is, through desireless actions (निष्काम-कर्म, Niṣkāma-Karma). Second, fickleness or vacillations of the heart is named Vikṣepa-Doṣa. Upāsanākāṇḍa can only remove it through worship. Third, the ignorance of the Paramānanda is called Āvaraṇa-Doṣa, and Jñānakāṇḍa can only burn it through knowledge. Jñānakāṇḍa being the last part of the Vedas, is known as Vedānta, that is, the Upaniṣads. Just as the removal of hunger is only possible by eating food and not by drinking water, and thirst is quenched only by drinking water and

---

1 Vedānta (वेदान्त) means "the end of the Vedas," and reflects ideas espoused in the Upaniṣads (उपनिषद्), specifically, knowledge and liberation.

2 Jīva (जीव) means the conscious element in the body who is the doer-enjoyer. It is the embodied Ātmā, i.e., the delimited Ātmā. It is the pure Ātmā on whom I-ness sense of the body, senses, mind and intellect are superimposed due to nescience. It has also been referred to as Jīvātmā (जीवात्मा), Dehī (देही), Śarīrī (शरीरी), Jīva-Sākṣī (जीव-साक्षी), Soul, or Spirit. Just as there is no distinction between the space enclosed in a pot and the pervasive space and upon the destruction of the pot is only the pervasive space, likewise there is no distinction between a pure Jīva and the Paramātmā (परमात्मा, the Supreme Being).

3 Asti-Bhāti-Priya (अस्ति-भाति-प्रिय) means the Existent-Conscious-Bliss. Asti (अस्ति) means the sense of perpetual existence, the sense of Astitva (अस्तित्व, existence, of being), the sense of Sat (सत्, real). Bhāti (भाति) means the sense of knowledge, illumination, wisdom, the sense of consciousness (भातित्व, Bhātitva). Priya (प्रिय) means the sense of happiness or Ānanda (आनन्द, bliss). Asti-Bhāti-Priya is synonymous with Saccidānanda (सच्चिदानन्द, Real Conscious Bliss), a compound word from Sat (सत्), meaning that which is the real, existent, or true essence, Cit (चित्), meaning the conscious element, and Ānanda (आनन्द) meaning bliss. All three are considered inseparable from the nature of the supreme imperishable Reality or the Brahman.

4 Mala (मल) means impurity, dirt.

5 Vikṣepa (विक्षेप) means vacillations, the tossing of the mind which obstructs concentration of the mind.

6 Āvaraṇa (आवरण) means the veil of ignorance.

not by food, in the same way, the three faults can only be removed by their own respective Kāṇḍa, and not by any other Kāṇḍa.

Just as the beginningless divine Vedas brought out from the breath (निःश्वास, Niḥśvāsa) of the Supreme Lord are Trikāṇḍātmaka, in the same way, having come out of the blessed mouth of Bhagavāna Śrī Kṛṣṇa, the same principles indeed support Śrīmad Bhagavad Gītā. In addition, for a discerning dispassionate seeker desirous of knowing, it provides spiritual guidance (उपदेश, Upadeśa) of knowledge. Once the fault of impurity is gone through desireless actions, the fault of vacillations is gone through worship, and through knowledge, the root ignorance of doership-ego (कर्तृत्व-अहंकार) in the body, mind, and senses of a seeker is burnt, as its reward, he does not remain a doer (कर्ता, Kartā) of the activities (कर्म, Karma) of the body but remains only an observer of those activities. In that state, doing everything through the body, he is not doing anything and is not in bondage to those activities (BG 3.27 - BG 3.28, BG 14.19 - BG 14.20, and BG 18.17). That is because the reach of Māyā (माया)[7]and all bondages are in the refuge of this delusional superimposition of the body on the Ātmā - the delusional imagination of the body as the Ātmā, Mithyā Dehābhimāna (मिथ्या-देहाभिमान), or Dehātmavāda (देहात्मवाद). As a clarifier of this tenet, Gītā is deemed as Vyavahārika (व्यवहारिक) Vedānta, that is, practical Vedānta. It is also known as Smṛti-Prasthāna (स्मृति-प्रस्थान), that is, the starting point or axiom of remembered traditions, and it is among the three canonical texts of Vedānta - Prasthāna-Trayī (प्रस्थान-त्रयी) having epistemic authority. The other two are the Upaniṣads, known as the Upadeśa-Prasthāna (उपदेश-प्रस्थान), that is, the injunctive scriptures, and the Brahma-Sūtra (ब्रह्म-सूत्र), known as the Sūtra-Prasthāna (सूत्र-प्रस्थान), the Nyāya-Prasthāna (न्याय-प्रस्थान) or the Yukti-Prasthāna (युक्ति-प्रस्थान), that is, the logical text or the axiom of logic. Therefore, through the knowledge of the Paramānanda, removing ignorance and freeing one from the mortal world of birth and death is the principal subject matter of Śrīmad Bhagavad Gītā. Desireless actions (Niṣkāma-Karma) through purity of the conscience are valuable in this knowledge. Still, it cannot ever be an independent path to liberation (मोक्ष, Mokṣa), as will be demonstrated hereafter.

In this current Rajoguṇī (रजोगुणी) Kali-Yuga (कलि-युग), with the influence of the Rajoguṇa not grasping this truth, some have deemed desireless actions devoid of knowledge as an independent path to achieving liberation. They have made Karma-Yoga (Niṣkāma-Karma) and the other, the Yoga of Knowledge and Realization (ज्ञान-योग, Jñāna-Yoga) two separate subject matters of Śrīmad Bhagavad Gītā. That is unconvincing and without any validity. Any book having two main subjects is neither seen nor heard. Of the two, one can be the main or principal and the other minor or secondary, but both cannot be equal. Can two independent rulers rule a country? One whose acts are desireless (निष्काम-कर्मी, Niṣkāma-Karmī), having oneness in his body, mind, and senses assumes all activities done through his body, mind, and senses as his own, and offers fruits of his Karma to the Lord, who he considers as someone separate from himself. Such a person with discriminating vision, with the body, mind, and senses separate from the Lord, with such conduct, how can he be free from the bondage of birth and death?

Though the fruit of the offering of fruits is a pious fruit (पुण्य-फल, Puṇya-Phala), by which purity of the conscience and fitness (अधिकार, Adhikāra) for knowledge is acquirable. Still, that status by itself cannot deliver liberation. The root of bondage is ignorance attached to the discriminating intellect. Desireless actions being themselves the work of ignorance, are not capable of cutting its root - the ignorance. There is a tenet in the kingdom of Prakṛti that fruit cannot cut the roots of a tree. To cut the roots of a tree, one needs an ax. Therefore, knowledge of oneness can only be the one ax that can cut ignorance. The offering of fruits by itself cannot ever remove ignorance, as desireless actions do not have appropriate tools in their toolbox

[7] Māyā (माया) is the delusive power (शक्ति, Śakti), the power of being, of the supreme imperishable Reality by which the supreme imperishable Reality appears in the space-time as the world that is neither immutable nor non-existent in the physical plane of nescience. It is the object of three kinds of knowledge: 1) according to revealed knowledge it is unreal, 2) according to reasoning it is indescribable, and 3) according to the perceptions of the empirical person, it is real. In common usage it is used to express delusion, unreality.

to cut them. The offering of fruits by itself accrues its fruits, and the root of birth and death is the result of accumulated impressions of Karma of many births (सञ्चित कर्म-संस्कार, Sañcita Karma-Saṃskāra).[8] As long as Karma-Saṃskāras are well and alive, where is freedom from birth and death?

Niṣkāma-Karma, by its nature, neither can burn doership-ego nor remove ignorance, then how can one expect liberation from it? However, accepting it as an independent means for liberation, there is grave harm, as now the Path of Knowledge is closed. It is, though, natural for one to move away from the Path of Knowledge when in the first place, one provides an equal status of knowledge to something else and then considers knowledge unacceptable. Not only that, but also when desireless actions do not remain desireless, then they will not be the real means for purity of the conscience. Purity of the conscience can only happen after loosening the ego and awakening humility. However, by giving desireless actions equal status as knowledge, one's ego becomes more assertive. In such a state, one cannot maintain a proper level like a student at a lower level claiming equivalency with a student at the highest level. How can he establish himself steadfast at that highest level? On the contrary, with such a claim, he may not be even fit to remain in the lower level, and the saying, "इतो नष्टस्ततो भ्रष्ट, here he is destroyed and again from there he is fallen" exemplifies the predicament.

My effort herein is to interpret the words of Bhagavāna Śrī Kṛṣṇa by their real intent and point out where some have formulated two independent paths of liberation by selectively ignoring verses and words that are not consistent with their views and misinterpreting verses and words suitable to their opinions. In the seven hundred verses, Bhagavāna did not intend to confuse anyone. If one correctly interprets the entire Śrīmad Bhagavad Gītā consistently, there is no ambiguity in the verses and words Bhagavāna has used. Every word and verse is consistent with the previous and the following verse from the beginning to the end. Herein for every verse, its connection and its relationship to the previous verse, and where there is a new occasion, its mutual connection is shown. I hope readers will carefully review the consistency of interpretations herein so that those who are followers of Gītā do not make up their minds at the outset and put a halt on their chosen path. I pray that with self-study, Gītā lovers hold Niṣkāma-Karma in its rightful place and move forward in becoming fit for the Path of Knowledge and Realization. I hope all those who are Gītā lovers will find this work helpful.

---

[8] In "accumulated impressions of Karma of many births, (सञ्चित कर्म-संस्कार, Sañcita Karma-Saṃskāra)" the term Sañcita (सञ्चित) means accumulated and the term Karma-Saṃskāra (कर्म-संस्कार) means a dynamic impression of righteous or unrighteous action. Collectively they are dynamic psychological imprints left in the subconscious by actions, whether conscious or unconscious, internal or external, desirable or undesirable. They influence a person's nature, response, and state of mind. These imprints are not merely passive vestiges of actions and intentions but dynamic forces constantly pushing a Jīva. These impressions wait to return to the conscious level of the mind, influencing the future in the form of expectations, sense of self-worth, habits, innate dispositions, and emotions, propelling one's life and generating future actions. They are referred to as behavioral traits either as default from birth or perfected over time through conscious shaping of the conscience.

INTRODUCTION

In my writing herein, I have used the International Alphabet of Sanskrit Transliteration (IAST) with diacritical markings. I am mindful that reading IAST words may discourage non-specialist readers because of their complications and confuse those whose prior alphabetic experience has been through English. However, I have attempted judicious use of IAST words in conjunction with standard English terms to read and comprehend quickly. In the end, a pronunciation guide of transliterated alphabets and a glossary of Vedantic terms is appended. All Vedantic words transliterated in English herein are with initial caps

In my early childhood, being educated in the Jesuit system where the medium of instruction was English, I was fortunate in the summer of 1962 to learn Saṃskṛta from Śrī Kāshirāma Śāstrī. In those earlier developmental years, I was blessed to be exposed to some great thinkers of the past, particularly Śrī Ādi Śaṅkarācārya, Śrī Rāmānujācārya, Śrī Vallabhācārya, and some of the modern era especially Svāmī Ātmānanda Muni of Puṣkara. He frequently came to our house in Ahmedabad and imparted his extensive knowledge of the Vedas, the Upaniṣads, and Śrīmad Bhagavad Gītā. My thinking and presentation herein have been greatly influenced by the words of Svāmī Ātmānanda Muni and Śrī Ādi Śaṅkarācārya. After I came to the United States in 1968, earned master's and doctoral degrees in electrical engineering, and had a successful career as a Senior Executive in the New Jersey state government for four decades, responsible for developing and implementing energy policies; my daughter Ratna completed her studies, earned an MBA, got married and successfully settled with a rewarding career; my son Ashish became a successful Radiation Oncologist; my obligations towards my family having met, a time came when I decided to redirect my thinking inwards. I spent ample time reviewing some significant contributions of Śrī Bāla Gaṅgādhara Tilaka, Māhātmā Gāndhī, Dr. Rādhākṛṣṇana, Svāmī Vivekānanda, Śrī Prabhupāda, Svāmī Cinmayānanda, Svāmī Śivānanda and quite a few more. As I started to compare their publications, I found that some interpreted Gītā to further their perspective. Where verses appeared to be inconsistent with their views, they treated them as minor and did not give due importance to their comments. The seven hundred verses, in eighteen chapters, came out from the Śrī-Mukha of Bhagavāna Śrī Kṛṣṇa, and I thought, why should there be any conflict between the words, verses, and chapters. There is no reason why Bhagavāna would want to confuse us. Correctly interpreted, every word should be consistent within the verse and with the verses before and after in the same chapter and previous and subsequent chapters.

With the lockdown of 2020 due to Covid-19, I found blessings in disguise. My longtime desire, at last, became a reality. At the beginning of March 2020, I started to pen my thoughts on the "Intent of Śrīmad Bhagavad Gītā," starting particularly with what was intended in the meaning of the term "Yoga" in Gītā. Is there a mutually harmonious connection between Gītā chapters and verses? What does Gītā mean by the term Yoga? In my writing, I have reviewed and provided comments on how the term Karma-Yoga is interpreted by some, which meets the test of their thinking, particularly in those Gītā verses where Karma-Yoga, Buddhi-Yoga, Yoga, and Yoga-Yukta are used. In other words, accepting their interpretation of verses, is there a harmonious connection between the words and their meanings in those verses or not? I would hope we keep in mind that whatever words were spoken in Gītā are all "Yathārtha (यथार्थ, accordant with reality," and there is not even an iota of "Arthavāda (अर्थवाद, empty praise)." Gītā has censured Arthavāda (see Gītā Chapter 2 verses BG 2.40 through BG 2.44). Therefore, in my analysis of the verses, it was only appropriate for me to accept the meanings of words accordant with reality. Acceptance of Arthavāda may be relevant only where there is no harmonious connection with Yathārtha words. Abandoning the relationship with Yathārtha words and accepting Arthavāda is like a mother leaving an adopted child with the wishful thinking of having her own.

It is often impossible to find terms in English that are semantically coextensive with Saṃskṛta terms. The word meanings of any language are forged by a cultural and philosophical framework of people who speak that language. Thus, Saṃskṛta words derived their meanings from a conceptual system of thought in India a few thousand years ago. Being much different from the western system of thought that has shaped the meanings of English words, there are unavoidable constraints in any interpretation work. Therefore, it is essential to return to the word's original meaning when expressed rather than using a standard modern dictionary to translate Saṃskṛta words. While I do not claim to be an expert in etymology, I have made a sincere effort to bring forth true or Yathārtha meanings of those terms. For example, there is no English word that accurately conveys the meaning of the word "Brahman (ब्रह्मन्)" derived from Brah (ब्रह्) "pervasive." In Vedānta, it represents the supreme imperishable Reality, the pure Self, the pure Ātma or the Paramātmā (परमात्मा).

The Brahman is formless and without attributes (निर्गुण, Nirguṇa), without distinctions (निर्विशेष, Nirviśeṣa), self-existent, absolute, and immutable, whence all existence arises, by which everything is sustained and into which everything ultimately dissolves. The Brahman is, by definition, super-sensuous. It is beyond comprehension or cognition. It cannot even be understood inferentially, for every inferential dynamic depends upon a repeatedly perceived concomitance between that which is to be proved and its characteristics (e.g., between fire and smoke). The Brahman associated with its potency, Māyā (शक्ति, Śakti), appears as the Lord (ईश्वर, Īśvara), the qualified Brahman, the creator, preserver, and destroyer of the world. The Brahman is outside time, space, and causality. The empirical world is completely dependent on Brahman. It is dependent and changing, but it is not non-existent in the physical plane of nescience. Changes in empirical order do not affect the integrity of the Brahman. The Brahman is real, and the world perceived as real is apparent, imagined, and unreal. Any change, duality, or plurality is an illusion. The empirical world is just a misapprehension of the real Brahman.

The same problem typically arises with other Vedantic terms as well. Accordingly, I am providing some basic Vedantic terms used hereafter for readers to comprehend the context of these words.

Ābhāsa (आभास) means inkling, perception, or a sense of the presence of something. A thing that does not have actual existence but is perceived as real in someone else's reality is known as Ābhāsa. A person's shadow is a person's Ābhāsa.

Adhikārī (अधिकारी) means a person endowed with the fourfold means (साधन-चतुष्टय, Sādhana-Catuṣṭaya) who is competent and eligible for knowledge.

Adhiṣṭhāna (अधिष्ठान) means ground, underlying truth, substratum, resting upon, or basis. A true thing on whose dependence delusion exists is known as Adhiṣṭhāna of that delusion. In a snake delusion in a rope, the rope is the Adhiṣṭhāna.

Adhyāsa (अध्यास) means superimposition, false attribution, or a sense of mistaken ascription of essential nature to something which does not belong to it. Delusion is known as Adhyāsa. There are two types of Adhyāsa: 1) Arthādhyāsa (अर्थाध्यास): Delusional thing is known as Arthādhyāsa, like the delusional snake in a rope, and 2) Jñānādhyāsa (ज्ञानाध्यास): Delusional knowledge is known as Jñānādhyāsa, like the knowledge of the snake.

Adhyasta (अध्यस्त) means a falsely cognized thing placed upon or wrongly ascribed. A delusional thing is Adhyasta, like a snake is Adhyasta in a rope.

Antaḥkaraṇa (अन्तःकरण) means the conscience, inner cause, or internal instrument in the subtle body (सूक्ष्म-शरीर, Sūkṣma-Śarīra). It consists of four components:

1. Manas (मनस्, Mind) is an inner instrument characterized by the disposition of developing thought and its variant (संकल्पविकल्पात्मक-वृत्ति, Saṃkalpavikalpātmaka-Vṛtti). It receives information from the external world with the help of the sense-organs and presents them to the intellect for decision-making.
2. Buddhi (बुद्धि, Intellect) is characterized by inner-disposition of decision-making (निश्चयात्मक-वृत्ति, Niścayātmaka-Vṛtti). It is derived from the root Budh (बुध्), which means to be awake, to observe, to know. Discriminative in nature, intellect is that which can discern real (सत्, Sat) from unreal (असत्, Asat), right from wrong, good from bad, piety from sin, and thereby provide a selection of a wise choice.
3. Citta (चित्त, Subconscious Mind) is characterized by inner-disposition of probing (अनुसंधानात्मक-वृत्ति, Anusaṃdhānātmaka-Vṛtti) within the mind and intellect. Active even in the state of deep sleep (सुषुप्ति-अवस्था, Suṣupti-Avasthā), it is the substratum where dynamic impressions (संस्कार, Saṃskāra) of actions (कर्म, Karma) are embedded. It is the recorder and holder of past impressions, reactions, and desires, whether remembered consciously or not.
4. Ahaṃkāra (अहंकार, Ego) is that which provides the conceit or conception of individuality, the sense of self. It is the inner disposition of I-ness (अभिमानात्मक-वृत्ति, Abhimānātmaka-Vṛtti) which identifies the Ātmā (Self) with the body as "I." The "I-ness" sense in the body, sense-organs, mind, and intellect.

Asti-Bhāti-Priya (अस्ति-भाति-प्रिय): Existent-Conscious-Bliss. Asti (अस्ति) means the sense of perpetual existence, the sense of Astitva (अस्तित्व, existence, of being), the sense of Sat (सत्, real). Bhāti (भाति) means the sense of knowledge, illumination, wisdom, the sense of consciousness (भातित्व, Bhātitva). Priya (प्रिय) means the sense of happiness or Ānanda (आनन्द, bliss). Asti-Bhāti-Priya is synonymous with Saccidānanda (सच्चिदानन्द, Real Conscious Bliss), a compound word from Sat (सत्), meaning that which is the real, existent, or true essence, Cit (चित्), meaning the conscious element, and Ānanda (आनन्द) meaning bliss. All three are considered inseparable from the nature of the supreme imperishable Reality or the Brahman.

Atiśayatā-Doṣa (अतिशयता-दोष) means a fault arising out of an attribute of more or less (न्यूनाधिकता, Nyūnādhikatā) in enjoyments. In the world, enjoyment of one may be greater than the second, and enjoyment of the second may be lesser than the third resulting in a mutual attribute of more or less enjoyment. There may be a pain in looking at one with greater enjoyment. While in looking at one with equal enjoyment, there may be jealousy. In contrast, there may be excessive pride in looking at one with lesser enjoyment. This way, these enjoyments are with Atiśayatā-Doṣa.

Ativyāpti-Doṣa (अतिव्याप्ति-दोष) means a fault wherein characteristics not only spread in the target but also in the non-target. For instance, describing the characteristics of a cow as cows have horns becomes an Ativyāpti-Doṣa because then characteristics also apply to female cows.

Avyāpti-Doṣa (अव्याप्ति-दोष) means a fault of insufficient pervasion. It is wherein characteristics do not spread entirely or in every target part. For instance, describing the characteristics of a cow as cows are brown becomes Avyāpti-Doṣa because the brown characteristics do not spread in the entire class of cows.

Bhāva (भाव) means emotion, sentiment. Any subjective process of arousing mental states or emotional waves originating in the mind in the form of a thought or resolve is called Bhāva. It can mean becoming, being, or existing. It can also mean nature or status.

Bheda (भेद) means distinction, discrimination, or differentiation. There are three kinds of distinctions:

1. Sajātīya-Bheda (सजातीय-भेद, homogeneous distinction): One cow has a homogeneous distinction from another cow.
2. Vijātīya-Bheda (विजातीय-भेद, heterogeneous distinction): A cow has a heterogeneous distinction from a horse.
3. Svagata-Bheda (स्वगत-भेद, intrinsic distinction): That by which one part of a substance is discriminated from another. Parts like hands, feet, or eyes in one's body have intrinsic distinctions.

Guṇa-Vibhāga (गुण-विभाग) means work or products of the constituents of Prakṛti. Collectively it includes the following: The five great elements (पञ्चभूत, Pañcabhūta): 1) earth (पृथ्वी, Pṛthvī), 2) water (आप, Āpa), 3) fire (अग्नि, Agni), 4) wind (वायु, Vāyu) and 5) space (आकाश, Ākāśa); 6) mind (मनस्, Manas); 7) intellect (बुद्धि, Buddhi); 8) ego (अहंकार, Ahaṃkāra) ; the five cognition organs (पञ्च-ज्ञानेन्द्रिय, Pañca-Jñānendriya): 9) skin (त्वक, Tvaka) with the sense of touch, 10) tongue (रसना, Rasanā) with the sense of taste, 11) eyes (चक्षु, Cakṣu) with the sense of sight, 12) nose (घ्राण, Ghrāṇa) with the sense of smell, 13) ears (श्रोत्र, Śrotra) with the sense of hearing; the five action-organs (पञ्च-कर्मेन्द्रिय, Pañca-Karmendriya): 14) mouth (वाक, Vāka) with the organ of voice, 15) hands (पाणि, Pāṇi) with the organ to receive, gather, collect (ग्रहण, Grahaṇa) and hold (धारण, Dhāraṇa), 16) feet (पाद, Pāda) with the organ to walk, move, locomotion (गमन, Gamana), 17) anus (पायु, Pāyu) with the organ of excretion, 18) genitals (उपस्थ, Upastha) with the organ of reproduction; the five vital breaths of air (पञ्च-प्राण, Pañca-Prāṇa): 19) Prāṇa-Vāyu (प्राण-वायु), 20) Apāna-Vāyu (अपान-वायु), 21) Samāna-Vāyu (समान-वायु), 22) Udāna-Vāyu (उदान-वायु), 23) Vyāna-Vāyu (व्यान-वायु) ; and the five objects of senses (पञ्च-विषय, Pañca-Viṣaya): 24) sound (शब्द, Śabda), 25) touch (स्पर्श, Sparśa), 26) form (रूप, Rupa), 27) taste (रस, Rasa), and 28) smell (गन्ध, Gandha).

Kāraṇa (कारण) means cause or reason. That which produces an act (कार्य, Kārya) is known as Kāraṇa. There are two types of Kāraṇa: 1) Upādāna-Kāraṇa (उपादान-कारण): Material cause. That which enters the work, without which the work cannot sustain, is known as Upādāna-Kāraṇa. Like clay is the Upādāna-Kāraṇa of a pot, and 2) Nimitta-Kāraṇa (निमित्त-कारण)): Instrumental cause. That which exists neutral before work and whose destruction does not destroy the work. Like the potter, the wheel, the stick is Nimitta-Kāraṇa of a pot.

Karma (कर्म) means action, act, or deed in general. From a Vedantic perspective, a good or bad activity that produces emotion (Bhāva, भाव) in humans is known as Karma.

Karma-Vibhāga (कर्म-विभाग) means mutual interaction among the products (गुण-विभाग, Guṇa-Vibhāga) of the constituents of Prakṛti.

Kārya (कार्य) means work, action, what is done, or the effect of a cause.

Mokṣa (मोक्ष) means liberation. Attainment of eternal (नित्य, Nitya) and immovable (अचल, Acala) happiness (सुख, Sukha) and complete (अत्यन्त, Atyanta) removal (निव्रुत्ति, Nivrutti) of pain and suffering (दु:ख, Duḥkha) is Mokṣa. Alternatively, attainment of the Brahman and freedom from the bondage of the Saṃsāra is Mokṣa, meaning liberation from the Saṃsāra of transmigrating lives and attainment of the supreme-bliss (Paramānanda).

Mumukṣu (मुमुक्षु) means one who has an intense desire for liberation.

Navadhā-Bhakti (नवधा-भक्ति) means the ninefold devotion consisting of: (1) listening to the holy scriptures (श्रवण, Śravaṇa), (2) chanting (कीर्तन, Kīrtana), (3) remembering teachings of the holy scriptures (स्मरण, Smaraṇa), (4) serving at the lotus-feet of the Lord (पाद-सेवन, Pāda-Sevana), (5) worshipping (अर्चन, Arcana), (6) bowing to the Lord (वन्दन, Vandana), (7) serving the Lord (दास्य, Dāsya), (8) friendship with the Lord (सख्य, Sakhya), and (9) surrender to the Lord (आत्म-निवेदन, Ātma-Nivedana).

Pariccheda (परिच्छेद) means limit, extent, or boundary. There are three types of Pariccheda: 1) Deśa-Pariccheda (देश-परिच्छेद) - Space bounded. That which exists in one place or region but not in others is

Deśa-Pariccheda, 2) Kāla-Pariccheda (काल-परिच्छेद) - Time differentiated. That which exists in one time but not in others is Kāla-Pariccheda, and 3) Vastu-Pariccheda (वस्तु-परिच्छेद) - Material distinction. That in which difference between class (जाति, Jāti) and individual (व्यक्ति, Vyakti) exists is Vastu-Pariccheda.

Pariṇāma (परिणाम) means transformation, result, or effect. That work which is produced by mutation (विकार, Vikāra) of the material cause is known as Pariṇāma, like yogurt is the Pariṇāma of milk.

Pariṇāmī-Upādāna (परिणामी-उपादान) means transforming cause. It is a cause that changes in the process of work like milk is the Pariṇāmī-Upādāna of yogurt.

Sādhana-Catuṣṭaya (साधन-चतुष्टय) means the fourfold means: 1) discernment (विवेक, Viveka). The ability to discern between the real and the unreal, between the permanent and the impermanent, between the Ātmā and the non-Ātmā; 2) dispassion (वैराग्य, Vairāgya) for pleasures of this world and of heavens; 3) the sixfold virtues (षट्-सम्पत्ति, Ṣaṭ-Sampatti): a) control of the mind (शम, Śama), b) restraint over the senses (दम, Dama), c) faith in the words of preceptors and scriptures (श्रद्धा, Śraddhā), d) absence of mental vacillations (समाधान, Samādhāna), e) desistance from the relinquishment of actions (कर्म-त्याग, Karma-Tyāga) and vile objects (उपराम, Uparāma), f) tolerance (तितिक्षा, Titikṣā) to bear dualities such as heat and cold, pleasure and pain, hunger and thirst and 4) intense desire for liberation (मुमुक्षुत्व, Mumukṣutva).

Sākṣī-Dṛṣṭā (साक्षी-द्रष्टा): The witness-observer. The immovable (अचल, Acala) and immutable (कूटस्थ, Kūṭastha) pure conscious element in the body that passively observes and illuminates actions and mutations of the body is known as Sākṣī-Dṛṣṭā. The words Sākṣī and Dṛṣṭā are synonymous.

Saṃsāra (संसार): The world of transmigrating lives. Saṃsāra is that which does Saṃsaraṇa (संसरण, passes through a succession of states, birth-rebirth of living beings). The terms Saṃsāra, Jagata, Prapañca, and world are synonymous.

Sattā (सत्ता): Reality, beingness, presence, or existence. Sattā (सत्ता) are of three types:

1. Vyavahārika-Sattā (व्यवहारिक-सत्ता): Ordinary or practical Reality. It is one where the determination of absence in the past, present, and future (त्रिकालाभाव-नि श्चय) cannot be made without Self-Realization (ब्रह्म-ज्ञान, Brahma-Jñāna). The conscious world (जाग्रत प्रपन्च) has ordinary Reality because, without Self-Realization, it is not realized as unreal.
2. Prātibhāsika-Sattā (प्रातिभासिक-सत्ता): Apparent or illusory Reality. It is one where the determination of absence in the past, present, and future (त्रिकालाभाव-निश्चय) can be made without Self-Realization. Dreamworld (स्वप्न प्रपन्च), an illusory snake has an apparent Reality because, upon removal of the defect (दोष) without Self-Realization, the snake can be realized as unreal.
3. Pāramārthika-Sattā (पारमार्थिक-सत्ता): Transcendental Reality. It is beyond time and space. It exists at all times - past, present, and future. The Brahman has transcendental Reality.

Ṣaḍvikāra (षड्विकार): The sixfold mutations. They are: 1) lust (काम, Kāma), 2) anger (क्रोध, Krodha), 3) greed (लोभ, Lobha), 4) delusion (मोह, Moha), 5) excessive pride (मद, Mada) and 6) envy (मत्सर, Matsara).

Upādhi (उपाधि) means an adjunct with discriminative attributes. From the Vedantic perspective, Upādhi refers to what separates some substance but does not enter or manifest in the separated substance. Like a pot that separates pot-enclosed space from the pervasive space but does not enter into the true nature of the space. The pot is the Upādhi of the intrinsic space. It can also mean designation, limitation, and condition related to time and space.

Upahita (उपहित) means placed within. A thing separated by an adjunct with discriminative attributes is known as Upahita. The space within the pot is Upahita in the pot.

Vivarta (विवर्त) means an apparent or an imagined thing. An apparent imagined (मिथ्या, Mithyā) thing perceived in and without mutating its real material cause (Upādāna) is the Vivarta of its material cause. A delusional snake in a rope is the Vivarta of the actual rope. A thing in the form of a Vivarta has neither reality nor the ability to produce mutation in its underlying substrate (Adhiṣṭhāna).

Vivartopādāna (विवर्तोपादान): A cause in which delusion is perceived. It is a compound word from Vivarta (विवर्त) and Upādāna (उपादान). It is a cause where real work is not created but is merely perceived. An actual rope is said to be the Vivartopādāna of a delusional snake because, in reality, the snake is not born though there is a perception that there is a snake.

WHAT IS THE OBJECT OF HUMAN PURSUIT?

Opinion about the object of human pursuit varies from person to person, region to region, and country to country. Some hold that the primary purpose of human life on this earth is to regain the God-given authority and dominion that one has lost by restoring fellowship with the Creator. Some hold a position that the main objective of life is to provide service to the needy and destitute. Some believe that the main aim of life is to protect the mother earth by protecting natural resources such as air, water, and land with sustainable actions. Some hold that life is to eat, drink and be merry. Some believe that the main objective of life is to become rich and famous. We would find as many views if an attempt were made to enumerate opinions of the current 2021 world population of 7.9 billion. Accordingly, I am limiting my comments to what is enunciated in various Vedic scriptures. Depiction of the purpose of life therein is to pursue Dharma (धर्म), Artha (अर्थ), Kāma (काम), and Mokṣa (मोक्ष).

What are Dharma, Artha, Kāma, and Mokṣa?

Dharma (धर्म) is derived from the root Dhṛ (धृ), meaning to hold, bear, carry, or support. धारणात् धर्मः - that which holds together or supports is Dharma. In this sense, Dharma encompasses all ethical, moral, social, and other values or principles and codes of conduct, which contribute to the well-being, sustenance, and harmonious functioning of individuals, societies, and nations and prevent their disintegration. Dharma thus signifies behaviors that are in accord with Ṛta (ऋत), the principle of the natural order which regulates and coordinates the operation of the world and everything within it. It is the principle that makes life and the world possible and includes religious duties, moral rights, laws, conduct that enable social order, virtues, the right way of living, and responsibilities of each individual that all beings must accept and respect to sustain harmony and order in the world. The term Dharma hereafter is referred to as righteousness. Where the word has other meanings such as duty, attribute, or nature, they are so identified. The most common usage of the term Dharma as "religion" is not used in my analysis, critique, and perspective provided hereafter.

Artha (अर्थ) means the instruments for the sustenance of life and incorporates wealth, career, activity to make a living, financial security, and economic prosperity. Its typical use is in the context of wealth, material, or worldly possessions. It is also used to express purpose or aim.

Kāma (काम) signifies lust, desire, passion, or pleasure of the senses. It is an internal force that produces an intense desire for something or circumstance while already having a significant amount of the desired object. It can take any form, such as the lust for sexuality, money, or power. It can take such mundane forms as the desire for food as distinct from the need for food or the passion for redolence when one lusts for a particular smell that brings back memories.

Mokṣa (मोक्ष) means liberation, summum bonum consisting in the total cessation of transmigratory life and its cause, the subject matter of the "Intent of Śrīmad Bhagavad Gītā."

Among them, Artha (wealth) and Kāma (desire) only give transient happiness, though, in the end, the result is only unhappiness. That is why they are not beneficial (श्रेय, Śreya) but are just dear (प्रेय, Preya). Though Dharma and Mokṣa are difficult when an effort is made, the results are excellent, so they are not just dear but beneficial.

> However, some argue that Artha is the foundation for Dharma and Kāma. Without prosperity and security in society or individually, moral life and sensuality become difficult. Poverty breeds vice and hate, while prosperity breeds virtues and love. However, all three are mutually connected. One should not cease enjoying life, virtuous behavior, or pursuit of wealth creation; excessive pursuit of anyone with complete rejection of the other two harms all three, including the one excessively pursued.

Notwithstanding varied arguments, what do we see when we observe the phenomenal world? We perceive that all beings are deliriously running around nonstop, incessantly, from an awake state to sleep and from birth to death (आसुप्तेरामृते, Āsupterāmṛte) singing the same song in unison, in their pursuit for "that thing" without which the Saṃsāra is nil. The quest for "that thing" is referred to in scriptures as Puruṣārtha (पुरुषार्थ) - पुरुषस्य अर्थ इति पुरुषार्थ, Puruṣasya Artha Iti Puruṣārtha, a compound word from Puruṣa (पुरुष, a person) and Artha (अर्थ, purpose). Thus, Puruṣārtha is the object of human pursuit, the objective of the desire of all living beings. A question here arises - what is that thing without contention has become the object of all beings? What is there to say? **It is happiness, happiness, and only happiness!** O, happiness! How succulent you are! You have kept your hands over the heads of all, sparing none. Having just come out of a mother's womb, even an infant laments for you with his quivering lips. You have stained everyone's bosom from birth. Trains are squealing, ships are sailing, armies are fighting, nightingales are crying, flower buds are blooming, lions are roaring, elephants are trumpeting, markets are in uproar, and everywhere one looks, humanity is running around insanely. What for is this all? Directly (साक्षात्, Sākṣāt) or by regular succession (परंपरा, Paraṃparā), knowingly or unknowingly, everyone's thoughts and prayers are aimed only at happiness in all their efforts.

Since everyone appears to be engaged in the enjoyment of worldly objects, it may lead one to conclude that Puruṣārtha is material enjoyment (विषय-भोग, Viṣaya-Bhoga). However, this thought is inappropriate, as no one likes enjoyment just for fun. Albeit, all beings unquestionably are seen immersed in that happiness through enjoyment. Through the enjoyment of objects, all beings anxiously look forward to embracing "that thing" that is only happiness and nothing but happiness, the bliss-form (सुख-स्वरुप, Sukha-Svarupa). However, when those objects no longer provide them happiness, they are discarded. One can reason - material enjoyments offer just a glimpse of that bliss form like a mirror to see one's face. As long as it continues to give a glimpse of that bliss form, one will embrace and hold it tight to one's chest. However, when it is no longer suitable to see one's face, it will be pelted with stones and discarded. The mirror is kept as long as it is good to see one's face. When the silver coating comes off, no one wants to keep the useless piece of glass. It is clear that the mirror is not beloved, but the face is. One can conclude that objects are not cherished, but happiness is. As long as things are coated with happiness and I-ness-ridden sense and can allow us to provide a glimpse of internal happiness, they are embraced. However, when the coating of happiness and I-ness-ridden sense disappears from them, they are immediately abandoned. In the past, Gopīcandra, Bhartṛhari, and others gave up their kingdoms, majesty, wealth, sons, and wives; Mahārānī Mīrābāī left her husband and palace life when she did not find them bliss-form. It is thus evident that material enjoyments are not beloved, but happiness is.

To some extent, every being is blessed with worldly enjoyment as an instrument in their quest for happiness. Yet, human gratification is not seen when one glances around. Rather more indulgence is seen. As more enjoyments are acquired, more is the conflagration of the flame for happiness. Hey, Lord! What disease did we catch that we would not even wish on our enemy? For a thirsty, one can see satisfaction and thirst-quenching in every drop consumed, but here, the matter is entirely different. Instead of lessened thirst, one sees aggravated thirst. What is the reason? The reason is evident. Material objects do not provide any degree of requisite happiness but, like the belly of a firefly, only show a glimpse of their beauty. Just as an enticer by a seducing wink standing far behind a sheer curtain makes her lover's heart highly excited for an embrace, enjoyments do not provide a genuine embrace to the lover. However, a glimpse alone fills the lover's heart with extreme pain and makes him squirm like a fish for an intimate rendezvous. Like an oblation of Ghī (घी, clarified butter) in fire, this fire of love burns so much that his distraught heart yearns for the limits of time and space from the Saṃsāra to be erased, and the embrace becomes so tight that there is no limit of time and space. How can this happen? Being limited, how can one meet the unlimited? Being insignificant, how can one embrace the significant? Unbathed, stinking, wearing dirty clothes, how can anyone shake hands with royalty?

So, if you are thinking of attaining eternal and immovable happiness not bounded by time and space, then throw away the worldly objects of intense craving and disposition. Hold in your hands a sword of knowledge (ज्ञान, Jñāna), and sharpen it on a grindstone of faith in a preceptor (गुरु, Guru) and scriptures (शास्त्र, Śāstra). With your body, mind, and wealth, take refuge in a true preceptor (सद्गुरु, Sadguru) and true scriptures (सच्छास्त्र, Sacchāstra) and through tactics shown by them become a skillful swordsman. With a firm determination, swing the sword at your neck, and then it is a victory for thee. Now, you provide light to the sun and the moon. The well-being of the stellar constellations and the world is all in your hands. With the opening of your eyes, the Saṃsāra is born, and with the closing of your eyes, Pralaya (प्रलय)[9] of the Saṃsāra is ipso facto (स्वतः सिद्ध, Svataḥ Siddha).

तद्विद्धि प्रणिपातेन परिप्रश्नेन सेवया |
उपदेक्ष्यन्ति ते ज्ञानं ज्ञानिनस्तत्त्वदर्शिन: || BG 4:34 ||

> Know That, with prostration, service, and exhaustive questioning. They, the wise knowers of the Truth, will impart knowledge to you.

श्रद्धावान् लभते ज्ञानं तत्पर: संयतेन्द्रिय: |
ज्ञानं लब्ध्वा परां शान्तिमचिरेणाधिगच्छति || BG 4:39 ||

> One with steady faith, ready with means, and who has restrained the senses acquires knowledge. Having acquired knowledge attains supreme peace immediately.

To acquire knowledge - faith, assertiveness, and subduedness of senses are necessary. The absence of even one will preclude the acquisition of knowledge. The knowledge herein is the Brahma-Jñāna, knowledge of the Ātmā, knowledge of the Brahman. While it is not something that can be attained instantly, a seeker must go through several steps (ब्रह्मविद्या, Brahmavidyā) toward the ultimate Realization.

What is Pratyakṣa-Jñāna, Parokṣa-Jñāna and Aparokṣa-Jñāna?

Vedantic philosophy provides three traditional kinds of knowledge (ज्ञान, Jñāna): Pratyakṣa (empirical), Parokṣa (indirect), and Aparokṣa (transcendental).

Pratyakṣa (प्रत्यक्ष) means that which is perceptible to the eyes or is visible. In general usage, it refers to being present, present before the eyes, within the range of sight, cognizable by any sense organ, distinct, evident, clear, direct, immediate, explicit, express, and corporeal. It is a mode of proof (प्रमाण, Pramāṇa). Pratyakṣa refers to the faculties of perception with which are connected thoughts (विचार, Vicāra), imagination (कल्पना,

---

9 Pralaya (प्रलय) is an eonic term for dissolution of the material world specified for different periods of time. In the dissolution, the material world merges into the unmanifest Prakṛti.

Kalpanā), and volition (प्रयत्न, Prayatna), which together as Cetasa (चेतस्) illuminate the mind (मनस्, Manas), the ordinary mental equipment of an individual, and give awareness or consciousness (चेतना, Cetanā). There are four types of valid perceptions: a) sense perception (इन्द्रिय-प्रत्यक्ष, Indriya-Pratyakṣa), b) mental perception (मनस्-प्रत्यक्ष, Manas-Pratyakṣa), c) self-consciousness (स्ववेदना-प्रत्यक्ष, Svavedanā-Pratyakṣa), and d) supernormal intuition (योग-प्रत्यक्ष, Yoga-Pratyakṣa).

Parokṣa (परोक्ष) is a compound word from Parā (परा), meaning beyond, and Akṣa (अक्ष), meaning eye, and so Parokṣa means beyond the eyes, beyond the range of sight. Therefore, it also means invisible, remote, or hidden. It refers to mediating knowledge or indirect cognition mediated by sensory-intellectual apparatus. The thought system's psychological insights that have evolved in the context of two levels of realities, empirical and transcendental, are gained through direct and indirect cognition of things in the world. A seeker gets basic knowledge of the Brahman, the Paramātmā, the Ātmā, Mokṣa, Jñāna, and Karma through scriptures such as the Vedas and Upaniṣads and true preceptors (Sadguru). Such objective knowledge is called Parokṣa and is indirect. At this stage, though he has a basic understanding that there is only one Ātmā in all beings, which is the Paramātmā, he does not have direct or transcendental knowledge to identify his Ātmā as the Paramātmā, the Brahman.

Aparokṣa (अपरोक्ष) means not invisible and refers to direct intuitive knowledge, the highest kind of knowledge. This knowledge is gained by a seeker by establishing a preceptor-pupil relationship with a spiritual guide who has already experienced that kind of knowledge (अपरोक्षानुभूति, Aparokṣānubhūti). Once the seeker becomes Jīvanmukta (जीवन्मुक्त),[10]he realizes and experiences that he is not separate from the Supreme Being, the Paramātmā, the Brahman, and that he is the Paramātmā, the Brahman. This knowledge of Self-Realization is called Aparokṣa or direct or transcendental knowledge. It is direct in that the knower does not experience anything other than the Paramātmā, the Brahman. His realization becomes evident from his behavior and how he views the Saṃsāra. Aparokṣa is without a variant when one recognizes the non-dual nature of the ever-realized Self (तत् त्वम् असि, Tat Tvam Asi. That thou art). It is the immediate knowledge gained through the practice of meditation by the removal of all thoughts (विकल्प, Vikalpa). It leads to the thoughtless state (निर्विकल्प, Nirvikalpa), which is the highest experience, the immediate realization of the Truth. It is the method of cessation from individual and collective perception leading to the position of neutrality. "सर्वं खल्विदं ब्रह्म, all this is the Brahman" is Parokṣa knowledge, but understanding, experiencing, and realizing "अहम् ब्रह्मास्मि, I am the Brahman" is Aparokṣa-Jñāna.

Vedānta explains the transition from Parokṣa-Jñāna to Aparokṣa-Jñāna with the famous tenth man story. The story goes thus: ten students tried to cross a high-flowing river. They went on a boat. After crossing the river, the gang leader started counting each of them. Every time he counted, he left himself out and counted the rest of them, and so he always got the number nine. That caused frustration in the gang. Each one counted in turn, and each time they repeated the same mistake of forgetting to count the person who counted. They thought that one among them had drowned in the river. Each time they counted, the tenth man was missing. The tenth man was always there, but they failed to count him and did not realize his presence. They started lamenting over his missing. A wise man came that way and enquired about their cause of worry during that time. Seeing their plight, he helped them to count. When the wise man counted, there were precisely ten people. He declared, "The tenth man is here." The students were surprised and, at the same time, happy about the wise man's declaration. The wise man said, "The tenth man is safely here, but ignorance hid him from your vision." This story from the scripture is precisely applicable to the transition of our knowledge. The Brahman is very much here. We are the Brahman; however, we are unaware of it. Ignorance is hiding our understanding.

---

[10] Jīvanmukta (जीवन्मुक्त) means one who has realized knowledge of the supreme imperishable Reality and is free from the bondage of the world of birth and death.

Parokṣa - In the example, the wise man came and took the responsibility of counting. In a detached manner, he counted and said, "The tenth man is here." This gave knowledge to the gang that all were safe and not missing. Likewise, when we read the scriptures, we get the knowledge that "ब्रह्मनअस्ति, Brahman Asti," the Brahman exists. Though we are relieved by knowing our true nature, we feel that the Brahman is somewhere, and we have to reach there or attain it. We do not think what the scriptures are telling about our nature.

Aparokṣa - In the example, when the wise man helped the students count, they realized that the tenth man was that left-out man, and he was with them all the time. After learning, when the gang leader counted again, he was quick to realize, "I am that tenth missing man." Likewise, when we progress towards our goal, we learn, "I am the Brahman" and "I am not a Saṃsārī (संसारी)." That is Aparokṣa-Jñāna.

Parokṣa consists in the intellectual assent to a stated proposition, and Aparokṣa consists in the actual realization of that proposition. In Parokṣa, there is a distinction between a subjective concept and its objective reality. That distinction is irrelevant in the case of Aparokṣa-Jñāna. A man is said to attain Parokṣa (indirect) wisdom when he knows (theoretically) that the Brahman exists. However, he is said to achieve direct cognition (साक्षात्कार, Sākṣātkāra) when he experiences and realizes that he is himself the Brahman. Then, he becomes Jīvanmukta. Vedānta conveys the Aparokṣa absolute in a Parokṣa way, which is valid because while referring to specific facts about the Brahman, Parokṣa does not refer to unrealities. Śrīmad-Bhāgavata 11th Canto, 21st Chapter, Verse 35 refers to the seers' indirect (Parokṣa) statements. The seers of the Vedas are found to speak variously about the Brahman in an indirect manner (Parokṣa-Vāda), such as, "The eye, O! Emperor is the supreme Brahman" or "This being who is in the right eye is named Indha. Though he is Indha, he is indirectly called Indra, for the deities have a fondness, as it were, for indirect names and hate to be called indirectly." Thus, Parokṣa is "this," and Aparokṣa is "that" of the Upaniṣads. Parokṣa wisdom or mediate knowledge, which is the correct perception, does not liberate a person from the Saṃsāra, but it is confirmed by Aparokṣa wisdom. Parokṣa-Vāda (indirect injunctions) of the Vedic seers indirectly leads one to the path of liberation Śrīmad-Bhāgavata 11th Canto, 3rd Chapter, Verse 44. As will be discussed later in (BG 8.12 - BG 8.13), Śrī Kṛṣṇa tells Arjuna about "That" which is to be "known," and about "That" by realizing which one attains immortality. That is Parokṣa wisdom by which a listener's attention is aroused, and the fruit of such knowledge is indicated. The fruit is the realization of the attributeless Brahman, the knowledge of the knowable beginningless, the knower of the field. The cognition that the Brahman exists but transcends all verbal expressions and cannot be expressed in terms of existence and non-existence. Ādi Śaṅkarācārya explains that Śrī Kṛṣṇa objectifies the "Acosmic" through the process of superimposition and sublation by designating the Brahman as the field-knower employing the adjunct field pluralized due to hands and feet. The Brahman is to be realized as existing. In Śrīmad Bhagavad Gītā, the Lord Vāsudeva Śrī Kṛṣṇa is addressed as Bhagavāna (भगवान).

What does Bhagavāna mean?

Viṣṇu Purāṇa, 6.5.78 defines Bhagavāna as -

उत्पत्तिं प्रलयं चैव भूतानामागतिं गतिम् |
वेत्तिं विद्यामविद्यां च स वाच्यो भगवानिति ||

He who understands creation and dissolution, appearance and disappearance of beings, knowledge, and ignorance should be called Bhagavāna.

The term Bhagavāna is a compound word from two disyllables Bhaga (भग) and Vāna (वान). The disyllable Vāna (वान) means possessor. Thus,

भगः अस्य अस्ति इति भगवान, that is, one who has Bhaga (भग) is Bhagavāna.

The term Bhaga (भग) is used in the scriptures to denote one of the Ādityas, the sun, the moon, the provider, the bestower, or opulence. However, definitive meaning is provided in Viṣṇu Purāṇa 6.5.74 -

ऐश्वर्यस्य समग्रस्य वीर्यस्य यशसः श्रियः।
ज्ञान-वैराग्ययोश्चैव षण्णां भग इतीरणा॥

Bhaga denotes six attributes "Total (समग्र), lordliness (ऐश्वर्य), power (वीर्य), renown (यशसः), splendor (श्रियः), knowledge (ज्ञान) and dispassion (वैराग्य).

1. Samagra-Aiśvarya (समग्र-ऐश्वर्य) means an attribute of the total, complete and absolute dominion or lordliness.
2. Samagra-Vīrya (समग्र-वीर्य) means an attribute of absolute power, the capacity to create, sustain, and resolve.
3. Samagra-Yaśasaḥ (समग्र-यशसः) means an attribute of absolute fame.
4. Samagra-Śriyaḥ (समग्र-श्रियः) means an attribute of absolute splendor.
5. Samagra-Jñāna (समग्र-ज्ञान means an attribute of complete knowledge.
6. Samagra-Vairāgya (समग्र-वैराग्य) means an attribute of total dispassion.

Vāsudeva Śrī Kṛṣṇa, one in Whom those six exist eternally, unimpeded, and in full measure, is addressed as Bhagavāna. He is the Supreme Lord Who knows "the origin, dissolution, appearance, and disappearance of living beings, and is aware of knowledge and ignorance."

WHAT IS BONDAGE? WHAT IS LIBERATION?

Reverting to the subject of human pursuit, absolute happiness not limited by time and space is the object of the life of all beings, and that is the supreme effort (Puruṣārtha). Attainment of eternal and immovable happiness and complete removal of sorrow is liberation (Mokṣa). Alternatively, attainment of the Brahman and freedom from the bondage of the Saṃsāra is Mokṣa, meaning liberation from the Saṃsāra of transmigrating lives and attainment of the supreme-bliss (Paramānanda). Acquisition of eternal happiness and complete removal of sorrow is desired by even an ordinary, and so all are, to some extent, desirers for liberation (Mumukṣu). Here a question arises - what is bondage (बन्धन, Bandhana)? From what does one want to be free (मुक्त, Mukta)? With some thought, it is clear that:

> "पुनरपि जननं पुनरपि मरणं पुनरपि जननी जठरे शयनम्, And, again birth and again death and again resting in the mother's womb is real bondage."[11]

That is, based on Karma, Jīva takes repeated births and deaths like a pot bound by a rope of impressions (वासना, Vāsanā)[12]going up and down in the Saṃsāra-well with an 8,400,000-cycle clock hanging over. In this Saṃsāra-well, the cycle that is driven by a farmer in the form of time (काल, Kāla) seldom ends. That is bondage, that is sorrow, and that is pain. Freedom from it is liberation. This can be understood as follows:

- Jīva takes birth and death because of his relationship with the Saṃsāra of I-ness (अहंता, Ahaṃtā) and mineness (ममता, Mamatā).
- The relationship with the Saṃsāra of I-ness and mineness is because of his relationship with the body (देह, Deha). In the deep-sleep (सुषुप्ति, Suṣupti) state, when the relationship of Jīva with the body is gone, then the Saṃsāra of I-ness and mineness disappears. With the analytic process of separation and connection (अन्वय-व्यतिरेक, Anvaya-Vyatireka),[13]it is clear that the relationship with the Saṃsāra is only possible due to the relationship with the body.

---

[11] Verse 21 of Ādi Śaṅkarācārya (आदि शंकराचार्य) "Bhaja Govindaṃ (भज गोविन्दं)" -
पुनः - again; अपि - and; जननं - birth; मरणं - death; जननी - mother; जठरे - in the womb; शयनम् - sleep, rest.

[12] Vāsanā (वासना) means impressions. They are inherent latencies and tendencies resulting from previous actions. They are assimilated with predispositions, tendencies, or propensities of the mind in the present due to past experiences. With continuous ongoing desires, subliminal traces or subtle fingerprints remain in mind. Thereby a state of constant agitation remains - always planning the future and thinking about the past, preventing one from living in a state of clarity that arises in the awareness of the eternal present moment. It can also mean desire.

[13] Anvaya-Vyatireka (अन्वय-व्यतिरेक) means an analytic process of "separation" and "connection," to indicate inference in which reason is co-present or is co-absent with the major term, as the pair of positive and negative instantiations representing both inductive and deductive reasoning. For instance, in the example of roses strung to form a garland, without the string which holds together the roses, there is no garland of roses is Anvaya, and the fact that the string is separate from the roses is Vyatireka.

- Relationship with the body is because of limited vision (परिच्छिन्न-दृष्टि, Paricchinna-Dṛṣṭi).
- Limited vision is discriminating vision (भेद-दृष्टि, Bheda-Dṛṣṭi).
- Discriminating-vision is born of ignorance (अज्ञान-जन्य, Ajñāna-Janya).

This matter can be clarified as follows. A Jīva, due to ignorance of his own true nature, sees himself as limited as the body and knows the Saṃsāra as something different and separate from himself. Due to this discriminating vision, bound by I-ness and mineness, he becomes desirous for happiness. Despite being infinitely blissful, fallen from his true nature, he becomes anxious for happiness. Those things whose impressions (Saṃskāras) reside within always become objects of desire. Due to his smell-Saṃskāra, a musk deer wanders from forest to forest looking for smell, not realizing that it emanates from his own navel. Similarly, like the musk deer, Jīva, despite being a repository of abundant happiness within, veiled by ignorance of not knowing it within, attracted by the smell of the supreme bliss, roams around in all directions for that happiness.

The desire for happiness is due to ignorance, which is real grief. By being limited, Jīva desires happiness due to I-ness and mineness, and with the "I am a doer" sense, becomes engaged in an activity. Because of discriminating vision, Jīva forms intellect that favors or likes some things and disfavors or dislikes some other things. Then, it forms fondness or attachment (राग, Rāga) with objects that are agreeable and develops hate or aversion (द्वेष, Dveṣa) with unfavorable objects. This way, he gets into bondage to the rules of Prakṛti (प्रकृति).[14]In the kingdom of Prakṛti, there is a well-established rule that attachment is the cause of piety (पुण्य, Puṇya) and aversion is the cause of sin (पाप, Pāpa). Due to ignorance, the Jīva desirous for happiness is caught in the bondage of doership-intellect (कर्तृत्व-बुद्धि, Karttṛtva-Buddhi) and by attachment or aversion produces piety or sin with the resultant fruit of pleasure or pain and is then put in the body-form jail as the cause (निमित्त, Nimitta) for the enjoyment of pleasure or pain. With the desire for happiness, he performs Karma through the body. Then for the enjoyment of the fruits of his Karma, he receives the body again; without a body, there is no enjoyment, which is why the body is known as Bhogāyatana.[15]This way, the flow from Karma to the body and from the body to Karma is moving so consistently that there is likely no end, even if there is Pralaya of the Saṃsāra. Not only a single Pralaya, but even after infinite Brahmās[16]have lived their lives, each ending in a Pralaya, the cycle of body and Karma of Jīva never ceases.

अव्यक्ताद्व्यक्तय: सर्वा: प्रभवन्त्यहरागमे |
रात्र्यागमे प्रलीयन्ते तत्रैवाव्यक्तसंज्ञके || BG 8.18 ||

At the arrival of the day, all beings originate from the Unmanifest; and when night falls, they dissolve in that same called the Unmanifest.

भूतग्राम: स एवायं भूत्वा प्रलीयते |
रात्र्यागमेऽवश: पार्थ प्रभवत्यहरागमे || BG 8.19 ||

Hey Arjuna! They are the same multitude of beings who, after repeated births, are helplessly dissolved at the fall of night and are born at the arrival of the day.

In this Saṃsāra, no power can show mercy on a Jīva and stop the malefic flow of body and Karma until he about turns towards his own true nature and with the fire of knowledge (ज्ञानाग्नि, Jñānāgni) burns his

---

[14] Prakṛti (प्रकृति) means nature. It is the primal matter with three different constituents known as " गुण, Guṇa" {Sattva (सत्त्व) or Sattvaguṇa (सत्त्वगुण), Rajas (रजस्) or Rajoguṇa (रजोगुण) and Tamas (तमस्) or Tamoguṇa (तमोगुण)}, whose equilibrium is the basis of all observed empirical Reality.

[15] Bhogāyatana (भोगायतन) means the one who partakes enjoyments. The gross body is the Bhogāyatana of an individual Jīva. Just as a householder lives in a house, a Jīva lives in the gross body.

[16] Brahmā (ब्रह्मा) is the creator part of the supreme Tri-Murti - Śiva, Viṣṇu, and Brahmā. According to Śiva Purāṇa 2.1.7 Brahmā was created by Lord Śiva (शिव) with Pārvatī (पार्वती) from his right limb through the umbilical lotus (पङ्कज) called Hiraṇmaya that sprang from the lake of the navel of the supreme Personality Lord Viṣṇu while sleeping.

ignorance-born doership-intellect and discriminating-vision. There is an established rule in the kingdom of Prakṛti, "As you sow, so shall you reap." A doer has to become an experiencer (भोक्ता, Bhoktā). Impressions of done deeds (Karma-Saṃskāras) always reside on the support of doership-intellect. As long as doership-intellect is present and is not burnt by realizing the eternal supreme-bliss, those Karma-Saṃskāras will bring a doer in the bondage of enjoyments. That is unavoidable. Why? Because the Supreme Being (Paramātmā) exists in doership, Karma, and resolves. When all activities are ongoing in the presence of the Supreme Being, then who is capable of doing it otherwise? While performing Karma, does one know that someone is watching what is being done? If one knows that someone is watching what one is doing, why would one do it? Who can steal the eyes of the observer? That someone is the divine vision.

The point is that the Supreme Being exists in Karma, so it cannot be without reward. It will make it face fruits, putting a doer in the bondage of enjoyership. In summary, the acquisition of the body is undoubtedly for the enjoyment of pain and sorrow. Even worldly happiness is painful because it is full of pain and suffering. The cause of pleasure and pain is the Saṃskāra of piety and sin. Piety and sin are due to attachment and aversion. The root of attachment and aversion is agreeable and disagreeable knowledge. The cause of agreeable and disagreeable knowledge is doer-intellect bound by I-ness and mineness. Doer-intellect is because of discriminating-vision, and discriminating-vision is due to the ignorance of one's true nature. That is, due to the discriminating vision, when through I-ness and mineness, a Jīva desires "I want to be happy," then desire for that happiness puts him in the bondage of doer-intellect and thrusts him into the flow of agreeable and disagreeable, attachment and aversion, piety and sin and thus birth and death, never finding a shore anywhere. That is bondage, and liberation is to be free from this bondage.

What are the types of Liberation?

Scriptures refer to five major kinds of liberation: 1) Sāyujya-Mukti (सायुज्य मुक्ति), 2) Sālokya-Mukti (सालोक्य-मुक्ति), 3) Sārṣṭi-Mukti (सार्ष्टि-मुक्ति), 4) Sāmīpya-Mukti (सामीप्य-मुक्ति) and 5) Sārupya-Mukti (सारुप्य-मुक्ति). Among the five, Sāyujya-Mukti is related to the Path of Knowledge (Jñāna-Mārga), and the other four are related to the Path of Devotion (Bhakti-Mārga).

In the Path of Knowledge, the oneness of the delimited Ātmā in the attributeless and formless Brahman through knowledge is called Sāyujya-Mukti. Delimited Ātmā means the pure Ātmā (Self) on whom I-ness sense of the body, senses, mind, and intellect are superimposed due to nescience.

The Path of Devotion relates to worship of the Brahman with attributes (Saguṇa-Brahman, the Supreme Personality). In the first enumerated liberation, known as Sālokya-Mukti, the devotee attains the abode of the Supreme Personality upon liberation. The devotee goes to live in the same sphere or world of the Supreme Personality. In the second type of liberation, known as Sārṣṭi-Mukti, the devotee receives the same lordliness (Aiśvarya) as the Supreme Personality. In the third type of liberation, known as Sāmīpya-Mukti, the devotee becomes a personal associate near the Supreme Personality. In the fourth type of liberation, known as Sārupya-Mukti, the devotee acquires the same form as the Supreme Personality, including Śaṃkha (a conch), Sudarśana-Cakra (a spinning disk-like weapon meaning "disk of auspicious vision"), Gadā (a sphere ended mace) and Padma (a lotus) except for Śrīvatsa (the abode of Śrī Lakṣmī), Bhṛgulatā (the footprint of Saptarṣi Bhṛgu) and Kaustubha-Maṇi (कौस्तुभ-मणि) {the fourth jewel that came out from the churning of the ocean of milk (क्षीर-सागर-मन्थन, Kṣīra-Sāgara-Manthana)} located on the chest of the Supreme Personality.

As will be elaborated in Chapter - 8, all liberations without knowledge under the Path of Devotion are limited by time and are subject to return to the mortal world of birth and death, the Punarāvṛtti (पुनरावृत्ति). Only under the Path of Knowledge, there is no Punarāvṛtti. In the Path of Devotion, under all liberations, upon depletion of piety impressions (Puṇya-Saṃskāras) carried to the higher worlds, the devotee returns to the mortal world. Depending upon whether they are without desires (निष्कामी, Niṣkāmī) or with desires (सकामी, Sakāmī) returns as Yoga-Bhraṣṭa (योग-भ्रष्ट) or not as Yoga-Bhraṣṭa respectively, as will be elaborated in Chapter 6.

Yoga-Bhraṣṭa means one who is fallen from Yoga, meaning one who has not attained union with oneness in the Supreme Personality. It means unsuccessful from both the Path of Karma and the Path of Knowledge, unsupported and deluded.

However, those in the Path of Devotion, like Caitanya Mahā Prabhu, have inspired devotees to execute pure devotional service out of spontaneous love for the Supreme Personality. These devotees never desire such liberation. They always want to remain in the service of the Lord. Some are indifferent to even Lord Śiva, immortality, and the Brahman. In their view, there is a constant sense of service in devotion, which they find liberation lacking. Whereas seekers of attaining oneness in the attributeless Brahman desire cessation of the process of birth and death. However, supra devotees are satisfied with remaining in the material world and executing devotional service. However, as will be further clarified, devotion is indeed necessary for one to be fit for knowledge.

In Śrīmad Bhāgavata, in the 3rd Canto, 29th Chapter, and 13th verse, when Kapila Muni upon questioned by his mother Devahūti (देवहूति) about devotion, he says that:

सालोक्यसार्ष्टिसामीप्यसारूप्यैकत्वमप्युत |
दीयमानं न गृह्णन्ति विना मत्सेवनं जनाः || भागवत 3.29.13 ||

उत् - Even ; दीयमानं - being offered, ; जनाः - pure devotees ; न - (do) not ; गृह्णन्ति - accept ; सालोक्य - living on the same sphere, ; सार्ष्टि - having the same lordliness, ; सामीप्य - being a personal associate, ; सारूप्य - having the same form ; एकत्वम् - oneness, ; विना - except, ; मत् - for My ; सेवनं - devotional service ; अपि - indeed.

Even being offered, pure devotees do not accept living on the same sphere, having the same lordliness, being a personal associate, having the same oneness form, except for My devotional service.

Intent - Such devotees do not desire oneness with the Supreme Lord, as desired by seekers and meditators. To become one with the Supreme Lord is beyond the dream of such devotees. To serve the Lord, some may accept higher spheres such as Vaikuṇṭha (वैकुण्ठ), but they will never accept merging into the Brahman effulgence. Such devotees are so fond of rendering service to the Supreme Lord that the five kinds of liberations are not vital to them.

What are the means for Liberation?

By reflecting on the nature of bondage, one can ascertain the means for liberation. Freedom is breaking the shackles of bondage, and that is why the means that can break the bonds of bondage can be the only means for liberation. The root of birth and death, pleasure and pain, and thus piety and sin is the ego of doership. That is the cause of all bondages. Saṃskāras of Karma, such as attachment and aversion, reside on the support of doership-ego. With the ego of "I am a doer," whatever emotions and efforts happen, good or evil, those emotions and efforts are like waves in an ocean that disappear later but leave seeds in the form of Saṃskāras in the heart where the doership-ego resides. Saṃskāras resides in a subtle state on the ego's dependence, who has become a doer of those emotions and efforts. Later those subtle Saṃskāras, in their time, become ready for fruition in the gross state, just like varieties of seeds hidden in the soil in subtle form germinate in a rainy season or the smallest subtle particles of the skin of frogs become alive when rains return to free the frogs from their shrouds and make their way up through the moist soil to the surface. Likewise, Karma-Saṃskāras becoming ready for fruition brings a doer helplessly into birth and death bondage. Whether good or evil, their enjoyment by necessity puts him in the bondage of the body. Due to the relationship with the body, Jīva has birth and death. In the Saṃsāra, there is no other grief equivalent to it. Because of the relationship with the body, there is repeated bondage of the infallible with fallible, the unlimited with limited, the pure with impure, the blissful with painful, the unborn with birth, and the imperishable with perishable. Learned preceptors have theorized that a Jīva is independent in doing Karma, whether he does or not. However, after doing Karma, he is not independent in enjoying fruits, whether he wants them. In enjoying fruits, Jīva is undoubtedly dependent and has to enjoy the fruits, whether good or evil.

> "नाभुक्तं क्षीयते कर्म कल्पकोटिशतैरपि, there is no depletion (क्षय, Kṣaya) of Karma without enjoyment (भोग, Bhoga) even if a billion Kalpa[17]pass."

> "अवश्यम्भावीभावानां प्रतिकारो भवेध्यदि । तदा दुःखैर्न लिप्येरन नलरामयुधिष्टिराः, if it is possible to stop events that are certainly going to happen in the future, (if it is possible to deplete fruits of Karma without enjoyment), then King Nakula, Dharmātmā Yudhiṣṭhira, and Bhagavāna Śrī Rāma would not have suffered pain in their mortal bodies."

Karma is only because of doership-ego, and birth and death are only because of Karma. Without burning doership, where is freedom from birth and death? The root of doership is discriminating vision, "अन्योऽसावन्योऽहमस्मि, he is one, I am other." Discriminating vision is because of ignorance of one's own true nature. Removal of ignorance can only be achieved by direct intuitive transcendental knowledge (Aparokṣa-Jñāna) of the supreme imperishable Reality attained through reason and discrimination between the real and the unreal. It is impossible if one hopes to remove ignorance by performing specific Karma. It is akin to someone trying to remove darkness using a weapon - an utterly futile effort. Darkness can only be removed by light.

Ignorance is like darkness. Stumbles of Karma are only in darkness. One is likely to stumble walking in darkness, not in light. Accordingly, when the darkness of ignorance covers a Jīva, he undergoes stumbles of Karma. When Karma is ignorance-born, how can it remove the darkness of ignorance? Anything produced due to Karma cannot stay steady but certainly, perish. With creation, there is deterioration and destruction. The Vedas and Upaniṣads have proffered:

> "तध्यथेह कर्मचितो लोकः क्षीयते एवमेवामुत्र पुण्यचितो लोकः क्षीयते, just as this Karma-created world is destroyed, in the same way, piety-world created by Karma is also destroyed."[18]

> "ऋते ज्ञानान्न मुक्तिः, without knowledge, there is no freedom."

> "ज्ञानादेव तु कैवल्यम्, only with knowledge liberation is possible."

> "नान्यः पन्था विध्यतेऽयनाय, for freedom there is no other path."

The path to liberation with Karma without knowledge is like an imaginary flower in the sky (खपुष्प, Khapuṣpa). The truth espoused in the Veda-Śāstra is that the creation of the Saṃsāra is due to delusional ignorance. A thing maybe something, but knowing it as something else is ignorance of contrary cognition. It is like cognizing a rope as a snake - this is ignorance. Can chants, incantations, or truncheon blow to kill a delusional snake lead to removing the snake? Removal of the snake is only possible by a truncheon if the snake is in the external space in reality. But, in the exterior area right in front is only the rope; the snake is undoubtedly not there. How can blows of a truncheon make it go away? There is the perception of a snake in the rope only because of faint darkness. If a lamp is lit to remove darkness, then the rope will be visible, and the determination of the absence of the snake at all times is established. In the snake-perception time, in reality, it was only the rope; the snake neither came from anywhere nor later on was destroyed. The snake was perceived only because of the ignorance of the rope. With the knowledge of the rope, both the being and non-being of the snake are proven as delusional. Likewise, due to the ignorance of one's true nature, there is the perception of the Saṃsāra (of I-you, birth-death, piety-sin, and pleasure-pain) in the Supreme Being, in the Paramātmā, in the Brahman.

---

[17] Kalpa (कल्प) means a day of Brahmā or 4.32 billion years.

[18] Chāndogya Upaniṣad (छान्दोग्य उपनिषद्) 8.1.6

Destroying it by only Karma is impossible. By only Karma, no one has ever removed it, nor will anyone be able to do it in the future. To remove ignorance, a fit person endowed, with the fourfold means (Sādhana-Catuṣṭaya), with the grace of preceptors and scriptures, and through effort, needs only to gain knowledge of one's own Ātmā. Then only the removal of the Saṃsāra of the transmigrating lives of birth and death is possible. The Saṃsāra, per se, is not born. Neither was there before its creation, nor would it be there after its destruction. It is perceived in the middle, only delusionally.

अव्यक्तादीनि भूतानि व्यक्तमध्यानि भारत |
अव्यक्तनिधनान्येव तत्र का परिदेवना || BG 2.28 ||

Hey Arjuna! All beings are unmanifest in the beginning, unmanifest in the end, and only manifest in the intermediate state. In these conditions, why lament?

Grief can only be of a thing that is real (Sat). There is no grief over an imagined thing. No one physically goes to grieve over the death of a family member in someone's dream. However, the objects of your grief are these bodies. In reality, they are unreal, only to see. That is why grief over this delusional world of bodies is unbecoming. There is no dispute that these bodies were not in any embodied form before their birth. But they were invisible. After their death, they will not be in any embodied form but become invisible. Things perceived only in the middle period and not before and after are like the dream world. They are like the snake in a rope, just a subject of delusion. Just as the snake and dream world, without pre and post-time, appear only in the middle, are unreal and illusory, in the same way, due to ignorance, the Saṃsāra of the bodies in its perception time delusionally appears real. In reality, it is only the existent Paramātmā. Why grieve for a thing that is not there but only delusional?

या निशा सर्वभूतानां तस्यां जागर्ति संयमी |
यस्यां जाग्रति भूता सा निशा पश्यतो मुनेः || BG 2.69 ||

A restrained ascetic is awake in that which is a night for all living beings. In which all living beings are awake, that is a night for the perceiver sage.

Regarding the Supreme Reality, all living beings are asleep. They are unconscious of the Supreme Reality. For them, the Supreme Reality has become unknown. For all living beings, the Supreme Reality is like night. In that ever-pure Supreme Reality, a self-restrained sage of stable wisdom is awake; he is conscious. In the Supreme Reality, his intellect is situated "is as is," he is established with I-ness and is entirely blissful. But those worldly enjoyment objects in whom all living entities are being conscious and are enjoying, in whom their intellect is becoming true (having an I-ness sense in them and holding them as true), the seer of the Supreme Reality is sleeping. For him, all these objects are equivalent to a night and are just nothing. In his view, all these objects are like imaginary flowers in space.

भ्रान्त्या प्रतीतः संसारो विवेकान्न तु कर्मभिः ।
न हि रज्जूरगारोपो घण्टाघोषान्निवर्तते ॥

Removal (Nivrutti) of the Saṃsāra perceived by delusion is only possible by the knowledge of the Ātmā, not by Karma. A snake perceived in a rope due to delusion cannot be removed by the tinkle of a bell. Its removal is only possible by illumination.

Thus, ignorance is the root of Karma. In no way can Karma remove it. Because ignorance is the root and Karma is the fruit, the fruit cannot oppose the root. Opposition to ignorance can only be an ax of knowledge, which can cut the source of ignorance and the fruits of action.

Earlier in the Introduction, there was a reference to the five Prāṇa (प्राण) in the definition of the products of the constituents of Prakṛti. Since the term Prāṇa is referred to at many locations, a brief understanding of Prāṇa is in order.

What is Prāṇa?

Prāṇa (प्राण) means vital breaths of air, life force, or energy. The foundation and essence of all life, energy, and vitality. It permeates the entire Saṃsāra and flows in everything. It is the connecting link between the Saṃsāra, the conscious element (चेतन, Cetana), and the mind. Life in the Saṃsāra is possible by the flow of Prāṇa in all living beings and performing vital functions. It regulates all physical processes, for example - breath, supply of oxygen, digestion, elimination, and much more. It infuses and vitalizes all matter by coalescing into atoms and sub-atomic particles, which become the basic building blocks of all matter, manifesting as the Saṃsāra. Prāṇa is distributed in the whole body through a network of channels known as Nāḍī (नाडी)[19]and centers known as Cakra (चक्र, wheel).

As depicted in the Vedas and Vedānta Śāstra under Tantra (तंत्र), there are seven centers (Cakra) in the subtle body arranged vertically along the Suṣumnā (सुषुम्ना) Nāḍī from its base to the top of the head and are symbolically mapped to specific human physiological capacity, seed syllable, sounds, Tanmātra,[20]deities, colors, and other motifs. Cakra is a center of energy (शक्ति, Śakti) as a vital force. They are seven in number: 1) Mūlādhāra (मूलाधार) situated at the anus, 2) Svādhiṣṭhāna (स्वाधिष्ठान) at the genitals, 3) Maṇipūra (मणिपूर) at the navel, 4) Anāhata (अनाहत) at the heart, 5) Viśuddha (विशुद्ध) at the throat, 6) Ājñā (आज्ञा) at the space between the eyebrows and 7) Sahasrāra (सहस्रार) at the top of the head. Corresponding to each Cakra in the astral body, there are plexuses in the physical body. A plexus is a center of interwoven nerves, arteries, and veins. The sacral plexus corresponds to the Mūlādhāra Cakra, the prostatic plexus to the Svādhiṣṭhāna Cakra, the solar plexus to the Maṇipūra Cakra, the cardiac plexus to the Anāhata Cakra, the laryngeal plexus to the Viśuddha Cakra and the cavernous plexus to the Ājñā Cakra. Each Cakra has control over a particular center in the gross body. The nervous, digestive, circulatory, respiratory, genital-urinary functions, and other body systems are controlled by an individual Cakra. The gross nerves and plexuses of the physical plane have a close relationship with the subtle ones. As physical centers are closely related to the astral centers, vibrations produced in the physical centers by prescribed Yogic methods have desired effects in the astral centers. Used as focal points for meditative visualizations, and with Prāṇāyāma, Mudrā, Bandha, Kriyā, and Mantra, the flow of Prāṇa through each Cakra can be manipulated to achieve enlightenment.

There are 72,000 channels (Nāḍī) in the body. Of these, there are three principal channels:

1. The Suṣumnā Nāḍī runs from the base of the spine to the crown of the head, passing through each Cakra. It is the channel through which Kuṇḍalinī (कुण्डलिनी) Śakti rises from its origin at the Mūlādhāra Cakra to the Sahasrāra Cakra at the crown of the head. In subtle body terms, the Suṣumnā Nāḍī is the path to enlightenment.
2. The Iḍā (इडा) Nāḍī begins and ends on the left side of the Suṣumnā. It is regarded as the lunar Nāḍī, calm and nurturing by nature, and is said to control all mental processes and the feminine aspects of our personality. The color of Iḍā is whitish like that of the full moon.
3. The Piṅgalā (पिङ्गला) Nāḍī, the solar Nāḍī, begins and ends to the right of the Suṣumnā. The Piṅgalā is reddish-orange color like that of the evening sun. It is warm and stimulating by nature, controls all vital bodily processes, and oversees masculine aspects of our personality.

---

[19] Nāḍī (नाडी) means the channels through which Prāṇa of the physical body, the subtle body and the causal body is said to flow. See Chāndogya Upaniṣad, verse 8.6.6. for Nāḍī System.

[20] Tanmātra (तन्मात्र) means rudimentary or subtle elements that are the primordial causes of the five great elements of physical manifestation known as the Pañcabhūta. The five Tanmātra are: 1) smell (गन्ध, Gandha) corresponding to earth (पृथ्वी, Pṛthvī), 2) taste (रस, Rasa) corresponding to water (आप, Āpa), 3) form (रुप, Rupa) corresponding to fire (अग्नि, Agni), 4) touch (स्पर्श, Sparśa) corresponding to wind (वायु, Vāyu) and 5) sound (शब्द, Śabda) corresponding to space (आकाश, Ākāśa).

The Caduceus, the symbol of modern medicine, is roughly similar to the relationships among the Iḍā, Piṅgalā, and Suṣumnā Nāḍī. The Iḍā and Piṅgalā Nāḍī spiral around the Suṣumnā Nāḍī like the double helix of our DNA, crossing each other at every Cakra. Eventually, all three meet at the Ājñā Cakra.

The body receives energy from Prāṇa and distributes it within, and then eliminates it. Persons with healthy and harmonious vibrations provide an aura that makes one feel the presence of good Prāṇa. Conversely, illness offers a hindrance to the flow of Prāṇa. When we take a physical breath, there is a corresponding movement in the subtle or astral spine. It flows up in the subtle spine in conjunction with inhalation and down with exhalation. This linkage between breath and the flow of Prāṇa is central to many meditation techniques. As one develops the ability to control breath, one can influence the flow of Prāṇa; thereby gaining harmony and health in both the body and the mind. Control of breath is known as Prāṇāyāma (प्राणायाम), a compound word from Prāṇa (प्राण), meaning breath and Āyāma (आयाम), meaning control. Prāṇa travels upward through the Iḍā Nāḍī. With this upward movement, breath is drawn into the lungs. As a result, the mind is drawn outwards to the world of the senses. The energy then travels downwards through the Piṅgalā Nāḍī. When the energy is going down, it is called the Apāna rather than the Prāṇa. This downward movement is accompanied by physical exhalation and signifies a rejection of external circumstances. One manifestation of this cycle is the association of inhalation with excitement and happiness and exhalation with defeat and depression. Happiness and sadness must always follow each other when the cause of each is the external circumstance, which is constantly changing. However, through Prāṇāyāma techniques, one can instead redirect energy through the Suṣumnā. When the level of energy in the Suṣumnā reaches the top of the spine and goes into the spiritual eye or Ājñā Cakra, it opens the eye of intuition and the intellect.

Through the exploration of the body and breath, ancient Yogīs discovered that the life force energy could be subdivided into energetic components called Vāyu (वायु). Vāyu means wind or air. Its root वा (Vā) means that which flows. Thus, Vāyu is an energetic force that moves in a specific direction to control bodily functions and activities. They all have very subtle yet distinct energetic attributes, including particular functions and directions of flow. Yogīs can control and cultivate these Vāyus by bringing their focus and awareness to them. Each Vāyu governs a specific area of the body and ideally functions in harmony with each other. Their subtle energetic movements affect and influence one's physical, emotional, and mental health and wellness. If a Vāyu becomes imbalanced, it can create disharmony through the complete energetic system of the body or can negatively affect its associated Cakra or organs linked to its location. Complete mastery of using Vāyus is not necessary to improve health, inward focus, and the ability to feel the subtleties within the body. Cultivating an essential awareness of one or more of the Vāyus can help deepen one's awareness of the body and the breath to achieve one's potential.

There are five major Vāyus in the body, known as Pañca-Prāṇa and are the primary currents of the vital force: 1) Prāṇa-Vāyu (प्राण-वायु), 2) Apāna-Vāyu (अपान-वायु), 3) Samāna-Vāyu (समान-वायु), 4) Udāna-Vāyu (उदान-वायु), and 5) Vyāna-Vāyu (व्यान-वायु).

1. The Prāṇa-Vāyu supplies the body with essential oxygen, and its energy flows from the nostrils to the heart level pervading the chest region. It translates as "forward moving air," and its flow is inwards and upwards. It nourishes the brain and the eyes and governs the reception of all things: food, air, senses, and thoughts. It is the total energy in the body. It directs and feeds into the other four Vāyus.
2. The Apāna-Vāyu influences the lower part of the body, from the navel to the soles of the feet. It translates as "air that moves away," and its flow is downwards and out. Its energy nourishes organs of digestion, reproduction, and elimination of all substances from the body, such as carbon dioxide, urine, and feces.
3. The Vyāna-Vāyu is situated in the heart and lungs and flows through the nerve channels of the entire body. It translates as "outward moving air," and its flow moves from the body's center to the periphery. It governs the circulation of all substances throughout the body, particularly an Nāḍī.

4. The Udāna-Vāyu is situated in the throat, and it has a circular flow around the neck and the head. It translates to "that which carries upward," and its flow moves upward from the heart to the head, the five senses, and the brain. It functions to "hold us up" and governs speech, self-expression, and growth. A weak or dysfunctional Udāna-Vāyu can manifest as speech difficulties, shortness of breath and disease of the throat, lack of self-expression, uncoordinated movement, or loss of balance. With the assistance of Udāna-Vāyu, the astral body separates itself from the physical body in the process of death. A strong Udāna-Vāyu eases the phase of death. With its control, the body becomes very light, and one may even gain the ability to levitate. External obstacles such as water, earth, or stones no longer provide obstruction when in control. Yogīs who sit or lie on a bed of nails possess the ability to control their Udāna-Vāyu. Yogīs who live in forests and remain unaffected by heat, cold, thorns, and insects are protected through the control of Udāna-Vāyu.
5. The Samāna-Vāyu is situated in the abdomen, with its energy centered in the navel. The Samāna-Vāyu translates to "balancing air." Its flow moves from the body's periphery to the center. It distributes the energy of nutrition throughout the body and governs digestion and assimilation of all substances: food, air, experiences, emotions, and thoughts. A weak or dysfunctional Samāna-Vāyu can manifest as poor judgment, low confidence, lack of motivation and desire, and digestion issues. We know that food influences our physical body and affects our psyche and consciousness. The attribute of our Prāṇa is directly associated with the quality of our food. Pure Sāttvika vegetarian food and the practice of Prāṇāyāma provide a healthy and balanced body for life. When Yogīs can control the Samāna-Vāyu, it manifests as a pure flame. Those in whom the Samāna-Vāyu is completely pure have a radiant aura, which is even noticeable by those who cannot see auras.

There are four areas in the human body where the flow of Prāṇa is particularly intensive - through the sole of each foot and the palm of each hand. The feet are closely related to the earth element and represent negative polarity. Therefore, one should never concentrate on the feet in meditation. Conversely, the energy of the palms originates from the heart. It is related to the air element and produces positive polarity.

How can Knowledge deplete Karma?

It is imperative to contemplate how depletion of Karma is possible through knowledge and the nature of that knowledge? It is a firm tenet of Vedānta that the Saṃsāra is created for the enjoyment of a Jīva. The creator of the Saṃsāra is only Jīva through his Karma. After establishing a garden just as a gardener tastes sweet-sour fruits, the creation of the Saṃsāra has no purpose other than for a Jīva to enjoy the fruits of his Karma - and so the Saṃsāra is only in the form of enjoyments. Having come into the bondage of doership, a Jīva bound by Prakṛti creates his own Saṃsāra to enjoy the fruits of Karma. That is why the Saṃsāra is said to be created by actions (कर्म-रचित, Karma-Racita).

तद्यथेह कर्मचितो लोकः क्षीयते
एवमेवामुत्र पुण्यचितो लोकः क्षीयते ।[21]

Whether this world or another world, created by Jīva based on his individual (piety and sin) acts, perish after giving its enjoyment of fruits (Phalabhoga).

The Paramātmā is singularly existent in 1) Karma, 2) the Saṃsāra (created by Karma), and 3) the enjoyments of fruits (of Jīva). The Paramātmā, unattached to any transformations, is the neutral observer of all these activities, similar to how the earth indifferently makes seeds hidden under the soil ready for fruition without being affected. Jīva, having come in the bondage of doership, remaining dependent on Prakṛti, constantly flows in the currents of birth and death. Even at the end of a Kalpa, Jīva, staying dependent on Prakṛti,

[21] Chāndogya Upaniṣad 8.1.6

merges into Prakṛti and not in the Paramātmā, as he is still in the bondage of doership. Later at the beginning of the next Kalpa, Jīva is thrown out of Prakṛti and, like a musk deer, roams around in all directions. In this regard, Śrī Kṛṣṇa Himself gives this command from His blessed mouth -

सर्वभूतानि कौन्तेय प्रकृतिं यान्ति मामिकाम् |
कल्पक्षये पुनस्तानि कल्पादौ विसृजाम्यहम् || BG 9.7 ||

> Hey Arjuna! At the end of a Kalpa, all beings merge in My Prakṛti. At the beginning of the next Kalpa, I create them again.

The reason for the merger in Prakṛti is that due to the doership-ego, the flow of Karma can never be calmed. When a Jīva, as an enjoyer, takes some Karma from the repository of accumulated past Karma (सञ्चित-कोश, Sañcita-Kośa) to the ready to be enjoyed repository (प्रारब्ध-कोश, Prārabdha-Kośa), with enjoyments, he also becomes a doer; and due to doership-ego, Karma-Saṃskāras are deposited in the Sañcita-Kośa. From seed to tree and tree to seed, the Sañcita-Kośa is never empty. It is always evergreen and complete, so there is the bondage of Prakṛti with Karma. In the present, unless Karma-born enjoyments end, meaning total depletion of Sañcita-Kośa, and future doership does not remain, then the Jīva can be free from the bondage of Prakṛti. Unfortunately, due to the sentiment of ignorance, there is neither freedom from doership nor freedom from enjoyments. Consequently, Jīva cannot be free from the bondage of Prakṛti. Just as a Jīva, performing Karma goes from the awake to the sleep state, and then after awaking back to his routine Karma, in the same way, he is thrown out from Prakṛti at the beginning of the next Kalpa.

प्रकृतिं स्वामवष्टभ्य विसृजामि पुनः पुनः |
भूतग्राममिमं कृत्स्नमवशं प्रकृतेर्वशात् || BG 9.8 ||

> Taking control of My own nature, I create again and again all of this multitude of beings helpless by the force of their nature.

न च मां तानि कर्माणि निबध्नन्ति धनञ्जय |
उदासीनवदासीनमसक्तं तेषु कर्मसु || BG 9.9 ||

> Hey Arjuna! Those actions do not bind Me. I stay indifferent and detached from those actions.

मयाध्यक्षेण प्रकृतिः सूयते सचराचरम् |
हेतुनानेन कौन्तेय जगद्विपरिवर्तते || BG 9.10 ||

> Hey Arjuna! Under My supervision, Prakṛti creates movable and stationary beings. For this reason, the world changes.

The intention here is that as long as a Jīva does not attain union with oneness in the Paramātmā through the knowledge of the Truth but remains separate from the Paramātmā as a doer of Karma, till then, dependent on the forces of his nature, helplessly moves around in the flow of birth and death for the enjoyment of fruits of Karma. Upon leaving the body, not finding oneness in the Paramātmā, merges in the lower nature (Aparā-Prakṛti). Again, for the enjoyment of fruits of accumulated Karma, Jīva comes out of the Aparā-Prakṛti, just as varied kinds of seeds hidden in the earth spring out in their time. Indeed, to the point that at the end of a Kalpa, Jīva does not merge in the Paramātmā but merges in Aparā-Prakṛti, and again at the beginning of the next Kalpa emanates from Aparā-Prakṛti. There is no end to the flow of the cycle of birth-death. That is similar to how as long as a seed is fit to provide fruits, the flow from seed to tree and tree to seed continues. The flow from Karma to body and body to Karma constantly continues as long as a Jīva, on the dependence of his nature, does not become pure by burning the dirt of Karma in the fire of knowledge. All these activities of Prakṛti happen only through the Paramātmā, Who continues to move those activities of Prakṛti without any desire. Without the power of the Paramātmā, Prakṛti is also unable to act on its own, and all these plays of Prakṛti happen on Its dependence.

भूमिरापोऽनलो वायुः खं मनो बुद्धिरेव च |
अहङ्कार इतीयं मे भिन्ना प्रकृतिरष्टधा || BG 7.4 ||

Earth, water, fire, wind, space, mind, intellect and ego are the distinct components of My eightfold nature.

अपरेयमितस्त्वन्यां प्रकृतिं विद्धि मे पराम् |
जीवभूतां महाबाहो ययेदं धार्यते जगत् || BG 7.5 ||

Hey Arjuna! That is My lower nature. Besides this, know My other higher life-form nature by which this world is upheld.

The above eightfold lower nature (Aparā-Prakṛti) is of the functional form (Kārya-Prakṛti) and is the transformation (विकृति, Vikṛti) of Prakṛti. However, separate from it, there is a higher nature (Parā-Prakṛti) of Mine, the Mulā (मूला) Prakṛti, which sustains the phenomenal world (Saṃsāra, Jagata). With its relationship, the conscious (Cetana) is named Jīva. Prakṛti in the deep-sleep state is called Parā-Prakṛti, and it is the transforming material cause or seed of the Saṃsāra. The same when it goes into the awake or the dream state, transforming the eightfold Aparā-Prakṛti creates the Saṃsāra.

The Paramātmā, without any mutation, is merely situated as the real witness-conscious and is the Vivartopādāna cause of the perceived Saṃsāra. Prakṛti transforming into the Saṃsāra is the transforming cause of the Saṃsāra. Additionally, Karma-Saṃskāras of a Jīva, as the cause, become the provider of inspiration to Prakṛti, and per his own Saṃskāras, the Jīva becomes an enjoyer. Just as a king's subordinates build palaces, gardens, and temples for his enjoyment on a mere clue, in a similar way, in the underlying truthiness of the Paramātmā, Parā-Prakṛti creates the Saṃsāra of enjoyments for the Jīva. Nevertheless, here there is not a bit of independent doership of Prakṛti. Her behavior is like an obedient servant dancing on the signals of the Jīva; the real doer is Jīva himself. He brings out his Prakṛti from within and creates the theater of Saṃsāra. After enjoying the play, he merges the entire Saṃsāra and Prakṛti in himself in the deep-sleep state and rests in the Paramātmā, just as a magician puts, after displaying his tricks, his illusions back in his pouch and reposes.

अत्र पितापिता भवति, मातामाता, लोका अलोकाः, देवा अदेवाः, वेदा अवेदाः । अत्र स्तेनोऽस्तेनो भवति, भ्रूणहाभ्रूणहा, चाण्डालोऽचण्डालः, पौल्कसोऽपौल्कसः, श्रमणोऽश्रमणः, तापसोऽतापसः, अनन्वागतं पुण्येनानन्वागतं पापेन, तीर्णो हि तदा सर्वाञ्छोकान्हृदयस्य भवति ॥[22]

Means (in that deep-sleep state) a father does not stay father. A mother does not stay mother, the world does not stay world, a Devatā does not stay Devatā, the Vedas do not stay Vedas, a thief does not stay thief, a murderer of a Brāhmaṇa does not stay murderer, a Cāṇḍāla (an outcast, a person of lowest and most despised of diverse casts born from a Śūdra father and a Brāhmaṇa mother) does not stay Cāṇḍāla, a Paulkasa (a person born from a Śūdra father and a Kṣatriya mother) does not stay Paulkasa, a Śramaṇa (one who performs acts of austerity, a monk, devotee, religious mendicant) does not stay Śramaṇa, and an ascetic does not stay an ascetic. (This form of his) is untouched by good work and unaffected by evil work, for he is then beyond all woes of his heart (all situated in oneness).

All distinctions remain here in the awake state, but there in the deep-sleep state, there is only unity in all. It is thus evident that all distinctions arise dependent on the enjoyments of individual Karma-Saṃskāras of Jīva. When those individual Karma-Saṃskāras become indifferent towards their enjoyments, then in the deep-sleep state, all differences evaporate, similar to camphor, which vanishes as soon as it is out of a closed container. Neither the place of enjoyment remains nor the Saṃsāra remains. Neither the enjoyments remain nor the enjoying body remains. Neither any class remains nor an individual remains. If the Saṃsāra, body,

[22] Bṛhadāraṇyaka Upaniṣad (बृहदारण्यक उपनिषद्) 4.3.22

and enjoyments existed without Karma-Saṃskāras, they should have been present when Karma-Saṃskāras were not awake but were in a state of ignorance. In the deep-sleep state, Karma-Saṃskāras remain in the state of ignorance, and that is why there is the merger of the Saṃsāra. When they awake in front of fruits, then from the deep-sleep state again, the Saṃsāra, enjoyments, and the enjoying body comes out. With this separation and connection, it is clear that the root of the Saṃsāra is the causal Karma-Saṃskāras of a Jīva and not any other cause. Without Karma-Saṃskāras, there is no other cause for the Saṃsāra. Jīva, with his own Karma-Saṃskāras, brings out his own Saṃsāra, like a spider who creates a web from silk within and ends up being caught in the web or like how a tiny seed of a banyan tree turns out into a massive tree. Jīva finds himself subordinated in the witnessing Paramātmā for the enjoyment of fruits of planted Karma-Saṃskāras. That is, Jīva, shrouded by ignorance, is himself the creator of pleasure and pain and is the enjoyer of fruits. To enjoy fruits of singular Karma-Saṃskāras, Jīva with discriminating doership-ego assumes different species (Yonis) such as deities, humans, animals, or aves. Except for the enjoyment of fruits, the nature of all is the same, like in the deep-sleep state where there is the oneness of all.

न कर्तृत्वं न कर्माणि लोकस्य सृजति प्रभु: |
न कर्मफलसंयोगं स्वभावस्तु प्रवर्तते || BG 5.14 ||

> The Lord creates neither doership nor actions nor conjunction of fruits of action in living beings. Instead, it is only nature that acts.

नादत्ते कस्यचित्पापं न चैव सुकृतं विभु: |
अज्ञानेनावृतं ज्ञानं तेन मुह्यन्ति जन्तव: || BG 5.15 ||

> The omnipresent Lord certainly does not take anyone's sin or piety. Knowledge is shrouded in ignorance, and therefore, all living beings are deluded.

The omnipresent Lord, meaning the pure Ātmā, does not take anyone's sin or piety. Sin or piety does not touch the pure Ātmā. Even though all sin and piety happen in its presence, none of them can taint it. Only due to ignorance, when a Jīva forgets his real omnipresent nature and, with the shrouding of discriminative knowledge, believes himself as a "bounded being" and thus doer of Karma and the Lord as the bestower of fruits, then based on the rules of Prakṛti, bounded by piety and sin, comes in the bondage of the enjoyership of fruits of happiness and grief. It is only due to this ignorance that all living beings are deluded. Only due to ignorance, the all-knowing Paramātmā is shrouded, by which, holding doership-ego, bound by his nature and falling in the bondage of enjoyership, a Jīva is deluded. The preceding shows that Karma-Saṃskāras of a Jīva create the Saṃsāra, and it is only there as a cause for the enjoyment of fruits. As long as Karma-Saṃskāras are present, there is no non-being of the Saṃsāra. As long as the Saṃsāra exists, where is freedom from birth and death? There cannot be an end of Karma-Saṃskāras without knowledge.

Without acquiring knowledge, when Jīva has enjoyed Prārabdha enjoyments and is on his deathbed, he becomes unaware (अचेत, Aceta) of the Saṃsāra. At that time, the senses, mind, and intellect get tired from the Saṃsāra and stop receiving signals from their respective objects. Then how can he see the Saṃsāra? The root of the Saṃsāra, the enjoyment impressions of Prārabdha, is already cut. They were the ones who had created them for his enjoyment, and their duty had already ended. Regardless of whether the body, family, or the Saṃsāra are on fire, anxious for the journey to the other world, he is ready to mount the horse (Prāṇa) by putting his feet on the stirrups. In this state, the senses, mind, and intellect become united in the bright space in the heart of the Jīva. Then, their functions cease, akin to when a king wants to travel, all his immediate subordinates desirous of going with him appear before him. At that time, all their relatives gather around him and reflect that now he has become unconscious, not speaking. The son says, "Hey, father! Why don't you love your beloved son?" The wife says, "Hey, love of my life! Who are you leaving me with?" However, he does not answer. Who is there to listen and speak? The servants who listen and speak are situated separately from the king. Who would bring the message there? It should not be understood that at this time, he is unconscious. He is indeed conscious (सचेत, Saceta) in his inner palace preparing for his trip, with his Sañcita-Kośa notepad open and busy making arrangements for necessities for travel (पाथेय, Pātheya) for his enjoyment. It is said in the Veda-Śāstra that when Prārabdha-Bhoga is fully depleted, then Jīva has a recollection of all past lives. However, it is impossible while being alive because the movie roll of Prārabdha is still mounted on the projector of enjoyments, so where is free time to turn around and see? However, when this movie roll ends, there is free time for remembering past lives. Together with the rules of Prakṛti, for the enjoyment of fruits, he then contemplates over all those Karma of past lives that have become dominant and suitable to give fruits. Then, he chooses for himself those enjoyments and type of life which he can enjoy under the rules of Prakṛti. Although no one would choose an inferior species such as a lion, snake, or scorpion, the influence of Māyā is such that in the frenzy of one's past Karma, one will unwittingly choose them, similar to how some prominent people under the influence of alcohol may decide to commit unacceptable deeds, never expected of them. Accordingly, in the bondage of Karma and a frenzy, he will choose what is in the fixed order of things (नियति, Niyati) of the rules of Prakṛti. Once he has taken his travel necessities, merging the ten senses, mind, and intellect in himself and taking complete accumulated Karma-Saṃskāras and new Prārabdha possessions mounts the horse (Prāṇa) for his trip to the next world and gees him up so fast that no one has any sight of him.

"येनेदं सर्वं विजानाति तं केन विजानियात्, the one who is the observer of all how can he be seen? "

Commensurate with what he had contemplated where he wanted to go and what enjoyments and Yoni he had chosen before departing from his kingdom, Udāna-Vāyu will make ready a new kingdom (body), new palace (heart), and his minister (intellect), companion (mind), servants (senses) and guards (Prāṇa) similar to how a dream-world is created. Then that king enters his palace, appoints his minister, companion, servants, and guards, and makes his own Saṃsāra of enjoyments.

यं यं वापि स्मरन्भावं त्यजत्यन्ते कलेवरम् |
तं तमेवैति कौन्तेय सदा तद्भावभावित: || BG 8.6 ||

Hey Arjuna! Even in the end, remembering whatever form one leaves the body, ever absorbed in that form, certainly acquires that.

Once again, activities of enjoyment and Karma commences. He tastes some sweet-sour fruits and sows more seeds in his heart with the desire to have more. As a result, the Karma (seed) and enjoyments (fruits) market remains warm and never cools down. It is the rule of Prakṛti that all efforts done by being a doer of Karma become seed-form, and when the seeds of Karma germinate, two shoots emerge, one in the form of enjoyments and the other in the form of desires (Vāsanā). The shoot of enjoyments immediately allows him to taste sweet-sour fruits and enjoyments of pleasure and pain. The second shoot of desires will leave in the heart of the doer aroma of impressions (Saṃskāras) and again put the doer in the bondage of enjoyment. Then, at the time of the enjoyment of fruits, it manifests as waves of desires in the doer's heart, and again the enjoyment of fruits makes him active in Karma. From that Karma, as previously depicted, present enjoyments and new desires will again arise. This way, Karma, from Karma to present enjoyments and future desires, from desires to Saṃskāras, from Saṃskāras to again desires for activity in Karma and from desires for Karma and again Karma, then enjoyments and desires and thus the flow of Karma is so consistent that it can never be calmed.

When Karma-Saṃskāras are still residual, how is it possible for the non-being of the body and the Saṃsāra? When all Karma are done in the witness of the existent Paramātmā, how is it conceivable for them not to give enjoyment? No matter how much anyone tries to hide them, can they be hidden from the one who observes and knows them? Is it possible to put salt in the eyes of the Trayambaka, the three-eyed Lord Śiva? Only a fool thinks that no one has seen him, but the observer is undoubtedly sitting in his heart, from where all desires, all resolves, and all efforts arise. How can there be a distance from It?

ईश्वर: सर्वभूतानां हृद्देशेऽर्जुन तिष्ठति || BG 18.61 ||

Hey Arjuna! The Lord is seated in the heart of all beings.

In all living beings, the Supreme Being sits in the bright space in the heart, a space for contemplation and immediate perception of the Brahman. When the enjoyment of the residual fruits of Karma is necessary, then the body and enjoyment materials are needed. Without enjoyment location and enjoyment materials, is enjoyment possible? When the body and the Saṃsāra are present, can birth and death be avoided? When birth and death are present, can there be an end to pain and sorrow? Therefore, for one who has an intense desire for liberation, depletion of Karma-Saṃskāras (the root of all evil) becomes their definite duty in the attainment of the Paramānanda.

Depletion of Karma is said to be of three types:

1. By the enjoyment of fruits (फलभोग, Phalabhoga).
2. By penance, expiation, or atonement (प्रायश्चित्त, Prāyaścitta).
3. By knowledge (ज्ञान, Jñāna).

First, depletion of Karma is always impossible with the enjoyment of fruits. Because with fruit-enjoyment where there is depletion of one Karma, at the same time, due to the presence of doership, performance of numerous new Karma will materialize, and that would be like a mustache getting heavier than the beard. Again, the enjoyment experienced was only of Prārabdha Karma in front. The repository of accumulated Karma (Sañcita-Kośa) is still sitting as it was and has not even come in front for enjoyment. So how can enjoyment of Sañcita-Kośa even happen in the present?

Second, depletion of Karma is unlikely with penance (Prāyaścitta). Its state is the same as fruit enjoyment. In scriptures, the efficacy of penance is enumerated only for sinful Karma. Nowhere in Śāstra can one find any statement articulating the depletion of pious Karma by penance. Therefore, for the enjoyment of pious Karma, the bondage of birth and death becomes unavoidable. Thus, penance cannot free one from the bondage of birth and death. In addition, where there is a penance of one sinful Karma, numerous new Karma of piety and sin will arise, as even emotional waves bursting in mind and intellect are also Karma. Whether they are good sentiments or evil, they all produce Saṃskāras of piety or sin. How can one stay without emotions as long as limited ego and doership are present? Furthermore, penance can only be of Prārabdha Karma, which is in front for enjoyment. Penance is impossible for those in Sañcita-Kośa that are not yet in front for enjoyment and are unknown. Thus, the cause of innumerable future births is certainly accumulated when depletion of accumulated Karma is not possible. What about Prārabdha Saṃskāras? Their depletion will happen after giving enjoyment; if not today, maybe tomorrow. Accordingly, complete depletion of Karma-Saṃskāras is neither possible by enjoyment nor penance. It is only possible by knowledge.

Therefore, if you desire complete depletion of Karma, then conflagrate a massive Jñānāgni in your heart, and there, burn all Karma of the past, present, and future, and let your ego melt. When you do not remain, who will be there for enjoyment? Can anyone bind the space? There is no other path.

अपि चेदसि पापेभ्य: सर्वेभ्य: पापकृत्तम: |
सर्वं ज्ञानप्लवेनैव वृजिनं सन्तरिष्यसि || BG 4.36 ||
यथैधांसि समिद्धोऽग्निर्भस्मसात्कुरुतेऽर्जुन |
ज्ञानाग्नि: सर्वकर्माणि भस्मसात्कुरुते तथा || BG 4.37 ||

Even if you are the most sinful of all sinners, you will undoubtedly cross over the entire ocean of sin with the boat of knowledge. Hey Arjuna! Just as a blazing fire turns firewood into ashes, the fire of knowledge reduces all actions into ashes

Freed from the delusional superimposition of the body on the Ātmā, a person, through the realization of Reality, happily crosses over the entire ocean on a boat without touching the water. That person who is situated in his own all-witness Ātmā embarking on the boat of knowledge, "I am not a doer-enjoyer of the constituents and duties of the body, mind, and senses, but always a witness-observer of their activities" - crosses over the entire ocean of sins easily. All actions and impressions (Saṃskāras) depend on the "I am a doer" ego, and all seeds of action blossom in this delusional egotistic earth. By burning delusional I-ness ego in the fire of knowledge, one who has found union in own Ātmā with oneness, all his accumulated past action seeds become seedless, and his current actions do not remain any cause as well.

What is the root of Karma?

I-ness ego in mind and intellect of Jīva is ongoing due to ignorance of his true nature. That is why, for anything done through the mind and intellect, he becomes the owner of its doership. Alongside the mind and intellect, Jīva has a oneness relationship (तादात्म्य, Tādātmya) with the body and senses. Consequently, he also becomes the owner of any activity appearing through them. In reality, the one in the form of "I" is the witness-conscious (Sākṣī-Cetana), illuminating the mind and intellect. It is in whose light, despite being insentient, they are becoming sentient; just like a piece of iron that is inanimate and without any light becomes illuminated by the contact with fire. The witness-conscious is indeed the true nature of Jīva. The light of knowledge in mind and intellect is not theirs, but indeed of the witness-conscious. The convincing measure of the aforementioned is that in the awake state, it is only when this witness-conscious provides its power to the mind, intellect, senses, and body that they can perform their respective functions, but in the dream state, when this witness-conscious abandons the bodily chariot and the sense-horses and has a relationship only with the mind and intellect, at that time the body and senses are removed from their posts just like servants who are not suitable to perform their duties when the king takes away their authority. Words may enter the ears but not heard; things may be in sight but not seen; materials with aroma may be next to the nose but olfactory sensations not felt; despite the relationship of sweets with taste, there is no taste, and neither materials soft as silk nor materials coarse as sandstones can provide sensation to the skin.

Moreover, they are dismissed when the witness-conscious abandons the mind and intellect in the deep-sleep state. There is neither any resolve nor any variant of the mind nor discrimination of the intellect. Then, in the awake state, like the sun, when that witness-conscious provides them its light, they become conscious, similar to how humans, animals, and birds all engage in their routines when the sun rises at dawn.

It is thus shown that in reality, the mind, intellect, senses, and body - all members of the family of ignorance (अविद्या, Avidyā)[23]who are insentient by nature are solely illuminated by the light of the witness-conscious. If they had their power and their own I-ness, then when the witness-conscious abandons them, their activities should have been ongoing, but that does not happen. It is thus clear that the "I," the one referred to as the Ātmā, is only the witness-conscious and not these insentient materials. Like the reflection of a face in a mirror, its power, consciousness, and I-ness are all mirrored in them, and they all, being gratified, get engaged in their activities. Because the mind and intellect are incredibly close to the witness-conscious, its I-ness and Ātmā-ness are manifest in the mind and intellect due to relational superimposition. Therefore, the mind and intellect are grasped in the form of "I" and in the form of the Ātmā. Delusion in a rope that "this is a snake," in reality, "this" form is only the rope, and the object of "this-ness (इदंता, Idaṃtā)" is also the rope, but because of delusory ignorance, relationship with this-ness of the rope is perceived in the snake. Accordingly, in the mind and intellect, a delusion is ongoing about the I-ness and Ātmā-ness of the witness-conscious.

---

[23] Avidyā (अविद्या) means ignorance, nescience. An elusive power (Śakti) in the Brahman which is sometimes regarded as one with Māyā and sometimes as different from it. It forms the condition of an individual Jīva and is otherwise called ignorance or impure-Māyā. It forms the causal body of a Jīva. It is the impure element.

Since there is a mutual nondifference (oneness) of the mind and intellect with the body and senses, through the mind and intellect, the I-ness ego of Jīva is also ongoing in the body and senses. Any emotion or effort that is manifest through the mind and intellect, or any act that is manifest through the body and senses with the knowledge of the mind and intellect, in all of them, Jīva shrouded by ignorance due to oneness attribution assumes ownership of "I am a doer." Any emotional wave or act produced through the mind and intellect or with the knowledge of the mind and intellect in the body or senses is defined as Karma.

भूतभावोद्भवकरो विसर्गः कर्मसञ्ज्ञितः || BG 8.3 ||

विसर्गः - activity ; भूत-भाव-उद्भव-करः - that produces sentiments in beings ; कर्म-संज्ञितः - is called "Karma."

Any activity that produces sentiments in beings is called Karma.

That is, a good or bad activity that produces sentiments (Bhāva) in human beings is defined as Karma. Any subjective process of arousing mental states or emotional waves originating in the mind and intellect in the form of a thought or resolve is called Bhāva. All activities of the body and senses, which are the direct result of the mind and intellect or occur in the knowledge of the mind and intellect being producers of emotions, are called Karma. The intention here is that all efforts that create enjoyments or impressions (Saṃskāras) are called Karma, and only in the mind and intellect those emotional activities can manifest and not anywhere else. Though after eating, myriads of actions happen within the body, such as feces, urine, blood, and muscles, they do not occur in the knowledge of the mind and intellect. They are neither the result of the mind and intellect nor do they create any good or bad impressions. Thus, they do not fall within the definition of Karma. Any Karma that arises through the mind, intellect, senses, and body in the form of activity must perish later. However, due to ignorance, Jīva develops a doership-ego in those activities, takes associated Karma-Saṃskāras within, and thus is bound by the enjoyment of fruits. As long as this ignorance-born doership-ego is present, Karma-Saṃskāras never ends because they are the root and support of all Karma. Until this root and support are entirely burnt, Karma-Saṃskāras can never be burnt. In reality, the pure Jīva is a non-doer, solely an observer, like a dancer who has received authority from a king, who performs various musicals with the help of her family, and the king is just the enjoyer. Similarly, having received power from Jīva, the mind, intellect, and their entire Avidyā family creates enjoyments and musicals (enjoyment-objects) on the stage (body) for the enjoyment of their king (Jīva). But in this musical, that witness-conscious forgetting his true nature is involved in the script of the dancer (and her family) in such a way that he forgets his reality and assumes the "I am a doer" ego in all of their activities and creative plays. Although he came only to see the musical, he got so enamored that instead of watching, he started to dance, and thus the market of hitting and getting hit became warm. Alas, grief! Extreme grief! O, Dancer! May you perish! You shrouded one on whose support you existed! You destroyed one who nurtured you! You threw scriptures at him, by whose grace you had obtained them! With your relationship, you put the unborn, the imperishable, into the bondage of birth and death. You turned the great into insignificant, the eternally pure to impure, and the blissful-quiescent nature into painful and restless! Confess! Who are you? From where have you come? What is your motive?

The response came -

"I am not something. Neither have I come from anywhere, nor do I have any motive. I am that groom's shadow only. Can a shadow be any different thing from the one with a shadow? In reality, I do not create any individualities separate from my groom, and I am he and he only. Do ocean waves keep separate reality from water, or do gold ornaments keep separate reality from gold? I am only my groom's shadow and his pride. I do not have any reality of my own. I am dancing only on the power of my groom, and the one making me with beingness and non-beingness is only my groom, whether he keeps me there or not. To the question - what am I? I have no voice. Only my groom can tell, so you should ask him what am I?"

Can shadow exist separate from a person? When does a person arrange for his shadow to remain with him? It always moves attached to him. Helpless with no place, how can she abandon him to go elsewhere? "I am my groom's shadow. Where can I stay away from my groom? Where do I have a place where I can abandon my groom and go elsewhere? On the contrary, without any arrangement, I move around with him. The answer needs to be elicited from you only to 'where have I come from?'."

Now remains the question of motive. What can be the answer? "Motive! Can there be any motive of my own? Has there been any motive for a devoted and virtuous wife? It is serving my husband with all my body and mind. Just for the pleasure of my husband, whether in the awake world or the sleep world, I instantaneously create varieties of mirror palaces so that he can be happy seeing his face in various intricate mirrors and enjoy his lovely face in different forms and showing his happiness honor me with the applause of claps that would further encourage me to vigorously dance on the beat of his claps and thereby please him more. Besides that, what else can be my motive? However, as I dance on a slight hint from my groom, my husband is so simple, gentle, and an embodiment of love that he becomes one with each of my creations without any discrimination. Therefore, because of his simplicity, in reality, he becomes a doer himself even though he is not doing anything, superimposing himself in my doership. Salutations! Salutations! Repeated Salutations for this simplicity and gentleness. Can one find such simplicity and gentleness anywhere in the Saṃsāra? Even the simplest space remains space after meeting a stone that is the grossest, or meeting water, fire, or wind that is very gentle does not become stone, water, fire, or wind. However, my husband is so simple that meeting an inanimate stone himself becomes inanimate, meeting fire becomes hot, meeting wind becomes mellow, and meeting water becomes liquid. Meeting attributes - becomes one with attributes, meeting acts - takes the form of acts, and meeting substance - himself becomes like a substance, without keeping even a tiny bit of own separate existence. Meeting far becomes far, meeting close becomes close. However, in reality, he is neither far nor close, neither hot nor cold, neither inanimate nor animate, and certainly not any attribute, act, or substance. Unique from all, he is as he was."

"तदेजति तन्नैजति तद्दूरे तद्वन्तिके । तदन्तरस्य सर्वस्य तदु सर्वस्यास्य बाह्यतः

He is walking, but not walking. He is farther than far, closer than close, within all and everything outside all."[24]

From a natural perspective, all kinds of Karma are ongoing because of the constituents of Prakṛti. Still, because of ego having acquired mental clouding, Jīva himself becomes the "doer I am." Though the true nature of Jīva is the pure witness-conscious, due to oneness with the mind, intellect, and senses, and attributing those Karma in himself, Jīva starts to yearn for their fruits and enjoyments. That is his bondage. Accordingly, the root and support of all Karma, all enjoyments, and the entire world of birth and death are solely this "I am a doer" self-ego. Until it is burnt, how can there be the end of enjoyments of Karma and the end of birth and death even with the passage of infinite Kalpas? The only possibility of burning it is in the fire of knowledge, never with Karma. Doership-ego is not any earthen pot or a substance that can be smashed into pieces with a truncheon, like removing dirt from clothes with soap or making a garment bright by dyeing it with a bright color. Neither can it be removed by acts of penance like those ordained for penance of sin, nor can it be removed using transforming acts like how gold can be converted into ornaments. In removing the doership-ego, separate from the supra, there is no use of Karma, and axiomatically, all of them cannot be successful by their nature. For Karma, there can be only five infra objectives:

1. Creation of a substance.
2. Destruction of a substance.

---

[24] Īśa Upaniṣad (ईश उपनिषद्) 5

3. Receipt of a substance.
4. Mutation of a substance. (Like the usefulness of fire in transforming wheat flour to bread.)
5. Attribution. (Like dirt removal attribute of garments.)

However, removal of the doership-ego is always impossible through these objectives of Karma. The point herein is that through Karma, there is no possible way to remove it. On the contrary, Karma will make it firmer because activity cannot be accomplished without a doer. Doership is the one and the only disease. How can dirt be removed by dirtying? That is like extracting butter from water. Those things born of ignorance can be removed by knowledge, those born without thought can be removed by analytic thinking, and those shown as born of darkness can only be removed by light and not with anything else.

There is a saga that in Uttarākhaṇḍa, in a deserted hilly location, there was a village of uncivilized people who had never seen darkness in their entire lifetime. They worked very hard during the day and at sunset went to sleep, and in the morning on sunrise, they would wake up and once again go to work. While wandering one day, one of them saw a cave full of darkness in the nearby mountain. Since he had never seen darkness in his life, being amidst darkness, he got petrified and ran to his village to get some men back to the cave. When the men came and saw darkness, they all got perplexed and thought amongst themselves that "definitely in this place a ghost has come who will kill us all when we go to sleep and so before others return to the village, we should move him away." Having thought so, they all started to beat up the ghost with their spears and arrows with bravery. Hours went by, and they all got exhausted, but the spirit had not even moved an inch. He was situated as he was. After some time, one elderly person came and advised, "this ghost is not going to move by weapons; to move him away, you need to donate. If you donate, he will go away by himself once he is pleased." Accepting the older person's advice, they all donated by their respective abilities, but he did not move. They were highly perplexed and started to think that he would eat their children and domestic animals if they did not find a way to remove him soon. One came up with the idea that chants and prayers may remove him if all unite and pray to the Lord. Accepting such an idea, they started to chant and pray, but to no avail. He was still there. Some travelers from a distant city happened to pass by and were amused to see what was happening. The travelers told them, "We know how to get rid of the ghost instantaneously. Just gather some oil, some old rags, and a long piece of a bamboo stick." Upon hearing this, the villagers became happy and gathered the requested items. The travelers took the rags, attached them to a bamboo stick, and made a torch. After fully immersing the rags in oil, they lit it, and when the torch was fully lit, they told the villagers, "Come follow us. We will remove the ghost right now." They all followed behind the brightly lit torch, and combed the entire cave, behold, the ghost was nowhere to be found, and finally, the villagers became happy and found peace.

While this darkness of ignorance is situated with firmness in the heart-form cave, and the business of activity is ongoing in the mind, intellect, senses, and body through the constituents of Prakṛti, sitting in the midst, Jīva has assumed himself as a doer, now how can this darkness be removed without the light of knowledge?

प्रकृते: क्रियमाणानि गुणै: कर्माणि सर्वश: |
अहङ्कारविमूढात्मा कर्ताहमिति मन्यते || BG 3.27 ||

In all ways, actions are being done by the constituents of Prakṛti only. However, one whose mind is deluded by egoism thinks, "I am a doer."

Whatever activities happen through all living beings happen only through the three constituents (Sattva, Rajas, and Tamas) of Prakṛti. However, one who has acquired mental clouding due to ego, right in the midst, believes "I am a doer." In summary, without the light of knowledge, the darkness-ignorance of presuming other's duties and Karma in oneself cannot be removed by Karma.

What is the root of Doership?

The root of the doership is the discriminating vision. Whenever there is a desire to acquire something unattainable and to remove antagonistic things, or there is a perception of mutation in one's self or someone else, and there is a desire to remove it or have it removed in others, it is then that the sentiment of doership arises in a Jīva, which is indeed due to discriminating-vision. When a Jīva knows his Ātmā limited by time and space as something else and the Saṃsāra as something else separate from himself, it is then that doership is born in him. Had Jīva, with pure Sāttvika knowledge, realized his Ātmā equally existent in the Saṃsāra of dissimilarities and as one immutable in all mutations, and had he seen himself only as one impartite Ātmā in all divided beings, then how can there be any doership possible?

सर्वभूतेषु येनैकं भावमव्ययमीक्षते |
अविभक्तं विभक्तेषु तज्ज्ञानं विद्धि सात्त्विकम् || BG 18.20 ||

> Know that knowledge to be Sāttvika by which one sees one undivided immutable existent in all separate living beings.

From the unmanifest to stationary and movable, there is only one undivided existent in all beings - the Supreme Reality. The Supreme Reality does not mutate by itself or through mutation of its attributes. It is one and the only cause of all beings. That knowledge by which all beings are perceived in the form of the Existent-Conscious-Bliss, the cause of all, such oneness knowledge ought to be known as Sāttvika, like waves or eddies though dissimilar are only water. Large, small, tall, short, formation, or destruction are modifications of waves and not water, which "is as is" in all states. How can a display of waves be beloved to one with only water vision? If oneness-vision was fully ripened, doership can't form, even if the purest act of public service is in front. That is because discriminating mutations would not be perceived in his Ātmā with his water vision. When Jīva has made a steadfast resolve, "In my Ātmā, the movable and immovable Saṃsāra, earth, mountains, trees are like a dream. They are only delusionally perceived, and there is no contact of them in my infinite Ātmā," then how can he become a doer and how can he be active in any Karma? Even if any unrestrained activity naturally manifests through his body and senses, they are only just for pastime. They cannot be with any sentiment of doership or a desire for reward. Thus, the root of doership is only the discriminating vision born of ignorance.

What is the cause of Discriminating-Vision?

Limited vision is the cause of discriminating vision. That is, knowing one's Ātmā is limited to only one region. When Jīva believes that he belongs only to one area, he knows others as separate from himself and thus sees the Saṃsāra of distinctions. Had Jīva, through Sāttvika knowledge, known his Ātmā as pervasive without limitations of time and space, then he would not have perceived the Saṃsāra with distinctions. Indeed, the pervasive ocean does not see any difference in itself from waves or eddies but sees them like water. The pervasive space does not distinguish itself from the earth, mountains, trees, forests, or habitations but sees them in the form of space. Even if a human staying separate from an ocean makes a resolve that the waves are separate from the ocean and staying separate from the space makes a resolve that the earth, mountains, or trees are separate from the space, the ocean or the space do not see these modifications in them. Thus, the cause of discriminating vision is knowing one's Ātmā in some limited form, and because of this limitation, Jīva has bondage to the mind, intellect, senses, and body. When Jīva cognizes his Ātmā is limited in time and space in as much time and space as the mind, intellect, senses, and body reside, then his Ātmā has a delusion of oneness with them. With such delusional cognition of oneness (तादात्म्याध्यास, Tādātmyādhyāsa), when in reality, there is no oneness with them, he adopts their nature. He is then entangled in the bondage of birth-death and doership-enjoyership. Had he in his ignorance not known his Ātmā limited by time and space at the time and space when and where the mind, intellect, and senses resided, but through knowledge known it as pervasive throughout all time and space, then he would not have had oneness of nature with the mind, intellect, and senses. Accordingly, if Jīva had no oneness delusion with them, then he would not have had bondage with birth-death and doership-enjoyership. Thus, it is evident that the root of all bondages and all distinctions is knowing one's Ātmā as something limited. That is ignorance. That is Avidyā. That is Māyā!

What is the reality of Discrimination and Limitation?

In reality, the pure Ātmā is ever free from time and material produced limitations as well as all homogeneous (सजातीय, Sajātīya), heterogeneous (विजातीय, Vijātīya) and intrinsic (स्वगत, Svagata) distinctions. All distinctions and limitations are merely delusional, not real (मायामात्र, Māyāmātra). Had these distinctions and limitations been real, their removal is not possible through knowledge but can only be accomplished by Karma. With knowledge, it is not possible to cut any material thing. The fruit of knowledge is to remove the ignorance in support of the thing. In reality, the Ātmā is ever stainless from all distinctions and limitations; all mutations are born of ignorance, and thus, their removal is only possible by Sāttvika knowledge.

यज्ज्ञात्वा न पुनर्मोहमेवं यास्यसि पाण्डव |
येन भूतान्यशेषेण द्रक्ष्यस्यात्मन्यथो मयि || BG 4.35 ||

> Hey Arjuna! Knowing That, you will not acquire delusion again, and by which you will completely see all beings in your Self and thus in Me.

With the influence of that knowledge, you will see the entire humanity, all living beings in your Ātmā, as your miraculous waves. With the creation and destruction of those waves in the ocean of your Ātmā, there is no increase or decrease, and you will know the oneness of your Ātmā and Me, the Paramātmā. In one pervasive space, when pots of various sizes, quantities, and shapes are present, due to those distinct adjuncts (Upādhi), the pervasive space taking the form of those adjuncts appears as if it had adjuncts of various sizes, quantities, and shapes similar to those of the pots. In a spherical adjunct, it appears as spherical. In a cylindrical adjunct, it appears as cylindrical. In a cubic adjunct, it appears as cubic. In a large adjunct, it appears as large. In a small adjunct, it appears as small, as many pot-enclosed spaces are perceived as there are adjuncts. Separateness and division of one adjunct from another are perceived as separateness and division of pot-enclosed spaces. Not only that, but with the creation of pots, the creation of pot-enclosed spaces, the destruction of pots, the destruction of pot-enclosed spaces, and the going and coming of the pots, the going and coming of the pot-enclosed spaces are seen. However, in the pure space, without the adjuncts of pots, there is neither any form nor shape, there is neither any number nor measure, there is neither separateness nor conjunction or division, there is neither creation nor destruction, and there is neither going nor coming. Rather, in all of these distinctions and limitations, the pure space "is as is." Only with the attributes of the adjuncts during the time of ignorance is there an imagination of the enclosed (Upahita) space. In reality, even in the presence of the adjuncts, there is no touch of the attributes of the adjuncts in the enclosed space. Not only does the space not see any kind of adjuncts in its form, but in the creation, sustentation, and destruction of the adjuncts sees nothing but itself and does not even have any ego of those adjuncts.

Correspondingly, the pervasive-distinctionless-conscious Ātmā is the only one existent in the various bodies, senses, consciences, and the immovable and movable external Saṃsāra. That conscious existent in those distinctly separate adjunct spaces is perceived as distinctly separate in those adjuncts; and joining with individual shapes of the adjunct appears of similar shape as the adjunct, like "I am tall," "I am short," "I am skinny," "I am fat," and so on. Joining with the adjunct of the senses is perceived with senses, like "I am with eyes," "I am blind," "I am without hands," and so on. Joining with the adjunct of the conscience, "I am with good intellect," "I am with poor intellect," "I am generous," and "I am stingy" are perceived. Joining with individual adjuncts of a class is perceived as possessing class, like "I am a human," "I am an animal," I am a bird," "I am a Brāhmaṇa," "I am a Kṣatriya," "I am a Vaiśya," "I am a Śūdra," and so on. Due to the distinction of the number of adjuncts, it is perceived as possessing numbers, like the number of humans on the earth is almost eight billion. With the adjuncts of separateness, conjunction, and division, it is seen as having separateness, conjunction, and division, like "I am separate, they are separate, I have conjunction with some, and I have a division with some." Thus, born with the birth of adjuncts and dead with the destruction of adjuncts, one with sixfold mutations (Ṣaḍvikāra) of the adjuncts, and with coming and going of the adjuncts, it is seen as one with the attributes of coming or going, like "I am born," "I am situated," "I am growing," "I am becoming resultant," "I am diminishing," "I am dying," "I am coming or going" and so on. However, without the adjuncts, the Ātmā does not have any shape, neither class nor any number, neither effect nor separateness, neither division nor conjunction, and neither going nor coming. By the abandonment of body adjuncts, it does not create any number; it is not one, nor is eight billion. By the abandonment of sense adjuncts, neither is it with eyes nor is it without eyes, it is neither with hearing ability nor is it deaf, it is neither with feet nor is it without feet, and so on. By the abandonment of the conscience adjuncts, it is neither with good intellect nor is it with poor intellect, neither is it endowed with reason nor is it destitute of reason. It is null related to all distinctions and limitations - always situated within itself "is as is." What is happening is that there is an imagined behavior of the adjunct-attributes in the Upahita witness-conscious only. There is never any touch of the adjuncts and their attributes in the Upahita witness-conscious. The Upahita witness-conscious does not see any adjuncts in its true nature. However, in all states of adjuncts (creation, sustentation, and destruction), it sees itself "is as is" and in no way is conscious of those adjuncts. In reality, it is only in the adjunct view that all adjuncts are perceived.

यथाकाशस्थितो नित्यं वायु: सर्वत्रगो महान् |
तथा सर्वाणि भूतानि मत्स्थानीत्युपधारय || BG 9.6 ||

Just as the mighty and moving everywhere wind always exists in the space; similarly, know that all beings exist in Me.

Just as the space is always immovably existent, and the great wind moving all over in the space cannot move it or even touch it, in the same way, all beings on My dependence acquiring birth, sustentation, and death cannot move Me nor any of their mutations touch Me. All successes of "being" and "not-being" happen with My support. However, I am dissociated from those being and not-being manifestations, and I do not see them in Me.

यथा सर्वगतं सौक्ष्म्यादाकाशं नोपलिप्यते |
सर्वत्रावस्थितो देहे तथात्मा नोपलिप्यते || BG 13.32 ||

Just as the all-pervading space is not stained due to its subtlety, so is the Self, present everywhere in the body, not stained.

The space is ubiquitous and subtle. The entire phenomenal world of pots and pans is created on its dependence. Without the subtle space, the creation of the phenomenal world is impossible. Again, the destruction of the phenomenal world also happens on the dependence on space. However, with the creation and destruction of the phenomenal world, there is no creation and destruction of space. The space is unstained by that creation and destruction. In the same manner, pervading everywhere in all bodies, the Ātmā is unstained by mutations (विकार, Vikāra) of the bodies, notwithstanding the fruition of all those mutations happens on the dependence of the Ātmā.

Having clarified the true nature of the witness-conscious Ātmā and adjuncts, we now need to examine the test of the tactic. The elucidation of the nature of real (Sat) and unreal (Asat) cannot be anything other than those things that permeate the entire space and all times (past, present, and future) as real, and those things that are in a limited space and limited time as unreal. Things that are in some space and not in some others and are in some time and not in some others by their nature possess the attribute of origination and destruction. With some deliberation, it is clear that whatever Saṃsāra of the great elements is standing is only graspable by the senses. Only the senses can cognize it. Without the senses, there is no awareness of it. If in the Saṃsāra there were no form-sensing cognitive-sense eyes, then there would not be any sense of form in any substance. If there were no taste-sensing cognitive-sense tongue, the taste would not make any difference. If there were no cognitive smell sense, there would not be any aroma smell. If there were no cognitive touch sense, there would not be any sense of contact. Again, if there were no cognitive sense like ears, then there would not be any sense of sound. The real measure of this is found in the deep-sleep state when the senses merge in their cause. There is a complete absence of the five objects of the senses. Had the five objects of senses been independent of the senses (इन्द्रिय-निरपेक्ष, Indriya-Nirapekṣa), then in the deep-sleep state, they would have been grasped when the senses are merged in their cause. However, all beings only grasp sense-dependent (इन्द्रिय-सापेक्ष, Indriya-Sāpekṣa) objects in the awake and dream state.

With the merger of the senses, nobody grasps sense objects in the deep-sleep state. Separate from the five objects of senses, viz., touch, taste, form, smell, and sound, one cannot find any other form of the Saṃsāra. The Saṃsāra is only "पञ्च-विषयात्मक, Pañca-Viṣayātmaka," consisting of the five objects of senses, and is only sense-dependent; and that too individually dependent. The form is only graspable by the eyes and not by the ears. Sound is only ear-graspable and not eye-graspable. They can individually grasp only their object and not grasp anyone else's object. Accordingly, in the Saṃsāra, without objects grasping senses, sense objects are absent at all times - past, present, and future. Those things that are perceived only in their ordinary operative time and not in other separate times, bounded by time and space, are apparent. They are not there. They are only delusional (Mithyā). In reality, even during their perception time, they are objects of delusional perception, like a snake (in a rope) is only perceived in its ordinary operative time. In reality, they are certainly not there.

Such delusive adjunct Saṃsāra is not capable of putting its mutational stain on its underlying support, the witness-conscious. A delusional thing, by its nature, is not something that can stay on its own support but is only delusionally perceived on the support of some reality, some truth (Satya). For instance, apparent silver is only perceived on the support of a real oyster shell. However, in reality, it is nothing. It is impossible to have a perception of a delusional thing unless there is a true, real thing under it. It is without any reality. It does not have its existence but appears to be real only because of the reality of its underlying support. Like the existenceless silver is only perceived as existent due to the existence of the oyster shell. In reality, it is null. The number zero (0) does not have any value, but it becomes valuable when added after one (1). By its nature, the Saṃsāra is ever-transforming and perishable. It can seldom be stable, so it is delusional (Mithyā) and is certainly not there. Indeed, it needs something immutable and imperishable underneath, on whose support the perception of the delusional Saṃsāra is possible. Without real underlying support, perception of the unreal is impossible. What can that be? It can only be the Trikālabādhya (त्रिकालबाध्य)[25]limitless true witness-conscious. Having acquired beingness with the power of the underlying witness-conscious, the adjunct-form Saṃsāra is perceived as real. However, it cannot have its reality. It cannot stain the underlying support by its mutation, just as the water of a mirage cannot wet the earth, an illusional snake cannot make a rope poisonous, or a wealthy person appearing in a dream as a beggar does not become poor. There is a tenet in the kingdom of Prakṛti that only substances of equal reality can be each other's helpers or opposers.

Substances of different realities cannot be mutual helpers or opposers. A dream fire cannot burn a live body, though it can be painfully hot for the dream body, but not for the live body. For the live body, the heat of the dream body cannot touch it. Accordingly, the adjunct-form Saṃsāra has practical or ordinary Reality, and its engagements are only in the ordinary operative time. However, the supporting witness-conscious

[25] Trikālabādhya (त्रिकालबाध्य) means one whose determination of unreality (मिथ्यात्व-निश्चय, Mithyātva-Niścaya) cannot be made in the past, present and future.

has transcendental Reality, is ipso facto (Svataḥ-Siddha) at all times - past, present, and future, and is the illuminator of all being and non-being of ordinary substances. Therefore, the ordinary adjunct substances being of dissimilar reality cannot stain the witness-conscious. Had there been any stain of the mutation of the adjunct on the underlying supporting witness-conscious, then there would not have been any perception of the adjunct later on; because a mutable thing at a later moment is always perishable, unlikely ever stable. Just as the flow of Gaṅgā transforms every moment, so do mutable things transform every moment, heading in the mouth of time, never to remain. With the mutations of the adjunct, if the underlying support had acquired a perishable attribute, who would be there to illuminate the adjunct? Who would prove the existence of the adjunct? One cannot prove the "non-being" of a thing with a "non-being" thing. Only a "being" thing can prove the "non-being" of a thing. The adjunct Saṃsāra is always perceived in the form of "is." Like the pot is, the space is, the earth is, the water is, etc. It is in a complete "non-being" form in its nature. Notwithstanding the Saṃsāra being of a "non-being" form, with the "being" of the supreme witness-conscious, it is perceived in the "being" form. For instance, a wave has a non-being form and does not have its reality by its nature. Notwithstanding being a non-being form, it is still perceived as a being form because of the reality of the being-form water. It is thus amply evident that the adjunct-form Saṃsāra has no taint on the underlying support witness-conscious but is perceived as real solely because of the reality of its underlying support and not because of its nature as its reality is but nil. For example, an anvil, remaining grounded and thus stationary, allows the making of various ornaments. However, if due to repeated blows it becomes ungrounded, then the creation of ornaments is impossible. This way, the witness-conscious Ātmā remains immutable and provides evidence of the adjunct-form Saṃsāra. It is thus clear that there is non-being of an unreal thing even if it is perceived because, in reality, it is not there; but only by its perception indicates that there is some real immovable thing. It is like an illusory snake that is not there, but its perception provides the presence of the real rope. There is truly no non-being of a real thing, even if it is not perceived through gross vision. It is always there. There is no non-being of the Ātmā at all times - past, present, and future and there is no being at any time of the Saṃsāra of distinctions and limitations.

नासतो विद्यते भावो नाभावो विद्यते सतः |
उभयोरपि दृष्टोऽन्तस्त्वनयोस्तत्त्वदर्शिभिः || BG 2.16 ||

There is no being of the unreal, and there is no non-being of the real. The truth about both is perceived by seers of Reality.

अविनाशि तु तद्विद्धि येन सर्वमिदं ततम् |
विनाशमव्ययस्यास्य न कश्चित्कर्तुमर्हति || BG 2.17 ||

However, know That (Self) to be imperishable by which all this is pervaded. None can destroy that Immutable (Self).

अन्तवन्त इमे देहा नित्यस्योक्ताः शरीरिणः |
अनाशिनोऽप्रमेयस्य तस्माद्युध्यस्व भारत || BG 2.18 ||

These bodies that perish are said to be of the eternal, imperishable, and indeterminable embodied Self. Therefore, hey, Arjuna! Fight.

An unreal thing is not present at any time. Its perception in the present time is like a snake in a rope, merely a delusion of the senses. In reality, it is not even present in its time of perception. There is no absence of the real thing at any time. A real thing not perceived due to the influence of delusion is still there "is as is," just as during the snake perception time, even if the rope is not perceived, it is still there. Various seers of the Truth have cogitated upon such subtlety of the real and unreal. Hence, one ought to know the imperishable thing by whom all this Saṃsāra is made complete. Without the imperishable, who can hold the perishable Saṃsāra? No one is competent to destroy the indestructible. All the bodies of the imperishable, indeterminable, and eternal Ātmā are perishable. They are only clues, and so Bhagavāna Śrī Kṛṣṇa guides Arjuna to stand up and fight and not to think about all the delusional bodies of relatives who are ready to fight him. Had the adjunct-form Saṃsāra been real, it should have been perceived in other states. However, it is perceived only in its own operative time. In the awake state, neither the dream-Saṃsāra remains nor the deep-sleep, and in the dream state, neither the awake-Saṃsāra remains nor the deep-sleep, and in the deep-sleep state, neither the awake nor the dream state remains. That is why all states are faltering. That thing which is sometimes there and sometimes not there, being time and space bounded, can only be unreal (Mithyā), and that is how by its nature, the Saṃsāra is. However, the Ātmā is present in all states. It is the observer and knower of all states and is the one that illuminates all states by its light. When a Jīva comes out of the dream and deep-sleep into the awake state, it provides an unmistakable witness of seeing and knowing all states. It says, "In the dream, I saw that the state was very erratic, sometimes I was an elephant, sometimes a horse, a sparrow, sometimes a billionaire, and in the deep sleep I saw that there was nothing, there was no element such as space and earth, there was no body, senses, mind, and intellect, there was nothing, there was only bliss and only bliss. In the awake state, I am seeing this whole Saṃsāra." From the above, it is clear that the observer of all three states is some one observer alone, and that can only be the witness-conscious Ātmā, who is present in all states, and who is providing direct evidence of observing in all states. It does not provide any hearsay account but a direct eyewitness account, immutable in all states. That is, it is observing and knowing. Distinct from it, the body, senses, mind, and intellect possessing the attributes of rising and setting cannot be observers but only remain as the observed scene. Had that observer been mutable from the mutations of the states, then those mutations should have been perceived in those states. However, that is not so. The pleasure and pain of the awake state do not remain in the dream state, and the pleasure and pain of the dream state do not stay in the awake state. It is thus clear that the Ātmā is only a witness and "is as is," without any mutations in all states. It is the Real, the Truth, and the omnipresent-pervasive in all space and time. The body, senses, mind, and intellect are like clothing. They have no adherence to it and are discarded when their own time comes. A person does not become the garment he wears. With the dilapidation of the garments, he does not become dilapidated.

Similarly, the Ātmā is distinct from the body, senses, mind, and intellect. It is immutable from their mutations. The body and senses are shed from it in the dream state like a person removes his coat and hangs it on a hook. The mind and intellect are also shed from it in the deep sleep state, like a person removing his work clothes and going to bed. If there had been any stain to the Ātmā from the awake body, senses, and thus pleasure and pain, they would have remained with him in the dream state and the deep-sleep state. If there had been any adherence to the mind and intellect, they would have remained in the deep-sleep state, but not all these remain.

न जायते म्रियते वा कदाचित नायं भूत्वा भविता वा न भूय: |
अजो नित्य: शाश्वतोऽयं पुराणो न हन्यते हन्यमाने शरीरे || BG 2.20 ||

This Self is never born and never dies at any time, nor having existed before again becomes non-existent. It is unborn, eternal, everlasting, and ever-new. It is not destroyed upon the destruction of the body.

वासांसि जीर्णानि यथा विहाय नवानि गृह्णाति नरोऽपराणि |
तथा शरीराणि विहाय जीर्णा न्यन्यानि संयाति नवानि देही || BG 2.22 ||

Just as a person discards worn clothes and takes new ones, so does the embodied Self, dumping dilapidated bodies, occupies other new ones.

The observer and knower of all states, who is unstained by all states, who is the dweller in all times and space, and who is free from all limitations of time and space is the Reality, and that is the Ātmā. The world of the body, senses, mind, and intellect is only a clue, and the Ātmā is the observer and knower of the being and non-being of the Saṃsāra and is dissociated from those being and non-being. Only by its light, all have become illuminated, and only by its being existent, all are perceived as existing. "सोऽहमस्मि, That I am." There is no distinction between the witness-conscious in the bodily space and the pervasive witness-conscious. Only because of the adjunct of the body, there is a con-adjunct imagination of distinction in the pervasive witness-conscious. In reality, there is only oneness. With an adjunct of a pot, the distinction between a pot-enclosed space and the pervasive space is imagined, but the adjunct-form pot has not separated the pot-enclosed space from the pervasive space. Indeed, there is always oneness between the pot-enclosed space and the pervasive space.

Depletion of Karma is possible through Knowledge

A fit one, endowed with the fourfold means (Sādhana-Catuṣṭaya), in whose pure heart the flow of analytic thought has flourished, whose "I-ness sense" from the body, senses, mind, and intellect has dissolved, and one who has found I-ness in his true witness-conscious Ātmā, his limited-vision, "I am only in this much time and space and not in other time and space" is removed on its own. When he finds only his Ātmā enjoying bliss in all-space, all-time, and all-material form waves, then, where is any room for discriminating-vision of he is someone, I am some other? With oneness vision, "आत्मैवेदं, all this is only the Ātmā," there is nothing left to be acquired nor anything to relinquish. Then, where is free time for doership, and what duty? It becomes necessary for the ghost of doership and duty to hang overhead as long as grasping and relinquishing intellect due to discriminating vision is present. However, with the influence of the analytic perspective, there is nothing about to happen left in the Ātmā. When one does not see anything mutable happen in the Ātmā and one does not find any reality of the Saṃsāra of I-you distinct from the Ātmā, then where is the place for grasping and relinquishing? When grasping and relinquishing are cleaned out, where is the free time for doership and duty? Doership and duty are produced by grasping and relinquishing intellect with I-ness in the limited body. However, with analytic thinking, when I-ness sense in the nescience world of the mind and intellect is burnt and when one is situated with firmness in the limitless true witness-conscious, the absence of grasping and relinquishing, it is natural for doership and duty to be burnt. It is like one awake from a dream who does not find any taint of doership in the Ātmā and does not see anything happening in the Ātmā, then why would the boat of Karma-Saṃskāras not sink? In the ignorance-sleep, doer and Karma are born of discriminating-vision, and they have become the substratum of Karma-Saṃskāra. However, when knowledge devoid of all discriminations is awakened, there is complete depletion of Karma and Karma-Saṃskāras on their own.

Delusional ignorance born I-ness ego holds the body, senses, mind, and intellect strung in its string just as beads threaded in a rosary stay together and cannot be separated. However, through knowledge, when the I-ness ego form string is broken, and "I," the witness-conscious is found situated with firmness in one's own Ātmā, the entire family of the body, senses, mind, and intellect is shattered just like beads of a rosary are scattered all over upon breaking of the thread. When causal acts and thus all activities of a doer and Karma become oppressed, then whether it is a cause, whether it is an act, whether it is a doer or whether it is Karma - all relationships are proven as apparent or illusory forms (Vivarta) of one's Ātmā. Then, devoid of relationships, all instruments that bring about action appear as miracles of the Ātmā. In a dream, a dreamer sees himself as a potter, a pot, a father, and a son and perceives causes and acts that have not occurred. The imagination of causes and acts is ignorance by itself. That is bondage. By analytic vision, it is successfully removed on its own. All efforts in the form of Karma happen through the work of Prakṛti (the body, mind, intellect, and senses). The delimited Ātmā, because of ignorance, is holding a delusional ego about those activities in itself. However, it realizes that it was never a doer when it sees with real vision with analytic thinking. It was solely ever-observer-witness and unnecessarily assumed doership of the business of others, got into the bondage of enjoyership, and thereby like a clock, was circling in the wheel of birth and death.

पुरुषः प्रकृतिस्थो हि भुङ्क्ते प्रकृतिजान्गुणान् |
कारणं गुणसङ्गोऽस्य सदसद्योनिजन्मसु || BG 13.21 ||

Puruṣa seated in Prakṛti experiences the constituents born of Prakṛti. Attachment to the constituents is only the cause of its birth in superior and inferior wombs.

उपद्रष्टानुमन्ता च भर्ता भोक्ता महेश्वरः |
परमात्मेति चाप्युक्तो देहेऽस्मिन्पुरुषः परः || BG 13.22 ||

Puruṣa seated in the body is unassociated with Prakṛti and is said to be the Close Observer, the Sanctioner, the Sustainer, the Experiencer, the Maheśvara, and the Paramātmā.

The Puruṣa sitting in Prakṛti is enjoying the constituents born of Prakṛti. His relationship with the constituents is only the reason for his taking birth in superior and inferior species. Staying extremely close to the activities of body, senses, mind, and intellect (instruments for Karma and enjoyments) and sitting dissociated in them, not doing anything, just being an observer, the Puruṣa is said to be the Close Observer (उपद्रष्टा, Upadraṣṭā), just as someone proficient in oblation science (यज्ञ-विद्या, Yajña-Vidyā) not performing oblations himself, just neutrally observes merits and faults in activities of oblations performed by family priests and institutors of oblations. Without being active in the activities of the conscience and senses, seen as agreeable, being a witness of the activities of the conscience and not ever preventing it, thereby providing real sanction, the Puruṣa is said to be the Sanctioner (अनुमन्ता, Anumantā), just as in his dance performance a lead actor provides beats to an actress giving his approval. With His power, holding and sustaining the body, the Puruṣa is said to be the Sustainer (भर्ता, Bhartā). Sense-objects related dispositions in the form of pleasure and pain of the conscience seem to be grasped through the perception of the Puruṣa. Instincts in the form of "I am happy, I am unhappy" occur only because of the proximity of the Puruṣa and so the term Bhartā. With some thought, one can see that the terms Observer, Sanctioner, Sustainer, and Experiencer are applied to the activities of Prakṛti because of the proximity of the witnessing Puruṣa. In reality, the Puruṣa, being the master of all, is called the Great Supreme Lord (महेश्वर, Maheśvara, Lord Śiva), and being the Ātmā of all, movable and immovable beings, and thus with own pure Saccidānanda form is called the Supreme Being (परमात्मा, Paramātmā). With the adjuncts of pots, just as there is no distinction and limitation of the space, in the same manner, with the adjuncts of bodies, there are no distinctions and limitations of the Puruṣa. It is ever and devoid of distinctions and limitations in its true nature.

Just as Bhasmāsura,[26] enamored with the dance of Mohinī,[27] began to dance with her and unwittingly put his hand over his head and thereby burnt himself to ashes, in the same way, enchanted by the dance of Prakṛti, the Puruṣa himself joins in the dance and on his own becomes bound to Prakṛti. However, when Jīva opens his third eye of knowledge, the entire Prakṛti and its family turn into ashes. All bondages are shattered like one awake from a dream finds himself ever-free and dissociated. Just as the creation and end of the fire, rain and storm in support of the space cannot heat the space, nor can it wet it, nor move it, in the same way, he comes to know that neither did he ever have any relationship nor will he ever have a relationship with all Karma, Karma-Saṃskāras and the five causes of Karma.

अधिष्ठानं तथा कर्ता करणं च पृथग्विधम् |
विविधाश्च पृथक्चेष्टा दैवं चैवात्र पञ्चमम् || BG 18.14 ||

---

[26] Bhasmāsura after years of penance to please Lord Śiva was granted his wish that he could turn anyone to ashes upon placing his palm on the head of the person.

[27] Mohinī is Lord Viṣṇu's female incarnation to free the Saṃsāra from the atrocities of demon Bhasmāsura.

The ground, the doer, various kinds of instruments, manifold distinct efforts, and the fifth is Daiva.

The five causes of Karma are:

1. Adhiṣṭhāna (अधिष्ठान, ground) - The body which is the support for the appearance of desires, knowledge, and actions.
2. Kartā (कर्ता, doer) - The delimited Ātmā who is a doer-enjoyer with an I-ness sense in the body. The delimited Ātmā, Jīva, Jīvātmā, and Soul are synonymous.
3. Karaṇa (करण, instrument) - Various kinds of instruments through which actions are performed are enumerated as A) the five cognitive senses (पञ्च-ज्ञानेन्द्रिय, Pañca-Jñānendriya): 1) skin (त्वक, Tvaka) with the sense of touch, 2) tongue (रसना, Rasanā) with the sense of taste, 3) eyes (चक्षु, Cakṣu) with the sense of sight, 4) nose (घ्राण, Ghrāṇa) with the sense of smell and 5) ears (श्रोत्र, Śrotra) with the sense of hearing, B) the five action faculties (पञ्च-कर्मेन्द्रिय, Pañca-Karmendriya): 1) mouth (वाक, Vāka) with the organ of voice, 2) hands (पाणि, Pāṇi) with the organ of grasping (Grahaṇa) and holding (Dhāraṇa), 3) feet (पाद, Pāda) with the organ of locomotion (Gamana), 4) anus (पायु, Pāyu) with the organ of excretion and 5) genitals (उपस्थ, Upastha) with the organ of reproduction, C) the mind and D) the intellect.
4. Ceṣṭā (चेष्टा, effort) - Manifold distinct efforts of Prāṇa (प्राण) such as in-breath, out-breath through which activities in the senses, mind, and intellect happen.
5. Daiva (दैव, the presiding deity) - Various presiding deities that control the mind and senses. The Adhideva (अधिदेव) of eyes is the sun-deity, the Adhideva of ears is the directions, and so on. The power of these presiding deities is known as Adhidaiva-Śakti (अधिदैव-शक्ति). The intention is that senses grasp their objects with the grace of these deities.

All activities in the form of Karma happen only due to the assistance of these five, and these five are the cause of Karma. A knower of the Truth who has known himself dissociated and untainted from these five experiences directly, "Even though these five are active on my support, I have no stain from them and that despite my giving power to all activities of Prakṛti, I am untainted from all of them."

न मां कर्माणि लिम्पन्ति न मे कर्मफले स्पृहा |
इति मां योऽभिजानाति कर्मभिर्न स बध्यते || BG 4.14 ||

Actions neither taint Me, nor do I have attachment to fruits of action. One who knows Me so, is also not bound by action.

न च मां तानि कर्माणि निबध्नन्ति धनञ्जय |
उदासीनवदासीनमसक्तं तेषु कर्मसु || BG 9.9 ||

Hey Arjuna! Those actions do not bind Me. I stay indifferent and detached from those actions.

प्रकृत्यैव च कर्माणि क्रियमाणानि सर्वशः |
यः पश्यति तथात्मानमकर्तारं स पश्यति || BG 13.29 ||

He who sees actions on all sides are solely done by Prakṛti, and the Self, as a non-doer, sees the Truth.

"To Me the all-witness, Karma does not touch Me, and I have no attachment to the fruits of Karma. Karma does not bind one who knows Me in My true nature. Hey Dhanañjaya! Creation and dissolution activities of Prakṛti do not bind Me the witness-conscious because like an indifferent I am situated in those Karma without attachment." Prakṛti does all Karma, and one who sees his own Ātmā, a non-doer, sees the Truth. Reaching such a state, a Jīvanmukta who has realized knowledge of the Ātmā and is free from the bondage of Māyā of the Saṃsāra, with the realization of the Reality whose "I am a doer, enjoyer, and Saṃsārī" knot in the heart that is part sentient and part insentient dissolves, all his doubts are removed, and all his Karma perish. Karma-Saṃskāras blossom only due to their dependence on ignorance-born delusional-doership and enjoyership-intellect. When the underlying delusional intellect is burnt by knowledge, all Karma-Saṃskāras are burnt on their own.

Just as -

भिद्यते हृदयग्रन्थिश्छिद्यन्ते सर्वसंशयाः ।
क्षीयन्ते चास्य कर्माणि तस्मिन्दृष्टे परावरे ॥[28]

> Knowing the Brahman, the knot in the heart is untied, all doubts are removed, and all Karma of that knower is destroyed.

It is only possible to burn all Karma-Saṃskāras by knowledge. There is no other approach to be free from Karma-Saṃskāras, nor will there be any. Freedom from Karma-Saṃskāras by enjoyment and penance is impossible, as previously discussed. Only by knowledge, Jīva can burn all Karma-Saṃskāras and be free from the bondage of birth and death and be free.

In this state, efforts of the body, senses, mind, and intellect of a Jīvanmukta knower do not stop. However, like roasted seeds, those efforts do not remain any cause for fruits. Activity in Karma, by its nature, is not the cause for bondage. Ignorance born doership and duty-bound intellect is the only bondage. Had only Karma been in the form of bondage and the cause for fruits, then Karma done in the states of animals, birds, insects, and infants in whom doership-intellect is not awake, should also bring fruits. "I am a doer," and duty-bound intellect is not yet awake in them, so Karma done in their species is not in bondage-form and does not become the cause for fruits.

Moreover, the Karma of that Jīvanmukta knower whose doership and duty-bound intellect were awake and burnt by knowledge is not the cause for bondage. Though a person whose doership and duty-bound intellect is awakened and has achieved progress but has not been burnt by knowledge, he is still under the bondage of Karma. The cause of bondage is solely doership and duty-bound intellect. Karma, by its nature, is not bondage-form. For the Jīvanmukta knower whose doership and duty-bound intellect is fully burnt through the knowledge of the Truth, with the dance of the body and senses, he does not remain a dancer. But, with his power, like a puppeteer, he is the one who makes the puppets (the body and senses) dance, and he stays "is as is." Thus, he is not doing anything, though all activities are happening with his support. Doer as he is, he is entirely a non-doer.

नैव किञ्चित्करोमीति युक्तो मन्येत तत्त्ववित् |
पश्यञ्शृण्वन्स्पृशञ्जिघ्रन्नश्नन्गच्छन्स्वपञ्श्वसन् || BG 5.8 ||
प्रलपन्विसृजन्गृह्णन्नुन्मिषन्निमिषन्नपि |
इन्द्रियाणीन्द्रियार्थेषु वर्तन्त इति धारयन् || BG 5.9 ||

> A knower of the Truth established in the Self even while seeing, hearing, touching, smelling, eating, walking, sleeping, breathing, talking, giving up, accepting, opening eyes, and closing eyes holds the view that senses are operating in their objects and thus believes "I am not even doing anything."

A knower of the Truth who has found union in the Paramātmā believes that the senses function in their respective objects. Situated in his witness form, even while doing everything, he remains a real non-doer. Even while engaging in activities such as seeing or hearing, he is not doing anything in reality. All his Karma is thus actionless, he has no doership-ego left, and his Karma does not remain the cause for fruits.

कर्मण्यकर्म यः पश्येदकर्मणि च कर्म यः |
स बुद्धिमान्मनुष्येषु स युक्तः कृत्स्नकर्मकृत् || BG 4.18 ||

[28] Muṇḍaka Upaniṣad (मुण्डक-उपनिषद्) 2.2.8

> One who sees non-action in action and who sees action in non-action is wise amongst all humans; he has attained union and has done everything.

One who is established with oneness in the witness-conscious is free from doership-ego. Due to the absence of doership, even though the flow of Karma through the body is ongoing, they do not become the cause for fruits, and they all become actionless. On the other hand, for one who has relinquished Karma holding doership-ego, because doership and desires are conjoined, there is a trueness sense of ego even in the relinquishment of Karma, so there is bondage of Karma. In truth, one who understands this is the real knower among all humans, he is the one who has realized union with the Paramātmā, and he has done everything. Even while doing everything in this state, the Jīvanmukta knower is a real non-doer. All his Karma becomes actionless, and knowing everyone his Ātmā, he is a real omniscient. While remaining active in Karma, he is the one in real Samādhī. He is a total renouncer.

SĀṄKHYA AND YOGA

For one, who is situated with oneness in the witness-conscious Ātmā and is without doership-ego, even though the flow of Karma through the body is ongoing, it does not become the cause for fruits, and all become non-action (Akarma). On the other hand, one who has relinquished Karma but is with doership-ego, because doership and impressions are conjoined, there is a trueness sense of ego even in the relinquishment of Karma, and so there is bondage of Karma. One who understands this in truth is a real knower among all beings, he is the one who has realized union with the Paramātmā, and he has done everything. In this state, the Jīvanmukta knower is a real non-doer (Akartā) even while doing everything. All his Karma becomes non-action, and knowing everyone as his Ātmā, is a real omniscient (सर्वज्ञ, Sarvajña). While remaining active in Karma, he is in real Samādhī (oneness). He is a total renouncer. Here, there is a real harmonious connection or coming together between knowledge and Karma. Even though he is doing everything, he is a renouncer of Karma and is a Niṣkāmī (one who has no desire or attachment). That is the oneness of Sāṅkhya and Yoga. That is the Yoga espoused in Gītā. Some have not grasped this intrinsic essence of Gītā - the oneness of Sāṅkhya and Yoga or the oneness of knowledge and Karma. They have shown disdain for such contemplative words as "knower (Jñānī) does not do any Karma, he is a non-doer (Akartā) and Karma-renouncer (Saṃnyāsī)" of Śrī Ādi Śaṅkarācārya in his Gītā Bhāṣya. Indeed, they have made a distinction between Sāṅkhya and Yoga and have shown them as separate and independent paths for the attainment of liberation.[29]The Yoga postulated by them is hereinafter referred to as Variant-Yoga, the Yoga of desireless actions (Niṣkāma-Karma).

They have depicted the distinction between the two paths as follows:

1. Sāṅkhya (Karma-Saṃnyāsa, the Path of Renunciation of Karma) - Forsaking worldly and Vedic Karma, leaving the householder stage (गृहस्थ-आश्रम, Gṛhastha-Āśrama), taking Saṃnyāsa {the fourth stage of life (संन्यास-आश्रम, Saṃnyāsa-Āśrama)}, and accepting only the Path of Renunciation (performing Karma only for the sustenance of life while renouncing all others, having abode in a secluded hut, observing sixfold virtues viz. control of the mind, restraint over the senses, faith in the words of preceptors and scriptures, absence of mental vacillations and thinking and contemplating on Vedānta to achieve the transcendental realization of own Brahman form). Such a path is named Sāṅkhya, Karma-Saṃnyāsa by them.
2. "(Variant) Yoga" - First, know the true nature of the Ātmā through scriptures, like Gītā Chapter 2, verses (BG 2.11 - BG 2.30), where Śrī Kṛṣṇa has elucidated that the Ātmā is unborn and eternal,

[29] Śrī Tilaka, Gītā Rahasya Pages 305-309, 311, 318, 324, 329-331, 336-337, 349, 351.

free from old age and death, does not perish with the destruction of the body, cannot be cut by weapons, cannot be burnt, cannot be wet, cannot be dry and so on. To achieve its realization, one needs to stay on the Path of Karma. That is, continue to do Karma without renouncing them, but do them only with a desireless sentiment (Niṣkāma-Bhāva), without any self-interest. At the same time, do those Karma without the ego of doership and keep equanimity of mind in the success or failure of fruits, but as a duty offer resultant fruits to the Lord. Additionally, do Karma only for public well-being and public service and continue them as long as one is alive. They call this (Variant) Yoga as Yoga or Karma-Yoga. They indicate that by doing Karma in such a way, the true nature of the Ātmā, as depicted in the verses (BG 2.11 - BG 2.30), becomes directly realized (Aparokṣa). Thus, according to them, by continuing to do Karma in this way, humans become free from the bondage of birth and death and achieve liberation, and then they do not have to take any more births. They believe that by following the above, even after direct intuitive knowledge of the Ātmā is attained, as a duty, the knower must continue activity in Karma as long as he is alive.

3. Though liberation is possible through Sāṅkhya, such a path does not do any good to the Saṃsāra and is prone to lead one to laziness and selfishness. Although both approaches have similar capabilities in attaining liberation and are independent, considering public well-being, their postulated Yoga (Variant-Yoga, Niṣkāma Karma-Yoga) path is the best, and that is the intent of Śrīmad Bhagavad Gītā in their view.

Some have postulated that Sāṅkhya and Yoga are separate and independent paths for liberation. Some have viewed both paths as independent but have opined that Yoga (Niṣkāma-Karma) is more productive for the benefit of the Saṃsāra. In contrast, some have considered that by Sāṅkhya, one gets indirect knowledge (Parokṣa Jñāna), and by Yoga attainment of direct intuitive knowledge (Aparokṣa-Jñāna). Moreover, some have pronounced Yoga as a means and Sāṅkhya (Karma-Saṃnyāsa) as something to be attained. Thus, several interpretations are prevalent regarding Sāṅkhya and Yoga discoursed in Gītā.

In my view expressed herein, I have been influenced by Ādi Śaṅkarācārya as well as Svāmī Ātmānanda. Contemplating upon their words, in Gītā 1) the meaning of the word Sāṅkhya (Karma-Saṃnyāsa) as the complete relinquishment of Karma and the meaning of the word Saṃnyāsa as the path of renunciation in the form of the fourth stage of life (Saṃnyāsa-Āśrama), and 2) the meaning of the word Yoga as doing Karma as a duty without any selfish motive for public well-being as long as one is alive and offering the resultant fruits to the Lord, is not proper and acceptable. Gītā has not espoused those as the best and faultless means of Karma, nor has it accepted that these two paths are separate. It is implausible that Gītā intended to treat these two paths independently to attain liberation. Gītā is not there to initiate conflict between activity and non-activity (Pravṛtti and Nivrutti), nor can such dispute be proven by the verses of Gītā. Moreover, the central tenet of Vedānta, of which Gītā is Prasthāna-Trayī, does not accept such views, as they are not consistent with the laws of Prakṛti nor support the shown approaches.

Following is my perspective on the intent of Gītā. Living in the kingdom of Prakṛti, Jīva can never be free from Karma.

न हि कश्चित्क्षणमपि जातु तिष्ठत्यकर्मकृत् |
कार्यते ह्यवशः कर्म सर्वः प्रकृतिजैर्गुणैः || BG 3.5 ||

No one can ever stay, even for a moment, without action. Unquestionably, all helplessly perform actions through the constituents born of Prakṛti.

Sattvaguṇa, Rajoguṇa, and Tamoguṇa are the three constituents of Prakṛti. From these three constituents, there is the creation of the intellect (Buddhi), the ego (Ahaṃkāra), the mind (Manas), the sense-organs (Indriya), and the entire sentient and insentient Saṃsāra. In creating the visible Saṃsāra, separate from the three constituents, there is no other cause. Sattvaguṇa results in knowledge. With Rajoguṇa, fickleness and agitation manifest. Tamoguṇa results in dense insentience. The three constituents together make the visible Saṃsāra. The three constituents are present in every movable, immovable, conscious, and insentient thing. No substance is without them. When every substance has a relationship with these three constituents, which are transformable, how can anything in the Saṃsāra stay without Karma, without activity? No living being for any moment can stay without Karma, but all engage in Karma through the constituents of Prakṛti by force.

Karma is always necessary for a Jīva. Done Karma puts a doer in the bondage of the body for the enjoyment of fruits of action. It is ordained in Vedānta that there is no other way to enjoy fruits without a gross body. Even the most outstanding pious Karma will unequivocally put a Jīva in the bodily jail to enjoy fruits. Therefore, the relationship of a Jīva with the body is the root of all pleasure and pain. It is only the relationship with the insentient body that makes the limitless-Ātmā limited, the unborn to born, the imperishable to perishable, the ever-blissful to unhappy, the ever-conscious to lifeless, the ever-pure to impure, the great to insignificant, the ever-free to bound, and the ever-satiated to one in the bondage of desires. Therefore, spiritual guidance showing an approach to doing Karma without getting into the bondage of enjoyment of fruits would be desirable. Lamentably Karma cannot be avoided by any means. Even if someone, by obstinacy or force, restraints the body and senses, how can he chain his mind? If mental activities (thoughts and their variants) stay on, then according to Gītā, it is not a relinquishment of Karma but is indeed Karma, and by falsely restraining the senses, he commits untruthful or fraudulent behavior. When actions are pervasive and unavoidable, then in such a situation -

कर्मेन्द्रियाणि संयम्य य आस्ते मनसा स्मरन् |
इन्द्रियार्थान्विमूढात्मा मिथ्याचार: स उच्यते || BG 3.6 ||

> Restraining the action-organs, a deluded one who sits thinking in the mind about sense objects is said to be a hypocrite.

Any effort or activity that has a relationship with the mind, that effort or activity is defined as Karma. Any effort that does not have conjunction (संसर्ग, Saṃsarga) with the mind is neither Karma nor does it have a fruit. With the movement of Prāṇa, numerous activities take place in the body whereby blood, flesh, fat, urine, feces, and others are created and discarded. However, due to the absence of their relationship with the mind, they are not within the definition of Karma. From this, it is clear that anything that happens through the mind is Karma, and not as commonly accepted, only that which occurs through action-organs. However, a deluded one who forcefully restrains action-organs keeps his mental activity open and dwells on sense objects. His activity of Karma is ongoing, which becomes the cause for good or bad fruits. One who forcibly restrains action-organs against the flow of nature is said to be a hypocrite because even though he appears as not doing Karma, he is indeed doing Karma.

With Karma present, without the enjoyment of fruits, where is freedom? If the enjoyment of fruits is present, where is freedom from the bondage of the body? When there is the bondage of the body, how can one stop the wheel of birth and death? Hey, Lord! How badly Jīva is entangled! How harsh and unsympathetic is Your rule that there is no way to be rescued. Jīva can neither free himself from Karma nor can he escape from birth and death. Let those who worry about public well-being sing songs of public good, but Jīva cries, "I am dead serious about my good. Hey, Paramātmā! Show me a path for my good. Blind as I am, I am badly caught in the hell of the four walls of Prakṛti. Hey, Maharṣis! Hey, Scriptures! Hey, Preceptors! Have mercy and show me some approach so I can be free. Do my good first because the public good is dependent on my good as I am blocking the path of the public good." It is like the movement of air in a given location - until the sun's heat makes air at a site lighter and moves it up in the sky, making room for colder air to take its place, there is no movement of air in the pervasive sky. Badly caught in a fishnet of Karma, Jīva is looking for that last straw of hope to be free. Is there any friend of the Lord who can save me from this predicament? In the form of Arjuna, the seeker cries in a loud tone, "Hey, Lord! Grief that is prevailing in my mind and senses at this time, not even the most cherished enjoyment of the Saṃsāra or enjoyments of the world of Brahmā can remedy the pain I am enduring."

कार्पण्यदोषोपहतस्वभावः पृच्छामि त्वां धर्मसम्मूढचेताः |
यच्छ्रेयः स्यान्निश्चितं ब्रूहि तन्मे शिष्यस्तेऽहं शाधि मां त्वां प्रपन्नम् || BG 2.7 ||

My innate nature is affected by cowardice, and my mind is confused about duty. I am asking you to tell me that which is decisively beneficial. Please guide me. I am your disciple and have surrendered to you.

न हि प्रपश्यामि ममापनुद्याद् यच्छोकमुच्छोषणमिन्द्रियाणाम् |
अवाप्य भूमावसपत्नमृद्धं राज्यं सुराणामपि चाधिपत्यम् || BG 2.8 ||

Even acquiring a prosperous kingdom on the earth free from enemies and supremacy over the deities, I do not see the approach which can remove my senses-drying grief.

Melting upon the lamentation of Jīva, Gītā descending next to Jīva, putting her hand over his shoulder and wiping his tears with a loving smile, says, "Wait! Do not be afraid. I am going to provide you with medication for your disease. Stop lamenting for a moment. Just remove vacillations of your mind, calm your heart and have faith in me." Anything contrary to this:

अश्रद्दधानाः पुरुषा धर्मस्यास्य परन्तप |
अप्राप्य मां निवर्तन्ते मृत्युसंसारवर्त्मनि || BG 9.3 ||

Hey Arjuna! Those who do not have faith in this righteousness, failing to attain Me, return to the mortal world of death.

"Endowed with faith when you have removed from your heart impurities of attachment and aversion and have become pure, just as how gold, when heated by the fire with the removal of impurities, becomes pure, listen to Me attentively, and with your pure intellect contemplate on My words, then your lamentation will abruptly cease, and then not only for yourself but also for others you will be peaceful."

Without the above-shown means, the status quo cannot be changed. It is therefore imperative to think about:

1. Who are you?
2. What is Karma, and who is its doer (Kartā)?
3. What is the bondage of Karma?

Before embarking further on, let us contemplate upon something fundamental that needs to be absorbed.

नासतो विद्यते भावो नाभावो विद्यते सतः | BG 2.16 |

There is no being of the unreal, and there is no non-being of the real.

In response to the first question, "Who are you?" if pointing your fingers at your chest, you pronounce, "That is who I am, standing right in front of you, what is there to question?", then based on the supra tenet your pronouncement is inappropriate. Let us elaborate on why.

The body and senses are never stationary at any time but are transforming every moment (Kṣaṇa-Pariṇāmī). As previously clarified, transformed things cannot be established as real (Sat), as those things are sometimes there and sometimes not there. Indeed, they are never there by their own nature but are only perceived illusorily. That is because they are perceived only in the middle and not in the time before and after. According to the tenet of Vedānta, a substance perceived only in the middle and not before or after is like a delusional snake in a rope - only delusional.

अव्यक्तादीनि भूतानि व्यक्तमध्यानि भारत |
अव्यक्तनिधनान्येव तत्र का परिदेवना || BG 2.28 ||

Hey Arjuna! All beings are unmanifest in the beginning, unmanifest in the end, and only manifest in the intermediate state. In these conditions, why lament?

Though one can never prove one's self illusory by one's conduct, one does accept oneself real as a doer and an enjoyer. However, the body and senses can be neither proven as doers nor established as enjoyers. The body is not an enjoyer because the body relationship is only limited to the current birth. Since it is cremated right upon death, getting the same body for enjoyment is impossible in rebirth. If the fruits of done Karma of the body were entirely enjoyed in the same body, rebirth would become without fruits. When the enjoyments of Karma are complete in the body in which they were done, meaning no Karma remains for enjoyment, then there should be no cause for the birth of the current body because there can be no other cause for the birth of the body except for the enjoyment of Karma done in the past. Thus, the body cannot be an enjoyer. The body is also not a doer because it is insentient by its nature. In an insentient thing, no act can happen on its own. Actions like movement can only occur in someone else's subordination, like a rock not having any motion of its own may acquire motion on the dependence of some conscious power. Its visible measure can be found in the dream and death states because, in these states, when the conscious power leaves the gross body and senses, it becomes like a corpse and cannot do anything. That is why the body and senses also cannot be doers. However, it is true that through them, acts can manifest, just as a knife used by a chef to chop onions does not make the blade a doer. It only remains an instrument (Karaṇa).

Further, that thing which is only an instrument cannot be a doer and certainly cannot be an enjoyer. When a person beheads someone with his sword, the sword does not become the experiencer, but the experiencer is that person who is the doer. In reality, the body and senses are the means in both doership and enjoyership of the doer-enjoyer and are not themselves doers and enjoyers. When a person using a knife cuts a melon, separates the skin from the pulp, and eats, he makes the knife an instrument in both doership and enjoyership. Likewise, the body and senses are instruments in the doership and enjoyership of a doer-enjoyer. In addition, it is not necessary that the instrument with which he becomes a doer is also the instrument with which he becomes an enjoyer. For instance, a person may use a spatula to make stir-fry vegetables but may use a fork to eat them.

Further, it is also not necessary to eat where one cooks. The person may cook in a kitchen but eat in the dining room. Similarly, a doer-enjoyer may perform Karma with his body but may enjoy with his mind and senses or perform Karma with his mind and senses but enjoy with the body. In addition, he may do Karma in this body, but the enjoyment of those Karma may be in this body or some other body. If one says, "Undoubtedly, I may not be the body and senses, but I am the conscience (the mind, intellect, Citta, and ego)." Even that is not befitting. The faults that apply to being the body and senses, all those faults are also attributed to being the conscience. The conscience is also insentient like the body and senses. Even in it, there is no activity of its own, but it is dancing on the choreography of some conscious power. When that conscious power abandons the conscience, its dancing stops. In the deep-sleep state, one gets its visible measure - when that conscious power leaves the conscience and goes into its abode, it also becomes like a corpse. There is neither thought nor variant of the mind, neither discrimination of the intellect nor probing of the Citta or I-ness of the ego. All of them in that state become useless, just as a locomotive is rendered useless without its engineer. However, as soon as the engineer enters the locomotive, it becomes useful for its desired function. Even the conscience is neither a doer nor an enjoyer but is merely an instrument of doership-enjoyership of that doer-enjoyer.

In summary, your true nature cannot be the body, the senses, or the conscience. All of them are nothing but instruments for your enjoyment, and none of them on their own are suitable to do any activity. Just as a sword stays motionless, unable to swing on its own, but in the hands of a conscious swordsman can swing all over, in the same way, whichever weapon you take in your hand (bestow your power), it becomes alive and commences activity. For instance, when the power of electricity meets different devices, activity occurs based on the nature of the individual insentient device. Electricity in a fan turns blades moving air with it, and the same electricity in a bulb provides light or in a refrigerator provides cooling to keep food fresh. Even though varied activities manifest based on individual devices, the one to make an insentient device alive is only the power of electricity. Only you are making the corpses alive. You have assumed their duties and become a doer of their acts due to your ignorance of being associated with them. That is your bondage, and it is only due to this ignorance that you have birth and death.

When a person walks in darkness, it is then that he stumbles, crashes into a wall, or falls in a ditch and injures his head, face, or knees. When you walk in the darkness of ignorance, not knowing your true nature, you assume the duties of others. Then you get stumbles of Karma and fall in the ditch of birth and death, where you can do nothing but cry or clench your teeth. Any activity happening in them is only due to your power at their root, though in reality, you have no union with them. You are dissociated from them. Iron shavings start dancing near a magnet, though the magnet is unattached. In the same way, only because of your presence and your beingness are all dancing. All you remain is only the observer of their dance. Due to your ignorance, uniting with them, you put yourself in the bondage of doership and enjoyership. Why is your union with them? Union is only possible between substances of the same reality and similar attributes. How is it possible for the union of substances of opposite reality and dissimilar attributes? How can an awake king ride an elephant in a dream? How can substances of different attributes such as fire and water have a relationship? They are only perceived in the awake state and in their ordinary operative time, but you are the one who is present in all states. As extensively discussed, you see all states and their being and non-being and provide eyewitness of seeing them visibly. They are all with insentient attributes, but you are conscious. They are all mutable, but you are immutable. Then how is it possible for the relationship of insentient with the conscious, mutable with the immutable, and apparent with the Real? Just as a dreamer has no adherence to dream mutations, you are dissociated from all of them.

All these bodies and senses are the work of Prakṛti. It is only in your existence that they are functioning through the constituents of Prakṛti in their activities. Doership is only of Prakṛti having received power from you. It is only operating for your enjoyment. Your doership is not a bit. The one who is a doer is always mutable, is always perishable, but you are imperishable in all states. You are always "as you are." When an army chief, accompanied by his army having secured power from a king, fights a war, all he is doing is his duty on behalf of his king. Though in operation, it may appear that the king is fighting the war, in actuality, the king may be resting in his palace. During the battle of the army chief, the king is a non-doer only. He has never moved from his position as a king. All doership and Karma are the creations of Prakṛti.

The time in which the operation of Prakṛti is attributed to you, even at that time, you remain in all respects a non-doer, never moved from your witness-conscious form. Thus, you are, in reality, neither a doer nor an enjoyer. The one who is a doer is also an enjoyer. No one may be a doer of a Karma whose enjoyment is enjoyed by someone else. In reality, there is no enjoyership in you. Only because of the imagined relationship with Prakṛti, there is an imagination of imagined enjoyment in you. Just as a quartz gem is seen as of the same color as a flower next to it, with a red flower, it appears as red, with a purple flower, it appears purple, but it is untainted from all colors and is always the same "is as is." Similarly, due to the imagined association with Prakṛti, doership-enjoyership of Prakṛti is imagined in you, but in reality, you are always "as you are."

कार्यकरणकर्तृत्वे हेतु: प्रकृतिरुच्यते |
पुरुष: सुखदु:खानां भोक्तृत्वे हेतुरुच्यते || BG 13.20 ||

Prakṛti is said to be the cause of actions, instruments, and doership. The Puruṣa is said to be the cause of the experience of pleasure and pain.

पुरुष: प्रकृतिस्थो हि भुङ्क्ते प्रकृतिजान्गुणान् |
कारणं गुणसङ्गोऽस्य सदसद्योनिजन्मसु || BG 13.21 ||

The Puruṣa seated in Prakṛti experiences the constituents born of Prakṛti. Attachment to the constituents is only the cause of its birth in superior and inferior wombs.

उपद्रष्टानुमन्ता च भर्ता भोक्ता महेश्वर: |
परमात्मेति चाप्युक्तो देहेऽस्मिन्पुरुष: पर: || BG 13.22 ||

The Puruṣa seated in the body is unassociated with Prakṛti and is said to be the Close Observer, the Sanctioner, the Sustainer, the Experiencer, the Maheśvara, and the Paramātmā.

Prakṛti is called the cause in all Karma, instruments of Karma, and doership. The Puruṣa (Jīvātmā) dwelling in the body-form city, immutable from the mutations of the body, is called the cause of the enjoyment of pleasure and pain. The Puruṣa is enjoying the constituents born of Prakṛti, having situated in Prakṛti with an imagined union. Union with the constituents of Prakṛti is only the cause for the Puruṣa to be born in superior or inferior life forms. In reality, the Puruṣa situated in the body is, in all ways, dissociated and untainted from Prakṛti and its constituents. Only because of being the observer of the constituents and Karma of Prakṛti, the Puruṣa is said to be the Close Observer (Upadraṣṭā). Just as a drummer without free will adjusts the meter and groove of his beats based on the dance of a performer, in the same way, without a free will in his own reality providing acquiescence to the constituents and Karma, the Puruṣa is said to be the Sanctioner (Anumantā). With His power, holding and sustaining the body, the Puruṣa is said to be the Sustainer (Bhartā). With His witnessing-light illuminating all enjoyments, the Puruṣa is said to be the Experiencer. Being the Lord of all deities, the Puruṣa is said to be the Great Supreme Lord (Maheśvara, Lord Śiva), and in reality, being pure from all adjuncts is said to be the Supreme Being (Paramātmā). You are the pure witness-conscious Ātmā. Despite residing in the body are not doing anything. Only with your light are you illuminating all activities of the body. Observer as you are, you illuminate all good and bad acts just as a self-illuminated lamp illuminates a house.

सर्वकर्माणि मनसा संन्यस्यास्ते सुखं वशी |
नवद्वारे पुरे देही नैव कुर्वन्न कारयन् || BG 5.13 ||

Mentally renouncing all actions and with a controlled conscience, the embodied certainly rests happily in the nine-gated city, neither doing nor causing others to do.

Dehī means the embodied Ātmā (Self), in which a (Yoga-Yukta) Yogī has become of the same form, mentally forsaking all actions, with a firm resolve, "Sense-organs are engaged in their objects, I, the witness, am not doing anything" is peacefully resting in the nine-gated city (body). He does not do anything by himself nor provides any inspiration to anyone but is only an observer of activities of the senses.

This way, "Who are you?", "Who is the doer?" and "What is bondage in Karma?" have been articulated. This knowledge is called Sāṅkhya. With the firmness of this knowledge, attaining a position in one's true nature, the witness-conscious Ātmā of all, and becoming one with it and losing I-ness in the body is called Yoga. In the Saṃsāra, there are only two things, one insentient and the other sentient. Knowing is only that sentient, the Real-Conscious-Bliss (Saccidānanda), the insentient everyone knows. Attaining that Saccidānanda Status is Yoga. Real Yoga was always with him. There was never a separation, just as there is ever union of waves with water and gold-ornaments with gold. Imagined separation occurs due to imagined ignorance, and the removal of that imagined ignorance born imagined separation through the discipline of Sāṅkhya is called Yoga. Union and disunion are only possible through the intellect. There is separation due to the insentience of the thoughtless I-ness conceited selfish intellect. There is union with subtle thought with the relinquishment of all attachments. That is why this Yoga is also called Buddhi-Yoga. Indeed, that is the Gītā set forth Sāṅkhya and Yoga. They are both one. They are only one instrument and provide only one fruit.

Refutation of deeming Sāṅkhya and Yoga as Independent Paths

The cognition of knowing "Who are you?", "Who is the doer?" and "What is the bondage of Karma?" is called Sāṅkhya. With the firmness of this knowledge, attaining a position in one's true witness-conscious Ātmā and becoming one with it, and losing I-ness sense in the body is called Yoga. Gītā has set forth

Sāṅkhya and Yoga as only one and not two independent paths. They are only one means and provide only one fruit. Contrary to the above, some have called renouncement of activity (Karma-Saṃnyāsa) as Sāṅkhya, and activity in Karma without desire for fruits and with doership and duty-bound intellect as Yoga or relinquishment of activity as Sāṅkhya and activity as Yoga. Such pronouncements are vacuous and nothing but unworthy imaginations. It is indeed surprising that they have deemed two separate paths that, despite being at odds with each other like day and night, as independent in the attainment of liberation. Because activity in Karma and non-activity in Karma being with the attributes of grasping and relinquishing are like a plus (+) and a minus (-), mutually in opposition. Thoughtfully, it is discerned that the desired thing is one, and its acquisition has two mutually opposite paths that are concurrent and independent. In other words, whether a seeker, based on his wish during the same time, goes by one opposing path of Sāṅkhya (Karma-relinquishment) or goes by a different opposing path of Yoga (Karma-activity), he will attain liberation. That is like telling someone going from Washington Crossing to Philadelphia that whether you face north and move or you face south and move, you will reach Philadelphia. Anyone giving such advice is called nothing but an unsteady. Direction has to be only one, though there can certainly be differences where one rests. Based on that logic, even Bhagavāna should be considered unsteady for having shown two contrary paths, Karma-activity and Karma-relinquishment, as independent, separate, and concurrent in attaining liberation.

How can one accept that? That can never be the intention of Bhagavāna, as there is no hint from him on the distinction between Sāṅkhya and Yoga. Just as there is no difference between the word Jala (water in standard terms) and Udaka (water offered in a ceremony of the dead), in His view, there is a non-difference between Sāṅkhya and Yoga. Imagined desireless actions (Niṣkāma-Karma) and imagined relinquishment of actions (Karma-Saṃnyāsa) are not agreeable to Him. His aim is towards solid desirelessness and solid renouncement. Solid desirelessness and solid renouncement can only remain as united. The proper conduct of either is possible only after reaching that state where the doer of Karma does not remain a doer and doership-ego with its root nescience is burnt in the fire of knowledge so that the relationship of I-ness and mineness in the body, senses, mind, and intellect is removed, leaving the body like a flute that without any doership becomes successful as a producer of melodic tones on the reality of that flutist - Lord Śrī Kṛṣṇa, the true witness-conscious. When that flute is handed to that flutist, then from that flute, melodic tones will come out naturally, as it was only the relationship with ego and selfishness that all tones were unmelodious.

योगयुक्तो विशुद्धात्मा विजितात्मा जितेन्द्रिय: |
सर्वभूतात्मभूतात्मा कुर्वन्नपि न लिप्यते || BG 5.7 ||
नैव किञ्चित्करोमीति युक्तो मन्येत तत्त्ववित् |
पश्यञ्शृण्वन्स्पृशञ्जिघ्रन्नश्नन्गच्छन्स्वपञ्श्वसन् || BG 5.8 ||
प्रलपन्विसृजन्गृह्णन्नुन्मिषन्निमिषन्नपि |
इन्द्रियाणीन्द्रियार्थेषु वर्तन्त इति धारयन् || BG 5.9 ||

> Established in the Self, one whose conscience is purified, whose mind and senses are correctly controlled, and whose Self has become the Self of all beings, even acting is not tainted.
>
> A knower of the Truth established in the Self even while seeing, hearing, touching, smelling, eating, walking, sleeping, breathing, talking, giving up, accepting, opening eyes, and closing eyes holds the view that senses are operative in their objects and thus believes "I am not even doing anything."

Having reached this state, due to the absence of doership-ego, even while performing unrestrained activities through the body and senses, he is a real non-doer, a Karma-renouncer, and a real desireless (Niṣkāmī). All his Karma is actionless (Akarma) and devoid of fruits. Due to the oneness relationship with the body, only the paltry ego is the doer of Karma and the enjoyer of fruits. When the ego is burnt in the fire of knowledge, who is the enjoyer of fruits? Who is the doer-enjoyer?

यस्य सर्वे समारम्भा: कामसंकल्पवर्जिता: |
ज्ञानाग्निदग्धकर्माणं तमाहु: पण्डितं बुधा: || BG 4.19 ||
त्यक्त्वा कर्मफलासङ्गं नित्यतृप्तो निराश्रय: |
कर्मण्यभिप्रवृत्तोऽपि नैव किञ्चित्करोति स: || BG 4.20 ||

Whose all initiations are without desire and resolve, and who has burnt all actions in the fire of knowledge, he is called a man of discrimination by the wise.

Always content, independent, having forsaken attachment to fruits of action, even though engaged in an activity, he is really not doing anything.

Thus, without abandoning the doership-ego, neither real Karma-Saṃnyāsa (Sāṅkhya) can be successful nor real Karma-(Yoga).

Karma-Saṃnyāsa, as depicted by some, is Injudicious

As long as the limited and discriminating vision is present in a seeker and the ego of I-ness and mineness in the body, he can be neither a Karma-Saṃnyāsī nor a Karma-Yogī. With ego remaining in the body, even if he has forsaken Karma, he is a doer and cannot attain Karma-Saṃnyāsa. He may have forcefully succeeded in holding back his insentient body, but the mind is a different question; all activities are still ongoing. In addition, those activities happening with ego in mind are Karma only.

मनः कृतं कृतं कर्म न शरीरकृतं कृतम्[30]

Karma done by the body is not only Karma, but Karma is also that which is done by the mind.

Even if he has done relinquishment of Karma, with ego present in the body, he surely becomes the doer of Karma-relinquishment. In the presence of ego, whatever activity of grasping or relinquishing happens, they all become Karma. Fruits are inevitable once Karma is done. With ego in the body, senses, mind, and intellect present, "I have done certain relinquishment, and this is the best effort" kind of sentiment should naturally emanate in the Karma-relinquisher. When I-ness is present in the body, senses, mind, and intellect, then whatever effort of relinquishment is happening through the body will have a doership-ego. That can happen only with the knowledge of the mind and intellect. When it is in the knowledge of the mind and intellect, it cannot remain without sentiments, as the emanations of sentimental waves are natural attributes of the mind. Where the limited and discriminating vision is present sentimental waves are unavoidable. Where there are sentimental waves, there, fruits are inevitable. They cannot be without fruits, whether good or evil. They are certainly there; it is the steady tenet of Prakṛti. Therefore, with the presence of ego in the body, no one can remain a Karma-relinquisher.

Variant-Yoga, as depicted by some, is Injudicious and Discordant

No one can remain desireless with I-ness sentiment remaining in the body, mind, and senses. So long as the limited vision is present in a seeker and he has spread himself only within his body and mind and nothing more than that, and his discriminating-vision of "अन्योऽसावन्योऽहमस्मि, he is one, I am other" is present then it is unavoidable for doership not to remain steady in Karma. Due to the presence of I-ness in the body, senses, mind, and intellect (which are the instruments of Karma), up to now, he has not known himself separate from them, then how can he be free from doership? Had he had this perceptible knowledge that "body I am not, nor am I senses, mind, or intellect, but I am that light in whose light they are all involved in their activities and without it, they are all insentient and null" - then undoubtedly, he could have been a

[30] Yoga-Vāsiṣṭha (योग-वासिष्ठ) 3.89.1

non-doer in the activities of body, senses, mind, and intellect. However, his I-ness sense is deeply entrenched in them through whom all acts of Karma occur, so how can it be said that he is detached from doership-attachment? If it can be said that indirectly through scriptures, he knew his true nature as "I am beyond the body, senses, mind, and intellect and I am their illuminator Ātmā" - due to that indirect knowledge, he is dissociated from doership-attachment; that perspective is not possible by any means. **The tenet of Vedānta is that indirect knowledge (Parokṣa-Jñāna) cannot be the opposer of ignorance. Only direct knowledge (Aparokṣa-Jñāna) can be the remover of ignorance.** Since doership-attachment is ignorance born, therefore until ignorance is removed, how can there be the absence of doership? Due to ignorance of his pure Ātmā, he knows himself as one who is tied within the boundaries of time and space, believes the rest of the Saṃsāra as something else, and does not know his own self - that is called ignorance. The result of this ignorance is definitely doer, duty, and Karma, and thus fruits - be they good or evil, but they cannot remain empty from the trio. Such is the profundity of ignorance. Ignorance can only be removed by direct intuitive analytic knowledge and never by other means. For instance, in a forest, at night, a person has a delusion of a snake and is extremely paranoid with fear. At the same time, a hiker who has true cognition and does not have a similar delusion sees the person in fear. With empathy, he tells him, "That is not a snake. It is only a rope." The person's fear will not be removed by those words until the hiker, using his flashlight, shows him directly, "See, this is not a snake. It is merely a rope." Before using the flashlight, with the words of the hiker, even though the deluded person got indirect knowledge of the rope, he cannot remove his ignorance of the rope. He cannot remove direct (Aparokṣa) knowledge of the snake. It remains as it was, and fear does not go. Only because of ignorance of the rope, there is direct (Aparokṣa) cognition of the snake and the paranoia of fear. Ignorance of the rope can be removed only by direct (Aparokṣa) knowledge of the rope, never by mere indirect knowledge. When the flashlight illumination makes the rope directly cognizant (Aparokṣa) to him, the snake's direct cognizance (Aparokṣa) is removed later. As a fruit, fear also does not remain. **The tenet of Vedānta is that one Parokṣa-Jñāna (indirect knowledge) is never able to remove other Aparokṣa-Jñāna (direct knowledge); only a second Aparokṣa-Jñāna can remove the first Aparokṣa-Jñāna.** Removal of direct cognizance of the snake is never going to be possible until there is direct cognizance of the rope. As the rope and the snake are in the same space, it is possible for indirect knowledge of the rope and direct knowledge of the snake in the same time and space because indirect knowledge does not oppose direct knowledge. However, direct knowledge of the rope and direct knowledge of the snake being mutually opposer cannot remain in the same time and space. Under this tenet and example, a Karma-Yogī active in desireless actions has I-ness sense directly in his body. His knowledge through scriptures that "I am not the body, I am the Ātmā" is indirect. As "I am the Ātmā" is indirect (Parokṣa) knowledge and "I am the body" is direct knowledge, both can remain in the same time and space. That is because one direct knowledge is not an opposer of another indirect knowledge. Thus, indirect knowledge through scriptures, "I am the Ātmā," until there is in one's Ātmā direct knowledge, "I am the ever, eternal, pure, awake free-form," how can it remove the I-ness sense that is direct (Aparokṣa) in the body? Only direct knowledge of the Ātmā is the opposer of the direct knowledge of the body because being mutually opposer, both direct knowledge cannot remain in one time and space. Only with direct knowledge of the underlying support (Adhiṣṭhāna) can one remove the imagined direct knowledge, like with the direct knowledge of the rope, direct knowledge of the snake is removed. But here, the underlying support of the body of that seeker is the existent Ātmā, and its direct knowledge is not there. Contrary to that, direct knowledge of the body is ongoing or always there. Direct knowledge of the body can only be removed when there is direct knowledge of the Ātmā, and thus the root ignorance and its fruit doership and enjoyership can be removed. However, our seeker (Niṣkāma-Karma Yogī) has not yet collected those accessories, so how can I-ness sense and doership-attachment in his body be removed? Therefore, even though he has only a sentimental resolve that "I am not a doer," he is indeed a doer, as the I-ness sense still exists in his body. Moreover, when doership and duty both are present, with his Karma, where can their fruits go? Even with the purity of his conscience, he has a sentiment that "I do not desire fruits of my Karma. I offer them all to the Lord," fruits for him are unavoidable. With ego present in the body, he is surely a doer of the sentiments. That is undeniable. When sentiments, doer of the sentiments, and duty all are present, and trueness is also present in them, what crime is committed by fruits? When the field (trueness sense in the body) is ready, the planter of seeds (doership-ego) is alive, the seeds (Karma) capable of germination are planted (seeds are not roasted in the fire of knowledge), and water (sentiments) is with sapidity, then where can fruits go? Even if the planter of seeds superfluously screams, "I do not want fruits," seeds have to sprout out from under the soil with force bringing forth fruits and helplessly giving the planter of seeds a taste of his fruits. Those who are afraid of fruits, why would they become planters of seeds? Thus, it is said that a Jīva is independent in doing Karma but is not independent in the enjoyment of resultant fruits. He is dependent. Yes, one's sentiments are exceptional, and in them is embedded sentiment of relinquishment. One will get good fruits, but it cannot be without fruits. Fruits are certainly in sentiments; there can be no fruits in the insentient Karma. If only Karma were the cause of fruits, then animals and birds should also get fruits of their done Karma, and even a knower whose sentiments are burnt should fall in the bondage of Karma. However, the tenet of Śāstra opines that because the ego is not awake in animals and birds, there are no fruits of Karma done in their species. As it relates to a knower, his sentiments having been awakened and burnt in the fire of knowledge and his Karma are not the cause of fruits. Therefore, the cause of fruits is only the sentiments. The cause of sentiments being doership-ego. If in the existence of doer, duty, and sentiments, the cause for not getting fruits is that the doer has relinquished the desire for fruits, then for the enjoyment of fruits of pain and suffering, even animals and birds are desireless; nobody has a sentiment to acquire pain and suffering. With the relinquishment of the desire for fruits, nobody should suffer pain and suffering. When a thief goes to rob, he goes after worshipping his revered deity and offers the enjoyment of fruits of pain to the Lord, but how can he be saved? You gorged yourself with sweets. Now, why are you afraid of nausea? In the presence of a doer, duty, and sentiments, Karma cannot remain without fruits. Yes, the resultant fruits can indeed be great because of the degree of relinquishment in his sentiments. Moreover, if the seeker has filled his heart with sentiments of fruit-relinquishment and not mere words, then fruits will also be exceptionally great, and he surely will become fit for the love and devotion of the Lord. He has completely dedicated himself to the Lord in his sentiments, but Yoga, in its true nature, is not possible merely by such gesture.

Mutual Discordance in the Variant-Yoga Components

The nature of Variant-Yoga (desireless actions), as proclaimed by some and as thoroughly explored in Sāṅkhya and Yoga, can have possibly three limbs:

1. Relinquishment of doership-attachment (कर्तृत्व-सङ्ग-त्याग, Karttṛtva-Saṅga-Tyāga)
2. Relinquishment of fruits of Karma (कर्म-फल-त्याग, Karma-Phala-Tyāga)
3. Duty-bound intellect (कर्तव्य-बुद्धि, Kartavya-Buddhi), "It is my duty to do certain Karma."

Two of the above, relinquishment of doership-attachment and relinquishment of fruits of Karma, are fully explored in "Karma-Saṃnyāsa, as depicted by some, is Injudicious" and "Variant-Yoga, as depicted by some, is Injudicious and Discordant." It is now imperative to ponder on the third limb, "Duty-bound intellect." Upon some thought, it is clear that the nature of all three limbs, as depicted by some, does not have concordance as postulated.

First, there is no concordance between "devoid of doership-attachment" and "with duty." Both sentiments, "I am not a doer" and "I have some duty," being mutually opposed, cannot stay in one support. When a Yogī, relinquishing attachment of doership, "I am not a doer of Karma," is active in his Karma, then on whom can the burden of duty be imposed? That is intuitively difficult to digest. When a doer is not present, then who can sustain duty? Contrary to that, one is indeed a doer on whom there is a duty. One can find the doer right beneath where there is a duty. When duty is present, backpedaling from doership accrues the fault of "वदतो व्याघात," that is, providing mutually adverse information, and is equivalent to saying, "मम मुखे जिह्वा नास्ति, I do not have a tongue in my mouth." If for the relinquishment of doership-attachment there was some other form propounded, that is not known and probably unthinkable. The word Karttṛtva (कर्त्तृत्व, duty) is tied to the word Kartāpana (कर्तापन, doership) that "I am a doer of Karma" and the meaning of the word Saṅga (सङ्ग) is attachment, association or relationship. The relinquishment (Tyāga) of the attachment of doership of Karma (I am a doer of Karma) is called relinquishment of doership-attachment. Therefore, the nature of relinquishment of doership-attachment can only be that "I am not a doer."

When there is no doer, then on whom one can impose duty? Without support, there cannot be something that can be placed (आधेय, Ādheya) on; just as without a supporting vessel, water cannot be contained. Here the Ādheya duty is present, but its supporting container, doership, is not. It is surprising how its concordance was ever depicted! The form of "Karttṛtva-Saṅga-Tyāga" may have been formulated like an institutor of sacrifice who holding water in his hand, makes a resolve to donate a cow. Likewise, believing doership-attachment as some substance, they may have resolved to relinquish it. Even if we accept that, there has to be some doer of that resolve. But here, relinquishment by its nature is without life. It is similar to the Ghī of the famous story of a weaver who died of hunger. His mother put some Ghī on his face and anus and cried, "My son did not die hungry, but died eating Ghī and excreting Ghī." Well, whatever is there, doer and duty are both mutually coupled. Without one, the other cannot remain. When one comes, the other automatically comes. When there is no doer, then on whom can there be a duty? When the person responsible for duty is no more, duty does not remain. There is no need to remove duty. Therefore, when there is no duty, then where is the doer? Only because of duty the term Kartā (doer) is named. When there is a doer, some duty comes into play, whether the duty is Sāttvika, Rājasika, or Tāmasika. When a limited and discriminating vision is born, then with the ego of "I am something," it is natural for the origination of desire and duty, "I become happy." Though in reality, he is bliss-form, all entanglements ensue because he forgot his true nature. With desire, it becomes necessary for doership to become assertive, "By whatever way, I get it," and with it, the duty also joins. Based on one's natural constituents, whether one makes one's duty Mokṣa, Dharma, Artha, Kāma, or anything, duty is steadfast with a doer. Even if it is believed for a moment that there is no duty, there is definitely a doer. Interestingly, when children play hide and seek games, even then, without duty, the doer remains without duty. It is not possible for the game without duty, as activities of hand and feet in the game will arise after duty is born in mind. Thus, it is impossible for a doer not to exist when there is a duty.

Second, there is no concordance between the relinquishment of doership-attachment and the relinquishment of fruits of Karma. If the relinquishment of fruits of Karma is a duty, then there has to be a doer of that fruit-relinquishment. When there is no doer, then the relinquishment of fruits of Karma does not have to be done; its relinquishment is ipso facto.

Concordance between the limbs of Variant-Yoga cannot be established with the kind of perspective provided by some. Here, "devoid of doership-attachment" and "with duty" are mutually discordant, and so concordance of the two is impossible. There, "relinquishment of doership-attachment" and "relinquishment of fruits of Karma" are also mutually discordant. In summary, with "duty" and "relinquishment of fruits of Karma" being present, the presence of a doer is necessary. Thus, their arrangement of limbs may be formulated as follows:

1. I am a doer of Karma.
2. Duty is ordained by the Lord on me, that I worship Him through my Karma.
3. Therefore, not desiring the fruits of my Karma, I offer them to the Lord.

Can Variant-Yoga, as depicted by some, provide Liberation?

Let us now look at whether the lifelong sole practice of Variant-Yoga can lead one to liberation and freedom from the Saṃsāra of transmigrating lives of birth and death or not? From the Vedantic perspective, there is no dispute that the cause of birth and death of a Jīva is due to the accumulated impressions of Karma (Sañcita Karma-Saṃskāras) done by the Jīva. Due to ignorance, when a Jīva knows himself as limited as something, the desire to be happy is born naturally. Jīva, with discriminating vision, knowing some things pleasure-yielding and some pain-yielding, forms favorable intellect in some things and antagonistic intellect in others. Jīva then desires the acquisition of favorable things and the relinquishment of unfavorable. Inspired by desire, he engages in Karma due to grasping and relinquishing intellect. Though done Karma disappears later on, their Saṃskāras stay in the refuge of the "I am a doer" ego and continue to remind their existence from time to time. Indeed, those Karma-Saṃskāras put a doer in the bondage of the body for the enjoyment of good and evil fruits. There, Jīva, on the one hand, enjoys the fruits of pleasure and pain of previously done Karma, but on the other hand, with the desire to be happy, engages in Karma again and thereby acquires more Karma-Saṃskāras. The ego of "I am a doer" is still present, and the desire, "I get pleasure and get such pleasure that it never ceases," is present. Therefore, activity in Karma cannot be avoided. That is the profundity of ignorance. Thus, Jīva can never be happy with Karma. On the contrary, Karma is the reason for his bondage. It puts a doer in the bondage of enjoyment of fruits. No matter how pure and good Karma is, it cannot remain without putting the doer in the bondage of the body for the enjoyment of fruits. However, those fruits are assuredly perishable in the end. He is anxious, "How can my desire for acquiring imperishable happiness be fulfilled with further Karma?" Anything that is made through Karma perishes. As per Śruti -

> "तद्यथेह कर्मचितो लोकः क्षीयते एवमेवामुत्र पुण्यचितो लोकः क्षीयते, just as this world created by Karma is destroyed, in the same way; piety-world created by Karma (after giving fruits) is also destroyed."

Happiness, being stricken with pain, in reality, is painful indeed. No matter how great the pleasures created by Karma are, in its end, they will transform into multifold pains, and that is a posteriori to all. Therefore, Karma can never be pleasure-yielding in its true nature, as it always ends in pain and suffering. The same intent is in Śrīmad Bhāgavata, 11th Canto, 10th Chapter Śrī Kṛṣṇa-Uddhava Saṃvāda.

Now, we need to examine the nature of Variant-Yoga and see whether, following such a path, Karma-Saṃskāras can be destroyed or not? The cause of birth and death is only Karma-Saṃskāras, and they reside in the refuge of the ego of "I am a doer" intellect. Without burning Karma-Saṃskāras, there is no other approach with which Variant-Yoga or any other means can provide freedom from birth and death because the seed of birth and death is only Karma-Saṃskāra. There are three accepted kinds of Saṃskāras of done Karma:

1. Saṃskāras of the Karma that is happening in the present are called Kriyamāṇa Karma-Saṃskāras or being done current impressions and whose memory continues to remain in the current life.
2. Saṃskāras of the Kriyamāṇa Karma of many previous births that are being deposited in the heart in the doership-ego are called Sañcita Karma-Saṃskāras, or accumulated impressions.
3. Of the Sañcita Karma-Saṃskāras, those ready for fruition and who have created the current body for the enjoyment of fruits are called Prārabdha Karma-Saṃskāras (ready to be experienced impressions).

Prārabdha Karma-Saṃskāras that are ready for fruition are depleted on their own after giving their fruits, whether one is a knower or an ignorant. Now what needs to be determined is whether, by following the postulated Variant Karma-Yoga, accumulated (Sañcita) and current (Kriyamāṇa) impressions (Saṃskāras) can be burnt or not? After some thought, it is clear that, based on the preceding, Variant Karma-Yoga can neither touch the repository of accumulated impressions nor the current. On the contrary, with such conduct, current Karma will continue to create its own Saṃskāra. Instead of emptying, it makes the Sañcita-Kośa evergreen and fuller. In the first place, this Karma-Yogī is conjoined with limited ego and discriminating vision, so I-ness sentiment becomes resident in the body, senses, mind, and intellect (which are the instruments of Karma). So, the sentiment, "I am a doer," which is the support of all Saṃskāras, exists and is all alive and not burnt. Variant-Yoga, by its practice alone, is not capable of burning the "I am a doer" sentiment, even if it is followed until the end of the life of Brahmā. Quite the reverse, by its practice, it makes doership-ego more assertive. That is because there is the presence of I-ness in whatever activities that are ongoing through the body, senses, mind, and intellect. The Yogī certainly knows himself as a doer of those activities. Because of the existence of trueness in those Karma, himself, and the body, he continues to accumulate within himself Saṃskāras, which are the cause of memory of those Karma.

Variant-Yoga can be divided into the following five limbs -

1. I am a doer of Karma.
2. I have certain Karma as my duty (Kartavya).
3. I am active in Karma, not for myself but for public well-being (Loka-Kalyāṇa).
4. I offer my Karma to the Lord.
5. I am equal in success and failure of whatever fruits there are or even not there.

We need to judiciously examine each limb to see if it can free the Yogī from doership-ego.

First, with a bit of introspection, it is clear that his vision is endowed with discrimination. In this vision: 1) doer is real, 2) duty is real, 3) instruments of Karma viz. the body, senses, mind, and intellect are real, 4) Karma is real, 5) fruits are real, 6) relinquishment of fruits are real, 7) Saṃsāra, for whose good he is doing Karma is real, 8) separate from him, the Lord, the Bestower of fruits is real, and 9) offering of fruits of Karma is also real. When all of them are real, how can Saṃskāras of done Karma be made unreal (Mithyā)? Indeed, they must be more real than real! When Karma-Saṃskāras are shown real, then why would fruits not be there? How can fruits be made unreal? Sure, one can be convinced that its fruits are highly elevated, but they are indeed perishable, and the fruits, by their nature, put one in the bondage of birth and death and are not the ones that can provide freedom.

Second, this Yogī is duty-bound, "I have certain Karma as my duty." The word Kartavya, ordinarily referred to as duty, is in the sense of scriptural injunctions (Vidhi), and so both terms Kartavya and Vidhi are synonymous. Śāstra has formulated the fruits of injunctive Karma as piety (Puṇya) and the fruits of prohibited (Niṣiddha) Karma as sin (Pāpa). When the creation of sin is definite in the fruits of prohibited Karma, no power can stop it. As the law of the Lord is so harsh, then how can there be no piety fruits of injunctive Karma? That would be a grave injustice, as this Yogī is holding all in trueness, be it the doer, duty, Karma, fruits, Saṃsāra, or the Lord. Alternatively, it could be understood this way. When he has made an activity in Karma his injunctive duty, then relinquishment of activity will become a non-duty, a prohibited act for him. Because it is forbidden, the relinquishment of Karma will become sinful for him. When Karma-relinquishment is sin, then why would Karma-activity be not piety? When Karma-activity becomes piety, it will bring its fruit, and the Yogī will have to come in the bondage of the body for its enjoyment.

Third, now the question that is left is about equanimity of mind. Whether he performs Karma with equanimity in the success and failure of the fruits? With a bit of thought, it is clear that he is not alike in Karma, whether he does or does not do. That is because Karma is a duty for him. Karma is a scriptural injunction for him. Hence, in the relinquishment of Karma, he is neither equal nor independent. Additionally, in the cause of public well-being, whether he does or not, he is also not equal, as Karma is an obligation for him for public well-being. He is also not equal in whether he offers his Karma to the Lord or does not offer, as the offering to the Lord is also a duty for him. "It is my pleasure whether I do Karma or not, whether I do them for the sake of public well-being or I do them for my good, or I do not do at all for anyone's sake, or whether I do it only as a pastime and it would be my joy whether I offer the fruits to the Lord or not" - in all of the above matters he is not equal, but undoubtedly unequal. When he is certainly unequal in all these matters and is in bondage, then how and from where can he have equanimity in only fruits? That cannot be grasped! Where will equanimity come when there is the bondage of duty from all over? Duty, by its nature, is discriminating. Without discrimination, the duty can never come into being. In reality, when someone creates a guise of equality, even though he has not reached natural non-artificiality and parity, such a ploy can only be understood as nothing but a play of an impersonator. The root of discrimination is only limited ego due to discriminating-vision, so establishing equality without melting the ego is impossible. Where there are distinctions and limitations, there go desires. When the limitations of the body bind the Yogī, it is natural for him to be with desires. When desires are present, how can there be equality? Artificial equality cannot remain without betrayal. If not today, then tomorrow. How long can a $100 counterfeit bill stay in circulation? Outwardly, one may sing songs of equality, "I am equal in success and failure of fruits," but from within, can discrimination hold itself in launching its arrow? Not, as its root, the limited ego is still present within. Thus, the Yogī is still far from real equanimity due to limited vision. Even if he has filled in his conscience sentiment of equanimity, such sentiment can neither burn current Karma-Saṃskāras nor can it even touch accumulated Karma-Saṃskāras. Being the Sāttvika result of the conscience, that sentiment of equanimity is itself the cause of its Saṃskāra.

Now remains the "I am a doer" ego, the root of all Karma-Saṃskāras. No approach for cutting it is found in the practice of the postulated Variant Karma-Yoga. On the contrary, holding the weight of duty, the firmness of ego is increased. Duty is certainly ignorance; as it is only due to ignorance, there is duty. When Jīva, in limited form, becomes something, duty gets on the top of his head forcibly. Upon duty reaching the top of his head, his limited ego becomes firmer. In other words, one can only be free from this I-ness sentiment when this ghost of duty is brought down by whatever means. Freedom from duty can happen only when I-ness sentiment comes down from the head because duty always follows I-ness sentiment. From I-ness sentiment, duty comes out. With duty, the I-ness sense gets firmer. This I-ness sentiment is only ignorance born. It is not born of any commencement or result. So, it can only be removed by knowledge, never by Karma. Only by knowledge, the knowledge that is not indirect knowledge (Parokṣa) but direct intuitive transcendental (Aparokṣa) knowledge of own Ātmā.

नाहं देहो नेन्द्रियाण्यन्तरङ्गं नाहंकारः प्राणवर्गो न बुद्धिः ।
दारापत्यक्षेत्रवित्तादिदूरः साक्षी नित्यः प्रत्यगात्मा शिवोऽहम् ॥[31]

I am not the body, not senses, not conscience, not ego, not Prāṇa, or not intellect. However, I am separate from woman, son et al. and field, wealth et al., the inner Self of all, the eternal witness Śiva only.

अपि चेदसि पापेभ्य: सर्वेभ्य: पापकृत्तम: |
सर्वं ज्ञानप्लवेनैव वृजिनं सन्तरिष्यसि || BG 4.36 ||
यथैधांसि समिद्धोऽग्निर्भस्मसात्कुरुतेऽर्जुन |
ज्ञानाग्नि: सर्वकर्माणि भस्मसात्कुरुते तथा || BG 4.37 ||
न हि ज्ञानेन सदृशं पवित्रमिह विद्यते |
तत्स्वयं योगसंसिद्ध: कालेनात्मनि विन्दति || BG 4.38 ||

Even if you are the most sinful of all sinners, you will undoubtedly cross over the entire ocean of sin with the boat of knowledge.

Hey Arjuna! Just as a blazing fire turns firewood into ashes, the fire of knowledge reduces all actions into ashes.

Unquestionably nothing exists here as purifying as knowledge, which in due time, upon attaining perfection in Yoga, the Yogī experiences in his own heart.

When you attain such direct realization of the Ātmā, whether they are doer, duty, Karma, accumulated or current Karma Saṃskāras - all are burnt, just as a blazing fire burns a heap of firewood and turns it into

---

[31] Ādi Śaṅkarācārya's "Advaita Pañcaratnam, अद्वैत पञ्चरत्नम्) 1

ashes. Then even while doing everything, you are a non-doer. All Karma is nothing but Akarma (non-action) and automatically without fruits. You are free from all injunctions and prohibitions. You are a true desireless, a true Karma-Yogī, and a personification of equality. Then, the body, senses, mind, and intellect move around in the flow of fate, like a clock, clicking periodically upon winding its key. Even while not doing anything with your reality, you will be doing everything; and yet not come into the bondage of duty. You would be standing separate from the body, senses, mind, and intellect and observing their play. They will be busy crying, but you will be laughing. They will be lamenting, but you will be enjoying. Thus, you will be the light that would illuminate the entire Saṃsāra.

आत्मा ब्रह्मेति निश्चित्य भावाभावौ च कल्पितौ ।
निष्कामः किं विजानाति किं ब्रूते च करोति किम्॥[32]

> Knowing one's Ātmā as the Brahman and the being and non-being Jagata as imaginary, for such a true desireless, what else would he have to know, what else would he have to say, or what else would he have to do?

Concluding, some have pronounced Variant Karma-Yoga as independent means for liberation. However, it can be a separate means for release only if it can burn accumulated and current impressions (Sañcita and Kriyamāṇa Karma-Saṃskāras). By its nature, it is shown that Variant-Yoga is not able to remove Kriyamāṇa Saṃskāras, let alone remove Sañcita Saṃskāras. Thus, when the said Variant-Yoga cannot be proven as an independent path for attaining liberation, opining two separate paths is nothing but fantasy. In reality, Jīva and Jagata are born of ignorance. Only ignorance remover knowledge can be the path. Desireless actions being the means for knowledge, though, can become a stepping-stone for that path, not an independent one!

Are Desireless-Actions of Variant-Yoga useful?

Variant-Yoga, as postulated by some, neither can burn current Karma nor accumulated Karma, though those ready for fruition Karma are burnt on their own after providing their fruits. Further, freedom from birth and death is not possible by just the practice of such Yoga. This does not mean that it is always a failure. No! How can that be? Indeed, it is the nectar for a fit Yogī, though only to a limit. Not that it is a magic wand that will free us. There is a tenet in the kingdom of Prakṛti that for one who is fit, every substance in a proper proportion may be fruitful at some times. However, for the same fit person, at some other times, it may be poisonous. Additionally, it may be suitable for one fit person, but it may be unsuitable for others.

While it may be beneficial in one proportion, it may be harmful if the proportion is increased. Medicine in proper balance may be helpful but harmful in increased proportion. Laxatives may be necessary for a sick person with a stomach ailment at once. However, continued use may acerbate stomach ailment and reduce gastric juices after the patient's bowels are cleaned, he has recovered and is healthy. Ghī may be beneficial for a healthy strong person. But for one who has a fever, it may make him weaker. Similarly, fertilizer in appropriate proportion can increase crop production, but excessive fertilizer will burn the crop. According to the said rule, in its time and proper balance, Niṣkāma-Karma-Yoga can also provide success to one who is qualified and competent. This Yoga intends that the aim is the only relinquishment in all righteous activities. All righteous acts practiced by a fit person require a gift of relinquishment in proper proportion based on his fitness. However, in the bondage of ignorance, holding doership-ego and duty, and seeking happiness, a person is active in Karma. For a materialistic person who is engaged in worldly enjoyments and who in his vain self-interest has made attaining worldly enjoyments or acquiring higher heavenly worlds his aim, for the removal of such person's vain self-interest and bondage of enjoyment, Śruti Bhagavatī, with her grace

---

[32] Aṣṭāvakra Gītā (अष्टावक्र गीता) 18.8

has censured worldly as well as heavenly enjoyments and has shown their fruits as perishable, possessing the faults of depletion (Kṣaya) and of the attribute of possessing more or less in enjoyments (Atiśayatā) and hence pain-yielding.

यामिमां पुष्पितां वाचं प्रवदन्त्यविपश्चित: |
वेदवादरता: पार्थ नान्यदस्तीति वादिन: || BG 2.42 ||
कामात्मान: स्वर्गपरा जन्मकर्मफलप्रदाम् |
क्रियाविशेषबहुलां भोगैश्वर्यगतिं प्रति || BG 2.43 ||
भोगैश्वर्यप्रसक्तानां तयापहृतचेतसाम् |
व्यवसायात्मिका बुद्धि: समाधौ न विधीयते || BG 2.44 ||

Hey Arjuna! The undiscerning who deems heaven as the highest goal, who is desire-ridden, who revels in the letter of the Vedas, and who declares "there is nothing more than this" utters flowery words of many actions replete with specific rites that give fruits of action in the form of birth and acquisition of enjoyments and power. Whose mind is carried away by those words and attached to enjoyments and power, his resolute intellect cannot situate with a steadfast concentration in the Self.

Further, Śruti Bhagavatī guided that you do Karma without keeping your self-interest in the forefront and do Karma for public well-being. This way, through your Karma, by offering your Karma to the Lord, provide service to the Lord and not be anxious for reward. Moreover, make a resolve in your Citta that -

कर्मण्येवाधिकारस्ते मा फलेषु कदाचन |
मा कर्मफलहेतुर्भूर्मा ते सङ्गोऽस्त्वकर्मणि || BG 2.47 ||

Your right is only in action, not in the fruit at any time. Do not be impelled by the fruits of actions. Do not have an attachment to non-action.

It is your right to do Karma. The reward is not a thing of your right but is only a thing of the right of the Lord. The act of offering one's Karma and fruits to the Lord is in itself a great fruit through which the grace of the Lord is obtained. They are stationary fruits, and in reality, worldly fruits are not real because being perishable, they are fruitless. Thus, for fruits, why would one become anxious and make oneself an unbeliever; and take the right of the Lord in one's hand? Why would we then have a begging attitude in front of the Lord when He is our father and is our benefactor? We are ignorant, but He being omniscient, knows everything for our well-being. Whatever pleasure and pain come from Him is always for our good because He is an auspicious personification, so how can evil manifest from Him? His grace is always in our best interest, whether it is a pleasure or pain. Only because of our foolishness and paltry intellect do we make the imagination of good or evil in His grace and become non-believers in Him - that is a great sin, the root of all sins.

When we are over-anxious about reward, our behavior becomes warped, and as a result, we are driven far from the reward. The desire for reward increases Rajoguṇa, which is the root of grief. Rajoguṇa is the only one that brings us a failure. In the presence of increased Rajoguṇa, our heart becomes unstable, and then success moves away from us. Many a time, attempting to pour liquid from a tiny bottle to another when our mind is worried about spillage, then because of Rajoguṇī worry, our hands will shake, and the liquid will spill out. However, worry-free and without fear, not even a single drop will spill out if we start pouring the liquid. It is a steady rule of Prakṛti that success is always due to Sattvaguṇa, and Sattvaguṇa always comes by the relinquishment of the desire for fruits.

For a materialistic person whose heart is filled with Rajoguṇa, Śruti Bhagavatī, showing compassion towards such a person, thought it impossible to abandon Karma suddenly. Citta of such a person is full of steam, and until the steam is not fully released, he cannot remain calm; similar to a patient who is under a lot of pain due to a boil filled with pus, he cannot get relief until the pus is removed. Only Karma can remove the steam of Rajoguṇa. Hence, someone should present a path to remove it. However, the tactic should be such that -

1. With the sentiment of fruit relinquishment in the activity of Karma, the agony of the desire for fruits does not become painful to him.
2. Pain in Karma changes into joy through a) pure sentiment of duty and b) public service and relinquishment of self-interest.
3. Karma changes into such devotion through firmness of the sentiment of offering to the lord that quiescence awakens in the Citta of the fit.

When the taste of peace is acquired, naturally, the fountainhead of devotion opens up. When the fountainhead of devotion becomes potent, then whether it is a duty or whether it is Karma, all of them are let go by him, just as a glass drops on its own from the hands of an intoxicated person. Śruti Bhagavatī and Prakṛti, being sentimental on Jīva, with deep compassion, created a composition of such desireless actions that here, it can provide an opportunity to remove the increased flow of Rajoguṇa. There, it can provide a chance to be free from the vain self-interest and enjoyment laced intellect and obtain a fitness for devotion because the fruit of Karma is only that the heart becomes pure from Rajoguṇa. For Śruti Bhagavatī, the removal of Rajoguṇa by Karma-Yoga and preparation of devotional fruit is intended. The same intent is clarified in Śrīmad Bhāgavata, 11th Canto, 11th Chapter verses 22 to 25 words of Bhagavāna in the beginning, the 20th Chapter verses 6 to 11 and Pippalāyana words 3rd Chapter verse 40. Through devotion, ego can be thinned, and with the fire of knowledge flown away, like a glacier, the melting and flowing in the form of water can be airborne as mist. Thus, by making judicious use of Variant-Yoga, fitness for knowledge can be earned with the purity of the conscience. However, by the practice alone of Variant-Yoga, neither knowledge can be acquired nor liberation. Variant-Yoga by regular succession with the removal of Rajoguṇa is helpful in the acquisition of knowledge and liberation. However, those who have made Variant-Yoga their only aim and believe that there is undoubtedly nothing further from this and have refused to go further are stopping the opening of the fountainhead of pure devotion. If they believe that this rest area is the desired location and have permanently set their camp, how can they move ahead? Because of improper use, the success of Variant-Yoga does not happen for them. One should not worry about how can public well-being happen with Karma-Yoga gone? It is only on the exaltation of the Ātmā that the good of the entire Saṃsāra is dependent. Until you are free from the disease, how can you make others without illness? Remaining a quack, instead of removing the sickness and pain of others, you may put their lives in danger. First, why don't you reach your destination, and then you will know where the good of the Saṃsāra lay? In the Saṃsāra, every substance is for relinquishment. There is nothing in the world to cling on to for good. Enjoyment is there to be free from enjoyment, activity in Karma is there to be free from the bondage of Karma, and duty is there to be free from duty. Even when the body is so clear about leaving, what can be the thing to hold on to? Though you have sworn to hold on to, and contrary to that, Prakṛti has tied everything to be freed. See! Who wins this war? That is not an imaginary whim. Evidence of the truthfulness of this tenet is provided through the words of Śrī Kṛṣṇa spoken to Uddhava in Śrīmad Bhāgavata. Śrī Kṛṣṇa of Śrīmad Bhagavad Gītā is the same Śrī Kṛṣṇa of Śrīmad Bhāgavata. Those interested in the evidence of the truthfulness of this tenet kindly refer to Śrīmad Bhāgavata 11th Canto, Chapters 10th, 11th, 12th, 13th, 14th, 19th, and 20th and contemplate with calm Citta.

Liberation and Public Well-being through the oneness of Sāṅkhya and Yoga

Only after burning one's limited ego in the fire of knowledge and attaining union with oneness in own Ātmā can true renunciation of Karma and true desireless Karma-Yoga or real Sāṅkhya and real Yoga be obtained. By abandoning doership delusion, whether it is accumulated or current, all Karma and Saṃskāras can be burnt. That is the only path to freedom from birth and death bondage. There is no other path, nor will there be. That is Yoga, and that is Sāṅkhya, which is the propounded subject of Gītā. Having risen to this state, a Yogī, even while doing, is a non-doer. All his Karma are Akarma and are similar to roasted seeds or burnt rope, which, while retaining their shape, in the case of roasted seeds, are not suitable for producing fruits, or in the case of burnt rope, not useful to tie anything. Relinquishment of any activity in its own form is not Karma-Saṃnyāsa, the way some have made a mockery of Karma-Saṃnyāsa. In the kingdom of Prakṛti, nobody can be motionless by their nature.

न हि कश्चित्क्षणमपि जातु तिष्ठत्यकर्मकृत् |
कार्यते ह्यवश: कर्म सर्व: प्रकृतिजैर्गुणै: || BG 3.5 ||

No one can ever stay, even for a moment, without action. Unquestionably, all helplessly perform actions through the constituents born of Prakṛti.

A real renouncer (Karma-Saṃnyāsī) is one who, through knowledge, detaches his Ātmā "is as is" from the body and born thereof all attachments, just as butter separated from yogurt cannot mix with watered buttermilk. In the same way, the Ātmā to not have any attachment with the body and remain unstained from it and born thereof all activities, just as a lotus leaf remains in water (BG 5.10), and I-ness and mineness and desire do not ever spring in the body (BG 3.30). Such a Yogī, in reality, is a true renouncer.

ब्रह्मण्याधाय कर्माणि सङ्गं त्यक्त्वा करोति य: |
लिप्यते न स पापेन पद्मपत्रमिवाम्भसा || BG 5.10 ||

Abandoning attachment, he who performs action dedicated to the Brahman is not tainted by sin as a lotus leaf by water.

Acquiring the above renunciation (Karma-Saṃnyāsa), Bhagavāna commands Arjuna to get up and engage in the war.

मयि सर्वाणि कर्माणि संन्यस्याध्यात्मचेतसा |
निराशीर्निर्ममो भूत्वा युध्यस्व विगतज्वर: || BG 3.30 ||

Renouncing all actions in Me with the mind in transcendent knowledge, having become free from expectations, mineness, and affliction, fight.

Bhagavāna tells Arjuna - "With analytic perspective renouncing all Karma in My Brahman-form, true nature that I am, in that form whether it is a doer, whether it is Karma or whether it is the body - all are delusional, imagined perceptions. Even though with My power, insentient as they are, all are dancing similar to how wooden puppets dance with the power of a puppeteer, I have no stain from them. Their mutations do not mutate Me, but I am the witness-observer of their activities." This way, "Hey, Arjuna! Directly realizing your Ātmā and forsaking desire and mineness without being afflicted, resolve that 'I am neither doing anything, nor anything is happening in me,' and fight."

That is real, alive, and awake Karma-Saṃnyāsa. That is the essence of Gītā and Vedānta. Motionlessness (निश्चेष्टता, Niśceṣṭatā) can never be the essence of Gītā and Vedānta, nor can it be proven by any measure or example. Were motionlessness the essence of Vedānta, then thoughtful contributions, those masterpieces of the two greatest epitomes of Vedantic thinking, Bhagavāna Vedavyāsa and Ādi Śaṅkarācārya, would never have been possible for ordinary beings, even in many lifetimes. The flow of energy that was moved by these remarkable beings and greats of the recent past, Śrī Kabīradāsa, Śrī Jñāneśvara Mahārāja, Śrī Svāmī Rāmadāsa, Guru Nānaka, Śrī Svāmī Vivekānanda, Śrī Svāmī Rāmatīrtha, Śrī Svāmī Ātmānanda, Śrī Svāmī Śivānanda, Śrī Svāmī Cinmayānanda and others who in brief periods have created awareness and miracle, is without a doubt, nothing but the fruit of Vedānta and Gītā-propounded Karma-Saṃnyāsa. They are all miracles of this Sāṅkhya and Yoga. Contrary to this, the form of Sāṅkhya and Yoga that some have formulated is artificial. It is like a lifeless mannequin that does not have Prāṇa and is merely a photo of the true Yoga, which is only good to see, but from which real success cannot be attained. By not doing anything, everything can be done. Instead of being a doer where everything done is always paltry (acts with faults). For such acts, to be faultless is impossible. When one becomes someone as a doer, fallen from one's true

Lordly form, the ruination of a paltry Jīva is inevitable. When a Jīva has limited himself, then anything he does is limited. It cannot be grand, and that which has become limited will be with fault. Contrary to this, when one is beyond the limited I-ness sense and has washed his hands from doer and duty, one's seat will be elevated from being a Jīva to being the Paramātmā. Then the fountainhead of energy from within will open up with a flow similar to a rapid mountain stream that turns into a large river. At that time, one will be completely pure and full of generosity. Anything done naturally, without any duty, will be only created by the Lord. The senses, mind, intellect, and the paltriest fiend ego have left, as these limbs have been fully dedicated to the Lord, who sits in them and is their controller. At that time, one's words will be Lordly words, and one's vision will be Lordly vision. At this stage, light from all limbs will emanate just as how sunlight comes out through wet garments. At that time, whatever acts manifest from these limbs, they will be grand and faultless and beneficial to all. In reality, duty is the bondage of Jīva. It is only because of duty that there is the assertiveness of ego, and it is because of ego that there are fruits of Karma, which is the cause of birth and death. Just as buckets of a water-wheel move around in a stream, sometimes up, sometimes down, like a Jīva-form bucket tied with duty-form rope moves around and around over the Saṃsāra-form stream is never able to be let loose. However, with the knowledge of one's true nature, when one can free oneself from the noose of duty, then who is the doer? What duty? Wherefrom birth and death? What Saṃsāra? Then you are the one beloved one. You are the one who is prayed. You are the one who is providing light to all. You are the one to provide energy to the sun. You are the one to grant coolness to the moon. You are the one to twinkle the stars, and even death will tremble with fear from you; what are birth and death then?

भीषाऽस्माद्वातः पवते । भीषोदेति सूर्यः ।
भीषाऽस्मादग्निश्चेन्द्रश्च । मृत्युर्धावति पञ्चम इति ।[33]

That is, the wind is moving because of his fear, the sun rises because of his fear, and because of his fear, the fire-deity and Indra are performing their acts, and fifth, death is running. That is the state in which one should conduct one's self.

Delimited Ātmā! Wake up in your true nature and see; there is never any duty. You are ever free from all duty. You are the light of all and the Lord of all in your witness-conscious form. Has there been any duty for a king? The obligation of duty is on his servants. The burden of duty is only on those bound by the Saṃsāra and whose eyes have not met yours, that is, those who have not found Yoga in you. Though everything is done under his authority, the king seated on his throne is unflinching in his supreme rest. Not doing anything himself, he is doing everything. Opposite to this, those who have duty on their backs, even though they may be active in Karma all the time, cannot do anything. Bound by duty, they cannot even move around. Being self-boundable, what can they do? Only those who are free can perform.

Just as a bull of an oilman rotating an oil extraction device after a whole day's travel is still at the same place in the evening as he was in the morning, in the same way, those who are under the burden of doership, what can they do? Duty does not even allow their napes to lift. At the beginning of Śrīmad Bhāgavata, 11th Canto, 21st Chapter, Śrī Kṛṣṇa tells Uddhava the same, "Duty in the form of injunctions and prohibitions is only for those extremely ignorant, the ones who remaining bound in the body make numerous wishes in their hearts, and influenced by those wishes expand their Karma all around, and thus always receive pain and suffering and flow forever in the Saṃsāra." Injunctions and prohibitions are for them so that after the relinquishment of a series of Karma, the flow of Karma can stop in a few Karma. Duty in the form of injunction and prohibition is not something real. It is only bondage for them so that they remain in its control. The same is spoken by Śrī Kṛṣṇa to Arjuna in BG 6.44 -

जिज्ञासुरपि योगस्य शब्दब्रह्मातिवर्तते ।

Even the seeker of Yoga certainly goes beyond the injunctions and prohibitions of the Vedas.

---

[33] Taittirīya Upaniṣad (तैत्तिरीय उपनिषद्) 2.8

Just as a river flowing within the bounds of its banks becomes one with the ocean and becomes free from the bondage of the banks, a Jīva-form river needs to flow within the bounds of the banks of injunctions and prohibitions of the Vedas to be awakened. Even when a seeker of this Yoga becomes free from duty, does one need to ask anything about this Yogī? Once he is awakened, why would there be any duty? Duty then would be a sin for him and detrimental to his real love. Well, can there be any rule in love?

In succinct terms, it is only through Karma-Saṃnyāsa, that is, where there is oneness between Sāṅkhya and Yoga, upon forsaking I-ness in the body "not doing anything," everything can be done. However, through Variant-Yoga, that is, where there is bondage with the body, and there is a duty but no desire for fruits, nothing is done while doing everything. It can neither give freedom from birth and death nor is it capable of accomplishing real public well-being (लोकसंग्रह, Lokasaṃgraha). Genuine public well-being can only be accomplished by the Yoga of situating with oneness in the Ātmā, like the greats of recent past, Śrī Kabīradāsa, Śrī Jñāneśvara Mahārāja, Śrī Svāmī Rāmadāsa, Guru Nānaka, Śrī Svāmī Vivekānanda, Śrī Svāmī Rāmatīrtha, Svāmī Ātmānanda, and others. Śrī Svāmī Rāmatīrtha, in his discourse on "Adhyātma-Śakti" in the USA around 1902-1904, made profound remarks. To wit - "The moment we stand up as improvers of the Saṃsāra, that very moment we become spoilers of the Saṃsāra." "Physician heal thyself," "Physician get your own treatment." According to Vedānta, the entire Saṃsāra is nothing else apart from the Lord. The entire Saṃsāra is complete, the entire Saṃsāra is the Brahman, the entire Saṃsāra is my own Ātmā, and the entire Saṃsāra is one alone. That being the case, if I accept some approach to improve the Saṃsāra and then come to know that you are downtrodden and see that you are in pain and suffering because of your paltry aspirations, I am instantly spoiling you, and I am being spoilt. By this method, I am accepting you as something separate from me. In reality, such a discriminating intellect is illusory. That is why Vedānta is saying, "Improvers! Those proclaiming themselves as improvers! You think that the Saṃsāra is full of sin. You think that the Saṃsāra is ugly. You think that you should curse at the Saṃsāra. That is all your delusional vision. Why should one believe that the Saṃsāra is so distressed that it needs help from you? Śrī Kṛṣṇa came, Mahāvīra Svāmī came, Bhagavāna Buddha came, Jesus Christ came, and many other knowers of the Reality came. They all did whatever they could to uplift and enlighten people, but do we see any improvement in the Saṃsāra? Even today, there is the same pain, the same suffering, and the same conflicts the Saṃsāra is found as it was. Today does anyone think that people are happier than in the past? Have all our cars, trains, airplanes, and amenities of modern Saṃsāra made us any happier? That is just like that fraction whose numerator and the denominator are increasing, that is, ½=2/4=4/8= 8/16 by form may look different from the prior one, it may look as if it is increasing, but in reality, the numerator and denominator are increasing at the same rate, with the fraction having never changed. Extending the logic, if our wealth has increased, then at the same time, our needs and expenditures have increased. In essence, this Saṃsāra is like a dog's tail. It can never stay straight. Those who rise with the desire to improve the Saṃsāra are deceiving themselves. They are making a big mistake in their effort to improve the Saṃsāra. What needs to be improved is not the Saṃsāra but oneself because it is only upon one's worsening that there is an appearance of worsening of the Saṃsāra. Do not make your focus outside yourself. Improve yourself. Know by conviction and experience your own real Lordliness. The moment you are complete by realizing the Lord, the exact moment the stream of life, power, and joy will flow forever. That is the only approach to spreading the Truth.

Nature of Karma

Let us first reflect upon the nature of Karma, its application, and its fruit. The nature of Karma, as depicted by Gītā, is --

भूतभावोद्भवकरो विसर्गः कर्मसञ्ज्ञितः || BG 8.3 ||

Activity that produces sentiments in beings is called Karma.

Good or bad activity that produces sentiments in beings is defined as Karma. The subjective processes of arousing mental states or emotional waves originating in the mind and intellect in the form of thoughts or resolves are called sentiments. Activities of the body and senses which directly result from the mind and intellect or occur in the knowledge of the mind and intellect being producers of emotions are called Karma. The intention here is that all those efforts that create enjoyments or impressions (Saṃskāras) are called Karma. Emotional activities can manifest only in the mind and intellect and not anywhere else. Without the mind and intellect, sentiments are not formed. Without sentiments, there is no cause for fruits. Though after eating, myriads of actions happen within the body, such as feces, urine, blood, and muscles, they do not happen in the knowledge of the mind and intellect. They are not the result of the mind and intellect, nor do they create any good or bad impressions. That is why they do not fall within the definition of Karma. That is the pervasive definition of Karma. Besides this, to call material relinquishment towards deities as Karma makes Karma extremely adulterated. Evidence of the trueness of the definition is that except for human life-form, Śāstra has not declared activities happening in other life-forms, such as animals, and birds, as the cause for the fruits of piety or sin. The reason for this is that even though innumerable activities are ongoing in these species, there being no awakened relationship of the mind and intellect in those activities, they do not become the cause for the creation of good or evil sentiments, and thus they do not become the cause for the fruits of piety or sin. In these species, the Sheath of Supreme Bliss (Ānandamaya-Kośa)[34]is not developed, and their intellect is like a dream, so they cannot arouse sentiments. Under the same rule, the Karma of a knower is not the cause for fruits. That is because with the maturity of knowledge in his activities, his discriminating vision having been burnt, his sentiments of good and evil are also burnt. Thus, activities that produce sentiments can only be defined as Karma and nothing else.

With this definition of Karma, all activities and all non-activities, whether they are in the form of grasping or relinquishing, are the direct result of the mind and intellect. Because they are happening in the knowledge of the mind and intellect, they produce sentiments and so fall in the definition of Karma. Further, whether it is an activity or a non-activity, both have a relationship with Prakṛti, and both are created in the kingdom of Prakṛti. Since the kingdom of Prakṛti is broad, the singularity of fitness is natural. If all living beings were only of one fitness, then there would be an absence of variegation of Prakṛti, and there would be no discriminating sentiments. How can that happen? In the kingdom of Prakṛti, singularity is necessary. When Prakṛti, by her nature, is Tri-constituted (Triguṇamayī), then due to the distinctions of the three constituents, there are innumerable distinctions in the kingdom of Prakṛti - what is there to be surprised? When there are distinctions in the root, distinctions in acts are natural. In this infinite creation of the Lord, it is impossible to find substances that are equal in nature and form, no matter where you look in the world. When there are distinctions between nature and form, the necessity of distinctions of fitness is also established. There must be a corresponding distinction in fitness based on individual nature. Fitness that a father has, a son does not have; fitness a son has, a mother does not have; fitness a mother has, women do not have; fitness a child has, a youth does not have; fitness a youth has, elderly do not have; fitness a Brāhmaṇa has, Kṣatriya does not have; fitness a Kṣatriya has, a Vaiśya and Śūdra does not have; fitness a Brahmacārī has, a householder does not have; fitness a householder has, a retired and a Saṃnyāsī does not have, and fitness a retiree and a Saṃnyāsī has, a householder does not have, and so on. There is nothing unsuccessful in the kingdom of Prakṛti. Everything is successful based on individual nature and fitness. Not only that, even Sankhiyā, a toxic Āyurvedic medicine based on a person's fitness, can be ambrosiac. When it is so, corresponding to one's fitness, it is inevitable for activity and non-activity to succeed. For someone, activity is fruitful, while for someone else, non-activity. If someone's non-activity is to be forsaken, then it may be necessary for someone else to relinquish activity. For whom activity is Karma, for them, non-activity is forbidden action

[34] Ānandamaya-Kośa (आनन्दमय-कोश) means the Sheath of Supreme Bliss. It is the innermost subtlest sheath of the Pañca-Kośa (पञ्च-कोश, the five sheaths that cover the Ātmā as described in Taittirīya Upaniṣad 2.1-5). When the mind and senses cease functioning in a deep sleep, it still stands between the finite world and the Ātmā. The sheath typically has its most total play during deep sleep, while it has only a partial manifestation in the dream and wakeful states. The Ānandamaya-Kośa is a reflection of the Ātmā as the Real-Conscious-Bliss (सच्चिदानन्द, Saccidānanda).

(Vikarma); and for whom a non-activity is Karma, activity is resolutely forbidden. When the kingdom of Prakṛti is Tri-constituted, then all Sāttvika, Rājasika, and Tāmasika activities can become Karma; not that only Rajoguṇī activities be accepted as Karma and Sattvaguṇī activities be removed from the bounds of Karma. Indeed, according to fitness, Rajoguṇī activity and Sattvaguṇī non-activity are all Karma. Keeping only Rajoguṇī activities in the definition of Karma and treating Sattvaguṇī non-activity as null of Karma and making it separate from the definition of Karma is nothing but empty stubbornness. If someone's mind is full of Rajoguṇa, then according to the rules of Prakṛti for him, only activity is acceptable, and non-activity is to be left. For instance, if the pus in a boil developed in someone's body is not removed, the boil can never be cured. On the contrary, the pus will spread in his body. So, it is vital to provide a path to take out the pus. Similarly, for a sick patient (in the form of the Saṃsāra) in whose heart (boil), Rajoguṇa and fickleness (pus) have developed, it is necessary to provide a path of activity to remove it. If Rajoguṇa is not offered a path to leave and stopped by non-activity, then that Rajoguṇī pus will not stop, but on its own, it will find some other way, by which non-activity will become defiled. Sickness will get worse. Desireless actions are articulated to remove this Rajoguṇī pus through a righteous path. However, in the kingdom of Prakṛti, every activity, finally after having itself satiated and exhausted, is there for change into non-activity. That is the stable rule of Prakṛti. There is nothing in the kingdom of Prakṛti that can remain steady. On the contrary, every activity is bound to change every moment. Hunger after satisfaction is there for non-activity only. Every enjoyment activity after clasping is there to move the hands away. Waking activity after fatigue is there for non-activity only. Sleeping activity after giving rest is for breaking only. Even the wheel of coming and going, birth and death, after creating agony in the heart, is entirely there for freedom only.

When it is so, how can one accept the Rajoguṇī activity of Karma to be steady? Accepting so is breaking the stable rule of Prakṛti. When the boil (heart) is cleaned after Rajoguṇī pus has come out, what charity is there in putting the pus back in? Pus was there to be removed from the inside, not the other way around or put back in from the outside. When the pus is removed, it is only necessary to apply Sāttvika ointment of peace on the boil (heart). Suppose a negligent physician leaves after making an overly excessive incision to remove a boil. Then instead of curing the boil, he may create additional boils in which pus is likely to be developed. For such a patient, an effort of non-activity can be only acceptable, and activity not acceptable. For some, activity may be acceptable in every state based on their fitness, and non-activity is not acceptable. Again, for some, non-activity may be acceptable in other states, and activity is not acceptable.

When such is the rule of Prakṛti, going against the rule, how can Bhagavāna become a negligent physician to define only efforts of activity as Karma and call non-activity as forbidden and null of Karma? It is not comprehendible that Gītā has come down to teach something contrary to the rules of Prakṛti. How is that possible? Neither Bhagavāna can be a negligent physician nor has Gītā come down to teach something contrary to the rules of Prakṛti, notwithstanding the lamentation of some in their Rajoguṇa inebriation. Gītā is explicit regarding this -

आरुरुक्षोर्मुनेर्योगं कर्म कारणमुच्यते |
योगारूढस्य तस्यैव शम: कारणमुच्यते || BG 6.3 ||

> Action is said to be the cause for a sage seeking ascension in Yoga. Having ascended in Yoga quiescence is said to be the cause for him.

For a seeker desiring to attain Yoga of situating with oneness in the Ātmā, Karma is called the cause. However, after having ascended, control of "resolves of doer and duty" is called the cause to remain steady in that state. Bhagavad Gītā is a broad, generous scripture. How can she set forth a subject with an adulterated perspective? Whatever she says, she says it with a complete pervasive vision for protecting the entire earth. Then how can Gītā utter words contrary to the rules of Prakṛti? Such as "Effort in activity is only Karma and effort in non-activity is an inferior and null Karma."

How can Gītā say that the lifelong activity of Rajoguṇī Karma is not there to be abandoned when the instruments of Karma (the body, senses, mind, and intellect) on their own time after being tired are there to rest? In the end, in the kingdom of Prakṛti, fatigue is present, and we find its clear evidence always in the deep-sleep state. Every living being, tired of activity, always goes into non-activity of the deep-sleep state. It is only due to the non-activity of deep sleep that energy for future activity is obtained. When the fruit of every activity is non-activity only, every fruit of grasping is determined in the kingdom of Prakṛti as relinquishment only, then how can non-activity be trampled upon? Indeed, if activity has gotten any respect, it is only because of its relationship with non-activity. Ice cream has gotten its sweetness only because of its association with sugar. Without it, there is no sweetness in ice cream. If desireless actions have earned some respect, it is only because of their relationship with the relinquishment of fruits. By strengthening the relationship of activity with relinquishment, they become more respected and a more potent cause for fruits. If that is so, how can Gītā make non-activity relinquishable, and how can that non-activity be trampled upon? True! It will not be trampled by itself, but those who want to crush it will stumble, and in the end, repeated stumbles will have to bow down before non-activity. It is clarified in Chapter 13, verses (BG 13.7 - BG 13. 11), and Chapter 18 verses (BG 18.47- BG 18.55) that total renunciation of all activities in the attainment of knowledge is the necessary means. That is acceptable and not unacceptable.

In essence, Gītā has not come down for respect or disrespect of either activity or non-activity, and it is not there for the acceptance of one and rejection of the other. However, from the perspective of Gītā, whether it is an activity or non-activity, based on their positions, both are respectful and successful and come into the definition of Karma. How can it be said that Gītā is there to give respect only to activity? Though she is aggressive in requesting sacrifice of the body, senses, mind, intellect, and ego, it is not proper for her to impose fitness on anything by limited I-ness. Then, where is mineness for external substances? The tenet of Gītā is that the "I-ness sense" in the body, senses, mind, and intellect should be torn, and the "I am a doer" sentiment should not arise in them. Only then, through Karma, can one become faultless, and one can be free from the bondage of Karma. Otherwise, there is no freedom from bondage. Just as there are differences in diseases, and there are differences in the nature of patients, based on disease and nature of the patients, distinction in medicine, distinction in dosage, distinction in drinking with or after taking medication, and distinction in diet and physical activity is necessary. If a physician gives the same medicine, the exact dosage, to all his patients, it will prove harmful. When the condition of gross body treatment is like this, why get surprised by distinctions in means and differences in paths dealing with subtle mental matters? A preceptor and scripture that shows only one path to all and does not keep the distinction of fitness will be harmful and impure. This way, those who grasp the intent of Gītā only in path distinctions, that is, take support of Gītā in respecting one path and disrespecting another path, are indeed destroyers of the pervasive and humanity saving Gītā. For a complete scripture like Gītā, how can one imagine it is active in accepting activity and relinquishing non-activity, especially when the fruit of all activities is only non-activity? Or, how can it be believed that from the perspective of Gītā, efforts in Rajoguṇī activity are only Karma, and efforts in Sattvaguṇī non-activity are not Karma?

Cause and Effect in the activity of Karma

What is the cause of activity in Karma, and what is its fruit? With some thought, it is clear that no external substance is the cause of activity in Karma. Neither can the Saṃsāra be the cause of activity in Karma, nor the enjoyment of fruits of Karma can be the cause of activity in Karma. Though external substances can be instrumental in Karma activity, they cannot become material causes (Upādāna). The material cause of any action does not reside outside the action. To find it, one must only look inside the act. That is the rule of Prakṛti. Just like clay, the material cause of a pot can be found only within the pot and not outside. To search for the material cause of activity in Karma, we should start from where the wave of activity in Karma originates, which can be found only in the heart of a doer. Now we need to see - what can be the thing in the heart that makes a doer active in Karma? The answer is clear. The thing with whose being in the heart activity in Karma is produced and with whose non-being there is no activity of Karma is certainly the material cause of activity in Karma. Haven't we all experienced that we become active in eating and drinking only when an urge of hunger and thirst first arises in the heart. When that urge is satisfied, then the activity of eating and drinking ceases on its own. Activity commences upon the rise of an impulse related to an activity. Upon the rise of walking-related urge, walking activity commences. Upon the rise of rest-related urge, rest-activity commences. With the satisfaction of all those urges, corresponding activity stops. Elsewhere, activities in voice, touch, and other sense-objects commence only when those sense-object-related urges have already arisen in the heart. When those sense-object-related urges are gone from the heart, then those corresponding sense-object-related activities automatically stop. Later on, even if those enjoyable objects are present right in front because of the absence of urge, those objects do not remain the cause of activity. It is thus evident that external substances are not the cause of activity but are only instrumental. Just as when hunger is satiated, even if the most delicious food is in front, it does not remain any cause of activity. Public service and public well-being virtuous activities commence only when in an earlier period, public service and well-being-related urges have already arisen in the heart. When those urges are gone from the heart, those activities stop automatically. Analytic thinking and activity in renunciatory Karma only commence when the reality-related mental waves first arise in the heart. With the removal of mental waves, renunciatory activities also stop. Therefore, the cause of activity in Karma is only disturbances in the heart, and securing freedom from disturbances is the fruit of Karma. With the vision for the salvation of humanity, there cannot be any other cause and fruit of activity in Karma. In all activities of Karma, only this cause and this fruit can be found, not any different. Acquiring desired things and forsaking undesired things can never be the fruit of Karma. Even though the acquisition of desired and relinquishment of undesired is helpful in the removal of disturbances in the heart, the direct fruit is only the relinquishment of fruits. Succinctly put, only relinquishment is the fruit of Karma; activity can never be the fruit of Karma.

Once again, reverting to the example of an edgy patient who has developed pus in a boil on his body, he gets peace only after the physician surgically removes the pus. The main reason for the patient's stability is the removal of pus. The physician and the surgical knife instruments helping remove pus are the minor cause, not major. If the pus from the boil goes away, peace can be obtained even without a physician. Peace cannot be attained even in the physician's presence if the pus does not disappear. In achieving peace, the major cause is the removal of pus. Likewise, the acquisition of desired and the relinquishment of undesired are also minor causes in providing peace; the major cause is the removal of disturbances. If through means such as thinking and dispassion one can achieve removal of vacillations, then even without the acquisition of desired and the relinquishment of undesired, one can obtain peace. The same situation is in means such as public service, whereby we are only doing a favor to ourselves by being active in public service. The major fruit of this activity is the purging of agony in the heart by the success of public service in providing peace. Public service helping purge agony is only a minor cause; the major cause is purging the agony only. In reality, by performing public service, we are not doing any favor to the public. On the contrary, there is favor of the people on us. The reasoning is simple. Had we not had the opportunity to do public service, that agony that is making us uncomfortable would not have been purged and would have remained undoubtedly painful. Indeed, we should be thankful to those who allow us the opportunity to serve as they help us to be free from pain.

There is a story of Abraham Lincoln, considered by many as a pure soul before he became the 16th President of the United States of America. While Lincoln was practicing law, he used to go from one town to another to try cases before different courts. In those days, there were no railroads, and traveling "on the circuit" (going around from court to court) was primarily done on horseback. One day, when several lawyers besides Mr. Lincoln were traveling in this way, they came to a very muddy place on the road, and at one side, near the rail fence, was a poor pig stuck fast and squealing as loud as possible. The men thought this very funny and laughed at the unfortunate pig, but Lincoln said,

"Let us stop and help the poor thing out,"

"Oh, Abe," said one, "You must be crazy! Wouldn't your clothes look pretty after lifting that dirty pig, wouldn't they?"

The others all poked fun at Lincoln, and so they rode on until they were out of sight and hearing of the suffering beast. Lincoln rode on with them also, but little by little, he went slower. He was thinking about the pig and the farmer who owned him. He thought, "What a pity for him to lose that pig; he can't afford it! It means shoes for his little children to wear next winter." Then the memory of that pitiful squeal kept ringing in his ears. So, after going quite a long distance with the other gentlemen, Lincoln turned his horse and rode back all alone to see if he could get the pig out. He found the poor thing still deeper than before in the mud and mire. Therefore, he took some rails from the fence and, putting them down by the squealing animal, made a safe footing to stand on. Then he took two other rails and, putting them under the pig, pried him up out of the mud until he could reach him with his hands. Then he took hold of him and placed him on the dry sand.

As the pig ran grunting off toward his home, Lincoln soon reached the next town and went straight to the courthouse to plead for his client. Upon seeing him in soiled clothes, those present were surprised and asked him what had happened? Upon his narration of the story, they all started to praise Lincoln profusely for his kindness and compassion. Thereupon Lincoln said, "Wait a minute! Do not praise me. I did not do any favor to anybody. Whatever I did was to take the pain out of my mind". That provides further corroboration that the fruit of Karma is only the removal of the disturbance in the heart, the removal of disturbances in the heart.

That is morality. That is the rule. In reality, whoever performs service of or favor on someone is performing service of and favor on themselves. Assisting others means doing a favor to oneself, just like a ball thrown at a wall returns to the thrower. The wall is only a means for the ball to return to the thrower. Without the assistance of the wall, the ball cannot return to the thrower. Favor to others is there only to return that favor, similar to the wall. Accordingly, the major fruit of every activity is one's good only. When milk is boiled, it becomes frothy and rises with steam production. But it settles down as soon as steam comes out by adding some cold water. As long as milk has contact with fire, steam will again be produced, and milk will rise and become frothy until the whole milk becomes condensed milk. Likewise, disturbances in the form of desires for the acquisition of desired and the relinquishment of undesired are born in the heart due to ignorance. These disturbances are called Vikṣepa (विक्षेप, vacillations) and are the main cause of activity in Karma. As long as desires are present in the heart, disturbances cannot be removed. However, disturbances also disappear when that steam (desires) is let out of the heart. In other words, desires are nothing but the vacillations (Vikṣepa) of the heart.

Removal of desires is either by:

1. Fulfillment of desires.
2. After extensive Karma, desires go when a Jīva is tired and disappointed in not getting the desired objects. Vacillations are removed with it.
3. Through thinking, dispassion, and knowledge, desires can be removed. Vacillations are removed with it.

Only by the above three the removal of desires and vacillations is possible. In the case of the first two, when desires come out of the heart, vacillations are removed; but the removal is only transitory. As soon as there is a conjunction with the fire of ignorance, they are reborn at a later time in other forms of desires and vacillations. That is similar to how the rise in boiling milk is reduced temporarily by pouring some cold water, but milk once again starts rising and frothing because of contact with fire. Opposite to the first two, the purged desires and vacillations provide steady peace under the third way. The essence is that the fruit of Karma is only the removal of vacillations. The actual acquisition of desired things can never be the fruit of Karma.

Major Levels of Vacillations and Distinctions of Doers

The fruit of Karma-inducing instruments is the removal of vacillations (Vikṣepa) arising in the heart and nothing else. While there are multitudes of vacillations, they can be broadly divided into six major levels by distinctions of doers.

1. In the first level are those persons who are iniquitous, "पामर, Pāmara." Though they bow down before scriptures and public morality, they are involved in arbitrary and unrestrained enjoyment of objects of pleasure and trample the interest of others for their self-interest. Vacillations in their hearts are "Deep-Rooted Tamogunī-Vikṣepa." Such individuals are also known as "निषिद्ध-सकामी, Niṣiddha-Sakāmī" who covet forbidden desire-ridden acts. They use whatever means they have to fulfill their self-interest, including the willingness to sacrifice everything, their body, mind, and wealth in the blazing fire of gratification. That is their only duty. They are ever engaged in removing vacillations resident in their heart through fulfilling that duty.
2. In the second level are those persons who are materialistic, "विषयी, Viṣayī." They only partake in enjoyments within the bounds of scriptures and public morality. Even though they are self-interested, they also look at the interest of those who are their acquaintances. Their self-interest is not based on trampling the welfare of their close contacts. That being their aim in life, they are always ready to fulfill their duty and are ever engaged in removing their vacillations. They are also known as "शुभ-सकामी, Śubha-Sakāmī," who covet "virtuous desire-ridden acts." Vacillations in their hearts are "Diminished Tamogunī-Vikṣepa." Where there is selfishness, there is Tamoguṇa. Though in such persons, it is diminished. If Jīva desires his good, it is the rule of Prakṛti that, like a compassionate mother, Prakṛti will always assist Jīva in uplifting him from lower level to higher level, just like a seed sown in the soil, with the union of fertile soil and water, develops sequentially to a sprout, twig, trunk, branch, flower and finally a fully ripened fruit.
3. In the third level are those persons who are "निष्काम-कर्मी, Niṣkāma-Karmī" who perform desireless-Karma. Although self-interested Tamoguṇa is not present in them, their hearts are filled with Rajoguṇa of activity in Karma. As provided in Chapter 14 verse (BG 14.12) -

   ......प्रवृत्तिरारम्भ: कर्मणामशम: स्पृहा |
   रजस्येतानि जायन्ते...... || BG 14.12 ||

   Activity, the commencement of actions, disquiet, and desire appear upon the dominance of the Rajoguṇa.

   Though their Rajoguṇa is not mixed with selfishness, having developed naturally has become the cause of desireless Karma activity. Rajoguṇa, with its relationship with the body and mind, does not let them stay stationary. However, forsaking selfishness, it flows with desireless sentiments of benevolence towards others with sentiments that:

a. I am a doer of Karma.
b. To be engaged in Karma for public well-being is my duty from the Lord.
c. That is why I am engaging in Karma, fulfilling that command by offering fruits of Karma to the Lord.

Vacillations in their hearts are "रजोगुणी-विक्षेप, Rajoguṇī-Vikṣepa." Characteristics of Rajoguṇa are activity, and that of Tamoguṇa is the insentience of selfishness. There is an activity in such seekers, but there is no selfish insentience, and so activity is only Rajoguṇī. With the fulfillment of this duty, they are engaged in the removal of the flow of vacillations resident in their hearts, and with it, as said in Chapter 18, verse BG 18.46 by their Karma, they worship the Lord -

यत: प्रवृत्तिर्भूतानां येन सर्वमिदं ततम् |
स्वकर्मणा तमभ्यर्च्य सिद्धिं विन्दति मानव: || BG 18.46 ||

> Through the performance of natural activities as worship, a human attains perfection - worshipping That from Whom all beings have proceeded and by Whom all this is pervaded.

With the worship of the Paramātmā through one's Karma, not just lighting of lamps, a human gets purity of the conscience. This Karma is indeed the preceding constituent part of worship. At this level, vacillations can be removed neither by virtuous desire-ridden Karma nor by relinquishment of Karma. Only desireless activity in Karma is the means for the removal of vacillations.

4. In the fourth level are those persons who are "निष्काम-भक्त, Niṣkāma-Bhakta." These are desireless devotees in whose hearts the fountainhead of the devotion of the manifest-form Lord (Saguṇa-Bhakti) has opened up through desireless-Karma. The Lord to whom Karma and fruits of Karma were offered in the third level, now at this level, their hearts are filled with a real love for the Lord, their longing for a divine experience of the Lord increases, and following the scriptures through Navadhā-Bhakti devote their lives entirely to the Lord as per BG 10.9 -

मच्चित्ता मद्गतप्राणा बोधयन्त: परस्परम् |
कथयन्तश्च मां नित्यं तुष्यन्ति च रमन्ति च || BG 10.9 ||

> With their mind fixed on Me, their lives surrendered to Me, enlightening one another and conversing about Me, they always find contentment and delight.

Sentiments in the Saṃsāra of such persons mostly melt. They see the entire Saṃsāra in the image of their revered deity, and their hearts are filled with nothing but real love for their revered deity. Sentiments of public well-being and benevolence towards others when they were Niṣkāma-Karmī in the third level are out of their hearts. When their hearts are overwhelmed with real love, they attain peace within their bosoms, and their fault-vision of virtues and vices (Guṇa-Doṣa) flows away. Fault vision is present until real love is not sprung. However, as soon as real love springs, it immediately puts a curtain over their fault-vision, and all faults of virtues and vices start to look like the finger snap of Bhagavāna Śrī Kṛṣṇa. Where is room for public well-being and benevolence towards others when there is no fault-vision? These predicaments exist only as long as their hearts are devoid of true love and their discriminating vision is firm. Only because of the firmness of discriminating vision, sentiments of good and evil manifest, and a pure vision is formed for all evil from the Saṃsāra to be removed and goodness established. The root cause of these predicaments is that the greenery of true love in the heart is becoming arid. There is a tenet in the kingdom of Prakṛti that no good or evil exists in the Saṃsāra. It is only in one's view. The Saṃsāra appears to one just as one's view. Therefore, when the rain of true love starts to fall on this lover, the saline soil of the fault of virtues and vices sweeps away. In the absence of the fault of vices and virtues, when the flood of love comes, tears in the form of love cannot be held in the heart but have to overflow out of the eyes. In such a state, where is room for benevolence towards others? That is the difference between desireless actions and devotion. Even though the duty of goodwill towards others and vacillations have been removed from the heart of this lover, in its place, the desire for a divine experience of the Lord has enclosed the heart. Vacillations in the hearts of such persons are "रजसत्त्वगुणी-विक्षेप, Rajasattvaguṇī-Vikṣepa." A person at this level is ready to remove such vacillations by listening to the holy scriptures, chanting, worshipping, and the meditation on the Lord's divine play forms. At this stage, desireless-Karma activity is not capable of removing his vacillations. Now, "I am a doer, and on me, there is some duty" having gone, "All-doer is only the Lord, I am not doing anything, I am only an occasion like a dancing puppet," such sentiments are awake in him. Due to the firmness of such pure sentiments, his sentiments of doership become soft. With the softness of doership, the duty that was firm in desireless activities becomes soft.

5. In the fifth level are those persons who are dispassionate seekers known as "वैराग्यवान-जिज्ञासु, Vairāgyavāna-Jijñāsu." In the fourth level, through the devotion of the Lord, objectless peace without any relationship of the worldly fickle enjoyable objects had arisen in the hearts of the discerning. With that peace, there was the development of Sattvaguṇa, and discrimination of real and unreal had formed a picture of unreality and transiency of the Saṃsāra in their eyes. When the drum starts to beat, the worldly attachment disappears from the hearts of such discerning, just like how an owl hides on his own upon sunrise. Dispassion has now surrounded their hearts from all sides. The entire Saṃsāra appears burning. There is no vision of trueness and beauty in any substance, and the limited enjoyment of the Saṃsāra seems to them devoid of pleasure.

(पुनरपि जननं पुनरपि मरणं पुनरपि जननी जठरे शयनम्)

"Again, birth and again death and again resting in the mother's womb" form of repeated coming and going is their suffering. The Peace that had aroused in their hearts by the worship of the Lord has set the fire ablaze in their hearts. Now, intense desire has developed for the peace that came about by closeness with the Lord to remain intact and for the true nature of the bliss-form Lord to be attained so that there is a complete absence of pain and suffering. With intense discernment, dispassion, and desire to know, the sixfold virtues such as mind control become successful with ease. As a rule, control of the mind, restraint of the senses from their objects, faith, desistance, and other attributes are deposited naturally. That is similar to pulling one leg of a four-legged stool; the remaining three are automatically drawn. Now, the only vacillations in their hearts are, "Where is this peace coming from? Where is its origin? How can it be obtained? What is my true nature? What is the true nature of the Paramātmā? Why was the Saṃsāra created? Who created the Saṃsāra? How was the Saṃsāra created?" There is only one thing at the root of the vacillations: the search for the Truth. Vacillations in their hearts are "सत्त्वगुणी-विक्षेप, Sattvaguṇī-Vikṣepa." Removing such vacillations is neither possible by desireless-Karma nor by only remembering teachings of the holy scriptures, meditation of the manifest-form Paramātmā. Only sitting and listening to enlightened knowers, listening to the scriptures that provide the Truth, contemplation, and profound repeated meditation can be helpful in the removal of such vacillations. There are no other possible means. Thus, at this stage, leaving all other activities aside, their only aim is to be active in these means.

6. In the sixth and the highest level are those great beings (Māhātmā) who are "तत्त्ववेत्ता-ज्ञानी, Tattva-Vettā Jñānī" knowers of the Reality. Such persons have successfully gone through difficult means of the fifth level and have made direct transcendental (Aparokṣa) resolve of oneness between their Ātmā and the Paramātmā. They have resolved that their Ātmā is a non-doer, a non-enjoyer, dissociated, unborn, and imperishable, and by witness-form have made their Ātmā directly experienced as the Ātmā of all. Once sugar cane juice is extracted, knowing that its rind is without juice is thrown away.

In the same way, gaining the Saccidānanda Brahman in their own Ātmā, perfectly existent in it, and knowing the mind, intellect, senses, body, and the entire visible Saṃsāra consisting of the five great elements pointless and essenceless, are abandoned like juiceless rind - and thus they become free, become Jīvanmukta even while being alive. They who have abandoned attachment-aversion and grasping-relinquishing duties are also free from the imagination of bondage and liberation. Though seen as doing everything through the body, remain non-doers. Seen as enjoying enjoyments and pleasure and pain through the body, they stay non-enjoyers and unstained from pleasure and pain. Even though they appear to be seen in the body until the end of the enjoyment of Prārabdha, they remain dissociated. In reality, only such great beings can be called Guṇātīta (गुणातीत) - those who are free from or beyond the constituents of Prakṛti, the transcendent sages. Although with the flow of Prārabdha, one can see an inkling of vacillations in them, with the maturity of such knowledge, "I am the dissociated Ātmā, only the observer of the world of the body, senses, mind, and intellect, I am not doing anything, and neither my true nature makes anything, nor any mutation can touch my form" they remain distant from all vacillations. Therefore, even though they are doing everything, they are not doing anything and are not in any bondage. The attainment of this state is indeed the major fruit of all means. Only after ascending to this state can one obtain real freedom from all bondages of doer and duty. With this knowledge, all accumulated and current Karma Saṃskāras are completely burnt. That is where there is unity in Sāṅkhya and Yoga. That is the propounded subject of Gītā; Bhagavāna's Upadeśa to Arjuna was to make him ascend in this state and fight.

The essence is that vacillations resident in the heart in lower levels make a Jīva active in Karma with the aim that through Karma, after fulfillment of desires, one can obtain freedom from them. Just as when one has an itch in some part of the body, hands naturally reach that spot to relieve the irritation. Indeed, vacillations are not eradicated. Vacillations of lower levels are such that once a desire is fulfilled, it goes away only momentarily but later on returns in some other form. Just as how there is the removal of darkness for a moment with a light flash from a firefly. However, darkness reappears, like how scratching provides temporary relief once stung by a bee, but the opposite happens - itch increases. Vacillations of lower levels, by their nature, can never be removed; instead, there is growth in them. In the Saṃsāra, irrespective of the level one is in, every living being is full of intense desire to be free from vacillations, which is natural. Thus, the main cause in the activities of every living being is only the removal of vacillations; even where, by one's error, instead of removing the vacillations, just the opposite happens, increases them. Be it desirable or undesirable, every being in every activity aims to be free from vacillations. However, Prakṛti here has filled the hearts with an intense desire to get rid of vacillations, and there through the activity of second and lower levels, on the one hand, has provided a path for the removal of vacillations, but on the other hand, as an imperceptible boil has filled with some other forms of vacillations. Moreover, when a Jīva is fatigued doing Karma of his level and does not see freedom from vacillations, fatigue becomes the cause for him to reach higher levels. Though his fatigue is from Karma, he is not tired of the desire for the removal of vacillations. However, his desires are increasingly growing in the search for means to get away from the vacillations, to be free. Under the pure heartedness rule of Prakṛti, she attracts a Jīva at lower levels, takes him to higher levels sequentially, makes him ascend in the Śiva-form, and then frees him from her bondage. All bondages and vacillations are only there to make him ascend in the witness-observer state so that they can be removed from their roots.

Based on the preceding, one can conclude that the fruit of activity in Karma is to take out the flow of Tamoguṇa and Rajoguṇa of Prakṛti, which is brimming in the heart of Jīva, being an impediment to the highest good and is taking him towards the Saṃsāra, by the good path and his heart be filled with Sattvaguṇa. Sattvaguṇa, being suppressed by Tamoguṇa and Rajoguṇa, cannot be awakened without removing Tamoguṇa and Rajoguṇa. With the rise of Sattvaguṇa, Karma becomes fruitless, and then there is the light of knowledge in Jīva, as Sattvaguṇa is in the form of light. Contrary to this, Tamoguṇa is like darkness, and Rajoguṇa is fickle, just as -

सत्त्वात्सञ्जायते ज्ञानं रजसो लोभ एव च |
प्रमादमोहौ तमसो भवतोऽज्ञानमेव च || BG 14.17 ||

With Sattvaguṇa, knowledge is born. Greed arises with Rajoguṇa, and negligence, delusion, and ignorance arise with Tamoguṇa.

Knowledge is born of Sattvaguṇa. Greed is born of Rajoguṇa, and negligence, delusion, and ignorance are born of Tamoguṇa. The main purpose of the desireless activity is that the flow of Rajoguṇa that is moving towards the Saṃsāra be diverted and moved towards the Lord through it. Moving towards the Lord, the flow of Rajoguṇa is diminished. It turns itself into Sattvaguṇa because now a relationship of relinquishment (of fruits) is formed. With relinquishment, Sattvaguṇa is awakened naturally, and with Sattvaguṇa, there is growth in relinquishment. Accordingly, with fruit-relinquishment and concomitant increased growth of Sattvaguṇa, it is possible to relinquish doership and duty through knowledge. To stop the flow of Jīva and harm (हिंसा, Hiṃsā), Śāstra has attached the relationship of harm with sacrifice so that even if harm is acceptable, then it should be done through sacrifice. Hiṃsā is said to be of three kinds: 1) mental as bearing malice; 2) verbal, as abusive language and 3) personal, as acts of violence. This way, to reduce the flow of Rajoguṇī Karma, its relationship with fruit relinquishment was attached so that with the growth of Sattvaguṇa, one can be free from Rajoguṇī Karma. It is thus clear that the fruit of Karma is only to remove both Tamoguṇa and Rajoguṇa and grow Sattvaguṇa. With the growth of Sattvaguṇa, Karma becomes fruitless; then, it is only through knowledge that the Paramātmā can be realized. It is impossible to realize the Paramātmā through Karma. Whatever is achieved through Karma is perishable, and an imperishable thing cannot be the object of Karma. It is therefore said -

कर्मणा बध्यते जन्तुर्विद्यया तु प्रमुच्यते ।[35]

A Jīva comes in bondage by Karma and is free by knowledge.

The attainment of the Paramātmā by Karma could be possible only if the Paramātmā were not omnipresent but separate from us and situated in some other space. However, when He is omnipresent and is within us, how can He be attained by Karma? In such a state, the only thing necessary is to remove the darkness of ignorance. That can only be done by the light of knowledge, never by Karma. Sure, Karma is necessary for collecting oil, wick, lamp, and matches to remove darkness, but only the light of the lamp can effectuate the removal of darkness. Likewise, there is the usefulness of Karma in the collection of accessories for knowledge, but after that, it becomes useless. Thus, desireless actions are useful in the removal of Rajoguṇa and the growth of Sattvaguṇa, but after the full development of Sattvaguṇa, they do not remain useful anymore. After the full development of Sattvaguṇa, when one is established with oneness in the Ātmā through knowledge, then any activity happening naturally in this great being is apparent Karma only. It is not done with doer or duty-bound intellect. There is no relationship of the constituents in those Karma. Indeed, when he has achieved by himself Guṇātīta status, what relationship do the constituents have with him? However, in that state, even though he is seen as doing Karma, in reality, he is only a non-doer. He is a renouncer of all commencements. He is a real Niṣkāmī. Coming out of the body, he is seated in his Ātmā with oneness. There, he does not see any attachment to his Karma. So, even while doing Karma through the body, he is indeed a non-doer.

तत्त्ववित्तु महाबाहो गुणकर्मविभागयो: |
गुणा गुणेषु वर्तन्त इति मत्वा न सज्जते || BG 3.28 ||

Hey Arjuna! On the contrary, one who knows the Truth about the distinction between the constituents of Prakṛti and their operations is not attached to action, knowing that the constituents operate amidst the constituents.

---

[35] Saṃnyāsopaniṣad (संन्यासोपनिषद्) 2.117

प्रकाशं च प्रवृत्तिं च मोहमेव च पाण्डव |
न द्वेष्टि सम्प्रवृत्तानि न निवृत्तानि काङ्‍क्षति || BG 14.22 ||
उदासीनवदासीनो गुणैर्यो न विचाल्यते |
गुणा वर्तन्त इत्येवं योऽवतिष्ठति नेङ्गते || BG 14.23 ||
समदु:खसुख: स्वस्थ: समलोष्टाश्मकाञ्चन: |
तुल्यप्रियाप्रियो धीरस्तुल्यनिन्दात्मसंस्तुति: || BG 14.24 ||
मानापमानयोस्तुल्यस्तुल्यो मित्रारिपक्षयो: |
सर्वारम्भपरित्यागी गुणातीत: स उच्यते || BG 14.25 ||

Hey Arjuna! With Sattvaguṇa light, with Rajoguṇa activity, and with Tamoguṇa delusion is produced. One who is beyond the constituents does not hate the constituents that are active and does not desire the constituents that are absent.

Seated indifferent, one is not disturbed by the constituents. Situated this way, one does not waver, knowing the constituents are only active.

Situated in own Self, one who is beyond the constituents is alike in pleasure and pain, alike in pleasant and unpleasant, treats equally clod, stone, and gold, and has equanimity in censure and praise.

One who is the same in honor and disgrace, equal towards friends and foes, and does not initiate any actions is called Guṇātīta.

Whatever natural activities happen in the body of such a great being, as they are not the cause of fruits, they always remain actionless. They are only apparent Karma, delusional only. Therefore, no injunctions such as engagement in acts of public well-being remain for such persons because, at that time, the entire Saṃsāra is like a dream to them. At this stage, all natural activities coming out through their bodies are ideal and in the public interest. However, individuals at a lower level with duty-bound intellect cannot accomplish them over many lifetimes. Indeed, it is Gītā's propounded objective to make one ascend in this state and perform the natural activity of Karma. Karma activity in the bondage of duty can never be the intent of Gītā, and Karma done accordingly can never be faultless because the one who is bound cannot free a bound one. The only one who is free can free one who is bound.

CRITIQUE

Is there a mutually harmonious connection between Gītā chapters and verses? At this point, we want to ascertain what does Gītā mean by the term Yoga? Further, we need to review to what extent the word Karma-Yoga interpreted by many meets the test of their thinking, particularly in those Gītā verses where Karma-Yoga, Buddhi-Yoga, Yoga, Yoga-Yukta is used. In other words, accepting their interpretation of verses, is there a harmonious connection between the words and their meanings in those verses or not? It is imperative to keep in mind that whatever words spoken in Gītā are all Yathārtha (accordant with reality), and there is not even an iota of Arthavāda (empty praise); on the contrary, Gītā has censured Arthavāda (see verses BG 2.40 through BG 2.44). Therefore, in the analysis of the verses, it would be only appropriate to accept the meanings of words accordant with reality. Acceptance of Arthavāda may be relevant only where there is no harmonious connection with Yathārtha words. Abandoning the relationship with Yathārtha words and accepting Arthavāda is like a mother leaving an adopted child with the wishful thinking of having her own child.

The Sāṅkhya Yoga - Chapter 2

एषा तेऽभिहिता साङ्ख्ये बुद्धिर्योगे त्विमां शृणु |
बुद्ध्या युक्तो यया पार्थ कर्मबन्धं प्रहास्यसि || BG 2.39 ||

This knowledge of Sāṅkhya has so far been imparted to you. Hey Arjuna! Listen to this knowledge on the subject of Yoga. Endowed with such knowledge, you will be completely free from the bondage of actions.

The intention is that the knowledge of Sāṅkhya that was spoken to you, "Your, mine, and these king's Ātmā, was there before and will remain in the future. With the destruction of bodies, this (Ātmā) does not perish." Just as "I am a child, I am a youth, I am an adult, I am old," various states of the gross body are imagined in the Ātmā by ignorance, in the same way, "I take birth, I die" various states of the subtle body are superimposed on the Ātmā. In reality, the Ātmā neither is born nor dies.

न त्वेवाहं जातु नासं न त्वं नेमे जनाधिपा |
न चैव न भविष्याम: सर्वे वयमत: परम् || BG 2.12 ||

It is certainly not so that I was not there at any time, nor you, or these kings. It is not so that we all will not be there from here onwards.

देहिनोऽस्मिन्यथा देहे कौमारं यौवनं जरा |
तथा देहान्तरप्राप्तिर्धीरस्तत्र न मुह्यति || BG 2.13 ||

Just as childhood, youth, and old age are imagined in the body, likewise acquisition of another body is imagined in the embodied Self. A person with fortitude is not deluded in that subject.

नासतो विद्यते भावो नाभावो विद्यते सत: |
उभयोरपि दृष्टोऽन्तस्त्वनयोस्तत्त्वदर्शिभि: || BG 2.16 ||

There is no being of the unreal, and there is no non-being of the real. The truth about both is perceived by seers of Reality.

अविनाशि तु तद्विद्धि येन सर्वमिदं ततम् |
विनाशमव्ययस्यास्य न कश्चित्कर्तुमर्हति || BG 2.17 ||

However, know That (Self) to be imperishable by which all this is pervaded. None can destroy that Immutable (Self).

अन्तवन्त इमे देहा नित्यस्योक्ता: शरीरिण: |
अनाशिनोऽप्रमेयस्य तस्माद्युध्यस्व भारत || BG 2.18 ||

These bodies that perish are said to be of the eternal, imperishable, and indeterminable embodied Self. Therefore, hey, Arjuna! Fight.

In reality, an unreal thing like the body is not there at any time. An unreal thing is never steady, but like a snake delusion in a rope, there is only a delusional perception, an apparent illusion of the body in the Ātmā. In reality, the real thing Ātmā does not perish any time. According to this tenet, the embodied Ātmā that is imperishable and indeterminable its bodies by nature have been called perishable. That is why hey, Bhārata! When the Ātmā does not perish, and the bodies never remain, you should fight the righteous war.

य एनं वेत्ति हन्तारं यश्चैनं मन्यते हतम् |
उभौ तौ न विजानीतो नायं हन्ति न हन्यते || BG 2.19 ||

One who knows it as a slayer and one who deems it can be slain; they both do not know this (Self). It neither kills nor is slain.

न जायते म्रियते वा कदाचित नायं भूत्वा भविता वा न भूय: |
अजो नित्य: शाश्वतोऽयं पुराणो न हन्यते हन्यमाने शरीरे || BG 2.20 ||

This Self is never born and never dies at any time, nor having existed before again becomes non-existent. It is unborn, eternal, everlasting, and ever-new. It is not destroyed upon the destruction of the body.

One who has known the Ātmā as one who kills or being killed they have indeed not known anything because, in reality, the Ātmā neither kills anyone nor is killed by anyone. It is neither born nor ever dies, and having once existed does not ever cease to be. On the contrary, it is unborn, eternal, everlasting, and ever-new and is not destroyed even when the body is destroyed.

वेदाविनाशिनं नित्यं य एनमजमव्ययम् |
कथं स पुरुष: पार्थ कं घातयति हन्ति कम् || BG 2.21 ||

Hey Arjuna! He who knows this Self as imperishable, eternal, unborn, and undecaying, how can such person cause anyone to be slain? Who can he kill?

A person who knows the Ātmā directly as unborn and destructible, “That I am,” then hey, Pārtha! Whom can that person kill? In his vision, there is nothing else but the Ātmā; just as in the formation and destruction of waves, water does not see its creation and destruction.

वासांसि जीर्णानि यथा विहाय नवानि गृह्णाति नरोऽपराणि ।
तथा शरीराणि विहाय जीर्णा न्यन्यानि संयाति नवानि देही || BG 2.22 ||

Just as a person discards worn clothes and takes new ones, so does the embodied Self, dumping dilapidated bodies, occupies other new ones.

Just as a person abandoning old garments wears other new clothes and with the destruction of old clothes does not see his destruction, in the same way, the Ātmā dumping old bodies occupy other new bodies; a person who knows the Ātmā transcendentally in such a way, he knows his Ātmā immutable in all bodies.

नैनं छिन्दन्ति शस्त्राणि नैनं दहति पावक: ।
न चैनं क्लेदयन्त्यापो न शोषयति मारुत: || BG 2.23 ||

Weapons cannot cut it, fire cannot burn it, water cannot wet it, and wind cannot dry it.

अच्छेद्योऽयमदाह्योऽयमक्लेद्योऽशोष्य एव च ।
नित्य: सर्वगत: स्थाणुरचलोऽयं सनातन: || BG 2.24 ||

This Self is unslashable, unburnable, unwettable, and undryable. It is eternal, all-pervasive, stable, immovable, and everlasting.

In reality, no weapons can cut the Ātmā, fire cannot burn it, water cannot wet it, and wind cannot dry it. The great elements are not able to influence the Ātmā. That is, the Ātmā does not get influenced by anyone. It is eternal, all-pervading, standing firmly, immovable, and always there.

अव्यक्तोऽयमचिन्त्योऽयमविकार्योऽयमुच्यते ।
तस्मादेवं विदित्वैनं नानुशोचितुमर्हसि || BG 2.25 ||

This Self is said to be unmanifest, imponderable, and immutable. Therefore, knowing such, it is not befitting for you to grieve.

This way, the Ātmā is called a non-object of the mind and senses and unchangeable. Knowing "That," there is no reason for your grief.

Harmonious connection through the intellect with the aforementioned Sāṅkhya knowledge is indeed called Yoga. Separation from the Ātmā is only due to ignorance-driven impure intellect and the "I am a doer" sentiment. Union in one's Ātmā is only possible through pure intelligence with knowledge, "I am not doing anything, I am not an enjoyer, but I am only the disassociated immutable witness-conscious." There is no other possible way for union in the Ātmā, as the Ātmā is not any substance in which, like two loops of handcuffs, a conjunctive union is possible. Only by this intellect, "I am a non-doer, non-enjoyer, disassociated and immutable," becoming established in the witness-conscious Ātmā, the bondage of Karma can be cut. The bondage of Karma is there as long as a Jīva forgets his witness-conscious form, becomes body-form, and becomes a doer of Karma. However, when Jīva knows itself separate from the body as an observer-witness of the body and Karma, then the bondage of Karma is automatically broken. A witness is never punishable, and that is the rule. Besides this, while holding duty-bound intellect, there is no other possible way to break the bondage of Karma, as the root of obligation is doership. With duty, doership becomes assertive. Accepting the thinking of some, if one remains active in Karma with duty-bound intellect, then that duty-bound intellect will make doership more powerful and keep one separate from one's Ātmā. No matter how many lifetimes pass in performing Karma, it will never keep one united. When a union is attained in the Ātmā, it is only achieved after abandoning duty-bound intellect. Duty-bound intellect keeps doership very tenacious and keeps impressions of done Karma profuse. So, by its nature, it cannot burn accumulated and current Karma-Saṃskāras. When Karma-Saṃskāras are profuse, then where is the case for breaking the bondage of Karma?

Contrary to those mentioned above, with the absence of doership and duty-bound intellect, through the realization of the Truth, the attainment of Buddhi-Yoga, "I am neither a doer nor an enjoyer, but I am the dissociated immutable witness-conscious Ātmā only," all Karma Saṃskāras be they accumulated or be they current are scorched to ashes providing freedom from their bondage immediately. This knower of the Truth cognizes himself separate from the body, senses, mind, and intellect as a non-doer, non-enjoyer, immutable Ātmā. This knower cognizes himself as only the witness-illuminator of the body, senses, mind, and intellect, so Karma cannot taint him. Just as the sun remains an untainted witness while illuminating the good and evil world, in the same way, this knower of the Truth, established in his Ātmā "is as is" illuminating the mutations and the activities of the body, himself remains immutable-untainted-witness, and while doing everything through the body is not bound by Karma. The meaningfulness of such words as "कर्मबन्धं प्रहास्यसि, you will cut the bondage of Karma" is impossible with desireless actions (Niṣkāma-Karma) propounded by some. However, only by the Yoga of establishing in own Ātmā with oneness can such words be made meaningful. If desireless-Karma is accepted as Yoga somehow, then after the spiritual guidance (Upadeśa) of Sāṅkhya, Upadeśa of such Yoga does not follow the bounds and propriety of Śāstra.

Moreover, Upadeśa of Bhagavāna to Arjuna without moral bounds is not befitting. Under Śāstra, Upadeśa of Sāṅkhya knowledge is an injunction towards one who is fit, an Adhikārī in whose heart, first, there is the removal of impurities of desire-ridden subtle impressions through desireless actions. After that, the heart has become pure from attachment and aversion through discernment and dispassion. After Sāṅkhya Upadeśa, Variant-Yoga could have been Karma-Yoga if Karma-Yoga had been accepted as an internal instrument of knowledge. But based on the bounds of Śāstra, Niṣkāma Karma (desireless actions) is an external instrument of knowledge, not internal. With the birth of dispassion through Niṣkāma-Karma, it becomes an opposer in listening and not a helper. Being an external instrument, it is not acceptable for listening and contemplation, but indeed is one to be abandoned. When Arjuna's despite towards enemies has evaporated with the influence of intense dispassion, the tree of despite whose roots were getting deeper and firmer towards those enemies right from childhood and whose result was the pitched battle of Kurukṣetra (BG 1.28 - BG 1.46, BG 2.4 - BG 2.8), then Upadeśa of desireless-Karma (Variant-Yoga), after having provided Sāṅkhya Upadeśa to such an attachment and aversion free Arjuna is not befitting anyway. Such a Upadeśa becomes nothing but an unworthy effort. How can attribution of such fault on the head of Bhagavāna be acceptable?

Furthermore, Arjuna's lifelong conduct had been righteous with desireless-sentiment. Bound by righteousness, even though he was mighty and well able, Arjuna could not do anything but witness the abject insult of Draupadī in the full court. Moreover, he faced grave dangers during exile in the forest. All of these were nothing but desireless-Karma, and as a result, intense dispassion had sprouted in him. That being his state, after Upadeśa of Sāṅkhya, to push him towards desireless-Karma does not measure up to any bounds of morality. Thus, the Yoga herein cannot be called Variant-Yoga (Niṣkāma Karma) by any means, but for the one established in the Ātmā with oneness, it can only be Jñāna-Yoga.

योगस्थः कुरु कर्माणि संगं त्यक्त्वा धनंजय ।
सिद्ध्यसिद्ध्योः समो भूत्वा समत्वं योग उच्यते ॥ BG 2.48 ॥

> Hey Arjuna! Becoming established in Yoga and relinquishing attachment perform actions with evenness in success and failure. Equanimity of intelligence is called Yoga.

Earlier, views of some regarding Yoga as activity in Karma holding duty-bound intellect and forsaking fruits of Karma was designated as Variant-Yoga. However, Variant-Yoga cannot fulfill the conditions of the above verse (BG 2.48). First, such a doership relationship in Karma, "I am a doer of Karma," is nothing but attachment. In the presence of duty-bound intellect, relinquishment of this attachment is impossible. When a Jīva knows himself as limited something else from the Ātmā, he becomes a doer of Karma. Doership is always born in the sentiment of limitation. With the birth of doership, the duty of injunctions and prohibitions comes out automatically, "Doing Karma, in some form is an injunction for me, and in some other form, it is forbidden for me. It is my duty to be active in all prescribed Karma and avoid all prohibited Karma." Such duty cannot stay independent of doership.

On the contrary, the result of doership is indeed this duty. Thus, relinquishing doership-attachment is always impossible in the presence of duty. Even if a Yogī is involved in Karma with such sentiments, "I am not a doer of Karma, some Karma is my duty, and I am offering all fruits of my Karma to the Lord," he remains a doer of Karma. In reality, the relinquishment of doership-attachment is not established. In the sentiments mentioned above, there is the presence of limitations. Despite limitations, even if the Yogī has sentiments of relinquishing doership-attachment, he becomes the doer of sentiments. When he has already become the doer of sentiments, he will be the enjoyer of the fruits of his pure sentiments. Fruits are not in insentient Karma. Sentiments of the conscience are the cause of fruits. As long as sentiments are present in any form and are not scorched in the fire of knowledge until then, said Variant-Yoga, cannot establish relinquishment of doership-attachment. Though expressed sentiments are pure and not the cause of the Saṃsāra, they can indeed advance the highest good. However, they cannot uproot doer-intellect to establish relinquishment of attachment by their presence. Second, in the presence of limited sentiments, doership-attachment, and duty-bound intellect, said Variant-Yoga is not capable of fulfilling what is said in verse (BG 2.48), "सिद्ध्यसिद्ध्योः समो भूत्वा, become equal in success and failure." Duty-bound intellect is the fruit of limited sentiments and doership-attachment. How can there be equanimity in success and failure when it is present? As explained earlier, duty-bound intellect is injunctive and prohibitive only.

Moreover, when the relationship of injunctions and prohibitions is sitting on the head of the said Yogī, where will equanimity in success and failure come from? That is unfathomable. Injunctions and prohibitions, by their nature, are unequal. Equality can only come when the bondage of injunctions and prohibitions is broken. But because this Yogī is holding duty-bound intellect, injunctions and prohibitions are attached to him. Even if the Yogī in his Karma has made a resolve, "I do not desire fruits of my done Karma, but offer all fruits of Karma to the Lord," still "सिद्ध्यसिद्ध्योः समः, equanimity in success and failure" cannot be established. Even if we accept that with his pure sentiments, he did not desire the fruits of his actions and offered them to the Lord, still, "Offering my fruits of actions to the Lord my conscience will be pure" - which itself is a fruit, and that fruit he has earned for himself. "What is my motive when I offer fruits of Karma to the Lord irrespective of whether such Karma makes my conscience pure or not?" - in such success and failure, he is not equal but unequal. Since the purity of the conscience is necessary and must be there, in this subject, he is an enjoyer of fruits and not a relinquisher of fruits. Though he is not with a desire for worldly enjoyments, he is not desireless. How can equanimity come in success and failure when desires are attached to his conscience? Desires are the cause of inequality, be it worldly or transcendental. As long as they are present in the conscience, they will not allow equanimity to enter. Desires and equanimity are like darkness and light, mutually averse. Thus, with limited sentiments, doership-attachment, and duty of injunctions and prohibitions remaining present, attaining equanimity in success and failure is like looking for a flower in space.

In contrast, a Yogī who has found union in his Ātmā, because of the removal of his limited sentiments, is not doing anything. He has neither any duty nor any fruits. He is dissociated from the instruments (the body, senses, mind, and intellect) of Karma and is sitting as its audience. Though doing everything with the body, he is a non-doer, just as the sun, with its rays illuminating different substances, remains untainted. Whatever activity in the Saṃsāra is observed, it is only due to the sun's illumination. However, the sun is dissociated from all the activities and is only the witness light. The Yogī, established in his Ātmā illuminating the doer, Karma, and fruits with his witness-light, is dissociated from all and untainted. Just as said in verse BG 2.48, he is, in reality, an attachment-relinquisher and is equal in success and failure. This status of establishment in the Ātmā is indeed the real equanimity, and the sentence "समत्वं योग उच्यते, equanimity of intelligence is called Yoga" is here completely established.

बुद्धियुक्तो जहातीह उभे सुकृतदुष्कृते |
तस्माद्योगाय युज्यस्व योग: कर्मसु कौशलम् || BG 2.50 ||

> One with equanimity of intelligence relinquishes both pious and sinful actions here. Therefore, you engage in Yoga. Yoga is the skill in actions.

Variant-Yoga with duty-bound intellect, as espoused by some, cannot provide freedom from piety and sin in this world, as provided in verse BG 2.50. Engaging in injunctions and abandoning prohibitions is called piety (Puṇya). Engaging in forbidden acts and abandoning injunctions is called sin (Pāpa). Separate from that, there is no other nature of piety or sin. Additionally, engaging in injunctive acts and abandoning forbidden acts is nothing but a duty. Being active in Karma with duty-bound intellect is an injunction for this Yogī, and relinquishing duty for him is a prohibited act. Therefore, the said Variant-Yoga because it is with duty, though not sinful, is definitely in the form of piety. So, Variant-Yoga cannot provide freedom from the bondage of piety and sin in this world. When duty (Kartavya) is the basis for us to do any Karma, then any Karma contrary to that will become misdeed (अकर्तव्य, Akartavya) for us.

When we engage in that misdeed, it should be one that will provide contrary results. If it is not in the form that gives contrary results, it is also not a misdeed. Since it is a misdeed for us, it is also the one that provides contrary results. This way, engaged in misdeed, if we get into the bondage of contrary results, then involved in duty, why wouldn't we get in the bondage of piety? Of course, we will. This kind of rule of the Lord is not plausible where one person doing non-prescribed Karma can become a partner in bad deeds, while a person doing ordained Karma cannot become a partner in good deeds. If there is such a rule, then it is unjust. A human remaining in the bondage of 1) limited sentiments, 2) doership, and 3) duty cannot be free from the bondage of good or bad deeds. Thus, according to this rule, a Yogī practicing Variant-Yoga being with the duty will become a partner in good deeds and thus cannot be faithful to the test of the verse BG 2.50.

Contrary to the above, a Yogī who has found union in his Ātmā, having come out of the body's limitations and is free from doership and duty sentiments, is neither doing anything nor is in the bondage of good or evil, pleasure or pain dualities. Indeed, he attains absolute freedom from the Saṃsāra. This Yogī, through the realization of the Truth, "is as is" situated in the Ātmā of all beings, untainted from all, similar to how Bhagavāna described his true nature (Svarupa) -

यथाकाशस्थितो नित्यं वायु: सर्वत्रगो महान् |
तथा सर्वाणि भूतानि मत्स्थानीत्युपधारय || BG 9.6 ||

> Just as the mighty and moving everywhere wind always exists in space; similarly, know that all beings exist in Me.

When a Yogī has found union in the true nature of the Lord with oneness, then what is his connection with good or evil? The bondage of good or evil was due to limited I-ness in the body, the "I am a doer" superimposition (Adhyāsa) that is completely burnt in the fire of knowledge. He is limitless as the witness-observer of all and dissociated from all. This Yogī, in reality, with the influence of this knowledge, while doing everything, is a non-doer. That is called skill in actions. Even after doing Karma, he does not come into the bondage of Karma. In the Saṃsāra, whatever happens, is only due to the powerful grace of the dissociated from all, the true witness-conscious Ātmā. Just as a fish residing in a water body does not drown but in a dissociated form continues to swim, similarly established in Karma, the Yogī is untainted from all Karma; and thus, is firmly skillful in actions. However, even with his sentiment of fruit-relinquishment, our Variant-Yogī remains deprived of being skillful in Karma, as he is in the bondage of limited sentiments and duty. Being the doer of relinquishment of fruits, he helplessly comes into the bondage of fruits, as the business of Prakṛti is such that he has not been able to free himself.

कर्मजं बुद्धियुक्ता हि फलं त्यक्त्वा मनीषिण: |
जन्मबन्धविनिर्मुक्ता: पदं गच्छन्त्यनामयम् || BG 2.51 ||

Wise men, united with equanimity of intelligence, relinquishing fruits of actions, are indeed liberated from the bondage of birth and attain the ambrosiac Status.

The fruits of Karma can only be relinquished when the doer, duty, Karma, and fruits appear as imagined waves (Vivarta) in the Ātmā. With the influence of beholding only one Ātmā in all beings (सर्वात्मैक्य-द्रष्टि, Sarvātmaikya-Dṛṣṭi), the pot of Karma-Saṃskāras drowns, and distinctions of cause and action, support and that being-supported are removed from his vision. Then, "एकमेवाद्वितीयम्, only one without a second" the underlying support (Adhiṣṭhāna) Ātmā appears as the perceived cause (Vivartopādāna) of all causes, actions, support and that being-supported. In the underlying support rope, the Vivartopādāna of the superimposed snake is only the rope. The superimposed snake is only the Vivarta of the Adhiṣṭhāna rope, which without producing any mutation in its Adhiṣṭhāna, arises and ends. Contrary to this, as long as "I am a doer of Karma, there is some duty on me, and I do not desire fruits of my Karma for myself but offer them all to the Lord," such discriminating cause and action, support and that being-supported form of rope wrapped around the neck of Jīva-form pot are hanging over the head of the Saṃsāra-form well, how can there be freedom from Karma-Saṃskāras, how can there be the relinquishment of fruits of Karma as said in verse BG 2.51?

Let us contemplate a little. When a Jīva covered with an ego as a doer becomes something, imposes on himself duty that is separate from himself, knows Karma as separate from himself, whose material cause (doer) he has become, sees fruits of Karma separate from himself, which fruits he does not desire for himself but offers to the Lord who is separate from himself, has become a doer of the relinquishment of fruits of Karma that is separate from himself, and is caught in the wheel of numerous discriminating sentiments of doership, duty, Karma, fruits of Karma and relinquishment of fruits that have put a neck-hold on him - with such ignorance born perspective how can he free himself from the Karma-Saṃskāra net? Discriminating sentiments are the cause of Saṃskāras. When Saṃskāras are alive, how can there be freedom from the fruits of Karma? The cause of fruits is those Saṃskāras only, which with numerous discriminating sentiments remain profuse and are not burnt in the fire of knowledge. When Saṃskāras and fruits are present, believing freedom from the bondage of birth and the supreme Status's attainment is nothing but mockery and equivalent to a pie in the sky. So, where is there an occasion for such? The emotional result of the conscience is called Bhāvanā or sentiment, and just as sentiments arise one by one in the conscience, they are illuminated by the witness-conscious Ātmā. Later on, when the sentiments dissolve in the conscience, their Saṃskāras stay in the conscience in the refuge of the witness-conscious. Accordingly, when the true witness-conscious exists in those Saṃskāras, how can they be without fruits? One can have pure sentiments, and their fruits can also be pure, but they cannot be without fruits.

In contrast, without I-ness sense in the body, a Yogī who has found union with oneness in his Ātmā and "is as is" has procured an absolute position in his own witness-conscious, though he is doing everything through the body, he is a non-doer. There is no doership, duty, Karma, fruits, and relinquishment of fruits in him. He is only the observer-witness of the entire doership. Just as -

सर्वभूतस्थितं यो मां भजत्येकत्वमास्थित: |
सर्वथा वर्तमानोऽपि स योगी मयि वर्तते || BG 6.31 ||

A Yogī established with oneness in Me, who worships Me existent in all beings, abides in Me alone however he behaves.

With this perspective, when he has no doership, where is free time for Karma-Saṃskāras? When Saṃskāras are not there, where are fruits? When there are no fruits, where is the bondage of birth? When there is no bondage of birth, who has known the supreme Status? That supreme Status is always attained. It is only because of false attribution (Adhyāsa) of birth that one is turning away, though situated in own Ātmā. In reality, the Yogī, forsaking the Karma's fruits, free from the bondage of birth, while alive, attains the supreme Status and is true to the test of the verse BG 6.31.

Having formulated the nature of this Yoga, Bhagavāna articulates in the following two verses how one can attain such Yoga.

यदा ते मोहकलिलं बुद्धिर्व्यतितरिष्यति |
तदा गन्तासि निर्वेदं श्रोतव्यस्य श्रुतस्य च || BG 2.52 ||

> When your intellect properly crosses the delusional morass, you will acquire dispassion from both what is to be heard and what is heard.

श्रुतिविप्रतिपन्ना ते यदा स्थास्यति निश्चला |
समाधावचला बुद्धिस्तदा योगमवाप्स्यसि || BG 2.53 ||

> When your intellect, bewildered by varied Vedic tenets, becomes steady and immovable in the Self, you will attain Yoga.

In the above verses BG 2.52 and BG 2.53, for the attainment of Yoga in the true nature of the Paramātmā, Bhagavāna has not held Karma as the cause. It is explicitly stated for the intellect to be 1) out of the delusional morass and 2) established steadfast in the true nature of the Paramātmā. In the Variant-Yoga, the presence of "I am a doer of Karma, there is some duty on me, and I do not desire fruits of my Karma for myself but offer them all to the Lord" can neither take the intellect away from the delusional morass nor can establish the intellect steadfastly in the true nature of the Paramātmā. On the contrary, it will enlarge the delusional morass.

The word "मोह, Moha" here stands for ignorance. Contrary knowledge is called ignorance. For instance, knowledge of a rope as a snake is called ignorance. Direct removal of ignorance is only possible by knowledge, never with Karma. The contrary knowledge of rope as a snake can only be removed by rope knowledge through illumination; no matter how many blows of truncheon are employed, removal of the apparent (Mithyā) snake is impossible. Here, in the Ātmā, devoid of doership-attachment, superimposing and making more assertive doership and duty is the root of the delusional morass. I-ness and mineness, attachment and aversion, pleasure and pain, or birth and death, are just branches of the root ignorance. Cognizing the dissociated immutable Ātmā as a mutable doer is the root of all ignorance. How can this root be uprooted through Karma? On the contrary, with Karma, it would become firmer. The cognition of doership in the devoid of doership Ātmā is nothing but contrary knowledge. It is only ignorance. The practice of the limb of Variant-Yoga to be active in Karma imposing duty and doership (that are mutually dependent) on oneself, with maturity, will naturally strengthen the delusional morass. Has darkness been ever removed by darkness? In the Ātmā, there is no doership-attachment. However, by Karma, we are making the attribution of doership and duty in the Ātmā more assertive. So instead of removing delusional morass, we are providing nourishment to it. Thus, the only possible way to remove the intellect from the delusional morass is through analytic thinking, cognizing the devoid of doership Ātmā as dissociated from them. "I am the unattached Ātmā. I have no association with the body. I am only their observer-witness. The body and senses may act by their nature, but I have no taint from them. I am neither a doer nor do I have any duty. I am only their audience" - that analytic thinking is the only one to provide freedom from the delusional morass (BG 5.8 - BG 5.9). If, in reality, there was any taint on the Ātmā from the ignorance of doership and duty, it could have been removed with Karma. However, it is a stable tenet of Gītā that the attributes of gross and subtle bodies cannot touch the Ātmā (BG 2.13). The Ātmā is imperishable. With the destruction of the body, it does not perish. Neither does it die nor does it kill. No mutation can touch it (BG 2.16 - BG 2.25). In such a state, when the Ātmā is ever-free from ignorance of doership and duty, and there is only an illusory perception of doership and duty in the Ātmā, then to remove the intellect from the delusional morass through Karma is impossible; it can only be removed by contemplation. Sure, there is a role for Karma. Through desireless

Karma, the impurity of malice in the heart can be purged so that the seed of pure knowledge can be planted in it. However, adding more fertilizer without planting seeds even after the soil has become pure will deprive one of obtaining fruits. With desireless actions, once the heart has become pure, what is necessary is to remove the delusional ignorance of doership and duty from the Ātmā through firm analytic thinking. Nevertheless, once the heart has become pure, the delusional morass will enlarge if we continue nourishing doership and duty. What is there to doubt? Once the heart has become pure, if there is a continuation of the practice of duty and doership, then whatever is put in the pure heart will quickly ripen. When the Variant-Yoga cannot remove the intellect from the delusional morass, where is the question of establishing the intellect steadfastly in the true nature of the Paramātmā? Only with the removal of ignorance can there be the possibility of an immovable Status, which is impossible in the presence of ignorance. Due to ignorance, doership and duty assumed by Jīva were detrimental to the steadfast establishment of the intellect in the Paramātmā. So, how can there be an immovable Status in the presence of doership and duty?

Yes, there is no question that according to the above method, through analytic thinking after having attained union in own Ātmā, Karma cannot put a Yogī in bondage. All his Karma remains Akarma (non-action) and, like roasted seeds, does not remain the cause for fruits. In reality, he is devoid of desire-resolves (काम-संकल्प-वर्जित, Kāma-Saṃkalpa-Varjita), for he has burnt all his Karma in the fire of knowledge. Active in Karma, he is not doing anything. He is equipoised in success and failure. Even while doing Karma, he does not come into the bondage of Karma. He is free from attachment (गतसङ्ग, Gatasaṅga), and he is established in knowledge (ज्ञानावस्थित, Jñānāvasthita) (BG 4.18 - BG 4.23).

Therefore, in the attainment of Yoga, there is no other use of Karma other than to clean the heart from the thorns of malevolence. It is impossible to harvest the fruit of Yoga attainment through Karma. That fruit can only be obtained by planting seeds of analytic thoughts. That is why Bhagavāna, in the verses (BG 2.52 - BG 2.53), has not articulated Karma as the cause for the attainment of Yoga. But the words of Bhagavāna are, "When your intellect will properly cross the delusional morass, then you will acquire dispassion from both what is to be heard and what is heard." The intention here is that the Truth of the Ātmā is so profound that "श्रुत्वाप्येनं वेद न चैव कश्चित्, having listened, certainly do not know it" (BG 2.29). Indeed, the mind and words have no reach to the Ātmā, and not reaching there remain only there where they were. Words cannot narrate that limitless thing because whatever is narrated through words is only for correlation and discrimination. Bhagavāna has articulated that with dispassion, through subtle intellect, one should grasp from words only the essence like grain and discard words as a husk. Even though the procurement of grain is through the husk, one cannot procure grain without the abandonment of the husk. Those desirous of grain have to forsake husk. From words when you will grasp the essence {directly expressed meaning (वाच्यार्थ, Vācyārtha) of the word} in the form of grain, and abandon husk knowing it worthless; and knowing words as without essence you will attain dispassion, then your bewildered intellect, filled with doubt after hearing various tenets of the Vedas, "This is real, or that is real," without a doubt you will attain the immovable Status in your Ātmā, and then you will attain Yoga. From this, it is clear that be it a measure of Gītā or a tactical measure, attainment of Yoga is only possible through knowledge.

What are the characteristics of a Sage of Stable Wisdom (Sthitaprajña)?

With the desire to know the characteristics of a Sthitaprajña (स्थितप्रज्ञ, a sage of stable wisdom) whose intellect is steadfastly established in the true nature of the Paramātmā, Arjuna asks Bhagavāna - "What are the characteristics of a sage of stable wisdom established with oneness in the Ātmā?" When we contemplate the characteristics of a sage of stable wisdom enumerated by Bhagavāna, it is clear that illumination of those characteristics cannot be done just by Karma. They can be enlightened only by analytic thinking (तत्त्व विचार, Tattva Vicāra). In the words of Bhagavāna (BG 2.55 - BG 2.58) - "Hey Pārtha! When one fully discards all desires of the mind and is mentally content only in the Ātmā, then he is called a sage of stable wisdom. A person is of stable wisdom when he is not mentally perturbed in grief, his longing for pleasure has ceased, and he is free from attachment, fear, and anger. His wisdom is stable, who neither rejoices nor hates obtaining whatever good or evil and is without attachment everywhere. When he withdraws his senses from their objects as a tortoise does his limbs from all sides, then his wisdom is stable."

From these characteristics, it is clear that relinquishment of desires and situating with equanimity are the only two that are necessary for the sage of stable wisdom, and both are mutually dependent. With the first, there is the attainment of the second; and with the second, there is the nourishment of the first. The cause of inequality is desires, so with the relinquishment of desires, attainment of equanimity becomes natural. With the awakening of equanimity, desires are abandoned naturally. Desires happen as the cause for attaining pleasure. Equanimity, by nature, is pleasure-yielding. That is why, when equanimity is attained, desires have no purpose. Whether you call relinquishment of desires or attainment of equanimity, they are only one and not two separates. Now, we need to see the cause of desires or inequality? With some thought, it becomes clear that, in the faultless and equanimous limitless Brahman, when due to ignorance some limited wave "अहमस्मि, I am" originates, then due to the assertiveness of I-ness, ego is produced.

With ego - the intellect, mind, senses, and body are born, and then due to the insentience of the ego, the I-ness sense becomes assertive in them. With it, the desire to "become happy" is born naturally. Then, with a discriminating vision, Jīva develops favorable intellect in some things and antagonistic intellect in some other things. Then due to attachment and aversion, with sentiments of grasping and relinquishing, Jīva, subdued by desires, becomes active in Karma. Holding doer-intellect, doing Karma Jīva gets into the bondage of birth and death. Thus, the cause of desires or inequalities is only the limited ego born of ignorance (of one's true nature). It is only ego from which all desires and inequalities are born. From it happens the bondage of Karma. That is the cause of birth and death. Therefore, until the ego is burnt, there is no freedom from desires and inequalities. By doing Karma, the limited ego cannot be removed. On the contrary, by doing Karma gets nourishment. As activity in Karma cannot happen without doership-ego, that doership-ego is bondage, so its removal is impossible through Karma. Its removal is only possible by knowing one's true nature. That is because its creation is only due to the ignorance of one's true nature, the ignorance of the witness-conscious Ātmā. Like an earthen pot, limited ego in the Ātmā is not such that blows of a club can eradicate it, as its creation is only delusional due to the ignorance of its own Ātmā. In the kingdom of Prakṛti, there is a tenet, "With whose ignorance what is produced, it can only be removed by the knowledge of that thing with whose ignorance it was produced." Like a snake born of ignorance of a rope can only be removed by knowledge of the rope. Accordingly, the cause of inequality, the limited ego, can only be removed by the knowledge of the Ātmā, never by Karma. Only with the removal of ego can one attain the state of Sthitaprajña. With the removal of ego, all desires and inequalities are naturally removed, and equanimity is attained. In the words of Gītā -

इहैव तैर्जित: सर्गो येषां साम्ये स्थितं मन: |
निर्दोषं हि समं ब्रह्म तस्माद् ब्रह्मणि ते स्थिता: || BG 5.19 ||

Even here, the world is won by them, whose mind is established in equanimity. Because the Brahman is faultless and equanimous, they are established with oneness in the Brahman.

एवं बुद्धे: परं बुद्ध्वा संस्तभ्यात्मानमात्मना |
जहि शत्रुं महाबाहो कामरूपं दुरासदम् || BG 3.43 ||

Hey Arjuna! Thus, controlling the intellect through the senses and the mind, and through the intellect knowing the one beyond - the Self, forsake the painfully controllable enemy in the form of desire.

Thus, relinquishing desires and establishing equanimity can only be successful by the knowledge of the Ātmā, never by Karma. That is the opinion of Gītā, and only through that is the attainment of the state of Sthitaprajña. In the two verses above (BG 5.19 and BG 3.43), to establish equanimity and win over the foe in the form of desire, Gītā has explicitly depicted knowledge of the Ātmā as the cause. If, from Gītā's perspective, Karma had been the cause for attaining equanimity and winning over the enemy (desire), it would have been explicitly stated, "You perform Karma. You will achieve equanimity and win over the enemy desire by only doing Karma." However, here it is stated, "Upon attainment of equanimity, the Saṃsāra can be won while alive. Equanimity is acquired upon attaining the Brahman Status." "Knowing the one beyond - the Ātmā, forsake the painfully controllable enemy in the form of desire." That does not mean that no Karma is happening through the body of the sage of stable wisdom. Natural activities are happening through his body, and many are happening, but they are not with any duty. With duty, doership is awakened first, and that doership is the one that separates one from the true nature of the Ātmā. However, all Karma of the Sthitaprajña is in the form of Akarma, non-action, actionless, and in his vision, both doer and Karma are the Brahman.

कर्मण्यकर्म य: पश्येदकर्मणि च कर्म य: ।
स बुद्धिमान्मनुष्येषु स युक्त: कृत्स्नकर्मकृत् || BG 4.18 ||

One who sees non-action in action and action in non-action is wise amongst all humans; he has attained union and has done everything.

This Sthitaprajña performs no Karma with duty-bound intellect. By Karma done with duty-bound intellect, no one can achieve the state of Sthitaprajña. The fruit of Karma done with duty-bound intellect is only that Karma done with desire is changed into Karma with the desireless sentiment, "I am offering the fruit of my Karma to the Lord and doing such Karma is my duty towards the Lord." The fruit of such sentiment is only that love for the Lord is awakened in the heart, by which the fountainhead of devotion can fully open. However, after devotion is born, it is necessary to abandon the sentiment of duty-bound intellect. Devotion cannot become ablaze if this sentiment is continually held as there is no rule in love, just as a person suffering from fever, fed with dry food, gets strength but becomes weaker if he is fed instead with Ghī. However, after being cured, if he is continued to be fed with dry food, it will make him weak, and therefore at that time, relinquishment of dry food is necessary for him.

Similarly, duty-bound intellect is necessary before devotion is born, but after devotion is born, it is necessary to forsake it. Upon devotion becoming ablaze, no injunctive duty remains. What is the fun of devotion if some injunctive thorn is there? If loving devotion is not there, then where is dispassion from objects? The fountainhead of Lordly devotion is the only one that can flow away attachment to objects. Love for objects can only go away from the heart when first, the heart is filled with Lordly love that is opposed to objects. In the kingdom of Prakṛti, there is a rule that the heart cannot remain without love at any time. It has to have some kind of love in it. For example, if the Gopis (गोपी) did not have undivided love for Bhagavāna, then they would not have been able to leave their families. If there were bondage of duty in their hearts, they would never have been instruments of undivided love. In front of love, duty was merely an object of mockery for them. If there is no dispassion from objects, how can relinquishment of desires be possible? If there is no relinquishment of desires, then where is equanimity? If there is no equanimity, how can there be the stability of wisdom? Accordingly, neither duty-bound intellect can be the cause for the stability of wisdom, nor through a sage of stable wisdom, any Karma is done with duty-bound intellect.

Bhagavāna, in addition, gave importance to the usefulness of self-control of the senses in the stability of wisdom. He clarified how the mind acquires the lowest depths of degradation without controlling the senses. With control of the senses, the kind of peace obtained is explained, and how analytic thinking is born in a peaceful mind leading to the attainment of stability of wisdom (BG 2.60 - BG 2.68). After that, the glory of the sage of stable wisdom is explained, "While he is in a deep state of sleep from all sides in the Saṃsāra, yet he is awake in his own Ātmā, and no worldly desires can produce any disturbance in his heart." Being without mineness and egotism, he attains supreme peace. That is known as the "Brāhmi-Sthiti." Its influence is such that if such a state is reached at the time of death, the bondage of birth is removed (BG 2.69 - BG 2.72).

Thus, with the critique of Chapter 2, it is clear that the intended meaning of the words Buddhi-Yoga or Yoga that is used here, duty-bound intellect is incapable of justifying the meanings thereof. Through duty-bound intellect, there is no attainment of the said Variant-Yoga, nor by said Variant-Yogī with duty-bound intellect activity in Karma is possible. Even though duty-bound intellect in a lower state by regular succession can be helpful in this Variant-Yoga, in other states, it can be obstructive in the said Variant-Yoga, and without abandoning it, Variant-Yoga is impossible to attain. In the attainment of union, there is no help from duty-bound intellect.

Duty is one bondage, in which under one rule, there is an injunction of remaining in bondage. Deviating even an inch can be declared forbidden for him. Bondage is always there on the necks of those animals tied to a post, those who require oversight in the absence of bondage. Tied to a post, they can move around in a limited space. Anything beyond is considered prohibited. Righteous-Śāstra showing mercy on humans and protecting them from negligence has tied them with righteousness rope (Śikhā-Sūtra)[36]to a post in the form of Vedic Karmakāṇḍa so that they are obliged to behave within the limits of the Vedas. In that Yajñopavīta, three threads of Triguṇa (Sattvaguṇa, Rajoguṇa, and Tamoguṇa) are used. The intention is that now they are tied by the constituents of Prakṛti, and so it is their duty to only move around within the bounds of the Vedic moral post to which they are tied. However, by this, it is not the intention of the Vedas to keep them tied forever. On the contrary, it is to make them free from bondage. How so? Preliminarily, the activity of Karma in the objects of enjoyment is ordained within the Vedic bounds. When a person desists enjoyment and accepts, "Here there is no happiness," first, that object, like "विषकुम्भं पयोमुखम्, poison pot with milk on the top" appears pleasant but is indeed full of grief and sorrow. Second, there is only labor in it. Eat as much as you sweat, but you are still indigent in the end. You receive fruits of enjoyment commensurate with a pious deed that you perform, not a bit more. Because Rajoguṇa is still present in him, he is tied with the bondage of duty-bound desireless actions to remove desire-ridden activity from him. Even though he desists enjoyments, due to the presence of Rajoguṇa in his heart cannot remain steady. That is why it is now necessary to divert him from the activity of enjoyments and tie him to a post in the form of Lordly offerings so that, on the one hand, he does not leap towards enjoyments and, on the other hand, he can become pure from Rajoguṇa. When his Rajoguṇa is removed, his heart is filled with Sattvaguṇa. In his steady pure conscience sentiment of a keen desire to know the Truth becomes ablaze, then Śāstra unties him from the knot of the rope (Śikhā and Sūtra) and provides freedom from all worldly duties because the fruit of all these bondages is only the desire to know the Truth. With the desire to know ablaze, there is no bondage for him. This fire has so much energy that once it is ablaze, it cannot become quiet until it turns the entire Saṃsāra into ashes. Thus, these words of Bhagavāna -

जिज्ञासुरपि योगस्य शब्दब्रह्मातिवर्तते || BG 6.44 ||

Even the seeker of Yoga certainly goes beyond the injunctions and prohibitions of Veda.

The fruit of righteousness and the bondage of Śāstra is only freedom. However, even before coming into bondage, those who have broken the bondage and who believe that breaking the Śikhā and Sūtra is freedom have indeed misplaced the true intent of Gītā.

The Karma Yoga - Chapter 3

Not understanding the real intent of the words of Bhagavāna in the second chapter, at the beginning of the third chapter, Arjuna casts a doubt, "Hey Janārdana! If you consider knowledge superior to Karma, then hey, Keśava! Why are you enjoining me in this fearful war? By words that seem confusingly mingled, my intelligence is bewildered, as it were. Therefore, tell me that one thing, after deciding, by which I may attain the highest good. Tell me whether performing Karma is better for me or knowledge in the form of relinquishment of action (Karma-Tyāga)." In reality, Bhagavāna had not said anything confusing or mingled. It was Bhagavāna's intent through preceptors and scriptures for Arjuna to know transcendentally (Aparokṣa) the true nature of the Ātmā, that is - "your Ātmā is ever-young, immortal, and immutable and whose nature is

[36] Śikhā-Sutra (शिखा-सूत्र) means the lock of hair on the crown and the Yajñopavīta (sacred thread).

the Real-Conscious-Bliss-form. The being and non-being transformations of the entire Saṃsāra born of the great elements and the body, senses, mind, and intellect though are transforming in support of the Ātmā, yet none of those transformations can touch the Ātmā." That is known as Sāṅkhya and with contemplation of this Sāṅkhya knowledge and attaining a transcendental position in the Ātmā, "I am the ever-free dissociated witness separate from the world of the body, senses, mind, and intellect, only their observer." There is a tenet in the kingdom of Prakṛti that no activity can succeed in darkness. There has to be some light for its success, and "I am the undiminished light through which activities of the body and others are successful, yet none of them can touch me - the conscious light." That is known as Yoga.

Except for those above, Bhagavāna intends that neither relinquishment of Karma is Sāṅkhya nor Karma activity with duty-bound intellect is Yoga. But through Sāṅkhya knowledge, attaining oneness position in one's Ātmā, separating one's self from and remaining only the observer of the activities of body, senses, mind, and intellect and knowing them essenceless, leaving them free, similar to when a magician in his show produces one of our enemies in front of us and yet we may not desire to hurt him, and thus with the resolve of unreality, making one's self free from all duties, is Yoga. That is where there is a true harmonious connection between knowledge and Karma. That is the supreme effort. That is where all animosities disappear, and the bondage of Karma is broken. Just as -

भिद्यते हृदयग्रन्थिश्छिद्यन्ते सर्वसंशयाः ।
क्षीयन्ते चास्य कर्माणि तस्मिन्दृष्टे परावरे ॥ MU[37] 2.2.8 ॥

Knowing the Brahman, the knot in the heart is untied, all doubts are removed, and all Karma of that knower is destroyed.

With realized cognition of the cause and action free Paramātmā, the "I-mine" knot in the heart of Jīva is untied, all doubts evaporate, and all his Karma are depleted, are reduced to null. However, when Arjuna could not grasp this intent of Bhagavāna, he had to come down and tell Arjuna - "Earlier in this world, twofold disciplines were set forth by Me. Among them for Sāṅkhyās, the discipline of knowledge (Jñāna-Yoga), and for Yogīs, the discipline of action (Karma-Yoga).

1. For those Sāṅkhya-Yogīs, whose fitness (Adhikāra) is in knowledge and whose heart has become pure from Tamoguṇa and Rajoguṇa - the discipline of the Yoga of Knowledge (Jñāna-Yoga), that is, the Path of Renunciation (Karma-Tyāgarupa Nivrutti Mārga).
2. For those Karma-Yogī, whose fitness is in Karma and from whose heart Tamoguṇa (sleep, negligence, laziness, aversion in Karma) is removed, but Rajoguṇa is still present, to remove the flow of Rajoguṇa by the best Śāstra supported path - the discipline of Karma-Yoga, that is, the Path of desireless actions accepting the Lordly command to perform Karma holding doer and duty-bound intellect, and not desiring fruits of Karma for one's self offer them to the Lord (BG 3.3).

In both paths, there is no relinquishment of Karma (activities of the body, senses, mind, and intellect) in its true nature because, without initiation of Karma, one cannot enjoy Naiṣkarmya." **Not to come in the bondage of Karma even after doing Karma, and scorching the seeds of Karma in the fire of knowledge and making Karma actionless (Akarma) and devoid of fruits is called "Naiṣkarmya."** In the success of Naiṣkarmya, Rajoguṇa is detrimental, and only Karma can remove it. Only after removing Rajoguṇa through Karma the attainment of Naiṣkarmya is possible. With Rajoguṇa present in the heart, Naiṣkarmya can't be attained. Accordingly, the necessity of Karma in the attainment of Naiṣkarmya is shown.

Further, only by renouncing Karma (Karma-Saṃnyāsa) the success of transcendentally realizing the witness-conscious Ātmā cannot be accomplished. Karma-Saṃnyāsa, in reality, is only the removal of Rajoguṇa (the

---

[37] Muṇḍaka Upaniṣad (मुण्डक-उपनिषद्) 2.2.8

cause of Karma) resident in the heart and not the relinquishment of Karma by force. When Rajoguṇa is removed from the heart through activity in Karma, Karma drops like a ripe fruit due to its absence. Forcibly abandoning Karma is not Karma-Saṃnyāsa. Be it Karma-Saṃnyāsa or Karma-Yoga; in both, Karma is useful. Looking from a pervasive perspective, there is no single moment when living beings can stay without Karma but helplessly do Karma through the three constituents (Sattva, Rajas, and Tamas) of Prakṛti. The Saṃsāra is born of Prakṛti, and the nature of all three constituents is transformative. In such a state, when a Jīva is boundable with Prakṛti, how can he stay without Karma? Tamoguṇa is in the form of ignorance. It makes a Jīva active in insentience. Rajoguṇa is in the form of fickleness. It makes the body, senses, mind, and intellect fickle. Sattvaguṇa is like illumination. It reduces external activities of the body, senses, mind, and intellect. It stimulates the mind and intellect in the activity of analytic thinking, moving one towards renunciation. Though analytic thinking is not a bodily Karma, it is indeed a mental and intellectual Karma (BG 3.4 - BG 3.5). In the kingdom of Prakṛti, no living being can be without Karma, and those who forcefully restrain only senses and continue to dwell on sense-objects in the mind are nothing but hypocrites (BG 3.6).

In contrast, those who, through mental control of their senses, forsake the desire for fruits while practicing Karma-Yoga are indeed superior (BG 3.7). Bhagavāna prods, "Following the law of your life (स्वधर्म, Svadharma) perform Karma prescribed by the injunctions of the scriptures. It is superior to do Karma than not do Karma of any kind, as even maintenance of bodily activities is not possible without Karma" (BG 3.8). When Karma cannot be forsaken anyway and engaging in Karma, one cannot avoid bondage; then, one should only perform sacrificial (Yajñārtha) Karma. That is Karma for the sake of Lord Viṣṇu abandoning doership-ego. By doing Karma for the sake of the Lord, one does not come in the bondage of Karma, as all other Karma puts one in bondage. The fruit of Karma for the sake of the Lord is to become fit for knowledge through purity of the conscience, and so Karma that is "for the sake of the Lord" is not in the form of bondage (BG 3.9).

In addition, Bhagavāna spoke to Arjuna about how ancient Karma was. In the beginning, Brahmā created humanity together with sacrifice and said - "By this sacrifice attain growth; let this be the provider of coveted objects of desire to you." Whatever is possible for you to get, the intent is that you can only get through your Karma. Without your Karma, even the Paramātmā cannot give you anything. As depicted in Śrīmad Bhāgavata 10th Canto Govardhana-Līlā, the same intent was conveyed to Nanda and others that without your Karma, even Indra cannot give you anything, so abandon ritualistic worship of Indra and perform worship in the form of Karma. So is the beginningless wheel of Karma and humanity moving - with Karma, humanity is born, and with humanity, Karma is born. From a gross perspective, know that with food there is the creation of living beings; with the rain, there is the production of food; with sacrifice, there is the creation of rain; with Karma, there is the creation of sacrifice; with the Vedas, there is the creation of Karma, and through the Paramātmā there is the creation of the Vedas.

Understand that through the Paramātmā, the Vedas were born. Through the Vedas, Karma. Through Karma, sacrifice. Through sacrifice, rain. Through rain, food. Through food, living beings. Through living beings once again in sequence Karma, sacrifice, rain, and food and through food again living beings, and through living beings again Karma, and from Karma again sequentially living beings. In such a manner, the flow from Karma to humanity and from humanity to Karma is moving from eternity. When this wheel of humanity and Karma is beginningless, then to turn away from Karma is like cutting off the Saṃsāra-Cakra. When the Paramātmā has created all the Vedas, Karma, and humanity, and the root of all is the Paramātmā, then without any dispute, the success of the fruits of the Vedas and Karma is the movement towards that root (the Paramātmā) and not towards the Saṃsāra of birth and death through Karma. In reality, through our conduct, we ought to make ourselves an example for the Saṃsāra to emulate; and, with the relinquishment of self-interest, make our lives benevolent. Achieving good for oneself and the Saṃsāra and assisting in moving the Saṃsāra-Cakra is the aim of Karma. However, abandoning this aim, some have made enjoyment of this or higher worlds their aim, and who are dwelling in the sense-objects, through their Karma, are becoming valueless, not only for themselves but also for the Saṃsāra. Indeed, their lives are worthless (BG 3.10 - 3.16). Thus, the beginninglessness of Karma and the goal and fruits of Karma is articulated by Bhagavāna.

At this stage, with some thought, it is clear that, in reality, the fruit of Karma is not the attainment of the Brahman because only a thing that is separate and unattained can be acquired through Karma. However, the Brahman is not different from oneself but is the contiguous one's Ātmā only - that is the drumbeat of the Vedas. In the Chāndogya Upaniṣad (छान्दोग्य उपनिषद्), at the end of the dialogue between Uddālaka and his son Śvetaketu, one of the four principal Mahāvākya "तत्त्वमसि श्वेतकेतो"[38]of the Vedas is propounded. "Hey, Śvetaketu! Because of oneness between the Brahman and your Ātmā, you are That (Brahman)." Moreover, from Brahmā to the minutest blade of grass, the Brahman exists in all moving and stationary beings. It is not separate from all.

Such one's true nature Brahman being "the Ātmā of all, (सर्वात्मा, Sarvātmā)" is not unattained but is ever-attained. Only because of ignorance is it perceived as unattained. Akin to a person with a pencil on his ears looking for it all over, when someone tells him, "It is on your ears." It is then that there is the acquisition of the pencil. In reality, even though possessed, the pencil was perceived as unacquired. As such, attainment of the Brahman is not possible through Karma; only through the cognition of the Brahman attainment of the Brahman be possible. The fruit of Karma can only be the removal of Rajoguṇī vacillations that are opposers of knowledge, as is extensively discussed in "Nature of Karma" and "Cause and Effect in the activity of Karma." Removal of the fault that is the opposer of knowledge is only the fruit of Karma. Bhagavāna also spoke that one who does not have this fault (Rajoguṇī vacillations), or who had the fault and is now purged, who delights in the Ātmā, who is content only in the Ātmā and is fully satisfied in the Ātmā, for him there is no duty. For that person in this Saṃsāra, there is neither any purpose for doing anything nor for not doing anything. He is free from all injunctions and prohibitions such as "certain Karma is my duty" or "relinquishment of Karma is my duty." Attaining what is to be attained, he has nothing left to accept or reject in the entire Saṃsāra. Doing Karma, there is no goal left to gain. That is true independence, freedom, or liberation (BG 3.17 - BG 3.18).

यस्त्वात्मरतिरेव स्यादात्मतृप्तश्च मानवः |
आत्मन्येव च सन्तुष्टस्तस्य कार्यं न विद्यते || BG 3.17 ||

> However, that person who solely rejoices in the Self, who is content in the Self, and who is satisfied solely in the Self, for him, there is no duty.

नैव तस्य कृतेनार्थो नाकृतेनेह कश्चन |
न चास्य सर्वभूतेषु कश्चिदर्थव्यपाश्रयः || BG 3.18 ||

> Here, for him, there is no purpose, either performing an action or not performing any action, and there is no selfish dependence on all living beings.

At this location, let us see what some believe. In their view, duty does not go away for a Variant-Yogī, if not for himself, in the interest of the Saṃsāra activity in Karma is his duty.[39]However, such a view is without attaining direct transcendental experience and remaining separate from the Ātmā. As such, the Variant-Yogī has a trueness sense in the Saṃsāra and cognizes it as separate from his own Ātmā, and when he sees something spoilt in the Saṃsāra, he assumes his duty to improve it. Alternatively, that Yogī earlier knew himself in bondage and now knows himself free from the bondage of the Saṃsāra, and sees the Saṃsāra separate from himself, still in bondage. When he knows the Saṃsāra, birth, and death, bondage and liberation, sin and piety as real, then he is neither content in the Ātmā nor delights in the Ātmā, and he is not satisfied. Self-contentment and self-satisfaction are where through the realization of the Truth, the entire Saṃsāra is perceived as waves of the ocean (the Ātmā), and in all waves like the ocean, only one Ātmā is seen enjoying the bliss. What is spoilt, and what is there to improve? Like Lord Śiva, when this Ātmā

---

[38] Chāndogya Upaniṣad (छान्दोग्य उपनिषद्) 6.8.7
[39] Śrī Tilaka, Gītā Rahasya Pages 307 - 309

opens its third eye, then it will know that there is nothing spoilt in the Saṃsāra, there is nothing suitable to improve in the Saṃsāra, and there is neither any bondage for anyone anytime nor liberation. Spoilage and improvement only happen within, by which we know ourselves as something separate from the Ātmā. Like a dream bringing out the Saṃsāra from within, we begin to imagine birth and death, bondage and liberation and piety and sin. This way, like a spider, one creates from within a web of resolves, but after creating it, gets caught in it. When a person sleeps peacefully and dreams until he comes out of the dream state and is awake, how can there be a non-being in his dream world? However, when he has knowledge awakened according to these words of Bhagavāna, he can directly realize his true nature and of the Saṃsāra. Just as -

या निशा सर्वभूतानां तस्यां जागर्ति संयमी |
यस्यां जाग्रति भूतानि सा निशा पश्यतो मुने: || BG 2.69 ||

A restrained ascetic is awake in that which is a night for all living beings. In which all living beings are awake, that is a night for the perceiver sage.

The Saṃsāra wheel in which all created beings are awake, that is, they have accepted its trueness, that Saṃsāra wheel for the self-contented has become null, like night. Then for the great being who has attained such a state, for him - what Saṃsāra? Who is spoilt, and who needs improvement? Whose birth and death? Whose bondage? Whose liberation? All these arrangements of birth and death were happening in the ignorance sleep, and the bondage of all duties was only up to that time. For a great being in whom knowledge has awakened and who has known his Ātmā in reality, wouldn't it be an injustice for someone to assign the bondage of duty? How can Bhagavāna impose an obligation on such a great being? We need to change our thinking! We need to let such a great being be free from the neck-hold of responsibility, let him enjoy real freedom. Bondage of duty should be really on the one who is in the bondage of the body. How can there be any bondage for such a self-contented great being? He is neither the body nor the senses, nor the mind nor the intellect, but beyond all of them, just their observer. He is just the conscious space. Can space be bound?

The necessity of Karma, the woven nature of Karma and humanity, and the epilogue of Karma (where Karma goes and achieves the end) have been postulated from an ordinary perspective. The intention is that only after attainment of self-contentment is there an end of Karma, and that is the epilogue of Karma. That is because there is a tenet in the kingdom of Prakṛti that one who has a beginning has an end. When all efforts in Karma after initiation are there to perish, then why wouldn't the flow of Karma not end after being initiated? Every effort is only for one to be happy, and from Brahmā to an ant, every living being is running around only for this happiness. Once the desired object is obtained for which the run around is going on, it is also natural that the run around will cease. When this self-contented has obtained steady happiness and peace, his Karma happens naturally, just as how a potter's wheel rotates a long time after the turning stick is separated from the wheel. That is the end of Karma. That is the epilogue of Karma. There is no duty left for him, whether he does Karma or not, but he has equanimity of mind in doing Karma or not doing Karma.

Then, Bhagavāna making Arjuna face Him tells - "Hey Arjuna! To acquire this contentment and delight in the Ātmā, where all Karma becomes Akarma and 'despite doing everything, really not doing anything,' you always perform the right Karma without attachment. Because after purity of the conscience is achieved, doing Karma with an unattached sentiment, there is the attainment of the Paramātmā" (BG 3.19).

तस्मादसक्त: सततं कार्यं कर्म समाचर |
असक्तो ह्याचरन्कर्म परमाप्नोति पूरुष: || BG 3.19 ||

Therefore, always perform duty-bound action properly without attachment. For, a person attains supreme (Status) by performing action without attachment.

In "कार्यं कर्म समाचर," Kāryam (कार्यम्) is an adjective of Karma (कर्म), meaning ought to be done Karma or natural Karma. Knowing that Janaka and others achieved supreme Status through Karma and looking at the welfare of humanity, performing Karma is befitting (BG 3.20). Setting one's conduct as an example for people to emulate is called Lokasaṃgraha, that is, public well-being or welfare of humanity. By this, it does not mean that by Karma, one can attain the Paramātmā. Only through purity of the conscience by regular succession can Karma become an instrument in the attainment of the Lord. King Janaka did not attain the Lord only by Karma but by its fruit - purity of the conscience. In his pure conscience, through spiritual guidance of the seven perfected sages (Sapta-Siddha) and his analytic thinking, Janaka attained supreme perfection as fully described in Yoga-Vasīṣṭha, Upaśama-Prakaraṇa, Janaka Ākhyāna.

Moreover, after perfection, whatever natural Karma Janaka did was nothing but Akarma. When ego melts away, there is no attachment of doership with Karma of persons like Janaka. Their Karma is done as playtime only for public well-being.

यद्यदाचरति श्रेष्ठस्तत्तदेवेतरो जन: |
स यत्प्रमाणं कुरुते लोकस्तदनुवर्तते || BG 3.21 ||

Whatever a great person does, other people also do. Whatever standard that great person sets, humanity follows.

From the perspective of public well-being, others follow and behave similarly to whatever conduct is exhibited by a great person. "Hey, Pārtha! Just look at Me. Even though there is no duty for Me in all three worlds and no unacquired thing for Me to acquire, I am engaged solely in action. If I do not ever engage tirelessly in action, humans will follow My path in all possible ways" (BG 3.22 - BG 3.23). "If I do not engage in actions, these worlds will perish, and I would become a doer of deficient actions and destroyer of humanity" (BG 3.24). "Just as an ignorant person acts with attachment, so should a wise person desiring the welfare of humanity perform actions without attachment" (BG 3.25). "A wise person should not create debility in the mind of an ignorant person who is attached to action. However, established in the Ātmā and performing all actions, he should have the ignorant perform actions." Not seeing any mutation in own Ātmā due to Karma, engage in Karma free from duty and doership, and have those ignorant persons engage in Karma (BG 3.26).

The intention in the verses (BG 3.19 - BG 3.26) is that in the verses BG 3.17 and BG 3.18, the epilogue and the end of Karma that Bhagavāna had articulated -

"One who rejoices and is content in one's Ātmā, no duty remains. Because neither does he want any fruit by doing Karma nor by not doing any Karma, he wants something. He is free from all injunctions and prohibitions and has no attachment whatsoever for any being."

In the next verse, BG 3.19, the words of Bhagavāna are -

"तस्मादसक्त: सततं कार्यं कर्म समाचर, that is why you should perform Karma without attachment."

Here the word "तस्मात्, Tasmāt" means "that is why" and is in the context of verses BG 3.17 and BG 3.18. In that connection, Bhagavāna provides his intent that the major fruit of Karma is the attainment of rejoicing and contentment in the Ātmā after the purging of Rajoguṇī vacillations resident in the heart. Public well-being is not the major fruit, but indeed minor fruit, because in the next verse, BG 3.20, Bhagavāna says -

"लोकसंग्रहमेवापि सम्पश्यन्कर्तुमर्हसि, also looking towards the welfare of the humanity, the performance of Karma is only proper for you."

From this, it is clear that Lokasaṃgraha is not the major fruit of Karma, but that Lokasaṃgraha also becomes one cause in the activity of Karma. It is depicted as an additional or rather second reason for activity in Karma. Had Lokasaṃgraha been the major reason in Bhagavāna's view, then first in verse BG 3.19 with the word "तस्मात्, Tasmāt," he would have added that and would have said, "that is why you must do Lokasaṃgraha."

But, not doing so, Bhagavāna has made a sequential connection of the word Tasmāt (तस्मात्, that is why) with rejoicing in the Ātmā (आत्म-रति, Ātma-Rati) which is the essence of Karma. He has provided Lokasaṃgraha as the second reason for activity in Karma by saying, "If one looks from the perspective of the welfare of mankind, then also you should engage in Karma." Accordingly, from the perspective of the Bhagavāna, there are only two causes and fruits of Karma -

1. The major cause is the removal of Rajoguṇī vacillations that are detrimental in rejoice (Ātma-Rati) and contentment in the Ātmā through desireless actions (Niṣkāma-Karma), and after removing them and becoming free from all duties through knowledge ascend in Ātma-Rati. Additionally, based on the fitness of the mind, sequentially with unselfishness, desireless righteous activity, desireless devotion, and acquiring intense dispassion towards worldly attachments through listening and contemplation of Vedānta, one should attain contentment and satisfaction in the Ātmā - this is the major fruit of Karma. That is the real meaning of "तस्मादसक्त: सततं कार्यं कर्म समाचर" which was associated in the verses BG 3.17 and BG 3.18. It is important to recall what was discussed in "Nature of Karma" that listening, contemplation of Vedānta, based on one's fitness being mental Karma fall within the meaning of unattached Karma, and under Kṣatriya duty, a righteous war (Dharma-Yuddha) is part of the righteous activity.
2. The minor cause of activity in Karma discussed earlier after attaining a position in the Ātmā with the realization of the Truth is that through a Jīvanmukta, only natural Karma is performed, and that too for Lokasaṃgraha only. He remains active in the cause of public good as playtime and not because of any duty. What is duty? Duty is that for which the Vedas impose on a doer some injunctions to engage in and some prohibitions not to engage in. Where there is neither an injunction nor any fault of contrary results imposed on a doer to engage in Karma, there is no duty on the doer, nor is there any fault of contrary results on the doer. Imposition of the obligation of Karma by the Vedas is always on those who have I-ness sense in the body due to discriminating-vision. The intention being, bound by duties of the injunctions of the Vedas, Jīva ought to engage in good and desireless activity for self-improvement. Sequentially, the I-ness sense becomes loose from the body. In the end, discriminating vision evaporates like camphor. With the oneness-vision, a realization of the existence of one Ātmā in all beings is attained. Then, the bondage of duty is cut on its own. There is no other purpose for the bondage of duty separate from this. When a Jīvanmukta has acquired realization of only one Ātmā in all beings through oneness-vision, when he has transcendentally (Aparokṣa) realized all living beings from Brahmā to a blade of grass as his Ātmā, when he has determined the entire Saṃsāra directly as a dream (null-form) in his Ātmā, how and why would any Śāstra impose any duty on him? By now, he is already beyond the bounds of Śāstra - and so which duty can he be tied? He could only tie himself to duty as long as he held the Saṃsāra with trueness sense and accepted the Saṃsāra as real. However, when he cognizes the Saṃsāra unreal, similar to a child who creates an army of clay, then how can he be tied to any duty? Children's joy is creating clay toys, having fun and games, and then kicking and smashing the toys back to their original status. Innocent as they are, they have mental independence - who can impose a duty on them? If a learned person, even if he thought he had a duty, is not free but is still in bondage. In the words of Bhagavāna Aṣṭāvakra -

ज्ञानामृतेन तृप्तस्य कृतकृत्यस्य योगिनः ।
नैवास्ति किंचित्कर्तव्यमस्ति चेन्न स तत्त्ववित ॥

One who is content with the ambrosia of knowledge, no residual duty remains for such a contented Yogī. He is not a knower of Truth if he sees any obligation in him.

Bhagavāna says in a mild tone, "लोकसंग्रहमेवापि सम्पश्यन्कर्तुमर्हसि, with a view towards Lokasaṃgraha it is right for you to do Karma, and not as a duty." In verse BG 3.21, Bhagavāna simply says and provides an argument that "because whatever behavior a great person exhibits and through his behavior whatever standard he sets, the Saṃsāra also behaves like that, and therefore it is proper for you to engage in Karma." Bhagavāna did not forcefully say, "Lokasaṃgraha is your duty, and you have to do it." Further, in verse BG 3.22, in a similar mild tone, Bhagavāna provides himself as an example and succinctly tells Arjuna, "Hey Pārtha! Even though there is no duty for Me in all three worlds and no unacquired thing for Me to acquire, I am engaged solely in Karma."

Whether as a tactic or as a measure, from an overall perspective, it is established that for a knower of the Truth, public well-being is not some injunctive duty, and there is no adverse impact for not engaging in Lokasaṃgraha. Had there been any negative impact, then Bhagavāna would have spoken about it when Arjuna was desisting war and Bhagavāna was preparing him to fight the righteous war. On the contrary, Bhagavāna is not presenting arguments from the perspective of Śāstra but is offering mild views from an ordinary perspective in the verses BG 3.23 and BG 3.24 -

यदि ह्यहं न वर्तेयं जातु कर्मण्यतन्द्रित: |
मम वर्त्मानुवर्तन्ते मनुष्या: पार्थ सर्वश: || BG 3.23 ||

> Indeed, Hey Arjuna! If I do not ever engage tirelessly in action, humans will follow My path in all possible ways.

उत्सीदेयुरिमे लोका न कुर्यां कर्म चेदहम् |
संकरस्य च कर्ता स्यामुपहन्यामिमा: प्रजा: || BG 3.24 ||

> If I do not engage in action, these worlds will perish, and I will become the doer of deficient action and the destroyer of all humanity.

Though Bhagavāna was providing arguments from an ordinary perspective, concomitantly, He was not binding Himself from any duty with an explicit statement in BG 3.22 that -

> "न मे पार्थास्ति कर्तव्यं त्रिषु लोकेषु किञ्चन, I do not have any duty in the three worlds."

A Lokasaṃgraha activity is only for a Jīvanmukta. Others cannot be fit for it. Further, not being a duty, Lokasaṃgraha is only a minor cause and not a major cause for activity in Karma. From Gītā-perspective, the major cause of activity in Karma is that based on one's fitness, one should move forward in the path of contentment and ascend in contentment in the Ātmā. From the perspective of Gītā, there can be only these two causes in the activity in Karma. Separate from them, desire-ridden activity is not acceptable to Gītā in the definition of Karma, and on the contrary, it is considered Vikarma, prohibited Karma.

Having clarified Lokasaṃgraha, Bhagavāna next shows a distinction in Karma between a knower and an ignorant. In the vision of a knower, there is no reality of Karma separate from his Ātmā.

> "कर्मण्यकर्म य: पश्येत्, one who sees non-action in action" (BG 4.18)

In his view, all efforts of Karma have become motionless and immutable in the form of the Brahman, and he does not see in his Ātmā any taint of the sixfold instruments of action (Ṣaṭ-Kāraka).[40]So how can he hold external attachments such as "I am a doer of Karma, and Lokasaṃgraha is a duty for me"? He is naturally free from all attachments, does not see any taint in himself from any of them, performs Karma without attachment, and engages in Lokasaṃgraha. From his perspective, in his Ātmā, even though he does not want to acquire anything or forsake anything through Karma, he does not intend through Karma to produce

[40] Ṣaṭa-Kāraka (षट-कारक) means the sixfold instruments of action: (1) doer (कर्ता, Kartā) of the act; (2) action (कर्म, Karma) meaning the activity of the act; (3) instruments (करण, Karaṇa) by which act is performed; (4) for whom act is performed (संप्रदान, Saṃpradāna); (5) from where act is performed (अपादान, Apādāna); and (6) in which act is performed (अधिकरण, Adhikaraṇa). A Kāraka relation means a relation between a noun and the verbal activity with which it is connected.

debility in the minds of the ignorant who are fit only for Karma. Through Karma, even those ignorant may be able to remove their increased Rajoguṇa and achieve this state, which would not be possible had they abandoned Karma. Therefore, it behooves a knower established in the Ātmā who does not see any mutation in his Ātmā to continue his engagement in Lokasaṃgraha.

Who is the doer of Karma in reality? With ignorance, how does the bondage of Karma happen? With knowledge, how can there be freedom from the bondage of Karma? Bhagavāna, in the following two verses, explains the intent -

प्रकृते: क्रियमाणानि गुणै: कर्माणि सर्वश: |
अहङ्कारविमूढात्मा कर्ताहमिति मन्यते || BG 3.27 ||

> In all ways, actions are being done by the constituents of Prakṛti only. However, one whose mind is deluded by egoism thinks, "I am a doer."

तत्त्ववित्तु महाबाहो गुणकर्मविभागयो: |
गुणा गुणेषु वर्तन्त इति मत्वा न सज्जते || BG 3.28 ||

> Hey Arjuna! On the contrary, one who knows the Truth about the distinction between the constituents of Prakṛti and their operations is not attached to action, knowing that the constituents operate amidst the constituents.

The intention here is to know where Karma is located and at which location Karma becomes blunted? In the Saṃsāra, there are only two main elements - one is Prakṛti, and the second is the Puruṣa, the witness-conscious Ātmā. Under Vedānta and Sāṅkhya precepts, the Saṃsāra is in the kingdom of Prakṛti and is a transformation of Prakṛti only. However, the immutable actionless Ātmā, which is the underlying support of Prakṛti, is all-pervading and is free from all mutations. Mutations always happen in those things that are gross and limited. Mutations can't exist in subtle limitless things because there is no freedom for mutations to exist due to their omnipresence. The pervasive space is free from all modifications because of its subtlety and pervasiveness. Though all modifications happen in support of the space, that is, the wind moves, the rain falls, the hurricanes blow dust, the sun radiates heat, and many such modifications occur depending on the pervasive space, the space does not move, does not get wet, does not get dirty or does not get heated. Because of its subtlety, though support for all modifications, the space sits changelessly "is as is." Likewise, the Ātmā, because of its all-pervasiveness and subtlety supporting all mutations of Prakṛti, is itself seated immutable.

Because it always exists in all of them, from Brahmā to a blade of grass, it is everyone's Ātmā. In all of them, the use of the word "I" or "Aham, अहम्" is for the Ātmā only, and it is grasped only with the word "I," that is, the use of the word "I" is only for that. It is impossible to use the word "I" for any insentient thing separate from the Ātmā because no one establishes themselves as "I am insentient" in their conduct. Still, all prove themselves "conscious" and great by their behavior. An insentient thing is sometimes there and sometimes not there, but based on individual conduct, no one can establish that "I am sometimes not there." Though there is a merger of all transformations of Prakṛti (the body, senses, and the conscience) in the deep-sleep state, "I am also at that time and observing non-being of all, my non-being did not happen" is proven by all in their experience. Thus, "I" is for the Ātmā only and not the insentient Prakṛti. In such an all-pervasive Ātmā, there is no possibility of any kind of mutation of Karma, any taint of Karma. With the transformation of Prakṛti, if the Ātmā itself becomes mutable, then a perception of it later is impossible because mutations themselves have a non-existent form. They cannot illuminate themselves. There must be something imperishable, immutable thing in the root of all modifications under whose support they are illuminated.

Different ornaments are created depending on immovable instruments such as an anvil or a stake of a goldsmith. If the instruments themselves become movable due to the making of the ornaments, then in their support, the creation of the modifiable ornaments is impossible. Accordingly, when the Ātmā is untouched by any mutation, then all mutations in the form of Karma should happen only in the kingdom of Prakṛti because there isn't any other third thing to whom Karma mutations can be attributed. Prakṛti, by its nature, is constituted of Sattva, Rajas, and Tamas constituents. In any state, when the three constituents are in equilibrium, the mutation in the form of Karma cannot originate. Just as when the three faults of the body viz. wind (वात, Vāta), bile (पित्त, Pitta), and phlegm (कफ, Kapha) remain in equilibrium, then the body stays in an unmodified disease-free healthy state. There is no transformation in Prakṛti in the equilibrium state of the constituents. In that state, the Saṃsāra stays merged as in a deep sleep, so no Karma happens even in that state. Karma can only occur in the transformation of Prakṛti when the three constituents lose equilibrium and agitation is activated in them. During the turmoil in the constituents, one of the three constituents becomes dominant in a Jīva, and the other two remain subdued. Jīva does Karma following the constituent that is dominant. In the words of Gītā, Karma, such as knowledge, light, and relinquishment, are effectuated by Sattvaguṇa. Rajoguṇa produces greed and fickleness, and Tamoguṇa creates negligence, delusion, ignorance, and laziness. Just as -

सत्त्वात्सञ्जायते ज्ञानं रजसो लोभ एव च |
प्रमादमोहौ तमसो भवतोऽज्ञानमेव च || BG 14.17 ||

> With Sattvaguṇa, knowledge is born. Greed arises with Rajoguṇa, and negligence, delusion, and ignorance arise with Tamoguṇa.

From this, it is established that in the "I-form" Ātmā, there is no taint from Karma, and there is no taint of Karma in the equilibrium state of Prakṛti. It is only in the non-equilibrium state of Prakṛti that Karma is produced per respective individual constituents. Thus, the Ātmā being immutable is not found as a doer, and also, being untainted is not seen to be touched by Karma. Only due to disturbance are the constituents found as doers, and it is only due to the constituents that there is the fruition of the transformations in the form of Karma. Now at this stage, we need to see **how the Ātmā, even though it is a non-doer (Akartā), is entangled in the bondage of Karma?** The resolution of this is based on the view above - the absence of discernment of the true nature of Prakṛti and the Ātmā. That is the root of this bondage. Through this ignorance, due to mutual "अन्योन्याध्यास, Anyonyādhyāsa" of the nature of Prakṛti and the Ātmā, the Puruṣa as Jīva comes into the bondage of Karma and clinging to piety-sin, birth-death and pleasure-pain moves around in a circle like a clock. That Anyonyādhyāsa, the delusion of one in the second and the delusion of the second in the first, is such that the I-ness attribute of the Ātmā is superimposed (Adhyasta) in Prakṛti, and doership of the constituents of Prakṛti is superimposed (Adhyasta) on the Ātmā. Thereby Jīva, by delusional ego, holds the constituent attributes of Prakṛti as "I am a doer" and comes into the bondage of doership-ego. This ignorance is indeed the root of all ills.

The perception of the ego of I-ness attribute of the Ātmā in the constituents and the perception of doership of the constituents in the Ātmā is known as "चिज्जड ग्रन्थि, Cijjaḍa Granthi," a knot that is sentient in some part and insentient in some part. Due to ignorance, with the I-ness ego in the mind, intellect, and Citta that are the transformations of the constituents of Prakṛti, Jīva holds the "I am a doer" ego in whatever activity that happens in the mind and intellect or whatever efforts that occur in the body and senses through the mind and intellect. Then, bound by the rules of Prakṛti, through good and evil Karma, accumulates righteous and unrighteous Saṃskāras, and for the enjoyment of their fruits bound by the body gets into the wheel of birth and death. Karma through the body, and the body through Karma - the flow of Karma and body continues. In such a state, as long as this knot is present and is not burnt through the fire of knowledge, fruit is acquired when he engages in Karma, holding a duty of some kind on himself, whether the Karma is desireless or desire-ridden. With the presence of the "I am a doer" ego in the constituents, he holds righteous and unrighteous Saṃskāras in himself, which cannot remain fruitless.

Where is Karma located? At which location does Karma become blunted? In addition, what kind of bondage does a Jīva have with Karma? That is explained previously. It is now imperative to think about Jīva, who is entangled in the evil net of Prakṛti, as to how to free him from the bondage of Karma? Answer is clear, without removing the part sentient and part insentient knot, there is no deliverance for Jīva because it is the root of all evil. Engaging in any sort of Karma to break this knot is like looking for a flower in space. Karma is the fruit of this knot, so engaging in Karma will instead provide nourishment to the knot. When the root of the disease is ascertained, it becomes natural to cut it. When he has fallen from his true nature and is inflicted with a disease of birth and death, the disease can be removed by only being established in the true nature of the Ātmā. In BG 15.2, Bhagavāna giving the comparison of a fig tree to the Saṃsāra has shown that the branches of the Saṃsāra-tree have spread up down all over, and it is only through Karma done in the human species its roots have spread down to the world below - अधश्च मूलान्यनुसन्ततानि कर्मानुबन्धीनि मनुष्यलोके. That is why, by Karma, it is impossible to cut this knot, which would be like removing dirt by dirt. Bhagavāna, in Chapter 15, verses BG 15.3, BG 15.4, and BG 15.5, provides an approach to cutting this tree -

अश्वत्थमेनं सुविरूढमूल मसङ्गशस्त्रेण दृढेन छित्त्वा || BG 15.3 ||
ततः पदं तत्परिमार्गितव्यं यस्मिन्गता न निवर्तन्ति भूयः || BG 15.4 ||
निर्मानमोहा जितसङ्गदोषा अध्यात्मनित्या विनिवृत्तकामाः |
द्वन्द्वैर्विमुक्ताः सुखदुःखसंज्ञै गच्छन्त्यमूढाः पदमव्ययं तत् || BG 15.5 ||

Cutting the deep-rooted fig tree with a strong weapon of detachment, then that "Status" ought to be sought, having gone from where there is no return.

Free from vanity and delusion, having overcome flaws of attachment, ever involved in the search for the Self, free from lust, liberated from dualities like pleasure and pain, such undeluded sages attain the imperishable "Status."

भिद्यते हृदयग्रन्थिश्छिद्यन्ते सर्वसंशयाः ।
क्षीयन्ते चास्य कर्माणि तस्मिन्दृष्टे परावरे ॥[41]

Knowing the Brahman, the knot in the heart is untied, all doubts are removed, and all Karma of that knower is destroyed.

Only through the transcendental realization of the Paramātmā, the knot in the heart is melted, all doubts are smashed, and all Karma is depleted. Such is the drumbeat of the Vedas -

"बध्यतेऽविध्यया जन्तुर्विध्यया तु प्रमुच्यते, because of ignorance there is bondage, and only with the knowledge there is freedom."

At this location, Bhagavāna tells Arjuna in BG 3.28, "Hey Arjuna! On the contrary, one who knows the Truth about the distinction between the constituents of Prakṛti and their operations is not attached to action knowing that the constituents operate amidst the constituents." Only through the knowledge of the Reality freedom from the bondage of Karma is acceptable to Bhagavāna.

Thus, from the measures of Upaniṣads and Gītā, it is clearly shown that the knot in the heart is the root of the bondage of Karma, and only through analytic thinking upon attaining a position in the Ātmā, it can be untied. Based on experience, it is also shown that as long as a Jīva immersed in ignorance imagines someone else's constituents and duties in himself and adheres to the impurity of doership of the constituents, how can he be free from the bondage of Karma? However, according to verse BG 15.5, when a Jīva acquiring fitness, leaving vanity and delusion, winning over faults of I-ness and mineness attachments, abandons all desires, being without dualities from pleasure and pain, in a solitary place does his accounting, then he will know, "There was never any taint of these constituents and Karma ever in me." Has space situated

[41] Muṇḍaka Upaniṣad (मुण्डक-उपनिषद्) 2.2.8

within a dirty swamp ever embraced muck? It is always unstained. In the same way, "There was never any taint of impurity of the constituents and Karma in my witness-conscious true nature." If a learned Paṇḍita intoxicated for whatever reason says, "I am not a Brāhmaṇa, I am a Cāṇḍāla," then under the influence of alcohol by his words, he does not become a Cāṇḍāla but remains a Brāhmaṇa only, and when he becomes sober, he considers himself Brāhmaṇa only. In the same way, even though possessed by ignorance, a Jīva may imagine attributes of the constituents of Prakṛti in himself. Yet, in reality, he "is" like space ever pure, and upon abandoning the frenzy of ignorance, he will know himself similarly dissociated. By whose presence actions are successful and, in whose absence, there are no actions - the one who is causal for actions. Where there is no visible knowledge of the cause, the cause can be inferred by such separation and connection (Anvaya-Vyatireka). For instance, where there is fire, there is smoke; and in the absence (Vyatireka) of fire, there is the absence of smoke, and so where there is smoke, its cause fire is thus inferable. Likewise, in the presence of the constituents, there is the fruition of Karma; and in the absence of the constituents, there is the absence of Karma, so the constituents are established as the doer of Karma. In both the awake and the dream states, based on the individual constituents, the flow of Sāttvika, Rājasika, and Tāmasika Karma goes on intact. In the presence of the constituents, activities of knowledge and action are not absent; indeed, there is no moment when there is no activity. The body, senses, mind, intellect, and Citta are involved in some form of activity all the time. However, when the constituents merge in their Prakṛti, all activities of knowledge and action suddenly stop in the deep-sleep state. Even though the constituents are absent, the I-form Ātmā is present and is the observer of the being and the non-being of the constituents and Karma. Whose visible witness is given by himself when he comes in the awake state, "At that time there were no constituents, there was no activity of knowledge and actions, and there were no mind, senses, and intellect transformations of the constituents, but I was there and enjoying objectless pleasure." Were the Ātmā the cause of the doer of Karma, then at that time, Karma should have been produced in it. Just as the sun in the form of light does not ever remain without light, in the same way, were the Ātmā in the form of a doer, then it should never remain without doership. From the logic above, it is clear that the Ātmā is never a doer. The doer is only the constituents. Further, even when the doership of the constituents is superimposed on the Ātmā, then also the Ātmā is not a doer but remains only as an observer. Constituents are the ones that make superimposition of their doership on the Ātmā. Just as when a king's army is fighting in a war, at that time, it is commonly said that the king is fighting, but the king may be really in his palace and may not be doing anything. He is only the power, and the army's war is only attributed to him. In the same way, the Ātmā is always on its own "is as is." During the activity time of the constituents, it does not ever become mutated. It remains only the observer of the constituents with its power, and in it, doership of the constituents is only attributed. Even the attribution is only from the constituent's perspective and not from the perspective of the Ātmā. For instance, in the space, the name pot-enclosed space and bringing of water are only from the perspective of the pot. It is not from the perspective of the space. From the perspective of space, there is neither the name pot-enclosed space nor the act of bringing water, but separate from the name, form, and act, it is the space only. Similarly, in the Ātmā, the name "witness" and the activity of power are only from the constituent's perspective. From the perspective of the Ātmā, in the absence of the constituents, there is neither the name "witness" nor any activity in the form of power in the Ātmā. If the Ātmā becomes mutable due to the mutations of the constituents, who would prove the existence of those mutations? Mutations themselves, being of perishable nature, on their own support, cannot prove themselves. Their proof is only possible by some immutable thing that remains untainted from those mutations, just as the proof of the mutation of fire and water is done in support of space, yet the space itself does not get heated by fire nor get wet by water. If space itself mutates due to the mutation of fire and water, how would there be proof of those mutations?

Summarizing -

नान्यं गुणेभ्य: कर्तारं यदा द्रष्टानुपश्यति |
गुणेभ्यश्च परं वेत्ति मद्भावं सोऽधिगच्छति || BG 14.19 ||

When the percipient sees no doer other than the constituents and knows Me beyond the constituents, he attains My form.

One who has become fit, through spiritual guidance of a preceptor and measures of the scriptures, his pure tactic and example with firm effort has separated himself (his Ātmā) from the constituents and Karma, such a knower of the Truth - "गुणा गुणेषु वर्तन्त इति मत्वा न सज्जते, is not attached to Karma knowing that the constituents operate amidst the constituents" (BG 3.28). "I am unattached untainted from them," knowing that he is not attached to the constituents and Karma and is not bound like a water hen in water.

Thus, a knower of the Truth who, knowing himself "is as is," has separated his Ātmā from the constituents and Karma of Prakṛti, that great warrior is indeed an absolute winner of the battle of the Saṃsāra, and in this life is free. He is Jīvanmukta. Only he is the one who has instantaneously attained freedom from the bondage of Karma. Even though engaged through the body in Karma, he is a real non-doer. Involved in unrestrained activities, he is a real Karma-Saṃnyāsī, a relinquisher of Karma - प्रवृत्तिरपि धीरस्य निवृत्तिफलभागिनी, the activity of a knower of the Truth is renunciatory only.[42]Seen with desire in the conscience, he is indeed a true desireless. In reality, he is free from all injunctive and forbidden duties. Indeed, all duties are there for one to attain such a state. After giving its fruit, duty itself becomes accomplished with its objective. Outside this, from Gītā's perspective, while holding doer-intellect, simply abandoning Karma is not Karma-Saṃnyāsa, and having such duty that "I am offering my Karma to the Lord" is indeed sentimental delusional fruit-relinquishment. It is not real Karma-Yoga. However, the knowledge of the Truth of the establishment in the Ātmā is real Karma-Saṃnyāsa, and that is the real Karma-Yoga, and that is the harmony between Sāṅkhya and Yoga. That is where apparent opposition of knowledge and Karma is removed, and true congruity happens. That is the real attainment of Yoga. That is for which Gītā has descended. Only when one has ascended in such a state can one bid farewell to the fruits of Karma, and this is the propounded subject of Gītā. Delusional sentimental fruit-relinquishment can never be the subject of Gītā, and neither can it give freedom from its fruit. Even though Gītā does not disrespect sentimental fruit-relinquishment and considers it a real instrument of Karma relinquishment, this cannot be the only fruit of Gītā - that much fruit of Gītā where those who have done the "end" is a grave mistake. A scripture that is content and focused only on one inferior instrument binds the doer of that instrument. For whom doors for other instruments are shut, it is degraded and unsuitable to be called an authentic scripture. Gītā is not such an unauthentic scripture. It is a vast ocean into which all instrumental rivers have entry. Commensurate with fitness, Gītā gives everyone opportunity, whether activity or non-activity. The fruit of all is real Karma-Saṃnyāsa. Having ascended in this Karma-Saṃnyāsa, Arjuna was advised to fight, just as -

मयि सर्वाणि कर्माणि संन्यस्याध्यात्मचेतसा |
निराशीर्निर्ममो भूत्वा युध्यस्व विगतज्वर: || BG 3.30 ||

Renouncing all actions in Me with the mind in transcendent knowledge, having become free from expectations, mineness, and affliction, fight.

In addition, Bhagavāna explaining the glory of this view that "only the constituents are engaged in their attributes, there is no taint of the constituents and Karma in Me the witness-conscious" said that even those who have not ascended "is as is" in the true nature, but accepting this view, without fault-finding intellect and with faith, are engaged in constant conduct, they will also be freed from the bondage of Karma. Contrary to this, those foolish persons who are not following this view, but have a fault-finding vision, that is, have no faith, "How can it be possible that there is no taint of the constituents and Karma in the Ātmā?" such persons whose Citta is devoid of that entire knowledge, know them as fallen from the auspicious path (BG 3.31 - BG 3.32).

---

[42] Aṣṭāvakra Gītā (अष्टावक्र गीता) 18.61

In the end, Bhagavāna summarizing the chapter, said - the question you posed to Me at the beginning of this chapter, "If you consider knowledge as superior to Karma, then Hey Keśava! Why are you enjoining me in this terrible Karma?" is improper. My intent is only in the congruity of knowledge and Karma and never abandoning Karma. Whether a knower or an ignorant, activities in the form of efforts always continue commensurate with individual nature. Even a knower engages in bodily and mental activities based on his nature. The fruit of knowledge is only that - based on the method above and thought, removing the bondage of doership from the Ātmā and attaining "is as is" steadfast position in own witness-conscious Ātmā, the bondage of Karma can be cut. To stop the flow of nature is not the fruit of knowledge. All beings, whether insentient, sentient, immovable, or movable, commensurate with their nature, all move in the natural flow, so why be stubborn? (BG 3.33).

When Prakṛti is so powerful, it is natural for the senses that are transformations of Prakṛti to attach to their favorable objects and to have an aversion to disliked objects. However, it would be beneficial for humans not to start barking like dogs by becoming themselves like the senses and thus becoming controlled by attachment and aversion. A Jīva falls from the path of the highest good (BG 3.34) because attachment and aversion are hindrances. To defeat attachment and aversion, Bhagavāna said - One's duty, even devoid of merits, is superior to a perfectly observed duty of others. Death is better in one's duty. The duty of others is fraught with danger. The conduct of responsibility of others, even if it is better, can only provide fear, just as a mother's breastfeeding is proper for a newborn, but food intake is fearful. Just as a mango seed, based on its fitness, fed by soil and fertilizer over a period, opens up into numerous states in the form of shoots, leaves, branches, trunks, flowers, and sweet ripe mangoes, however without the soil and fertilizer even fed with other better substances there is no production of mangoes. Based on fitness, even when one's law of life (Svadharma) is without merit, its conduct uplifts a Jīva day by day, subdues attachment and aversion, makes him ascend in the witness-conscious state, and makes him as Śiva. So is the meaning of the word "Dharma" -

धारणाद्धर्मत्याहुर्धर्मो धारयते प्रजाः ।
यत्स्याद्धारणसंयुक्तं स धर्म इति कथ्यते ॥

Whatever is held together based on fitness, holding together and putting into practice is called Dharma (धर्म, righteousness). Indeed, such a Dharma is holding together the Saṃsāra. That which holds together is certainly Dharma, as said in BG 3.35. Action, not just words, is Dharma.

After that, on Arjuna's question, "Then, even not wishing by what is this person impelled to sin, as if enjoined forcibly?" What is that power that gets him involved in evil Karma? In response, Bhagavāna said, "Born of the constituent Rajas, it is this desire and this anger. Know this voraciously eating greatly sinful desire as the foe in this world."

Desires are of three kinds based on the three constituents of Prakṛti -

1. Sāttvika desire - a subtle covering like smoke obscuring fire,
2. Rājasika desire - a medium covering like dust covering a mirror, and
3. Tāmasika desire - a dense covering like an amnion protecting an embryo, hardly visible.

In the form of desire, the foe which resides in the senses, mind, and intellect covers the knowledge of Jīva. Hence, it can be caught by gaining control over its residence (the senses), though it cannot be killed. However, the foe can be destroyed from the root by the direct experience of the Ātmā, which is beyond the senses, mind, and intellect (BG 3.36 - BG 3.43).

An extensive critique of this chapter and critical evaluation of the Variant-Yoga that espouses, "I have some duty and not desiring for myself I offer fruits of my Karma to the Lord" does not pass the test of the intent of the chapter. In conclusion, by its nature, the Variant-Yoga cannot provide freedom from the bondage of

Karma, nor can it provide freedom from birth and death or can be the propounded subject of Gītā. Though it can be a second path to become steady in the Vāstavika-Yoga (वास्तविक-योग), but definitely cannot be the propounded subject of Gītā.

The Jñāna Karma Saṃnyāsa Yoga - Chapter 4

At the beginning of the chapter Bhagavāna said - "इमं विवस्वते योगं प्रोक्तवानहमव्ययम्, I imparted this immutable Yoga to Vivasvān (at the beginning of the Kalpa)." Having said so, Bhagavāna showed a regular succession of Yoga, "Vivasvān told it to Manu and Manu told it to Ikṣvāku, and this way by regular succession all royal sages came to know. Due to a long lapse of time, Yoga has disappeared from this world. That same ancient Yoga is being imparted to you today by Me because you are My devotee and friend, and this Yoga has supreme profundity."

The word "इमं, this" indicates the Yoga spoken earlier. That is, the Yoga that was articulated in the second chapter and also enunciated at the end of the third chapter in the form of total renunciation of all actions (all actions including doership-conceit, सर्व-कर्म-संन्यास, Sarva-Karma-Saṃnyāsa) in own Ātmā." The intention in "अव्ययम् योगम्, immutable Yoga" cannot be the Variant-Yoga of desireless actions (Niṣkāma Karma-Yoga). That is because, in the Variant-Yoga, the doer is with a beginning (सादि, Sādi), duty is with a beginning, and Karma is also with a beginning. Things that are with a beginning, it is also necessary that they all end. When doer, duty, and Karma are all with beginning and end, how can the fruits produced by them be imperishable? Fruits being with end, their end has to be definite, and therefore desireless actions cannot be called immutable Yoga. In immutable Yoga, the witness-conscious of a Jīva is always in union with the pure Ātmā. There is never a separation, just as there is no separation of gold ornaments with gold and waves with water. Only during the period of ignorance, like waves in the ocean water, in the body, there is a delusion of separation due to ego of I-ness and mineness when a Jīva perceives, "The Ātmā is unattained by me. By attaining it, I can become happy." Through knowledge, immutable Yoga is attained by removing I-ness and mineness ignorance from the body and transcendentally realizing own witness-conscious Ātmā as eternal, pure, awake, dissociated, and separate from the body. Thus, removing delusion, through knowledge, even during the delusional period, there is the success of immovable steady Yoga. That is the immutable Yoga. It is the one that was told to Vivasvān, the sun-deity, at the beginning of the Kalpa (BG 4.1 - BG 4.3).

On this, Arjuna, not understanding the immutable Yoga and not cognizing the true nature of Bhagavāna, questioned - "Your birth is later. Birth of Vivasvān was prior. How do I know that you imparted this Yoga in the beginning?" (BG 4. 4). You are right in front of me, clearly visible to my eyes in a human body. How do I know that your birth was before Vivasvān? How can I determine that you told this Yoga at the beginning of the Kalpa? In response, Bhagavāna said, "Just as innumerable waves originate and merge in an ocean, yet there is no transformation in the nature of water, such as creation or destruction, water on its own 'is as is.' It is the nature of water to be wavy. In the nature of water, waves are only imagined. In reality, waves cannot touch the water. Likewise, in your and My Ātmā, unending waves of birth and Karma arise and set, but in our Ātmā, there is no taint of those birth and Karma. Those birth and Karma waves are apparent or illusory perceptions in our Ātmā. There is no reality of a shadow separate from one with the shadow. There is no entry of the shadow in the true nature of the one with shadow. A shadow is only an illusory perception of the one whose shadow it is. Accordingly, separate from the Ātmā, there is no reality of birth and Karma, and the entry of birth and Karma cannot happen in the true nature of the Ātmā, which is why birth and Karma are only illusory perceptions of the Ātmā. Thus, there is no touch of them in our Ātmā; our Ātmā on its own 'is as is.' Because I know the Ātmā in its true nature, I can recall those births and Karma simply as miracles of the Ātmā, but because you have not acquired knowledge of yourself, you cannot remember those births and Karma in their true nature. Even though I am the unborn and immutable Ātmā, and the underlying (Adhiṣṭhāna) Lord of all beings, subordinating My nature, I incarnate by My Māyā on the earth." Additionally, Bhagavāna described the cause and time when he incarnates on the earth (BG 5.8).

After that, Bhagavāna explained, "The one, who truly knows My divine births and Karma, cognizes that all those births and Karma are illusorily perceived in Me, the Ātmā of all (Sarvātmā), and they have no taint in Me. I am unborn, even though I am seen as taking birth. Indeed, I am a non-doer (Akartā), even though I am perceived as doing everything (सर्व-कर्ता, Sarva-Kartā) - knowing so in truth, with the influence of such knowledge, that person after abandoning the body after death attains Me only. It is the glory of My knowledge that many devotees purified with the austerity of knowledge, whose attachment, fear, and anger purged, and who took refuge in Me, attained My true nature" (BG 4.9 - BG 4.10).

Providing knowledge of His true nature, Bhagavāna further said, "A Jīva has a perception of things in accordance and commensurate with whatever sentiment he has. A Jīva perceives Me based on his sentiments. With whatever sentiment one worships Me, I worship that person accordingly. To the extent that even those desire-ridden persons who worship deities with a desire to acquire fruits of Karma, commensurate with their Karma, I am the one who is the bestower of the fruits in the form of their revered deity in the human world. I am the one who provides the fruits, whichever revered deity they worship, based on their sentiment, in the form of their revered deity. By the distinctions of the constituents and Karma, a fourfold functional class system (चतुर-वर्ण, Catura-Varṇa)[43]was created by My power to sustain humanity. Know that all-witness as I am, though non-doer and immutable, I am the all-doer with My power." The intention is, "Even though fruition of all Karma happens in My witness, neither Karma can taint Me nor do I have an attachment to fruits of Karma. One who knows Me the Ātmā of all 'is as is,' with the influence of such knowledge, he does not fall into the bondage of Karma. Knowing My true nature, earlier, many seekers of liberation have engaged themselves in Karma. That is why you should also cognize your true nature, 'my Ātmā is untainted from all kinds of constituents and Karma,' and engage in Karma done through regular succession" (BG 4.11 - BG 4.15).

Based on the words above of Bhagavāna, freedom from the bondage of Karma is dependent on the transcendental realization (Sākṣātkāra) of one's Ātmā. Variant-Yoga that "certain Karma is my duty, and I offer their fruits to the Lord" by its nature is not sufficient to provide freedom from the bondage of Karma. If, from Gītā's perspective, Variant-Yoga was indeed able to free one from the bondage of Karma, it would have been clearly stated as causal in bondage and liberation at someplace. However, nowhere in Gītā the nature of such Yoga is described, nor has it been shown as one that can provide freedom from the bondage of Karma.

To describe the nature of Karma and Akarma, Bhagavāna further said - "Hey Arjuna! What is Karma (action), and what is Akarma (non-action)? In this subject, even a person endowed with the ability of true reasoning and discernment is confused. I will tell you the true nature of Karma, Akarma, and Vikarma (forbidden action), knowing which you will be free from the bondage of the Saṃsāra - as the path of Karma is profound (BG 4.16 - BG 4.17). That person who sees Akarma in Karma and Karma in Akarma is wise, and he is the one who has attained Yoga. He is Yoga-Yukta." With the melting of doership-ego, a person established through knowledge in his Ātmā does not see any taint from Karma in his Ātmā and does not find any mutation of Karma in his true nature. While doing everything through the body, such a knower of the Truth is a non-doer, and he only sees non-action in action. Contrary to that, with the doership-ego still present, a person who is only holding back activities of the body, such person's thoughts and variants due to I-ness ego in the body is with sentiments and become the cause of fruits. His Akarma (relinquishment of Karma) being with fruits is Karma only. However, a knower of the Truth of Karma and Akarma, who has found union in My true nature, and who has done everything, all his Karma are indeed Akarma, that is, know that they are not the cause of fruits. That is, so far, the discussion on the nature of Akarma. In seeking the attainment

---

[43] Catura-Varṇa (चतुर-वर्ण) means the fourfold functional class system of the society. Śrīmad Bhagavad Gītā provides the classification in terms of four major functions necessary for sustainability of the humanity: 1) education, entrusted to the Brāhmaṇa, 2) security, entrusted to the Kṣatriya, 3) commerce, entrusted to the Vaiśya and 4) labor, entrusted to the Śūdra. The innate attributes of a Brāhmaṇa (ब्रह्म-प्रकृति, Brahma-Prakṛti) are provided in BG 18.42; a Kṣatriya (क्षात्र-प्रकृति, Kṣātra-Prakṛti) are in BG 18.43, a Vaiśya (वैश्य-प्रकृति, Vaiśya-Prakṛti) and a Śūdra (शूद्र-प्रकृति, Śūdra-Prakṛti) are in BG 18.44.

of the true nature of Akarma, whatever fitness-based instruments are used, they being the cause of real fruits, are all called Karma. Opposite of this, keeping enjoyment perspective in front, whatever sacrifice and desire-ridden Karma are performed, they being perishable, know all of them as Vikarma or Niṣiddha-Karma (prohibited acts) (BG 4.18).

Having thus described the nature of Akarma, Karma, and Vikarma, Bhagavāna then provides the unique characteristics of that Akarmī (अकर्मी), the one who is established in the Ātmā through knowledge, who though doing everything is not doing anything -

यस्य सर्वे समारम्भा: कामसंकल्पवर्जिता: |
ज्ञानाग्निदग्धकर्माणं तमाहु: पण्डितं बुधा: || BG 4.19 ||

> Whose all initiations are without desire and resolve, and who has burnt all actions in the fire of knowledge, he is called a man of discrimination by the wise.

In the Variant-Yoga, one who understands, "Doing Karma is my duty and not desiring resultant fruits for myself I offer them to the Lord," is not accordant with the characteristics above. He is neither successful as "काम-संकल्प-वर्जित, without desires and resolves" nor is he successful in having "ज्ञानाग्निदग्धकर्मा, all Karma burnt in the fire of knowledge." "I am a doer of Karma. It is my duty to do Karma, and relinquishment of Karma is a non-duty for me" being with such resolves he cannot be "संकल्प-वर्जित, without resolves." Moreover, he does not see the fruits of his Karma as burnt seeds but sees them as hale and hearty in plenty. He does not desire to taste the fruits but readily offers them to some special entity separate from himself. Undoubtedly, there has to be the fruit of the offering of the fruits in such a condition. Therefore, he cannot be without desires either. When the doer, duty, Karma, and fruits are all present individually separate, and with oneness-vision are not sacrificed in the fire of the knowledge of the Ātmā, then how can they become "ज्ञानाग्निदग्धकर्मा, all Karma burnt in the fire of knowledge"? Especially when he is grasping all of them as individually separate with a discriminating vision, and his trueness sense is present in the discriminating vision.

In contrast, a Yogī who is Yoga-Yukta in his own Ātmā, whose I-ness and mineness superimposition (Adhyāsa) from the body is removed, is not doing anything, does not see any duty in himself, and does not know any fruits of Karma. The body, senses, mind, and intellect are merely engaged delusionally in their respective functions with his power while resting "is as is" in his true nature. As doership, duty, and fruits of Karma are not present, in reality, he is successful without desires and resolves, and he is directly successful in all his Karma burnt in the fire of knowledge.

त्यक्त्वा कर्मफलासङ्गं नित्यतृप्तो निराश्रय: |
कर्मण्यभिप्रवृत्तोऽपि नैव किञ्चित्करोति स: || BG 4.20 ||

> Always content, independent, and having forsaken attachment to fruits of action, even though engaged in an activity, he is really not doing anything.

Given the above, a Variant-Yogī is bound by the fruits of the offering of fruits of Karma and is neither a relinquisher of fruits of Karma nor is he free from duty attachment. That is because he is still a doer of the offering of fruits of Karma. His knowing the Lord separate from himself and offering the Lord only sentimental fruits of action makes him distant from being ever content in the Paramānanda because his discriminating vision makes him far away even to touch the Paramānanda. Accordingly, when he is far from the Paramānanda, how can he not be dependent on the Saṃsāra? Being in the bondage of duty, being a doer, and being active in Karma, how can he be a non-doer of any kind?

In contrast, our Yogī established with oneness in the Ātmā (Yoga-Yukta), free from the attachments of doership through analytic thinking (Tattva-Sākṣātkāra), "is as is" always content in own Paramānanda-form. Being always content, he is indeed not dependent on the Saṃsāra as he does not see anything suitable to depend on. He has no I-ness and mineness superimposition in the body. Indeed, he is not doing anything despite doing everything through the illusory perceived body. Thus, he is a real relinquisher of the fruits of Karma.

निराशीर्यतचित्तात्मा त्यक्तसर्वपरिग्रहः |
शारीरं केवलं कर्म कुर्वन्नाप्नोति किल्बिषम् || BG 4.21 ||

> Free of expectations, having abandoned all possessions, one who controls the mind and body and performs only bodily activities incurs no sin.

A Variant-Yogī has not known himself as separate from the body and the mind. He is experiencing oneness (Tādātmya) with the mind, and because of the ignorance of his true nature, he has become one with the duties of their duties and the doer of their Karma. With the bondage of ignorance present in such a state, he cannot be free from expectations (Nirāśī) and win over the mind and the body; the root of all bondages is only ignorance. The mind and the body are only their results. For this Variant-Yogī, the root bondage is still "as is" present, not yet broken, with the consequence that he sees himself with duty and thus puts himself in its bondage. Then how can he be a winner over the mind and body? With his mind remaining in substances, he cannot be without expectations. With the presence of ignorance, the root of all sins, he cannot be free from sin. Remaining in the bondage of duty, freedom from ignorance is impossible. In such a state, whatever Karma he does, he is bound to get their fruits. Though he does not deserve evil fruits, he still accrues piety fruits due to his sentiment of fruit-relinquishment. Since piety fruits have not gone anywhere, he has to come in the bondage of the body as a result thereof. When the fruits of his Karma are in the bondage of the body, then "कुर्वन्नाप्नोति किल्बिषम्, does not acquire sin even while doing Karma" is not successful for such a Variant-Yogī.

In contrast, a Yoga-Yukta Yogī, who is sitting with oneness in the Ātmā, free from the world of the mind and body, is indeed a real winner, as he does not see any reality of theirs in his Ātmā. He does not see any reality of any substance in his Ātmā. His trueness sense in substances is gone, and he is free from expectations. With the removal of the superimposition of duty, he is not a partner in any sin or piety (Kilbiṣa) even though he is doing everything through the body.

यदृच्छालाभसन्तुष्टो द्वन्द्वातीतो विमत्सरः |
समः सिद्धावसिद्धौ च कृत्वापि न निबध्यते || BG 4.22 ||

> One who is content with what is obtained on its own accord, beyond dualities, unenvious and equal in success and failure, is not bound despite performing actions.

A Variant-Yogī with doership-ego and bondage of duty present in his body cannot be without dualities (द्वन्द्वातीत), cannot be satisfied with whatever is obtained on its own accord (यदृच्छालाभसन्तुष्ट) or cannot be equal in success and failure (समः सिद्धि असिद्धि). Though he has a sentiment of being so, it is clear that his sentiment results from his conscience and ignorance. That sentiment is sentimental only and not real. Being tied with ego in the body, for him not to be in bondage after doing Karma cannot be established. However, our Yoga-Yukta Yogī, because he has uprooted the root of all dualities, the I-ness and mineness superimposition, is without dualities, and is satisfied with whatever is obtained on its own accord, is without envy, and is equal in success and failure. Due to his awakened knowledge, although he is involved in all kinds of activities, as if in a dream, they do not bind him. Just as -

गतसङ्गस्य मुक्तस्य ज्ञानावस्थितचेतसः |
यज्ञायाचरतः कर्म समग्रं प्रविलीयते || BG 4.23 ||

> All actions of a liberated whose mind is established in knowledge and devoid of attachments performed as a sacrifice are destroyed.

From the above words of Bhagavāna, it is clear that a Yoga-Yukta Yogī who has found union in the Ātmā, among all these attributes, has auspicious attributes. He, in reality, is the one who sees Akarma in Karma and, while doing everything, is always liberated from the bondage of Karma. In contrast, there is an insufficient extent of all attributes in our Variant-Yogī. None of them are sufficient.

In addition, from verses BG 4.24 to BG 4.32, Bhagavāna articulated the varied natural activities of all those Yogīs whose actions have become a sacrifice and have taken the form of the Brahman. In verse BG 4.33, depicting the glory of the sacrifice of knowledge, Bhagavāna commanded - "Hey Parantapa! The sacrifice of knowledge is superior to the sacrifice of materials. Hey Pārtha! All actions entirely end in knowledge." Upon acquiring knowledge, whatever is not done also becomes done. What are the instruments for acquiring knowledge? One can gain knowledge by approaching knowers of the Truth with prostration (Daṇḍavat-Praṇāma),[44]their service, and without deceit repeatedly questioning. Those knowers will impart knowledge to you (BG 4.34) by such virtuous conduct. What is the fruit of knowledge? By acquiring that knowledge, you will not be deluded like this again "I am the killer of Bhīṣma, Droṇa, and others, or they will die." However, by the influence of that knowledge, you will know all beings as miracles of your Ātmā. The glory of that knowledge is so pervasive that, even if you are the most sinful of all sinners, you will undoubtedly cross over the entire ocean of sin with the boat of knowledge. Just as a blazing fire turns firewood into ashes, the fire of knowledge turns all Karma into ashes. In this Saṃsāra, unquestionably, there is nothing purifying like knowledge, nor will there be; that knowledge can be experienced in due time by one's effort upon attaining union in the Ātmā (BG 4.35 - BG 4.38). Who is fit (Adhikārī) for that knowledge? It is said - One with steady faith, who is ready with means, and who has restrained the senses, acquires knowledge. Having acquired knowledge attains supreme peace immediately. In contrast, an ignorant person, who is without faith and is skeptical, such a person falls from the path of the highest good. There is no happiness for such a person either in this world or the next (BG 4.39 - 4.40).

At the end of the chapter, Bhagavāna concludes - Having attained the knowledge of the Ātmā, whose doubts have gone, that is, all doubts such as the "Ātmā is a doer of Karma, or there is a taint of Karma in the Ātmā" having been removed, one who has known his Ātmā just like a walnut within one's grip "is as is" as -

1. I, in the form of the Ātmā, am neither a doer of any kind of Karma nor any kind of mutation through Karma can touch my Ātmā,
2. Gross and subtle bodies through the constituents of Prakṛti are doers of Karma. I am immovable and immutable. Only their observer,
3. Though they all dance with my power, like a magnet, they cannot touch me.

Through transcendental realization (Tattva-Sākṣātkāra), having attained union with oneness in own Ātmā, total renunciation of all Karma is effectuated. In other words, while the body is engaged in all kinds of activities, one who does not see taint of them in his Ātmā, such a person, in reality, is a complete Karma-Saṃnyāsī. For the one who has renounced all actions by Yoga, whose doubts have been destroyed by knowledge, and who is sitting in the Ātmā with oneness, there is no bondage of Karma (BG 4.41). That is why Hey Bhārata! This doubt in your heart, "I, Arjuna, am the killer of Bhīṣma, Droṇa, and others, and Bhīṣma and others will die," is only born of ignorance. In reality, you Arjuna as a killer, Bhīṣma and others as being killed, and all activities of killing and being killed are all miracle waves of your Ātmā. Your Ātmā is untainted "is as is," like an ocean in the creation and destruction of waves. Cutting this doubt asunder with a sword of knowledge and removing the doership-ego situate with oneness in your Ātmā and stand up to fight. Being active in this way - righteousness (Dharma), prosperity (Artha), desire (Kāma), and liberation (Mokṣa), all four will prove to be your game of left hand (BG 4.42).

Thus, with the critique of this chapter, like a mirror, it is clear that some who have espoused Variant-Yoga as the propounded subject of Gītā, "It is my duty to do Karma and I offer the fruits of all Karma to the Lord,"

---

44 Daṇḍavat-Praṇāma (दण्डवत्-प्रणाम) is a process of paying respectful obeisance and total surrender by lying fully prostrate on the ground like a stick.

does not pass the test of the words of Gītā of the chapter. Neither is it a faultless procedure of Karma nor, by its nature, can free a doer from the bondage of Karma. In contrast, the true coming together of knowledge and Karma is the propounded subject of Gītā. Indeed, the faultless procedure from the perspective of Gītā is to ascend to that state where a doer does not remain a doer, duty does not remain duty, Karma does not remain Karma, and fruit does not remain fruit. But where a doer becomes non-doer, Karma becomes Akarma (non-action), the fruit becomes fruitless, and there is the complete sacrifice of all duties - the end of all duties. Under the view of Gītā, this is the only faultless procedure of Karma, and accordingly, Arjuna was commanded to rise in that state and wage war.

The Yoga of Renunciation - Chapter 5

Not grasping the intent of the congruity of knowledge and Karma that Bhagavāna expressed in the fourth chapter, at the beginning of this chapter, Arjuna again questions - "Hey Kṛṣṇa! You praise renunciation of action (Karma-Saṃnyāsa), and again, (Karma) Yoga. Of the two, tell me decisively that one which is more beneficial" (BG 5.1).

In reality, no distinction between the two was ever intended by Bhagavāna. On the contrary, until now, Bhagavāna is articulately showing the mutual connection of Knowledge and Karma, Sāṅkhya and Yoga, Karma-Saṃnyāsa and Karma-Yoga. The one who is discriminating is only the doership-ego. When a Jīva, falling from the true nature of the Ātmā, is caught in the chokehold of ignorance and holds "I am a doer" ego, then sometimes he has a sentiment to relinquish Karma (Saṃnyāsa) and at some other times to relinquish fruits (Karma-Yoga). However, due to the doership-ego with sentiments present, in reality, both of them have their fruits, Because there are fruits where there are sentiments. Contrary to that, through the realization of the Truth, when the arrow of ignorance is taken out, and the dirt of doership-ego is removed, with the melting of the superimposition of the I-ness and mineness in the gross and subtle bodies, all of his Karma become Akarma, and all of his fruits become fruitless. With the awakening of knowledge, he is now awake in his true Ātmā and "is as is" dissociated from the gross and subtle bodies (the doers and enjoyers of Karma and fruits). However, not understanding such intent of Bhagavāna, Arjuna questions again.

On this, Bhagavāna acknowledging Arjuna's view and with a superficial connection (अध्याहार, Adhyāhāra)[45]between Sāṅkhya and Yoga, responded - yes, "Hey Pārtha! Both Karma-Saṃnyāsa and Karma-Yoga are providers of freedom. However, of the two, Karma-Yoga has importance over Karma-Saṃnyāsa." It would be helpful to recall that **real Karma-Saṃnyāsa is renunciation of doership-ego through knowledge.** Here, Bhagavāna provided importance to Karma-Yoga as opposed to Karma-Saṃnyāsa, with the view that only through Karma-Yoga means one can ascend to the goal of Karma-Saṃnyāsa and not without it. A Karma-Yogī, who does not hate anyone nor has any desire for anything, should be understood as an ever-Saṃnyāsī. Know that the root of the bondage of the Saṃsāra is attachment and aversion, and thus all desirous dualities. One free from these dualities quickly becomes free from bondage (BG 5.2 - BG 5.3). It is essential to recognize that a Karma-Yogī is compared to a Karma-Saṃnyāsī. If a Karma-Yogī, by nature, were believed to be superior to a Karma-Saṃnyāsī, he would not be compared to a Karma-Saṃnyāsī. A great is never compared to an insignificant, but a little is always compared to a great. From this, it is clear that **a Karma-Yogī by nature is not superior to a Karma-Saṃnyāsī but is important from an instrumental perspective.**

If, in Bhagavāna's view, the distinction between Sāṅkhya and Yoga was agreeable by nature, then immediately in the following two verses, BG 5.4 and BG 5.5, He would not have shown non-difference between Sāṅkhya and Yoga, and would not have called those expressing difference between them as "with the intellect of a

---

[45] The term "Adhyāhāra" herein means superficially connecting, that is, mentally not having distinction between Sāṅkhya and Yoga, but superficially imagining distinction.

child." However, in reality, the distinction between them is indeed unacceptable to Bhagavāna, and it was only to express respect for Arjuna's view He had said so. Then immediately coming to the point, He says - "Hey, Pāṇḍava! Unwise persons call Sāṅkhya and Yoga individually separate, not persons of discrimination. One who is situated properly even in one acquires the fruit of both." Ultimately ascending to such a state, where attaining a position in the Ātmā, doership-ego is removed, there is unity between Karma-Saṃnyāsa and Karma-Yoga (relinquishment of fruits). The supreme Status that can be achieved by Sāṅkhya can also be achieved by Yoga. Thus, one who knows Sāṅkhya and Yoga as one really perceives (BG 5.4 - BG 5.5).

At this juncture, those with variant views attributing distinctions in the form and path between Sāṅkhya and Yoga have expressed the unity of Bhagavāna's words "साङ्ख्ययोगौ पृथग्बाला: प्रवदन्ति" in many different ways.

1. Some have said that in the path of renunciation (Saṃnyāsa), even viewing knowledge as central, attainment of knowledge (Sāṅkhya) is not possible without Karma (Yoga). Albeit, when Karma is done in the path of Karma-Yoga, it is done with knowledge. That is, it is done with the relinquishment of fruits. Accordingly, when in the path of Saṃnyāsa (Sāṅkhya) there is the necessity of Karma (Yoga), and in the path of Karma (Yoga) there is the necessity of knowledge (Sāṅkhya), then it is reasonable to accept oneness between them. In other words, oneness between the two is made, keeping both paths independent and accepting the need for one on the other.
2. Others have said that Saṃnyāsa (Sāṅkhya) is in the intellect, not in external acts of relinquishment of Karma or fire, and thus relinquishing desire for fruits and resolves, those who do injunctive Karma should be called real Saṃnyāsī. In Yoga, they have internalized the sentiment of Sāṅkhya.

However, not understanding the Truth, in reality, their above words are indeed improper and lamentable -

1. In the first group, in the success of Sāṅkhya believing Yoga as instrumental, and in the success of Yoga believing Sāṅkhya as instrumental, what is established is only dependence and "अन्योऽन्याश्रयता, state of mutual dependence," which by all means is improper. A thing that is a means for a second thing, how can that first thing be the goal of the second thing? When Yoga is accepted as causal in the success of Sāṅkhya, accepting Sāṅkhya as causal in the success of Yoga is nothing more than a play of the intelligence of a child, just like, someone would embrace fire as the cause of smoke and smoke as the cause of the fire. Even if one accepts such a notion that they each are the cause of one another, what one sees is mutual dependence between cause and effect and not oneness. Here the words of Bhagavāna are -

   > "Unwise persons call Sāṅkhya and Yoga individually separate, not persons of discrimination. One who is situated properly even in one acquires fruit of both (BG 5.4)."

   This means that one who is fully established in Yoga, his Sāṅkhya (Karma-Saṃnyāsa) is established (Yukta), and one who is fully established in Sāṅkhya, his Yoga (relinquishment of fruits) is established on its own. Thus, to Bhagavāna oneness of both by nature is acceptable and not as a means and end. However, quite the opposite, under the Variant-Yoga, there is a distinction in the form of means and end, and there is the necessity of a person risen in any one of them on the other. Thus, a person risen in one does not get the fruits of both, failing the test of the words of Bhagavāna in the verse BG 5.4. What is proven is only the distinction between the two and not the oneness of both.
2. In the second group, though mutual dependence between Sāṅkhya and Yoga has not been espoused, Sāṅkhya is mixed in the nature of Yoga. They have not kept any independent reality of Sāṅkhya but have indeed lost the true nature of Sāṅkhya. Sāṅkhya, in its true nature, does not remain in the picture. There is only Yoga, and only Yoga is left. Of the two, when there is an absence of one, then where is the oneness between the two? But the words of Bhagavāna are -

   > "One who is fully established in either acquires the fruits of both. The supreme Status attained by Sāṅkhya can also be reached by Yoga (BG 5.4 - BG 5.5).

According to this group, of two paths, one of them is not there for one to arise. Only Yoga is left. Sāṅkhya is not there at all. In obligatory Karma, they have accepted only relinquishment of the fruits as the nature of Sāṅkhya, and that is the nature of Yoga. In such a state, how can one attach congruity to the words of Bhagavāna in the verse BG 5.5, "The supreme Status attained by Sāṅkhya can also be reached by Yoga," when according to this group, there is no separate reality of Sāṅkhya? From the words of Bhagavāna, one cannot assume to chokehold Sāṅkhya and mix it with Yoga. On the contrary, from the words of Bhagavāna, for both, their separate reality is established, have clearly shown oneness between the two, and have been told that in this state, the position that can be attained by Sāṅkhya can also be achieved by Yoga. Even if we accept the view of this group, their espoused Variant-Yoga, by its nature, is not suitable for one to attain the supreme Status, as is said by Bhagavāna in the verses (BG 5.4 - BG 5.5).

It is extensively covered in various places in "Variant-Yoga, as depicted by some, is Injudicious and Discordant" and "Can Variant-Yoga, as depicted by some, provide Liberation?" that "I am a doer of Karma, there is some duty on me, and I offer the fruits of my Karma to the Lord" is indeed rooted in ignorance because these are by nature with many sentiments and distinctions. For a Variant-Yogī, even when current Karma cannot provide freedom from the enjoyments of fruits, then how it can burn accumulated impressions (Sañcita Karma-Saṃskāras) of many lives? It cannot be said that those who have postulated such Variant-Yoga believe that by such a Yoga, in some form, there can be real depletion of accumulated and current Karma. Has anyone provided some measure and tactic in support thereof? However, it is clear that in the immutable Ātmā of a Jīva, there cannot be any mutation of doership and duty (BG 2.19 - BG 2.25). Only when a Jīva falls from the true nature of the Ātmā and comes in the bondage of the body, then with discriminating-vision and I-ness ego in the body he is caught in the web of doership, and for the enjoyment of his done Karma, he has to take birth. Hence, the uninterrupted flow from Karma to body and body to Karma commences.

All of them being discriminative adjuncts of ignorance can only be removed by knowledge of the Ātmā. There is no relinquishment of anything in the nature of the said Variant-Yoga. There is no relinquishment of doership, duty, and Karma, but all adjuncts of ignorance such as doership are present in their locations. There is only the relinquishment of fruits, which is nothing but sentimental. There are plenty of fruits in the presence of doership and duty because of the sentiment of fruit-relinquishment. Just because of that, he cannot ever be without fruits. There is a rule in the kingdom of Prakṛti that the more the sentiments of fruit relinquishment with a given effort, the more is the commensurate growth in fruits. Sure, freedom from fruits was possible in that state when doership and duty could have been removed through knowledge, thereby gaining independence from bondage. However, the entire family of Prakṛti and ignorance are present here. How can there be hope for freedom from bondage? If you hold a snake too close to yourself feeding milk, you had better be careful that you are not bit or killed! If you hope to save yourself from the poison, take refuge in that Lord (witness-conscious). He is the one who can break all those inclinations of the limited ego like the fangs of Kāliya-Nāga[46] (BG 7.14). When the said Variant-Yoga is not capable of freeing one from the fruits of current Karma, then hoping that it can eliminate accumulated Karma-Saṃskāras is undoubtedly a grave mistake. It is simply nothing but deceiving or being deceived. Thus, when the said Variant-Yoga is not capable of depleting Karma, then by its nature, it is blunted in attaining the supreme Status following the words of Bhagavāna. It is thus evident that in whatever form oneness between Sāṅkhya and Yoga is presented by these commentators - they are discordant.

The real oneness of Sāṅkhya (Karma-Saṃnyāsa) and Yoga (Niṣkāma-Karma, relinquishment of fruits) propounded by Bhagavāna is only possible by reaching that state where doership-ego, the one discriminating

[46] The story of Kāliya-Nāga (कालिय-नाग), a dreaded multi-fanged serpent in the river Yamunā is provided in the 16th Chapter of the 10th Canto of the Śrīmad Bhāgavata Purāṇa.

between the two, is gone through the knowledge of the Ātmā by attaining a position in the Ātmā and I-ness sense in the body, senses, mind, and intellect (the instruments of Karma) is burnt in the fire of knowledge. There is a harmonious connection between the natural relinquishment of Karma (Saṃnyāsa, Sāṅkhya) and the relinquishment of fruits (Yoga) reaching that state. In the previous state, when he was in the bondage of the body due to ignorance, he had assumed duties of their duties and was a doer of their Karma. However, through knowledge, he is now dissociated from those duties and Karma. He is their observer, only the witness. When he is no longer a doer of duties and Karma of the body but only an observer, he is a one hundred percent renouncer, a Karma-Saṃnyāsī, and a real desireless Yogī, a Niṣkāmī. With the removal of doership superimposition, he is no longer a doer. He is a Karma-Saṃnyāsī ipso facto, and in reality, he is a relinquisher of fruits. Like a potter's wheel in motion, the body and senses are moving based on their respective functions, and with the awakening of knowledge, he has no taint from any of them. While doing everything through the body, because of his unattachment, he is now a non-doer Karma-Saṃnyāsī, and even though he is seen as with desires, he is desireless, a Niṣkāmī. Desires and Karma are the attributes of the body, senses, mind, and intellect, and now he is no longer their doer but merely an observer. That is why Bhagavāna has said, "Only a child (an unwise) calls Sāṅkhya and Yoga individually separate, not a knower of the Truth Paṇḍita."

In contrast, one who remains in the bondage of doership and retains sentiments of "relinquishment of Karma" and "relinquishment of fruits" is like a stage show character, unreal only. In addition, Bhagavāna said - Without attaining union in own Ātmā, Karma-Saṃnyāsa is hard because, in the presence of doership-bound intellect, even relinquishment of Karma due to the ego of relinquishment becomes Karma and becomes the cause of fruits. However, one who is free from doership-ego and has attained union in his Ātmā, such a contemplative person, immediately attains the Parabrahma, the Brahman, the Paramātmā (BG 5.6).

Having shown oneness between Sāṅkhya and Yoga, now Bhagavāna in both meanings uses the word Yoga - Hey Pāṇḍava! One who is Yoga-Yukta in the Ātmā, whose conscience is pure, who has wholly subdued his mind and senses and in whom the Ātmā of Brahmā to the minutest particle has become his Ātmā, such a person because of his unattachment is not tainted by Karma even while he is engaged in Karma. With this realization of the Truth, "Senses are functioning in their respective fields, but I am neither a sense organ nor sense-organs are mine," with sense-organs seeing, hearing, smelling, eating, walking, and grasping objects, "I am not doing anything, I am only an observer of the senses, and their objects" remains untainted by them. A person who "is as is," with the realization of the Truth, renouncing doership-attachment, "I am a doer of Karma," with the offering of Karma to the supreme imperishable Reality (Brahmārpaṇa) is engaged in Karma; such a person, like a lotus-leaf, is not tainted by piety or sin. Yogīs abandoning doership superimposition, devoid of ego, engage in Karma through the body. Based on the above, those who are united (Yukta) in their true nature (Ātmā), relinquishing fruits of Karma, achieve steady peace. But, those who are not united (Ayukta) due to their attachment to the desire for fruits fall into the bondage of Karma. Such Yogīs mentally relinquishing all Karma, with a firm resolve, "I, witness-conscious, am neither doing anything, nor anything is happening in me," happily dwells in the city (body) of nine gates, themselves not doing anything nor having anything done (BG 5.6 - BG 5.13).

From the preceding words of Bhagavāna, it is clear that only a Yogī who is Yoga-Yukta in his own Ātmā is capable of fulfilling all those goals. In contrast, because he has doership and duty-bound intellect, there is an insufficiency of the above attributes in a desireless performer (Niṣkāma-Karmī). Duty-bound intellect cannot come without doership-intellect, and without ego in the body, doership-intellect is impossible. In the bondage of I-ness in the body, when he is with doership and duty, then he cannot be with a pure conscience (विशुद्धात्मा, Viśuddhātmā) and cannot be one who has subdued his senses (जितेन्द्रिय, Jitendriya). Stuck in the sludge of ego in the body with duty-bound intellect, how can he be pure in the conscience? His I-ness sense is still in the mind and senses, and he has become a doer of their duties and Karma. How can he be

Jitendriya? How can he subdue his mind and senses when he becomes like the senses and has the ego of their duties and Karma? In such a state, how can he know the Ātmā of all beings as his Ātmā? How can he remain unattached from the activities of the mind and senses when he has become a doer of their actions due to duty-bound intellect (BG 5.7 - BG 5.9)? The only cause of duty-bound intellect is that he has assumed doership of those activities, "I am a doer of all these activities" - except that there cannot be any cause of duty-bound intellect. If he had not become a doer of the activities of the body and senses, then duty would not have mounted on him. However, in such a state, when there is a presence of I-ness in the senses, and there is a presence of doer and duty (the accessories of the bondage of Karma in the activities of the senses), then how can he be dissociated from all Karma, and like lotus-leaf remain untainted from piety and sin (BG 5.10)? No matter how much he laments and resolves, "I am not a doer. I do not desire fruits," fruits must spring out forcibly. It is the tenet of the Lord that a doer has to become an enjoyer, and with whatever sentiment Karma is done, one has to enjoy commensurate fruits. With his sentiment of fruit-relinquishment, this Yogī gets more fruits, but he cannot be ever fruitless.

In addition, Bhagavāna, in His own words, made it clear that - Hey Kurunandana! Paramātmā does not create any kind of doership in a Jīva, nor does he create Karma in a Jīva and does not even create conjunction with fruits, but all of these are nothing but imaginations of Prakṛti, who have received power from the Paramātmā, is showing her performance. In reality, the omnipresent Paramātmā does not accept any sin or piety of a Jīva. It is only because of ignorance that the knowledge of the Paramātmā, that light of the Paramātmā is covered, and hence a Jīva is deluded. In other words, because of the curtain of ignorance between a Jīva and the Paramātmā, even though there is real oneness, he imagines separation between him and the Paramātmā. Due to that separation because of the "I am a doer" ego, he gets deluded by being entangled in the bondage of unreal piety and sin. However, those who have removed the curtain of ignorance through knowledge of the Ātmā, for them that knowledge undoubtedly shines like the sun, whereby their doership delusion becomes quiet (BG 5.14 - BG 5.16).

From the words above of Bhagavāna, it is clear that doership, Karma, and fruits are only born of ignorance. It is only through the realization of the Ātmā that its removal is possible. Any kind of Karma cannot remove doership, and attaining union in the Ātmā is not possible by any kind of Karma. However, a union can be achieved only through knowledge after removing doership. Now, Bhagavāna describes the fruits and characteristics of the one whose delusion of doership has become quiet as follows - one whose sins are purged by knowledge, whose intellect, mind, and faith have become of the same form as the pure Ātmā (as due to delusion of doership his true nature had become of the contrary form) such a person after leaving the body achieves final exemption from life (अपुनरावृत्ति, Apunarāvṛtti). He reaches a Status whereby he does not return to the mortal world, achieves liberation while alive, and becomes a Jīvanmukta. Such a Paṇḍita holding equanimity with his witness-vision sees everything equally, irrespective of whether it is a learned Brāhmaṇa, a cow, an elephant, a Cāṇḍāla, or a dog. He only sees his Ātmā in all those forms, those beings. Such a person whose mind is existent in equanimity has indeed conquered the Saṃsāra in this life. Brahman is equanimous and faultless. He is established with oneness in the Brahman. That is why he is one with a pure conscience and has subdued his senses. Such a steady-intellect knower of the Brahman, who is established with oneness in the Brahman, does not rejoice in acquiring nice things, nor does he have apprehension about receiving disliked things.

A person without attachment to external objects acquires happiness born of meditation of the Lord in the conscience. He who is Yoga-Yukta in the Brahman enjoys eternal happiness (BG 5.17 - BG 5.21). In verses BG 5.22 and BG 5.23, having described external objects as pain-yielding and perishable, the necessity of bearing the forces of desire and anger is described. Then Bhagavāna said - Hey Pāṇḍava! This way, having found oneness in his own Ātmā, without consideration of external objects, a person who is happy in his Ātmā, who has found rest in the Ātmā, and who is shining in his Ātmā, such a Yogī being Brahman-form attains the Brahman. All of whose sins are purged, one who has subdued his mind and is engrossed in the well-being of all, such a Yogī acquires Nirvāṇa-Brahma - oneness in the Brahman with liberation from the worldly cycle of birth and death. Those who are free from desire and anger and who have conquered their Citta, such knowers of the Ātmā, only see the Brahman that is quiet all over. Forsaking external objects, one who has turned inwards, has conquered the mind and intellect and is free from desire, fear, and anger, such a sage who continuously strives for liberation is always free (BG 5.24 - BG 5.28).

From the words above of Bhagavāna, it is clear that these attributes are insufficient in a Variant-Yogī (Niṣkāma-Karmī). Based on the attributes of a Variant-Yogī that these commentators have described, it is quite evident that a Variant-Yogī has not known himself as separate from the body, senses, mind, and intellect. Due to duty-bound intellect, even now, he sees himself in oneness with them and thus is bound by them. Had he known himself separate transcendentally (Aparokṣa), there would never have been any cause for duty-bound intellect. Duty-bound intellect is always applicable to limited I-ness. What can duty do to the limitless form? Due to the attribute of limitation, he is with discriminating-vision. In such a state, how can he be "तद्बुद्धि, Tadbuddhi,"[47]"तन्निष्ठ, Tanniṣṭha,"[48] and "तत्परायण, Tatparāyaṇa,"[49]and take advantage of Apunarāvṛtti (BG 5.17)? "अन्योऽसावन्योऽहमस्मि, he is one, I am other" in this discriminating vision, he has trueness sense. How can he be equal to a Brāhmaṇa, Cāṇḍāla, or a dog when he is not separate from the body and does not know himself as anything else separate from the body (BG 5.18)? Remaining in oneness with the body, no matter how much he boasts about his equanimity, it is not real, but only unreal sentimentally. Because I-ness sense in the body is directly intuitive (Aparokṣa), and knowledge, "I am a Brāhmaṇa, Cāṇḍāla or a dog," that knowledge is indirect (Parokṣa) through preceptors and scriptures. As extensively discussed in "Variant-Yoga, as depicted by some, is Injudicious and Discordant," indirect (Parokṣa) knowledge is not in opposition to direct intuitive (Aparokṣa) knowledge. Only one direct intuitive (Aparokṣa) knowledge can be opposer to another direct intuitive (Aparokṣa) knowledge. With discriminating intellect present, he cannot exist with oneness in the Brahman, nor can he conquer the Saṃsāra while alive. He cannot remain without joy or sorrow in liked or disliked things, nor can he enjoy eternal happiness. He cannot remain unattached to external objects because he has not yet acquired a sense of untrueness concerning mirage-like external objects. He still has a trueness sense in them (BG 5.18 - BG 5.21).

In contrast, by the realization of the Truth, a Yogī who is Yoga-Yukta in his own Ātmā has known himself "is as is" separate from the body and has determined the world of the body, senses, mind, and intellect as illusory perceptions and miracles of his Ātmā. With the creation and end of those perceptions, he does not see any touch of those mutations in his Ātmā. His discriminating vision has fully melted, and now he only beholds the delusional world in the Brahman form. He is a Samadarśī (समदर्शी). He is a Tadbuddhi, Tanniṣṭha, and Tatparāyaṇa. He has, in reality, conquered the Saṃsāra in this life. When he does not see any reality of the Saṃsāra separate from his Ātmā, he is unattached and without joy and sorrow from external objects. In the end, Bhagavāna says, "Knowing Me, the Supreme Lord of all worlds, the enjoyer of sacrifices and austerities, and friend of all beings, peace is attained."

Thus, from the critique of this chapter, it is clear that the nature of Variant-Yoga that some have depicted does not meet the test of this chapter. It cannot be established that our Variant-Yogī has attributes that a Yogī should have as described in the chapter, and achieving union by Karma cannot be proven either. However, it is also clear that only through knowledge it is possible to have a union in the Ātmā. Certainly, having attained Yoga through knowledge, he becomes free from doership, Karma, and fruits. Nothing can put him in bondage. Accordingly, how some have postulated oneness between Yoga and Sāṅkhya is not judicious.

---

[47] Tadbuddhi (तद्बुद्धि) means whose intellect has become That (Brahman) form.
[48] Tanniṣṭha (तन्निष्ठ) means whose firm faith is placed in That (Brahman) form.
[49] Tatparāyaṇa (तत्परायण) means who is oriented towards That (Brahman) form.

The Yoga of Meditation - Chapter 6

In response to Arjuna's question at the beginning of the fifth chapter, Bhagavāna explained the oneness between Sāṅkhya and Yoga, and the same is reinforced here at the beginning of the sixth chapter -

अनाश्रित: कर्मफलं कार्यं कर्म करोति य: |
स संन्यासी च योगी च न निरग्निर्न चाक्रिय: || BG 6.1 ||

> Not depending on the fruits of action, he who performs ought to be done acts is a renouncer and a Yogī, not the one who abandons fire and actions.

Doership-ego is the support of fruits of Karma. Forsaking doership-ego, a person who does Karma based on one's nature is a Saṃnyāsī and a Yogī. One who just abandons fire and activities is not a Saṃnyāsī. The term "कार्यम्, Kāryam" in "कार्यम् कर्म करोति य:" is an adjective of the term Karma (कर्म) and not a verb. Therefore, the meaning of the words "कार्यम् कर्म" cannot be taken as "doing Karma is a duty," but the proper meaning can only be "Karma that is proper to engage in" or intrinsic Karma, natural Karma. That which is called Saṃnyāsa ought to be known as Yoga. Because without renunciation of doership-ego, by simply abandoning only fire and activities, one cannot become a Saṃnyāsī, in the same way, without renouncing resolves such as "I am a doer of Karma, and I have certain duty on me," no one can be a Yogī either (BG 6.2).

The intention here is that real renunciation is necessary for both, whether it is Saṃnyāsa or Yoga. It is impossible to succeed in activities from either Saṃnyāsa or Yoga holding vain sentiment of renunciation. Merely relinquishing fire and activity while holding doership-ego is not a real Saṃnyāsa. It is only an apparent illusory Saṃnyāsa. Keeping a doership-ego and simply having a sentiment of renunciation of fruits is neither true renunciation of fruits nor true Yoga. In the sentiment of renunciation of fruits, when a doer of the sentiment is still present, renunciation of fruits cannot happen. However, for the doer of this sentiment, because the sentiment is with renunciation, its result is growth in fruits and not the absence of fruits. The reason is that the root of fruits, the doership-ego, has not been uprooted, and the absence of fruits is impossible in the presence of the root. For instance, grafting a fruit tree, as long as its roots are present, does not become fruitless; on the contrary, it bears more fruits. Likewise, in the presence of a doership-ego, the sentiment of renunciation of fruits does not remain fruitless but assures more fruits. Therefore, be it Saṃnyāsa or Yoga, real renunciation is necessary for either of them. In other words, the root doership-ego needs to be beheaded by the sword of knowledge. Firmly established in one's Ātmā, when the relationship of I-ness in the body, senses, mind, and intellect is broken, then even when he is engaged in fire and activity with the body, that great person is a relinquisher of fire, and a real Karma-Saṃnyāsī. One who relinquishes fire is the one who has given up fires. Fires here mean auxiliaries of rituals. One who abandons actions is the one who is free from activities like penances and charities that are not associated with fire. With the removal of I-ness sentiment from the body, even without the sentiment of renunciation of fruits, he is a real relinquisher of fruits and a real Yogī. Even though the body, senses, mind, and intellect are engaged in their respective activities, there is no activity of Karma in the witness-conscious in which he is sitting with oneness. Only because of ignorance, there was an imagined superimposition of doership in him. He has no desire for fruits because separate from his witness-conscious there is complete non-existence of duality (द्वैत, Dvaita). The desire for fruits would have occurred if he had become Dvaita, something separate from the witness-conscious. Only because of the force of ignorance and superimposition of imagined Dvaita is he cooking the means of unreal desire for fruits and relinquishment of fruits. That is why Bhagavāna has said in verse BG 6.1, "न निरग्नि: न च अक्रिय:" relinquishing fire and activity one does not become a Saṃnyāsī and in the verse BG 6.2 "न ह्यसंन्यस्तसङ्कल्पो योगी भवति कश्चन" without renunciation of resolves (Saṃkalpa Saṃnyāsa) one cannot become a Yogī either. The intent in renouncing resolves is only about the root resolve, "I am a doer of Karma. I have some duty"; here, renouncing that resolve alone is expected. All other resolves are its branches. Through knowledge, only after attaining oneness in the Ātmā, renunciation of resolves depends on this realization of the Truth that "I am not the body, senses, mind, and intellect, they are not mine, but

I am their witness-observer, and I am untainted by them - they are all miraculous waves of my true nature." Therefore, whether it is Saṃnyāsa or Yoga, from both sides, the real relinquishment of the "I am a doer" sentiment is agreeable to Bhagavāna, and it is with this relinquishment that there is oneness between the two. With the success of this relinquishment, even though his body, senses, mind, and intellect are engaged in their respective activities, because of his I-ness ego not remaining in them, he is neither a doer of their actions nor an enjoyer of the fruits of those actions. Due to his immutability, he is Karma-Saṃnyāsī in their activities. Even without any sentiment of relinquishment of fruits, he is without any desire for them and thus is indeed a relinquisher of the fruits.

Bhagavāna clarifies the words Saṃkalpa-Saṃnyāsa (resolve-renunciation) used for a Yogī in verse BG 6.1 in the following two verses - Hey Pāṇḍava! For a contemplative person who has a desire to ascend in Yoga, Karma done with duty-bound intellect and desireless sentiment is the cause for the attainment of Yoga. But after ascending in Yoga, restraint of all resolves such as doership and duty, that is, quiescence is the cause of situating in Yoga (BG 6.3). Even though desireless-Karma by tradition is the cause in the attainment of Yoga, it is not a direct cause. The direct cause is the restraint of resolves such as doership and duty. Just as a surgical knife used on a boil to remove pus and thereby cure the ailment is considered a cause by tradition, not a direct cause, the direct cause can only be the application of appropriate ointment. Likewise, in the cure of the disease of the Saṃsāra, desireless actions by tradition have been called the cause of the removal of the Rajoguṇī boil. It is not a direct cause. The Direct cause can only be the resolve restraining ointment. Now, Bhagavāna describes the attributes of the one who has ascended in Yoga (योगारुढ, Yogāruḍha) in the following manner - When a Yogī does not get attached to sense-objects as "I am an enjoyer of the objects of the senses," and is not attached to Karma as "I am a doer of Karma," then the renouncer of all resolves of doership and enjoyership is called Yogāruḍha (BG 6.4).

Having shown oneness between Saṃnyāsa and Yoga and having described the attributes of a Yogī, Bhagavāna now describes useful means in the attainment of Yoga and says - "The main duty of this Yogī is to elevate himself on his own, and not drown himself in the worldly ocean. Only he can be his friend, and he can be his enemy. When that person with his strength subdues his mind, he can be his friend, but when he lets his mind flow away in the worldly ocean, he becomes his own enemy" (BG 6.5 - BG 6.6). When he becomes his friend, the entire Saṃsāra becomes his friend, and then the preceptors and scriptures can be his helper. However, when he becomes his enemy, the whole Saṃsāra becomes his enemy, and the preceptors and scriptures cannot elevate him. One whose mind is calm in dualities such as heat and cold, pleasure and pain, honor and disgrace, that is, one who sees the cause of all these dualities internally and not externally in friends and foes, such a person who has subdued his mind, one with a peaceful conscience is fit for the divine experience (BG 6.7). Having been fully equipped with means, one whose mind is content with knowledge and realized knowledge (Vijñāna, the direct experience of understood knowledge) and who has uniquely subdued his senses, whose I-ness and mineness in the body, senses, mind, and intellect has wholly melted, such an immutably established Yogī for whom a clod, stone or gold are alike, he is said to be Yukta (युक्त, established), he has found oneness in the Paramātmā (BG 6.8). Hence, one who is established in equanimity, such a Yogī, has sameness of intellect towards the goodhearted, friends, foes, neutrals, mediators, antagonists, relatives, pious, and sinners. Without any distinction, he knows the Ātmā of everyone as his Ātmā and sees all of them as miracles of his Ātmā, and that is why he excels (BG 6.9).

This way, instruments in the attainment of Yoga and where he needs to reach have been described in everyday terms. Now instruments are described uniquely for the attainment of the state mentioned above - One who has subdued his mind and senses, forsaken desire and possessions, and residing alone in a secluded place ought to constantly engage in the query of the Ātmā. It should be accomplished as follows: first, setting one's seat in a clean place neither too high nor too low on which sacred grass, deerskin, and cloth are placed one over the other. After that, sitting on that seat, controlling activities of the mind and senses, with the mind concentrated on a single point, engage in Yoga for self-purification. Holding the body, head, and neck even and motionless, become steady, and without looking at directions, focus eyesight on the tip of the nose (BG 6.10 - BG 6.13). By doing so, that is, sight focused on the tip of the nose, the fruit is indeed the query of the Ātmā through concentration (एकाग्रता, Ekāgratā). Concentration on the nose tip is not the result in itself. That was the description of external conduct and posture for a Yogī. Now Bhagavāna describes cognitive behavior: "Established in a vow of celibacy, fearless, with quiet conscience and united, restraining the mind one ought to sit with the mind concentrated on Me and devoted to Me. Thus, a Yogī with a controlled mind (who is a seeker of Yoga) who is constantly involved in the query of the true nature of the Ātmā acquires My Status. The Status where peace is attained through ultimate liberation[50]from material existence" (BG 6.14 - BG 6.15). That was the description of a sound mental state. Now Bhagavāna describes the requisite food intake and behavior: "That Yoga is not for a Yogī who overeats or does not eat at all; it is neither for a Yogī who sleeps a lot and certainly not for a Yogī who stays awake a lot. A Yogī whose eating and recreation are guided, whose efforts in Karma are judicious and whose sleep and waking is restrained, achieves Yoga that removes sorrow" (BG 6.16 - BG 6.17). It is important to keep in mind that the term Yogī in the above discussion is about a person who possesses the fourfold means (Sādhana-Catuṣṭaya) and who has an intense desire to know how to attain oneness in his own Ātmā. **When the uniquely concentrated mind becomes steadfast in the Ātmā and becomes unattached from all desires, at that time, he is Yoga-Yukta. He has found oneness in his Ātmā.** Just as a lamp flame remains unflickering in a wind-free location, such a comparison of the concentrated mind united in the Ātmā of a Yogī is known. That state, in which through the practice of Yoga, the controlled mind ceases from all sides, and with the transcendental realization of his Ātmā becomes content in his Ātmā, in that state only, through the one that is beyond the senses - the subtle intellect, he experiences that infinite bliss. Established in that state, the Yogī is not moved from the true nature of the Ātmā. There is no other higher gain for him having gained such a state. The Yogī is not shaken by the most profound sorrow when established in that state. The state where there is the absence of conjunction with sorrow is known by the name Yoga. That Yoga ought to be decidedly practiced with an undespondent mind (BG 6.18 - BG 6.23). Having thus described the perfected state of Yoga, now in the attainment of this state, useful means are again described - "Completely abandoning all desires born of resolves, and controlling the senses from all sides with the mind, very slowly through resolute intellect, withdraw the mind, and then having made the mind established in the Ātmā, think not even of anything. When the fickle and unsteady mind wanders in whatsoever, withdrawing it from there, have it confined in the Ātmā alone. Whose mind is completely peaceful, whose Rajoguṇa is subdued and who is sinless, such a Yogī certainly acquires supreme bliss in the form of the Brahman. A sinless Yogī, always united in the Ātmā, easily enjoys infinite bliss in the form of Brahman-attainment" (BG 6.24 - BG 6.28).

Given the above words of Bhagavāna in the verses (BG 6.5 - BG 6.28), it should be now clear that external desireless actions done with duty-bound intellect (Variant-Yoga) are not at all helpful in the attainment of Yoga (union with oneness in the Ātmā). Although, by regular succession, desireless actions can be helpful in the removal of increased Rajoguṇa that is a deterrent in Yoga, yet, in the attainment of Yoga, it has no usefulness. If, from the perspective of Bhagavāna, the Niṣkāma-Karma was indeed useful, then at this location, there is no reason why some indication of it would not have been provided, mainly when seat, food, recreation, waking, and sleeping - all useful means are fully discussed without missing anything. Indeed, there is a full sequential discussion of all useful elements. Here, one ought to wonder how can there be a mention of Niṣkāma-Karma? Especially when it has a clear opposition to the above means and accessories. What is necessary at this location is internal Sattvaguṇa without vacillations. However, duty-bound Niṣkāma-Karma, as its grace, gifts vacillations to the heart. How can it even be mentioned? From the perspective of Bhagavāna, attainment of Yoga is only possible through analytic thinking (Tattva-Cintana). That is why

[50] Ultimate liberation (परम निर्वाण, Parama Nirvāṇa) means attainment of eternal and immovable happiness and complete removal of pain and suffering. Alternatively, attainment of the Brahman and freedom from the bondage of Saṃsāra, meaning liberation from the Saṃsāra of transmigrating lives and attainment of the eternal supreme-bliss (परमानन्द, Paramānanda).

only those means that are useful in analytic thinking are articulated: 1) control over the mind and senses, 2) relinquishment of desires and possessions, 3) residing alone in a solitary place, 4) clean place, 5) stability of seat, 6) holding the body, head, and neck even and motionless, 7) focusing the eyesight on the tip of the nose, 8) fearless and serene conscience, 9) practice of celibacy, 10) the mind concentrated and devoted to the Supreme Reality, the Paramātmā, and 11) guided eating, recreation, sleeping and staying awake (BG 6.10 - BG 6.17).

In summary, attainment of Yoga is only possible through analytic thinking because the distinction of Jīva from own Ātmā is born of ignorance only. It is imagined, not real. This ignorance-born distinction can only be removed by knowledge, not by any activity in the form of Karma. It is impossible to remove that distinction by Karma; just as darkness can only be removed by illumination, it is impossible to remove darkness by blows of a truncheon. Ignorance remover knowledge is only in analytic thinking, and analytic thinking is only possible in a highly focused mind and not in a duty-bound agitated mind. That is why, through Niṣkāma-Karma, with the removal of Rajoguṇa, those eleven means described earlier are extremely useful for the concentration of the mind. At this location, if Niṣkāma-Karma were useful in the concentration of the mind, then Bhagavāna would have mentioned it. Indeed, Niṣkāma-Karma at this location is not only entirely unuseful but impedes concentration. How can then it be even mentioned? Just as a constipated patient may be given a laxative to clean his bowels, he must stop the laxatives after his system is clean. If the laxatives are continued even after the cure, it can be harmful to the patient. In the same way, to reduce the force of Rajoguṇa, in the beginning, Niṣkāma-Karma is necessary, but once Sattvaguṇa has emerged, then forcing Rajoguṇa in the form of Niṣkāma-Karma from outside is harmful. Only those earlier described means could be helpful in the concentration, by which the fire of knowledge can be set ablaze and the garbage of ignorance, the discriminating sentiment is incinerated. Of course, after attaining oneness in one's own Ātmā, removing the distinction between Jīva and the Paramātmā, and experiencing oneness with the Ātmā, Karma is no longer in bondage-form for that Yogī, he is entirely untainted from Karma, and all his Karma becomes Akarma.

However, as said earlier, to achieve a position in Yoga, one needs those eleven means only. Any external Karma is then an impediment. Just as curing a disease, it is necessary to intake proper and abandon improper, but after being disease-free, the relationship between proper and improper is naturally broken. Before attaining a position in Yoga, external Karma impeded the attainment of Yoga. Once Yoga is attained, external Karma does not pose any impediment. The way external Niṣkāma-Karma is shown as the means for liberation by some, and their opinion that only Niṣkāma-Karma can be called Yoga, or only Niṣkāma-Karma is an independent path for liberation and that it cannot be ever abandoned, is indeed their fallacy. Shouldn't they have paid close attention to those words of Bhagavāna? It is surprising that when Bhagavāna laid out the entire spectrum of means at this location, He forgot to mention these Variant-Yoga advocates' highest aim and Niṣkāma-Karma as the only independent means to achieve liberation.

Many have said that verses (BG 6.5 - BG 6.28), where Bhagavāna has described the means, are not for Karma-Yoga but Haṭha-Yoga (हठ-योग). Their assertion is not valid either. First, if we look at the occasion, it is not related to the cessation of Prāṇa (प्राण-निरोध, Prāṇa-Nirodha) type Haṭha-Yoga. At the beginning of the fifth chapter, in response to the doubt expressed by Arjuna, Bhagavāna clearly showed the oneness between Saṃnyāsa and Yoga. At the beginning of the sixth chapter, in the verses (BG 6.1 - BG 6.4), Bhagavāna once again discusses the same oneness. Further, from verses (BG 6.5 - BG 6.28), Bhagavāna describes the means for attaining the same Yoga, whose oneness is with Saṃnyāsa. There is no subject of Haṭha-Yoga, separate from what is described above. At no place has Bhagavāna indicated that "This is the description of the renunciation-Yoga and now listen to the subject of Haṭha-Yoga." If Bhagavāna was describing Haṭha-Yoga, then the flow of Prāṇa-Vāyu, Apāna-Vāyu, and Prāṇāyāma should have been presented, which are the major limbs of Haṭha-Yoga, and without them, any discussion of Haṭha-Yoga is indeed incomplete. However, here instead of the discussion on all of these Haṭha-Yoga related necessary topics, Bhagavāna indifferently talks about Āsana (आसान, seat) and that too in common terms. It is possible that with the discussion of Āsana, the ears of those individuals may have perked up, and they may have made a firm assertion that now Bhagavāna is describing Haṭha-Yoga. However, they should also reflect that the relationship of Āsana is also with the concentration of the mind, which is necessary for analytic thinking (Tattva-Cintana), and food, recreation, and other means described have a direct relationship with mental concentration - the valuable means for analytic thinking. If Bhagavāna was describing Haṭha-Yoga, then other limbs of Haṭha-Yoga such as Netī, Dhautī, Yama, and Niyama should also have been sequentially discussed, but here in the discussion of other limbs, there is satiety only. Thus, the subject matter herein is not related to Haṭha-Yoga. Suppose there was no use of the above means such as Āsana, food, or recreation (BG 6.10 - BG 6.17) in the concentration of the mind for analytic thinking. Then there is a possibility for the assertion that there is a discussion of Haṭha-Yoga. However, in analytic thinking, all of these means are used. The occasion is also analytic thinking, and so about-facing from all and meddling Haṭha-Yoga in between is a vacuous obstinacy.

Additionally, the fruits of the means described by Bhagavāna in the verses (BG 6.10 - BG 6.17), Haṭha-Yoga cannot achieve. The purpose of Haṭha-Yoga is the cessation of Prāṇa by force (Haṭha). The nature of bodily functions is such that whatever activities are ongoing in the body, mind, and senses are directly influenced by the Prāṇa-Vāyu; it is only on a horse in the form of Prāṇa that the equestrian in the form of mind rides. If the flow of Prāṇa is stopped, then commensurately, the mind also stops, similar to how equestrian stops moving when the horse is stopped by pulling his reigns. When the activity of the mind is stopped, there is a feeling of happiness, just like a tired person, upon resting experiences with the removal of fatigue. In the awake state, the cause of agitations in a Jīva are the resolves of the mind only. So, happiness acquired by removing resolves lasts only as long as the mind is confined. In the deep-sleep state, when the mind merges in ignorance, the activity of the mind is confined, and there is an experience of happiness. However, during mental confinement, no knowledge or thought remains. There is a complete absence of knowledge or thought. In a pure Sāttvika mind, it would have been possible for knowledge or thought to exist. However, at that time, it is inanimate, similar to a surgery patient who is inanimate as long as he is not out of anesthesia. Then, who is there to think or have knowledge? Doer of thought or knowledge is not present at that time. Nevertheless, just as a surgery patient experiences his anguish after he is out of anesthesia, the mental snake starts hissing attachment and aversion in the same way with the flow of Prāṇa restarting. With the stoppage of the flow of Prāṇa, the mental snake becomes motionless similar to how cold makes a snake stationary. However, as soon as cold turns into warmth by the sun's heat, the snake again starts to hiss, as his venom was never removed. He was only made motionless. Likewise, with the stoppage of the flow of Prāṇa, the mind is made inactive for some time in this Yoga, but with the heat of the Saṃsāra befalling on him, the same attachment and aversion reappear in him. The venom in the form of the trueness of the Saṃsāra is not removed.

Therefore, Haṭha-Yoga, where Prāṇa is stopped by force, is not the one in its true nature that can give any kind of steady peace. Steady peace can only come through analytic knowledge, under whose influence this extremely large Saṃsāra, while standing, remains like a burnt rope, whose shape is there but is without any reality. Just as in space, with its support, the infinite Saṃsāra of mountains, land, oceans, gardens, palaces, and houses are situated, but by becoming like space, with space vision, if there is a search of the entire Saṃsāra, then not even an iota of them can be grasped. Similarly, in support of the underlying substrate conscious, the entire stationary and movable Saṃsāra of the great elements is firmly observable, that Saṃsāra, with the entry into the true nature of the substrate and observed from the vision of the substrate, "न भूतो न भविष्यति, not in the present not in future," is absent at all times - past, present, and future. Then, intact Samādhī (oneness with the Ātmā) is achieved while alive. That is real Samādhī in the form of knowledge, from which rising is never possible. With the maturity of knowledge of the Truth, the Yogī does not see any touch of the conscience, varied internal tendencies, or the external world that is the object of those tendencies in his witness-conscious Ātmā. Thus, with the absence of the duality (Dvaita), he also has Samādhī in ordinary vacillations in the past, present, and future. In contrast, those who have presumed to call cessation of Prāṇa as Samādhī, that being without knowledge, is simply mental restraint and mental restraint is a unique state of ignorance. At that time, the merger of the mind is only possible in its material cause (Upādāna) ignorance only, just as the merger of an earthen pot is only possible in its material cause, clod or lump of earth. That is because its root ignorance is not burnt through knowledge. There is still trueness of ignorance, and with the ignorance present, the merger of the mind is impossible in the Adhiṣṭhāna Ātmā.

Samādhī, through cessation of Prāṇa by its nature being a unique state of ignorance, has a rising form, and in the rising, there is a delusion of Samādhī. Therefore, at this location, Bhagavāna has articulated the purpose and the fruit of Yoga in the verses BG 6.8, BG 6.9, BG 6.18, BG 6.19, BG 6.20, BG 6.21, BG 6.22 and BG 6.23, and Haṭha-Yogī in no way is capable of making them successful. He is neither content with knowledge and realized knowledge nor is he immutable in the activities of the senses (BG 6.8), as he has not attained a position in the witness-conscious Ātmā through knowledge. Separate from the witness of the entire Saṃsāra, he is devoid of his reality. Not having acquired intuitive transcendental (Aparokṣa) knowledge, he neither sees a clod, stone, or gold equally nor has equanimity among the good-hearted, friends, foes, neutrals, mediators, antagonists, relatives, pious, and sinners (BG 6.9). Having trueness of discriminating intellect in all materials, he cannot be desireless (BG 6.18). Not having oneness with the witness-conscious Ātmā his mind cannot stay motionless like a lamp flame (BG 6.19). Engaged in beholding the Ātmā, he cannot be content (BG 6.20). He has not acquired that absolute bliss beyond the senses, established wherein he cannot be moved from the Reality (BG 6.21). Neither has he earned that highest gain, situated in which he would never have been movable even in the time of most profound sorrow (BG 6.22). This way, he remains deprived of all of these attributes and fruits because, through the cessation of Prāṇa, all he has done is only restrained his mind. With pure Sāttvika intellect, following the words of preceptors and scriptures through tactics and thoughts, he has not known himself separate as a witness of his own three bodies - gross, subtle, and causal, and three states - awake, dream, and deep sleep. In contrast, through the realization of the Truth, a Yogī free from doership and enjoyership who is established with oneness in his Ātmā as a witness of the three bodies and the three states has a vision of sameness indeed and "is as is" immutable in the activities of the body. Because of his direct experience of the Saṃsāra as not having its reality, he is without any desires. He is content in his own Ātmā, so he does not see any other higher gain. Because of a firm determination that "pleasure and pain are attributes of the conscience, there is no taint of them in me," he is unmoved by even the deepest sorrows.

Accordingly, a duty-bound desireless Variant-Yogī can neither be the meaning of the above name Yogī nor Haṭha-Yogī can be the meaning of Yogī. From Gītā's perspective, only through the realization of the Truth, one who has found Yoga (oneness) in own Ātmā is the intended Yogī, and he is the one who meets the test of all words of Bhagavāna, and not the other two. The limbs Yama, Niyama, Dhāraṇā, and Dhyāna of Pātañjala Aṣṭāṅga-Yoga (Haṭha-Yoga) are helpful in analytic thinking, though for a weak seeker are not unsanctioned by Vedānta and Gītā, yet the subject of varied Ātmā of Pātañjala-Yoga (पातञ्जल-योग) is not acceptable to Gītā. Because in this chapter in the verses (BG 6.29 - BG 6.32), **Bhagavāna has accepted only one Ātmā residing in all living beings and not multifold Ātmā.** From this perspective, Jñāna-Yoga, Yoga of Knowledge, can only be the propounded subject of Gītā. Any other Yoga cannot be the propounded subject of Gītā.

In the four verses (BG 6.29 - 6.32), Bhagavāna has described the nature of that Yogī who, based on the above-described Yoga, is Yoga-Yukta - one who sees his Ātmā as the underlying support (Adhiṣṭhāna), not only in his body, but in all movable and immovable beings, and perceives all beings in his Ātmā as dreamlike illusory, such a Yogī with equal vision everywhere is Yoga-Yukta. "I am not lost to him who beholds Me everywhere and everything in Me, and neither is he lost to Me." In his vision, the entire Saṃsāra becomes a mirror to show My face, and he does not become invisible to Me. "A Yogī established in Me with oneness worships Me, the Parameśvara situated in all beings as their Ātmā. In whatever way he acts, the Yogī is only rejoicing in Me. Hey Arjuna! Just as how an ignorant has an I-ness vision of his body as the Ātmā, a Yogī with sameness sentiment embraces all objects everywhere in the form of the Ātmā, be they pleasure or pain. That Yogī excels, that is My opinion."

From the nature above of the Yogī, it is clear that whether it is a duty-bound Variant-Yogī or a Haṭha-Yogī, neither of the two have wherewithal here because a duty-bound Variant-Yogī due to his delusion of the body as his Ātmā is with discriminating-vision and a Haṭha-Yogī is without analytic thought. Only a Yogī, through the realization of the Truth becoming free from the ego of the body as the Ātmā and free from doership and duty, established with oneness in the Ātmā, can meet the test of all words of Bhagavāna heretofore discussed.

Upon Bhagavāna's words above, knowing the usefulness of control of the mind in the attainment of Yoga and understanding it to be difficult, Arjuna questions - "Hey Madhusūdana! This Yoga You have spoken with equanimity; I do not see its steady-state due to mental fickleness. Hey Śrī Kṛṣṇa! Mind is so fickle, agitating, strong and unyielding, that I deem its control extremely difficult like the wind" (BG 6.33 - BG 6.34). On this, Bhagavāna replied - "Hey, Mahābāhu! Undoubtedly, the mind being restless is difficult to control. However, hey, Kaunteya! With practice and dispassion, it can be held. One whose mind is not under control, for him, attainment of this Yoga is difficult; but for one whose mind is under control, through sacrifice and the approach mentioned above he can attain this Yoga, that is My opinion" (BG 6.35 - BG 6.36).

The intention here is that as long as a person has equanimity of vision in a sense object, until then, due to attachment-bound intellect, it becomes necessary for the mind to run around. Pleasure-bound intellect in a sense-object is ignorance-born delusional and not real, and accepting the painful sense-objects as pleasure-yielding is indeed a contrary delusion. The delusion of pleasure-bound intellect in the sense-objects can be removed by discerning thoughtfulness. With the absence of pleasure-bound intellect, when dispassion of seeing fault in them is produced, the mind naturally ceases from the objects. With the emergence of desistance in those objects, mind control is automatically achieved. Only attachment to objects is the cause of fickleness. The term Abhyāsa (practice) is not intended by Bhagavāna to mean the practice of the cessation of Prāṇa, which by its nature cannot truly stop the mind. Though, after extensive effort in stopping the Prāṇa, even if the mind is stopped for some time, upon the restarting of Prāṇa, the mind once again "as it was" runs after objects because the delusion of pleasure-bound intellect in objects was not removed through the practice of discernment and thinking. Only the flow of the mind was stopped. In such a state, once the flow of the mind restarts, the running around of the mind becomes necessary due to the presence of pleasure-bound intellect. Hence, cessation of Prāṇa cannot become the real means for restraining the mind. Only discernment and thinking can be the real means because removing the delusion of pleasure-bound intellect in the sense-objects makes it possible to achieve dispassion in seeing faults. That is the Abhyāsa that is acceptable to Bhagavāna.

In addition, Arjuna expressed his doubt that the path of Yoga is very hard to understand. It may not be possible to attain it in this lifetime. If it is not reached in this lifetime, what would be one's destination?" Arjuna again asked - "Hey Kṛṣṇa! A seeker of a feeble effort whose mind has deviated away from Yoga, but who has faith in it, failing to attain perfection in Yoga, to what destination he goes?" On this, Bhagavāna consoled him that there is no bad end for such a person, but after being Yoga-Bhraṣṭa, that is being unsuccessful in Yoga, he is reborn and continues his movement forward with force in the path of Yoga (BG 6.37 - BG 6.44). When efforts for the sake of Yoga are not fruitless, a Yogī perfected through many births, purified from sins, endeavoring with great effort, attains the supreme destination. A Yogī established with oneness in his own Ātmā is deemed superior to an ascetic, even superior to a knower of the scriptures. So, a Yogī is superior to a doer. Therefore, Hey Arjuna! You become only a Yogī. That is, free from doership and enjoyership, attain a position in the Ātmā. Even among all Yogīs, one who of steady faith, through the conscience with oneness in Me, worships Me, in My opinion, he is the most united (BG 6.45 - BG 6.47).

Accordingly, with the critique of this chapter Variant-Yoga of doership and duty-bound intellect cannot be established as the propounded subject of Gītā. Neither its practice for providing freedom from the bondage of Karma can be proven, nor can such nature of Yoga be confirmed through the words of Gītā. In contrast, through knowledge with the removal of doership and duty-bound intellect, the Yoga of attaining a oneness position in one's own Ātmā is established as the propounded subject of Gītā. It is the only one by its nature capable of providing direct, immediate liberation from the bondage of Karma. At the end of this chapter, its unbeatableness was articulated.

The Yoga of Knowledge and Realization - Chapter 7

At the beginning of the chapter, Bhagavāna said - "Hey Pārtha! With your mind fixed on Me and in My refuge practicing Yoga, hear how you will know Me completely without any doubt. I shall tell you this knowledge completely together with its realization, knowing which, nothing else more remains here to be known. Among thousands of humans, only some strive for perfection. Even among the striving perfected ones, only some know Me in Truth" (BG 7.1 - BG 7.3).

In the first verse of the chapter, Bhagavāna made a resolve to reveal the means and fruit of Yoga for the fit one (Adhikārī) in Yoga with the mind attached to the Lord, and in the second and third verses, the cause of Yoga that is knowledge (ज्ञान, Jñāna) and realized knowledge (विज्ञान, Vijñāna). From this, one can infer that in the opinion of Bhagavāna, only knowledge is acceptable as the cause of Yoga and not Karma. In accordance with the perspective of some, if Karma was the cause of Yoga from Bhagavāna's view, then at this location, Bhagavāna should have articulated Karma instead of knowledge and should have said, "I shall tell you this Karma completely by which in this Saṃsāra there would be nothing left to either do or to receive." However, such words would have been spoken had Karma been agreeable to Bhagavāna as the cause of Yoga. Only knowledge is acceptable to Bhagavāna as a cause, then why would He postulate Karma? That is why only knowledge is discussed until the end of the chapter.

First, Bhagavāna articulated His eightfold lower Nature (Aparā-Prakṛti), and then separate from it, He described His higher Nature (Parā-Prakṛti) that supports Jīva and underlies the Saṃsāra. Further, He said that these two are the womb of all beings, and I am the creator and dissolver of the world. There is nothing else beyond Me. This Saṃsāra is threaded in Me like gems in a string (BG 7.4 - BG 7.7). Then, Bhagavāna described His true witness-conscious form existent in all beings as sapidity in water, brilliance in the sun and the moon, sound in space, and articulated - "The threefold constituents Sattva, Rajas, and Tamas of Prakṛti (whose transformation is the Saṃsāra) exists only with My support. However, bewildered by those constituents, the Saṃsāra does not know Me - the immutable, Who is beyond them (BG 7.8 - BG 7.13). Undoubtedly, this Māyā, the divine delusive power of Mine consisting of the three constituents, is hard to cross over. Those who surrender to Me alone cross over this Māyā. Instead of adoring this Māyā, those who worship Me will overcome it." Then, Bhagavāna described four kinds of persons of virtuous conduct who worship Him: 1) an afflicted (आर्त, Ārta), 2) a seeker of material gain (अर्थार्थी, Arthārthi), 3) a seeker of knowledge (जिज्ञासु, Jijñāsu) and 4) a knower (ज्ञानी, Jñānī).

Further, Bhagavāna said, "Among them, a knower, in My opinion, is My very Ātmā. For, with a steadfast mind he is established in Me alone, the abode unparalleled" (BG 7.14 - BG 7.19). After that, Bhagavāna describing His all-pervasive form, said, "Deprived of knowledge due to those desires, the afflicted and the seekers of material gain worship other deities following all observances impelled by their nature. I certainly bestow their steady devotion towards whatever form of a deity they seek to worship with faith upon those devotees. They who are engaged in worship with that faith, undoubtedly in the deity-form, receive those fruits granted by Me only." That is, "It is only I in the form of those deities who fulfills their desires. Though everything that occurs is due to Me, these devotees who are not My direct clients do not reach Me but reach only those deities they worship and receive their desired fruits, which are perishable indeed" (BG 7.20 - BG 7.23). Then Bhagavāna described His true nature, "The undiscriminating ones, not knowing My immutable unsurpassable supreme nature, believe that I, the unmanifest, have acquired limited individuality." That is, "Though I am beyond the reach of the senses, ignorant people not knowing My true immutable supreme nature behold Me as a limited individual." In reality, "Veiled by My Yoga-Māyā, I am not enlightened to the deluded in My unborn and immutable-form. Whatever appears as manifested, in reality, it is only My unmanifest form. Knowing Me as a limited human being is merely a delusion of the senses. Being the witness of all beings, I know all beings in the past, present, and future, but they do not know Me. That is why all beings, not knowing Me, deluded by the dualities of desire and aversion, acquire birth and death. However, those pious persons, whose sins have been purged, free from duality delusion, steadfastly worship Me. Accordingly, in my support, those who perform a sacrifice to be free from old age and death come to know the entire Adhyātma, Karma, Adhibhūta, Adhidaiva, and Adhiyajña as the Brahman. Just as waves, eddies, and bubbles are miracles of water and are water, in the same way, the entire Karma, Adhyātma, and Adhidaiva are miracles of the Brahman and are only the Brahman. At the time of death, those who know Me in the Brahman-form know them as having a steadfast mind in Me." They are Yoga-Yukta.

As espoused by some, Karma cannot be proven for one to achieve Yoga. Accordingly, with the critique of this chapter, Yoga cannot be established as said Variant-Yoga (with duty and without desire for fruits). At the beginning of the chapter, Bhagavāna vowed to provide knowledge and realized knowledge as the cause of the attainment of Yoga. Articulating that knowledge and His true nature and showing the dependence of Yoga on that knowledge, Bhagavāna ended the chapter.

The Yoga of the Supreme Imperishable Reality - Chapter 8

At the end of the seventh chapter, when Bhagavāna mentioned Brahman, Adhyātma, Karma, Adhibhūta, Adhidaiva, and Adhiyajña, at the beginning of this chapter, Arjuna inquires about their attributes and asks, "At the time of death, how are You to be known by one with a steadfast mind" (BG 8.1 - BG 8.2)? On this, Bhagavāna described the nature of each of them and said, "At the end time, one who remembering Me alone departs leaving the body, he acquires My Status, there is no doubt in that. Even in the end, remembering whatever form one leaves the body, ever absorbed in that form, certainly acquires that. Therefore, at all times, remember Me and fight. Dedicating your mind and intellect to Me, you will undoubtedly attain Me only." That is, absorbed in whatever sentiment one leaves the body; one acquires the abode based on that sentiment. That is why one ought to think of the Lord at all times (BG 8.3 - BG 8.7). After that, Bhagavāna described his attributeless-form (Nirguṇa) that is appropriate to remember at the time of death and told the correct procedure of meditating thereupon and said, "One who constantly thinks of Me, does not behold anything else except for Me the all-witness, for that ever-established Yogī, I am easily attainable, and for him, there is no need for meditation procedures. Only after attaining Me those great beings who have acquired supreme perfection can become free from this ephemeral painful world of coming and going. Without attaining Me, even if one reaches all other worlds up to the world of Brahmā, they have to certainly return to the Saṃsāra" (BG 8.8 - BG 8.16). Then, He described the measure of day and night of Brahmā and said, "Without attaining Me, during Brahmā's sleep all living beings merge in the Unmanifest (Māyā), and during the waking state of Brahmā all living beings reappear; no one is free from this cycle of the Saṃsāra. Beyond that Unmanifest, there is another eternal unmanifest Reality. That is called the Unmanifest and the Imperishable. That is My supreme abode, attaining which none returns." That is, attaining that Status, there is the final exemption from life, freedom from the cycle of birth and death (Apunarāvṛtti). That Supreme Personality can only be reached by undivided (अनन्य, Ananya) devotion based on knowledge. Undivided devotion (अनन्य-भक्ति, Ananya-Bhakti) is really to know transcendentally one's self and the Saṃsāra in the form of the Brahman (BG 8.17 - BG 8.22). Those Yogīs who have ascended in Yoga, who have not yet attained the Supreme Personality with undivided devotion, who have not been Yoga-Yukta, who have not yet attained oneness in their own Ātmā, and are active through the means of Yoga, for them, the paths of

Uttarāyana[51]and Dakṣiṇāyana[52]after death were described. Uttarāyana is the path of light, and Dakṣiṇāyana is the path of darkness. Uttarāyana or the six months of the sun's movement northwards, the bright fortnight of the moon, bright part of the day are all characterized by light. Light is symbolic of knowledge, while darkness is symbolic of ignorance. Dakṣiṇāyana, the six months of the sun's southward movement, the dark fortnight of the moon, and night have the commonality of darkness.

Further, Bhagavāna told Arjuna, "A Yoga-Yukta Yogī who truly knows these two paths does not get confused. That is why hey, Arjuna! At all times, you become Yoga-Yukta." The intention here is that a Yogī who knows directly, "These two paths are only in the kingdom of Prakṛti, there is no path in my Ātmā," incinerates all paths, all worlds, and destinations by his fire of knowledge and, like a roaring lion, breaks through the cage of Prakṛti and achieves freedom, he does not have to go anywhere (BG 8.23 - BG 8.27). In the end, pronouncing the glory of Yoga, the chapter was concluded, "Whatever fruit of piety that is spoken in the scriptures to accrue from the study of the Vedas, of sacrifices, and charity, a Yogī knowing all these, transcends them and certainly attains that supreme primeval Abode" (BG 8.28).

With the critique of this chapter, based on the words of Bhagavāna, the nature of Yoga as postulated by some (with duty and without desire for fruits) cannot be proved. In the last two verses of the chapter, the glory of Yoga is described, "Truly knowing these two paths, no Yogī is deluded and enjoying the fruits of the Vedas and sacrifice attains supreme primeval Abode." The Variant-Yogī does not meet that test because, retaining duty-bound intellect, he is a doer of Karma and is a holder of the sentiments of relinquishment of fruits of Karma. His sentiment is only concerning the relinquishment of fruits due to his doer and duty-bound intellect. So, departing from either of the two paths, he will be undoubtedly bewildered. Freedom from the bondage of the paths could only have been acquired had he severed his bondage from Prakṛti, as these paths are in the kingdom of Prakṛti and are associated with Prakṛti only. Bondage with Prakṛti could only have been severed had he experienced the transcendental realization of the Ātmā. The oneness in the Ātmā would have shed all distinctions of doership and duty on their own, just as a goblet of wine falls from a drunk's hands. However, the Variant-Yogī is with discriminating vision and by doership is bound in the bondage of Prakṛti. Though it is true that his duty is not desire-ridden (Sakāma) and is desireless (Niṣkāma), therefore, as established by Śāstra, he will acquire the path of Dakṣiṇāyana, the path of darkness, the path of ignorance. Having fallen from Yoga, he will continue rotating in the cycle of life and death. As provided in the verses (BG 6.37 - BG 6.45), after taking birth, he will again move forward with great effort in Yoga and depart through Uttarāyana, the path of light, the path of knowledge; he will not be reborn. Only a Yogī who has direct intuitive knowledge (Aparokṣa Jñāna) of the Brahman and whose undivided worship of the attributeless Oṃ (ॐ) as the Brahman has become ripe depart through Uttarāyana. As described in Māṇḍukya Upaniṣad, Yogīs with direct intuitive knowledge in the world of Brahmā attain liberation from the body (Videha-Mokṣa) and are not reborn in the Saṃsāra. However, our Variant-Yogī is with discriminating intellect and is a desireless doer, not one who worships the attributeless, so he cannot be fit (Adhikārī) for the path of Uttarāyana. He is only fit for the path of Dakṣiṇāyana. Accordingly, the one worthy of the spoken glory of the Yoga can be only a Yogī who is established with oneness in the Ātmā. He is the one who has come out of the bondage of Prakṛti. He is the one who sees all beings as miracles of his own Ātmā, and while alive, he is free from all bondages. In his view, there is no path, destination, desired world, or no coming, going, and being the existent of all, is untouched by all. The world of the body, senses, mind, and intellect

---

[51] Uttarāyana (उत्तरायन) means the movement of the sun towards the north. It is a compound word from Uttara (उत्तर) meaning north and Ayanam (अयनम्) meaning movement, path. This movement begins to occur a day after the winter solstice which occurs around December 21 and continues for a six-month period through to the summer solstice around June 21.

[52] Dakṣiṇāyana (दक्षिणायन) means movement of the sun towards the south. It is a compound word from Dakṣiṇa (दक्षिण) meaning south and Ayanam (अयनम्) meaning movement, path. This movement begins to occur a day after summer solstice around June 21 and continues for a six-month period through to the winter solstice which occurs around December 21.

is dancing on his authority, but he is a non-doer. All duties get fulfilled through him, but he is free from duty, and he has attained the supreme Status beyond everything.

The Yoga of the Royal Knowledge of Royal Profundity - Chapter 9

At the beginning of the ninth chapter, Bhagavāna vowed to articulate the Yoga glorified with means and fruits at the end of the eighth chapter and said, "Hey, the one without a vision of seeing faults! I shall tell you, this most profound knowledge with realized knowledge, Knowing which you will be liberated from the evil (the grief-stricken world)." The knowledge described as royal knowledge of royal profundity, Bhagavāna said, "is the best, extremely pure, directly realizable, righteous, easy in practice, and imperishable. However, those who do not have faith in this righteousness, failing to attain Me, return to the mortal world of death" (BG 9.1 - BG 9.3).

From the words above of Bhagavāna, it is clear that this Yoga of royal knowledge is attainable by knowledge only and not Karma achievable. It is spoken of as one that provides a direct result, is a giver of imperishable fruit, and is easy in practice. Just as the knowledge of rope immediately removes the delusion of the snake and fear, thereby providing the direct result. Removal of a delusional snake is impossible by Karma, such as club blows. With the knowledge of the Ātmā, the underlying support of all, the delusion of the Saṃsāra is gone. There is the complete absence of sorrow, and without any effort, like a person awakened from a dream, imperishable Yoga is attained instantaneously. Akin to a billionaire, who upon waking up sees his steady belongings intact and in his possession, when earlier in his dream he had become a pauper and was grief-stricken with the loss of his wealth, in the same way, with knowledge, Jīva awakens in own Ātmā and attains the imperishable Yoga, which is indeed impossible with Karma. Accordingly, this knowledge is direct, imperishable, fruit yielder, and easy to practice.

In addition, Bhagavāna described His form and said - "This Jagata (जगत) is complete with Me, and is situated only in My support. Despite My being the underlying support of the entire Jagata, there is no taint of the Jagata on Me. I am untouched by the Jagata. Just as the wind cannot touch the space even though it moves around in and in support of the space, in the same way, I am untainted from the Jagata (BG 9.4 - BG 9.6). At the end of a Kalpa, by not attaining Me, all beings merge in My Prakṛti. At the beginning of the next Kalpa, I again create them from My Prakṛti. Taking control of My nature, I create again and again this entire multitude of beings, helpless by the force of their nature. Those actions do not bind Me, as I stay indifferent and detached in those actions" (BG 9.7 - BG 9.10). After that, Bhagavāna described four kinds of beings -

1. Confused beings who, not knowing My transcendent status, deride Me, the Great Supreme Lord of beings holding a human body. All desires, Karma, and knowledge are vain for such ignorant demonic-natured humans.
2. Great beings who worship Me know Me as the imperishable and the origin of all beings. They are constantly involved in My devotional musical recitals with undivided minds.
3. Knowers who, through the sacrifice of knowledge, worship Me as one in all varied forms in this Saṃsāra. They worship Me as the Ātmā of all beings (Sarvātmā), like only one water in numerous waves of the ocean. Here Bhagavāna described accessories for the sacrifice of knowledge and said, "I am this world's father, mother, sustainer, grandfather, object to know the sacred syllable Oṃ (ॐ), Ṛk-Veda, Sāma-Veda, Yaju-Veda, destination, nourisher, master, witness, abode, refuge, friend, origin, sustentation, dissolution, a repository of all accumulated actions and the imperishable seed. I am the Vedic rite. I am the sacrifice. I am the ancestral oblation. I am the medicinal herbs and plants. I am the Vedic hymn. I am the clarified butter. I am the fire, and I am the oblation. I radiate heat. I rain, attract, and then release. I am indeed immortality and death, and real and unreal."
4. Desire-ridden beings who desire Me, the bliss form, in the form of objects of enjoyment through sacrifice. With the influence of piety, they enjoy divine opulence in the world of the deities and, upon

expending all piety, again return to the mortal world. Thus, those desire-ridden certainly return to the cycle of birth and death (BG 9.11 - BG 9.21).

The four kinds of humans - a confused, a seeker, a knower, and a desire-ridden discussed heretofore, perform sacrifices in varied ways based on their sentiments to attain the bliss-form Lord. In the words of Bhagavāna, "Because of distinctions in their sentiments, they acquire different ends, even though they all have Me as their goal. Those who worship Me, thinking of Me with an undivided mind, I am attained directly, and I provide their Yoga-Kṣema. I provide what they do not have and preserve what they have. Those devotees, who faithfully worship other deities, are also, in reality, worshipping Me because it is only I who am in the form of those deities. However, their worship is not per Śāstra. In all of the desire-ridden sacrifices, I am indeed the Adhiyajña and the enjoyer. However, those active in desire-ridden sacrifices do not truly know Me because of their desires, so they fall again in the Saṃsāra-Cakra of birth and death. In summary, with whatever sentiment individuals worship Me, I am attained by them in the same form as their sentiment. Those striving for the deities, attain My deity-form; those striving for the ancestors, attain My ancestor-form; those striving for the spirits, attain My spirit-form and those striving for the Saccidānanda attain My direct supreme imperishable-form" (BG 9.22 - BG 9.25).

In addition, Bhagavāna described a simple procedure for His worship and said, "A pure-minded devotee even if he offers with devotion as little as a leaf, a flower, a fruit or water, I accept it with love. That is why whatever is done, eaten, donated, sacrificed, and austerities performed; why shouldn't they be offered to Me? Not only that, but even one's doership-sentiment should be offered to Me. With united mind, through renunciatory Yoga, that is, with the mind in union with Me through renunciation, you will be free from the bondage of good and evil Karma, and being free you will attain Me" (BG 9.26 - BG 9.28). Then Bhagavāna said - "I am the same towards all beings. To Me, no one is hateful nor dear. However, those who worship Me devotionally are in Me, and I am in them in mutual oneness. To the extent that, even if an extremely evil person worships Me with undivided devotion, he should indeed be deemed worthy, for he is of a correct resolution. He soon becomes righteous and attains lasting peace. That is why, hey Arjuna! My devotees never perish. Seeking refuge in Me, who may be even of inferior birth like women, Vaiśya and Śūdra certainly reach the supreme abode. Then, what is there to say about a pious Brāhmaṇa and a devout royal sage? Therefore, acquiring this pleasureless transitory world, worship Me only. Set your mind on Me, be My devotee, worship Me, and pay obeisance unto Me. Thus, moving towards Me and established in Me, you will attain Me, the Paramātmā" (BG 9.29 - BG 9.34).

In this chapter, to attain union in His true nature, Bhagavāna articulated knowledge of His pure, true nature dissociated from the Saṃsāra and described His undivided worship. According to the words of Bhagavāna, for the attainment of Yoga, duty-bound intellect was neither pronounced as causal nor found its entry in the true nature of Yoga. On the contrary, right in the first verse, Bhagavāna enunciated knowledge and realized knowledge as causal to free one from the painful Saṃsāra. In reality, the presence of duty-bound intellect, instead of providing union, only provides separation (Viyoga) from the Ātmā. As long as duty-bound intellect is present, neither undivided devotion can be accomplished, nor knowledge as Sarvātmā (the Ātmā of all beings) is acquired. That is because duty-bound intellect, by its nature, is incapable of dissolving the "I am a doer" ego. On the contrary, it makes it firmly steady, and this "I am a doer" ego is the biggest impediment in Yoga. The sentiment, "I have some duty," cannot remove the doership-ego from the root. However, like the effect of watering, it is the one that keeps it evergreen, which is the root of all evil. Even though desireless duty-bound intellect can remove the root of desire-ridden duty, it impedes undivided devotion and knowledge of being the Ātmā of all. Just as desireless duty is necessary for freedom from desire-ridden duty, undivided devotion, and knowledge of being the Ātmā of all, renunciation of desireless duty-bound intellect is also required.

The Yoga of the Divine Manifestations - Chapter 10

At the beginning of the tenth chapter, Bhagavāna, in the cause of attaining Yoga, described knowledge of His true nature and said - "Hey Mahābāhu! Listen to My supreme words once again, which with the desire for your good I shall tell you the beloved one. Neither the mass of deities nor the great seers know My origin. I am the origin of all the deities and the great seers in all respects. Who knows Me the unborn, beginningless and the Great Supreme Lord of the worlds, he, the undeluded among mortals, is released from all sins. Intelligence, knowledge (of the Ātmā), non-delusion (absence of confusion, clarity of thought), forgiveness (to remain undisturbed towards even offenders), truthfulness (of speech), restraint of senses, control of the mind, pleasure, pain, being, non-being, fear, fearlessness, nonviolence, equanimity, contentment, austerity, charity (of material for the sake of the Lord), renown, infamy - from Me alone all these manifold sentiments arise in beings. In the past, the seven great seers, the four (Kumāras), and the Manu were born of thought (Saṃkalpa) with My mental power. In the world, all these are their progeny. The entire cause of the causes and action is indeed I only, though I do not have any cause of Myself and in their being and not-being I am situated 'is as is.' He who truly knows these divine manifestations and Yoga of Mine is established through steadfast Yoga. I am the origin of everything, and everything properly moves on through Me. Deeming so, the wise worship Me with devout faith. With their mind fixed on Me, their lives surrendered to Me, enlightening one another and conversing about Me, they always find contentment and delight. To them who are constantly established in Me and lovingly worship Me, I give them the Yoga of discernment by which they come to Me. Moved by compassion alone, I, existent in their hearts, destroy their darkness of ignorance with a lustrous flame of knowledge" (BG 10.1 - BG 10.11).

From the words above of Bhagavāna, it is clear that the Yoga (union with oneness) in the true nature of Bhagavāna is only possible by the knowledge of the Truth (तत्त्व-ज्ञान, Tattva-Jñāna) of His true nature; there is no room here for any desireless actions to achieve the same. Had desireless actions been agreeable to Bhagavāna for directly attaining Yoga in His true nature, there would have been some indication at this location. However, from His side, there is only satiety, and there is a clear pleading that in this Yoga, there is no direct usefulness of desireless actions. Again, those who have fitness in this heretofore described Yoga are the ones who have always dedicated their mind and Prāṇa to Bhagavāna; only duty-bound intellect and relinquishment of fruits have not been deemed sufficient (BG 10.1). Such paltry relinquishment is not the one that provides satisfaction to Bhagavāna. On the contrary, He wants the sacrifice of the mind and Prāṇa to attain oneness in the Ātmā. Only upon achieving such a state the darkness of ignorance can be destroyed by the light of knowledge and not by Karma (BG 10.10 - BG 10.11).

Listening to the words of Bhagavāna, Arjuna was satisfied, his incomprehension removed, and expressing his gratitude with faith said, "Hey Bhagavāna! You are the supreme Brahman, the supreme abode, the supreme sanctification, the divine Personality, the primordial Supreme Lord, the unborn, and the all-pervading." Again, Arjuna said, "Divine sage Nārada, Asita, Devala, Vyāsa, and all other seers have described You as such, and You Yourself are indeed articulating the same to me." That is why "Hey Keśava! Whatever You are telling me, I deem all that to be true. Indeed, neither the deities nor the demons know your manifestation. Only You know Yourself by Yourself." While the eyes can see a form, You cannot be known by any instruments. The fruit of knowledge is the removal of ignorance only. Knowing You cannot be the fruit of knowledge. Upon removal of ignorance through knowledge, You can be known and not by any instrument. This way, You are not the subject of Phala-Vyāpti (फल-व्याप्ति), but only the matter of Vṛtti-Vyāpti (वृत्ति-व्याप्ति) only. Phala-Vyāpti means the cognition of knowing some substance in a separate form from one's own through measures such as the senses. Vṛtti-Vyāpti means knowledge wherein the inner disposition does not become an object shaped like a pot. The only motive of the inner disposition is to disrupt the conduct of the one in support of the object, and the object becomes self-luminous by its illumination.

The purpose of the inner-disposition in the form of the Ātmā (आत्माकार-वृत्ति, Ātmākāra-Vṛtti) is not to illuminate the Ātmā, but only to disrupt the conduct of ignorance that resides in support of the Ātmā. That is why knowledge has the form of Vṛtti-Vyāpti because the Ātmā is self-illuminated by its light; it is not an object of any disposition. "Hey, Bhagavāna! You alone are capable of completely articulating Your divine manifestations, by which manifestations You are existent pervading all these worlds. Hey Yogeśvara! How can I always know You? Hey blessed Lord! In what form are You to be meditated upon by me? Hey Janārdana! Once again, recount in detail Your Yoga and manifestations as I am not content hearing Your ambrosiac words" (BG 10.12 - BG 10.18).

On this Bhagavāna showing compassion towards those who are not capable of knowing His form of all-forms (Sarvarupa), described the more prominent manifestations in the verses (BG 10.19 - BG 10.38) practical to know His various forms, so that by the contemplation of Bhagavāna in those major manifestations they can have a divine experience of His multiple forms. In the end, Bhagavāna said, "Hey Arjuna! That which is the seed of all beings, I am. There is no mobile or stationary being who can exist without Me. Hey Parantapa! There is no end to My divine manifestations. What is stated by Me is only illustrative of the extent of My manifestations. Whatever majestic, prosperous, or powerful being there is, know it to be only born of a part of My splendor. Hey Arjuna! What is your motive for knowing this extensively? I am existent holding this entire world in only one part of Mine" (BG 10.39 - BG 10.42).

In this chapter, Bhagavāna provided knowledge of His true nature, and for those who are unable to see Bhagavāna in all of His forms, he described his major manifestations. The intention is that in support of those manifestations, seeing Bhagavāna in those manifestations, they can free themselves from their limited I-ness ego and attain Yoga of oneness in the true nature of Bhagavāna. Nothing of the Variant-Yoga is found in this chapter. Neither is it considered in the class of means nor is it accepted in the class of fruits.

The Yoga of the Vision of the Cosmic-Form - Chapter 11

Listening to the Yoga of the Divine Manifestations of Bhagavāna in the tenth chapter, Arjuna's mind became cheerful, and offering his prayers said, "This ignorance of mine is removed by those supreme profound words (named 'Adhyātma') spoken by You for my good. Hey, the lotus-eyed! Indeed, the origin and dissolution of all beings and Your imperishable magnanimity have also been heard by me extensively from You. Hey Parameśvara! It is so as You have described Yourself, yet hey, the Supreme Personality! I desire to see that Lordly form of Yours. Hey, Lord! If You so deem possible by me to see, then, hey, the Lord of Yoga! Show me that immutable-form of Yours" (BG 11.1 - BG 11.4).

On this, Bhagavāna accepting Arjuna's prayer, said, "Hey Arjuna! Behold My forms in hundreds and thousands of various kinds, divine, and of various colors and shapes. Behold the (twelve) Ādityas, the (eight) Vasus, the (eleven) Rudras, twin Aśvanī Kumāras, the (forty-nine) Marutas, and many hitherto unseen astonishing forms. Here, now behold the entire world of moving and stationary beings assembled in one place in My body and whatever else you desire to see. However, it is impossible to see Me with just these eyes of yours. Therefore, I am giving you divine vision to behold My Yoga and Lordliness" (BG 11.5 - BG 11.8). Having said so, Śrī Yogeśvara Hari showed Arjuna His Supreme Lordly form. Sañjaya described the glory of that form to Dhṛtarāṣṭra (BG 11.9 - BG 11.14). Having received the divine sight, Arjuna, upon seeing those divine forms of Bhagavāna, started to describe each of them to Bhagavāna and said, "Hey Deva! I see in Your Cosmic-Form innumerable astonishing forms" and with obeisance said, "Hey, best of the deities! Tell me who are You with this fierce-form? My salutations to You. Be gracious, I desire to know Your primordial-form; for, I do not comprehend Your activity" (BG 11.15 - BG 11.31). On this, Bhagavāna said, "I am the dominant world dissolving time, active here annihilating the worlds. Among all these warriors standing in opposing armies, except you, none will remain. Therefore, stand up. Conquering the foes, you secure honor and enjoy a prosperous kingdom. Indeed, they all have already been slain by Me. Hey, skillful bowman! Be only an occasion" (BG 11.32 - BG 11.34).

Listening to such words of Bhagavāna, the diademed Arjuna, bowing with joined palms, trembling, even fearful, and expressing respect, spoke again in a faltering voice, "Unaware of this majesty of Yours, taking You as a friend, out of affection or carelessness, such presumptuous words as Hey Kṛṣṇa, Hey Yādava, Hey Sakhā that were spoken by me in their front or also when alone, at recreation, resting, sitting, and eating. You were disrespected in jest, for which hey the infallible One! I am begging forgiveness for all those transgressions from You, the Immeasurable." This way, with numerous prayers for forgiveness, Arjuna said, "Hey, Lord of the deities! Having seen what is unseen, I am becoming exuberant, and my mind is distressed with fear. Hey, Lord! Reveal to me only that familiar form of Yours with four arms. Hey, the abode of the world! Be gracious" (BG 11.35 - BG 11.46).

Upon this, Bhagavāna said, "By the power of My Yoga and with My grace, this supreme, brilliant, primal, and infinite Cosmic-Form of Mine is revealed to you, which none, but you, have ever beheld before. Neither by the study of the Vedas, sacrifices, charities, and severe austerities, nor by ceremonial acts can I be seen in this form by anyone in the human world except you. Be not distressed and confused beholding such ghastly form of Mine. Rid of fear and mentally pleased, you behold that very form of Mine with four arms." After that, Bhagavāna gave solace to the fear-struck Arjuna and returned in His gentle two-armed form BG 11.47 - BG 11.50).

Beholding the gentle two-armed human form of Bhagavāna, Arjuna became peaceful and regained his composure. Then, Bhagavāna said, "Hey Arjuna! This extremely hard to behold the form of Mine, which you have seen, even deities perpetually crave to see that form, but they do not see it. As you have seen Me, I am neither possible to be seen by the study of Vedas nor by the practice of austerities nor by giving charities and not by performing sacrifices. It is only possible to know truly, see, and enter My form by undivided devotion. That is why, hey, Pāṇḍava! He attains Me, who is free from all attachments, whose actions are only to attain Me, who through all efforts is moving towards Me, who worships Me alone, and who is free from malice towards all beings" (BG 11.51 - BG 11.55).

In this chapter, to enter His true nature and attain Yoga (union with oneness) in the Ātmā, Bhagavāna enunciated only undivided devotion as a means. There was also an absence of the Variant-Yoga in the form of duty-bound intellect. Besides that, in verse BG 11.48, a refutation of Karma was found, wherein Bhagavāna said, "With sacrifice (Karma), austerity, no one can see this form of Mine." It is important to remember that undivided devotion and knowledge of the Truth, like seed and its sprout, being mutual means and end, have oneness only. There is no mutual distinction. Though duty-bound intellect and undivided devotion, like darkness and illumination, are mutually in opposition, both cannot exist at one time in one substrate (अधिकरण, Adhikaraṇa).

The Yoga of Devotion - Chapter 12

At the end of the eleventh chapter, Bhagavāna described the glory of His undivided worship in knowing, seeing, and entering in His manifest form. Listening to such majesty, at the beginning of this chapter, Arjuna questioned, "Thus, those ever-united devotees who always worship You (the manifest-form) and those who worship the Imperishable, the Unmanifest - among them who knows Yoga best? (BG 12.1).

Bhagavāna, responding, said, "Fixing their minds on Me, ever united, I deem those who worship Me with absolute faith as the best Yogīs." In the attainment of the attributeless-form, the manifest-form devotion being a necessary means, a devotee is referred to as Yuktatama (युक्ततम), best Yogī. "However, those who worship the Imperishable, the Ineffable, the Unmanifest, the Omnipresent, the Unthinkable, the Immutable, the Immovable, and the Unwavering, fully controlling all senses, with equanimity of mind everywhere, and devoted to the welfare of all beings, indeed attain Me. Toil is greater for those whose minds are attached to the unmanifest form. The unmanifest objective is acquired with great pain by the embodied (for those who consider their body the Ātmā)." It should be kept in mind that those who are not yet fit (Adhikārī) to attain this unmanifest-form, for them, as a means, the manifest-form devotion is prescribed. "However, those who worship surrendering all actions to Me (including doership, and not just fruits of action), moving towards Me, meditating with an undivided union in Me alone, and with the mind fixed on Me, hey Arjuna! I quickly become the one to deliver them from the ocean of the mortal world of death. That is why hey, Arjuna! Fix your mind on Me alone, and let your discerning be absorbed in Me. After that, you will dwell in Me alone, without any doubt" (BG 12.2 - BG 12.8).

The intention of the words of Bhagavāna herein is that due to the I-ness ego in the body, it is challenging to enter into the unmanifest form of Bhagavāna that is beyond the senses. With propitiation, through the devotion of pure love of the manifest form, the I-ness ego in the body quickly melts away. Indeed, there is such an attraction in love that a lover immediately sacrifices himself for his beloved one. When there is so much attraction in the delusional worldly love for a spouse or children that one loses oneself for the loved ones during the state of love, what is there to say about totally losing oneself where there is a true love for the Paramātmā? Because with the manifest-form love, offering one's self is easy. Only through self-surrender entry into the unmanifest form is possible. That is why the manifest-form devotion is called Yuktatama. That does not mean that the manifest and the unmanifest-form worships are separate paths for attaining Bhagavāna. There is only one path, just the difference in steps. It is difficult to step up to the unmanifest-form step without stepping on the manifest-form step. That is why manifest-form devotion is called the best, and unmanifest-form devotion is called the most difficult.

In addition, Bhagavāna said, "If you cannot concentrate your mind steadfastly on My manifest-form, then through repeated efforts, instill a desire for knowledge to attain My manifest-form. That is, begin the flow of inner thoughts repeatedly in My manifest form. Again, if you are not able to practice this way, then move towards doing Madartha-Karma (मदर्थ-कर्म, Karma for My sake), that is, Bhagavadartha-Karma (भगवदर्थ-कर्म). You will acquire perfection in the form of purity of the conscience by doing Karma for My sake" (BG 12.9 - BG 12.10). In verse BG 12.10, "Karma for My sake" refers to becoming active in listening to the holy scriptures (Śravaṇa), musical recitations of religious hymns, Mantras and praise of the Lord (Kīrtana), remembering teachings of the sacred scriptures (Smaraṇa), worshipping (Arcana), and bowing to the divine (Vandana) and others in the ninefold limbs of devotion (Navadhā-Bhakti). That was expressed step-wise for those whose mind and intellect following verse BG 12.8 cannot be steady in the manifest form of Bhagavāna, and following verse BG 12.9 to make the mind and intellect steady in the manifest form of Bhagavāna cannot even make repeated efforts. This shows that the fruit of Bhagavadartha Karma is the practice mentioned above, the cause for fixing the mind and intellect on the manifest form of Bhagavāna. The fruit of practice is the steadiness of the mind and intellect through meditation (Dhyāna) in the manifest form. The fruit of the steadiness of the mind and intellect in manifest form is the entry in the attributeless form upon looseness of the I-ness ego in the body, the Vāstavika-Yoga.

After that, Bhagavāna said, "In the effort of the Yoga of attaining Me, if you cannot do this, that is, you cannot even do Karma for My sake then winning over your mind renounce all fruits of your Karma, do not retain any fruit (BG 12.11). The intention here is that a person who cannot even do Bhagavadartha Karma, as provided in verse BG 12.10, renouncing fruits of Karma per verse BG 12.11 is the lowest step. He should at least conquer his mind; not let it wander towards the Saṃsāra, and not keep any Saṃsāra related fruits - the Variant-Yoga. When the fruit relinquishment is connected to the Saṃsāra, it can automatically convert into Bhagavadartha-Karma.

With the articulation of the steps, Bhagavāna clarified, "Knowledge {indirect knowledge (Parokṣa-Jñāna) of the true nature of Bhagavāna} is better than practice (Abhyāsa). Dhyāna (as provided in BG 12.8, keeping the mind and intellect fixed on the true nature of Bhagavāna) is better than knowledge. Only with the indirect knowledge of a thing is the success of meditation on it possible. When there is indirect knowledge of the true nature of Bhagavāna, then only by that indirect knowledge is meditation possible. Relinquishment of fruits of Karma is better than meditation. With this relinquishment, supreme peace can be attained. Here in BG 12.12, relinquishment of fruits of Karma is not the sought after (इष्ट, Iṣṭa) relinquishment of fruits of Karma of verse BG 12.11, which is described as the lowest among the sequential order of the means. Bhagavāna has considered the relinquishment of fruits of BG 12.11 in a lower category than meditation, repeated efforts, and Bhagavadartha Karma, as described in the verses BG 12.8, BG 12.9, and BG 12.10. Then how can this relinquishment of fruits be called better than meditation? It can neither be superior to meditation nor can it be the result of meditation, and as is said in this verse, immediate peace cannot be attained by it. However, here the meaning of the words "relinquishment of fruits of action, Karma-Phala-Tyāga" ought to be opined as "the total renunciation of all actions (Sarva-Karma-Saṃnyāsa)" that is articulated in BG 12.6, "Surrender all doership, actions and thus fruits of action to Me the manifest-form Supreme Lord." That Sarva-Karma-Saṃnyāsa can be the only one that can be superior to meditation because only with repeated meditation efforts in the manifest form of Bhagavāna can the form become firm in the heart. As a result, in the passion of true love, the connection of I-ness and mineness in the body and senses naturally breaks; and after its success, peace is attained. Thus, this Karma-Phala-Tyāga, that is, Sarva-Karma-Saṃnyāsa of verse BG 12.6, is superior to meditation.

Additionally, Bhagavāna, in the verses (BG 12.13 - BG 12.19), described characteristics of that Yogī who, based on the approaches above, has acquired peace and is dear to Bhagavāna. In the end, Bhagavāna said, "Moving towards Me, indeed, those devotees who follow these immortal virtues set forth above with faith are extremely dear to Me (BG 12.20).

Accordingly, in the critique of this chapter, even here, Variant-Yoga was not shown to be the propounded subject of Gītā. On the contrary, under the hierarchy articulated to enter the true nature of Bhagavāna, this Variant-Yoga is established as the lowest sixth step, and that is this way -

For attaining oneness in the true nature of Bhagavāna, the last step is the worship of the unmanifest attributeless form. In its absence,

1. "Sarva-Karma-Saṃnyāsa" in the manifest form of Bhagavāna, that is, offering one's doership to Bhagavāna through oneness Yoga (BG 12.6). In its absence,
2. With meditation fixing the mind and intellect steadfast on the manifest form of Bhagavāna (BG 12.8). In its absence,
3. With the desire to attain Bhagavāna, the practice of meditation (BG 12.9). In its absence,
4. Stay absorbed in Bhagavadartha Karma. Be ready to listen to the holy scriptures (श्रवण, Śravaṇa), chant (कीर्तन, Kīrtana), and remember the teachings of the sacred scriptures (स्मरण, Smaraṇa) et al. (BG 12.10). In its absence,
5. Move towards the relinquishment of fruits of Karma (BG 12.11).

This way, the lowest sixth step of the means remaining, the Variant-Yoga cannot become an independent Gītā propounded subject.

The Yoga of the Field and the Knower of the Field - Chapter 13

In the twelfth chapter, responding to the query of Arjuna, Bhagavāna articulated worship of His manifest form and the stepwise means to attain Him. In this chapter, Bhagavāna gets active in enunciating the fruit of His manifest-form worship, which is the entry into His unmanifest form. No one can directly describe that unmanifest form by words. Its articulation is only possible by attributing an adjunct with discriminative attributes (Upādhi). With the adjunct of the body, Bhagavāna is describing His unmanifest form and says - "Hey Kaunteya! This body is called the field (क्षेत्र, Kṣetra). Him, who knows the field, is called the field-knower (क्षेत्रज्ञ, Kṣetrajña) by its knowers. Know Me as the field-knower in all the fields. I believe that the knowledge of the field and the field-knower is the real knowledge." That is, know Me the unmanifest-form, the attributeless as the field-knower that illuminates the field.

The intention herein is that it is impossible to know any substance in darkness. Its knowledge is only possible by some form of light. Even in the absence of illumination from inanimate objects such as the sun, the light that provides the cognition of knowing that "this is the body" or "I am the body" is only the Ātmā - the field-knower, the unmanifest-form, which is existent in the body. Such knowledge of the field and the field-knower, the determination of the insentient field part as absent at all times, and holding only the conscious field-knower part is deemed as knowledge of the unmanifest-form of the Lord (BG 13.1 - BG 13.2). After that, Bhagavāna vowed to briefly describe the nature of the field and the field-knower. His discourse provided the seers, the Vedas, and Brahma-Sūtra as the validation. The great elements (Pañcabhūta), the ego, the intellect, the unmanifest, the ten senses and the one (mind), and the five objects of the senses totaling twenty-four elements are described by Bhagavāna as the nature of the field. In addition, He briefly described the transformations of the field viz., desire, antipathy, pleasure, pain, the aggregate (gross body), consciousness (enlightening disposition of the conscience), and sustentation (the power to hold the body and senses) (BG 13.3 - BG 13.6). Having thus described the nature of the field and the field-knower, to realize them directly, Bhagavāna then told the required attributes.

1. Humility,
2. Unostentatiousness,
3. Non-violence (not to hurt anyone through the body, mind, or speech),
4. Forgiveness (remaining undisturbed towards offenders),
5. Simplicity (straightforwardness and absence of crookedness in all mental and vocal conduct related to eating, drinking, or clothing),
6. Service of the preceptor (with faith and devotion, service of the preceptor with the body, mind, and wealth to procure his grace),
7. Purity (cleanliness within and outside),
8. Steadfastness (diverting the conscience from worldly activities and exclusively pursuing the path leading to liberation),
9. Self-control (imposing discipline on the body, mind, and senses when they function against one's genuine interest and confining activities in the righteous path),
10. Dispassion (aversion towards the worldly objects of the senses),
11. Relinquishment of ego,
12. Repeated perception of evil and pain in birth, death, old age, and disease,
13. Absence of attachment and excessive love for children, wife or home,
14. Constant even-mindedness in the acquisition of desired and undesired things,
15. Unwavering undivided devotion to the Lord (from this, it is shown that undivided devotion in the manifest form is the means for the knowledge of the unmanifest form),
16. Residing in a solitary place due to aversion to masses,
17. Constant pursuit for transcendent knowledge of the Ātmā and
18. Perception of the content of knowledge of the Truth.

All these being the means of knowledge are in the form of knowledge. Thus, what is other than that is ignorance. Accordingly, eighteen instruments of knowledge were described (BG 13.7 - BG 13.11).

The position, "1) Gītā is an activity-oriented scripture and does not provide an opportunity for non-activity (Nivrutti), 2) one can achieve knowledge of the Ātmā by remaining in activity only, and 3) by performing desireless actions (Niṣkāma-Karma) direct realization of the Ātmā is possible, and it is an independent path for the direct transcendental (Aparokṣa) knowledge," held by those should contemplate on the above words spoken by Bhagavāna. If Gītā is an activity-dominant scripture, if from Gītā's perspective, non-activity ought to be relinquished and if by being engaged in activity from the perspective of Bhagavāna, the direct transcendental realization of the Ātmā is possible, then why did Bhagavāna articulate this renunciation-dominant eighteen means for the knowledge of His unmanifest form? It is also not so that Bhagavāna has described these eighteen means as alternatives, like how some have made Sāṅkhya (Nivrutti) and Yoga (Pravṛtti) two alternative paths for liberation. However, Bhagavāna has made it explicitly clear in verse BG 13.11 - "एतज्ज्ञानमिति प्रोक्तमज्ञानं यदतोऽन्यथा, all this is said to be knowledge (the means for knowledge), and everything else that is contrary is ignorance." In such a state, how can these means be deemed as alternatives? One must accept that these are all agreeable to Bhagavāna as exclusive means. One can say that by engaging in an activity, one can accomplish the practice of all these means, and one should put these means into practice while remaining engaged in an activity. However, Bhagavāna, by His words in the verse BG 13.10, has clearly said, "विविक्तदेशसेवित्वमरतिर्जनसंसदि, residing in solitary place while not having a fondness for masses of people." How can that be possible by remaining engaged in an activity, and what can its reconciliation be? Secondly, there is no dispute that without the direct realization of the unmanifest form of Bhagavāna (meaning, without being established with oneness in the unmanifest form), liberation is not possible at all. If liberation were dependent on the knowledge of the manifest form, then Arjuna, who always had direct knowledge of the manifest form of Bhagavāna, yet his darkness of ignorance was present. In addition, if manifest-form direct knowledge were sufficient in attaining liberation, then for Dhruva and Prahlāda, in addition to their direct knowledge of the manifest form, there was no need for the direct knowledge of the unmanifest-form. However, even with the manifest-form knowledge, Bhagavāna had to give Upadeśa of Gītā to Arjuna, and also for Dhruva and Prahlāda, in addition to the manifest-form knowledge, they had to acquire knowledge of the unmanifest-form to attain the unmanifest-form realization. From this, it is clear that for liberation, direct realization of the unmanifest form is the only direct means, which is possible only with knowledge. If desireless actions with duty-bound intellect were agreeable to Bhagavāna for the unmanifest-form realization, then it was necessary for Bhagavāna to postulate, either within these eighteen means or separate from them, a nineteenth means of Niṣkāma-Karma. However, it is not even considered in the list of means by Bhagavāna. Nor has Bhagavāna spoken of it as a separate means as an alternative, but He has clearly said that anything other than the eighteen means is ignorance. Accordingly, Niṣkāma-Karma is not proven by any measure as a direct means for liberation based on the words of Bhagavāna. Nevertheless, desireless actions by regular succession can be the means for liberation. Its fruit is only the purity of the conscience. After that, it is not to be practiced but is to be left. To color a dirty garment, it is necessary to clean it with soap. However, continued use of soap is not necessary once the dirt is removed. All that is necessary is to immerse the garment in color. At that time, soap was not helpful but was an impediment. In the same way, desireless actions of duty-bound intellect as a means through regular succession after the purity of the conscience is only to be abandoned. That is why Bhagavāna has not emphasized it in the list of means. However, these eighteen means are useful for knowledge. They are not to be abandoned but are the ones to be practiced. Direct realization of the unmanifest form depends on repeated pure thought practice by a penetrating and introverted intellect. That is only possible by complete renunciation, which is only possible in solitude, not in the hassle of the Saṃsāra. At that time, activity in the form of desireless actions is not helpful in the practice of focusing intellect inwards but indeed detrimental. These eighteen means are not detrimental in focusing inwards but are helpful. Though it is quite a different thing for a seer of the Truth after realization of the Truth, when an activity does not remain activity and non-activity does not remain non-activity. In that state, he is established in the form of the all-witness, dissociated from activity and non-activity, remains transcendental to material existence, and is entirely free from duty and doership. Though his body, senses, mind, and intellect are engaged in their activities, he remains immovable and immutable. While ignorant persons, based on their sentiments, may perceive activity and non-activity in the existence and non-existence of efforts of this great being, in reality, the great being "is as is" established in himself, immovable and dissociated indeed. That is why neither any means nor end remains, or any helpful and detrimental bondage applies. However, for a seeker, before the realization of the Truth, acceptability of the eighteen renunciatory means and the abandonability of the activity of desireless actions were necessary. That is akin to a patient, once cured of the disease, who is not bound by a dietary and activity regimen, though he needed to follow that same regimen in the presence of disease.

In addition, in the verses (BG 13.12 - BG 13.17), Bhagavāna described the unmanifest-form Parabrahma (supreme Brahman) that is knowable through knowledge and said - "Hey Arjuna! This field (where one attains the Parabrahma), knowledge (how it is acquired), and the knowable (the Parabrahma) is spoken to you briefly." The intention here is that the field is insentient and mutable, and by its nature, even not being is perceived as real due to the reality of the field-knower. All mutations are perceived on the dependence of the field-knower that is untouched by them. Hey Arjuna! Know Me as that field-knower. Knowing so truly, My devotee attains My form (BG 13.18). It should be noted that here Bhagavāna has articulated the attainment of His form only by knowledge and not by Karma.

Further, Bhagavāna providing knowledge of Prakṛti and the Puruṣa, said, "Know Prakṛti (the field) and the Puruṣa (the field-knower, the Jīvātmā) as beginningless." That is, the Saṃsāra is only because of the relationship between the two. "Know that among them, anything that has the constituents and transformations is all born of Prakṛti. In the form of activity (observable activities), instruments (the body, senses, and mind), and in the form of doership, whatever is seen or known, Prakṛti is the cause. Being associated with Prakṛti, superimposing the constituents and Karma of Prakṛti in himself due to ignorance, the Puruṣa situated in Prakṛti enjoys the constituents born of Prakṛti. Thus, due to ignorance having united with Prakṛti, the Puruṣa is called the cause in the enjoyment of pleasure and pain." In reality, the Puruṣa dwelling in the body is like the space, untainted from its constituents and transformations. Being the observer of the constituents and transformations, the Puruṣa is named Upadraṣṭā, Anumantā, Bhartā, et al. In reality, the Puruṣa is free from all attachments, the Brahman-form. Then, describing the fruits of knowledge, Bhagavāna said, "One who thus knows the Puruṣa and Prakṛti with its constituents, though engaged in activity in all ways, is not born again" (BG 13.19 - BG 13.23).

At this point, it is essential to contemplate the clear words of Bhagavāna. **Only due to ignorance of one's true nature and the superimposition of the constituents and actions of Prakṛti in one's self that the Puruṣa comes in the bondage of birth and death. It is only due to ignorance that there is the manifestation of activity in Karma.** In such a state, how can activity in Karma remove that ignorance? When Karma is the fruit of ignorance, how can the fruit dig out its root? Only knowledge is needed to remove ignorance. Upon the knowledge of the Truth, even though natural Karma happens through the body of a knower, as his I-ness sense in the body is burnt, his doership-ego does not remain in those Karma. His trueness sense in Karma does not remain, and all of his Karma remain only illusory. However, the Variant-Yogī has a trueness sense in Karma, and it is made firmer with duty-bound intellect. Thus, Variant-Yoga is not an opposer of ignorance but indeed a helper.

In addition, Bhagavāna described the activities of those seers of the Truth who have known themselves "as they are," dissociated and ever-free from Prakṛti and the field, and said, "Some perceive the Ātmā seated in the heart by pure and subtle intellect with meditation, others with Sāṅkhya-Yoga and some others with Karma-Yoga (having become free from doership and duty). However, with the influence of the knowledge mentioned above, there is no distinction in their resolve, even in the presence of discrimination in their conduct. They do not see anything changing in their true nature and become free from all injunctions-prohibitions and all grasping-relinquishing. Other persons who do not know their Ātmā this way, for them Bhagavāna commanded that with faith if they worship, meditate upon the Ātmā having listened to its true nature from other seers of the Truth, such persons engrossed in listening also overcome death (BG 13.24 - BG 13.25).

In the end, Bhagavāna providing the essence, said, "Hey, best of the descendants of Bharata! Whatever being is born, either stationary or moving, know it to be due to the union of the field and the field-knower. He, who sees the unperishable Supreme Lord equally existent in all perishable beings, sees truly. Indeed, beholding the Lord equally existing everywhere, one does not injure the Ātmā by the self and thus attains the supreme goal. He who sees, on all sides, actions are solely done by Prakṛti and the Ātmā, as a non-doer, sees the Truth. When one perceives a diverse variety of beings existent in one Supreme Being and from Whom plurality is spreading, he becomes the Brahman. Hey Kaunteya! Though existent in the body, the beginningless, attributeless, and imperishable Supreme Being neither acts nor is stained. Hey Bhārata! Just as the one sun illuminates this entire world, so does the field's Owner illuminates the whole field (BG 13.23 - BG 13.33).

Here, the sameness of the field-knower, the Ātmā, the Puruṣa, and the Paramātmā is articulated. The enunciated place and the direction a seeker needs to reach were also provided. In the end, Bhagavāna said that those persons who, with their eyes of knowledge, separate the mixture of the field and the field-knower through Haṃsa-Vṛtti[53]with Kṣīra-Nīra-Viveka[54]and separate their Ātmā from the bondage of Prakṛti, they attain the supreme Status (BG 13.34).

Based on the critique of this chapter, Variant-Yoga's duty-bound intellect is neither established as a direct means for knowledge nor for a knower having attained knowledge duty in Karma activity is found. On the contrary, excluding this Variant-Yoga amongst the real means of knowledge, it can be inferred that after purity of the conscience, Bhagavāna has hinted at avoiding it. If it was agreeable as a direct means of knowledge, there is no reason why Bhagavāna would not have provided even a small clue? But at the end of the chapter, separating one's Ātmā from the duty born of Prakṛti is the only real perspective articulated. It is only on this that liberation is dependent.

The Yoga of the Threefold Constituents - Chapter 14

In the thirteenth chapter, Bhagavāna articulated His unmanifest-form, knowledge of the Puruṣa and the field-knower (Kṣetrajña), and instructed to separate the combination of the field and the field-knower through the eyes of knowledge. In this chapter, Bhagavāna describes how to determine the absence of Prakṛti and its constituents at all times and says, "Again, I shall state the highest and the best knowledge among all forms of knowledge, mastering which all sages after leaving the body have attained the supreme perfection. Resorting to this knowledge, those who have attained My form are not born at the time of the manifestation of the world and are not distressed at the time of its dissolution. My womb is the Mahat-Brahma, wherein I place My conscious seed. Thence, the creation of all beings materializes. Whatever forms arise from all kinds of wombs, their womb is the great Brahman. I am the father, provider of the seed." Whatever beings are born in the four wombs: 1) sweat-born (स्वेद-जा, Sveda-Jā), 2) germination-born (उद्भिज-जा, Udbhija-Jā), 3) egg-born (अण्ड-जा, Aṇḍa-Jā) and 4) placenta-born (जरायु-जा, Jarāyu-Jā), the womb that holds the embryo is the Tri-constituted Prakṛti, and I am the impregnating father. The intention here is that separate from Me, Prakṛti does not have any reality. It is without any reality of its own. Only holding My conscious seed, it creates all beings. Born of Prakṛti are the three constituents Sattva, Rajas, and Tamas, who, with their conjunction, bind the imperishable Jīvātmā, the Kṣetrajña, the Puruṣa, or the Ātmā in the body. Sattvaguṇa being the purest, is illuminating and healing. It binds with attachment to pleasure and knowledge. Rajoguṇa is in the form of deep desire that creates thirst and passion. It binds the Jīvātmā with attachment to action. Tamoguṇa is born of ignorance. It deludes all beings and binds them with negligence, laziness, and sleep.

[53] Haṃsa-Vṛtti (हंस-वृत्ति) means best welfare attitude towards all. Haṃsa (हंस) means a swan. It is said that a swan has the ability of drinking milk from a mixture of milk and water by separating milk and discarding water. That is, changing bad attitude to good attitude, even after hearing or seeing bad thing about anyone.

[54] Kṣīra-Nīra-Viveka (क्षीर-नीर-विवेक) means a wisdom that provides complete and clear distinction between real and unreal, good and bad. It is said that a swan is endowed with such a wisdom, he can drink Kṣīra (क्षीर, milk) from a mixture of milk and water leaving behind Nīra (नीर, water).

Sattvaguṇa unites in pleasure, Rajoguṇa in action and shrouding knowledge Tamoguṇa unites in negligence (BG 14.1 - BG 14.10).

This way, the nature and characteristics of the three constituents were enunciated by Bhagavāna. Then, with the conjunction of the constituents, the destination in the world and form of existence attained by a Jīvātmā at the time of death were described. Additionally, whatever Karma and fruits happen with the conjunction of the constituents during the lifetime were described. Then, Bhagavāna said, "Know that for a Jīvātmā, birth and death, inferior and superior destination, Karma and its fruits of pleasure and pain, whatever is acquired, in its root as the cause are the constituents only." When a Jīvātmā knows in Truth, "Only the constituents are the doers and the enjoyers, I am not doing anything, but I am beyond the constituents without attachment and untainted," such a knower, free from the three constituents that are the cause of the creation of the body, enjoys the Paramānanda, free from birth, death, old age and disease (BG 4.12 - BG 14.20).

Here one needs to think that a great being who has known himself dissociated, non-doer, and in the form of a witness of the constituents, and thus the work of the constituents (which is the body), how can duty bind him as some have deemed? It is only due to the association of the constituents and the body that there is an imagination of duty with delusional ignorance. If he sees duty in himself, he is not beyond the constituents (Guṇātīta) and is neither free from the body nor free from birth, death, old age, and disease. In reality, a great being beyond the constituents due to his disassociation is free from all duties. Whatever natural Karma (without any duty) is happening through the body, he is not their doer but just an observer.

On this, Arjuna asked, "Hey Lord! What are the characteristics of those who have transcended the three constituents? How do they behave? How do they go beyond the three constituents? (BG 14.21). In response, Bhagavāna said, "With Sattvaguṇa enlightenment, Rajoguṇa activity, and Tamoguṇa delusion is produced. One who is beyond the constituents does not hate the constituents that are active and does not desire the constituents that are absent. Seated indifferent, one is not disturbed by the constituents, one does not waver knowing the constituents are only active." Because of his disassociation, such a person remains equal in the transformations of the constituents, viz., pleasure and pain, pleasant and unpleasant, gold and stone, censure and praise, honor and dishonor, and meeting friends and foes. With his resolve, "The body, senses, mind, and intellect are acting in their duties, and I am separate from them a non-doer and thus an observer," he has abandoned all Karma. Even while perceived as a doer, he is a non-doer. A person who is the same in honor and disgrace, equal towards friends and foes, and does not initiate any actions is called a Guṇātīta" (BG 14.22 - BG 14.25).

Bhagavāna, thus, articulated the self-experienced attributes of a Guṇātīta great being and showed that "One who with unwavering devotional Yoga worships Me, transcending the constituents, becomes fit to be like Brahman. Indeed, I am the substrate of the Brahman, the Immortal, the Imperishable, the eternal Righteousness, and the pure Bliss" (BG 14.26 - BG 14.27).

Accordingly, based on the words of Bhagavāna, the only approach for freedom from the bondage of the constituents and its transformations, viz., birth and death, pleasure and pain, and the body, is shown as "the Yoga of establishing with oneness in the Ātmā through knowledge," and unwavering devotion is articulated as the direct means for knowledge. Niṣkāma-Karma with duty-bound intellect is neither accepted as a means to attain the attribute of being beyond the constituents nor is it found in the characteristics of a great being beyond the constituents. Accordingly, in the critique of this chapter, Variant-Yoga does not meet the requisite test of the chapter.

The Yoga of the Supreme Personality - Chapter 15

One can infer a cause by seeing an activity; like seeing smoke on a mountain, one can infer the presence of fire. In the same way, with the sight of the Saṃsāra, knowledge of the causal Supreme Being is provided by Bhagavāna in this chapter with His words - This Saṃsāra is like a fig tree. Unlike other trees, its roots go upwards (ऊर्ध्वमूल, Ūrdhva-Mūla) and not downwards (अधःमूल, Adhaḥ-Mūla). Paramātmā, who is the root (मूल, Mūla), is subtler than the subtle (सूक्ष्माति-सूक्ष्म, Sūkṣmāti-Sūkṣma) and omnipresent (सर्व-व्यापी, Sarva-Vyāpī) and thus beyond the best (परात्पर, Parātpara). That is why the Saṃsāra-tree is called with roots upwards.

The Saṃsāra-tree is not stable, yet ignorant persons call it imperishable. Just as the beauty of a tree is in its leaves, the beauty of this Saṃsāra-tree is in the leaf-form Vedas. They provide the location of the root, the peaceful and supreme bliss Paramānanda. One who knows this tree "is as is" has found its roots. He is the knower of the Vedas. Nourished by the three constituents and the buds in the form of sense objects, viz., touch, taste, and others, the fully grown branches of this tree are spread all over up and down, and in the human life-form, its roots have gone extensively deep down by Karma. The seed of the Saṃsāra is Karma only, and Karma done in the human species puts a Jīva in bondage. However, if one contemplates, its form is not perceived as seen through gross vision. On the contrary, it has no creation, destruction, or sustentation, only like a dream, it has come out illusory. Firmly rooted, nourished by Karma, this Aśvattha (अश्वत्थ, fig) tree ought to be cut by a strong weapon of detachment, and one ought to properly seek that Status, acquiring which there is no birth and death again. In addition, one ought to take refuge in that primeval Supreme Personality alone, whence this eternal activity has emanated (BG 15.1 - BG 15.4).

Here Bhagavāna has made it clear -

1. This Saṃsāra-tree called imperishable is ephemeral and illusory,
2. Karma in human life is the seed of the Saṃsāra. There are no fruits of Karma in other life-forms, Only Karma by humans provide fruits, and for their enjoyment, they create the Saṃsāra of birth and death. Again, Karma of a Jīva is unending, and indeed with those Karma, the root of the Saṃsāra has become firm, and whose branches of enjoyment are spreading up-down and all over in the life-forms of deities, humans, animals, birds, and others,
3. Karma is only due to ignorance. Whatever is happening through ignorance is indeed illusory, and so if one sees with a vision of wisdom, there is no taint of Karma in the Ātmā, just as activities in a dream have no impact in the awake state. With the vision of wisdom, the Saṃsāra born of Karma has no creation, sustentation, and destruction in the Ātmā. Such a form of the Saṃsāra was thus depicted,
4. Karma, done with attachment, "I am a doer of Karma," makes the Saṃsāra-tree firmly rooted. Then to cut its roots, a strong weapon of detachment is needed. Desireless actions with duty-bound intellect are blunt in cutting its roots, and as such, it cannot be even called a weapon of detachment because it makes the doership delusion (the root of the Saṃsāra) firmer.
5. Cutting the roots (Karma) of the Saṃsāra-tree by the weapon of detachment, one ought to seek that real supreme Status, the Brahman, in whose refuge the Saṃsāra is perceived as real even though it is not real, and by Whom this beginningless activity is spread, and in Whom there is no taint of it. Bhagavāna has clearly shown that one can only be free from the cycle of birth and death by attaining that supreme Status.

Next, Bhagavāna describes the nature of the weapon of detachment by which the roots (Karma) of the Saṃsāra-tree can be cut, and the search for that supreme Status can be done. Free from vanity and delusion, having overcome the flaws of attachment, ever searching the Ātmā, free from lust, liberated from dualities like pleasure and pain, such undeluded (sages) attain the imperishable Status (BG 15.5).

With the formulation of the "detachment weapon," articulating fitness for the nature of knowledge, Bhagavāna describes His true nature, "The sun does not illuminate it, neither the moon nor the fire. Gone where one does not return, that is My supreme Abode. My eternal part alone, becoming a Jīva in the Saṃsāra, attracts senses with the mind as the sixth situated in Prakṛti. When a Jīva leaves the body and acquires a second body, grasping the six senses takes them to a new body, like fragrance by the wind from flowers. The deluded do not see a Jīva leaving, staying, or experiencing through association with the constituents. Only the one with the eyes of wisdom perceives." In the body, sustentation of the senses, their enjoyment, conjunction with the constituents, and leaving the body, whatever activities manifest, they all happen because of the power of the Jīva. However, the Jīva is unattached and only their observer. He is limitless without their limitations. He appears limited only because of their adjuncts and remains untainted by them. Such was the oneness between a Jīva and the Paramātmā depicted. Then Bhagavāna said, "My brilliance is not only in the body, but the luminosity in the sun which illuminates the entire world, the brilliance which is in the moon and the fire, know them to be Mine alone. Entering into the earth, I sustain all beings with My power. Becoming moon, I nourish all medicinal herbs and plants with My sapidity. Becoming the fire of digestion and residing in the body of living beings, together with inhalation and exhalation, I digest fourfold foods. Situated in the heart of all, I enlighten memory, knowledge, and forgetfulness. Through all Vedas, I alone am to be known. I am the knower of the Vedas and the cause of Vedānta" (BG 15.6 - BG 15.15).

Accordingly, from verse BG 15.12 up to here, both far and near, Bhagavāna described his pervasiveness and being the Ātmā of all and said, "In the world, there are two persons (groups of adjuncts), the perishable and the imperishable. All beings are said to be perishable, and the imperishable is Māyā. Distinct from these is the Supreme Personality, said to be the Paramātmā. Entering the three worlds, the imperishable Lord sustains all. Since I surpass the perishable and am exalted above the imperishable, both in common speech and in the Vedas, I am celebrated as the Puruṣottama. The undeluded who knows Me the Puruṣottama thus, he the all-knowing adores Me in all sentiments, sees Me in all activities." In the end, Bhagavāna said, "Thus, this most profound Śāstra is spoken by Me. Hey descendent of Bharata! Knowing it, one becomes wise and contented." Liberation in the form of contentment is dependent directly on experiencing this knowledge. Without it, attaining contentment is impossible through actions only and is like a flower in the sky (BG 15.19 - BG 15.20).

From the critique of this chapter, it is thus clear that, for attaining the Paramātmā and freedom from the Saṃsāra of birth and death, knowledge is the only means and that, as articulated in verse BG 15.5, can only be attained by abandoning vanity, delusion, attachment, and thus dualities such as desire and by moving towards the Ātmā. Karma is not useful by any means. On the contrary, it is the one that makes the root of the Saṃsāra firmer.

The Yoga of the Attributes - Divine and Demonic - Chapter 16

The knowledge of Gītā is complete in the fifteenth chapter, and no additional knowledge remains. In this chapter, the accumulation of helpful divine attributes (दैवी-सम्पत्ति, Daivī-Sampatti) and the abandonment of detrimental demonic attributes (आसुरी-सम्पत्ति, Āsurī-Sampatti) is articulated in attaining the heretofore-articulated knowledge.

First, the divine attributes were described in the verses (BG 16.1 - BG 16.3), "Fearlessness, mental purity, uniquely establishing in knowledge and Yoga, charity, restraint of senses, the performance of sacrifices, self-study of the scriptures, austerity, simplicity, non-violence, truthfulness, absence of anger, renunciation, tranquility, absence of fault-finding, kindness towards living beings, uncovetousness, gentleness, shyness, steadiness, splendor, forgiveness, fortitude, cleanliness, benevolence and humility, hey Arjuna! These are of those born with divine attributes."

Attributes ordinarily found in a person born with demonic attributes are hypocrisy, arrogance, excessive vanity, anger, harshness, and ignorance. Then, it is shown that divine attributes are deemed for liberation and demonic attributes for bondage (BG 16.4 - BG 16.5). After that, Bhagavāna extensively described demonic attributes and said, "Those who are hateful, cruel, impious, and vile humans, I repeatedly cast down in the Saṃsāra in demonic wombs only. The deluded, having acquired demonic wombs birth after birth, not attaining Me, go to lower than that lowest state indeed (BG 16.6 - BG 16.20).

Bhagavāna then described threefold gates of hell - lust, anger, and greed, the destroyers of own Ātmā and said, "Released from these three doors of darkness, a person who conducts for his good attains the supreme goal. Discarding scriptural injunctions who behaves in own licentious arbitrary way he attains neither perfection nor happiness or the supreme goal." In the end, Bhagavāna said, "Therefore, Śāstra shall be your guide regarding what should or should not be done. Knowing said injunctions of Śāstra, you ought to perform it here (BG 16.21 - BG 16.24).

In this chapter, Bhagavāna articulated divine attributes that are helpful and demonic attributes that are detrimental to knowledge and commanded activity in virtuous conduct for the accumulation of divine attributes. In virtuous behavior, what is a duty? What is a misdeed? Here, Śāstra is shown as a measure for such determination. Karma is neither voiced as a direct cause in liberation nor duty of Karma is imposed on a knower. Variant-Yoga is not even considered in the accumulation of divine attributes. In contrast, the Yoga of Knowledge and Relinquishment is shown as a significant component in the accumulation of divine attributes. Only through bodily, material, and mental relinquishments can all limbs of divine attributes be acquired.

The Yoga of the Threefold Faith - Chapter 17

At the end of the sixteenth chapter, Bhagavāna, in the cause of accumulation of divine attributes, commanded to do Karma following the procedures of the scriptures. At the beginning of this chapter, Arjuna asked, "Hey Śrī Kṛṣṇa! Abandoning scriptural procedures, those who worship only with faith, what is their status - Sāttvika (the cause of goodness, purity, and virtuosity), Rājasika (the cause of activity, fickleness, and agitation), or Tāmasika (the cause of the sixfold mutations viz. lust, anger, greed, delusion, excessive pride and envy)? (BG 17.1). In response, Bhagavāna said, "Indeed, threefold is the faith of embodied beings according to past impressions - Sāttvika, Rājasika, and Tāmasika. Listen to those classifications." Prakṛti is constituted of the three constituents, and all embodied are created from Prakṛti. Whatever constituent is dominant in the conscience, correspondent to the extent of that dominance, one's faith is. That is because faith is an attribute of the conscience (Antaḥkaraṇa) and is dependent on the good and bad impressions of previous lives. To whatever extent the conscience is endowed with impressions, in accordance with that extent, a person is endowed with faith, and thus his natural sentiments. Further, in accordance with that faith and sentiments, he acquires the body, class, and family. That is why this transmigratory life is largely dependent on the faith of individuals. All humans are endowed with some form of faith, and they are as their faith is. Their nature is like their faith. According to this rule, persons with the Sāttvika faith worship deities, those with the Rājasika faith worship semi-deities and evil demons, and persons with the Tāmasika faith worship evil spirits and ghosts. Those who perform stern austerities not ordained by the scriptures but with hypocrisy and egotism, and who by the force of lust and attachment torture organs of the body and Me situated in the conscience, know those ignorant persons to be with demonic resolve. Because there are no fruits where procedures of Śāstra are absent, there is only an increase in self-ego (BG 17.2 - BG 17.6).

This way, conduct contrary to the procedures of Śāstra is criticized, and describing three kinds of faith, Bhagavāna said, "Food dear to all is of three kinds and so is sacrifice, austerity, and charity." Accordingly, commensurate with the Tri-constituted faith, three kinds of food, viz., Sāttvika, Rājasika, and Tāmasika, are described in the verses (BG 17.8 - BG 17.10), and three kinds of sacrifices are described in the verses (BG 17.11 - BG 17.13). Dividing the austerities into three by bodily, verbal, and mental distinctions, threefold attributes are described in the verses based on the threefold constituents (BG 17.14 - BG 17.19). Threefold charities are provided in the verses (BG 17.20 - BG 17.22). After that, providing the essence of the procedures of Śāstra said that with the designation of the threefold syllables "ॐ तत् सत्, Oṃ Tat Sat," the nature of the Brahman, free of Māyā, can be pointed out. Even though the Brahman is without name form, with these threefold syllables, the designation of the Brahman is made for the initiation of the sentiments of a devotee. That is why at the beginning of the creation, Brāhmaṇa (Adhyātma), Veda (Adhideva), and Yajña (Adhibhūta) were created with this name indication. Thus, a knower of the Vedas, when he initiates acts of sacrifice, charity, and austerity enumerated in the Vedas, always commences with the utterance of "ॐ Oṃ" - the designation of the Paramātmā. Abandoning desires, a person seeking liberation performs various acts of sacrifice, charity, and austerity with the name-indication of "तत्, Tat." In true good sentiments, the name "सत्, Sat" is enjoined, and thus in praiseworthy acts, the name "सत्, Sat" is also used. Sustentation of humans in sacrifice, charity, and austerity is called "सत्, Sat." Additionally, Karma as an offering to the Lord is called "सत्, Sat." That is, all activities that have a relationship with the "सत्, Sat" Paramātmā are all called "सत्, Sat" because they are the ones that take a doer towards the Reality (BG 17.23 - BG 17.27).

This way, the Brahman free from Māyā is defined with threefold syllables "ॐ तत् सत्, Oṃ Tat Sat." The activities of sacrifice, charity, and austerity with the sentiment of offering to the Brahman with the application of the threefold syllables have indeed been called the essence of Śāstra procedures. In the end, Bhagavāna said that without faith, without Sāttvika faith, whatever sacrifice, charity, and austerity are performed, or whatever Karma is done, being non-conforming with Śāstra are all "असत्, Asat" and has no fruit here in this world or other worlds (BG 17.28).

In this chapter, in response to the query of Arjuna, Bhagavāna described the nature and fruits of austerity and penance not conforming with Śāstra and spoke about the nature, distinction, and fruits of the threefold faiths. Bhagavāna articulating the nature and essence of Śāstra procedures useful in the divine attributes and disparaging faithless and non-conforming austerity, penance ended the chapter.

Niṣkāma-Karma is the direct means for liberation, or after knowledge, there is a duty of Karma - such postulations are not found in any place in this chapter. Though desireless sacrifice, charity, and austerity are described in this chapter, their direct fruit is only the accumulation of divine attributes observing Śāstra procedures and not liberation, as is evident by the congruity of verses in chapters sixteen and seventeen.

The Yoga of Liberation and Renunciation - Chapter 18

The entire science of Śrīmad Bhagavad Gītā is provided in this chapter, and so it is indeed an epilogue. Listening to the discussion on renunciation (संन्यास, Saṃnyāsa) and relinquishment (Tyāga) at various locations in previous chapters, and knowing renunciation and relinquishment as the core subject, Arjuna asked Bhagavāna the last question, "Hey Mahābāho! I would like to know the distinction between renunciation and relinquishment separately" (BG 18.1). Responding, Bhagavāna said that on this subject, there are distinctly separate opinions -

1. Some wise say relinquishment (Tyāga) of Karma prompted by desire is "renunciation, Saṃnyāsa."
2. Many thoughtfully competent declare not abandoning Karma but forsaking all fruits of Karma as "relinquishment, Tyāga."
3. Some intellectuals declare Karma has flaws. Therefore, all Karma ought to be relinquished.
4. Others declare that acts of sacrifice, charity, and austerity should not be relinquished (BG 18.2 - 18.3).

Then Bhagavāna said, "Hear My opinion on the subject of relinquishment. Relinquishment is declared to be of three kinds." The meanings of the words Tyāga (relinquishment) and Saṃnyāsa (renunciation) are identical. That is why the response is given only in terms of Tyāga (relinquishment). Bhagavāna has used these two words as synonyms throughout His Upadeśa. "Acts of sacrifice, charity, and austerity should not be relinquished but should certainly be performed. Sacrifice, charity, and austerity indeed purify wise men. However, even these activities should be performed without attachment and expectation of rewards. Hey Arjuna! That is My firm and most valid opinion. To renounce obligatory acts is not proper. Their renunciation due to ignorance is said to be Tāmasika. Due to fear of bodily distress, if actions are relinquished as painful, such relinquishment is Rājasika. A reward does not accrue by performing such relinquishment. Ordained acts (Niyata-Karma) performed as ought to be done, giving up attachment and fruit, such relinquishment is deemed Sāttvika (BG 18.4 - BG 18.9).

Addressing the views of those who consider the relinquishment of desirable Karma as Saṃnyāsa, or the relinquishment of all Karma as Tyāga, believing all Karma by their nature are with flaws, it is the definite view of Bhagavāna that ordained acts (Niyata-Karma) performed with duty-bound intellect, as ought to be done giving up attachment and fruit, such relinquishment is deemed Sāttvika. Contrary to this, abandoning Karma due to fear of distress to the body or abandoning them, thinking them to be worthless, is not real relinquishment. But such relinquishment is only Rājasika or Tāmasika, and that relinquishment does not have any fruit. Since the fruit of a Sāttvika relinquishment is the purity of the conscience, without it, just abandoning Karma is like leaving dirty garments without using soap. In such a state, how can anyone dye the garment with color? Indeed, without staining with the color of knowledge on the attire of the conscience, there is no success. That is why Bhagavāna has disregarded Rājasika and Tāmasika relinquishments and has respected Sāttvika relinquishment. However, He is not satisfied with only this and immediately directs His focus in the following two verses. He says, "Hey Bhārata! One who has transcended the body and is established with oneness in the Paramātmā and all of whose 'I am a doer, and duty' doubts gone, such an intelligent knower of the Truth neither hates unmeritorious Karma nor is attached to meritorious Karma." He has a sight that sees only one Ātmā in all beings (सर्वात्म-द्रष्टि, Sarvātma-Dṛṣṭi), his sight of discriminating between good and evil has gone, and he is an all-relinquisher (सर्व-त्यागी, Sarva-Tyāgi) (BG 18.10). However, for one who has I-ness in the body, one who has superimposed the body on the Ātmā and in whom doership and duty-bound intellect are present, for such an embodied being, it is impossible to abandon all Karma completely. For the one who considers his body as the Ātmā, first, complete relinquishment of Karma cannot happen. Ego remaining, even if there is a relinquishment of activities of the body and senses, the activity of the mind continues, which will have its fruits. Second, with desireless actions, the conscience that needs to be pure remains deprived. The I-ness ego in the body remaining, one who is a relinquisher of the fruits of action should be deemed as a relinquisher, Tyāgi (BG 18.11). There are three kinds of fruits - bad, good, and mixed for those who are not all-relinquishers, who are not free from doership and duty. The bad fruit of Karma is hell and the acquisition of birth in the wombs of animals, birds, or insects. The good fruit of Karma is the acquisition of birth in the wombs of deities. The fruit of mixed Karma is birth in the human womb. However, there is never any fruit for those all-relinquishing Saṃnyāsī who have transcended the body and, through the realization of the Truth, are free from doership and duty (BG 18.12).

Further, Bhagavāna showed that with the body, mind, or speech, whatever injunctive and prohibitive Karma a person initiates, there are five causes of success enunciated by the tenets of Vedānta -

1. Adhiṣṭhāna (अधिष्ठान, ground) - The body that is the support for the appearance of desire, knowledge, and actions.
2. Kartā (कर्ता, doer) - The delimited Ātmā who is a doer-enjoyer with an I-ness sense in the body. The delimited Ātmā, Jīva, Jīvātmā, and Soul are synonyms.
3. Karaṇa (करण, instrument) - Various kinds of instruments through which actions are performed, such as A) the five cognitive senses (पञ्च-ज्ञानेन्द्रिय, Pañca-Jñānendriya): 1) skin (त्वक, Tvaka), 2) tongue (रसना, Rasanā), 3) eyes (चक्षु, Cakṣu), 4) nose (घ्राण, Ghrāṇa) and 5) ears (श्रोत्र, Śrotra), B) the five action faculties (पञ्च-कर्मेन्द्रिय, Pañca-Karmendriya): 1) mouth (वाक, Vāka) with the faculty of voice, 2) hands (पाणि, Pāṇi) with the faculty of grasping (Grahaṇa) and holding (Dhāraṇa), 3) feet (पाद, Pāda) with the faculty of locomotion (Gamana), 4) anus (पायु, Pāyu) with the faculty of excretion and 5) genitals (उपस्थ, Upastha) with the faculty of reproduction, C) the mind and D) the intellect.
4. Ceṣṭā (चेष्टा, effort) - The manifold distinct efforts of the Prāṇa (प्राण) such as in-breath and out-breath through which activities in the senses, mind, and intellect happen.
5. Daiva (दैव, the presiding deity) - Various presiding deities that control the mind and senses. The Adhideva (अधिदेव) of eyes is the sun-deity, the Adhideva of ears is the directions, and so on. The power of these presiding deities is known as Adhidaiva-Śakti (अधिदैव-शक्ति). The intention is that senses grasp their objects with the grace of these deities.

Whatever Karma a human does with his body, mind, and speech, whether just or unjust, there can be only these five causes in their execution (BG 18.13 - BG 18.15). Despite the five direct causes, because of imperfect intellect, a human only sees his Ātmā as a doer, and that feeble-minded is not the one who sees the Truth. In reality, the doer of Karma is those five causes above, but due to ignorance, he believes own Ātmā as a doer. The ignorance, "I am a doer," is the bondage for a Jīva. Opposite of this, through the knowledge of the Truth, by becoming established in own witness-conscious Ātmā, one whose "I am a doer" sentiment has gone, and whose intellect is not tainted by doership-sentiment, such a person even killing the entire Saṃsāra is not killing anyone and does not remain in the bondage of Karma. As his I-ness sense in the five direct causes of Karma is removed, and now he is not the doer of their acts, but established in his own witness-conscious, he is now just an observer of those acts. It is axiomatic that a seer-observer of a show is not responsible for the actions of others that he observes. Indeed, the one responsible is the one who is the doer (BG 18.16 - BG 18.17).

It is thus clear from the above words of Bhagavāna as is spoken in the verse BG 18.12 that, from the threefold fruits of Karma viz. bad, good, and mixed, only this seer-witness is free. He is an all-relinquisher, and he is a renouncer, a Saṃnyāsī. With the influence of the realization of the Truth, even though he appears as doing everything through his body, he is not doing anything. He is a non-doer. Contrary to this, that Sāttvika-relinquisher, as said in verse BG 18.9, is active in Karma through the duty-bound intellect and is the doer of relinquishment of the fruits of Karma, is neither an all-relinquisher nor can he be free from the threefold fruits. Though he is free from bad and mixed fruits, he is indeed a partner in good fruits.

Bhagavāna providing various views regarding Tyāga (relinquishment) and Saṃnyāsa (renunciation), disregarded views of those who deem relinquishment of all Karma as Saṃnyāsa or those who deem relinquishment of desire-ridden Karma as Saṃnyāsa. Among the two, one engaged in Karma with duty-bound intellect but abandoning attachment and fruits is depicted as a Sāttvika-relinquisher. Even greater respect is provided to those transcendent sages (Guṇātīta) who transcend the constituents, are free from doership-sentiment, and only engage in Karma as observers. Whether accumulated or current, they are free from all bondages of Karma and are deemed real Saṃnyāsī by Bhagavāna. That is indeed Karma-Saṃnyāsa.

In addition, Bhagavāna showed that the knower, knowledge, and knowable (to be known) are impellers of Karma. With the relationship between these three, the desire for activity in Karma is born. With the relationship of a doer, act, and means, Karma is created. So, these three are the collective accessories of Karma (BG 18.18). Then, from distinctions of the constituents, Bhagavāna articulated three kinds of knowledge in the verses (BG 18.20 - BG 18.22), threefold Karma in the verses (BG 18.23 - BG 18.25), and threefold doers in the verses (BG 18.26 - BG 18.28). Then, separately from the triple distinctions of the constituents, intellect, and resolve in the verses (BG 18.29 - BG 18.35), threefold pleasure in the verses (BG 18.36 - BG 18.39) are described and showed that when the entire Saṃsāra is the transformation of Prakṛti, there cannot be anything sentient or insentient on the earth, heavens, and deities that can be without these three constituents. With threefold distinctions, duties, and activities of Brāhmaṇa, Kṣatriya, Vaiśya, and Śūdra are described in the verses (BG 18.40 - BG 18.44).

After that, Bhagavāna stated that a person based on fitness could attain purity of the conscience through the worship of the Paramātmā in the form of desireless actions. Worship of the Paramātmā from Whom all beings have proceeded and by Whom everything pervaded. Bhagavāna indicated that compared to a correctly performed duty of others, own duty, even defective is better. Because, by engaging in Karma based on own intrinsic nature, one does not incur sin. Even if natural Karma is with flaws, it should not be abandoned. All Karma is with flaws, just as fire is with the flaw of smoke. Though, with the removal of smoke, a non-smoke fire can be obtained; obtaining a non-smoke fire is not possible in the absence of smoke. In the same way, by natural Karma, the conscience with flaws can be made without defects, just as a pus-filled boil can be made disease-free by removing pus.

Similarly, by natural Karma, the conscience can be made pure by removing the Rajoguṇī-pus from the conscience. A person putting natural Karma in his conduct, with desireless Karma making his conscience pure, freeing himself from all attachments and desires and subduing his mind through renunciation of doership, attains the supreme perfection of Naiṣkarmya - that is, actionlessness or freedom from reaction (BG 18.45 - BG 18.49). The intention here is that a Jīva who is moving in the flow of Prakṛti, at least by putting innate flawed Karma in his conduct, step by step uplifting himself, free from attachment, subduing his mind and senses, free from doership-sentiment and establishing with oneness in the witness-conscious Ātmā attains Naiṣkarmya perfection. Once he reaches that state, even though he may be doing everything yet, he remains a non-doer.

Further, Bhagavāna said, "Hey Arjuna, Know from Me briefly how having acquired fitness, one attains the Brahman - the supreme consummation of knowledge."

A tranquil-minded person who -

- is united with a dispassionately pure intellect,
- has controlled his mind with resolve,
- has abandoned sound and other objects,
- has destroyed attachment and aversion,
- dwells lonely,
- eats lightly,
- controls the body, mind, and speech,
- is ever engaged in meditation-Yoga,
- resorts to dispassion,
- has relinquished egoism, force, arrogance, lust, anger, and accumulation of possessions,

such a person who is tranquil and without mineness is fit for the status of the Brahman. "Becoming the Brahman, a tranquil-minded person neither grieves nor desires. With equanimity towards all beings, he gains supreme devotion unto Me - I Who am existent in all beings equally, like water in waves. By that devotion, he comprehends Me in truth as to what My extent is and Who I am. Then knowing Me in truth, he immediately enters into Me. Though always performing all actions, being in My refuge, he attains eternal immutable Status by My grace. That is why, hey, Dhanañjaya! Taking support of Jñāna-Yoga, mentally surrendering all actions to Me, having oriented towards Me, always be one with your mind on Me." Be with the resolve, "I am neither the body, senses, mind, and intellect nor the doer of their activities. I am only the witness-observer of their activities." This way, "With your mind fixed on Me; you will overcome all obstacles by My grace. But, if due to ego, you do not listen to My words, then you will perish." As long as separation from the Lord and doership and duty exist, all obstacles continue with him until then. However, through the knowledge of the Truth by attaining a oneness position in the Lord and becoming free from the bondage of doership and duty, there is "the end" of all obstacles (BG 18.50 - BG 18.58). Again, Bhagavāna said, "Resorting to ego if you think that 'I will not fight,' your decision is erroneous. Your nature will force you to engage. By delusion what you do not desire to do, bound by your natural activities, you will helplessly do" (BG 18.59 - BG 18.60). The intention here is that since one's innate attributes are so mighty that it is impossible to navigate against the flow of one's nature, and any insistence on doing so is nothing but delusional ego. Therefore, a person's duty is to abandon all efforts contrary to nature, engage in activities according to one's nature, become established in own witness-conscious form through the realization of the Truth, and separate own Ātmā from own nature. Accordingly, one ought to become free from the bondage of Prakṛti, just like diverting a river's flow to construct a dam on the river and thereby have control over it. By following one's nature, a person, through the realization of the Truth by separating his Ātmā from his nature, can assert control over nature and become independent from nature. By this rule, "Hey Arjuna! The Lord is seated in the heart of all beings and, having mounted on a machine in the form of Māyā, moves around all beings by His power. Himself, not doing anything, only by His nearness, moves around all beings bound by Māyā based on their Karma. That is why, hey Bhārata! With all sentiments, surrender unto His refuge alone. By His grace, you will attain supreme peace and eternal Status. Only by attaining oneness in Him, with His grace, you can acquire supreme peace and thus the eternal Status" (BG 18.61 - BG 18.62). Then Bhagavāna said, "This way, the most profound of the profound knowledge is imparted by Me to you. Again, listen to My extremely profound supreme words. Because you are very dear to Me, I will say what is good for you. Your mind should leave the thinking mode and become one in Me; from that objective, you should be My devotee. Through knowledge, only worship Me, and only pay obeisance unto Me. This way, losing yourself, you will attain only Me, and this, I am making a true promise to you. That is why giving up all duties, seek refuge in Me alone. Grieve not; I shall free you from all sins." Again, the root of all sins is doership delusion. With the amnesia of own true witness-conscious form, when a Jīva comes into the bondage of the body, then holding duty becomes a doer of their activities, and for the enjoyment of fruits of those Karma has to come in the bondage of the body. However, with the realization of the Truth, becoming established with oneness in the Ātmā, when he separates himself "is as is" from the body, and becoming free from doership-sentiment becomes just a witness-observer of the activities of the body, then just like a person awake from a dream he becomes immediately free from all sins. That is the propounded subject of Gītā, and it is only here that there is a harmonious connection between knowledge and Karma (BG 18.63 - BG 18.66). In addition, in the verses (BG 18.67 - BG 18.71), Bhagavāna articulated the magnanimity of Gītā and asked Arjuna, "Hey Arjuna, the conqueror of wealth! Have you heard this with a concentrated mind? Has your confusion, born of ignorance, been destroyed?" On this, Arjuna replied, "Hey, Śrī Kṛṣṇa, the infallible one! With Your grace, my confusion is dispelled, and I have regained memory. Being free from doubts, I shall obey Your command." After that, Sañjaya described to King Dhṛtarāṣṭra the glory of the dialogue between Śrī Kṛṣṇa and Arjuna and the amazement of the Cosmic Form of Bhagavāna ended Gītā (BG 18.72 - BG 18.77).

In this chapter, upon the question of Arjuna, "I would like to know the distinction between Tyāga (relinquishment) and Saṃnyāsa (renunciation) separately, Bhagavāna holding oneness between Tyāga and Saṃnyāsa articulated different opinions on the subject of Saṃnyāsa. In whose opinion Saṃnyāsa is a relinquishment of desire-ridden Karma, or in the opinion of others that by nature relinquishment of all Karma is Saṃnyāsa, Bhagavāna disregarding them, called that relinquishment as Sāttvika and excellent by which ordained (Niyata) Karma with duty-bound intellect can be put into one's conduct, and attachment to fruits can be abandoned. However, the best relinquishment that is agreeable to Bhagavāna is, through the realization of the Truth, the burning of doership-ego in the five means of Karma (as detailed in verse BG 18.14) and establishing with oneness in own witness-conscious Ātmā and remaining only as an observer of the five means. Accordingly, becoming free from doership-attachment, and engaging in those intrinsic natural Karma, is the best relinquishment acceptable to Bhagavāna. After that, based on distinctions of the three constituents - knowledge, Karma, doer, intellect, resolve, pleasure, and distinctions of the four functional classes of the society (Catura-Varṇa) were articulated. Bhagavāna then said humans should not abandon their righteousness but engage in natural Karma. With the purity of the conscience, attain that supreme Naiṣkarmya perfection. Acquiring the supreme consummation of knowledge, attain the supreme devotion of Bhagavāna. By that supreme devotion, knowing Bhagavāna with oneness in His true nature is achieved. Then such a person even doing all kinds of Karma attains that eternal imperishable Status and his Sarva-Karma-Saṃnyāsa is ipso facto successful.

Variant-Yoga (with duty and without fruits) is the propounded subject of Gītā, Variant-Yoga is the direct means for liberation, or there is a duty of Karma on a knower - none of that is established in the critique of this chapter.

EPILOGUE

Some who embrace the position that Karma-Yoga is to be active in Karma, holding duty-bound intellect for activities towards public well-being (Lokasaṃgraha) and not desiring fruits of Karma for oneself offer them to the Lord. That is the direct means for liberation, or after attaining knowledge, the conduct of such Karma-Yoga is an obligation for a knower, and that is the propounded subject of Gītā. Based on the critique of the entire Bhagavad-Gītā, the said view as a direct means for liberation was neither established nor was it found as the propounded subject of Gītā. Following is the essence of the subject matter presented:

1. Any human's highest effort (Parama Puruṣārtha) is to attain liberation.
2. The true nature of liberation is attaining eternal and immovable happiness and the complete removal of pain and suffering.
3. Repeatedly taking birth and dying is the bondage.
    a. Accumulated impressions of righteous and unrighteous actions (Karma-Saṃskāras) done with doership-intellect is the cause of birth and death.
    b. Karma-Saṃskāras arise due to the relationship with the Saṃsāra of I-ness, mineness, and theirness.
    c. The relationship of the Saṃsāra of I-ness, mineness, and theirness is due to ego in the body. Due to the ego in the body, there is doership-intellect.
    d. The ego in the body is due to limited vision.
    e. The limited vision is discriminating in nature. That is, viewing own and another's cause and effect to be different and distinct.
    f. Discriminating-vision is born of ignorance (false knowledge).
4. Thus, the root of bondage is only ignorance. Ignorance can only be removed by knowing the true nature of one's Self (Ātmā). The direct means for liberation is the transcendental knowledge (Aparokṣa-Jñāna) of own Ātmā.
5. Depletion (Kṣaya) of Karma-Saṃskāras (the cause of birth and death) is possible in three ways, 1) by the enjoyment of fruits (Phalabhoga), 2) through penance (Prāyaścitta), and 3) the intuitive realization (Sākṣātkāra) of the Ātmā. Among them, enjoyment of fruits and penance cannot altogether remove all Karma-Saṃskāras because where it is possible to reduce any Karma-Saṃskāra by enjoyment and penance, many new Karma-Saṃskāras are born. Only the "fire of knowledge (Jñānāgni)" can easily burn all Karma-Saṃskāras completely (BG 4.37).
6. a. Through the knowledge of the Ātmā, an intuitive realization of the Ātmā happens.
    b. With the intuitive realization of the Ātmā, there is a resolve of complete absence in the past, present, and future of the limited and discriminating vision that is born of ignorance.

c. With the resolve of the absence of limited and discriminating vision, there is a resolve of the absence of the "दहोऽहम्, I am a body" ego.
d. With the resolve of the absence of the ego in the body, the "I am a doer" delusion is gone.
e. With the removal of the doership delusion, whether accumulated past Karma (Sañcita) or current Karma (Kriyamāṇa, being done Karma), there is depletion of all Karma-Saṃskāras That is because all Karma-Saṃskāras exist in support of the "I am a doer" intellect.

7. A Jīva suffers stumbles of Karma only in the darkness of ignorance. That is why Karma is not an opposer of ignorance because the root of Karma is ignorance, and Karma is indeed the fruit of ignorance. Hence, Karma cannot shear its root ignorance. Only the light of knowledge can remove the darkness of ignorance, removing the pain and suffering of the stumbles of Karma.
8. "I have certain duties and not desiring fruits of my Karma, I offer them to the Lord," that conduct of a Karma-Yogī can neither incinerate accumulated Karma-Saṃskāras nor make current Karma fruitless. Doing Karma in such a manner, that is, the Variant Karma-Yoga, doership, and duty-bound intellect continue to exist. Indeed doership-intellect is the support of Karma-Saṃskāras. That is why such intelligence cannot burn Karma-Saṃskāras. Thus, the conduct of Karma-Yoga in the said manner by its nature cannot free one from the bondage of birth and death anyway.
9. "I am not a doer of Karma; I am unattached, and I have a certain duty" that kind of arrangement of the components of the Variant Karma-Yoga is not sound. In the presence of duty, the existence of a doer is necessary; without a doer, the duty cannot happen. The conduct of said Variant Karma-Yoga can only remove the flow of Rajoguṇa residing in the heart by an excellent path, and through purity of the conscience can run the fountainhead of devotion. The usefulness of Karma-Yoga in attaining liberation can only be to this extent. After that, by burning doership delusion through knowledge, liberation is possible with the rising of devotion and dispassion. The said Variant Karma-Yoga is not capable of burning doership delusion anyway.
10. Based on the above, through knowledge, upon realizing the Truth, a person attains oneness in his witness-conscious Ātmā. Attaining oneness, that knower of the Truth becomes "is as is" dissociated from the body, senses, mind, and intellect. In this state, he does not remain a doer of the body's activities but is just their observer, like a spectator of a drama. With the doership delusion having disappeared, all his Karma become Akarma (non-action) and, like roasted seeds, are incapable of producing Saṃskāras.
11. Even though being active in Karma through the body only, such a knower of the Truth remains a Karma-Saṃnyāsī. Through the realization of the Ātmā, he remains "is as is" dissociated from the body's activities. Now he is not a doer of the body's actions but is their observer and does not see any taint from Karma in his own witness-conscious. Even though he is doing Karma through his body, he is a real Karma-Saṃnyāsī. When he is not a doer of Karma, he is also not an enjoyer of the fruits. All his Karma without doership and enjoyership remain without fruits and, like roasted seeds, cannot be the cause of fruits. Thus, a knower of the Truth is, in fact, a relinquisher of the fruits, a true Karma-Yogī. The name Karma-Tyāga is Karma-Saṃnyāsa, and the name Karma-Phala-Tyāga (relinquishment of fruits of Karma) is Karma-Yoga. This way, these two subjects, only through the knowledge mentioned above, become firmly successful. Thus, the propounded subject of Gītā is the oneness of Karma-Saṃnyāsa and Karma-Yoga.
12. Contrary to this, holding duty-bound intellect, the sentiment of relinquishment of fruits of Karma cannot free one from the fruits of Karma. The cause of fruits of Karma is not the insentient Karma, but only the sentiments. Because the sentiments of 1) relinquishment of fruits of Karma and 2) being a doer are present, Karma cannot be without fruits. However, since the sentiments are renunciatory, their fruits are also more, but they can never be without fruits. In the oneness of the above Karma-Saṃnyāsa and Karma-Yoga, the sentiment of fruit-relinquishment being instrumental, Gītā does not disrespect this relinquishment of fruits. However, only this much cannot be the propounded subject of Gītā.

13. Through knowledge, without attaining oneness in own witness-conscious Ātmā, Karma-Yoga in the form of relinquishment of the fruits is not successful. The sentiment of relinquishment of the fruits has its fruit, and in fact, it does not accomplish Karma-Yoga. Additionally, without attaining oneness in own Ātmā, there cannot be the success of Karma-Saṃnyāsa. In the presence of doership-intellect, even if one has relinquished Karma, one becomes a doer of the relinquishment of Karma. Moreover, when one has become a doer of the relinquishment of Karma, Karma-Saṃnyāsa cannot be successful. Without attaining oneness in own witness-conscious Ātmā, neither Karma-Yoga nor Karma-Saṃnyāsa can be successful.
14. From the perspective of Gītā, efforts that create sentiments are defined as Karma (BG 8.3). From this perspective, whether it is an activity (Pravṛtti) form effort or a non-activity (Nivrutti) form effort, all of them come in the definition of Karma. In such a state, some believe that activity form efforts are only Karma and non-activity form efforts are null and inferior forms of Karma are not judicious. Whether it is activity or non-activity, Gītā provides due respect to either of them based on fitness. Of the two, Gītā has no intent to hold one and leave the other. However, Gītā aims to reach that exalted state where the opposition between activity and non-activity is gone, and there is oneness between the two.
15. The cause of activity in Karma can neither be the enjoyment of external substances nor can the righteous actions such as public well-being make a Jīva engage in Karma. All of these external substances are only minor instrumental causes in the activity of Karma; the primary cause of activity in Karma is only the vacillations (Vikṣepa) resident in the heart. Whatever substance-related vacillations are born in the heart, they make a Jīva active in the correspondent activity of Karma. That is why the leading cause of activity in Karma is the vacillations resident in the heart only. Removal of vacillations is the only fruit.
16. Removal of the vacillations is possible in three ways -
    a. Fulfillment of the desires.
    b. Not acquiring the desired object, a Jīva gets tired and becomes disappointed.
    c. Through thinking, dispassion, and knowledge when a Jīva removes desires from his heart.

    Vacillations removed by the first two provide only transitory peace. Both desires and vacillations are reborn with the conjunction of the fire of ignorance. Removal of the vacillations by the third way provides stable peace.
17. Though there are infinite types of vacillations, they can be broadly divided into five levels -
    a. Deep-Rooted Tamogunī-Vikṣepa, which resides in the hearts of iniquitous (Pāmara) persons who remain absorbed in enjoyments transgressing the bounds of Śāstra.
    b. Diminished Tamogunī-Vikṣepa, which resides in the hearts of virtuous desire-ridden persons who remain absorbed in enjoyments within the bounds of Śāstra.
    c. Rajoguṇī Vikṣepa resides in the hearts of desireless doers who remain absorbed in Karma with the sentiment of offering to the Lord.
    d. Rajasattvaguṇī Vikṣepa resides in the hearts of desireless loving devotees who are aspirants for the divine experience of the manifest-form Lord.
    e. Sattvaguṇī Vikṣepa resides in the hearts of the dispassionate and seekers of the Truth who are aspirants for the realization of the Reality.
18. Lower-level vacillations make a human engage in Karma to obtain freedom from vacillations. However, with the satisfaction of desires, even though a human becomes free from those vacillations for a moment, vacillations return in some other form. Indeed, vacillations are not removed from the root. Certainly, the desire for the complete removal of vacillations is natural in all beings. Prakṛti, on the one hand, has filled the hearts of humans with an intense desire to get rid of vacillations. Still, on the other hand, through the activity of lower levels, where she has provided a path for the removal of vacillations, she fills vacillations of some other form. When a human gets tired of doing Karma at his level but does not get freedom from vacillations, then that fatigue is the only one that

lifts him to higher levels. Because the fatigue is of Karma only, he does not get tired of the desire to remove vacillations. That is the pure-hearted rule of Prakṛti by which humans are taken from lower levels to higher levels.

19. Thus, the fruit of activity in desireless Karma is that the flow of Tamogunī and Rajoguṇī vacillations of Prakṛti, which are brimming in the hearts of humans, being impediments in the higher good, be taken out through a promising path and replaced with Sattvaguṇa. As Tamoguṇa and Rajoguṇa suppress Sattvaguṇa, it cannot be awakened without removing Tamoguṇa and Rajoguṇa. With the rise of Sattvaguṇa, Karma becomes fruitless, and then, there is a light of knowledge in the human. The Paramātmā, Who is omnipresent and existent in our hearts, is shrouded only due to ignorance and so unattainable through Karma. Thus, reaching this state, for the attainment of the Paramātmā, ignorance remover knowledge is the only useful one. Through knowledge, when oneness in the Ātmā is established, only natural activities arise for such a great being. Only natural actions arise, and all Karma are done illusorily. That is because they are not done with any kind of doership and duty-bound intellect, and they do not have any relationship with the constituents of Prakṛti. When the great being has attained the status of Guṇātīta, then all his Karma is naturally Akarma (non-action).
20. Accordingly, making one ascend in this state and engaging in the natural activity of Karma is the propounded subject of Gītā.

Establishing Oneness in the Ātmā through Concentration of the Mind

What is the true nature of the mind? Upon contemplation, one can realize that the mind is emotional (भावात्मक, Bhāvātmaka). One cannot find any other form separate from emotions because when the mind becomes without emotions, it does not remain anything by its nature. In the nullity of emotions, the state of mind is the state of deep sleep (Suṣupti-Avasthā) or dissolution (Laya). Had the mind been any independent form other than without emotions, it should be known when emotions are absent. Clear evidence is in the awake and dream state when the mind engages with innumerable emotional waves. It is then that its true nature is realized. However, emotions are dissolved in a deep sleep, so one cannot find their true nature. Hence, it is evident that "the mind is only emotional." Without emotions, the mind does not have any form.

So, what are emotions? Any wave in the mind in the form of a thought or resolve is called emotion. Even if one thinks about the world, the world has no independent state separate from emotions. Whatever emotions one has, one's world is likewise. Indeed, not only in this world, whether it is this world or the next, the creation of all worlds is dependent on the individual emotions of a Jīva. Without the emotions of a Jīva, there is no success (Siddhi) in this or other worlds. In the four kinds of species, 1) germination-born, 2) sweat-born, 3) egg-born, and 4) placenta-born, sequentially, as there is the growth of emotions, so does their world grow. It is only from the sight of gradual want of emotions that, compared to humans, the worlds of animals, birds, and insects are sequentially insignificant. Only due to the deficiency of emotions, the world of humans is trivial compared to the world of the deities. The world of humans is limited to the seven continents, but the world of the deities goes beyond the seven seas and the seven Dvipas (द्विप). In the world, whatever substances (Dravya), attributes (Guṇa), and acts (Kriyā) are there, they all exist based on individual emotions. Those substances, attributes, and acts are not material but mental based on individual emotions. That is why one thing that is pungent for one is mixed for another. An item may be hot for one but cold for someone else. A thing may be good and pious for one, but it may be evil and sinful for others. The only cause is the singularity of emotions in all these singularities. It is said - "भवोऽयं भावनामात्र न कश्चित् परमार्थतः, this world is only emotional, does not have any form of the higher good." A proportional form of the world becomes for the individual based on individual emotions. For a desire-ridden (Sakāmī), it takes the form of enjoyment. For a desireless (Niṣkāmī), it elevates one; for a devotee, it takes the shape of the image of the Lord; for a dispassionate, it takes the form of fire. And for a wise, it takes the state of the supreme-bliss (Paramānanda).

"The Saṃsāra is created for our enjoyment only. That is why we must partake enjoyments" such is the view of a desire-ridden, and with this view, he sees the world and behaves. "This world has gone bad. It is our duty to make it better" such is the view of a desireless, and he holds the world with this view. "This world is in the image of the Lord, in all forms He provides a glimpse of His Self" such is the view of a desireless devotee, and with the same perspective, he sees the world. "This world is extremely sorrowful and is like the heat of the fire of Pralaya. Falling into the repeated cycle of birth and death is great pain. I need to free myself by any means" such is the view of a dispassionate, and with such a view, he sees the world. "This world by its nature was never created but is the miracle of my Ātmā. It is a Vivarta of my Ātmā, and its nature is the Paramānanda only" such is the view of a Self-Realized knower of the Truth, and with that emotion, he sees the world.

Accordingly, we can conclude that one cannot find the nature of the mind or the world without emotions. One can say that between the mind and the world, there are only emotions, which establish both, by which there is the connection of the two, and by whose dissolution, both the mind and the world dissolve.

So, what is the concentration of the mind? How should it be achieved? What is its fruit? Notwithstanding varied perspectives on the subject, making the mind devoid of emotions by efforts through the control of breath and Āsana (Prāṇa-Nirodha and Kriyātmaka Ceṣṭā} is not the concentration of the mind based on my Vedantic perspective. This state of mind is in the deep-sleep and merger state, which is not the cause of any real fruit. Because without emanation of pure emotions (शुद्ध-भावोद्गार, Śuddha-Bhāvodgāra), action-based mental restraint is just like the development of sore reddish skin due to pus remaining in a boil. Such a skin state cannot be considered good but bad for a smart physician. The real good state of mind is where emotions with desires are removed and replaced with desireless ones through pure unselfish renunciatory thought and action.

After that, with the influence of desireless thoughts, the purpose of life is moved from the world and targeted with firmness towards the highest good (Paramārtha). This way, getting rid of worldly desires and inclinations (Kāmanā and Vāsanā), engage the flow of pure devotional love and make the mind immovable in only one emotion. That, in reality, is the concentration of the mind, by which faults of impurity and vacillations are verily removed. Once the faults are removed, a steady peace is acquired, just as there is a sigh of relief upon the removal of pus. In contrast, about facing this path, if mental restraint is accomplished through action-based efforts, as the faults are still present, all efforts continue to clean the band-aid instead of cleaning the wound. The underlying disease continues to persist, and there is no hope for curing the wound. However, with action-based efforts, even if it is possible to control the mind (dissolution of the mind) for a short time, in the next rising time, because the faults of impurity and vacillations are still present, "is as is," they cannot provide any steady peace. That is because without the creation of pure emotions, only through the control of Prāṇa, the mind is stopped, just as an equestrian is stopped by blocking a horse. Accordingly, such a mind control technique cannot give peace right at the root. It can neither remove the faults nor the root of the Saṃsāra, the limited ego anyway. On the contrary, it is quite possible that with faults remaining and in the absence of pure emotions, mental restraint may make the ego of mental restraint firmer and provide further nourishment. Such an ego then blocks the path of the highest good. He neither believes in the words of holy persons and real scriptures nor accepts their approaches, but indeed reaffirms the predicament of removing a cat but bringing in a camel. In contrast, in the flow of pure devotional loving emotions, there is such power that by their influence, it throws out impurity and vacillations from the heart, shakes the root of the limited ego, and provides steady peace.

In the world, love is only one thing that can make all kinds of self-sacrifices. There is nothing else that has such capability. When love for wife and children can lose itself during enjoyment time, it should not be surprising that pure Sāttvika love related to the highest good can sacrifice the limited ego right at the root. In Śrīmad Bhāgavata Purāṇa, there is an episode during Rāsa-Līlā when Śrī Kṛṣṇa disappeared from the Gopis. At that time, in the hearts of all Gopis, emotions of devotional love (Prema-Bhakti) sprang out by which they lost their selves and, in various divine plays, saw themselves in the form of Śrī Kṛṣṇa. Some in Śrī Kṛṣṇa were restraining Kāliya-Nāga by dancing over his fangs, and some were making flutes from their garments and reverberating the entire Vraja with musical notes. That is indeed the emotional Samādhī, which is the fruit of all other Samādhī. It is the real control of mental dispositions (Vāstavika Citta-Vṛtti Nirodha). The one that cleanses the heart from worldly attachment and aversion (Rāga-Dveṣa) and fills with true, steadfast dispassion (Vairāgya). It is through this dispassion the flow of analytic thought (Tattva-Vicāra) emanates, and then "यत्र यत्र मनो याति तत्र तत्र समाधाय:, where ever mind goes there is Samādhī" in such form, there is the attainment of natural (Sahaja) Samādhī. Without the aforementioned emotional Samādhī, natural Samādhī is difficult. There is so much potency in emotional Samādhī that it melts one but also all who are in close contact. When Uddhava went to Vraja to provide spiritual guidance, he was emotionally struck by the pure devotional love of the Gopis, and all his knowledge disappeared. Control of Prāṇa can never produce such influence, even in a dream. That is the reason why, whether it is the Vedas, whether it is the Upaniṣads, whether it is Smṛti or whether it is Purāṇa - all true scriptures (Sacchāstra) are indifferent in discussing action-based stoppage of Prāṇa. Were these efforts substantial firm means in the highest good, and the fact that the scriptures mentioned above do not discuss such means, wouldn't that indicate incompleteness of those scriptures? However, those scriptures do not accept these action-based efforts as a firm means to achieve the highest good. As such, there is no substance in the world without fruits. Such action-based efforts can work to control the highly extroverted mind like an uncontrolled horse. Only after controlling the mind, as its fruit, is there emanation of pure emotions (Śuddha-Bhāvodgāra). Without purity of emotions, there cannot be purity of the mind. There cannot be the concentration of the mind without the concentration of emotions produced through the emanation of pure emotions. Just as iron can be cut by iron, following the approach above, only through the purity and concentration of the emotions, with the awakening of the "Truth discerning emotions," the emotional Saṃsāra can be freed. There is no other path to freedom. "नान्यः पन्था विध्यतेऽयनाय, there is no other path towards freedom" (Śruti).

Those who desire to know the Truth ought to contemplate the above words and select their path. Keeping the importance of the emanation of emotions and purity of emotions at the forefront, several prayers aid in the emanation of pure emotions. One ought to memorize the Universal Prayer and recite it daily in the morning and at night with a calm mind contemplating the words while meditating on one's revered deity. At the point where the mind becomes steady, one ought to cease.

Several other prayers are also provided that may be added based on individual shortcomings.

Universal Prayer

Oṃ(ॐ) Tat Sat

O, Lord! With undivided supreme faith and without expectation, I beseech thee for Your grace to endow me with wisdom and power not to hurt anyone mentally, verbally, or bodily by my thoughts, words, and deeds.

O, Lord! With undivided supreme faith and without expectation, I beseech Thee for Your grace to endow me with a tongue that utters only unoffending, truthful, pleasant, and beneficial words.

O, Lord! With undivided supreme faith and without expectation, I beseech Thee for Your grace to endow me with a resolve to abandon lust, anger, and greed.

O, Lord! With undivided supreme faith and without expectation, I beseech Thee for Your grace to endow me with a resolve to partake only foods that promote longevity, purity, power, health, happiness, satisfaction and are savory, stable, and pleasing to the heart.

O, Lord! With undivided supreme faith and without expectation, I beseech Thee for Your grace to endow me with the sixfold virtues, 1) control of the mind, 2) restraint over the senses, 3) faith in the words of the preceptors and the scriptures, 4) absence of mental vacillations, 5) desistance from the relinquishment of actions and vile objects, and 6) tolerance to bear dualities such as heat and cold, pleasure and pain, hunger and thirst. O, Lord! Grant me a resolve to remain in Your knowledge and Your undivided devotion.

Prayer to relinquish Gratification of the Sense-Objects

O, Lord! With Your limitless grace, You have bestowed upon us this life - the gateway of liberation to attain You. It is a pity that we have squandered our lives instead of relinquishing the poison of gratification of sense objects. The gratification of the sense objects is not the fruit of this human birth, but the tranquility of the mind is. These gratifications are like Trojan horses; they may look great and innocent, but they are evil and painful. Repeatedly taking birth, enduring pain throughout the lifetime and in death - at the root of all these evils, there is no cause other than for this Self in the past to have been mentally caught in cognizing all these pain-yielding sense-objects as pleasure-yielding. Desired objects become poisonous when acquired; they never remain pleasure-yielding. All that poison is now manifesting in varied forms of pain and suffering. In the presence of desires, bound by these pains, this imperishable Self is tormented by enjoyments. Even when there are no desires, this Self is in agony.

O, Lord! It is a pity that we have enjoyed the poison believing it to be ambrosia, and have about-faced Your ambrosiac lotus-feet. Instead of higher worlds, we have bought hell. The water of a mirage looks excellent but is not fit to quench thirst. Running after it does nothing but intensify thirst. Likewise, running after false pleasures of sense-gratification, believing them real instead of providing happiness, increases our pain and suffering.

O, Lord! It is a pity we looked for peace where there was no peace and about-faced from Your bliss-form lotus-feet. Having lost everything, we are now at your doorstep. You are kind; we are pathetic. O, Father! Forgive us for our offenses and bestow Your true power so that in the refuge of Your bliss-form lotus-feet, we can crossover the painful worldly ocean and attain imperishable peace.

O, Lord! O, Loving towards devotees! O, Protector of those who surrender! We surrender to Thee. We are impure; You are the Purifier. Do not depart seeing our vices. Make Your Purifier name successful. Your vision towards us will not elevate us. You are with equi-vision all over. Just as the pure Gaṅgā taking a dirty stream under her refuge and merging it makes it pure Gaṅgā, in the same way, see towards Yourself and uplift us.

O, Lord! With Your limitless grace, we now cognize that the cause of pain and suffering in the mortal world is nothing but the mineness of substances that cause our pain. Wealth, wife, and children, in reality, are not ours. Before coming in these bodies, they were in some form and were Yours only. When we are not in these bodies, they will still be in some form, and Yours only, in the middle, knowing them as ours, we made ourselves grief-stricken. Those things that are not ours before and do not remain ours after, how can they be ours in the middle? In the middle, they should be only of the One in Whom they stay before and after. In the middle, they were given to us as bailment. In error, breaching Your trust of the bailment, we became Your offenders. Now we genuinely offer Your things at Your lotus feet. O, Lord! Bestow upon us intellectual power so that we never believe them to be ours. With an undivided devotional love, we serve You. Whatever command You give to our intellect, we will genuinely obey them. Whatever we eat, be that Your consecrated offerings. Whatever we drink, be that the ambrosia of Your lotus feet. Wherever we walk, be that Your circumambulation. Whatever we do with our hands, be that in Your service. Whatever we see with the eyes, be that only Your true nature, and whatever the ears hear, be that only Your glory.

Prayer to relinquish Attachment

O, Lord! You are merciful. You are the embodiment of mercy. We, Your offenders, are Your children. O, Father! Forgive us for our offenses. Our error was that we believed Your substances - wealth, wife, and children as ours. Just as pilgrims gather in an Inn at night, in the same way, Your family has gathered, all will depart by their paths at sunrise. However, this ignorant mind with mineness has seized them, and with this offense, it is suffering. Now I am genuinely offering them at Your lotus feet. When I was not in this body, these substances were in some form and only Yours. When I am not in this body, they will also be Yours only. I committed a significant offense in the middle by considering them as mine.

Hey, Mind! Be cautious now. You have made me extremely unhappy. You have bound yourself like a monkey, grabbing a fistful of substances. Forsaking them, surrender to the bliss-form Lord, by which you and I both can acquire peace. Now, sunrise is about to happen, and travel is imminent.

O, Lord! I am stuck in the dilemma of the mortal world. I have no support to stand on. Give me the support of Your lotus feet. Have mercy, give me Your power and purify my intellect so that I shall never think of Your substances as mine in the future. O, Lord, these enjoyments were also available to us in inferior life forms. That is why the reward of the human life-form cannot be these enjoyments. However, the only real fruit of this mortal life is only at Your lotus feet, which we are still deprived of. Help our boat crossover the worldly ocean. Look at our grey hairs and bestow upon us strength so that whatever we do is for Your sake. Whatever we eat, be that Your consecrated offerings. Whatever we drink, be that the ambrosia of Your lotus feet. Wherever we walk, be that Your circumambulation. Whatever we do with our hands, be that in Your service. Whatever we see with the eyes, be that only Your true nature, and whatever the ears hear, be that only Your glory. O, Lord! All these relatives are because of their relationship with the body. How will the relatives accompany me when the body will not accompany me? The real relationship was only with You, which we forgot. I died an orphan. The mind cheated me. O, Lord! Be graceful. Protect me from this evil.

Prayer to be Desireless

O, Lord! The gratification of the sense objects is not the fruit of this human birth, but the tranquility of the mind is. O, Lord! We have acquired these enjoyments of the sense objects in infinite life forms. We have not acquired peace; instead, they have made the mind increasingly fickle, like pouring oil over fire. What hope can we have to acquire peace in the future with their union? Pity we were looking for peace where there is no peace and have remained about-faced deprived of the bliss-form lotus-feet of Yours. You are kind; we are pathetic. O, Father! Forgive us for our offenses and bestow Your true power to crossover the painful worldly ocean and attain imperishable peace in the refuge of Your bliss-form lotus-feet.

O, Lord! With Your limitless grace, we now cognize that the cause of pain and suffering in the mortal world is nothing but the mineness in substances that become the cause of our pain. Wealth, wife, and children, in reality, are not ours. Before coming in these bodies, they were in some form and were Yours only. When we are not in these bodies, they will still be in some form, and Yours only, in the middle, knowing them as ours, we made ourselves grief-stricken. Those things that are not ours before and do not remain ours after, how can they be ours in the middle? In the middle, believing them to be ours is robbery. The bailment of someone before, of the same someone after, is indeed of the same someone in the middle. Anyone who claims authority over it in the middle is a thief. In the middle, seizing possession, it does not become his. In the middle, if cash can be ours, then whatever cash of the Bank in the authority of the cashier should be his. In the middle, if children by exercising authority can be ours, then in the land of a landowner, the produce from the seeds sown by a farmer should be of the farmer. In the middle, by exercising authority over the wife, she becomes ours, then the cows of an owner in the hands of one who tends them should be his. In reality, all these substances are Yours only - in the past, present, and future.

In the middle, owning them, we made ourselves unhappy. O, Lord! Bestow upon us intellectual power so that we never believe them to be ours, and as devoted servants, serve Your family with desireless sentiment without considering gain or loss. Whatever command You give to our intellect, we will genuinely obey them. Whatever we utter through our mouths, we only speak the truth. Whatever we do, we do it only for the good of all beings. Whatever we eat, be that Your consecrated offerings. Whatever we drink, be that the ambrosia of Your lotus feet. Wherever we walk, be that Your circumambulation. Whatever we do with our hands, be that in Your service. Whatever we see with the eyes, be that only Your true nature, and whatever the ears hear, be that only Your glory.

Prayer to remove Vacillations

O, Lord! Forgive us for our trespasses. Our error was that we believed Your substances as ours and exercised our authority over them. Now, we truly offer Your things at Your lotus feet. When we were not in these bodies, these substances were in some form and only Yours. When we are not in these bodies, they will be Yours only. I committed a big offense in the middle by considering them as mine. Those things that are not ours before and do not remain ours after, in the middle believing them to be ours, is a breach of Your trust in the bailment. Show mercy on us, make our intellect pure, and bestow Your power so that we would never commit the same offense. Grief is that despite You are the one to do or have it done, we have unseated You from Your throne in our hearts, and we have become doers and Lord by ourselves. Whatever we hope for does not ever happen. Whatever happens, only those remain that You wish. This mind is ignorant. Erroneously unsatisfied with Your wish and unnecessarily meddling in the middle, burns in the fire of anxiety. Hey, naive Mind! Why don't you trust your Lord? The all-pervading Lord who sustains the entire mortal world, why would He not sustain you? With this offense, hey, Sinner! You have strung a noose around your neck; no one else is around to do so. With this fault of yours, will you find rest neither here nor there!

O, Lord! This mental monkey has badly shaken this bodily tree and does not allow staying put. This ghost is firmly behind us, one who has kept us about-faced from Your lotus feet. O, Lord! We are defeated; we beg for mercy at Your lotus feet. Please withdraw this Māyā of Yours. In reality, even grief is one of Your messengers for our good only. If we properly follow Your command, there is no cause for grief. The root of grief is I-ness and mineness in the mortal world. No cause for grief remains by truly offering this I-ness and mineness at Your lotus feet. At Your wish, our aim is only to be content and oneness with You. You are extremely kind; Who over-looking our actions does not miss Your Own actions. O, Lord! The enjoyments of the mortal world in which we are trapped were acquired by us even in inferior life forms. The reward of human life is not the enjoyment of sense objects, but only the undivided devotion at Your lotus feet is the major fruit of human life, which we are still deprived of. O, Lord! Please show mercy on us and help our sinking boat cross over. Kindly bestow upon us Your true power so that we do not grasp by the relationship with the body any substance of the mortal world but directly hold every substance with Your relationship. Whatever we do, be that for Your worship. Whatever we eat, be that Your consecrated offerings. Whatever we drink, be that the ambrosia of Your lotus feet. Wherever we walk, be that Your circumambulation. Whatever we do with our hands, be that in Your service. Whatever we see with the eyes, be that only Your true nature. Whatever the ears hear, be that only Your glory, and whatever we utter, be they all Your recitals. O, Lord! Let all difficulties of the mortal world not produce cowardice in us.

Prayer to remove Grief

O, Lord! You are benevolent, the embodiment of benevolence and the ocean of benevolence. How can any bad thing happen through You, the all-benevolent? How can darkness emanate from the sun? We are wrong that we perceive good and bad in Your acts. Just as a pediatrician with a minor incision removes pus in a boil on a child's body, the child disregarding the favor, cannot stop crying. O, Lord! To remove our worldly disease, with Your compassion from time to time, You grace our hearts with an incision. But we, with our stupidity, misconstrue Your favor as disfavor and thereby become Your offenders.

O, Lord! By Your grace now, we have realized that You, except Yourself, have no mineness in any worldly substance. You do not wish the mind to be trapped in any substance other than You. O, Lord! Bliss-yielding is only Your lotus feet. However, when this Self, in his error abandoning Your bliss-form lotus feet, grasps some substance in the mortal world as pleasure-yielding and forms mineness; it is then that he acquires grief. If the substances were ours, they would not deceive us, but their deceit proves that it was our mistake to think of them as ours and thus got deceived. When we were not in these bodies, these substances were in some form and only Yours. When we are not in these bodies, they will be Yours only. In the middle, believing them to be ours is Your theft. It is a breach of Your trust in the bailment. Those things that are not ours before and do not remain ours after, how can they be ours in the middle? They were always Yours. They never leave You. Though they have separated from us, they have not left Your kingdom. In reality, our things perish, but Yours never perish.

O, Lord! Hopelessly we are at Your front door. Kindly blow Your graceful breath where You have made an incision. O, Lord! Bestow upon us pure undivided devotion at Your tranquil lotus feet. O, Lord! Bestow true power in our hearts so that we never make the same mistake, and except Your lotus-feet, do not have mineness in any other substance. That we serve Your family without mineness and not be tainted by grief and happiness of the family. The enjoyments of the mortal world are pain-yielding. O, Lord! Bless me that we never about-face from Your lotus feet and never face such grief in the future. Whatever command You give to our intellect, we will truly obey them. Whatever we do with our bodies, be that in Your service. Whatever we eat, be that Your consecrated offerings. Whatever we drink, be that the ambrosia of Your lotus feet. Wherever we walk, be that Your circumambulation. Whatever we do with our hands, be that in Your service. Whatever we see with the eyes, be that only Your true nature, and whatever the ears hear, be that only Your glory.

Prayer to control Anger

O, Lord! The gratification of the sense objects is not the fruit of this human birth, but the tranquility of the mind is. O, Lord! We have acquired these enjoyments of the sense objects for infinite life forms. We have not acquired peace; instead, they have made the mind increasingly fickle, like pouring oil over fire. What hope can we have to acquire peace in the future with their union? Pity we were looking for peace where there is no peace and have remained about-faced deprived of the bliss-form lotus-feet of Yours. You are kind; we are pathetic. O, Father! Forgive us for our offenses and bestow Your true power so that we can crossover the painful worldly ocean and attain imperishable peace in the refuge of Your bliss-form lotus feet.

O, Lord! With Your limitless grace, we now cognize the cause of pain and suffering in the mortal world as nothing but the mineness of substances. They are the cause of our pain. Wealth, wife, and children, in reality, are not ours. Before coming in these bodies, they were in some form and were Yours only. When we are not in these bodies, they will still be in some form, and Yours only. In the middle, knowing them as ours, we made ourselves grief-stricken. O, Lord! Bestow upon us intellectual power so that we never believe them to be ours, and as devoted servants, serve Your family with desireless sentiment without considering gain or loss. Whatever command You give to our intellect, we will genuinely obey them. Whatever we utter through our mouths, we only speak the truth. Whatever we do, we do it only for the good of all beings. Whatever we eat, be that Your consecrated offerings. Whatever we drink, be that the ambrosia of Your lotus feet. Wherever we walk, be that Your circumambulation. Whatever we do with our hands, be that in Your service. Whatever we see with the eyes, be that only Your true nature, and whatever the ears hear, be that only Your glory.

O, Lord! When this evil anger manifests in our hearts, we become impure in the mind and body. We are defeated in its front. Please protect us. We surrender at Your lotus feet. Hey, Mind! You about-face from your true preceptor Lord within and become an unbeliever whenever you are in its influence.

Knowing loss, if we come under the influence of this evil, then we are non-believers. Loss or gain is not something that is ours, as no substance ever remains ours. Duty is ours, so we do it. If anyone inflicts loss to our family, the true preceptor Lord will settle the matter. In the eyes of that Trayambaka, no one can put salt. What was our need to go beyond our duty and make our priceless mind impure for these trifles and attach mineness in the family by being about-faced from the true preceptor? Without mineness, there is no anger. Thoughtfully analyzed, the cause of this loss is our being mentally trapped in these objects during some time in the past and being about-faced from the Lord. In return, the Lord manifesting in this form has whipped us. Now, we are running to take revenge on that opponent. We ought to regain our senses. We are bourgeoning our mistake and producing cause for being whipped more.

Knowing dishonor, we are only dishonored if we become angry; we cognize our body as our Self and have an ego. Those who have an ego in the skin are lowly. The preceptor within has repeatedly guided us that we are not the body but the pure Self. By our becoming body-form, and as body-form becoming angry is a real disrespect of the words of the preceptor within, great disbelief. Calmly behold that we will only acquire the lowest depths of degradation by disrespecting such pure words. With this evilness, we ought to suffer. We are running to take revenge on the opposer.

O, Lord! With the grace of Your lotus feet, save us from this evil. O, Lord! Bestow upon us strength to win over this enemy so that we are never touched by it.

Prayer for Total Renunciation

O, Lord! This Māyā of Yours weirdly spread all over is by no means possible to be untangled. As we untangle, it becomes more tangled. O! How badly we are trapped. Like a monkey, Your Māyā has made us dance around. We are tired. We cannot dance anymore. By Your grace, when our eyes were enlightened, we realized that we were still robbed. That which we thought was enjoyment turned out to be disease. That which we thought was ambrosia turned out to be poison. There is no end to Your Māyā; we cannot behold the end of the cycle of birth and death. O, Lord! Be graceful. Withdraw your Māyā. It is Your game, but it is our death. It is Your laughter, but it is our pain and suffering. O, Lord! Show mercy. If You want to play your game, bless us with a vision that we are just their observers. Here in this theater of the mortal world, being actors, we cannot bear being beaten up in fights. O, Lord! Impart us knowledge of Gītā that You gave to Arjuna so that we can also become one to do everything without doing anything. Why are You being so miserly? You showered the sun with light all twelve months. You will not be deprived of anything by gracing us with twenty-four hours of our happiness.

O, Lord! We are anxious to behold You, the One Whose infinite grace is making the insignificant Māyā appear as infinite. Now, I cannot even say two things, I take care of Your family and behold Your blissful face. You are my beehive to procure honey. You are my abode and my cane. If You desire, may You take care of Your family! Where is my livelihood from them? O, Lord! Be graceful, kindly bestow Your intellectual power so that we can cognize Your form of all-forms “is as is.” Whatever we do with our bodies, be that in Your service. Whatever we eat, be that Your consecrated offerings. Whatever we drink, be that the ambrosia of Your lotus feet. Wherever we walk, be that Your circumambulation. Whatever we do with our hands, be that in Your service. Whatever we see with the eyes, be that only Your true nature, and whatever the ears hear, be that only Your glory.

Prayer for restraining Ego

O, Lord! You are benevolent, the embodiment of benevolence and the ocean of benevolence. How can any bad thing happen through You, the all-benevolent? How can darkness emanate from the sun? We are wrong that we perceive good and bad in Your acts. Just as a pediatrician with a minor incision removes pus in a boil on a child's body, the child cannot stop crying, disregarding the favor. O, Lord! To remove our worldly disease, with Your compassion from time to time, You grace our hearts with an incision. But we, with our stupidity, misconstrue Your favor as disfavor and thereby become Your offenders.

O, Lord! Having stumbled from all sides, we have now resolved that there is no other grief in the mortal world than the rise of paltry ego in any form - that is indeed the grief. Like the restraint of the multi-fanged Kāliya-Nāga, chafing its fangs is but one pleasure. The deep hole of grief springs out hurdles of birth and death. O, You ego! The real enemy of this Self, you are the one to create the riptide world in the infinite calm ocean and are the one to drown this Self in it. First, due to ignorance separate from Your true nature, this Self becomes something in I-form. Knows the rest of the mortal world separate from own Self and with discriminating-vision forms favorable disposition in some and unfavorable disposition in some others. Then becomes anxious in things of favorable disposition with attachment intellect and unfavorable things with aversion intellect. With this attachment and aversion, due to doership-intellect, falls in the bondage of piety and sin. Like a clock, it falls in the circle of birth and death, roaming around up and down. With analytic thinking, it should be realized that there is not an iota of doership in this Self. O, Lord! You are the doer-holder of everything. Knowing whatever activity is happening and meddling in between with "I am a doer" ego, this Self puts a noose around his neck. That remains the only purpose and nothing else. After eating, myriads of activities happen in the body, such as feces, urine, blood, muscles, and other states through which the ingested food goes through that are not perceptible to this Self. However, under all states and activities like water in waves, You are existent. Without Your existence, no activity can arise. Then, whatever activity is happening in his knowledge, there is no other attachment except for assuming his ego. For the legs in walking, the hands in moving, the eyes in seeing and for thinking, infinite efforts happen through endless channels in the body and mind with whom he has no relationship. However, under all those efforts, You are seated. In every mental activity, there is only Your light.

Hey, paltry ego! Now I have realized you are essenceless and there to harm me. Your being is there to destroy my conduct and destroy my highest good. You enter, and my obstacles arise. You have inflicted pain and suffering in the body-form burrow seated like a snake with your hissing. Now I know who my robber is. You are the one to rob me of my self-wealth.

O, Lord! Bestow upon us Your power whereby we can defeat this evil enemy, become undivided devotees of Your lotus-feet, and we can attain real peace. Whatever we do with our body, be that in Your service. Whatever we eat, be that Your consecrated offerings. Whatever we drink, be that ambrosia of Your lotus feet. Wherever we walk, be that Your circumambulation. Whatever we do with our hands, be that in Your service. Whatever we see with the eyes, be that only Your true nature, and whatever the ears hear, be that only Your glory. Know everyone's Self as own Self. Know not anyone insignificant. When we know someone insignificant, then You become insignificant. In reality, You reside there and provide Your glimpse there as well. In reality, with ignorance, that thing is not disrespected, but we become offenders of Your insult with our conduct. O, Lord! Grace us so that we never commit such an error.

Prayer to strengthen Mental Power

O Antaryāmi, the Lord resident within! O my true witness-conscious! O my Ātmā! O the Ātmā of All! You are the all-doer. Except You, who else is in the Saṃsāra who can be grasped as a doer? You are the granter of all pleasure and pain. All Your efforts are for our good. Grief is Your Mahāprasāda, which You bestow upon Your lovers only. A pot maker mixes clay with water, shapes, dries, and bakes it in a kiln for a few days to make a finished earthen pot. What good is an unbaked pot? How can it hold water? Even a small impact of feet can break it into pieces. O, Lord! O, my Ātmā! With mercy, You are toiling to bake our heart-form pots on the kiln of grief and suffering so that these hearts do not shatter with minor stumbles; so that they become capable of holding the ambrosia of Paramānanda. Thankful are we, O, the embodiment of benevolence! We are grateful for Your cleverness.

O, Lord! O all-witness! Bake at moderate temperatures. At very high temperatures, there is a fear of breaking the pots. At this time, we are still Your young children, not yet fit to qualify for Your tests. Sure, if Your grace continues this way, no big deal, we will be cent percent fit. You just be merciful; with Your kindness, everything will be successful. With Your grace, this grief is just a flower. It is nothing but Your loving playfulness. Are You not existent in bloody red eyes and lightning-like harsh words? If You are, then why is there grief for us? Why don't You bestow upon us that vision by which we can have a glimpse of You? You are the one to do or have done everything. You are the one to make us dance. We are only puppets. What good is being brave when weapons are not used on the battlefield? What good is the doership-ego when "perceiving vision" is not bestowed at the right time? Hiding behind bloody red eyes, what is the use in hurting? O Lord! I beseech Thee to grant me mental power so that I can attain steadfast union with oneness in Your unmanifest form and enjoy eternal and immovable supreme-bliss.

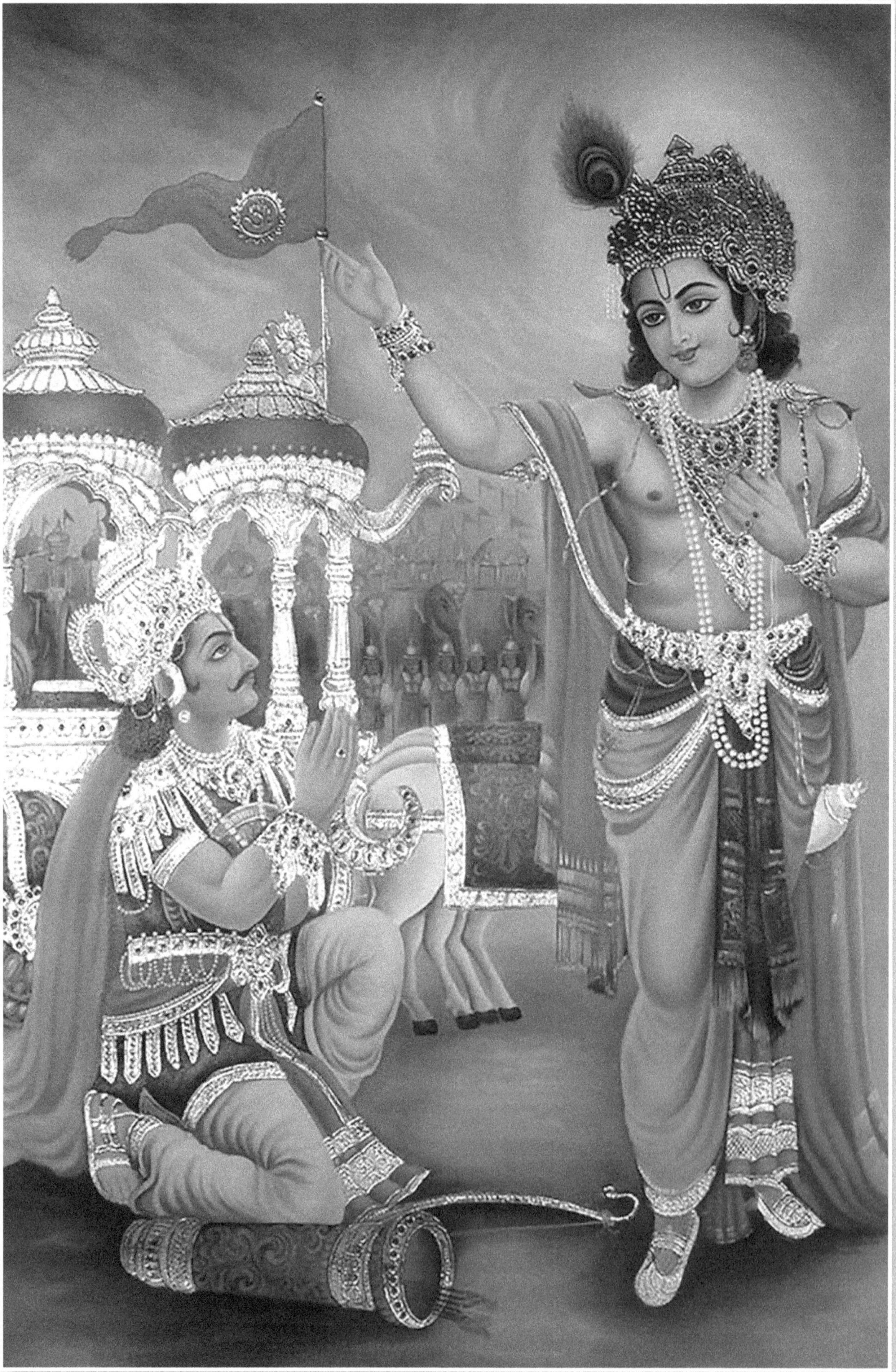

CHAPTER 1

THE DESPONDENCY OF ARJUNA

धृतराष्ट्र उवाच
धर्मक्षेत्रे कुरुक्षेत्रे समवेता युयुत्सवः |
मामकाः पाण्डवाश्चैव किमकुर्वत सञ्जय || BG 1.1 ||
धृतराष्ट्र उवाच - Dhṛtarāṣṭra said -

सञ्जय - Hey Sañjaya! ; धर्म-क्षेत्रे - On the righteousness land ; कुरु-क्षेत्रे - Kurukṣetra, ; समवेताः - having assembled ; युयुत्सवः - with the desire to fight, ; किम् - what ; अकुर्वत - did ; मामकाः - my ; च - and ; एव - also ; पाण्डवाः - Pāṇḍu's (sons do)?

Dhṛtarāṣṭra said -

Hey Sañjaya! On the righteousness land Kurukṣetra, having assembled with the desire to fight, what did my and Pāṇḍu's sons do?

सञ्जय उवाच
दृष्ट्वा तु पाण्डवानीकं व्यूढं दुर्योधनस्तदा ।
आचार्यमुपसङ्गम्य राजा वचनमब्रवीत् || BG 1. 2 ||
सञ्जय उवाच - Sañjaya said -

तदा - At that time, ; दृष्ट्वा - having seen ; पाण्डव-अनीकम् - the Pāṇḍava army ; व्यूढम् - in battle formation, ; तु - then ; राजा - King ; दुर्योधनः - Duryodhana, ; उपसङ्गम्य - having approached ; आचार्यम् - the preceptor (Droṇācārya), ; अब्रवीत् - spoke (these) ; वचनम् - words.

Sañjaya said -

At that time, having seen the Pāṇḍava army in battle formation, King Duryodhana, having approached the preceptor (Droṇācārya), spoke these words.

पश्यैतां पाण्डुपुत्राणामाचार्य महतीं चमूम् ।
व्यूढां द्रुपदपुत्रेण तव शिष्येण धीमता || BG 1.3 ||

आचार्य - Hey preceptor! ; पश्य - Observe ; एताम् - this ; महतीम् - immense ; चमूम् - army ; पाण्डु-पुत्राणाम् - of Pāṇḍu's sons, ; व्यूढाम् - (set) in battle formation ; तव - (by) your ; धीमता - intelligent ; शिष्येण - disciple ; द्रुपद-पुत्रेण - (Dhṛṣṭadyumna), the son of Drupada.

Hey preceptor! Observe this immense army of Pāṇḍu's sons, set in battle formation by your intelligent disciple (Dhṛṣṭadyumna), the son of Drupada.

अत्र शूरा महेष्वासा भीमार्जुनसमा युधि
युयुधानो विराटश्च द्रुपदश्च महारथः || BG 1.4 ||

अत्र - In this ; युधि - war, ; भीम -च -अर्जुन-समाः - like Bhīma and Arjuna, ; शूराः - (there are many) brave warriors ; महा-इषु-आसाः - with large bows, (such as), ; युयुधानः - Yuyudhāna (Sātyaki), ; विराटः - Virāṭa, ; च - and ; महारथः - Mahārathī ; द्रुपदः - (King) Drupada,

धृष्टकेतुश्चेकितानः काशिराजश्च वीर्यवान् |
पुरुजित्कुन्तिभोजश्च शैब्यश्च नरपुङ्गवः || BG 1.5 ||

च - And ; च - also, ; धृष्टकेतुः - Dhṛṣṭaketu, ; चेकितानः - Cekitāna, ; वीर्यवान् - heroic ; काशिराजः - King of Kāśī, ; पुरुजित् - Purujit, ; कुन्तिभोजः - Kuntibhoja, ; च - and ; नर-पुङ्गवः - best among men ; शैब्यः - Śaibya,

युधामन्युश्च विक्रान्त उत्तमौजाश्च वीर्यवान् |
सौभद्रो द्रौपदेयाश्च सर्व एव महारथाः || BG 1.6 ||

च - And ; च - also, ; विक्रान्तः - gallant ; युधामन्युः - Yudhāmanyu, ; वीर्यवान् - heroic ; उत्तमौजाः - Uttamaujā, ; सौभद्रः - (Abhimanyu) son of Subhadrā, ; च - and ; द्रौपदेयाः - the (five) sons of Draupadī, ; सर्वे - all (of them) ; एव - indeed (are) ; महारथाः - great warriors.

In this war, like Bhīma and Arjuna, there are many brave warriors with large bows, such as Yuyudhāna, Virāṭa, Mahārathī[55]King Drupada, Dhṛṣṭaketu, Cekitāna, heroic King of Kāśī, Purujit, Kuntibhoja, best among men Śaibya, gallant Yudhāmanyu, heroic Uttamaujā, (Abhimanyu) son of Subhadrā, and the (five) sons[56]of Draupadī, all are great warriors.

अस्माकं तु विशिष्टा ये तान्निबोध द्विजोत्तम |
नायका मम सैन्यस्य संज्ञार्थं तान्ब्रवीमि ते || BG 1.7 ||

द्विज-उत्तम - Hey (Droṇācārya), the best of the twice-born! ; तु - Again, ; निबोध - note ; तान् - them, ; मम - my ; विशिष्टाः - distinguished ; नायकाः - leaders ; ये - who ; अस्माकम् - (are in) our ; सैन्यस्य - army. ; ब्रवीमि - I will narrate ; तान् - them ; ते - (for) your ; संज्ञार्थं - complete understanding.

Hey (Droṇācārya), the best of the twice-born![57]Note the distinguished leaders of our army. I will narrate them for your complete understanding.

(Among them, first -)

भवान्भीष्मश्च कर्णश्च कृपश्च समितिञ्जयः |
अश्वत्थामा विकर्णश्च सौमदत्तिस्तथैव च || BG 1.8 ||

भवान् - Yourself, ; च - and ; भीष्मः - Bhīṣma, ; च - and ; च - also ; कर्णः - Karṇa, ; समितिञ्जयः - victorious in battle ; कृपः - Kṛpācārya, ; च - and ; तथा - similarly ; एव - also ; अश्वत्थामा - Aśvatthāmā, ; विकर्णः - Vikarṇa, ; च - and ; सौमदत्तिः - (Bhūriśravā) son of Saumadatta.

---

[55] Mahārathī (महारथी) means a great warrior. One who has mastery over all forms of weapons, battle formations and combat skills. Such a warrior is said to have the ability to single handedly match the strength of ten thousand ordinary warriors.

[56] The five sons of Draupadī are: Prativindhya (प्रतिविन्ध्य from Yudhiṣṭhira), Sutasoma (सुतसोम from Bhīma), Śrutakarmā (श्रुतकर्मा from Arjuna), Śatānīka (शतानीक from Nakula) and Śrutasena (श्रुतसेन from Sahadeva).

[57] Here one who is twice born is addressed as Dvija (द्विज). Animals that are born from eggs are believed to be born twice, once when the egg is produced and the second time when the eggs are out, like birds etc. Also, Yajñopavīta Saṃskāra (one of the sixteen rites of passage in a person's life) is considered a second birth, hence a person such as a Brāhmaṇa wearing Yajñopavīta (यज्ञोपवीत, sacred thread) is called a Dvija.

Yourself, Bhīṣma, Karṇa, victorious in battle Kṛpācārya, Aśvatthāmā, Vikarṇa and (Bhūriśravā) son of Saumadatta.

(Besides them, there are -)

अन्ये च बहव: शूरा मदर्थे त्यक्तजीविता: |
नानाशस्त्रप्रहरणा: सर्वे युद्धविशारदा: || BG 1.9 ||

च - And ; बहवः - many ; अन्ये - other ; शूराः - brave warriors ; नाना-शस्त्र-प्रहरणाः - armed with various weapons, ; सर्वे - all ; युद्ध-विशारदाः - (are) skillful in battle ; त्यक्त-जीविताः - (and) prepared to lay down their lives ; मदर्थे - for my sake.

And many other brave warriors armed with various weapons, all are skillful in battle and prepared to lay down their lives for my sake.

(The essence is that -)

अपर्याप्तं तदस्माकं बलं भीष्माभिरक्षितम् |
पर्याप्तं त्विदमेतेषां बलं भीमाभिरक्षितम् || BG 1.10 ||

अस्माकम् - Our ; बलम् - army, ; तत् - that ; भीष्म-अभिरक्षितम् - is carefully guarded by Bhīṣma, ; अपर्याप्तम् - (is) invincible (by all means). ; तु - However, ; इदम् - this ; बलम् - army ; एतेषाम् - of theirs ; भीम-अभिरक्षितम् - protected by Bhīma ; पर्याप्तम् - (is) easy to win.

Our army, carefully guarded by Bhīṣma, is invincible. However, their army protected by Bhīma is easy to win.

अयनेषु च सर्वेषु यथाभागमवस्थिता: |
भीष्ममेवाभिरक्षन्तु भवन्त: सर्व एव हि || BG 1.11 ||

च - And ; एव - so ; सर्वे - all ; भवन्तः - (of) you, ; अवस्थिताः - stationed ; यथा-भागम् - (in) respective control ; सर्वेषु - of all ; अयनेषु - battlefronts, ; हि - undoubtedly, ; अभिरक्षन्तु - protect ; एव - only ; भीष्मम् - Bhīṣma (from all sides).

All of you stationed in respective control of all battlefronts protect only Bhīṣma.

(In this manner, Duryodhana clearly showed the battle readiness state of both armies to Droṇācārya. Sañjaya is now telling King Dhṛtarāṣṭra that, listening to those words spoken by Duryodhana to Droṇācārya -)

तस्य सञ्जनयन्हर्षं कुरुवृद्ध: पितामह: |
सिंहनादं विनद्योच्चै: शङ्खं दध्मौ प्रतापवान् || BG 1.12 ||

उच्चैः - In a loud tone, ; कुरु-वृद्धः - the elder among the Kauravas, ; प्रतापवान् - the mighty ; पितामहः - grandfather (Bhīṣma), ; सञ्जनयन् - arousing ; हर्षम् - joy ; तस्य - (in the heart of) that (Duryodhana), ; विनद्य-सिंहनादम् - roared like a lion ; दध्मौ - (and) blew (his) ; शङ्खम् - conch.

In a loud tone, the elder among the Kauravas, the mighty grandfather (Bhīṣma), arousing joy in (Duryodhana), roared like a lion and blew his conch.

तत: शङ्खाश्च भेर्यश्च पणवानकगोमुखा: |
सहसैवाभ्यहन्यन्त स शब्दस्तुमुलोऽभवत् || BG 1.13 ||

ततः - After that, ; शङ्खाः - conches ; च - and ; भेर्यः - drums, ; च - and ; पणव-आनक-गोमुखाः - small drums, large kettledrums, and blow horns (and various other musical instruments) ; अभि-अहन्यन्त - blared forth ; सहसा - altogether, ; एव - and ; सः - that ; शब्दः - sound ; अभवत् - was ; तुमुलः - highly tumultuous.

After that, conches, drums, small drums, large kettledrums, and blow horns blared forth, and that sound was highly tumultuous.

ततः श्वेतैर्हयैर्युक्ते महति स्यन्दने स्थितौ |
माधवः पाण्डवश्चैव दिव्यौ शङ्खौ प्रदध्मतुः || BG 1.14 ||

ततः - After that, ; स्थितौ - seated (in a) ; महति - large ; स्यन्दने - chariot ; युक्ते - yoked by ; श्वेतैः - white ; हयैः - horses, ; माधवः - Mādhava (Śrī Kṛṣṇa, the slayer of demon Madhu) ; च - and ; पाण्डवः - Pāṇḍava (Arjuna) ; एव - also ; प्रदध्मतुः - blew (their) ; दिव्यौ - divine ; शङ्खौ - conches.

After that, seated in a large chariot yoked by white horses, Śrī Kṛṣṇa and Arjuna blew their divine conches.

पाञ्चजन्यं हृषीकेशो देवदत्तं धनञ्जयः |
पौण्ड्रं दध्मौ महाशङ्खं भीमकर्मा वृकोदरः || BG 1.15 ||

हृषीकेशः - Hṛṣīkeśa (Śrī Kṛṣṇa, the Lord of the senses, blew the great conch named) ; पाञ्चजन्यम् - Pāñcajanya, ; धनञ्जयः - Dhanañjaya (Arjuna, the conqueror of wealth) ; देवदत्तम् - (blew the great conch named) Devadatta, ; भीम-कर्मा - (and Bhīma,) the performer of formidable acts ; वृक-उदरः - and having a belly of a wolf, ; दध्मौ - blew ; महा-शङ्खम् - the great conch ; पौण्ड्रम् - (named) Pauṇḍra.

Śrī Kṛṣṇa blew Pāñcajanya, Arjuna blew Devadatta, and Bhīma, the performer of formidable acts and having a belly of a wolf, blew the great conch Pauṇḍra.

अनन्तविजयं राजा कुन्तीपुत्रो युधिष्ठिरः |
नकुलः सहदेवश्च सुघोषमणिपुष्पकौ || BG 1.16 ||

राजा - King ; युधिष्ठिरः - Yudhiṣṭhira, ; कुन्ती-पुत्रः - son of Kuntī, ; अनन्तविजयम् - (blew his conch) Anantavijaya, ; नकुलः - (while) Nakula ; च - and ; सहदेवः - Sahadeva (blew) ; सुघोष - Sughoṣa (and) ; मणि-पुष्पकौ - Maṇipuṣpaka.

King Yudhiṣṭhira, son of Kuntī, blew his conch Anantavijaya, while Nakula and Sahadeva blew Sughoṣa and Maṇipuṣpaka.

काश्यश्च परमेष्वासः शिखण्डी च महारथः |
धृष्टद्युम्नो विराटश्च सात्यकिश्चापराजितः || BG 1.17 ||
द्रुपदो द्रौपदेयाश्च सर्वशः पृथिवीपते |
सौभद्रश्च महाबाहुः शङ्खान्दध्मुः पृथक् || BG 1.18 ||

पृथिवी-पते - Hey (King Dhṛtarāṣṭra,) the Lord of the land! ; परम-इषु-आसः - The supreme bowmen ; काश्यः - King of Kāśī, ; च - and ; महारथः - the great warrior ; शिखण्डी - Śikhaṇḍī, ; च - and ; धृष्टद्युम्नः - Dhṛṣṭadyumna, ; च - and ; विराटः - Virāṭa, ; च - and ; अपराजितः - invincible ; सात्यकिः - Sātyaki, ; च - and ; द्रुपदः - Drupada, ; द्रौपदेयाः - (and the five) sons of Draupadī, ; च - and ; महा-बाहुः - (Abhimanyu) the mighty-armed ; सौभद्रः - son of Subhadrā, ; सर्वशः - all (of them) ; दध्मुः - blew ; पृथक् पृथक् - (their) individual ; शङ्खान् - conches.

Hey King Dhṛtarāṣṭra! The supreme bowmen King of Kāśī, great warrior Śikhaṇḍī, Dhṛṣṭadyumna, Virāṭa, invincible Sātyaki, Drupada, the sons of Draupadī, and (Abhimanyu) the mighty-armed son of Subhadrā, all blew their conches.

स घोषो धार्तराष्ट्राणां हृदयानि व्यदारयत् |
नभश्च पृथिवीं चैव तुमुलोऽभ्यनुनादयन् || BG 1.19 ||

च - And ; सः - that ; तुमुलः - explosive ; घोषः - sound, ; अभ्यनुनादयन् - reverberating (in) ; नभः - the sky ; च - and ; पृथिवीम् - the earth, ; एव - indeed ; व्यदारयत् - shattered ; हृदयानि - the hearts ; धार्तराष्ट्राणाम् - of Duryodhana and others.

That explosive sound, reverberating in the sky and the earth, shattered the hearts of Duryodhana and others.

अथ व्यवस्थितान्दृष्ट्वा धार्तराष्ट्रान् कपिध्वजः |
प्रवृत्ते शस्त्रसम्पाते धनुरुद्यम्य पाण्डवः ||BG 1.20 ||
हृषीकेशं तदा वाक्यमिदमाह महीपते |

महीपते - Hey (King Dhṛtarāṣṭra,) the Lord of the land! ; अथ - After that, ; दृष्ट्वा - seeing ; धार्त्रराष्ट्रान् - the sons of Dhṛtarāṣṭra ; व्यवस्थितान् - standing ready ; प्रवृत्ते - to commence ; शस्त्र-सम्पाते - the use of weapons, ; पाण्डवः - Pāṇḍava (Arjuna, the son of Pāṇḍu seated on a) ; कपि-ध्वजः - monkey-bannered (chariot) ; तदा - then ; उद्यम्य - lifting ; धनुः - his bow ; आह - said ; इदम् - these ; वाक्यम् - words ; हृषीकेशम् - to Hṛṣīkeśa (Śrī Kṛṣṇa, the Lord of the senses).

Hey King Dhṛtarāṣṭra! After that, seeing the sons of Dhṛtarāṣṭra standing ready to commence the use of weapons, Arjuna, seated on a monkey-bannered chariot, then lifting his bow, said these words to Śrī Kṛṣṇa, the Lord of the senses.

अर्जुन उवाच -
सेनयोरुभयोर्मध्ये रथं स्थापय मेऽच्युत || BG 1.21||
अर्जुनः उवाच - Arjuna said -

अच्युत - Hey Acyuta (Śrī Kṛṣṇa, the infallible One)! ; स्थापय - Position ; मे - my ; रथम् - chariot ; मध्ये - in the middle ; उभयोः - of both ; सेनयोः - armies.

Arjuna said -

Hey Śrī Kṛṣṇa, the infallible One! Position my chariot in the middle of both armies.

यावदेतान्निरीक्षेऽहं योद्धुकामानवस्थितान् |
कैर्मया सह योद्धव्यमस्मिन् रणसमुद्यमे || BG 1.22 ||

यावत् - so that ; अहम् - I ; निरीक्षे - (may adequately) see ; एतान् - them ; अवस्थितान् - (those who are) standing ; योद्धु-कामान् - with a desire to fight ; अस्मिन् - in this ; रण-समुद्यमे - war effort, ; सह - with ; कैः - whom ; मया - I ; योद्धव्यम् - ought to fight,

so that I may adequately see them, those who are standing with a desire to fight in this war effort, with whom I ought to fight,

(Moreover -)

योत्स्यमानानवेक्षेऽहं य एतेऽत्र समागताः ।
धार्तराष्ट्रस्य दुर्बुद्धेर्युद्धे प्रियचिकीर्षवः || BG 1.23 ||

अहम् - I ; अवेक्षे - (want) to see ; एते - those ; प्रिय-चिकीर्षवः - well-wishers ; दुर्बुद्धेः - (of) evil-minded ; धार्तराष्ट्रस्य - Duryodhana ; ये - who ; समागताः - have assembled ; अत्र - here ; योत्स्यमानान् - to fight ; युद्धे - in (this) war.

I want to see those well-wishers of evil-minded Duryodhana who have assembled here to fight in this war.

सञ्जय उवाच |
एवमुक्तो हृषीकेशो गुडाकेशेन भारत |
सेनयोरुभयोर्मध्ये स्थापयित्वा रथोत्तमम् || BG 1.24 ||
भीष्मद्रोणप्रमुखतः सर्वेषां च महीक्षिताम् |
उवाच पार्थ पश्यैतान्समवेतान्कुरूनिति || BG 1.25 ||
सञ्जय उवाच - Sañjaya said -

भारत - Hey (King Dhṛtarāṣṭra,) the descendent of Bharata! ; एवम् - Upon so ; उक्तः - spoken ; गुडाकेशेन - by (Arjuna) the one who has conquered sleep, ; हृषीकेशः - Hṛṣīkeśa (Śrī Kṛṣṇa), ; स्थापयित्वा - standing ; रथ-उत्तमम् - the best of chariots ; मध्ये - in the middle ; उभयोः - of both ; सेनयोः - armies ; प्रमुखतः - facing ; भीष्म-द्रोण - Bhīṣma, Droṇa, ; च - and ; सर्वेषाम् - all ; महीक्षिताम् - kings, ; उवाच - said ; इति - so ; पार्थ - "Hey (Arjuna,) the son of Pṛthā! ; पश्य - See ; एतान् - these ; समवेतान् - assembled ; कुरून् - Kauravas."

Sañjaya said -

Hey King Dhṛtarāṣṭra! Upon spoken by Arjuna, Śrī Kṛṣṇa, standing the best of chariots in the middle of both armies facing Bhīṣma, Droṇa, and all kings, said - "Hey Arjuna! See these assembled Kauravas."

तत्रापश्यत्स्थितान् पार्थ: पितृ नथ पितामहान् |
आचार्यान्मातुलान्भ्रातृ न्पुत्रान्पौत्रान्सखींस्तथा |
श्वशुरान्सुहृदश्चैव सेनयोरुभयोरपि || BG 1.26 ||

अथ - After that, ; तत्र - there ; पार्थः - Pārtha (Arjuna) ; एव - indeed ; अपश्यत् - saw ; पितॄन् - fathers, ; पितामहान् - grandfathers, ; आचार्यान् - teachers, ; मातुलान् - maternal uncles, ; भ्रातॄन् - brothers, ; पुत्रान् - sons, ; पौत्रान् - grandsons, ; श्वशुरान् - fathers-in-law, ; तथा - and ; सखीन् - friends, ; च - and ; अपि - also ; सुहृदः well-wishers ; स्थितान् - standing ; उभयोः - in both ; सेनयोः - armies.

Arjuna saw fathers, grandfathers, teachers, maternal uncles, brothers, sons, grandsons, fathers-in-law, friends, and well-wishers standing in both armies.

तान्समीक्ष्य स कौन्तेय: सर्वान्बन्धूनवस्थितान् |
कृपया परयाविष्टो विषीदन्निदमब्रवीत् || BG 1.27 ||

आविष्टः - Overwhelmed by ; परया - extreme ; कृपया - compassion ; विषीदन् - (and) deep sorrow, ; समीक्ष्य - seeing ; सर्वान् - all ; तान् - those ; बन्धून् - relatives ; अवस्थितान् - standing (ready to fight), ; सः - that ; कौन्तेयः - Kaunteya (Arjuna, the son of Kuntī) ; अब्रवीत् - said ; इदम् - this.

Overwhelmed by extreme compassion and deep sorrow, seeing all those relatives standing, Arjuna said this.

अर्जुन उवाच |
दृष्ट्वेमं स्वजनं कृष्ण युयुत्सुं समुपस्थितम् |
सीदन्ति मम गात्राणि मुखं च परिशुष्यति || BG 1.28 ||
वेपथुश्च शरीरे मे रोमहर्षश्च जायते || BG 1.29 ||
अर्जुन उवाच - *Arjuna said -*

कृष्ण - Hey Śrī Kṛṣṇa! ; दृष्ट्वा - Seeing ; इमम् - these ; स्वजनम् - relatives ; समुपस्थितम् - assembled ; युयुत्सुम् - eager to fight, ; मम - my ; गात्राणि - limbs ; सीदन्ति - are sinking, ; च - and ; मुखम् - (my) face ; परिशुष्यति - is drying up, ; च - and ; मे - my ; शरीरे - body ; वेपथुः - is shaking, ; च - and ; रोम-हर्षः जायते - (my) hairs are standing on end.

Arjuna said -

Hey Śrī Kṛṣṇa! Seeing these relatives assembled eager to fight, my limbs are sinking, my face is drying up, my body is shaking, and my hairs are standing on end.

(Besides this -)

गाण्डीवं स्रंसते हस्तात्त्वक्चै व परिदह्यते |
न च शक्नोम्यवस्थातुं भ्रमतीव च मे मन: || BG 1.30 ||

गाण्डीवम् - Gāṇḍīva ; स्रंसते - is slipping ; हस्तात् - from (my) hand, ; च - and ; एव - also ; त्वक् - (my) skin ; परिदह्यते - is burning, ; शक्नोमि न - I cannot ; अवस्थातुम् - to stand steady, ; च - and ; मे - my ; मनः - mind (is) ; च - also ; भ्रमति इव - wandering (around confused).

Gāṇḍīva is slipping from my hand, my skin is burning, I cannot stand steady, and my mind is wandering.

निमित्तानि च पश्यामि विपरीतानि केशव |
न च श्रेयोऽनुपश्यामि हत्वा स्वजनमाहवे || BG 1.31 ||

केशव - Hey Keśava (Śrī Kṛṣṇa, the one with long hairs)! ; च - Also, ; न अनुपश्यामि - I do not foresee ; श्रेयः - any good ; हत्वा - in killing ; स्वजनम् - my relatives ; आहवे - on the battlefield. पश्यामि च - I also see ; विपरीतानि - contrary ; निमित्तानि - portents.

Hey Keśava! I do not foresee any good in killing my relatives on the battlefield. I also see contrary portents.

(In such a situation -)

न काङ्क्षे विजयं कृष्ण न च राज्यं सुखानि च |
किं नो राज्येन गोविन्द किं भोगैर्जीवितेन वा || BG 1.32 ||

कृष्ण - Hey Śrī Kṛṣṇa! ; न - (I do) not ; काङ्क्षे - desire ; विजयम् - victory, ; च - and ; राज्यम् - kingdom, ; च - and (also, I do) ; न - not (desire) ; सुखानि - happiness. ; गोविन्द - Hey Govinda (Śrī Kṛṣṇa, the one who tends cows)! ; नः - For us, ; किम् - what (are the benefits) ; राज्येन - from the kingdom, ; भोगैः - enjoyments, ; वा - or ; जीवितेन - (even) being alive? ; किम् - what (benefits will accrue)?

Hey Śrī Kṛṣṇa! I do not desire victory, kingdom, or happiness. Hey Govinda! What are the benefits from the kingdom, enjoyments, or even being alive? What benefits will accrue?

(Because -)

येषामर्थे काङ्क्षितं नो राज्यं भोगाः सुखानि च |
त इमेऽवस्थिता युद्धे प्राणांस्त्यक्त्वा धनानि च || BG 1.33 ||

येषाम् - (For) whose ; अर्थे - sake ; नः - we ; काङ्क्षितम् - have coveted ; राज्यम् - the kingdom, ; भोगाः - enjoyments, ; च - and ; सुखानि - happiness - ; त्यक्त्वा - forsaking ; इमे - those (desires) ; धनानि - for wealth ; च - and ; प्राणान् - life, ; ते - they ; अवस्थिताः - are standing ; युद्धे - to fight.

For whose sake we have coveted the kingdom, enjoyments, and happiness - forsaking desires for wealth and life, they are standing to fight.

(Who are they? -)

आचार्याः पितरः पुत्रास्तथैव च पितामहाः |
मातुलाः श्वशुराः पौत्राः श्यालाः सम्बन्धिनस्तथा || BG 1.34 ||

आचार्याः - Preceptors, ; पितरः - fathers, ; पुत्राः - sons, ; पौत्राः -grandsons, ; च - and ; पितामहाः - grandfathers (all these are close relatives), ; तथा - and ; एव - similarly ; मातुलाः - maternal uncles, ; श्वशुराः - fathers-in-law, ; श्यालाः - brothers-in-law, ; तथा - and (also other) ; सम्बन्धिनः - relatives.

Preceptors, fathers, sons, grandsons, grandfathers, maternal uncles, fathers-in-law, brothers-in-law, and other relatives.

(That is why -)

एतान्न हन्तुमिच्छामि घ्नतोऽपि मधुसूदन |
अपि त्रैलोक्यराज्यस्य हेतोः किं नु महीकृते || BG 1.35 ||

मधुसूदन - Hey Madhusūdana (Śrī Kṛṣṇa, the slayer of demon Madhu)! ; अपि - Though (they may) ; घ्नतः - slay (me), ; न - (I do) not ; इच्छामि - wish ; हन्तुम् - to kill ; एतान् - them, ; अपि हेतोः - (not) even for ; त्रैलोक्य-राज्यस्य - the kingdom of the three worlds, ; नु - then ; किम् - why ; महीकृते - for some little land?

Hey Madhusūdana! Though they may slay me, I do not wish to kill them, not even for the kingdom of the three worlds, then why for some little land?

निहत्य धार्तराष्ट्रान्नः का प्रीतिः स्याज्जनार्दन |
पापमेवाश्रयेदस्मान्हत्वैतानाततायिनः || BG 1.36 ||

जनार्दन - Hey Janārdana (Śrī Kṛṣṇa, the one who inflicts pain on evil persons)! ; का - What ; स्यात् - is ; नः - our ; प्रीतिः - benefit ; निहत्य - by slaying ; धार्तराष्ट्रान् - the sons of Dhṛtarāṣṭra? ; हत्वा - By killing ; एतान् - these ; आततायिनः - Ātatāyī, ; अस्मान् - we ; आश्रयेत् - will be incur ; पापम् - sin ; एव - only.

Hey Janārdana! What is our benefit by slaying the sons of Dhṛtarāṣṭra? By killing these Ātatāyī,[58]we will incur sin only.

तस्मान्नार्हा वयं हन्तुं धार्तराष्ट्रान्स्वबान्धवान् |
स्वजनं हि कथं हत्वा सुखिनः स्याम माधव || BG 1.37 ||

तस्मात् - Therefore, ; न अर्हाः - it is inappropriate ; वयम् - for us ; हन्तुम् - to slay ; स्वबान्धवान् - our relatives, ; धार्तराष्ट्रान् - the sons of Dhṛtarāṣtra. ; माधव - Hey Mādhava (Śrī Kṛṣṇa)! ; हि - For ; कथम् - how ; स्याम - can we be ; सुखिनः - happy ; हत्वा - by killing ; स्वजनम् - our relatives?

Therefore, it is inappropriate for us to slay our relatives, the sons of Dhṛtarāṣṭra. Hey Mādhava! How can we be happy by killing our relatives?

यद्यप्येते न पश्यन्ति लोभोपहतचेतसः |
कुलक्षयकृतं दोषं मित्रद्रोहे च पातकम् || BG 1.38 ||

यदि-अपि - Yet, ; एते - these (people), ; लोभ-उपहत-चेतसः - whose conscience is overpowered by greed, ; न - do not ; पश्यन्ति - see ; दोषम् - the evil ; कुल-क्षय-कृतम् - arising from the downfall of the family ; च - and ; पातकम् - the sin ; मित्र-द्रोहे - of being hostile towards friends.

Yet, these people, whose conscience is overpowered by greed, do not see the evil arising from the downfall of the family and the sin of being hostile towards friends.

(However -)

कथं न ज्ञेयमस्माभिः पापादस्मान्निवर्तितुम् |
कुलक्षयकृतं दोषं प्रपश्यद्भिर्जनार्दन || BG 1.39 ||

जनार्दन - Hey Janārdana (Śrī Kṛṣṇa)! ; प्रपश्यद्भिः - Recognizing ; दोषम् - the evil ; कुल-क्षय-कृतम् - arising from the family's downfall, ; कथम् - why ; अस्माभिः - should we ; न - not ; ज्ञेयम् - try ; निवर्तितुम् - to save ; अस्मान् - ourselves from these ; पापात् - sins?

Hey Janārdana! Recognizing the evil arising from the family's downfall, why should we not try to save ourselves from these sins?

(Now, Arjuna describes the six evils arising from the family's downfall. It is evident that -)

कुलक्षये प्रणश्यन्ति कुलधर्माः सनातनाः |
धर्मे नष्टे कुलं कृत्स्नमधर्मोऽभिभवत्युत || BG 1.40 ||

*कुल-क्षये - (**First**), with the family's downfall, ; सनातनाः - all long-standing ; कुल-धर्माः - family traditions and duties ; प्रणश्यन्ति - will be destroyed. ; उत - (**Second**), also ; नष्टे - with the destruction ; धर्मे - of traditions and duties, ; कृत्स्नम् - the entire ; कुलम् - family ; अभिभवति - will become ; अधर्मः - unrighteous.*

---

[58] Ātatāyī (आततायी) means a heinous crime committer. It is used on an armed person who kills an unarmed person, or one who uses poison to kill.

(***First***), with the family's downfall, all long-standing family traditions and duties[59] will be destroyed. (***Second***) with the destruction of traditions and duties, the entire family will become unrighteous.

अधर्माभिभवात्कृष्ण प्रदुष्यन्ति कुलस्त्रियः |
स्त्रीषु दुष्टासु वार्ष्णेय जायते वर्णसंकरः || BG 1.41 ||

*कृष्ण - (**Third**), Hey Śrī Kṛṣṇa! ; कुल-स्त्रियः - Women of the family ; प्रदुष्यन्ति - will become immoral ; अधर्म-अभिभवात् - with the influence of unrighteousness. ; वार्ष्णेय - (**Fourth**) Hey Vārṣṇeya (Śrī Kṛṣṇa, the descendent of Vṛṣṇi)! ; दुष्टासु - From immoral ; स्त्रीषु - women, ; वर्ण-सङ्करः - (children) of mixed functional classes ; जायते - will be born.*

(**Third**), Hey Śrī Kṛṣṇa! Women of the family will become immoral with the influence of unrighteousness. (**Fourth**) Hey Vārṣṇeya! From immoral women, children of mixed functional classes will be born.

सङ्करो नरकायैव कुलघ्नानां कुलस्य च |
पतन्ति पितरो ह्येषां लुप्तपिण्डोदकक्रियाः || BG 1.42 ||

*सङ्करः - (**Fifth**, those) children of mixed functional classes ; एव - will indeed ; कुल-घ्नानाम् - take those destroyers of family ; च - and ; कुलस्य - (the remaining) family ; नरकाय - into hell. ; पितरः - (**Sixth**), departed ancestors ; एषाम् - whose ; लुप्त-पिण्ड-उदक-क्रियाः - "Piṇḍodaka-Kriyā" has vanished ; हि - will undoubtedly ; पतन्ति - fall.*

(**Fifth**), those children of mixed functional classes will take those destroyers of family and the remaining family into hell. (**Sixth**), departed ancestors whose Piṇḍodaka Kriyā[60] has vanished will undoubtedly fall.

(This way -)

दोषैरेतैः कुलघ्नानां वर्णसंकरकारकैः |
उत्साद्यन्ते जातिधर्माः कुलधर्माश्च शाश्वताः || BG 1.43 ||

शाश्वताः - Long-standing ; जाति-धर्माः - class duties ; च - and ; कुल-धर्माः - family traditions and duties ; उत्साद्यन्ते - are ruined ; एतैः - by these ; दोषैः - flaws ; कुल-घ्नानाम् - of the destroyers of the family ; वर्णसंकर-कारकैः - that create mixed functional classes.

Long-standing class duties and family traditions and duties are ruined by the flaws of the destroyers of the family that create mixed functional classes.

(Additionally -)

उत्सन्नकुलधर्माणां मनुष्याणां जनार्दन |
नरकेऽनियतं वासो भवतीत्यनुशुश्रुम || BG 1.44 ||

जनार्दन - Hey Janārdana (Śrī Kṛṣṇa)! ; अनुशुश्रुम - We have heard ; इति - that ; मनुष्याणाम् - people ; उत्सन्न-कुल-धर्माणाम् - whose family traditions and duties have been ruined ; वासः भवति - reside ; नरके - in hell ; अनियतम् - for an indefinite time,

Hey Janārdana! We have heard that people whose family traditions and duties have been ruined reside in hell for an indefinite time.

अहो बत महत्पापं कर्तुं व्यवसिता वयम् |
यद्राज्यसुखलोभेन हन्तुं स्वजनमुद्यताः || BG 1.45 ||

अहो बत - What a pity! ; यत् - That ; वयम् - we ; व्यवसिता - are determined ; कर्तुम् - to commit ; महत् - a grievous ; पापम् - sin, ; राज्य-सुख-लोभेन - (and) with the greed for the kingdom and its pleasures, ; उद्यताः - we are ready ; हन्तुम् - to slaughter ; स्वजनम् - (even) our own family.

---

59 Duties mean Nitya-Karma (नित्य-कर्म, daily obligatory duties, rituals) and Naimittika-Karma (नैमित्तिक-कर्म, occasional duties, rituals).
60 Piṇḍodaka-Kriyā (पिण्डोदक-क्रिया) means the performance (क्रिया, Kriyā) of the offering of a round mass generally of rice (पिण्ड, Piṇḍa) and water (उदक, Udaka) in a ritual to pay homage to the departed ancestors.

What a pity! We are determined to commit a grievous sin, and with the greed for the kingdom and its pleasures, we are ready to slaughter even our own family.

(The evil sentiment that has arisen in me, in its place -)

यदि मामप्रतीकारमशस्त्रं शस्त्रपाणय: |
धार्तराष्ट्रा रणे हन्युस्तन्मे क्षेमतरं भवेत् || BG 1.46 ||

भवेत् - It would be ; क्षेमतरम् - better ; मे - for me ; यदि - (even) if ; शस्त्र-पाणयः - the armed ; धार्तराष्ट्राः - sons of Dhṛtarāṣṭra ; हन्युः - killed ; माम् - me ; अशस्त्रम् - unarmed ; अप्रतीकारम् - (and) unretaliating ; रणे - on the battlefield ; तत् - then.

It would be better for me even if the armed sons of Dhṛtarāṣṭra killed me unarmed and unretaliating on the battlefield.

(That is, though it is sinful to kill an unarmed and unretaliating person, it would be more beneficial for me to be killed as a fruit of my evil sentiment.)

सञ्जय उवाच |
एवमुक्त्वार्जुन: सङ्ख्ये रथोपस्थ उपाविशत् |
विसृज्य सशरं चापं शोकसंविग्नमानस: || BG 1.47 ||
सञ्जयः उवाच - Sañjaya said -

अर्जुनः - Arjuna ; उक्त्वा - having said ; एवम् - so ; सङ्ख्ये - on the battlefield, ; शोक-संविग्न-मानसः - (his) mind anxious with grief, ; विसृज्य - abandoning ; चापं - (his) bow ; सशरम् - with arrows, ; उपाविशत् - sat down ; रथ-उपस्थे - in the rear of the chariot.

Sañjaya said -

Arjuna, having said so on the battlefield, his mind anxious with grief, abandoning his bow with arrows, sat down in the rear of the chariot.

ॐ तत्सदिति श्रीमद्भगवद्गीतासूपनिषत्सु ब्रह्मविद्यायां योगशास्त्रे

श्रीकृष्णार्जुनसम्वादे अर्जुनविषादयोगो नाम

प्रथमोऽध्याय: || 1 ||

Oṃ Tat Sat

In the Śrīmad Bhagavad Gītā Upaniṣad

The Yoga Science of the Knowledge of Self-Realization

The Discourse of Lord Śrī Kṛṣṇa and Arjuna

This First Chapter

Yoga Named - The Despondency of Arjuna

Clarification

The first chapter is in the form of an introduction to the subject. How was the opportunity afforded for the Upadeśa (spiritual guidance) of Śrīmad Bhagavad Gītā? It is said that King Bhagīratha (भगीरथ) had brought down the material (अधिभौतिक, Adhibhautika) Gaṅgā from the heavens to the earth and thereby provided deliverance to sixty thousand sons of King Sāgara. In the same manner, how can Arjuna, by bringing Gaṅgā to the surface of the earth in the form of transcendent knowledge (Adhyātma) of Gītā, uplift innumerable children of mother earth? This chapter formulates that.

When the armies of Kauravas and Pāṇḍavas had assembled on the battlefield of Kurukṣetra for the Mahābhārata War, at that time, Maharṣi Vedavyāsa came to the blind King Dhṛtarāṣṭra in Hastināpura. He said, "If you desire to witness the battle, I will give you a divine vision to see it directly (Pratyakṣa) while sitting here in the palace." Dhṛtarāṣṭra joining his palms, prayed, "Hey Lord! Whether it is Duryodhana or Yudhiṣṭhira, both are my children. With my own eyes, I do not have enough courage to see the deaths of my children. However, if you deem it appropriate, then grace Sañjaya, my charioteer (Sārathī), with divine vision. He will verbally narrate the war as he sees it." Lord Vedavyāsa accepted the prayer, gave divine vision to Sañjaya, and left. Now, Sañjaya sitting in Hastināpura, provides an instantaneous account, word by word, of what is happening on the battlefield.

Dhṛtarāṣṭra asked, "Hey Sañjaya! On the righteousness land (धर्मक्षेत्र, Dharmakṣetra) Kurukṣetra, having assembled with the desire to fight, what did my and Pāṇḍu's sons do?" Going to Kurukṣetra was the purpose (Nimitta) of the war and indeed to wage war, then this question, "What did my and Pāṇḍu's sons do?" sounds incongruent. Still with a lingering doubt in his mind that it is quite possible that by going to Kurukṣetra, my sons may have been influenced by its righteousness, and realizing vacuity (असारता, Asāratā) of the Saṃsāra may have forsaken ill will and may have embraced each other and thereby there was no reason for the war. It is this doubt in the mind of Dhṛtarāṣṭra that has raised his question, and that is why the adjective "धर्मक्षेत्र, Dharmakṣetra" is given to the battlefield Kurukṣetra.

In response, Sañjaya told Dhṛtarāṣṭra that, at that time, having seen the Pāṇḍava army in battle formation, Duryodhana went to preceptor Droṇācārya and spoke these words, "Hey Ācarya ! Observe this immense army of Pāṇḍu's sons, set in battle formation by your intelligent disciple Dhṛṣṭadyumna, son of Drupada," and then recited the names all principal warriors (Mahārathī). It should be noted that "Your intelligent disciple Dhṛṣṭadyumna has set the battle formation of the Pāṇḍava army" is a sarcastic statement, implying that the warfare knowledge learned from you is being used against you. The intention herein is to arouse agitation in the mind of Droṇācārya and to recall his past animosity.[61]After that, Duryodhana, reckoning the names of the prominent chiefs of his army, recognized Droṇācārya first, the intention being to arouse superiority in the mind of Droṇācārya. Then Duryodhana gave comfort to Droṇācārya, saying that, protected by grandfather Bhīṣma, our army is invincible from all sides; however, the army that Bhīma protects is easy to win over. Then he implored all of them, stationed in respective control of all battlefronts, to protect only Bhīṣma from all sides.

Listening to the words of Duryodhana towards Droṇācārya, grandfather Bhīṣma, arousing joy in the heart of Duryodhana, in a loud tone, roared like a lion and blew his conch. With that, conches, drums, small drums, large kettledrums, blow horns, and various other musical instruments blared forth all together, and that sound was highly tumultuous. After that, Śrī Kṛṣṇa, the five Pāṇḍavas, the five sons of Draupadī, and other kings on their side also blew their conches. That explosive sound shattered the heart of Duryodhana and reverberated in the sky and the earth.

---

[61] In childhood, when King Drupada and Droṇācārya were co-students, Drupada would often tell Droṇa that upon his coronation, he would give him part of his Kingdom, and both would spend the rest of their lives as co-equals. Upon completing their education, at some point in time, Drupada became King. However, here Droṇa spent his time in dire poverty. One day Aśvatthāmā, son of Droṇa, seeing other children drinking milk came home crying. Not having any milk at home, Droṇa took some rice, crushed them, and after mixing it with water gave it to his son as milk and satisfied him. However, Droṇa was highly distraught with his conduct. Impelled by love for his son, he went to King Drupada for monetary assistance to remove his poverty. King Drupada, in his excessive kingly vanity, instead of fulfilling his own promise, disrespected Droṇa. As a result, Droṇa developed longstanding anger towards Drupada and subsequently focused his efforts on teaching weaponry to the Pāṇḍavas and Kauravas. Upon completion of education, Pāṇḍavas and Kauravas were commanded by Droṇa to capture Drupada as Guru-Dakṣiṇā. The Pāṇḍavas won over Drupada, captured him, and brought him to Droṇa. Droṇa took half of the Kingdom and set Drupada free. Feeling extremely powerless, Drupada made a mental resolve to slay Droṇa and to accomplish that initiated a sacrifice (Yajña) to acquire a son who would fulfill his resolve. Therefrom, as the fruit of the sacrifice, son Dhṛṣṭadyumna was born, who later on learned weaponry from Droṇa and who accepted Droṇa as his preceptor. That same Dhṛṣṭadyumna is now standing in opposition to Droṇācārya, setting up battle formation for the Pāṇḍavas as their chief and ready to slay Droṇācārya. Here, Duryodhana intends to incite Droṇācārya to recall his past animosity against Drupada that was embedded in his heart.

After seeing Duryodhana, Arjuna lifted his bow and asked Śrī Kṛṣṇa, "Hey, Śrī Kṛṣṇa, the infallible One! Position my chariot in the middle of both armies to see who has come to fight and with whom I ought to fight? I want to properly see all those well-wishers of evil-minded Duryodhana who have gathered here to fight." Thereupon so spoken by Arjuna, Śrī Kṛṣṇa took the chariot and positioned it in the middle of both armies and said, "Hey Arjuna! See these assembled Kauravas." Arjuna saw fathers, grandfathers, teachers, maternal uncles, brothers, sons, grandsons, friends, fathers-in-law, and well-wishers standing in both armies. Seeing all of those relatives standing ready to fight, overwhelmed by extreme compassion and deep sorrow, he said, "Hey, Śrī Kṛṣṇa! Seeing these relatives assembled eager to fight, my limbs are sinking, my face is drying up, my body is shaking, and my hairs are standing on end. Gāṇḍīva is slipping from my hand, my skin is burning, I cannot stand steady, and my mind is wandering. Hey Śrī Kṛṣṇa! I also see contrary portents. I do not foresee any good in killing relatives on the battlefield. Hey Śrī Kṛṣṇa, I do not desire victory, kingdom, or happiness. What is the benefit from the kingdom, enjoyments, or even being alive? What benefits will accrue? For whose sake we have coveted the kingdom, enjoyments, and happiness, they are none other than these teachers, fathers, sons, grandsons, grandfathers, maternal uncles, fathers-in-law, brothers-in-law, and other relatives, who are all standing ready to fight forsaking desires for wealth and life. Therefore, even if we acquire all we have coveted, they will be nothing but like cremation grounds. Because real joy is in the enjoyment of luxury with all relatives, not like an iniquitous (Pāmara) person who would kill and enjoy blood-stained opulence. Hey Śrī Kṛṣṇa! Though they may slay me, I do not wish to kill them, not even for the kingdom of the three worlds, then why for some little land? Hey Śrī Kṛṣṇa! What is our benefit by slaying the sons of Dhṛtarāṣṭra? We will incur sin only by slaying these Ātatāyī (heinous crime committers). Therefore, it is inappropriate for us to slay the sons of Dhṛtarāṣṭra. Hey Śrī Kṛṣṇa! How can we be happy by slaying our relatives? Yet, these people, whose conscience is overpowered by greed, do not see the evil arising from the family's downfall and the sin of being hostile towards friends. Hey Śrī Kṛṣṇa! Recognizing the evil arising from the family's downfall, why should we not try to save ourselves from these sins?" Listen -

1. All long-standing family traditions and duties will be destroyed with the family's downfall. The debt (ऋण, Ṛṇa) of a householder towards deities, seers, and ancestors will vanish. When there is no one in the family to take the name and offer water, then who will pay off this obligation?
2. With the destruction of long-standing family traditions and duties, in the absence of righteousness (Dharma), unrighteousness (Adharma) will take over. In the absence of one, it becomes necessary for the second to take over, similar to how night takes over when the day ends.
3. When the bugle of unrighteousness starts making its call and greed for objects of enjoyment takes hold, women of the family will become immoral. Righteousness is the only thing that, like a guard, checks the thief's (in the form of greed) entry and does not allow him to enter the family. With the vanishing of righteousness, the thief's entry into the family and looting of the wealth of piety is like a piece of cake.
4. From immoral women, with the evil of the downfall of the family, there will be a rise in the birth of children of mixed functional classes (वर्णसंकरता, Varṇasaṃkaratā).
5. For those destroyers of family, falling into hell is inevitable. In addition, the children of mixed functional classes are undoubtedly there who will take the remaining family and themselves to hell.
6. Moreover, departed ancestors will undoubtedly fall with the vanishing of Piṇḍodaka-Kriyā due to the children of mixed functional classes.

With these mixed functional class-producing evils of the destroyers of family, destruction of themselves, their family, women, and ancestors is definite. By these flaws of the destroyers of the family, long-standing class duties and family traditions and duties will be ruined. We have heard that people whose family traditions and duties are ruined reside in hell for an indefinite time. Knowing those family-destroying faults, why should we not try to save ourselves from these sins?

What a pity! We are determined to commit a grievous sin, and with greed for the kingdom and its pleasures, we are ready to slaughter even our own family. In place of the evil sentiment in my heart, it would be better for me even if the armed sons of Dhṛtarāṣṭra killed me unarmed and unretaliating on the battlefield. Then, having said so on the battlefield, his mind anxious with grief, abandoning his bow with arrows, Arjuna sat down in the rear of the chariot.

Accordingly, in this chapter, the cause (Nimitta) of Arjuna's grief was articulated, by which, in the form of Gītā, the transcendent knowledge Gaṅgā incarnated. After this, Sañjaya describes to Dhṛtarāṣṭra the way dialogue between Lord Śrī Kṛṣṇa and Arjuna happened in the next chapter.

CHAPTER 2

THE SĀṄKHYA YOGA

सञ्जय उवाच |
तं तथा कृपयाविष्टमश्रुपूर्णाकुलेक्षणम् |
विषीदन्तमिदं वाक्यमुवाच मधुसूदनः || BG 2.1 ||
सञ्जय उवाच - Sañjaya Said -

तम् - (Seeing) him (Arjuna) ; तथा - this way ; आविष्टम् - overwhelmed with ; कृपया - compassion, ; अश्रु-पूर्ण - tearful ; आकुल-ईक्षणम् - with distressed eyes, ; विषीदन्तम् - (and) despondent, ; मधुसूदनः - Madhusūdana (Śrī Kṛṣṇa, the slayer of demon Madhu) ; उवाच - spoke ; इदम् - these ; वाक्यम् - words.

Sañjaya said -

(Seeing) Arjuna overwhelmed with compassion, tearful with distressed eyes, and despondent, Śrī Kṛṣṇa spoke these words.

श्रीभगवानुवाच |
कुतस्त्वा कश्मलमिदं विषमे समुपस्थितम् |
अनार्यजुष्टमस्वर्ग्यमकीर्तिकरमर्जुन || BG 2.2 ||
श्रीभगवान् उवाच - Śrī Bhagavān said -

अर्जुन - Hey Arjuna! ; कुतः - Whence ; इदम् - this ; अनार्य-जुष्टम् - ignoble, ; अस्वर्ग्यम् - unheavenly, ; अकीर्तिकरम् - (and) disgraceful ; कश्मलम् - ignorance ; समुपस्थितम् - arisen ; त्वा - in you ; विषमे - at this critical juncture?

Śrī Bhagavān said -

Hey Arjuna! Whence this ignoble, unheavenly, and disgraceful ignorance arisen in you at this critical juncture?

Intent - There are only three perspectives to test the appropriateness and acceptability of any action (क्रिया, Kriyā) -

1. Best individuals practice it.
2. It would take one to higher abodes.
3. It would assist in establishing a good name.

Likewise, the true nature of righteousness (Dharma) is - "यतोऽभ्युदय निश्रेयसिद्धि स धर्म, actions that elevate one in this world and are helpful for liberation in the other world is called Dharma." Here, however, the words of Bhagavāna are that from all three perspectives, your desistance in the battle is nothing more than the cause for your downfall. Such desistance is neither respectable for a noble person nor helpful in this world or other worlds. From the perspective of Bhagavāna (भगवद्-दृष्टि, Bhagavad-Dṛṣṭi), the evil due to the ruination of the family that was spoken by Arjuna is not respectful but is one that deserves disrespect. Due to the fear of family ruination, if an evil family was allowed to blossom and its wicked thorns nurtured, the entire earth would be engulfed in sins. Then, the limits of morality would disappear, and punishment by a Kṣatriya king would become meaningless. Indeed, the purpose of the incarnation of Bhagavāna as provided in BG 4.8 would be of no use.

In contrast, killing an evil person is for his good and the world. Because, here in the kingdom of Prakṛti, the seeds of sins that he was sowing by handfuls and whose bad results are inevitable, he can be free; and there, the world would become safer from his atrocities. The slaying of an evil person can be an example for himself and the world. However, that was only an ignorance-born delusion of Arjuna with a contrary sentiment of unrighteousness (Adharma) in righteousness (Dharma) and righteousness in unrighteousness. Loss or gain, sin or piety towards a righteous goal is always seen from a collective perspective (समष्टि-दृष्टि, Samaṣṭi-Dṛṣṭi). From a collective perspective, a loss is a loss, and gain is gain. From an individual perspective (व्यष्टि-दृष्टि, Vyaṣṭi-Dṛṣṭi), there is no such bargain for loss or gain and sin or piety. From a righteous point of view, if good comes to a family by killing the evil one, then killing that one person is an act of piety.

For the interest of a community, a family, for the good of a region, a district, and the good of the world, a country ought to be sacrificed, and not all those acts are sinful but indeed pious. In a righteous war, hesitation by Arjuna in killing unrighteous family members is contrary to Kshatriya's duty, and unrighteousness is its direct result. "With the destruction of the family, women of the family will become immoral, and children of mixed functional classes will be born," all of these are nothing but Arjuna's delusional imaginations. They are not direct consequences of the destruction of the family but are indeed indirect, and not definite, but indefinite. If they were actual fruits of family ruination, then with the destruction of the family, such influence should have been visible in the Kauravas. However, there is no historical indication of such an effect in the Kaurava lineage. In the world, what is adored is righteousness and not worldly relationships. Relationships with relatives are limited to the current body, which is only in the awake state. In the sleep state, there is no such relationship. However, the association of righteousness is in all forms of existence and all conditions. Therefore, the behavior of Arjuna is one that no noble person would emulate. If Arjuna abandons the righteous war, then ignorance-based desisting being contrary to the duty of a Kṣatriya cannot be considered an act of piety. He gave more importance to the delusional dream-like unreal worldly relationships and did not sacrifice them for true righteousness. However, the plea of Dharma is that, for true righteousness, all temporal relationships should be broken like a blade of grass. Therefore, this desistance should be sinful. When it is sinful, it will drop one from higher worlds. In this world, it would bring infamy and nothing else. Thus, the statement of Bhagavāna that this ignorance of yours "अनार्यजुष्टमस्वर्ग्यमकीर्तिकरम्, is not commendable for noble persons, will not take you to heavens and will not produce recognition in this world." That was articulated from a righteous perspective. From realizing the Supreme Reality (Pāramārthika-Dṛṣṭi), Bhagavāna will articulate further.

(That is why -)

क्लैब्यं मा स्म गमः पार्थ नैतत्त्वय्युपपद्यते |
क्षुद्रं हृदयदौर्बल्यं त्यक्त्वोत्तिष्ठ परन्तप || BG 2.3 ||

पार्थ - Hey Pārtha (Arjuna)! ; मा स्म गमः - Yield not to ; क्लैब्यम् - unmanliness. ; एतत् - It ; न - is not ; उपपद्यते - befitting ; त्वयि - you. ; परन्तप - Hey Parantapa (Arjuna, the terror of foes)! ; उत्तिष्ठ - Stand up, ; त्यक्त्वा - forsaking ; क्षुद्रम् - the lowly ; हृदय-दौर्बल्यम् - weakness of the heart (to fight).

Hey Arjuna! Yield not to unmanliness. It is not befitting you. Hey, the terror of foes! Stand up, forsaking the lowly weakness of the heart.

Intent - Arjuna understood that the reason and grief he had expressed not to fight as provided at the end of the first chapter is accordant with righteousness, and Bhagavāna will sanction his views. Bhagavāna will accept as proper and will say, "Undoubtedly with the ruination of family, evils such as women of the family becoming immoral, birth of children of mixed functional classes (वर्णसंकर प्रजा, Varṇasaṃkara Prajā), mockery of family traditions and duties (कुलधर्म, Kuladharma) and duties of the class in which one is born (जातिधर्म, Jātidharma), and ruination of ancestors will take hold. That would be extremely catastrophic. Good that you awoke early and became cautious. Such a battle is never right." However, here, Bhagavāna said something completely unexpected, and to such an extent that to the mighty Arjuna, holder of the great bow Gāṇḍīva, a whip in the form of the word "unmanly" was flung.

(With his ears perking up, astonished Arjuna said -)

अर्जुन उवाच |
कथं भीष्ममहं सङ्ख्ये द्रोणं च मधुसूदन |
इषुभिः प्रतियोत्स्यामि पूजार्हावरिसूदन || BG 2.4 ||
Arjuna said -
अर्जुनः उवाच - Arjuna said -

मधुसूदन - Hey Madhusūdana (Śrī Kṛṣṇa)! ; कथम् - How ; योत्स्यामि अहम् - can I fight ; प्रति - against ; भीष्मम् - (Pitāmaha) Bhīṣma ; च - and ; द्रोणम् - (Ācarya) Droṇa ; इषुभिः - with arrows ; सङ्ख्ये - on the battlefield? ; अरि-सूदन - Hey Arisūdana (Śrī Kṛṣṇa, the slayer of foes)! ; पूजा-अर्हौ - (They both) are worthy of my reverence.

Hey Madhusūdana! How can I fight against Pitāmaha Bhīṣma and Ācarya Droṇa with arrows on the battlefield? Hey Arisūdana! They both are worthy of my reverence.

Intent - Even if it is accepted that slaying evil Duryodhana is morally correct, how can we behead grandfather Bhīṣma and Droṇācārya? They both deserve our reverence; our duty is to pay homage at their feet.

(That is why -)

गुरूनहत्वा हि महानुभावान् श्रेयो भोक्तुं भैक्ष्यमपीह लोके |
हत्वार्थकामांस्तु गुरूनिहैव भुञ्जीय भोगान् रुधिरप्रदिग्धान् || BG 2.5 ||

अपि - Indeed, ; श्रेयः - it would be better ; भोक्तुम् - to live ; भैक्ष्यम् - on alms ; इह - in this ; लोके - world ; अहत्वा - rather than killing ; महानुभावान् - honorable elders ; गुरून् - (- our) preceptors. ; हि - Because ; हत्वा - by killing ; गुरून् - the preceptors, ; इह - here (in this world), ; तु - certainly (we will) ; एव - only ; भुञ्जीय - be enjoying ; अर्थ-कामान् - material and sensual ; भोगान् - enjoyments ; रुधिर-प्रदिग्धान् - stained (by their) blood.

Indeed, it would be better to live on alms in this world rather than killing honorable elders - our preceptors. Because by killing the preceptors, we will only be enjoying material and sensual enjoyments stained by their blood.

Intent - The term Mahānubhāvān (महानुभावान्) is an adjective of Guru (गुरु, preceptor). It means that one ought to emulate the conduct of these "preceptors with great experience," such as honorable elders Bhīṣma and Droṇa. Under Vedantic philosophy, the purpose of human birth is to pursue Dharma (धर्म, righteousness, moral values), Artha (अर्थ, wealth, economic values), Kāma (काम, desire, psychological values) and Mokṣa (मोक्ष, liberation, spiritual values). Among them, Artha (wealth) and Kāma (desire) only give transient happiness, though, in the end, their result is only unhappiness, that is why they are not beneficial (श्रेय, Śreya) but are just dear (प्रेय, Preya). Though Dharma and Mokṣa are difficult during the effort, the results are excellent, so they are not just dear but beneficial. Arjuna, at this time, disregarding what is agreeable, is keen on knowing and has said that by slaying the preceptors, the maximum that can happen is for some time in this world we will get pleasure from material and sensual enjoyments (अर्थकामान् भोगान्). In this world, with the acquisition of the kingdom, all we will get is economic opulence such as land, wealth, and sensual enjoyments. However, the result of slaying the preceptors will be horrendous. Instead of killing them, it would be better for us to live on alms rather than take pleasure in those blood-stained enjoyments.

न चैतद्विद्म: कतरन्नो गरीयो यद्वा जयेम यदि वा नो जयेयु: |
यानेव हत्वा न जिजीविषाम स्तेऽवस्थिता: प्रमुखे धार्तराष्ट्रा: || BG 2.6 ||

च - And (we) ; न - do not ; विद्मः - know ; एतत् - that, ; कतरत् - which ; गरीयः - is better ; नः - for us (to fight or not to fight) ; यत् वा - whether (by fighting,) ; जयेम - we will win ; यदि वा - or ; जयेयुः - they will win ; नः - over us. ; एव - Indeed, ; न - (we do) not ; जिजीविषामः - wish to live ; हत्वा - by killing ; यान् - those (relatives -) ; ते - they ; धार्तराष्ट्राः - the sons of Dhṛtarāṣṭra ; अवस्थिताः - who are standing ; प्रमुखे - in front (to kill or be killed).

We do not know which is better for us, whether we will win or they will win over us. Indeed, we do not wish to live by killing those sons of Dhṛtarāṣṭra who are standing in front.

Intent - Either these people will conquer us, or we will defeat them and enjoy material and sensual enjoyments. It is not the direct consequence of war, but only an indirect, and not definite, but indeed indefinite. While "killing those sons of Dhṛtarāṣṭra we do not even want to live, yet they are all standing right in front of us ready to kill or be killed," - is the evident malefic result of the war. On this subject, "my mind is confused whether for us fighting the war is better or abandoning the war is better."

(That is why -)

कार्पण्यदोषोपहतस्वभाव: पृच्छामि त्वां धर्मसम्मूढचेता: |
यच्छ्रेय: स्यान्निश्चितं ब्रूहि तन्मे शिष्यस्तेऽहं शाधि मां त्वां प्रपन्नम् || BG 2.7 ||

अहम् - I am ; ते - Your ; शिष्यः - disciple ; प्रपन्नम् - (and have) surrendered ; त्वां - to You. ; शाधि - (Please) guide ; माम् - me. ; स्वभावः - (My innate) nature ; उपहत - is affected ; कार्पण्य-दोष - by cowardice ; धर्म-सम्मूढ-चेताः - (and my) mind is confused about duty. ; पृच्छामि - I am asking ; त्वाम् - You to ; ब्रूहि - tell ; मे - me ; तत् - that ; यत् - which ; स्यात् - is ; निश्चितम् - decisively ; श्रेयः - beneficial.

I am Your disciple and have surrendered to You. Please guide me. My innate nature is affected by cowardice, and my mind is confused about duty. I am asking You to tell me that which is decisively beneficial.

Intent - Based on those above, from my perspective, war appears to be disastrous, and here, desisting war, You indicate that they are both ruinous. That is why, with a dilemma of fighting the war is my duty or abandoning the war is my duty, my mind has become "किंकर्तव्यविमूढ, confused about what to do." With my inability to decide, cowardice has engulfed my mind, and as a result, my Kṣatriya nature is ruined. I am surrendering to You as Your disciple; please guide me on what is beneficial.

न हि प्रपश्यामि ममापनुद्याद् यच्छोकमुच्छोषणमिन्द्रियाणाम् |
अवाप्य भूमावसपत्नमृद्धं राज्यं सुराणामपि चाधिपत्यम् || BG 2.8 ||

हि - Because ; अपि - even ; अवाप्य - acquiring ; ऋद्धम् - a prosperous ; राज्यम् - kingdom ; भूमौ - on the earth, ; असपत्नम् - free from enemies ; च - and ; अधिपत्यम् - supremacy over ; सुराणाम् - the deities, ; (अहम्) - (I) ; न - do not ; प्रपश्यामि - see (the approach) ; यत् - which ; अपनुद्यात् - can remove ; मम - my ; इन्द्रियाणाम् - senses- ; उच्छोषणम् - drying ; शोकम् - grief.

Even acquiring a prosperous kingdom on the earth, free from enemies and supremacy over the deities, I do not see the approach which can remove my senses-drying grief.

Intent - Arjuna opened up his heart before Śrī Kṛṣṇa and kicked out this and other worlds' desirable material and sensual enjoyments. In addition, ardently becoming thirsty for the beneficial righteousness (Dharma) and liberation (Mokṣa), he surrendered to Bhagavāna with a disciple sentiment. Here, an occasion was described of one who is fit (Adhikārī) to be cleansed in the Gaṅgā of transcendent knowledge of Gītā.

सञ्जय उवाच |
एवमुक्त्वा हृषीकेशं गुडाकेश: परन्तप |
न योत्स्य इति गोविन्दमुक्त्वा तूष्णीं बभूव ह || BG 2.9 ||
सञ्जयः उवाच - Sañjaya said -

परन्तपः - Hey (King Dhṛtarāṣṭra,) the terror of foes! ; गुडाकेशः - Guḍākeśa (Arjuna), ; उक्त्वा - having said ; एवम् - so ; हृषीकेशम् - to Hṛṣīkeśa (Śrī Kṛṣṇa), ; ह - clearly ; उक्त्वा - saying ; गोविन्दम् - to Govinda (Śrī Kṛṣṇa), ; न - "I will not ; योत्स्ये - fight," ; इति - thus ; बभूव - became ; तूष्णीम् - silent.

Sañjaya said -

Hey King Dhṛtarāṣṭra! Arjuna, having said so to Śrī Kṛṣṇa, clearly saying to Śrī Kṛṣṇa, "I will not fight," then became silent.

Intent - I will not fight until clarity on what is beneficial for me is not provided to me.

तमुवाच हृषीकेश: प्रहसन्निव भारत |
सेनयोरुभयोर्मध्ये विषीदन्तमिदं वच: || BG 2.10 ||

भारत - Hey Bhārata (King Dhṛtarāṣṭra, the descendent of Bharata)! ; हृषीकेशः - Hṛṣīkeśa (Śrī Kṛṣṇa) ; उवाच - spoke ; इदम् - these ; वचः - words ; प्रहसन् इव - with a wry smile ; तम् - to him, (who sat) ; विषीदन्तम् - despondently ; मध्ये - in the middle ; उभयोः - of both ; सेनयोः - armies.

Hey King Dhṛtarāṣṭra! Śrī Kṛṣṇa spoke with a wry smile these words to him, who sat despondently in the middle of both armies.

Intent - The use of the word "प्रहसन्, wry smile" expresses a perspective that there is no validity in the thought process of Arjuna. By holding a non-thing as a real thing, his grief is like that of an upset child. Upon this, Bhagavāna knowing that Arjuna had humbly sought his refuge, became sentimental and gave this spiritual guidance.

श्रीभगवानुवाच |
अशोच्यानन्वशोचस्त्वं प्रज्ञावादांश्च भाषसे |
गतासूनगतासूंश्च नानुशोचन्ति पण्डिता: || BG 2.11 ||
श्रीभगवान् उवाच - Śrī Bhagavān said -

त्वम् - (Hey Arjuna!) You ; अन्वशोचः - grieve for those (preceptors and relatives) who call ; अशोच्यान् - for no grief ; च - and ; भाषसे - speak ; प्रज्ञा-वादान् - words of wisdom. (However,) ; पण्डिताः - the wise ; न - neither ; अनुशोचन्ति - grieve for ; गतासून् - one whose life has gone (like an arrow that has left the bow), ; च - nor ; अगतासून् - whose life has not yet gone (like the water of divine offering because of its necessity).

Śrī Bhagavān said -

You grieve for those who call for no grief and speak words of wisdom. However, the wise neither grieve for one whose life has gone nor whose life has not yet gone.

Intent - There can be only three causes (Nimitta) at the root of Arjuna's grief -

1. Through war, the Ātmā of Bhīṣma and others will perish.
2. Through war, the bodies of Bhīṣma and others will perish.
3. Through war, with the slaying of relatives and preceptors, the righteousness of Arjuna will perish.

Bhagavāna articulates to Arjuna that from all three causes, your grief is unfounded.

First, your grief due to the fear of destruction of the Ātmā of Bhīṣma and others is not valid because the Ātmā is ever young (अजर, Ajara) and immortal (अमर, Amara). None of the five great elements (महाभूत, Mahābhūta)[62]can influence it. When wind cannot dry it, fire cannot burn it, and water cannot wet it - how can weapons that are the products of the great elements destroy it? (BG 2.12, BG 2.13, BG 2.16, BG 2.17, BG 2.19 - BG 2.25).

Second, your grief due to the bodies of Bhīṣma and others is also not valid. Bodies, by their nature, are never stable, just as water poured on a filter is never stable. Indeed, one cannot behold the minutest moment when the body is the same as before, but indeed, the body on its own is destroyed every moment. There are between 50 and 75 trillion cells in the human body. Each type of cell has its life span. Every seven to ten years, every cell in the body is replaced by a new cell. Red blood cells live for about four months, while white blood cells live for more than a year. Skin cells live about two to three weeks. Colon cells die in four days. Sperm cells have three days, while brain cells typically last an entire lifetime (neurons in the cerebral cortex, for example, are not replaced when they die).

No power in the world can stop the flow of destruction of the body. "That is this body" that you are feeling is indeed a fallacy, just as saying to Gaṅgā and an evening lamp flame that "this is the same Gaṅgā I had bathed in yesterday" and "this is the same lamp flame" I had lit in the morning. In reality, they are never the same, but every moment with extreme velocity, they are moving in the flow of destruction, which by no means can be seized. That is why your grief for the body does not hold water. Even if you do not slay these bodies, no power can keep them. In addition, from a transcendental perspective, bodies are never there at any time, they are perceived in the Ātmā due to nescience, just as silver is perceived in an oyster shell, but in reality, it is not there. Your grief from the body's perspective is not valid either (BG 2.16, BG 2.18, BG 2.27, and BG 2.28).

Third, if you grieve because of the fear of the demise of righteousness, even then, your grief is not appropriate. From a righteous perspective, you must fight and not run away from it, as your side is the side of the truth (Satya), and fighting on the side of the truth is your duty as a Kṣatriya. In reality, righteousness is one unique thing that, when faced, becomes the duty of everyone to sacrifice all worldly relationships. Righteousness is something for the world beyond. Temporal relationships are of this world and not of the world beyond. It is one's duty to sacrifice this world for the world beyond. However, sacrificing the world beyond for this world can never be a duty. It is said that King Bali (बलि) for his preceptor, Prahlāda (प्रह्लाद) for his father, Vibhīṣaṇa (विभीषण) for his brother, Bhagavāna Paraśurāma (परशुराम) for his mother, and the Gopis for their husbands, exhibited contempt. Yet all those acts were proven accordant with righteousness. From a righteousness perspective, your desisting the battle is unrighteous and not righteous.

Fourth, from a practical perspective, fighting is a duty for you. Because if you die, the doors of heavens are open for you; and if you win the battle, then the enemy free kingdom is awaiting you. For you, both of your hands are full of goodies. Opposite to this, by your delusion, if you abandon the battle, lasting infamy will embrace you, and songs of your infamy will sound everywhere. Dishonor is worse than death for one who is highly regarded (BG 2.31 - BG 2.37).

---

[62] Mahābhūta (महाभूत) known as the great elements are five in number: 1) earth (पृथ्वी, Pṛthvī), 2) water (आप, Āpa), 3) fire (अग्नि, Agni), 4) wind (वायु, Vāyu) and 5) space (आकाश, Ākāśa). Because they pervade all transformations of Prakṛti they are called "great, Mahāna" and being the cause of the Pañcīkṛta of the Pañcabhūta they are subtle. Pañcīkṛta means done by Pañcīkaraṇa (पञ्चीकरण), which is an action by which anything is constituted of the five elements (1/2 of one and 1/8 of other four elements). Mahābhūta is also known as Pañca-Mahābhūta (पञ्च-महाभूत) or Pañcabhūta (पञ्चभूत).

From all perspectives, your desisting is only "अनार्यजुष्टमस्वर्ग्यमकीर्तिकरम्, not commendable for a noble person," and indeed, there is no basis for your grief. You speak like a wise Paṇḍita,[63]but only because of ignorance, you are grieving for the Ātmā, body, and righteousness, all of which ought not to be grieved. The wise do not grieve for those whose Prāṇa have left, who are dead, and those who are still alive; they never grieve with fear of the loss of Prāṇa. Because Ātmā of both is ever young and immortal, with the destruction of the body, it is never destroyed, and nor will be. Moreover, bodies of both never ever stay stable.

The creation and destruction of the bodies occur due to accumulated impressions of actions (Karma-Saṃskāras) of a Jīva. External substances are not the material cause (Upādāna-Kāraṇa) in the birth and death of the body but are only the instrumental cause (Nimitta-Kāraṇa). The material cause in the birth and end of the body is the Jīva's own Karma-Saṃskāras. In the "being" or "non-being" of any act, the main reason is its material cause. External instruments are not primary but indeed minor. They are just like "squeezing one who is asleep," only an excuse. Without Karma-Saṃskāras of a Jīva, no power can destroy the body. Because of this thought, the wise do not grieve for either. Accordingly, Bhagavāna clearly articulated the inappropriateness of Arjuna's grief by any measure. Now he explains this at length.

{In reality, Ātmā is eternal (Nitya), and so to grieve is not proper -}

न त्वेवाहं जातु नासं न त्वं नेमे जनाधिपा |
न चैव न भविष्याम: सर्वे वयमत: परम् || BG 2.12 ||

तु - It is ; एव - certainly ; न (एवम्) - not (so that) ; अहम् - I (in the form of the Ātmā) ; न आसम् - was not there ; जातु - at any time, (nor) ; त्वम् - you (in the form of the Ātmā) ; न (आसी:) - were not (there at any time, or) ; इमे - these ; जनाधिपा:- kings (in the form of the Ātmā) ; न (आसन्) - were not (there at any time), ; च - and ; एव - also ; न (एवम्) - it is not (so that) ; वयम् - we ; सर्वे - all (in the form of the Ātmā) ; न - will not ; भविष्याम: - be there ; अत: - from here ; परम् - onwards.

It is certainly not so that I was not there at any time, nor you, or these kings. It is not so that we all will not be there from here onwards.

Intent - Bhagavāna, with his arms raised and an unwavering determination, said that it is certainly not so that My, yours, or all these king's Ātmā was not there in the past or it will not be there in the future. However, it is definite that My, yours, and everyone's Ātmā were always there and will always be there. With the destruction of the body, if it is deemed that the "Sat-Svarupa"[64]Ātmā is also destroyed, then no fruit of good or evil Karma performed in the body should remain. In that case, there will be an occurrence of Kṛtanāśa-Doṣa (कृतनाश-दोष), the incurrence of fault when done Karma is destroyed without giving its fruits. In addition, there is no tenet of Śāstra that fruits of good or evil acts done in the current body are also acquired in the same body. Though those activities later on cease, the righteous and unrighteous impressions reside in the heart, in the witness of the Ātmā. These Karma-Saṃskāras, upon their due time, awake (उद्बुद्ध, Udbuddha) and become the cause for pleasure and pain of the Jīva in the current life or the next. If with the destruction of the body, the Ātmā was destroyed, then the fruition of Karma-Saṃskāras of done good or evil acts would be impossible. No "real" thing is left as support or substrate for the Karma-Saṃskāras in whose existence, Karma-Saṃskāras can be fruitful. Insentient Karma-Saṃskāras can't become fruitful on their own. However, one can observe the presence of numerous life forms and experiences of various kinds of innumerable and mutually singular pleasures and pains. At the root of such singularities (विलक्षणता, Vilakṣaṇatā), singular Karma-Saṃskāras of Jīva can only be held as causal, and no other cause can be found at the root of these singularities. Without any reason, if Jīva is deemed to acquire these singular enjoyments and life forms,

---

[63] Paṇḍita (पण्डित) means man of discrimination, one with wisdom. It is derived from Paṇḍ (पण्ड्) meaning knowledge of the Ātmā (Self) and so a Paṇḍita is one who has the knowledge of the Ātmā.

[64] Sat-Svarupa (सत् स्वरुप) means true-form, whose nature is in the form of Sat (सत्, true, real or existent)

then they will receive "अकृताभ्यागम-दोष, Akṛtābhyāgama-Doṣa," the fault incurred when one receives fruits without doing anything. In other words, to be in the bondage of fruits without performing Karma is considered contrary to the rules. Therefore, it is opined that for a Jīva, his impressions of Karma are causal. Again, the fruition of these Karma-Saṃskāras can only happen when the substrate of these Karma-Saṃskāras is deemed as some immovable Trikālabādhya[65]real thing. Just as in support of the immovable earth, numerous seeds face their fruits; without the support of the earth, the ability of seeds to germinate, grow and bear fruits is impossible in null space. In the same way, without the support of some real immovable thing, the fruition of Karma-Saṃskāras in vacuity is impossible.

Again, that real thing in whose support Karma-Saṃskāras have become fruitful should be the same as when Karma was done. Because in whose oversight and power Karma is performed, that has to be the support of Karma-Saṃskāras. Only through its support at later time arousal of Karma-Saṃskāras and the resultant production of fruits is possible. It is impossible that Karma is done in someone's support, Karma-Saṃskāras in some others, and fruits in someone else's. For instance, in a quarrel between two people, a third person sees what is happening. As a witness of the incident and based on his account, that person can allow judgment of appropriate penalty. However, if the observer of the incident is not the one to testify, how can there be reasonable penalty judgment based on the testimony of a fourth person who did not even witness the incident?

Further, one cannot accept that the real thing was born simultaneously as the Karma was done. Had it been born simultaneously as Karma, it would cease to exist with the cessation of activities. Had it ceased to exist when activities ceased, it could not have been the support of Karma-Saṃskāras and fruits. That is why acceptance of its eternal pre-existence (नित्य-प्राक्-सिद्धत्व, Nitya-Prāk-Siddhatva) before the performance of Karma is necessary. If it is proper for that real thing to exist before the execution of Karma, however that real thing may have been created with the birth of that body in which Karma was performed - that argument does not hold water. The acquisition of the body is a fruit of some Karma done in prior existence (पूर्वकृत-कर्म, Pūrvakṛta-Karma). That real thing is the underlying support for both those Karma performed in a previous life and the Karma-Saṃskāras. Without it, the fruition of the fruit of acquiring the body is impossible.

In addition, one cannot say that the real thing also perishes when Karma-Saṃskāras perish after giving their fruits. Had the real thing died with the perishing of Karma-Saṃskāras, then like Karma-Saṃskāras, it should also be born. Had it been born, it could not have been the support of Karma, Karma-Saṃskāras, and fruits; because those things that are perishable, its birth is necessary. By the argument above, a thing that has birth and end cannot be the support of Karma, Karma-Saṃskāras, and fruits.

With the direct observation of the acquisition by Jīva of various wombs and mutual singular pleasure and pain experiences of Jīva, this subject becomes clear that there is some single Trikālabādhya, unborn (अज, Aja), imperishable (अविनाशी, Avināśī) existent thing in whose support, own Karma-Saṃskāras of a Jīva become fruitful. It does not perish with the destruction of the body, Karma, and fruits. That real thing cannot be anything other than the Ātmā. Separate from the Ātmā - the gross body (स्थूल-शरीर, Sthūla-Śarīra), the subtle body (सूक्ष्म-शरीर, Sūkṣma-Śarīra)[66]and the causal body (कारण-शरीर, Kāraṇa-Śarīra) being Anātmā (अनात्मा)[67]cannot be real and neither in their support, there is the fruition of Karma-Saṃskāras. Though subtle and causal bodies can be a support (Adhikaraṇa) of the Karma-Saṃskāras and their fruits, they cannot become their underlying Reality (Adhiṣṭhāna). Just as a pot can be a support in holding water, but it

[65] Trikālabādhya (त्रिकालबाध्य) means one whose determination of unreality (मिथ्यात्व-निश्चय, Mithyātva-Niścaya) cannot be made in past, present and future.

[66] The subtle body (सूक्ष्म-शरीर, Sūkṣma-Śarīra) is an aggregation of the following nineteen subtle elements: five subtle action faculties (Pañca-Karmendriya), five subtle sense faculties (Pañca-Jñānendriya), five vital breaths of air (Pañca-Prāṇa), the mind, intellect, Citta and ego.

[67] Anātmā (अनात्मा) means that which is not the Ātmā.

cannot be its Adhiṣṭhāna, the Adhiṣṭhāna of water is the space enclosed in the pot in whose support water is situated. This way, Bhagavāna articulated that My, yours, and Ātmā of all of these people were always there and will always be there. With the destruction of the bodies, it does not perish.

There is no cognition of "not-being." However, "I was born, I will die," such direct awareness of birth and death in the embodied Self[68] is experienced by all. With the presence of a doubt that if the delimited Self were not born or dead, then such cognition should not happen, Bhagavāna explains -

देहिनोऽस्मिन्यथा देहे कौमारं यौवनं जरा |
तथा देहान्तरप्राप्तिर्धीरस्तत्र न मुह्यति || BG 2.13 ||

यथा - Just as ; कौमारम् - childhood, ; यौवनम् - youth, ; जरा - (and) old age (- the states of the gross body that "I am a child, I am a youth, or I am old") ; (कल्पयते) - (are imagined) ; अस्मिन् - in this ; देहे - body, ; तथा - likewise ; देहान्तरप्राप्तिः - acquisition of another body (- the states of the subtle body that "I am born, I die") ; (कल्पयते) - (is imagined by ignorance) ; देहिनः - in the embodied Self (but in reality, the embodied Self is neither born nor dies). ; धीरः - A person with fortitude ; न - is not ; मुह्यति - deluded ; तत्र - in that subject.

Just as childhood, youth, and old age are imagined in the body, likewise acquisition of another body is imagined in the embodied Self. A person with fortitude is not deluded in that subject.

Intent - Conjunction (संयोग, Saṃyoga) of the subtle body and the gross body is called birth (जन्म, Janma), and their disjunction (वियोग, Viyoga) is called death (मरण, Maraṇa). The Ātmā is separate from these two bodies, and it is their underlying support (as their Adhiṣṭhāna). If due to the "being" and "not-being" of these two bodies, existence and non-existence happen in that real Adhiṣṭhāna, and if due to the conjunction and disjunction type of transformations of these two bodies, there is a transformation in the Adhiṣṭhāna, then the formation of "being" and "not-being" and conjunction and disjunction type of transformations in these two bodies is impossible. An unreal (Mithyā) thing cannot exist in support of an unreal thing. An unreal thing can only exist in support of something real - just as how in support of an actual rope, an illusory snake is perceived. Both bodies bounded by time and space are caused. Being caused, they are unreal, insentient, and effect. The existence of anything unreal, insentient, and effect is impossible on its support but is only possible on the support of some real and conscious cause. If by the "being" and "not-being" of both bodies (which are unreal, insentient, and effect), the real and conscious cause had become existent and non-existent, and due to their conjunctive and disjunctive transformations, that real conscious cause had also become mutable, then being "existent and non-existent" and mutable, the real conscious form would also be an effect. Being an effect, it would also be unreal and insentient. In addition, when something is unreal, insentient, and effect, it cannot be the cause and underlying support of the two bodies. Even in our physical world, with the creation and destruction of any activity, we cannot find the creation and destruction of its cause. For instance, with the creation and destruction of pots, we cannot see the creation and destruction of its cause clay.

Even if a more pervasive thing in time and space is deemed as the underlying support of both bodies, that also does not hold water. Because no matter how much more pervasive in time and space the thing is, in the end, being pervasive in time and space, it is caused. Being caused, it is unreal, insentient, and effect only. Then how can it be the underlying support of these bodies? In support of nullity, the existence of nullity is impossible.

---

[68] The embodied Self or the delimited Self is the conscious element in the body who is the doer-enjoyer. It is variously referred to as Jīva (जीव), Jīvātmā (जीवात्मा), Dehī (देही), Śarīrī (शरीरी), Jīva-Sākṣī (जीव-साक्षी), Soul, or Spirit. It is the pure Ātmā on whom I-ness sense of the body, senses, mind and intellect are superimposed due to nescience. Just as there is no distinction between the space enclosed in a pot and the pervasive space and upon the destruction of the pot is only the pervasive space, likewise there is no distinction between the pure Jīvātmā and the Paramātmā (the Supreme Being).

If, in support of nullity, the existence of these two bodies is accepted, that is also not valid. Because nullity is like "not-being." These two bodies are directly experienced as existing. The creation of "not-being" from "being" is impossible. In support of nullity, there cannot be "being" or "not-being" of these two bodies. The existence of both bodies is not possible, nor a thing that is more pervasive in time and space can be held as their cause and underlying support. Only one real conscious immovable thing, one that cannot be determined unreal in past, present, and future, can be causal and the underlying support of both bodies and that real thing remains immovable and immutable from "being and not-being" and "conjunction and disjunction" of the two bodies. If that real thing becomes mutable from the mutations of these bodies, then the fruition of transformations of these bodies is impossible in its dependence. That is similar to how an immovable fixed Anvil of a goldsmith supports the ability to create an ornament. If the Anvil is not set but is movable, then the creation of ornaments is impossible.

Even though birth and death happen due to the conjunction and disjunction of subtle and gross bodies in support of the true witness-conscious Ātmā, there is no birth or death of the Ātmā. "I am a child," "I am a youth," and "I am elderly," these child, youth, and elderly states are only of the gross body and not even of the subtle body. The states of the gross body are imagined in the Ātmā due to ignorance. Likewise, due to ignorance, conjunction and disjunction based birth and death of the two bodies (gross and subtle) are also imagined in the Ātmā. A quartz crystal placed over a red flower appears red because of the conjunctive relationship, yet despite the appearance of the redness of the flower in the quartz crystal, it is "as it was." With the imagined sense of oneness (Tādātmya) of both bodies with the Ātmā, the conjunctive and disjunctive forms of birth and death of both bodies are imagined in the Ātmā due to ignorance. However, the Ātmā on its own "is as is," indeed, unborn and imperishable only. Knowing so, a steadfast person does not see in his Ātmā the birth and death of the two bodies and does not get bewildered. The conjunction and disjunction of gross and subtle bodies in the form of birth and death is thus shown as not being of the Ātmā.

(Now, objects of senses that inflict dualities such as heat and cold, pleasure and pain in both of these bodies, and their impossibility in the Ātmā is articulated -)

मात्रास्पर्शास्तु कौन्तेय शीतोष्णसुखदु: खदा: |
आगमापायिनोऽनित्यास्तांस्तितिक्षस्व भारत || BG 2.14 ||

कौन्तेय - Hey Kaunteya (Arjuna)! ; मात्रा-स्पर्शाः - Contacts of senses with their objects ; शीत-उष्ण-सुख-दुःखदाः - cause cold and heat, pleasure and pain. ; तु - Indeed, ; आगम-अपायिनः - (they) come and go (and) ; अनित्याः - do not last. (Therefore,) ; तितिक्षस्व - endure ; तान् - them, ; भारत – hey, the descendent of Bharata!

Hey Arjuna! Contacts of senses with their objects cause cold and heat, pleasure and pain. Indeed, they come and go and do not last. Therefore, endure them, hey, the descendant of Bharata!

Intent - The objects of senses, whose contact dualities such as cold and heat, pleasure and pain are produced, are creatable and destructible, are transient, and do not last. They cannot touch your Ātmā and are indeed dreamlike; only felt during the period of their manifestation. Because these objects are creatable and destructible, they can never stay steady, but every moment they move away in the flow of time, just as how the flow of Gaṅgā moves towards the ocean with high speed. Objects are never the same as they were moments earlier. The sense, "They are these objects," is illusory, similar to the misapprehension when seeing a lamp flame the following morning and having the feeling, "That is the same lamp flame that was lit in the evening." When cognition of objects happens only during contact with senses, and their existence is found only during the time of comprehension, then they are all mental only. Therefore, when all objects are transient and not everlasting, why should there be any doubt regarding the transitory and non-lasting nature of dualities such as cold and heat born of their contact? Though cognition of these objects and their contact-born dualities such as pleasure and pain happen in support of the real and underlying substrate Ātmā, they do not touch the Ātmā. The Ātmā is always dissociated. Accordingly, when the dualities are temporary and mere perceptions and do not have reality, then Hey Arjuna! You ought to endure them.

(Why should these dualities be endured? That, Bhagavāna explains -)

यं हि न व्यथयन्त्येते पुरुषं पुरुषर्षभ |
समदु:खसुखं धीरं सोऽमृतत्वाय कल्पते || BG 2.15 ||

हि - Because, ; पुरुष-ऋषभ - Hey Puruṣa-Ṛṣabha (Arjuna, the excellent one with the might of a bull)! ; पुरुषम् - A person ; यम् - who ; सम-दुःख-सुखम् - is equal in pain and pleasure, ; न - (and) not ; व्यथयन्ति - distressed ; एते - by them (- the contact of senses and their objects), ; सः - he ; धीरम् - with fortitude ; कल्पते - is understood (to be fit) for ; अमृतत्वाय - immortality.

Hey Arjuna! A person who is equal in pain and pleasure and not distressed by them, he with fortitude is fit for immortality.

Intent -The cause of dualities such as pleasure and pain is discriminating vision (Bheda-Dṛṣṭi). When a person sees himself separate from the entire Saṃsāra and understands the whole Saṃsāra as separate from himself, and with inanimateness of ignorance perceives discriminating-vision as real, then with favorable intelligence (अनुकूल-बुद्धि, Anukūla-Buddhi) forms attachment in some and with antagonistic intelligence (प्रतिकूल-बुद्धि, Pratikūla-Buddhi) forms aversion in others. Moreover, it is with this attachment and aversion (राग-द्वेष, Rāga-Dveṣa) that he perceives dualities such as pleasure and pain, heat and cold, and so on. Accordingly, the root cause of these dualities is grasping the unreal I-you kind of Saṃsāra as real. That is, holding something other than what it is (अन्यथा-ग्रहण, Anyathā-Grahaṇa). A thing maybe something, but cognizing it as something else is called Anyathā-Grahaṇa. For instance, there may be a rope right in front, but perceiving it as a snake is called Anyathā-Grahaṇa. At the root of all these unreal dualities, there is the trueness sense of Anyathā Grahaṇa only. In reality, this I-you and so forth Saṃsāra does not arise in the existent Ātmā by some initiation or transformation but is only perceived due to ignorance, just as a dream. With trueness sense in the unreal Saṃsāra, there is the formation of pleasure and pain and so forth dualities through favorable and unfavorable, attachment and aversion. Though these dualities and their subject matters are illusory (Māyāmātra) but as assertiveness of trueness sense grows in them, then with their relationship distress grows increasingly. As a result, individuals fall farther and farther away from their true nature.

Contrary to this, one who endures these dualities with untrueness-sense (Mithyā-Buddhi) in them, thinking that these are unreal, and is not agitated, comes closer to his true Ātmā. That is why, Bhagavāna articulated that one with fortitude and discernment (Viveka) who is equal in dualities like pleasure and pain and so forth, who considers such dualities as unreal and who does not get distressed is fit for liberation - the state of immortality. The reality of the Ātmā and the unreality of the body and related to that birth and death, external objects of senses, and dualities like pleasure and pain born of contact with those objects, are thus articulated.

{Now, for the aforementioned discerning person with fortitude, Bhagavāna describes the truth of the nature of the real (सत्, Sat) and the unreal (असत्, Asat) -}

नासतो विद्यते भावो नाभावो विद्यते सत: |
उभयोरपि दृष्टोऽन्तस्त्वनयोस्तत्त्वदर्शिभि: || BG 2.16 ||

विद्यते - There is ; न - no ; भावः - being ; असतः - of the unreal (thing anytime), ; तु - and ; विद्यते - there is ; न - no ; अभावः - non-being ; सतः - of the real (thing anytime.) ; अन्तः - The truth ; अनयोः - about ; उभयोः - both ; अपि - also ; दृष्टः - is perceived ; तत्त्व-दर्शिभिः - by seers of Reality.

There is no being of the unreal, and there is no non-being of the real. The truth about both is perceived by seers of Reality.

Intent - Unreal thing by its nature is not there. There is no presence of the unreal thing at any time, even if it is perceptible by gross sight. A real thing, by its nature, is not absent at any time. Even if it is not perceptible by a physical view, there is no absence of a real thing. It is always there. Such truth about both the real and unreal is known to the seers of Reality (Tattva-Darśī). The intention here is that perception (true knowledge) is always of the real (Sat). The perception of an unreal thing is like a space flower, incredibly impossible. A thing that is not there, how can there be a perception of such an invisible thing? How can there be his perception when there is no son of a barren woman (a wild impossibility)? That is why the object of perception in the past, present, and future is only a real thing. An unreal thing cannot be the object of any perception; it can only be the object of delusion (Bhrama). Like the sun, a real thing is perceptible before and after the delusion. Due to the influence of delusion, even if it is not perceived in its true nature in the delusional middle time, what is there is only that real thing. There is no non-being of the real thing even in the delusional time. In the delusional time, even if correct vision is absent, there is no non-being of the real thing. Suppose the real thing does not remain in the delusional location. It is impossible to delude the unreal thing because the perception of where "there is nothing" there "there is something" is impossible. In underlying null support, the existence of delusion is not possible. Only the delusional thing indicates the presence of real underlying support.

As an example, one can see that there is no non-being of an actual rope at all times (past, present, and future), and at all times, there is no being of an unreal snake in that real underlying support. Before and after the delusion of the snake, the rope in its perception time is perceptible. Only in the delusional middle-time, the real rope is otherwise grasped (Anyathā-Grahaṇa) as a snake, though it "is as is" only the real rope in the delusion location. At that time, there was never an absence of the real rope. If the real rope is not there in the delusion location, then the delusion of the unreal snake becomes impossible. In the snake delusion time, "this (इदं, Idaṃ)" is understood ordinarily as the real rope only. However, due to faint darkness and fault of eyes, it is not known uniquely, yet in the delusional knowledge of "this is the snake," the object of "this-ness (इदंता, Idaṃtā)" is the real rope only. If "this" real rope is unknown in the delusion time, then the delusion of the snake is not possible. In the delusional middle time, "this" is ordinarily understood as the rope. Even if it is not perceived uniquely due to the influence of delusion, it is still the real rope. With the influence of delusion, even though there is a loss of real vision, still the real thing at that time did not disappear anywhere, and it is there "is as is," there is no non-being. With the influence of delusion, even in the delusion time when the snake is grasped otherwise (Anyathā-Grahaṇa), then also at that time, there is no beingness of the unreal snake, and like a space flower, it is absent in the real rope.

From this thought and example, at all times (past, present, and future), there is never non-being of the existent Ātmā, even if it is not perceived due to ignorance. It is always there. There is never any "being" of the unreal body, body-related birth and death, sense-organs and their objects, and the dualities born of them, such as pleasure and pain. With the influence of ignorance, even if their appearance is perceived, their real existence is absent. The body, senses, mind, and intellect are bound by space, time, and material (देश, काल, वस्तु-परिच्छेद्य, Deśa, Kāla, Vastu Paricchedya)[69]and causable and perishable. They are not there before their creation and do not remain after their destruction. They are perceived only in the middle time. Indeed, they are not even the objects of any perception in the middle time. They are only objects of delusion. Those things perceived only in the middle and not before or after are like a snake in a rope. In reality, they are not there; they are only objects of delusion. However, the existent Ātmā is in the past, present, and future, before the birth of the body and after its destruction, and indeed, it is there in the body during the time of delusion.

---

[69] Deśa-Paricchedya (देश-परिच्छेद्य) means one that is bounded by space, that which is in one space and not in another. Kāla-Paricchedya (काल-परिच्छेद्य) means one that is bounded by time, that which is in one time and not in another. Vastu-Paricchedya (वस्तु-परिच्छेद्य) means one where distinction between things or material exists. Just as a pot is distinguished from a cloth and vice a versa, both the pot and cloth being distinguishable are Vastu-Paricchedya.

1. Before the world of the body, senses, mind, and intellect, the existence of the eternal and immutable Ātmā is definite. If it was not there at any time, then being creatable and perishable, it would be delusional. Then it would not be able to provide a perception of the delusional body, senses, mind, and intellect.
2. The existence of the Ātmā is definite in the non-beingness of the world of the body, senses, mind, and intellect. That is because when it is impossible for sustentation (स्थिति, Sthiti) of the body in nullity, then its non-beingness is also impossible in nullity. Its non-beingness is definite only in whose support their creation and maintenance happen. The creation and sustentation of a pot depend on clay, and its dissolution is also in clay. In the same way, the birth and sustentation of the body, senses, mind, and intellect depend on the pure Ātmā, and their dissolution (Laya) is definitely in support of the Ātmā. The Existence of the immutable Ātmā is thus proven in the non-being of the body, senses, mind, and intellect.
3. In the delusional time of the body, the "body is," "birth is," "death is," "object is," "happiness is," "pain is," "sorrow is not there," and "pain is but pleasure is not" - and in other forms of "being" and "non-being" delusions, only the Ātmā is perceived in the "is," form, and as everyone's beingness. The Ātmā, the existent common in all (सत्ता-सामान्य, Sattā-Sāmānya) pervades all being and non-being delusions. If the common in all existent Ātmā were not in the location of perception of being and non-being delusions, how can the world's perception be possible? Perception of "there is something" where "there is nothing" is impossible. In support of nullity, it is impossible to have a perception of the being or non-being of a thing. However, a thing may be perceived as something else, like a thing might be a rope but may be perceived as a snake. However, it is impossible to have a perception where "there is nothing" there "something is there." Perception of the body and senses cannot be in support of nullity. Its perception is possible only in support of the existent common to all. Therefore, in the perception-time and location of the body and senses, the Ātmā is perceived in the "is" form and as existent in all delusional beings and non-beings. In the perception time of the delusion, there is no absence of the Ātmā. However, in all perceptions of the body and senses, the object of perception in the form of "is" is only the Ātmā existent common in all. In their delusion, the body and senses, despite "not-being," are grasped otherwise. In "this is a snake" delusion, only the rope is grasped as "this." The snake, though not even existing, was grasped otherwise.

Accordingly, the existent Ātmā is there before and after the perception of the body, senses, mind, and intellect delusions. In the middle time, due to ignorance and the absence of correct-vision, even though the existent Ātmā is not perceived, it does not disappear. Even if the body, senses, mind, and intellect are perceived otherwise (Anyathā-Grahaṇa) with incorrect vision, they still do not exist. Like a space flower, their extreme non-beingness is in the existent Ātmā. Accordingly, Bhagavāna articulated the true nature of real (Sat) and unreal (Asat), "There is no being of unreal, and there is no non-being of real."

{Now, in the following verses, Bhagavāna enunciates the real (Sat) and unreal (Asat) separately -}

अविनाशि तु तद्विद्धि येन सर्वमिदं ततम् |
विनाशमव्ययस्यास्य न कश्चित्कर्तुमर्हति || BG 2.17 ||

तु - However, ; विद्धि - know ; तत् - That (Self) ; अविनाशि - to be imperishable ; येन - by which ; सर्वम् - all ; इदम् - this ; ततम् - is pervaded. ; न कश्चित् - None ; कर्तुम् अर्हति - can ; विनाशम् - destroy ; अस्य - that ; अव्ययस्य - Immutable (Self).

However, know That (Self) to be imperishable by which all this is pervaded. None can destroy that Immutable (Self).

Intent - Imperishable is that "एकमेवाद्वितीयम्, only one without a second"[70] Ātmā by which this entire world of the threefold limitations is pervaded. There is no space where it is not there, there is no time when it is not

[70] Chāndogya Upaniṣad (छान्दोग्य उपनिषद्) 6.2.1

there, and there is nothing in which it is not there. Even though it is in all space, that space does not bind it. Even though it is at all times, it cannot be slashed at any time. Even though it exists in all individual things, nothing can discriminate it. The great elements (Mahābhūta) and materials that are the transformations of the great elements cannot destroy it. No material in the world can ruin it, because it is the existent power in all materials. Then how can those materials make their existence vanish? An inanimate piece of iron with the power of fire can incinerate external substances but is incapable of burning (removing) its existent fire. A pair of tongs with the power of a hand can pick up other materials but cannot pick up the hand. An ax can shear many materials but is incapable of shearing its iron head that provides its power. In the same way, space, time, and material can destroy all materials but cannot even touch the existent Ātmā. That is why, as said by Bhagavāna - "Whatever separate from the Ātmā that is the Anātmā, such Anātmā is not capable of destroying the imperishable Ātmā." Here destruction means non-perception or non-being.

(In contrast -)

अन्तवन्त इमे देहा नित्यस्योक्ताः शरीरिणः |
अनाशिनोऽप्रमेयस्य तस्माद्युध्यस्व भारत || BG 2.18 ||

इमे - (By their own nature,) these ; देहाः - bodies ; अन्तवन्तः - that perish ; उक्ताः - are said to be ; नित्यस्य - of the eternal, ; अनाशिनः - imperishable, (and) ; अप्रमेयस्य - indeterminable ; शरीरिणः - embodied Self. ; तस्मात् - Therefore, ; भारत - hey, Bhārata (Arjuna, the descendent of Bharata)! ; युध्यस्व - fight.

These bodies that perish are said to be of the eternal, imperishable, and indeterminable embodied Self. Therefore, hey, Arjuna! Fight.

Intent - Those things that cannot be validated by the ears, eyes, and other sense-organs and by the six measures (षट्-प्रमाण, Ṣaṭ-Pramāṇa)[71]are called indeterminable (अप्रमेय, Aprameya). These bodies with discriminative attributes, adjuncts of the eternal, imperishable, and indeterminable Ātmā, are perishable by nature. The terms eternal (नित्य, Nitya) and imperishable (अनाशिनः, Anāśinaḥ) are not tautologous, as eternity and perishability are of two types. For example, a body that is reduced to ashes and not perceptible is said to have perished. It is also said to have perished when, though existent, it has undergone a significant change due to disease and other reasons. The two expressions Nitya and Anāśinaḥ rule out both these types of destructions as regards the Ātmā. Bodies are not the same at any time or space and are always perishable. No power can save them from destruction, as they are always morsels of time. If one can catch time, then maybe bodies can be held. However, no one in the world has conquered time; everyone has accepted defeat from time.

Under the dagger of time, the entire animate and inanimate Saṃsāra-Cakra (संसार-चक्र, the worldly cycle) is moving around. Still, with the destruction of these adjunct bodies, the within (Upahita) witness Ātmā does not perish. Just as in the pervasive space with discriminative attributes of numerous varied-sized pots, the imagination of pot-enclosed spaces is made, and with the creation and destruction of pots, there is only an illusion of the creation and breaking of pot-enclosed spaces. With the creation of a pot, there is a creation of a "pot-enclosed space," and with the destruction of the pot, there is the destruction of the "pot-enclosed space." Thus, with a pot with discriminative attributes, there is an illusion of creating and destroying pot-enclosed space in the pervasive space. However, in reality, the pervasive space on its own "is as is"; there is neither any plurality nor creation or destruction. Due to ignorance, there is a delusion of plurality in the Ātmā

[71] Ṣaṭa-Pramāṇa (षट्-प्रमाण) means the six measures that provide correct knowledge and the truth: 1) perception (प्रत्यक्ष, Pratyakṣa), 2) inference (अनुमान, Anumāna), 3) comparison and analogy (उपमान, Upamāna), 4) postulation, derivation from circumstances (अर्थापत्ति, Arthāpatti), 5) non-perception, negative cognitive proof (अनुपलब्धि, Anupalabdhi) and 6) word, testimony of past or present reliable experts (शब्द, Śabda).

with the plurality of bodies in the world. With birth and death of the bodies, there is an imagination of plurality of the Ātmā taking birth and dying. In reality, with the distinctions of bodies, there is no distinction in the pervasive Ātmā. With the creation or destruction of the bodies, there is never any creation or destruction of the Ātmā. **That is why, Bhagavāna, in this verse, has clearly stated that there is only one imperishable Ātmā (Self) in all of these bodies.** The word Śarīriṇaḥ (शरीरिणः) is only singular, and there is no usage of plurality in the word.

Accordingly, the words of Bhagavāna are that your desisting war with the fear of destruction of the Ātmā and bodies is not proper. No one can kill the imperishable Ātmā, and by nature, perishable bodies cannot be kept by anyone. You should recall your Kṣatriya duty and fight.

(In the following seven verses, Bhagavāna articulates the true nature of the Ātmā very distinctly -)

य एनं वेत्ति हन्तारं यश्चैनं मन्यते हतम् |
उभौ तौ न विजानीतो नायं हन्ति न हन्यते || BG 2.19 ||

यः - One who ; वेत्ति - knows ; एनम् - it ; हन्तारम् - as a slayer ; च - and ; यः - one who ; मन्यते - deems ; एनम् - it ; हतम् - can be slain; ; तौ - they ; उभौ - both ; न - do not ; विजानीतः - know ; अयम् - this (Self). ; न - (In reality, it) neither ; हन्ति - kills ; न - nor ; हन्यते - is slain.

One who knows it as a slayer and one who deems it can be slain; they both do not know this (Self). It neither kills nor is slain.

Intent - Now, looking at the cause of Arjuna's grief, Bhagavāna describes the true nature of the Ātmā. The cause of Arjuna's grief was this ignorance, "I the Arjuna-form Ātmā will be a slayer of the reverential Bhīṣma-form Ātmā, the reverential Droṇa-form Ātmā and the Ātmā of Duryodhana and other relatives. The Ātmā of other reverential beings and relatives will perish, and the women-form Ātmā will become immoral, and as a result, mixed functional class Ātmā will be born. There will be the downfall of the ancestor-form Ātmā, and with the disappearance of class duties and family duties, the Ātmā of the entire family will go to hell for an indefinite time. The cause of all these evils will be the Ātmā of Arjuna." At the root of all of these causes of grief is the grasping otherwise (Anyathā-Grahaṇa) of the Ātmā as possessing distinctions and limitations (Bheda and Pariccheda), even though the Ātmā itself is without distinctions and limitations.

There are three things in the adjunct-form bodies -

1. Gross body (Sthūla-Śarīra) in which physical activities in the form of birth and death manifest.
2. Subtle body (Sūkṣma-Śarīra), the one with the ego of doership and enjoyership of Karma of the gross body.
3. The dissociated witness-observer Ātmā, by whose "beingness" and thus power, activities such as slaying and being slain in the gross body and doership-enjoyership ego in the subtle body manifest. The one dissociated from all killing and being slain acts and doership-enjoyership ego. The one, **free from all distinctions (सर्व-भेद-विनिर्मुक्त, Sarva-Bheda-Vinirmukta), only one Ātmā in all gross and subtle bodies and all movable and immovable entities.** The entire space, time, and material (देश-काल-वस्तु, Deśa-Kāla-Vastu) and all substances, attributes, and acts (द्रव्य-गुण-कर्म, Dravya-Guṇa-Karma) acquire creation, sustentation, and dissolution (उत्पत्ति-स्थिति-लय, Utpatti-Sthiti-Laya) in it. Still, it is dissociated from all of them. In other words, unassociated as it is with everything, they are all born, maintained, and end in it. In the sky, the sun radiates heat; there is rain, storms, and tornadoes. Though all these activities happen in the sky, the sky itself does not get heated, wet, or dirty but is always pure. Even though all of these activities are happening in the sky, assuming the form of the sky and seeing from the perspective of the sky, nothing is happening in it.

Similarly, even though all activities in the gross and subtle body occur in support of the pervasive Ātmā and indeed happen in the Ātmā, in the pervasive Ātmā, there is no taint of any of those activities. **The true nature (Vāstavika Svarupa) of all beings is the all-pervasive Ātmā that is free from all distinctions.** However, Jīva, not knowing his true nature, imagines distinctions and manifoldness of the Ātmā based on the distinctions and manifoldness of bodies; and with Anyonyādhyāsa (अन्योन्याध्यास, delusion of one in second and delusion of second in the first) superimposes the gross and subtle bodies on the Ātmā. Imagines the gross and subtle bodies as the Ātmā or the Self. Imagines in the dissociated Ātmā the activities of the gross and subtle bodies of slaying and being slain and doership and enjoyership. Bound by the rules of Prakṛti, due to this ignorance, he flows away in the stream of sin and piety, and birth and death until he attains transcendental knowledge of his own pervasive Ātmā and situates with oneness in it.

Now, Bhagavāna focusing on the pervasive and free from all distinctions Ātmā, and recalling the cause of Arjuna's grief, gives him Upadeśa, "Hey Arjuna! By having I-you ego in the gross and subtle body and imagining distinctions in the 'free from all distinctions' Ātmā, you understand yourself as a slayer of the Ātmā and also the Ātmā of Bhīṣma and others as being slain. Born of ignorance, this is indeed your delusion. There is no birth or sustentation of Arjuna, Bhīṣma, and other bodies in the Ātmā, nor slaying and being a slain-like activity or I-you type doership-enjoyership ego. One who knows the dissociated Ātmā as a slayer, or one who deems the pervasive Ātmā as being slain, both are mistaken. In reality, the Ātmā is neither a slayer nor one to be slain."

(Next, the pervasive Ātmā that is beyond all states is described -)

न जायते म्रियते वा कदाचित नायं भूत्वा भविता वा न भूय: |
अजो नित्य: शाश्वतोऽयं पुराणो न हन्यते हन्यमाने शरीरे || BG 2.20 ||

अयम् - This (Self is) ; न - never ; जायते - born ; वा - and ; न - never ; म्रियते - dies ; कदाचित् - any time, ; न वा - nor ; भूत्वा - having existed before ; भूय: - again ; अभविता - becomes non-existent. ; अयम् - It is ; अज: - unborn, ; नित्य: - eternal, ; शाश्वत: - everlasting, ; पुराण: - (and) ever-new. ; न हन्यते - (It) is not destroyed ; हन्यमाने - upon the destruction of ; शरीरे - the body.

This Self is never born and never dies at any time, nor having existed before again becomes non-existent. It is unborn, eternal, everlasting, and ever-new. It is not destroyed upon the destruction of the body.

Intent - Had it possessed the states of birth and death, the pervasive Ātmā could have been a slayer or be slain. However, it is beyond (अतीत, Atīta) the three states of 1) being born, 2) dying, and 3) becoming non-existent, having existed before. Within these three states are the sixfold material transformations (षड्-भावविकार, Ṣaḍ-Bhāva-Vikāra).[72]That is, the Ātmā is dissociated from the three states and the sixfold material transformations. They cannot touch it. In verse, the two transformations, viz., taking birth and dying, are explicitly negated in the nature of the Ātmā. Also, in the sentence "nor having existed before again becomes non-existent," the remaining four transformations should also be understood as negated. Only a thing bound by time and space can come in the bondage of the three states and transformations. However, the one not bound by time and space, how can it be in the bondage of the three states and transformations? If with the distinctions of the bodies, there were distinctions of the Ātmā, then definitely the Ātmā could have been bound by space and time and could have become one with the three states and transformations. However, with the distinctions of the bodies, there is no distinction in the Ātmā. So how can the three states and the transformations bind it?

---

[72] Ṣaḍ-Bhāva-Vikāra (षड्-भावविकार) means the sixfold transformations of the material world: 1) to be born (जायते, Jāyate), 2) to remain (अस्ति, Asti), 3) to result into (विपरिणमते, Vipariṇamate), 4) to grow (वर्धते, Vardhate), 5) to decay (अपक्षीयते, Apakṣīyate) and 6) to die (विनश्यति, Vinaśyati).

Additionally, with the distinctions of the bodies, distinctions in the Ātmā could have happened if the bodies were of equal Reality with the Ātmā. However, these bodies are matters of ordinary Reality (Vyavahārika-Sattā).[73]They are perceived only in the awake state and during the perception time of their activities. They are not perceived in the sleep state. In contrast, the Ātmā has transcendental Reality (Pāramārthika-Sattā)[74]and illuminating all states (awake, dream, or deep-sleep) "is as is" dissociated from all states. Only substances of equal Reality can be mutual helpers or opposers; substances of contrary Reality cannot be helpers or supporters. Just as the thirst of ordinary Reality can be satisfied by normal water but cannot be satisfied by the water of a mirage, and similarly, a live person can be burnt by the fire of ordinary Reality, however fire of a dream even though is perceived in support of a live person, cannot touch him, let alone burn him. The world of the body, senses, mind, and intellect, like a dream, is only felt during the time of ignorance; with the awakening of knowledge, its absence at all times (त्रिकालाभाव, Trikālābhāva) is directly established. All seers of the Truth and the Veda-Śāstra are witnesses to this direct experience or realization. Therefore, with its relationship, how can the unreal world of the body, senses, mind, and intellect create distinctions in the pure Ātmā? When the unreal world of the body, senses, mind, and intellect is incapable of creating distinctions in the Ātmā, then in the impartite, one alone and unbounded Ātmā, how can the three states and the transformations arise? How can it be a doer-enjoyer of slaying and being slain activity when it is free from these states and transformations?

The pervasive Ātmā being free from all distinctions and limitations is unborn, eternal, everlasting, and ever-new. That is why with the destruction of bodies, it does not perish; just as with the destruction of pots, space is not destroyed.

(Now, the impossibility of the activity of slaying and being slain is described in a seer of the Reality -)

वेदाविनाशिनं नित्यं य एनमजमव्ययम् |
कथं स पुरुष: पार्थ कं घातयति हन्ति कम् || BG 2.21 ||

पार्थ – Hey Pārtha (Arjuna)! ; स: - He ; य: - who ; वेद - knows ; एनम् - this (Self as) ; अविनाशिनम् - imperishable, ; नित्यम् - eternal, ; अजम् - unborn, (and) ; अव्ययम् - undecaying, ; कथम् - how can ; पुरुष: - (such) person ; कम् घातयति - cause anyone to be slain? ; कम् - Who can he ; हन्ति - kill?

Hey Arjuna! He who knows this Self as imperishable, eternal, unborn, and undecaying, how can such person cause anyone to be slain? Who can he kill?

Intent - In the above verses, completely free from all distinctions and limitations, only one pervasive Ātmā in all bodies in dissociated form is articulated. Moreover, the way the three states and six transformations do not touch the Ātmā is clearly described. One, who directly realizes the Ātmā, determines the absence of the gross and subtle body and their attributes in his Ātmā at all times. One who has burnt his I-ness sense in the gross and subtle body by the fire of knowledge; meaning, one who has burnt his superimposition of the gross and subtle body on the Ātmā and who is situated with I-ness "is as is" in own Ātmā. One who has broken the cage of doership and enjoyership and has become completely free from all duties. In all unreal adjunct-form bodies, one who sees his Ātmā untainted from distinctions and transformations, with the creation or destruction of bodies does not see birth or death in his Ātmā, and separate from his Ātmā does not see any existence of bodies; just as an ocean, separate from itself, does not see any existence of waves or eddies and with the creation and destruction of such waves or eddies does not see creation and destruction in itself, but only sees creation and destruction as miracles of its own nature. "Hey Arjuna! This

[73] Vyavahārika-Sattā (व्यवहारिक-सत्ता) means ordinary or practical Reality. It is one where the determination of absence in the past, present, and future (त्रिकालाभाव-निश्चय) cannot be made without Self-Realization (ब्रह्म-ज्ञान, Brahma-Jñāna). The conscious world (जाग्रत प्रपन्च) has ordinary Reality because, without Self-Realization, it is not realized as unreal.

[74] Pāramārthika-Sattā (पारमार्थिक-सत्ता) means transcendental Reality. It is one that is beyond time and space. It exists at all times - past, present and future. The Brahman has transcendental Reality.

way, one who has cognized his Ātmā "is as is" unborn, eternal and undecaying, how can he have someone slain or who can he kill?" The delusional perspective of slaying and being slain is there as long as a Jīva, having fallen from the pervasive Ātmika-ocean, has I-ness sense in some body-form waves separate from himself and with unreal imagination of body-form waves get into attachment with some and aversion with others. With attachment and aversion (Rāga-Dveṣa), he has taken upon himself the bondage of sin, piety, birth, and death due to ignorance. Days of happiness showed their back that very moment when that mistake was made. Immersed in the dream of ignorance, no matter how many resolutions a Jīva may make, the untouched Ātmā "is as is" does not see any growth or decay in itself. In all those body-form waves, he knows attachment and aversion, and born from them, creation and destruction are miracles of his blissful nature, and though situated in all of them, he is dissociated from all. Only by this analytic thinking can one truly situate with oneness in own pervasive Ātmā "is as is" dissociated from the body, senses, mind, and intellect and their activities. The body, senses, mind, and intellect bound by their innate attributes may themselves conduct activities in whatever way, yet that knower of the Reality situated in his true nature remains only an observer of all those activities and does not see any growth or decay in his real nature.

A person who has dissociated this eternal, unborn, and undecaying Ātmā from all bodies transcendentally, "सोऽहमस्मि, that I am," how can such a person have someone slain, or how can he kill someone? He does not see in himself any mutation of slaying, getting someone killed, or being slain.

(Now Bhagavāna describes the disassociation of the bodies from the Ātmā -)

वासांसि जीर्णानि यथा विहाय नवानि गृह्णाति नरोऽपराणि |
तथा शरीराणि विहाय जीर्णा न्यन्यानि संयाति नवानि देही || BG 2.22 ||

यथा - Just as ; नरः - a person ; विहाय - discards ; जीर्णानि - worn ; वासांसि - clothes ; गृह्णाति - (and) takes ; नवानि - new ; अपराणि - ones (and by this conduct does not see any increase or decrease in him), ; तथा - so does ; देही - the embodied Self, ; विहाय - dumping ; जीर्णानि - dilapidated ; शरीराणि - bodies, ; संयाति – occupies ; अन्यानि - other ; नवानि - new ones (and in doing so, there is no increase or decrease in it).

Just as a person discards worn clothes and takes new ones, so does the embodied Self, dumping dilapidated bodies, occupies other new ones.

Intent - When a person discards old worn-out garments and replaces them with new ones, he does not see his destruction with the destruction of old garments, does not see his creation by the replacement of new garments, does not see the making of new garments his creation, damaging of garments his damage, dirtying of garments his dirtying and cleanliness of garments his cleanliness. Every day the condition of the garments changes, but he does not feel that "something in me is changing." In the same way, Ātmā does not see the sixfold mutations of the body in itself and does not itself become mutable by the transformations of the body. The Ātmā is dissociated from 1) the gross, subtle, and causal bodies,[75] 2) the awake, dream,

---

[75] Explanation of the three bodies, three states and five sheaths is as follows -

1. The state of the gross body (Sthūla Śarīra) is the awake state (Jāgrata Avasthā) and the Sheath of Food (Annamaya-Kośa). The gross body increases or decreases by its relationship with food.
2. The state of the subtle body (Sūkṣma-Śarīra) is the dream state (Svapna Avasthā). The subtle body keeps its activity also in the dream state. It is divided into the Sheath of the Vital Breaths of Air (Prāṇamaya-Kośa), the Sheath of the Mind (Manomaya-Kośa) and the Sheath of Discernment (Vijñānamaya-Kośa). The five subtle action faculties (Karmendriya) and the five Prāṇa are called the Sheath of the Vital Breaths of Air. The five subtle cognitive senses (Jñānendriya) and the mind are called the Sheath of the Mind. The five subtle cognitive senses (Jñānendriya) and the intellect are called the Sheath of Discernment.
3. The state of the causal body (Kāraṇa Śarīra) is the deep-sleep state (Suṣupti Avasthā) and the Sheath of Supreme Bliss (Ānandamaya-Kośa). The conscious element with ignorance (अविद्या-विशिष्ट-चेतन, Avidyā-Viśiṣṭa-Cetana) is known as the Supreme Bliss Sheath (Ānandamaya-Kośa), where the cause of vacillations (Vikṣepa) - the intellect, mind and senses all become dissolved (Laya) in their cause (Upādāna) nescience (Avidyā).

and deep sleep states, and 3) the five sheaths, just as how a person donning garments is dissociated from the garments. He may wear a shirt, jacket, and coat but does not become the shirt, jacket, or coat. Even though the Ātmā is seated as a witness in the gross, subtle, and causal bodies, in the awake, dream, and deep sleep states and the five sheaths, still, it is neither the gross body, the subtle body, or the causal body and also not the three states or the five sheaths. It is dissociated from the three bodies, the three states, and the five sheaths. With their creation or destruction and contraction or expansion, it does not see its creation or destruction and contraction or expansion.

In the pervasive space, when innumerable pots are created and destroyed, there is no creation and destruction of pot-enclosed space with their relationship. The space "is as is," dissociated from the creation and destruction of the pots. Likewise, the Ātmā abandoning old bodies and taking new bodies does not see its creation and destruction and is dissociated from that creation and destruction. One who has known his Ātmā dissociated from the body and who has made complete non-existence (अत्यन्ताभाव, Atyantābhāva) of the body in his Ātmā, "Separate from my Ātmā there is no existence of the body in the past, present, and future," such a knower of the Truth, being eternal and imperishable, does neither grieve for the Ātmā nor for the extremely insignificant bodies and is not the doer-enjoyer of killing and being killed acts.

(Now, Bhagavāna describes the eternal and immutable nature of the Ātmā -)

नैनं छिन्दन्ति शस्त्राणि नैनं दहति पावकः |
न चैनं क्लेदयन्त्यापो न शोषयति मारुतः || BG 2.23 ||

शस्त्राणि - Weapons ; न - cannot ; छिन्दन्ति - cut ; एनम् - it, ; पावकः - fire ; न - cannot ; दहति - burn ; एनम् - it, ; आपः - water ; न - cannot ; क्लेदयन्ति - wet ; एनम् - it, ; च - and ; मारुतः - wind ; न - cannot; शोषयति - dry (it).

Weapons cannot cut it, fire cannot burn it, water cannot wet it, and wind cannot dry it.

Intent - The Ātmā can only be a doer and enjoyer of the activities of killing or being killed when something can make it mutable with its relationship or it is a substance (Dravya), has attributes (Guṇa), or is one who acts (Kriyāvāna). However, neither the great elements nor any material created by the great elements can influence it. Then how can it be mutable or be a doer and enjoyer of killing and being killed acts? If it were separate from something, then it could have come under the influence of that thing. However, it sits inside everything as its reality, so how can they influence it? There is nothing that can destroy its Ātmā; they are only able to destroy other things that are separate from the Ātmā. The potency of the power with which it can destroy things other than itself, that potency is nothing but the potency of its power; with what potency can it destroy its power?

No earth weapons can cut this Ātmā. Neither can fire burn it, nor water can wet it, or wind can dry it. Fire can burn substances separate from itself but cannot burn itself. Water can wet other substances separate from itself but cannot wet itself. Wind can dry substances separate from itself but cannot dry itself. When weapons, fire, water, and wind cannot cut, burn, wet, or dry their gross form, how can they cut, burn, wet, or dry the conscious element seated within and subtler than the subtle? Never! The Ātmā can be a substance, have attributes, or be one who acts if only it is bound by space, time, and material. Only a bounded or limited thing can be a substance, have attributes, and one that can act. An unbounded thing cannot be a substance, have attributes, or be one that can act. Time for activity is only when any space or time is empty from it. The Ātmā can possess attributes only with a material distinction because only within distinguishable materials can attributes reside. Moreover, it can be a substance only if it were the support of actions and attributes. However, it is beyond space, time, and material and is a substrate of all substances, attributes, and acts; it is beyond all of them.

The Ātmā being the substrate support of all transformations is itself seated eternal and immutable and is not a doer and enjoyer of killing and being killed acts.

(Now, again, Bhagavāna describes the nature of the Ātmā -)

अच्छेद्योऽयमदाह्योऽयमक्लेद्योऽशोष्य एव च |
नित्य: सर्वगत: स्थाणुरचलोऽयं सनातन: || BG 2.24 ||

अयम् - This (Self is) ; अच्छेद्य: - unslashable, ; अदाह्य: - unburnable, ; अक्लेद्य: - unwettable, ; च - and ; एव - indeed, ; अयम् - it ; अशोष्य: - is undryable. ; अयम् - It is ; नित्य: - eternal, ; सर्वगत: - all-pervasive, ; स्थाणु: - stable, ; अचल: - immovable, (and) ; सनातन: - everlasting (then how can anyone have any influence on it?)

This Self is unslashable, unburnable, unwettable, and undryable. It is eternal, all-pervasive, stable, immovable, and everlasting.

Intent - The Ātmā can be neither a subject of slashability nor the subject of the acts of burnability, wettability, or dryability. That is why, the Ātmā is called Acchedya (अच्छेद्य, unslashable), Adāhya (अदाह्य, unburnable), Akledya (अक्लेद्य, unwettable), and Aśoṣya (अशोष्य, undryable). The subject of slashing and burning acts can only manifest in a region separate from the acts of slashing and burning. Because of its ubiquity, it is within the acts of slashing and burning. Indeed, those acts have no power of their own. The capability of all these acts of slashing and burning is borrowed from the Ātmā - the repository of all power. Without it, they are all just null. How can all those activities of slashing and burning be done on the Ātmā? Never. The Ātmā, not being a subject of the acts of slashing, burning, and others, is eternal, all-pervasive, stable, immovable, and everlasting.

If the nature of the Ātmā is expressed only with the term "नित्य, Nitya (eternal)," then the smallest subtle particles (परमाणु, Paramāṇu) in the earth, water, light, and wind are also eternal. Therefore, the meaning of the term Nitya in them makes it an Ativyāpti-Doṣa, a fault wherein the characteristics spread in the target and non-target. For instance, describing the characteristics of a cow as cows have horns becomes an Ativyāpti-Doṣa, because the characteristics then apply to female cows as well. For the removal of this fault, the term "सर्वगत, Sarvagata (all-pervasive)" is used; smallest subtle particles may be eternal but are not all-pervasive.

When the term Sarvagata is used for the nature of the Ātmā, then space is also all-pervasive (Sarvagata), so the meaning of the term Sarvagata for space also makes it an Ativyāpti-Doṣa. For the removal of this fault, the term "स्थाणु, Sthāṇu (stable)" is used. Even though space is Sarvagata, it is only perceived in the awake state, region, and time. In the dream and deep-sleep state, and in the dream and deep-sleep region and time, it is not perceived; there is non-being of the space. Space is not such that it can remain steady (Sthira). It is therefore not stable (Sthāṇu). However, the Ātmā is present in all states.

Again, suppose only Sthāṇu (stable) is used for the nature of the Ātmā. In that case, there is Avidyā (nescience, ignorance) that can remain steady, which is present in the awake, dream, and deep-sleep states and creation, sustentation, and dissolution. Therefore, the use of the term Sthāṇu in Avidyā makes it an Ativyāpti-Doṣa, and hence for the removal of this fault, the use of the term "अचल, Acala (immovable)" is made. Even though Avidyā is present in all three states, it is not immovable but is always in the movable form. Only with knowledge (Jñāna) can it be determined absent at all times. However, the Ātmā is everlasting and immovable (Sanātana and Acala) and is situated eternal, immovable, and unrestricted in all states, in all things, in all substances, attributes, and acts (Dravya-Guṇa-Karma), in all regions, and time (Deśa-Kāla) and all creation, sustentation and dissolution (Utpatti-Sthiti-Nāśa). Such was the description of the Ātmā articulated.

अव्यक्तोऽयमचिन्त्योऽयमविकार्योऽयमुच्यते |
तस्मादेवं विदित्वैनं नानुशोचितुमर्हसि || BG 2.25 ||

अयम् - This (Self) ; उच्यते - is said to be ; अव्यक्त: - unmanifest (not a subject of the senses), ; अयम् - it ; अचिन्त्य: - is imponderable (not a matter of the mind), ; अयम् - (and) it ; अविकार्य: - is immutable. ; तस्मात् - Therefore, ; विदित्वा - knowing ; एनम् - it ; एवम् - such, ; न - (it is) not ; अर्हसि - befitting for you ; अनुशोचितुम् - to grieve.

This Self is said to be unmanifest, imponderable, and immutable. Therefore, knowing such, it is not befitting for you to grieve.

Intent - The Ātmā is situated so subtly and immovably that it cannot be made an object of the senses. Though it is immovably seated in the senses, the senses cannot reach it; all they can do is make external substances their objects. Indeed, they cannot even make themselves as objects, just as the eyes cannot see themselves but only see external objects. Have we all not experienced that when an extremely minute particle is close under the eyelids, we ask someone else - "Can you please see if there is anything in my eyes?" The Ātmā is the ear of the ears, the skin of the skin, the eyes of the eyes, the taste of taste, and the smell of smell! Therefore, how can these senses see it or know it? Situated in the ears, it hears, situated in the skin it touches, situated in the eyes it sees, situated in the tongue it tastes, and situated in the nose it smells. Having attained their objective from the Ātmā, all these senses grasp sense objects such as sound (Śabda), touch (Sparśa), form (Rupa), taste (Rasa), and smell (Gandha). Although it is the witness-form power of these five senses, it is beyond their range. How can these senses make the Ātmā, who is beyond the reach of the senses, their object? Being non-object (अविषय, Aviṣaya) of the senses, it is called "अव्यक्त, Avyakta (unmanifest)."

The Ātmā not being the object of thinking (Cintana) is called "Acintya, imponderable." The mind can only think about substances that are separate from it. It is not capable of pondering over that illuminating Reality by whose existence there is the existence of the mind and whose existence mental activity is ongoing. A sword empowered by a hand can slash other things but is not capable of slashing the hand that is holding it. The light of a lit wick can illuminate other objects but cannot illuminate its internal light. The mind has no power of its own nor any illumination of its own. Only with the power of the true witness-conscious the mind appears real (Sat) though unreal (Asat). With the light of the conscious Reality, even though the mind is insentient appears sentient. Even though the Ātmā is shining in the activity of the mind, it is not the object of mental activity, just as electricity in a luminaire makes it active in illuminating surroundings, but reversing itself cannot illuminate electricity. That is why the Ātmā is called "Acintya, imponderable." The Ātmā, existent in the mind, intellect, and senses, is the one who sees and knows everything, but with what sense faculty can it be perceived? How can the mind and intellect know it? येनेदं सर्वं विजानाति तं केन विजानायादिति, by whom all this is known, how can it be known?

The Ātmā, because of its ever-immovability (Nitya-Acalatā) being unmanifest (Avyakta) and imponderable (Acintya), is called "Avikārī, immutable." With the mutations of the body, such as birth and death, the Ātmā does not become mutable. "Hey Arjuna! Knowing your Ātmā this way, there is no occasion for your grief. Because, in your Ātmā, the entire world of Arjuna, Bhīṣma, Droṇa, and others is like waves in the waters of an ocean that are created and destroyed, yet they cannot produce any mutation in the form of creation or destruction in the Ātmā."

The I-ness sense in the gross and subtle bodies and the sentiment of doership and enjoyership in the Ātmā that is free from doership and enjoyership - such contrary sentiments that were the cause of Arjuna's grief, were resolved through the knowledge of the reality by Bhagavāna.

(Now, Bhagavāna accepting Arjuna's lowest perspective, articulates the impossibility of grief and delusion -)

अथ चैनं नित्यजातं नित्यं वा मन्यसे मृतम् |
तथापि त्वं महाबाहो नैवं शोचितुमर्हसि || BG 2.26 ||

महा-बाहो - Hey (Arjuna,) the mighty armed! ; च - Even ; अथ - if ; त्वम् - you ; मन्यसे - think that ; एनम् - it (the Self is) ; नित्य-जातम् - perpetually born ; वा - and ; नित्यम् - perpetually ; मृतम् - dies, ; तथा अपि - still, ; अर्हसि - (You) ought ; न - not ; शोचितुम् - to grieve ; एवम् - this way.

Hey Arjuna! Even if you think that the Self is perpetually born and dies, You ought not to grieve this way.

Intent - In reality, based on the view above, the Ātmā is eternal (Nitya), ever-young (Ajara), immortal (Amara), unborn (Aja), and imperishable (Avināśī). However, even for a moment, if one accepts your lowest perspective that Ātmā of Bhīṣma, Droṇa, and others are always going to be born and always going to die, then also, hey, Arjuna! Your grief that "with the destruction of the family, women of the family will become immoral, children of mixed functional classes will be born, and the downfall of ancestors will occur" is not proper.

(In the next verse, Bhagavāna describes the inappropriateness of Arjuna's grief from this perspective -)

जातस्य हि ध्रुवो मृत्युर्ध्रुवं जन्म मृतस्य च ।
तस्मादपरिहार्येऽर्थे न त्वं शोचितुमर्हसि ॥ BG 2.27 ॥

मृत्युः - Death ; ध्रुवः - is inevitable ; जातस्य - for one born; ; च - and ; मृतस्य - for one who dies, ; जन्म - birth ; हि - is indeed ; ध्रुवम् - certain. ; तस्मात् - That is why, ; अपरिहार्ये - in this unavoidable ; अर्थे - sequence, ; त्वम् - you ; अर्हसि - ought ; न - not ; शोचितुम् - to grieve.

Death is inevitable for one born, and for one who dies, birth is indeed certain. That is why, in this unavoidable sequence, you ought not to grieve.

Intent - If the Ātmā is considered endowed with the attribute of perpetual birth and death, then whatever is created, its death is certain, and one who has died, his birth is also certain. It is not so that one can achieve liberation by dying, and the bondage of birth and death can be cut. If it is so deemed, then "कृतनाश, Kṛtanāśa" Doṣa will incur. That is, a fault incurred when done deeds (Karma) become fruitless without enjoying their fruits. In addition, if deeds become fruitless (Niṣphala) without enjoying the fruits of done deeds, then without any cause, why a Jīva would be in the jail of present life? There cannot be freedom from the cycle of birth and death by just dying. However, it is certain to be born again after dying, just as it is the nature of water to go down and fire to go up. No power can change this nature. Your view that the Ātmā, by its nature, has the attribute of always taking birth and death, so birth and death cannot be avoided, then what is the purpose of your grief that there will be the destruction of family duties and class duties by the end of the relatives? All these people subdued by their nature of dying will die, then why are you putting your feet of duty in between? The cause of their death is only their nature. Therefore, you are not the cause of their deaths but only the instrument (Nimitta). Instrumental cause is always dependent on the underlying cause, not independent. Just as seeds are the underlying cause in fruits' formation and not the farmer. The farmer is only the instrument. In reaping fruits, he is not independent but is dependent on the fruit's underlying cause - the seeds. Without the seeds, the farmer cannot independently harvest fruits; but even without the farmer, if there is the right conjunction of earth and seeds, there can also be the production of fruits. Just as someone who falls while dozing blames a person sitting next to him that you did not support my head, in the same way, these people, by their mortal nature, have to die. You are in the middle like "the excuse of the dozer of falling," just an instrument only, not a killer. You do not need to grieve with your deeming the Ātmā of Bhīṣma, Droṇa, and other relatives as endowed with the attributes of taking birth and dying.

{Now, Bhagavāna articulates how the perceptible (Vyakta) world of the bodies is delusional (Ābhāsa-Mātra) -}

अव्यक्तादीनि भूतानि व्यक्तमध्यानि भारत ।
अव्यक्तनिधनान्येव तत्र का परिदेवना ॥ BG 2.28॥

भारत - Hey Bhārata (Arjuna, the descendent of Bharata)! ; भूतानि - All beings (are) ; अव्यक्तादीनि - unmanifest (without the body before birth) in the beginning, ; अव्यक्तनिधनानि - unmanifest (without the body after death) in the end, ; एव – (and) only ; व्यक्तमध्यानि - manifest in the intermediate state (with the body). ; तत्र - In these (conditions), ; का - why ; परिदेवना - lament?

Hey Arjuna! All beings are unmanifest in the beginning, unmanifest in the end, and only manifest in the intermediate state. In these conditions, why lament?

Intent - Grief can only be for a real thing. Only knowing something real, there is an activity of grief. There is no grief over an imaginary thing. No one physically goes to grieve over the death of a family member in someone's dream. However, the objects of your grief are these bodies. They are unreal, not real, only to see, not accordant with reality. That is why your grief over this delusional world of the bodies is unbecoming. There is no dispute that these bodies before their birth were not in any embodied form but were invisible, and after their death, they will not be in any embodied form but will become invisible. Then those things that are perceived only in the middle period and not in periods before and after are like a dream world and like a snake in the rope, just the subject of delusion. Just as a snake in a rope and dream-world, without pre and post-time, appear only in the middle are unreal and illusory, so is this awake world. There is no uniqueness in it. Just as a dream world in its time appears real, in the same way, this world of the bodies in its time seems real. Therefore, a thing that is not there, only delusional, why grieve?

{The real (Sat) Ātmā in whose support this unreal (Asat) appears as real, Bhagavāna describes its astonishing form -}

आश्चर्यवत्पश्यति कश्चिदेन माश्चर्यवद्वदति तथैव चान्य: |
आश्चर्यवच्चैनमन्य: शृणोति श्रुत्वाप्येनं वेद न चैव कश्चित् || BG 2.29 ||

कश्चित् - Some (knowers of the Self) ; पश्यति - behold ; एनम् - it (the Self) ; आश्चर्यवत् - with astonishment. ; च - And ; तथा एव - similarly ; अन्यः - some (knowers of the Self) ; वदति - speak (about its truth to seekers) ; आश्चर्यवत् - with wonder. ; च - And ; अन्यः - others (seekers) ; शृणोति - listen about ; एनम् - it (the Self) ; आश्चर्यवत् - with amazement, ; च - and ; कश्चित् - some (seekers) ; अपि - also, ; श्रुत्वा - having heard, ; एव - certainly ; न - do not ; वेद - know ; एनम् - it.

Some behold the Self with astonishment. Some speak about it with wonder. Others listen about it with amazement, and some, having heard, certainly do not know it.

Intent - The Ātmā is astonishing. Whatever is seen or heard, everything is in it, but no one can touch it. It is everyone's reality and Prāṇa, yet it is untainted. This Ātmā is so simple that it is perceived just like that, despite it being "is as is" on its own, with whatever it associates. Associating with an attribute it is perceived with an attribute, associating with a substance it is perceived as a substance, associating with an act it is perceived with an act, and yet it is beyond attributes, substances, and acts, just as how a quartz crystal appears as of the same color as a flower underneath. With a red flower, the crystal appears red; with a violet flower, it appears violet, and so on, but it does not have any color of its own and is dissociated from any color but "is as is" without any taint. The Ātmā with whatever intelligence, mental state, sentiment, substance, and thought it associates with, corresponding to those adjuncts it is so perceived. It is one "Cintāmaṇi and Kalpavṛkṣa,"[76] one in whose refuge, whatever sentiment and thought a Jīva makes, there is fruition through it. Some say the world is created by time, some say it is created from the smallest subtle particle, some deem Prakṛti as the material cause of the world, some say without actions (Karma), all this is useless, and so the cause of the world is Karma, and some depict the creation of the world from the conscious element with its Māyā (Māyā-Viśiṣṭa Cetana). Some hold the world is created from twenty-five elements (Tattva), and some say, "No, there are only thirty-three elements." Some believe the number is nineteen, some seventeen, while some say fifteen, and some other thirteen, eleven, seven, or five only. Some say liberation is achieved by action. Some believe liberation is from knowledge. While some believe liberation is from knowledge and action. Some say the action is the means for knowledge and so on. Even though this entire unrest is happening in the Ātmā, all intelligence is non-intellectual, all mental states are renunciatory, all

[76] Cintāmaṇi (चिन्तामणि) means a wish fulfilling jewel and Kalpavṛkṣa (कल्पवृक्ष) means a wish fulfilling divine tree.

sentiments are non-sentimental, and all thoughts are null. It is the one who is in intelligence, mental states, sentiments, and thoughts. All of them are successful only by its grace, yet it is unique. Based on individual perceptions, only through it, awareness of the world and various causes happen; except it, who else is there under whose support there can be awareness of cause and actions? There cannot be awareness in nullity. Still, there is neither the world nor the causes or any element in its form. There are neither twenty-five elements nor nineteen or seventeen. In reality, it is the element of all elements. Besides it, everything else is non-elemental. In it, there has never been any bondage nor any liberation. One thing may be beautiful to one but ugly for another, and a thing favorable to one may be unfavorable to another. One that illuminates all - beautiful and ugly, favorable and unfavorable, instincts and objects, is free from all.

Some knowers of the Truth behold the Ātmā with astonishment. Some knowers of the Truth speak about the Ātmā to other keen seekers of knowledge with wonder, and some who are fit (Adhikārī) listen about the Ātmā in amazement. However, even beholding, speaking, or listening, nobody knows it. The object of beholding, speaking, and listening can be only that thing that is separate from one, just as pots and pans can be seen, spoken, and heard about because they are separate from the perceiver. However, the Ātmā is not separate from one, but being the Ātmā of all is exceptionally impartite and is the true nature of all. Own true nature being always acquired (नित्य-प्राप्त, Nitya Prāpta) is not a matter of activity of beholding, speaking, or listening. That is why the Ātmā is not an object of beholding, speaking, or listening. Indeed, to attain the ever-attained Ātmā is not a fruit of beholding, speaking, or listening. However, directly or through succession, removing the self-ignorance that resides in the refuge of the Ātmā is the only fruit of these means. Just as with the knowledge of "the tenth person (Daśama Puruṣa),"[77]only the ignorance of the "tenth" is removed, and not the gain of the "tenth." Because being one's true nature, it is always attained. Even though it is always attained, it is perceived as unattained only due to ignorance.

(Now, concluding the Sāṅkhya knowledge, Bhagavāna says -)

देही नित्यमवध्योऽयं देहे सर्वस्य भारत |
तस्मात्सर्वाणि भूतानि न त्वं शोचितुमर्हसि || BG 2.30 ||

भारत - Hey Bhārata (Arjuna)! ; अयम् - This ; देही - embodied Self (residing) ; सर्वस्य - in all ; देहे - bodies ; नित्यम् - is eternally ; अवध्यः - indestructible. ; तस्मात् - Therefore, (not only for Bhīṣma, Droṇa, and others, but also) ; सर्वाणि - for all ; भूतानि - beings, ; त्वम् - you ; अर्हसि - ought ; न - not ; शोचितुम् - to grieve.

Hey Arjuna! This embodied Self in all bodies is eternally indestructible. Therefore, for all beings, you ought not to grieve.

Intent - The Ātmā that is in the bodies of all living beings is always unslayable. Not only the Ātmā that is in the bodies of Bhīṣma, Droṇa and all relatives that are here on the battlefield but also the Ātmā in no one can be slain. Even the personified time cannot kill the Ātmā, as time itself is dancing to the tune of the Ātmā.

---

[77] Story of "Daśama Puruṣa, tenth person" goes thus: ten students tried to cross a high flowing river. They went on a boat. After crossing the river, to ensure safety, the leader of the gang started to count each one of them. Every time he counted, he left himself and counted the rest of them, and so he always got the number nine. This caused frustration in the gang. Each one counted in turn and each time they repeated the same mistake of forgetting to count the person who counted. By ignorance, they thought that one among them drowned in the river. Each time they counted the tenth man was missing. All the time the tenth man was very much there, but they failed to count him and they did not realize his presence. They started lamenting over his missing. During that time a wise man came that way and enquired about their cause of worry. Seeing their plight, he helped them to count. When the wise man counted, there were exactly ten people. He declared that 'the tenth man is here'. The students were surprised and at same time happy about the wise man's declaration. The wise man said, 'the tenth man is very much here safely but he was hidden from your vision by ignorance'. With the measure of words (Śabda-Pramāṇa) "the tenth" was not gained, because it being his own form (Svarupa) was always there. With the measure of the words there was only removal (Nivrutti) of ignorance (Ajñāna) of the "tenth". This way the fruit (Phala) of knowledge (Jñāna) is only the removal of ignorance, not attainment of the Ātmā.

It is the power of time; it is beyond the reach of time. Therefore, with the slaying of bodies, it cannot be slain. In reality, separate from the Ātmā, the world of the body, senses, mind, and intellect has no existence. Only with the power of the existent Ātmā, even though they are unreal, they appear as real, and in the Ātmā, they are just delusional. It is no different from how the destruction of waves does not destroy the ocean, or the destruction of gold ornaments does not destroy gold. In the same way, with the slaying of the bodies, the Ātmā is not destroyed. Just as a snake in a rope is delusional, and the delusional snake, in reality, is still a rope, in the same way, this delusional world of the body, senses, mind, and intellect is only the Ātmā.

Accordingly, hey Arjuna! The object of your grief and delusion - the Ātmā, always unslayable, never dies. Therefore, for not only Bhīṣma, Droṇa, and the relatives here on the battlefield, but also no living being, it is befitting for you to grieve. Bodies being always perishable are not even there. Their birth, existence, death, and "killing and being killed" activity, doership, and enjoyership sentiments in the Ātmā are only dreamlike and delusional. Thus, there is no cause for your grief and delusion based either on the perspective of the Ātmā or the body.

(Now, Bhagavāna describes the inappropriateness of his grief from the perspective of duty -)

स्वधर्ममपि चावेक्ष्य न विकम्पितुमर्हसि |
धर्म्याद्धि युद्धाच्छ्रेयोऽन्यत्क्षत्रियस्य न विद्यते || BG 2.31 ||

च अपि - Indeed, ; अवेक्ष्य - considering ; स्वधर्मम् - the law of your own life, ; अर्हसि - (you) ought ; न - not ; विकम्पितुम् - to be perturbed. ; हि - For, ; विद्यते - there is ; न - no ; श्रेयः - greater good ; क्षत्रियस्य - for a Kṣatriya. ; अन्यत् - other than ; धर्म्यात् - the righteous ; युद्धात् - war.

Indeed, considering the law of your own life, you ought not to be perturbed. There is no greater good for a Kṣatriya other than the righteous war.

Intent - Hey, Arjuna! If there is a doubt in your mind, "Accepted that Ātmā does not ever die and bodies are transitory, but where is my moral duty to carry the burden over my back of killing these relatives? Even if I accept that their bodies are continuously perishing and will perish, and no power can stop their destruction, where is the goodness in my heart that, with my own hands, I am ready to behead those relatives and preceptors who are worthy of my worship and enjoy the luxury of the kingdom stained by their blood? Holding such cruelty, where is my righteousness?"

Hey Arjuna! This doubt of yours is misplaced. Considering your duty as a Kṣatriya, to abandon the battle and be disturbed is not befitting you, but from a righteous perspective, you must fight. When a pus-filled boil develops in any part of a person's body, making him sick, a physician must remove the pus from the boil with a scalpel. If the physician desists in this act or shows mercy, he is straying away from his responsibilities. He is answerable for that desistance; the act is not an act of mercy but is indeed unmerciful. Because by doing so, he is destroying that part of the body and other connected components, providing an opportunity for more pain and suffering. Similarly, on the earth, in the body of Prakṛti, when pus-filled boils in the form of cruel sinners are born, it becomes the duty of a righteous Kṣatriya to clean those boils with a sharp sword. On the one hand, due to their relationship with other parts of Prakṛti, there is no pain and suffering in those other parts, and on the other hand, removing the faulty pus may become beneficial for them. If a righteous Kṣatriya desists from his duty due to cowardice or shows mercy, then definitely, with this cowardice, he will fall from his responsibility, will be answerable for his desistance, and his mercy will be unmerciful. The purpose of a Kṣatriya life is that wherever there is an increase in unrighteousness on the earth, there, without procrastinating, it becomes the duty to punish those evil persons with proper punishment. Accordingly, protecting the land in the righteous sacrifice, a righteous Kṣatriya is ready even to sacrifice his own life. When ordinary persons cannot rectify the situation, I have to incarnate on the earth to provide treatment to those faulty parts of Prakṛti (BG 4.6 - BG 4.8).

Therefore, hey, Arjuna! It is your moral duty to clean the pus-filled boils like Duryodhana that have developed in the body of Prakṛti. It becomes your duty to slay Duryodhana and anyone else in the war that has joined the side of unrighteousness. You will fall from your duty if you turn your face away from your responsibility due to unreal dreamlike worldly relationships. More significant than this righteous battle, there is no other better good for a Kṣatriya to conduct. Abandoning the war, on the contrary, will be unrighteous for you indeed.

(Now, from a righteousness and practical perspective, Bhagavāna describes the duty to fight in the following seven verses -)

यदृच्छया चोपपन्नं स्वर्गद्वारमपावृतम् |
सुखिन: क्षत्रिया: पार्थ लभन्ते युद्धमीदृशम् || BG 2.32 ||

पार्थ - Hey Pārtha (Arjuna)! ; सुखिन: - (Only) fortunate ; क्षत्रिया: - Kṣatriya ; लभन्ते - acquire, ; उपपन्नं - reached ; यदृच्छया - on its own, ; च - and ; अपावृतम् - open ; स्वर्ग-द्वारम् - gateway to heaven ; ईदृशम् - as ; युद्धम् - (this) war.

Hey Arjuna! Only fortunate Kṣatriya acquire, reached on its own, open gateway to heaven as this war.

Intent - Moral obligation is more potent for a human than worldly obligations. Acquisition of the human body is only to satisfy this obligation, as it can only be satisfied in this species. Attainment of this and other worlds and enjoyment and liberation is achieved only upon the complete satisfaction of this obligation. Therefore, to pay off this debt, every single moment, a human has to be ready and be prepared to sacrifice his life. The body and body-related relationships in this world are only in the awake state, but the relationship of righteousness is in both worlds and all three states (awake, dream, and deep sleep). These worldly relationships and enjoyments are just desired, meaning they feel good for only some time, but in the end, they are filled with sorrow. In contrast, righteousness is not just desired but is indeed beneficial. In both worlds, it is a giver of real happiness. Accordingly, upon facing righteousness and the material world, giving more importance to the unreal body and body-related relationships and only holding them as real is not an act of piety but is indeed sinful. Facing such a predicament, one ought to show total disdain towards the body and body-related relationships. One ought to bow down towards righteousness, which is the real duty of a human being.

"Hey Arjuna! For you, this by chance, what has come unsought, as if the doors of the heavens have opened up on their own, in which you can sacrifice the body (in which there is I-ness and the relatives in whom there is mineness), you will be able to become debt-free (उऋण, Uṛṇa) from your moral obligation. Therefore, you obey the law of your life (Svadharma) because only a fortunate Kṣatriya gets the opportunity of such righteous war."

(What is beneficial in the war was discussed, now, the harm that is in not fighting is described -)

अथ चेतत्त्वमिमं धर्म्यं संग्रामं न करिष्यसि |
तत: स्वधर्मं कीर्तिं च हित्वा पापमवाप्स्यसि || BG 2.33 ||

अथ चेत् - On the other hand, if ; त्वम् - you ; न - do not ; करिष्यसि - engage ; इमम् - in this ; धर्म्यम् - righteous ; सङ्ग्रामम् - war, ; तत: - then ; अवाप्स्यसि - you will incur ; पापम् - sin ; हित्वा - sacrificing (both) ; स्वधर्मम् - the law of your life ; च - and ; कीर्तिम् - fame.

If you do not engage in this righteous war, you will incur sin by sacrificing both the law of your life and fame.

Intent - Leaving aside an iniquitous (Pāmara) person, in the world and in whatever level of vacillations a person is, Karma is viewed from these three perspectives:

1. By performance of Karma, to accumulate righteousness.
2. By performance of Karma, to become safe from sin and,
3. In this world, to gain fame.

In such persons, even if all three perspectives are not present in any Karma, at least one of these three perspectives is present. If there is an absence of these three perspectives in any Karma, that person falls in the category of a Pāmara (iniquitous) person. It was Bhagavāna's statement to Arjuna that all three perspectives are absent in his desistance from the righteous war.

1. By abandoning the war, you cannot attain righteousness.
2. By abandoning the war, you cannot be safe from sin. But will acquire it, as the desistence is not favorable to the flow of Prakṛti, but is unfavorable. In this desistance, there is no other reason but your delusion. Delusion is the root of all sins - an accepted tenant of all Śāstra. Thus, this desistance is the producer of sin.
3. Destruction of fame is evident.

(Now, in the following three verses, Bhagavāna articulates the attendant infamy -)

अकीर्तिं चापि भूतानि कथयिष्यन्ति तेऽव्ययाम् |
सम्भावितस्य चाकीर्ति र्मरणादतिरिच्यते || BG 2.34 ||

च - And, ; भूतानि - people ; अपि - (will) also ; कथयिष्यन्ति - narrate ; ते - your ; अव्ययाम् - everlasting ; अकीर्तिम् - infamy. ; च - And, ; सम्भावितस्य - for one highly regarded, ; अकीर्तिः - dishonor ; अतिरिच्यते - is worse ; मरणात् - than death.

People will narrate your everlasting infamy. For one highly regarded, dishonor is worse than death.

Intent - Not only those who are Kṣatriya but also the entire population will sing about your infamy. Death would be better for you instead; in death, there will be some pain only at the time of death (the departure of Prāṇa). However, for the entire lifetime, you will have to listen to this infamy with your ears and bear them, which would be worse than the pain of death for one highly regarded for virtues like righteousness and bravery.

भयाद्रणादुपरतं मंस्यन्ते त्वां महारथाः |
येषां च त्वं बहुमतो भूत्वा यास्यसि लाघवम् || BG 2.35 ||

महारथाः - Great warriors ; मंस्यन्ते - will believe that ; त्वाम् - you ; उपरतम् - withdrew ; रणात् - from the battlefield ; भयात् - due to fear, ; च - and ; त्वम् - you ; यास्यसि - will ; लाघवम् - fall in esteem ; येषाम् - among whom ; भूत्वा - you are ; बहु-मतः - highly regarded.

Great warriors will believe that you withdrew from the battlefield due to fear, and you will fall in esteem among whom you are highly regarded.

Intent - Nobody will say that Arjuna left the war paying respect to elders and preceptors and expressing his love for his relatives. However, the only thing that will be discussed is "Gāṇḍīva was there only for show, but when the time came, Arjuna ran away, and the duty[78]that he had taken up at the court of King Virāṭa, he was indeed just fit for that. Hey Arjuna! Even though you are highly regarded among all great warriors, they will all belittle you."

(This way -)

अवाच्यवादांश्च बहून्वदिष्यन्ति तवाहिताः |
निन्दन्तस्तव सामर्थ्यं ततो दुःखतरं नु किम् || BG 2.36 ||

तव - Your ; अहिताः - foes ; वदिष्यन्ति - will hurl ; बहून् - many ; अवाच्य-वादान् - unspeakable words ; निन्दन्तः - denouncing ; तव - your ; सामर्थ्यम् - competence. ; च - And, ; नु - then ; किम् - what can be ; दुःखतरम् - more hurtful ; ततः - than that?

---

[78] During the thirteenth year of incognito exile of the Pāṇḍavas, Arjuna teaches dance and music as a eunuch Bṛhannalā and dresses as a woman in the court of King Virāṭa.

Your foes will hurl many unspeakable words denouncing your competence. What can be more hurtful than that?

Intent - From all perspectives, transcendental, righteousness, and practical, it is beneficial for you to fight.

हतो वा प्राप्स्यसि स्वर्गं जित्वा वा भोक्ष्यसे महीम् |
तस्मादुत्तिष्ठ कौन्तेय युद्धाय कृतनिश्चयः || BG 2.37 ||

वा - Either ; प्राप्स्यसि - you will gain ; स्वर्गम् - heaven ; हतः - being slain ; वा - or ; भोक्ष्यसे - enjoy ; महीम् - the world ; जित्वा - by winning. ; तस्मात् - Therefore, ; कौन्तेय - hey, Kaunteya (Arjuna)! ; उत्तिष्ठ - Stand up, ; कृत-निश्चयः - determined ; युद्धाय - to fight.

Either you will gain heaven being slain or enjoy the world by winning. Therefore, hey, Arjuna! Stand up, determined to fight.

Intent - By engaging in the war, you will have goodies in both hands; there is benefit in living and honor in dying. However, in the war, proper caution becomes your duty so that you can become fit for liberation.

सुखदुःखे समे कृत्वा लाभालाभौ जयाजयौ |
ततो युद्धाय युज्यस्व नैवं पापमवाप्स्यसि || BG 2.38||

कृत्वा - Look ; समे - with equanimity on ; सुख-दुःखे - pleasure and pain, ; लाभ-अलाभौ - gain and loss, ; जय-अजयौ - victory and defeat, ; ततः - and then ; युज्यस्व - engage ; युद्धाय - in the war. ; एवम् - This way (you will) ; न - not ; अवाप्स्यसि - incur ; पापम् - sin.

Look with equanimity on pleasure and pain, gain and loss, victory and defeat, and then engage in the war. This way, you will not incur sin.

Intent - An act may be the same, but with distinctions in views and sentiments, distinctions in sin and piety manifest. If in the war engagement, had Arjuna had this view and sentiment, "In this war, I will win over my relatives, my fame will increase, I will get all the benefits of the kingdom and will get the ability to enjoy the attendant opulence" and acted with that desire, then from worldly perspective engaging in the war being selfish and killing revered ones and relatives would be the creator of sin. However, abandoning this self-interested perspective and keeping a righteous view in the forefront, if Arjuna were to engage in the war with this sentiment, "With pleasure or pain I have no attachment to the former or aversion to the latter, I have no motive in gain or loss and whether I am victorious or lose the battle - so what? All I want is to satisfy my moral obligation, which is the only aim of my life. At this time, Prakṛti is asking me to pay off this obligation, which I am prepared to satisfy every moment and in every which way. Whatever may happen to me in the kingdom of Prakṛti, so what? On the world stage, Prakṛti is displaying her performance. All I have to do is follow the duties assigned to me. What is my motive for gain or loss and victory or defeat?" Then, he would not be a partner in any sin. Therefore, the words of Bhagavāna are that by abandoning the aforementioned worldly perspective and the desire for pleasure-pain and gain-loss, engage in the war with a righteous view. You will not incur sin because it is the selfish desire at the root of all evil.

(Up to here, Bhagavāna resolved the grief and delusion of Arjuna from the perspectives of the Ātmā, body, and righteousness. His duty to engage in the war was articulated from righteousness and practical perspectives, and withdrawing from the battlefield was shown to incur sin and invite infamy. However, in the kingdom of Prakṛti, no Karma remains empty from sin or piety. If any action is not sinful, then it has to be pious, and a pious deed with its relationship will put a Jīva in the bondage of birth and death. That is why, now, Bhagavāna describes that Yoga, situated in which one can acquire freedom from the bondage of Karma of both sin and piety, and located in which the doer of Karma becomes a non-doer and Karma becomes non-action.)

एषा तेऽभिहिता साङ्ख्ये बुद्धिर्योगे त्विमां शृणु |
बुद्ध्या युक्तो यया पार्थ कर्मबन्धं प्रहास्यसि || BG 2.39 ||

एषा - This ; बुद्धि: - knowledge ; साङ्ख्ये - of the Sāṅkhya (regarding the discrimination between the body and the Self) ; अभिहिता - has (so far) been imparted ; ते - to you. ; तु - Again, ; पार्थ - hey Pārtha (Arjuna, the son of Pṛthā)! ; शृणु - Listen ; इमाम् (बुद्धिम्) - to this (knowledge) ; योगे - on the subject of Yoga (whereby union of Jīva and the Self can be attained). ; युक्त: - Endowed with ; यया - such ; बुद्ध्या - knowledge, ; प्रहास्यसि - you will be completely free from ; कर्मबन्धम् - the (piety and sin form) bondage of actions.

This knowledge of the Sāṅkhya has so far been imparted to you. Hey Arjuna! Listen to this knowledge on the subject of Yoga. Endowed with such knowledge, you will be completely free from the bondage of actions.

Intent - From the aforementioned moral perspective, Arjuna was instructed to fight the war with equanimity of mind in pleasure or pain and gain or loss. Even though engagement in the war with a moral perspective does not become the cause for sin, nevertheless, it will be a cause for piety. That is because the fruit of every righteous act is removing sin and gaining piety. In addition, if the fruits of pious deeds are not completely expended, then the bondage of Karma cannot be eliminated because even piety for its enjoyment puts a Jīva in the bondage of the body, and thereby it becomes inevitable for the Jīva to suffer pain in the form of birth and death. Therefore now, Bhagavāna provides the knowledge of that Yoga by which freedom from the bondage of sinful and pious Karma is acquired. That discerning Sāṅkhya knowledge related to the body and the Ātmā that Bhagavāna had provided earlier, by its transcendental realization (Aparokṣa-Jñāna),

- burning I-ness in the body, senses, mind, and intellect,
- burning "I am a doer" sense in the activities of the body,
- situating with oneness in the true witness-conscious Ātmā, and
- only remaining observer of those activities -

that is called Yoga, which is espoused in the Gītā. Only by the realization (Sākṣātkāra) of this knowledge union with oneness in the true witness-conscious Ātmā is possible. How so? It is only due to the absence of this knowledge that there is a disjunction (Viyoga) from the true witness-conscious Ātmā due to ignorance. Therefore, only with the realization of this knowledge is it possible to remove the bondage of Karma. With discriminating vision, due to doership-ego in the body, the bondage of Karma manifest. Through the Reality vision (Tattva-Dṛṣṭi), when the I-ness sense from the body is removed, and one is situated with I-ness in the true witness-conscious Ātmā, where is the bondage of Karma? To whom? Because the true witness-conscious Ātmā is never a doer, only an observer. When it is not a doer, it is not an enjoyer either. Only due to I-ness in the body, unreal doership and enjoyership become the root of the bondage of Karma. Accordingly, with Self-Realization upon acquiring a position in own Ātmā, attainment of Yoga is successful. The bondage of Karma perishes with the uprooting of doership and enjoyership. In this verse, Bhagavāna has articulated that only through knowledge the bondage of Karma can be eradicated - "Endowed with such knowledge you will be completely free from the bondage of Karma."

In contrast, for those who view only desireless actions as Yoga, such a view is not real Yoga but is an apparent Yoga and is not the one that can provide freedom from the bondage of Karma. The nature of Yoga, in their view, is -

1. I am a doer of Karma.
2. Performing Karma is my duty from the Lord.
3. Not desiring the fruits of my Karma, I only perform Karma that is in my power.
4. With equanimity of mind in success or failure, I perform Karma as an offering to the Lord.

It is clear from this Yoga perspective that first, there is the presence of a discriminating perspective, which is the root of the bondage of Karma. Second, there is the presence of duty and with it follows doership, so there cannot be freedom from the bondage of enjoyership. Third, there is a sentiment of relinquishing fruits of action, so it cannot be a sin-producer but is undoubtedly the cause for piety. Fourth, with the presence of doership root, having only the sentiment of relinquishment of the fruits, there is no absence of the fruits. On the contrary, there is growth in the fruits. When roots are live, by grafting a mango tree, fruits are not destroyed from the tree. Instead, there is an increase in mango yield. In this Yoga, since the holder of the sentiment of relinquishing fruits of actions is present, he has not disappeared anywhere, and therefore instead of the absence of fruits, there is their growth. Accordingly, through this Yoga, when current actions (Kriyamāṇa-Karma) continue to produce fruits, where is the question of the removal of accumulated actions (Sañcita-Karma)? That is why, by its nature, this Yoga is not capable of cutting the bondage of Karma. However, through this Yoga, with the purity of the conscience, by dispassion (Vairāgya), one can become fit for knowledge, but by its real nature, it can never be the provider of freedom from the bondage of actions.

The Yoga, "to situate with oneness in the true witness-conscious Ātmā (Self) through the realization of the Truth (Tattva-Sākṣātkāra)" in the subsequent discussion, will be addressed as Yoga, Jñāna-Yoga, Buddhi-Yoga, Vāstavika-Yoga, and Tātvika-Yoga. The Desireless-Action-Yoga (Niṣkāma-Karma-Yoga) depicted by some commentators will be addressed as Variant-Yoga.

(Now, Bhagavāna describes the fruit of this Yoga -)

नेहाभिक्रमनाशोऽस्ति प्रत्यवायो न विद्यते |
स्वल्पमप्यस्य धर्मस्य त्रायते महतो भयात् || BG 2.40 ||

अस्ति - There is ; न - no ; अभिक्रम-नाशः - loss of (seed or) commencement (like a sown seed in a field whether it is fruitful or not) ; इह - in this (knowledge), ; न - nor ; विद्यते - there is ; प्रत्यवायः - (any) fault that may provide contrary results (Viparīta-Phalarupa-Doṣa, such as a medicine that may provide an opposite or negative reaction in a disease treatment). ; स्वल्पम् - Even a little (conduct) ; अस्य - of this ; धर्मस्य - righteous law ; अपि - can ; त्रायते - provide deliverance from ; महतः - the great ; भयात् - fear (of birth and death).

There is no loss of commencement in this knowledge, nor is there any fault that may provide contrary results. Even a little of this righteous law can give deliverance from the great fear.

Intent - Once this Yoga commences, the person dies before achieving the ultimate goal, then whatever is completed does not become fruitless. However, it stays in the form of a seed in the heart and sprouts out in the next life. It does not end without ripening the fruit of liberation, which is why in this Yoga, there is no loss of seed. Just as in desire-ridden acts (Sakāma-Karma), such as sacrifices (Yajña), not done as prescribed, there is a failure to get desired fruits. If there is unfavorable conduct by mistake, the fault that provides contrary results (Viparīta-Phalarupa Doṣa) is incurred. In this Yoga, there is neither failure in getting the fruits nor incurrence of the fault of contrary results, but even with a little conduct or practice of this Yoga, there is deliverance from the great fear of birth and death. Just as a person awake from a dream gets freedom from the pain suffered in a dream and experiences calmness, in the same way, the moment a person, through the Sāṅkhya-knowledge, freed from I-ness and mineness of the body becomes awakened (प्रबुद्ध, Prabuddha) in the true witness-conscious Ātmā and experiences directly, "I am neither the body, nor the senses, nor the mind or the intellect; and neither are they mine, all I am is the undiminished light, in whose illumination their being and non-being activities materialize and in whom they and their attributes have no association," that very moment, the great fear of birth and death of Jīva disappears. The truth is that the true witness-conscious Ātmā is entirely free from the evil of doership-enjoyership and birth-death. Only due to ignorance, with discriminating and limited vision and having I-ness sense in the unreal body, Jīva is attached to dreamlike doership and enjoyership and thus birth and death, which upon awakening of knowledge is immediately removed. Therefore, in this verse, it is said that even a little practice of this Yoga provides deliverance from the great fear of birth and death because the very moment this transcendental knowledge is realized, that very instant freedom is achieved.

In the Variant-Yoga, even if it is accepted that there is no loss of seed (or commencement) and there is no fault of contrary results, however, as is said in the above verse, its little practice by its nature is not capable of providing deliverance from the fear of birth and death. Indeed, it is not at all able to provide deliverance from birth and death. Why? Because the fruit of the Variant-Yoga is only the purification of the inner conscience and nothing more. It is only in the purified conscience with the awakening of knowledge and attaining a position in the true witness-conscious Ātmā that deliverance is possible. Due to ignorance, having fallen from own true witness-conscious Ātmā, there was this great fear. This great birth and death fear has not arisen that some actions can avoid. If, in reality, it was born, then the Variant-Yoga would have been helpful, and Vāstavika-Yoga would have been fruitless, but this great fear is born of ignorance. The Variant-Yoga is action and sentiment-dominant with discriminating-vision and duty and doership-bound intellect and not reality-dominant with non-discriminating-vision. It is primarily based on activities and sentiments and is laced with discriminating-vision and duty and doership-bound intellect and not based on the fundamental reality with oneness-vision. In such a state, being action and sentiment-dominant, it can neither give freedom from duty and doership-bound intellect nor burn accumulated and current impressions of actions (Sañcita and Kriyamāṇa Karma-Saṃskāras) which are the cause of birth and death. In reality, sentiment dominance cannot even remove current impressions. Then where is the question of accumulated impressions? The fruit is not in the insentient Karma. Laced with duty and doership-bound intellect, only the sentiment is the real cause of fruits. Therefore, when the cause of fruits (sentiments) is present, how can current impressions become fruitless? When one accepts that sentiments are excellent, their fruits have to be excellent, not the absence of fruits. Freedom from fruits can be obtained only when a position beyond the reach of the sentiments is acquired. When accumulated and current impressions of actions are present, accepting freedom from the great fear of birth and death is nothing but a vacuous fantasy. Thus, this Variant-Yoga cannot remove the great fear at any time, but with the practice of Vāstavika-Yoga, freedom from the great fear is possible. **Therefore, Variant-Yoga cannot be understood as the intent in the two verses (BG 2.39 - BG 2.40); only Vāstavika-Yoga is the intended meaning of the term Yoga in these verses.**

(Now, in this Yoga, means are briefly expressed -)

व्यवसायात्मिका बुद्धिरेकेह कुरुनन्दन |
बहुशाखा ह्यनन्ताश्च बुद्धयोऽव्यवसायिनाम् || BG 2.41 ||

कुरु-नन्दन - Hey (Arjuna,) the joy of the Kurus! ; इह - In this (Yoga path), ; हि - there is only ; एका - one ; व्यवसाय-आत्मिका - resolute ; बुद्धिः - intellect (that only the Self is eternally blissful, and everything else is without essence). ; बुद्धयः - The intellect of ; अव्यवसायिनाम् - the irresolute (desire-ridden) ; बहु-शाखाः - is multi-branched ; च - and ; अनन्ताः - endless.

Hey Arjuna! In this Yoga, there is only one resolute intellect. The intellect of the irresolute is multi-branched and endless.

Intent - In the verse, the term व्यवसायात्मिका-बुद्धि (Vyavasāyātmikā-Buddhi) should not be understood as professional or occupational intellect but should be understood as a resolute intellect (निश्चयात्मक-बुद्धि, Niścayātmaka-Buddhi). In his resolve, a person who is fit for this Yoga, there is only one eternally blissful Ātmā. Everything else separate from it is without any meaning (असार, Asāra) and indeed filled with grief. His intellect can discern between real and unreal, right and wrong (सार-असार विवेक, Sāra-Asāra Viveka). It is certainly resolute, and that intellect is only one. He has made only the attainment of the eternal blissful Ātmā his goal in all of his activities. With the awakening of his discerning intellect, the other three means: 1) dispassion (Vairāgya), 2) the sixfold virtues (Ṣaṭ-Sampatti),[79] and 3) desire for liberation (मुमुक्षुत्व, Mumukṣutva)

---

[79] The sixfold virtues (षट्-सम्पत्ति, Ṣaṭa-Sampatti) are enumerated as: a) control of the mind (शम, Śama), b) restraint over the senses (दम, Dama), c) faith in the words of the preceptors and scriptures (श्रद्धा, Śraddhā) d) absence of mental vacillations (समाधान,

should be known within because their root is only discernment (Viveka). Just as branches, leaves, flowers, and fruits come out on their own from the root, in the same fashion, with discernment taking hold, the other three are automatically established. Accordingly, a keen desirer for liberation endowed with the four means (Sādhana-Catuṣṭaya) should be considered fit for this Yoga. Contrary to this, a desire-ridden person with irresolute intellect has multifold and unending desires. No matter what, every being, in every effort, is looking for happiness but is unable to make a mental resolve, "Only the Ātmā is eternally blissful." These desire-ridden persons look for happiness in numerous objects of enjoyment devoid of happiness. In addition, subordinated by their desires, they look for happiness sometimes in children or wealth. If kicked from there, they look for happiness in women, sometimes in alcohol, cars, or fame and honor. Like "Falling from the frying pan into the fire," their minds are full of infinite desires. Accordingly, in this Yoga, "Only the Ātmā is eternally blissful" - such discerning resolute intellect is articulated as the primary means in the Yoga path.

(Now, up until the other world, Bhagavāna criticizes those objects of pleasure that are detrimental in this Yoga -)

यामिमां पुष्पितां वाचं प्रवदन्त्यविपश्चित: |
वेदवादरता: पार्थ नान्यदस्तीति वादिन: || BG 2.42 ||
कामात्मान: स्वर्गपरा जन्मकर्मफलप्रदाम् |
क्रियाविशेषबहुलां भोगैश्वर्यगतिं प्रति || BG 2.43 ||
भोगैश्वर्यप्रसक्तानां तयापहृतचेतसाम् |
व्यवसायात्मिका बुद्धि: समाधौ न विधीयते || BG 2.44 ||

पार्थ - Hey Pārtha (Arjuna)! ; अविपश्चित: - The undiscerning ; स्वर्गपरा: - (who deems) heaven as the highest goal, ; कामात्मान: - (who is) desire-ridden, ; वेदवादरता: - (who) revels in the letter of the Vedas, ; वादिन: - (and) who declares ; न अन्यत् अस्ति इति - "there is nothing more than this," ; प्रवदन्ति - utters ; याम् इमाम् - these kinds of ; पुष्पिताम् - flowery ; वाचम् - words ; क्रियाविशेषबहुलाम् - of many actions replete with specific rites ; जन्मकर्मफलप्रदाम् - that give fruits of action in the form of birth ; भोगैश्वर्यगतिं प्रति - (and) acquisition of enjoyments and power. ; तयापहृतचेतसाम् - Whose mind is carried away by those (words) ; भोगैश्वर्यप्रसक्तानाम् - (and) attached to enjoyments and power, ; व्यवसायात्मिका - (his) resolute ; बुद्धि: - intellect ; न विधीयते - cannot situate ; समाधौ - with a steadfast concentration (in the Self)?

Hey Arjuna! The undiscerning who deems heaven as the highest goal, who is desire-ridden, who revels in the letter of the Vedas, and who declares "there is nothing more than this," utters flowery words of many actions replete with specific rites that give fruits of action in the form of birth and acquisition of enjoyments and power. Whose mind is carried away by those words and attached to enjoyments and power, his resolute intellect cannot situate with a steadfast concentration in the Self?

The intent of verses (BG 2.42 - BG 2.43) - The glory of the enjoyments and power described in the Vedas, in reality, is not to glorify the enjoyments and power of the higher worlds. Nor is the intention that the fruits of human life are limited only to attain heavenly enjoyments and power. Because the enjoyments in their attainment time are with the fault of more or less (Atiśayatā-Doṣa), and so in their presence, they are mixed with the pains of jealousy, excessive pride, and hate. Being with the fault of destruction (Kṣaya-Doṣa), in their end-time, they are painful. What is there to doubt? Where there is a glorification of the enjoyments of heaven in the words of the Vedas, it is merely empty praise (Arthavāda). They are spoken with compassion towards those desire-ridden persons, who in this world are engrossed in the accumulation of enjoyments and have made them their only objective of life. Showing compassion towards such persons, the Vedas have

---

Samādhāna), e) desistance from relinquishment of actions (Karma-Tyāga) and vile objects (उपराम, Uparāma), f) tolerance to bear dualities such as heat and cold, pleasure and pain, hunger and thirst (तितिक्षा, Titikṣā) and 4) intense desire for liberation (मुमुक्षुत्व, Mumukṣutva).

described the glory of the enjoyments and power of heaven and said that if you are making enjoyments as the goal of your life, then try to achieve the enjoyments of heaven, which is far greater than the enjoyments of this world.

However, in describing the enjoyments of heaven, the Vedas did not disclose that by such a charade of heavenly enjoyments, the intention was to encourage riddance of desires of the enjoyments of this world. There is no intention of the Vedas in the reality of the statement, "Enjoyments of the heaven are pleasure-yielding." It is no different from a mother wishing to give a bitter medicine to a sick child for his cure, but the child hearing about the medicine runs away. When the mother entices the child by showing him some soft sweets and tells him she would give him sweets if he takes medicine. Likewise, the desire of Śruti-Bhagavatī is to feed her children suffering from the disease of enjoyments with the bitter medicine of renunciation. However, her children sick from the disease of enjoyment are running away from the bitter medicine of renunciation. So, she sings about the glory of sweets that are enjoyments of heaven. Just as the result of medicine is not sweets, but a cure for the disease, in the same way, the glory of the enjoyments of heaven is not in its reality. However, the intent of Śruti-Bhagavatī is in the renunciation of worldly enjoyments and desires and acquiring a cure from the disease of birth and death. That is known as "sweet tongue justice." However, those desire-ridden undiscerning persons not understanding the real intent of Śruti-Bhagavatī, believe as true those vacuous words of praise, "Stop, there is nothing else better than this; the only fruit of human life is the acquisition of the enjoyments of the heaven." In addition, they engage or get others engaged in many actions replete with rites whose fruit is nothing but birth and death, and a Jīva in its frenzy remains a pauper as he was.

Therefore, until heaven, enjoyments are like a disease, and being with the faults of destruction and the attribute of more or less are only pain-yielding and the cause of the transmigrating world of birth and death. Pleasure-yielding is only the Ātmā. Now, the impediments in Yoga are described.

The intent of verse (BG 2.44) - An owl perceives the sun as darkness due to the flaw of vision. When the sun is like darkness in the sight of an owl, then it is unlikely for it to have a fondness for the sun. For attaining the sun, first, in its intellect, there has to be a resolution that the sun is illuminating. Then fondness has to arise for the sun. After that, there has to be a desire for its attainment, and there has to be the means for its attainment. Only then can it attain the sun. In attaining the sun, first, it must have a firm resolve in its mind, "The sun is illuminating." In contrast, if its intellect is enlightened only in darkness, it can never move towards the sun.

Similarly, for the attainment of the blissful Ātmā, first, it is necessary for the intellect of a Jīva to firmly resolve, "The Ātmā is blissful, and the world is painful." After that, he has to have a fondness for the Ātmā, a keen desire to know it, and acquire the means for its attainment, and only then is it possible for its attainment. However, like an owl, a person in whose negative intellect, darkness is light, and enjoyments and power are pleasure-yielding, for him establishing in the Ātmā with oneness is impossible. Therefore, Bhagavāna states that - by flowery words whose minds have been enamored and who are attached to enjoyments and power, such persons do not have a resolute intellect that the Ātmā is pleasure-yielding, they do not have a fondness in the Ātmā, or keen desire to know it and neither do they have the means nor can they attain the position in the blissful Ātmā.

(Accordingly, Bhagavāna criticizing pain-yielding enjoyments guides Arjuna to attain Yoga in the form of situating with oneness in the blissful Ātmā -)

त्रैगुण्यविषया वेदा निस्त्रैगुण्यो भवार्जुन |
निर्द्वन्द्वो नित्यसत्त्वस्थो निर्योगक्षेम आत्मवान् || BG 2.45 ||

अर्जुन - Hey Arjuna! ; वेदाः - All (Karma-Kāṇḍātmaka) Vedas ; त्रैगुण्य-विषयाः - have (the world created by) three constituents (of Prakṛti) as their object. ; भव - (You) be ; निस्त्रैगुण्यः - free from the three constituents, ; निर्द्वन्द्वः - free from dualities (of pleasure and pain, success and failure), ; निर्योगक्षेमः - without (desire for) gain and preservation, ; नित्य-सत्त्वस्थः - always remain in virtuosity, ; आत्मवान् - and focused on the Self.

Hey Arjuna! All the Vedas have the three constituents as their object. You be free from three constituents, free from dualities, without desire for gain and preservation, always remain in virtuosity, and focused on the Self.

Intent - Those parts of the Vedas (Śruti-Bhagavatī) which relate to ceremonial acts and sacrificial rites (कर्म-काण्डात्मक, Karma-Kāṇḍātmaka) only make the Saṃsāra created by the three constituents of Prakṛti as their object. Heaven and other worlds are also the creation of these three constituents. Being the work of those constituents, they cause pleasure and pain and birth and death. Whatever the constituents create is subject to creation and destruction and possesses the attribute of mutation. The work of the constituents cannot be immutable because the constituents themselves are mutable. That is why, Arjuna, you become free from the three constituents (Nistraiguṇya), and be situated in the attributeless (Guṇātīta) supreme Status by abandoning I-ness and mineness from the mind, intellect, senses, and the gross body. Intellect is the work of Sattvaguṇa.[80]The mind and the senses are the work of Rajoguṇa,[81]and the gross body is the work of Tamoguṇa.[82]The root of all dualities is the illusory I-ness sense in the body, senses, mind, and intellect. Due to ignorance, with I-ness sense in them, humans assume duties (Dharmī) of their duties (Dharma) and become doers (Karmī) of their deeds (Karma) and thus become bound by all dualities. With the thought of Sāṅkhya-knowledge, get out of this ego of I-ness and mineness (Ahaṃtā-Mamatā) from the body, senses, mind, and intellect and become free from dualities (Nir-Dvandva) and be situated in the eternal thing - in the true nature of the Ātmā. Free from the worry of providing what is not and preserving what is possessed (Yoga-Kṣema), become focused on the true nature of the Ātmā. Maintain the thought, "I am neither the body, nor the senses, nor the mind or the intellect, but I am that underlying support in whose refuge all these illusory bodies are perceived."

From this, it is clear that in Variant-Yoga, there is insufficient pervasion (Avyāpti-Doṣa) of all of these characteristics because laced with doership and duty-bound intellect, the I-ness sense in the body is definite. When there is an I-ness sense in the body, the Yogī can't become free from the three constituents and the dualities. Though sentimentally, he is equal in pleasure or pain and success or failure, he cannot be duality free with ego in the dualistic body. In such a state, how can he always remain situated in an eternal thing or be without worry of gain and preservation and focused on the Ātmā? Though his sentiment is pure and is helpful in the Vāstavika-Yoga, from the perspective of Gītā, a sentimental alone Yoga cannot be Yoga. Only Tātvika-Yoga is Yoga.

(The same thing is eminently articulated by glorifying that Yoga by which all bondages are broken -)

यावानर्थ उदपाने सर्वत: सम्प्लुतोदके |
तावान्सर्वेषु वेदेषु ब्राह्मणस्य विजानत: || BG 2.46 ||

विजानत: - For a knower ; ब्राह्मणस्य - of the Brahman (who has realized the ultimate Truth), ; यावान् - (there is) as much ; अर्थ: - purpose ; सर्वेषु - in all ; वेदेषु - Vedas ; तावान् - as there is ; उदपाने - (for a person) in a small pond ; सम्प्लुतोदके - (upon acquisition of a large reservoir) wholly filled with water ; सर्वत: - from all sides.

For a knower of the Brahman, there is as much purpose in all Vedas as there is for a person in a small pond upon acquisition of a large reservoir wholly filled with water from all sides

[80] Sattvaguṇa (सत्त्वगुण) is the first of the three constituents of Prakṛti or constituent attributes of all material substances. It predominates in the deities (देव, Deva). It is the cause of goodness, purity and virtuosity.
[81] Rajoguṇa (रजोगुण) is the second of the three constituents of Prakṛti or constituent attributes of all material substances. It predominates in humans and is the cause of activity. It produces fickleness (Cañcalatā) and agitation (Kṣobha).
[82] Tamoguṇa (तमोगुण) is the last of the three constituents of Prakṛti or constituent attributes of all material substances. It predominates in demons (असुर, Asura). It is the cause of the sixfold mutations (षड्विकार, Ṣaḍvikāra): 1) lust (काम, Kāma), 2) anger (क्रोध, Krodha), 3) greed (लोभ, Lobha), 4) delusion (मोह, Moha), 5) excessive pride (मद, Mada) and 6) envy (मत्सर, Matsara).

Intent - Just as a person, upon finding a small water body, may be able to drink water but cannot do other things like bathing, but upon finding a larger water body, he may be able to take a bath but not swim. However, when he finds an extremely large reservoir brimming to its edge, he can now drink, swim, boat, and do many more things. Then he does not need any small pond or reservoir. In the same way, following the Veda enjoined desire-ridden acts, there is the acquisition of some enjoyments and power of this world. With other desire-ridden acts, there is the acquisition of more enjoyments and power of the next world. Yet there is no attainment of objectless happiness (Nir-Viṣayaka Sukha) beyond which there is no other happiness. However, one who has attained the Brahman bliss, the ocean of bliss, and who is situated in it, for such a knower of the Brahman, that is, for a Brāhmaṇa, there is no use or need for the Veda enjoined deeds and produced from there enjoyments and power. He has acquired that ocean of bliss, with whose infinitesimal component all enjoyments and power of both worlds are happening, and all beings are alive. It should be acknowledged that there is no splendor in the enjoyments and power of both worlds. Just by the existence of that blissful Brahman, all these non-splendorous appear with splendor, which this Brāhmaṇa has realized. Therefore, just as finding a filled large water reservoir, there is no need for a small pond; in the same way, this Brāhmaṇa has achieved his real goal and therefore does not need the Vedas.

The flow of Gaṅgā, remaining within the bounds of two banks, meets the ocean and becomes the ocean; after that, for her, there are no limitations of the banks. The limitations of the banks were there so that they could be removed upon meeting the ocean. Similarly, the flow of a Jīva-form river is guided to remain within the limits of two banks of regulative injunctions and prohibitions (Vidhi-Niṣedha) of the Vedas so that without any hindrance, it can merge into the Brahman-ocean and become Brahman, and on its own become unlimited and be free from the injunctions and prohibitions of the Vedas. Just as grain is obtained from the husk, and without a husk, it is impossible, but after obtaining grain, there is no use for the husk, and it is abandoned as worthless. In the same way, attainment of the ocean of bliss happens through the Vedas. Without the Veda enjoined deeds, attainment of the Brahman is impossible, yet after attainment of the Brahman, there is no use for the Vedas. It is no different from the need for a physician and medicine until the patient is cured, but once cured, both physician and medicine on their own become unuseful.

From verses (BG 2.39 - BG 2.46), Vāstavika-Yoga, its fruit, and useful resolute intellect (Vyavasāyātmika-Buddhi) in its attainment are articulated. Further, criticizing the enjoyments and power of both worlds that are detrimental to the attainment of Vāstavika-Yoga is articulated. The glory of that Vāstavika-Yoga is described wherein, establishing oneness in the Ātmā, a Yogī being uninterested in the world and the Vedas becomes free from all bondages. Now, Bhagavāna addressing the concern of Arjuna, "Engaging in war, women of the family will become immoral and so on," articulates this duty to remove his worry related to the consequences of the war -

कर्मण्येवाधिकारस्ते मा फलेषु कदाचन ।
मा कर्मफलहेतुर्भूर्मा ते सङ्गोऽस्त्वकर्मणि || BG 2.47 ||

ते - Your ; अधिकारः - right ; एव - is only ; कर्मणि - in action (Karma), ; मा - (your right is) not ; फलेषु - in the fruit ; कदाचन - at any time. ; ते - You ; मा - do not ; भूः - be ; कर्मफलहेतुः - impelled by the fruits of action, (the fruit is a thing of the right for me the Lord only) ; मा - (and at the same time) do not ; अस्तु - have ; सङ्गः - an attachment ; अकर्मणि - to non-action.

Your right is only in action, not in the fruit at any time. Do not be impelled by the fruits of actions. Do not have an attachment to non-action.

Intent - Hey, Arjuna! At least, your right in performing Karma based on your law of life (Svadharma) is that you engage in the war as your duty. War engagement is a thing that is within your power, but the result is not something within your power. The result will be as is about to happen in Prakṛti. It is not your duty to look at whether by engaging in the war there will be the acquisition of bad consequences such as women of the family becoming immoral, the birth of mixed functional class children, etc. Whatever results Prakṛti has orchestrated for the future, the responsibility squarely rests on the back of Prakṛti, not on you. You should only look at your present righteous duty. You should not look at the results, and indeed, you should not even have a whiff of attachment to the results because the one focused on the results falls from his righteous duty. At the time of "hitting the mark," if there is a desire to reap the reward in the mind of a bowman, then due to that Rajoguṇī desire, it is very likely that his hand will shake, and he will miss his mark. That is why your eyes should not be on the fruits. You should also not have an attachment to withdraw from action, as the relinquishment of duty-bound Karma is not Sāttvika but is indeed Tāmasika (BG 18.7) with only bad and not good results. You should only have your sight on righteous duty and hand over to Prakṛti your body as if it were a machine.

(Accordingly, Bhagavāna articulated the obligation of duty-bound Karma without any desire for the fruits. Prodding Arjuna not just to stand there, Bhagavāna glorified Yoga-Yukta Karma -)

योगस्थः कुरु कर्माणि संगं त्यक्त्वा धनंजय ।
सिद्ध्यसिद्ध्योः समो भूत्वा समत्वं योग उच्यते ॥ BG 2.48 ॥

धनञ्जय - Hey Dhanañjaya (Arjuna)! ; भूत्वा - Becoming ; योगस्थः - established in Yoga (and) ; त्यक्त्वा - relinquishing ; सङ्गम् - (doership) attachment ; कुरु - perform ; कर्माणि - actions ; समः - with evenness ; सिद्ध्यसिद्ध्योः - in success and failure. ; समत्वम् - Equanimity of intelligence ; उच्यते - is called ; योगः - Yoga.

Hey Arjuna! Becoming established in Yoga and relinquishing attachment perform actions with evenness in success and failure. Equanimity of intelligence is called Yoga.

Intent - Based on the preceding, when Karma is a duty and forsaking Karma is a misdeed, Arjuna! You should situate with oneness in the true nature of your Ātmā and be engaged in Karma, and be free from doership-sense by disassociating from the body, senses, mind, and intellect. The root of all dissimilarities and bondages is the "I am a doer" ego in the body. With the sentiment of relinquishment of fruits of action, there is the purging of Rajoguṇa, by which Karma becomes without fault and successful, and there is no provision of contrary results. Because of the presence of the "I am a doer" ego in the body, there is a pious fruit, which in its existence becomes the cause of the Saṃsāra. However, performing Karma with the knowledge, "I am not the body, nor the senses, nor the mind or the intellect, but am that witnessing light in whose illumination they are all active, that is why I am not a doer but merely an observer" the bondage of Karma is broken. This knowledge is not any lone sentiment, and that is the truth. In reality, a witness is not a doer but only an observer. Accordingly, when the association with the body is removed, who would get the fruits? Moreover, what fruit? The cause of the fruits was the I-ness sense in the body. How can a witness get good or evil fruits? Even in an ordinary public perspective, a witness is not subject to punishment. By the influence of this knowledge, equanimity happens naturally in the success and failure of the fruits. The cause of attachment to the fruits is the I-ness ego, which is removed by this knowledge like an impurity. Water situated equally in different waves is the very existence of all waves. The existent common in all (Sattā-Sāmānya) Ātmā equally existing in all is the very existence of one's self. Situating with oneness in that Sattā-Sāmānya is called Yoga.

(Thus, was articulated the unbeatableness of Yoga-Yukta Karma, now extreme lowness of desire-ridden action is described -)

दूरेण ह्यवरं कर्म बुद्धियोगाद्धनञ्जय |
बुद्धौ शरणमन्विच्छ कृपणाः फलहेतवः || BG 2.49 ||

धनञ्जय - Hey Dhanañjaya (Arjuna)! ; बुद्धि-योगात् - (Compared to) Jñāna-Yoga, ; कर्म - (desire-ridden) action ; दूरेण - is extremely ; अवरम् - inferior. ; अन्विच्छ - (Therefore,) seek ; शरणम् - refuge ; बुद्धौ - in the equanimity of intelligence. ; हि - For ; कृपणाः - wretched (are they) ; फल-हेतवः - (who) seek fruits.

Hey Arjuna! Compared to Jñāna-Yoga, desire-ridden action is extremely inferior. Therefore, seek refuge in the equanimity of intelligence. For wretched are they who seek fruits.

Intent - Desires are the result of Rajoguṇa, and Rajoguṇa, by its nature, is fickle. With Rajoguṇī desires remaining in desire-ridden Karma, the mind becomes fickle during the period of desire-ridden activity. There is indeed cause for fear with the thought that results may be unfruitful. Besides this, where there is desire, there is wretchedness. Accordingly, during their time of the conduct, desire-ridden Karma cannot be the cause for happiness due to fickleness, fear, and wretchedness but are indeed the cause for pain. There is a tenet in the kingdom of Prakṛti that as long as the heart is filled with Rajoguṇī desires and fear, they will not allow Karma to be successful. Only failure will be its lot because both are impediments to success. Under the rules of Prakṛti, whenever there is the success of Karma, it happens when Rajoguṇa leaves the heart and is replaced by Sattvaguṇa or when the mind is without any hope for the desire for fruits. When there is the acquisition of fruits of Karma, even then, only that much fruit is obtained as much labor is expended, nothing more than the effort. That is why desire-ridden Karma cannot be any cause for piety. Piety fills the conscience with purity. Therefore, desire-ridden Karma is indeed labor and only labor. If any fruit is obtained, by its nature, it will be perishable, which in its time of destruction will be the cause of manifold pain instead of providing happiness. To enjoy the fruits of good or evil things obtained by those actions, they will put a Jīva in the bondage of birth and death. Accordingly, desire-ridden actions in their commencement and end cause grief and only grief.

In contrast, Yoga-Yukta actions are just pastimes in the present because of the absence of desires. Due to the absence of Rajoguṇa, they are not impediments to the success of fruits, and free from doership-ego, they are not the cause for the bondage of birth and death. This way, Buddhi-Yoga in all three states is blissful. In its comparison, desire-ridden actions are extremely inferior.

The conduct of Karma is shown in three ways -

1. Actions performed as a duty without the desire for results (Verse BG 2.47 - Variant-Yoga)
2. Actions performed relinquishing attachment to doership having attained oneness in the Ātmā (Verse BG 2.48 - Tātvika-Yoga)
3. Actions performed with the desire for fruits (Verse BG 2.49)

Among them, desire-ridden actions (Sakāma-Karma) are depicted as the most inferior, and Yoga-Yukta Karma unbeatable.

(Now the glory of this Yoga-Yukta Karma is further articulated -)

बुद्धियुक्तो जहातीह उभे सुकृतदुष्कृते |
तस्माद्योगाय युज्यस्व योग: कर्मसु कौशलम् || BG 2.50||

बुद्धि-युक्तः - One with equanimity of intelligence ; जहाति - relinquishes ; उभे - both ; सुकृत-दुष्कृते - pious and sinful actions ; इह - here (in this world). ; तस्मात् - Therefore, ; युज्यस्व - engage ; योगाय - in Yoga. ; योगः - Yoga ; कौशलम् - is the skill ; कर्मसु - in actions.

One with equanimity of intelligence relinquishes both pious and sinful actions here. Therefore, you engage in Yoga. Yoga is the skill in actions.

Intent - Due to the ignorance of the true nature of own Ātmā, a person with discriminating-vision who has I-ness sense in the body, senses, and mind assumes their duties and becomes a doer of their activities. When such a person with doership-intellect with whatever sentiment engages in Karma incurs piety or sin according to his good or evil sentiments. In the incurrence of piety or sin, there cannot be any other cause separate from this. However, this Vāstavika-Yogī, who has an evenness of intelligence, through analytic vision, setting ablaze the fire of knowledge in his heart incinerates ignorance and born from them discriminating-vision. Free from I-ness ego in the body, senses, and mind, he is now situated with I-ness in the all-pervading witness-conscious Ātmā. Now he is not a doer of the actions of the body, senses, and mind or possess their duties, but free from all duty and doership-intellect is merely the observer-witness of the duties and actions of the body, senses, and mind. Sentiment not remaining in his Karma, he is not tainted by sin or piety. In a mucky ditch, the space within does not get dirty but "is as is" without dirt. In the same manner, with his pure vision, he always remains pure from the dirt of sin and piety and also, in this world, obtains freedom from sin and piety. In their sleep of ignorance, others with impure vision imagine sin and piety in themselves, others, and even in the Vāstavika-Yogī mentioned above. However, the Vāstavika-Yogī, with his pure analytic vision, has made sin and piety run away from this Saṃsāra; just as with sunrise, one cannot find darkness where it went. Because of his disassociation, even while doing everything with his body, he is a non-doer only and does not come into the bondage of Karma of any kind. This skill in Karma is named Yoga.

In contrast, a Variant-Yogī has discriminating and ignorance-vision. He is with duty-bound intelligence. He has assumed I-ness sense in the body, senses, and mind and is the doer of their activities and has assumed their duties. However, there is a difference; his duty, not being selfish, possesses the sentiments of fruit-relinquishment. Accordingly, in the presence of all ingredients of ignorance, he cannot become free from the bondage of sin and piety merely with the sentiments of forsaking fruits. His sentiments are pure. They are not sinful but are pious. However, such a state continues until going through this Yoga he moves towards and situates in Vāstavika-Yoga.

(Its special discussion follows -)

कर्मजं बुद्धियुक्ता हि फलं त्यक्त्वा मनीषिण: |
जन्मबन्धविनिर्मुक्ता: पदं गच्छन्त्यनामयम् || BG 2.51 ||

मनीषिण: - Wise men, ; बुद्धि-युक्ता: - united with equanimity of intelligence, ; त्यक्त्वा - relinquishing ; फलम् - the fruits ; कर्मजम् - of action, ; हि - are indeed ; जन्म-बन्ध-विनिर्मुक्ता: - liberated from the bondage of birth (and) ; गच्छन्ति - attain ; अनामयम् - the ambrosiac ; पदम् - Status.

Wise men, united with equanimity of intelligence, relinquishing fruits of action, are indeed liberated from the bondage of birth and attain the ambrosiac Status.

Intent - Fruits are not in inanimate Karma, but the sentiments of a doer are the cause for fruits. Whatever form of sentiment there is, be it acquiring or relinquishing, its fruit corresponds with the sentiment. There will be corresponding lowly grievous fruit when there is a selfish sentiment of acquiring. Conversely, there will be blissful fruit when there is an unselfish relinquishing sentiment. The cause of fruits is only sentiments and not just Karma. If just Karma were the cause of fruits, there have to be fruits for even birds and animals of good or evil actions done in their species. However, nowhere in Śruti-Smṛti scriptures is any discussion about the fruits of actions performed in those species. The reason is that though actions performed in those species are unrestrained, there are no sentiments in those actions, and therefore they cannot be any cause for fruit. Sentiments are attributes of the conscience, and in those species, because of incomplete development of the five sheaths (पञ्च-कोश, Pañca-Kośa)[83]of the conscience, the conscience is not awake but is in a dream or deep-sleep state. In the unawake conscience, actions performed in those species are devoid of sentiments,

[83] Pañca-Kośa (पञ्च-कोश) means the five sheaths that cover the Ātmā as described in Taittirīya Upaniṣad (2.1-5), from gross to fine are: 1) the Sheath of Food (अन्नमय-कोश, Annamaya-Kośa), 2) the Sheath of the Vital Breaths of Air (प्राणमय-कोश, Prāṇamaya-Kośa) consisting of the five action faculties viz. mouth, hands, feet, anus and the genitals and five vital breaths of air viz. Prāṇa, Apāna, Samāna, Udāna and Vyāna, 3) the Sheath of the Mind (मनोमय-कोश, Manomaya-Kośa) consisting of the five cognitive senses viz. skin, tongue, eyes, nose and ears, and mind, 4) the Discernment Sheath (विज्ञानमय-कोश, Vijñānamaya-Kośa) consisting of the five cognitive senses and the intellect and 5) the Sheath of Supreme Bliss (आनन्दमय-कोश, Ānandamaya-Kośa)

and therefore there are no fruits from them. From this, it is shown that fruits are only due to sentiments of the conscience; Karma, by its nature, is not the cause for any fruits.

Wise men who have come out of the morass of the body, senses, and the conscience through their analytic thinking established in the equanimity of intelligence while alive and awake sit with oneness in the all-pervading witness-conscious Ātmā. Dissociated from the conscience and its duties, they do not hold any sentiments, as they have incinerated all of them in the fire of knowledge. They remain only in shape form, like a burnt rope. They are not suitable for any bondage. That is why, free from sentiments, they are the only ones free from the fruits of Karma. They are the ones dissociated from the body and who, while alive and awake, are liberated from the bondage of birth "जन्मबन्धविनिर्मुक्त" and have attained the ambrosiac absolute Status.

Opposite of the above, a Variant-Yogī being a doer of the duties and actions of the conscience is with the sentiments of relinquishment of fruits of action. He is the doer of that relinquishment of fruits. In such a state, he cannot be free from the fruits of Karma. However, becoming endowed with the means mentioned above, and through Tātvika-Yoga becoming dissociated from the conscience and its duties and situating in the Status beyond the reach of the sentiments, he can obtain freedom from the fruits of actions, but not in his current state.

There may be a lingering doubt that he does not just have a sentiment of fruit relinquishment. He has also abandoned the sentiment of "I am a doer" and has a pure sentiment of "the all-doer is the Lord, I am not doing anything." Then, where is the fruit for him?

Response - He is not dissociated from the body, senses, and the conscience through the realization of the Truth and established in the all-pervading witness-conscious Ātmā. That is why he sees a distinction between himself and the Lord. With oneness in the conscience, he has become the doer of the sentiment, "I am not doing anything, the all-doer is the Lord," so he cannot become completely free from fruits. Albeit he has excellent sentiments and as a result, fruits will also be purer and more, they cannot be devoid of fruits. This sentiment is very close to Vāstavika-Yoga, yet attaining liberation from the fruits of actions can only happen when he reaches that Status. Camping here will not do the job.

(Now, in the following two verses, Bhagavāna describes how and relinquishing which impediments one can establish with equanimity of intelligence -)

यदा ते मोहकलिलं बुद्धिर्व्यतितरिष्यति |
तदा गन्तासि निर्वेदं श्रोतव्यस्य श्रुतस्य च || BG 2.52 ||

यदा - When ; ते - your ; बुद्धिः - intellect ; व्यतितरिष्यति - properly crosses ; मोह-कलिलम् - the delusional morass, ; तदा (त्वम्) - then (you) ; गन्तासि - will acquire ; निर्वेदम् - dispassion ; श्रोतव्यस्य - from (both) what is to be heard ; च - and ; श्रुतस्य - what is heard.

When your intellect properly crosses the delusional morass, you will acquire dispassion from both what is to be heard and what is heard.

Intent - The delusional morass impedes situating with oneness in the own true Ātmā. Only freedom from the delusional morass can make union in the Ātmā possible. Superimposing doership and duty, "I am a doer, and there is some duty on me" on the Ātmā, which is free from doership and duty, and imagining association of the body, senses, mind, and intellect with the Ātmā (that is dissociated from them), is indeed the root of the delusional morass. It is only because of this that the sense of I-ness in the body and mineness in the relationships of the body is born. As a result, due to discriminating vision, in some, there is favorable and in others unfavorable intellect. Then there is attachment to favorite things and aversion to unfavorable things. With attachment and aversion, there is the birth of all travesties - sin and piety, birth and death, pleasure and pain. All these evils are branches of the delusional morass - the root. Only by cutting this root with an ax of knowledge is freedom from these travesties possible. It is impossible to cut the root by Karma. Accordingly, Arjuna! When you cross over this delusional morass properly, you will attain union in the Ātmā.

Then whatever you have heard about the nature of the Ātmā or whatever you ought to hear, you will find them all pale, and then you will obtain dispassion. No "word" or "meaning" can reach the Ātmā, the Self, and not having reached there, all words and meanings remain near only.

श्रुतिविप्रतिपन्ना ते यदा स्थास्यति निश्चला |
समाधावचला बुद्धिस्तदा योगमवाप्स्यसि || BG 2.53 ||

यदा - When ; ते - your ; बुद्धिः - intellect, ; श्रुति-विप्रतिपन्ना - bewildered by (listening to) varied Vedic tenets, ; स्थास्यति - becomes ; निश्चला - steady (and) ; अचला - immovable ; समाधौ - in the Self, ; तदा - then ; अवाप्स्यसि - you will attain ; योगम् - Yoga (of situating with oneness in the Self).

When your intellect, bewildered by varied Vedic tenets, becomes steady and immovable in the Self, you will attain Yoga.

Intent - One Śruti says something, the other something else. In the same way, in the words of Smṛti and sages, one can see mutual differences. Even though, from a gross perspective, mutual differences are perceived among the words of Śruti, Smṛti, and sages, from a subtle perspective, there is no mutual difference among them. The intent in all of their teachings is only "ब्रह्म सत्यं जगन्मिथ्या जीवो ब्रह्मैव नापरः Brahma is real (Satya), the world (Jagata) is unreal (Mithyā), and Jīva is Brahma-form indeed, and not different." When your mind is bewildered listening to various tenets, "this is true, or that is true," possessing means and through subtle analytic thinking removing all distinctions, becomes steady and immovable in your Ātmā and does not see anything happening in the Ātmā, you will attain oneness in the Ātmā and will cross over the delusional morass. From this, it is clear that only with an intellect endowed with the fourfold means (discernment, dispassion, the sixfold virtues, and intense desire for liberation), with analytic thinking, one can attain union with oneness in the Ātmā; with Karma, one cannot reach that place.

अर्जुन उवाच |
स्थितप्रज्ञस्य का भाषा समाधिस्थस्य केशव |
स्थितधीः किं प्रभाषेत किमासीत व्रजेत किम् || BG 2.54 ||
अर्जुनः उवाच - Arjuna said -

केशव - Hey Keśava (Śrī Kṛṣṇa)! ; का - What are ; भाषा - the characteristics ; स्थितप्रज्ञस्य - (of a sage) of stable wisdom ; समाधिस्थस्य - situated with oneness in the Self? ; स्थितधीः - One who is situated (with stable wisdom), ; किम् - how (does he) ; प्रभाषेत - talk, ; किम् - how (does he) ; आसीत - sit (and) ; किम् - how (does he) ; व्रजेत - walk?

Arjuna said -

Hey Keśava! What are the characteristics of a sage of stable wisdom situated with oneness in the Self? One who is situated with stable wisdom, how does he talk, sit and walk?

{Until the end of the chapter, Bhagavāna describes the characteristics of a sage of stable wisdom (Sthitaprajña) with means -}

श्रीभगवानुवाच |
प्रजहाति यदा कामान्सर्वान्पार्थ मनोगतान् |
आत्मन्येवात्मना तुष्टः स्थितप्रज्ञस्तदोच्यते || BG 2.55 ||
श्रीभगवानुवाच - Śrī Bhagavān said -

पार्थ - Hey Pārtha (Arjuna)! ; यदा - When ; प्रजहाति - (one) entirely discards ; सर्वान् - all ; कामान् - desires ; मनोगतान् - of the mind ; आत्मना - (and is) mentally ; तुष्टः - content ; आत्मनि - in the Self ; एव - alone (and not in any worldly materials), ; तदा - then (he) ; उच्यते - is called ; स्थितप्रज्ञः - (a sage) of stable wisdom.

Śrī Bhagavān said -

Hey Arjuna! When one entirely discards all desires of the mind and is mentally content in the Self alone, he is called a sage of stable wisdom.

Intent - Desires happen when the desired object is separate from one and appears real. With an unreality sense in desired objects, how can there be desire? Just as a person awake from a dream does not anytime wish for desirable objects of the dream, he has realized that the desirable thing of the dream was not separate from him and was not real, and he was becoming a desirable thing with his imagination. The sage of stable wisdom (Sthitaprajña) is awake in his own Ātmā. Like a dream, his trueness sense of desirable objects is gone, and he has made a direct resolve, "This entire world is my imagination; there is nothing separate from me." Accordingly, his desire is automatically removed with the absence of desirable things. The blissful is content in his Ātmā mentally and not through any worldly materials. His pleasure-driven intellect in worldly materials was illusory, which had evaporated by attaining the status of oneness in the Ātmā.

दुःखेष्वनुद्विग्नमनाः सुखेषु विगतस्पृहः |
वीतरागभयक्रोधः स्थितधीर्मुनिरुच्यते || BG 2.56 ||

मुनिः - A sage ; उच्यते - is said to be ; स्थितधीः - of stable wisdom (when he) ; अनुद्विग्न-मनाः - is not mentally perturbed ; दुःखेषु - in grief, ; विगत-स्पृहः - (his) longing has ceased ; सुखेषु - for pleasure, ; वीत-राग-भय-क्रोधः - (and) he is free from attachment, fear, and anger.

A sage is of stable wisdom when he is not mentally perturbed in grief, his longing for pleasure has ceased, and he is free from attachment, fear, and anger.

Intent - Pleasure and attachment are produced with the acquisition of favorable things. With the acquisition of unfavorable things, fear and anger are produced. They are only due to the ignorance of own true nature and I-ness sense in the body. However, a sage of stable wisdom, having attained oneness in the Ātmā, has directly burnt in the fire of knowledge his sense of "देहोऽहम्, I am a body." In his perspective, there is neither any favorable thing nor any unfavorable. He has resolved, "All objects and in them, favorable and unfavorable intellect are merely miracles of my Ātmā." As a result, he has no distress, longing, attachment, fear, or anger. From acquiring illusory pleasure or pain, he is never movable from his nature.

यः सर्वत्रानभिस्नेहस्तत्तत्प्राप्य शुभाशुभम् |
ना यः सर्वत्र अनभिस्नेहः तत् तत् प्राप्य शुभ-अशुभम् || BG 2.57 ||

तस्य - His ; प्रज्ञा - wisdom ; प्रतिष्ठिता - is stable (in the Self); ; यः - who ; प्राप्य - obtaining ; तत् तत् - whatever ; शुभ-अशुभम् - good or evil, ; न - neither ; अभिनन्दति - rejoices ; न - nor ; द्वेष्टि - hates, ; अनभिस्नेहः - and is without attachment ; सर्वत्र - everywhere.

His wisdom is stable; who obtaining whatever good or evil, neither rejoices nor hates, and is without attachment everywhere.

Intent - His good or evil sentiment is burnt in the absence of trueness sense in his own body. From an attachment or aversion perspective, he does not have any attachment to anything as his intellect is firmly situated in the Ātmā. The body, senses, and the good or evil sentiment in them and attachment or aversion mental state were only the expansion of the intellect removed by his analytic perspective.

यदा संहरते चायं कूर्मोऽङ्गानीव सर्वशः |
इन्द्रियाणीन्द्रियार्थेभ्यस्तस्य प्रज्ञा प्रतिष्ठिता || BG 2.58 ||

च - And, ; यदा - when ; अयम् - he ; संहरते - withdraws ; इन्द्रियाणि - (his) senses ; इन्द्रिय-अर्थेभ्यः - from their objects ; इव - as ; कूर्मः - a tortoise ; अङ्गानि - does his limbs ; सर्वशः - from all sides, ; तस्य - (then) his ; प्रज्ञा - wisdom ; प्रतिष्ठिता - is stable (in the Self).

When he withdraws his senses from their objects as a tortoise does his limbs from all sides, then his wisdom is stable.

Intent - Expansion of activities in individual objects with the attachment of the senses happens only during a time when there is a pre-fixed sense of trueness and delight in them. Whenever an individual's sense of trueness and delight in whichever object is removed, the attachment and activity in those objects are naturally contracted. That is the scripture-accepted rule. However, for this sage of stable wisdom, the fountainhead of all delightful things, the Existent-Conscious-Bliss Ātmā is already attained, by which both the sense of trueness and delight in objects has evaporated. Just as the sweetness in sweets comes from its relationship with sugar, without sugar, the same is unsavory. There is no sweetness in objects. Only due to their relationship with the Ātmā, though they are all without trueness and delight, they appear as if they had trueness and delight sense. He has separated and held the Existent-Conscious-Bliss Ātmā like milk from a mixture of milk and water with his Haṃsa-Vṛtti and has abandoned objects viewing them as worthless like water. In such a state, like the limbs of a tortoise, his activity in the objects of senses is naturally withdrawn forever. The intellect of such a person is steadfastly fixed on the Ātmā.

In the above four verses, the self-realized characteristics of a sage of stable wisdom were articulated, which are natural for persons who have realized the Ātmā and for a seeker achievable by effort. The essence of the four verses (BG 2.55 - BG 2.58) is summarized next.

Just as a musk-deer, not knowing the presence of musk in his navel, charmed by its smell, wanders around from forest to forest looking for that smell, similarly, a Jīva within whom the eternal blissful Ātmā is existent, but due to ignorance not knowing it within, attracted by its smell roams around looking for it in the world and objects of the senses. However, for one who has found the fountainhead of bliss within, through the grace of preceptors and scriptures and own efforts, the desire to obtain happiness in the sense objects is naturally removed. No force or means are required to separate him from those objects of senses, and no acquired unwanted things have to be relinquished by any force with the fear that they will become the cause of bondage. Just as a sugar cane juice extractor provides juice discarding bagasse, a Sthitaprajña, in his discerning intellect, separates and holds the real essence of the perceptible world, the real essence by whose existence all these unreal (Asat) appear as real (Sat) and discards the perceptible world knowing it as useless bagasse. His attachment, fear, and anger in perceptible substances are burnt, just as a burnt rope remains only in shape but is not useful to tie. Through the realization of the Truth, his I-ness sense in the body has gone, and he does not have any more desires and attachment to the conscience's favorable good and blissful tendencies, nor does he anguish or hate unfavorable bad and grievous tendencies. Now, in favorable and unfavorable tendencies, free from anguish and desires knowing them without essence, as an indifferent, becomes their observer as a witness.

{Next, Bhagavāna describes the difference between a sage of stable wisdom (Sthitaprajña) and a seeker -}

विषया विनिवर्तन्ते निराहारस्य देहिनः ।
रसवर्जं रसोऽप्यस्य परं दृष्ट्वा निवर्तते || BG 2.59 ||

विषयाः - Objects, ; रसवर्जम् - but not the taste for them, ; विनिवर्तन्ते - may leave ; देहिनः - for a person ; निराहारस्य - who does not feed on them, ; अस्य - but for him (the Sthitaprajña), ; दृष्ट्वा - with the realization ; परम् - of the supreme (Self), ; अपि - even ; रसः - his taste ; निवर्तते - leaves.

Objects, but not the taste for them, may leave for a person who does not feed on them, but with the realization of the supreme Self, even his taste leaves.

Intent - Earlier, attributes of a sage of stable wisdom were described - that he is without distress in times of grief, and without longing in times of happiness, he has forsaken all mental desires, he is without attachment or aversion in the acquisition of good or evil, and he has withdrawn from all sense-objects.

The said characteristics can also be found in those controlling the mind and senses by practicing restraints and observances (Yama-Niyama). As there is exceeding pervasion (Ativyāpti) of those characteristics in a seeker, to remove the Ativyāpti-Doṣa, it is made clear in this verse that for the one who does not engage in the enjoyment of sense-objects, his sense-objects depart. Still, his taste in them does not leave. Even though he has restrained his mind and senses and is perceived as having no longing or distress in times of happiness or grief, such a seeker is free from desires, without attachment or aversion, and has withdrawn his senses from sense objects; however, he has not resolved, "Happiness and grief are only illusory like a flower in the space, and desirable objects and desires are only perceived dreamlike." Just as a brave soldier considering enemies on the battlefield as real is steadfast in his battle, a seeker considering his mind and senses, his dispositions of happiness and grief, attachments and aversions and sense-objects such as touch, taste, smell as enemies, restrains them knowing them as separate from him and real and hence is involved in a battle with them. In contrast, for a Sthitaprajña, his taste in sense-objects and his trueness sense in mind and senses and thus happiness and grief are all gone. What is tasteful and real (Sat) in them and with whose illumination they were perceived as tasteful and real, he has acquired that essence of the ocean of taste. Thus, what he thought was tasteful and real, now knowing it as worthless, has forsaken his I-ness and mineness in them. In addition, knowing them as only perceptions, he has become unfearful, just as, even if a magician in his tricks may make one of our enemies appear before us, yet knowing them unreal, we would have no desire to fight.

(So far, characteristics of a sage of stable wisdom are depicted, now senses that are impediments in this Yoga, their restraint is articulated next -)

यततो ह्यपि कौन्तेय पुरुषस्य विपश्चित: |
इन्द्रियाणि प्रमाथीनि हरन्ति प्रसभं मन: || BG 2.60||

हि - Indeed, ; कौन्तेय - Hey Kaunteya (Arjuna)! ; प्रमाथीनि - The agitating ; इन्द्रियाणि - senses ; प्रसभं - forcibly ; हरन्ति - take over ; अपि - even ; मनः - the mind of ; यततः - an endeavoring ; विपश्चितः पुरुषस्य - discerning person.

Hey Arjuna! The agitating senses forcibly take over even the mind of an endeavoring discerning person.

Intent - One whose mind is not steadfastly fixed on the Ātmā but who is active in the discernment of essence and non-essence and sees faults in the sense objects; such an intelligent person is known as a "विपश्चित, Vipaścita." Bhagavāna has explicitly clarified that it is necessary to have full restraint of the senses in attaining stability of wisdom (Sthitapragnyatā). The mind can only be fixed immovably on the Ātmā when the senses are not fixed on external objects. If their focus is outward, the mind can't be immovable. Because when the senses are extroverted, they forcibly take over the mind. For instance, if the flow in all pipes is stopped in a reservoir with five pipes, water in the reservoir can remain immovable. However, even if one of the pipes is open, it will give an immediate pathway for water to drain and agitate the entire reservoir. With that analogy, there are five pipes of cognitive senses in the reservoir of the conscience (full of water in the form of the mind). If the senses are closed outwards, the mind can stay immovable and be in front of the Ātmā. But out of the five senses, even if one sense becomes outward, it will immediately provide a pathway for the mind to leave and agitate the entire conscience. In such a state, for the mind to stay immovably fixed on the Ātmā is extremely unlikely. Therefore, endeavoring to control them becomes a duty. The senses are highly turbulent and forcibly take over the mind of an intelligent person.

(Bhagavāna provides help of His manifest-form devotion in the restraint of the senses -)

तानि सर्वाणि संयम्य युक्त आसीत मत्परः |
वशे हि यस्येन्द्रियाणि तस्य प्रज्ञा प्रतिष्ठिता || BG 2.61 ||

संयम्य - Restraining ; सर्वाणि - all ; तानि - of them (senses), ; आसीत - sit ; युक्तः - (with the mind) concentrated ; मत्परः - on Me. ; हि - For, ; यस्य - one whose ; इन्द्रियाणि - senses ; वशे - are under control; ; तस्य - his ; प्रज्ञा - wisdom ; प्रतिष्ठिता - is stable.

Restraining all senses, sit with the mind concentrated on Me. One whose senses are under control; his wisdom is stable.

Intent - To concentrate the mind steadfastly on the Ātmā, earlier, the stubborn nature of the senses and the necessity of restraint over the senses are described. In this verse, the approach to restraint is shown. Bhagavāna says that it is possible to restrain the senses by taking some kind of support. Without support, how can there be restraint over the senses? Just as the help of a stake and a rope is necessary to restrain an animal, to restrain the senses, there is a need for some kind of support. Here, Bhagavāna provides Himself as the support and says, "Make My manifest-form the stake and My worship the rope as your duty in the restraint of your senses." Activities of the senses in external objects happen due to their desire for happiness; activity is never for any desire for grief. However, from a thoughtful view, pleasure-sense in objects is illusory. Because first, the acquisition of objects happens at the cost of many hardships and faults. Second, even obtained objects remain the cause for attachment and aversion due to their fault of yielding more or less in enjoyments. Third, because of their attribute of perishability, they are indeed the reason for fear. Therefore, all three states of objects are grievous. "With repeated practice and thoughtfulness seeing fault in objects, and through listening, chanting, recalling and other forms of devotions of My manifest play-forms (Līlā-Vigraha), one ought to search for My manifest-form." Happiness is acquired effortlessly, free of attachment and aversion, without worldly objects. Then, the state of mind and senses become immovable like a rat who just ate mercury. All external activities are forsaken on their own, just as the flow of Gaṅgā never goes towards the Himālaya. Seeing fault in sense objects and in the refuge of devotion, one who has kept all senses under control, his mind can be fixed immovably on the Ātmā.

(By incessant thinking of sense objects, how the intellect of a person falls is described in the following two verses -)

ध्यायतो विषयान्पुंसः सङ्गस्तेषूपजायते |
सङ्गात्सञ्जायते कामः कामात्क्रोधोऽभिजायते || BG 2.62 ||
क्रोधाद्भवति सम्मोहः सम्मोहात्स्मृतिविभ्रमः |
स्मृतिभ्रंशाद् बुद्धिनाशो बुद्धिनाशात्प्रणश्यति || BG 2.63 ||

पुंसः - A person ; ध्यायतः - thinking about ; विषयान् - objects ; उपजायते - (first) develops ; सङ्गः - an attachment ; तेषु - to them (that they are pleasure-yielding). ; सङ्गात् - (Second) from attachment, ; कामः - desire ; सञ्जायते - arises (that I should acquire them by any means). ; कामात् - From (that) desire (when there are obstacles in acquiring those objects), ; क्रोधः - anger ; अभिजायते - is born.

क्रोधात् - From anger ; भवति - arises ; सम्मोहः - delusion, ; सम्मोहात् - (and then) from delusion ; स्मृति-विभ्रमः - ensues memory failure (as to "what is my duty?") ; स्मृति-भ्रंशात् - With memory failure, ; बुद्धि-नाशः - intelligence is destroyed ; प्रणश्यति - (and that person) perishes ; बुद्धि-नाशात् - with the destruction of intelligence.

A person thinking about objects develops an attachment to them. From attachment, desire arises. From desire, anger is born.

From anger arises delusion, and from delusion ensues memory failure. With memory failure, intelligence is destroyed, and that person perishes with the destruction of intelligence.

The intent of verses (BG 2.62 - BG 2.63) - If the direction of the mind is not focused towards the Lord seeing fault in objects, then it becomes unavoidable for that person not to contemplate on sense objects. The nature of the mind is such that it cannot remain without support. For instance, water, with its attribute of fluidity, needs a path to flow. If an appropriate course is not provided, it will break the barrier and find its way to flow. If the flow of mind is not directed to contemplate and focus on the Lord, it will move towards enjoying sense objects. When the flow of mind moves towards worldly pleasures, how he falls is described stepwise -

1. By contemplating, one develops a fondness for sense objects that are undoubtedly beautiful and elegant.
2. With a fondness for objects, the desire develops to procure them by any means.
3. Where there is desire, in the kingdom of Prakṛti, obstacles are definite to follow; like where a carcass is decaying, there vultures and jackals are drawn naturally. When obstacles arise, it becomes necessary for agitation to occur in mind. For instance, when the flow of a river faces large rocks, water hitting it splashes all over. Similarly, when there is a hindrance in acquiring some desirable objects, an outburst of anger is definite.
4. With anger, delusion (mental blurring) occurs. There is no sense of good or evil, right or wrong.
5. With delusion, there is a failure of memory. That is - who am I? What is my duty? Where is my good? Such memory and thinking become blinded.
6. With the failure of memory, intelligence is destroyed. It becomes unsuitable for discerning between good and evil, right and wrong.
7. Finally, with the destruction of intelligence, the person falls from his beneficial path and perishes.

Accordingly, by unrestrained contemplation of sense objects, a person moves towards his destruction, just as how a stubborn child slipping from roof stairs falls to the ground.

(Now, the benefits that accrue from restraint are described in the following two verses -)

रागद्वेषवियुक्तैस्तु विषयानिन्द्रियैश्चरन् |
आत्मवश्यैर्विधेयात्मा प्रसादमधिगच्छति || BG 2.64 ||

तु - However, ; विधेय-आत्मा - a self-controlled (person), ; आत्म-वश्यैः - with self-restrained ; इन्द्रियैः - senses ; राग-द्वेष-वियुक्तैः - free from attachment and aversion, ; चरन् - enjoying ; विषयान् - objects, ; अधिगच्छति - attains ; प्रसादम् - purity of the conscience.

A self-controlled person, with restrained senses free from attachment and aversion, enjoying objects, attains purity of the conscience.

Intent - When trained horses are reigned by an intelligent charioteer, protecting both the chariot and its occupants from potholes and thorns, he can safely take them to their destination. In the same way, when senses in the form of horses are trained, they are the enjoyers of objects free of attachment and aversion and operate under the control of a charioteer (intellect). Without any obstacle, it will make the person fit for "तद्विष्णोः परमं पदम्, that highest status of Lord Viṣṇu," and such a person with self-controlled mind attains purity of the conscience. Just as a lake gets dirty in the rainy season, but later on in a cooler period becomes cleaner, independent and outward-facing senses cause impure conscience. Senses, by their nature, are the result of Rajoguṇa and make the conscience fickle by their relationship. With the restraint of Rajoguṇī senses, Sattvaguṇa naturally arises. With the arising of Sattvaguṇa, there is indeed purity of the conscience. Only a person with such pure conscience is suited for Self-Realization.

प्रसादे सर्वदुःखानां हानिरस्योपजायते |
प्रसन्नचेतसो ह्याशु बुद्धिः पर्यवतिष्ठते || BG 2.65 ||

प्रसादे - Upon attaining purity, ; सर्व-दुःखानाम् - all sorrows ; अस्य - of this (qualified) ; उपजायते - are ; हानिः - destroyed. ; हि - Indeed, ; बुद्धिः - the intellect ; प्रसन्न-चेतसः - of such serene-minded ; आशु - quickly ; पर्यवतिष्ठते - becomes steadfast.

Upon attaining purity, all of his sorrows are destroyed. The intellect of such serene-minded quickly becomes steadfast.

Intent - The cause of all sorrows is only the extroverted mind and senses. Extroverted senses are the enemies of human beings. First, when they become their enemies, the entire world becomes their enemy. By winning over these internal enemies, the whole world can be conquered. By conquering them, there is serenity in the conscience, like the one attained when Mandarācala (मन्दराचल) Mountain came out after the churning of the ocean of Milk (Kṣīra-Sāgara-Manthana). Accordingly, all sorrows vanish with the independence of the senses and calming of the conscience. For such a serene-minded person, with the removal of obstacles, his intellect quickly becomes properly steadfast in the Ātmā.

(Next, the faults of uncontrolled senses are described -)

नास्ति बुद्धिरयुक्तस्य न चायुक्तस्य भावना |
न चाभावयत: शान्तिरशान्तस्य कुत: सुखम् || BG 2.66 ||

अस्ति - There is ; न - no ; बुद्धि: - (Self-related) intellect ; अयुक्तस्य - for an unsteady, ; च - and ; न - (there is) no ; भावना - (Self-related) sentiment (that I attain the Self) ;अयुक्तस्य - for (that) unsteady. ; अभावयत: - For the one without sentiments ; न - (there is) no ; शान्ति: - peace, ; च - and ; अशान्तस्य - for one without peace, ; कुत: - where is ; सुखम् - happiness?

There is no Self-related intellect for an unsteady, and there is no Self-related sentiment for that unsteady. For the one without sentiments, there is no peace, and for one without peace, where is happiness?

Intent - There is neither wisdom nor sentiments in the heart of an uncontrolled person. For a person without sentiments, there is no peace, then where is happiness? For the one who is focused on attaining the supreme objective (Paramārtha-Parāyaṇa), it is necessary in the first place to have control over the senses. In a vacillating heart, in the absence of control, there is no discerning intellect that can discriminate between what is true and what is false, what is good and what is evil, or what is real and unreal? When there is no discerning intellect, then in the enjoyment-bound intellect, how can there be the pure sentiment with faith towards preceptors and scriptures? When there is no pure sentiment, then with enjoyment bound sentiment present, how can there be peace in the heart? When the heart is wavering and fickle, then how can the face of real bliss of the Ātmā be visible? An uncontrolled person can never acquire happiness by any means.

इन्द्रियाणां हि चरतां यन्मनोऽनुविधीयते |
तदस्य हरति प्रज्ञां वायुर्नावमिवाम्भसि || BG 2.67 ||

हि - Indeed, ; चरताम् - (among) the wandering ; इन्द्रियाणाम् - senses, ; तत् - that (one sense) ; अनु - with ; यत् - which ; मन: - the mind ; विधीयते - engages ; हरति - carries away ; अस्य - his ; प्रज्ञाम् - wisdom, ; इव - just as ; वायु: - (how) the wind (carries away) ; नावम् - a boat (of its course) ; अम्भसि - in the water.

Among the wandering senses, that one sense with which the mind engages carries away his wisdom, just as how the wind carries away a boat in the water.

Intent - Senses that are extroverted toward objects destroy everything about this person. The mind is also taken in those object regions by the senses with whatever objects the senses are after. Just as a swindler takes a wealthy person into a forest with pretense and steals him, in the same way, the senses take the mind into the forest of object enjoyments with pretense and steal the wealth of Self-perception. With fondness and attachment, when there is a union of the mind and senses with enjoyable objects, then it also makes the intellect bewildered, just as the wind, with its force, hurls a boat in the water. In the ocean of the world, the force of the wind in the form of the senses takes the boat of intellect way off course from its path to the highest objective. When the mind and intellect all have become about-faced (are moving in the wrong direction), then how can there be anything beneficial for this person? Even if only one sense becomes greedy for its objects, everything of this person is destroyed due to the absence of control.

(Having shown harm due to uncontrolled senses and benefit due to control over senses, now Bhagavāna reverts to the earlier occasion -)

तस्माद्यस्य महाबाहो निगृहीतानि सर्वशः ।
इन्द्रियाणीन्द्रियार्थेभ्यस्तस्य प्रज्ञा प्रतिष्ठिता || BG 2.68 ||

तस्मात् - Therefore, ; महा-बाहो - Hey Mahābāho (Arjuna, the mighty-armed)! ; यस्य - Whose ; इन्द्रियाणि - senses ; सर्वशः - are entirely ; निगृहीतानि - withdrawn ; इन्द्रिय-अर्थेभ्यः - from sense objects, ; तस्य - his ; प्रज्ञा - intellect (in the Self) ; प्रतिष्ठिता - is stable.

Therefore, Hey Arjuna! Whose senses are entirely withdrawn from sense objects, his intellect is stable.

Intent - Only such a self-restrained person is fit for the stability of wisdom, and his intellect can become immovably steady in the Ātmā.

(Now, describing again the nature of a sage of stable wisdom who has relinquished all desires, ends the chapter -)

या निशा सर्वभूतानां तस्यां जागर्ति संयमी ।
यस्यां जाग्रति भूतानि सा निशा पश्यतो मुनेः || BG 2.69 ||

संयमी - A restrained ascetic ; जागर्ति - is awake (he has found oneness) ; तस्यां - in that {supreme Truth (Paramārtha-Tattva)} ; या - which ; निशा - is a night ; सर्वभूतानां - for all living beings (all living beings are null and sleeping regarding that supreme Truth). ; यस्यां - In which ; भूतानि - (all) living beings ; जाग्रति - are awake (are active with trueness-sense), ; सा - that (worldly cycle of birth and death) ; निशा - is a night ; पश्यतः - for the perceiver ; मुनेः - sage (for him there is the absence of the worldly cycle of birth and death in the past, present, and future).

A restrained ascetic is awake in that which is a night for all living beings. In which all living beings are awake, that is a night for the perceiver sage.

Intent - For all living beings, that Supreme Reality is like night. Regarding that Supreme Reality, all living beings are asleep, are unconscious of that Reality, and for whom the Supreme Reality has become unknown. In that ever-pure supreme bliss Reality, a self-restrained sage of stable wisdom is awake; he is conscious. In that Reality, his intellect is situated "as is." He is situated in that Reality with I-ness and is thoroughly enjoying it. But those worldly enjoyment objects in whom all living beings are being conscious and are enjoying, and in whom their intellect is becoming true or having an I-ness sense, those objects which they are holding as true, from those objects the seer of the Reality is sleeping. For him, all these objects are equivalent to a night and are just nothing, meaning, in his view, all these objects are like an imagined flower in the space.

आपूर्यमाणमचलप्रतिष्ठं समुद्रमापः प्रविशन्ति यद्वत् ।
तद्वत्कामा यं प्रविशन्ति सर्वे स शान्तिमाप्नोति न कामकामी || BG 2.70 ||

यद्वत् - Just as ; आपः - water (from various rivers) ; प्रविशन्ति - enters ; अचल-प्रतिष्ठम् - an immovably established ; समुद्रम् - ocean ; आपूर्यमाणम् - filled from all sides (without creating any disturbance), ; तद्वत् - in the same way ; यम् - in whom (the sage of stable wisdom in whose ocean-like heart) ; सर्वे - all ; कामाः - desires ; प्रविशन्ति - enter (without creating agitation), ; सः - he ; आप्नोति - attains ; शान्तिम् - peace ; न - and not ; काम-कामी - the one who desires sense objects.

Just as water enters an immovably established ocean filled from all sides, in the same way in whom all desires enter, he attains peace and not the one who desires sense objects.

Intent - When there is a discriminating intellect in one's self, in desirable-objects separate from one's self, and desire-ridden dispositions of the conscience, and also there is trueness sense in the discriminating intellect, then with trueness sense of the discriminating intellect, desires become the cause for disturbance in the heart. In contrast, by Self-Realization, when the oneness position is established in the Ātmā (the underlying support of all of them), and all these desires, the desirer and desirable objects appear only as waves in the Ātmā, then these three trueness senses are burnt, and they remain only in the imaginary state. In such a state, illusory desires with their awakening do not become the cause for disturbance in the heart. Accordingly, one whose heart has become immovably solemn, like an ocean, filled with direct intuitive knowledge, "I am not a desire, there is no desirable object in me, and I am not a doer of desire," in that ocean of heart even though numerous rivers of desires enter, yet they cannot produce any agitation. Such a sage of stable wisdom attains peace and not the one who has desires for sense objects.

विहाय कामान्य: सर्वान्पुमांश्चरति नि:स्पृह: |
निर्ममो निरहङ्कार: स शान्तिमधिगच्छति || BG 2.71 ||

सः - He (who) ; चरति - moves around ; निर्ममः - without mineness ; निरहङ्कारः - (and) without I-ness ; विहाय - relinquishing ; सर्वान् - all ; कामान् - desires ; निःस्पृहः - (and) free from yearnings, ; यः - that ; पुमान् - person ; अधिगच्छति - attains ; शान्तिम् - peace.

He who moves around without mineness and I-ness relinquishing all desires and free from yearnings, that person attains peace.

(Now, articulating the result of the stability of wisdom, the chapter is concluded -)

एषा ब्राह्मी स्थिति: पार्थ नैनां प्राप्य विमुह्यति |
स्थित्वास्यामन्तकालेऽपि ब्रह्मनिर्वाणमृच्छति || BG 2.72 ||

पार्थ - Hey Pārtha (Arjuna)! ; एषा - That is ; स्थितिः - the state ; ब्राह्मी - of the Brahman. ; प्राप्य - Attaining ; एनाम् - it, ; न - (one does) not ; विमुह्यति - get deluded (in the worldly cycle of birth and death). ; अपि - Even if ; स्थित्वा - (one is) situated ; अस्याम् - in this (state) ; अन्तकाले - at the time of death, ; ऋच्छति - (one) attains ; ब्रह्म-निर्वाणम् - Nirvāṇa-Brahma.

Hey Arjuna! That is the state of the Brahman. Attaining it, one does not get deluded. Even if one is situated in this state at the time of death, one attains Nirvāṇa-Brahma.[84]

ॐ तत्सदिति श्रीमद्भगवद्गीतासूपनिषत्सु ब्रह्मविध्यायां योगशास्त्रे

श्रीकृष्णार्जुनसम्वादे सांख्ययोगो नाम

द्वितीयोऽध्याय: || BG 2 ||

Oṃ Tat Sat

In the Śrīmad Bhagavad Gītā Upaniṣad

The Yoga Science of the Knowledge of Self-Realization

The Discourse of Lord Śrī Kṛṣṇa and Arjuna

This Second Chapter

Yoga Named - The Sāṅkhya Yoga

Clarification

In the first chapter, when deluded and grief-stricken Arjuna abandoned his weapons and became confused about his duty and not understanding his benefit, at the beginning of this chapter, he surrenders to Bhagavāna (BG 2.4 - BG 2.7), who then separates Arjuna's grief in three causes, and provides resolution for each cause and explains that irrespective of whether it is related to the body, the Ātmā or to righteousness there is no reason for his grief. If there is grief from the perspective of the Ātmā of Bhīṣma and others, then the Ātmā of all living beings is unborn and imperishable. Weapons can never slash it. If there is grief from a bodily

[84] Nirvāṇa-Brahma (निर्वाण-ब्रह्म) means oneness in the Brahman with liberation from the worldly cycle of birth and death.

perspective, all living beings' bodies are always unsteady and ephemeral. No power in the Saṃsāra can keep them. If they are grieved from a righteousness perspective, then it is not befitting because when there is a moral dilemma, it becomes one's duty to sacrifice worldly relationships. From a practical and transcendental perspective, it is his duty to engage in the war (BG 2.11 - BG 2.13). Not only that, but desisting the war would destroy both of his worlds, this and the other world; and by engaging in the war, either winning or dying, under either scenario, it would be indeed beneficial to him (BG 2.33 - BG 2.38).

In addition, Bhagavāna articulated, with means, the Yoga of situating with oneness in own pure Ātmā, whereby a doer (Kartā) of deeds (Karma) becomes a non-doer (Akartā) and all Karma become Akarma (non-action). Sāṅkhya-knowledge is provided to Arjuna up to verse BG 2.30. Through its transcendental realization, burning I-ness ego in the body, senses, mind, and intellect and situating with oneness in own true witness-conscious Ātmā and burning the "I am a doer" ego in the activities of the body and senses, and remaining their observer only, is articulated as Yoga. The fruit of the Yoga described is such that there is no destruction of commencement in the Yoga. In this life, whatever means are acquired, they do not become fruitless (Niṣphala), and one does not acquire contrary results. However, even a little practice will protect one from the great fear of birth and death (BG 2.39 - BG 2.40).

"One whose nature is pure bliss is only the Ātmā" such resolute intellect is formulated as the primary means (Sādhana) in this Yoga. In addition, intellect that is irresolute and with desires is shown as opposer in this Yoga, and up to heaven, desire-ridden objects of enjoyment were criticized (BG 2.41- BG 2.44). Then glorifying this Yoga, Bhagavāna said that a knower of the Brahman rises above the Veda prescribed desire-ridden Karma and enjoyment and opulence born from those Karma, and has no purpose in injunctions and prohibitions (Vidhi-Niṣedha) of the Vedas (BG 2.45 - BG 2.46). After that, describing desireless actions (Niṣkāma-Karma), the excellence of Yoga-Yukta Karma is articulated. With Yoga-Yukta Karma, association with doership is forsaken, equanimity of the mind is established, freedom from pious and sinful fruits is obtained, the bondage of birth and death is cut, and an ambrosiac supreme Status is attained.

In contrast, desire-ridden Karma is shown as the most inferior, and the desire for fruits is depicted as miserable and distressful (BG 2.47 - BG 2.51). In addition, in the verses (BG 2.52 - BG 2.53), those main impediments were described, which in this Yoga are obstacles. Then Bhagavāna said that - when your intellect will cross over the "I am a doer" ego and doership delusional morass, you will absorb the truth in the words of Śāstra. Accordingly, when your bewildered intellect, listening to varied Veda-tenets, remains steady and immovable in your own Ātmā, then you will attain the Yoga of oneness in the witness-conscious Ātmā.

On this, upon Arjuna's desire to know the characteristics of a sage of stable wisdom (Sthitaprajña), Bhagavāna articulated the characteristics of the one whose intellect is immovably situated in the Ātmā and provided the difference between a Sthitaprajña and a seeker (BG 2.54 - BG 2.59). Then, the outward-facing senses that are the obstacles in this Yoga are described, and it is shown that the stability of wisdom (Sthitapragnyatā) is only dependent on the control of the senses (BG 2.60 - BG 2.61). Moreover, thinking about sense objects, how a person first develops fondness, deep desire, anger, and finally acquires his downfall is sequentially described (BG 2.62 - BG 2.63). After that, through the restraint of the senses and with the attainment of purity of the conscience, how the absence of grief and steadiness of intellect is achieved is described. Showing harm with unrestrained senses and benefit with restrained senses, the dependence of the stability of wisdom on the restraint of the senses is provided (BG 2.64 - BG 2.68).

Ending the chapter, Bhagavāna described the nature and glory of that knower of the Reality Sthitaprajña as - "Awake in that, which is the night for all living beings. In which living beings are awake, that is the night for the perceiver sage. He is asleep concerning the Saṃsāra and is awake in his Ātmā and the entire Saṃsāra in his view is null." In the heart of this knower of the Ātmā, no worldly desire can enter and make his nature changeable. Being without I-ness and mineness, he attains supreme peace. At the time of death, if a Jīva is situated in this Brāhmi-state, he attains Nirvāṇa-Brahma and is not subject to birth and death (BG 2.69 - BG 2.72).

In this chapter, first, Sāṅkhya knowledge and then the Yoga of the steadfast establishment with oneness in the true witness-conscious Ātmā is described by which the bondage of Karma is cut at the root, and all actions become non-action. Then in this Yoga, its means, obstacles, glory, and the characteristics of a Yogī were described. On this, Arjuna, not grasping the real intention of Bhagavāna, understood that Bhagavāna is praising knowledge in the form of abandonment of actions. "He is asleep concerning the Saṃsāra," "Like the rivers in the ocean, desires cannot produce any disturbance in his heart," "Abandoning all desires, becoming free from I-ness and mineness, he is moving around," and so on. Arjuna thought, for me, it will happen for good. I will effortlessly get rid of this killing field. But Bhagavāna intended to describe the exalted glory of that Yogī, who by the splendor of Tātvika-Yoga is assertively situated in his own true witness-conscious Ātmā and by its influence views the entire Saṃsāra and his mind, senses, and body as null, like one just awoke from a dream. He becomes so dissociated from the activities of body, senses, and mind that all his efforts become natural and, in his view, nothing is happening, and even killing the entire Saṃsāra, he is not killing anyone and does not come into any bondage. It was never the intention of Bhagavāna to abandon actions in their true nature. By this Yoga, becoming free from the association of doership and duty, Bhagavāna intended that one ought to engage in Karma with unattached natural activities. Actions by their nature are not the cause for the bondage of a Jīva. The cause is the "I am a doer" sense, doership and duty only, born of ignorance. However, Arjuna, not grasping this, doubtfully asks Bhagavāna at the beginning of the third chapter -

Chapter 3

The Karma Yoga

अर्जुन उवाच |
ज्यायसी चेत्कर्मणस्ते मता बुद्धिर्जनार्दन |
तत्किं कर्मणि घोरे मां नियोजयसि केशव || BG 3.1 ||
अर्जुनः उवाच - Arjuna said -

जनार्दन - Hey Janārdana (Śrī Kṛṣṇa)! ; चेत् - If ; ते - you ; मता - consider ; बुद्धिः - knowledge ; ज्यायसी - superior to ; कर्मणः - action, ; तत् - then ; केशव - hey, Keśava (Śrī Kṛṣṇa)! ; किम् - Why ; नियोजयसि - are you enjoining ; माम् - me ; घोरे - in this fearful ; कर्मणि - action (of war)?

Arjuna said -

Hey Śrī Kṛṣṇa! If you consider knowledge superior to action, then hey, Keśava! Why are you enjoining me in this fearful war?

व्यामिश्रेणेव वाक्येन बुद्धिं मोहयसीव मे |
तदेकं वद निश्चित्य येन श्रेयोऽहमाप्नुयाम् || BG 3.2 ||

वाक्येन - By words ; व्यामिश्रेण इव - that seem confusingly mingled, ; मे - my ; बुद्धिं - intelligence ; मोहयसि इव - is bewildered, as it were. ; वद - (Therefore,) tell (me) ; तत् - that ; एकं - one (thing), ; निश्चित्य - after deciding, ; येन - by which ; अहम् - I may ; आप्नुयाम् - attain ; श्रेयः- the highest good.

By words that seem confusingly mingled, my intelligence is bewildered, as it were. Therefore, tell me that one thing, after deciding, by which I may attain the highest good.

Intent - Tell me whether Karma (performing action) is better for me or knowledge in the form of relinquishment of action.

{When Arjuna, not grasping the intent of the words of Bhagavāna, raised the above question, then Bhagavāna making a superimposition (अध्यारोप, Adhyāropa),[85] guided him through this way -}

---

[85] Adhyāropa (अध्यारोप) means superimposition of the unreal on the real, like the false perception of a snake in a rope which is not a snake. Here, while keeping in mind a major objective to prove, to discuss a minor subject is also called Adhyāropa. For instance, someone needs buttermilk, and keeping that in mind asking his friend - Do you have cows? Do they give milk? Do you convert milk to yogurt? Do your extract butter? Such words are called Adhyāropa.

श्रीभगवानुवाच |
लोकेऽस्मिन्द्विविधा निष्ठा पुरा प्रोक्ता मयानघ |
ज्ञानयोगेन साङ्ख्यानां कर्मयोगेन योगिनाम् || BG 3.3 ||
श्रीभगवान् उवाच - Bhagavān said -

अनघ - Hey Anagha (Arjuna, the sinless one)! ; पुरा - Earlier (from the beginning of the creation) ; अस्मिन् - in this ; लोके - world, ; द्विविधा - twofold ; निष्ठा - disciplines ; प्रोक्ता - were set forth ; मया - by Me. ; साङ्ख्यानाम् - (Among them) for Sāṅkhyās (the followers of the "Path of Renunciation") ; ज्ञान-योगेन - the discipline of knowledge (Jñāna-Yoga), ; योगिनाम् - (and) for Yogīs (the followers of the "Path of Activity"), ; कर्म-योगेन - the discipline of action (Karma-Yoga).

Hey Arjuna! Earlier in this world, twofold disciplines were set forth by Me. Among them for Sāṅkhyās, the discipline of knowledge (Jñāna-Yoga), and Yogīs, the discipline of action (Karma-Yoga).

Intent - The term "पुरा प्रोक्ता, Purā Proktā" does not mean the two disciplines or faiths spoken in the earlier chapter. The intention is that the Lord promulgated these two disciplines from the beginning of the world's creation. For one who is fit for knowledge, by desireless actions whose faults of impurity and vacillations are purged, who is free from Rajoguṇa and in whose pure conscience, with the awakening of discernment and dispassion, a keen desire to know the Reality is awakened, for such a dispassionate seeker the discipline of knowledge is articulated. But for the one who is fit only for Karma, due to the influence of Rajoguṇa who cannot remain without engaging in Karma and because of the flow of Rajoguṇa whose mind cannot stay steady in thinking about the Reality, for such a Yogī, the discipline of Niṣkāma Karma-Yoga is articulated as the best path for the removal of Rajoguṇa. The firm resolve of the Citta is called "Niṣṭhā."

{It is evident that success of Naiṣkarmya (नैष्कर्म्य, actionlessness)[86] knowledge without Karma is impossible -}

न कर्मणामनारम्भान्नैष्कर्म्यं पुरुषोऽश्नुते |
न च संन्यसनादेव सिद्धिं समधिगच्छति || BG 3.4 ||

पुरुषः - A person ; न - cannot ; अश्नुते - achieve ; नैष्कर्म्यं - actionlessness (knowledge) ; अनारम्भात् - without initiating ; कर्मणाम् - actions. ; च - Moreover, ; सिद्धिम् - perfection (purity of the conscience) ; न - cannot ; समधिगच्छति - be achieved ; संन्यसनात् एव - by merely renouncing (actions).

A person cannot achieve actionlessness without initiating actions. Moreover, perfection cannot be achieved by merely renouncing actions.

Intent - When a knower of the Reality, upon realization of his own Ātmā, becomes dissociated from the body, then he does not remain a doer of the activities of the body but just their observer and does not see anything happening in his Ātmā through actions. Ascending in the status of the Ātmā, not being the cause for fruits, Karma that occur naturally through the body are called Naiṣkarmya or Akarma. Without the initiation of Karma, the success of Naiṣkarmya is impossible. Only through Karma is its success possible. How so? Because of discriminating and limiting vision, in the beginning, this person in the frenzy of Prakṛti is covered by the I-ness ego in the body and so is naturally shrouded by Tamoguṇa and Rajoguṇa. With I-ness and mineness, surrounded by selfishness and desires, he remains endowed with the faults of impurity and vacillations. With desireless actions and devotion until his faults of impurity and vacillations are removed,

---

[86] Naiṣkarmya (नैष्कर्म्य) means actionlessness, freedom from reaction, or that which does not produce experience of the resultant action, or exemption from acts and their consequences. It is not to come in bondage of actions even after performing actions and scorching the seeds of actions in the fire of knowledge (ज्ञानाग्नि, Jñānāgni) and making it actionless and without fruits.

how can he enjoy the aforementioned Naiṣkarmya enjoyment? Devotion, a mental activity, falls within the meaning of Karma. For instance, when there is pus in a boil on the body until the pus is removed, how can there be calmness? Until the impurities and vacillations residing in the heart are removed and replaced with desireless actions and devotion, how can there be ownership in this Naiṣkarmya peace? Withholding them internally, it is impossible to attain liberation by simply forsaking Karma. By the method mentioned above, only with Karma, the success of Naiṣkarmya and liberation can be achieved, not by abandoning Karma before commencement. However, at the root of all activities, the aim is in true non-activity (Nivrutti) compared to activity (Pravṛtti). Abandonment of activity before beginning activity does not remain any cause for fruit. For instance, for a hungry, only after the activity of eating the removal of hunger is successful. Before the activity of eating, retirement cannot be any cause for the fruit. Accordingly, there can be a success in non-activity of actions only by activity in actions. Abandoning actions before the commencement of actions does not become a cause for Naiṣkarmya and liberation.

(Usefulness of Karma is shown towards the highest objective. Now from a practical viewpoint, Bhagavāna shows the potency of Karma -)

न हि कश्चित्क्षणमपि जातु तिष्ठत्यकर्मकृत् |
कार्यते ह्यवश: कर्म सर्व: प्रकृतिजैर्गुणै: || BG 3.5 ||

हि - For, ; न कश्चित् - no one ; जातु - can ever ; तिष्ठति - stay, ; अपि - even ; क्षणम् - for a moment, ; अकर्मकृत् - without action. ; हि - Unquestionably, ; सर्व: - all ; अवश: - helplessly ; कार्यते - perform ; कर्म - actions (according to their nature) ; गुणै: - through the constituents ; प्रकृतिजै: - born of Prakṛti .

No one can ever stay, even for a moment, without action. Unquestionably, all helplessly perform actions through the constituents born of Prakṛti.

Intent - Sattvaguṇa, Rajoguṇa, and Tamoguṇa are the three constituents of Prakṛti. From these three constituents, there is the creation of ego, intellect, mind, sense-organs, and the entire sentient and insentient Saṃsāra. In creating the visible Saṃsāra, separate from the three constituents, there is no other cause. Sattvaguṇa results in knowledge. With Rajoguṇa, fickleness and agitation are produced, and Tamoguṇa results in dense insentience. The three constituents together produce the visible Saṃsāra. The three constituents are present in every movable, immovable, sentient and insentient thing. No substance is without them. When every substance has a relationship with these three constituents, which are transformable, how can anything in the Saṃsāra stay without Karma and activity? Never. Accordingly, no living being for any moment can stay without Karma, but all are forced to engage in Karma through the constituents of Prakṛti.

(When Karma is pervasive and unavoidable, then in such a situation -)

कर्मेन्द्रियाणि संयम्य य आस्ते मनसा स्मरन् |
इन्द्रियार्थान्विमूढात्मा मिथ्याचार: स उच्यते || BG 3.6 ||

संयम्य - (Forcefully) restraining ; कर्म-इन्द्रियाणि - (only) the action-organs, ; विमूढात्मा - a deluded person ; य: - who ; आस्ते - sits ; स्मरन् - thinking ; मनसा - in mind ; इन्द्रियार्थान् - about sense-objects, ; स: - he ; उच्यते - is said to be ; मिथ्याचार: - a hypocrite.

Restraining the action-organs, a deluded one who sits thinking in mind about sense objects is said to be a hypocrite.

Intent - Any effort or activity that has a relationship with the mind; that effort or activity is named Karma. Any effort that does not have a conjunction with the mind is neither Karma nor does it have a fruit. With the movement of Prāṇa, numerous activities take place in the body whereby blood, flesh, fat, urine, feces, and others are created and discarded. However, due to the absence of their relationship with the mind, they are not within the definition of Karma. From this, it is clear that anything that happens through the mind is Karma and not as commonly accepted as "only that which happens through action-organs." However, a deluded one who forcefully restraining action-organs keeps his mental activity open and dwells on sense objects; his business of Karma is ongoing, which becomes the cause for good or bad fruits. One who forcibly restrains action-organs against the flow of nature is called a hypocrite (दम्भी, Dambhī) because even though he appears as not doing Karma, he is indeed doing Karma.

यस्त्विन्द्रियाणि मनसा नियम्यारभतेऽर्जुन |
कर्मेन्द्रियैः कर्मयोगमसक्तः स विशिष्यते || BG 3.7 ||

तु - However, ; नियम्य - controlling ; इन्द्रियाणि - the sense-organs ; मनसा - with the mind, ; असक्तः - unattached, ; यः - one who ; आरभते - commences ; कर्म-योगम् - Karma-Yoga (with the sentiment of offering to the Lord) ; कर्म-इन्द्रियैः - through action-organs, ; अर्जुन - hey Arjuna! ; सः - He ; विशिष्यते - excels.

Controlling the sense-organs with the mind, unattached, one who commences Karma-Yoga through action-organs, hey Arjuna! He excels

Intent - From the hypocrite-relinquisher of actions, that person is superior with a sentiment of offering to the Lord, mentally forsaking attachment and aversion from sense-objects and without attachment to the results, instead of holding back action-organs engages in Karma-Yoga. This movement of his is agreeable with Prakṛti because, in the kingdom of Prakṛti, action-organs are not the cause of bondage, as they are created only for their functionalities. The cause for bondage is the mental attachment and aversion, which he has already abandoned. Now unattached as he is, with the sense of offering to the Lord, he is engaged in Karma, by which here in his conscience purity is taking hold, and there the flow of Rajoguṇa is being removed. That was only the fruit of Karma.

(That is why -)

नियतं कुरु कर्म त्वं कर्म ज्यायो ह्यकर्मणः |
शरीरयात्रापि च ते न प्रसिद्ध्येदकर्मणः || BG 3.8 ||

त्वं - You ; कुरु - perform ; नियतम् - prescribed (by Śāstra) ; कर्म - acts ; हि - because ; कर्म - an action ; ज्यायः - is superior ; अकर्मणः - to inaction. ; च अपि - Besides, even ; ते - your ; शरीर-यात्रा - life in the body ; न - is not ; प्रसिद्ध्येत् - possible ; अकर्मणः - without action.

You perform prescribed acts because an action is superior to inaction. Besides, even your life in the body is not possible without action.

Intent - There is a creation of Karma even when the action-organs are held back. Additionally, there is an increase in the untruthfulness fault (मिथ्याचारित्व-दोष, Mithyācāritva-Doṣa). Therefore, based on the law of one's life, Karma prescribed by scriptural injunctions ought to be performed. Thus, with the performance of obligatory acts, one is saved from the untruthfulness fault, and through purity of the conscience, Karma becomes Akarma. Scriptural injunctions are there to get one involved in an activity based on individual fitness and to take one naturally towards renunciation. It is better to perform Karma than not to engage in Karma. Instead of holding the impurity fault within, it is better to let it out, by which there is no internal decay. Indeed, everyday sustenance of the body cannot be accomplished without Karma, then how can one live without Karma?

From the words of Bhagavāna, Karma cannot be abandoned, and by doing Karma, it becomes unavoidable for a Jīva to come in its bondage. That is so as the cause of bondage is Karma. Whether it is activity or non-activity, they all have their reward. In such a state, what is the destination for a Jīva?

(Upon arousal of such doubt, Bhagavāna says -)

यज्ञार्थात्कर्मणोऽन्यत्र लोकोऽयं कर्मबन्धन: |
तदर्थं कर्म कौन्तेय मुक्तसङ्ग: समाचर || BG 3.9 ||

अयम् - This ; लोक: - world ; कर्म-बन्धन: - (comes in) the bondage of action ; कर्मण: - by (engaging in) acts ; अन्यत्र - other than ; यज्ञार्थात् - for the sake of sacrifice (that is, for the sake of the Lord). ; कौन्तेय - (That is why,) hey Kaunteya (Arjuna)! ; मुक्त-सङ्ग: - Free from attachment, ; समाचर - engage ; कर्म - (in) activities ; तदर्थम् - as a sacrifice.

This world comes in the bondage of action by engaging in acts other than for the sake of sacrifice. That is why, hey Arjuna! Free from attachment, engage in activities as a sacrifice.

Intent - In the verse, "Yajñārtha (यज्ञार्थ, for the sake of sacrifice)," the term Yajña means the Lord Viṣṇu as confirmed in Taittirīya Saṃhitā (तैत्तिरीय संहिता)1.7.4.4. Accordingly, the first sentence ought to be understood as "This world comes in the bondage of Karma by engaging in Karma other than for the sake of Lord Viṣṇu." Holding a sentiment of self-interest and mineness, activity or renunciation, whatever Karma a person performs, its reward is the Saṃsāra. Moreover, they will put this person in the bondage of the Saṃsāra, even if they are done with the hope of attaining higher worlds. Karma performed for the enjoyment of fruits puts a person in the bondage of birth and, upon completion of the enjoyment of fruits, puts him in the mouth of death. These actions do not assist in freeing a Jīva from the bondage of birth and death.

In contrast, the Karma that is done without the Saṃsāra related selfish and mineness sentiments, but done only with a sentiment of offering to the Lord and without attachment to the fruits does not put a doer in the bondage of the Saṃsāra. The cause of bondage is always self-interest and mineness. Karma, in its form, is never the cause of bondage. However, this Yajñārtha-Karma, that is, current desireless actions by its performance, makes the conscience pure and, later, with the grace of the Lord, makes the person fit for knowledge. The person ascending in Yoga attains oneness in his Ātmā and enjoys Naiṣkarmya. Accordingly, Yajñārtha-Karma by regular succession is helpful in the freedom from the bondage and is not the cause for bondage.

From verses (BG 3.5 - BG 3.9), the unavoidability of Karma and opposition to Karma is formulated, and now Bhagavāna shows the state of having no beginning (अनादिता, Anāditā) of Karma and the woven nature of the world and Karma.

सहयज्ञा: प्रजा: सृष्ट्वा पुरोवाच प्रजापति: |
अनेन प्रसविष्यध्वमेष वोऽस्त्विष्टकामधुक् || BG 3.10 ||

पुरा - At the beginning (of the Kalpa), ; प्रजापति: - Prajāpati (Brahmā), ; सृष्ट्वा - having created ; प्रजा: - humanity ; सह-यज्ञा: - together with sacrifice, ; उवाच - said - ; अनेन - "By this (sacrifice), ; प्रसविष्यध्वम् - attain growth; ; एष: - (let) this ; अस्तु - be ; इष्ट-कामधुक् - a provider of coveted objects of desire ; व: - to you."

In the beginning, Prajāpati, having created humanity together with sacrifice, said - "By this sacrifice attain growth; let this be a provider of coveted objects of desire to you."

Intent - In the verse, the epithet Kāmadhuk (कामधुक्) is the same as Kāmadhenu (कामधेनु) - the divine cow of Indra, the king of the deities of the heaven. To the one in possession, Kāmadhenu is said to provide all coveted objects of desire. Sacrifice, charity, austerity, and other good deeds which are performed targeting deities with good sentiments are all sacrifices, and those sacrifices are indeed in the form of Karma. Whether and whoever acquires, enjoyment or liberation are all obtained through Karma. Without sacrifice in the form of Karma, even Brahmā cannot give himself anything. The creation of the world by Brahmā is also dependent on the Karma of a Jīva. Creating action predominant (Karma-Pradhāna) sacrifice together with the world, Brahmā told humanity that you further procreate and acquire enjoyments and liberation, whatever you desire with this sacrifice of Karma (a sacrifice that is the provider of coveted objects of desire).

This way, the state of no beginning of Karma was postulated, and the pervasiveness of Karma was shown in the acquisition of desire-ridden and desireless fruits.

(Then Brahmā said -)

देवान्भावयतानेन ते देवा भावयन्तु वः |
परस्परं भावयन्तः श्रेयः परमवाप्स्यथ || BG 3.11 ||

भावयत - Satisfy ; देवान् - the deities ; अनेन - through this (sacrifice). ; ते - (Then) those ; देवाः - deities ; भावयन्तु - will satisfy ; वः - you. ; परस्परं - Mutually ; भावयन्तः - satisfying (each other, through purity of the conscience) ; अवाप्स्यथ - you will acquire ; परम् - the highest ; श्रेयः - good.

Satisfy the deities through this sacrifice. Then those deities will satisfy you. Mutually satisfying each other, you will acquire the highest good.

Intent - Whatever perishable gross manifestations there are, the controlling divine power (Adhidaiva-Śakti) is called "Devatā," the deity who controls every individual body (Vyaṣṭi-Śarīra), action-organs, cognition organs, mind, intellect, and I-ness ego of all individual beings based on their deeds, just as an engineer runs a locomotive. Every sense organ has its separate deity. For instance, the deity of the eyes is the sun-deity (Sūryadeva); the deity of the mind is the moon-deity (चन्द्रमा, Candramā). For every sense organ in the individual body, the deity of its respective aggregate sense-organs (Samaṣṭi-Indriya) is the sense organ of the Cosmic Form. To wit, the sun-deity, who is the controller of the aggregate eyes, is the eyes of the Cosmic-Form, and similarly, the moon-deity, who is the controller of the collective minds, is the mind of the Cosmic-Form. At the beginning of the Kalpa, Brahmā creating humanity together with sacrifice said that with this sacrifice satisfy the deities, and the satisfied deities will satisfy you, similar to how by offering one seed to the earth, many fruits can be obtained. In the absence of the earth, obtaining fruits is impossible. The deity who is the substrate of the collective worlds (Samaṣṭi-Brahmāṇḍa), offering the seed in the form of Karma to him, you will attain a great reward, not otherwise. Karma offered to the deities will be oblatory, and satisfying the deities will satisfy you. By succession, you will attain the highest good.

(This way -)

इष्टान्भोगान्हि वो देवा दास्यन्ते यज्ञभाविताः |
तैर्दत्तानप्रदायैभ्यो यो भुङ्क्ते स्तेन एव सः || BG 3.12 ||

देवाः - (Those) deities, ; यज्ञ-भाविताः - satisfied through sacrifice, ; हि - will undoubtedly ; दास्यन्ते - bestow ; भोगान् - the enjoyments ; वः - you ; इष्टान् - seek. ; सः - He ; एव - is definitely ; स्तेनः - a thief ; यः - who ; भुङ्क्ते - (solely) enjoys ; तैः - their ; दत्तान् - bestowed (wealth, children, and other enjoyments) ; अप्रदाय - without any offerings ; एभ्यः - to those (deities).

Those deities, satisfied through sacrifice, will undoubtedly bestow the enjoyments you seek. He is a thief who solely enjoys their bestowed enjoyments without any offerings to those deities.

यज्ञशिष्टाशिनः सन्तो मुच्यन्ते सर्वकिल्बिषैः |
भुञ्जते ते त्वघं पापा ये पचन्त्यात्मकारणात् || BG 3.13 ||

ते - Those ; सन्तः - righteous ; यज्ञ-शिष्ट-अशिनः - (who) partake in leftovers of the sacrifice ; मुच्यन्ते - are released ; सर्व-किल्बिषैः - from all sins. ; पापाः - The sinful ; ये - who ; पचन्ति - cook ; आत्म-कारणात् - (only) for their own sake (is like) ; भुञ्जते - eating ; अघं - sin ; तु - indeed.

Those righteous who partake in leftovers of the sacrifice are released from all sins. The sinful who cook for their own sake is like eating sin indeed.

Intent - Offering them with gratitude, through whom there is the acquisition of enjoyments, and enjoying those enjoyments as their grace, as well as sharing with other living entities, is indeed virtuous behavior of a righteous person. To keep this moral behavior steady, and with that goal in mind, there is the formulation of the five great sacrifices (पञ्च-महायज्ञ, Pañca-Mahāyajña)[87]and the occasional (नैमित्तिक, Naimittika) sixteen rites of passage in human life (षोडश-संस्कार, Ṣoḍaśa-Saṃskāra).[88]Keeping this virtuous behavior steady, a person can make progress in this world and the next. In contrast, by abandoning this virtuous behavior, he can be deprived of both worlds. There is no doubt about that. In actuality, during enjoyment, forgetting, and moving away from whom there is the acquisition of enjoyments, and solely enjoying it without sharing with other living beings is indeed a lowly ungrateful animalistic behavior and is highly loathsome. Undoubtedly, this is the reason for many kinds of grief and poverty.

Thus, the way there was the promulgation of action-form sacrifice together with the world, and the way how a person with good desire and disposition can acquire sought after enjoyments through sacrifice, and once obtained, the way how enjoyments are to be enjoyed after offering, that sequence was briefly articulated.

(The interwoven nature of Karma and humanity is described in the following three verses -)

अन्नाद्भवन्ति भूतानि पर्जन्यादन्नसम्भवः |
यज्ञाद्भवति पर्जन्यो यज्ञः कर्मसमुद्भवः || BG 3.14 ||

अन्नात् - From food ; भवन्ति - are born ; भूतानि - living beings; ; अन्न-सम्भवः - food originates ; पर्जन्यात् - from rain. ; पर्जन्यः - Rain ; भवति - arises ; यज्ञात् - from sacrifice, ; यज्ञः - (and) sacrifice ; कर्म-समुद्भवः - is born of action.

From food are born living beings; food originates from rain. Rain arises from sacrifice, and sacrifice is born of action.

कर्म ब्रह्मोद्भवं विद्धि ब्रह्माक्षरसमुद्भवम् |
तस्मात्सर्वगतं ब्रह्म नित्यं यज्ञे प्रतिष्ठितम् || BG 3.15 ||

विद्धि - Know that ; कर्म - action ; ब्रह्म-उद्भवं - is born of the Vedas; ; ब्रह्म - the Vedas ; अक्षर-समुद्भवम् - are born of the Imperishable (Reality). ; तस्मात् - Therefore, ; सर्वगतं - the all-pervasive ; ब्रह्म - Vedas ; नित्यं - are always ; प्रतिष्ठितम् - existent ; यज्ञे - in sacrifice.

Know that action is born of the Vedas; the Vedas are born of the Imperishable (Reality). Therefore, the all-pervasive Vedas are always existent in sacrifice.

एवं प्रवर्तितं चक्रं नानुवर्तयतीह यः |
अघायुरिन्द्रियारामो मोघं पार्थ स जीवति || BG 3.16 ||

एवं - This way, ; पार्थ - hey Pārtha (Arjuna)! ; सः - One ; यः - who ; न - does not ; अनुवर्तयति - follow ; प्रवर्तितम् - the moving ; चक्रम् - wheel ; इह - here (in this world, that is, does not lend his hand in moving the worldly wheel), ; इन्द्रिय-आरामः - who rejoices in sense-objects, ; अघायुः - living in sin, ; जीवति - lives ; मोघम् - in vain.

---

[87] Pañca-Mahāyajña (पञ्च-महायज्ञ) means the five great sacrifices: 1) the worship of divine entities (देव-यज्ञ, Deva-Yajña), 2) the worship of knowledge (ब्रह्म-यज्ञ, Brahma-Yajña), 3) the worship of ancestors (पितृ-यज्ञ, Pitṛ-Yajña), 4) the worship of living entities (भूत-यज्ञ, Bhūta-Yajña) and 5) the worship of guests (अतिथि-यज्ञ, Atithi-Yajña).

[88] Ṣoḍaśa-Saṃskāra (षोडश-संस्कार) means the sixteen rites of passage in a human being's life as described in Vedic Scriptures: 1) Garbhādhāna-Saṃskāra (गर्भाधान-संस्कार), 2) Puṃsavana-Saṃskāra (पुंसवन-संस्कार), 3) Sīmaṃtonnayana-Saṃskāra (सीमंतोन्नयन-संस्कार, 4) Jātakarma-Saṃskāra (जातकर्म-संस्कार), 5) Nāmakaraṇa- Saṃskāra (नामकरण-संस्कार), 6) Niṣkramaṇa-Saṃskāra (निष्क्रमण-संस्कार), 7) Annaprāśana-Saṃskāra (अन्नप्राशन-संस्कार), 8) Cūḍākaraṇa-Saṃskāra (चूडाकरण-संस्कार), 9) Karṇavedha-Saṃskāra (कर्णवेध-संस्कार), 10) Vidyārambha-Saṃskāra (विद्यारंभ-संस्कार), 11) Upanayana-Saṃskāra (उपनयन-संस्कार), 12) Vedārambha-Saṃskāra (वेदारंभ-संस्कार), 13 Keśāṃta-Saṃskāra (केशांत-संस्कार), 14) Samāvartana-Saṃskāra (समावर्तन-संस्कार), 15) Vivāha-Saṃskāra (विवाह-संस्कार) and 16) Antyeṣṭi-Saṃskāra (अन्त्येष्टि-संस्कार).

Hey Arjuna! One who does not follow the moving wheel in this world, who rejoices in sense-objects, living in sin, lives in vain.

The intent of verses (BG 3.14 - BG 3.16) - By the way above, through sacrifice (in the form of Karma), the wheel of the creation of humanity is continuing by the production of rain and food. With rain and food, there is the creation of four kinds of lives: 1) sweat-born, 2) germination-born, 3) egg-born, and 4) placenta-born. Through humans, there is the performance of Karma (sacrifice). Thus, through humanity, Karma, and through Karma, humanity, the entwining has been ongoing from the beginning of the world.

Karma is born of the Vedas, and the Vedas are born of the Brahman (the Reality, the Paramātmā). That is why the Vedas that illuminate all matters are always seated in sacrifice. Just as clay exists in a clod of clay and earthen pots, in the same way, the Paramātmā manifesting in the form of sacrifice creates the Saṃsāra, and so service towards sacrifice is indeed service of the Paramātmā.

A person who does not take part in moving the worldly cycle (Saṃsāra-Cakra) of sacrifice and humanity and who has made his aim of life to remain engrossed in the delight of sense-objects, the life of such an iniquitous person who covets prohibited desire-ridden acts does not remain any cause for fruits other than the cause for sin. He has neither assisted in moving the Saṃsāra-Cakra through good desire-ridden actions nor made efforts for his good through desireless actions. His life is only the cause for the growth of sins. All he is doing is sowing handfuls of seeds of grief, which is why for him, death is better.

In response to the question of Arjuna, up to here, the unavoidability of Karma, the necessity of Karma, the state of having no beginning of Karma (Anāditā), and the interwoven nature of humanity and Karma were articulated. Moreover, criticizing those iniquitous (Pāmara) individuals who rejoice in sense objects and praising those good desire-ridden individuals who, through sacrifice, are involved in the well-being of themselves and the Saṃsāra. However, due to desires, their fruit is only the Saṃsāra. Yet compared to the ones who rejoice in the sense objects (इन्द्रियारामी, Indriyārāmī), they are far better because they are forging ahead towards desirelessness. Only that person is on the path of cutting the bondage of the Saṃsāra who (per BG 3.9) is engaged in actions for the sake of the Lord (Bhagavadartha-Karma) with desireless sentiments and without attachment to fruits.

{Reaching that location where freedom from the bondage of Karma is achieved, and there is an end (पर्यवसान, Paryavasāna) of Karma is provided in the following two verses -}

यस्त्वात्मरतिरेव स्यादात्मतृप्तश्च मानवः |
आत्मन्येव च सन्तुष्टस्तस्य कार्यं न विद्यते || BG 3.17 ||

तु - However, ; यः - that ; मानवः - person (who) ; एव - solely ; आत्म-रतिः - rejoices in the Self, ; च - and (who) ; आत्म-तृप्तः - is content in the Self, ; च - and (who) ; स्यात् - is ; सन्तुष्टः - satisfied ; एव - solely ; आत्मनि - in the Self, ; तस्य - for him, ; विद्यते - there is ; न - no ; कार्यम् - duty.

However, that person who solely rejoices in the Self, who is content in the Self, and who is satisfied solely in the Self, for him, there is no duty.

नैव तस्य कृतेनार्थो नाकृतेनेह कश्चन |
न चास्य सर्वभूतेषु कश्चिदर्थव्यपाश्रयः || BG 3.18 ||

इह - Here (in this world), ; तस्य - for him, ; न - (there is) no ; अर्थः - purpose, ; एव - indeed (either) ; कृतेन - performing (an action that he wants to gain something, or) ; अकृतेन - not performing (any action) ; न कश्चन - (there is) not any (purpose, that he will incur sin), ; च - and ; अस्य - for this (person) ; कश्चित् न - there is no ; अर्थ-व्यपाश्रयः - selfish dependence ; सर्व-भूतेषु - on all living beings.

Here, for him, there is no purpose, either performing an action or not performing any action, and there is no selfish dependence on all living beings.

The intent of verses (BG 3.17 - BG 3.18) - That knower of the Ātmā is free from these two grasping and relinquishing-form of injunctions, "Performing Karma is a duty for me" or "Relinquishing Karma is a duty for me." Bondage of Karma and duty of Karma are there for the freedom from bondage and duty, not for the bondage to keep ongoing. For instance, the bondage of the banks in the flow of a river is there so that the river can become one with the ocean and become free from the bondage of the banks. Or a patient is kept in the bondage of medicine and dietary regimen so that once cured, he can be free from medicine and dietary regimen, not that he remain in their bondage for a lifetime. In essence, in the kingdom of Prakṛti, all bondages, after satisfying their goal, are there for freedom from them. According to this rule, a person who is content in his own Ātmā is naturally free from all bondages, not by any effort. That is similar to how infants naturally stop breastfeeding when they start eating solid food upon the development of teeth. By this, though, it is not the intent that he becomes without Karma, but he becomes without duty. Just as an infant's limbs move naturally and not by any duty, in the same way, for this Yogī, content in the Ātmā, all his efforts are natural and not for the fulfillment of any duty. Bondage of duty was there until the Ātmā confined by I-ness ego (Paricchinna Ahaṃkāra) had become a doer. However, from the analytic perspective, when the doer and I-ness sense disappear, where is duty? What is acquirable? Not seeing one's self separate from own Ātmā and the entire Saṃsāra and seeing them all as miracles of the Ātmā, that is "Ātma-Trupti," that is contentment in the Ātmā.

(Through Karma, only by becoming pure from impurity and vacillations can one achieve contentment in the Ātmā. Therefore, to ascend in that state, Bhagavāna is showing the necessity of Karma -)

तस्मादसक्तः सततं कार्यं कर्म समाचर |
असक्तो ह्याचरन्कर्म परमाप्नोति पूरुषः || BG 3.19 ||

तस्मात् - Therefore, (to ascend in that state, you) ; सततम् - always ; समाचर - properly perform ; कार्यम् - duty-bound ; कर्म - action ; असक्तः - without attachment. ; हि - For, ; पूरुषः - a person ; आप्नोति - (with the purity of the conscience) attains ; परम् - the supreme (Status) ; आचरन् - by performing ; कर्म - action ; असक्तः - without attachment.

Therefore, always perform duty-bound action properly without attachment. A person attains the supreme (Status) by performing action without attachment.

Intent - Through Karma, without attachment, upon the conscience becoming pure, one can ascend to Naiṣkarmya. Where there is no obligation of Karma and all Karma becomes Akarma.

(On this subject, Bhagavāna provides an example -)

कर्मणैव हि संसिद्धिमास्थिता जनकादयः |
लोकसंग्रहमेवापि सम्पश्यन्कर्तुमर्हसि || BG 3.20 ||

जनक-आदयः - Janaka and other kings ; हि - have certainly ; आस्थिताः - attained ; संसिद्धिम् - complete perfection ; कर्मणा - through action ; एव - alone. ; अपि - Moreover, ; सम्पश्यन् - looking towards ; लोक-सङ्ग्रहम् - the welfare of humanity, ; कर्तुम् - the performance of action ; एव - is only ; अर्हसि - proper for you.

Janaka and other kings have certainly attained complete perfection through action alone. Moreover, looking towards the welfare of humanity, the performance of action is only proper for you.

Intent -The major fruit of this unattached activity in Karma is acquiring complete perfection where action becomes non-action, and the example provided was of King Janaka. Another purpose of Karma activity is the welfare of humanity or public well-being (Lokasaṃgraha). Arjuna was told that even looking at the welfare of humanity; it is proper for you to engage in Karma.

(Now, in Lokasaṃgraha, the purpose of Karma is shown -)

यद्यदाचरति श्रेष्ठस्तत्तदेवेतरो जनः |
स यत्प्रमाणं कुरुते लोकस्तदनुवर्तते || BG 3.21 ||

यत् यत् - Whatever ; श्रेष्ठः - a great person ; आचरति - does, ; इतरः - other ; जनः - people ; एव - also (do) ; तत् तत् - that. ; यत् - Whatever ; प्रमाणम् - standard ; सः - that (great person through his behavior) ; कुरुते - sets, ; लोकः - humanity ; अनुवर्तते - follows ; तत् - that.

Whatever a great person does, other people also do. Whatever standard that great person sets, humanity follows.

Intent - Thorough one's good behavior to be an example and provide guidance to humanity is called Lokasaṃgraha. That is why, for great people, even if there is no obligation to engage in Karma, it still becomes an emulation measure for humanity to continue performing Karma, by which there can be the well-being of humanity.

(On this, Bhagavāna gives an example of Himself -)

न मे पार्थास्ति कर्तव्यं त्रिषु लोकेषु किञ्चन |
नानवाप्तमवाप्तव्यं वर्त एव च कर्मणि || BG 3.22 ||

पार्थ - Hey Pārtha (Arjuna)! ; न अस्ति - (Even though) there isn't ; किञ्चन - any ; कर्तव्यम् - duty ; मे - for Me ; त्रिषु - in all three ; लोकेषु - worlds ; च - and ; न - (there is) no ; अनवाप्तम् - unacquired (thing) ; अवाप्तव्यम् - (proper for Me) to acquire, ; वर्ते - (yet I am) engaged ; एव - solely ; कर्मणि - in action.

Hey Arjuna! Even though there is no duty for Me in all three worlds and no unacquired thing to acquire, I am engaged solely in action.

यदि ह्यहं न वर्तेयं जातु कर्मण्यतन्द्रितः |
मम वर्त्मानुवर्तन्ते मनुष्याः पार्थ सर्वशः || BG 3.23 ||

हि - Indeed, ; पार्थ - Hey Pārtha (Arjuna)! ; यदि - If ; अहम् - I ; न - do not ; जातु - ever ; वर्तेयम् - engage ; अतन्द्रितः - tirelessly ; कर्मणि - in action, ; मनुष्याः - humans ; अनुवर्तन्ते - (will) follow ; मम - My ; वर्त्म - path ; सर्वशः - in all possible ways.

Indeed, Hey Arjuna! If I do not ever engage tirelessly in action, humans will follow My path in all possible ways.

उत्सीदेयुरिमे लोका न कुर्यां कर्म चेदहम् |
संकरस्य च कर्ता स्यामुपहन्यामिमाः प्रजाः || BG 3.24 ||

चेत् - If ; अहम् - I ; कुर्याम् - do ; न - not ; कर्म - (engage in) action, ; इमे - these ; लोकाः - worlds ; उत्सीदेयुः - will perish, (and I) ; स्याम् - will become ; कर्ता - the doer ; संकरस्य - of deficient action ; च - and ; उपहन्याम् - the destroyer ; इमाः - of all ; प्रजाः - humanity.

If I do not engage in action, these worlds will perish, and I will become the doer of deficient action and the destroyer of all humanity.

Intent - Even if there is no obligation of Karma on a wise person, from the perspective of public well-being, it is appropriate for him to stay involved in Karma. A wise person has no duty to perform because he has reached his goal of life being a knower of the Ātmā. On this subject, Bhagavāna provides Himself as an example, and the way there is harm to the world by the abandonment of Karma by wise persons was described. In verse, the Saṃkara (संकर) part of Saṃkarasya (संकरस्य) is an adjective of Karma (कर्म), Karma-Saṃkaratā (कर्म-संकरता) meaning inferior or deficient action (कर्म-हीनता, Karma-Hīnatā). By not performing

Karma, I shall be the doer of deficient action. That is, I shall confuse the classes by My failure to perform by the scriptures, thereby causing harm to them.

(With the same intention, to engage others in Karma, Bhagavāna in the following two verses gives His advice -)

सक्ता: कर्मण्यविद्वांसो यथा कुर्वन्ति भारत |
कुर्याद्विद्वांस्तथासक्तश्चिकीर्षुर्लोकसंग्रहम् || BG 3.25 ||

भारत - Hey Bhārata (Arjuna)! ; यथा - Just as ; अविद्वांस: - an ignorant person ; कुर्वन्ति - performs ; कर्मणि - acts ; सक्ता: - with attachment, ; तथा - so (should) ; विद्वान् - a wise person ; चिकीर्षु: - desiring ; लोक-सङ्ग्रहम् - the welfare of humanity ; कुर्यात् – engage in activity ; असक्त: - without attachment.

Hey Arjuna! Just as an ignorant person acts with attachment, so should a wise person desiring the welfare of humanity engage in activity without attachment.

न बुद्धिभेदं जनयेदज्ञानां कर्मसङ्गिनाम् |
जोषयेत्सर्वकर्माणि विद्वान्युक्त: समाचरन् || BG 3.26 ||

विद्वान् - A wise person ; न जनयेत् - should not create ; बुद्धि-भेदम् - debility in the mind ; अज्ञानाम् - of an ignorant person ; कर्म-सङ्गिनाम् - who is attached to action. ; युक्त: - (However,) established (in the Self and) ; समाचरन् - properly performing ; सर्व-कर्माणि - all activities, ; जोषयेत् - (he) should have (the ignorant) perform (actions).

A wise person should not create debility in the mind of an ignorant person who is attached to action. However, established in the Self and properly performing all activities, he should have the ignorant perform actions.

Intent - The natural flow of a river is always towards the ocean, and upon merging with the ocean, it is retired on its own. The flow should always be left alone to move at its pace because it always moves towards its goal. If an obstacle is put right in the middle and the flow is obstructed, that flow moves away from its real goal. According to the same rule, in the kingdom of Prakṛti, the flow of all activities on their own is towards the ocean of renunciation. In the end, moving at its own pace, all activities will be retired in renunciation.

Activity in Karma, of those ignorant persons who have an attachment to them, moving at its own pace, upon ripening, is there only to be retired in that actionlessness (Naiṣkarmya) ocean, Self-contentment (Ātma-Trupti as per verse BG 3.17). All actions (Karma) become non-action (Akarma), and all duties become successful and become contented. However, if the flow of the activity of Karma is broken midway, then it will be sinful because by doing so, the flow is deprived of reaching its real goal. Therefore, for a wise person, even though there is no duty, still from a public welfare perspective, in the interest of an ignorant person who is only fit for actions, he should also assume such a role as an older person playing with a child becomes a child making a childlike face and feeding the child.

The main aim of Karma is contentment in the Ātmā (Ātma-Trupti) only. Naiṣkarmya, described in the verses (BG 3.17 - BG 3.18), can only be acquired by unattached Karma and never by abandoning action. However, a minor purpose of Karma is public well-being. The wise have fitness in public well-being activity, not as any duty, but just for playtime with public well-being-vision.

{Bhagavāna shows in the following two verses how there is Karma bondage with ignorance and how there is freedom from bondage through knowledge. At the beginning of this chapter, a doubt was expressed by Arjuna, and addressing that up to here, Bhagavāna comes to the significant point and describes Karma established in knowledge (Jñāna-Yukta), that is Yoga-Yukta Karma -}

प्रकृते: क्रियमाणानि गुणै: कर्माणि सर्वश: |
अहङ्कारविमूढात्मा कर्ताहमिति मन्यते || BG 3.27 ||

सर्वश: - In all ways, ; कर्माणि - actions ; क्रियमाणानि - are being done ; गुणै: - by the (three) constituents ; प्रकृते: - of Prakṛti (only. However,) ; अहङ्कार-विमूढात्मा - one whose mind is deluded by egoism ; मन्यते - thinks, ; अहम् कर्ता - "I am a doer" ; इति - as such.

In all ways, actions are being done by the constituents of Prakṛti only. However, one whose mind is deluded by egoism thinks, "I am a doer."

Intent - Sattva, Rajas, and Tamas are the three constituents of Prakṛti. Whatever activities happen through all living beings happen only through these three constituents. With Tamoguṇa, there is the activity of negligence (प्रमाद, Pramāda), delusion (मोह, Moha), laziness (आलस्य, Ālasya), and sleep (निद्रा, Nidrā). With Rajoguṇa, there is the activity of fickleness (चञ्चलता, Cañcalatā), passion (राग, Rāga), greed (लोभ, Lobha), and attachment (आसक्ति, Āsakti) in Karma. With Sattvaguṇa, there is the activity of purity (निर्मलता, Nirmalatā), happiness (सुख, Sukha), knowledge (ज्ञान, Jñāna), illumination (प्रकाश, Prakāśa), and tranquility (शान्ति, Śānti). Whatever activity (स्फुरण, Sphuraṇa) is created in the body, mind, and senses of a person; all those activities happen through the three constituents based on their attributes. Nothing separate from the constituents is the reason for the activity in the body, mind, and senses. At whatever time, whatever constituent is aroused, based on that, commensurate activity in the body, mind, and senses manifest. However, the Ātmā is never the doer of these constituents and actions, but dissociated from these constituents and actions is only their witnessing-observer. Despite that, one whose mind is enamored with ego, with the ego of "I am a doer," believes his Ātmā as the doer of all these activities. With this unreal doership sense, there is the bondage of enjoyership for this person. In reality, influenced by respective constituents, the body, mind, and senses are active in their respective activities; one has no connection with the other. Only due to the delusional ego, he has beaded the body, mind, and senses in his thread of ignorance like the beads of a garland and thus has become the doer of their duties and actions. Only this ignorance is the cause of this person's bondage.

(Next, Bhagavāna provides an approach to get rid of this ignorance -)

तत्त्ववित्तु महाबाहो गुणकर्मविभागयो: |
गुणा गुणेषु वर्तन्त इति मत्वा न सज्जते || BG 3.28 ||

महाबाहो - Hey Mahābāho (Arjuna)! ; तु - On the contrary, ; तत्त्ववित् - one who knows the Truth ; गुणकर्मविभागयो: - about the distinctions between the constituents of Prakṛti (Guṇa-Vibhāga) and their operations (Karma-Vibhāga), ; न सज्जते - is not attached (to action), ; मत्वा - knowing ; इति - that ; गुणा: - the constituents ; वर्तन्ते - operate ; गुणेषु - amidst the constituents.

Hey Arjuna! On the contrary, one who knows the Truth[89] about the distinction between the constituents of Prakṛti and their operations is not attached to action, knowing that the constituents operate amidst the constituents.

Intent - That knower of the Truth (Tattva-Vettā), who has directly known his Ātmā dissociated from the body, realizes -

"The body, senses, mind, and intellect are active in their respective objects. I am not a doer of their activities, but I am the undiminished light (अलुप्त प्रकाश, Alupta Prakāśa) in whom through the constituents all 'being' and 'non-being' activities of the body are ongoing, but there is no taint in me from any of them."

---

[89] The direct realization (Sākṣātkāra) of one's Ātmā as disassociated from the constituents of Prakṛti and their operations (गुणकर्मविभाग, Guṇakarmavibhāga) is called knowing the "Tattva, Truth."

Believing so in these constituents of Prakṛti and their operations, he is not attached (आसक्त, Āsakta) with I-ness doership-sentiment and is not tainted.

(However, to those ignorant who do not know this Truth -)

प्रकृतेर्गुणसम्मूढा: सज्जन्ते गुणकर्मसु |
तानकृत्स्नविदो मन्दान्कृत्स्नविन्न विचालयेत् || BG 3.29 ||

कृत्स्नवित् - The all-knowing (Sarvajña) ; न विचालयेत् - ought not to agitate ; तान् - those ; मन्दान् - dimwit ; अकृत्स्नविदः - partial knowers ; गुण-सम्मूढाः - deluded by the constituents ; प्रकृतेः - of Prakṛti ; सज्जन्ते - (who are) attached ; गुण-कर्मसु - to the products of the constituents.

The all-knowing ought not to agitate those dimwit partial knowers deluded by the constituents of Prakṛti who are attached to the products of the constituents.

Intent - Deluded by the constituents of Prakṛti, those who are attached to the work (products, effects) of the constituents (Guṇa-Karma), being in oneness with the body, know themselves as doers, such dim-witted with improper perspective (असम्यगदर्शी, Asamyagadarśī) ought not to be agitated by those all-knowing with the proper perspective. The all-knowing are the ones who have realized the pure Ātmā. The reason being, by Karma, with the removal of the impurity fault, they can be with proper perspective (सम्यगदर्शी, Samyagadarśī) and not by abandoning Karma.

(Now, Bhagavāna aiming towards Arjuna articulates action established in knowledge -)

मयि सर्वाणि कर्माणि संन्यस्याध्यात्मचेतसा |
निराशीर्निर्ममो भूत्वा युध्यस्व विगतज्वर: || BG 3.30 ||

संन्यस्य - Renouncing ; सर्वाणि - all ; कर्माणि - actions ; मयि - in Me (Paramātmā) ; अध्यात्मचेतसा - (with) the mind in transcendent knowledge (that "I am neither a doer nor an enjoyer,") ; भूत्वा - having become ; निराशीः - free from expectations, ; निर्ममः - without mineness, ; विगतज्वरः - (and) without affliction, ; युध्यस्व - fight.

Renouncing all actions in Me with the mind in transcendent knowledge, having become free from expectations, mineness, and affliction, fight.

Intent - Just as in support of space, there is the creation and destruction of substances, attributes, and acts (द्रव्य-गुण-कर्म, Dravya-Guṇa-Karma), but no mutation touches the space, in the same way, the entire operation of the constituents and actions cannot touch the Ātmā, even though they are happening in support of the Ātmā. Directly realizing one's Ātmā and attaining union with oneness is, in reality, total renunciation of all actions (Sarva-Karma-Saṃnyāsa). Only by this transcendent knowledge (Aparokṣa-Jñāna), the knowledge of the Ātmā attained through the process of reason and discrimination between the real and the unreal; there is the success of Sarva-Karma-Saṃnyāsa. Separate from this, "Renounce all actions, and fight," how can these two opposite activities stay together equally in one support and in one time-series position (कालावच्छिन्न, Kālāvacchinna) like day and night? Therefore, "Arjuna with your mind in transcendent knowledge, 'I am not a body, this body is not mine, I am not a doer, I am not an enjoyer, but I am the light in whose illumination there is the fruition of the existence of the body and doership-enjoyership,' offering Sarva-Karma-Saṃnyāsa in Me the witness-conscious Ātmā of all (Sarvātmā), becoming dissociated from the body and free from the desire for fruits and mineness of kingdom and relatives, without affliction, fight."

There is a doubt here that "I am offering not only my fruit but all of my actions to the Lord." With such a sentiment, there should be a success of Sarva-Karma-Saṃnyāsa.

Resolution - First, the relinquishment is sentimental and not real. Because sentiments are matters of the kingdom of Māyā and are the work of ignorance, it is like washing dirt with dirt. Second, even if he has a sentiment of Sarva-Karma-Saṃnyāsa, he has not relinquished this sentiment, and both sentiment and doer of the sentiment are present. Thus, when both sentiment and doer of the sentiment are present, the success of Sarva-Karma-Saṃnyāsa is not possible because the cause of fruit is only sentiment. However, the sentiment is pure, and therefore, it is helpful in the fruition of true Sarva-Karma-Saṃnyāsa, but by its nature, it cannot make Sarva-Karma-Saṃnyāsa successful.

ये मे मतमिदं नित्यमनुतिष्ठन्ति मानवा: |
श्रद्धावन्तोऽनसूयन्तो मुच्यन्ते तेऽपि कर्मभि: || BG 3.31 ||

ये - Those ; मानवा: - humans (who) ; नित्यम् - invariably ; अनुतिष्ठन्ति - abide ; इदम् - by this ; मतम् - doctrine ; मे - of Mine (that Ātmā is not a doer-enjoyer, but the entire doer and enjoyership is in the constituents of Prakṛti), ; श्रद्धावन्त: - with faith ; अनसूयन्त: - (and) free from seeing faults, ; ते - they ; अपि - (are) also ; मुच्यन्ते - liberated ; कर्मभि: - from actions (in due time with direct realization of this knowledge).

Those humans who invariably abide by this doctrine of Mine, with faith and free from seeing faults, are also liberated from actions.

Intent - For those persons who have not yet accomplished Sarva-Karma-Saṃnyāsa through the realization of the Truth, but those who have faith in My opinion, "In reality in our dissociated Ātmā, there is no taint from actions of any kind" and free from seeing faults are always undertaking and practicing, they will also be liberated from the bondage of Karma by the influence of faith and practice through transcendent knowledge attaining union with oneness in the Ātmā.

ये त्वेतदभ्यसूयन्तो नानुतिष्ठन्ति मे मतम् |
सर्वज्ञानविमूढांस्तान्विद्धि नष्टानचेतस: || BG 3.32 ||

तु - However, ; ये - those ; अचेतस: - devoid of discrimination ; सर्व-ज्ञान-विमूढान् - (and) deluded of all knowledge ; अभ्यसूयन्त: - seeing fault ; एतत् - in this ; मतम् - doctrine ; मे - of Mine ; न - (do) not ; अनुतिष्ठन्ति - follow (it), ; विद्धि - know ; तान् - them ; नष्टान् - ruined.

However, those devoid of discrimination and deluded of all knowledge seeing fault in this doctrine of Mine do not follow it, know them ruined.

Intent - In contrast, those who do not have faith in My words, who do not follow it but instead have a faulty perspective, "How can it be possible that Ātmā is not a doer and there is no taint of action on it? How can we believe that?" Know that there is only ruination for them.

(This way, describing the state of no beginning and unavoidability of Karma, in the end, Bhagavāna described Yoga-Yukta Karma by which the bondage of Karma is cut at the root and Sarva-Karma-Saṃnyāsa is attained.

In the epilogue of this chapter, in response to the doubt expressed by Arjuna, "If knowledge is superior to Karma, then why are you enjoining me in this fearful war?" Bhagavāna makes it clear that contrary to what you have understood, My intention is not in relinquishment of Karma in its true nature, but -)

सदृशं चेष्टते स्वस्या: प्रकृतेर्ज्ञानवानपि |
प्रकृतिं यान्ति भूतानि निग्रह: किं करिष्यति || BG 3.33 ||

अपि - Even ; ज्ञानवान् - wise persons ; चेष्टते - act ; सदृशम् - in accordance ; स्वस्या: - with their ; प्रकृते: - nature. ; भूतानि - All living beings ; यान्ति - conform (to their own) ; प्रकृतिम् - nature. (Then,) ; किम् - what (can anyone's) ; निग्रह: - repression ; करिष्यति - do?

Even wise persons act in accordance with their nature. All living beings conform to their own nature. Then, what can anyone's repression do?

Intent - The impressions (Saṃskāras) of previously done pious and sinful deeds manifesting in the current life are referred to as Prakṛti or nature. Based on individual nature, it is natural for all activities that are substances of the kingdom of Prakṛti to manifest in the body and senses. Even a wise person in the bondage of nature acts according to his nature, and all living beings behave based on their nature, then what can anyone's repression do? Restraint against one's nature is nothing but a delusional effort. The real effort is that through analytic thinking, one ought to make own Ātmā dissociated from the body and senses so that the bondage of action is removed.

(When Prakṛti is so powerful and unavoidable, the human effort will be fruitless, and even Śāstra will be meaningless. Upon the possibility of such a doubt, Bhagavāna articulates what ought to be the effort of a person -)

इन्द्रियस्येन्द्रियस्यार्थे रागद्वेषौ व्यवस्थितौ |
तयोर्न वशमागच्छेत्तौ ह्यस्य परिपन्थिनौ || BG 3.34 ||

राग-द्वेषौ - Attachment and aversion ; इन्द्रियस्य - of the senses ; व्यवस्थितौ - are situated ; इन्द्रियस्य - in the sense ; अर्थे - objects. ; न - Do not ; आगच्छेत् - be ; वशम् - swayed ; तयोः - by them, ; हि - for ; तौ - they are ; अस्य - his ; परिपन्थिनौ - swindlers (in his beneficial path).

Attachment and aversion of the senses are situated in the sense objects. Do not be swayed by them, for they are swindlers.

Intent - Just as a swindler staying together with a person with pretense steals wealth, in the same way, attachment and aversion sit in the heart of a Jīva, making trueness sense firmer in untrue things and deluding him steals his wealth of discrimination. Therefore, with the power of discernment and thought, one should not be swayed by attachment and aversion. Even though every sense organ naturally has an attachment to favorable objects and aversion to unfavorable objects, staying with them, one ought not to become like the sense-organs, but by analytic thinking make oneself separate from them. To achieve one's good, one ought to at least conduct based on one's nature because only by behavior according to one's nature can one suppress attachment and aversion.

श्रेयान्स्वधर्मो विगुण: परधर्मात्स्वनुष्ठितात् |
स्वधर्मे निधनं श्रेय: परधर्मो भयावह: || BG 3.35 ||

विगुणः - (Even) devoid of merits, ; स्वधर्मः - one's duty ; श्रेयान् - is superior ; स्वनुष्ठितात् - to a perfectly observed ; परधर्मात् - duty of others. ; निधनम् - Death ; श्रेयः - is better ; स्वधर्मे - in one's duty; ; परधर्मः - the duty of others ; भय-आवहः - is fraught with danger.

Even devoid of merits, one's duty is superior to a perfectly observed duty of others. Death is better in one's duty; the duty of others is fraught with danger.

Intent - The conduct of one's duty is favorable to Prakṛti. Here the meaning of Prakṛti is the law of the Lord. Natural efforts corresponding to one's nature are there to uplift a Jīva, even though they may be devoid of merits or have faults. However, efforts in opposition to Prakṛti, even though they may be excellent, are indeed opposer to the good of a Jīva. Just as feeding non-oily food is consistent with the nature of a patient suffering from fever even if he is weak, still by gaining strength at some point in time, he can also digest Ghī. However, if he were fed Ghī when he had a fever, instead of it being nourishing, it would become the cause of his weakness. Accordingly, it is better to die being active in one's law of life. Because by dying this way, one's conduct of own duty in future births can uplift one further, just as a child falling asleep reading his first lesson upon waking the next day starts reading only the second lesson. The essence is that by walking in step with the flow of one's nature, one can control own nature; like walking with the flow of a river and providing a path to flow, a dam can be built and thereby control it. Those actions performed under the Śāstra prescribed functional class duties in which there is, to some extent relationship of mental, verbal, bodily, and material relinquishment, and which are naturally grasped by the mind; only those actions are called "conducted following one's duty." Only with the conduct of one's duty attachment and aversion can be suppressed. That is because, based on one's fitness, in this conduct of one's duty (स्वधर्म-आचरण, Svadharma-Ācaraṇa) relinquishment (Tyāga) is placed, and only relinquishment is the key to suppress attachment and aversion.

(On this, Arjuna with this doubt, "Everyone desires happiness, no one desires sorrow. Therefore, all are desirer of good, yet why is a human drawn towards sinning, and thus sorrow?" questions -)

अर्जुन उवाच |
अथ केन प्रयुक्तोऽयं पापं चरति पूरुषः |
अनिच्छन्नपि वार्ष्णेय बलादिव नियोजितः || BG 3.36 ||
अर्जुनः उवाच - Arjuna said -

वार्ष्णेय - Hey Vārṣṇeya (Śrī Kṛṣṇa, the descendent of Vṛṣṇi)! ; अथ - Then, ; अपि - even ; अनिच्छन् - not wishing, ; केन - by what ; अयं - is this ; पूरुषः - person ; प्रयुक्तः - impelled ; चरति - to commit ; पापम् - sin, ; इव - as if ; नियोजितः - enjoined ; बलात् - forcibly (to do so)?

Arjuna said -

Hey Śrī Kṛṣṇa! Then, even not wishing, by what is this person impelled to commit sin, as if enjoined forcibly?

श्रीभगवानुवाच |
काम एष क्रोध एष रजोगुणसमुद्भवः ||
महाशनो महापाप्मा विद्ध्येनमिह वैरिणम् || BG 3.37 ||
श्रीभगवान् उवाच - Śrī Bhagavān said -

रजः गुण-समुद्भवः - Born of the constituent Rajas (of Prakṛti), ; एषः - (it is) this ; कामः - desire ; एषः - (and which converts into) this ; क्रोधः - anger. ; विद्धि - Know ; एनम् - this ; महा-अशनः - voraciously eating (that is, one which is insatiable with enjoyments) ; महा-पाप्मा - greatly sinful ; (कामः) - (desire) ; वैरिणम् - as the foe (of the Jīva) ; इह - in this world.

Śrī Bhagavān said -

Born of the constituent Rajas, it is this desire and this anger. Know this voraciously eating greatly sinful desire as the foe in this world.

Intent - Seeing obstacles in achieving a goal, this desire (Kāma) turns into anger (Krodha), which is why anger is only a second state of desire. Even though all seek happiness, with the flow of Rajoguṇa, this desire blinds them from where their real good (वास्तविक-कल्याण, Vāstavika-Kalyāṇa) is.

(How does this desire enshroud a Jīva? -)

धूमेनाव्रियते वह्निर्यथादर्शो मलेन च |
यथोल्बेनावृतो गर्भस्तथा तेनेदमावृतम् || BG 3.38 ||

यथा - Just as ; वह्निः - fire ; आव्रियते - is obscured ; धूमेन - by smoke, ; आदर्शः - a mirror (is covered) ; मलेन - by dust, ; च - and ; यथा - just as ; गर्भः - an embryo ; आवृतः - (is) covered ; उल्बेन - by the amnion, ; तथा - so (is) ; इदम् - this (knowledge) ; आवृतम् - shrouded ; तेन - by that (desire).

Just as fire is obscured by smoke, a mirror by dust, and an embryo by the amnion, knowledge is shrouded by desire.

Intent - The shrouds of desire consists of three kinds: 1) a subtle covering like smoke obscuring fire, 2) a medium covering like dust covering a mirror, and 3) a dense covering like the amnion covering an embryo, hardly visible.

आवृतं ज्ञानमेतेन ज्ञानिनो नित्यवैरिणा |
कामरूपेण कौन्तेय दुष्पूरेणानलेन च || BG 3.39 ||

कौन्तेय - Hey Kaunteya (Arjuna)! ; ज्ञानम् - Knowledge ; आवृतम् - is covered ; एतेन - by it (who is) ; नित्यवैरिणा - a perpetual enemy ; ज्ञानिनः - of the wise, ; कामरूपेण - (whose) form is desire ; च - and ; दुष्पूरेण अनलेन - like fire insatiable.

Hey Arjuna! Knowledge is covered by it who is a perpetual enemy of the wise, whose form is desire and like fire insatiable.

(That is why Jīva cannot see it's good. To catch the enemy, one ought to find out where he lives and so Bhagavāna provides his address as to where he dwells -)

इन्द्रियाणि मनो बुद्धिरस्याधिष्ठानमुच्यते |
एतैर्विमोहयत्येष ज्ञानमावृत्य देहिनम् || BG 3.40 ||

इन्द्रियाणि - The senses, ; मनः - mind, (and) ; बुद्धिः - intellect ; उच्यते - have been called ; अस्य - its ; अधिष्ठानम् - residence. ; एतैः - Through them, ; आवृत्य - shrouding ; ज्ञानम् - knowledge, ; एषः - it ; विमोहयति - deludes ; देहिनम् - the embodied Self.

The senses, mind, and intellect have been called its residence. Through them, shrouding knowledge, it deludes the embodied Self.

Intent - Desire does not let a Jīva see what is good for him.

(What is the benefit of catching desire? -)

तस्मात्त्वमिन्द्रियाण्यादौ नियम्य भरतर्षभ |
पाप्मानं प्रजहि ह्येनं ज्ञानविज्ञाननाशनम् || BG 3.41 ||

तस्मात् - Therefore, ; भरतर्षभ - Hey Bharatarṣabha (Arjuna, the excellent one amongst the descendants of Bharata)! ; त्वम् -You ; हि - (can) certainly ; प्रजहि - slay ; एनं - this ; ज्ञान-विज्ञान-नाशनम् - knowledge and realization destroyer ; पाप्मानम् – sinful (desire) ; नियम्य - by controlling ; इन्द्रियाणि - the senses ; आदौ - first.

Therefore, Hey Arjuna! You can certainly slay this knowledge and realization destroyer sinful desire by controlling the senses first.

Intent - In the verse, the term Prajahi (प्रजहि, slay), this sinful "desire" means to fully give up this wicked craving that destroys knowledge and realization. Through preceptors and scriptures, the discernment (Viveka) of Ātmā-Anātmā is called knowledge (Jñāna), and to experience it uniquely is called realization (Vijñāna). Know that the senses, mind, and intellect are the three entrances of the fort of the enemy in the form of desire. This and the next world can be won by claiming authority over them.

(This way -)

इन्द्रियाणि पराण्याहुरिन्द्रियेभ्य: परं मन: |
मनसस्तु परा बुद्धिर्यो बुद्धेः परतस्तु स: || BG 3.42 ||

आहुः - They say ; पराणि - beyond are ; इन्द्रियाणि - the senses (superior and subtle), ; मनः - the mind ; परम् - is beyond ; इन्द्रियेभ्यः - the senses, ; तु - and ; बुद्धिः - the intellect ; परा - is beyond ; मनसः - the mind. ; तु - However, ; यः - that ; परतः - which is extremely beyond ; बुद्धेः - the intellect ; सः - is That (Self).

They say beyond are the senses, the mind is beyond the senses, and the intellect is beyond the mind. However, that which is extremely beyond the intellect is That (Self).

Intent - Senses are beyond the visible world and the body. They are superior to both and are within and subtle. By controlling the senses, the entire Saṃsāra can be controlled, just as by acquiring control over musical instruments, control over "tunes" coming out of those instruments can be achieved. When senses become enemies of a Jīva, then the entire Saṃsāra becomes his enemy, just as when senses become like uncontrolled horses and arbitrarily roam around into the objects of enjoyment, then the entire weaponized Saṃsāra becomes his enemy. Mind is beyond the senses, and control over the mind can be acquired by having control over the senses, just as a horse-rider can be held by holding the horse. Intellect is beyond the mind. By holding the mind-form horse, the intellect-form rider can also be held. And, that which is beyond the intellect is the Ātmā. By having control over the senses, mind, and intellect, the enemy in the form of desire can be caught and then, with the realization of the Ātmā (Ātma-Sākṣātkāra), it can be incinerated. Accordingly, by acquiring control over the senses, mind, and intellect, arrest of the enemy in the form of desire and with the knowledge of the Ātmā, cutting it off from the root, is described, and now this subject is described with clarity.

एवं बुद्धेः परं बुद्ध्वा संस्तभ्यात्मानमात्मना |
जहि शत्रुं महाबाहो कामरूपं दुरासदम् || BG 3.43 ||

महाबाहो - Hey Mahābāho (Arjuna)! ; एवम् - Thus, ; संस्तभ्य - controlling ; आत्मानम् - the intellect ; आत्मना - through the mind and senses, (and) ; बुद्धेः - through the intellect ; बुद्ध्वा - knowing ; परम् - the one beyond (- the Self), ; जहि - forsake ; दुरासदम् - the painfully controllable ; शत्रुम् - enemy ; काम-रूपम् - in the form of desire.

Hey Arjuna! Thus, controlling the intellect through the mind and senses, and through the intellect knowing the one beyond - the Self, forsake the painfully controllable enemy in the form of desire.

Intent - By having control over the mind, senses, and intellect, the enemy in the form of desire can be subdued but not slew. Only through the realization of the Ātmā, establishing with oneness in the Ātmā, that enemy can be incinerated. When this Lord Śiva opens his third eye of knowledge, this enemy in the form of desire is instantaneously incinerated. With some thought, it is clear that only discriminating vision is found as causal at the root of all desires. When the desired object is seen as something separate from oneself, then due to attachment, there is a desire to acquire it, and with aversion, naturally, there is a desire for abandonment. Desire is an attribute of the mind and intellect. By suppressing the mind and intellect, the attribute is also suppressed. As long as discriminating intellect is present and the desired thing appears separate from oneself, desire with its roots cannot be destroyed. However, through knowledge, when the ignorance of discriminating vision is burnt and separate from own Ātmā, nothing is left. Then, with the absence of the desired thing, desire in its true nature also disappears. With the substrate knowledge, there is the complete removal of the delusional thing, just as knowledge of the rope immediately removes the delusion of a snake. Accordingly, the Ātmā is the substrate of all desired things and desire, and by its transcendental realization, the absence of the desire-form enemy is possible.

ॐ तत्सदिति श्रीमद्भगवद्गीतासूपनिषत्सु ब्रह्मविद्यायां योगशास्त्रे

श्रीकृष्णार्जुनसम्वादे कर्मयोगो नाम

तृतीयोऽध्यायः || BG 3 ||

Oṃ Tat Sat

In the Śrīmad Bhagavad Gītā Upaniṣad

The Yoga Science of the Knowledge of Self-Realization

The Discourse of Lord Śrī Kṛṣṇa and Arjuna

This Third Chapter

Yoga Named - The Karma Yoga

Clarification

At the end of the second chapter, Bhagavāna described the characteristics of a sage of stable wisdom (Sthitaprajña), saying the "Saṃsāra-Cakra in which all living beings are awake, a Sthitaprajña is asleep; and that Supreme Reality (परमार्थ-तत्व, Paramārtha-Tattva) in which all living entities are asleep (Aceta) he is awake, that is, he is enjoying its bliss" (BG 2.69). At that time, Arjuna understood that Bhagavāna was praising empty knowledge of Karma relinquishment. At the beginning of the third chapter, questioned Bhagavāna, "If you consider knowledge superior to action, why are you enjoining me in this fearful war?" (BG 3.1 - BG 3.2).

The intention of Bhagavāna from the characteristics above of a Sthitaprajña was to indicate the glory of this Yoga, which is so great that by its influence, this vast world of the five great elements (Pañcabhūta) even standing right in front becomes void and that Yogī sits so steadfast in his Ātmā that no power in the Saṃsāra can agitate him from that position. His relationship of the doer, ego, and mineness with the body, senses, mind, and intellect is so far removed that even while performing Karma through his body, he does not see himself as a doer (Kartā) or does not see anything happening in his own Ātmā. Nevertheless, natural activities happen through his body just as a wound clock continues to tic-tac until its fixed time. Thus, even while doing everything, he is not doing anything.

However, upon this question of Arjuna, Bhagavāna surmised that Arjuna had not absorbed His intent. Then setting foot on the ground, Bhagavāna gave him Upadeśa, "Hey Arjuna! As you have understood, I have never intended to suggest the relinquishment of Karma in its true nature. In this Saṃsāra, two kinds of disciplines have been spoken by Me in the past, one Sāṅkhya-discipline and the other Yoga-discipline. There is no intention of Bhagavāna to show distinction, but by the superimposition of distinctions (Bheda-Adhyāropa), his real intent is to show oneness connection (Abheda-Samanvaya). To acquire status in either discipline, relinquishment of actions (Karma-Tyāga) will not do, and in the kingdom of Prakṛti, relinquishment of actions in their true nature is impossible. The only movement of hand-feet is not action (Karma), but emotional waves originating in the mind are also Karma. When that is the case, holding-back hands, feet, and other action-organs, one who mentally ponders over sense objects is not a relinquisher of action (Karma-Tyāgi) but is a hypocrite. Showing the unavoidability of Karma, Bhagavāna glorified conduct of desireless actions (Niṣkāma-Karma) compared to delusional relinquishment of action (Mithyā Karma-Tyāga), by which freed from untruthfulness (मिथ्याचारित्व, Mithyācāritva), the flow of Rajoguṇa is removed. With the flow of Rajoguṇa removed, purity of the conscience is achieved, and with the grace of the Lord, fitness for knowledge is acquired. That is the fruit of Karma (BG 3.3 - BG 3.6).

Stating the unavoidability of Karma, Bhagavāna formulated the state of having no beginning and showed that Brahmā concomitantly created both humanity and sacrifice in the form of Karma. Therefore, as long as the Saṃsāra is present, how can one be free from Karma? Albeit, it becomes the duty of every human through the sacrifice of Karma to satisfy the deity who is the power controlling the Saṃsāra. Being satisfied, the deity will not only do good to the Saṃsāra but will do him good. Then, that wheel of sacrifice is described by the production of rain and food, and with food, the creation of humanity. Through Karma, humanity, through humanity, Karma - the beginningless wheel that is ongoing is described. Bhagavāna criticized those Niṣiddha-Sakāmī who are engrossed in the delight of sense objects coveting forbidden desire-ridden acts, who neither through desireless-Karma have acquired the grace of the Lord to become fit for knowledge nor through good desire-ridden Karma have assisted in moving the Saṃsāra-Cakra (BG 3.10 - BG 3.16).

Bhagavāna showed that in the kingdom of Prakṛti, there is no way to be free from Karma. Nevertheless, those brave hearts who broke the bars of the cage of Prakṛti and staking the flag of their blissful form became content in the Paramānanda; for them, there is no duty. By doing something or not doing anything, there is nothing to gain or relinquish. Activity in Karma is only to gain or relinquish something. To acquire that real independence, where all duties are like how jackals show their backs when in front of lions, always engage in Karma with the unattached sentiment because with unattached Karma, humans can attain the Paramātmā. This way, the end of Karma is shown only in self-contentment and through unattached Karma steps in achieving are shown, providing an example of King Janaka (BG 3.17 - BG 3.19).

After that, for a knower of the Truth, in the absence of obligation and attainableness, how to remain active in activity related to the welfare of humanity is depicted. How there is harm to the Saṃsāra by their not engaging in action and how there is a benefit to the Saṃsāra by their engaging in action, that cause and effect are described, and in that regard, Bhagavāna gave himself as an example (BG 3.20 - BG 3.26).

In reality, Karma cannot be avoided anyway. Such power of Karma and how a person with attachment to the body comes in the bondage of Karma, and how a knower of the Truth who is dissociated remains untainted by Karma is clarified, and Arjuna is advised, "With your mind in transcendent knowledge, completely renouncing your entire Karma, without any affliction, fight. A person who has faith in these words of Mine and puts them in practice; they are freed from the bondage of Karma. However, for those who do not have faith in this opinion of Mine, 'our Ātmā is non-doer (Akartā) and non-enjoyer (अभोक्ता, Abhoktā)' but instead sees a fault in it, their ruination is definite" (BG 3.27 - BG 3.32). After that, in the epilogue of the chapter, Bhagavāna told Arjuna, "As you understood, My intent was never in the relinquishment of Karma, but My intention is only in this Yoga-Yukta Karma, by which there is the success of the real and pure Sarva-Karma-Saṃnyāsa because whether it is a wise person or an ignorant, neither of them can do without Karma." Attachment and aversion that the senses have in their objects have been called swindlers in the path of the highest good, and suppressing them through the conduct of the law of one's nature is commanded (BG 3.33 - BG 3.35).

After that, upon Arjuna's question, "Even not wishing, by what is this person impelled to sin, as if enjoined forcibly?" Bhagavāna shows that produced by Rajoguṇa, this desire is the enemy of Jīva. Like the fire that is never satisfied with offerings, this desire shrouds knowledge by which Jīva fails to see his good. Its dwellings were shown as the senses, mind, and intellect and explained that this desire-form enemy could be defeated by restraining them, though it cannot be slain. However, the one that is beyond the intellect, the Ātmā; by its direct realization, it can be incinerated with its roots (BG 3.36 - BG 3.39).

To the deluded Arjuna with debility in Karma, in this chapter, Bhagavāna explained the depth of Karma. The power of Karma, the unavoidability of Karma, the state of no beginning of Karma, the close relationship of Saṃsāra and Karma, the necessity of Karma in the cause of human welfare (Lokasaṃgraha), and the injunction of Lokasaṃgraha are described. It is clarified that in reality, only through the constituents of Prakṛti, all this activity of Karma is ongoing. In the true witness-conscious Ātmā, there is no taint from any of them. Due to ego, those whose minds are deluded superimpose doership-ego in their Ātmā and freely put themselves in the bondage of enjoyership. However, through Self-Realization, understanding this subject as it is, "In my real true nature, there is never any taint of Karma. I am only the observer-witness of Prakṛti and born of Prakṛti constituents and actions. All constituents and actions of Prakṛti are only miracles and wave-forms of my Ātmā, just as an ocean does not get wet by its waves. Likewise, there is nothing separate from me like doership and action, and there is no association of them in me" - this is indeed Karma-Saṃnyāsa in the Lord. To abandon Karma in its true nature is not Karma-Saṃnyāsa. That is where there is a true mutual connection (Yathārtha Samanvaya) between Sāṅkhya and Yoga. Engaging in this true and solid Karma-Saṃnyāsa Bhagavāna gives Upadeśa to Arjuna to fight. (BG 3.30).

Thus, to the deluded Arjuna, describing the true nature of relinquishment of action (Karma-Tyāga), Bhagavāna ended the chapter. Now, at the beginning of the fourth chapter, Bhagavāna discusses the Yoga of situating with oneness in the Ātmā that was already formulated at the end of the second chapter. The beginningless succession (Anādi-Paramparā) and imperishability (Avyayatā) of that Yoga are described this way -

CHAPTER 4

THE JÑĀNA KARMA SAṂNYĀSA YOGA

श्रीभगवानुवाच |
इमं विवस्वते योगं प्रोक्तवानहमव्ययम् |
विवस्वान्मनवे प्राह मनुरिक्ष्वाकवेऽब्रवीत् || BG 4.1 ||
श्रीभगवान् उवाच - Śrī Bhagavān said -

अहम् - I ; प्रोक्तवान् - imparted ; इमम् - this ; अव्ययम् - immutable ; योगम् - Yoga ; विवस्वते - to Vivasvān (the sun-deity, at the beginning of the creation). ; विवस्वान् - Vivasvān ; प्राह - told ; मनवे - it to (his son) Manu, (and) ; मनुः - Manu ; अब्रवीत् - told ; इक्ष्वाकवे - it to Ikṣvāku.

Śrī Bhagavān said -

I imparted this immutable Yoga to Vivasvān. Vivasvān told it to Manu, and Manu told it to Ikṣvāku.

Intent - Here in "इमं अव्ययम् योगम्" (this immutable Yoga), the term "इमं, this" indicates the Yoga spoken earlier. That is, the Yoga that was articulated in the second chapter and also enunciated at the end of the third chapter in the form of total renunciation of all actions (Sarva-Karma-Saṃnyāsa) in own Ātmā." The term "अव्ययम्, immutable" signifies ancient succession. The term "योग, Yoga" does not refer to the relinquishment of fruits of action (Karma-Phala-Tyāga) by a desireless seeker of knowledge who holds doership and duty-bound intellect because it is not immutable. For such a seeker, his fruit being only the purity of his conscience is indeed mutable because anything that has a fruit cannot be immutable. However, through the realization of the Truth, with the mutual connection between Sāṅkhya and Yoga, that is, with oneness in the relinquishment of action (Karma-Tyāga) and the relinquishment of fruits (Phala-Tyāga) where there is a oneness of Jīva in own Ātmā, that is this immutable Yoga. From the highest objective, Jīva does not have any distinction from the Brahman. Only with the discriminative-adjunct of ignorance is there a distinction-imagination of the discriminative-adjunct (Sopādhika-Bheda). Through knowledge, upon the adjunct opposed, there is the attainment of the ever-continuous immovable Yoga. The intention in "I told it to Vivasvān (sun-deity)" is to indicate, "I was the one to manifest the Yoga, not the writer of the Yoga," which is why this Yoga is without beginning (अनादि, Anādi). Thus, this Yoga is depicted as unborn (अज, Aja) and immutable (अव्यय, Avyaya).

एवं परम्पराप्राप्तमिमं राजर्षयो विदुः |
स कालेनेह महता योगो नष्टः परन्तप || BG 4.2 ||

परन्तप - Hey Parantapa (Arjuna)! ; राजर्षयः - Royal sages ; विदुः - have known ; इमम् - this (Yoga) ; एवम् – thus ; परम्पराप्राप्तम् - acquired through regular succession (from one to the other). ; महता - (Due to) a long lapse ; कालेन - of time ; सः - that ; योगः - Yoga ; नष्टः - has disappeared ; इह - from this world (the traditional succession is broken).

Hey Arjuna! Royal sages have known this Yoga acquired through regular succession. Due to a long lapse of time that Yoga has disappeared from this world.

Intent - Here, the term Naṣṭa (नष्ट) is not interpreted as "to perish" but means becoming covered or hidden.

स एवायं मया तेऽद्य योगः प्रोक्तः पुरातनः |
भक्तोऽसि मे सखा चेति रहस्यं ह्येतदुत्तमम् || BG 4.3 ||

सः - That ; अयम् एव - same ; पुरातनः - ancient ; योगः - Yoga ; प्रोक्तः - is being imparted ; ते - to you ; अद्य - today ; मया - by Me ; हि - because ; असि - (you) are ; मे - My ; भक्तः - devotee ; च - and ; सखा - friend, (and here) ; एतत् - this (Yoga) ; उत्तमम् - has supreme ; रहस्यम् - profundity ; इति - as such.

That same ancient Yoga is being imparted to you today by Me because you are My devotee and friend, and this Yoga has supreme profundity.

(On this with a doubt -)

अर्जुन उवाच |
अपरं भवतो जन्म परं जन्म विवस्वतः |
कथमेतद्विजानीयां त्वमादौ प्रोक्तवानिति || BG 4.4 ||
अर्जुनः उवाच - Arjuna said -

भवतः - Your ; जन्म - birth ; अपरम् - is later; ; जन्म - (and) the birth ; विवस्वतः - of Vivasvān (the sun-deity) ; परम् - was prior (in the beginning of creation). ; कथम् - (Therefore,) how ; विजानीयाम् - do I know ; इति - that ; त्वम् - You ; प्रोक्तवान् - imparted ; एतत् - this Yoga ; आदौ - (to the sun-deity) in the beginning (of the creation)?

Arjuna said -

Your birth is later; the birth of Vivasvān was prior. How do I know that You imparted this Yoga in the beginning?

श्रीभगवानुवाच |
बहूनि मे व्यतीतानि जन्मानि तव चार्जुन |
तान्यहं वेद सर्वाणि न त्वं वेत्थ परन्तप || BG 4.5 ||
श्रीभगवान् उवाच - Śrī Bhagavān said -

अर्जुन - Hey Arjuna! ; बहूनि - Many ; जन्मानि - births ; तव - of yours ; च - and ; मे - Mine ; व्यतीतानि - have gone. ; परन्तप - Hey Parantapa (Arjuna)! ; अहम् - I ; वेद - know ; तानि - them ; सर्वाणि - all, ; त्वम् - (but) you ; न - do not ; वेत्थ - know (yours).

Śrī Bhagavān said -

Hey Arjuna! Many births of yours and Mine have gone. Hey Parantapa! I know them all, but you do not know yours.

Intent - Arjuna! Your thinking power is shrouded by the impressions (Saṃskāras) of piety and sin, so you do not know your past lives. However, I have an eternal, pure, conscious, free nature (Nitya-Śuddha-Buddha-Mukta-Svabhāva), so I know all of those lives, as My thinking power is not shrouded.

{When You are the all-knowing (Sarvajña), eternal Supreme Lord of pure nature, then how does your birth happen without the Saṃskāras of piety and sin? Upon such a doubt, Bhagavāna says -}

अजोऽपि सन्नव्ययात्मा भूतानामीश्वरोऽपि सन् |
प्रकृतिं स्वामधिष्ठाय सम्भवाम्यात्ममायया || BG 4.6 ||

अपि - Although ; सन् - being ; अजः - the unborn ; अव्यय-आत्मा - immutable Self ; अपि - and ; सन् - being ; ईश्वरः - the Lord ; भूतानाम् - of all living beings, ; अधिष्ठाय - subordinating ; स्वाम् - My own ; प्रकृतिम् - nature, ; सम्भवामि - (I) incarnate ; आत्म-मायया - by My Māyā.

Although being the unborn immutable Self and the Lord of all living beings, subordinating My own nature, I incarnate by My Māyā.

Intent - The birth of all living beings happens naturally based on their piety and sin impressions (Saṃskāras) on the dependence of Prakṛti. I take birth or appear to become embodied. However, My birth does not occur on the reliance of Prakṛti by some piety or sin Saṃskāras. I incarnate by My Māyā subordinating My nature. I manifest by My "power of being. This power of being is all-pervasive and consists of the three constituents of Prakṛti. The entire Saṃsāra is subject to the laws of Prakṛti. However, deluded by it, they do not know their own Ātmā, the Self, Me Vāsudeva. Thus, as it were, I am born, by My power of being, imaginary play like, and not in fact. Unlike all living beings, the fruit of My birth is not enjoyments of happiness and sorrow.

(When does the birth of the Lord happen?)

यदा यदा हि धर्मस्य ग्लानिर्भवति भारत |
अभ्युत्थानमधर्मस्य तदात्मानं सृजाम्यहम् || BG 4.7 ||

भारत - Hey Bhārata (Arjuna)! ; यदा यदा - Whenever ; भवति - there is ; ग्लानिः - a decline ; धर्मस्य - in righteousness ; अभ्युत्थानम् - (and) a rise ; अधर्मस्य - in unrighteousness, ; तदा - then ; हि - only ; अहम् - I ; सृजामि - manifest ; आत्मानम् - Myself.

Hey Arjuna! Whenever there is a decline in righteousness and a rise in unrighteousness, then only I manifest Myself.

(What is the purpose of His birth?)

परित्राणाय साधूनां विनाशाय च दुष्कृताम् |
धर्मसंस्थापनार्थाय सम्भवामि युगे युगे || BG 4.8 ||

सम्भवामि - I am born ; युगे युगे – age after age ; परित्राणाय - to protect ; साधूनाम् - the virtuous, ; विनाशाय - eradicate ; दुष्कृताम् – evil, ; च - and ; धर्म-संस्थापन-अर्थाय - establish righteousness..

I am born age after age to protect the virtuous, eradicate evil, and establish righteousness.

Intent - Piety of the virtuous and sin of the evil together personifying create My body. Moreover, protection of the virtuous, destruction of the evil, and establishment of righteousness is the only purpose for creating This body. Separate from this, in the creation of This body, I do not have any purpose, nor is there any reward for Me.

(Now, Bhagavāna describes the divinity of His birth and actions -)

जन्म कर्म च मे दिव्यमेवं यो वेत्ति तत्त्वतः |
त्यक्त्वा देहं पुनर्जन्म नैति मामेति सोऽर्जुन || BG 4.9 ||

अर्जुन - Hey Arjuna! ; यः - One, who ; वेत्ति - knows ; एवम् - thus ; मे - My ; दिव्यम् - divine ; जन्म - birth ; च - and ; कर्म - actions ; तत्त्वतः - truly {that the existent Self (Paramātmā) illusory perceived as born, is not born, and seen as performing actions, is not doing anything}, ; एति न - does not take ; जन्म - birth ; पुनः - again ; त्यक्त्वा - after abandoning ; देहम् - the body. ; सः - He ; एति - attains ; माम् - Me (only with the influence of true knowledge).

Hey Arjuna! One, who thus knows My divine birth and actions truly, does not take birth again after abandoning the body. He attains Me only.

Intent - I, the all-witness, eternal, unborn, and actionless, though perceived as born, am not born. Perceived as performing Karma, I am indeed not doing anything, and even when Karma are perceived as being done by Me, they do not touch Me. Even though those births and Karma are dreamlike perceived in the kingdom of Māyā on My dependence, there is no taint of those births and Karma in Me - that is the divinity of My births and Karma. The one who truly knows Me, the Ātmā of all (Sarvātmā), and own Ātmā in oneness, that is, one who has directly experienced truly, "Just as in support of space, with the manifestation of hurricanes, tornadoes, rain or heat there is not an iota of touch in the space, in the same way, in support of the Asti-Bhāti-Priya Ātmā, all births and Karma even though are illusory perceived do not touch the Ātmā, the Ātmā dissociated from the body, senses, mind, and intellect, that I am," such a person even while alive is free, and once he leaves the body does not retake birth, but attains Me only.

(Knowing You so, is anyone liberated? -)

वीतरागभयक्रोधा मन्मया मामुपाश्रिता: |
बहवो ज्ञानतपसा पूता मद्भावमागता: || BG 4.10 ||

बहव: - Many (devotees who are) ; वीत-राग-भय-क्रोधा: - free from attachment, fear, and anger, ; मन्मया: - absorbed in Me, ; उपाश्रिता: - have taken refuge ; माम् - in Me, ; पूता: - (and) purified ; ज्ञान-तपसा - by the austerity of knowledge ; आगता: - have attained ; मद्भावम् - My status.

Many who are free from attachment, fear, and anger, absorbed in Me, have taken refuge in Me, and purified by the austerity of knowledge have attained My status.

Intent - Many devotees free from attachment, fear, and anger becoming pure from the austerity of knowledge have attained My status. Separate from knowledge, no other austerity can make a Jīva pure to attain union with oneness in the Ātmā. Only this knowledge, making one pure, can provide that oneness in the Ātmā, "I am the eternal, pure, conscious, free nature - dissociated from the body, senses, mind, and intellect." Further, only the fit for this knowledge is free from attachment, fear, and anger and moving towards the Lord.

(While many with this austerity of knowledge have attained My status, yet others also -)

ये यथा मां प्रपद्यन्ते तांस्तथैव भजाम्यहम् |
मम वर्त्मानुवर्तन्ते मनुष्या: पार्थ सर्वश: || BG 4.11 ||

यथा - In whatever manner ; ये - they ; प्रपद्यन्ते - surrender to ; माम् - Me (the Parameśvara), ; अहम् - I ; एव - certainly ; भजामि - oblige ; तान् - them ; तथा - accordingly. ; पार्थ - Hey Pārtha (Arjuna)! ; सर्वश: - In all respects, ; मनुष्या: - humans ; अनुवर्तन्ते - follow ; मम - My ; वर्त्म - path.

In whatever manner they surrender to Me, I certainly oblige them accordingly. Hey Arjuna! In all respects, humans follow My path.

Intent - With whatever sentiment one surrenders, approaches or worships Me, I oblige that person accordingly. All humans follow My path. All of their activities are successful only with My support. The intention is that I, the Existent-Conscious-Witness common in all, even though I am without adjuncts, acquire whatever sentimental-adjuncts living beings have and become just like that adjunct for them. For instance, even though wind and fire do not have any shape, they take a similar shape when they meet with a long, wide, crooked, or straight discriminative-adjunct of wood or location. "वायुर्यथैको भुवनं प्रविष्टो रुपं रुपं प्रतिरुपो बभूव, even as one air has entered into the world, but it shapes itself to the forms it meets."[90]Accordingly, upon animosity approach of Rāvaṇa (रावण) and others, in the form of an enemy; upon worship with the sentiment of a son by King Daśaratha (दशरथ), in the form of a son; upon worship by Arjuna and Sudāmā (सुदामा) with the sentiment of a friend, in the form of a friend; for those with desire in the form of desire; for desired-ridden in the form of sought after objects; for desireless in the form of peace and those worshiping in oneness-sentiment, I assume the form of the Ātmā. For evil persons in the form of Kali-Yuga, virtuous persons in Sat-Yuga, desire-ridden persons in enjoyments, dispassionate in the form of endurance like fire, and a wise in the bliss form are established. Even though the Saṃsāra has no form of its own, still by their individually separate perspective, I appear to them in the Saṃsāra accordingly. This way, all living beings are following My path only. That is, the destination of all is only Me. The destination of all living beings is only for happiness, and so with whatever sentiment they worship Me, for them, I assume the same form.

(According to this rule -)

काङ्‌ क्षन्त: कर्मणां सिद्धिं यजन्त इह देवता: |
क्षिप्रं हि मानुषे लोके सिद्धिर्भवति कर्मजा || BG 4.12 ||

इह - In this ; मानुषे - human ; लोके - world, ; काङ्क्षन्तः - desiring ; सिद्धिम् - fruition ; कर्मणाम् - of (their) actions, ; यजन्ते - (those who) worship ; देवताः - deities, ; सिद्धिः - (for them) the success ; कर्मजा - of actions ; हि - certainly ; भवति - happens ; क्षिप्रम् - quickly (through Me).

In this human world, desiring fruition of actions those who worship deities, the success of actions certainly happens quickly.

Intent - Seeking to obtain success in fruits of action, people offer sacrifices or worship deities like Indra and Agni. Success is quickly gained by those who worship their revered deity. For those desire-ridden persons who worship deities, only I, the Ātmā of all, assume the form of their revered deity following their sentiment. Only I appear before them in the form of their desired thing, similar to how it is only gold that appears in gold ornaments, whether it is a ring, necklace, or any other ornament.

चातुर्वर्ण्यं मया सृष्टं गुणकर्मविभागश: |
तस्य कर्तारमपि मां विद्ध्यकर्तारमव्ययम् || BG 4.13 ||

गुण-कर्म-विभागशः - According to the distinctions of the constituents and actions (of Prakṛti), ; चातुर्वर्ण्यम् - the fourfold functional class system ; सृष्टम् - was created ; मया - by Me. ; अपि - Indeed, ; विद्धि - know ; माम् - Me ; अव्ययम् - the immutable ; अकर्तारम् - (and) non-doer ; तस्य - (as) their (meaning the four classes Brāhmaṇa, Kṣatriya, Vaiśya, and Śūdra) ; कर्तारम् - creator.

According to the distinctions of the constituents and actions, the fourfold functional class system was created by Me. Indeed, know Me the immutable and non-doer as their creator.

Intent - In reality, I am imperishable and non-doer. By becoming a doer, I cannot remain imperishable because how can he remain imperishable in one with the mutation of doership? However, despite being a non-doer, only by My power does this entire creation manifest in the kingdom of Prakṛti, and thus there is the attribution of doership in Me. Just as the creation of the whole world is on the support of the existence of space, which "is as is" not doing anything by itself, in the same fashion, in the kingdom of Prakṛti, with the distinctions of the constituents and actions, creation of the fourfold functional class system (Catura-Varṇa) is only with My power.

[90] Kaṭha Upaniṣad (कठ उपनिषद्) 2.2.10

(Even though everything is being fruitful through Me, yet in reality -)

न मां कर्माणि लिम्पन्ति न मे कर्मफले स्पृहा ।
इति मां योऽभिजानाति कर्मभिर्न स बध्यते || BG 4.14 ||

कर्माणि - Actions ; न - neither ; लिम्पन्ति - taint ; माम् - Me, ; न - nor (do) ; मे - I (have) ; स्पृहा - an attachment ; कर्मफले - to the fruits of action. ; सः यः - One who ; अभिजानाति - knows ; माम् - Me ; इति - so ; न - (is also) not ; बध्यते - bound ; कर्मभिः - by action.

Actions neither taint Me, nor do I have an attachment to the fruits of action. One who knows Me so is also not bound by action.

Intent - Just as in the space and its support, all creations manifest, but there is no taint of them on the space; in the same way, all doers, actions, and means are all successful in My presence, Me the all-witnessing Ātmā of all, yet they do not taint Me. One who knows Me transcendentally as "I am That Who is the all-witnessing Ātmā of all" is not bound by action.

एवं ज्ञात्वा कृतं कर्म पूर्वैरपि मुमुक्षुभिः ।
कुरु कर्मैव तस्मात्त्वं पूर्वैः पूर्वतरं कृतम् || BG 4.15 ||

कर्म - Actions ; अपि - were ; कृतम् - performed ; मुमुक्षुभिः - by seekers of liberation ; पूर्वैः - in the past, ; ज्ञात्वा - knowing ; एवम् - Thus (I, the Supreme Lord, am not tainted by action, do not have an attachment to the fruits of action, and one who transcendentally knows Me as such is also not bound by action). ; तस्मात् - Therefore, ; त्वम् - you ; कुरु - perform ; कर्म - actions ; कृतम् - done ; पूर्वतरम् - traditionally ; पूर्वैः - by ancestors ; एव - only.

Actions were performed by seekers of liberation in the past, knowing Thus. Therefore, you perform actions done traditionally by ancestors only.

Intent - Knowing that there is no taint of Karma in Me the Ātmā of all, and knowing that Karma does not bind one who knows in fact as such, in the past to know Me in such a way, Karma was performed by seekers of liberation. Therefore, Arjuna, you perform Karma done through tradition by your ancestors. It should be remembered that worship and analytic thinking for one who is fit are also Karma. This way, Bhagavāna described his divine births and actions and provided the fruit of knowing Him.

{Now, Bhagavāna describes the nature of action (Karma) and actionlessness (Akarma) -}

किं कर्म किमकर्मेति कवयोऽप्यत्र मोहिताः ।
तत्ते कर्म प्रवक्ष्यामि यज्ज्ञात्वा मोक्ष्यसेऽशुभात् || BG 4.16 ||

किम् - What is ; कर्म - an action? ; किम् - What is ; अकर्म - a non-action? ; इति - Thus, ; अत्र - on this (subject), ; अपि - even ; कवयः - the wise ; मोहिताः - are deluded. ; प्रवक्ष्यामि - (Therefore,) I shall tell ; ते - you ; तत् - that (Truth of) ; कर्म - action, ; ज्ञात्वा - knowing ; यत् - which, ; मोक्ष्यसे - you will be free ; अशुभात् - from the evil (of the worldly wheel of birth and death).

What is an action? What is a non-action? Thus, on this, even the wise are deluded. Therefore, I shall tell you that action, knowing which, you will be free from the evil.

Intent - What is "that" Bhagavāna is referring to in "I shall tell you that"? It is the knowledge of the Truth or the true principle of Karma. Additionally, what is the evil referred to here? Evil is the worldly wheel of birth and death of transmigrating lives.

कर्मणो ह्यपि बोद्धव्यं बोद्धव्यं च विकर्मणः ।
अकर्मणश्च बोद्धव्यं गहना कर्मणो गतिः || BG 4.17 ||

कर्मणः - The (true nature) of action ; बोद्धव्यम् - should be known; ; च - and ; विकर्मणः - forbidden action ; बोद्धव्यम् - should be known, ; च - and ; अपि - also ; अकर्मणः - inaction ; बोद्धव्यम् - should be known. ; हि - For, ; गतिः - the path of ; कर्मणः - action ; गहना - is profound.

The true nature of action should be known; forbidden action should be known, and inaction should be known. For, the path of action is profound.

Intent - One ought to know scripturally enjoined and forbidden (Niṣiddha) acts. In addition, one ought to know inaction, meaning nullity of action (idleness or immobility), as opposed to the term non-action (अकर्म, Akarma), which has a specific meaning related to Naiṣkarmya. One ought to know all three types of actions, good, bad, and doing nothing. The path of action is profound, which means that the truth or reality of action is hard to understand.

(Bhagavāna now describes their true nature -)

कर्मण्यकर्म य: पश्येदकर्मणि च कर्म य: |
स बुद्धिमान्मनुष्येषु स युक्त: कृत्स्नकर्मकृत् || BG 4.18 ||

य: - One who ; पश्येत् - sees ; अकर्म - non-action (stainlessness from action) ; कर्मणि - in action (action done without doership-ego), ; च - and ; य: - who (sees) ; कर्म - action ; अकर्मणि - in non-action (relinquishment of action done with ego), ; बुद्धिमान् - (is) wise ; मनुष्येषु - amongst all humans; ; स: - he has ; युक्त: - attained union (in the Self) ; कृत्स्नकर्मकृत् - (and) has done everything.

One who sees non-action in action and action in non-action is wise amongst all humans; he has attained union and has done everything.

Intent - {आत्मैवेदं सर्वम्, the Ātmā is this entire (observable world)}[91] - that knowledge when it becomes firmly realized in a person, then his limited I-ness is burnt. With the removal of I-ness in the body, senses, mind, and intellect, he is situated with I-ness in his own witnessing Ātmā. Such a person sees the entire world of substances, attributes and acts as the Ātmā and separate from the Ātmā does not see any existence in them, just as how a pawnbroker's gold perspective in rings, earrings, necklaces, and other ornaments is direct. All efforts in his body, mind, and senses happen naturally for such a person. He does not see any taint of them in his Ātmā and knows that nothing is happening, just like a dream world. That is the vision of action (Karma) in non-action (Akarma). In contrast, a person with I-ness sense in the body who though renounces external bodily activities, yet is continuously pondering over sense-objects and also his trueness sense in the Saṃsāra is present, that is, he sees the Saṃsāra as real, that person even though is not doing anything is doing everything and is actually in the bondage of action. That is because he is with impressions and sentiments, and in this non-action (Akarma), that is, relinquishment of action, he sees action. One who knows so is indeed a wise person, he is the one who has attained union in his own Ātmā, and he has done everything. Such a knower of the Truth is contented (कृतकृत्य, Kṛtakṛtya), and for him, there is no duty.

(Now Bhagavāna describes in the following five verses the true nature of a Yogī who sees non-action in action -)

यस्य सर्वे समारम्भा: कामसंकल्पवर्जिता: |
ज्ञानाग्निदग्धकर्माणं तमाहु: पण्डितं बुधा: || BG 4.19 ||

यस्य - Whose ; सर्वे - all ; समारम्भा: - initiations (of actions) ; वर्जिता: - are without ; काम - desire (and) ; संकल्प - resolve, ; दग्ध - (and who has) burnt ; कर्माणम् - all actions ; ज्ञानाग्नि - in the fire of knowledge, ; तम् - he ; आहु: - is called ; पण्डितम् - a man of discrimination ; बुधा: - by the wise.

Whose all initiations are without desire and resolve, and who has burnt all actions in the fire of knowledge, he is called a man of discrimination by the wise.

[91] Chāndogya Upaniṣad (छान्दोग्य उपनिषद्) 7.25.2

Intent - The cause in the initiation of Karma is only desire (काम, Kāma) and resolve (संकल्प, Saṃkalpa), and the root of desires and resolves is the limited ego (Paricchinna Ahaṃkāra). With the influence of ignorance, when a person imagines himself as something separate from his own real Ātmā, then a desire is born. With the desire, there is the formation of a resolve to acquire the desired object. However, when the fire of knowledge becomes ablaze, it incinerates ignorance. With the maturity of knowledge, "I am everything," the seat of I-ness dislodging from the limited ego fastens in his own Ātmā. Then he only sees his own Ātmā, which is the authority of the entire cause and Karma, and then the perceptible threesome born of ignorance, that is, 1) doer in the form of ego, 2) cause in the form of desire, and resolve and 3) Karma, all become loose. Then, whether it is a doer, a cause in the form of resolves, or Karma, he only sees the underlying support of the threesome - his Ātmā. Moreover, the doer and Karma are perceived as illusory waves of his own Ātmā, and the desires and resolves remain like roasted seeds. Accordingly, one whose Karma is burnt in the fire of knowledge and is devoid of desires and resolves is called a "Paṇḍita, a man of discrimination" by the wise.

त्यक्त्वा कर्मफलासङ्गं नित्यतृप्तो निराश्रय: |
कर्मण्यभिप्रवृत्तोऽपि नैव किञ्चित्करोति स: || BG 4.20 ||

नित्यतृप्त: - Always content (in the Self), ; निराश्रय: - independent, ; त्यक्त्वा - (and) having forsaken ; कर्मफलासङ्गम् - (doership-ego in actions and) attachment to the fruits of action, ; अपि - even though ; अभिप्रवृत्त: - engaged ; कर्मणि - in an activity, ; स: - he ; एव - (is) really ; न - not ; करोति - doing ; किञ्चित् - anything.

Always content, independent, and having forsaken attachment to the fruits of action, even though engaged in an activity, he is really not doing anything.

Intent - Through the transcendental realization of the Ātmā, a Yogī is always content in his own Ātmā. He who is dissociated from the body, mind, and senses, free from "I am a doer" doership-ego, forsaken the fruits of Karma, and is without instrumental dependence on the desired fruits of both worlds, even though he is engaged in the activities of the body is not doing anything. Just as a person awake from a dream does not see any taint in himself, in the same way, one who has ascended to Reality sees non-action in action.

निराशीर्यतचित्तात्मा त्यक्तसर्वपरिग्रह: |
शारीरं केवलं कर्म कुर्वन्नाप्नोति किल्बिषम् || BG 4.21 ||

निराशी: - Free of expectations, ; त्यक्त-सर्व-परिग्रह: - having abandoned all possessions, ; यत-चित्त-आत्मा - (one who) controls the mind and body ; कुर्वन् - (and) performs ; केवलम् - only ; शारीरम् - bodily ; कर्म - activities ; आप्नोति - incurs ; न - no ; किल्बिषम् - sin.

Free of expectations, having abandoned all possessions, one who controls the mind and body and performs only bodily activities incurs no sin.

Intent - By the above perspective, removing the I-ness sense from the mind and body and situating with I-ness in the all-witness Ātmā is indeed winning over or controlling the mind and body. Only due to the trueness sense in substances is there an entry of expectations. However, attaining a position in the all-witness underlying support of all, substances that are the objects of expectations appear dreamlike. When such substances do not exist, where do expectations have any place? Thus, this Yogī is naturally free from expectations. With whose relationship, devoid of happiness-yielding objects perceived as happiness-yielding, such possession of accumulative enjoyment materials are naturally abandoned by attaining the blissful Ātmā. A Yogī, engaged only in bodily activities, does not acquire sin. He does not come in the bondage of birth and death. "शारीरं केवलं कर्म, only bodily activities" does not just mean Karma that is only for the sustenance of the body. Acceptance of such interpretation does not provide a harmonious connection with BG 4.19 "यस्य सर्वे समारम्भा, whose all initiations" and BG 4.20 "कर्मण्यभिप्रवृत्तोऽपि, even though engaged in action." It is not so that a person bound by the injunction of engaging only in activities for the sustenance of the body as a duty can become a seer of non-action in action. However, the intention is that due to the absence of ego, even engaging without any duty in natural activities through the body and senses, such a person does not come into the bondage of sin or piety. Because the root of bondage and sin-piety is only ego, which is burnt through the fire of knowledge, and the body and senses move ahead like a locomotive on the tracks of ready-for-fruition past actions (प्रारब्ध, Prārabdha, that portion of accumulated past actions now ready to materialize or to be enjoyed). That is the meaning of "शारीरं केवलं कर्म, only bodily activities." The term "शारीरं, Śārīraṃ" does not mean only the gross body but also includes the subtle body. The reason is that without the conjunction of the subtle body, it is impossible for Karma in the gross body alone. Additionally, the term "किल्बिषम्, Kilbiṣam" signifies both sin and piety because even piety is the cause of bondage, it is also a form of sin.

यदृच्छालाभसन्तुष्टो द्वन्द्वातीतो विमत्सरः ।
समः सिद्धावसिद्धौ च कृत्वापि न निबध्यते || BG 4.22 ||

यदृच्छा-लाभ-सन्तुष्टः - (One who is) content with what is obtained on its own accord, ; द्वन्द्व-अतीतः - beyond dualities (such as happiness and grief, heat and cold), ; विमत्सरः - unenvious, ; समः - (and) equal in ; सिद्धौ - success ; च - and ; असिद्धौ - failure, ; न - (is) not ; निबध्यते - bound ; अपि - despite ; कृत्वा - performing (actions).

One who is content with what is obtained on its own accord, beyond dualities, unenvious and equal in success and failure, is not bound despite performing actions.

Intent - Instruments of enjoyment in the form of the body, mind, and senses, substances of enjoyment and with their relationship through favorable and unfavorable mental states of dualities like pleasure and pain, heat and cold - they all retain influence and put a Jīva in bondage as long as delusional I-ness sense in the body is present. However, when this relationship of I-ness sense is broken, and a seat is procured in the true witness-conscious Ātmā, then seeing the absence of the existence of objects of desire, that Yogī naturally becomes "यदृच्छालाभसन्तुष्ट, content with whatever is obtained on its own accord" and not seeing the existence of dualities automatically becomes "द्वन्द्वातीत, free from dualities." "All this is my miracle" with such a view becomes devoid of "मत्सर, envy" because the cause of envy is discriminating-perspective. Thus, removing the "I am a doer" sentiment, equanimity in success and failure is naturally established. By the influence of the fire of knowledge, they all remain only delusional in their true nature with the incineration of the trueness sentiment in the enjoyer body, the enjoyment substances, and the fruits of pleasure and pain. He does not see any taint from any of them in his Ātmā and does not see anything happening from them in his Ātmā. Accordingly, even when performing an activity, he is not bound. Though in the view of other ignorant persons, he may appear as if he is doing and enjoying, in reality, he is a non-doer and sees non-action in action.

गतसङ्गस्य मुक्तस्य ज्ञानावस्थितचेतसः ।
यज्ञायाचरतः कर्म समग्रं प्रविलीयते || BG 4.23 ||

समग्रम् - All ; कर्म - actions ; मुक्तस्य - of a liberated ; ज्ञान-अवस्थित-चेतसः - whose mind is established in knowledge ; गत-सङ्गस्य - (and) devoid of attachments ; आचरतः - performed ; यज्ञाय - as a sacrifice ; प्रविलीयते - are destroyed.

All actions of a liberated whose mind is established in knowledge and devoid of attachments performed as a sacrifice are destroyed.

Intent - All his actions are in the form of sacrifice (Yajña). The term Yajña here means the pervasive Lord Viṣṇu. Waves in an ocean can be distinguished from other waves. However, waves as water cannot be distinguished from the ocean's water. In the same way, being situated in the Ātmā of all, the Yogī is naturally free from all attachments. A person free from such sentiments as "I am a doer" and "I have some duty" in whatever action he is naturally engaged becomes like a sacrifice, like offerings to the Lord. They all become the Brahman form.

(For a Yogī situated in the Ātmā, various activities in the form of sacrifice that occur naturally based on earlier nature are described next -)

ब्रह्मार्पणं ब्रह्म हविर्ब्रह्माग्नौ ब्रह्मणा हुतम् |
ब्रह्मैव तेन गन्तव्यं ब्रह्मकर्मसमाधिना || BG 4.24 ||

अर्पणं - Instruments (such as wooden ladles) of sacrifice ; ब्रह्म - are the Brahman. ; हविः - Offerings suitable for oblation in the consecrated fire (such as Ghī, milk, curd, sugar, saffron, grains, coconut, perfumed water, incense, seeds, petals, and herbs) ; ब्रह्म - are the Brahman. ; हुतम् - Votive rituals (performed by) ; ब्रह्मणा - a Brahman-form doer ; ब्रह्म-अग्नौ - in the Brahman-form fire (is the Brahman). ; तेन - (Accordingly,) that ; गन्तव्यम् - which is to be obtained ; ब्रह्म-कर्म-समाधिना - by the one absorbed in the Brahman-form action ; एव - is indeed ; ब्रह्म - the Brahman.

Instruments of sacrifice are the Brahman. Offerings suitable for oblation in the consecrated fire are the Brahman. Votive rituals performed by a Brahman-form doer in the Brahman-form fire is the Brahman. That which is to be obtained by the one absorbed in the Brahman-form action is indeed the Brahman.

Intent - There are sixfold instruments (षट-कारक, Ṣaṭ-Kāraka) that bring about any activity: (1) doer (कर्ता, Kartā) of the act, (2) action (कर्म, Karma) meaning the activity of the act, (3) instruments (करण, Karaṇa) by which action is performed, (4) for whom the act is performed (संप्रदान, Saṃpradāna), (5) from where the act is performed (अपादान, Apādāna), and (6) in which the act is performed (अधिकरण, Adhikaraṇa). For the one who is absorbed in the Brahman-form action, his Brahman-sight is always in the sixfold instruments that are the cause of his activity in Karma, just as how to a knower of rope, his rope-vision remains in the objects of illusion, like the snake or stick. The use of the term Yajña is to express these instruments as a metaphor in the form of fire (Agni) and offerings (Havi). The term Yajña means the pervasive Lord Viṣṇu. For such a Yogī, all his efforts are naturally in the form of the Brahman. Compounding of "ब्रह्मकर्मसमाधिना, Brahmakarmasamādhinā" is this way, ब्रह्म एव कर्म > ब्रह्मकर्म, तस्मिन् ब्रह्मकर्मणि समाधि (एकत्वद्रष्टि) यस्यासौ ब्रह्मकर्मसमाधि, तेन "ब्रह्मकर्मसमाधिना". One who sees with oneness-sight only the Brahman in all Karma, all his efforts are in the form of Brahman.

दैवमेवापरे यज्ञं योगिनः पर्युपासते |
ब्रह्माग्नावपरे यज्ञं यज्ञेनैवोपजुह्वति || BG 4.25 ||

अपरे - (Some) other ; योगिनः - Yogīs ; पर्युपासते - offer ; यज्ञम् - sacrifice ; दैवम् - to deities ; एव - alone. ; अपरे - Other (Yogīs) ; उपजुह्वति - perform ; यज्ञं - sacrifice ; यज्ञेन - through the sacrifice (of knowledge) ; ब्रह्म-अग्नौ - in the fire of the Brahman ; एव - alone.

Some Yogīs offer sacrifice to deities alone. Others perform sacrifice through the sacrifice of knowledge in the fire of the Brahman alone.

Intent - The intention is that free from obligation, based on their own nature, some knowers of the Truth naturally conduct sacrifice in the form of devotion to deities. Examples are Puruṣottama Maryādā Śrī Rāma and King Janaka, to name a few. To perform "यज्ञं यज्ञेन, sacrifice through sacrifice" in the "fire of knowledge (Brahmāgni)" means to perform the sacrifice of knowledge in the form of "सर्वं खल्विदं ब्रह्म, all this is the Brahman" and incinerate the sacrifice (Yajña). Take the knowledge above to its highest level and wash your hands from "doing something or not doing something." Here the example is Bhagavāna Dattātreya (दत्तात्रेय).

श्रोत्रादीनीन्द्रियाण्यन्ये संयमाग्निषु जुह्वति |
शब्दादीन्विषयानन्य इन्द्रियाग्निषु जुह्वति || BG 4.26 ||

अन्ये - Others ; जुह्वति - offer ; श्रोत्र-आदीनि - hearing and other ; इन्द्रियाणि - senses (as a sacrifice) ; संयम-अग्निषु - in the fire of restraint. ; अन्ये - Others ; जुह्वति - offer ; विषयान् - objects (like) ; शब्द-आदीन् - sound and others (as a sacrifice) ; इन्द्रिय-अग्निषु - in the fire of the senses

Others offer hearing and other senses in the fire of restraint. Others offer objects like sound and others in the fire of the senses.

Intent - Offering (sacrificing) the senses in the fire of restraint means restraining the senses from their respective sense-objects and making them independent. The offering of objects like sound and others in the fire of the senses means only accepting the objects of the senses without taste, following the injunctions of the scriptures. Here the example is Jaḍabharata (जडभरत).

सर्वाणीन्द्रियकर्माणि प्राणकर्माणि चापरे |
आत्मसंयमयोगाग्नौ जुह्वति ज्ञानदीपिते || BG 4.27 ||

अपरे - Others ; जुह्वति - offer ; सर्वाणि - all ; इन्द्रिय-कर्माणि - activities of the senses ; च - and ; प्राण-कर्माणि - the activities of the vital breaths of air ; आत्म-संयम-योग-अग्नौ - in the fire of Yoga of self-restraint ; ज्ञान-दीपिते - blazed by knowledge.

Others offer all activities of the senses and vital breaths of air in the fire of Yoga of self-restraint blazed by knowledge.

Intent - With the direct realization of the Ātmā as "अहम् ब्रह्मास्मि, I am the Brahman" those who have set ablaze the fire of knowledge and incinerated "देहोऽहम्, I am a body," "कर्ताभोक्ताहम्, I am a doer-enjoyer" and other forms of I-ness sense in the body and are situated in their Ātmā in oneness, are the ones referred to in the verse. That is, "I am dissociated from the body, senses, and vital breaths of air. I am not the one with duties (धर्मी, Dharmī) of their duties (धर्म, Dharma), but I am an observer-witness (Dṛṣṭā-Sākṣī)," - through such pure knowledge they have found rest in own Ātmā. Such Yogīs sacrifice activities of the senses and vital breaths of air in the fire of self-restraint; they just become observers of activities of the senses and vital breaths of air. That is indeed the offering of the activities of the senses and vital breaths of air in the fire of Yoga of self-restraint.

द्रव्ययज्ञास्तपोयज्ञा योगयज्ञास्तथापरे |
स्वाध्यायज्ञानयज्ञाश्च यतयः संशितव्रताः || BG 4.28 ||

तथा - Similarly, ; अपरे - other ; यतयः - ascetics ; संशितव्रताः - observe strict vows, ; द्रव्य-यज्ञाः - (some) sacrifice material possessions (in the cause of the highest good); ; तपो-यज्ञाः - (some) perform austerity (in the form of restraint of the senses), ; योग-यज्ञाः - (some perform (Aṣṭāṅga)-Yoga, ; च - and ; स्वाध्याय-ज्ञान-यज्ञाः - some perform self-study (of the Self-related scriptures such as listening, contemplating)

Similarly, other ascetics observe strict vows, some sacrifice material possessions; some perform austerity, some perform (Aṣṭāṅga)-Yoga[92], and some perform self-study.

Intent - Through the realization of the Ātmā, those who have found union in their own Ātmā, who are without doership-sentiment, such seers, even while engaged in various kinds of activities by their individual earlier nature, only see non-action in action. Among them, some in the path of the highest good perform the sacrifice of perishable material possessions, some perform austerities, some engage in the performance of the eightfold (Aṣṭāṅga) Yoga, some study the Vedas and self-study the scriptures related to the Lord and some perform the sacrifice of knowledge in the form of teaching of the Reality, and others are involved in the writing of spiritual texts.

---

92 Aṣṭāṅga-Yoga (अष्टाङ्ग-योग) means the Yoga consisting of eight limbs: 1) moral codes (यम, Yama), 2) observances (नियम, Niyama), 3) postures (आसन, Āsana), 4) breath-control (प्राणायाम, Prāṇāyāma), 5) sense-control (प्रत्याहार, Pratyāhāra), 6) concentration (धारणा, Dhāraṇā), 7) meditation (ध्यान, Dhyāna) and 8) absorption into the Reality (समाधि, Samādhī).

अपाने जुह्वति प्राणं प्राणेऽपानं तथापरे |
प्राणापानगती रुद्ध्वा प्राणायामपरायणा: || BG 4.29 ||

अपरे - Others ; जुह्वति - place ; प्राणम् - the in-breath ; अपाने - in the out-breath ; अपानम् - (and) the out-breath ; प्राणे - in the in-breath, ; तथा - and ; रुद्ध्वा - holding ; प्राण-अपान-गती - the movement of the in and out-breaths ; प्राणायाम-परायणाः - are absorbed in breath control.

Others place the in-breath in the out-breath and the out-breath in the in-breath, and holding the movement of the in and out-breaths are absorbed in breath control.

Intent - Breath control (प्राणायाम, Prāṇāyāma) is of three kinds. First, the merger (लय, Laya) of the in-breath (प्राण-वायु, Prāṇa-Vāyu) in the out-breath (अपान-वायु, Apāna-Vāyu) is called "पूरक, Pūraka." It is essentially breathing in. Prāṇa-Vāyu supplies the body with essential oxygen, and its energy flows from the nostrils to the heart level pervading the chest region. It translates as "forward moving air," and its flow is inwards and upwards. It nourishes the brain and eyes and governs the reception of all things: food, air, senses, and thoughts. It is the fundamental energy in the body and directs and feeds into the other four breaths 1) Apāna-Vāyu, 2) Samāna-Vāyu (समान-वायु), 3) Udāna-Vāyu (उदान-वायु), and 4) Vyāna-Vāyu (व्यान-वायु). Second, the merger of the out-breath (Apāna-Vāyu) with the in-breath is called "रेचक, Recaka." It is essentially exhaling breath. Apāna-Vāyu influences the lower part of the body, from the navel to the soles of the feet. It translates as "the air that moves away," and its flow is downwards and out. Its energy nourishes the organs of digestion, reproduction, and elimination of all substances from the body: carbon dioxide, urine, stool, et al. Third, the holding (निरोध, Nirodha) of the movement of Prāṇa-Vāyu and Apāna-Vāyu is called "कुम्भक, Kumbhaka" essentially it is the time between inhale and exhale. This way, absorbed in Prāṇāyāma, many Yogīs remain dissociated from the body, and senses continue to move the bellows of Prāṇa-Vāyu and Apāna-Vāyu. In Yogavāsiṣṭha (योगवासिष्ठ), Nirvāṇa-Prakaraṇa in the Bhuśaṇḍivāsiṣṭha (भुशण्डिवासिष्ठ) Saṃvāda, the life of Bhuśaṇḍi is an example here.

अपरे नियताहारा: प्राणान्प्राणेषु जुह्वति |
सर्वेऽप्येते यज्ञविदो यज्ञक्षपितकल्मषा: || BG 4.30 ||

अपरे - Others ; नियत-आहाराः - with regulated diets ; जुह्वति - sacrifice their ; प्राणान् - vital breaths of air ; प्राणेषु - in the vital breaths of air. ; अपि - Also, ; सर्वे - all ; एते - of those ; यज्ञ-क्षपित-कल्मषाः - whose sins are destroyed by the sacrifice (of knowledge) ; यज्ञविदः - are knowers of (the Brahman in the form of) the sacrifice.

Others with regulated diets sacrifice their vital breaths of air in the vital breaths of air. All of those whose sins are destroyed by the sacrifice are knowers of the sacrifice.

Intent - Whose sins are destroyed by the sacrifice of knowledge are the knowers of the sacrifice. That is, they are the knowers of the Brahman.

(Thus, in the above seven verses, various natural activities of the knowers of the Reality are described. Now, their fruit and from a pervasive viewpoint, Bhagavāna describes the importance of sacrifice -)

यज्ञशिष्टामृतभुजो यान्ति ब्रह्म सनातनम् |
नायं लोकोऽस्त्ययज्ञस्य कुतोऽन्य: कुरुसत्तम || BG 4.31 ||

यज्ञ-शिष्ट-अमृत-भुजः - Partaking ambrosial remains of these sacrifices ; यान्ति - (they) attain ; सनातनम् - the eternal ; ब्रह्म - Brahman. ; कुरुसत्तम - Hey Kurusattama (Arjuna, the best of the descendants of the Kurus)! ; अयम् - This ; लोकः - world ; न अस्ति - is not (happiness-yielder) ; अयज्ञस्य - for a non-sacrificer. ; कुतः - How ; अन्यः - can other (worlds) be (happiness-yielder)?

Partaking ambrosial remains of these sacrifices, they attain the eternal Brahman. Hey Arjuna! This world is not for a non-sacrificer. How can others be?

Intent - With sentiments of sacrifice, enjoying the bliss of the Brahman, those Yogīs certainly attain the eternal Brahman. Hey Arjuna! From a pervasive perspective, relinquishment is indeed sacrificing. In whatever effort there is a relationship of bodily, mental, vocal, or material relinquishment, they all become a sacrifice. One ought to understand that without the relationship of relinquishment, there is no success of any sacrifice. Accordingly, for one who is a non-relinquisher, a non-sacrificer, when happiness is impossible for him in this world, then how can one even hope that there will be happiness in the other world?

एवं बहुविधा यज्ञा वितता ब्रह्मणो मुखे |
कर्मजान्विद्धि तान्सर्वानेवं ज्ञात्वा विमोक्ष्यसे || BG 4.32 ||

एवम् - Thus, ; बहुविधाः - manifold ; यज्ञाः - sacrifices ; वितताः - are spread in ; मुखे - the mouth (words) of ; ब्रह्मणः - the Brahman (the Vedas). ; विद्धि - Know that ; सर्वान् - all of ; तान् - them ; कर्मजान् - are born of action (that is, produced through the acts of the body, mind and speech). ; ज्ञात्वा - Knowing ; एवम् - so, ; विमोक्ष्यसे - (you) will be liberated (from the bondage of the Saṃsāra).

Thus, manifold sacrifices are spread in the words of the Vedas. Know that all of them are born of action. Knowing so, you will be liberated.

Intent - Those sacrifices described earlier, they and many other kinds of sacrifices are provided in the Vedas. However, the success of those sacrifices happens only through the acts of the body, senses, vital breaths of air, mind, and intellect. That is why all those sacrifices are born of the body and senses. The Ātmā is dissociated from all these activities of sacrifice. Knowing so own Ātmā as dissociated, non-doer, and non-enjoyer, attaining union with oneness in it, you will be free from the bondage of the Saṃsāra. You will be liberated from the cycle of birth and death.

श्रेयान्द्रव्यमयाद्यज्ञाज्ज्ञानयज्ञ: परन्तप |
सर्वं कर्माखिलं पार्थ ज्ञाने परिसमाप्यते || BG 4.33 ||

परन्तप - Hey Parantapa (Arjuna)! ; ज्ञान-यज्ञः - The sacrifice of knowledge ; श्रेयान् - is superior ; यज्ञात् - to the sacrifice ; द्रव्यमयात् - of materials. ; पार्थ - Hey Pārtha (Arjuna)! ; सर्वम् - All ; कर्म - actions ; अखिलम् - entirely ; परिसमाप्यते - end ; ज्ञाने - in knowledge.

Hey Arjuna! The sacrifice of knowledge is superior to the sacrifice of materials. Hey Pārtha! All actions entirely end in knowledge.

Intent - Whatever sacrifices are produced through materials; all are born of Karma. The fruit of all those sacrifices is not liberation but making one endowed with the means to become fit for knowledge. That is the fruit of all material sacrifices. Compared to material sacrifices, the sacrifice of knowledge is superior because it is the only real cause for liberation. Without knowledge, material sacrifice alone cannot assist in attaining liberation. Accordingly, all Karma, after making one fit for knowledge, become free from their fruits.

(Now Bhagavāna describes the means to acquire knowledge -)

तद्विद्धि प्रणिपातेन परिप्रश्नेन सेवया |
उपदेक्ष्यन्ति ते ज्ञानं ज्ञानिनस्तत्त्वदर्शिन: || BG 4:34 ||

विद्धि - Know ; तत् - That (knowledge by approaching preceptors), ; प्रणिपातेन - with prostration, ; सेवया - (their) service, ; परिप्रश्नेन - (and) exhaustive questioning. ; ते - (Then) they, ; ज्ञानिनः - the wise ; तत्त्व-दर्शिनः - knowers of the Truth, ; उपदेक्ष्यन्ति - will impart ; ज्ञानम् - knowledge (to you).

Know That, with prostration, service, and exhaustive questioning. They, the wise knowers of the Truth, will impart knowledge to you.

Intent - First, acquiring the fourfold means (Sādhana-Catuṣṭaya), one ought to take refuge in a preceptor. Second, with a long prostration (Daṇḍavat Praṇāma) and without guile, serve him and acquire his grace. Third, with a sentiment of deep desire to learn and an unargumentative intellect, repeatedly question him, "Bhagavāna! How did Jīva get into the bondage of the grievous Saṃsāra? How can he be free?" Melting with your respectful conduct, the wise knower of the Truth will give you spiritual guidance of knowledge. Your effort will not be fruitful through a teacher who just knows the scriptures, but only a wise knower who has realized the Truth can assist you to attain knowledge of the Truth.

(Now, in the following four verses, the fruit of that knowledge is provided -)

यज्ज्ञात्वा न पुनर्मोहमेवं यास्यसि पाण्डव |
येन भूतान्यशेषेण द्रक्ष्यस्यात्मन्यथो मयि || BG 4.35 ||

पाण्डव - Hey Pāṇḍava (Arjuna)! ; ज्ञात्वा - Knowing ; यत् - That (knowledge, you will) ; न - not ; यास्यसि - acquire ; मोहम् - delusion ; पुनः- again (that these relatives are mortal and I am the one to kill them), ; एवम् - (and) thus ; येन - by which (knowledge you will) ; अशेषेण - completely ; द्रक्ष्यस्यि - see ; भूतानि - all beings ; आत्मनि - in your Self ; अथो - and thus ; मयि - in Me (in oneness).

Hey Arjuna! Knowing That, you will not acquire delusion again, and by which you will completely see all beings in your Self and thus in Me.

Intent - Hey, Arjuna! When you situate in the sacrifice of knowledge, you will not be deluded that "I will be the slayer of Bhīṣma and Droṇa, or Bhīṣma and Droṇa are slayable and so on." However, with the influence of that knowledge, you will see the entire humanity, all living beings, in your Ātmā as your miraculous waves. With the creation and destruction of those waves in the ocean of your Ātmā, there is no increase or decrease, and you will know the oneness of your Ātmā and Me, the Paramātmā.

अपि चेदसि पापेभ्यः सर्वेभ्यः पापकृत्तमः |
सर्वं ज्ञानप्लवेनैव वृजिनं सन्तरिष्यसि ||BG 4.36 ||

अपि - Even ; चेत् - if ; असि - you are ; पापकृत्तमः - the most sinful of ; सर्वेभ्यः - all ; पापेभ्यः - sinners, ; सन्तरिष्यसि एव - you will undoubtedly cross over ; सर्वं - the entire ; वृजिनं - ocean of sin. ज्ञानप्लवेन - with the boat of knowledge.

Even if you are the most sinful of all sinners, you will undoubtedly cross over the entire ocean of sin with the boat of knowledge.

Intent - Just as a person on a boat happily crosses over the entire ocean without touching the water, freed from the delusional superimposition of the body on the Ātmā, through the realization of the Reality, that person situated in his own all-witness Ātmā embarking on the boat of knowledge "I am not a doer-enjoyer of the duties and actions of the body, but always the witness-observer of their activities," crosses over the entire ocean of sins easily. Just as the space sitting in a dirty pond does not become dirty or the space sitting in an ocean does not become saline, in the same way, the Ātmā dissociated from the body's activities is always pure, in which this Yogī has found oneness.

यथैधांसि समिद्धोऽग्निर्भस्मसात्कुरुतेऽर्जुन |
ज्ञानाग्निः सर्वकर्माणि भस्मसात्कुरुते तथा || BG 4.37 ||

अर्जुन - Hey Arjuna! ; यथा - Just as ; समिद्धः - a blazing ; अग्निः - fire ; कुरुते - turns ; एधांसि - firewood ; भस्मसात् - into ashes, ; तथा - similarly, ; ज्ञानाग्निः - the fire of knowledge ; कुरुते - reduces ; सर्वकर्माणि - all actions ; भस्मसात् - into ashes.

Hey Arjuna! Just as a blazing fire turns firewood into ashes, similarly, the fire of knowledge reduces all actions into ashes.

Intent - All actions and impressions (Saṃskāras) remain in support of the "I am a doer" sense, and all seeds of activities blossom in this delusional egotistic earth. This Yogī burns that delusional I-ness sense by the fire of knowledge, and he finds union in his Ātmā with oneness. Without the supporting earth, all his accumulated past action seeds become seedless, and his current actions do not remain any cause.

(That is why -)

न हि ज्ञानेन सदृशं पवित्रमिह विद्यते |
तत्स्वयं योगसंसिद्धः कालेनात्मनि विन्दति || BG 4.38 ||

हि - Unquestionably ; न - nothing ; विद्यते - exists ; इह - here (in this world) ; पवित्रम् - as purifying ; सदृशं - as ; ज्ञानेन - knowledge (that makes a doer-enjoyer Jīva the all-witness), ; तत् - which (knowledge) ; कालेन - in due time, ; योगसंसिद्धः - upon attaining perfection in Yoga, ; विन्दति - (the Yogī) experiences ; स्वयम् - in (his) own, ; आत्मनि - heart.

Unquestionably nothing exists here as purifying as knowledge, which in due time, upon attaining perfection in Yoga, the Yogī experiences in his own heart.

Intent - For instance, even if gold is washed in an ocean or various kinds of soaps are used on it, nothing can remove impurities from the gold. If that gold is heated in the fire, it can be made pure, and its actual value can be fetched. However, a Jīva (doer of sin and piety, the enjoyer of happiness and pain, and holder of birth and death) can't be made pure through Karma, charity, sacrifice, austerity, or other worldly means even over many, many lives. Only the fire of knowledge can instantaneously incinerate his roots of doership and enjoyership, sin and piety, birth and death, and turn insignificant into the Supreme Lord, eternally sinless, eternally blissful, unborn, imperishably pure. That is why there is nothing like knowledge in this world.

(Having described the glory of knowledge and fruits, now Bhagavāna describes who is fit for the knowledge -)

श्रद्धावान् लभते ज्ञानं तत्परः संयतेन्द्रियः |
ज्ञानं लब्ध्वा परां शान्तिमचिरेणाधिगच्छति || BG 4:39 ||

श्रद्धावान् - One with steady faith, ; तत्परः - ready with means, ; संयत-इन्द्रियः - (and) who has restrained the senses ; लभते - acquires ; ज्ञानम् - knowledge. ; लब्ध्वा - (Then) having acquired ; ज्ञानम् - knowledge ; अधिगच्छति - attains ; पराम् - supreme ; शान्तिम् - peace ; अचिरेण - immediately.

One with steady faith, ready with means, and who has restrained the senses acquires knowledge. Having acquired knowledge attains supreme peace immediately.

Intent - Having immovable trust in the words of preceptors and scriptures is called "Śraddhā, faith." To be ready with means for knowledge is called "Tatparatā, readiness." Just as a person mounted on a horse, the moving of senses on its own is called "Jitendriyatā, subduedness of the senses." Only a seeker of liberation attains knowledge in whose conscience all these three are together. Even the absence of any one of the three makes the attainment of knowledge difficult, just as it is impossible to make a "Mahā-Prasāda" without any one of the ingredients flour, Ghī, or sugar. Acquiring that knowledge, he immediately attains supreme peace in his true nature, the Paramānanda, the supreme-bliss, just as a person on waking becomes free from his painful dream and attains himself.

अज्ञश्चाश्रद्दधानश्च संशयात्मा विनश्यति |
नायं लोकोऽस्ति न परो न सुखं संशयात्मनः || BG 4.40 ||

अज्ञः - The ignorant, ; च - and ; अश्रद्दधानः - the devoid of faith, ; च - and ; संशय-आत्मा - the skeptical self ; विनश्यति - perish (from the path of the highest good). ; अस्ति - There is ; न - neither ; अयं - this ; लोकः - world ; न - nor ; परः - the next world ; न - or ; सुखं - happiness ; संशयात्मनः - for the skeptical self.

The ignorant, the devoid of faith, and the skeptical perish. There is neither this world nor the next world or happiness for the skeptical.

Intent - Though the good of an ignorant and one without faith is difficult, their good can happen. However, the good of a skeptical person is impossible, and know him fallen from both worlds.

(At the beginning of the chapter, the Yoga that was described, Bhagavāna, concludes the chapter with the same -)

योगसंन्यस्तकर्माणं ज्ञानसञ्छिन्नसंशयम् |
आत्मवन्तं न कर्माणि निबध्नन्ति धनञ्जय || BG 4.41 ||

धनञ्जय - Hey Dhanañjaya (Arjuna)! ; कर्माणि - Actions ; न - do not ; निबध्नन्ति - bind ; योग-संन्यस्तकर्माणं - the one who has renounced all actions by Yoga, ; ज्ञानसञ्छिन्नसंशयम् - whose (all doership and enjoyership) doubts have been destroyed by knowledge, ; आत्मवन्तं - (and) who is situated in the Self.

Hey Arjuna! Actions do not bind the one who has renounced all actions by Yoga, whose doubts have been destroyed by knowledge, and who is situated in the Self.

Intent - One who has attained union with oneness in his Ātmā and has forsaken all actions, such a person because of his detachment, even while doing everything through the body, he is not doing anything. With the knowledge of the oneness of own Ātmā and the Paramātmā, one who has destroyed all doubts of doership and enjoyership, for such a knower of the Ātmā all accumulated past and current good and bad Karma cannot put him in bondage.

तस्मादज्ञानसम्भूतं हृत्स्थं ज्ञानासिनात्मन: |
छित्त्वैनं संशयं योगमातिष्ठोत्तिष्ठ भारत || BG 4.42 ||

भारत - Hey Bhārata (Arjuna)! ; तस्मात् - Therefore, ; आत्मन: - with own ; ज्ञान-असिना - sword of knowledge, ; छित्त्वा - cutting asunder ; एनम् - this ; अज्ञान-सम्भूतम् - born of ignorance ; संशयम् - doubt (that I am a slayer and they are going to be slain) ; हृत्स्थम् - (that is) sitting in the heart, ; आतिष्ठ - situate in ; योगम् - Yoga, (and) ; उत्तिष्ठ - stand up (to fight).

Hey Arjuna! Therefore, with own sword of knowledge, cutting asunder this born of ignorance doubt that is sitting in the heart, situate in Yoga, and stand up to fight.

Intent - Hey, Arjuna! The doubt in your heart, "I, Arjuna, am a performer of an act of slaying, and Bhīṣma and others are mutations of death-form mutations," is only born of ignorance. Cut this doubt with your sword of knowledge and understand that there is no separation of the Ātmā from the Paramātmā. Only due to ignorance, with delusional I-ness sense in the body, senses, mind, and intellect, is there imagination of separation. In reality, there is no separation. There is always oneness. Like with an adjunct of a pot, the separateness of pot-enclosed space and the pervasive space is imagined. But in reality, the pot by its relationship cannot confine the space, and with the creation or destruction of the pots, there is no creation or destruction of the space. You have this delusion that "I am a slayer, and they are the ones who will be slain" due to ignorance in imagining the actions of the body in your Ātmā. With the birth or death of the body, the Ātmā does not take birth or die, and there cannot be any separation from the pervasive conscious element (Cetana), the Paramātmā. Therefore, situating in Yoga through knowledge stand up to fight.

ॐ तत्सदिति श्रीमद्भगवद्गीतासूपनिषत्सु ब्रह्मविद्यायां योगशास्त्रे

श्रीकृष्णार्जुनसम्वादे ज्ञानकर्मसंन्यासयोगो नाम

चतुर्थोऽध्याय: || BG 4 ||

Oṃ Tat Sat

In the Śrīmad Bhagavad Gītā Upaniṣad

The Yoga Science of the Knowledge of Self-Realization

The Discourse of Lord Śrī Kṛṣṇa and Arjuna

This Fourth Chapter

Yoga Named - The Jñāna Karma Saṃnyāsa Yoga

Clarification

At the beginning of the fourth chapter, Bhagavāna described Tātvika-Yoga, the Yoga of situating with oneness in own Ātmā, which is formulated in the second and third chapters, and that Yoga is described as immutable. There is never any separation of Jīva from the Paramātmā, and indeed, there will never be. However, in the middle, due to ignorance (Ajñāna), there is an imagination of delusional separation (Mithyā-Viyoga). Through knowledge, when this ignorance is burnt, it is realized that naturally, the union is always attained and infinite without beginning (Anādi-Ananta). For instance, when an ocean wave having ego of its external shapes such as height or weight forgets its inner nature of water and clashing with similar waves becomes distressed by the beating, it becomes eager for oneness with water. When, through some means, it acquires an internal perspective, that inside out everywhere it is only water, and removes its I-ness in the waveform, then it will experience that its separation from the water was never possible because all waves are nothing but miracles of water, then where is the beating? All this was the play of water. Accordingly, describing this Yoga as immutable, its succession was shown. At the beginning of the creation, having first manifested through Bhagavāna, it was articulated how it was passed on through successive generations. Bhagavāna said that over a period, this Yoga disappeared. However, I will tell you about this Yoga (BG 4.1 - BG 4.3).

On this, Arjuna expressed his doubt, "Your birth is later; the birth of Vivasvān (sun-deity) was prior. How do I know that you imparted this Yoga in the beginning?" In response, Bhagavāna said that there had been many births of yours and Mine, you do not know them, but I know them all. Unlike all living beings, My birth does not happen to enjoy happiness and grief, the fruits of acts of piety and sin. However, unborn and immutable as I am, whenever there is a decline in righteousness, I incarnate for the establishment of righteousness, subordinating Prakṛti (BG 4.4 - BG 4.8). However, appearing as if I am being born, I am unborn, appearing as engaging in Karma, I am a non-doer. One who truly knows My form as such, they also become free. Many fit and endowed with the fourfold means (Sādhana-Catuṣṭaya) have become free with the influence of this knowledge. Those with desire and those who are desireless, with whatever sentiment they worship me, the fruition of their sentiments happen in My presence. Additionally, all other activities and arrangements of the functional classification system of the society according to the distinctions of the constituents and actions have been successful through Me, yet none of those actions taint Me. Karma does not bind those who truly know My divine births and Karma; knowing so, many seekers of liberation in the past had engaged themselves in Karma (BG 4.9 - BG 4.15).

In addition, Bhagavāna commanded that the movement of Karma is very profound, and even the wise get deluded on the subject - What is an action? What is a non-action? The nature of action and non-action was articulated this way. Through the realization of the Reality (Tattva-Sākṣātkāra) attaining union with oneness in their own Ātmā, those who are free from I-ness sense in the body, mind, and senses and who perform natural activities through them are free from doership-ego. Even while engaged in activities, they are non-doers. However, those who, without removing ego in the body, mind, and senses, have renounced only bodily activities, even while not doing anything they, come into the bondage of Karma (BG 4.16 - BG 4.18).

After that, Bhagavāna described the nature of those Yogīs who, while doing everything, are still non-doers, who have burnt all actions in the "fire of knowledge," who see non-action in action (Akarma-Darśī), and those unattached persons whose every effort has become like sacrifice (BG 4.19 - BG 4.23). Then, Bhagavāna formulated various natural sacrificial efforts of those Yogīs who partake in the leftover ambrosia of the blissful Brahman. In the end, amongst all material sacrifices, the superiority of the sacrifice of knowledge is described, upon whose fruition all Karma become successful. Then, the means for the success of that sacrifice of knowledge is described, and its fruit is discussed, by whose influence the most sinful can effortlessly cross over the ocean of sin. All of their Karma is incinerated with the fire of knowledge, just as how fire burns firewood (BG 4.24 - BG 4.32). After that, the attributes of persons fit for this knowledge and those who are not fit for this knowledge are provided (BG 4.33 - BG 4.40). Additionally, Bhagavāna said that a person who has attained union in the Ātmā, who has renounced all Karma, who sees Akarma (non-action) in Karma (action) and all his separation and doubts are removed by knowledge, for such a Yogī situated in the Ātmā, Karma does not bind (BG 4.41 - BG 4.42).

Describing the same "Yoga of situating with oneness in own Ātmā" in which even while doing everything, "doing nothing" remains, Bhagavāna ended the chapter. In the third chapter, in verse BG 3.30, it was articulated that "With the mind in transcendent knowledge that 'I am neither a doer nor an enjoyer,' completely renouncing your entire actions in My Paramātmā-form, being one without any desire, without any mineness, and without any affliction, fight." That same Yoga is affirmed in this chapter. Listening to the glory of sometimes action (BG 4.12 - BG 4.17) and sometimes knowledge (BG 4.18 - BG 4.39), Arjuna becomes confused and, at the beginning of the fourth chapter, expresses his doubt that sometimes You are praising renouncing action (Karma-Saṃnyāsa) (BG 4.41) and then sometimes Yoga (BG 4.42), that is why, among the two that which is beneficial, only that you tell me. In reality, there was never any intention of Bhagavāna to show any distinction between the two, but only the oneness in relinquishment of actions (Sāṅkhya) and Yoga was His main aim. Holding the "I am a doer I-ness" sense and abandoning action is not a real Karma-Saṃnyāsa, but it is only a delusional Karma-Saṃnyāsa. It is like keeping watering the roots of a plant but at the same time breaking its leaves.

A true Karma-Saṃnyāsa is one where actions are made without fruits (Niṣphala) through knowledge attaining union with oneness in the Ātmā and uprooting the root doership-ego. Maintaining doership-intellect, only sentimental relinquishment of fruits (Phala-Tyāga), "I do not desire fruits of action" is not a real Karma-Yoga based on the view of the Lord, but is only a delusional Yoga. By maintaining doership and duty, even if there is a sentiment of fruit-relinquishment, just as is arranged by the rules of the Lord, its fruit is definite. The doer has to become an enjoyer. There is a fruit of relinquishment of fruit, which is though great. If only with the lack of sentiments of relinquishing fruits, actions are without fruit (Phala-Śūnya), then even sinners do not have any sentiments of experiencing sorrowful fruits. Indeed no one desires to suffer grief, so just by a mere desire not to have fruits, all of them should not suffer grief. In the existence of doership and duty, relinquishing the desire for fruits does not give freedom from the enjoyment of the fruits. Even if the fruit is the acquisition of birth in excellent families, fruit is still there. That is why from Bhagavāna's view, it is not a real Yoga. However, the true Yoga of desireless actions (Niṣkāma Karma-Yoga) is one where through knowledge, attaining union in own Ātmā, the root of doership-intellect is burnt. Then imagined actions can make the Yoga of desireless actions successful.

This way, by the Yoga of situating with oneness in the Ātmā, the main aim of Bhagavāna is to maintain unity between Karma-Saṃnyāsa and Karma-Yoga. Not grasping this purpose of Bhagavāna once again, Arjuna questions -

Chapter 5

The Yoga of Renunciation

अर्जुन उवाच |
संन्यासं कर्मणां कृष्ण पुनर्योगं च शंससि |
यच्छ्रेय एतयोरेकं तन्मे ब्रूहि सुनिश्चितम् || BG 5.1 ||
अर्जुन उवाच - Arjuna said -

कृष्ण - Hey (Śrī) Kṛṣṇa! (You) ; शंससि - praise ; संन्यासम् - renunciation ; कर्मणाम् - of action ; च - and ; पुनः - again ; योगम् - (Karma) Yoga. ; एतयोः - Of the two, ; ब्रूहि - tell ; मे - me ; सुनिश्चितम् - decisively ; तत् - that ; एकम् - one ; यत् - which is ; श्रेयः - more beneficial.

Arjuna said -

Hey Śrī Kṛṣṇa! You praise renunciation of action, and again, (Karma) Yoga. Of the two, tell me decisively the more beneficial one.

Intent - Not understanding the oneness between renunciation and Yoga, and understanding renunciation of actions (Karma-Saṃnyāsa) and performance of actions (Karma-Yoga) separate like darkness and illumination, Arjuna is asking Bhagavāna - "Hey Bhagavāna! 'All actions entirely end in knowledge,' 'the fire of knowledge (Jñānāgni) reduces all actions into ashes,' 'nothing exists here as purifying as knowledge' (BG 4.33 - BG 4.38) and 'who has renounced all actions by Yoga' (BG 4.41) and other such words where You praise knowledge in the form of renunciation of actions and then at other times 'situate in Yoga, stand up to fight' (BG 4.42) You are praising 'Yoga.' That is why please tell me decisively the more beneficial one among the two."

"Arjuna. You are confused. Up till now, you have not understood My intention" - Bhagavāna did not think it appropriate to use such exacting words, and indeed, it is not relevant to use such words that would hurt the feelings of a pupil.

(Keeping the main intention in the forefront and accepting Arjuna's discriminating vision and following his understanding, Bhagavāna says -

श्रीभगवानुवाच |
संन्यासः कर्मयोगश्च निःश्रेयसकरावुभौ |
तयोस्तु कर्मसंन्यासात्कर्मयोगो विशिष्यते || BG 5.2 ||
श्रीभगवान् उवाच - Śrī Bhagavān said -

संन्यासः - Renunciation (of actions) ; च - and ; कर्म-योगः - Karma-Yoga, ; उभौ - both ; निःश्रेयसकरौ - are beneficial. ; तु - However, ; तयोः - of the two, ; कर्म-योगः - Karma-Yoga ; विशिष्यते - has importance ; कर्म-संन्यासात् - over renunciation of actions.

Śrī Bhagavān said -

Renunciation of actions and Karma-Yoga, both are beneficial. However, of the two, Karma-Yoga has importance over renunciation.

Intent - In the first part of the verse, Bhagavāna keeping his aim in the forefront, declared both of them beneficial because, in reality, both are only one. In the second part of the verse, keeping in mind the discriminating vision of Arjuna, who sees a difference between the two, provided importance to Karma-Yoga to make the means more assertive. If, as a means, Karma-Yoga is deemed superior to renunciation of actions (Karma-Saṃnyāsa), then with some thinking, it is evident that such a perspective cannot be proven. Because Karma-Yoga can only be superior to renunciation if renunciation and Karma-Yoga are separate paths or independent. It is not so. From the perspective of central scriptural tenets, there is no distinction between the two. There is only oneness (Abheda), just as was provided in the fourth chapter, and is clarified in this chapter verses (BG 5.4 - BG 5.5). Both are not independent of the superimposition of the unreal on the real (Adhyāropa). When through Yoga of desireless actions (Niṣkāma Karma-Yoga) one can ascend to renunciation of actions (Sāṅkhya, Karma-Saṃnyāsa), how can means be superior to the end? Even if both are deemed mutually indifferent and independent, desireless actions cannot provide liberation independently. How can Karma-Yoga be considered superior? Accordingly, “Karma-Yoga being easier as a means is superior to renunciation of actions” is inconsistent with experience. However, based on fitness, there is the importance of Karma-Yoga. For those not inclined toward renunciation, desireless actions are important, just as a patient with fever is only fit to eat dry food and not Ghī, which would be difficult to digest.

(Now, Bhagavāna glorifies Karma-Yoga from discriminating-vision between renunciation and Yoga.)

ज्ञेय: स नित्यसंन्यासी यो न द्वेष्टि न काङ्क्षति |
निर्द्वन्द्वो हि महाबाहो सुखं बन्धात्प्रमुच्यते || BG 5.3 ||

महाबाहो - Hey Mahābāho (Arjuna)! ; सः - He ; यः - who ; न - neither ; द्वेष्टि - hates (anyone) ; न - nor ; काङ्क्षति - desires (anything) ; ज्ञेयः - should be known ; नित्य-संन्यासी - as a perpetual renouncer. ; हि - For, ; निर्द्वन्द्वः - free from dualities (such as hate-love), ; सुखम् - (he is) easily ; प्रमुच्यते - liberated ; बन्धात् - from bondage (of the world).

Hey Arjuna! He who neither hates nor desires should be known as a perpetual renouncer. For, free from dualities, he is easily liberated from bondage.

Intent - The root of all bondages is the ego of doership and enjoyership. All other bondages such as birth and death are its branches only. A person who does not hate unfavorable objects nor desires favorable objects easily frees himself from those bondages of doership and enjoyership. It is only hate and desire that makes those bondages of doership and others firm; with their absence, they all become loose. Accordingly, when a person, free from dualities such as hate and desire, engages in action, he can easily acquire knowledge because hate and desire are detrimental to knowledge acquisition. As there is a sentiment of relinquishing fruits in desireless actions, neither hate nor desire is present. That does not mean that by independent desireless actions, bondage is broken. However, bondage becomes loose by engaging in actions without hate and desire. Through knowledge, one can easily become free from bondage; that is the only intention here. The sentence “He who neither hates nor desires should be known as a perpetual renouncer (Nitya-Saṃnyāsī)” does not mean that he is the directly expressed meaning (वाच्यार्थ, Vācyārtha) of the term Nitya-Saṃnyāsī and the term Nitya-Saṃnyāsī is used for him. However, whatever relinquishment of hate or desire he has done, the intention is only in the glory of that much relinquishment. For instance, recognizing in part the glory of the bravery of Devadatta (देवदत्त), it is said, "Devadatta is a lion," there, the directly expressed meaning of the term lion is used for Devadatta. It should be noted that the term Saṃnyāsa (renunciation) is not used in Gītā in the sense of the fourth stage of life (चतुर्थाश्रम, Caturthāśrama or Saṃnyāsa-Āśrama),[93]but, through the realization of the Truth, complete freedom from I-ness sense in the body, senses, mind, and intellect is Saṃnyāsa in the language of Gītā, irrespective of the stage of life it is attained. Many holding Saṃnyāsa as the Caturthāśrama are engaged in refutation and confrontation based on sectarianism, which is a grave error.

(Next, holding the main tenet Bhagavāna provides oneness between Saṃnyāsa and Yoga -)

साङ्ख्ययोगौ पृथग्बाला: प्रवदन्ति न पण्डिता: |
एकमप्यास्थित: सम्यगुभयोर्विन्दते फलम् || BG 5.4 ||

बाला: - Unwise persons ; प्रवदन्ति - call ; साङ्ख्य-योगौ - Sāṅkhya and Yoga ; पृथक् - individually separate, ; न - not ; पण्डिता: - persons of discrimination. ; सम्यक् - (One who is) appropriately ; आस्थित: - situated ; अपि - even ; एकम् - in one ; विन्दते - acquires ; फलम् - the fruit ; उभयो: - of both (in the form of liberation).

Unwise persons call Sāṅkhya and Yoga individually separate, not persons of discrimination. One who is appropriately situated even in one acquires the fruit of both.

Intent - In reality, Sāṅkhya and Yoga are one. There is the only difference in name, not in form. Those who imagine distinction are with the intellect of a child. They do not understand the subtle depth. Those who are knowers of the Truth do not presume any difference between the two. Just as clarified in Chapter 4 - Clarification, holding doership-ego mere relinquishment (Tyāga) of Karma is not Karma-Saṃnyāsa. With the existence of the "ego of relinquishment," that relinquishment has its fruit. Moreover, holding a doership ego, desireless Karma is not Yoga because being a doer of actions, even if there is a sentiment that "I do not desire fruits of my action and I offer them all to the Lord," still has its fruits. When a doer of the deed exists, and the sentiment is alive, then where can fruits go? Impressions of actions (Karma-Saṃskāras) permanently reside in the refuge of a doer and give fruits according to whatever sentiment the deeds are done, which is the Lord's rule. Where neither doership-ego nor sentiments are burnt, how can impressions of actions be made without fruits? Where can fruits go? It is true that with a sentiment of relinquishment of fruits, its fruit has to be excellent, but it cannot be without any fruits.

In contrast, with the burning of doership-ego, even when the body's activities may be ongoing like a machine, activities cannot be the cause of fruits due to the absence of the doer. That is because there is no sentiment in them, nor do they create impressions (Saṃskāras). There is no doer, sentiments, and impressions of Karma. Where are the fruits? And to whom? Even while engaged in Karma, he is a true Karma-Saṃnyāsī and a true Karma-Yogī. Accordingly, through the Yoga of establishing in the Ātmā with oneness and the burning of doership-ego, both Karma-Saṃnyāsa and Karma-Yoga are attained. Neither can be attained without it. There is congruity and oneness between both reaching this stage. One, who truly knows so, is called a Paṇḍita. Free from doership-ego, one who is fully situated in either Yoga (Pravṛtti, activity) or Sāṅkhya (Nivrutti, renunciation) attains the fruit of liberation. It should be noted that here Sāṅkhya and Saṃnyāsa denote the same meaning. Even though the question was raised regarding Saṃnyāsa and Yoga, the response was provided with the words Sāṅkhya and Yoga.

In contrast, those who have held Yoga and Sāṅkhya as means and end (Sādhana-Sādhya) or through tradition with the oneness of fruits have grasped both as one, are with an intellect of a child. Only the mutual

---

[93] Saṃnyāsa-Āśrama (संन्यास-आश्रम) means the last stage of life marked by renunciation of material desires and prejudices, represented by a state of disinterest and detachment from material life, generally without any meaningful property or home, and focused on liberation, peace and simple spiritual life. Anyone could enter this stage after completing the Brahmacarya stage of life.

distinction between means and end is seen. How can there be a oneness between cause and fruit? If, by tradition, their oneness is accepted with the oneness of fruits, then sacrifice, charity, and austerity, being traditional means for knowledge, should also be accepted with oneness with Sāṅkhya. Further, those who accept Sāṅkhya and Yoga as mutually indifferent and independent and hold oneness among the two should be known as even more ignorant than those with an intellect of a child. Perform action (Yoga) and relinquish action (Sāṅkhya) are both mutually like being and not-being and have a distinction like a day and night. There cannot be any oneness among them and cannot have one fruit of mutually opposite paths.

यत्साङ्ख्यैः प्राप्यते स्थानं तद्योगैरपि गम्यते |
एकं साङ्ख्यं च योगं च यः पश्यति स पश्यति || BG 5.5 ||

स्थानम् - (The supreme) Status (that is, liberation), ; यत् - which ; प्राप्यते - is acquired ; साङ्ख्यैः - by a Sāṅkhya-Saṃnyāsī, ; तत् - it ; अपि - is also ; गम्यते - reached ; योगैः - by a Karma-Yogī. ; स - (Only) he ; पश्यति - perceives (really) ; यः - who ; पश्यति - perceives ; साङ्ख्यम् - Sāṅkhya ; च - and ; योगम् - Yoga ; एकम् - as one.

The Status, which is acquired by a Sāṅkhya-Saṃnyāsī, is also reached by a Karma-Yogī. Only he perceives who perceives Sāṅkhya and Yoga as one.

Intent - When there is oneness in Sāṅkhya and Yoga, then the supreme Status that is acquired through them is also the same. Because without attaining union with oneness in own Ātmā, Karma-Saṃnyāsa is entirely impossible. Even if the body's efforts are abandoned, mental activities still continue, and they will have their fruits. However, attaining union in the Ātmā, there is always Karma-Saṃnyāsa, even in the presence of unrestrained activities. Moreover, they do not have any fruits because now he does not see anything happening in his Ātmā, similar to how a person awake from a dream does not know any taint in him from the activities of the dream. Additionally, without a union in the Ātmā, even relinquishment of fruits is impossible. As is clarified earlier, with doer-sense remaining, fruit is definite. However, attaining Tātvika-Yoga, both relinquishments of actions and fruits materialize. Accordingly, one who sees both in their true nature as one sees it indeed.

संन्यासस्तु महाबाहो दुःखमाप्तुमयोगतः |
योगयुक्तो मुनिर्ब्रह्म नचिरेणाधिगच्छति || BG 5.6 ||

महाबाहो - Hey Mahābāho (Arjuna)! ; संन्यासः - Renunciation ; दुःखम् - is hard ; आप्तुम् - to achieve ; अयोगतः - without establishing in the Self. ; तु - However, ; मुनिः - a sage ; योग-युक्तः - who is established in Yoga ; नचिरेण - immediately ; अधिगच्छति - attains ; ब्रह्म - the Brahman.

Hey Arjuna! Renunciation is hard to achieve without establishing in the Self. However, a sage who is established in Yoga immediately attains the Brahman.

Intent - As clarified earlier, it is difficult to renounce actions (Karma-Saṃnyāsa) without establishing oneself in the Ātmā with oneness. Without Tātvika-Yoga, because of the presence of the doer, even relinquishment of actions (Karma-Tyāga) has its fruit, and so it cannot truly achieve Karma-Saṃnyāsa. However, a sage who is established (has found union with oneness) in his own Ātmā, without any delay, attains the Brahman. If the term Yoga is interpreted as the Yoga of desireless actions (Niṣkāma Karma-Yoga) and distinct from Sāṅkhya (Saṃnyāsa, renunciation), that is, "क्रम-समुच्चय, Krama-Samuccaya"[94]is deemed, then there is no real congruity with the above words of Bhagavāna. Because, in the first place, a desireless action Yogī is not a contemplative (मननशील, Mananaśīla) sage. He is a doer (कर्मी, Karmī) with a discriminating-vision of a doer and duty-bound intellect. Second, as this verse says, a desireless action Yogī cannot attain the Brahman

[94] Krama-Samuccaya (क्रम-समुच्चय) is a view that first with desireless-actions (Niṣkāma-Karma), purity of the conscience (Antaḥkaraṇa) is achieved, and thereafter with knowledge liberation can be attained.

immediately without any delay. Because of his discriminating vision between Sāṅkhya (Saṃnyāsa) and Yoga, he has to ascend in Sāṅkhya through Yoga, and then through Sāṅkhya he has to attain the Brahman.

Further, deeming Yoga as an independent path, that is, accepting "सम-समुच्चय, Sama-Samuccaya,"[95]he cannot attain the Brahman immediately as described in this verse because he still maintains a discriminating-vision of doer and duty. Then, where is the immediate attainment of the Brahman? Immediate attainment of the Brahman is procured only by the one who realizes the supreme imperishable Reality, cuts doership and duty bondages of Prakṛti, and becomes Jīvanmukta while alive. Just as a person awake from a bad dream acquires his true nature, a sage established in the Ātmā (Yoga-Yukta) upon awakening of knowledge, without delay, attains Brahman. Thus, it is clear that the meaning of the word Yoga is the Yoga of the highest objective of attaining union with oneness in the Brahman and that such Yoga has oneness with Saṃnyāsa. The oneness between Sāṅkhya (Saṃnyāsa) and Yoga is articulated in the three verses above. **From here on, in all the remaining chapters, the oneness of the two is expressed with the word Yoga by Bhagavāna.**

योगयुक्तो विशुद्धात्मा विजितात्मा जितेन्द्रियः |
सर्वभूतात्मभूतात्मा कुर्वन्नपि न लिप्यते || BG 5.7 ||

योगयुक्तः - Established in the Self, ; विशुद्धात्मा - one whose conscience is purified, ; विजितात्मा जितेन्द्रियः - whose mind and senses are properly controlled, (and) ; सर्वभूतात्म-भूतात्मा - whose Self has become the Self of all beings, (such a knower of the Truth,) ; अपि - even ; कुर्वन् - acting ; न - is not ; लिप्यते - tainted.

Established in the Self, one whose conscience is purified, whose mind and senses are properly controlled, and whose Self has become the Self of all beings, even acting is not tainted.

Intent - Because a desireless action Yogī is with duty-bound intellect, he cannot be said to be free from the delusional superimposition of the body on the Ātmā (देहाध्यास, Dehādhyāsa). In such a state, he cannot directly experience the Ātmā of all living beings as his Ātmā, and because of his doership-ego, he cannot remain untainted while engaging in Karma. That is why one who is free from I-ness in the body and is established in his Ātmā with oneness is the real meaning of the term Yoga-Yukta and only in him do all these words come true.

(Engaging in Karma, with what knowledge and sentiments do such a person remain untainted? -)

नैव किञ्चित्करोमीति युक्तो मन्येत तत्त्ववित् |
पश्यञ्शृण्वन्स्पृशञ्जिघ्रन्नश्नन्गच्छन्स्वपञ्श्वसन् || BG 5.8 ||
प्रलपन्विसृजन्गृह्णन्नुन्मिषन्निमिषन्नपि |
इन्द्रियाणीन्द्रियार्थेषु वर्तन्त इति धारयन् || BG 5.9 ||

तत्त्ववित् - A knower of the Truth ; युक्तः - established in the Self ; अपि - even (while) ; पश्यन् - seeing, ; शृण्वन् - hearing, ; स्पृशन् - touching, ; जिघ्रन् - smelling, ; अश्नन् - eating, ; गच्छन् - walking, ; स्वपन् - sleeping, ; श्वसन् - breathing, ; प्रलपन् - talking, ; विसृजन् - giving up, ; गृह्णन् - accepting, ; उन्मिषन् - opening (eyes), ; निमिषन् - (and) closing (eyes), ; धारयन् - holds (the view) ; इति - that ; इन्द्रियाणि - senses ; वर्तन्ते - are operating ; इन्द्रियार्थेषु - in their objects ; इति - (and) thus ; मन्येत् - believes ; न - "(I am) not ; एव - even ; करोमि - doing ; किञ्चित् - anything."

A knower of the Truth established in the Self even while seeing, hearing, touching, smelling, eating, walking, sleeping, breathing, talking, giving up, accepting, opening eyes, and closing eyes, holds the view that senses are operating in their objects and thus believes "I am not even doing anything."

[95] Sama-Samuccaya (सम-समुच्चय) is a view that desireless-actions (Niṣkāma-Karma) and knowledge are two independent and equal strength paths in the attainment of liberation, one not dependent on the other

Intent - "I, the witness-form Ātmā, am not doing anything. I am not the senses, the senses are not mine, and I am not a doer of their activities. However, I am the existent light in whose presence all of their being and not-being activities are successful. None of those activities taint me," holding such direct firmness, a knower of the Truth keeps his senses and their activities dissociated and immutable. Engaging in activities through the sense-organs is not doing anything and is not bound.

ब्रह्मण्याधाय कर्माणि सङ्गं त्यक्त्वा करोति य: |
लिप्यते न स पापेन पद्मपत्रमिवाम्भसा || BG 5.10 ||

त्यक्त्वा - Abandoning ; सङ्गम् - (doership) attachment, ; सः - he ; यः - who ; करोति - performs ; कर्माणि - action ; आधाय - dedicated to ; ब्रह्मणि - the Brahman (in accordance with BG 4.24) ; न - is not ; लिप्यते - tainted ; पापेन - by sin ; इव - as ; पद्मपत्रम् - a lotus leaf (untouched) ; अम्भसा - by water.

Abandoning attachment, he who performs action dedicated to the Brahman is not tainted by sin as a lotus leaf by water.

Intent - A person abandoning attachment to doership performs Karma with the intent of offering to the Brahman is not tainted by sin or piety, like a lotus leaf untouched by water. What is the "offering of Karma to the Brahman (ब्रह्मार्पण, Brahmārpaṇa)"? On this subject, in BG 4.24, it is articulated that through analytic thinking (Tattva-Vicāra) on the sixfold instruments of activities (Ṣaṭ-Kāraka) becoming one (Abheda) with the Brahman, by merging in the Brahman and becoming the Brahman is indeed the true Brahmārpaṇa of Karma. The Brahman is not some personified (मूर्तिमान, Mūrtimāna) thing nor action or any personified substance that it can be offered to some personified deity in the form of fruits or flowers. Yes, there can be a sentimental offering, "I, a performer of Karma, am offering my Karma to the Brahman." However, as is said in the second part of this verse, such a sentimental offering does not keep one untainted from sin or piety, like a lotus leaf. That is because the performer of actions is offering Karma (that is separate from himself) to the Brahman (that is someone separate from himself) and is accumulating sentiments of performed actions and offerings. Then, how can he be without any fruits? Though he cannot be tainted by sin in these fruits, he is tainted by piety. "He is not tainted by sin" should be understood as not tainted by both piety and sin, not just sin.

Accordingly, as long as the doer (Kartā), actions (Karma), and sentiments (Bhāvanā) all three are not burnt in the fire of knowledge, till then, real Brahmārpaṇa of actions is not possible nor like a lotus leaf untaintability of piety or sin is possible. Because in sentimental Brahmārpaṇa, there is the fruit of the sentiments with the presence of doer and sentiments.

कायेन मनसा बुद्ध्या केवलैरिन्द्रियैरपि |
योगिन: कर्म कुर्वन्ति सङ्गं त्यक्त्वात्मशुद्धये || BG 5.11 ||

त्यक्त्वा - Abandoning ; सङ्गम् - (doership) attachment, ; योगिनः - Yogīs ; कुर्वन्ति - engage in ; कर्म - action ; केवलैः - only through ; इन्द्रियैः - the senses, ; मनसा - mind, ; बुद्ध्या - intellect, ; कायेन - (and) body ; अपि - only ; आत्म-शुद्धये - for self-purification.

Abandoning attachment, Yogīs engage in action only through the senses, mind, intellect, and body for only self-purification.

Intent - "Yogīs engage in action only for self-purification (आत्म-शुद्धि, Ātma-Śuddhi)." What is self-purification? With some thought, it is clear that only removal of malicious impressions (Durvāsanā) and replacement with the flow of good impressions in the conscience is not self-purification. However, becoming one without any inner impressions (निर्वासनिक, Nirvāsanika) is indeed real self-purification because impressions (Vāsanā) themselves are born of ignorance and are delusional. With ego, superimposition of the impressions on the self is itself "self-impurity." Thus, removing ego through analytic thinking and seeing own Ātmā dissociated and only one in all beings (Sarvātmā-Dṛṣṭi) can be the only self-purification. Yogīs, established in the Ātmā (Yoga-Yukta), engage in actions only through the body, senses, mind, and intellect; however, the ego does not stay with them. Like a rosary string, the ego-string holding the body-senses beads had separated him from the Ātmā. Through analytic thinking, the ego string is broken, and the body-senses beads disperse all over. Now, the Ātmā is only their observer. That is self-purification, and it is only with this perspective all Yogīs engage in Karma.

युक्तः कर्मफलं त्यक्त्वा शान्तिमाप्नोति नैष्ठिकीम् |
अयुक्तः कामकारेण फले सक्तो निबध्यते || BG 5.12 ||

त्यक्त्वा - Forsaking ; कर्म-फलं - actions and thus fruits, ; आप्नोति - (one) acquires ; नैष्ठिकीम् - steady ; शान्तिम् - peace ; युक्तः - by being established in the Self. ; कामकारेण - Impelled by desires (and) ; सक्तः - attached ; फले - to fruits, ; निबध्यते - (one) is bound ; अयुक्तः - by not being established in the Self.

Forsaking actions and thus fruits, one acquires steady peace by being established in the Self. Impelled by desires and attached to fruits, one is bound by not being established in the Self.

Intent - A transcendent Yogī who has attained union with oneness in the Ātmā (Yoga-Yukta) is a real relinquisher (Yathārtha-Tyāgi) of actions and fruits. One who has incinerated doership and other sentiments is the one who achieves steady peace (नैष्ठिक-शान्ति, Naiṣṭhika-Śānti). Relinquishment of the fruits of action of a desireless seeker is sentimental, and so it is not entirely devoid of fruits. Nevertheless, its fruits are excellent. However, there being a remainder of fruits, he cannot achieve steady peace as said in the above verse. Even though he is not established in the Ātmā, he is on the right path, yet fruits bind him as the sentiment of fruit-relinquishment is present. That is why desireless action performers cannot be called Yukta. They cannot be called "established in the Ātmā." Only a Tātvika-Yogī is called Yukta, one who is free from the association of the body, actions, and fruits, and he is the one who can attain steady peace.

सर्वकर्माणि मनसा संन्यस्यास्ते सुखं वशी |
नवद्वारे पुरे देही नैव कुर्वन्न कारयन् || BG 5.13 ||

मनसा - Mentally ; संन्यस्य - renouncing ; सर्वकर्माणि - all actions (and) ; वशी - with a controlled conscience, ; देही - the embodied ; एव - certainly ; आस्ते - rests ; सुखम् - happily ; नवद्वारे - in the nine-gated ; पुरे - city, ; न - neither ; कुर्वन्न - doing ; न - nor ; कारयन् - causing (others) to do.

Mentally renouncing all actions and with a controlled conscience, the embodied certainly rests happily in the nine-gated city, neither doing nor causing others to do.

Intent - Dehī (देही) means the embodied Ātmā (Self), in which the (Yoga-Yukta) Yogī has become of the same form, mentally forsaking all actions, with a firm resolve, "Sense-organs are engaged in their objects, I, the witness, am not doing anything" is peacefully resting in the nine-gated city (body). He does not do anything by himself nor provides any inspiration to anyone but is only the observer of the activities of the conscience and senses. It is indeed conquering them by becoming dissociated from the conscience and senses and knowing them as without existence (Sva-Sattā-Śūnya).

(Engaged in Karma with whatever sentiment and thought a Yoga-Yukta Yogī remains untainted. It is articulated from verses (BG 5.7 - BG 5.13).

(Next, Bhagavāna shows that in reality, doership and Karma are not created but are only born of ignorance -)

न कर्तृत्वं न कर्माणि लोकस्य सृजति प्रभुः |
न कर्मफलसंयोगं स्वभावस्तु प्रवर्तते || BG 5.14 ||

प्रभुः - The Lord ; सृजति - creates ; न - neither ; कर्तृत्वं - doership ; न - nor ; कर्माणि - actions ; न - nor ; कर्मफलसंयोगं - conjunction of the fruits of action ; लोकस्य - in living beings. ; तु - Instead (by the power of the Lord), ; स्वभावः - (it is only) nature ; प्रवर्तते - that acts (in these activities).

The Lord creates neither doership nor actions nor conjunction of the fruits of action in living beings. Instead, it is only nature that acts.

Intent - "I am a doer, performance of certain Karma is my duty, and there have to be some fruits, or I do not desire fruits" - all these are extensions of discriminating vision and are born of ignorance. They are all born of ignorance. They are only in the kingdom of Prakṛti and indeed the products of nature. Therefore, they have neither been created by the Lord nor do they have any touch on the true nature of the Lord. In addition, only in the light of the Lord, Prakṛti is dancing in all these forms, and she is the one joining and disjoining doership, doer, and thus conjunction of the fruits.

(In reality -)

नादत्ते कस्यचित्पापं न चैव सुकृतं विभु: |
अज्ञानेनावृतं ज्ञानं तेन मुह्यन्ति जन्तव: || BG 5.15 ||

विभु: - The omnipresent Lord ; एव - certainly ; न - (does) not ; आदत्ते - take ; कस्यचित् - anyone's ; पापम् - sin ; न - or ; सुकृतं - piety. ; ज्ञानम् - Knowledge ; आवृतम् - is shrouded ; अज्ञानेन - in ignorance, ; च - and ; तेन - therefore, ; जन्तव: - all living beings ; मुह्यन्ति - are deluded.

The omnipresent Lord certainly does not take anyone's sin or piety. Knowledge is shrouded in ignorance, and therefore, all living beings are deluded.

Intent - The omnipresent Lord, the pure Ātmā, does not take anyone's sin or piety. Sin or piety do not touch the Ātmā. Even though all sin and piety happen in its presence, none of them can taint it. Only due to ignorance when a living being forgets his real omnipresent form and with the shroud of discriminative knowledge believes himself as a limited being and thus doer of Karma and the Lord as the bestower of fruits, then based on the rules of Prakṛti, bounded by piety and sin, comes in the bondage of the enjoyership of fruits of happiness and grief. It is only due to this ignorance that all living beings are deluded.

ज्ञानेन तु तदज्ञानं येषां नाशितमात्मन: |
तेषामादित्यवज्ज्ञानं प्रकाशयति तत्परम् || BG 5.16 ||

तु - However, ; येषाम् - whose ; अज्ञानम् - ignorance ; तत् - of that ; आत्मन: - Self ; नाशितम् - is destroyed ; ज्ञानेन - by knowledge; ; तेषाम् - their ; ज्ञानम् - knowledge ; प्रकाशयति - illuminates ; तत् - that ; परम् - supreme (Brahman) ; आदित्यवत् - like the sun.

Whose ignorance of the Self is destroyed by knowledge; their knowledge illuminates the supreme Brahman like the sun.

Intent - Through discriminative knowledge of the Ātmā, ignorance of the "I am a doer of Karma and thus worldly enjoyer of happiness and grief and the Lord is the enjoyer of my pious and sinful fruits" is destroyed. Their knowledge illuminates their Ātmā, just as in the sun's light, all things appear as they are, and there is no doubt in their nature. Likewise, through discriminative knowledge of the Ātmā, they directly experience their Ātmā "is as is" without any doubt. They transcendentally realize, "I am neither a doer nor an enjoyer, but I am eternal, pure, awake, and free-nature."

(Accordingly, through discriminative knowledge, those persons whose doership and other delusions have been removed and who have found union in own Ātmā, next up till verse BG 5.21, their characteristics, fitness, and rewards are formulated -)

तद्बुद्धयस्तदात्मानस्तन्निष्ठास्तत्परायणा: |
गच्छन्त्यपुनरावृत्तिं ज्ञाननिर्धूतकल्मषा: || BG 5.17 ||

तत्-बुद्धय: - Whose intellect has become That (Brahman) form, ; तत्-आत्मान: - whose mind has become That (Brahman) form, ; तत्-निष्ठा: - whose firm faith is placed in That (Brahman) form, ; तत्-परायणा: - who is oriented towards That

(Brahman) form, ; ज्ञान-निर्धूत-कल्मषाः - (and) whose sins are annihilated by knowledge ; गच्छन्ति - proceed ; अपुनरावृत्तिम् - to that Status from where one does not return.

Whose intellect has become That form, whose mind has become That form, whose firm faith is placed in That form, who is oriented towards That form, and whose sins are annihilated by knowledge proceed to that Status from where one does not return.

Intent - In the verse, what is "That?" It is the supreme imperishable Reality, the Brahman. Only due to the shroud of doership-delusion is there an accumulation of piety and sin in the conscience through I-ness and mineness. When that doership-delusion born of ignorance becomes quiet through knowledge, the mind, intellect, and all of their efforts become Brahman-form. Those with firm faith in the Brahman, whose sins are purged, attain liberation in the form of final exemption from the transmigratory life of birth and death. They achieve a Status from which one does not return (Apunarāvṛtti-Mokṣa) and, while alive, become free from the bondage of the world of birth and death (जीवन्मुक्त, Jīvanmukta). The root of all sins is doership-delusion, from which they have found solid freedom.

विद्याविनयसम्पन्ने ब्राह्मणे गवि हस्तिनि |
शुनि चैव श्वपाके च पण्डिताः समदर्शिनः || BG 5.18 ||

पण्डिताः - Men of discrimination ; सम-दर्शिनः - see equally ; ब्राह्मणे - a Brāhmaṇa ; विद्या-विनय-सम्पन्ने - endowed with knowledge and humility, ; गवि - a cow, ; हस्तिनि - an elephant, ; च - and ; शुनि - a dog, ; च - and ; एव - even ; श्वपाके - an outcast.

Men of discrimination see equally a Brāhmaṇa endowed with knowledge and humility, a cow, an elephant, a dog, and even an outcast.

Intent - There cannot be equanimity of vision by holding trueness in the external name-forms. However, with the maturity of the knowledge of the Truth (Tattva-Jñāna), when external name-forms of a discerning person disappear from vision and reside in the sight of the Asti-Bhāti-Priya Ātmā, then he sees in all name-forms only That one form and all name-forms appear as miracles of That one form. Asti-Bhāti-Priya Ātmā is the reality of everyone and by which all appear as real. A goldsmith's vision is only in the gold of the ornaments, or a knower of water only sees water in waves or eddies. Such a vision is called seeing things equally (Sama-Dṛṣṭi).

Similarly, a discerning person holding an equanimous Brahman vision sees, in all distinct name forms, a Brāhmaṇa, a cow, an elephant, a dog, and even an outcast, the Brahman. All causes of dissimilarities in external name forms disappear from his vision. In the verse, the term Śvapāke (श्वपाके) means an outcast generally referred to as a Cāṇḍāla (चाण्डाल).[96]In contrast, holding trueness in the external name forms those who have maintained equanimity in behavior only; they are deprived of real peace born of equanimity, fall prey to distinctions born of attachment and aversion, and move farther away from the Brahman, the real Truth.

इहैव तैर्जितः सर्गो येषां साम्ये स्थितं मनः |
निर्दोषं हि समं ब्रह्म तस्माद् ब्रह्मणि ते स्थिताः || BG 5.19 ||

एव - Even ; इह - here (in this life), ; सर्गः - the world ; जितः - is won ; तैः - by them, ; येषाम् - whose ; मनः - mind ; स्थितम् - is established ; साम्ये - in equanimity. ; हि - Because ; ब्रह्म - the Brahman ; निर्दोषम् - is faultless ; समम् - (and) equanimous, ; तस्मात् - so ; ते - they ; स्थिताः - are established (with oneness) ; ब्रह्मणि - in the Brahman.

Even here, the world is won by them, whose mind is established in equanimity. Because the Brahman is faultless and equanimous, they are established with oneness in the Brahman.

---

[96] Cāṇḍāla (चाण्डाल) means an outcast, a person of lowest and most despised of mixed functional class born from a Śūdra father and a Brāhmaṇa mother. It is also used to describe dog eaters.

Intent - The material world and the root of all grief is only discriminating-vision. Because of discriminating-vision, living beings are bound in the grief-stricken bondage of the material world due to attachment and aversion (Rāga-Dveṣa). Indeed, that discriminating vision is born of ignorance. The wise have burnt their ignorance with discriminating knowledge. They have abandoned wave-vision and accepted water-vision and now have attained union in the Brahman, which is faultless and equanimous. Therefore, they have conquered the material world while being alive. Through their analytic perspective, they are established with equanimity in the material world of dissimilarities, and none of the distinctions can now touch them.

न प्रहृष्येत्प्रियं प्राप्य नोद्विजेत्प्राप्य चाप्रियम् |
स्थिरबुद्धिरसम्मूढो ब्रह्मविद् ब्रह्मणि स्थित: || BG 5.20 ||

असम्मूढः - An undeluded ; च - and ; स्थिर-बुद्धिः - steady intellect ; ब्रह्मवित् - knower of the Brahman, ; स्थितः - established ; ब्रह्मणि - in the Brahman (with oneness by the influence of knowledge), ; न - neither ; प्रहृष्येत् - rejoices ; प्राप्य - in obtaining ; प्रियम् - (what is) pleasant ; न - nor ; उद्विजेत् - is disturbed ; प्राप्य - obtaining ; अप्रियम् - (what is) unpleasant.

An undeluded and steady intellect knower of the Brahman, established in the Brahman, neither rejoices in obtaining what is pleasant nor is disturbed obtaining unpleasant.

Intent - Pleasantness, and unpleasantness are not in materials (वस्तुगत, Vastugata). A thing that may appear pleasant at one time may become unpleasant at some other time. If pleasantness and unpleasantness were in materials, then the above should not happen. From this, it is clear that pleasantness is only in the favorable inclination of the conscience, and unpleasantness is in the unfavorable inclination of the conscience. Because the relationship with objects creates these inclinations, there is a perception of pleasantness and unpleasantness in objects. However, a steady intellect knower of the Brahman, established with oneness in the Brahman, is dissociated from the conscience and inclinations of the conscience. Hence, he is neither elated nor riled but is just the observer of these pleasant and unpleasant inclinations.

बाह्यस्पर्शेष्वसक्तात्मा विन्दत्यात्मनि यत्सुखम् |
स ब्रह्मयोगयुक्तात्मा सुखमक्षयमश्नुते || BG 5.21 ||

असक्त-आत्मा - Whose conscience is unattached ; बाह्य-स्पर्शेषु - to external contacts (enjoyments born of contact with senses), ; विन्दति - acquires ; यत् - that ; सुखम् - bliss ; आत्मनि - (which is) in the Self. ; सः - He ; ब्रह्म-योग-युक्तात्मा - who is established with oneness in the Brahman ; अश्नुते - enjoys ; अक्षयम् - undecaying ; सुखम् - bliss.

Whose conscience is unattached to external contacts acquires bliss in the Self. He who is established with oneness in the Brahman enjoys undecaying bliss.

Intent - External contacts are external objects with which the senses contact. They are enjoyments born of contact with the senses. A person who is not attached to external objects acquires happiness within the Ātmā through meditation. That person, established in the Brahman through Yoga with oneness, enjoys imperishable happiness. ब्रह्मणि योगेन युक्त आत्मा यस्यासौ, स "ब्रह्मयोगयुक्तात्मा", one whose Ātmā is established with oneness in the Brahman is called "Brahma-Yoga-Yukta-Ātmā."

(Enjoyable things are impediments in this Yoga -)

ये हि संस्पर्शजा भोगा दु:खयोनय एव ते |
आद्यन्तवन्त: कौन्तेय न तेषु रमते बुध: || BG 5.22 ||

कौन्तेय - Hey Kaunteya (Arjuna)! ; ये - Those ; भोगाः - enjoyments ; संस्पर्शजाः - born of contacts (of the senses with objects) ; हि - are definitely ; दुःख-योनयः - the source of sorrow ; एव - (and) indeed ; ते - they ; आदि अन्तवन्तः - have a beginning and an end. ; बुधः - A wise ; न - does not ; रमते - take delight ; तेषु - in them.

Hey Arjuna! Those enjoyments born of contacts are the source of sorrow and have a beginning and an end. A wise does not take delight in them.

Intent - There is no doubt that enjoyments born of the union of objects and senses have a beginning and an end. Those things that are not at the beginning and not in the end are not in the middle. In the middle, just as in a dream, they are only the subject of a delusional perception. Knowing so, a wise person does not delight in them. The mind is trapped in enjoyments only because of the mistake of knowing them true and steady; however, there is not an iota of trueness or steadiness in them. The flow of sorrow oozes out with their relationship only because of this ignorance.

शक्नोतीहैव य: सोढुं प्राक्शरीरविमोक्षणात् |
कामक्रोधोद्भवं वेगं स युक्त: स सुखी नर: || BG 5.23 ||

इह - Here (in this world), ; प्राक् - before ; शरीर-विमोक्षणात् - leaving the body, ; यः - (one) who ; एव - is indeed ; शक्नोति - capable ; सोढुम् - of bearing ; वेगम् - the forces ; काम-क्रोध-उद्भवम् - born of desire and anger, ; सः - that ; नरः - person ; सुखी - is happy, ; सः - (and) he ; युक्तः - is united (in the Self).

Here, before leaving the body, one who is capable of bearing the forces born of desire and anger, that person is happy, and he is united.

Intent - A person who, while alive, is not moved by the forces of desire and anger and remains dissociated from them is the one who has attained union in his own Ātmā. During the existence of the body, one who has conquered his mind in such a way is the one who is fit to attain union in the Ātmā. He is a Yogī, and he is a happy person.

योऽन्त:सुखोऽन्तरारामस्तथान्तर्ज्योतिरेव य: ।
स योगी ब्रह्मनिर्वाणं ब्रह्मभूतोऽधिगच्छति || BG 5.24 ||

यः - (Abandoning attachment to objects, one) who ; अन्तः-सुखः - (has found) inner happiness, ; अन्तः-आरामः - (who) rests within ; तथा - and ; एव - who undoubtedly ; अन्तः-ज्योतिः - illuminates within, ; यः - such ; योगी - a Yogī ; ब्रह्म-भूतः - becoming the Brahman, ; अधिगच्छति - attains ; ब्रह्म-निर्वाणम् - the Nirvāṇa-Brahma.

One who has found inner happiness, who rests within and who undoubtedly illuminates within, such a Yogī becoming the Brahman, attains the Nirvāṇa-Brahma

Intent - A person, without dependence on happiness in external objects, who attains objectless bliss of the Ātmā, like a hungry who becomes satisfied and content upon eating, in the same way, becomes satisfied and content with the bliss of the Ātmā, rests in own Ātmā. Further, with the maturity of knowledge, he is self-illuminated in his own Ātmā. He is established with oneness in the Ātmā. Such a Yogī, free from the superimposition of the body on the Ātmā (Dehādhyāsa) becoming the Brahman attains the bliss of the Brahman, attains Nirvāṇa-Brahma (निर्वाण-ब्रह्म, oneness in the Brahman with liberation from the worldly cycle of birth and death).

(Who is fit for the above State? Bhagavāna explains -)

लभन्ते ब्रह्मनिर्वाणमृषय: क्षीणकल्मषा: |
छिन्नद्वैधा यतात्मान: सर्वभूतहिते रता: || BG 5.25 ||

ऋषयः - Seers, ; क्षीण-कल्मषाः - whose sins have been purged, ; छिन्न-द्वैधाः - whose (duality) doubts have been removed, ; यत-आत्मानः - who have their inner sense controlled, ; रताः - (and) who are engrossed ; सर्व-भूतहिते - in the welfare of all beings, ; लभन्ते - acquire ; ब्रह्म-निर्वाणम् - the Nirvāṇa-Brahma.

Seers, whose sins have been purged, whose doubts have been removed, who have their inner sense controlled, and who are engrossed in the welfare of all beings, acquire the Nirvāṇa-Brahma.

Intent - Success of all these means is only possible through knowledge; there is no place for Karma here. Only through knowledge purging of the remaining sins is possible. Through penance (Prāyaścitta) and other means purging of the sins without remainder is impossible (BG 4.36 - BG 4.37). Unarguably, only knowledge is useful to remove doubts of dualities. In a victory over the mind and intellect, only knowledge can be the true cause. However, they can be restrained through austerity and others, yet they cannot be won over. Through knowledge, becoming dissociated from the mind and intellect, complete victory with their roots is possible. Doubts are removed through knowledge and the purging of sin. Victory over the mind and intellect and the well-being of all beings is natural, and such seers can attain the bliss-form Brahman. Even though Karma and austerity are helpful in victory over the mind and intellect, purging of sin and victory over the mind and intellect in real terms is only possible to be achieved through knowledge.

कामक्रोधवियुक्तानां यतीनां यतचेतसाम् |
अभितो ब्रह्मनिर्वाणं वर्तते विदितात्मनाम् || BG 5.26 ||

यतीनाम् - (For) self-restrained ascetics, ; काम-क्रोध-वियुक्तानाम् - who are free from desire and anger, ; यत-चेतसाम् - who have conquered their mind, ; विदित-आत्मनाम् - (and) who have known the Self, ; ब्रह्म-निर्वाणं - (only) the Nirvāṇa-Brahma ; वर्तते - operates ; अभितः - from all sides.

For self-restrained ascetics, who are free from desire and anger, who have conquered their mind and who have known the Self, only the Nirvāṇa-Brahma operates from all sides.

Intent - From all sides, only the bliss-form Brahman is visible to the self-restrained ascetics. To them, entire material existence appears as a miracle of the Brahman. In addition, they are only sipping the ambrosiac bliss of the Brahman from a goblet of inclinations born of the union of the senses and their objects. Wherever their mind goes, there they have oneness with the Brahman, there they have Samādhī.

(Now, describing the tenet with means, Bhagavāna ends the chapter -)

स्पर्शान्कृत्वा बहिर्बाह्यांश्चक्षुश्चैवान्तरे भ्रुवोः |
प्राणापानौ समौ कृत्वा नासाभ्यन्तरचारिणौ || BG 5.27 ||
यतेन्द्रियमनोबुद्धिर्मुनिर्मोक्षपरायणः |
विगतेच्छाभयक्रोधो यः सदा मुक्त एव सः || BG 5.28 ||

कृत्वा - Keeping ; बाह्यान् - external ; स्पर्शान् - contacts (objects of enjoyment) ; बहिः - out (of the heart), ; च - and ; चक्षुः - (with) the eyes (focused) ; अन्तरे - between ; भ्रुवोः - the eyebrows ; समौ कृत्वा - (and) equalizing ; प्राण-अपानौ - the in-breath and out-breath ; नास-अभ्यन्तर-चारिणौ - that moves within the nostrils, ; सः - one ; यः- who is ; मोक्ष-परायणः - a liberation bound ; मुनिः - sage ; यत-इन्द्रिय-मनः-बुद्धिः - who has conquered the senses, mind, and intellect ; विगत-इच्छा-भय-क्रोधः - (and) is free from desire, fear, and anger, ; एव - is certainly ; सदा - ever ; मुक्तः - free ; एव - indeed.

Keeping external contacts out, with the eyes focused between the eyebrows and equalizing the in-breath and out-breath that moves within the nostrils, a liberation-bound sage who has conquered the senses, mind, and intellect and is free from desire, fear, and anger, is certainly ever free.

Intent - The I-ness sense in the mind, intellect, and senses is the root of bondage. In "non-thing" external objects, when "thing" sense is firm, then due to ignorance, there is a desire for unacquired things. Through discriminating vision, fear is born, and with an unfavorable perspective, anger is born. With desire, fear, and anger, this ego becomes firmer. Thus, bondage gets even firmer. However, a liberation bound sage has removed all of his attachment from non-thing external objects from his heart and has made the flow of in-breath (Prāṇa-Vāyu) and out-breath (Apāna-Vāyu) even and has focused his glance between his eyebrows, and is engaged in the search for the existent bliss-form Ātmā. He is indeed ever-free. With realizing his own bliss-form Ātmā, he immediately knows the bondage-form external objects as non-things. Dissociated from desire, fear, and anger, he becomes free from the senses, mind, and intellect.

(Now, Bhagavāna describes, with fruit, the true nature of ought to know Brahman -)

भोक्तारं यज्ञतपसां सर्वलोकमहेश्वरम् |
सुहृदं सर्वभूतानां ज्ञात्वा मां शान्तिमृच्छति || BG 5.29 ||

ज्ञात्वा - Knowing ; माम् - Me, ; सर्व-लोक-महेश्वरम् - the Supreme Lord of all worlds, ; भोक्तारम् - the enjoyer ; यज्ञ-तपसाम् - of sacrifices and austerities, (and) ; सुहृदम्- friend ; सर्व-भूतानाम् - of all beings, ; शान्तिम् - peace ; ऋच्छति - is attained.

Knowing Me, the Supreme Lord of all worlds, the enjoyer of sacrifices and austerities, and friend of all beings, peace is attained.

Intent - Existing right beneath all sacrifices and austerities in witness-form, I am the enjoyer of all sacrifices and austerities. In contrast, a living being having an enjoyership-ego cannot be a real enjoyer of sacrifices and austerities. With I-ness sense in enjoyments, he has only conjunction with those enjoyments, not oneness, just as one wave has conjunction with other waves, not oneness. However, being their "Ātmā" water has oneness with all waves. Accordingly, enjoyership conceited Jīva has distinctly separate connections with sacrifices, austerities, and enjoyments. That is why in truth, he cannot be their enjoyer. I, the all-witness, like one water in various waves, with natural oneness, I am their enjoyer because oneness is necessary for the reality of enjoyments. Being the supporting reality of the entire humanity, I am the Supreme Lord of Brahmā and other deities. In the closeness of My "form of being Ātmā of all (Sarvātma-Svarupa)," whoever desires whatever, with My power, they acquire them. For instance, when a thief desires to steal, the fulfillment of his desire is done under My support. However, due to his evil desire, in its retaliation, My Prakṛti gives him a harsh punishment and beats him so that he is brought back on the right path. In the form of My Prakṛti, I am a friend of all living beings. I am the enjoyer of all sacrifices and austerities, the Maheśvara, and friend of all beings in this form. Knowing Me so, a sage who is moving towards liberation attains peace. The intention is to know My true nature as "doing everything (Sarva Kartā) but in reality, not doing anything (Akartā)," peace is possible. In attaining His true nature, Bhagavāna described the usefulness of knowability and not an obligation.

ॐ तत्सदिति श्रीमद्भगवद्गीतासूपनिषत्सु ब्रह्मविद्यायां योगशास्त्रे

श्रीकृष्णार्जुनसम्वादे कर्मसंन्यासयोगो नाम

पंचमोऽध्यायः || BG 5 ||

Oṃ Tat Sat

In the Śrīmad Bhagavad Gītā Upaniṣad

The Yoga Science of the Knowledge of Self-Realization

The Discourse of Lord Śrī Kṛṣṇa and Arjuna

This Fifth Chapter

Yoga Named - The Yoga of Renunciation

Clarification

Not understanding the subtle depth of oneness of renunciation (Karma-Saṃnyāsa) and Karma-Yoga that Bhagavāna is discussing in previous chapters, at the beginning of this chapter, Arjuna questioned - "Hey Śrī Kṛṣṇa! You praise renunciation of action, and again, (Karma) Yoga. Of the two, tell me decisively that one which is more beneficial" (BG 5.1). In reality, Bhagavāna did not previously describe two paths among which

Arjuna could have been told to leave one and accept the other. However, all along, Bhagavāna is suggesting one thing only, "Merely renouncing Karma in the form of efforts is not any Karma-Saṃnyāsa." Yes, what needs to be left is that delusional doership I-ness, which in the ignorance of own "non-doer true witness-form" is stuck in the middle with the ego of doership. Indeed, all efforts happen through the transformations of the constituents of Prakṛti, and I, the witness with My power, provide a beat for Prakṛti to show her dances for My pastime and as long as I desire. When I get tired, I close the trunk of Prakṛti and rest in My eternal bliss form. Who are you the doership-ego to meddle in between?

When Jīva, at some point in time, awakens from his ignorance-sleep and finds oneness in the Ātmā, then where is Karma-Yoga of fruit-relinquishment? Have activities of a dream ever bound anyone by which one has to resolve to renounce the fruits? Where is the fruit of relinquishment when there is no real Karma? All along, Bhagavāna has indicated that, through knowledge, upon burning of doership I-ness, relinquishment of actions and relinquishment of fruits become one. However, when Arjuna did not grasp this intention of Bhagavāna, then Bhagavāna did not think it appropriate to tell the Gāṇḍīvadhārī beloved pupil Arjuna "You are stupid." By saying so, there was a possibility of harming him mentally, and therefore keeping Arjuna's dilemma in the forefront, Bhagavāna said, "Hey Arjuna! In reality, renunciation (Saṃnyāsa) and Karma-Yoga, are both freedom providers. However, among the two, instead of relinquishing Karma, Karma-Yoga is superior." By engaging in Karma, a person can experience the oneness of the two in due course. However, when a feeble-minded person against his qualification or fitness abandons Karma, he is like a dog of a laundryman, neither of the house nor the pier. Bhagavāna amplified that a person who engages in actions without desire and hate should be known as a perpetual renouncer (Nitya-Saṃnyāsī) because such a person is free of dualities (Nir-Dvandva) and quickly becomes free from bondage (BG 5.2 - BG 5.3). Then, Bhagavāna said that those who have an intellect of a child not knowing the truth between Sāṅkhya and Yoga call them separate. However, a knower of the Truth does not because properly establishing in one is indeed establishing in both. The ultimate status that Sāṅkhya can procure, the same can be reached by Yoga. The one, who sees both in oneness, sees truly (Yathārtha). Without attaining union in own Ātmā, renunciation of actions (Karma-Saṃnyāsa) is difficult. Because when doership remains, even relinquishment of actions being with the ego of relinquishment becomes Karma (BG 5.4 - BG 5.6).

Showing oneness between Sāṅkhya and Yoga, Bhagavāna said, "A person who is established with oneness in the Ātmā (Yoga-Yukta) and has removed doership-ego becomes the Ātmā of all living beings and even while doing everything he is not tainted. Such a knower of the Truth making efforts through the senses does not see those sense-activities in himself, and all his doership and actions become offerings to the Brahman (Brahmārpaṇa) through knowledge and just like a lotus leaf (by water) is not tainted by any fruits." Such Yogīs only engage in actions through the body, senses, mind, and intellect without any doership-sentiment. Accordingly, those Yoga-Yukta achieve steady peace (Naiṣṭhika-Śānti) and gain freedom from Karma and fruits. However, a person who is not united (Ayukta) is bound as he is attached to fruits. A Yoga-Yukta, mentally abandoning all Karma, holding a firm resolve, "I, the witness-conscious, am not doing anything, and I am not having the body do anything," happily rests in the nine-gated city (body) (BG 5.7 - BG 5.13).

If duty (Karttṛtva), action (Karma), and fruits (Phala) are not in the Ātmā, then where are they? Resolving this question, Bhagavāna showed that gaining power from the true witness-conscious Ātmā and in its light, this dancer in the form of Māyā is playing the game of joining and separating Karma and fruits. Otherwise, the true witness-conscious takes neither anyone's piety nor sin. Knowledge of Jīva is shrouded only because of ignorance in the form of Māyā. By it, Jīva is deluded and puts himself in the bondage of doership and enjoyership. Due to ignorance (of Jīva), operations of Māyā are attributed to the head of the true witness-conscious. However, one whose ignorance is destroyed by the knowledge of the Ātmā and in whom the cover of Māyā is lifted, to him, the immovable omnipresent Ātmā "is as is" appears in all these efforts of Māyā. Just as a face is seen once dirt is removed from a mirror, in the same way, with the removal of the dirt of ignorance, doership and duty all vanish (BG 5.14 - BG 5.16).

In addition, Bhagavāna described the true nature of those Yogīs, whose doership-delusion has calmed and who are united in their own Ātmā. Whose mental activities are all towards the Ātmā achieve a status from which one does not return (Apunarāvṛtti-Mokṣa) and, while alive, become free from the bondage of the world of birth and death; become Jīvanmukta. They see equally a Brāhmaṇa, a cow, a dog, an elephant, and an outcast. Established in the Brahman, they conquer the material world by becoming free from all bondage in this life. Such persons do not rejoice in the acquisition of favorable things nor are distressed upon receiving unfavorable things. For such a person's happiness sense in external sense-objects disappears, and they experience undecaying happiness within (BG 5.17 - BG 5.21). Accordingly, describing the true nature of Yogīs, Bhagavāna showed attachment to external objects as a major obstacle in this Yoga and indicated that those who can bear the forces of desire and anger are united; they attain the Nirvāṇa-Brahma. They only see the Brahman all over from all sides. Further, Bhagavāna described various means useful in this Yoga, such as forsaking external objects, gazing between the eyebrows and equalizing the flow of in-breath and out-breath, victory over the senses, mind, and intellect, constant striving for liberation and abandonment of desire, fear and anger (BG 5.22 - BG 5.28). Concluding the chapter, describing His ought to be known true nature, Bhagavāna said that one who knows My true nature as the enjoyer of all sacrifices and austerities, Maheśvara and friend of all beings, such a person attains peace (BG 5.29).

This chapter describes the oneness between Sāṅkhya and Yoga, the characteristics of a Yogī, the glory of Yoga, and the useful means in Yoga. Then again, at the beginning of the sixth chapter Bhagavāna strengthens the oneness of Sāṅkhya and Yoga.

CHAPTER 6

THE YOGA OF MEDITATION

श्रीभगवानुवाच |
अनाश्रित: कर्मफलं कार्यं कर्म करोति य: |
स संन्यासी च योगी च न निरग्निर्न चाक्रिय: || BG 6.1 ||
श्रीभगवान् उवाच - Śrī Bhagavān said -

अनाश्रितः - Not depending ; कर्म-फलम् - on the fruits of action (that is, without doership-intellect, which is the support of the fruits of action), ; सः - he ; यः - who ; करोति - performs ; कार्यम् - ought to be done ; कर्म - acts ; संन्यासी - (is) a renouncer ; च - and ; योगी - a Yogī, ; च - and ; न - not ; निरग्निः - (the one who) abandons fire ; च - and ; न - not (the one who) ; अक्रियः - abandons actions.

Śrī Bhagavān said -

Not depending on the fruits of action, he who performs ought to be done acts is a renouncer and a Yogī, not the one who abandons fire and actions.

Intent - Fruits of Karma are dependent on the doership-intellect. The impressions (Saṃskāras) of done Karma depend on the "I am a doer" intellect, which in due time, becomes ready for fruition, irrespective of whether they are done with desire-ridden or desireless sentiments. Where there is a sentiment, there is a corresponding fruit, and sentiments always reside in the doership-intellect. The fruits of action depend on the doership-intellect. "Not depending on the fruits of action" means through the knowledge of the Truth forsaking the doership intellect the performance of ought to be done, Karma. "The body, mind, and senses act in their duties. I am not a doer of their activities but their witness-observer," with such direct transcendent knowledge, one who performs natural Karma is indeed a renouncer (Karma-Saṃnyāsī). He is a Karma-Yogī. The intention here is that as he is dissociated from the body, doing everything through the body, he is indeed not doing anything. Being a non-doer, he does not come in the bondage of fruits. He is a true renouncer (Saṃnyāsī), a true Yogī. Holding doership-ego, no one becomes a renouncer just by forsaking household fires and rituals. One who "abandons fire" has given up fires, the auxiliaries to rituals. One who "abandons actions" is free from activities like penances and charities that are not associated with fire. Even if such a renouncer abandons fire and actions because he has an I-ness sense in renunciation, he cannot achieve Karma-Saṃnyāsa.

{This way, non-distinction (Abheda) of renunciation (Saṃnyāsa) from Yoga was shown. Next, Bhagavāna shows non-distinction of Yoga from renunciation -}

यं संन्यासमिति प्राहुर्योगं तं विद्धि पाण्डव |
न ह्यसंन्यस्तसङ्कल्पो योगी भवति कश्चन || BG 6.2 ||

पाण्डव - Hey Pāṇḍava (Arjuna)! ; विद्धि - Know ; तम् - that ; यम् - which ; इति - (they) so ; प्राहुः - call ; संन्यासम् - "Renunciation" ; योगम् - as Yoga. ; हि - For ; न कश्चन - no one ; भवति - becomes ; योगी - a Yogī ; असंन्यस्त-सङ्कल्पः - without forsaking resolves (such as "I am a doer").

Hey Arjuna! Know that which they call "Renunciation" as Yoga. No one becomes a Yogī without forsaking resolves.

Intent - What is called "Renunciation, Saṃnyāsa," hey Arjun! Know it as Yoga, just as an urn is known as a vase also. There is only a difference in words between urn and vase and not in the meaning. In the same way, there is only a word difference between Tātvika-renunciation and Tātvika-Yoga; there is no difference in the meaning. Holding doership-intellect, no one becomes a renouncer (Saṃnyāsī) by merely abandoning fire and actions. Similarly, having doership and duty-bound intellect, only with a sentiment of fruit-relinquishment, one does not become a Yogī (one who is desireless, Niṣkāmī). There is no freedom from just a sentiment of fruit-relinquishment. Because of doer-sentiment, there is a fruit of the sentiment of fruit-relinquishment. Therefore, no one becomes a Yogī until there is renunciation of resolves (Saṃkalpa-Saṃnyāsa). Indeed, "I am a doer, and I have certain duties" is the root resolve of all resolves; all other resolves are its branches. Becoming a Yogī is not possible without removing this root resolve. Removing this resolve from its roots by the realization of the Truth and determining the absence in the past, present, and future of doership and duty-bound intellect, both renunciation and Yoga become one. And then there is a true success of both. With the absence of doership-intellect and disassociation from the body, mind, and senses, even while engaged in actions, he is a true renouncer (Karma-Saṃnyāsī) and does not have a sentiment of fruit-relinquishment; he is a fruit relinquisher (Phala-Tyāgi).

(Where Karma is useful and where it is not useful and an impediment, that is next articulated -)

आरुरुक्षोर्मुनेर्योगं कर्म कारणमुच्यते |
योगारूढस्य तस्यैव शमः कारणमुच्यते || BG 6.3 ||

कर्म - (Desireless) action ; उच्यते - is said ; कारणम् - to be the cause ; मुनेः - for a (contemplative) sage ; आरुरुक्षोः - seeking ascension ; योगम् - in Yoga. ; योग-आरूढस्य - Having ascended in Yoga, ; शमः - quiescence ; उच्यते - is said ; कारणम् - to be the cause ; तस्य - for him ; एव - indeed.

Action is the cause for a sage seeking ascension in Yoga. Having ascended in Yoga, quiescence is the cause for him.

Intent - For a contemplative sage who has a desire to ascend in the Tātvika-Yoga (of establishing union with oneness in the Ātmā), engaging in Karma with such desireless sentiments, "1) I am a doer of Karma, 2) to be active in certain Karma is my duty from the Lord, 3) obeying the command of the Lord I am engaging in Karma per my fitness so that through Karma I can worship the Lord, 4) not desiring fruits of Karma I offer them to the Lord and 5) I will remain equal in success and failure of the fruits of Karma" is said to be the cause in the attainment of Yoga. However, having ascended in Yoga, for the same sage, cessation (उपशम, Upaśama) of the above five limbed desireless actions (Niṣkāma-Karma) is the cause. The intention here is that for a seeker of Yoga, performing to be done acts with desireless sentiment is extremely helpful; without it, he cannot attain Yoga. However, having ascended in Yoga, renunciation of duty and doership-sentiment are equally necessary for the same sage. If he continues to hold duty and doership-resolves, he cannot steadfastly establish himself in Tātvika-Yoga. An arrow must be loaded on a bow, and the bowstring pulled to hit a target. Without pulling the bowstring, the arrow may not reach the target. However, for hitting the target after pulling the bowstring, it is also necessary to release it. If the string stays drawn and is not released, the target will not be penetrated. Therefore, it is necessary to fill the heart with a pure desireless ego of doership and duty to remove the impure ego. However, once the impure ego is gone, it is equally necessary for the pure ego to go. Because if it remains, it will become an impediment in Yoga; just as how after soap removes dirt from clothes, the soap must be washed clean.

(How does a Yogī know that "I have ascended in Yoga"? Bhagavāna describes that -)

यदा हि नेन्द्रियार्थेषु न कर्मस्वनुषज्जते |
सर्वसंकल्पसंन्यासी योगारूढस्तदोच्यते || BG 6.4 ||

यदा - When (a sage is) ; न - no ; अनुषज्जते - (longer) attached ; कर्मसु - to actions (that "I am a doer of actions") ; हि - (and) also ; न - not ; इन्द्रिय-अर्थेषु - to sense objects (that "I am an enjoyer of the sense-objects"), ; तदा - then ; सर्व-संकल्प-संन्यासी - (he) the renouncer all (doer-enjoyer) resolves ; उच्यते - is said to have ; योग-आरूढः - ascended in Yoga.

When a sage is no longer attached to actions and sense objects, the renouncer of all resolves is said to have ascended in Yoga.

Intent - When a sage is no longer attached to the sense-objects that "I am an enjoyer of all these sense-objects" and to Karma that "I am a doer of all these Karma," through the realization of the Truth, then free from doership and enjoyership, the renouncer of all resolves, is said to be Yogāruḍha, meaning he has ascended in Yoga. The absence of resolves in its true nature is not renunciation of resolves (Saṃkalpa-Saṃnyāsa), but in an earlier state when he was a doer of resolves, at that time, had he remained just a witness, that would have been a real renunciation of resolves.

(Therefore, for the attainment of the Yogāruḍha state, one ought to -)

उद्धरेदात्मनात्मानं नात्मानमवसादयेत् |
आत्मैव ह्यात्मनो बन्धुरात्मैव रिपुरात्मनः || BG 6.5 ||

उद्धरेत् - Elevate ; आत्मानम् - the self ; आत्मना - by self. ; न - Do not ; आत्मानम् - let the self ; अवसादयेत् - fall (drown in the worldly ocean). ; हि - For, ; आत्मा - the self ; एव - is indeed ; बन्धुः - a friend ; आत्मनः - of the self, ; आत्मा - (and) the self ; एव - alone is ; रिपुः - an enemy ; आत्मनः - of the self.

Elevate the self by self. Do not let the self fall. For, the self is indeed a friend of the self, and the self alone is an enemy of the self.

Intent - Elevate the self, that is, elevate your mind, intellect, and senses drowned in the worldly ocean by your mind, intellect, and senses. Do not let your mind, intellect, and senses drown in the worldly ocean. For the good of Jīva, it is necessary for four graces (कृपा, Kṛpā) to come together: 1) grace of the Lord (Īśvara-Kṛpā), 2) grace of a preceptor (Guru-Kṛpā), 3) grace of the scriptures (Śāstra-Kṛpā) and 4) grace within (Ātma-Kṛpā). Grace within (Ātma-Kṛpā) is an earnest desire in the conscience of one who is fit, "by whatever means I become free from the worldly ocean." Success is not achieved even when the other three are ready for fruition if grace within is not awakened. Suppose grace within is awakened in reality (Yathārtha), then even when the other three are not perceptible, they are bound to move towards the fit, just as a butterfly is naturally attracted to fire. In this verse, "One ought to elevate the self by self and not let the self fall," clarifies the intent. In self-elevation, Ātma-Kṛpā, being within, is a material and leading cause. The remaining three graces being external are instrumental and minor. The pre-eminence of material cause (Upādāna) compared to an instrumental cause (Nimitta) is axiomatically agreeable to all. Just as with iron, one can cut iron; with one's mind and intellect, one can elevate one's mind and intellect because the mind and intellect introverting are their friends and extroverting are their enemies. First, when they become their enemies, the rest of the world becomes enemies of Jīva. However, when they become friends, the world as a whole becomes Jīva's friend. They are the ones who imagine external non-things as things and form sentiments of trueness in untrue things. And through attachment and aversion, they create their enemies. However, with the support of right-vision (Yathārtha-Dṛṣṭi), when all selfishness and desires are forsaken, they are also the ones who make themselves their friends.

(With what attributes the Ātmā is a friend and with what attributes the Ātmā is an enemy? That Bhagavāna describes -)

बन्धुरात्मात्मनस्तस्य येनात्मैवात्मना जित: |
अनात्मनस्तु शत्रुत्वे वर्ते तात्मैव शत्रुवत् || BG 6.6 ||

येन आत्मना - By that self (mind) ; आत्मा - (whose) self (a conglomerate of the body, senses, mind, and intellect) ; जितः - is subdued, ; तस्य - his ; आत्मा - self (mind) ; एव - indeed is ; आत्मनः - his own ; बन्धुः - friend. ; तु - However, (in contrast) ; अनात्मनः - an extroverted ; आत्मा - self (mind) ; एव - indeed ; वर्तेत - operates ; शत्रुवत् - as an enemy ; शत्रुत्वे - with animosity.

By that self whose self is subdued, his self indeed is his own friend. However, an extroverted self indeed operates as an enemy with animosity.

Intent - "By that self whose self is subdued" means by the mind whose Ātmā in the form of a conglomerate of the body, senses, mind, and intellect is subdued. One who has subdued his senses, mind, and intellect from attachment to external delusional (Mithyā) objects, that person is his friend. However, in contrast, a person who has trapped his senses, mind, and intellect in external objects is like a person who has become his enemy, and then the entire world becomes his enemy.

जितात्मन: प्रशान्तस्य परमात्मा समाहित: |
शीतोष्णसुखदु:खेषु तथा मानापमानयो: || BG 6.7 ||

जित-आत्मनः - One who has subdued the self (a conglomerate of the body, senses, mind, and intellect), ; प्रशान्तस्य - who is serene ; शीत-उष्ण-सुख-दुःखेषु - in (dualities such as) cold and heat, pleasure and pain, ; तथा मान-अपमानयोः - and in honor and disgrace, ; समाहितः - is fit to unite (in) ; परमात्मा - the supreme Brahman.

One who has subdued the self, serene in cold and heat, pleasure and pain, honor and disgrace, is fit to unite in the supreme Brahman.

Intent - Based on the above, becoming his friend, a person who sees reasons for his pleasure and pain, honor and disgrace only within, such a person who has subdued his mind and has a peaceful conscience is fit for the divine experience (Paramātmā-Darśana) everywhere.

ज्ञानविज्ञानतृप्तात्मा कूटस्थो विजितेन्द्रिय: |
युक्त इत्युच्यते योगी समलोष्टाश्मकाञ्चन: || BG 6.8 ||

योगी - That Yogī ; इति - is thus ; उच्यते - said ; युक्तः - to be established (in Yoga) ; ज्ञान-विज्ञान-तृप्त-आत्मा - whose conscience is content in knowledge and realized knowledge, ; कूटस्थः - (who is) immutable, ; विजित-इन्द्रियः - (who has) subdued his senses, (and) ; सम-लोष्ट-अश्म-काञ्चनः - for whom a clod, stone, and gold are all alike.

That Yogī is said to be established in Yoga whose conscience is content in knowledge and realized knowledge, immutable, subdued his senses, and for whom a clod, stone, and gold are all alike.

Intent - Understanding the substance spoken in the scriptures is called "Jñāna, knowledge," and experiencing it directly (Aparokṣa), the understood subject of the scriptures is called "Vijñāna, realized knowledge." A Yogī who is content in knowledge and realized knowledge, who through analytic perspective is immutable and dissociated from the body, who does not see their duties and activities in himself and separate from own Ātmā does not see their existence, and who has subdued his senses is called Yukta (established). He has already attained union in his own Ātmā, so should be known. Then he only holds a clod, a stone or gold, and other dissimilar things in the form of the Ātmā, and knows, like silver in an oyster shell, all material things as subjects of delusional perception in his Ātmā alone.

सुहृन्मित्रार्युदासीनमध्यस्थद्वेष्यबन्धुषु |
साधुष्वपि च पापेषु समबुद्धिर्विशिष्यते || BG 6.9 ||

विशिष्यते - He excels ; सम-बुद्धिः - whose intellect is the same (towards) ; सुहृत् - good-hearted, ; मित्र - friends, ; अरि - foes, ; उदासीन - neutrals, ; मध्यस्थ - mediators, ; द्वेष्य - antagonists, ; बन्धुषु - relatives, ; साधुषु - pious, ; च - and ; अपि - even ; पापेषु - sinners.

He excels whose intellect is the same towards good-hearted, friends, foes, neutrals, mediators, antagonists, relatives, pious, and sinners.

Intent - A performer of unselfish acts for the benefit of others is called a "Suhṛda (सुहृद, good-hearted)," affectionate one is called a "Mitra (मित्र, friend)," one who harms is called an "Ari (अरि, foe)," one who does not take sides is called an "Udāsīna (उदासीन, neutral)," one who maintains the interest of both opposing sides is called a "Madhyastha (मध्यस्थ, mediator)," one who is an antagonist is called a "Dveṣī (द्वेषी)." One who is a relative is called a "Bandhu (बन्धु)." Additionally, one who behaves following the scriptures (Śāstra) is called a "Sādhu (साधु), a Puṇyātmā (पुण्यात्मा, a pious, righteous being)," and one who behaves contrary to the scriptures is called a "Pāpī (पापी, a sinner, an unrighteous)." A Yogī is the most splendid who does not perceive merits and demerits (Guṇa-Doṣa) in the Ātmā of those righteous and unrighteous but only sees the attributeless and immutable Brahman. He is the one who excels.

(In the attainment of Yoga, one who is fit was described, and where he has to reach was provided. Special means are described next -)

योगी युञ्जीत सततमात्मानं रहसि स्थित: |
एकाकी यतचित्तात्मा निराशीरपरिग्रह: || BG 6.10 ||

स्थितः - Residing ; एकाकी - alone ; रहसि - in a secluded place, ; यत-चित्त-आत्मा - with the mind and body in control ; निराशीः अपरिग्रहः - (and) free from desires and possessions (of objects of enjoyment), ; योगी - a Yogī ; सततम् - (ought to) constantly ; युञ्जीत - engage ; आत्मानम् - in Self-query.

Residing alone in a secluded place, with the mind and body in control and free from desires and possessions, a Yogī ought to constantly engage in Self-query.

Intent - Establishing the equanimity mentioned earlier is only possible through constant contemplation to attain union in the Ātmā, that is, the Self-query (आत्मानुसन्धान, Ātmānusandhāna). Residing alone in a secluded place, abandoning extroversion of the senses and keeping them under restraint, and giving up desires and possessions are valuable means of Self-query.

शुचौ देशे प्रतिष्ठाप्य स्थिरमासनमात्मन: |
नात्युच्छ्रितं नातिनीचं चैलाजिनकुशोत्तरम् || BG 6.11 ||

प्रतिष्ठाप्य - Setting ; आत्मनः - one's ; आसनम् - seat ; शुचौ - in a clean ; देशे - place ; न - neither ; अति-उच्छ्रितम् - too high ; न - nor ; अति-नीचम् - too low ; चैल-अजिन-कुश-उत्तरम् - (on which) sacred grass, deerskin, and cloth are placed one over the other.

Setting one's seat in a clean place neither too high nor too low on which sacred grass, deerskin, and cloth are placed one over the other.

तत्रैकाग्रं मन: कृत्वा यतचित्तेन्द्रियक्रिय: |
उपविश्यासने युञ्ज्याद्योगमात्मविशुद्धये || BG 6.12 ||

उपविश्य - Sitting ; तत्र - on that ; आसने - seat ; युञ्ज्यात् - engage ; योगम् - in Yoga ; आत्म-विशुद्धये - for self-purification ; यत-चित्त-इन्द्रिय-क्रियः - by controlling the activities of the mind and senses, ; मनः - (with) the mind ; एकाग्रम् कृत्वा - concentrated on a single point.

Sitting on that seat engage in Yoga for self-purification by controlling the activities of the mind and senses with the mind concentrated on a single point.

Intent - Engage in Yoga for self-purification means engaging in Self-query.

(External means are described. Now, how the body should be postured is provided -)

समं कायशिरोग्रीवं धारयन्नचलं स्थिरः |
सम्प्रेक्ष्य नासिकाग्रं स्वं दिशश्चानवलोकयन् || BG 6.13 ||

धारयन् - Holding ; काय-शिरः-ग्रीवम् - the body, head, and neck ; समम् - even ; च - and ; अचलम् - motionless, ; स्थिरः - become steady, ; अनवलोकयन् - (and) without looking at ; दिशः - directions, ; सम्प्रेक्ष्य - focus eyesight on ; स्वम् - own ; नासिक-अग्रं - the tip of the nose.

Holding the body, head, and neck even and motionless, become steady, and without looking at directions, focus eyesight on the tip of the nose.

Intent - By doing so, that is, eyesight focused on the tip of the nose, the fruit is indeed Self-query through concentration. Concentration on the nose tip is not the result in itself.

(Next, how the mind should be is discussed -)

प्रशान्तात्मा विगतभीर्ब्रह्मचारिव्रते स्थितः |
मनः संयम्य मच्चित्तो युक्त आसीत मत्परः || BG 6.14 ||

स्थितः - Established ; ब्रह्मचारि-व्रते - in a vow of celibacy, ; विगत-भीः - fearless, ; प्रशान्त-आत्मा - with serene conscience, ; युक्तः - (and) united (in Me), ; संयम्य - restraining ; मनः - the mind, ; आसीत - sit ; मत्-चित्तः - with the mind concentrated on Me ; मत्-परः - (and) devoted to Me.

Established in a vow of celibacy, fearless, with serene conscience and united, restraining the mind, sit with the mind concentrated on Me and devoted to Me.

Intent - An extroverted mind is not suitable for Self-query, only the introverted one. That is why, in the introverted mind, Bhagavāna depicts the nature of a helpful mind. First, become calm and fearless by being free of desires and thirsts for the material world because the cause of unrest and fear is desire and thirst. Through the observance of celibacy, restrain your mind and concentrate on Me. Leaving worldly dependence, take My support because the mind cannot stay without any support. Discarding substances of Rajoguṇa increase Sattvaguṇa and move towards Me. Only such a mind is suitable for Self-query.

युञ्जन्नेवं सदात्मानं योगी नियतमानसः |
शान्तिं निर्वाणपरमां मत्संस्थामधिगच्छति || BG 6.15 ||

एवं - Thus, ; नियत-मानसः - with a steady mind, ; योगी - a Yogī ; सदा - (who is) constantly ; युञ्जन् - engaged ; आत्मानम् - (in the query) of the Self ; अधिगच्छति - acquires ; शान्तिम् - peace ; मत्-संस्थाम् - abiding in Me ; निर्वाण-परमाम् - (in the form of) Ultimate Liberation.

With a steady mind, a Yogī who is constantly engaged in the query of the Self acquires peace abiding in Me in the form of Ultimate Liberation.

(Now diet, recreation, such useful means in this Yoga are described -)

नात्यश्नतस्तु योगोऽस्ति न चैकान्तमनश्नतः |
न चाति स्वप्नशीलस्य जाग्रतो नैव चार्जुन || BG 6.16 ||

अर्जुन - Hey Arjuna! ; तु - However, ; योगः - Yoga ; अस्ति - is ; न - not ; अश्नतः - (for one who) eats ; अति - too much ; च - and ; न - not ; अनश्नतः - (for one who) does not eat ; एकान्तम् - at all. ; च - And ; न - (it is) neither ; स्वप्न-शीलस्य - (for one who) sleeps ; अति - a lot ; च - and ; एव - certainly ; न - not ; जाग्रतः - (for one who) stays awake a lot.

Hey Arjuna! Yoga is not for one who overeats or does not eat at all. It is neither for one who sleeps a lot and certainly not for one who stays awake a lot.

युक्ताहारविहारस्य युक्तचेष्टस्य कर्मसु |
युक्तस्वप्नावबोधस्य योगो भवति दुःखहा || BG 6.17 ||

आहार-विहारस्य - Whose eating and recreation ; युक्त - are guided, ; चेष्टस्य - whose efforts ; कर्मसु - in actions ; युक्त - are judicious, ; स्वप्न-अवबोधस्य - (and) whose sleep and waking are ; युक्त - restrained, ; भवति - achieves ; योगः - Yoga ; दुःखहा - that removes sorrow.

Whose eating and recreation are guided, whose efforts in actions are judicious, and whose sleep and waking are restrained, achieves Yoga that removes sorrow.

Intent - When this Yoga is achievable only through thoughtful practice and thoughts can only happen in Sattvaguṇī inclination, it is imperative and necessary that diet, recreation, waking, and sleeping activities are reasonable. Because being irregular, all these activities increase Rajoguṇa and Tamoguṇa, impeding this Yoga.

(When does such a Yogī endowed with proper attributes become united? -)

यदा विनियतं चित्तमात्मन्येवावतिष्ठते |
निःस्पृहः सर्वकामेभ्यो युक्त इत्युच्यते तदा || BG 6.18 ||

यदा - When ; विनियतम् - the uniquely controlled ; चित्तम् - mind ; अवतिष्ठते - rests ; एव - solely ; आत्मनि - in the Self, ; निःस्पृहः - without cravings ; सर्व-कामेभ्यः - for all (objects of) desire ; तदा - then (one) ; उच्यते - is said to be ; युक्तः - united (in Yoga) ; इति - as such.

When the uniquely controlled mind rests solely in the Self without cravings for objects of desire, one is said to be united in Yoga.

Intent - It is when the mind is withdrawn from all sides of the world and is entirely situated in one's own Ātmā. With the maturity of Self-query, it does not have any existence of its own separate from the Ātmā. All inclinations of the mind, like a mirror, become merely to show the face of own Ātmā. All distinct results of the mind are perceived as "the distinctionless existent common in all (Nirviśeṣa Sattā-Sāmānya)." With the firmness of knowledge, all existences (material world) remain like the water of a mirage. The mind on its own becomes desireless from cravings for all delusionally perceived substances. Upon acquiring such a state, it should be known that the Yogī has become Yoga-Yukta. He has attained oneness in his own Ātmā.

(Now, a metaphor of that mind in oneness is provided -)

यथा दीपो निवातस्थो नेङ्गते सोपमा स्मृता |
योगिनो यतचित्तस्य युञ्जतो योगमात्मनः || BG 6.19 ||

यथा - Just as a ; दीपः - lamp flame ; न - does not ; इङ्गते - flicker ; निवातस्थः - in a windless location, ; सा - such ; उपमा - comparison ; स्मृता - is known ; योगिनः - of a Yogī ; यत-चित्तस्य - whose mind is controlled ; युञ्जतः - (and) who is engaged ; आत्मनः - in Self-query ; योगम् - Yoga.

Just as a lamp flame does not flicker in a windless location, such comparison is known of a Yogī whose mind is controlled and who is engaged in Self-query Yoga.

Intent - Like the flame of a lamp in a windless location, the mind of a Yogī is immovably situated in the Ātmā, and from there, it does not move.

यत्रोपरमते चित्तं निरुद्धं योगसेवया |
यत्र चैवात्मनात्मानं पश्यन्नात्मनि तुष्यति || BG 6.20 ||
सुखमात्यन्तिकं यत्तद्बुद्धिग्राह्यमतीन्द्रियम् |
वेत्ति यत्र न चैवायं स्थितश्चलति तत्त्वत: || BG 6.21 ||
यं लब्ध्वा चापरं लाभं मन्यते नाधिकं तत: |
यस्मिन्स्थितो न दु:खेन गुरुणापि विचाल्यते || BG 6.22 ||
तं विद्याद् दु:खसंयोगवियोगं योगसञ्ज्ञितम् |
स निश्चयेन योक्तव्यो योगोऽनिर्विण्णचेतसा || BG 6.23 ||

यत्र - Where ; योग-सेवया - through the practice of Yoga, ; निरुद्धम् - the restrained ; चित्तम् - mind ; उपरमते - withdraws (from objects), ; च - and ; यत्र - where ; पश्यन् - beholding ; आत्मानम् - the Self ; आत्मना - through the (pure) intellect, ; तुष्यति - is content ; आत्मनि - in the Self ; एव - alone; यत्र - where ; अयम् - this (Yogī) ; वेत्ति - experiences ; तत् - that ; अतीन्द्रियम् - beyond the senses ; आत्यन्तिकम् - absolute ; सुखम् - bliss ; यत् - which ; बुद्धि-ग्राह्यम् - is grasped by the intellect ; एव - alone, ; च - and ; स्थितः - established wherein ; न - is not ; चलति - moved ; तत्त्वतः - from the Reality; लब्ध्वा - having gained ; यम् - that (Self), ; ततः - which (one) ; मन्यते - deems ; न - no ; अपरम् - other ; लाभम् - gain ; अधिकम् - greater, ; च - and ; स्थितः - established ; यस्मिन् - in which ; अपि - even ; गुरुणा - the most profound ; दुःखेन - sorrow ; न - does not ; विचाल्यते - shake him; तम् - That (state) ; दुःख-संयोग-वियोगम् - where there is the absence of conjunction with sorrow ; विद्यात् - should be known ; योग-संज्ञितम् - by the name Yoga. ; सः - That ; योगः - Yoga ; निश्चयेन - ought to be decidedly ; योक्तव्यः - practiced ; अनिर्विण्ण-चेतसा - with an undespondent mind.

Where through the practice of Yoga, the restrained mind withdraws from objects, and where beholding the Self through the pure intellect is content in the Self alone; where the Yogī experiences that beyond the senses absolute bliss which is grasped by the intellect alone, and established wherein is not moved from the Reality; having gained that, which one deems no other gain greater, and established in which even the most profound sorrow does not shake him. That state where there is the absence of conjunction with sorrow should be known by the name Yoga. That Yoga ought to be decidedly practiced with an undespondent mind.

The intent of verses (BG 6.20 - BG 6.23) - The state articulated in the above four verses is known by Yoga, where sorrow has no reach. It becomes a duty for humans to achieve that Yoga because without it, there is no other means, nor will there be, for the freedom from the grief-stricken material world of birth and death. As proclaimed in the Vedas, "नान्यः पन्था विध्यतेऽयनाय, there is no other path towards freedom," and so the aim of human life should be this Yoga. Through analytic thinking, establishing with oneness in own Ātmā is the meaning of the word Yoga, where renunciation of actions (Karma-Saṃnyāsa) and performance of actions (Karma-Yoga) harmoniously merge. Neither separate from this, desireless actions (Niṣkāma-Karma) nor can Haṭha-Yoga be the meaning of the term Yoga because though they can be means for Tātvika-Yoga, they cannot themselves be the end, and they, by their practice, cannot free one from the conjunction with the grievous material world. **The term Yoga only means "establishing with oneness in the Ātmā."**

(Having thus described Yoga, now in the attainment of this state, useful means are again described in the following five verses -)

संकल्पप्रभवान्कामांस्त्यक्त्वा सर्वानशेषत: |
मनसैवेन्द्रियग्रामं विनियम्य समन्तत: || BG 6.24 ||
शनै: शनैरुपरमेद्बुद्ध्या धृतिगृहीतया |
आत्मसंस्थं मन: कृत्वा न किञ्चिदपि चिन्तयेत् || BG 6.25 ||

अशेषतः - Completely ; त्यक्त्वा - abandoning ; सर्वान् - all ; कामान् - desires ; संकल्प-प्रभवान् - born of resolves ; विनियम्य - (and) controlling ; इन्द्रिय-ग्रामम् - the entire group of senses ; समन्ततः - from all sides ; मनसा - with the mind ; एव - alone; शनैः शनैः - very slowly ; धृति-गृहीतया - through a resolute ; बुद्ध्या - intellect ; उपरमेत् - withdraw (the mind from desires), ; कृत्वा - (and then) having made ; मनः - the mind ; आत्म-संस्थम् - established in the Self, ; चिन्तयेत् - think ; न - not ; अपि - even ; किञ्चित् - of anything.

Completely abandoning all desires born of resolves and controlling the senses from all sides with the mind, very slowly through a resolute intellect withdraw the mind, and then having made the mind established in the Self, think not even of anything.

The intent of verses (BG 6.24 - BG 6.25) - Establishment of the mind in the Ātmā is accomplished by removing it here from worldly matters and joining it there in the Ātmā, just as an onion sapling is removed from one location and planted in a designated location where it can grow. An extroverted mind is detrimental to this. Only an introverted mind can be instrumental. With this intention, a command is given to forsake without any remainder all resolve-born desires and withdraw from all sides the entire group of senses. Accordingly, when the mind withdraws both internally and externally, then with a resolute intellect, the establishment of the mind in the Ātmā is inevitable. When the mind establishes in the Ātmā, all thinking becomes unnecessary.

यतो यतो निश्चरति मनश्चञ्चलमस्थिरम् |
ततस्ततो नियम्यैतदात्मन्येव वशं नयेत् || BG 6.26 ||

एतत् - (When) this ; चञ्चलम् - fickle (and) ; अस्थिरम् - unsteady ; मनः - mind ; निश्चरति - wanders ; यतः यतः - in whatsoever (worldly matters), ; नियम्य - withdrawing it ; ततः ततः - from there, ; नयेत् - have it ; वशं - confined ; आत्मनि - in the Self ; एव - alone.

When the fickle and unsteady mind wanders in whatsoever, withdrawing it from there, have it confined in the Self alone.

Intent - For ages, wandering of the mind in worldly objects has been ongoing. Not being established in the Ātmā, repeated wandering of the mind toward material objects is natural because of the strength of practice through the ages. Accordingly, Bhagavāna commanded that the fickle mind be withdrawn from wherever it wanders and joined in the Ātmā. Through analytic vision perceiving worldly objects as illusory, just as the water of a mirage, one ought to remove their attachment from the mind and instead join the mind in the Ātmā because the mind cannot remain without dependence.

(Now Bhagavāna describes its fruit -)

प्रशान्तमनसं ह्येनं योगिनं सुखमुत्तमम् |
उपैति शान्तरजसं ब्रह्मभूतमकल्मषम् || BG 6.27 ||

प्रशान्त-मनसम् - Whose mind is completely peaceful, ; शान्त-रजसम् - whose Rajoguṇa is subdued, ; अकल्मषम् - (and) who is sinless, ; एनम् - such ; योगिनम् - a Yogī ; हि - certainly ; उपैति - acquires ; उत्तमम् - the supreme ; सुखम् - bliss ; ब्रह्म-भूतम् - in the form of the Brahman.

Whose mind is completely peaceful, whose Rajoguṇa is subdued, and who is sinless, such a Yogī certainly acquires the supreme bliss of the Brahman.

युञ्जन्नेवं सदात्मानं योगी विगतकल्मषः |
सुखेन ब्रह्मसंस्पर्शमत्यन्तं सुखमश्नुते || BG 6.28 ||

एवम् - Thus, ; विगत-कल्मषः - a sinless ; योगी - Yogī, ; सदा - always ; युञ्जन् - united ; आत्मानम् - in the Self, ; सुखेन - easily ; अश्नुते - enjoys ; अत्यन्तम् - the infinite ; सुखम् - bliss ; ब्रह्म-संस्पर्शम् - in the form of Brahman attainment.

A sinless Yogī, always united in the Self, easily enjoys the infinite bliss of Brahman attainment.

(In the following four verses, Bhagavāna describes the attributes of a Yogī who has attained the Brahman -)

सर्वभूतस्थमात्मानं सर्वभूतानि चात्मनि |
ईक्षते योगयुक्तात्मा सर्वत्र समदर्शन: || BG 6.29 ||

सम-दर्शनः - With equality of vision ; सर्वत्र - everywhere, ; योग-युक्त-आत्मा - one who is established in Yoga, ; ईक्षते - beholds (with oneness) ; आत्मानम् - the Self ; सर्व-भूतस्थम् - in all beings ; च - and ; सर्व-भूतानि - all beings ; आत्मनि - in the Self.

With equality of vision everywhere, one who is established in Yoga beholds the Self in all beings and all beings in the Self.

Intent - Equality of vision means Brahma-Dṛṣṭi (ब्रह्म-दृष्टि, seeing everything as the Brahman). Terms Sama-Dṛṣṭi (सम-दृष्टि, seeing everything equally) and Ekatva-Dṛṣṭi (एकत्व-दृष्टि, seeing everything in oneness) are also used to express the same intent of seeing everything as the Brahman alone. A Yogī who has attained oneness in the Ātmā beholds the Ātmā in all beings and does not see any entity-form in them. Unlike how milk and sugar become a mutual mixture, he does not see a mixture of living beings and the Ātmā. However, similar to the underlying support rope in an illusory snake, the Yogī sees his Ātmā as the underlying support in all living beings. That which is grasped as a snake is only a rope; the snake is never there. Those understood as movable and immovable-form beings are only the Ātmā, and what is perceived is "there are no beings." In addition, he sees in his Ātmā all beings in the form of a Vivarta, just as there is no snake-ness in the illusory snake. He sees all living beings without their existence as imagined objects of false perception. There is only one Ātmā; such is his matured perspective.

यो मां पश्यति सर्वत्र सर्वं च मयि पश्यति |
तस्याहं न प्रणश्यामि स च मे न प्रणश्यति || BG 6.30 ||

अहं - I am ; न - not ; प्रणश्यामि - lost ; तस्य - to him ; यः - who ; पश्यति - beholds ; माम् - Me ; सर्वत्र - everywhere (in all beings just as water in waves) ; च - and ; पश्यति - beholds ; सर्वम् - everything (all beings) ; मयि - in Me (just as ripples in water), ; च - and ; न - neither ; सः - is he ; प्रणश्यति - lost ; मे - to Me.

I am not lost to him who beholds Me everywhere and everything in Me, and neither is he lost to Me.

Intent - Based on the preceding, a Yogī who sees Me, the all-witness Ātmā of all (Sarvātmā), as the underlying support everywhere and sees all living beings as a Vivarta imagined in Me the Sarvātmā, I am not invisible from his sight, and he is never invisible from My sight. Just as a person with certain blindness visualizes everywhere green on the coming of spring, in the same way, being blinded from the worldly vision, he sees Me the Sarvātmā everywhere in his Ātmā. Then he is only My Ātmā, so how can he hide from Me? Earlier, he had hidden Me under his ignorance.

सर्वभूतस्थितं यो मां भजत्येकत्वमास्थित: |
सर्वथा वर्तमानोऽपि स योगी मयि वर्तते || BG 6.31 ||

योगी - A Yogī, ; आस्थितः - established ; एकत्वम् - with oneness (in Me) ; यः - who ; भजति - worships ; माम् - Me (the Supreme Lord) ; सर्व-भूत-स्थितम् - existent in all beings (as their Self), ; वर्तते - abides ; मयि - in Me ; अपि - alone ; सर्वथा - however ; सः - he ; वर्तमानः - behaves.

A Yogī established with oneness in Me, who worships Me existent in all beings, abides in Me alone however he behaves.

Intent - One whose vision of beholding living beings (भूत-दृष्टि, Bhūta-Dṛṣṭi) and the vision of beholding the phenomenal world (प्रपञ्च-दृष्टि, Prapañca-Dṛṣṭi) is gone and is full of a vision of beholding the existence of only one Ātmā in all beings (सर्वात्मैक्य-द्रष्टि, Sarvātmaikya-Dṛṣṭi), such a Yogī, established in Me with oneness, worships Me the Ātmā existent in all beings. Through his Sarvātmaikya-Dṛṣṭi, he sees only Me everywhere. Then, in whatever manner he may act, with the influence of his analytic perspective, Yogī is always abiding in Me. For him, there are no scriptural injunctions or prohibitions. The intention is that just as all waves are only in the form of water, all living beings are nothing but the Brahman, their underlying support. With this direct realization perspective, even when such Yogī may act through the body somehow, he is rejoicing in Me alone. Only because of the influence of this perspective remains free from all sin and piety bondages.

आत्मौपम्येन सर्वत्र समं पश्यति योऽर्जुन |
सुखं वा यदि वा दु:खं स योगी परमो मत: || BG 6.32 ||

अर्जुन - Hey Arjuna! ; आत्मा-उपम्येन - In his analogy, ; योगी - a Yogī ; यः - who ; पश्यति - beholds ; सर्वत्र - everywhere ; सुखम् वा - happiness ; यदि वा - or ; दुःखम् - sorrow ; समम् - alike ; सः - he ; मतः - is deemed ; परमः - the most splendid.

Hey Arjuna! In his analogy, a Yogī who beholds everywhere happiness or sorrow alike is deemed the most splendid.

Intent - Just as an ignorant person has I-ness sense in the body, in the same way, one who has Ātmā-vision in all movable and stationary beings and mental states such as happiness and sorrow, such Yogī is deemed as the most splendid. One whose vision is without distinctions in all beings like one gold-vision in various gold ornaments, whose attachment to favorable dispositions and aversion to unfavorable dispositions is removed, and "in the form of the conscience I am an enjoyer, worldly objects are to be enjoyed by me, and with their relationship all dispositions related to happiness and sorrow are enjoyments" in the trio of enjoyer (Bhoktā), to be enjoyed (Bhogya) and enjoyments (Bhoga) one whose sentiments of cause and action (Kāraṇa and Kārya) is removed and in the trio, only one Ātmā-vision has become firm, that Yogī is indeed the best.

(Listening to this unique glory of Yoga, knowing himself as unfit, Arjuna being aghast, questions Bhagavāna -)

अर्जुन उवाच |
योऽयं योगस्त्वया प्रोक्त: साम्येन मधुसूदन |
एतस्याहं न पश्यामि चञ्चलत्वात्स्थितिं स्थिराम् || BG 6.33 ||
अर्जुन उवाच - Arjuna said -

मधुसूदन - Hey Madhusūdana (Śrī Kṛṣṇa)! ; अयं - This ; योगः - Yoga ; यः - that ; प्रोक्तः - is spoken ; त्वया - by You ; साम्येन - with equanimity, ; अहं - I ; न - do not ; पश्यामि - see ; एतस्य - its ; स्थिराम् - steady- ; स्थितिम् - state ; चञ्चलत्वात् - due to (mental) fickleness.

Arjuna said -

Hey Śrī Kṛṣṇa! This Yoga that is spoken by You with equanimity, I do not see its steady-state due to mental fickleness.

चञ्चलं हि मन: कृष्ण प्रमाथि बलवद्दृढम् |
तस्याहं निग्रहं मन्ये वायोरिव सुदुष्करम् || BG 6.34 ||

कृष्ण - Hey Śrī Kṛṣṇa! ; मनः - The mind is ; हि - so ; चञ्चलम् - fickle, ; प्रमाथि - agitating, ; बलवत् - strong, ; दृढम् - (and) unyielding ; अहम् - (that) I ; मन्ये - deem ; तस्य - its ; निग्रहम् - control ; सुदुष्करम् - extremely difficult, ; इव - like (controlling) ; वायोः - the wind.

Hey Kṛṣṇa! The mind is so fickle, agitating, strong, and unyielding that I deem its control extremely difficult, like controlling the wind.

Intent - The mind is extremely fickle. It is agitating, one that can make the body and senses agitated and helpless. It is so strong that it is impossible to be subdued by anyone. It is unyielding and impossible to slash. Controlling such a mind is like trying to control the wind. Extremely difficult.

श्रीभगवानुवाच |
असंशयं महाबाहो मनो दुर्निग्रहं चलम् |
अभ्यासेन तु कौन्तेय वैराग्येण च गृह्यते || BG 6.35 ||
श्रीभगवान् उवाच - Śrī Bhagavān said -

महाबाहो - Hey Mahābāho (Arjuna)! ; असंशयम् - Undoubtedly, ; मनः - the mind ; चलम् - (being) restless ; दुर्निग्रहम् - is difficult to control. ;तु - However, ; कौन्तेय - hey, Kaunteya (Arjuna)! ; अभ्यासेन - With practice ; च - and ; वैराग्येण - dispassion (in the form of seeing fault in objects), ; गृह्यते - it can be held.

Śrī Bhagavān said -

Hey Arjuna! Undoubtedly, the mind being restless is difficult to control. However, hey, Kaunteya! With practice and dispassion, it can be held.

Intent - Flow of homogeneous inclinations (Sajātīya-Vṛtti) is named Abhyāsa (practice) and becoming devoid of passion (Vigatarāga) in visible and invisible objects through the repeated vision of seeing fault (Doṣa-Dṛṣṭi) in them is called Vairāgya (dispassion). The mind is fickle and is difficult to be controlled, yet it cannot be said that it is not suitable to be controlled. It can be controlled through the strength of practice and dispassion. It has become fickle on its own because of attachment (Rāga) created by the influence of ignorance and practice of trueness-vision (Samyaka-Dṛṣṭi) in objects. In the kingdom of Prakṛti, practice is one major thing where corresponding to the strength of one's practice, one's form and nature are molded. That is why with the practice of a vision of seeing worldly objects as untrue and with faults, the mind can be controlled.

असंयतात्मना योगो दुष्प्राप इति मे मतिः |
वश्यात्मना तु यतता शक्योऽवाप्तुमुपायतः || BG 6.36 ||

इति - It is thus ; मे - My ; मतिः - opinion that ; असंयत-आत्मना - for one whose mind is uncontrolled, ; योगः - (this) Yoga ; दुष्प्रापः - is hard to achieve. ; तु - However, ; वश्य-आत्मना - for one whose mind is controlled, ; शक्यः - it is possible ; अवाप्तुम् - to achieve ; यतता - by striving ; उपायतः - (with aforementioned proper) means.

It is My opinion that for one whose mind is uncontrolled, Yoga is hard to achieve. However, for one whose mind is controlled, it is possible to achieve by striving with proper means.

Intent - As formulated in the verses (BG 6.10 - BG 6.28), this Yoga can be achieved with an approach of Self-query. Self-query can only be accomplished in a controlled, concentrated mind, never in an agitated mind. That is why Bhagavāna has described attainment of this Yoga as possible by one who is self-controlled (Saṃyatātmā) and has declared one who is not self-controlled (Asaṃyatātmā) as not fit to achieve this Yoga.

(From Arjuna's perspective, situating in this Yoga is difficult. If one engages in this Yoga, it is unlikely that he can achieve this Yoga in one life due to how extremely difficult it is. Further, if someone is active in this Yoga but leaves the body before achieving it or his mind is bewildered, then in that state, what destination does he end up in? This doubt grew in Arjuna's mind, and getting anxious, questioned Bhagavāna -)

अर्जुन उवाच ।
अयतिः श्रद्धयोपेतो योगाच्चलितमानसः ।
अप्राप्य योगसंसिद्धिं कां गतिं कृष्ण गच्छति || BG 6.37 ||
अर्जुन उवाच - Arjuna said -

कृष्ण - Hey Śrī Kṛṣṇa! ; अयतिः - A seeker of a feeble effort ; योगात्-चलित-मानसः - whose mind has deviated away from Yoga ; श्रद्धया उपेतः - (but) who has faith in it, ; अप्राप्य - failing ; योग-संसिद्धिम् - to attain perfection in Yoga (in the end time), ; काम् - to what ; गतिम् - destination ; गच्छति - (he) goes?

Arjuna said -

Hey Śrī Kṛṣṇa! A seeker of a feeble effort whose mind has deviated away from Yoga but who has faith in it, failing to attain perfection in Yoga, to what destination he goes?

कच्चिन्नोभयविभ्रष्टश्छिन्नाभ्रमिव नश्यति ।
अप्रतिष्ठो महाबाहो विमूढो ब्रह्मणः पथि || BG 6.38 ||

महाबाहो - Hey Mahābāho (Śrī Kṛṣṇa)! ; कच्चित् - Whether ; उभय-विभ्रष्टः - having fallen off from both sides {that is, the supreme objective (Paramārtha) and the worldly objective (Saṃsārī)}, ; अप्रतिष्ठः - unsupported ; विमूढः - (and) deluded ; पथि - in the path ; ब्रह्मणः - of the Brahman, ; न नश्यति - does he not perish ; इव - like ; छिन्न-अभ्रम् - a scattered cloud?

Hey Śrī Kṛṣṇa! Whether having fallen off from both sides, unsupported and deluded in the path of the Brahman, does he not perish like a scattered cloud?

Intent - Having fallen from both sides means having fallen from the path of action (Karma) and the path of knowledge (Jñāna). Does he not perish?

एतन्मे संशयं कृष्ण छेत्तुमर्हस्यशेषतः ।
त्वदन्यः संशयस्यास्य छेत्ता न ह्युपपद्यते || BG 6.39 ||

कृष्ण - Hey Śrī Kṛṣṇa! ; अर्हसि - You ought to ; छेत्तुम् - dispel ; एतत् - this ; संशयम् - doubt ; मे - of mine ; अशेषतः - completely. ; हि - But for ; त्वत् - You, ; न - none ; अन्यः - other ; उपपद्यते - can be found ; छेत्ता - to dispel ; अस्य - this ; संशयस्य - doubt.

Hey Śrī Kṛṣṇa! You ought to dispel this doubt of mine completely. But for You, none other can be found to dispel this doubt.

श्रीभगवानुवाच ।
पार्थ नैवेह नामुत्र विनाशस्तस्य विद्यते ।
न हि कल्याणकृत्कश्चिद्दुर्गतिं तात गच्छति || BG 6.40 ||
श्रीभगवान् उवाच - Śrī Bhagavān said -

पार्थ - Hey Pārtha (Arjuna)! ; एव - Certainly, ; तस्य - his ; विनाशः - destruction ; विद्यते - is ; न - neither ; इह - in this world ; न - nor ; अमुत्र - in the other world. ; हि - For, ; तात - hey, beloved! ; कश्चित् - Any ; कल्याण-कृत् - doer of good ; न - (does) not ; गच्छति - acquire ; दुर्गतिम् - a bad end.

Śrī Bhagavān said -

Hey Arjuna! Certainly, his destruction is neither in this world nor in the other world. For, hey, beloved! Any doer of good does not acquire a bad end.

Intent - Just as the conjunction of light with darkness and fire with water is not possible, in the same way, for a doer of the good engaged in attaining the Brahman, conjunction with a bad end is unlikely.

प्राप्य पुण्यकृतां लोकानुषित्वा शाश्वती: समा: |
शुचीनां श्रीमतां गेहे योगभ्रष्टोऽभिजायते || BG 6.41 ||

योग-भ्रष्टः - Fallen from Yoga, ; प्राप्य - (upon rebirth) acquiring ; लोकान् - the worlds ; पुण्य-कृताम् - of the righteous ; उषित्वा - (and) residing (therein) ; शाश्वतीः - long-lasting ; समाः - years ; अभिजायते - (is) reborn ; गेहे - in the home ; शुचीनाम् - of a pure ; श्रीमताम् - and prosperous householder.

Fallen from Yoga, upon acquiring the worlds of the righteous and residing therein for long-lasting years, is reborn in the home of a pure and prosperous householder.

अथवा योगिनामेव कुले भवति धीमताम् |
एतद्धि दुर्लभतरं लोके जन्म यदीदृशम् || BG 6.42 ||

अथवा - Or, ; एव - certainly ; भवति - takes birth ; कुले - in the family ; धीमताम् - of a wise ; योगिनाम् - Yogī. ; हि - Indeed, ; जन्म - a birth ; ईदृशम् - like ; यत् - that ; लोके - in this world, ; एतत् - that ; दुर्लभतरं - is rare.

Or, certainly takes birth in the family of a wise Yogī. Indeed, a birth like that in this world is rare.

Intent - If in the conscience of a Yoga-Bhraṣṭa there is some residual impression of enjoyment (Bhoga-Vāsanā) left, and suppressing them he was active in the path of Yoga but was not able to attain it, then in such a state, it becomes necessary for him to take birth in a prosperous (Śrīmāna) family. However, if he is without impressions (Nirvāsanika), but died before attaining Yoga, then in that state, he is born in the family of an impoverished wise Yogī. Such a birth in this world is rare because there he easily acquires all the means for Yoga and in the same life easily attains Yoga, just as in the presence of materials such as oil, wick, and lamp only by striking matchstick darkness is removed.

तत्र तं बुद्धिसंयोगं लभते पौर्वदेहिकम् |
यतते च ततो भूय: संसिद्धौ कुरुनन्दन || BG 6.43 ||

कुरुनन्दन - Hey Kurunandana (Arjuna)! ; तत्र - There ; लभते - (he naturally) acquires ; तम् -that ; बुद्धि-संयोगम् - conjunction of intellect ; पौर्व-देहिकम् - related to the previous body (life) ; च - and, ; ततः - after that, ; भूयः - (he) again ; यतते - endeavors ; संसिद्धौ - for perfection.

Hey Arjuna! There he acquires the conjunction of intellect related to the previous life and, after that, again endeavors for perfection.

Intent - Just as a person on a pilgrimage on his way at nightfall rests in a camp and waking up in the morning embarks on his journey towards his destination, in the same way, a Yoga-Bhraṣṭa also taking new birth moves ahead with vigor on the path of Yoga attainment.

पूर्वाभ्यासेन तेनैव ह्रियते ह्यवशोऽपि स: |
जिज्ञासुरपि योगस्य शब्दब्रह्मातिवर्तते || BG 6.44 ||

एव - Indeed, ; सः - he ; हि - too ; अवशः - is helplessly ; ह्रियते - pulled ; तेन - by that ; पूर्व-अभ्यासेन - past practice (on the path towards liberation). ; अपि - Even ; जिज्ञासुः - a seeker ; योगस्य - of Yoga ; अपि - certainly ; अतिवर्तते - goes beyond ; शब्द-ब्रह्म - the injunctions and prohibitions of the Vedas.

Indeed, he is helplessly pulled by that past practice. Even a seeker of Yoga certainly goes beyond the injunctions and prohibitions of the Vedas.

Intent - In his previous life, whatever practice he had done on the path towards liberation, in the current birth, he is attracted to move forwards only with the strength of that past practice. Just as a person writing falls to sleep but upon waking resumes where he left, in the same way, when a seeker of knowledge of Yoga becomes free from the injunctions and prohibitions (Vidhi-Niṣedha) of Varṇāśrama (वर्णाश्रम) proclaimed in the Vedas, then a Yogī who is free from all injunctions and prohibitions, what is there to say? Fruit of injunctions and prohibitions of the Vedas was the desire only to know, which though, after giving its fruit, achieved its objective.

प्रयत्नाद्यतमानस्तु योगी संशुद्धकिल्बिषः |
अनेकजन्मसंसिद्धस्ततो याति परां गतिम् || BG 6.45 ||

तु - Again, (in this birth), ; अनेक-जन्म-संसिद्धः - perfected through many births, ; योगी - a Yogī, ; संशुद्ध-किल्बिषः - who is purified from sins, ; यतमानः - endeavoring ; प्रयत्नात् - with great effort, ; ततः - thereafter ; याति - attains ; पराम् - the supreme ; गतिम् - destination.

Perfected through many births, a Yogī, who is purified from sins, endeavoring with great effort, thereafter attains the supreme destination.

Intent - A seeker of Yoga, little by little over many lives accumulating piety impressions (Puṇya-Saṃskāras) related to the attainment of the Paramātmā, with their influence in the last birth having become more effortful and purer from all sins, attains the supreme abode.

(Describing the unbeatableness of Yoga, Bhagavāna concludes the chapter -)

तपस्विभ्योऽधिकोयोगी ज्ञानिभ्योऽपिमतोऽधिकः|
कर्मिभ्यश्चाधिकोयोगी तस्माद्योगीभवार्जुन|| BG 6.46 ||

योगी - A Yogī ; मतः - is deemed ; अधिकः - superior ; तपस्विभ्यः - to an ascetic, ; च - and ; अपि - even ; अधिकः - superior ; ज्ञानिभ्यः - to a knower of the scriptures, ; योगी - (and so) a Yogī ; अधिकः - is superior ; कर्मिभ्यः - to a doer (Karma-Yogī who acts by the scriptures). ; तस्मात् - Therefore, ; अर्जुन - hey Arjuna! ; भव - (You) become ; योगी - a Yogī (only).

A Yogī is deemed superior to an ascetic, even superior to a knower of the scriptures, and so a Yogī is superior to a doer. Therefore, hey Arjuna! You become a Yogī only.

Intent - The fruits of austerity, self-study of the scriptures related to the Lord, desire-ridden, and desireless-Karma, either directly or through succession with the realization of the Truth, is only this Yoga of establishment with oneness in the Ātmā. It is the goal of all instruments, deemed the most superior. It is the goal of human life and the highest effort (Parama-Puruṣārtha). Thus, Bhagavāna commanded Arjuna to ascend in this Yoga.

योगिनामपि सर्वेषां मद्गतेनान्तरात्मना |
श्रद्धावान्भजते यो मां स मे युक्ततमो मतः || BG 6.47 ||

अपि - Even ; सर्वेषाम् - among all those ; योगिनाम् - Yogīs, ; यः - who ; श्रद्धावान् - of steady faith ; अन्तः-आत्मना - through the conscience ; मत् गतेन - with oneness in Me ; भजते - worship ; माम् - Me, ; मे - in My ; मतः- opinion, ; सः - he ; युक्ततमः - is the most united.

Even among all Yogīs, who of steady faith through the conscience with oneness in Me worship Me, in My opinion, he is the most united.

Intent - One who sees in all his mental states (Vṛtti) only Me the all-witness (Sarva-Sākṣī), in My opinion, he is the superior Yogī. That is, "यत्र यत्र मनो याति तत्र तत्र समाधाय, where ever his mind goes, there is his "Samādhī" - oneness with the Brahman.

ॐ तत्सदिति श्रीमद्भगवद्गीतासूपनिषत्सु ब्रह्मविध्यायां योगशास्त्रे

श्रीकृष्णार्जुनसम्वादे ध्यानयोगो नाम

षष्ठोऽध्यायः || BG 6 ||

Oṃ Tat Sat

In the Śrīmad Bhagavad Gītā Upaniṣad

The Yoga Science of the Knowledge of Self-Realization

The Discourse of Lord Śrī Kṛṣṇa and Arjuna

This Sixth Chapter

Yoga Named - The Yoga of Meditation

Clarification

In response to the query of Arjuna in the fifth chapter, Bhagavāna had clarified the oneness (Abheda) between renunciation (Saṃnyāsa) and Yoga, which at the beginning of this chapter, Bhagavāna reaffirms and indicates that a person who performs ordained acts as duty, abandoning doer-intellect, he is indeed a renouncer (Karma-Saṃnyāsī), and he is a Karma-Yogī. Holding doer-intellect and renouncing fires that are the auxiliaries to rituals and activities like penances, charities, and others that are not associated with fire, one does not become a renouncer. When doer-intellect is present, even if activities and fire are abandoned, he still becomes a doer of the ego of relinquishment (Tyāga). With the ego of relinquishment, he deposits within himself impressions (Saṃskāras) of the act of renunciation. When there is an accumulation of impressions, those impressions will not remain without bringing him into the bondage of birth and death to enjoy the fruits of action. For the enjoyment of his fruits of piety, his state is like "falling from a frying pan into the fire" or "coming out of a well and falling into a ditch." Even though the fruits of relinquishment are excellent, in the end, whatever results of Karma there are, they do perish. They are not the ones that can remain steady. When they are perishable, even if they are great, long-lasting, stationary opulence, they do not give pleasure because of the fear of their destruction. When they are perishable, they remain deprived and nothing but deprived. When a true kingdom can be acquired, why not attempt to acquire it? A hungry always remains hungry no matter how many dreams he has of delightful meals. Can the six tastes (Ṣaṭ-Rasa)[97]of a dream ever remove hunger? Abandoning actions while holding doer-intellect, with a sentiment of fruit-relinquishment, there is no deliverance or freedom. Can one be free from the thorns of a rose bush by just plucking leaves while keeping the roots intact? If you desire to get rid of the thorns, then with full force, give a blow with an ax of knowledge, then tell whether all the visible thorns have quickly changed into roses or not.

When the root in the form of doership I-ness is uprooted, then it is Saṃnyāsa, and it is Yoga. Just as in, Udaka is this and Jala is that; the underlying meaning of the words is only water. When there is freedom from I-ness (Aham), donning the crown of knowledge when one sits on the throne of own witness-conscious and I-ness is hung, then bells will ring not only in the kingdom of the body but in the entire phenomenal world. Then, whether it is the sun, or whether it is the moon, or whether they are the stars, in all of them there is his brilliance, and all of them will run away fearful of him. Then, he is the doer-holder of everything, yet he is not doing anything; all fruits materialize only by him, yet he is untainted and desireless. When a king is crowned, his deputy, heads of the army, commerce, revenue, other departments, their subordinates, and employees who have received authority from the king are actively engaged in fulfilling their responsibilities. At that time, does the king have to run after them? Everything occurs because of his authority, but he is a non-doer (Akartā Karma-Saṃnyāsī); all fruits materialize because of his grace, yet he is a Karma-Yogī (desireless, Niṣkāmī). With the establishment of oneness in the Ātmā, what is known as Saṃnyāsa should also be known as Yoga. Holding doer-intellect by abandoning only actions, one does not become a Saṃnyāsī (a relinquisher of actions, Karma-Tyāgi). With resolves of doership and duty remaining, one does not become a Yogī (a relinquisher of fruits, Phala-Tyāgi). With doership-intellect remaining, when the ghost of obligation is hovering over the head, "I have some obligation," in its frenzy, various branches of resolves spring out, which have their fruits and by which doership-intellect becomes further unyielding. Therefore, without renouncing duty, no one can become without resolves (Saṃnyasta-Saṃkalpī). Without establishing oneself with oneness in own Ātmā, no one can get rid of duty, and doership resolves. Without establishing oneself with oneness in own witness-conscious, one cannot become a Yogī. Essence is that in the existence

---

[97] Ṣaṭa-Rasa (षट्-रस) means six tastes: 1) sweet (मधुर, Madhura), 2) salty (लवण, Lavaṇa), 3) bitter (तिक्त, Tikta), 4) sour (अम्ल, Amla), 5) pungent (कटु, Kaṭu) and 6) astringent (कषाय, Kaṣāya).

of doership-intellect, neither Saṃnyāsa can be achieved nor Yoga. When freedom from doership-intellect is acquired, both are established in oneness-form (BG 6.1 - BG 6.2).

In addition, Bhagavāna said that for a seeker of Yoga though in previous states, desireless actions were said to be the cause, yet to establish in the forward Yogāruḍha state, relinquishment of those actions is said to be the cause. In the presence of duty and doership-sentiments, it is impossible to become Yogāruḍha. Then, Bhagavāna describing the attributes of a Yogāruḍha, said that when a sage is no longer attached to sense objects, "I am an enjoyer of all these sense-objects," and actions, "I am a doer of all these actions," through the realization of the Truth (Tattva-Sākṣātkāra), free from doership and enjoyership the renouncer (of all resolves) is said to be Yogāruḍha, meaning he has ascended in Yoga (BG 6.3 - BG 6.4). **From this point onwards in Gītā, there is no distinction between Saṃnyāsa and Yoga, and both are referred to as Yoga in oneness. To be established with oneness in own witness-conscious is the meaning of the word Yoga and this Yoga is the propounded subject of Gītā. Neither is Haṭha-Yoga the meaning of Yoga nor desireless actions (Niṣkāma-Karma-Pravṛtti) of a seeker is the meaning of the word Yoga.** Though the Yoga of desireless actions by Gītā-perspective is not disrespectful, it is indeed highly regarded, but it is not the propounded subject. From the top of a peak, Gītā is the one looking where there is no doer, no duty, no actions, and no Saṃsāra, but all of these are fruitful by it, but nothing happens in it. That is the real Karma-Yoga, and that is the real Karma-Saṃnyāsa.

After that, articulating means (Sādhana) to attain that state, Bhagavāna said that in the first place, a human should make his mind his friend and not his enemy by extroverting it in the material world (BG 6.5 - BG 6.6). Such a person with a controlled mind is described as fit (Adhikārī) for Self-Realization (Ātma-Sākṣātkāra). Then, Bhagavāna describing the vision of seeing everything with equanimity (Sama-Dṛṣṭi) of a knower of the Truth, said that such a Yogī sees no difference in sentiments between a stone and gold, friend and foe and other dualities (BG 6.7 - BG 6.9). In addition, for situating in this Yoga, Bhagavāna described useful means such as residing alone in a lonely place, renunciation of desires and accumulation of material things, clean location, type of seat, control of the mind and senses, holding the head and body even and motionless, eyesight on the tip of the nose, mental calmness, fearlessness, practice of celibacy, devotion towards the Lord, guided diet, recreation, sleep and wake state and others (BG 6.10 - BG 6.19). After that, Bhagavāna described a Yoga-Yukta and compared him to a lamp flame in a windless location, and said that when the uniquely controlled mind rests solely in the Ātmā without cravings for objects of desire, then one is said to be united in Yoga (BG 6.18 - BG 6.19). In that state, through the practice of Yoga, one with a controlled mind is content in the Ātmā, experiencing it. He experiences the highest bliss with the intellect beyond the senses; having attained such a state, he does not deem anything else greater to gain and is not agitated by the most profound sorrow. Such a state is depicted as Yoga (BG 6.20 - BG 6.23). For the attainment of such a state, emphasis such as completely abandoning all resolve-born desires, holding back the entire group of senses from all sides through the mind, through despondent intellect very slowly withdrawing from all objects and establishing the mind in the Ātmā was provided. With such an approach, by calming Rajoguṇa, attainment of the supreme bliss of the Brahman was described (BG 6.24 - BG 6.28). Then from verses (BG 6.29 - BG 6.32), attributes of a Yogī established in such a form were extensively provided.

On this Arjuna, understanding such a Yoga extremely difficult to achieve and that control of the mind was extremely necessary and unavoidable, questioned Bhagavāna on how to control the mind? Because like the wind, it is difficult to control (BG 6.33 - BG 6.34). On this, Bhagavāna described dispassion in objects and practice of discernment between real and unreal as the cause for the control of the mind, and a person without control of the mind was shown definitely as not fit for Yoga (BG 6.35 - BG 6.36). After that, Arjuna again questioned a person with feeble effort whose mind has deviated from Yoga but has faith in it, failing to attain Yoga; what destination does he go to? (BG 6.37 - BG 6.39). On this, Bhagavāna described the destination of a Yoga-Bhraṣṭa and said that for such a person, there could not be a bad end (अधोगति, Adhogati), but in future births, he would move forward in the path of Yoga. Through the practice of earlier births, being attracted more and more to Yoga, an endeavoring Yogī, purified by becoming sinless, attains the supreme destination (BG 6.40 - BG 6.45). In the end, describing the unbeatableness of a Yogī from an ascetic, a knower of the scriptures, and a Karma-Yogī concluded the chapter (BG 6.46 - BG 6.47).

At the beginning of the chapter reaffirming the oneness between Saṃnyāsa and Yoga, the means of Yoga attainment, the approach to restraining the mind, the importance of Yoga, and the attributes of a Yogī are described. Then, upon query of Arjuna, means for the control of the mind, its utility, the end of a Yoga-Bhraṣṭa are described, and the unbeatableness of Yoga is articulated. In the last six chapters, formulating the nature of Sāṅkhya and Yoga, their oneness is reaffirmed.

CHAPTER 7

THE YOGA OF KNOWLEDGE AND REALIZATION

श्रीभगवानुवाच |
मय्यासक्तमना: पार्थ योगं युञ्जन्मदाश्रय: |
असंशयं समग्रं मां यथा ज्ञास्यसि तच्छृणु || BG 7.1 ||
श्रीभगवान् उवाच - Śrī Bhagavān said -

पार्थ - Hey Pārtha (Arjuna)! ; आसक्त-मनाः - With your mind fixed ; मयि - on Me ; मत् - (and) in My ; आश्रयः - refuge ; युञ्जन् - practicing ; योगम् - Yoga, ; शृणु - hear ; तत् - that ; यथा - how ; ज्ञास्यसि - you will know ; माम् - Me ; समग्रम् - completely ; असंशयम् - without any doubt.

Śrī Bhagavān said -

Hey Arjuna! With your mind fixed on Me and in My refuge practicing Yoga, hear how you will know Me completely without any doubt.

Intent - The term Samagraṃ (समग्रं, complete) means in all forms (Sarvarupa), cause and action (Kāraṇa-Kārya), adjective and its referent (Viśeṣaṇa-Viśeṣya), support and that which is supported (Ādhāra-Ādheya) all of these I am, that is what Bhagavāna is referring to.

ज्ञानं तेऽहं सविज्ञानमिदं वक्ष्याम्यशेषत: |
यज्ज्ञात्वा नेह भूयोऽन्यज्ज्ञातव्यमवशिष्यते || BG 7.2 ||

अहम् - I ; वक्ष्यामि - shall tell ; ते - you ; इदम् - this ; ज्ञानम् - knowledge ; अशेषतः - completely ; सविज्ञानम् - with its realization, ; ज्ञात्वा - knowing ; यत् - which ; न - nothing ; अन्यत् - else ; भूयः - more ; अवशिष्यते - remains ; इह - here (in this world) ; ज्ञातव्यम् - to be known.

I shall tell you this knowledge completely with its realization, knowing which nothing more remains to be known.

The intent of verses (BG 7.1 - BG 7.2) - Attraction of the mind towards the Lord and a life moving towards Him (Bhagavat-Parāyaṇa) are the primary reasons for success in Yoga. Contrary to that, he cannot reach there, whose mind is attracted to the world and moving towards it (Saṃsāra-Parāyaṇa). Perceiving the Lord in all forms and knowing only the Lord as of all forms is the fruit of Yoga. To know the form of the Ātmā through preceptors and scriptures is called knowledge (Jñāna), and to directly experience it is called realization (Vijñāna). Bhagavāna is formulating knowledge based on experience, knowing that there is nothing else remaining to know in the world. One who knows the true nature of gold knows rings, bangles, necklaces, and all other complete works of gold. The direct attainment of Yoga was elucidated only through knowledge and not through Karma.

(Next, Bhagavāna describes the difficulty in acquiring this knowledge -)

मनुष्याणां सहस्रेषु कश्चिद्यतति सिद्धये |
यततामपि सिद्धानां कश्चिन्मां वेत्ति तत्त्वत: || BG 7.3 ||

सहस्रेषु - Among thousands of ; मनुष्याणाम् - humans ; कश्चित् - only some ; यतति - strive ; सिद्धये - for perfection (of this knowledge). ; अपि - Even ; यतताम् - among the striving ; सिद्धानाम् - perfected ones, ; कश्चित् - only some ; वेत्ति - know ; माम् - Me ; तत्त्वत: - in Truth.

Among thousands of humans, only some strive for perfection. Even among the striving perfected ones, only some know Me in Truth.

Intent - First, no one makes an effort to attain Me due to the influence of Māyā. Instead, like a thirsty deer looking for water in the mirage of a desert, all are running in worldly efforts. Among thousands of persons, only a handful make an effort to attain Me. Then, even among those striving to attain Me, there may be one who may come to know Me truly. That is similar to how there are uncountable forests. There may be only a few forests with elephants. One can even find herds of elephants, but to find an elephant with a pearl on its head is rare.

(Next Bhagavāna formulates knowledge and realization -)

भूमिरापोऽनलो वायु: खं मनो बुद्धिरेव च |
अहङ्कार इतीयं मे भिन्ना प्रकृतिरष्टधा || BG 7.4 ||

भूमि: - Earth, ; आप: - water, ; अनल: - fire, ; वायु: - wind, ; खं - space, ; मन: - mind, ; बुद्धि: - intellect, ; च - and ; अहङ्कार: - ego, ; इति - as such ; इयम् - these ; एव - indeed (are) ; भिन्ना - the distinct (components of) ; मे - My ; अष्टधा - eightfold ; प्रकृति: - nature (Prakṛti).

Earth, water, fire, wind, space, mind, intellect, and ego are the distinct components of My eightfold nature.

Intent - Here, it is essential to keep in mind that the five great elements (Pañcabhūta): 1) earth, 2) water, 3) fire, 4) wind, and 5) space) should be understood in their rudimentary forms (Tanmātra) rather than their gross forms. Mind refers to the cause of the mind, viz., the ego (अहंकार, Ahaṃkāra). Intellect refers to the cause of the ego, the Mahat. Ego is that which provides conceit or conception of individuality, the sense of self. It is the inner disposition of I-ness (अभिमानात्मक-वृत्ति, Abhimānātmaka-Vṛtti) which identifies the Ātmā (Self) with the body as "I." The "I-ness" sense in the body, sense-organs, mind, and intellect.

अपरेयमितस्त्वन्यां प्रकृतिं विद्धि मे पराम् |
जीवभूतां महाबाहो ययेदं धार्यते जगत् || BG 7.5 ||

महाबाहो - Hey Mahābāho (Arjuna)! ; इयम् - That (eightfold Prakṛti) ; अपरा - is (My insentient) lower nature. ; तु - However, ; इत: - besides this, ; विद्धि - know ; मे - My ; अन्याम् - other ; पराम् - higher (causal, root) ; जीवभूताम् - life-form ; प्रकृतिम् - nature ; यया - by which ; इदम् - this ; जगत् - world ; धार्यते - is upheld.

Hey Arjuna! That is the My lower nature. Besides this, know My other higher life-form nature by which this world is upheld.

The intent of verses (BG 7.4 - BG 7.5) - Those mentioned above eightfold lower nature (Aparā-Prakṛti) is of the functional form (Kārya-Prakṛti), which is the transformation (Vikṛti) of Prakṛti. However, separate from it, there is a higher nature (Parā-Prakṛti) of Mine, the Mulā (मूला) or root life-form Prakṛti which transforms into the eightfold lower nature and creates the phenomenal world (Saṃsāra, Jagata). With its relationship, the conscious (Cetana) is named Jīva. Prakṛti in the deep-sleep state is called the Parā-Prakṛti, and it is the transforming material cause or seed of the Saṃsāra. The same when it goes into the awake or the dream-state, transforming the eightfold Aparā-Prakṛti creates the Saṃsāra.

एतद्योनीनि भूतानि सर्वाणीत्युपधारय |
अहं कृत्स्नस्य जगत: प्रभव: प्रलयस्तथा || BG 7.6 ||

उपधारय - Know ; इति - that ; एतत् - this ; योनीनि - two (Parā-Prakṛti and Aparā-Prakṛti) is the womb of ; सर्वाणि - all ; भूतानि - beings, ; अहम् - (and) I am ; प्रभवः - the creator ; तथा - and ; प्रलयः - dissolver ; कृत्स्नस्य - of the entire ; जगतः - world.

Know that this dual Prakṛti is the womb of all beings, and I am the creator and dissolver of the entire world.

Intent - All living beings emanate from these dual Prakṛti. These two are the birthplace (Yoni-Sthāna) of all living beings, the material cause that is transformed (Pariṇāmī-Kāraṇa). Further, the dance of Prakṛti in the form of creation and destruction of the world that happens in whose illumination, that underlying existent support (Adhiṣṭhāna-Sattā) is none other than Me. I am the Vivartopādāna-cause of its creation and destruction, the cause in which delusional creation and destruction are perceived.

मत्त: परतरं नान्यत्किञ्चिदस्ति धनञ्जय |
मयि सर्वमिदं प्रोतं सूत्रे मणिगणा इव || BG 7.7 ||

धनञ्जय - Hey Dhanañjaya (Arjuna)! ; अस्ति - There is ; न अन्यत् - nothing ; किञ्चित् - else ; परतरं - beyond ; मत्तः - Me. ; सर्वम् - All ; इदम् - this (world) ; प्रोतम् - is threaded ; मयि - in Me ; इव - like ; मणिगणाः - gems ; सूत्रे - in a string.

Hey Arjuna! There is nothing else beyond Me. All this is threaded in Me like gems in a string.

Intent - Prakṛti and the world that is the work of Prakṛti are nothing without Me because all these are only perceptions of Me and only My miracle. That is why in all forms, I am the one shining. Just as earrings, necklaces, and other ornaments are nothing other than gold, they are all perceptions and miracles of gold, and in all of them, only gold is shining. So is the entire world threaded in Me.

(Now, Bhagavāna briefly provides his attribute of having all forms and being the Ātmā of all -)

रसोऽहमप्सु कौन्तेय प्रभास्मि शशिसूर्ययो: |
प्रणव: सर्ववेदेषु शब्द: खे पौरुषं नृषु || BG 7.8 ||

कौन्तेय - Hey Kaunteya (Arjuna)! ; अहम् - I ; अस्मि - am ; रसः - sapidity ; अप्सु - in water, ; प्रभा - brilliance ; शशि-सूर्ययोः - in the sun and the moon, ; प्रणवः - the sacred syllable Oṃ (ॐ) ; सर्व-वेदेषु - in all Vedas, ; शब्दः - sound ; खे - in the space, (and) ; पौरुषम् - humanness ; नृषु - in the humans.

Hey Arjuna! I am sapidity in water, brilliance in the sun and the moon, the sacred syllable Oṃ (ॐ) in all Vedas, sound in the space, and humanness in the humans.

Intent - The essence of water is called “Rasa, sapidity,” and in Me, that sapid thread, water is beaded. Similarly, the brilliance that is in the sun and the moon, that I am, by which they all shine. All the Vedas are strung in Me in the form of Oṃ (ॐ), which is the essence of all Vedas. In Me, the entire space is woven in the form of sound (Śabda). In addition, in the humans, I am in the form of their humanness; in that humanness-form Me, all humans shine.

पुण्यो गन्ध: पृथिव्यां च तेजश्चास्मि विभावसौ |
जीवनं सर्वभूतेषु तपश्चास्मि तपस्विषु || BG 7.9 ||

अस्मि - I am ; पुण्यः - pure ; गन्धः - fragrance ; पृथिव्याम् - in the earth, ; च - and ; तेजः - brilliance ; विभावसौ - in fire, ; च - and ; अस्मि - I am ; जीवनम् - life ; सर्व-भूतेषु - in all beings, ; च - and ; तपः - austerity ; तपस्विषु - in ascetics.

I am pure fragrance in the earth, brilliance in fire, life in all beings, and austerity in ascetics.

Intent - The essence of the earth is pure fragrance, and in that fragrance-form Me, the entire earth is pervaded. In the same way, the essence of fire is brilliance, and in that brilliance-form Me, fire is illuminating. I am in the form of life in all beings, by Whom all living beings are alive, and in ascetics, I am situated in the form of austerity.

बीजं मां सर्वभूतानां विद्धि पार्थ सनातनम् |
बुद्धिर्बुद्धिमतामस्मि तेजस्तेजस्विनामहम् || BG 7.10 ||

पार्थ - Hey Pārtha (Arjuna)! ; विद्धि - Know ; माम् - Me ; सनातनम् - (as) the eternal ; बीजम् - seed (the root cause) ; सर्वभूतानाम् - in all beings. ; अहम् - I ; अस्मि - am ; बुद्धिः - the intellect ; बुद्धिमताम् - of the intelligent (and) ; तेजः - the brilliance ; तेजस्विनाम् - of the brilliant.

Hey Arjuna! Know Me as the eternal seed in all beings. I am the intellect of the intelligent and the brilliance of the brilliant.

बलं बलवतां चाहं कामरागविवर्जितम् |
धर्माविरुद्धो भूतेषु कामोऽस्मि भरतर्षभ || BG 7.11 ||

भरतर्षभ - Hey Bharatarṣabha (Arjuna, the excellent one amongst the descendants of Bharata)! ; बलवताम् - Of the strong, ; अहम् - I ; अस्मि - am ; बलम् - the strength ; काम-राग-विवर्जितम् - devoid of (worldly) desire and attachment; ; च - and ; भूतेषु - in beings, (I am) ; कामः - the desire ; धर्म-अविरुद्धः - not opposed to righteousness.

Hey Arjuna! Of the strong, I am the strength devoid of desire and attachment; and in beings, I am the desire not opposed to righteousness.

Intent - Attachment and desire-laced strength are Tāmasika and demonic (Āsurī). With its relationship, there is an increase of I-ness in the body. In contrast, with the relinquishment of I-ness and mineness in materials, faith in the words of preceptors and scriptures, relinquishment of happiness-sense in objects of enjoyment, belief in the existence of other worlds (Āstikatā in Paraloka), and other forms, it is only I, the (Sāttvika and devoid of desire and attachment) divine strength existent in those individuals with divine attributes. By that strength, they attain Me. In addition, "We ought not to be sorrowful and selfish, be free from the sorrowful mortal world and be partners in liberation" and so forth - in all such forms, I am the desire consistent with righteousness, by which Jīva moves towards Me.

ये चैव सात्त्विका भावा राजसास्तामसाश्च ये |
मत्त एवेति तान्विद्धि न त्वहं तेषु ते मयि || BG 7.12 ||

ये - Whatever ; भावाः - things are ; एव - indeed ; सात्त्विकाः - Sattvaguṇī ; च - and ; ये - whatever (things are) ; राजसाः - Rajoguṇī, ; च - and ; तामसाः - Tamoguṇī ; विद्धि - know ; इति - that ; तान् - all of them ; मत्तः - originate from Me ; एव - alone. ; तु - Though ; ते - they ; मयि - are in Me, ; अहं - I am ; न - not ; तेषु - in them.

Whatever things are Sattvaguṇī, Rajoguṇī, and Tamoguṇī, know that all originate from Me alone. Though they are in Me, I am not in them.

Intent - The perceived phenomenal world consists of the three constituents known as the cause of the world's creation. However, in reality, the causal perception is nothing but delusionary. Whether they are the constituents or their work (the phenomenal world), they all originate from Me. Even though they arise from Me and are dependent on My support, I am not reliant on their support. Indeed, even in My support, they are only delusionary and by My power are only clues. In reality, they are without their existence. Just as a flag on a palace indicates the king's presence, in the same way, the three constituents and beingness within them indicate the presence of Me, the one existent common in all, but they do not have any existence of their own.

(Even though I am everyone's form and Ātmā, despite that -)

त्रिभिर्गुणमयैर्भावैरेभि: सर्वमिदं जगत् |
मोहितं नाभिजानाति मामेभ्य: परमव्ययम् || BG 7.13 ||

मोहितम् - Deluded by ; एभिः - these ; भावैः - substances ; त्रिभिः गुणमयैः - consisting of the three constituents, ; इदम् - this ; सर्वम् - entire ; जगत् - world ; न - does not ; अभिजानाति - know ; माम् - Me, ; अव्ययम् - the immutable (Reality Who is) ; परम् - beyond ; एभ्यः - them.

Deluded by substances consisting of the three constituents, the entire world does not know Me, the immutable Who is beyond them.

Intent - All these substances are nothing but Triguṇamayī. They consist of the three constituents of Prakṛti viz. Sattvaguṇa, Rajoguṇa and Tamoguṇa. Wherever there is a perception of their presence, there, in reality, I am existent. Not having their existence, their perception is impossible without Me. Just as without one (1), zero (0) cannot exist, and zero (0) by its nature is nothing, being nothing by itself in support of one (1), there is a realization of value. In the same way, the Triguṇātmaka substances, by their nature, are not there. Even being in non-existent form, in support of My existence, they are perceived as existing. Despite that, the entire world is deluded by the transformations of the three constituents such as attachment, aversion, and so forth. Due to their vision of seeing fault and being deprived of discriminating power, they fail to cognize Me as beyond and other than the constituents. They only see the Triguṇamayī manifestations, just as how a person who has jaundice, even though things are not yellow, sees everything yellow.

(What is the cause of this, and how can it be removed? -)

दैवी ह्येषा गुणमयी मम माया दुरत्यया |
मामेव ये प्रपद्यन्ते मायामेतां तरन्ति ते || BG 7.14 ||

हि - Undoubtedly, ; एषा - this ; दैवी - divine ; माया - delusive power (Māyā) ; मम - of Mine ; गुणमयी - consisting of the three constituents ; दुरत्यया - is hard to cross over. ; ते - Those ; ये - who ; प्रपद्यन्ते - surrender ; माम् - to Me ; एव - alone, ; तरन्ति - cross over ; एताम् - this ; मायाम् - Māyā.

Undoubtedly, this divine delusive power of Mine consisting of the three constituents is hard to cross over. Those who surrender to Me alone cross over this Māyā.

Intent - It is difficult to overcome this divine delusive power of Mine. Why? Because Jīva is deluded by its influence, instead of cognizing Me, he only sees the Triguṇamayī Māyā. However, those persons with the intelligence of seeing one Ātmā in all (Sarvātma-Bhāva), who are in front of Me and surrender to Me, only they are the ones who can overcome this Māyā. When a Jīva is facing away from Me, he is shrouded by this Māyā, just as there is a covering of darkness in the absence of the sun.

न मां दुष्कृतिनो मूढा: प्रपद्यन्ते नराधमा: |
माययापहृतज्ञाना आसुरं भावमाश्रिता: || BG 7.15 ||

अपहृत-ज्ञानाः - Deprived of knowledge ; आश्रिताः - (and) dependent ; आसुरम् - on demonic ; भावम् - dispositions ; मायया - due to Māyā - ; दुष्कृतिनः - evildoers, ; मूढाः - deluded, ; नर-अधमाः - (and) the vilest among humans ; न - do not ; प्रपद्यन्ते - surrender to ; माम् - Me.

Deprived of knowledge and dependent on demonic dispositions due to Māyā - evildoers, deluded, and the vilest among humans do not surrender to Me.

Intent - Where there are evil deeds, delusion, and demonic possessions, the dancer in the form of Māyā becomes prominent, and with her influence, meditation and knowledge move away. When meditation and knowledge have moved away, how can they come to My refuge? When they do not have My refuge, then shrouded by ignorance even though I am eternally shining like the sun, I am invisible from their view, just as in the sight of an owl, the sun appears as a sphere of darkness.

(Then who acquires Your refuge? -)

चतुर्विधा भजन्ते मां जना: सुकृतिनोऽर्जुन |
आर्तो जिज्ञासुरर्थार्थी ज्ञानी च भरतर्षभ || BG 7.16 ||

अर्जुन भरतर्षभ - Hey Arjuna, the excellent one amongst the descendants of Bharata! ; चतुः-विधाः - (There are) four kinds of ; जनाः - persons ; सुकृतिनः - of virtuous acts ; भजन्ते - (who) worship ; माम् - Me: ; आर्तः - an afflicted (with pain), ; जिज्ञासुः - a seeker of knowledge (with desire to know Me), ; अर्थार्थी - a seeker of material gain, ; च - and ; ज्ञानी - a knower (who is established in knowledge).

Hey Arjuna, the excellent one amongst the descendants of Bharata! There are four kinds of persons of virtuous acts who worship Me: an afflicted, a seeker of knowledge, a seeker of material gain, and a knower.

Intent - There are four kinds of people who worship the Lord:

1. Ārta (आर्त) - One who is disease-stricken, who does not possess desired objects, or who is in pain due to fear of thieves, wild animals, and others.
2. Arthārthi (अर्थार्थी) - One who desires material gain such as wealth, children, and others.
3. Jijñāsu (जिज्ञासु) - One who is endowed with fourfold means (Sādhana-Catuṣṭaya), who understands the Lord as the ultimate objective and has a keen desire to attain Him.
4. Jñānī (ज्ञानी) - One who has cognized the true nature of the Lord "is as is."

Accordingly, in the world, there are four kinds of persons who worship the Lord following their fondness, and they are all virtuous because, in their view, the Lord is unbeatable (सर्वोत्कृष्ट, Sarvotkṛṣṭa) and loving towards those who have surrendered (शरणागत-वत्सल, Śaraṇāgata-Vatsala).

तेषां ज्ञानी नित्ययुक्त एकभक्तिर्विशिष्यते |
प्रियो हि ज्ञानिनोऽत्यर्थमहं स च मम प्रिय: || BG 7.17 ||

तेषाम् - Among (them), ; ज्ञानी - a knower (Jñānī), ; नित्य-युक्तः - ever established (in Me) ; एक-भक्तिः - (and) exclusively devoted, ; विशिष्यते - excels. ; हि - For, ; अहम् - I am ; अत्यर्थम् - exceedingly ; प्रियः - dear ; ज्ञानिनः - to a knower ; च - and ; सः - he ; प्रियः - (is) dear to ; मम - Me.

A knower, ever established and exclusively devoted, excels. I am exceedingly dear to a knower, and he is dear to Me.

Intent - The object of ultimate love is only the Ātmā. In the world, whoever loves whatever, does it only from the perspective of their happiness. However, a knower with analytic thinking has cognized Me directly (Aparokṣa) as his Ātmā. That is why I am exceedingly dear to him. He being My Ātmā, is certainly dear to Me.

(Aren't the other three dear to You? -)

उदारा: सर्व एवैते ज्ञानी त्वात्मैव मे मतम् |
आस्थित: स हि युक्तात्मा मामेवानुत्तमां गतिम् || BG 7.18 ||

एव - Indeed ; सर्वे - all ; एते - these ; उदाराः - are generous. ; तु - However, ; ज्ञानी - a knower ; मे - in My ; मतम् - opinion ; एव - (is My) very ; आत्मा - Self. ; हि - For, ; सः - he ; आस्थितः - is situated ; युक्त-आत्मा - with a steadfast mind ; माम् - in Me ; एव - alone, ; अनुत्तमाम् गतिम् - the abode unparalleled.

Indeed, all are generous. However, a knower, in My opinion, is My very Self., For, he is situated with a steadfast mind in Me alone, the abode unparalleled.

Intent - All these devotees are generous, and though they are dear to Me, a knower is indeed My very Ātmā. He has relinquished everything and has exhausted his confined I-ness sense and thus the entire world in Me. He is established with oneness in Me in all sentiments - the supreme destination beyond which there is nothing better. It is a tenet of the scriptures that whoever gives up personal selfishness and mineness to whoever becomes correspondingly dear to the other. That is why that relinquishment is love. Here a knower has not left anything for Me. He has given up all his I-ness and mineness and has surrendered to Me, holding a sense of seeing one Ātmā in all. Thus, he is the one who crosses over the Māyā.

बहूनां जन्मनामन्ते ज्ञानवान्मां प्रपद्यते |
वासुदेव: सर्वमिति स महात्मा सुदुर्लभ: || BG 7.19 ||

अन्ते - At the end of ; बहूनाम् - (efforts of) many ; जन्मनाम् - births, (in the last birth) ; ज्ञानवान् - a knower ; सर्वम् - (realizing) "all this is ; वासुदेवः - Vāsudeva" ; इति - as such ; प्रपद्यते - attains ; माम् - Me. ; सः - Such ; महात्मा - a great soul ; सुदुर्लभः - is extremely rare.

At the end of many births, a knower realizing "all this is Vāsudeva" attains Me. Such a great soul is extremely rare.

Intent - A seeker after many births wherein impressions of knowledge-acquisition are accumulated, upon maturity of knowledge in the last birth, becoming knowledgeable and upon the realization of the Truth attains Me, establishes with oneness in Me. For a seeker active in the path of attaining the Lord, there is no bad end. However, in every such birth, with increasing knowledge-impressions, a Yoga-Bhraṣṭa seeker, the one who is fallen from Yoga as discussed in (BG 6.40 - BG 6.45), in the last birth attaining direct transcendent knowledge becomes free. What is the nature of this knowledge by which the Lord can be attained (Bhagavat-Prāpti)? It is said - The object of the mind and the senses (I, you, whatever movable and immovable and thus gross and subtle phenomenal world is) are all the Lord Vāsudeva. Without the Lord, there is no existence of the phenomenal world. The phenomenal world has no touch on the true nature of the Lord, just as there is no existence of the world without space, and the world cannot touch space. Great souls who know their true nature transcendentally are indeed rare, and they are the ones who cross over the Māyā.

{Among the four devotees, a knower is described. Seekers of knowledge accumulating knowledge-impressions at some point in time through the attainment of the Lord will overcome the Māyā. Next, Bhagavāna describes the remaining two: an afflicted (Ārta) and a seeker of material gain (Arthārthi) -}

कामैस्तैस्तैर्हृतज्ञाना: प्रपद्यन्तेऽन्यदेवता: |
तं तं नियममास्थाय प्रकृत्या नियता: स्वया || BG 7.20 ||

हृत-ज्ञानाः - (The afflicted and seekers of material gain) deprived of knowledge, ; प्रपद्यन्ते - worship ; अन्य-देवताः - other deities (to acquire their grace) ; तैः तैः - with those ; कामैः - (enjoyment) desires ; आस्थाय - following ; तम् तम् - those ; नियमम् - observances ; नियताः - impelled by ; स्वया - their own ; प्रकृत्या - nature.

(Those afflicted and seekers of material gain) deprived of knowledge, worship other deities with those desires following observances impelled by their nature.

Intent - Afflicted and seekers of material gain whose discerning power is gone surrender to other deities with desires for wealth, children, etc., obeying all observances based on their nature. As discussed in verse BG 7.15, when those who bow down before scriptures and public morality but get involved in arbitrary and unrestrained enjoyment of objects of pleasure and trample the interests of others for their self-interest are in all respects away from Me, then those afflicted who desire to be free from problems and those who desire objects of enjoyment are also not in front of Me. However, due to their varied desires, having lost their discerning power, they strive to please other deities. With the force of Rajoguṇī desires, and their hearts being disturbed, there is no formation of thought, "I am only bliss-form Ātmā of all, and I am extremely close and full in their hearts." In the absence of this discernment, happiness sense in desired objects becomes firmer, and inspired by their Rajoguṇī nature, for the satisfaction of desires, they are ready to worship those deities with whose grace they have hope of acquiring their wishes. They adopt whatever rules prescribed in worshiping those deities and thus remain deprived of Me - the real bliss form.

(Though due to their ignorance, they do not see Me, yet fruition of all of their wishes materialize only through Me, and that is this way -)

यो यो यां यां तनुं भक्तः श्रद्धयार्चितुमिच्छति |
तस्य तस्याचलां श्रद्धां तामेव विदधाम्यहम् || BG 7.21 ||

अहम् - I ; एव - indeed ; विदधामि - bestow upon ; यः यः - those ; भक्तः - (desire-ridden) devotees ; तस्य तस्य - their ; अचलाम् - steady ; श्रद्धाम् - devotion ; याम् याम् - (towards) whatever ; तनुम् - form of deity ; ताम् - that ; इच्छति - (they) seek ; अर्चितुम् - to worship ; श्रद्धया - with faith.

I indeed bestow upon those devotees their steady devotion towards whatever form of deity that they seek to worship with faith.

Intent - Whether it is worldly or transcendental, the success of any fruit is mainly on faith; without faith, no deity can give anything. That is why faith is the main deity. Indeed, I, "the Ātmā of all," am situated in the heart of that devotee in the form of faith towards that deity, by which he can worship that deity. If I do not provide My power in the form of faith in his heart, then he would not be fit to worship that deity, even an iota. Even being in front of that deity, the deity would not be able to provide any fruit to the devotee who has no faith.

स तया श्रद्धया युक्तस्तस्याराधनमीहते |
लभते च ततः कामान्मयैव विहितान्हि तान् || BG 7.22 ||

सः - He ; ईहते - engages ; तस्य - in their ; आराधनम् - worship ; युक्तः - with ; तया - that ; श्रद्धया - faith (bestowed by Me), ; च - and ; हि - undoubtedly, ; ततः - in the deity-form ; लभते - receives ; तान् - those ; कामान् - fruits ; विहितान् - granted ; मया - by Me ; एव - only.

He engages in their worship with that faith and undoubtedly, in the deity-form, receives those fruits granted by Me only.

Intent - Everything is fruitful through Me only. Here, faith in the hearts of devotees is established only through Me, and there, based on their sentiment in the form of the deity in whom they have faith, it is only I who am in their front. In reality, when there is nothing besides Me, then in whatever way they worship those deities, those devotions reach Me, the all-witness Ātmā of all, and the success of fruition is only through Me. Here, their sentiment takes the form of the deity with My power, and there, their sentiment itself takes the form of fruits with My power. This way, I make the inanimate sentiment live by My power, and everything happens through Me only. However, due to their ignorance, they believe themselves to be the worshippers of their worshipped-deity (Ārādhya-Deva) and believe that the fruition of their wishes is due to their revered deity. Due to their ignorance, they remain deprived of Me, the Ātmā of all.

अन्तवत्तु फलं तेषां तद्भवत्यल्पमेधसाम् |
देवान्देवयजो यान्ति मद्भक्ता यान्ति मामपि || BG 7.23 ||

तत् - That ; फलम् - fruit (of action) ; तेषाम् - of those ; अल्प-मेधसाम् - feeble-minded ; भवति - is ; अन्तवत् - finite. ; देव-यजः - Worshippers of deities ; यान्ति - go to ; देवान् - deities; ; तु - however, ; मत् - My ; भक्ताः - devotees ; यान्ति - attain ; माम् - Me ; अपि - alone.

That fruit of those feeble-minded is finite. Worshippers of deities reach deities; however, My devotes attain Me alone.

Intent - Only because of this ignorance, not understanding this subject truly, "Everything is fruitful through Me only, and it is only I, who am in the form of all those deities (who are delusionally perceived in Me the witness existent in all forms)" - all efforts of those feeble-minded are unsuccessful. Their running around for happiness is wasteful, as all beings are seen looking for complete happiness in all their efforts. However, due to the want of knowledge, those feeble-minded only acquire sorrow and poverty even with their efforts. In reality, being the work of Māyā, whether it is a deity, the world of the deities, or whether it is enjoyments, they are all ephemeral and, in their end, provide only grief. This way, those who worship deities reach deities. However, a devotee who is a seeker of knowledge and thus knower attains Me the eternal immutable Ātmā of all.

From (BG 7.15 to BG 7.23), four types of devotees are described: an inflicted, a seeker of material gain, a seeker of knowledge, and a knower. Among them, a seeker of knowledge and a knower are the ones who can overcome Māyā and be fit for realizing the Lord in all forms.

(Next, Bhagavāna describes - why the ordinary does not come in My refuge?)

अव्यक्तं व्यक्तिमापन्नं मन्यन्ते मामबुद्धयः |
परं भावमजानन्तो ममाव्ययमनुत्तमम् || BG 7.24 ||

अबुद्धयः - The undiscriminating ones, ; अजानन्तः - not knowing ; मम - My ; अव्ययम् - immutable, ; अनुत्तमम् - unsurpassable, ; परम् - supreme ; भावम् - nature, ; मन्यन्ते - believe (that) ; माम् - I, ; अव्यक्तम् - the unmanifest (one beyond the mind and senses), ; आपन्नम् - have acquired ; व्यक्तिम् - (limited) individuality.

The undiscriminating ones, not knowing My immutable, unsurpassable, supreme nature, believe that I, the unmanifest, have acquired limited individuality.

Intent - In reality, I am unmanifest. I do not have any individuality and am not graspable by the mind and senses. The mind and senses can grasp only manifest everyday things with attributes. Attributeless (Nirviśeṣa) common things being imperceptible cannot be grasped by them. However, only the attributeless unmanifest-form is present under those "to be grasped and one who grasps" individuals with attributes whose forms are fruitful on its dependence. Only on its support being and not-being, birth and end of all individuals materialize. The attributeless imperceptible witness-conscious is immovable and immutable in those being and non-being of individuals with attributes, just as being and non-being of ornaments such as necklaces and bangles being dependent on the common and without attributes gold. In the being and non-being forms of necklaces and bangles, the common form of gold remains immovable and immutable. Despite being attributeless, common, and imperceptible-form and being existent in the awareness sense of individuals, those undiscriminating individuals do not know My immutable supreme nature. Guided by their senses, they believe Me as a perceptible limited individual. Based on their inclinations, they worship only some perceptible forms, such as Rāma, Kṛṣṇa, et al., and thus do not surrender to Me the all-witnessing Ātmā of all. Though Rāma-Kṛṣṇa et al. are play-forms (Līlā-Vigraha) of Me, the Ātmā of all, and their worship is a middle step towards My refuge, but believing that step as the desired (उद्दिष्ट, Uddiṣṭa) destination set their final camp and do not move forwards towards Me.

(When You are in all individuals and everyone's Ātmā, then why are you not visible to all? -)

नाहं प्रकाशः सर्वस्य योगमायासमावृतः |
मूढोऽयं नाभिजानाति लोको मामजमव्ययम् || BG 7.25 ||

योग-माया-समावृतः - Veiled by (the delusive power of) My Yoga-Māyā, ; अहम् - I ; न - do not ; प्रकाशः - manifest ; सर्वस्य - to all. ; अयम् - (That is why,) this ; मूढः - deluded ; लोकः - world ; अभिजानाति - knows ; माम् - Me ; न - not, ; अजम् - the unborn ; अव्ययम् - (and) immutable.

Veiled by My Yoga-Māyā, I do not manifest to all. This deluded world knows Me not, the unborn and immutable.

Intent - Veiled by his various roles, an actor is unknown to the audience other than the roles he is playing. Yet, those various roles do not hide his perspective and do not remain hidden from some clever individuals. Hidden by the delusive power (Māyā) of the union of the three constituents, even though I am present in all forms, yet to all ordinary individuals, I am not perceptible. However, that Yoga-Māyā cannot hide My vision and cannot hide Me from those knowers of the Truth who know My true nature. Yet, firmly situated in the hearts and sights of deluded, ignorant beings of the world, Yoga-Māyā makes their sights outwards and does not let them turn inwards. As a result, they only see the external delusional world and do not cognize Me with their vision of seeing faults. That is like a confused monkey in front of a clean mirror, but because of his faulty vision only sees his image as another monkey and does not see the mirror. Even though I am present in front of deluded beings in all forms - inside, outside, and everywhere, I am not cognized by them due to their vision of seeing faults. Not seeing Me the unborn immutable, they only see the world of their imagination.

वेदाहं समतीतानि वर्तमानानि चार्जुन |
भविष्याणि च भूतानि मां तु वेद न कश्चन || BG 7.26 ||

अर्जुन - Hey Arjuna! ; अहम् - I ; वेद - know ; भूतानि - all beings ; समतीतानि - of the past, ; च - and ; वर्तमानानि - present ; च - and ; भविष्याणि - future (as My own true nature). ; तु - However, ; न - no ; कश्चन - one (except a knower) ; वेद - knows ; माम् - Me (as such).

Hey Arjuna! I know all beings of the past, present, and future. However, no one knows Me.

Intent - Despite My true nature being existent in those beings' knowledge, vision, and effort, they do not know Me because of Māyā. However, I know all beings of the past, the present, and the ones to come into being in the future. Wherever their vision goes, I, the Ātmā of all, illuminate all names and forms at that location hidden from their sight. However, they only see names and forms delusionally through the lens of their vision empowered with Māyā. In the delusional (Mithyā) names and forms the One that is shining, and with Whose awareness everything is being made aware of, their eyes do not reach. Even though I know all beings of all times, they do not know Me, the Ātmā of all in their own Ātmā, and continue to maintain I-ness in the body.

(With what impediments are You not known this way? -)

इच्छाद्वेषसमुत्थेन द्वन्द्वमोहेन भारत |
सर्वभूतानि सम्मोहं सर्गे यान्ति परन्तप || BG 7.27 ||

भारत - Hey Bhārata (Arjuna)! ; परन्तप - The terror of foes! ; सर्व-भूतानि - All beings ; सर्गे - (right) from creation ; यान्ति - are subject to ; सम्मोहम् - confusion ; द्वन्द्व-मोहेन - by the duality delusions ; इच्छा-द्वेष-समुत्थेन - born of attachment and aversion.

Hey Arjuna, the terror of foes! All beings right from creation are subject to confusion by the duality delusions born of attachment and aversion.

Intent - Due to the ignorance of own true nature of being the all-witness Ātmā of all, an I-ness sense is formed in the body. With I-ness sense in the body, there is the formation of discriminating-vision. With a discriminating vision, one develops a favorable inclination toward some things and, in some other things, an antagonistic inclination. As a result, attachment to objects of favorable inclination and aversion towards objects of antagonistic inclination develops. Due to attachment and aversion through I-ness and mineness, duality delusions such as happiness and sorrow, gain and loss, lust and anger are formed. Indeed, confused by these dualistic delusions, all beings are subjugated to mental clouding right from the beginning.

येषां त्वन्तगतं पापं जनानां पुण्यकर्मणाम् |
ते द्वन्द्वमोहनिर्मुक्ता भजन्ते मां दृढव्रता: || BG 7.28 ||

तु - However, ; येषाम् - those ; जनानाम् - persons ; दृढ-व्रताः - with steadfast resolve ; पापम् - whose sins ; अन्तगतम् - are purged ; पुण्य-कर्मणाम् - act virtuously (and) ; द्वन्द्व-मोह-निर्मुक्ताः - are free from the duality delusions ; ते - they ; भजन्ते - worship ; माम् - Me.

However, those with steadfast resolve whose sins are purged act virtuously and are free from the duality delusions worship Me.

Intent - One whose resolve is, "Bliss-form is only the Lord, worldly enjoyments are in the form of a disease, repeated births and deaths are lasting diseases, and only through undivided (Ananya) refuge in the Lord there is a possibility of curing this disease," such persons are called of steadfast resolve (दृढव्रती, Dṛḍhavratī). Such virtuous steadfast devotees whose sins are purged, free from the duality delusions such as lust and anger, attachment and aversion, worship Me. They surrender to Me. Sin is purged with pious acts, just as darkness with illumination. With freedom from sins, freedom from the duality delusions is acquired. With the removal of dualities, moving towards the Lord is achieved. Having moved towards the Lord, through the attainment of the Lord, one achieves freedom from the cycle of birth and death.

जरामरणमोक्षाय मामाश्रित्य यतन्ति ये |
ते ब्रह्म तद्विदु: कृत्स्नमध्यात्मं कर्म चाखिलम् || BG 7.29 ||

आश्रित्य - Surrendering ; माम् - to Me ; ते - they ; ये - who ; यतन्ति - strive ; जरा-मरण-मोक्षाय - for release from old age (and) death ; विदुः - come to know ; कृत्स्नम् - the entire ; अध्यात्मम् - "Adhyātma" ; च - and ; अखिलम् - complete ; कर्म - "Karma" ; तत् - as that ; ब्रह्म - Brahman.

Surrendering to Me, they who strive for release from old age and death come to know the entire "Adhyātma" and complete "Karma" as that Brahman.

साधिभूताधिदैवं मां साधियज्ञं च ये विदु: |
प्रयाणकालेऽपि च मां ते विदुर्युक्तचेतस: || BG 7.30 ||

अपि - Together ; साधिभूत - with "Adhibhūta" ; च - and ; अधिदैवम् - "Adhidaiva" ; च - and ; साधियज्ञम् - with "Adhiyajña" ; ये - (those) who ; प्रयाणकाले - at the time of death ; विदुः - know ; माम् - Me (in the Brahman-form), ; विदुः - know ; ते - them ; युक्त-चेतसः - (as) having steadfast mind ; माम् - in Me.

Together with "Adhibhūta," "Adhidaiva," and "Adhiyajña," those who at the time of death know Me in the Brahman-form, know them as having a steadfast mind in Me.

The intent of verses (BG 7.29 - BG 7.30) - As described in and under verse BG 7.28, one who has moved towards Me steadfastly strives to be free from the grief of birth and death. Such a person knows the entire Adhyātma, Adhidaiva, Adhibhūta, Adhiyajña, and Karma - the entire existence of the phenomenal world as Me the Brahman. That is, Adhyātma, Adhidaiva et al. are all the Brahman-form, just as gold rings, gold-necklaces are all varied forms of gold and "I am that Brahman." At the time of death, one who knows transcendentally (Aparokṣa) oneness of the Brahman and the Ātmā (ब्रह्मात्मैक्य, Brahmātmaikya), such a person has steadfast mind Yukta-Citta with oneness in the Ātmā, has attained union (Yoga) in Me, and is Yoga-Yukta. With the influence of this direct transcendent knowledge, he does not take birth again.

ॐ तत्सदिति श्रीमद्भगवद्गीतासूपनिषत्सु ब्रह्मविध्यायां योगशास्त्रे

श्रीकृष्णार्जुनसम्वादे ज्ञानविज्ञानयोगो नाम

सप्तमोऽध्यायः || BG 7 ||

Oṃ Tat Sat

In the Śrīmad Bhagavad Gītā Upaniṣad

The Yoga Science of the Knowledge of Self-Realization

The Discourse of Lord Śrī Kṛṣṇa and Arjuna

This Seventh Chapter

Yoga Named - The Yoga of Knowledge and Realization

Clarification

In this chapter, Bhagavāna described His attribute of being the Ātmā of all beings (सर्वात्मता, Sarvātmatā) and the attribute of being in all diverse forms (Sarvarupatā) in the cause of attaining union (Yoga) with oneness in His true nature. In the first two verses, Bhagavāna formulated knowledge and realized knowledge (Jñāna and Vijñāna), knowing which He can be known in all forms and knowing that nothing else remains to be known in this world. Bhagavāna indicated extreme difficulty acquiring that knowledge (BG 7.1 - BG 7.3). Then Bhagavāna described the birthplace of the world as a whole and said that from where the world originates is indeed My Nature (Prakṛti) divided into Parā and Aparā, two components. Though My Prakṛti is not separate from Me, just as a person's shadow is not separate from him, I do not become Prakṛti just as a person himself does not become his own shadow. I am beyond Prakṛti and beyond the Saṃsāra that is the transformed result of Prakṛti, yet nothing is beyond Me, just as space follows all yet remains dissociated from all.

Further, Bhagavāna indicated that the entire Saṃsāra is threaded in Me just as beads in a rosary are (BG 7.4 - BG 7.7). After that, Bhagavāna briefly described how He pervades the great elements (Pañcabhūta), the Vedas, the three constituents of Prakṛti, and their work (the world), and said that they all being His shadow, are dependent on Him. However, He is not dependent on them (BG 7.8 - BG 7.12). Then, He explained that even though I pervade all, the world deluded by substances consisting of the three constituents does not know Me, the immutable Who is beyond them. Even though this world is of non-existent form, it appears as of existent form. Just as a pair of tongs with the power of hands can lift external objects but cannot grasp the hand, in the same way, with Whose existence the three constituents have a presence, they are unable to know that "Existent." Difficulty in overcoming His Māyā is a major reason for this ignorance. Only by exclusively surrendering unto Him is shown as the way to overcome this Māyā (BG 7.13 - BG 7.14).

After that, Bhagavāna described those confused evildoers and vilest among humans, whose knowledge is gone due to Māyā and are dependent on demonic dispositions, do not surrender to Him. For such persons, an effort to cross over the Māyā is impossible. Leaving them aside, there are four kinds of devotees: 1) an afflicted (Ārta), 2) a seeker of material gain (Arthārthi), 3) a seeker of knowledge (Jijñāsu), and 4) a knower (Jñānī), who by with their nature surrender to Bhagavāna. Among them, a knower is depicted as the dearest to Bhagavāna. Exclusively devoted to Bhagavāna, he is always situated with oneness and is the only one fit to overcome Māyā. Second, a seeker of knowledge with the effort of many lives, knowing the entire world in the form of the Lord Vāsudeva attaining the Lord will overcome Māyā (BG 7.15 - BG 7.19). Because the discerning power of an afflicted and a seeker of material gain is lost, they surrender to other deities based on their nature due to their varied desires. However, I am the one who establishes their faith in those deities based on their desires. Endowed with such faith, they can worship those deities, and I come in front of them in the very form of that deity. Indeed, I, in the form of that deity who provides desired fruits, yet those blinded by desire do not see Me. Because of this ignorance, even doing everything, they remain deprived of attaining Me the eternal bliss-form, and thus these feeble-minded acquire only perishable fruits. This way, the nature of four kinds of devotees is described, among whom a knower and a seeker of knowledge attaining the Lord are articulated as the ones who are fit to overcome Māyā (BG 7.20 - BG 7.23).

When You are eternal bliss-form and are the Ātmā of all, why do beings abandoning You move towards other deities? In front of such a doubt, Bhagavāna made it clear that such unwise persons who have I-ness in the body and senses and, as a result, who have become prey to the vision of discrimination and confinement become focused only on visible material things that are objects of the mind and senses. Such feeble-minded persons believe Me as a worldly person and a divine physical entity. That is why they do not see Me, the one who resides in the eyes and sees everything; and does not attain Me, who is always situated in the heart. That is why veiled by My Māyā, I, the unborn and immutable, am not visible to ordinary beings. Beings do not know Me the Ātmā of all, yet I know all past, present, and future beings. Due to ignorance, fondness of attachment to desire, and dualities born of despite, all beings not knowing Me stay in the cycle of sorrowful birth and death. However, those pious persons whose sins are purged, such steadfast devotees free from the dualities of attachment and aversion, worship Me alone. Therefore, those persons who desire to be free from old age and death, moving towards Me, endeavoring come to know the entire Adhyātma, Adhidaiva, Adhibhūta, Adhiyajña, and all Karma in the form of Brahman. Indeed, up to the time of death, those who know Me, know them as Yoga-Yukta, and with the influence of this knowledge, they do not take birth again.

Accordingly, in this chapter on the attainment of Yoga, Bhagavāna described His true nature, and at the beginning of the chapter, the promise he had made to describe all of His forms is articulated. At the beginning of the eighth chapter Arjuna not knowing the true nature of the Brahman, Adhyātma, Adhidaiva, Adhibhūta, Adhiyajña, and Karma, asks Bhagavāna -

CHAPTER 8

THE YOGA OF THE SUPREME IMPERISHABLE REALITY

अर्जुन उवाच |
किं तद्ब्रह्म किमध्यात्मं किं कर्म पुरुषोत्तम |
अधिभूतं च किं प्रोक्तमधिदैवं किमुच्यते || BG 8.1 ||
अधियज्ञ: कथं कोऽत्र देहेऽस्मिन्मधुसूदन |
प्रयाणकाले च कथं ज्ञेयोऽसि नियतात्मभि: || BG 8.2 ||
अर्जुन उवाच - Arjuna said -

पुरुषोत्तम - Hey Puruṣottama (Śrī Kṛṣṇa, the Supreme Personality)! ; किम् - What is ; तत् - that ; ब्रह्म - Brahman? ; किम् - What is ; अध्यात्मम् - Adhyātma? ; किम् - What is ; कर्म - Karma? ; किम् - What has ; प्रोक्तम् - been called ; अधिभूतम् - Adhibhūta? ; च - And ; किम् - what is ; उच्यते - called ; अधिदैवम् - Adhidaiva?

मधुसूदन - Hey Madhusūdana (Śrī Kṛṣṇa)! ; अत्र - Here ; देहे - in the body, ; कः - who ; कथम् - (and) how is ; अस्मिन् - this ; अधियज्ञः - Adhiyajña? ; च - And ; प्रयाण-काले - at the time of death, ; कथम् - how are ; असि - You ; ज्ञेयः - to be known ; नियत-आत्मभिः - by one with a steadfast mind?

Arjuna said -

Hey Puruṣottama[98]! What is that Brahman? What is Adhyātma? What is Karma? What is called Adhibhūta? What is called Adhidaiva?

Hey Madhusūdana! Here in the body, who and how is this Adhiyajña? At the time of death, how are You to be known by one with a steadfast mind?

श्रीभगवानुवाच |
अक्षरं ब्रह्म परमं स्वभावोऽध्यात्ममुच्यते |
भूतभावोद्भवकरो विसर्ग: कर्मसञ्ज्ञित: ||BG 8. 3 ||
श्रीभगवान् उवाच - Śrī Bhagavān said -

ब्रह्म - The "Brahman" is ; परमम् - the supreme, ; अक्षरम् - the imperishable. ; स्वभावः - Intrinsic nature ; उच्यते - is called ; अध्यात्मम् - "Adhyātma." ; विसर्गः - Activity ; भूत-भाव-उद्भव-करः - that produces sentiments in beings ; कर्म-संज्ञितः - is called "Karma."

[98] Śrī Kṛṣṇa is here addressed as Puruṣottama (पुरुषोत्तम, the supreme Personality). Puruṣottama is a compound word from Puruṣa (पुरुष) meaning Personality and Uttama (उत्तम) meaning best, highest or supreme.

Śrī Bhagavān said -

The "Brahman" is the supreme, the imperishable. Intrinsic nature is called "Adhyātma."[99] Activity that produces sentiments in beings is called "Karma."

Intent - That which is the supreme, the imperishable is the Brahman. In the Nyāya (न्याय) doctrine, space and time are deemed as substances that always exist (Nitya-Dravya) and are known as imperishable (Akṣara). In the Sāṅkhya doctrine, Prakṛti (Nature) is deemed as all-pervading (विभु, Vibhu) in imperishable form. However, in Whom, space and all-pervading Prakṛti becomes completely null, such imperishable, that is, imperishable of those imperishable is the Brahman.

Intrinsic nature (स्वभाव, Svabhāva) is called Adhyātma. That which is created without any cause is called Svabhāva. The cause (Pariṇāmī-Upādāna) that transforms into the power of knowledge and action (Jñāna-Śakti, Kriyā-Śakti) is called Adhyātma. That is why Prakṛti is called Adhyātma.

Good or bad activity that produces sentiments (Bhāva) in beings is defined as Karma. Any subjective process of arousing mental states or emotional waves originating in the mind and intellect in the form of a thought or resolve is called Bhāva. Activities of the body and senses directly resulting from the mind and intellect, or occurring in the knowledge of the mind and intellect being producers of emotions, are called Karma. The intention here is that all those efforts that create enjoyments or impressions (Saṃskāras) are called Karma. Only in the mind and intellect, those emotional activities can manifest and not anywhere else. Though after eating, myriads of actions happen within the body, such as feces, urine, blood, or muscles, they do not happen in the knowledge of the mind and intellect. They are not the result of the mind and intellect, nor do they create any good or bad impressions; they do not fall within the definition of Karma. Thus, this is the pervasive definition of Karma. Separate from this to only call material relinquishment towards deities as Karma is to make Karma extremely adulterated.

अधिभूतं क्षरो भाव: पुरुषश्चाधिदैवतम् |
अधियज्ञोऽहमेवात्र देहे देहभृतां वर || BG 8.4 ||

क्षर: - Perishable (with creation destruction attributes) ; भाव: - elements ; अधिभूतम् - are called "Adhibhūta." ; पुरुष: - Puruṣa (the one resting in the body) ; अधिदैवतम् - is called "Adhidaiva," ; च - and ; देह-भृताम् वर - hey, (Arjuna) the best among the embodied! ; अत्र - Here ; देहे - in the body, ; अहम् - I am ; एव - indeed ; अधियज्ञ: - "Adhiyajña."

Perishable elements are called "Adhibhūta." Puruṣa is called "Adhidaiva," and hey, Arjuna, the best among the embodied! Here in the body, I am indeed "Adhiyajña."

Intent - Whatever perishable elements there are, whatever visible mortal world there is, being endowed with the property of creation and destruction is called Adhibhūta. Situated in every entity endowed with the property of creation and destruction (उत्पत्ति-नाश-धर्मी, Utpatti-Nāśa-Dharmī), there is a conscious-divine-power (चेतन-देव-शक्ति, Cetana-Deva-Śakti) referred to as Puruṣa (Personality) by whose grace all mutations, all activities of knowledge and actions of the senses and conscience materialize, that Personality is called Adhideva. In addition, all activities of doing and enjoying that manifest in the body are in the form of sacrifice and are for the enjoyment of the Jīvātmā. The materialization of all enjoyment type sacrifices happens in support of the Antaryāmi - "सो मनसोन्तर यमयति एष त आत्मा अन्तर्याम्यमृत:, the one who is sitting within the

[99] The five cognitive sense-organs (पञ्च-ज्ञानेन्द्रिय, Pañca-Jñānendriya): 1) skin (त्वक, Tvaka), 2) tongue (रसना, Rasanā), 3) eyes (चक्षु, Cakṣu), 4) nose (घ्राण, Ghrāṇa) and 5) ears (श्रोत्र, Śrotra); the five action-organs (पञ्च-कर्मेन्द्रिय, Pañca-Karmendriya): 1) mouth (वाक, Vāka) for voice, 2) hands (पाणि, Pāṇi) for grasping, receiving, gathering, collecting (Grahaṇa) and holding (Dhāraṇa), 3) feet (पाद, Pāda) for walking, moving, locomotion (Gamana), 4) anus (पायु, Pāyu) for excretion and 5) genitals (उपस्थ, Upastha) for reproduction; the mind (मनस्, Manas); the intellect (बुद्धि, Buddhi); the subconscious mind (चित्त, Citta) and ego (अहंकार, Ahaṃkāra) - these fourteen are called "Adhyātma". All knowledge and actions manifest through them.

conscience (Antaḥkaraṇa) controlling all is your Antaryāmi ambrosiac Ātmā."[100] This Antaryāmi support (अधिष्ठाता, Adhiṣṭhātā) Adhiyajña in this body, is I alone.

(This way, Bhagavāna responded to six questions. In response to the seventh question, "At the time of death, how are You to be known by one with a steadfast mind?" Bhagavāna elaborates until the end of the chapter. -)

अन्तकाले च मामेव स्मरन्मुक्त्वा कलेवरम् |
य: प्रयाति स मद्भावं याति नास्त्यत्र संशय: || BG 8.5 ||

च - Moreover, ; स: - he ; य: - who ; प्रयाति - departs, ; मुक्त्वा - leaving ; कलेवरम् - the body ; स्मरन् - remembering ; माम् - Me ; एव - alone ; अन्त-काले - in the end time (of death), ; याति - acquires ; मत् - My ; भावम् - status. ; अस्ति - There is ; न - no ; संशय: - doubt ; अत्र - about that.

He who departs, leaving the body remembering Me alone in the end time, acquires My status. There is no doubt about that.

Intent - A person who, in his end-time, leaves his body thinking of Me, the Real-Conscious-Bliss (Saccidānanda, omnipresent Ātmā of all), he directly attains the Brahman status; there is no doubt about it. Because that knower of the Truth, while alive, has attained Me, just like a walnut within one's grip (करामलकवत, Karāmalakavata). His vision never disappears from Me. The Real-Conscious-Bliss is only the true nature of a Jīva. Only due to ignorance in the middle there was a contrary notion, so where is the place for any doubt?

(One whose vision does not perceive Me, that person -)

यं यं वापि स्मरन्भावं त्यजत्यन्ते कलेवरम् |
तं तमेवैति कौन्तेय सदा तद्भावभावित: || BG 8.6 ||

वा - Or, ; कौन्तेय - hey Kaunteya (Arjuna)! ; अपि - Even ; अन्ते - in the end (time of death), ; स्मरन् - remembering ; यं यं - whatever ; भावम् - form ; त्यजति - (one) leaves ; कलेवरम् - the body, ; सदा - ever ; तद्भावभावित: - absorbed in that form, ; एव - certainly ; एति - acquires ; तं तं - that.

Hey Arjuna! Even in the end, remembering whatever form one leaves the body, ever absorbed in that form, certainly acquires that.

Intent - Jīva is an embodiment of sentiments, and the world is full of sentiments. That is why "याद्रशी भावना यस्य सिद्धिर्भवति ताद्रशी, just as how firm one's sentiment is such becomes his form." The tenet of Vedānta is that the mover of one's fate (Prārabdha) is Jīva itself. In the end, whatever sentiment a Jīva has, his future destination and acquisition of enjoyments happen based on that sentiment. The existent Paramātmā is present in sentiments, so they cannot be unsuccessful. However, sentiments do not manifest accidentally in any unexpected form in the end time. Sentiments are molded with the practice of whatever firm thoughts and actions one is engaged in throughout one's lifetime. Following this rule, if in the lifetime of a steady minded person, the object of subtle intellect, that is, the inclinations do not unite in My real all-witness form and its practice does not materialize, then in whatever sentiment he is immersed, be it with attributes or without attributes (Saguṇa or Nirguṇa), with the strength of that sentiment, in the end, leaving his body remembering that sentiment attains that very form.

---

[100] Bṛhadāraṇyaka Upaniṣad (बृहदारण्यक उपनिषद्)

(Accordingly, when sentiments at the end time are the foremost -)

तस्मात्सर्वेषु कालेषु मामनुस्मर युध्य च |
मय्यर्पितमनोबुद्धिर्मामेवैष्यस्यसंशयम् || BG 8.7 ||

तस्मात् - Therefore, ; सर्वेषु - at all ; कालेषु - times, ; अनुस्मर - remember ; माम् - Me ; च - and ; युध्य - fight. ; अर्पित-मनः-बुद्धिः - Dedicating (your) mind and intellect ; मयि - to Me, ; असंशयम् - (you will) undoubtedly ; एष्यसि - attain ; माम् - Me ; एव - only.

Therefore, at all times, remember Me and fight. Dedicating your mind and intellect to Me, you will undoubtedly attain Me only.

Intent - That is why just as is described in BG 8.5, at all times, you ought to think only about Me, the all-witness Ātmā of all, and ought to practice the same so firmly that even while engaged in the dangerous war - "I, Arjuna am a slayer, these Duryodhana and others will be slain, and I have a certain relationship with them" such doership-enjoyership association with the body would never arise. However, acquired on its own without any desire, not by any obligation, engaging naturally in the law of own life (Svadharma), your inclination ought to remain steadfast, "In my Ātmā there is no slayer Arjuna, there is no Duryodhana who is going to be slain, there is no war, there is no cause for the war, there is no action of killing, there are no slayable bodies, nor are there any weapons in the form of instruments to kill. But all these are miracles of my Ātmā and are only illusory waves in which though I appear as the Ātmā and shinning, yet in my true from there is no creation, destruction of these perceptions, nothing has happened, nor anything will happen." With the maturity of this knowledge, dedicating your body, senses, mind, and intellect, you will undoubtedly attain Me. Holding doer-intellect, offering the mind and intellect to Bhagavāna, is not a true dedication. This offering is only sentimental, not real. Its fruit is only the purity of the conscience, not the attainment of the Lord. However, here the words of Bhagavāna are "मामेवैष्यस्यसंशयम्, you will undoubtedly attain Me," by which the aforementioned total dedication should be understood only in the form of knowledge.

Those steady minded Yogīs who, in the end, leave their bodies contemplating Bhagavāna through knowledge attain immediate liberation (सध्यो-मुक्ति, Sadhyo-Mukti). However, in the words of Śruti, "द्रश्यते त्वग्र्यया बुद्धया सूक्ष्मया सूक्ष्मदर्शीभिः, (the subtle element, Ātma-Tattva) can only be perceived by seers of subtlety through the subtle and sharp intellect."

{Those steadfast minded Yogīs whose intellect through knowledge has not penetrated that subtle element, for them through attributeless meditation (Nirguṇa-Dhyāna) Bhagavāna describes sequential liberation (Krama-Mukti) -}

अभ्यासयोगयुक्तेन चेतसा नान्यगामिना |
परमं पुरुषं दिव्यं याति पार्थानुचिन्तयन् || BG 8.8 ||

पार्थ - Hey Pārtha (Arjuna)! ; अभ्यास-योग-युक्तेन - (A Yogī,) with a steadfast discipline in the practice (of) ; अनुचिन्तयन् - (constantly) thinking ; चेतसा - with a mind ; न अन्य-गामिना - that does not move towards any other (thing), ; याति - attains ; परमम् - the supreme ; दिव्यम् - divine ; पुरुषम् - Personality.

Hey Arjuna! (A Yogī), with a steadfast discipline in the practice of constantly thinking with a mind that does not move towards any other, attains the supreme divine Personality.

Intent - Following the above approach of BG 8.7, if a steady minded Yogī is not able through knowledge to dedicate his mind and intellect to the Lord, then through the practice of the discipline of the "Yoga of Meditation" by thinking with a mind that does not wander anywhere else, in the end, leaving the body attains the Supreme Personality. Repetition of homogeneous inclinations related to the Lord and abandonment of heterogeneous inclinations is called Abhyāsa-Yoga or Dhyāna-Yoga.

(Endowed with what attributes he attains the Supreme Personality -)

कविं पुराणमनुशासितार मणोरणीयांसमनुस्मरेद्यः |
सर्वस्य धातारमचिन्त्यरूप मादित्यवर्णं तमसः परस्तात् || BG 8.9 ||
प्रयाणकाले मनसाचलेन भक्त्या युक्तो योगबलेन चैव |
भ्रुवोर्मध्ये प्राणमावेश्य सम्यक् स तं परं पुरुषमुपैति दिव्यम् || BG 8.10 ||

यः - Who ; अनुस्मरेत् - meditates on the ; कविम् - omniscient, ; पुराणम् - beginningless ancient ; अनुशासितारम् - controller of all, ; अणोः अणीयांसम् - subtler than the subtle, ; धातारम् - sustainer ; सर्वस्य - of all, ; अचिन्त्य-रूपम् - imponderable in form, ; आदित्य-वर्णम् - resplendent like the sun, ; परस्तात् - beyond ; तमसः - the delusional darkness (attains the same form of the supreme divine Personality);

प्रयाण-काले - in the end time, ; योग-बलेन - through the power of Yoga, ; युक्तः - with ; भक्त्या - devotion ; च - and ; अचलेन - a steady ; मनसा - mind ; सम्यक् - properly ; आवेश्य - establishing ; प्राणम् - the vital breaths of air ; मध्ये - in the middle of ; भ्रुवोः - the eyebrows, (meditating) ; सः - he ; उपैति - attains ; तम् - that ; परम् - supreme ; दिव्यम् - divine ; पुरुषम् - Personality ; एव - indeed.

Who meditates on the omniscient, beginningless ancient controller of all, subtler than the subtle, sustainer of all, imponderable in form, resplendent like the sun, beyond the delusional darkness; in the end time, through the power of Yoga, with devotion and a steady mind properly establishing the vital breaths of air in the middle of the eyebrows, he attains the supreme divine Personality.

The intent of verses (BG 8.9 - BG 8.10) - In the discipline of knowledge (Jñāna-Mārga), in the end, it is not necessary to have the mental state concentrated on the form of the one to be meditated (Dhyeya), nor is there any injunction in the end time that if there is no Brahman-form mental-state, there will be an obstacle in the immediate liberation (Sadhyo-Mukti) of a knower. A knower is liberated concomitantly with realized knowledge. With the realization of the distinction free Brahman in his resolve, there is no distinction between the Ātmā and Anātmā, the Jīvātmā and the Brahman. That is why - "यत्र यत्र मनो याति तत्र तत्र समाधायः:, wherever the mind goes there is Samādhī," and so is his natural oneness with the Brahman. That is similar to how a goldsmith with a natural perspective of gold in varied ornaments such as necklaces or rings does not see any other distinctions in the ornaments.

Nevertheless, concerning meditation (Dhyāna), it is not so. Indeed, it is indispensable for the Dhyāna-Yogī in the end time to remain with the mental state concentrated on the Dhyeya. Even if one accepts that a Dhyāna-Yogī who is following the discipline of practicing meditation on the Dhyeya during his entire lifetime, in the end time, if his mental state does not remain in that form, then a doubt remains regarding his attainment of the Dhyeya-form. However, as is said in BG 8.6, in the end-time, whatever form of sentiment he has, he will acquire that form; here, the example of Jaḍabharata[101]is apt. Since the root ignorance of the Dhyāna-Yogī has not been burnt with knowledge yet, he is still in the bondage of Prakṛti. Indeed, there is a rule in Prakṛti, "Sentiment, in the end, is the next destination." That is the major difference between knowledge (Jñāna) and meditation (Dhyāna). Here Bhagavāna stated that for a Dhyāna-Yogī at the time of death, he ought to have an immovable mental state concentrated on the form of Dhyeya and articulated the use of the strength of both devotion and Yoga. In verse, the word Yoga is in reference to breath control Yoga, and the fruit of that Yoga is control of the Prāṇa, and with control of the breath, control over the mind can be achieved. Additionally, the fruit of devotion through love is the attachment of the mind in the form

[101] Jaḍabharata was a great dispassionate soul, who in earlier birth worshipped Bhagavāna while living alone in a small hut in a remote forest. In that life, he did not acquire knowledge. During that time, he become very fond of a small fawn. During his end time, he departed remembering that little fawn, by the influence of which he was born in the species (Yoni) of deer, and then in later births acquiring knowledge attained liberation.

of the Dhyeya. That is why diverting the mind from wandering all over through Yoga and through devotion joining it in the Dhyeya, both being fruits, are successful. Accordingly, first making the mind steady in the lotus-heart and establishing the vital breaths of air between the eyebrows through the Suṣumnā-Nāḍī, a Yogī with proper steadfast meditation upon "कविं पुराणम् .., omniscient, beginningless ancient" form attains the supreme divine Personality.

(With means, in the next three verses, this subject is elaborated -)

यदक्षरं वेदविदो वदन्ति विशन्ति यद्यतयो वीतरागाः |
यदिच्छन्तो ब्रह्मचर्यं चरन्ति तत्ते पदं संग्रहेण प्रवक्ष्ये || BG 8.11 ||

वेद-विदः - Veda-knowers ; वदन्ति - call ; यत् - that (Status) ; अक्षरम् - the "Imperishable." ; इच्छन्तः - Seeking ; यत् - which ; यत् यतयः - the endeavoring ascetics ; वीत-रागाः - free of attachments ; चरन्ति - (and) observing ; ब्रह्मचर्यम् - celibacy ; विशन्ति - enter. ; तत् - That ; पदम् - Status ; सङ्ग्रहेण - (I shall) briefly ; प्रवक्ष्ये - tell ; ते - you.

Veda-knowers call that (Status) the "Imperishable." Seeking which the endeavoring ascetics free of attachments and observing celibacy enter. That Status, I shall briefly tell you.

Intent - Knowers of the Vedas call that Status the "Imperishable," the imperishable Brahman described in BG 8.3. In this verse, fitness for the attainment of that Status is discussed. In the words of Bhagavāna, those who are endeavoring ascetics, whose attachment and aversion are gone, and through the practice of celibacy who have conquered their mind and senses, only such steady-minded ascetics are qualified for that Status who the knowers of the Vedas call the "Imperishable."

(In the end time, the sequence of thinking of a steadfast minded on the Brahman is described -)

सर्वद्वाराणि संयम्य मनो हृदि निरुध्य च |
मूर्ध्न्याधायात्मनः प्राणमास्थितो योगधारणाम् || BG 8.12 ||
ओमित्येकाक्षरं ब्रह्म व्याहरन्मामनुस्मरन् |
यः प्रयाति त्यजन्देहं स याति परमां गतिम् || BG 8.13 ||

संयम्य - Controlling ; सर्व-द्वाराणि - all gateways of the senses, ; निरुध्य - confining ; मनः - the mind ; हृदि - in the heart, ; आधाय - placing ; आत्मनः - one's ; प्राणम् - vital breaths of air ; मूर्ध्नि - in the head ; च - and ; आस्थितः - establishing ; योग-धारणाम् - in yogic concentration,

यः - one who ; प्रयाति - departs ; त्यजन् - abandoning ; देहम् - the body ; व्याहरन् - intoning ; इति - the ; एक-अक्षरम् - monosyllable ; ओम् - "Oṃ, ॐ" (representing) ; ब्रह्म - the Brahman ; अनुस्मरन् - (and) thinking of ; माम् - Me (the Paramātmā), ; सः - he ; याति - attains ; परमाम् - the supreme ; गतिम् - destination.

Controlling all gateways of the senses, confining the mind in the heart, placing one's vital breaths of air in the head and establishing in yogic concentration, one who departs abandoning the body intoning the monosyllable "Oṃ ॐ" representing the Brahman and thinking of Me, he attains the supreme destination.

The intent of verses (BG 8.12 - BG 8.13) - Contact of the mind with external objects is only through the sense-organs, which cause vacillations. That is why control of the sense gateways is articulated. Additionally, to be free from internal resolves and alternatives (Saṃkalpa-Vikalpa), a command is given to confine the mind in the heart. The connection of the mind is with Prāṇa, that is, the breath. Mind moves only by mounting on the Prāṇa-form horse, so establishing the breath in the head is deemed necessary by which the mind can be appropriately stopped. Accordingly, establishing yogic concentration (Yoga-Dhāraṇā), concentration in breath control, and steadying the vital breaths of air there, one ought to constantly think of Me by intoning Oṃ (ॐ), the monosyllable representing Me the Brahman. The way of worshipping Oṃ (ॐ) in the form of Brahman is described in Māṇḍukya Upaniṣad (माण्डूक्य उपनिषद्) and Vicāra Sāgara (विचार सागर) at the end of section five. This Dhyāna-Yoga is in the form of mental merger (Laya-Cintana) and is for those persons with weak intelligence or for those with impediments of subtle desires that do not allow entry into knowledge, and also for those seekers with faith who have restrained their senses through the guidance of preceptors and scriptures and who have subdued their subtle desires and have become dispassionate regarding worldly objects. Such a Dhyāna-Yogī, in the end, contemplating on Oṃ (ॐ) in the form of the Brahman, leaving his body through the Uttarāyana path, attains the world of Brahmā (Brahmaloka). That is detailed in BG 8.24 of this chapter. There he becomes truth-loving Satyakāma, the one whose resolves become fact (Satya-Saṃkalpa) and with Brahmā attains Sāyujya-Mukti, becomes one with Brahmā. In that world, in the absence of Rajoguṇa and Tamoguṇa and with the maturity of Sattvaguṇa, without preceptors and scriptures, he attains knowledge. Until the total dissolution of the manifest world, he enjoys divine opulence. At the time of total dissolution (Pralaya), he becomes liberated from the body (Videha-Mukta) together with Brahmā through knowledge and does not return to the mortal world. That is called sequential liberation Krama-Mukti. This way, sequential liberation was articulated from verses (BG 8.8 - BG 8.13).

अनन्यचेता: सततं यो मां स्मरति नित्यश: |
तस्याहं सुलभ: पार्थ नित्ययुक्तस्य योगिन: || BG 8.14 ||

पार्थ - Hey Pārtha (Arjuna)! ; अनन्य-चेताः - Not thinking of anyone else, ; यः - (one) who ; नित्यशः - forever ; सततम् - constantly ; स्मरति - remembers ; माम् - Me, ; अहं - I am ; सुलभः - easily attained ; तस्य - by that ; नित्य-युक्तस्य - ever-established ; योगिनः - Yogī.

Hey Arjuna! Not thinking of anyone else, one who forever constantly remembers Me, I am easily attained by that ever-established Yogī.

Intent - One whose mental state is exclusively in Me, the Ātmā of all, and in whose sight the visible mortal world is null, such single-minded Yogī in all his mental states always worships Me alone. A Yogī who follows the discipline of knowledge and becomes of the same form with oneness as his Ātmā, I am easily attained. While alive, he is liberated. After leaving his body, he does not have to go anywhere. Śruti, "न तस्य प्राणा उत्क्रामन्ति तत्रैव समविलीयन्ते, Prāṇa of that (knower of the Truth) does not leave, but in death merges there only."

(What is the fruit of attaining Me? -)

मामुपेत्य पुनर्जन्म दु:खालयमशाश्वतम् |
नाप्नुवन्ति महात्मान: संसिद्धिं परमां गता: || BG 8.15 ||

गताः - Having acquired ; परमाम् - supreme ; संसिद्धिम् - perfection ; उपेत्य - attaining ; माम् - Me, ; महात्मानः - great beings (Māhātmā) ; न - do not ; आप्नुवन्ति - acquire ; अशाश्वतम् - ephemeral ; पुनः-जन्म - rebirth, ; दुःख-आलयम् - the abode of grief.

Having acquired supreme perfection attaining Me, great beings do not acquire ephemeral rebirth, the abode of grief.

Intent - Those great beings (Māhātmā), who have acquired perfection in the form of liberation, attaining Me, do not return to the transitory world full of grief.

आब्रह्मभुवनाल्लोका: पुनरावर्तिनोऽर्जुन |
मामुपेत्य तु कौन्तेय पुनर्जन्म न विद्यते || BG 8.16 ||

अर्जुन - Hey Arjuna! ; आब्रह्म-भुवनात् - Up to the world of Brahmā (Brahmaloka), ; लोकाः - people (of all worlds) ; पुनः-आवर्तिनः - are reborn. ; तु - However, ; कौन्तेय - hey, Kaunteya (Arjuna)! ; उपेत्य - Attaining ; माम् - Me, ; विद्यते - there is ; न - no (more) ; पुनः-जन्म - rebirth.

Hey Arjuna! Up to the world of Brahmā, all people are reborn. However, hey, Kaunteya! Attaining Me, there is no more rebirth.

Intent - Only through knowledge, by attaining Me, freedom from rebirth and thus freedom from returning to the mortal world of birth and death (Punarāvṛtti) is possible. But for that, there is no other approach, and there never will be. Without attaining Me, even if the world of Brahmā (ब्रह्मलोक, Brahmaloka) is acquired, still in the end, even from there, there will be a return to the mortal world. As discussed in the Intent of BG 8.13, there is no return (Apunarāvṛtti) from Brahmaloka for those Dhyāna-Yogī who in their lifetime have done unyielding practice of attributeless Ahaṃgraha-Dhyāna (अहंग्रह-ध्यान)[102]and in the end-time remaining absorbed in this meditation and through the mental merger (Laya-Cintana) have acquired Saṃskāra of knowledge and have left their bodies. Separate from them, those persons who, through the influence of sacrifice, charity and austerity, have attained Sālokya-Mukti in Brahmaloka are also subject to Punarāvṛtti and have to return to the mortal world. Because by performing Karma, whatever is made, its destruction is definite. That is why "क्षीणे पुण्ये मर्त्यलोकं विशन्ति, with the depletion of action-born pious impressions, return (to the mortal world) from Brahmaloka is definite." In such persons, there are no Saṃskāras of knowledge, no such fitness of the sixfold virtues (Ṣaṭ-Sampatti) such as discernment and dispassion, nor any accessories of knowledge such as preceptors and scriptures. That is why, without impressions, fitness, and accessories, where is knowledge? Without knowledge, where is liberation? In such a state, even Brahmaloka is limited by time in the end. Then, how can there be freedom from Punarāvṛtti?

(How is Brahmaloka limited by time? -)

सहस्रयुगपर्यन्तमहर्यद्ब्रह्मणो विदुः ।
रात्रिं युगसहस्रान्तां तेऽहोरात्रविदो जनाः || BG 8.17 ||

ते - Those ; जनाः - persons ; (ये) - (who) ; विदुः - know ; यत् - that ; अहः - a day (Kalpa) ; ब्रह्मणः - of Brahmā ; सहस्र-युग-पर्यन्तम् - lasts one thousand (Mahā) Yuga, ; रात्रिम् - (and) a night ; युग-सहस्र-अन्ताम् - last one thousand (Mahā) Yuga ; अहोरात्र-विदः - know day and night (the truth regarding the measurement of time).

Those persons who know that a day (Kalpa) of Brahmā lasts one thousand (Mahā) Yuga[103]and a night last one thousand (Mahā) Yuga know day and night.

Intent - In a single day of a human, many small worms experience their entire lifetime. In a single day-night of a Devatā (deity), humans experience a whole year. In a day of Brahmā, fourteen Manu and fourteen Indra sequentially experience their lifetime. In a single Ghaṭī (घटी)[104]of Lord Viṣṇu, a thousand Brahmā sequentially experience their lifetime. In a single Pala (पल)[105]of Maheśvara, a thousand Viṣṇu sequentially experience their lifetime. In half a Pala of Śakti, a thousand Maheśvara sequentially experience their lifetime. Just as -

चतुर्युगसहस्राणि दिनमेकं पैतामहम् ।
पितामहसहस्राणि विष्णोर्घटिकमेव च ॥
विष्णोरेकसहस्राणि पलमेकंमाहेश्वरम् ।
महेश्वरसहस्राणि शक्तेर्धपलं भवेत् ॥

When the "conscious-element" by inanimateness forgetting one's consciousness appears in some manifest form, it is bound by the limitation of time. When it is bound by time, it is limited no matter how long it is. Anything

---

102 Ahaṃgraha-Dhyāna (अहंग्रह-ध्यान) means a meditation in which a meditator identifies himself with the higher Self, the Brahman or the supreme Personality and meditates to become one with that source.

103 Mahā-Yuga (महा-युग) consists of 4,320,000 years of humans, comprised of: Sat-Yuga (सत्-युग)1,728,000 years, Tretā-Yuga (त्रेता-युग) 1,296,000 years, Dvāpara-Yuga (द्वापर-युग) 864,000 years and Kali-Yuga (कलि-युग) 432,000 years. In one Mahā-Yuga, there are 12,000 years of Devatā. A day of Brahmā, also known as a Kalpa consists of 1000 Mahā-Yuga or 4.32 billion years of humans and 12 million years of Devatā. One-hundred-year lifetime of Brahmā is equal to 311,040,000,000,000 human years.

104 Ghaṭī (घटी) consists of 24 minutes. There are 2.5 Ghaṭī in an hour.

105 Pala (पल) consists of 24 seconds. There are 2.5 Pala in a minute.

connected with it perishes. It is also unavoidable for a perished thing in time to reappear in a changed form. Bound by time, this conscious one goes into the cycle of coming and going until it attains its real supreme unmanifest form. The order of time (Kāla-Niyati) is fixed in individual species with birth. Had time its own true nature, then what is described above, from the time of Śakti to the time of small worms, sequentially such amazing differences, like a mountain from a mole, would not have happened. However, time, in reality, is unlimited (अमर्यादित, Amaryādita). Only when a Jīva takes birth based on his Karma in whatever Yoni, then the limit of time is also based on that Yoni; in its own form, time is not limited. Until a Jīva becomes free from its manifest form and attains its supreme unmanifest form, it cannot be free from the bondage of time. It is only with the manifest form that time comes out and puts Jīva in its bondage. In its true nature, had time been limited, then a day of Brahmā should appear as one day of Devatā, humans or worms, and not a day of Brahmā as 4,320,000,000 human years and of Devatā as 12,000,000 years. Thus, it is clear that being in a manifest form without knowledge, even if Brahmaloka is attained, Punarāvṛtti is unavoidable because Brahmaloka is also limited by time. One who knows so in truth is the one who has known time in its true element.

(What happens in a day and night of Brahmā without attaining Me? -)

अव्यक्ताद्व्यक्तय: सर्वा: प्रभवन्त्यहरागमे |
रात्र्यागमे प्रलीयन्ते तत्रैवाव्यक्तसंज्ञके || BG 8.18 ||

अहरागमे - At the arrival of the (Brahmā's) day, ; सर्वा: - all ; व्यक्तय: - beings (stationary and movable) ; प्रभवन्ति - originate ; अव्यक्तात् - from the Unmanifest (Māyā of Brahmā's sleep-state); ; रात्र्यागमे - (and) when (Brahmā's) night falls, ; प्रलीयन्ते - (they) dissolve ; तत्र - (in) that ; एव - same ; अव्यक्तसंज्ञके - called the Unmanifest.

At the arrival of the day, all beings originate from the Unmanifest; and when night falls, they dissolve in that same called the Unmanifest.

Intent - The sleep-state of Brahmā, which is the state of equipoise of the three constituents of Prakṛti, is named "अव्यक्त, Avyakta (Unmanifest)." The Saṃsāra of the movable and immovable beings is created only due to the imbalance (विषमता, Viṣamatā) of the three constituents. With equilibrium (समता, Samatā) of the three constituents, there is the dissolution of the Saṃsāra. Without the attainment of the Lord, in the awake time of Brahmā, all movable and immovable beings originate from this Unmanifest and, in the sleep-state of Brahmā, dissolve in the same Unmanifest. They do not achieve any kind of freedom from birth and death.

भूतग्राम: स एवायं भूत्वा प्रलीयते |
रात्र्यागमेऽवश: पार्थ प्रभवत्यहरागमे || BG 8.19 ||

पार्थ - Hey Pārtha (Arjuna)! ; स: - They (are) ; अयम् - this ; एव - same ; भूतग्राम: - multitude of beings (who,) ; भूत्वा भूत्वा - after repeated births, (are) ; अवश: - helplessly ; प्रलीयते - dissolved ; रात्र्यागमे - at the fall of (Brahmā's) night ; प्रभवति - (and) are born ; अहरागमे - at the arrival of the (Brahmā's) day.

Hey Arjuna! They are the same multitude of beings who, after repeated births, are helplessly dissolved at the fall of night and are born at the arrival of the day.

Intent - Without attaining the Lord, at no time and by no means freedom from returning to the mortal world (Punarāvṛtti) can be achieved.

(By whose attainment, freedom from Punarāvṛtti is achieved, its true form is described. -)

परस्तस्मात्तु भावोऽन्योऽव्यक्तोऽव्यक्तात्सनातन: |
य: स सर्वेषु भूतेषु नश्यत्सु न विनश्यति || BG 8.20 ||

तु - However, ; पर: - beyond ; तस्मात् - that ; अव्यक्तात् - Unmanifest, ; स: - (there is) that ; अन्य: - other ; सनातन: - eternal ; अव्यक्त: - unmanifest ; भाव: - Reality. ; य: - It ; न - (does) not ; विनश्यति - perish ; नश्यत्सु - upon the destruction ; सर्वेषु - of all ; भूतेषु - beings.

However, beyond that Unmanifest, there is another eternal unmanifest Reality. It does not perish upon the destruction of all beings.

Intent - The true nature of the Unmanifest (Avyakta) discussed in the previous two verses is not the supreme Unmanifest because, with the realization of the Truth, even its absence can be established at all times, just as with the knowledge of the rope there is absence determination of the illusory snake. However, beyond that Unmanifest, unique from that, there is another eternal unmanifest Reality, which does not perish even after the destruction of all beings. Knowing the eternal unmanifest Reality, the Unmanifest of (BG 8.18) is also established as null-form, similar to how waves are without any essence becoming one with water.

अव्यक्तोऽक्षर इत्युक्तस्तमाहु: परमां गतिम् |
यं प्राप्य न निवर्तन्ते तद्धाम परमं मम || BG 8.21 ||

तम् - That ; उक्तः - called ; अव्यक्तः - "the Unmanifest," (and) ; अक्षरः - "the Imperishable," ; इति - thus ; आहुः - they say ; परमाम् - is the supreme ; गतिम् - destination. ; तत् - That ; मम - is My ; परमम् - supreme ; धाम - abode, ; प्राप्य - attaining ; यम् - which ; न - none ; निवर्तन्ते - returns.

That called "the Unmanifest" and "the Imperishable," they say is the supreme destination. That is My supreme abode, attaining which none returns.

Intent - It is called the Unmanifest, the Imperishable, and is known as the highest destination. That is My supreme abode. There is no returning to the cycle of birth and death by attaining it.

(Approach to attain it is discussed next -)

पुरुष: स पर: पार्थ भक्त्या लभ्यस्त्वनन्यया |
यस्यान्त:स्थानि भूतानि येन सर्वमिदं ततम् || BG 8.22 ||

पार्थ - Hey Pārtha (Arjuna)! ; सः - That ; परः - supreme ; पुरुषः - Personality ; यस्य अन्तः-स्थानि - within whom situated are ; भूतानि - all beings ; तु - (and) again ; येन - by whom ; सर्वम् - all ; इदम् - this (world) ; ततम् - is pervaded ; लभ्यः - is attainable by ; अनन्यया - undivided ; भक्त्या - devotion (established in knowledge).

Hey Arjuna! That Supreme Personality within whom situated are all beings and again by whom all this is pervaded is attainable by undivided devotion.

Intent - That Supreme Personality (Paramātmā), situated in the animate and inanimate adjunct city (body), can be attained only through undivided devotion (Ananya-Bhakti). Here **undivided devotion means devotion established in the knowledge, "सर्वं खल्विदं ब्रह्म, all this is Brahman only,"** and only with direct intuitive knowledge, it is attainable. The intention here is that the One that is the cause of all, in That highest cause dissolving one's confined I-ness is the undivided devotion, and its success can only happen with the above knowledge. Just as earrings or necklaces exist in gold and gold is complete in them all, in the same way, all beings exist in the Paramātmā, and in all, the Paramātmā is complete.

Accordingly, in the verses (BG 8.14 - BG 8.22), only through the realization of the Truth the impossibility of returning to the mortal world of birth and death was articulated. Without knowledge, all persons were shown subject to Punarāvṛtti, and the flow of rebirth was depicted as continuous (अखण्ड, Akhaṇḍa).

(Now, those Dhyāna-Yogīs who are fit for Krama-Mukti to attain the Brahman through devotion to "Oṃ, ॐ" as the Brahman, for them, the path ahead is articulated -)

यत्र काले त्वनावृत्तिमावृत्तिं चैव योगिन: |
प्रयाता यान्ति तं कालं वक्ष्यामि भरतर्षभ || BG 8.23 ||

भरतर्षभ - Hey Bharatarṣabha (Arjuna)! ; यत्र - Where, ; प्रयाताः - departing ; काले - at the time (through the path) ; योगिनः - (when) Yogīs ; यान्ति - acquire (the state of) ; अनावृत्तिम् - non-return ; च - or ; आवृत्तिम् - (the state of) return, ; तु - again ; वक्ष्यामि - I shall describe ; तम् - that ; कालम् - time (path) ; एव - also.

Hey Arjuna! Departing at the time when Yogīs acquire the state of non-return or the state of return, I shall describe that time.

Intent - The term Kāla (काल) here does not mean the time but a path. Those paths where non-return (Apunarāvṛtti) or return (Punarāvṛtti) materialize based on the path taken under the control of whichever deity has authority at that time. Apunarāvṛtti and Punarāvṛtti are not in terms of time but are dependent on the means. It is not the intention that those who leave their bodies during Uttarāyana time all acquire Apunarāvṛtti, whereas those who leave their bodies during Dakṣiṇāyana acquire Punarāvṛtti. However, the intention is that those who are fit for the world of Brahmā departing through the brilliant Uttarāyana path acquire the world of Brahmā, and those who are fit for the world of the deities departing through the smoky Dakṣiṇāyana path will acquire the world of the deities irrespective of the time they depart, they go only by the path based on their fitness.

अग्निर्ज्योतिरहः शुक्लः षण्मासा उत्तरायणम् |
तत्र प्रयाता गच्छन्ति ब्रह्म ब्रह्मविदो जनाः || BG 8.24 ||

तत्र - There, ; प्रयाताः - departing (through the path under the authority of the presiding deities of) ; अग्निः - fire, ; ज्योतिः - light, ; अहः - daytime, ; शुक्लः - the bright (fortnight of the moon), ; षण्मासाः - (and) of six months ; उत्तर-अयनम् - of northern solar movement, ; ब्रह्मविदः जनाः - knowers of the Brahman (who worship the Brahman in the form of "Oṃ, ॐ") ; गच्छन्ति - attain ; ब्रह्म - the Brahman.

Departing (through the path under the authority of the presiding deities of) fire, light, daytime, the bright fortnight, and six months of northern solar movement, knowers of the Brahman attain the Brahman.

Intent - As stated in the verses (BG 8.8 - BG 8.13), those Dhyāna-Yogīs who are worthy of sequential liberation (Krama-Mukti), leaving their bodies through the paths under the authority of presiding deities at the time, attain Brahmaloka. Subsequently, through knowledge of the Brahman, attain the Brahman as defined in verse BG 8.13 and thus do not return to the mortal world of birth and death (Punarāvṛtti).

धूमो रात्रिस्तथा कृष्णः षण्मासा दक्षिणायनम् |
तत्र चान्द्रमसं ज्योतिर्योगी प्राप्य निवर्तते || BG 8.25 ||

तत्र - There, (departing through the path under the authority of the presiding deities of) ; धूमः - smoke, ; रात्रिः - night, ; कृष्णः - dark (fortnight of the moon), ; तथा - and ; षण्मासाः - six months ; दक्षिण-अयनम् - of southern solar movement), ; योगी - (a desireless Karma-)Yogī ; प्राप्य - acquires ; चान्द्रमसम् ज्योतिः- the moonlight (and) ; निवर्तते - returns.

(Departing through the path under the authority of the presiding deities of) smoke, night, dark fortnight, and six months of southern solar movement, a Karma-Yogī acquires the moonlight and returns.

Intent - Whose Karma is desire-ridden (Sakāmī) cannot be a Yogī. However, one whose actions are desireless (Niṣkāmī) can be a Yogī. For such a Yogī of desireless action, attainment of Brahmaloka is impossible because he has neither done Ahaṃgraha Brahma-worship nor has he done mental merger (Laya-Cintana). That is why under BG 6.41, after enjoying his piety impressions (Saṃskāras) in the world of the deities, he returns to the mortal world as a Yoga-Bhraṣṭa.

शुक्लकृष्णे गती ह्येते जगतः शाश्वते मते |
एकया यात्यनावृत्तिमन्ययावर्तते पुनः || BG 8.26 ||

हि - Certainly, ; एते - these two - ; शुक्ल-कृष्णे - the bright and the dark (Uttarāyana and Dakṣiṇāyana) ; गती - paths ; मते - have been deemed ; जगतः - (in) the world ; शाश्वते - from time immemorial. ; एकया - (Of the two,) by (means of) one (through the bright path), ; याति - (one) goes ; अनावृत्तिम् - and does not return; ; अन्यया - by the other (through the dark path, one) ; आवर्तते - comes back ; पुनः - again.

Certainly, these two - the bright and the dark paths have been deemed in the world from time immemorial. By means of one, one goes and does not return; by the other, one comes back again.

Intent - These paths, Bright and Dark (Śukla and Kṛṣṇa or Devayāna and Pitṛyāna or Uttarāyana and Dakṣiṇāyana), have been accepted in the world forever, by which there is no return (Apunarāvṛtti) through one and return (Punarāvṛtti) through the other.

(Next describing the glory of Jñāna-Yoga, Bhagavāna ends the chapter -)

नैते सृती पार्थ जानन्योगी मुह्यति कश्चन |
तस्मात्सर्वेषु कालेषु योगयुक्तो भवार्जुन || BG 8.27 ||

पार्थ - Hey Pārtha (Arjuna)! ; जानन् - Knowing ; एते - these two ; सृती - paths, ; न कश्चन - no ; योगी - Yogī ; मुह्यति - is deluded. ; तस्मात् - Therefore, ; अर्जुन - hey, Arjuna! ; सर्वेषु - At all ; कालेषु - times, ; भव - be ; योग-युक्तः - established in Yoga.

Hey Pārtha! Knowing these two paths, no Yogī is deluded. Therefore, hey, Arjuna! At all times, be established in Yoga.

Intent - Knowing these two paths are, "In the kingdom of Māyā, there is no path in my true nature," no Yogī who knows the Truth is deluded by these paths. They are not attached to these paths and, with the strength of their knowledge, like a roaring lion, break open the cage of Prakṛti and become free while alive. Therefore, Arjuna, you always stay established in Yoga. Through the realization of the Truth, you become established in your Ātmā in oneness.

वेदेषु यज्ञेषु तपःसु चैव दानेषु यत्पुण्यफलं प्रदिष्टम् |
अत्येति तत्सर्वमिदं विदित्वा योगी परं स्थानमुपैति चाद्यम् || BG 8.28 ||

यत् - Whatever ; पुण्य-फलम् - fruit of piety ; प्रदिष्टम् - that is spoken (in the scriptures to accrue from the study) ; वेदेषु - of the Vedas, ; यज्ञेषु - sacrifices, ; तपःसु - austerities, ; च - and ; दानेषु - charities, ; योगी - a Yogī (who is established with oneness in the Self) ; विदित्वा - knowing ; सर्वम् - all ; इदम् - these (causes of fruits) ; अत्येति - transcends them ; च - and ; एव - certainly ; उपैति - attains ; तत् - that ; परम् - supreme ; आद्यम् - primeval ; स्थानम् - Abode.

Whatever fruit of piety that is spoken (in the scriptures to accrue from the study) of the Vedas, sacrifices, austerities, and charities, a Yogī knowing all these transcends them and certainly attains that supreme primeval Abode.

Intent - The intention here is that, knowing his own Ātmā, he establishes himself in that supreme Status, from where all pious deeds and fruits come out and where he does not remain a doer or an enjoyer of pious deeds and fruits.

ॐ तत्सदिति श्रीमद्भगवद्गीतासूपनिषत्सु ब्रह्मविध्यायां योगशास्त्रे

श्रीकृष्णार्जुनसम्वादे अक्षरब्रह्मयोगो नाम

अष्टमोऽध्यायः || BG 8 ||

Oṃ Tat Sat

In the Śrīmad Bhagavad Gītā Upaniṣad

The Yoga Science of the Knowledge of Self-Realization

The Discourse of Lord Śrī Kṛṣṇa and Arjuna

This Eighth Chapter

Yoga Named - The Yoga of the Supreme Imperishable Reality

Clarification

At the end of the seventh chapter, listening to these words, "in the end time one who knows the entire Adhyātma (complete Karma, Adhidaiva, Adhibhūta, and Adhiyajña) as Me in the Brahman-form and 'that Brahman I am' - with the direct realization (Tattva-Sākṣātkāra) knowing so own Ātmā, know them as Yoga-Yukta," Arjuna asked seven questions to know the true nature of Adhyātma, Adhidaiva and others (BG 8.1 - BG 8.2). In response, Bhagavāna described the nature of the Brahman, Karma, Adhyātma, Adhibhūta, Adhidaiva, and Adhiyajña (BG 8.3 - BG 8.4). Bhagavāna responded to six questions. In response to the seventh question, "At the time of death, how are You to be known by one with a steadfast mind?" Bhagavāna said that in the end time, those who leave their bodies thinking of Me, the Real-Conscious-Bliss (Saccidānanda, omnipresent Ātmā of all), directly attain the Brahman status; there is no doubt about it. Others, remembering whatever sentiments they have been immersed in, acquire that same sentimental form upon leaving their bodies. Bhagavāna divided steady-minded Yogīs in the end time into two types based on their fitness, one following the discipline of knowledge (Jñāna-Yogī) and the other following the practice of meditation (Dhyāna-Yogī). Among them, giving prominence to a Jñāna-Yogī, Bhagavāna said that at all times, you ought to contemplate on Me, the all-witness Ātmā of all, so that even while engaging in dangerous things such as war, doership sense does not arise in you. Offering your mind and intellect to Me this way, you will undoubtedly attain Me. Accordingly, Bhagavāna commanded Arjuna to become steadfast in Jñāna-Yoga with this major approach (BG 8.5 - BG 8.7). However, for those who cannot enter into Jñāna-Yoga due to mental weakness, for them, Bhagavāna articulated Dhyāna-Yoga, through which attainment of the supreme divine Personality is attained. Then the form to be meditated on (Dhyeya) of that attributeless Brahman is stated, and an approach to how one should meditate at the end time. Additionally, worship of Oṃ (ॐ) as the Brahman is articulated, by which a Yogī attaining Brahmaloka becomes worthy of sequential liberation Krama-Mukti (BG 8.8 - BG 8.13).

After that, Bhagavāna indicated that attaining Him is easy for a Jñāna-Yogī whose mind is exclusively in Him alone, in whose mental dispositions there is nothing other than the Lord, and from whose heart all distinctions have evaporated like camphor. Accordingly, no injunctions such as closing eyes, nose, or ears remain for that ever-established Yogī. All these bondages are there as long as things appear separate from their true nature. However, upon establishing a state of seeing one Ātmā in all (Sarvātmaikya-Dṛṣṭi), then what is there to open and what is there to close? When everything is seen as a miracle of one's own Ātmā, what has the mind really known? What is there to stop it? This way, through immediate liberation (Sadhyo-Mukti), freedom from rebirth and freedom from the ephemeral repository of grief are depicted. In the absence of knowledge and devotion above, up to Brahmaloka, all are shown subject to return to the mortal world of birth and death (Punarāvṛtti) because all worlds are limited by time (BG 8.14 - BG 8.17). Further, it is shown that without attaining Me, upon the coming of the day of Brahmā, all beings emanate from the Unmanifest (Avyakta) Māyā, and upon nightfall, all dissolve in that Unmanifest. All beings repeatedly take birth and die. They are never free from "time" anyway (BG 8.18 - BG 8.19). Only the supreme unmanifest Reality is shown as the one that could free one from this bondage of time, a form beyond the unmanifest Māyā, and does not perish even upon the destruction of all beings. It is described as Avyakta, Akṣara, Parama-Gati, and Parama-Dhāma. Only through its attainment freedom from the cycle of birth and death is described. The possibility of attaining it is formulated through exclusive devotion established in knowledge (BG 8.20 - BG 8.22).

After that, before attaining this supreme unmanifest Reality, the way those Yogīs go through those paths whereby they acquire Apunarāvṛtti and Punarāvṛtti, that is, those separate paths Bright and Dark (Śukla and Kṛṣṇa or Devayāna and Pitṛyāna or Uttarāyana and Dakṣiṇāyana) are articulated. Among them, those Dhyāna-Yogī who leave their bodies through the devotion of attributeless Ahaṃgraha worship to attain Brahmaloka through the Uttarāyana path is described, and in that world, through knowledge, Apunarāvṛtti is articulated. However, for those duty-bound desireless devotes (Niṣkāmī) who leave their bodies worshipping the Lord, the Dakṣiṇāyana path is described to acquire the world of the deities (स्वर्गलोक, Svargaloka) and being Yoga-Bhraṣṭa their Punarāvṛtti is depicted. However, those desire-ridden (Sakāmī) who acquire Svargaloka through sacrifices, austerities, or charities after enjoying the opulence of Svarga return empty as they were and not as Yoga-Bhraṣṭa (BG 8.23 - BG 8.26).

In the end, describing the glory of Tattva-Yoga ended the chapter and said - Hey Arjuna! One who is established with oneness in My all-witness form that Yogī does not go anywhere, but like a roaring lion breaks the cage of the bondage of Prakṛti, acquires liberation, and becomes free while alive because both these paths are only in Prakṛti and do not come and go anywhere else. Whosoever is in the bondage of Prakṛti and joining with Prakṛti engages in good or evil acts, for them to enjoy the fruits of those acts, they have to come and go. The rule of nature is, "One who serves gets its fruits." However, this Yogī is not doing anything. Perceived as engaged in Karma, he is a non-doer, and joining Prakṛti is not deluded. Just like a king, he has become the Lord of Prakṛti; the kingdom of Prakṛti is operating in his grace, and yet he is untainted. That is why Arjuna! You become Yoga-Yukta. Fruit of piety described in the study of the Vedas, of sacrifice, austerity, and charity, this Yogī crosses over those fruits. Being free from doership conceit and having become Ātmā of all (Sarvātmā) attains the Supreme Primeval Abode.

Accordingly, responding to the question of Arjuna, "in the end time, how am I attained," Bhagavāna clarified and described the paths of Uttarāyana and Dakṣiṇāyana and their ends. In the end, providing the unbeatableness of a Yogī who is established in his own Ātmā glorified Tattva-Yoga and ended the chapter. Next, Bhagavāna formulates that knowledge and realized knowledge (Jñāna-Vijñāna) which materializes Tātvika-Yoga in the next chapter.

CHAPTER 9

THE YOGA OF THE ROYAL KNOWLEDGE OF ROYAL PROFUNDITY

श्रीभगवानुवाच |
इदं तु ते गुह्यतमं प्रवक्ष्याम्यनसूयवे |
ज्ञानं विज्ञानसहितं यज्ज्ञात्वा मोक्ष्यसेऽशुभात् || BG 9.1 ||
श्रीभगवान् उवाच - Śrī Bhagavān said -

अनसूयवे - Hey (Arjuna,) the one without a vision of seeing faults! ; प्रवक्ष्यामि - I shall tell ; ते - you ; इदम् - this ; गुह्यतमम् - most profound ; ज्ञानम् - knowledge ; विज्ञान-सहितम् - with realized knowledge, ; ज्ञात्वा - knowing ; यत् - that ; मोक्ष्यसे - you will be liberated ; अशुभात् - from the evil, ; तु - indeed.

Śrī Bhagavān said -

Hey Arjuna! I shall tell you this most profound knowledge with realized knowledge, knowing that you will be liberated from the evil.

Intent - The knowledge that was described in previous chapters and at the end of the eighth chapter whose unbeatableness through the Vedas, sacrifice, austerity, and others was articulated, with the intention of restating that same knowledge in this verse, the term "इदम्, this" is used. Here, a seeker who does not see faults is described as fit for this knowledge. Its fruit is described as liberation from evil, freedom from the bondage of the grievous world. Accordingly, describing the one who is fit for this knowledge, Bhagavāna articulates that knowledge with experienced knowledge, which he had vowed to tell Arjuna. In this verse, Bhagavāna addresses Arjuna as one devoid of the attribute of faultfinding (असूया, Asūyā).

राजविद्या राजगुह्यं पवित्रमिदमुत्तमम् |
प्रत्यक्षावगमं धर्म्यं सुसुखं कर्तुमव्ययम् || BG 9.2 ||

इदम् - This ; राज-विद्या - Royal Knowledge (supreme of all knowledge), ; राज-गुह्यम् - of Royal Profundity (knowing which nothing remains hidden) ; उत्तमम् - is the best, ; पवित्रम् - extremely pure, ; प्रत्यक्ष - directly ; अवगमम् - realizable, ; धर्म्यम् - righteous (the life-force of all righteousness), ; सुसुखम् - easy ; कर्तुम् - in practice, ; अव्ययम् - (and) imperishable (in fruits).

This Royal Knowledge of Royal Profundity is the best, extremely pure, directly realizable, righteous, easy in practice, and imperishable.

Intent - Knowing which, there is nothing else to know. Knowing which, everything unknown becomes known, so this highly illuminating Brahman-knowledge is called Rājavidyā (Royal Knowledge). The intention of the term Rājaguhya (Royal Profundity) is that this profound knowledge is not directly perceptible through the sense-organs but is like the molasses of a dumb, realizable by eating only. It is only to be self-experienced (स्वसंवेध्य, Svasaṃvedhya) and not realized by the experience of someone else (परसंवेध्य, Parasaṃvedhya). By knowing it, nothing can remain hidden from it; that is why it is called Rājaguhya. This best knowledge is extremely pure. By knowing it, sins accumulated over many lives and class fault perish immediately, like removing darkness by light, and a Jīva becomes Śiva.

The result is direct, like cash, and not like debt accrual from sacrifice, austerity, or charity. Such knowledge is directly experienceable, just as a person awake from the betrayal of a dream becomes directly free. In the same manner, through this knowledge, there is immediate freedom from the grief of the mortal world. It is not in opposition to anyone. This knowledge is righteous because it is in the form of non-opposition. It is unlike worldly enjoyments obtained through lots of pain, and even after acquiring, they are short-lived like a bolt of lightning. However, it is easy in practice, and its result is imperishable, as it is not attained through some sacrifice or austerity. It is only attained through discriminative analytical thinking. It does not perish after attaining. That is why it is imperishable. It is 1) a giver of direct result, 2) easy in means, and 3) is always there. All these things materialize with ease, something that is not in others. Therefore, this knowledge is proper to have faith in.

अश्रद्दधाना: पुरुषा धर्मस्यास्य परन्तप |
अप्राप्य मां निवर्तन्ते मृत्युसंसारवर्त्मनि || BG 9.3 ||

परन्तप - Hey Parantapa (Arjuna)! ; पुरुषा: - (Those) persons, ; अश्रद्दधाना: - who do not have faith ; अस्य - in this ; धर्मस्य - (transcendent) righteousness, ; अप्राप्य - failing to attain ; माम् - Me, ; निवर्तन्ते - return ; मृत्युसंसारवर्त्मनि - to the mortal world of (birth and) death.

Hey Arjuna! Those who do not have faith in this righteousness, failing to attain Me, return to the mortal world of death.

Intent - Faith is primary in the acquisition of this knowledge. Even though this knowledge is sense-imperceptible, those who have faith in it acquire it just like a walnut within one's grip through the strength of their effort. However, those who do not have faith never attain Me. Bound by Karma, based on their individual Karma, like a clock, they move round and round in the circle of birth and death of the mortal world. Without faith, there cannot be any activity in that which is imperceptible to the mind and intellect. Without activity, there cannot be an effort (Puruṣārtha). Without effort, how can there be its acquisition? In the cause (Nimitta) of this knowledge, faith is articulated as primary in the means and accessories (Sādhana-Sāmagrī). With faith, the rest of the means and accessories automatically are attracted.

(Thus, articulating fitness, fruit, object, and means, Bhagavāna describes that knowledge -)

मया ततमिदं सर्वं जगदव्यक्तमूर्तिना |
मत्स्थानि सर्वभूतानि न चाहं तेष्ववस्थित: || BG 9.4 ||

इदम् - This ; सर्वम् - entire ; जगत् - world ; ततम् - is pervaded ; मया - by Me ; अव्यक्त-मूर्तिना - in (My) unmanifest form. ; सर्व-भूतानि - All beings ; मत्-स्थानि - exist in Me (under My support). ; च - However, ; अहम् - I am ; न - not ; अवस्थित: - existing (dependent) ; तेषु - on them.

This entire world is pervaded by Me in My unmanifest form. All beings exist in Me. However, I am not dependent on them.

Intent - Just as an earthen pot is complete with clay and a gold ornament is complete with gold; there is no part of the pot or the ornament without its material cause (Upādāna). Similarly, this entire world is pervaded by Me, the unmanifest Saccidānanda. Though the perception of all these beings happens in My support,

I am not dependent on them. Just as the perception of gold ornaments happens on the dependence of its material cause gold; ornaments themselves do not have their existence. They are only perceived due to the existence of gold; gold is perceived by itself, not by any of its transformations. Likewise, perception of all beings happens in My support; however, I am not dependent on them. Living beings do not have their existence, they are aware only because of My awareness, and it is only in My support, the support of the existent common in all, that they have awareness. However, their awareness is illusory. It is just like how there is an illusory appearance of a snake on the dependence of a rope. The snake does not have its existence; it only appears because of the existence of its underlying support, the rope. Before the creation of beings, their sustentation, and after their destruction, I am "is as is"; not ever touched by any transformations. Despite being the existent common in all beings, I am dissociated from them all.

(Because of this disassociation, in reality -)

न च मत्स्थानि भूतानि पश्य मे योगमैश्वरम् |
भूतभृन्न च भूतस्थो ममात्मा भूतभावनः || BG 9.5 ||

भूतानि - All beings ; न - do not ; मत्-स्थानि - exist in Me. ; पश्य - (However,) behold ; ऐश्वरम् - the supreme power of ; मे - My ; योगम् - Yoga ; च - that despite ; भूत-भावनः - creating all beings ; च - and ; भूत-भृत् - sustaining all beings, ; मम - My ; आत्मा - Self ; न - does not ; भूत-स्थः - reside in beings (but is entirely dissociated from them).

All living beings do not exist in Me. However, behold the supreme power of My Yoga that despite creating and sustaining all beings, My Self does not reside in beings.

Intent - A delusional thing (Vivarta), even though perceived on the dependence of its underlying support (Adhiṣṭhāna), cannot touch its Adhiṣṭhāna. The Adhiṣṭhāna itself remaining "is as is" provides the perception of the delusional thing but does not change in the form of the delusional thing. A poisonous snake delusionally appearing in a rope does not make the rope poisonous, or the water of a mirage does not wet the earth. In the same way, I, the Ātmā of all, sustaining all living beings with My power, even though existent in all living beings as a witness, do not acquire the form of living beings. Behold this supreme power of My Yoga that doing everything, I am not doing anything (Akartā), and I am untainted by all. A question here arises why the Lord refers to "My Self?" Just as one expresses "one's self" with the superimposition of I-ness in the conglomerate of the body, mind, and senses, in the same way, the Lord uses "My Self" in common parlance, not like how the deluded world fails to note that the Ātmā cannot have another as its Ātmā.

(Next, Bhagavāna clarifies the meaning of the two verses mentioned above with an example -)

यथाकाशस्थितो नित्यं वायुः सर्वत्रगो महान् |
तथा सर्वाणि भूतानि मत्स्थानीत्युपधारय || BG 9.6 ||

यथा - Just as ; महान् - the mighty ; सर्वत्रगः - (and) moving everywhere ; वायुः - wind ; नित्यम् - always ; स्थितः - exists ; आकाश - in the space; ; तथा - similarly, ; उपधारय - know ; इति - that ; सर्वाणि - all ; भूतानि - beings ; मत्स्थानि - exist in Me.

Just as the mighty and moving everywhere wind always exists in the space; similarly, know that all beings exist in Me.

Intent - Just as the space is always immovably existent, and the mighty wind moving all over in the space cannot move it or even touch it, in the same way, all beings in My dependence acquiring birth, sustentation, and death cannot move Me nor any of their mutations touch Me. All successes of being and not-being happen with My support. However, I am dissociated from those being and not-being manifestations, and I do not see them in Me.

(When You are immovable and dissociated from all beings, then from what are all beings born, and where do they dissolve? -)

सर्वभूतानि कौन्तेय प्रकृतिं यान्ति मामिकाम् |
कल्पक्षये पुनस्तानि कल्पादौ विसृजाम्यहम् || BG 9.7 ||

कौन्तेय - Hey Kaunteya (Arjuna)! ; कल्पक्षये - At the end of a Kalpa, ; सर्वभूतानि - all beings ; यान्ति - merge ; मामिकाम् - in My ; प्रकृतिं - Prakṛti. ; कल्पादौ - At the beginning of (the next) Kalpa, ; अहम् - I ; विसृजामि - create ; तानि - them ; पुनः - again (from My Prakṛti).

Hey Arjuna! At the end of a Kalpa, all beings merge in My Prakṛti. At the beginning of the next Kalpa, I create them again.

प्रकृतिं स्वामवष्टभ्य विसृजामि पुनः पुनः |
भूतग्राममिमं कृत्स्नमवशं प्रकृतेर्वशात् ||BG 9.8 ||

अवष्टभ्य - Taking control of ; स्वाम् - My own ; प्रकृतिम् - nature, ; विसृजामि - I create ; पुनः पुनः - again and again ; कृत्स्नम् - all ; इमम् - (of) this ; भूत-ग्रामम् - multitude of beings ; अवशम् - helpless ; वशात् - by the force ; प्रकृतेः - of their nature.

Taking control of My own nature, I create again and again all of this multitude of beings helpless by the force of their nature.

The intent of verses (BG 9.7 - BG 9.8) - As long as a Jīva does not attain union with oneness in Me through the knowledge of the Truth, but remains separate from Me as a doer of Karma, till then, dependent on the forces of his nature, helplessly moves around in the flow of birth and death for the enjoyment of fruits of Karma. Upon leaving the body, not finding oneness in Me, merges in My lower Nature (Aparā-Prakṛti), consisting of the three constituents. Again, for the enjoyment of fruits of accumulated actions, a Jīva comes out of My Aparā-Prakṛti, just as varied kinds of seeds hidden in the earth spring out in their time. Indeed, to the point that at the end of a Kalpa, Jīva does not merge in Me but merges in Prakṛti, and again at the beginning of the next Kalpa emanates from Prakṛti. There is no end to the flow of the cycle of birth and death. Like how as long as a seed is fit to provide fruits, the flow from seed to tree and from tree to seed continues. Accordingly, as long as a Jīva does not become pure by burning the dirt of Karma by the fire of knowledge, until then, on the dependence of his nature, the flow from Karma to body and body to Karma continues constantly. All activities of Prakṛti happen through Me, and I continue to move those activities of Prakṛti without any desire. Without My power, Prakṛti is also unable to act on its own, and all these plays of Prakṛti happen on My dependence.

(Would piety and sin produced from the relationship of those distinct creations not taint You Parameśvara? -)

न च मां तानि कर्माणि निबध्नन्ति धनञ्जय |
उदासीनवदासीनमसक्तं तेषु कर्मसु || BG 9.9 ||

धनञ्जय - Hey Dhanañjaya (Arjuna)! ; तानि - Those ; कर्माणि - actions ; न - do not ; निबध्नन्ति - bind ; मां - Me. ; आसीनम् - (I) stay ; उदासीनवत् - indifferent ; च - and ; असक्तं - detached ; तेषु - from those ; कर्मसु - actions.

Hey Arjuna! Those actions do not bind Me. I stay indifferent and detached from those actions.

Intent - On the dependence of the pervasive space, activities such as cold waves, heat waves, and rain happen, yet the space does not become hot, cold, or wet. In the same way, all activities of Prakṛti in the form of creation and dissolution happen on My dependence, yet they do not bind Me. However, in all these activities of Prakṛti, I am existent in them indifferent and without any attachment. Neither do I have a desire for fruits, nor is there any doership-ego in them. That is why those Karma do not bind Me. Therefore, one should understand that all those who are free from doership-ego and thus attachment to fruits are not in the bondage of Karma.

(How do You stay neutral while engaged in Karma and not be bound? -)

मयाध्यक्षेण प्रकृतिः सूयते सचराचरम् |
हेतुनानेन कौन्तेय जगद्विपरिवर्तते || BG 9.10 ||

कौन्तेय - Hey Kaunteya (Arjuna)! ; मया - Under My ; अध्यक्षेण - supervision, ; प्रकृतिः - Prakṛti ; सूयते - creates ; सचराचरम् - movable and stationary (beings). ; अनेन - (For) this ; हेतुना - reason, ; जगत् - the world ; विपरिवर्तते - changes (in all states).

Hey Arjuna! Under My supervision, Prakṛti creates movable and stationary beings. For this reason, the world changes.

Intent - Just as iron shavings dance on the power of a magnet, yet in all those dances, the magnet is immutable. Similarly, on the dependence of My supportive power, Prakṛti creates the movable and stationary mortal world. However, I am detached from those activities. Without Me, no activity of Prakṛti can be successful. Those activities still do not taint Me. From this supportive cause of Mine, the world becomes transformed, and accordingly, without any doership, I remain neutral in those actions.

(Despite that-)

अवजानन्ति मां मूढा मानुषीं तनुमाश्रितम् |
परं भावमजानन्तो मम भूतमहेश्वरम् || BG 9.11 ||

अजानन्तः - Unaware ; मम - of My ; परम् - transcendent ; भावम् - status, ; मूढाः - the confused ; अवजानन्ति - deride ; माम् - Me, ; भूत-महेश्वरम् - the Great Supreme Lord of beings ; आश्रितम् - holding ; मानुषीम् - the human ; तनुम् - body.

Unaware of My transcendent status, the confused deride Me, the Great Supreme Lord of beings holding the human body.

Intent - They do not understand that this body of Mine, the Great Supreme Lord of all beings, is without any impressions of actions (Karma-Saṃskāras). It is only delusional (Māyāmātra) and is the cause to protect the virtuous, eradicate the evil and establish righteousness. It is not for the enjoyment of any happiness or grief. Not knowing so, they consider Me as an insignificant, ordinary human being. Holding the causal body, in reality, I am untainted from all; and am situated indifferent in the imbroglio of Prakṛti.

मोघाशा मोघकर्माणो मोघज्ञाना विचेतसः |
राक्षसीमासुरीं चैव प्रकृतिं मोहिनीं श्रिताः || BG 9.12 ||

विचेतसः - (For) the contrary-minded ; श्रिताः - (who) hold ; मोहिनीम् - deceptive, ; आसुरीम् – demonic, ; च - and ; राक्षसीम् - evil ; प्रकृतिम् - nature, ; एव - indeed (their) ; मोघ-आशाः - hopes are vain, ; मोघ-कर्माणः - actions are fruitless, ; मोघ-ज्ञानाः - (and) cognitions are vain.

For the contrary-minded who hold deceptive, demonic, and evil nature, their hopes are vain, actions are fruitless, and cognitions are vain.

Intent - All hopes, actions, and cognitions are worthless for such confused persons. Because the fruits of their hopes, actions, and cognitions are neither happiness and peace of this world nor the next, they are the ones who have assertively grasped only visible sense-perceptible existence as real. They have not realized, "Whatever sense-perceptible substances there are, they are all unreal (Māyā); underneath them, there is only one immovable immutable by whose existence the unreal appears as real" - not knowing so and grasping the delusional sight with assertiveness in the frenzy of demonic and evil nature they have become the ones who consider their body as the Ātmā (Dehātmavādī) and in whose conduct there is only to eat, drink and be merry.

(However, those who are with the faith and are engaged in the path of liberation with devotion to the Lord, such -)

महात्मानस्तु मां पार्थ दैवीं प्रकृतिमाश्रिताः |
भजन्त्यनन्यमनसो ज्ञात्वा भूतादिमव्ययम् || BG 9.13 ||

पार्थ - Hey Pārtha (Arjuna)! ; तु - However, ; महात्मानः - great beings, ; आश्रिताः - resorting to (their) ; दैवीम् - divine ; प्रकृतिम् - nature, ; ज्ञात्वा - knowing ; माम् - Me ; अव्ययम् - the imperishable (and) ; भूतादिम् - the origin of all beings, ; भजन्ति - worship Me ; अनन्य-मनसः - with an undivided mind.

Hey Arjuna! Great beings, resorting to their divine nature, knowing Me the imperishable and the origin of all beings, worship Me with an undivided mind.

Intent - "The mortal world is without any essence. In this essenceless world, only the Lord is the real essence" discerning so, great beings depending on their divine nature, possessing the attributes of control of the mind, restraint over the senses, faith, compassion, generosity and other forms of good attributes, worship Me with an undivided mind. That is, "true bliss-form is only the Lord," holding such a resolve, they have made Me their only goal in life and have known Me as the imperishable and the original cause of all beings. With this form, they have assertively held that just as how pervasive fire does not lose its pervasiveness for whatever reason by manifesting in unique locations and unique forms. In the same way, I, the omnipresent Ātmā of all, if I manifest in some unique form, then My omnipresence is not lost, and I do not fall from My existent common-form.

(Knowing so, how do they worship the Lord? -)

सततं कीर्तयन्तो मां यतन्तश्च दृढव्रताः |
नमस्यन्तश्च मां भक्त्या नित्ययुक्ता उपासते || BG 9.14 ||

दृढ-व्रताः - With firm resolve, ; सततम् - always ; कीर्तयन्तः - singing divine glories ; माम् - of Me, ; नित्य-युक्ताः - ever established (in Me) ; च - and ; यतन्तः - striving (for Me, they) ; उपासते - worship ; माम् - Me ; नमस्यन्तः - with obeisance ; च - and ; भक्त्या - devotion.

With firm resolve, always singing divine glories of Me, ever established and striving, worship Me with obeisance and devotion.

Intent - "Only the exclusive surrender at the lotus-feet of the Lord provides a stable boat to cross over the grief-stricken worldly ocean. Other than that, there is no other approach, nor will there be, even with the passing of millions of Kalpa." They are the ones who have made such a firm resolve, who are moving towards Me, always established in Me, sing My glories, and worship Me paying obeisance with great devotion.

{This way, in the verses (BG 9.11 - BG 9.12), the conduct of an iniquitous (Pāmara) and in (BG 9.13 - BG 9.14), the conduct of a seeker is described.}

(Next up to verse (BG 9.19), Bhagavāna describes the conduct of a knower of the Truth -)

ज्ञानयज्ञेन चाप्यन्ये यजन्तो मामुपासते |
एकत्वेन पृथक्त्वेन बहुधा विश्वतोमुखम् || BG 9.15 ||

च अपि - Additionally, ; अन्ये - others ; एकत्वेन - with oneness ; यजन्तः - devotion ; उपासते - worship ; माम् - Me ; विश्वतोमुखम् - manifesting in the world ; पृथक्त्वेन - distinctly ; बहुधा - in various forms ; ज्ञान-यज्ञेन - through the sacrifice of knowledge.

Others with oneness devotion worship Me manifesting in the world distinctly in various forms through the sacrifice of knowledge.

Intent - The "sacrifice of knowledge" means the knowledge whose content is "the Lord is the sacrifice." Some worship Me with this sacrifice, giving up other forms of worship. That knowledge treats Me as the one. The Brahman is the only one. Just as only one water appears in different forms, such as waves, ripples, or eddies, they are all only water from an analytic perspective. In the same way, I, the Ātmā, due to discriminating vision, appear in the world in varied forms, yet from an analytic perspective, I exist without distinctions in common form. Such is the way knowers devotionally worship Me in oneness through the sacrifice of knowledge

(In their view -)

अहं क्रतुरहं यज्ञ: स्वधाहमहमौषधम् |
मन्त्रोऽहमहमेवाज्यमहमग्निरहं हुतम् || BG 9.16 ||

अहम् - I am ; क्रतुः - the Vedic rite (Śrauta Karma). ; अहम् - I am ; यज्ञः - the (five great) sacrifice(s Smārta Karma). ; अहम् - I am ; स्वधा - the ancestral oblation (food given in the cause of ancestors). ; अहम् - I am ; औषधम् - the medicinal herbs and plants. ; अहम् - I am ; मन्त्रः - the Vedic hymn, ; अहम् - I am ; आज्यम् - the clarified butter (Ghī), ; अहम् - I am ; अग्निः - the fire, (and) ; एव - indeed ; अहम् - I am ; हुतम् - the oblation.

I am the Vedic rite. I am the sacrifice. I am the ancestral oblation. I am the medicinal herbs and plants. I am the Vedic hymn, I am the clarified butter, I am the fire, and I am the oblation.

Intent - An imagined thing that is perceived in the real underlying support, separate from it, the imagined thing does not have any existence of its own but is only in the form of the underlying support, just as an imagined snake is in its Adhiṣṭhāna rope. In Me (the substrate of all, the Brahman), the world which is perceived, not having its separate existence, is indeed in the form of Me, the Brahman. To behold everything in the form of the Adhiṣṭhāna Brahman is the real sacrifice of knowledge. Thus, in the view of those knowers of the Truth, all Vedic rites (Śrauta Karma) and sacrifices (Smārta Karma), the food given in the cause of ancestors (the ancestral oblation, Svadhā), medicinal herbs and plants, Vedic hymns (Mantra) and others are all Me in the form of the Brahman only.

पिताहमस्य जगतो माता धाता पितामह: |
वेद्यं पवित्रमोङ्कार ऋक्साम यजुरेव च || BG 9.17 ||
गतिर्भर्ता प्रभु: साक्षी निवास: शरणं सुहृत् |
प्रभव: प्रलय: स्थानं निधानं बीजमव्ययम् || BG 9.18 ||

एव - Indeed, ; अहम् - I am ; अस्य - this ; जगतः - world's ; पिता - father, ; माता - mother, ; धाता - sustainer (the dispenser of the fruits of action), ; पितामहः - grandfather, ; वेद्यम् - object to knowing ; पवित्रम् - the sacred ; ओङ्कारः - syllable Oṃ (ॐ), ; ऋक् - Ṛk-Veda, ; साम - Sāma-Veda, ; च - and ; यजुः - Yaju-Veda.

गतिः - destination, ; भर्ता - nourisher, ; प्रभुः - master, ; साक्षी - witness, ; निवासः - abode, ; शरणम् - refuge, ; सुहृत् - friend, ; प्रभवः - origin, ; स्थानम् - sustentation, ; प्रलयः - dissolution, ; निधानम् - the repository of all impressions of accumulated actions, ; अव्ययम् - (and) the imperishable ; बीजम् - seed.

Indeed, I am this world's father, mother, sustainer, grandfather, object to knowing the sacred syllable Oṃ (ॐ), Ṛk-Veda, Sāma-Veda, Yaju-Veda, destination, nourisher, master, witness, abode, refuge, friend, origin, sustentation, dissolution, the repository of all accumulated actions, and the imperishable seed.

The intent of verses (BG 9.17 - BG 9.18) - Here in this world and the next, all mental and bodily efforts of all beings happen on whose dependence, I am that father, the mother, the grandfather, the dispenser of the fruits of action (Dhātā), the sacred syllable Oṃ (ॐ), the Rig, Sāma and Yaju Vedas. I am the destination of all. I am the nourisher of all (Bhartā), the master of all (Prabhu), and the witness of the good and bad deeds of all (Dṛṣṭā). I am everyone's supporting abode (Nivāsa), the refuge that removes the grief of all who surrender (Śaraṇa), and a friend who is always engaged in doing good to others without anything in return (Suhṛta). I am everyone's origin, sustentation, and dissolution. I am the repository of Sañcita Karma (Nidhāna), and I am indeed the imperishable seed. The gist of verses BG 9.16, BG 9.17, and BG 9.18 is that all these discriminative states being adjuncts of the Saṃsāra are attributed to Me, Who is beyond all states. Knowers of the Truth (Tattva-Vettā) see Me beyond all states and worship Me through the sacrifice of knowledge.

तपाम्यहमहं वर्षं निगृह्णाम्युत्सृजामि च |
अमृतं चैव मृत्युश्च सदसच्चाहमर्जुन || BG 9.19 ||

अर्जुन - Hey Arjuna! ; अहम् - (In the form of the sun) I ; तपामि - radiate heat. ; अहम् - I ; वर्षम् - rain. ; निगृह्णामि - I attract ; च - and ; उत्सृजामि - (then) release. ; अहम् - I am ; एव - indeed ; अमृतम् - immortality ; च - and ; मृत्युः - death, ; च - and ; सत् - real (as "is" form) ; च - and ; असत् - unreal (as "not" form).

Hey Arjuna! I radiate heat. I rain. I attract and then release. I am indeed immortality and death, and real and unreal.

Intent - In the form of the sun radiating heat, raining, after raining attracting or drying up water and after that abandoning or releasing water in the form of rain - all these activities happen through Me. Hey Arjuna! Amṛta (immortality) and Mṛtyu (death), as well as Sat (real) and Asat (unreal), are all I. Whatever favorable inner-disposition substances there are of beings, they are Amṛta, and unfavorable inner-disposition objects are Mṛtyu. Only I am in all those favorable and unfavorable inner-disposition substances. In addition, whatever is grasped as Sat and Asat, described as "is" form and "is not" form, it is I who am in those being and not-being forms. Whatever duality results that are perceptible in the form of favorable and unfavorable, being and not-being, they all are perceived in My dependence, yet they do not touch Me. That is similar to how paintings are made in support of a wall, yet the paintings do not really touch the wall.

{Accordingly, the sacrifice of knowledge of a knower of the Truth with his analytic perspective is described. Now, Bhagavāna describes how a good desire-ridden (Śubha-Sakāmī) person worships -}

त्रैविद्या मां सोमपाः पूतपापा यज्ञैरिष्ट्वा स्वर्गतिं प्रार्थयन्ते |
ते पुण्यमासाद्य सुरेन्द्रलोक मश्नन्ति दिव्यान्दिवि देवभोगान् || BG 9.20 ||

त्रै-विद्याः - Knowers of the three Vedas {Ṛk-Veda (ऋक्-वेद), Yaju-Veda (यजु-वेद) and Sāma-Veda (साम-वेद)}, ; सोमपाः - drinkers of Somarasa, ; पूत-पापाः - purged of sins, ; यज्ञैः - through sacrifice ; इष्ट्वा - worshipping ; माम् - Me ; प्रार्थयन्ते - pray ; स्वर्गतिम् - for the way to heaven (Svarga). ; पुण्यम् - (As a fruit of their) piety, ; आसाद्य - attaining ; सुरेन्द्र-लोकम् - the world of Indra, ; ते - they ; अश्नन्ति - partake in ; दिव्यान् - the divine ; देव-भोगान् - enjoyments of the deities ; दिवि - in heaven.

Knowers of the three Vedas, drinkers of Somarasa, purged of sins, through sacrifice worshipping Me pray for the way to heaven. As a fruit of their piety, attaining the world of Indra, they partake in the divine enjoyments of the deities in heaven.

Intent - Knowers of the three Vedas, that is, knowers of Ṛk-Veda (ऋक्-वेद), Yaju-Veda (यजु-वेद), and Sāma-Veda (साम-वेद). Svarga means heaven, the world of deities presided by Indradeva. The intention in this verse is that those desire-ridden (Sakāmī) persons who worship Indra and other deities through Agniṣṭoma[106]and

[106] Agniṣṭoma-Yajña (अग्निष्टोम-यज्ञ) means a five-day sixteen priest sacrifice offered to Indra to attain the world of Indra (Svarga, heaven).

other sacrifices, in reality, are worshipping Me, the Paramātmā existent in the form of those deities. However, in the flow of their desires, they do not see Me there but only see Indra and other deities that are objects of their desire. Accordingly, they only see themselves worshipping those deities based on their inner dispositions and remain with their faces turned away from Me, the real true nature that is existent and seen in the form of those deities. Hence, they remain deprived of the eternal fruit and remain recipients of only transitory fruits.

(Next, Bhagavāna describes ignorance driven fruit that desire-ridden persons acquire -)

ते तं भुक्त्वा स्वर्गलोकं विशालं क्षीणे पुण्ये मर्त्यलोकं विशन्ति |
एवं त्रयीधर्ममनुप्रपन्ना गतागतं कामकामा लभन्ते || BG 9.21 ||

भुक्त्वा - Enjoying ; तम् - that ; विशालम् - vast ; स्वर्ग-लोकम् - world of the deities, ; क्षीणे - upon exhaustion of ; पुण्ये - piety, ; ते - they ; विशन्ति - return to ; मर्त्य-लोकम् - the world of the mortals. ; एवम् - Thus, ; काम-कामाः - desiring enjoyment, ; अनुप्रपन्नाः - the followers ; त्रयी-धर्मम् - of (desire-ridden rites prescribed in) the three Vedas ; लभन्ते - acquire ; गत-आगतम् - repeated going and coming.

Enjoying the vast world of the deities, upon exhaustion of piety, they return to the world of the mortals. Thus, desiring enjoyment, the followers of the three Vedas acquire repeated going and coming.

Intent - Just as a person desirous of enjoyment visits a foreign place with certain monetary assets, but upon depletion of his wealth, returns back home empty-handed, in the same fashion, a desire-ridden person with his accumulated piety enjoyment assets acquires the world of the deities and upon depletion of his assets falls back in the mortal world empty-handed.

(This way, four kinds of humans - an iniquitous, a desire-ridden, a seeker, and a knower are described who worship Bhagavāna based on their sentiments}.

(Next, Bhagavāna describes various fruits -)

अनन्याश्चिन्तयन्तो मां ये जनाः पर्युपासते |
तेषां नित्याभियुक्तानां योगक्षेमं वहाम्यहम् || BG 9.22 ||

ये - Those ; जनाः - devotees ; पर्युपासते - who worship ; चिन्तयन्तः - thinking ; माम् - of Me ; अनन्याः - alone, ; तेषाम् - for them, ; नित्य-अभियुक्तानाम् - who are ever established, ; अहम् - I ; वहामि - carry on their ; योग-क्षेमम् - Yoga-Kṣema (provide what they do not have and preserve what they have).

Those devotees who worship thinking of Me alone, for them, who are ever established, I carry on their Yoga-Kṣema.

Intent - In the term Yoga-Kṣema, Yoga means the acquisition of a thing that is not possessed, and Kṣema means preservation of what is acquired. Those who have offered everything, including their body, mind, senses, and Prāṇa to Me and have not kept anything for themselves, for such ever-established with oneness in Me alone (Ananya), I carry on their Yoga-Kṣema, just as an infant who is dependent on his mother, the mother carries on his Yoga-Kṣema, that is, takes on the responsibility of every need of the infant. I am equally responsible for not only worldly Yoga-Kṣema but also transcendental Yoga-Kṣema.

येऽप्यन्यदेवता भक्ता यजन्ते श्रद्धयान्विताः |
तेऽपि मामेव कौन्तेय यजन्त्यविधिपूर्वकम् || BG 9.23 ||

कौन्तेय - Hey Kaunteya (Arjuna)! ; अपि - Additionally, ; ये - those ; भक्ताः - devotees (who) ; अन्विताः - with ; श्रद्धया - faith ; यजन्ते - worship ; अन्य-देवता - other deities ; ते - they ; अपि - (are) indeed ; यजन्ति - worshipping ; माम् - Me ; एव - only, ; अविधि-पूर्वकम् - (though) not according to (Vedic) injunctions (but in ignorance).

Hey Arjuna! Those devotees who with faith worship other deities, they are indeed worshipping Me only, though not according to injunctions.

Intent - Even when they are worshipping those deities by keeping them in front, there, in reality, I, the Ātmā of all and support of all, am present. Only I, who appear in the form of the deities according to their sentiments. Just as a deer with water sentiment sees water in a desert mirage, in the same way, even though devotees have a divine disposition towards their deities, in reality, it is only I who am there. In such a state, whatever rituals and worship they are performing with their deities in mind, worship is only towards Me because, in truth, I am there. Since their sentiment is not towards Me, such rituals and worship are performed merely in ignorance and not the Veda ordained.

(This way, even though -)

अहं हि सर्वयज्ञानां भोक्ता च प्रभुरेव च |
न तु मामभिजानन्ति तत्त्वेनातश्च्यवन्ति ते || BG 9.24 ||

च - Also, ; हि - decisively ; अहम् - I am ; एव - indeed ; भोक्ता - the enjoyer ; च - and ; प्रभुः - master ; सर्व-यज्ञानाम् - of all sacrifices. ; तु - However, ; ते - they (the desire-ridden) ; न - do not ; अभिजानन्ति - recognize ; माम् - Me ; तत्त्वेन - in truth. ; अतः - Therefore, ; च्यवन्ति - they fall.

Decisively, I am indeed the enjoyer and master of all sacrifices. However, they do not recognize Me in truth. Therefore, they fall.

Intent - Accordingly, in all manner, I am the enjoyer and master of all those sacrifices of desire-ridden persons and am existent as witness-observer in their chants, oblations, consecrated fires, deities, and activities. However, due to the influence of desires, their eyes do not meet the One Who sees all, and they do not know Me in truth. That is why they fall and acquire rebirth. In summary, by not attaining Yoga (oneness) in My true nature and holding doership sense commensurate with their sentiments in whatever they do, they receive correspondent fruit through Me.

(It is this way -)

यान्ति देवव्रता देवान्पितॄ न्यान्ति पितृव्रताः |
भूतानि यान्ति भूतेज्या यान्ति मद्याजिनोऽपि माम् || BG 9.25 ||

देव-व्रताः - Those who resolve for deities ; यान्ति - go to ; देवान् - the deities, ; पितृ-व्रताः - those who resolve for ancestors ; यान्ति - go to ; पितॄन् - the ancestors, ; भूत-इज्याः - (and) those who resolve for spirits ; यान्ति - go to ; भूतानि - the spirits. ; मत् याजिनः - Those who are My devotees ; यान्ति - attain ; माम् - Me ; अपि - only.

Those who resolve for deities go to the deities, those who resolve for ancestors go to the ancestors, and those who resolve for spirits go to the spirits. Those who are My devotees attain Me only.

Intent - Whatever resolve one makes in My refuge, by that resolve, there is the attainment of fruit through Me. In their varied resolves, I, the all-witness Ātmā of all, am existent, and it is only with My existence in them that all of their resolves become ready for fruition, just as, with the existence of the earth, seeds become ready for sprouting. In Me, those who resolve for deities, whose discipline and devotion are oriented towards deities, attain the deities. Those who resolve for ancestors attain the ancestors, and those who resolve for spirits attain the spirits. However, those who in Me, resolve for Me only and are free from contrary sentiments, such true devotees of Mine certainly attain Me, as that is the Truth, and so they are not in the bondage of rebirth.

(This way, Bhagavāna described His true nature in various types of humans with varied sentiments, resolves, means and fruits.)

(Next, Bhagavāna describes an easy approach to attaining His true nature -)

पत्रं पुष्पं फलं तोयं यो मे भक्त्या प्रयच्छति |
तदहं भक्त्युपहृतमश्नामि प्रयतात्मन: || BG 9.26||

यः - Whoso ; भक्त्या - with devotion ; प्रयच्छति - offers ; मे - Me ; पत्रम् - a leaf, ; पुष्पम् - a flower, ; फलम् - a fruit, ; तोयम् - or water; ; अहम् - I ; अश्नामि - accept ; तत् - that ; भक्ति-उपहृतम् - devotional offering ; प्रयत आत्मनः - (of the) pure-minded (devotee).

Whoso with devotion offers Me a leaf, a flower, a fruit, or water; I accept that devotional offering of the pure-minded devotee.

Intent - In attaining Me, only love towards Me is important, not substances. If substances are less, even a leaf or a flower, and if they are not available, even a handful of water is sufficient for Me. However, devotion and love towards Me ought to be plenty because I am not an acceptor of substances; love is My true nature, so I only accept love. Substances are only instrumental (Nimitta-Mātra) in the offering of love. Just as candy is wrapped in paper, the value is not of the paper but the candy only. A gift given with devotional love by a pure-hearted lover, I enjoy it with love. Only love towards Me is the one that provides the capability to discard worldly I-ness and mineness to attain Me.

(This way, offering your love to Me in the form of a leaf or a flower or even a handful of water then -)

यत्करोषि यदश्नासि यज्जुहोषि ददासि यत् |
यत्तपस्यसि कौन्तेय तत्कुरुष्व मदर्पणम् || BG 9.27 ||

कौन्तेय - Hey Kaunteya (Arjuna)! ; यत् - Whatever ; करोषि - you do, ; यत् - whatever ; अश्नासि - you eat, ; यत् - whatever ; जुहोषि - you sacrifice, ; यत् - whatever ; ददासि - you donate, ; यत् - (and) whatever ; तपस्यसि - austerities you perform, ; कुरुष्व - do ; तत् - them ; अर्पणम् - as offerings ; मत् - to Me.

Hey Arjuna! Whatever you do, eat, sacrifice, donate and perform austerities; do them as offerings to Me.

Intent - To whatever extent, through devotional love a devotee forsakes for Me, he moves closer to Me. Through the influence of exclusive love for Me, I am attained without any doubt when there is total relinquishment. Relinquishment is indeed My value. That is why Arjuna! Whatever actions you perform, whatever you eat, whatever oblations you perform, charities you give, or any austerities you perform, you offer them only to Me. To the extent, "I am a doer of Karma, or I am offering these fruits to the Lord," even those doership-sentiments you offer to Me. That is Sarva-Tyāga (total relinquishment), and only through this attaining Me is possible. It is only due to the doership-ego that there is separation from Me. The natural state of establishment with oneness in Me (Yoga) is attained with its removal.

(Upon the accomplishment of total relinquishment -)

शुभाशुभफलैरेवं मोक्ष्यसे कर्मबन्धनै: |
संन्यासयोगयुक्तात्मा विमुक्तो मामुपैष्यसि || BG 9.28 ||

एवम् - Thus, ; मोक्ष्यसे - you will be released ; कर्म-बन्धनैः - from the bondage of action ; शुभ-अशुभ-फलैः - with their good and evil fruits. ; विमुक्तः - Liberated, ; संन्यास-योग-युक्त-आत्मा - with the mind established in the Self through the Yoga of Renunciation, ; उपैष्यसि - you will attain ; माम् - Me.

Thus, you will be released from the bondage of action with their good and evil fruits. Liberated, with the mind established in the Self through the Yoga of Renunciation, you will attain Me.

Intent - Thus, through probing of the Truth, establishing the mind in one's all-witness true nature and becoming free from doership ego is indeed Sarva-Tyāga (total relinquishment), and that is Tātvika-Yoga.

One whose mind is established with oneness in the Ātmā through the Yoga of Renunciation (Saṃnyāsa-Yoga) is capable of becoming free from the bondage of the fruits of good and evil acts. Becoming free from the bondage of Karma, he can attain the Lord. Without fulfillment of this Sarva-Tyāga, freedom from the bondage of Karma is like a flower in the sky. Without it, with duty-bound intellect, whatever offerings of the fruits of Karma are done, though they will not put one in the bondage of evil fruits, still, they will put one in the bondage of good fruits and will keep the Jīva separate from his real true nature (Vāstavika-Svarupa). A Jīva is only separate from his true nature due to the bondage of the good and evil fruits of Karma.

The dissolution (Samāsa) of "संन्यासयोगयुक्तात्मा" is this way - संन्यास: चासौ योग संन्यासयोग । तेन संन्यासयोगन ब्रह्मणि युक्त: आत्मा चित्त यस्य तव स त्वं 'संन्यासयोगयुक्तात्मा' With that Yoga of Renunciation (Saṃnyāsa-Yoga) whose mind is established in the Ātmā (Brahman).

(Next, Bhagavāna describes until the end of the chapter the form for one to be established and the procedure to become established -)

समोऽहं सर्वभूतेषु न मे द्वेष्योऽस्ति न प्रिय: |
ये भजन्ति तु मां भक्त्या मयि ते तेषु चाप्यहम् || BG 9.29 ||

अहम् - I am ; समः - the same ; सर्व-भूतेषु - towards all beings. ; मे - To Me, ; न - no (one) ; अस्ति - is ; द्वेष्यः - hateful ; न - nor ; प्रियः - dear. ; तु - However, ; ये - those who ; भजन्ति - worship ; माम् - Me ; भक्त्या - devotionally ; ते - they ; मयि - are in Me, ; च - and ; अहम् - I am ; अपि - also ; तेषु - in them.

I am the same towards all beings. To Me, no one is hateful nor dear. However, those who worship Me devotionally are in Me, and I am in them.

Intent - Just as the pervasive space exists equally everywhere, in the same way, I pervade equally in all movable and immovable beings created from the great elements (Mahābhūta), and I am their Ātmā. Being the Ātmā of all, I do not have a fondness or despite for anyone. Other than the Ātmā, in anything else known, there is fondness due to favorable intellect and hatred due to unfavorable intellect. Own Ātmā is not the cause for fondness or despite for anyone. Nevertheless, those who worship Me with undivided love are in Me, and I am in them. The intention here is that I am always there in them; I did not come into them from somewhere else. However, they have suppressed Me under their meager ego, so they are not in Me even though I am in them. However, when they worship Me with undivided knowledge-based devotion, they attain Yoga (union) in Me and establish oneness.

(Next, Bhagavāna describes His eternal purity -)

अपि चेत्सुदुराचारो भजते मामनन्यभाक् |
साधुरेव स मन्तव्य: सम्यग्व्यवसितो हि स: || BG 9.30 ||

चेत् - Even ; अपि - if ; सु-दुः-आचारः - an extremely evil person (abandoning his evil conduct) ; भजते - worships ; माम् - Me ; अनन्य-भाक् - with undivided devotion, ; सः - he ; एव - (should) indeed ; मन्तव्यः - be deemed ; साधुः - worthy, ; हि - for ; सः - he ; सम्यक् - (is of) the right ; व्यवसितः - resolution.

Even if an extremely evil person worships Me with undivided devotion, he should indeed be deemed worthy, for he is of the right resolution.

Intent - Just as the pervasive space situated in a cesspool does not get touched by the smell of the cesspool and always remains pure, in the same way, I, the all-witness Ātmā, existent in all beings with the equal sentiment, am not tainted by anyone's good or evil behavior. According to this principle, even a person who was evil in the past should be deemed worthy of virtuous conduct (Sādhu) if he frees himself from those evil dispositions and worships Me with exclusive devotion. Just as a gold bracelet stuck in the muck does not change its attribute; removing it from the muck, it "is as is" only gold and fetches its true value. If the Jīva is cleansed from the mire of evil with the water of exclusive devotion, "all this is Vāsudeva," washes his meager ego and becomes pure; he ought to be deemed as a real virtuous being. As he has made a resolve in his conscience, "I am the eternal, pure, true nature without doership and enjoyership."

क्षिप्रं भवति धर्मात्मा शश्वच्छान्तिं निगच्छति ।
कौन्तेय प्रतिजानीहि न मे भक्त: प्रणश्यति ॥ BG 9.31 ॥

क्षिप्रम् - (He) soon ; भवति - becomes ; धर्म-आत्मा - righteous ; निगच्छति - (and) attains ; शश्वत् - lasting ; शान्तिम् - peace. ; प्रतिजानीहि - Make a firm resolve (that), ; कौन्तेय - hey Kaunteya (Arjuna)! ; मे - My ; भक्तः - devotees ; न - never ; प्रणश्यति - perish.

He soon becomes righteous and attains lasting peace. Make a firm resolve that, hey Arjuna! My devotees never perish.

Intent - Leaving behind evil conduct, those who have become pure through exclusive worship of Me, and with the influence of that worship becoming free from I-ness ego in the body and having become one with Me the all-witness, indeed acquire My attributes and attain eternal peace. A witness is always without impurity and is never tainted by the good or evil mutations of the body and others. Accordingly, hey Arjuna! You make a resolve that My devotees never fall from grace. Those devotees who are on the path towards Me do not suffer a wrong end. However, they naturally move towards Me, just as how the flow of Gaṅgā is naturally towards the ocean.

(Thought of functional class has no role in attaining Me -)

मां हि पार्थ व्यपाश्रित्य येऽपि स्यु: पापयोनय: ।
स्त्रियो वैश्यास्तथा शूद्रास्तेऽपि यान्ति परां गतिम् ॥ BG 9.32 ॥

पार्थ - Hey Pārtha (Arjuna)! ; व्यपाश्रित्य - Seeking refuge ; माम् - in Me, ; ये - one who ; स्युः – may be ; अपि - even ; पाप-योनयः - of inferior birth, ; स्त्रियः - (like) women, ; वैश्याः - Vaiśya, ; तथा - and ; शूद्राः - Śūdra, ; ते - they ; हि - indeed ; अपि - also ; यान्ति - reach ; पराम् - the supreme ; गतिम् - abode.

Hey Arjuna! Seeking refuge in Me, one who may be of inferior birth like women, Vaiśya and Śūdra, indeed also reach the supreme abode.

Intent - The intention is that there is no taint of functional class (Varṇa) or other categories in My true nature. The distinctions of caste, creed, and color are only in the kingdom of Prakṛti, and that too is only limited to the gross body; this distinction does not remain in the subtle body. Those who surrender to Me by coming out of the kingdom of Prakṛti are naturally free from the distinctions and attain the supreme abode, irrespective of who they are.

किं पुनर्ब्राह्मणा: पुण्या भक्ता राजर्षयस्तथा ।
अनित्यमसुखं लोकमिमं प्राप्य भजस्व माम् ॥ BG 9.33 ॥

पुनः - Then, ; किम् - what (is there to say about) ; पुण्याः - pious ; ब्राह्मणाः - Brāhmaṇa ; तथा - and ; भक्ताः - devout ; राजर्षयः - royal sages? ; प्राप्य - (Therefore,) acquiring ; इमम् - this ; असुखम् - pleasureless ; अनित्यम् - transitory ; लोकम् - world ; भजस्व - worship ; माम् - Me (only).

Then, what is there to say about pious Brāhmaṇa and devout royal sages? Therefore, acquiring this pleasureless transitory world, worship Me only.

Intent - When those of inferior birth can attain My supreme abode, then those who by nature are pious, such as Brāhmaṇa and royal sages, moving towards Me indeed attain My supreme abode; what is there to doubt about? Hey Arjuna! Having acquired through difficulties and many pieties, this rare human body, which is transitory and painful by its nature, even Indra and others desire to acquire, being the only means to reach the supreme abode you worship Me, the Supreme Lord only.

(In summary, hey, Arjuna! -)

मन्मना भव मद्भक्तो मद्याजी मां नमस्कुरु |
मामेवैष्यसि युक्त्वैवमात्मानं मत्परायण: || BG 9.34 ||

मत्-मनाः - Set your mind on Me, ; भव - be ; मत्-भक्तः - My devotee, ; मत्-याजी - worship Me (and) ; नमस्कुरु - pay obeisance ; माम् - unto Me. ; एवम् - Thus, ; एष्यसि - (you will) attain ; माम् - Me, ; एव - the ; आत्मानम् – Self, ; मत्-परायणः - moving towards Me (and) ; युक्त्वा - established in Me.

Set your mind on Me, be My devotee, worship Me, and pay obeisance unto Me. Thus, you will attain Me, the Self, moving towards Me and established in Me.

Intent - Separate from Me the all-witness, the unreal existence that was mentally imagined due to ignorance, with the determination of absence at all times through knowledge be one with oneness in Me with your mind fixed on Me. Just as in all gold ornaments, there is only gold; in the same way, in all beings free from distinction, I am the "एकमेवाद्वितीयम्, only one without a second,"[107]be with such firm resolve and in all your efforts worship only Me. With this resolve, directly seeing Me, the Ātmā of all, in you and others, pay obeisance unto Me. Becoming My devote and having moved towards Me, attaining union in your Ātmā, you will attain Me. To become established in Me, neither past evil deeds can be impediments nor any functional class-related limits. However, being free from all evil acts, with the mind fixed on Me and moving towards Me, is the only key to attaining union with oneness in Me. A great example of the truthfulness of this is the sage Vālmīki.

ॐ तत्सदिति श्रीमद्भगवद्गीतासूपनिषत्सु ब्रह्मविध्यायां योगशास्त्रे

श्रीकृष्णार्जुनसम्वादे राजविद्याराजगुह्ययोगो नाम

नवमोऽध्याय: || BG 9 ||

Oṃ Tat Sat

In the Śrīmad Bhagavad Gītā Upaniṣad

The Yoga Science of the Knowledge of Self-Realization

The Discourse of Lord Śrī Kṛṣṇa and Arjuna

This Ninth Chapter

Yoga Named - The Yoga of the Royal Knowledge of Royal Profundity

Clarification

In the first two verses of this chapter, Bhagavāna described the glory of His Yoga of Knowledge (Jñāna-Yoga) and addressed it as Rājavidyā (Royal Knowledge) of Rājaguhya (Royal Profundity). In the third verse, Bhagavāna articulated faith as the primary instrument and, in the verses (BG 9.4 - BG 9.6), described with an example that true nature, knowing which, a union can be attained in it. Then, in the absence of the attainment of that union, Bhagavāna described the order of how all beings run around for innumerable eons in the form of coming and going, repeated cycles of rebirths in the kingdom of Prakṛti. Additionally, Bhagavāna showed that even at the end of the Kalpa, they could not be free from this coming and going,

[107] Chāndogya Upaniṣad (छान्दोग्य उपनिषद्) 6.2.1

and at the beginning of the next Kalpa helplessly have to take birth on the dependence of Prakṛti. Further, He explained, "though all these activities of Prakṛti happen in My power and under My supervision, those acts do not bind Me. That is because I am existent in those acts without doership-ego and remain detached from them. Under My supervision, Prakṛti creates the movable and stationary mortal world, and the world moves around in the cycle of being and not-being" (BG 9.7 -9.10).

Next, Bhagavāna described four kinds of humans who worship based on their disposition. First, among the four, a knower of the Truth (Tattva-Vettā Jñānī) is declared the best. With his proper perspective being devoid of distinctions in the manifold visible mortal world, he is the one who only worships the Lord through the sacrifice of knowledge. In his pure view, all Vedic rites (Śrauta-Karma) and sacrifices (Smārta-Karma), the food given in the cause of ancestors (the ancestral oblation, Svadhā), medicinal herbs and plants, Vedic hymns (Mantra) and others are all the Brahman. Moreover, in his view, everyone's destination, master, witness, abode, refuge, friend, origin, and dissolution, and the father and mother of the world is the Lord only. Whatever is grasped in the world in the form of real and unreal (Sat and Asat) and immortality and death (Amṛta and Mṛtyu), in his view, all is the Brahman only. The world born of delusion has moved away from his perspective, and all he sees is only the Brahman everywhere. Second, those seekers of knowledge, who, on the dependence of their divine nature, believe the Lord as the origin and end of all beings, worship with undivided (Ananya) devotion, always singing the glory of the Lord, worshiping and paying obeisance to the Lord are described. Third, those desire-ridden (Sakāmī) are described who, through sacrifices ordained in the three Vedas, worship the Lord to acquire the opulence of the world of the deities (Svargaloka) and being about-faced from the true bliss-form Lord look for Bhagavāna in the unreal perishable enjoyments of Svarga. Having fallen from the true path, upon depletion of piety, they are dropped back into the mortal world and remain fit for only coming and going in the eternal cycle of rebirths. Fourth, the confused iniquitous (Mūḍha-Pāmara) are described who, on the dependence of their demonic and evil nature, not knowing the existence of the Lord existing in all beings, only see the Lord in prohibited enjoyments (Niṣiddha-Bhoga). Enjoyment objects that are not blissful are sensed as blissful and beautiful because of the existence of the blissful and beautiful Lord. Not looking for the Lord there, through their gross eyes grasp only those objects as blissful; because of this ignorance, instead of being happy attain lots of grief (BG 9.11 - BG 9.21).

This way, describing four kinds of humans, Bhagavāna indicated that though the object of the efforts of all is I, the blissful, yet those who worship Me exclusively and conduct themselves following the true path, I take the responsibility in their Yoga-Kṣema, acquisition of things that are not possessed, and preservation of what is acquired. Moreover, those who, based on their sentiments, worship other deities, sacrifices, ancestors, and spirits, they, in reality, are worshipping Me only. Based on their sentiments, I come in their front in those forms, and other than Me, there is nothing that can stand before them. However, because their sentiment is not in Me, they do not attain Me, and by their sentiments, they fall into the repeated cycle of birth and death (BG 9.22 - BG 9.25). To attain His true nature, Bhagavāna described devotional love as the instrument by which there is relinquishment (Tyāga) of I-ness and mineness. Accordingly, total relinquishment (Sarva-Tyāga) is described as His true value. By which acquiring renunciation, the Lord can be attained, and the Jīva can become free from the bondage of good and evil acts (BG 9.26 - BG 9.28). Then articulating His equanimity, ever-purity, and the beingness of the Ātmā of all, Bhagavāna said that no matter how evil a person is, if he worships Me with undivided devotion, he should be considered a virtuous person. He has abandoned his I-ness and mineness in the body. Establishing himself in the Ātmā, he attains eternal peace. To such extent that surrendering to Me, even those of inferior birth can attain the supreme abode, as the witness-conscious Ātmā is everywhere eternally pure. The bondage of all faults and sins stays only as long as a Jīva remains about-faced from the all-witness true nature. Then what is there to question about a pious Brāhmaṇa and royal sages? That is why, in the transitory and devoid of happiness life of a human, worship is the essence. In the end, Bhagavāna gave Upadeśa to Arjuna that through all efforts setting the mind in Me, attain union with oneness in the Ātmā (BG 9.29 - BG 9.34). Accordingly, the glory of His Yoga, its true nature, and means and fitness for its attainment are articulated.

Chapter 10

The Yoga of the Divine Manifestations

(In the ninth chapter, Bhagavāna described His Yoga. The subject being abstruse (दुर्विज्ञेय, Durviejñeya), it is once again described in this chapter. With the term "भूय, again," - the connection is made between the current chapter and what was articulated previously.)

श्रीभगवानुवाच |
भूय एव महाबाहो शृणु मे परमं वच: |
यत्तेऽहं प्रीयमाणाय वक्ष्यामि हितकाम्यया || BG 10.1 ||
श्रीभगवान् उवाच - Śrī Bhagavān said -

महाबाहो - Hey Mahābāho (Arjuna)! ; शृणु - Listen ; मे - to My ; परमम् - supreme ; वचः - words ; भूयः एव - once again, ; यत् - which ; हित-काम्यया - with the desire for (your) good ; अहम् - I ; वक्ष्यामि - shall tell ; ते - you ; प्रीयमाणाय - the beloved one.

Śrī Bhagavān said -

Hey Arjuna! Listen to My supreme words once again, which with the desire for your good I shall tell you the beloved one.

Intent - Words proven beneficial only in this world cannot be declared supreme. However, supreme words are those through which benefits of other worlds are acquired. Bhagavāna, desirous to do good to Arjuna, spoke such supreme words.

(What are those supreme words? -)

न मे विदु: सुरगणा: प्रभवं न महर्षय: |
अहमादिर्हि देवानां महर्षीणां च सर्वश: || BG 10.2 ||

न - Neither ; सुर-गणाः - the mass of deities ; न - nor ; महर्षयः - the great seers ; विदुः - know ; मे - My ; प्रभवम् - origin. ; हि - For, ; अहम् - I am ; आदिः - the origin of all ; देवानाम् - the deities ; च - and ; महर्षीणाम् - the great seers ; सर्वशः - in all respects.

Neither the mass of deities nor the great seers know My origin. I am the origin of all the deities and the great seers in all respects.

Intent - The term "प्रभवं, Prabhavaṃ" means might, power as well as origin. Hence, the intention is that these deities like Indra and others and the great seers like Bhṛgu and others know neither My might nor origin.

Just as gold-ornaments do not know gold or waves do not know water, in the same way, holding I-ness ego in their being divinity or being seer, neither the deities nor the great seers know Me. Only by losing their I-ness sense and attaining oneness in Me, "कारणं कारणानाम्, the cause of the causes," I can be known and attained. Irrespective of whether they are deities or great seers, they cannot know Me holding their own identity because, in all respects, I am the "the original cause," the one without any cause.

(This way -)

यो मामजमनादिं च वेत्ति लोकमहेश्वरम् |
असम्मूढ: स मर्त्येषु सर्वपापै: प्रमुच्यते || BG 10.3 ||

यः - Who ; वेत्ति - knows (in truth) ; माम् - Me ; अजम् - the unborn, ; अनादिम् - beginningless ; च - and ; लोक-महेश्वरम् - the Great Supreme Lord of the worlds, ; सः - he, ; असम्मूढः - the undeluded ; मर्त्येषु - among the mortals, ; प्रमुच्यते - is released ; सर्व-पापैः - from all sins.

Who knows Me the unborn, beginningless and the Great Supreme Lord of the worlds, he, the undeluded among the mortals, is released from all sins.

Intent - By the way above, one who knows in truth, "the sixfold transformations (Ṣaḍ-Bhāva-Vikāra, in the form of birth, sustentation, growth, decay, result, and end) even though materialize on the dependence of the Paramātmā, yet there is no taint of those transformations on the Paramātmā, and they are all illusory in the kingdom of Prakṛti. Just as the creation and destruction of ornaments materialize on the dependence of gold and yet it does not taint gold, in the same way, the Paramātmā is my Ātmā," directly knowing own Ātmā as the Brahman, such a person free from I-ness sense in the body, undoubtedly, becomes free from all sins. The root of all sins is the I-ness sense in the body. It is from this limited ego that all sins emanate. It is the root of all sins. There is a discriminating vision due to the I-ness sense in the body. With discriminating vision, there is the formation of attachment and aversion. With attachment and aversion, there is the creation of sins. However, this ego is like a hunch on his back. All that is needed is a firm kick of knowledge to make it straight so that he can be back in his real unlimited form and be completely free from all sins.

{How am I the Great Supreme Lord (Maheśvara) of all worlds? -}

बुद्धिर्ज्ञानमसम्मोह: क्षमा सत्यं दम: शम: |
सुखं दु:खं भवोऽभावो भयं चाभयमेव च || BG 10.4 ||
अहिंसा समता तुष्टिस्तपो दानं यशोऽयश: |
भवन्ति भावा भूतानां मत्त एव पृथग्विधा: || BG 10.5 ||

बुद्धिः - Intelligence (deciding instinct, inner-disposition that resolves), ; ज्ञानम् - knowledge (cognition of the Self and other elements), ; असम्मोहः - non-delusion (absence of confusion, clarity of thought), ; क्षमा - forgiveness (absence of agitation when abused or offended), ; सत्यम् - truthfulness (utterance of true words as experienced and heard), ; दमः - restraint of the senses, ; शमः - control of the mind, ; सुखम् - pleasure, ; दुःखम् - pain, ; भवः - being (creation), ; अभावः - non-being (dissolution), ; भयम् - fear, ; च - and ; अभयम् - fearlessness ; एव - also; ; च - and

अहिंसा - nonviolence (non-infliction of injury to any being), ; समता - equanimity (level-headedness, steadiness of the mind), ; तुष्टिः - contentment (satisfaction in whatever is obtained), ; तपः - austerity (self-control of the body, senses, and others), ; दानम् - charity (based on the capacity to donate wealth as an offering to the Lord), ; यशः - renown (fame acquired with righteousness), ; अयशः - infamy (disrepute acquired due to unrighteousness) - ; पृथक्-विधाः - (all these) manifold ; भावाः - sentiments ; भवन्ति - arise ; भूतानाम् - in beings ; मत्तः - from Me ; एव - alone.

Intelligence, knowledge, non-delusion, forgiveness, truthfulness, restraint of the senses, control of the mind, pleasure, pain, being, non-being, fear, fearlessness, nonviolence, equanimity, contentment, austerity, charity, renown, infamy - all these manifold sentiments arise in beings from Me alone.

Intent - "Intelligence" means deciding instinct, inner-disposition that resolves, "knowledge" implies cognition of the Ātmā and other elements, "non-delusion" means the absence of confusion or clarity of thought, "forgiveness" means the absence of agitation when abused or offended, "truthfulness" means utterance of true words as experienced and heard, restraint of senses, control of the mind, pleasure, pain, "being" means creation, "non-being" means dissolution, fear, fearlessness, "nonviolence" means non-infliction of injury to any being, "equanimity" means level-headedness or steadiness of the mind, "contentment" means satisfaction in whatever is obtained, "austerity" means self-control of the body and senses, "charity" means based on capacity donating wealth as an offering to the Lord, "renown" means fame acquired with righteousness, "infamy" means disrepute acquired due to unrighteousness - all these manifold sentiments arise in beings from Me alone.

Just as varied forms of gold ornaments are created on the dependence on gold, and with the creation and destruction of the ornaments, gold does not change from its true nature; and stays "is as is." In the same way, in all beings, varied sentiments arise and die only due to Me, the existent common in all. However, with the creation and destruction of those unique sentiments, there is no change in My true nature. Only with My existence, I, illuminating those being and non-being sentiments, remain in My true nature "is as is." I am the Great Supreme Lord (Maheśvara) of all.

महर्षयः सप्त पूर्वे चत्वारो मनवस्तथा |
मद्भावा मानसा जाता येषां लोक इमाः प्रजाः || BG 10.6 ||

पूर्वे - In the past, ; सप्त - the seven ; महर्षयः - great seers, ; चत्वारः - the four (Kumāras), ; तथा - and ; मनवः - the Manu ; जाताः - were born ; मानसाः मत् भावाः - of My mental sentiments, ; लोके - (and) in the world, ; इमाः - all these are ; येषाम् – the whose ; प्रजाः - progeny.

In the past, the seven great seers, the four (Kumāras), and the Manu were born of My mental sentiments, and in the world, all these are the whose progeny.

Intent - The seven great seers (सप्तर्षि, Saptarṣi)[108]and the Manu, from whom this entire humanity has originated, were born of thought (Saṃkalpa) with My sentimental power. The entire cause of the causes and actions is indeed I only, though I do not have any cause of Myself and in their being and not-being I am situated "is as is." However

एतां विभूतिं योगं च मम यो वेत्ति तत्त्वतः |
सोऽविकम्पेन योगेन युज्यते नात्र संशयः || BG 10.7 ||

यः - Who ; तत्त्वतः - truly ; वेत्ति - knows ; एताम् - these ; विभूतिम् - divine manifestations ; च - and ; योगम् - Yoga ; मम - of Mine; ; सः - he, ; अविकम्पेन - through steadfast ; योगेन - Yoga, ; युज्यते - is established (with oneness in Me). ; अत्र - Here, ; न - (there is) no ; संशयः - doubt.

Who truly knows these divine manifestations and Yoga of Mine; he, through steadfast Yoga, is established. Here, there is no doubt.

---

[108] Saptarṣi (सप्तर्षि) collectively refers to the seven great seers (Maharṣi) of each Manvantara. Currently we are in the Vaivasvata-Manvantara (वैवस्वत-मन्वन्तर) with the following seven Maharṣi: Maharṣi Kaśyapa (कश्यप), Maharṣi Atri (अत्रि), Maharṣi Vasīṣtha (वसीष्ठ), Maharṣi Viśvāmitra (विश्वामित्र), Maharṣi Gautama (गौतम), Maharṣi Jamadagni (जमदग्नि) and Maharṣi Bhāradvāja (भारद्वाज) as cited in Bṛhadāraṇyaka Upaniṣad (बृहदारण्यक उपनिषद्) 2.2.6

Intent - One who knows My divine manifestations, "the entire mortal world is My miracle only and separate from Me all this is nothing, just as waves or eddies are miracles of water and separate from water, they are nothing." One who knows My Yoga-form, "everything materializes only through Me, though nothing happens in Me," such a knower of the Truth attains steadfast union with oneness in Me that it never parts. In reality, Yoga is not something to make anew. It is permanently established. However, born of ignorance, it is the discriminating vision by which there is a perception of separation. Through knowledge, such perception is removed, and ever-attained Yoga is steadfastly established. It is impossible to attain this Yoga through Karma only. That is just like how a wave remains separate from water because of its wave conceit. It gains its ever-existing oneness in water by losing its wave conceit through knowledge.

(This way, Bhagavāna described His divine manifestations and Yoga. Who is fit for attaining this Yoga? That is described next -)

अहं सर्वस्य प्रभवो मत्त: सर्वं प्रवर्तते |
इति मत्वा भजन्ते मां बुधा भावसमन्विता: || BG 10.8 ||

मत्वा - Deeming ; इति - that ; अहम् - I am ; प्रभवः - the origin ; सर्वस्य - of all ; सर्वम् - (and) all ; प्रवर्तते - move on properly ; मत्तः - through Me, ; बुधाः - the wise ; भजन्ते - worship ; माम् - Me ; भाव-समन्विताः - with devout faith.

Deeming that I am the origin of all and all move on properly through Me, the wise worship Me with devout faith.

Intent - Understanding, "in its true nature this world is without any essence and worthless, only through the existence of the One with value, the Lord, it is perceived as of value. That is why, in this valueless world, the search for the valuable Paramātmā ought to be the only aim of our lives," a wise person does not become extroverted towards the mortal world (Saṃsāra-Parāyaṇa) but becomes oriented towards the Lord and endowed with devout faith worships the Lord.

मच्चित्ता मद्गतप्राणा बोधयन्त: परस्परम् |
कथयन्तश्च मां नित्यं तुष्यन्ति च रमन्ति च || BG 10.9 ||

मत् चित्ताः - With (their) mind fixed on Me, ; च - and ; मत् गत-प्राणाः - lives surrendered to Me, (such devotees with undivided devotion) ; बोधयन्तः - by enlightening (My reality) ; परस्परम् - to one another ; च - and ; कथयन्तः - conversing ; माम् - about Me, ; नित्यम् - (they) always ; तुष्यन्ति - find contentment ; च - and ; रमन्ति - delight.

With their mind fixed on Me, their lives surrendered to Me, enlightening one another and conversing about Me, they always find contentment and delight.

Intent - Making the Lord as the only aim of life, in every action and every breath thinking only of the Lord, getting rid of worldly perspective from the mind, and deeming transcendental loss as loss and transcendental gain as gain - in such forms analyzing from transcendental perspective gain and loss, happiness and grief, and growth and decay is the meaning of the words "मच्चित्त, Maccitta" and "मद्गतप्राण, Madgataprāṇa." Such persons with their mind fixed on Me, enlightening My reality to one another, and conversing about Me remain contented in Me and always delight in Me.

(What kind of assistance do I provide to My devotees to attain Me? That is discussed in the following two verses -)

तेषां सततयुक्तानां भजतां प्रीतिपूर्वकम् |
ददामि बुद्धियोगं तं येन मामुपयान्ति ते || BG 10.10 ||

तेषाम् - To them ; सतत-युक्तानाम् - who are constantly established in Me ; प्रीति-पूर्वकम् - and lovingly ; भजताम् - worship Me, ; ददामि - I give ; तम् - them ; बुद्धि-योगम् - the Yoga of Discernment ; येन - by which ; ते - they ; उपयान्ति - come ; माम् - to Me.

To them who are constantly established in Me and lovingly worship Me, I give them the Yoga of Discernment by which they come to Me.

तेषामेवानुकम्पार्थमहमज्ञानजं तम: |
नाशयाम्यात्मभावस्थो ज्ञानदीपेन भास्वता || BG 10.11 ||

अनुकम्पार्थम् - Moved by compassion ; एव - alone (for those devotees), ; अहम् - I, ; आत्म-भावस्थ: - existent in their hearts, ; नाशयामि - destroy ; तेषाम् - their ; तम: - darkness ; अज्ञानजम् - of ignorance ; भास्वता - with a lustrous ; ज्ञान-दीपेन - flame of knowledge.

Moved by compassion alone, I, existent in their hearts, destroy their darkness of ignorance with a lustrous flame of knowledge.

The intent of verses (BG 10.10 - BG 10.11) - Moving towards the Lord, becoming united and based on the above manner offering own mind and life to the Lord is the duty of a fit person. His ultimate effort ends reaching there. Only with the compassion of the Lord, a qualified person moves forward. It is like the Pole star that provides a direction of the path. For a fit person, the compassion of the Lord is necessary and unavoidable. Existent in his heart, with a lustrous flame of knowledge, arousing emotional waves of pure thought of the truth of the Brahman in his Sāttvika intellect, his darkness of ignorance is removed, which without the compassion of the Lord is unattainable by any other means. That is indeed the compassion of the omnipresent, omnipotent, omniscient Lord. With the acquisition of the right means, such as own firm power and a favorable wind, one can cross over an ocean by a boat, in the same way, by a resolute effort exclusively moving towards the Lord and with a favorable wind of compassion of the Lord, both provide the ability to the fit to cross over the worldly ocean. The grace of a preceptor and grace of the Lord is not different, but only one. There is a difference in words but not in the meaning.

(Listening to the words of Bhagavāna, Arjuna was satisfied and, expressing his gratitude, said -)

अर्जुन उवाच |
परं ब्रह्म परं धाम पवित्रं परमं भवान् |
पुरुषं शाश्वतं दिव्यमादिदेवमजं विभुम् || BG 10.12 ||
अर्जुन उवाच - Arjuna Said -

भवान् - (Hey Lord!) You are ; परम् - the supreme ; ब्रह्म - Brahman, ; परम् - the supreme ; धाम - abode, ; परमम् - the supreme ; पवित्रम् - sanctification, ; शाश्वतम् - the eternal ; दिव्यम् - divine ; पुरुषम् - Personality, ; आदिदेवम् - the primordial Supreme Lord (origin of all beings), ; अजम् - the unborn, ; विभुम् - (and) the all-pervading.

Arjuna Said -

You are the supreme Brahman, the supreme abode, the supreme sanctification, the eternal divine Personality, the primordial Supreme Lord, the unborn, and the all-pervading.

Intent - Hey Lord! You are the supreme Brahman. You are the supreme abode, the provider of opportunity to all. You are the supreme sanctification, the illuminator of all good and evil yet untainted. You are the divine eternal Personality, residing immutably in all body-form cities yet remaining detached from creation and destruction. Moreover, You are the origin of all deities and all beings. You are the unborn and the all-pervading.

आहुस्त्वामृषय: सर्वे देवर्षिर्नारदस्तथा |
असितो देवलो व्यास: स्वयं चैव ब्रवीषि मे || BG 10.13 ||

देवर्षि: - Devine sage ; नारद: - Nārada, ; असित: - Asita, ; देवल: - Devala, ; व्यास: - Vyāsa, ; तथा - and ; सर्वे - all (other) ; ऋषय: - seers ; आहु: - have described ; त्वाम् - You (as such), ; च - and ; स्वयम् - You Yourself ; एव - (are) indeed ; ब्रवीषि - articulating (the same) ; मे - to me.

Divine sage Nārada, Asita, Devala, Vyāsa, and all other seers have described You as such, and You are indeed articulating the same to me.

सर्वमेतदृतं मन्ये यन्मां वदसि केशव |
न हि ते भगवन्व्यक्तिं विदुर्देवा न दानवा: || BG 10.14 ||

केशव - Hey Keśava (Śrī Kṛṣṇa)! ; यत् - Whatever ; माम् - You ; वदसि - are telling me, ; मन्ये - I deem ; सर्वम् - all ; एतत् - that ; ऋतम् - to be true. ; भगवन् - Hey Lord! ; हि - Indeed, ; न - neither ; देवाः - the deities ; न - nor ; दानवाः - the demons ; विदुः - know ; ते - Your ; व्यक्तिम् - manifestation.

Hey Keśava! Whatever You are telling me, I deem all that to be true. Hey Lord! Indeed, neither the deities nor the demons know Your manifestation.

Intent - Whatever You are commanding me, I deem it true. In reality, neither the deities nor the demons know Your origin.

(However -)

स्वयमेवात्मनात्मानं वेत्थ त्वं पुरुषोत्तम |
भूतभावन भूतेश देवदेव जगत्पते || BG 10.15 ||

पुरुषोत्तम - Hey Puruṣottama (Śrī Kṛṣṇa)! ; भूत-भावन - The cause of all beings! ; भूत-ईश - The Supreme Lord of all beings! ; देव-देव - The Lord of all deities! ; जगत्-पते - The Lord of the world! ; एव - Only ; त्वम् - You ; स्वयम् - Yourself ; वेत्थ - know ; आत्मानम् - the Self, ; आत्मना - by Yourself.

Hey Puruṣottama! The cause of all beings! The Supreme Lord of all beings! The Lord of all deities! The Lord of the world! Only You know the Self, by Yourself.

Intent - In other words, You cannot be the object of cognition of knowing some object in separate form from one's own through senses, just as how knowledge of pots and pans happens through the external disposition of the senses such as eyes. However, with the absence of all inner tendencies at all times, You Self-illuminate, just as the sun removing darkness illuminates by its illumination.

(That is why -)

वक्तुमर्हस्यशेषेण दिव्या ह्यात्मविभूतय: |
याभिर्विभूतिभिर्लोकानिमांस्त्वं व्याप्य तिष्ठसि || BG 10.16 ||

हि - Indeed, ; अर्हसि - (You alone) are capable ; अशेषेण - of completely ; वक्तुम् - articulating ; दिव्याः आत्म-विभूतयः - Your divine manifestations, ; याभिः - by which ; विभूतिभिः - manifestations ; त्वम् - You ; तिष्ठसि - are existent ; व्याप्य - pervading ; इमान् - all these ; लोकान् - worlds.

Indeed, You alone are capable of completely articulating Your divine manifestations, by which manifestations You are existent pervading all these worlds.

कथं विद्यामहं योगिंस्त्वां सदा परिचिन्तयन् |
केषु केषु च भावेषु चिन्त्योऽसि भगवन्मया || BG 10.17 ||

योगिन् - Hey Yogin (Śrī Kṛṣṇa, the Lord of Yoga)! ; सदा - Ever ; परिचिन्तयन् - contemplating ; कथम् - how can ; अहम् - I ; विद्याम् - know ; त्वाम् - You? ; च - Additionally, ; भगवन् - hey, blessed Lord! ; केषु केषु - In what ; भावेषु - (manifestation) form ; असि - are you ; चिन्त्यः - to be meditated upon ; मया - by Me?

Hey Yogin! Ever contemplating how can I know You? Hey blessed Lord! In what form are you to be meditated upon by Me?

Intent - Not knowing Your true nature, tell me about all those divine manifestations contemplating on whom I can know You.

(That is why -)

विस्तरेणात्मनो योगं विभूतिं च जनार्दन |
भूय: कथय तृप्तिर्हि शृण्वतो नास्ति मेऽमृतम् || BG 10.18 ||

जनार्दन - Hey Janārdana (Śrī Kṛṣṇa)! ; भूयः - Once again, ; कथय - recount ; विस्तरेण - in detail ; आत्मनः - Your ; योगम् - Yoga ; च - and ; विभूतिम् - manifestations ; हि - as ; मे - I ; अस्ति - am ; न - not ; तृप्तिः - content ; शृण्वतः - hearing Your ; अमृतम् - ambrosiac (words).

Hey Janārdana! Once again, recount in detail Your Yoga and manifestations as I am not content hearing Your ambrosiac words.

श्रीभगवानुवाच |
हन्त ते कथयिष्यामि दिव्या ह्यात्मविभूतय: |
प्राधान्यत: कुरुश्रेष्ठ नास्त्यन्तो विस्तरस्य मे || BG 10.19 ||
श्रीभगवान् उवाच - Śrī Bhagavān said -

कुरु-श्रेष्ठ - Hey Kuru-Śreṣṭha (Arjuna, the best of the descendants of the Kurus)! ; हन्त - Now ; कथयिष्यामि - I shall articulate ; ते - to you ; प्राधान्यतः - the more prominent of ; दिव्याः आत्म-विभूतयः - My divine manifestations, ; हि - as ; अस्ति - there is ; न - no ; अन्तः - end ; मे - to My ; विस्तरस्य - enormity.

Śrī Bhagavān said -

Hey Arjuna! Now I will articulate to you the more prominent of My divine manifestations, as there is no end to My enormity.

(Among them, you listen to the first manifestation -)

अहमात्मा गुडाकेश सर्वभूताशयस्थित: |
अहमादिश्च मध्यं च भूतानामन्त एव च || BG 10.20 ||

गुडाका-ईश - Hey Guḍākeśa (Arjuna)! ; सर्व-भूत-आशय-स्थितः - Existent in the hearts of all beings, ; अहम् - I am ; आत्मा - the Self, ; च - and ; एव च - indeed, ; अहम् - I am ; आदिः - the beginning, ; मध्यम् - the middle, ; च - and ; अन्तः - the end ; भूतानाम् - of all beings.

Hey Arjuna! Existent in the hearts of all beings, I am the Self, and indeed, I am the beginning, the middle, and the end of all beings.

Intent - Existent in the hearts of all beings, that is, resident in all beings, I am the Ātmā of all beings to be meditated upon. One not competent to do so may meditate upon the manifestations described after this. I am the beginning, the cause, or the origin of all beings. I am their middle, state of sustentation, and their end, dissolution.

आदित्यानामहं विष्णुर्ज्योतिषां रविरंशुमान् |
मरीचिर्मरुतामस्मि नक्षत्राणामहं शशी || BG 10.21 ||

अहम् - I am ; विष्णुः - Viṣṇu ; आदित्यानाम् - among the (twelve) Ādityas. ; अहम् - I ; अस्मि - am ; अंशुमान् - the radiant ; रविः - sun ; ज्योतिषाम् - among the luminosities, ; मरीचिः - Marīci ; मरुताम् - among the wind-deities, ; शशी - (and) the moon ; नक्षत्राणाम् - among the stars.

I am Viṣṇu among the Ādityas. I am the radiant sun among the luminosities, Marīci among the wind-deities, and the moon among the stars.

वेदानां सामवेदोऽस्मि देवानामस्मि वासवः |
इन्द्रियाणां मनश्चास्मि भूतानामस्मि चेतना || BG 10.22 ||

वेदानाम् - Among the Vedas, ; अस्मि - I am ; सामवेदः - Sāma-Veda; ; देवानाम् - among the deities, ; अस्मि - I am ; वासवः - Indra; ; इन्द्रियाणाम् - among the senses, ; अस्मि - I am ; मनः - the mind; ; च - and ; भूतानाम् - among beings, ; अस्मि - I am ; चेतना - intelligence.

Among the Vedas, I am Sāma-Veda; among the deities, I am Indra; among the senses, I am the mind; and among beings, I am intelligence.

Intent - Cetanā (चेतना) here means intelligence rather than the ordinary meaning of consciousness.

रुद्राणां शङ्करश्चास्मि वित्तेशो यक्षरक्षसाम् |
वसूनां पावकश्चास्मि मेरुः शिखरिणामहम् || BG 10.23 ||

च - And, ; अस्मि - I am ; शङ्करः - Shankar, ; रुद्राणाम् - among the (eleven) Rudras; ; वित्त-ईशः - I am Kubera, ; यक्ष-रक्षसाम् - among the Yakṣas and Rākṣasas; ; पावकः - I am fire, ; वसूनाम् - among the (eight) Vasus; ; च - and ; अहम् - I ; अस्मि - am ; मेरुः - Meru, ; शिखरिणाम् - among the mountains.

I am Shankar, among the Rudras; I am Kubera, among the Yakṣas and Rākṣasas; I am fire, among the Vasus; and I am Meru, among the mountains.

पुरोधसां च मुख्यं मां विद्धि पार्थ बृहस्पतिम् |
सेनानीनामहं स्कन्दः सरसामस्मि सागरः || BG 10.24 ||

पार्थ - Hey Pārtha (Arjuna)! ; विद्धि - Know ; माम् - Me ; बृहस्पतिम् - as Bṛhaspati, ; मुख्यम् - the chief ; पुरोधसाम् - among the priests. ; सेनानीनाम् - Among army commanders, ; अहम् - I am ; स्कन्दः - Skanda; ; च - and ; सरसाम् - among lakes, ; अस्मि - I am ; सागरः - the ocean.

Hey Arjuna! Know Me as Bṛhaspati, the chief among the priests. Among army commanders, I am Skanda; and among lakes, I am the ocean.

(Skanda is another name for the commander of the army of the deities Kārtikeya, son of Lord Śiva.)

महर्षीणां भृगुरहं गिरामस्म्येकमक्षरम् |
यज्ञानां जपयज्ञोऽस्मि स्थावराणां हिमालयः || BG 10.25 ||

अहम् - I ; अस्मि - am ; भृगुः - Bhṛgu, ; महर्षीणाम् - among the great seers; ; एकम् - mono- ; अक्षरम् - syllable (Oṃ, ॐ), ; गिराम् - among utterance; ; जप-यज्ञः - repetitive chants (of the names of divine manifestations), ; यज्ञानाम् - among sacrifice; ; अस्मि - (and) I am ; हिमालयः - Himālaya, ; स्थावराणाम् - among immovable objects.

I am Bhṛgu, among the great seers; the mono-syllable (Oṃ, ॐ), among utterance; repetitive chants, among sacrifice; and I am Himālaya, among immovable objects.

Intent - In the verse, sacrifice (Yajña) means an oblation, an observance, or an act in general for the propitiation of a deity. The simplest of all sacrifices is Japa-Yajña, or the repetitive chanting of any of the holy names of the divine Personality, Vedic hymns, or Mantra. In Japa-Yajña, the intoning of the chants is distinguished by four types: 1) Vaikharī (वैखरी, Mantra chanting with a high tone), 2) Madhyamā (मध्यमा, Mantra chanting without the lips moving so that it is inaudible to anyone), 3) Paśyantī (पश्यन्ती, Mantra chanting heartily without the tongue moving and the mind engrossed in the meaning of the chant), and 4) Parā (परा, Mantra chanting with inner-disposition steady in the meaning of the chant providing bliss and the intellect becoming steadfast in the Ātmā). In ritualistic sacrifices, several rules are applicable, all of which need to be meticulously followed. However, in Japa-Yajña, there are no rules. It can be done anywhere and anytime and is very purifying.

अश्वत्थ: सर्ववृक्षाणां देवर्षीणां च नारद: |
गन्धर्वाणां चित्ररथ: सिद्धानां कपिलो मुनि: || BG 10.26 ||

अश्वत्थः - (I am) the holy fig ; सर्व-वृक्षाणाम् - among all trees, ; नारदः - Nārada ; देवर्षीणाम् - among the divine seers, ; चित्ररथः - Citraratha ; गन्धर्वाणाम् - among the divine minstrels, ; च - and ; कपिलः मुनिः - sage Kapila ; सिद्धानाम् - among the perfected sages.

I am the holy fig among all trees, Nārada among the divine seers, Citraratha among the divine minstrels, and sage Kapila among the perfected sages.

Intent - Sage Kapila is referred to as Siddha or the perfected sage. Right from birth, a person, who has attained abundant righteousness (Atiśaya Dharma), knowledge (Jñāna), dispassion (Vairāgya), and lordliness (Aiśvarya), is called a "सिद्ध, Siddha."

उच्चै:श्रवसमश्वानां विद्धि माममृतोद्भवम् |
ऐरावतं गजेन्द्राणां नराणां च नराधिपम् || BG 10.27 ||

अश्वानाम् - Among horses, ; विद्धि - know ; माम् - Me ; उच्चैःश्रवसम् - as Uccaiḥśrava ; अमृत-उद्भवम् - born of ambrosia; ; गजेन्द्राणाम् - among the lordly elephants, ; ऐरावतम् - Airāvata; ; च - and ; नराणाम् - among humans, ; नराधिपम् - their ruler.

Among horses, know Me as Uccaiḥśrava born of ambrosia; among the lordly elephants, Airāvata; and among humans, their ruler.

आयुधानामहं वज्रं धेनूनामस्मि कामधुक् |
प्रजनश्चास्मि कन्दर्प: सर्पाणामस्मि वासुकि: || BG 10.28 ||

आयुधानाम् - Among weapons ; अहम् - I ; अस्मि - am ; वज्रम् - the thunderbolt (of Indra); ; धेनूनाम् - among cows, ; अस्मि - I am ; कामधुक् - the wish-granting cow (Kāmadhenu); ; अस्मि - I am ; प्रजनः - the progenitor ; कन्दर्पः - Kandarpa (Kāmadeva, the deity of love); ; च - and ; सर्पाणाम् - among serpents, ; वासुकिः - (I am) Vāsuki.

Among weapons, I am the thunderbolt of Indra; among cows, I am the wish-granting cow Kāmadhenu; I am the progenitor Kandarpa; and among serpents, I am Vāsuki.

Intent - Vajra, the thunderbolt of Indra, was created from the bones of the great seer Dadhīci (दधीचि) to kill the demon Vṛtrāsura (वृत्रासुर). The wish-granting cow Kāmadhenu of the great seer Vasīṣṭha was endowed with the power of yielding objects of desire. Kandarpa, the Kāmadeva (कामदेव), the divinity of love, is responsible for the force of attraction between the opposite sexes that facilitates the continuance of humanity through procreation.

अनन्तश्चास्मि नागानां वरुणो यादसामहम् |
पितृणामर्यमा चास्मि यम: संयमतामहम् || BG 10.29 ||

च - And, ; अहम् - I ; अस्मि - am ; अनन्तः - Ananta (Śeṣanāga) ; नागानाम् - among the cobras, ; वरुणः - Varuṇa ; यादसाम् - among the water-deities, ; अर्यमा - Aryamā ; पितॄणाम् - among the ancestors, ; च - and ; संयमताम् - among the subduers, ; अहम् - I ; अस्मि - am ; यमः - Yama (the deity of death)

I am Ananta among the cobras, Varuṇa among the water-deities, Aryamā among the ancestors, and among the subduers, I am Yama.

Intent - Ananta, known as Śeṣanāga (शेषनाग), is the ten thousand hooded divine cobra on whom Lord Viṣṇu rests. Aryamā, worshipped as the head of ancestors, is the third son of Aditi, the daughter of Prajāpati Dakṣa. Yamarāja (यमराज), the deity of death, arranges to take Jīvātmā from its mortal frame after death. He dispenses justice on behalf of the divine Personality for the actions of Jīvātmā in the current life, granting punishment or reward in the next life without deviating from his duties, however gruesome and painful they are. He reflects the glory of the divine Personality as the perfect dispenser of justice.

प्रह्लादश्चास्मि दैत्यानां काल: कलयतामहम् |
मृगाणां च मृगेन्द्रोऽहं वैनतेयश्च पक्षिणाम् || BG 10.30 ||

अहम् - I ; अस्मि - am ; प्रह्लादः - Prahlāda ; दैत्यानाम् - among the demons, ; च - and ; कालः - time ; कलयताम् - among the reckoners, ; च - and ; मृगेन्द्रः - lion ; मृगाणाम् - among the animals, ; च - and ; अहम् - I am ; वैनतेयः - (Garuḍa) the son of Vinatā ; पक्षिणाम् - among the birds.

I am Prahlāda among the demons, time among the reckoners, lion among the animals, and I am (Garuḍa) the son of Vinatā among the birds.

Intent - Daitya is a class of demons held to be implacable enemies of the deities. They are the descendants of Diti (daughter of Prajāpati Dakṣa) and Saptarṣi Kaśyapa. Prahlāda, the son of the mighty demon king Hiraṇyakaśipu (हिरण्यकशिपु), was one of the greatest devotees of Lord Viṣṇu. Garuḍa (गरुड़), the son of Vinatā, is the divine vehicle of Lord Viṣṇu.

पवन: पवतामस्मि राम: शस्त्रभृतामहम् |
झषाणां मकरश्चास्मि स्रोतसामस्मि जाह्नवी || BG 10.31 ||

पवताम् - Among purifiers, ; अहम् - I ; अस्मि - am ; पवनः - the wind; ; शस्त्र-भृताम् - among the bearers of weapons, ; रामः - (I am Lord Śrī) Rāma; ; झषाणाम् - among aquatic creatures, ; अस्मि - I am ; मकरः - crocodile; ; च - and ; स्रोतसाम् - among rivers, ; अस्मि - I am ; जाह्नवी - Gaṅgā.

Among purifiers, I am the wind; among the bearers of weapons, I am Rāma; among aquatic creatures, I am crocodile; and among rivers, I am Gaṅgā.

सर्गाणामादिरन्तश्च मध्यं चैवाहमर्जुन |
अध्यात्मविद्या विद्यानां वाद: प्रवदतामहम् || BG 10.32 ||

अर्जुन - Hey Arjuna! ; अहम् - I am ; आदिः - the beginning, ; अन्तः - the end, ; च - and ; एव - indeed ; मध्यम् - the middle ; सर्गाणाम् - of all creations. ; विद्यानाम् - Among knowledge, ; अहम् - I am ; अध्यात्म-विद्या - the knowledge of the Self; ; च - and ; प्रवदताम् - among (Vāda, Jalpa, Vitaṇḍa, and Saṃvāda) discussions, ; वादः - (I am) Vāda (that determines the truth).

Hey Arjuna! I am the beginning, the end, and the middle of all creations. Among knowledge, I am the knowledge of the Self; and among discussions, I am Vāda.

Intent - Hey, Arjuna! I am the origin, existence, and dissolution of everything. In BG 10.20, the origin and end are mentioned in terms of living beings. Here the reference is to the creation as a whole. Of the knowledge, the knowledge of the Brahman promoting liberation is pre-eminent - I am that. The term Pravadatā (प्रवदता) means discussions or arguments. Among discussions, I am Vāda (वाद) that determines the truth, that which provides a logical conclusion to the discussion. The discussions are of four kinds: 1) Saṃvāda (संवाद), 2) Vāda (वाद), 2) Jalpa (जल्प), and 4) Vitaṇḍa (वितण्ड).

- Saṃvāda is a discussion between a teacher and his student, as in Śrī Kṛṣṇa-Arjuna Saṃvāda in Śrīmad Bhagavad Gītā. The student does not argue with the teacher but questions his understanding for clarification. This type of discussion can occur only when the student surrenders himself completely at the feet of the teacher.

- Vāda is the discussion between two equals to settle what the truth is. Both come to the table for discussion with an open mind, and the discussion is based on some accepted measure of authority. For Vedānta, the measures are specifically the Prasthāntrayi - the Vedas, Bhagavad Gītā, and Brahma-Sūtra. There are judges to ensure that discussion proceeds along with accepted standards. It proceeds until one accepts the other's arguments. Sometimes the discussions can take days - as in the famous debate between Ādi Śaṅkarācārya and Mandana Miśrā, which was supposed to have lasted for 18 days until Mandana Miśrā accepted defeat and became a disciple of Śaṅkarācārya. Mandana Miśrā's wife, Bhārati, a scholar herself, had served as a judge for that Vāda.
- Jalpa is where each discusser comes to the table with a preconceived notion that he is right and the other fellow is wrong. The other fellow also comes with the same idea. It is a type of wrangling where both parties try to establish their position without any rules or regulations. They provide unjustifiable arguments and reasons with full confidence to establish their position. In the Nyāya-Sūtra, Jalpa is described as defending or attacking a proposition through quibbles, futilities, and other processes.
- Vitaṇḍa is a kind of an argument in which the opponent does not try to establish his own opinion but only tries to refute the exponent's view. In Vitaṇḍa, each party-exponent or opponent tries to win by refuting the other's opinion.

अक्षराणामकारोऽस्मि द्वन्द्वः सामासिकस्य च |
अहमेवाक्षयः कालो धाताहं विश्वतोमुखः || BG 10.33 ||

अहम् - I am, ; अकारः - "A" ; अक्षराणाम् - among the letters, ; द्वन्द्वः - Dvandva (the additive) ; सामासिकस्य - among the compounds, ; अक्षयः - the imperishable ; कालः - time, ; धाता - sustainer of all, ; च - and ; विश्वतोमुखः - facing all directions of the world, ; अहं - I ; एव - alone ; अस्मि - am (the Lord).

I am "A" among the letters, Dvandva (the additive) among the compounds, the imperishable time, sustainer of all, and facing all directions of the world, I alone am the Lord.

मृत्युः सर्वहरश्चाहमुद्भवश्च भविष्यताम् |
कीर्तिः श्रीर्वाक्च नारीणां स्मृतिर्मेधा धृतिः क्षमा || BG 10.34 ||

अहम् - I am ; सर्व-हरः - the all-destroying ; मृत्युः - death ; च - and ; उद्भवः - (I am) the origin ; भविष्यताम् - of things yet to happen. ; च - Additionally, ; नारीणाम् - in women, (I am) ; कीर्तिः - fame, ; श्रीः - prosperity, ; वाक् - speech, ; स्मृतिः - memory, ; मेधा - intelligence, ; धृतिः - endurance, ; च - and ; क्षमा - forgiveness.

I am the all-destroying death and the origin of things yet to happen. In women, I am fame, prosperity, speech, memory, intelligence, endurance, and forgiveness.

Intent - All-destroying death destroys everything, material possessions, and life. Fame (कीर्ति, Kīrti), prosperity (श्री, Śrī), speech (वाक्, Vāk), memory (स्मृति, Smṛti), intelligence (मेधा, Medhā), endurance (धृति, Dhṛti), and forgiveness (क्षमा, Kṣamā) are the seven wives of the deities. The seven attributes with feminine names are also popular, and so from both perspectives, they are divine manifestations of the Lord.

बृहत्साम तथा साम्नां गायत्री छन्दसामहम् |
मासानां मार्गशीर्षोऽहमृतूनां कुसुमाकरः || BG 10.35 ||

तथा - Also, ; अहम् - I am ; बृहत्-साम - Bṛhat-Sāma ; साम्नाम् - among the melodies of Śruti, ; गायत्री - Gāyatrī meter ; छन्दसाम् - among the Vedic meters, ; मार्गशीर्षः - Mārgaśīrṣa ; मासानाम् - among the months, ; ऋतूनाम् - (and) among seasons, ; अहम् - I am ; कुसुमाकरः - spring, when flowers abound.

I am Bṛhat-Sāma among the melodies of Śruti, Gāyatrī meter among the Vedic meters, Mārgaśīrṣa among the months, and among seasons, I am spring, when flowers abound.

द्यूतं छलयतामस्मि तेजस्तेजस्विनामहम् |
जयोऽस्मि व्यवसायोऽस्मि सत्त्वं सत्त्ववतामहम् || BG 10.36 ||

छलयताम् - Of the cheats, ; अहम् - I ; अस्मि - am ; द्यूतम् - the game of dice; ; तेजस्विनाम् - of the brilliant ; अस्मि - I am ; तेजः - the brilliance; ; जयः - (of the victorious I am) the victory; ; व्यवसायः - (of the resolute I am) the resolve; ; सत्त्ववताम् - (and) of the virtuous ; अहम् - I ; अस्मि - am ; सत्त्वम् - the virtue.

Of the cheats, I am the game of dice; of the brilliant, I am the brilliance; I am the victory; I am the resolve; and of the virtuous, I am the virtue.

वृष्णीनां वासुदेवोऽस्मि पाण्डवानां धनञ्जयः |
मुनीनामप्यहं व्यासः कवीनामुशना कविः || BG 10.37 ||

अहं - I ; अस्मि - am ; वासुदेवः - Vāsudeva (Śrī Kṛṣṇa) ; वृष्णीनाम् - among the Vṛṣṇi descendants, ; धनञ्जयः - (you) Arjuna ; पाण्डवानाम् - among the Pāṇḍavas, ; अपि - also ; व्यासः - Vedavyāsa ; मुनीनाम् - among the sages, ; कविः - (and) seer ; उशना - Uśanā ; कवीनाम् - among the seers.

I am Vāsudeva Śrī Kṛṣṇa among the Vṛṣṇi descendants, Arjuna among the Pāṇḍavas, Vedavyāsa among the sages, and seer Uśanā among the seers.

{Uśanā is also known as seer Śukrācārya (शुक्राचार्य).}

दण्डो दमयतामस्मि नीतिरस्मि जिगीषताम् |
मौनं चैवास्मि गुह्यानां ज्ञानं ज्ञानवतामहम् || BG 10.38 ||

दमयताम् - Of those who punish, ; अस्मि - I am ; दण्डः - the rod; ; जिगीषताम् - of those who seek victory, ; अस्मि - I am ; नीतिः - justice. ; गुह्यानाम् - Of secrets, ; अस्मि - I am ; मौनम् - the silence, ; च - and ; अहम् - I am ; एव - indeed ; ज्ञानम् - knowledge ; ज्ञानवताम् - of the knowers.

Of those who punish, I am the rod; of those who seek victory, I am justice. Of secrets, I am the silence, and I am indeed knowledge of the knowers.

Intent - Here, rod (दण्ड, Daṇḍa) means the power to subdue.

यच्चापि सर्वभूतानां बीजं तदहमर्जुन |
न तदस्ति विना यत्स्यान्मया भूतं चराचरम् || BG 10.39 ||

अर्जुन - Hey Arjuna! ; च - And, ; अपि - also ; तत् - that ; यत् - which ; बीजम् - is the seed (root cause) ; सर्व-भूतानाम् - of all beings, ; अहम् - I am. ; अस्ति - There is ; न - no ; तत् - such ; चर-अचरम् - mobile or stationary ; भूतम् - being ; यत् - who ; स्यात् - can exist ; विना - without ; मया - Me.

Hey Arjuna! That which is the seed of all beings, I am. There is no mobile or stationary being who can exist without Me.

Intent - Whatever root cause of beings is, that I am. Whether it is a movable or immovable substance, it cannot exist without Me. There cannot be any substance without beingness, and I am that beingness in them.

नान्तोऽस्ति मम दिव्यानां विभूतीनां परन्तप |
एष तूद्देशतः प्रोक्तो विभूतेर्विस्तरो मया || BG 10.40 ||

परन्तप - Hey Parantapa (Arjuna)! ; अस्ति - There is ; न - no ; अन्तः - end ; मम - to My ; दिव्यानाम् - divine ; विभूतीनाम् - manifestations. ; एषः - This, ; प्रोक्तः - (what) is stated ; मया - by Me ; तु - is only ; उद्देशतः - illustrative of ; विस्तरः - the extent ; विभूतेः - of (My) manifestations.

Hey Arjuna! There is no end to My divine manifestations. What is stated by Me is only illustrative of the extent of My manifestations.

Intent - Of the vast number of manifestations, I have only stated a limited number of divine manifestations for an illustrative purpose. No one should wonder, "Only these many manifestations" are there of the Lord, the Ātmā of all.

यद्यद्विभूतिमत्सत्त्वं श्रीमदूर्जितमेव वा |
तत्तदेवावगच्छ त्वं मम तेजोंऽशसम्भवम् || BG 10.41 ||

यत् यत् - Whatever ; विभूतिमत् - majestic, ; श्रीमत् - prosperous, ; वा - or ; ऊर्जितम् - powerful, ; सत्त्वम् - being (there is), ; त्वम् - you ; अवगच्छ - know ; तत् तत् - it to be ; एव - only ; सम्भवम् - born of ; अंश - a part ; मम - of My ; तेजः - splendor.

Whatever majestic, prosperous, or powerful being there is, know it to be only born of a part of My splendor.

अथवा बहुनैतेन किं ज्ञातेन तवार्जुन |
विष्टभ्याहमिदं कृत्स्नमेकांशेन स्थितो जगत् || BG 10.42 ||

अथवा - Or, ; अर्जुन - Hey Arjuna! ; किम् - What is ; तव - your (motive) ; ज्ञातेन - for knowing ; एतेन - this ; बहुना - extensively? ; अहम् - (Just understand that) I am ; स्थितः - existent, ; विष्टभ्य - holding ; इदम् - this ; कृत्स्नम् - entire ; जगत् - world ; एक-अंशेन - in (only) one part (of Mine).

Hey Arjuna! What is your motive for knowing this extensively? I am existent, holding this entire world in only one part of Mine.

ॐ तत्सदिति श्रीमद्भगवद्गीतासूपनिषत्सु ब्रह्मविद्यायां योगशास्त्रे

श्रीकृष्णार्जुनसम्वादे विभूतियोगो नाम

दशमोऽध्यायः || BG 10 ||

Oṃ Tat Sat

In the Śrīmad Bhagavad Gītā Upaniṣad

The Yoga Science of the Knowledge of Self-Realization

The Discourse of Lord Śrī Kṛṣṇa and Arjuna

This Tenth Chapter

Yoga Named - The Yoga of the Divine Manifestations

Clarification

The true nature of Yoga that Bhagavāna articulated in the ninth chapter, to restate the same, Bhagavāna attracts Arjuna's attention and says - Hey Arjuna! Listen to My supreme words once again, which with the desire for your good I shall tell you the beloved one. Neither divine entities nor the great seers know My power and origin, for, in all respects, I am the "the original cause," yet I do not have My cause. All these deities and the worlds are My miracles and manifestations. Just as the manifestation in the form of waves or eddies is the glory and miracle of the ocean, or just as creation or destruction in the form of pots is the posture of clay, in the same way, all deities, great seers, and the worlds are My divine manifestations and miracles only. Just as the moon's brilliance is not separate from the moon or the sparkling of diamonds is not different from the diamonds, in the same way, the miracles in the form of the worlds are not separate from Me. One who knows Me, the Great Supreme Lord of the world "is as is," unborn, and thus beginningless, he, the wise among humans, established with oneness in Me, becomes free from all sins.

Further, Bhagavāna stated that the manifold sentiments such as intelligence, knowledge, non-delusion, forgiveness, truthfulness, restraint of the senses, control of the mind, pleasure, pain, being, non-being, fear, fearlessness, nonviolence, equanimity, contentment, austerity, charity, renown, as well as the seven great seers and the Manu from whom this perishable world has originated, are all My miracles. Then Bhagavāna said that the one who knows My divine manifestations and Yoga, according to the manner above, attains immovable union in Me (BG 10.1 - BG 10.7). After that, Bhagavāna described the exclusive sentiments of those competent persons who are fit to know Him in this manner. For such persons, Bhagavāna expressed His compassion and how they are graced with an intellectual union, discerning intellect to attain Him, and residing in their hearts how their darkness of ignorance is destroyed with a lustrous flame of knowledge (BG 10.8 - BG 10.11).

Hearing the words of Bhagavāna, Arjuna experienced calmness of mind, his heart brimmed with happiness, bowing down his head and respecting the words of Bhagavāna with his hands on his chest said - "You are the supreme Brahman, the supreme abode, the supreme sanctification, the divine Personality, the primordial Supreme Lord, the unborn, and the all-pervading. Divine seer Nārada and other seers and sages have described You in the same way as You have described Yourself. Whatever You are telling me, I believe every word of Yours to be true. In reality, neither the deities nor the demons know Your true nature. Only You know Yourself by Yourself. That is why, You alone are capable of completely articulating Your divine manifestations, by which manifestations You are existent pervading all these worlds. Hey Yogeśvara! Not knowing Your real true nature, always meditating on You, how can I know You? In what form are You to be meditated upon by Me? Once again, recount in detail Your Yoga and manifestations as I am not content hearing Your ambrosiac words" (BG 10.12 - BG 10.18).

Listening to the above words of Arjuna, Bhagavāna was pleased just as a farmer sowing the best seeds is pleased with the hope of a good yield. Then filled with happiness, Bhagavāna said to Arjuna - "Hey Arjuna! I will articulate the more prominent of My divine manifestations to you, as there is no end to My extent. No one else can describe all of My manifestations completely because how can one find the end of My infinite divine manifestations? Where can there be the end of the vastness of My power?" The essence of the words of Bhagavāna is that through the mind, intellect, and senses, whatever is known by visible (Pratyakṣa), inference (Anumāna), and other measures, they all are My miracles and manifestations, and separate from Me, they have no existence of their own. Just as gold ornaments are nothing separate from gold, they are only miracles of gold. Just as an ocean cannot get wet from waves, the entire material world existing in My support cannot taint Me, and I am "as I am" in Myself even in the being or not-being of the world. Just as an actor does not see any taint in himself from the varied roles he plays in various performances, in the same way, even seen in the form of material manifestations of the world, I am "as I am" in Myself.

However, not grasping this intention of Bhagavāna, Arjuna asked Bhagavāna to describe those divine manifestations on whose support he could steady his mind and constantly meditating can know His existent form common in all. On this, commensurate with the mental competency of Arjuna, Bhagavāna described those prominent manifestations for Arjuna to see. To behold each of His forms so that he can ultimately realize the existent form common in all of Bhagavāna. In the scriptures, where there is an injunctive articulation of the worship of Śāligrāma (शालिग्राम) in the form of Lord Viṣṇu, the intention of the scriptures is only that even in a tiny stone existence of the all-pervading Lord Viṣṇu is visualized. Then, earth, mountains, rivers, and the four germination-born, sweat-born, egg-born, and placenta-born sentient and insentient beings have to be the forms of Lord Viṣṇu, not that only a tiny stone is Lord Viṣṇu. In such a way, Bhagavāna identified His existence and power in all beings. Visualizing such power of Bhagavāna in those prominent divine manifestations, one can know the true nature of Bhagavāna in the entire world and oneself.

Accordingly, in the verses (BG 10.20 - BG 10.38) describing various forms of His divine manifestations, Bhagavāna said - Hey Arjuna! Know that I am existent in the hearts of all beings and illuminate everyone's dispositions of pleasure and pain with My light, where there is neither the light of the sun nor electricity. However, there with My witnessing light, I illuminate all knowledge. Whatever visible luminosities are seen from gross eyes, I am the one that is shining like the sun. Among the stars, in the form of the moon, I calm down the hearts of all. In the form of the mind, I agitate all bodies among all senses. I am the intelligence that provides discriminative power to make choices in all beings. In the form of fire, activities of humanity happen only through Me. In the form of Meru, I am in a deep sleep, covered with the blanket of insentience among the mountains. In the form of the ocean, I am smiling among water bodies. Among the great seers, know Saptarṣi Bhṛgu as My miracle. He is the one who had kicked wealth and opulence with total relinquishment (Sarva-Tyāga). Among utterances, know Me as the monosyllable Oṃ (ॐ), that is A (अकार, Akāra), U (उकार, Ukāra), and M (मकार, Makāra). When a child is born, he cries with अ अ अ (a a a) or उ उ उ (u u u) or म म म (m m m). This way, all voices (Vāṇī), whether verbal or musical, their root is Oṃ (ॐ); and that I am. Among sacrifices (Yajña) in the form of chants, I am the most easily practiced Japa-Yajña, the repetitive chanting of any of the holy names of the divine Personality, Vedic hymns, or Mantra. Among stationary entities, I am Himālaya cooling everyone. Among trees, I am the holy fig. Among divine seers, forever playing melodies of happiness, I am the divine seer Nārada. Among the divine minstrels (Gandharva) who fascinate all with their music, I am Citraratha. Among perfected sages, I am sage Kapila. Among horses, in the form of Uccaiḥśrava born of ambrosia churning (Amṛta-Manthana); and among lordly elephants, in the form of Airāvata, with My all-pervasive neighing and trumpeting, I caution all. See, I am everywhere! In the form of their ruler, I restrain the evildoers among humans. Among weapons, in the form of a thunderbolt (Vajra), I provide evidence of My unslayability. In the form of Kāmadhenu, I materialize the desires of all. Among serpents, in the form of Vāsuki, and cobras (Nāga) in the form of Ananta (Śeṣanāga), I hiss My power and brilliance and thereby express My existence. Among ancestors as Aryamā, and among those who subdue in the form of Yama (the deity of death), I protect and restrain humanity. Among demons, in the form of Prahlāda, I provide a glimpse of My true love. I am that uncountable time among those who reckon every moment of creation and destruction. Among animals, in the form of a lion, I introduce My incomparable strength, and among birds, in the form of Garuḍa, I provide My beauty to all eyes. Among purifiers, in the form of wind, and those who bear arms, as Lord Śrī Rāma, I prove My bounds of morality and propriety (Maryādā). Among rivers, in the form of Gaṅgā, I flow with the thunder of Oṃ (ॐ). I am the beginning, middle, and end of creation. Among knowledge, I am Vedānta knowledge that leads one to know My true nature directly. Among letters, I am the beginning letter "A" (अकार, Akāra), among the compounds, I am the compound named Dvandva (the additive), and I am the imperishable time. In the Cosmic-Form manifestation (Virāṭa-Rupa), I am the sustainer of all, and in the form of death, I am the one to take away everything. In women, I am fame, prosperity, speech, memory, intelligence, endurance, and forgiveness. Among the melodies of Śruti, I am Bṛhat-Sāma, among Vedic meters, I am Gāyatrī meter, among months I am Mārgaśīrṣa, and among seasons, I am spring, when flowers abound. Among the Vṛṣṇi descendants, I am Vāsudeva Śrī Kṛṣṇa, among the Pāṇḍavas, I am you Arjuna, also I am Vedavyāsa among sages, and Uśanā (Śukrācārya) among the seers. Of those who subdue, I am the rod. Of those who seek victory, I am justice. I am the silence of secrets, and I am indeed knowledge of the knowers. In such forms, Bhagavāna described His prominent manifestations and said that whatever is described in the form of Asti (अस्ति, being) or Nāsti (नास्ति, not-being), I am the seed or root cause of all those beings. Nothing mobile or immovable can exist without Me because there cannot be anything without beingness and that beingness of all, I am.

The intention is - Arjuna, do not think that I come in the form of these divine manifestations by becoming effect. No, never! I am "as I am" without any mutations. These different manifestations provide a vision of Me, the existent common in all. They are there only to provide a glimpse and are only mirror-stationary, in which the one and only, I, entering, provide a glimpse of My varied forms, and yet stay "is as is" without any mutations. The attribute of a mirror is to touch an image and not the object. In a small mirror, the image appears small. In a large mirror, the image appears large. All the while, the object remains "is as is." Or just as the pervasive space with an adjunct of a large pot, a small pot, or a cup appears like those conditioned spaces, the pervasive space "is as is." In an insentient form, I appear insentient. In a sentient form, I appear sentient. In a movable form, I appear as movable, and in a stationary form, I appear as stationary - though I am without those sentient, insentient, movable, and immovable attributes, I am only in Myself "is as is."

Accordingly, Hey Arjuna! There is no end to My divine manifestations. What I told you is illustrative of the extent of My powers. Just as one entering a mirror palace seeing own face in multifaceted mirrors becomes entranced, in the same way from Brahmā to a small blade of grass, the entire Cosmic-Form manifestation is My mirror palace. In it, I, the beautiful among beautiful and young among the young, am existent in My eternal bliss, enjoying seeing My face in these varied mirrors. Whatever majestic, prosperous, or powerful exists, know it to be only born of a part of My splendor. What is your motive for knowing this extensively? I am existent, holding this entire world in only one part of Mine. The world as a whole is My miracle.

CHAPTER 11

THE YOGA OF THE VISION OF THE COSMIC-FORM

(Listening to the "Yoga of Divine Manifestations" of Bhagavāna in the tenth chapter, Arjuna's mind became cheerful, and offering his prayers -)

अर्जुन उवाच ।
मदनुग्रहाय परमं गुह्यमध्यात्मसञ्ज्ञितम् ।
यत्त्वयोक्तं वचस्तेन मोहोऽयं विगतो मम || BG 11.1 ||
अर्जुन उवाच - Arjuna said -

अयम् - This ; मोहः - ignorance ; मम - of mine ; विगतः - is removed ; यत् तेन - by those ; परमम् - supreme ; गुह्यम् - profound ; वचः - words ; अध्यात्म-संज्ञितम् - named "Adhyātma" (transcendent knowledge of the Self) ; उक्तम् - spoken ; त्वया - by You ; मत् अनुग्रहाय - for my good.

Arjuna said -

This ignorance of mine is removed by those supreme profound words named "Adhyātma" spoken by You for my good.

Intent - "Adhyātma" means the transcendent knowledge of the Brahman (Ātmā). The knowledge of the true nature of the Ātmā that You preached, by it, my ignorance, "I am a doer," is destroyed, and I have come to know that You are the doer of everything.

भवाप्ययौ हि भूतानां श्रुतौ विस्तरशो मया ।
त्वत्तः कमलपत्राक्ष माहात्म्यमपि चाव्ययम् || BG 11.2 ||

कमल-पत्र-अक्ष - Hey (Śrī Kṛṣṇa,) the lotus-eyed! ; हि - Indeed, ; भव-अप्ययौ - the origin and dissolution ; भूतानाम् - of all beings ; च - and ; अव्ययम् - ; (Your) imperishable ; माहात्म्यम् - magnanimity ; अपि - (have) also ; श्रुतौ - been heard ; विस्तरशः - extensively ; मया - by me ; त्वत्तः - from You.

Hey, the lotus-eyed! Indeed, the origin and dissolution of all beings and Your imperishable magnanimity have also been heard by me extensively from You.

एवमेतद्यथात्थ त्वमात्मानं परमेश्वर ।
द्रष्टुमिच्छामि ते रूपमैश्वरं पुरुषोत्तम || BG 11.3 ||

परमेश्वर - Hey Parameśvara (Śrī Kṛṣṇa, the Supreme Lord)! ; एवम् - It is so ; यथा - as ; त्वम् - You ; आत्थ - have described ; आत्मानं - Yourself, (yet) ; पुरुषोत्तम - Hey, Puruṣottama (Śrī Kṛṣṇa, the Supreme Personality! ; इच्छामि - I desire ; द्रष्टुम् - to see ; एतत् - that ; ऐश्वरम् - Lordly ; रूपम् - form ; ते - of Yours.

Hey Parameśvara! It is so as You have described Yourself, yet hey, the Supreme Personality! I desire to see that Lordly form of Yours.

मन्यसे यदि तच्छक्यं मया द्रष्टुमिति प्रभो |
योगेश्वर ततो मे त्वं दर्शयात्मानमव्ययम् || BG 11.4 ||

प्रभो - Hey Prabho (Śrī Kṛṣṇa, Lord)! ; यदि - If ; त्वम् - You ; इति - so ; मन्यसे - deem ; शक्यम् - possible ; मया - by me ; द्रष्टुम् - to see, (that form of Yours), ; ततः - then ; योगेश्वर - Hey Yogeśvara (Śrī Kṛṣṇa, the Lord of Yoga)! ; दर्शय - Show ; मे - me ; तत् - that ; अव्ययम् - immutable ; आत्मानम् - form (of Yours).

Hey Lord! If You so deem possible by me to see, then hey Yogeśvara! Show me that immutable form of Yours.

(Upon Arjuna's such prayer -)

श्रीभगवानुवाच |
पश्य मे पार्थ रूपाणि शतशोऽथ सहस्रशः |
नानाविधानि दिव्यानि नानावर्णाकृतीनि च || BG 11.5 ||
श्रीभगवान् उवाच - Śrī Bhagavān said -

पार्थ - Hey Pārtha (Arjuna)! ; पश्य - Behold ; मे - My ; रूपाणि - forms ; शतशः - in hundreds ; अथ - and ; सहस्रशः - thousands ; नाना-विधानि - of various kinds, ; दिव्यानि - divine, ; च - and ; नाना-वर्ण-आकृतीनि - of multiple colors and shapes.

Śrī Bhagavān said -

Hey Arjuna! Behold My forms in hundreds and thousands of various kinds, divine, and of multiple colors and shapes.

पश्यादित्यान्वसून् रुद्रानश्विनौ मरुतस्तथा |
बहून्यदृष्टपूर्वाणि पश्याश्चर्याणि भारत || BG 11.6 ||

भारत - Hey Bhārata (Arjuna)! ; पश्य - Behold (in Me) ; आदित्यान् - (the twelve) Ādityas, ; वसून् - (the eight) Vasus, ; रुद्रान् - (the eleven) Rudras, ; अश्विनौ - both Aśvinī (Kumāras), ; मरुताः - (the forty-nine) Marutas, ; तथा - and ; पश्य - behold ; बहूनि - many ; अदृष्ट-पूर्वाणि - hitherto unseen ; आश्चर्याणि - astonishing forms.

Hey Arjuna! Behold the Ādityas, the Vasus, the Rudras, both Aśvanī Kumāras, the Marutas, and many hitherto unseen astonishing forms.

Intent - The Cosmic Form of the Lord contains marvels on the earth and marvels in the higher spheres, never before seen together in this manner. The Lord reveals that the celestial deities are tiny fragments of His divine Cosmic-Form. He shows the twelve Ādityas, eight Vasus, eleven Rudras, two Aśvanī Kumāras, as well as the forty-nine Marutas within Himself.

The twelve Ādityas (आदित्य) are the sons of Aditi (the daughter of Prajāpati Dakṣa) enumerated as 1. Dhātā (धाता), 2. Mitra (मित्र), 3. Aryamā (अर्यमा), 4. Śukra (शुक्र), 5. Varuṇa (वरुण), 6. Aṃśa (अंश), 7. Bhaga (भग), 8. Vivasvān (विवस्वान्), 9. Pushā (पूषा), 10. Savitā (सविता), 11. Tvaṣṭā (त्वष्टा) and 12. Vāmana (वामन).

The eight Vasus (वसु) are the children of Aditi (the daughter of Prajāpati Dakṣa) and Saptarṣi Kaśyapa, enumerated as 1. Dhara (धर), 2. Dhruva (ध्रुव), 3. Soma (सोम), 4. Ahaḥ (अहः), 5. Anila (अनिल), 6. Anala (अनल), 7. Pratyūṣa (प्रत्यूष) and 8. Prabhāsa (प्रभास).

The eleven Rudras (रुद्र) are enumerated as 1. Hara (हर), 2. Bahurūpa (बहुरूप), 3. Trayambaka (त्रयम्बक), 4. Aparājita (अपराजित), 5. Vṛṣākapi (वृषाकपि), 6. Śambhu (शम्भु), 7. Kapardī (कपर्दी), 8. Raivata (रैवत), 9. Mṛgavyādha (मृगव्याध), 10. Śarva (शर्व) and 11. Kapālī (कपाली).

The twin Aśvanī Kumāras are associated with medicine and health and are generally known as the physicians of the deities. They are born of Prabhā (प्रभा) and Vivasvat (विवस्वत्), the sun-deity.

The forty-nine Marutas (मरुत, wind deities) are enumerated as Sattvajyoti (सत्त्वज्योति), Āditya (आदित्य), Satyajyoti (सत्यज्योति), Tiryagjyoti (तिर्यग्ज्योति), Sajyoti (सज्योति), Jyotiṣmān (ज्योतिष्मान्), Harita (हरित), Ṛtajit (ऋतजित्), Satyajit (सत्यजित्), Suṣeṇa (सुषेण), Senajit (सेनजित्), Satyamitra (सत्यमित्र), Abhimitra (अभिमित्र), Harimitra (हरिमित्र), Kṛta (कृत), Satya (सत्य), Dhruva (ध्रुव), Dhartā (धर्ता), Vidhartā (विधर्ता), Vidhāraya (विधारय), Dhvānta (ध्वान्त), Dhuni (धुनि), Ugra (उग्र), Bhīma (भीम), Abhiyu (अभियु), Sākṣipa (साक्षिप), Īdṛk (ईदृक्), Anyādṛk (अन्यादृक्), Yādṛk (यादृक्), Pratikṛt (प्रतिकृत्), Ṛk (ऋक्), Samiti (समिति), Saṃrambha (संरम्भ), Idṛkṣa (ईदृक्ष), Puruṣa (पुरुष), Anyādṛkṣa (अन्यादृक्ष), Cetasa (चेतस), Samitā (समिता), Samidṛkṣa (समिदृक्ष), Pratidṛkṣa (प्रतिदृक्ष), Maruti (मरुति), Sarata (सरत), Deva (देव), Dish (दिश), Yajuḥ (यजुः), Anudṛk (अनुदृक्), Sāma (साम), Mānuṣa (मानुष) and Viś (विश्).

इहैकस्थं जगत्कृत्स्नं पश्याद्य सचराचरम् |
मम देहे गुडाकेश यच्चान्यद्द्रष्टुमिच्छसि || BG 11.7 ||

गुडाकेश - Hey Guḍākeśa (Arjuna)! ; इह - Here, ; अद्य - now ; पश्य - behold ; कृत्स्नम् - the entire ; जगत् - world ; सचर-अचरम् - of moving and stationary (beings) ; एकस्थम् - assembled in one place ; मम - in My ; देहे - body, ; च - and ; यत् - whatever ; अन्यत् - else ; इच्छसि - you desire ; द्रष्टुम् - to see.

Hey Arjuna! Here, now behold the entire world of moving and stationary beings assembled in one place in My body and whatever else you desire to see.

न तु मां शक्यसे द्रष्टुमनेनैव स्वचक्षुषा |
दिव्यं ददामि ते चक्षु: पश्य मे योगमैश्वरम् || BG 11.8 ||

तु - However, ; न शक्यसे - (it is) impossible ; द्रष्टुम् - to see ; माम् - Me ; एव - (with) just ; अनेन - these ; स्व-चक्षुषा - eyes of yours. ; ददामि - (Therefore,) I am giving ; ते - you ; दिव्यम् - a divine ; चक्षुः - vision ; पश्य - to behold ; मे - My ; योगम् - Yoga (and) ; ऐश्वरम् - Lordliness.

However, it is impossible to see Me with just these eyes of yours. Therefore, I am giving you a divine vision to behold My Yoga and Lordliness.

सञ्जय उवाच |
एवमुक्त्वा ततो राजन्महायोगेश्वरो हरिः |
दर्शयामास पार्थाय परमं रूपमैश्वरम् || BG 11.9 ||
सञ्जय उवाच - Sañjaya said -

राजन् - Hey King (Dhṛtarāṣṭra)! ; उक्त्वा - Having said ; एवम् - so, ; ततः - after that, ; महा-योग-ईश्वरः - the great Lord of Yoga ; हरिः - Śrī Hari (Kṛṣṇa) ; दर्शयामास - showed (His) ; परमम् - supreme ; ऐश्वरम् - Lordly ; रूपम् - form ; पार्थाय - to Arjuna.

Sañjaya said -

Hey King Dhṛtarāṣṭra! Having said so, after that, the great Lord of Yoga Śrī Hari showed His supreme Lordly form to Arjuna.

अनेकवक्त्रनयनमनेकाद्भुतदर्शनम् |
अनेकदिव्याभरणं दिव्यानेकोद्यतायुधम् || BG 11.10 ||
दिव्यमाल्याम्बरधरं दिव्यगन्धानुलेपनम् |
सर्वाश्चर्यमयं देवमनन्तं विश्वतोमुखम् || BG 11.11 ||

अनेक-वक्त्र-नयनम् - (With) numerous faces and eyes, ; अनेक-अद्भुत-दर्शनम् - numerous astonishing sights, ; अनेक-दिव्य-आभरणम् - (wearing) numerous divine ornaments, ; दिव्य-अनेक-उद्यत-आयुधम् - numerous divine weapons uplifted (in the hands),

दिव्य-माल्य-अम्बर-धरम् - wearing divine garlands and vestments, ; दिव्य-गन्ध-अनुलेपनम् - anointed with divine fragrances, ; सर्व-आश्चर्यमयम् - all astonishing, ; देवम् - resplendent, ; अनन्तम् - endless, ; विश्वतोमुखम् - (and) with faces on all sides.

With numerous faces and eyes, numerous astonishing sights, numerous divine ornaments, numerous divine weapons uplifted in the hands, wearing divine garlands and vestments, anointed with divine fragrances, all astonishing, resplendent, endless, and with faces on all sides.

दिवि सूर्यसहस्रस्य भवेद्युगपदुत्थिता |
यदि भा: सदृशी सा स्याद्भासस्तस्य महात्मन: || BG 11.12 ||

दिवि - In the sky, ; भाः - the brilliance ; भवेत् - (that) can happen ; युगपत् - by the simultaneous ; उत्थिता - rising ; सूर्य-सहस्रस्य - of thousand suns, ; सा - such (brilliance) ; स्यात् यदि - can seldom be ; सदृशी - equal ; तस्य - to that ; भासः - brilliance ; महात्मनः - of the mighty Self.

In the sky, the brilliance of the simultaneous rising of thousand suns can seldom be equal to the brilliance of the mighty Self.

तत्रैकस्थं जगत्कृत्स्नं प्रविभक्तमनेकधा |
अपश्यद्देवदेवस्य शरीरे पाण्डवस्तदा || BG 11.13 ||

तदा - Then ; तत्र – there ; शरीरे - in the body ; देव-देवस्य - of the Lord of the deities, ; पाण्डवः - Pāṇḍava (Arjuna) ; अपश्यत् - saw ; कृत्स्नम् - the entire ; जगत् - world ; प्रविभक्तम् - divided ; अनेकधा - in manifold ways ; एकस्थम् - in one place.

There in the body of the Lord of the deities, Arjuna saw the entire world divided in manifold ways in one place.

तत: स विस्मयाविष्टो हृष्टरोमा धनञ्जय: |
प्रणम्य शिरसा देवं कृताञ्जलिरभाषत || BG 11.14 ||

ततः - Then ; सः - that ; विस्मय-आविष्टः - filled with astonishment ; हृष्ट-रोमा - (and) hairs standing on end, ; धनञ्जयः - Dhanañjaya (Arjuna) ; अभाषत - spoke ; देवम् - to the Lord, ; शिरसा - (his) head ; प्रणम्य - bowed ; कृत-अञ्जलिः - (and) hands folded.

Then filled with astonishment and hairs standing on end, Arjuna spoke to the Lord, his head bowed and hands folded.

अर्जुन उवाच |
पश्यामि देवांस्तव देव देहे सर्वांस्तथा भूतविशेषसङ्घान् |
ब्रह्माणमीशं कमलासनस्थमृषींश्च सर्वानुरगांश्च दिव्यान् || BG 11.15 ||
अर्जुनः उवाच - Arjuna said -

देव - Hey Deva (Śrī Kṛṣṇa, the Lord)! ; पश्यामि - I am seeing ; तव - in Your ; देहे - body ; सर्वान् - all ; देवान् - the deities, ; भूत-विशेष-सङ्घान् - groups of exceptional (mobile and stationary) beings, ; तथा - and ; कमल-आसनस्थं - seated on the lotus ; ईशम् - Lord ; ब्रह्माणम् - Brahmā ; च - and ; सर्वान् - all ; ऋषीन् - the seers ; च - and ; दिव्यान् - divine ; उरगान् - serpents.

Arjuna said -

Hey Lord! I am seeing in Your body all the deities, groups of exceptional beings, and seated on the lotus Lord Brahmā, all the seers and the divine serpents.

Intent - I am beholding all the deities, Indra and the rest, groups of exceptional beings mobile and stationary in varied shapes, the four-faced Lord Brahmā seated on the lotus, also the seer Vasīṣtha and the rest, and the divine serpent Vāsuki and the rest.

अनेकबाहूदरवक्त्रनेत्रं पश्यामि त्वां सर्वतोऽनन्तरूपम् |
नान्तं न मध्यं न पुनस्तवादिं पश्यामि विश्वेश्वर विश्वरूप || BG 11.16 ||

विश्वेश्वर - Hey Viśveśvara (Śrī Kṛṣṇa, the Lord of the world)! ; पश्यामि - I see ; त्वाम् - You ; अनेक-बाहु-उदर-वक्त्र-नेत्रम् - with many hands, bellies, faces, (and) eyes ; सर्वतः - in all directions. ; पुनः - Again, ; विश्वरूप – hey, Viśvarūpa (Śrī Kṛṣṇa, the Cosmic-Form)! ; पश्यामि - I see ; न - no ; आदिम् - beginning, ; न - no ; अन्तम् - end, ; न - (and) no ; मध्यम् - middle ; तव - in Your ; अनन्त-रूपम् - infinite form.

Hey, the Lord of the world! I see You with many hands, bellies, faces, and eyes in all directions. Again, hey, the Cosmic-Form! I see no beginning, no end, and middle in Your infinite form.

किरीटिनं गदिनं चक्रिणं च तेजोराशिं सर्वतो दीप्तिमन्तम् |
पश्यामि त्वां दुर्निरीक्ष्यं समन्ताद् दीप्तानलार्कद्युतिमप्रमेयम् || BG 11.17 ||

पश्यामि - I see ; त्वाम् - You ; किरीटिनम् - adorned with a diadem, ; गदिनम् - (spherical-end) mace, ; च - and ; चक्रिणम् - (spinning) discus, ; तेजो-राशिम् - an aura of brilliance ; दीप्तिमन्तम् - radiating ; सर्वतः - everywhere ; द्युतिम् - (with) a glow ; दीप्त-अनल - (of) the blazing fire ; अर्क - (and) the sun ; समन्तात् - in all directions ; दुर्निरीक्ष्यम् - challenging to see ; अप्रमेयम् - (and) indeterminable.

I see You adorned with a diadem, mace, and discus, an aura of brilliance radiating everywhere with a glow of the blazing fire and the sun in all directions, challenging to see and indeterminable.

Intent - Your brilliant form is indeterminable. (Aprameya) means that it is not a subject of validation by the senses, such as the eyes. The discus referred to is the Lord's Sudarśana Cakra.

(That is why seeing the power of Your Yoga -)

त्वमक्षरं परमं वेदितव्यं त्वमस्य विश्वस्य परं निधानम् |
त्वमव्ययः शाश्वतधर्मगोप्ता सनातनस्त्वं पुरुषो मतो मे || BG 11.18 ||

त्वम् - You are ; परमम् अक्षरम् - the supreme Imperishable (Parabrahma), ; वेदितव्यम् - worthy of being known. ; त्वम् - You ; अस्य - are ; परम् - the supreme ; निधानम् - underlying support ; विश्वस्य - of the world. ; त्वम् - You, ; अव्ययः - the immutable, ; शाश्वत-धर्म-गोप्ता - are the protector of eternal righteousness. ; मे - In my ; मतः -opinion, ; त्वम् - You are ; सनातनः - the everlasting ; पुरुषः - Personality.

You are the supreme Imperishable, worthy of being known. You are the supreme underlying support of the world. You, the immutable, are the protector of eternal righteousness. In my opinion, You are the everlasting Personality.

Intent - Here, "परमम् अक्षरम्" means the supreme Imperishable Parabrahma. The Brahman is worthy of being known by seekers of liberation.

अनादिमध्यान्तमनन्तवीर्यमनन्तबाहुं शशिसूर्यनेत्रम् |
पश्यामि त्वां दीप्तहुताशवक्त्रं स्वतेजसा विश्वमिदं तपन्तम् || BG 11.19 ||

अनादि-मध्य-अन्तम् - Without beginning, middle, and end, ; पश्यामि - I see ; त्वाम् - You ; अनन्त-वीर्यम् - endowed with inexhaustible energy, ; अनन्त-बाहुम् - innumerable arms, ; शशि-सूर्य-नेत्रम् - the moon and the sun as eyes, ; दीप्त-हुताश-वक्त्रम् - mouth like blazing fire, ; स्व-तेजसा - (and) with Your brilliance ; तपन्तम् - burning ; इदम् - this ; विश्वम् - world.

Without beginning, middle, and end, I see You endowed with inexhaustible energy, innumerable arms, the moon and the sun as eyes, mouth like blazing fire, and Your brilliance burning the world.

द्यावापृथिव्योरिदमन्तरं हि व्याप्तं त्वयैकेन दिशश्च सर्वा: |
दृष्ट्वाद्भुतं रूपमुग्रं तवेदं लोकत्रयं प्रव्यथितं महात्मन् || BG 11.20 ||

महात्मन् - Hey Mahātman (Śrī Kṛṣṇa, the mighty Being)! ; इदम् - This ; द्यावा-पृथिव्योः अन्तरम् - entire space between the heavens and the earth ; च - and ; सर्वाः - all ; दिशः - directions ; हि - is indeed ; व्याप्तम् - pervaded ; त्वया - by You ; एकेन - alone. ; लोक-त्रयम् - All three worlds ; प्रव्यथितम् - are struck with fear ; दृष्ट्वा - seeing ; इदम् - this ; अद्भुतम् - amazing ; उग्रम् - fierce ; रूपम् - form ; तव - of Yours.

Hey Mahātman! This entire space between the heavens and the earth and all directions is pervaded by You alone. All three worlds are struck with fear seeing this amazing fierce form of Yours.

(Earlier, Arjuna doubted, "Either we will defeat them, or they will defeat us." Bhagavāna, through His Cosmic Form, resolved this doubt of Arjuna by showing the death of Kauravas and the definite victory of Pāṇḍavas. Seeing this form, Arjuna said -)

अमी हि त्वां सुरसङ्घा विशन्ति केचिद्भीता: प्राञ्जलयो गृणन्ति |
स्वस्तीत्युक्त्वा महर्षिसिद्धसङ्घा: स्तुवन्ति त्वां स्तुतिभि: पुष्कलाभि: || BG 11.21 ||

अमी - These ; सुर-सङ्घाः - groups of deities ; विशन्ति - are entering ; त्वाम् - into You, ; हि - indeed, ; केचित् - some ; भीताः - frightened ; प्राञ्जलयः - with hands folded ; गृणन्ति - are worshipping (You, and) ; महर्षि-सिद्ध-सङ्घाः - hosts of great seers and perfected beings ; उक्त्वा - exclaiming ; स्वस्ति - "Let there be the well-being of all" ; इति - as such, ; स्तुवन्ति - are extolling ; त्वाम् - You ; स्तुतिभिः - with hymns ; पुष्कलाभिः - rich in contents.

Groups of deities are entering into You, some frightened with hands folded are worshipping, and hosts of great seers and perfected beings exclaiming "Let there be the well-being of all," are extolling You with hymns rich in contents.

(I see that -)

रुद्रादित्या वसवो ये च साध्या विश्वेऽश्विनौ मरुतश्चोष्मपाश्च |
गन्धर्वयक्षासुरसिद्धसङ्घा वीक्षन्ते त्वां विस्मिताश्चैव सर्वे || BG 11.22 ||

ये - They, ; रुद्र-आदित्याः - the Rudras, Ādityas ; च - and ; वसवः - Vasus, ; साध्याः - Sādhyās, ; विश्वे - Viśvedevas, ; अश्विनौ - both Aśvanī Kumāras, ; च - and ; मरुतः - Marutas, ; च - and ; उष्मपाः - ancestors, ; च - and ; गन्धर्व-यक्ष-असुर-सिद्ध-सङ्घाः - groups of Gandharvas, Yakṣas, Asuras, and Siddhas ; सर्वे - are all ; वीक्षन्ते - gazing ; त्वाम् - at You ; विस्मिताः - in amazement, ; एव - indeed.

The Rudras, Ādityas, Vasus, Sādhyās, Viśvedevas, both Aśvanī Kumāras, Marutas, ancestors, and groups of Gandharvas, Yakṣas, Asuras, and Siddhas are all gazing at You in amazement, indeed.

Intent - Rudras, Ādityas, and the rest are gazing at You in utter amazement.

Sādhyās (साध्या) are a group of twelve deities, the sons of Sādhyā (the daughter of Prajāpati Dakṣa) and Dharma, and are enumerated as 1. Manas (मनस्), 2. Anumantā (अनुमन्ता), 3. Prāṇa (प्राण), 4. Nara (नर), 5. Apāna (अपान), 6. Vīryavān (वीर्यवान्), 7. Naya (नय), 8. Haya (हय), 9. Haṃsa (हंस), 10. Nārāyaṇa (नारायण), 11. Vibhu (विभु) and 12. Prabhu (प्रभु).

Viśvedevas (विश्वेदेव) are a group of ten deities known as the protectors of humans and guardians of the world. They are the sons of Viśvā (the daughter of Prajāpati Dakṣa) and Dharma and are enumerated as 1. Vasu (वसु), 2. Satya (सत्य), 3. Kratu (क्रतु), 4. Dakṣa (दक्ष), 5. Kāla (काल), 6. Kāma (काम), 7. Dhṛti (धृति), 8. Kuru (कुरु), 9. Purūravas (पुरूरवस्) and 10. Mādravasa (माद्रवस).

The Gandharvas (गन्धर्व) are generally known as minstrels with superb musical skills and are married to Apsarā (अप्सरा) in the world of the deities. They act as messengers between the deities and the humans.

In the Vedic times, marriages contracted by mutual consent and without formal rituals were known as "Gandharva Vivāha."

The Yakṣas (यक्ष) are a broad class of semi-divine beings, usually benevolent and inoffensive disposition, but sometimes mischievous or capricious, connected with water, fertility, trees, forest, treasure, and wilderness. They are described as attendants of Kubera, the deity of wealth, and employed in guarding his gardens and treasures

The Asuras (असुर) are descendants of Diti and Danu (daughters of Prajāpati Dakṣa) and Saptarṣi Kaśyapa. Descendants of Diti are Daitya and of Danu are Dānava. In perpetual hostility with the deities (Sura), they are demons of the first order.

The Siddhas (सिद्ध) are perfected sages who have accomplished or fulfilled their objective. Right from birth, a person, who has attained abundant righteousness (Atiśaya Dharma), knowledge (Jñāna), dispassion (Vairāgya), and lordliness (Aiśvarya), is called a "Siddha."

रूपं महत्ते बहुवक्त्रनेत्रं महाबाहो बहुबाहूरुपादम् |
बहूदरं बहुदंष्ट्राकरालं दृष्ट्वा लोका: प्रव्यथितास्तथाहम् || BG 11.23 ||

महा-बाहो - Hey Mahābāho (Śrī Kṛṣṇa, the mighty-armed)! ; दृष्ट्वा - Seeing ; ते - Your ; महत् - immense ; रूपम् - form ; बहु-वक्त्र-नेत्रम् - with many mouths and eyes, ; बहु-बाहु-ऊरु-पादम् - many arms, thighs and feet, ; बहु-उदरम् - many bellies, ; बहु-दंष्ट्रा-करालम् - (and) many terrifying teeth, ; लोकाः - the worlds ; तथा - and ; अहम् - I ; प्रव्यथिताः - are consternated.

Hey Śrī Kṛṣṇa! Seeing Your immense form with many mouths, eyes, arms, thighs, feet, bellies, and terrifying teeth, the worlds and I are consternated.

नभ:स्पृशं दीप्तमनेकवर्णं व्यात्ताननं दीप्तविशालनेत्रम् |
दृष्ट्वा हि त्वां प्रव्यथितान्तरात्मा धृतिं न विन्दामि शमं च विष्णो || BG 11.24 ||

विष्णो - Hey Lord Viṣṇu! ; दृष्ट्वा - Seeing ; त्वाम् - You ; नभः-स्पृशम् - touch the sky, ; दीप्तम् - glowing ; अनेक-वर्णम् - with many forms, ; व्यात्त-आननम् - with open mouths, ; दीप्त-विशाल-नेत्रम् - (and) enormous blazing eyes, ; प्रव्यथित-अन्तर-आत्मा - with fear in the heart; ; हि - indeed, ; विन्दामि - (I) find ; न - neither ; धृतिम् - patience ; च - nor ; शमम् - peace.

Hey Lord Viṣṇu! Seeing You touch the sky, glowing with many forms, open mouths, and enormous blazing eyes, with fear in the heart; indeed, I find neither patience nor peace.

दंष्ट्राकरालानि च ते मुखानि दृष्ट्वैव कालानलसन्निभानि |
दिशो न जाने न लभे च शर्म प्रसीद देवेश जगन्निवास || BG 11.25 ||

दृष्ट्वा एव - Having indeed seen ; ते - Your ; दंष्ट्रा-करालानि - terrifying teeth ; च - and ; मुखानि - mouths ; काल-अनल-सन्निभानि - blazing like the all-consuming fire of dissolution, ; न - I cannot ; जाने - find ; दिशः - my bearings ; च - and ; न - cannot ; लभे - find ; शर्म - peace. ; देवेश – Hey Deveśa (Śrī Kṛṣṇa, the Lord of the deities)! ; जगत्-निवास - The abode of the world! ; प्रसीद - Be gracious.

Having indeed seen Your terrifying teeth and mouths blazing like the all-consuming fire of dissolution, I cannot find my bearings and cannot find peace. Hey, the Lord of deities! The abode of the world! Be gracious.

(The doubt about losing to those warriors that I had has now gone. Because I see that -)

अमी च त्वां धृतराष्ट्रस्य पुत्रा: सर्वे सहैवावनिपालसङ्घै: |
भीष्मो द्रोण: सूतपुत्रस्तथासौ सहास्मदीयैरपि योधमुख्यै: || BG 11.26 ||
वक्त्राणि ते त्वरमाणा विशन्ति दंष्ट्राकरालानि भयानकानि |

केचिद्विलग्ना दशनान्तरेषु सन्दृश्यन्ते चूर्णितैरुत्तमाङ्गैः || BG 11.27 ||

एव - Indeed ; त्वाम् - (into) You (enter) ; सर्वे - all ; अमी - these ; पुत्राः - sons ; धृतराष्ट्रस्य - of Dhṛtarāṣṭra ; सह - together with ; असौ - their ; अवनिपाल-सङ्घैः - allied group of kings, ; भीष्मः - Bhīṣma, ; द्रोणः - Droṇa, ; च - and ; सूत-पुत्रः - Karṇa, ; तथा - and ; अपि - also ; सह - with ; योध-मुख्यैः - the leading warriors ; अस्मदीयैः - on our side,

ते - they ; सन्दृश्यन्ते - are seen ; त्वरमाणाः - rapidly ; विशन्ति - entering (Your) ; वक्त्राणि - mouths ; भयानकानि - with fearsome ; दंष्ट्रा-करालानि - terrifying teeth, ; केचित् - some ; चूर्णितैः - crushed ; उत्तम-अङ्गैः - with their heads (and others) ; विलग्नाः - stuck ; दशन-अन्तरेषु - in between the teeth.

All these sons of Dhṛtarāṣṭra, together with their allied group of kings, Bhīṣma, Droṇa, and Karṇa, and the leading warriors on our side, are seen rapidly entering Your mouths with fearsome, terrifying teeth, some crushed with their heads and others stuck in between the teeth.

(How are they entering Your mouths? -)

यथा नदीनां बहवोऽम्बुवेगाः समुद्रमेवाभिमुखा द्रवन्ति |
तथा तवामी नरलोकवीरा विशन्ति वक्त्राण्यभिविज्वलन्ति || BG 11.28 ||

यथा - Just as ; बहवः - many ; अम्बु-वेगाः - torrents ; नदीनाम् - of rivers ; द्रवन्ति - rush ; अभिमुखाः - towards ; समुद्रम् - the ocean ; एव - alone; ; तथा - in the same way, ; अमी - these ; नर-लोक-वीराः - heroes among humans ; विशन्ति - enter ; तव - Your ; अभिविज्वलन्ति - exceptionally blazing ; वक्त्राणि - mouths.

Just as many torrents of rivers rush towards the ocean alone; in the same way, these heroes among humans enter Your exceptionally blazing mouths.

यथा प्रदीप्तं ज्वलनं पतङ्गा विशन्ति नाशाय समृद्धवेगाः |
तथैव नाशाय विशन्ति लोकास्तवापि वक्त्राणि समृद्धवेगाः || BG 11.29 ||

यथा एव - Just as ; पतङ्गाः - moths ; समृद्ध-वेगाः - with great speed ; विशन्ति - enter ; प्रदीप्तम् - a blazing ; ज्वलनम् - fire ; नाशाय - for self-destruction; ; तथा - in the same way, ; लोकाः - people ; अपि - too ; समृद्ध-वेगाः - with great speed ; विशन्ति - enter ; तव - Your ; वक्त्राणि - mouths ; नाशाय - to perish.

Just as moths with great speed enter a blazing fire for self-destruction, in the same way, people too with great speeds enter Your mouths to perish.

(I see that You -)

लेलिह्यसे ग्रसमानः समन्ताल्लोकान्समग्रान्वदनैर्ज्वलद्भिः |
तेजोभिरापूर्य जगत्समग्रंभासस्तवोग्राः प्रतपन्ति विष्णो || BG 11.30 ||

विष्णो - Hey Lord Viṣṇu! ; लेलिह्यसे - You are licking (and) ; ग्रसमानः - devouring ; समग्रान् - the entire ; लोकान् - world (of beings) ; समन्तात् - from all sides ; ज्वलद्भिः - (in Your) blazing ; वदनैः - mouths. ; समग्रम् - The whole ; जगत् - world ; प्रतपन्ति - is being scorched ; तव - by Your ; तेजोभिः - brilliance ; आपूर्य - filled with ; उग्राः - fierce ; भासः - radiance.

Hey Lord Viṣṇu! You are licking and devouring the entire world of beings from all sides in Your blazing mouths. The whole world is being scorched by Your brilliance filled with fierce radiance.

(That is why hey Lord! Kindly -)

आख्याहि मे को भवानुग्ररूपो नमोऽस्तु ते देववर प्रसीद |
विज्ञातुमिच्छामि भवन्तमाद्यं न हि प्रजानामि तव प्रवृत्तिम् || BG 11.31 ||

आख्याहि - Tell ; मे - me, ; कः - who are ; भवान् - You ; उग्ररूपः - with this fierce form? ; नमः - (My) salutations ; ते अस्तु - to You. ; देववर - Hey, Devavara (Śrī Kṛṣṇa, the best of the deities)! ; प्रसीद - Be gracious. ; इच्छामि - I desire ; विज्ञातुम् - to know ; भवन्तम् - Your ; आद्यम् - primordial form. ; हि - For, ; न - (I do) not ; प्रजानामि - comprehend ; तव - Your ; प्रवृत्तिम्- activity.

Tell me, who are You with this fierce form? My salutations to You. Hey, the best of the deities! Be gracious. I desire to know Your primordial form. For, I do not comprehend Your activity.

(Upon Arjuna's such plea -)

श्रीभगवानुवाच |
कालोऽस्मि लोकक्षयकृत्प्रवृद्धो लोकान्समाहर्तुमिह प्रवृत्तः |
ऋतेऽपि त्वां न भविष्यन्ति सर्वे येऽवस्थिताः प्रत्यनीकेषु योधाः || BG 11.32 ||
श्रीभगवान् उवाच - Śrī Bhagavān said -

अस्मि - I am ; प्रवृद्धः - the dominant ; लोक-क्षय-कृत् - world dissolving ; कालः - time, ; प्रवृत्तः - active ; इह - here, ; समाहर्तुम् - annihilating ; लोकान् - the worlds. ; सर्वे - (Among) all ; ये - these ; योधाः - warriors ; अवस्थिताः - standing ; प्रत्यनीकेषु - in opposing armies, ; अपि ऋते - except ; त्वाम् - you, ; न - none ; भविष्यन्ति - will (remain).

Śrī Bhagavān said -

I am the dominant world dissolving time, active here, annihilating the worlds. Among all these warriors standing in opposing armies, except you, none will remain.

Intent - As the dominant time, I dissolve the worlds. Even if you do not fight, all these warriors of opposing sides like Bhīṣma, Droṇa, and Karṇa who rouse your fear will perish.

तस्मात्त्वमुत्तिष्ठ यशो लभस्व जित्वा शत्रून्भुङ् क्ष्व राज्यं समृद्धम् |
मयैवैते निहताः पूर्वमेव निमित्तमात्रं भव सव्यसाचिन् || BG 11.33 ||

तस्मात् - Therefore, ; उत्तिष्ठ - stand up (for the war). ; जित्वा - Conquering ; शत्रून् - the foes, ; त्वम् - you ; लभस्व - secure ; यशः - fame ; भुङ्क्ष्व - (and) enjoy ; समृद्धम् - a prosperous ; राज्यम् - kingdom. ; एव - Indeed, ; एते - they all ; पूर्वम् - have already ; निहताः - been slain ; मया - by Me. ; सव्य-साचिन् - (That is why) hey, skillful bowman! ; भव - Be ; एव - only ; निमित्त-मात्रम् - an occasion (for the end of your foes).

Therefore, stand up. Conquering the foes, you secure honor and enjoy a prosperous kingdom. Indeed, they all have already been slain by Me. Hey, skillful bowman! Be only an occasion.

Intent - Therefore, you stand up to fight the war and win honor by defeating the greats like Bhīṣma, Droṇa, and Karṇa. By winning the war, you will enjoy the opulence of the kingdom. Know that all of these warriors have already been slain by Me; just be an occasion. Bhagavāna addresses Arjuna as Savyasācin (सव्यसाचिन्), meaning one who is a skillful bowman, one who can ambidextrously shoot arrows.

द्रोणं च भीष्मं च जयद्रथं च कर्णं तथान्यानपि योधवीरान् |
मया हतांस्त्वं जहि मा व्यथिष्ठा युध्यस्व जेतासि रणे सपत्नान् || BG 11.34 ||

त्वम् - You ; जहि - slay ; द्रोणम् - Droṇa, ; च - and ; भीष्मम् - Bhīṣma, ; च - and ; जयद्रथम् - Jayadratha, ; च - and ; कर्णम् - Karṇa, ; तथा - and ; अपि - also ; अन्यान् - other ; योध-वीरान् - warriors ; हतान् - (already) slain ; मया - by Me. ; युध्यस्व - Fight, ; मा - do not ; व्यथिष्ठाः - be afraid ; रणे - on the battlefield. ; जेता असि - You will conquer ; सपत्नान् - the foes.

You slay Droṇa, Bhīṣma, Jayadratha, Karṇa, and other warriors already slain by Me. Fight, do not be afraid on the battlefield. You will conquer the foes.

Intent - Bhagavāna singles out those major warriors who had aroused fear in Arjuna's heart. Arjuna was fully aware of the abilities of his preceptor Droṇācārya, who was feared because of his proficiency in archery and supernatural weapons. Grandfather Bhīṣma had the boon of withstanding death until he chose himself. He was a master of supernatural weapons and was invincible; not even Lord Paraśurāma could defeat him. Similarly, Jayadratha and Karṇa were exceptionally brave, skillful, and fierce fighters. Still, Bhagavāna prodded Arjuna to stand up and fight, as He already slew these men by the time.

सञ्जय उवाच |
एतच्छ्रुत्वा वचनं केशवस्य कृताञ्जलिर्वेपमान: किरीटी |
नमस्कृत्वा भूय एवाह कृष्णं सगद्गदं भीतभीत: प्रणम्य || BG 11.35 ||

सञ्जय उवाच - Sañjaya said -

श्रुत्वा - Listening ; एतत् - to such ; वचनम् - words ; केशवस्य - of Keśava (Śrī Kṛṣṇa), ; किरीटी - the diademed (Arjuna), ; नमस्कृत्वा - bowing ; कृत-अञ्जलिः - with joined palms, ; वेपमानः - trembling, ; एव - even ; भीत-भीतः - fearful, ; प्रणम्य - (and) expressing respect, ; आह - spoke ; भूयः - again ; कृष्णम् - to Śrī Kṛṣṇa ; सगद्गदम् - in a faltering voice.

Sañjaya said -

Listening to such words of Keśava, the diademed Arjuna, bowing with joined palms, trembling, even fearful, and expressing respect, spoke again to Śrī Kṛṣṇa in a faltering voice.

Intent - Arjuna spoke in a faltering voice, showing that he was in the grip of fear and was influenced by Lord Śrī Kṛṣṇa. His words were indistinct and low pitch as he was fearful with his throat choked.

अर्जुन उवाच |
स्थाने हृषीकेश तव प्रकीर्त्या जगत्प्रहृष्यत्यनुरज्यते च |
रक्षांसि भीतानि दिशो द्रवन्ति सर्वे नमस्यन्ति च सिद्धसङ्घा: || BG 11.36 ||

अर्जुन उवाच - Arjuna said -

हृषीकेश - Hey Hṛṣīkeśa (Śrī Kṛṣṇa)! ; भीतानि - Fearful ; रक्षांसि - demons ; द्रवन्ति - are running away ; दिशः - in (all) directions, ; च - and ; सर्वे - all ; सिद्ध-सङ्घाः - groups of perfected beings ; नमस्यन्ति - are bowing (down before You). ; स्थाने - It is befitting ; जगत् - (that) the world ; प्रहृष्यति - is rejoicing ; च - and ; अनुरज्यते - being enamored ; तव प्रकीर्त्या - in extolling Your name (and glory).

Arjuna said -

Hey Hṛṣīkeśa! Fearful demons are running away in all directions, and all groups of perfected beings are bowing. It is befitting that the world is rejoicing and being enamored in extolling Your name and glory.

कस्माच्च ते न नमेरन्महात्मन् गरीयसे ब्रह्मणोऽप्यादिकर्त्रे |
अनन्त देवेश जगन्निवास त्वमक्षरं सदसतत्परं यत् || BG 11.37 ||

महात्मन् - Hey Mahātman (Śrī Kṛṣṇa, the mighty Being)! ; कस्मात् - Why (should they) ; न - not ; नमेरन् - bow down ; ते - to You, ; गरीयसे - the supreme, ; आदि-कर्त्रे - the primal cause of ; अपि - even ; ब्रह्मणः - Brahmā? ; त्वम् - You (are) ; अनन्त - limitless, ; देवेश - the Lord of the deities, ; जगत् निवास - the abode of the world ; च - and ; यत् - that (which is) ; सत् - real (and) ; असत् - unreal ; तत् परं - (and) even beyond, ; अक्षरम् - the imperishable (Parabrahma).

Hey, the mighty Being! Why should they not bow down to You, the supreme, the primal cause of even Brahmā? You are limitless, the Lord of the deities, the abode of the world, and that which is real and unreal and even beyond, the Imperishable.

Intent - In the verse You are that which is the real (सत्, Sat) and the unreal (असत्, Asat), You are cognized in "is" and "is not" form. In reality, as knowers of the Vedas declare, You are beyond these adjuncts. You are the Imperishable Brahman. There are two types of cognitions in the sphere of cognitive experiences: 1) cognition of the real (सत्, Sat) and 2) cognition of the unreal (असत्, Asat). The cognition of a thing that is not mutable is real, whereas the cognition of a thing that is mutable is unreal. Therefore, the distinction between real and unreal solely rests on cognitions. In the entire sphere of experiences, both cognitions with an identical substrate is existent in all.

Here the intent is not about the cognition of something in nature, such as of "red rose," but that of the "rose is" or the "pot is," or the "cloth is." The cognition of the "rose is," or the "pot is," or the "cloth is," is mutable. However, the cognition of the Reality or "सत्, Sat" is not. Therefore, the objects of the cognitions of rose, pot, cloth, and the like are unreal, being mutable. In contrast, the object of the cognition of the "real, सत्, Sat" being immutable is not so. The unreal, which has no "being," such as heat or cold, and their cause, has no true existence. The affected states, such as heat or cold, are unreal when measured against valid cognition. They are only variable transformations. When scrutinized, a pot and the like are not seen apart from its material cause clay. Therefore, as effects, they are unreal. Similarly, not being cognizable apart from their causes, all transformations are unreal. Pots and the like are unreal because they are unknown before their creation and after their destruction. The same holds good for things like clay, the cause of pots, and the like, for these causes are not known apart from their causes. When the pot perishes, and the cognition of the pot proves mutable, the cognition of the real does not mutate. It is still available for other objects like cloth, rose, et al. The cognition of the real has as its content only the adjective. The cognition of the real, whose content is the adjective "सत्, Sat," will not have "that" as its referent, for an adjective without a substantive is illogical.

त्वमादिदेव: पुरुष: पुराणस्-त्वमस्य विश्वस्य परं निधानम् |
वेत्तासि वेद्यं च परं च धाम त्वया ततं विश्वमनन्तरूप || BG 11.38 ||

त्वम् - You ; असि - are ; आदिदेवः - the primal Lord (cause of all), ; पुराणः - the ancient ; पुरुषः - Personality. ; त्वम् - You are ; परम् - the supreme ; निधानम् - refuge ; अस्य - of this ; विश्वस्य - world, ; वेत्ता - knower of all ; च - and ; वेद्यम् - (the One ought) to be known, ; च - and ; परम् - the supreme ; धाम - Abode. ; अनन्त-रूप - Hey, limitless! ; विश्वम् - (This) world is ; ततम् - pervaded ; त्वया - by You.

You are the primal Lord, the ancient Personality. You are the supreme refuge of this world, knower of all, the One ought to be known, and the supreme abode. Hey, limitless! This world is pervaded by You.

Intent - You are the primal Lord, the primal cause of all, the ancient, everlasting, eternal Personality (Puruṣa) dwelling in the nine-gated city (the body). You are the underlying support, the abode of the world, wherein the world merges at dissolution. You are the knower of all, and the One all ought to strive to know. You pervade all over. You are existent in all.

वायुर्यमोऽग्निर्वरुण: शशाङ्क: प्रजापतिस्त्वं प्रपितामहश्च |
नमो नमस्तेऽस्तु सहस्रकृत्व: पुनश्च भूयोऽपि नमो नमस्ते || BG 11.39 ||

त्वम् - You are ; वायुः - Vāyu, the wind-deity; ; यमः - Yama, the death-deity; ; अग्निः - Agni, (the fire-deity;) ; वरुणः - Varuṇa, (the water-deity;) ; शशाङ्कः - Candramā, (the moon-deity;) ; प्रजापतिः - Prajāpati, (the Lord of humanity;) ; च - and ; प्रपितामहः - even the great grandfather. ; ते अस्तु - To You, ; नमः नमः - Salutations! Salutations! ; सहस्र-कृत्वः - A thousand times, ; भूयः - again ; च - and ; अपि - yet ; पुनः - again, ; नमः नमः - Salutations! Salutations!

You are Vāyu, the wind-deity; Yama, the death-deity; Agni, the fire-deity; Varuṇa, the water-deity; Candramā, the moon-deity; Prajāpati, the Lord of humanity, and even the great grandfather. To you, Salutations! Salutations! A thousand times, again and yet again, Salutations! Salutations!

Intent - Prajāpati, or the progenitor of the humanity, are the seven great seers (सप्तर्षि, Saptarṣi) and the Manu, from whom this entire humanity has originated. You are the father of even their fathers, and even the father of Brahmā is what is intended. Here the repeated acts of "Salutations" are expressed by the suffix Krutvah (कृत्वः). The use of the words "again and yet again" depicts the sentiment of inadequacy felt by Arjuna because of his reverence, love, and sense of astonishment.

नमः पुरस्तादथ पृष्ठतस्ते नमोऽस्तु ते सर्वत एव सर्व |
अनन्तवीर्यामितविक्रमस्त्वं सर्वं समाप्नोषि ततोऽसि सर्वः || BG 11.40 ||

त्वम् - You (have) ; अनन्त-वीर्य - infinite power, ; अमित-विक्रमः - boundless courage, ; समाप्नोषि - (and) hold within ; सर्वम् - the entire (world). ; ततः - Therefore, ; असि - You are ; सर्वः - the Entirety. ; सर्व - Hey, the Entirety! ; नमः - Salutations! ; ते - To You ; पुरस्तात् - from front ; अथ - and ; पृष्ठतः - rear, ; एव - and indeed ; नमः - Salutations! ; ते अस्तु - To You ; सर्वतः - from all sides.

You have infinite power, boundless courage, and hold within the entire world. Therefore, You are the Entirety. Hey, the Entirety! Salutations! To You from front and rear, and indeed Salutations! To You from all sides.

Intent -The term Sarva (सर्व) generally means all. Here it means the all-pervading form "the All," "the Entirety." There is no iota of space where the Lord does not exist, so the salutations are expressed in all directions where the Lord pervades. Your powers are infinite, meaning Your ability is infinite. Your courage or energy is without any bounds. Even powerful men fail to exercise their power to defeat foes. However, Your power is infinite and energy limitless, and You permeate the entire world. That is why You are "the All, the Entirety."

सखेति मत्वा प्रसभं यदुक्तं हे कृष्ण हे यादव हे सखेति |
अजानता महिमानं तवेदं मया प्रमादात्प्रणयेन वापि || BG 11.41 ||
यच्चावहासार्थमसत्कृतोऽसि विहारशय्यासनभोजनेषु |
एकोऽथवाप्यच्युत तत्समक्षं तत्क्षामये त्वामहमप्रमेयम् || BG 11.42 ||

अजानता - Unaware ; इदम् - of this ; महिमानम् - majesty ; तव - of Yours, ; मत्वा - taking you ; इति - as ; सखा - a friend, ; अपि - also ; प्रणयेन - out of affection ; वा - or ; प्रमादात् - carelessness, ; इति - such ; प्रसभम् - presumptuous (words as) ; हे कृष्ण - "Hey Kṛṣṇa," ; हे यादव - "Hey Yādava," ; हे सखा - "Hey Sakhā," ; यत् - that ; उक्तम् - were spoken ; मया - by me

तत् समक्षम् - in their front ; अथवा - or ; अपि - even ; एकः - (when) alone, ; विहार - (at) recreation, ; शय्या - resting, ; आसन - sitting, ; च - and ; भोजनेषु - eating. ; असि - (You) were ; असत्कृतः - disrespected ; अवहासार्थम् - in jest, ; यत् - for which ; अच्युत - hey, the infallible One! ; अहम् - I am ; क्षामये - begging forgiveness ; तत् - for all those transgressions ; त्वाम् - from You, ; अप्रमेयम् - the Immeasurable.

Unaware of this majesty of Yours, taking you as a friend, out of affection or carelessness, such presumptuous words as "Hey Kṛṣṇa," "Hey Yādava," "Hey Sakhā," that were spoken by me in their front or when alone, at recreation, resting, sitting, and eating. You were disrespected in jest, for which hey, the infallible One! I am begging forgiveness for all those transgressions from You, the Immeasurable.

Intent - Taking you as a friend, being of the same age, due to ignorance, I addressed you as "Kṛṣṇa" or "Yādava" (the descendant of the royal clan of Yadu) or "Sakhā" (friend). Ignorance of what? Ignorance of the majesty of this Cosmic Form of the Lord. I addressed You in such a manner due to carelessness or affection, not knowing Your true nature.

पितासि लोकस्य चराचरस्य त्वमस्य पूज्यश्च गुरुर्गरीयान् |
न त्वत्समोऽस्त्यभ्यधिकः कुतोऽन्यो लोकत्रयेऽप्यप्रतिमप्रभाव || BG 11.43 ||

अप्रतिम-प्रभाव - Hey, the unsurpassed power! ; त्वम् - You ; असि - are ; पिता - the father ; अस्य - of this ; लोकस्य - world ; चर-अचरस्य - of movable and immovable (beings), ; गरीयान् - a pre-eminent ; गुरुः - teacher, ; च - and ; अपि - indeed ; पूज्यः - worthy of worship. ; अस्ति - There is ; न - none ; अन्यः - other ; त्वत् समः - like You ; लोक-त्रये - in the three worlds. ; कुतः - How can there be ; अभ्यधिकः - one greater?

Hey, the unsurpassed power! You are the father of this world of movable and immovable beings, a pre-eminent teacher, and worthy of worship. There is none other like You in the three worlds. How can there be one greater?

Intent - None else can be even equal to You, let alone anyone being greater in all three worlds. The Lord is addressed as "अप्रतिम-प्रभाव, Apratima-Prabhāva," where Apratima means matchless or unsurpassed and Prabhāva means might or power. An analog is equivalent. Here the Lord has no analog and thus is of matchless might or unsurpassed power.

तस्मात्प्रणम्य प्रणिधाय कायं प्रसादये त्वामहमीशमीड्यम् |
पितेव पुत्रस्य सखेव सख्यु: प्रिय: प्रियायार्हसि देव सोढुम् || BG 11.44 ||

तस्मात् - Therefore, ; प्रणम्य - bowing ; प्रणिधाय - and prostrating ; कायम् - (my) body (at Your feet), ; ईड्यम् - hey, worthy of invocation, ; ईशम् - Lord! ; अहम् - I ; त्वाम् - (implore) You ; प्रसादये - for Your grace. ; देव - Hey, Lord! ; अर्हसि - You should ; सोढुम् - bear (my offenses) ; इव - just as ; पिता - a father (does) ; पुत्रस्य - of his son, ; इव - like ; सखा - a friend (does) ; सख्युः - of his friend, ; प्रियः - (and) a lover (does) ; प्रियायाः - of his beloved.

Therefore, bowing and prostrating my body at Your feet, hey, worthy of invocation, Lord! I implore You for Your grace. Hey, Lord! You bear my offenses just as a father does of his son, a friend does of his friend, and a lover does of his beloved.

अदृष्टपूर्वं हृषितोऽस्मि दृष्ट्वा भयेन च प्रव्यथितं मनो मे |
तदेव मे दर्शय देवरूपं प्रसीद देवेश जगन्निवास || BG 11.45 ||

दृष्ट्वा - Having seen ; अदृष्ट-पूर्वम् - what is unseen, ; अस्मि - I am ; हृषितः - becoming exuberant, ; च - and ; मे - my ; मनः - mind ; प्रव्यथितम् - is distressed ; भयेन - with fear. ; देव - (Therefore,) Hey, Lord! ; दर्शय - Reveal ; मे - to me ; एव - only ; तत् - that ; रूपम् - (familiar) form (of Yours). ; देवेश - Hey, Lord of the deities! ; जगत्-निवास - Hey, the abode of the world! ; प्रसीद - Be gracious.

Having seen what is unseen, I am becoming exuberant, and my mind is distressed with fear. Hey, Lord! Reveal to me only that familiar form of Yours. Hey, Lord of the deities! Hey, the abode of the world! Be gracious.

किरीटिनं गदिनं चक्रहस्त- मिच्छामि त्वां द्रष्टुमहं तथैव |
तेनैव रूपेण चतुर्भुजेन सहस्रबाहो भव विश्वमूर्ते || BG 11.46 ||

सहस्र-बाहो - Hey thousand-armed Being! ; अहम् - I ; इच्छामि - wish ; द्रष्टुम् - to see ; त्वाम् - You ; एव - only ; तथा - in that (form) ; किरीटिनम् - adorned with a diadem, ; गदिनम् - carrying a (spherical-end) mace, ; चक्र-हस्तम् - (and) holding the (spinning) discus in hand. ; विश्व-मूर्ते - Hey Cosmic-Form! ; भव - (Kindly) assume ; एव - only ; तेन - that ; रूपेण - form ; चतुः-भुजेन - with four arms.

Hey thousand-armed Being! I wish to see You only in that form adorned with a diadem, carrying a mace, and holding the discus in hand. Hey Cosmic-Form! Assume only that form with four arms.

(Knowing that Arjuna is fear struck, Bhagavāna withdrew His Cosmic Form and spoke affectionate words consolingly -)

श्रीभगवानुवाच |
मया प्रसन्नेन तवार्जुनेदं रूपं परं दर्शितमात्मयोगात् |
तेजोमयं विश्वमनन्तमाद्यं यन्मे त्वदन्येन न दृष्टपूर्वम् || BG 11.47 ||
श्रीभगवान् उवाच - Śrī Bhagavān said -

अर्जुन - Hey Arjuna! ; आत्म-योगात् - By the power of My Yoga ; मया - (and) with My ; प्रसन्नेन - grace, ; इदम् - this ; परम् - supreme, ; तेजोमयम् - brilliant, ; आद्यम् - primal, ; अनन्तम् - (and) infinite ; विश्वम् - Cosmic- ; रूपम् - Form ;

मे - of Mine ; दर्शितम् - revealed ; तव - to you, ; यत् - which ; न - none ; त्वत्-अन्येन - but you; दृष्ट-पूर्वम् - have (ever) beheld before.

Śrī Bhagavān said -

Hey Arjuna! By the power of My Yoga and with My grace, this supreme, brilliant, primal, and infinite Cosmic-Form of Mine revealed to you, which none but you have ever beheld before.

Intent - Prasannena (प्रसन्नेन), meaning by grace, expresses the mood of benevolence towards Arjuna. In such a mood, the divine Cosmic Form was revealed by the power or competence of the Yoga of Bhagavāna.

न वेदयज्ञाध्ययनैर्न दानै- र्न च क्रियाभिर्न तपोभिरुग्रै: |
एवंरूप: शक्य अहं नृलोके द्रष्टुं त्वदन्येन कुरुप्रवीर || BG 11.48 ||

कुरु-प्रवीर - Hey Kuru-Pravīra (Arjuna, the heroic among the Kurus)! ; न - Neither ; वेद-अध्ययनैः यज्ञ- by studies of the Vedas and sacrifices ; न - nor ; दानैः - by charities, ; च - and ; न - nor ; उग्रैः - by severe ; तपोभिः - austerities ; न - nor ; क्रियाभिः - by rituals, ; शक्यः - can ; अहम् - I ; द्रष्टुम् - be seen ; एवं-रूपः - in this form ; अन्येन - by anyone ; नृ-लोके - in the human world ; त्वत् - (except) you.

Hey Arjuna! Neither by studies of the Vedas and sacrifices, charities, severe austerities, or rituals can I be seen in this form by anyone in the human world except you.

Intent - I cannot be seen in the Cosmic Form as you have seen by studies of the Vedas, by correct performance of sacrifices, charities, rituals like Agnihotra enjoined by the scriptures, or by severe austerities by anyone else other than you in this human world. In verse, Arjuna is addressed as Kuru-Pravīra (कुरु-प्रवीर), meaning the heroic among the Kurus.

मा ते व्यथा मा च विमूढभावो दृष्ट्वा रूपं घोरमीदृङ्ममेदम् |
व्यपेतभी: प्रीतमना: पुनस्त्वं तदेव मे रूपमिदं प्रपश्य || BG 11.49 ||

ते - You ; मा - Be not ; व्यथा - distressed ; च - and ; मा - be not ; विमूढ-भावः - confused ; दृष्ट्वा - beholding ; इदम् - this ; ईदृक् - such ; घोरम् - ghastly ; रूपम् - form ; मम - of Mine. ; व्यपेतभीः - Rid of fear ; प्रीत-मनाः - (and) mentally pleased, ; त्वम् - you ; प्रपश्य - behold ; पुनः - again ; तत् - that ; इदम् एव - this very ; रूपम् - form ; मे - of Mine (with four arms).

Be not distressed and confused beholding such ghastly form of Mine. Rid of fear and mentally pleased, you behold that very form of Mine (with four arms).

सञ्जय उवाच |
इत्यर्जुनं वासुदेवस्तथोक्त्वा स्वकं रूपं दर्शयामास भूय: |
आश्वासयामास च भीतमेनं भूत्वा पुन: सौम्यवपुर्महात्मा || BG 11.50 ||
सञ्जय उवाच - Sañjaya said -

तथा - (Having) thus ; इति - so ; उक्त्वा - spoken ; अर्जुनम् - to Arjuna, ; वासुदेवः - Lord Vāsudeva (Śrī Kṛṣṇa) ; भूयः - once more ; दर्शयामास - revealed ; स्वकम् - His ; रूपम् - (familiar) form (with four arms) ; च - and, ; भूत्वा - assuming ; पुनः - again ; सौम्य-वपुः - the gentle human form (with two arms), ; महात्मा - the mighty Being ; आश्वासयामास - solaced ; एनम् - the one ; भीतम् - fear struck.

Sañjaya said -

Having spoken to Arjuna, Lord Vāsudeva once more revealed His familiar form (with four arms) and, assuming again the gentle human form (with two arms), the mighty Being solaced the one fear struck.

अर्जुन उवाच |
दृष्ट्वेदं मानुषं रूपं तव सौम्यं जनार्दन |
इदानीमस्मि संवृत्त: सचेता: प्रकृतिं गत: || BG 11.51 ||
अर्जुन उवाच - Arjuna said -

जनार्दन - Hey Janārdana (Śrī Kṛṣṇa)! ; दृष्ट्वा - Seeing ; इदम् - this ; सौम्यम् - gentle ; मानुषम् - human ; रूपम् - form ; तव - of Yours, ; इदानीम् - now ; अस्मि - I ; संवृत्तः - have regained ; सचेताः - my equanimity ; गतः - (and) regained ; प्रकृतिम् - my own nature.

Arjuna said -

Hey Janārdana! Seeing this gentle human form of Yours, now I have regained my equanimity and my own nature.

श्रीभगवानुवाच |
सुदुर्दर्शमिदं रूपं दृष्टवानसि यन्मम |
देवा अप्यस्य रूपस्य नित्यं दर्शनकाङ्क्षिण: || BG 11.52 ||
श्रीभगवान् उवाच - Śrī Bhagavān said -

इदम् - This ; सुदुर्दर्शम् - extremely hard to behold ; रूपम् - the form ; मम - of Mine, ; यत् - which ; दृष्टवान् असि - you have seen; ; अपि - even ; देवाः - deities ; नित्यम् - perpetually ; दर्शन-काङ्क्षिणः - crave to see ; अस्य - that ; रूपस्य - form.

Śrī Bhagavān said -

This extremely hard to behold the form of Mine, which you have seen; even deities perpetually crave to see that form.

नाहं वेदैर्न तपसा न दानेन न चेज्यया |
शक्य एवंविधो द्रष्टुं दृष्टवानसि मां यथा || BG 11.53 ||

एवम्-विधः - The way ; यथा - as ; दृष्टवान् असि - you have seen ; माम् - Me, ; अहम् - I am ; न - neither ; शक्यः - possible ; द्रष्टुम् - to be seen ; वेदैः - by (the study of) the Vedas ; न - nor ; तपसा - by (the practice of) austerities ; न - nor ; दानेन - by (giving of) charities ; च - and ; न - not ; इज्यया - by (the performance of) sacrifices.

The way you have seen Me, I am neither possible to be seen by the study of the Vedas nor by the practice of austerities nor by giving of charities and not by the performance of sacrifices.

भक्त्या त्वनन्यया शक्य अहमेवंविधोऽर्जुन |
ज्ञातुं द्रष्टुं च तत्त्वेन प्रवेष्टुं च परन्तप || BG 11.54 ||

परन्तप - Hey, the terror of foes, ; अर्जुन - Arjuna! ; तु - Only ; एवम्-विधः - this way, ; अनन्यया - by undivided ; भक्त्या - devotion, ; अहम् - I ; शक्यः - am possible to be ; तत्त्वेन - truly ; ज्ञातुम् - known, ; च - and ; द्रष्टुम् – seen, ; च - and ; प्रवेष्टुम् - entered (for union in My form).

Hey, the terror of foes, Arjuna! Only this way, by undivided devotion, am I possible to be truly known, seen, and entered.

Intent - Here, Bhagavāna talks about devotion, but that devotion should be "Ananya," undivided, exclusive, only one and none other. Such devotion is attained when by all means of cognition, only the Lord Vāsudeva is known. The term Praveśa (प्रवेष) means to enter. Here it is in reference to the union with oneness in the Lord.

मत्कर्मकृन्मत्परमो मद्भक्तः सङ्गवर्जितः |
निर्वैरः सर्वभूतेषु यः स मामेति पाण्डव || BG 11.55 ||

पाण्डव - Hey Pāṇḍava (Arjuna)! ; सः - He ; एति - attains ; माम् - Me, ; यः - who is ; सङ्ग-वर्जितः - free from all attachments, ; मत्-कर्म-कृत् - whose actions are only to attain Me, ; मत्-परमः - who (through all efforts) is moving towards Me, ; मत्-भक्तः - who worships Me alone, ; निर्वैरः - (and) who is free from malice ; सर्व-भूतेषु - towards all beings,

Hey Arjuna! He attains Me, who is free from all attachments, whose actions are only to attain Me, who through all efforts is moving towards Me, who worships Me alone, and who is free from malice towards all beings.

ॐ तत्सदिति श्रीमद्भगवद्गीतासूपनिषत्सु ब्रह्मविद्यायां योगशास्त्रे

श्रीकृष्णार्जुनसम्वादे विश्वरूपदर्शनयोगो नाम

अकादशोऽध्यायः || BG 11 ||

Oṃ Tat Sat

In the Śrīmad Bhagavad Gītā Upaniṣad

The Yoga Science of the Knowledge of Self-Realization

The Discourse of Lord Śrī Kṛṣṇa and Arjuna

This Eleventh Chapter

Yoga Named - The Yoga of the Vision of the Cosmic-Form

Clarification

In the tenth chapter, listening to the divine manifestations and Yoga of Bhagavāna, Arjuna found solace in his heart. At the beginning of this chapter, Arjuna expressed his gratitude to Bhagavāna and said, "My ignorance is removed by the supreme profound words about the transcendent knowledge of the Brahman (Ātmā, Self) that You spoke compassionately to me. Undoubtedly, I have realized that You are the origin and dissolution of all beings." Arjuna then implored Bhagavāna, "I desire to see Your Lordly form. If You deem possible by me to see, then show me Your immutable Cosmic-Form" (BG 11.1 - BG 11.5).

Upon Arjuna's prayer, Bhagavāna revealed his Cosmic-Form. So that in Arjuna's heart, real dispassion could take hold, replacing I-ness and mineness that was getting assertive by directly knowing the world as the morsel of time and ephemeral, and he can become dispassionate. Doership inebriety that he is the slayer of all the warriors can change into sobriety, and it becomes crystal clear in his mind that in all activities, there is not an iota of his doership. Only the Lord of the time sitting in everyone's heart, orchestrates all dances. Inspired by the Lord, all kinds of beings rapidly enter the fierce mouth of the Cosmic-Form, just as numerous torrents of rivers rush towards the ocean. The intention is for Arjuna to directly become dispassionate from the world and forsake doership sense to find Yoga, the union with oneness in the true nature of the Lord. With that aim, accepting the prayer of Arjuna Bhagavāna said, "Yes, hey Arjuna! See my hundreds and thousands of divine forms in various colors and shapes. See the Ādityas, Vasus, Rudras, twin Aśvanī Kumāras, Marutas, and many never seen before astonishing forms here in My body assembled in one place, the movable and immovable entire world, and whatever else you desire to see that also you see. However, it is impossible to see Me with your physical eyes; that is why I am giving you divine vision so that you can see My Yoga and Lordliness" (BG 11.5 - BG 11.8).

Having said so, Bhagavāna showed his Supreme Lordly form to Arjuna, and Sañjaya narrated the glory of that form to Dhṛtarāṣṭra (BG 11.9 - BG 11.13). After that, beholding the Cosmic-Form, astonished Arjuna, with both hands folded, head bowed, paying homage, said, "Hey Lord! I see in Your body all the deities, hosts of mobile and stationary beings, seated on the lotus Lord Brahmā, and all the seers and the divine serpents. I see You from all sides with innumerable arms, bellies, faces, and eyes in Your infinite form. I see Your Cosmic-Form with no beginning, no end, and middle." As he saw the amazing forms, Arjuna described them to Bhagavāna. To ease his fear, Bhagavāna started to directly show the demise of all those warriors from whom Arjuna feared being defeated. Seeing that, Arjuna said, "All the sons of Dhṛtarāṣṭra together with their allied assembly of kings and Bhīṣma, Droṇa, Karṇa, and that with leading warriors of our side are also seen rapidly entering Your mouths just as moths enter a blazing fire with great speed for self-destruction. Some are crushed with their heads, and others are stuck between the teeth. You are licking and devouring the entire world of beings from all sides in Your blazing mouths. Tell me, who are You with this fierce form? I desire to know Your primordial form because I do not comprehend this activity of Yours" (BG 11.14 - BG 11.31).

On this, Bhagavāna said, "I am the dominant world dissolving time. At this time, I am active in annihilating the world. No one except you will remain with all those warriors standing in opposing armies. Therefore, you stand up for the war, conquer the foes, secure honor, and enjoy the opulent kingdom. I have already slain them all. Hey, skillful bowman! You only be an occasion for the end of the foes. Slay Droṇa, Bhīṣma, Jayadratha, Karṇa, and other warriors. They are already slain by Me. Fight, do not be afraid on the battlefield. You will conquer the foes" (BG 11.32 - BG 11.34).

Here, the essence is that when a Jīva, due to ignorance of his true nature, in the frenzy of confined I-ness sense, becomes a doer of Karma, then all those efforts in the form of Karma perish at that time. However, impressions (Saṃskāras) in the form of seeds remain in the doer's heart. Just as many seeds in the earth shoot out in due time, in the same way, impressions of Karma residing in the heart in imperceptible form, dependent on time, manifest in perceptible form and produce to be experienced fruits and accessories for the experience. Through his own Karma, a Jīva is himself the material cause of his enjoyment. External elements such as region, time, or things cannot cause those enjoyments. However, they are all instruments in producing fruits of enjoyment, but never the cause. By rule, the material cause must remain in the act. Separate from the act, a cause cannot exist. Just as clay, the cause of the earthen pot always remains in the pot, not separate from the pot. The Jīva, because of his mistake of not seeing within himself the cause of his enjoyments such as happiness and grief, holds those external instruments which are perceptible through the physical senses as "these are the causes of my happiness and grief." Because of this mistake of causal sense in non-causal things, he develops attachment and aversion to things. With his attachment and aversion, he creates Saṃskāras of sin and piety. In reality, when accumulated impressions of past Karma become ready for fruition in the present, it is then that they create these external materials in the form of instruments. This way, all activities happen on the dependence of time in the witness of the existent Paramātmā.

Following this tenet, for those relatives who are to be slain by Arjuna, in reality, Arjuna is not the cause of their deaths. Only their own Karma Saṃskāras are the cause of their deaths. Arjuna is only the instrument (Nimitta), and his own Karma Saṃskāras have created that instrument. Alternatively, the assembler of all these joining and breaking is only the time-deity, with whose spinning discus of time (Kāla-Cakra) all these unions and relationships materialize. However, due to his unreal (Mithyā) doership I-ness, Arjuna unnecessarily became a doer, "I only am the slayer of Bhīṣma and others." Now, Bhagavāna is showing His "time-form" (Kāla-Svarupa), making it visible that this chess game was created by Him based on the individual actions of beings. Arjuna, assuming unreal doership I-ness, is caught in the time cycle by his foolishness. If he wants to save himself from this time cycle, then it is in his interest that he forsakes his doership I-ness; making his body, senses, mind, and intellect like inanimate string puppets and placing them in the Lord's hands; and sitting therein, the Lord, the witness-conscious through His time-cycle will make them dance as He wishes, to which he should consent. This way, he can be naturally free from the bondage of time and actions and attain union in the witness-conscious with oneness.

Listening to the words of Bhagavāna, Arjuna, bowing with joined palms, trembling, fearful, and expressing respect, provided salutations from the front and rear and salutations from all sides and spoke to Śrī Kṛṣṇa in a faltering voice, "Unaware of this majesty of Yours, taking you as a friend, out of affection or carelessness, such presumptuous words as 'Hey Kṛṣṇa,' 'Hey Yādava,' 'Hey Sakhā' that I spoke in their front or even when alone, at recreation, resting, sitting, and eating. You were disrespected in jest, for which hey the infallible One! I am begging forgiveness for all those transgressions from You, the Immeasurable." After that, he said, "Having seen what hitherto is unseen, I am becoming exuberant, and my mind is distressed with fear. Hey Lord! Reveal to me only that familiar form of Yours with four arms" (BG 11.35 - BG 11.46). On this, once more Bhagavāna revealed his familiar form with four arms, and then assuming the gentle human-form with two arms, the mighty Being solaced the fear struck Arjuna and said, "The Cosmic-Form of Mine extremely hard to behold, which you have seen, even deities perpetually crave for the vision of that form. As you have seen Me, I am neither possible to be seen by studies of the Vedas nor by the practice of austerities nor by giving of charities and not by the performance of sacrifices. Only through undivided devotion can I be truly known, seen and entered for union in My form" (BG 11.47 - BG 11.54). The intention here is that limited I-ness sense impedes the true entry for union with oneness in the form of the Lord. That entry can only happen through love and undivided devotion to the Lord. Sacrifice, austerity, and charity cannot melt this impediment; however, they increase doership I-ness in the absence of devotion. Even though hubris of sacrifice, austerities, and others are better than excessive pride related to worldly wealth or children, without the conjunction of undivided devotion to the Lord (Ananya Bhagavad-Bhakti), it is nothing but plain hubris, which is like "falling from a frying pan into the fire," only puts one in the bondage of the heavens and others and keeps one away from the real bliss. Only love is one such pure thing capable of embracing I-ness sentiment in the world. When transitory and imaginary love for women and others makes one lose I-ness during the period of love, then where is the doubt that eternal true love can uproot I-ness sentiment? There is such an attraction and magnetism in love that it is proper even if it sacrifices the insignificant I-ness sentiment. Just as a wave cannot fathom the ocean's depth even if it desires, losing itself as a wave and becoming an ocean can fathom its depth.

In the same way, when a devotee, through his undivided devotion, loses his insignificant I-ness sense in the Lord, then becoming the Lord-form, he can enter with oneness in the Lord. That is why, without devotion, entry into the true nature of the Lord is impossible. The Vedas, sacrifices, austerities, and others cannot enter here without devotion. At the end of the chapter, guidance was given in the form of a binding string, "Hey Arjuna! One who is free from all attachments, whose actions are only to attain Me, who through all efforts is moving towards Me, who worships Me alone and who is free from malice towards all beings, he attains Me" (BG 11.55).

Bhagavāna articulating undivided devotion (Ananya- Bhakti) as the means to attain union with oneness in His true nature ended the chapter.

Chapter 12

The Yoga of Devotion

अर्जुन उवाच |
एवं सततयुक्ता ये भक्तास्त्वां पर्युपासते |
ये चाप्यक्षरमव्यक्तं तेषां के योगवित्तमा: || BG 12.1 ||
अर्जुन उवाच - Arjuna said -

एवम् - Thus, ; ये - those ; सतत-युक्ताः - ever-united ; भक्ताः - devotees (who) ; पर्युपासते - (continually) worship ; त्वाम् - You (the manifest-form) ; च - and ; अपि - also ; ये - those (others who worship) ; अक्षरम् - the Imperishable, ; अव्यक्तम् - the Unmanifest (attributeless Brahman) - ; तेषाम् - among them ; के - who ; योग-वित्तमाः - knows Yoga best?

Arjuna said -

Thus, those ever-united devotees who always worship You (the manifest-form) and those others who worship the Imperishable, the Unmanifest - among them who knows Yoga best?

Intent - The word Evam (एवम्, thus) connects the last verse of the eleventh chapter to the first verse of this chapter. Arjuna is questioning Bhagavāna that there are those devotees whose acts are only for the sake of Your manifest-form (Saguṇa-Svarupa), all of whose efforts are to move towards You, who is free from all attachments, who worship You alone and who are free from malice towards all beings. Then others worship Your attributeless-form (Nirguṇa-Svarupa), the Brahman that is unmanifest, adjunctless, and beyond the range of the senses. Of the two, who is the best knower of Yoga? In earlier chapters, from the second to the ninth chapter, the glory of the worship of the Brahman - the supreme imperishable Reality, the imperishable devoid of adjuncts, the unmanifest form is sung. In the eleventh chapter, undivided devotion to the manifest form is articulated as the cause for seeing, knowing, and entering. That is why, now, this question of Arjuna is proper.

श्रीभगवानुवाच |
मय्यावेश्य मनो ये मां नित्ययुक्ता उपासते |
श्रद्धया परयोपेतास्ते मे युक्ततमा मता: || BG 12.2 ||
श्रीभगवान् उवाच - Śrī Bhagavān said -

आवेश्य - Fixing (their) ; मनः - minds ; मयि - on Me, ; नित्य-युक्ताः - ever united, ; ते - those ; ये - who ; उपासते - worship ; माम् - Me ; उपेताः - with ; परया - absolute ; श्रद्धया - faith ; मताः - are deemed ; मे - by Me ; युक्ततमाः - as the best Yogīs.

Śrī Bhagavān said -

Fixing their minds on Me, ever united, those who worship Me with absolute faith are deemed by Me as the best Yogīs.

Intent - Beginning from the second chapter until the ninth chapter, Bhagavāna is describing the glory of His all-witness, Ātmā of all, beyond the range of the senses, unmanifest-form and by attaining union with oneness in that form, freedom from the mortal world of birth and death is narrated. In this verse, a devotee of his manifest form endowed with absolute faith is declared the best Yogī. The question of Arjuna was, "One who worships Your imperishable, unmanifest, all-witnessing, attributeless-form and those who worship your manifest-form, that is, that which falls within the range of the senses, of the two who is the best Yogī?" In response, Bhagavāna said, "One endowed with absolute faith, setting or concentrating the mind on My form with attributes, ever united in Me, worships Me; he is the best Yogī." If these words are believed true literally and in reality, then until the ninth chapter, whatever Bhagavāna has described, His unmanifest, imperishable, Ātmā of all forms - all that becomes vacuous and meaningless. However, in reality, it is not so. The intention is that first, without fixing the mind steadfast on a form with attributes, it is extremely difficult to enter into the unmanifest form and, indeed, impossible. That is because the mind is a puppet of name-form, and name-form is caught in the mortal world. It is not possible for it to abruptly enter the One that is nameless and formless. Just as iron can be cut by iron, and poison can be destroyed by poison, in the same way, with the assistance of the name-form attribute of Bhagavāna and with absolute faith, steadying the mind on the name-form attribute of Bhagavāna, the mind can be removed from the name-form world. Just as water with the union of extreme cold acquires inanimateness of ice, and until it melts and flows from the sun's heat, it cannot fly in the form of mist.

In the same way, the mind has become inanimate by its conjunction with the name-form world. Until it becomes steady on the one with attributes - name, form, power, and Līlā of Bhagavāna, and through devotional warmth, with the love of Bhagavāna, becomes liquid like water and flows, until then it cannot be flown like mist in the fire of the knowledge of the unmanifest-form of Bhagavāna. Situating in the unmanifest and imperishable form of Bhagavāna, it is only the mind that is the impediment. When the mind becomes steadfast on the manifest form of Bhagavāna and comes out of the name-form world, then positioning in the unmanifest form is not difficult. When flowers of a mango tree bloom, there is no doubt about the formation of mangoes and subsequent ripening. By the laws of nature, fruits always follow flowers; upon blooming of flowers, fruits automatically form and manifest.

In the same way, the flower is the devotion of the manifest form, and the fruit is the devotion of the unmanifest form. Upon developing and fully forming the flower of the devotion of the manifest form, the devotion to the unmanifest form will develop. By the laws of nature, like the fruit, it follows right behind the manifest-form devotion.

On the contrary, if manifest-form devotion is abandoned, it is impossible to fix the mind on the unmanifest form even if one desires. Indeed, Bhagavāna himself, in the fifth verse of this chapter, states, "अव्यक्ता हि गतिर्दु:खं देहवद्भिरवाप्यते, for a person caught in I-ness and mineness of the body and senses, the unmanifest-form objective is acquired with great pain." Thus, it is only through the devotion to the manifest form that it is possible to steady the mind on the unmanifest form. Therefore, a devotee of the manifest form is called the best Yogī or "युक्ततम, Yuktatama" because, through the manifest-form devotion, he can ascend to the unmanifest form, which is the primary aim. A devotee who has ascended in the unmanifest form is Yuktatama on his true nature. It is not the intention here that compared to unmanifest-form devotion, a devotee of manifest-form by his nature is independently Yuktatama. According to the science of Āyurveda, Ghṛta or Ghī increases longevity, and thus it is known as "आयुष्य, Āyuṣya." There, it is not the intent that Ghī itself is Āyuṣya. However, it being the cause of Āyuṣya or longevity, it is described in the form of Āyuṣya. In the same way, being an aid in the devotion of the unmanifest form, the devotee of the manifest form is expressed in terms of Yuktatama-form, not by his own independent form.

(Next, other kinds of devotees of unmanifest-form are described -)

ये त्वक्षरमनिर्देश्यमव्यक्तं पर्युपासते |
सर्वत्रगमचिन्त्यञ्च कूटस्थमचलन्ध्रुवम् || BG 12.3 ||
सन्नियम्येन्द्रियग्रामं सर्वत्र समबुद्धय: |
ते प्राप्नुवन्ति मामेव सर्वभूतहिते रता: || BG 12.4 ||

तु - However, ; ये - those ; पर्युपासते - who worship (with oneness in Me, the attributeless Brahman), ; अक्षरम् - the Imperishable, ; अनिर्देश्यम् - the Ineffable, ; अव्यक्तम् - the Unmanifest, ; सर्वत्रगम् - the Omnipresent, ; अचिन्त्यम् - the Unthinkable, ; कूटस्थम् - the Immutable, ; अचलम् - the Immovable, ; च - and ; ध्रुवम् - the Unwavering,

सन्नियम्य - fully controlling ; इन्द्रिय-ग्रामम् - all senses, ; सम-बुद्धयः - with equanimity of the mind ; सर्वत्र - everywhere, ; रताः - (and) devoted ; सर्व-भूत-हिते - to the welfare of all beings, ; एव - indeed ; ते - they ; प्राप्नुवन्ति - attain ; माम् - Me (the Saccidānanda).

However, those who worship the Imperishable, the Ineffable, the Unmanifest, the Omnipresent, the Unthinkable, the Immutable, the Immovable, and the Unwavering, fully controlling all senses, with equanimity of the mind everywhere, and devoted to the welfare of all beings, indeed attain Me.

The intent of verses (BG 12.3 - BG 12.4) - Bhagavāna is describing the adjectives of the attributeless-form, the unmanifest-form. The one that cannot be destroyed in the past, present, and future is called the Imperishable. Not being the object of the senses, mind, and intellect, it is called the Unmanifest, the Ineffable, and the Unthinkable. It is the Unmanifest because it is not revealed by any means of cognition. Being the Unmanifest, it is the Ineffable as it is beyond the range of words and is not capable of being described. Indeed, only those things known by instruments such as the senses are thinkable by the mind. The Imperishable, being the opposite of this, is thus called the Unthinkable. Like the all-pervading and limitless space, the Imperishable is called the Omnipresent. The term Kūṭastha (कूटस्थ) means the Immutable. Kūṭa (कूट) is referred to as externally attractive but internally defective, often having false form, false evidence, and so on. Another meaning of the term Kūṭa is an anvil, a firm base on which a blacksmith forges hot iron, and so the term Kūṭastha can mean something that is fixed, changeless as an anvil. In Vedānta, what is variously known as Māyā, Avyakta, and what has, within it, numerous seeds of empirical life like nescience are also said to be Kūṭa. Thus, Kūṭa is Māyā, by whose existence the real is cognized. In that Kūṭa Māyā, the Imperishable is situated as a witness and the underlying support (Adhiṣṭhātā), and so it is called Kūṭastha, the Immutable. Further, situated immovably in the mutable Māyā, the Imperishable is called the Immovable, and being Immovable, it is called the Unwavering.

Those Yogīs, who are fully controlling, withdrawing all the senses from the sense-objects, with equanimity of the mind in dualities such as pleasure and pain at all times everywhere, worship My unmanifest-form in oneness, they who are devoted to the welfare of all beings, attain My form - the all-witness Ātmā of all. Bhagavāna declared the devotee of the manifest form as the best Yogī (Yuktatama) because through the devotion of the manifest form, he can become eligible and competent to ascend into the devotion of the unmanifest form. However, Bhagavāna did not explicitly say, “He, meaning the manifest-form devotee, attains Me.” That is because such a devotee with only the strength of his manifest-form devotion cannot attain Bhagavāna. Only through a regular succession of the unmanifest-form devotion can he become fit for the attainment of Bhagavāna. However, for this unmanifest-form devotee, Bhagavāna has explicitly said, “He attains Me, indeed.” From this, it is clear that manifest-form devotion is the means, and unmanifest-form devotion is the end and the fruit. Control of all senses, equanimity of the mind everywhere at all times, and dedication to the welfare of all beings are the three means that Bhagavāna has formulated for the unmanifest-form devotion.

Activities of the senses in their objects naturally happen with attachment and aversion through favorable and unfavorable intelligence. There, activities that are free from favorable and unfavorable intelligence and devoid of attachment and aversion are done with the control of the senses. Abandoning ornament perspective and only seeing ornament as gold, having a oneness-vision of the underlying truth in all beings is called "equanimity of the mind (समबुद्धि, Samabuddhi)," that is, the sameness of cognition. Samabuddhi is of two kinds, emotional (भावनामय, Bhāvanāmaya) and the other consisting knowledge (ज्ञानमय, Jñānamaya). Emotional Samabuddhi is the means, and Jñānamaya is the fruit. Here the intention is related to the emotional equanimity of the mind. Abandoning a worldly perspective and dedication to the welfare of all beings with a transcendental perspective is called "सर्वभूतहिते रताः" Accordingly, all three are mutually dependent. With control of the senses, equanimity of the mind is nourished; and with equanimity of the mind, control of the senses is nourished. With control of the senses and equanimity of the mind, dedication to the welfare of all beings is nourished. With a dedication to the welfare of all beings, control of the senses and equanimity of the mind are nourished. Just as the Prāṇa is dependent on the body, and the body is dependent on Prāṇa, in the same way, the three are mutually dependent.

(The toil, the impediment in the path of unmanifest devotion, is next described -)

क्लेशोऽधिकतरस्तेषामव्यक्तासक्तचेतसाम् |
अव्यक्ता हि गतिर्दुःखं देहवद्भिरवाप्यते || BG 12.5 ||

क्लेशः - Toil ; अधिकतरः - is greater ; तेषाम् - for those ; अव्यक्त-आसक्त-चेतसाम् - whose minds are attached to the unmanifest form. ; हि - For, ; अव्यक्ता - the unmanifest ; गतिः - objective ; अवाप्यते - is acquired ; दुःखम् - with great pain ; देहवद्भिः - by the embodied.

Toil is greater for those whose minds are attached to the unmanifest form. For, the unmanifest objective is acquired with great pain by the embodied.

Intent - By the way above, those involved in fixing their minds on the unmanifest form (beyond the range of the senses) have lots of toils in their means. Because, for the concentration of the mind on the unmanifest form, control of the senses and equanimity of the mind everywhere are the necessary means. However, those who are caught in the material I-ness and mineness of the world, those who have known the body as themselves, those who have mineness sense in the relationships of the body and whose activities related to the sense-objects are with attachment and aversion, for such embodied beings the unmanifest goal is extremely difficult. With trueness-sense attached to the I-ness and mineness of the body and senses, neither control of the senses nor equanimity of the mind can be successful. Accordingly, when control of the senses and equanimity of the mind is not successful, and with the potency of the enemy in the form of the senses and imbalanced intelligence remaining, how can the mind be situated steadfast on the unmanifest form? In such a state, the flow of the mind and the senses must be directed towards the manifest form of Bhagavāna, by which the mind can be detached from the name-form world and attached to the name-form of the manifest form of Bhagavāna. Then naturally, without attachment to worldly objects, control of the senses and equanimity of the mind can become successful. With successful control of the senses and equanimity of the mind, activity and positioning of the mind in the unmanifest form can become possible. It is established that activity in the unmanifest form is impossible for those who have I-ness in the body.

ये तु सर्वाणि कर्माणि मयि संन्यस्य मत्परः |
अनन्येनैव योगेन मां ध्यायन्त उपासते || BG 12.6 ||
तेषामहं समुद्धर्ता मृत्युसंसारसागरात् |
भवामि नचिरात्पार्थ मय्यावेशितचेतसाम् || BG 12.7 ||

तु - However, ; ये - those who ; उपासते - worship ; संन्यस्य - surrendering ; सर्वाणि - all ; कर्माणि - actions (including doership and not only just fruits of action) ; मयि - to Me (the manifest-form), ; मत्-परः - moving towards Me, ; ध्यायन्तः - meditating ; अनन्येन - with an undivided ; योगेन - union ; माम् - in Me ; एव - alone,

आवेशित-चेतसाम् - (and) with the mind fixed ; मयि - on Me (the manifest-form), ; पार्थ - hey, Pārtha (Arjuna)! ; अहम् - I ; न चिरात् - quickly ; भवामि - become ; समुद्धर्ता - the one to deliver ; तेषाम् - them ; मृत्यु-संसार-सागरात् - from the ocean of the mortal world of death.

However, those who worship surrendering all actions (including doership) to Me, moving towards Me, meditating with an undivided union in Me alone, and with the mind fixed on Me, hey, Arjuna! I quickly become the one to deliver them from the ocean of the mortal world of death.

The intent of verses (BG 12.6 - BG 12.7) - With I-ness in whatever activities that are ongoing in the body, senses, mind, and intellect, knowing one's self as not a doer, but making a resolve, "Whatever activities that are ongoing through the body there is not even an iota of their doership; the doer-holder of everything is Bhagavāna only. He, the Antaryāmi sitting inside, like a puppeteer, is making the insentient body dance." **With such a resolve, surrendering all doership and thus actions to the manifest-form Supreme Lord are here the total renunciation of all actions (Sarva-Karma-Saṃnyāsa).** In the above manner, with Sarva-Karma-Saṃnyāsa, one absorbed in Bhagavāna is successful in an undivided union. With an undivided union, meditation is successful, and with meditation, there is the nourishment of Sarva-Karma-Saṃnyāsa. Just as in classical music, Rāga Tāla (राग ताल) nourishes Megha (मेघ), and Rāga Megha nourishes Tāla. In the same way, by Sarva-Karma-Saṃnyāsa, meditation; and by meditation, Sarva-Karma-Saṃnyāsa are mutually nourished. In the visible world, "Except for Bhagavāna, there is nothing else of real essence," such resolute determination is called undivided union. Through this undivided union, moving the flow of thoughts in the manifest form of Bhagavāna is called meditation. Accordingly, with Sarva-Karma-Saṃnyāsa in Me (the manifest-form Supreme Lord), those devotees absorbed in Me through undivided union worship Me meditating with their minds fixed on Me; I quickly deliver them from the ocean of the mortal world of death. In other words, through undivided union providing freedom from the worldly attachments and making the devotees fit for the goal of the unmanifest form, I quickly make them attain My real all-witness form.

मय्येव मन आधत्स्व मयि बुद्धिं निवेशय |
निवसिष्यसि मय्येव अत ऊर्ध्वं न संशय: || BG 12.8 ||

आधत्स्व - Fix ; मनः - your mind ; मयि - on Me (the manifest-form) ; एव - alone, ; बुद्धिम् - (and let your) discerning ; निवेशय - be absorbed ; मयि - in Me. ; अतः - There ; ऊर्ध्वम् - after ; निवसिष्यसि - you will dwell ; मयि - in Me ; एव - alone, ; न - without ; संशयः - any doubt.

Fix your mind on Me alone, and let your discerning be absorbed in Me. After that, you will dwell in Me alone, without any doubt.

Intent - Now, summarizing both kinds of devotion and the subject of means and end, Bhagavāna states the essence. To attain My unmanifest form, first, fix your mind on My manifest form, and let your discerning intellect be established steadfast in Me alone. With the strength of the manifest-form devotion, you will reside in My unmanifest-form. In that, there is no doubt.

अथ चित्तं समाधातुं न शक्नोषि मयि स्थिरम् |
अभ्यासयोगेन ततो मामिच्छाप्तुं धनञ्जय || BG 12.9 ||

अथ - If (you are) ; न - not ; शक्नोषि - able ; समाधातुम् - to concentrate ; चित्तम् - your mind ; स्थिरम् - steadfastly ; मयि - on Me, ; ततः - then ; धनञ्जय - hey Dhanañjaya (Arjuna)! ; अभ्यास-योगेन - Through the practice of repeated efforts, ; इच्छ - seek ; आप्तुम् - to attain ; माम् - Me.

If you cannot concentrate your mind steadfastly on Me, then hey, Arjuna! Through the practice of repeated efforts, seek to attain Me.

Intent - Withdrawing the mind from all sides and repeatedly fixing it on one support is called Abhyāsa. Withdrawing your mind from worldly matters, make repeated efforts to unite it in My manifest form. With the strength of this practice, you will become capable of concentrating your mind on Me.

अभ्यासेऽप्यसमर्थोऽसि मत्कर्मपरमो भव |
मदर्थमपि कर्माणि कुर्वन्सिद्धिमवाप्स्यसि || BG 12.10 ||

असि - (If you) are ; अपि - even ; असमर्थः - unable ; अभ्यासे - in repeated efforts, ; भव - then become ; मत्-कर्म-परमः - devoted to performing acts for My sake. ; अपि - Even ; कुर्वन् - by performing ; कर्माणि - acts ; मत्-अर्थम् - for My sake, ; अवाप्स्यसि - you will achieve ; सिद्धिम् - perfection (in the form purity of the conscience).

If you are even unable in repeated efforts, then become devoted to performing acts for My sake. Even by performing acts for My sake, you will achieve perfection.

Intent - What are the acts for My sake (मदर्थ-कर्म, Madartha-Karma) or Bhagavad-Artha-Karma (भगवद्-अर्थ-कर्म)? Those means that are firmly imbibed in one's conduct to attain union with oneness in Bhagavāna are called acts for the sake of Bhagavāna. What are they? They are: 1) With deep love and with a leaf, a flower, or even water, the performance of service (सेवा, Sevā), worship ritual (पूजा, Pūjā),[109]offering ceremony (आरती, Āratī),[110]invocation (स्तुति, Stuti), eight limb long prostration (साष्टांग दण्डवत्-प्रणाम, Sāṣṭāṅga Daṇḍavat-Praṇāma)[111]and circumambulation of Bhagavāna, 2) knowing the devotees of Bhagavāna as the form of Bhagavāna performing their service, paying them homage with humility and repeated salutations in order to acquire their grace, 3) keeping the temple of Bhagavāna clean and tidy, 4) for the sake of Bhagavāna, constructing or getting built temples, water wells, step-wells and gardens, 5) always listening to the devotional stories of Bhagavāna, 6) melodiously reciting the names, attributes and divine plays (लीला, Līlā) of Bhagavāna, 7) always chanting and have others chant the names, Mantra of Bhagavāna, and 8) getting involved in mutual spiritual discussion with others and becoming tranced in love of Bhagavāna with throat choking up and hairs standing on end. If you cannot meditate upon Me through repeated efforts, then become devoted to doing acts for My sake. Thus, doing acts for My sake, Rajoguṇa, which impedes repeated efforts will vanish. With the departure of Rajoguṇa, per verses BG 12.8 and BG 12.9, you can become absorbed in meditation through repeated efforts. Accordingly, with the strength of My manifest-form devotion, and through control of the senses and equanimity of the mind, you will acquire perfection in the attainment of My unmanifest-form.

अथैतदप्यशक्तोऽसि कर्तुं मद्योगमाश्रितः |
सर्वकर्मफलत्यागं ततः कुरु यतात्मवान् || BG 12.11 ||

अथ - If ; असि - you are ; अशक्तः - unable ; कर्तुम् - to do ; अपि - even ; एतत् - this (acts for My sake), ; ततः - then ; यत-आत्मवान् - self-controlled, ; आश्रितः - resorting to ; मत्-योगम् - My Yoga, ; कुरु - do ; सर्व-कर्म-फल-त्यागम् - relinquish all fruits of action.

If you cannot do even this, then self-controlled, resorting to My Yoga, relinquish all fruits of action.

Intent - If, per verse BG 12.10, you cannot even perform acts for My sake, then intending to attain Me, by withdrawing your mind and senses from the worldly objects of enjoyment, relinquish all fruits of your actions. That is, do not perform actions with the world as the objective. However, whatever natural acts you perform, offer the fruits, that is, the results of those acts to Me. With this activity of desireless actions, you will become fit to do Karma for My sake through the purity of your conscience. Then, from the previous sequential order, you will attain Me through repeated efforts and meditation.

---

109 Pūjā (पूजा) means a worship ritual performed to offer devotional homage and prayer.

110 Āratī (आरती) means an offering ceremony in which lights with wicks soaked in Ghī are lit and songs sung praising the deity.

111 Sāṣṭāṅga Daṇḍavat-Praṇāma (साष्टांग दण्डवत्-प्रणाम) means eight limb long prostration where two toes, two knees, chest, forehead and two palms joined and stretched above the head touch the ground in the process of paying respectful obeisance and total surrender.

(This way, from verses BG 12.6 to BG 12.11, the sequential order from the highest to the lowest about the manifest-form devotion is stated. Now, from the lowest to the highest order of superiority is described -)

श्रेयो हि ज्ञानमभ्यासाज्ज्ञानाद्ध्यानं विशिष्यते |
ध्यानात्कर्मफलत्यागस्त्यागाच्छान्तिरनन्तरम् || BG 12.12 ||

ज्ञानम् - Knowledge ; श्रेयः - is superior ; अभ्यासात् - to repeated efforts (as provided in the verse BG 12.9). ; ध्यानम् - Meditation ; विशिष्यते - is superior ; ज्ञानात् - to knowledge. ; कर्म-फल-त्यागः - Relinquishment of (actions including doership and thus) fruits of action ; (विशिष्यते) - is superior ; ध्यानात् - to meditation. ; हि - For, ; त्यागात् - with relinquishment, ; अनन्तरम् - immediate ; शान्तिः - peace (is acquired).

Knowledge is superior to repeated efforts. Meditation is superior to knowledge. Relinquishment of (actions including doership and thus) fruits of action is superior to meditation. For, with relinquishment, immediate peace is acquired.

Intent - Compared to repeated efforts of listening to devotional narrations of Bhagavāna (Kathā), chanting and recitation of melodious hymns, names, attributes, and Līlā (Kīrtana) about acts for My sake, Madartha-Karma of verse BG 12.10, the indirect (Parokṣa) knowledge of the form of Bhagavāna is superior. That is because the fruit of listening to devotional narrations and chanting is only that the indirect knowledge of the manifest form of Bhagavāna becomes firm in the heart. In terms of means, all accept the superiority of fruits or results. Compared to repeated efforts of acts for My sake, Madartha-Karma, such as listening to devotional narrations and chants, indirect knowledge is called superior. Then compared to an indirect knowledge of Bhagavāna, meditation is called superior because the thing whose meditation is desired, it is necessary to have its indirect knowledge. If there is no indirect knowledge of a thing, its meditation is always impossible. Accordingly, meditation being the fruit of indirect knowledge, it is called superior to knowledge. After that, compared to meditation, relinquishment of (actions including doership and thus) fruits of action is called superior. **Here relinquishment of fruits of action is not the sought after (इष्ट, Iṣṭa) relinquishment of fruits of actions of verse BG 12.11, which is described as the lowest among the sequential order of the means. Because it can neither be superior to meditation nor can it be the result of meditation, and as said in this verse, immediate peace cannot be attained by it. However, here the meaning of the words "relinquish fruits of action (Karma-Phala-Tyāga)" ought to be opined as "total renunciation of all actions (Sarva-Karma-Saṃnyāsa)" that is articulated in BG 12.6 - "Surrender all doership, actions and thus fruits of action to Me the manifest-form Supreme Lord." That Sarva-Karma-Saṃnyāsa can be the only one that can be superior to meditation because only with repeated meditation efforts in the manifest form of Bhagavāna does the form become firm in the heart. As a result, in the passion of true love, the connection of I-ness and mineness in the body and senses naturally breaks; and after its success, peace is attained. That is why this Karma-Phala-Tyāga, that is, the said Sarva-Karma-Saṃnyāsa of verse BG 12.6, is superior to meditation.** By this Sarva-Karma-Saṃnyāsa, control of the senses and everywhere equanimity of the mind becoming successful provides peace in the form of activity in the unmanifest-form. Accordingly, characteristics of those devotees ought to be narrated, whose Sarva-Karma-Saṃnyāsa is successful through meditation and with the maturity of the manifest-form devotion who have become fit for the unmanifest-form devotion. Now, Bhagavāna describes their characteristics until the end of the chapter -

अद्वेष्टा सर्वभूतानां मैत्रः करुण एव च |
निर्ममो निरहङ्कारः समदुःखसुखः क्षमी || BG 12.13 ||
सन्तुष्टः सततं योगी यतात्मा दृढनिश्चयः |
मय्यर्पितमनोबुद्धिर्यो मद्भक्तः स मे प्रियः || BG 12.14 ||

अद्वेष्टा - (A Yogī who is) devoid of hate ; सर्व-भूतानां - towards all beings, ; मैत्रः - friendly (without any selfish motive) ; च - and ; करुणः - (without any purpose) compassionate, ; निरहङ्कारः - without egoism (and) ; निर्ममः - mineness (sense of possession), ; सम-दुःख-सुखः - same in pleasure and pain, ; क्षमी - forgiving, ; एव - indeed,

योगी - A Yogī, ; यः - who (is) ; सततम् - always ; सन्तुष्टः - satisfied, ; यत-आत्मा - self-disciplined, ; दृढ-निश्चयः - steadfast resolve, ; अर्पित-मनः-बुद्धिः - (and who) has surrendered his mind and intellect ; मयि - to Me; ; सः - that ; मत्-भक्तः - devotee of Mine ; प्रियः - is dear ; मे - to Me.

(A Yogī who is) devoid of hate towards all beings, friendly and compassionate, without egoism and mineness, same in pleasure and pain, forgiving, always satisfied, self-disciplined, steadfast resolve, and who has surrendered his mind and intellect to Me; that devotee of Mine is dear to Me.

The intent of verses (BG 12.13 - BG 12.14) - At the root of all faults, I-ness and mineness related to the body, mind, and senses remain the cause. In addition, it has also stretched its kingdom in all pleasure and pain dualities. However, by surrendering this I-ness and mineness at the feet of Bhagavāna, all beings become glimpses of the manifold forms of Bhagavāna. Thereafter, sameness in pleasure and pain is naturally established. Then, where is the question of hating anyone? There is no reason for being angry or taking revenge on offenders because one only sees Bhagavāna pinching with love in the form of that offender. In the heart of such a gentle-minded devotee, friendliness towards happy beings and compassion towards unhappy beings are formed. Then such a devotee, who has surrendered his mind and intellect at the feet of Bhagavāna, naturally becomes ever-satisfied, self-disciplined, and steadfast resolve and thus becomes dear to Bhagavāna. However, a knower is indeed the Ātmā of Bhagavāna, "ज्ञानी त्वात्मैव मे मतम्" (BG 7.18). He cannot be called dear, but only a devotee is dear to Bhagavāna. That is because only a thing separate from the Ātmā can be an object of love; Ātmā cannot be the object of love, as the Ātmā in its true nature is indeed love. That is why, in this chapter, from verse BG 12.13 to BG 12.20, those characteristics described can be only of those devotees who worship Bhagavāna with undivided faith, whose manifest-form devotion having matured based on BG 12.6, Sarva-Karma-Saṃnyāsa is successful and who have become fit to enter into the unmanifest-form.

यस्मान्नोद्विजते लोको लोकान्नोद्विजते च यः |
हर्षामर्षभयोद्वेगैर्मुक्तो यः स च मे प्रियः || BG 12.15 ||

यः - Who ; मुक्तः - is free from ; हर्ष-अमर्ष-भय-उद्वेगैः - elation, jealous anger, fear, and anxiety, ; च - and ; यस्मात् - from whom ; लोकः - the world ; न - is not ; उद्विजते - distressed ; च - and ; यः - who ; न - is not ; उद्विजते - distressed ; लोकात् - from the world, ; सः - he ; प्रियः - is dear ; मे - to Me.

Who is free from elation, jealous anger, fear, and anxiety, and from whom the world is not distressed and who is not distressed from the world, he is dear to Me.

अनपेक्षः शुचिर्दक्ष उदासीनो गतव्यथः |
सर्वारम्भपरित्यागी यो मद्भक्तः स मे प्रियः || BG 12.16 ||

सः - That ; मत्-भक्तः - devotee of Mine ; प्रियः - is dear ; मे - to Me ; यः - who is ; अनपेक्षः - without expectations, ; शुचिः - pure, ; दक्षः - adept, ; उदासीनः - indifferent, ; गत-व्यथः - unworried, ; सर्व-आरम्भ-परित्यागी - (and) relinquisher of all initiations.

That devotee of Mine is dear to Me who is without expectations, pure, adept, indifferent, unworried, and relinquisher of all initiations.

The intent of verses (BG 12.15 - BG 12.16) - Becoming afflicted with anger seeing someone progress means the person has a jealous-anger (अमर्ष, Amarṣa). Elation, jealous-anger, fear, anxiety, and all such tendencies are formed due to I-ness and mineness related to the body. Because this devotee is without those causes, he has become naturally free from those evil tendencies and has become dear to Bhagavāna. Similarly, all expectations and initiations of actions happen for the sake of the happiness of this world or the next. However, when the blissful Bhagavāna becomes resident in the heart and eyes of the devotee, the devotee is naturally free from expectations and is a relinquisher of initiations of all activities related to this and the next world. Again, all partisanships, fear, or hardships happen due to the connection with the world. However, with the mind surrendered at the feet of Bhagavāna, indifference and fearlessness from the world are acquired automatically, and thus purity and skill naturally serve the devotee. Among the various duties, one who immediately determines the real duty is called an adept (दक्ष, Dakṣa).

यो न हृष्यति न द्वेष्टि न शोचति न काङ्‍क्षति |
शुभाशुभपरित्यागी भक्तिमान्य: स मे प्रिय: || BG 12.17 ||

भक्तिमान् - A devotee ; यः - who ; न - neither ; हृष्यति - elates ; न - nor ; द्वेष्टि - hates ; न - nor ; शोचति - grieves ; न - or ; काङ्‍क्षति - desires ; यः - (and) who is ; शुभ-अशुभ-परित्यागी - a relinquisher of good and evil, ; सः - he ; प्रियः - is dear ; मे - to Me.

A devotee who neither elates nor hates nor grieves or desires and who is a relinquisher of good and evil, he is dear to Me.

Intent - Because of the like and dislike states of mind, tendencies of elation, hate, grief, and desire are formed by the influence of grasping and relinquishing dispositions. However, with the beating of the drum of equanimity remaining in the heart of this devotee, all those evil tendencies leave their seat from the heart. A devotee, free from the cause of imbalance, that is, free from dualities such as good and evil, is dear to Me.

सम: शत्रौ च मित्रे च तथा मानापमानयो: |
शीतोष्णसुखदु:खेषु सम: सङ्गविवर्जित: || BG 12.18 ||
तुल्यनिन्दास्तुतिर्मौनी सन्तुष्टो येन केनचित् |
अनिकेत: स्थिरमतिर्भक्तिमान्मे प्रियो नर: || BG 12.19 ||

समः - (A devotee who is) same towards ; मित्रे - friend ; च - and ; शत्रौ - foe, ; मान-अपमानयोः - honor and dishonor; ; च - and ; समः - same in ; शीत-उष्ण-सुख-दुःखेषु - cold and heat, pleasure and pain; ; तथा - and ; सङ्ग-विवर्जितः - free from all attachments,

तुल्य-निन्दा-स्तुतिः - alike in criticism and praise ; मौनी - has control over speech, ; सन्तुष्टः - content ; येन केनचित् - in whatever is received, ; अनिकेतः - unattached to abode, ; स्थिर-मतिः - (and) steady-minded - ; भक्तिमान् - (such a) devoted ; नरः - person ; प्रियः - is dear ; मे - to Me.

(A devotee who is) same towards friend and foe, honor and dishonor; same in cold and heat, pleasure and pain; free from all attachments, alike in criticism and praise, has control over speech, content in whatever is received, unattached to abode, and steady-minded - such a devoted person is dear to Me.

The intent of verses (BG 12.18 - BG 12.19) - The meaning of "सङ्ग-विवर्जित, free from all attachments" is not to grasp anything with bodily ego and mineness, but all objects of I-ness and mineness should be grasped only through the relationship with Bhagavāna. Here the term Maunī (मौनी) is not in the normal sense of one who is silent, but one who has control over his speech, control over the words that are uttered from his mouth. To be satisfied with whatever is received for the sustenance of the body, such as for eating, drinking, covering, resting, or sleeping, is called "सन्तुष्टो येन केनचित्, Santuṣṭo Yena Kenacit." The term Aniketa (अनिकेत) means one who does not have mineness in abode, who is unattached to abode, one who does not build a structure to live in, but like a snake, one who lives in the abodes built by others. Accordingly, with the aforementioned mental equanimity, one who is alike in dualities such as friend and foe, honor and dishonor, cold and heat and pleasure and pain, and whose mind is steadfastly fixed on the true nature of Bhagavāna, is dear to Bhagavāna.

(In the end, concluding the chapter, Bhagavāna said -)

ये तु धर्म्यामृतमिदं यथोक्तं पर्युपासते |
श्रद्दधाना मत्परमा भक्तास्तेऽतीव मे प्रिया: || BG 12.20 ||

मत्-परमाः - Moving towards Me, ; तु - indeed, ; ये - those ; भक्ताः - devotees (who) ; पर्युपासते - follow ; इदम् - these ; धर्म्य-अमृतम् - immortal virtues ; यथा उक्तम् - set forth above ; श्रद्दधानाः - with faith ; अतीव - (are) extremely ; प्रियाः - dear ; मे - to Me.

Moving towards Me, indeed, those devotees who follow these immortal virtues set forth above with faith are extremely dear to Me.

Intent - Just as is described in the verses (BG 12.13 - BG 12.19), devotees who follow this ambrosia of righteousness (धर्म्यामृत, Dharmyāmṛta), starting from the spiritual guidance of "अद्वेष्टा सर्वभूतानां, Adveṣṭā Sarvabhūtānāṃ" up to here, what is articulated, all these being the life force of all righteousness, are permeated by righteousness. The fruit of all righteousness is that only, and being the cause of immortality is like ambrosia. Those moving towards Bhagavāna with complete faith in the above set forth virtues leading to immortality, even if they have not yet attained it, but with devout faith who are ready to attain its success, such devotes are extremely dear to Bhagavāna. Just as a student who has complete faith in the words of his teacher and is prepared to follow his words, he is dear to his teacher, in the same way, as a devotee who has complete faith in the words of Bhagavāna and deems Bhagavāna as the supreme goal and is prepared to conduct himself by those words, he is extremely dear to Bhagavāna.

ॐ तत्सदिति श्रीमद्भगवद्गीतासूपनिषत्सु ब्रह्मविध्यायां योगशास्त्रे

श्रीकृष्णार्जुनसम्वादे भक्तियोगो नाम

द्वादशोऽध्यायः || BG 12 ||

Oṃ Tat Sat

In the Śrīmad Bhagavad Gītā Upaniṣad

The Yoga Science of the Knowledge of Self-Realization

The Discourse of Lord Śrī Kṛṣṇa and Arjuna

This Twelfth Chapter

Yoga Named - The Yoga of Devotion

Clarification

In the eleventh chapter, upon the plea of Arjuna, Bhagavāna revealed to Arjuna His Cosmic-Form and said that neither through studies of the Vedas and sacrifices nor through the performance of charities or austerities I could be seen and known the way you have seen Me. However, a devotee can only truly know, see, and enter My form through undivided devotion. At the beginning of this chapter, Arjuna raised a question, "Those ever-united devotees who always worship You (the manifest-form) and those others who worship the Imperishable, the Unmanifest - among them who knows Yoga best? (BG 12.1).

In response, Bhagavāna said, "Fixing their minds on Me, ever united, I deem those who worship Me with absolute faith as the best Yogīs." A newborn child dear to the mother is breastfed. Upon gaining strength, the child can digest dairy and other non-liquid foods at some point in time. For the child to digest other foods, first, it was necessary and unavoidable to be breastfed. In such a sense, Bhagavāna called his manifest-form devotee the best because in attaining the ultimate goal of union with oneness in the unmanifest-form, it is necessary for him to go through this manifest-form devotion, as without going through such a state, the ultimate goal cannot be achieved. Just as a pilgrim, who is Haridvāra bound for a holy bath in the Gaṅgā, even when he is miles away, he is still known as the pilgrim of Haridvāra, and in that sense, this devotee of the manifest form is called the best, not with the perspective that the manifest-form worship in its true nature is the final destination (BG 12.2). Then on the subject of the unmanifest-form devotion, Bhagavāna said, "Those who worship My imperishable unmanifest-form, they attain Me indeed, that is, without any other steps they directly attain Me, in it, there is no doubt. However, the unmanifest-form devotion is fraught with greater toil, because for embodied beings, with I-ness in the body, attainment of the unmanifest-form is extremely difficult" (BG 12.3 - BG 12.5). As long as there is I-ness in the body, total renunciation of all actions (all actions including doership-conceit, Sarva-Karma-Saṃnyāsa) in the manifest form and undivided devotion to the manifest form is commanded by Bhagavāna, and those devotees are assured quick deliverance from the ocean of the mortal world of death (BG 12.6 - BG 12.7). For the manifest-form devotees, Bhagavāna said, "I deliver them," however, for the unmanifest-form devotees, the knowers, it was not said so in the verse BG 12.4, but definite words were spoken, "They indeed attain Me." From this, it is clear that a devotee, through the compassion of Bhagavāna, becomes fit for knowledge, and devotion is an orderly step towards knowledge.

Accordingly, for meditation on the manifest form, Bhagavāna articulated fixing the mind steadfastly on the manifest form. In its absence, Bhagavāna commanded to make repeated efforts inquisitively. Inability in making repeated efforts, Bhagavāna commanded doing Madartha-Karma (acts for the sake of Bhagavāna), and even if that is not possible, then with desireless sentiment to relinquish all fruits of action (BG 12.8 - BG 12.11). In concluding all the steps, Bhagavāna said, "Compared to repeated efforts in the acts for My sake, indirect knowledge (Parokṣa-Jñāna) of My manifest-form is superior. Compared to such knowledge, meditation is superior. Compared to meditation, total renunciation of all actions (all actions including doership-conceit, Sarva-Karma-Saṃnyāsa) is superior, and through such renunciation by uniting with oneness in the unmanifest-form, immediate peace is acquired (BG 12.12). After that, in the verses (BG 12.13 - BG 12.20), the characteristics of those devotees with undivided faith were narrated, whose meditation becoming matured, Sarva-Karma-Saṃnyāsa in the manifest form becomes successful, and who become fit for the devotion of the unmanifest-form. The above characteristics of devotees are effort achieved. However, through devotion upon realizing the Truth, they are naturally possessed (Svabhāva-Siddha) by a knower.

Accordingly, in this chapter, articulating the Yoga of Devotion as a useful means to attain union in the unmanifest form, Bhagavāna concluded the chapter.

Chapter 13

The Yoga of the Field and the Knower of the Field

{In the twelfth chapter, in response to the question of Arjuna, Bhagavāna narrated worship of His manifest-form stepwise. It was stated that the fruit of the manifest-form devotion is entry into the unmanifest-form. Here in this chapter, Bhagavāna engages Himself to articulate that unmanifest form. Because the unmanifest form is beyond the reach of words and the mind (अवाङ्मनसगोचर, Avāṅmanasagocara), no one is capable of describing it through words and speech, which is why assignment of an adjunct with discriminative attribute (Upādhi) is made to describe it. Ordinarily, most beings have an I-ness sense in the body; that is why Bhagavāna holding an adjunct of the body as the "field, Kṣetra," and removing that attribute part, articulates the adjunctless (निरुपाधिक, Nirupādhika) without distinction (निर्विशेष, Nirviśeṣa) element as the "field-knower, Kṣetrajña."}

श्रीभगवानुवाच |
इदं शरीरं कौन्तेय क्षेत्रमित्यभिधीयते |
एतद्यो वेत्ति तं प्राहु: क्षेत्रज्ञ इति तद्विद: || BG 13.1 ||
श्रीभगवान् उवाच - Śrī Bhagavān said -

कौन्तेय - Hey Kaunteya (Arjuna)! ; इदम् - This ; शरीरम् - body ; अभिधीयते - is called ; क्षेत्रम् - the "field" ; इति - as such. ; तम् - The One ; यः - who ; वेत्ति - knows ; एतत् - it (the field) ; प्राहुः - is called ; क्षेत्रज्ञः - the "field-knower" ; इति - as such ; तत्-विदः - by its knowers.

Śrī Bhagavān said -

Hey Arjuna! This body is called the "field." The One who knows the field is called the "field-knower" by its knowers.

Intent - The term body does not mean just the gross body, but the intent is in the gross, the subtle, and the causal bodies and the five sheaths that cover the Ātmā. Just as varieties of seeds sown on a farm, becoming ready upon their own time, shoot out, in the same way, types of seeds in the form of actions sown in the field of the body, upon their own time, become ready for fruition. That is why this body is given the name of the "field (क्षेत्र, Kṣetra)." One who knows this body, in other words, is illumining it, is called the "field-knower (क्षेत्रज्ञ, Kṣetrajña)" by those wise knowers of the Truth. That which illuminates the object and notion that "I am a body" or "this is my body" is called the field-knower. In the darkness, one cannot have cognition of anything. Awareness of an object is possible only in the presence of some illumination. The comprehension of "I am not there" does not happen to anyone, from an ant to even Brahmā. However, in the wake, dream, or deep sleep state, continuous cognition of "I am" remains, even if it is the darkness of dissolution of the world.

The light that illuminates this cognition and objects is called the field-knower by knowers of the Truth. If the meaning of the word field-knower is deemed as the one, who has I-ness sense in the body, the delimited Ātmā, then it is not judicious. That is because even an ordinary person holds the perspective of I-ness in the body. That is why the sense of I-ness in the body cannot be the object of the standpoint of a knower. However, the witness in the body can be the only object of a knower's perspective. Here, it is the statement of Bhagavāna, "One who knows the field, it is called the field-knower by a knower of the Truth," further clarified in the next verse, "Know Me as that field-knower." That is why the meaning of the word Kṣetrajña instead of the one with I-ness sense in the body should be understood as the witness in the body as proper.

क्षेत्रज्ञं चापि मां विद्धि सर्वक्षेत्रेषु भारत |
क्षेत्रक्षेत्रज्ञयोर्ज्ञानं यत्तज्ज्ञानं मतं मम || 13.2 ||

च - Moreover, ; अपि - also ; भारत - hey Bhārata (Arjuna)! ; विद्धि - Know ; माम् - Me ; क्षेत्रज्ञम् - as the field-knower ; सर्व-क्षेत्रेषु - in all fields. ; यत् - It ; मम - is My ; मतम् - opinion ; तत् - that ; ज्ञानम् - the knowledge ; क्षेत्र-क्षेत्रज्ञयोः - of the field and the field-knower ; ज्ञानम् - is the real knowledge,

Hey Arjuna! Know Me as the field-knower in all fields. It is My opinion that the knowledge of the field and the field-knower is the real knowledge.

Intent - In all body-form fields, the existent light, in whose presence all body-form fields are perceived as existing even though they are non-existent, and being without real beingness and insentient are illuminated and conscious, know Me that alone as the field-knower. Just as a cloth separate from yarn, earthen pots distinct from clay, or gold ornaments separate from gold, do not have any existence of their own, only because of the presence of their material cause even being non-existent appear as existent. In reality, cloth, pots, or ornaments are without their existence (Svasattā-Śūnya). They are only word-form usage. One cannot find any meaning thereof in their material cause of yarn, clay, or gold.

In the same way, in the presence of the witness-conscious (Sākṣī-Cetana), unreal bodies appear as real because of the one Who is there, and in Whose witness-conscious they are holding names such as body. However, one cannot find anything in the form of a body. Know Me as the sole existing field-knower in all these bodies. Just as in numerous waves, there is only one water; water does not become diverse due to the multitudinous waves. In the same way, in all fields, I am the only field-knower. Multitudinous of the fields do not make Me the field-knower diverse.

Accordingly, to truly know the field and the field-knower is to know, "The body, being non-existent, insentient and thus grievous, is absent in the past, present, and future time; only in the present, like a snake in a rope, is the subject of delusional perception." In reality, the visible world grasped by the mind and the sense-organs is the Real-Conscious-Bliss field-knower; just as in the rope, the delusional snake is only the rope. Knowing the form of the field and the field-knower, one indeed knows My true nature. That is real knowledge.

(Described briefly, now Bhagavāna narrates in detail -)

तत्क्षेत्रं यच्च यादृक्च यद्विकारि यतश्च यत् |
स च यो यत्प्रभावश्च तत्समासेन मे शृणु || BG 13.3 ||

शृणु - Listen ; मे - to Me ; समासेन - briefly, ; तत् - about ; यत् - what ; तत् - that ; क्षेत्रम् - field is, ; च - and ; यादृक् - (what) it is like, ; च - and ; यत् विकारि - with what transformations (it is) ; च - and ; यतः - with what causes ; यत् - it is. ; च - Also, ; यः - what ; सः - that (field-knower) (is), ; च - and ; यत् प्रभावः - with what powers (it is).

Listen to Me briefly about what that field is, what it is like, with what transformations and causes it is. Also, what that (field-knower) is, and with what powers it is.

Intent - In reality, there is no intent to articulate the non-existent, insentient, and grievous field and its transformations. However, they indicate that Saccidānanda field-knower. The non-existent, insentient, and grievous field is enunciated to know its form. In its presence, all these transformations appear as real even though they are unreal, and in whom they are sensed and whose miracle they are, "यस्मिन्सर्वं यतः सर्वं यः सर्वं सर्वतश्च यः, in whom all this is, by whom all this is, who is all this and who is all else,"[112] so that through them the field-knower can be known. A love letter is held close to the heart and eyes because it brings a message from the beloved. The purpose is not in the letter but in the beloved one. In the same way, being the one to show the image of the field-knower, all these field transformations are lauded. However, the real purpose is in that Saccidānanda alone, not in these unreal perceptions.

(Now Bhagavāna lauds the truth of the field and field-knower to stimulate the intelligence of the listeners -)

ऋषिभिर्बहुधा गीतं छन्दोभिर्विविधैः पृथक् |
ब्रह्मसूत्रपदैश्चैव हेतुमद्भिर्विनिश्चितैः || BG 13.4 ||

गीतम् - It is sung ; बहुधा - variously ; ऋषिभिः - by seers ; विविधैः - in numerous ; पृथक् - distinct ; छन्दोभिः - (Vedic) hymns ; च - and, ; एव - indeed, ; विनिश्चितैः - determined ; हेतुमद्भिः - in the reasoned ; ब्रह्म-सूत्र-पदैः - words of the Brahma-Sūtra.

It is sung variously by seers in numerous distinct Vedic hymns and, indeed, determined in the reasoned words of the Brahma-Sūtra.

Intent - Being sung variously by seers such as Vasīṣṭha in distinct hymns such as those of the Ṛk-Veda, does not mean that the field-knower is diverse. The diversity is only concerning the field characterized by adjuncts with discriminative attributes and not regarding the field-knower. The intention is to articulate the form of the field-knower without distinction, and beyond the reach of words and mind, the fields with adjuncts of varied kinds are assigned. But in the end, the absence determination of the assigned discriminating attributes at all times and uncovering the field-knower from all those attributes is the only purpose of all seers and scriptures to reveal the true nature of the field-knower.

(In the following two verses, the field is briefly formulated -)

महाभूतान्यङ्ककारो बुद्धिरव्यक्त मेव च |
इन्द्रियाणि दशैकं च पञ्च चेन्द्रियगोचराः || BG 13.5 ||

महा-भूतानि - The great elements, ; अहङ्कारः - the ego, ; बुद्धिः - the intellect, ; च - and ; अव्यक्तम् - the unmanifest ; एव - too, ; इन्द्रियाणि दश - the ten senses ; च - and ; एकम् - the one (mind), ; च - and ; पञ्च - the five ; इन्द्रिय-गोचराः - objects of the senses.

The great elements, the ego, the intellect, the unmanifest, the ten senses and the one (mind), and the five objects of the senses.

Intent - The great elements are five in number and are known as Pañca-Mahābhūta (पञ्च-महाभूत), enumerated as 1) earth (पृथ्वी, Pṛthvī), 2) water (आप, Āpa), 3) fire (अग्नि, Agni), 4) wind (वायु, Vāyu) and 5) space (आकाश, Ākāśa). Because they permeate all mutations of Prakṛti, they are called great (Mahāna), and being the cause of the Pañcīkṛta[113] of the Pañca-Mahābhūta, they are subtle.

The cause of the great elements is 6) the ego (अहंकार, Ahaṃkāra). It is the "I-ness" sense in the body (देह, Deha), the sense-organs (इन्द्रिय, Indriya), the mind (मनस्, Manas) and the intellect (बुद्धि, Buddhi).

---

[112] Yoga-Vāsiṣṭha (योग-वासिष्ठ) 6.59.2

[113] Pañcīkṛta (पञ्चीकृत) means done by Pañcīkaraṇa (पञ्चीकरण), which is an action by which anything is constituted of the five elements (1/2 of one and 1/8 of other four elements)

The cause of the ego is 7) the intellect characterized by inner-disposition of decision-making (Niścayātmaka-Vṛtti). It is derived from the root Budh (बुध्), which means, "be awake, observe, to know." Discriminative in nature, intellect can discern real (Sat) from unreal (Asat), right from wrong, good from bad, piety from sin, and thereby provide a selection of a wise choice.

The cause of the intellect is 8) the Avyakta (अव्यक्त, unmanifest) or that what is not manifest, the unevolved, the state of Prakṛti that is devoid of transformations. It is also known as Māyā (माया) or Śakti (शक्ति, power) of the Supreme Lord as expressed in BG 7.14 - "My Māyā is hard to cross over." The term Eva (एव, too) is inserted to express the delimitation of Prakṛti to the realm of the eight-fold Prakṛti depicted above.

Of the ten senses, the five cognitive senses (पञ्च-ज्ञानेन्द्रिय, Pañca-Jñānendriya) enumerated are: 9) skin (त्वक, Tvaka), 10) tongue (रसना, Rasanā), 11) the eyes (चक्षु, Cakṣu), 12) nose (घ्राण, Ghrāṇa), 13) ears (श्रोत्र, Śrotra); and the five action-organs or the Pañca-Karmendriya (पञ्च-कर्मेन्द्रिय) are: 14) mouth (वाक, Vāka) with the faculty of voice, 15) hands (पाणि, Pāṇi) with the faculty of grasping (Grahaṇa) and holding (Dhāraṇa), 16) feet (पाद, Pāda) with the faculty of locomotion (Gamana), 17) anus (पायु, Pāyu) with the faculty of excretion and 18) genitals (उपस्थ, Upastha) with the faculty of reproduction.

Moreover, "and the one" or the eleventh faculty 19) is the mind (मनस्, Manas) that receives all sensory inputs, interprets, and desires. The essence is perception and cognition.

In addition, the five objects of the senses (पञ्च-विषय, Pañca-Vishay) enumerated are: 20) sound (शब्द, Śabda), 21) touch (स्पर्श, Sparśa), 22) form (रूप, Rupa), 23) taste (रस, Rasa) and 24) smell (गंध, Gandha). This way, the field is designated as altogether of 24 elements (तत्त्व, Tattva).

(Now, the transformations of the field are briefly narrated -)

इच्छा द्वेष: सुखं दु:खं सङ्घातश्चेतना धृति: |
एतत्क्षेत्रं समासेन सविकारमुदाहृतम् || BG 13.6 ||

इच्छा - Desire, ; द्वेषः - antipathy, ; सुखम् - pleasure, ; दुःखम् - pain, ; सङ्घातः - the aggregate (of the body and senses), ; चेतना - consciousness, ; धृतिः - (and) sustentation (meaning the power to sustain the body and senses) - ; एतत् - these ; समासेन - briefly ; उदाहृतम् - are said to be ; क्षेत्रम् - the field ; सविकारम् - with its transformations.

Desire, antipathy, pleasure, pain, the aggregate, consciousness, and sustentation - these briefly are said to be the field with its transformations.

Intent - Desire is an attribute of the conscience (Antaḥkaraṇa) seeking to acquire seen or heard objects that yield pleasure. Being an object of knowledge, it is part of the field. When met again, those things are experienced as the cause of pain; the desire to abandon them or hate them is called antipathy (Dveṣa). That is also an object of knowledge and hence part of the field. Similarly, the agreeable mental state (Anukūla-Vṛtti) is named pleasure (Sukha), and the antagonistic mental state (Pratikūla-Vṛtti) is named pain (Duḥkha), both being knowable are part of the field. The aggregate (सङ्घात, Saṅghāta) means the assembly of the body and senses. Just as a heated iron rod manifests fire, in the same way, the state of the conscience illuminated by the light of the conscious within is called awareness or consciousness (Cetanā). That, too, being knowable is part of the field. Sustentation (Dhṛti) means the power that holds or sustains the body and senses; it is also part of the field, being knowable. These attributes of the conscience and subject to creation and destruction have been called transformations (Vikāra). Thus, the field and its transformations are set forth briefly.

The intention is that the field of twenty-four elements and its transformations such as desire, antipathy, pleasure, or pain by Whom they are illuminated, under Whose support their creation, sustentation, and destruction occur, and Who knotting these insentient twenty-four elements makes them conscious, and then makes various transformations in them, that field-knower is real, existent and that is the only truth. All these others are its miracle and unreal (अतत्त्व, Atattva). This knowledge is not just for verbalizing but is for experiencing transcendentally. By talking and listening about immortality, one does not become immortal. One ought to drink it, experience it.

(For the ambrosiac knowledge, what kind of heart should one have? Bhagavāna describes in the following five verses -)

अमानित्वमदम्भित्वमहिंसा क्षान्तिरार्जवम् |
आचार्योपासनं शौचं स्थैर्यमात्मविनिग्रहः || BG 13.7 ||

अमानित्वम् - Humility, ; अदम्भित्वम् - unostentatiousness, ; अहिंसा - non-violence (not to hurt anyone through the body, mind, or speech), ; क्षान्तिः - forgiveness, ; आर्जवम् - simplicity (of the body, mind, and speech), ; आचार्य-उपासनम् - service to the teacher, ; शौचम् - purity (cleanliness of the body and the mind), ; स्थैर्यम् - steadfastness (of the conscience), ; आत्म-विनिग्रहः - self-control (of the body, mind, and senses),

Humility, unostentatiousness, non-violence, forgiveness, simplicity, service to the teacher, purity, steadfastness, self-control,

Intent - To exhibit one's superior attributes boastfully is called conceit; its absence is called humility (अमानित्व, Amānitva). Showing the best attributes that one does not possess is called hypocrisy (दम्भ, Dambha); its absence is called unostentatiousness. Not hurting or injuring any living being is called non-violence (अहिंसा, Ahiṃsā). Remaining undisturbed towards offenders is called forgiveness (Kṣamā). In all mental and vocal conduct related to eating, drinking, or clothing, straightforwardness, and absence of crookedness are called simplicity (आर्जव, Ārjava). With faith and devotion, the service of a teacher with the body, mind, and wealth to procure his grace is called service to the teacher (आचार्य-उपासना, Ācarya-Upāsanā). Nourishing oneself through a pure diet from pure materials rightfully procured and cleaning the defilements of the body through water and soil are all external cleanliness, and purity from attachment and aversion transformations is called internal cleanliness. This way, purity (शौच, Śauca) includes internal and external cleanliness. Diverting the conscience from worldly activities and exclusively pursuing the path leading to liberation is called steadfastness (स्थैर्य, Sthairya). Imposing discipline on the body, mind, and senses when they function against one's real interest and confining activities in the righteous path is called self-control (आत्म-विनिग्रह, Ātma-Vinigraha).

(Moreover -)

इन्द्रियार्थेषु वैराग्यमनहङ्कार एव च |
जन्ममृत्युजराव्याधिदुःखदोषानुदर्शनम् || BG 13.8 ||

वैराग्यम् - aversion ; इन्द्रिय-अर्थेषु - to sense objects, ; च एव - as well as ; अनहङ्कारः - an absence of egoism, ; जन्म-मृत्यु-जरा-व्याधि-दुःख-दोष-अनुदर्शनम् - repeated perception of evil and pain in birth, death, old age, and disease,

aversion to sense objects, as well as an absence of egoism, repeated perception of evil and pain in birth, death, old age, and disease,

Intent - Perceiving evil and reflecting upon the pain in birth, first during confinement in the womb and then during exit from the womb through the vagina. In the same way, perceiving evil and reflecting on the pain in the separation of the Prāṇa from the body at the time of death and the pain of leaving loved ones. Perceiving evil and reflecting on the loss of attributes of life such as loss of mobility, a decline in intellectual power, enfeeblement of energy, and many other pains of old age and perceiving evil and reflecting on the pain in the various diseases in the body. In childhood, pain from lack of strength and agility; in youth, pain related to lust and other changes ought to be perceived as evil and their pain reflected upon. All these, viz. birth, death, old age, and disease being the instruments of pain, are called pain. Accordingly, repeatedly seeing evil in all these pains, and with such perception, attachment and egoism related to sense grasped objects ought to be forsaken.

असक्तिरनभिष्वङ्ग: पुत्रदारगृहादिषु |
नित्यं च समचित्तत्वमिष्टानिष्टोपपत्तिषु || BG 13.9 ||

असक्तिः - absence of attachment (and) ; अनभिष्वङ्गः - lack of excessive love ; पुत्र-दार-गृह-आदिषु - for son, wife, home, and others, ; च - and ; नित्यम् - constant ; सम-चित्तत्वम् - even-mindedness ; उपपत्तिषु - in the acquisition of ; इष्ट - desired (and) ; अनिष्ट - undesired (things).

absence of attachment and lack of excessive love for son, wife, home, and others, constant even-mindedness in the acquisition of desired and undesired things,

Intent - Worldly love towards wife, son, or home is called (सक्ति, Sakti), and its absence is called (असक्ति, Asakti). More profound love is called (आसक्ति, Āsakti). Excessive love is called (अभिष्वङ्ग, Abhiṣvaṅga); like deeming pleasure and pain of wife and son as own. Lack of this excessive love is called (अनभिष्वङ्ग, Anabhiṣvaṅga). The term Putra (पुत्र, son) should be understood as children. Additionally, a lack of change in mental-state of happiness in the acquisition of the desired thing and unhappiness in the acquisition of an undesired thing is called even-mindedness (समचित्तता, Samacittatā). In other words, abandonment of excessive attachment and mineness in desired objects and remaining even-minded in acquiring desired and undesired.

मयि चानन्ययोगेन भक्तिरव्यभिचारिणी |
विविक्तदेशसेवित्वमरतिर्जनसंसदि || BG 13.10 ||

मयि - My ; अव्यभिचारिणी - unwavering ; अनन्य-योगेन - undivided ; भक्तिः - devotion (in accordance with BG 12.6), ; विविक्त-देश-सेवित्वम् - resorting to solitary places, ; च - and ; अरतिः - aversion ; जन-संसदि - to human masses,

My unwavering undivided devotion, resorting to solitary places, aversion to human masses,

Intent - The undivided devotion that Bhagavāna had narrated in verse BG 12.6, that undivided devotion of the manifest-form (Bhagavāna Vāsudeva) is here the unwavering (अव्यभिचारिणी, Avyabhicāriṇī) devotion. A place that is naturally pure, or is made pure by cleaning and is free from snakes, tigers, and other animals and insects in forests, riverbanks, or temples, in such solitary places, one whose nature is to reside is known as one who resorts to solitary places (विविक्तदेशसेवित्वम, Viviktadeśasevitvama). In addition, to be averse to all beings attached to sense objects.

अध्यात्मज्ञाननित्यत्वं तत्वज्ञानार्थदर्शनम् |
एतज्ज्ञानमिति प्रोक्तमज्ञानं यदतोऽन्यथा || BG 13.11 ||

अध्यात्म-ज्ञान-नित्यत्वम् - constant pursuit for the transcendent knowledge of the Self, ; तत्त्व-ज्ञान-अर्थ-दर्शनम् - (and) perception of the content of the knowledge of the Truth - ; एतत् - all this is ; प्रोक्तम् - said to be ; ज्ञानम् - knowledge. ; इति - Thus, ; अतः - what is ; अन्यथा - other than ; यत् - that, ; अज्ञानम् - is ignorance.

constant pursuit for the transcendent knowledge of the Self, and perception of the content of the knowledge of the Truth - all this is said to be knowledge. Thus, what is other than that, is ignorance.

Intent - From verse BG 13.7 to here, means (Sādhana) for acquiring knowledge were articulated. All these instruments of knowledge are lauded as knowledge (Jñāna), and everything else contrary is said to be ignorance (Ajñāna). Knowledge related to Adhyātma means spiritual or transcendent knowledge of the Ātmā. A steadfast fixation of the mind on it and the perception of the content of the real knowledge through these means, with the aim of liberation in the form of desistance from the world, ought to be sought. A vessel ought to be appropriate for what it is intended to hold. Pañcāmṛta[114]placed in a smelly container, makes even something pure impure. In the same way, for pure knowledge, the vessel in the form of the heart should be such that there is no foul smell of worldly dirt. If the heart is filled with knowledge that is fetid with conceit, hypocrisy, vanity, violence, impatience, or crookedness, that person will become just a verbal knower who, for himself and thus the world, instead of being serene, will prove to be disturbed and will remain the holder of Āsurī (आसुरी, demonic) wealth.

(Accordingly, in a pure conscience, those things that are appropriate to search are next articulated -)

ज्ञेयं यत्तत्प्रवक्ष्यामि यज्ज्ञात्वामृतमश्नुते |
अनादिमत्परं ब्रह्म न सत्तन्नासदुच्यते || BG 13.12 ||

प्रवक्ष्यामि - I shall (now) set forth ; तत् - that ; यत् - which is ; ज्ञेयम् - knowable - ; अनादिमत् - the beginningless ; परम् - the supreme ; ब्रह्म - Brahman; ; ज्ञात्वा - knowing ; यत् - which, ; अश्नुते - one attains ; अमृतम् - immortality. ; तत् - It ; उच्यते - is said to be ; न - neither ; सत् - existent ; न - nor ; असत् - non-existent.

I shall now set forth that which is knowable - the beginningless supreme Brahman; knowing which, one attains immortality. It is said to be neither existent nor non-existent.

Intent - The knowable (Jñeya) is what ought to be known. I will tell you completely the knowable through the means above. By knowing it, what fruit is acquired? One, who knows it, attains immortality. In other words, by knowing it directly, freedom from the bondage of birth and death is acquired, and the ambrosiac supreme-bliss (Paramānanda) is attained. How can supreme bliss be attained just by its knowledge? The Paramānanda is the Ātmā of all beings. However, due to ignorance, grasping it as something other than what it is in the form of I-you phenomenal world, living beings acquire doership and enjoyership and the pains of birth and death. A rope, in whom there is no fear, a deluded person grasping it otherwise as a snake is beset with fear. However, with direct intuitive knowledge of the rope, immediately, the object in the form of the snake and fear disappear completely. In the same manner, with direct intuitive knowledge of the Paramānanda, the object in the form of the phenomenal world and born there of doership and enjoyership and thus their fruits, the pains such as birth and death disappear completely. That is why its attainment is impossible through Karma. Only through direct intuitive knowledge has attainment of the Paramānanda and its experience been articulated.

What is that thing which is knowable? The beginningless (अनादिमत्, Anādimat) attributeless supreme Brahman (परब्रह्म, Parabrahma). It is called beginningless (Anādi) because it constantly exists, without the limits of time and space and birth. In other words, it cannot be proven by past, present, and future time, though all three times are realized through it. Because the Parabrahma is beyond the reach of words and the mind, and being without duality (निर्द्वन्द्व, Nirdvandva), no words can enter it, meaning it transcends all verbal expressions. Anything known through verbal expressions is dualistic; words do not have reach in non-duality. Only class, attributes, acts, or relationships are known through words. However, the Parabrahma has neither any class nor any attributes, and it is neither an act nor a relationship. That is why for the sake of enlightening its form, the use of prohibited contrary words is made - "The Parabrahma is said to be neither existent (सत्, Sat) nor non-existent (असत्, Asat)." A thing can only be called existent when something non-existent is present that is separate and equivalent to it. In an ocean, other than water - waves or eddies cannot be grabbed; they are all nothing but a deception of the eyes. Likewise, separate from the Parabrahma, in the Parabrahma, no phenomenal world is found. In Parabrahma, when there is no non-existent thing separate from it, how can that Parabrahma be called existent? The use of the term existent

---

[114] Pañcāmṛta (पञ्चामृत) means a mixture of cow milk, curd, honey, sugar, and Ghī used as an offering at a worship ritual (Pūjā) and distributed to the devotees as Prasāda.

is only to uncover it from non-existent. When the non-existent phenomenal world appears existent by the existence of the Parabrahma, how can it be called non-existent? Additionally, the term non-existent is also used to uncover it from the existent. Separate from the Parabrahma, there is nothing existent, then how can it be called non-existent, and how can the meaning of the term non-existent reach it? If separate from Parabrahma there was anything existent, then the Parabrahma could have been called non-existent to uncover that existent. Thus, it cannot be called either existent or non-existent. Due to the inability of words existent and non-existent to reach it, it cannot be called null either. For instance, there is neither existence nor nonexistence of the name-form gold-ring in gold. When a goldsmith makes a gold ring, during the time of the existence of the gold ring, gold is still gold; it "is as is." When the goldsmith melts the gold ring, during the non-existence of that gold ring, gold is still gold; it "is as is." Though the being and non-being of the name-form gold-ring happen on the dependence of gold, in the nature of gold, there is no stain of beingness and non-beingness of the name-form gold-ring. Though the terms existent and non-existent, and their meanings depend on the Parabrahma, there is no stain in its form from those terms and their meanings. The terms existent and non-existent, and their meanings are merely the use of name-form to explain the material cause (वाचारम्भण, Vācārambhaṇa).[115]In essence, everything is the Parabrahma alone; there is not even an iota of existence or non-existence in it. The knowable is not a subject of comprehension from the word "existent." Being beyond the range of the word existent (सत्, Sat), a doubt lingers regarding its non-existence. To remove this doubt, Bhagavāna next states -

सर्वत: पाणिपादं तत्सर्वतोऽक्षिशिरोमुखम् |
सर्वत: श्रुतिमल्लोके सर्वमावृत्य तिष्ठति || BG 13.13 ||

तत् - That (Parabrahma has) ; पाणि-पादम् - hands, feet ; सर्वतः - on all sides; ; अक्षि-शिरः-मुखम् - eyes, heads, mouths ; सर्वतः - on all sides; ; श्रुतिमत् - ears ; सर्वतः - on all sides; ; तिष्ठति - stands ; आवृत्य - covering ; सर्वम् - all ; लोके - in this world.

That Parabrahma has hands, feet, eyes, heads, mouths, and ears on all sides; stands covering all in this world.

Intent - The knowable field-knower Parabrahma has "hands, feet, eyes, heads, mouths and ears" on all sides. That is, the existence of the field-knower Parabrahma can be comprehended by the sense organ adjuncts of all living beings. The power that drives individual activities of the body, senses, mind, and intellect is derived from the Parabrahma. In the phenomenal world, separate from it, there is no one else with whose power this insentient world can dance. Indeed, the power of all powers is the Parabrahma. In this world, innumerable organs, viz. hands, feet, eyes there are, are the Parabrahma's alone. It is indeed the hand of all hands, the eye of all eyes, the ear of all ears, the life force of all life forces, and the mind of all minds.

According to Śruti, "श्रोत्रस्य श्रोत्रं मनसो मनो यद्,[116]who is the ear of the ear (who gives to the ear the power of hearing), who is the mind of the mind (who gives to the mind the power of thinking)." Separate from it, the paltry ego, like a cat sitting in the body-form den, continues meowing "me," "me," and other than holding the "I am a doer" conceit in the activities of the body and senses, it has no other doership of its own. Whatever the eyes see, in that vision activity, numerous electric signals produced by the photoreceptors in the retina pass through the optic nerves to the brain, turning them to the perceived images. The paltry ego does not have an iota of connection in those activities. However, the knowable's conscious power is present in every nerve and activity, like water in the waves. With some thought, it can be seen that when this conscious power leaves the gross body and moves into the sleep state, keeping a relationship only with the mind and intellect and continues to illuminate them, at that time, activities of the body and senses immediately stop.

---

[115] Vācārambhaṇa (वाचारम्भण) is the use of name-form to explain the material cause. For instance, the name-form "gold-chain" provides knowledge of gold as the material cause.

[116] Kena Upaniṣad (केन उपनिषद्) 1.2

Even if tasty things are in the mouth, things with aroma are near the nose, and the relationship of the sense faculties with their respective objects is present, yet they cannot sense their objects. The tongue can taste neither food nor the nose experience aroma. From this, it is evident that only through the power of this conscious the sense faculties are capable of functioning in their respective activities; there is no doership of ego. Binding oneself to enjoy the fruits of action is the only purpose of doership-ego and nothing else. Except for the power of the conscious, there cannot be anything that can make the puppets (in the form of the phenomenal world) dance.

The I-ness in this paltry ego is borrowed from the perception of the power of the conscious; it does not even have its own I-ness. When the conscious field-knower removes its perception from the ego in the deep-sleep state, I-ness disappears. The conscious field-knower is the only power of the body, senses, and mental activities. Moreover, just as it controls one body, the controller of the aggregate bodies, senses, minds, and intellects is Parabrahma. “It is from all sides with hands, feet, eyes, heads, mouths, and ears, and it stands pervading all.” In other words, despite it being existent in all these adjuncts of the sense faculties, it is without any adjunct. To clarify that it does not become one with adjunct, Bhagavāna states in the next verse.

(This Parabrahma -)

सर्वेन्द्रियगुणाभासं सर्वेन्द्रियविवर्जितम् |
असक्तं सर्वभृच्चैव निर्गुणं गुणभोक्तृ च || BG 13.14 ||

सर्व-इन्द्रिय-गुणाभासम् - Illuminating all sense-organs and their functions, ; एव - indeed (the Parabrahma) ; सर्व-इन्द्रिय-विवर्जितम् - (is) devoid of all sense-organs; ; च - and ; सर्व-भृत् - sustaining all ; असक्तम् - (is) unattached, ; च - and ; गुण-भोक्तृ - experiencing the constituents (of Prakṛti) ; निर्गुणम् - (is) beyond the constituents.

Illumining all sense-organs and their functions (the Parabrahma) is devoid of all sense-organs; sustaining all is unattached, and experiencing the constituents is beyond the constituents.

Intent - In the previous verse, the Parabrahma was described to have hands, feet, eyes, heads, mouths, and ears from all sides. One should not deduce that the Parabrahma is like Rāvaṇa, a unique person with many heads and mouths. In this verse, it is made clear that the Parabrahma is the one who illuminates all sense-organs and their functions and their objects, and itself is without sense-organs. Senses and their objects by their nature are probable (कदाचित्क, Kadācitka), meaning they are existent sometimes (कदाचित्, Kadācit) and non-existent at other times. Ears, skin, or other sense-organs and their corresponding objects, sound, and touch are present in the awake but not in the sleep state. The mind-intellect (the inner-conscience) and their objects, thoughts, and resolves are present in the awake and sleep states but not in the deep-sleep state. A thing that is present sometimes and not present at other times, without beginning and end, present only in the middle, like the water of a desert mirage, is illusory only. Perception of the illusory inkling can happen only on the dependence of the time-unbounded existent underlying support. The mind, intellect, and external sense instruments such as the ears, skin, and objects being probable are only imaginary. However, the eternal, immovable, and immutable Parabrahma is the existent underlying substrate of the senses and their objects, Who is present in the wake, sleep, and deep-sleep states, Who illuminates the being and non-being of these senses and their objects with its power, and Who is beyond their reach. Being the instrument of knowledge, just as the sense-organs are external instruments, in the same way, the mind and intellect being inner conscience, here they ought to be understood as within the meaning of the word sense-organs. The Parabrahma, with its power sustaining the entire movable and immovable world, like a mirror in various images, is beyond them. Even while experiencing the constituents of Prakṛti, being the support of Sattva, Rajas, and Tamas and their transformations such as pleasure, pain, or delusion, the Parabrahma is beyond them. Thus, the knowable Parabrahma is described as dissociated from all adjuncts and discriminative attributes.

{The power of the knowable in the body and sense adjuncts is described. In such a state, that knowable Parabrahma, remaining limited in those adjuncts, may be space-bounded, bringing forth such insufficient pervasion doubt in mind, Bhagavāna states -}

बहिरन्तश्च भूतानामचरं चरमेव च |
सूक्ष्मत्वात्तदविज्ञेयं दूरस्थं चान्तिके च तत् || BG 13.15 ||

तत् - It is ; बहिः - outside ; च - and ; अन्तः - inside ; भूतानाम् - all beings, ; अचरम् - stationary ; च - and ; चरम् - movable, ; च - and ; एव - indeed ; दूरस्थम् - far ; च - and ; अन्तिके - near. ; सूक्ष्मत्वात् - (Yet, due to its) subtleness, ; तत् - it ; अविज्ञेयम् - is not known.

It is outside and inside all beings, stationary and movable, and far and near. Yet, due to its subtleness, it is not known.

Intent - Parabrahma is not only in the body and senses alone. However, it is also in all stationary and mobile beings. Just as the yarn is behind cloth and clay is behind a pot, in the same way, the Parabrahma is behind all beings. All moving and stationary beings are naturally perceived as existing, though in all those beings, the only pervasive existent is the Parabrahma. It illuminates all substances like living beings and all moving and non-moving activities with its existent power. All substances, attributes, and acts are experienced only in "is" form; no substance is perceived in "is not" form. Thus, the Parabrahma, because of its pervasiveness, exists as the power in all substances, attributes, and moving and non-moving beings. From an analytic perspective, only the Parabrahma is perceived in moving and non-moving beings. In other words, like a snake in a rope, there is illusory cognizance of all moving and non-moving beings in its support. In living beings and whatever external space there is, the Parabrahma pervades. Pervasive as it is, it is not known to ignorant humans because of its subtleness. Just as Collyrium applied in the eyes, being extremely close, cannot be seen by the eyes in the same manner because of its subtleness. Even though the Parabrahma is existent with oneness in the senses, mind, and intellect, they cannot grasp it. Thus, it is farther than the farthest for ignorant humans, being unknown. However, for the one who has transcendentally realized the Ātmā, it being his Ātmā is nearer than the nearest. Alternatively, one can say that it is pervading everywhere farther from the farthest and nearer than the nearest.

(From those above, though the Parabrahma being devoid of space limitation pervades all space, yet like the distinction of a pot and cloth, the Parabrahma too may be materially distinct and divided, and even being all-pervasive, except for the past and the future one to remain only in the present, maybe time differentiated, one that exists in one time and not in another. Bringing forth such doubt in mind, Bhagavāna states -)

अविभक्तं च भूतेषु विभक्तमिव च स्थितम् |
भूतभर्तृ च तज्ज्ञेयं ग्रसिष्णु प्रभविष्णु च || BG 13.16 ||

स्थितम् - Existent ; भूतेषु - in all beings, ; अविभक्तम् - (it is) undivided ; इव - (though perceived) as ; विभक्तम् - divided. ; च - And, ; तत् - That ; ज्ञेयम् - knowable ; भूत-भर्तृ - is the sustainer of all beings (in the form of Lord Viṣṇu), ; च - and ; ग्रसिष्णु - annihilator (of all in the form of Lord Śiva), ; च - and, ; प्रभविष्णु - creator (of all in the form of Lord Brahmā) ; च - too.

Existent in all beings, it is undivided, though perceived as divided. The knowable is the sustainer, annihilator, and creator of all beings.

Intent - The Parabrahma, even though it seems divided in all beings, in reality, is existent undivided. It is impartite. Though there are distinctions between a pot and a cloth or a pot and a hut, the mutual distinctions are only in terms of form. They are all with mutual material distinctions. Yet, there is only one Parabrahma pervading with its power behind all those material distinctions. There is no distinction of anyone in the existent common in all. In it, they are all in oneness. Just as one wave is distinct from another wave, but water, none have a difference; all separate beings with their relationship cannot divide that Parabrahma. With its relationship, just as the dream world cannot divide the awake world, all beings by their relationship cannot divide the Parabrahma. Thus, the Parabrahma is depicted as being devoid of material distinctions.

Creation, sustentation, and destruction of all beings happen on the dependence of that knowable Parabrahma. Just as the creation, existence, and merger of a delusional and imagined snake happen on the reliance of a rope, the rope "is as is" before, middle, and after, in the same way, at the beginning, middle, and end of all beings, the Parabrahma is existent immovably in the past, present, and future. So, it is devoid of time differentiation as well. Thus, the Parabrahma is articulated as existent in an undivided form devoid of the threefold time, space, and material distinctions.

(Being present everywhere, if it does not become visible, is It darkness? With such doubt in mind, Bhagavāna says -)

ज्योतिषामपि तज्ज्योतिस्तमस: परमुच्यते |
ज्ञानं ज्ञेयं ज्ञानगम्यं हृदि सर्वस्य विष्ठितम् || BG 13.17 ||

तत् - That (Parabrahma) ; परम् - is beyond (dissociated from) ; तमसः - darkness (Māyā) ; अपि - and ; उच्यते - is said to be ; ज्योतिः - the light ; ज्योतिषाम् - of all lights. ; विष्ठितम् - Existent in ; सर्वस्य - everyone's ; हृदि - heart, (it illuminates) ; ज्ञानम् - intuitive knowledge ; ज्ञेयम् - and the knowable objects of knowledge. ; ज्ञानगम्यम् - (It is only) attainable by knowledge (of the Truth).

That Parabrahma is beyond darkness and is said to be the light of all lights. Existent in everyone's heart, it illuminates intuitive knowledge and the knowable objects of knowledge. It is only attainable by knowledge.

Intent - In the previous verse, the Parabrahma is described as the "existent" devoid of time, space, and material limitations. Now it is described in the conscious form. The Parabrahma is the light of the lights of the sun, moon, and fire. That is to say, the sun, the moon, or fire have no light of their own. Inanimate as they are, they are all illuminated by the light of the Parabrahma, just as a piece of iron itself is inanimate, yet the light of the fire appears with light. The Parabrahma is beyond darkness (Tamas). It is dissociated from ignorance and Māyā and is the one to illuminate them. Here, knowledge means intuitive knowledge (वृत्ति-ज्ञान, Vṛtti-Jñāna), and the knowable objects of knowledge (the knowable phenomenal world) are illuminated by it. In all hearts, it is existent in the form of the Ātmā, and only through the realized knowledge of the Ātmā, it can be attained.

(Summarizing the aforementioned, Bhagavāna says -

इति क्षेत्रं तथा ज्ञानं ज्ञेयं चोक्तं समासत: |
मद्भक्त एतद्विज्ञाय मद्भावायोपपद्यते || BG 13.18 ||

इति - Thus, ; क्षेत्रम् - the field ; तथा - and ; ज्ञानम् - knowledge ; च - and ; ज्ञेयम् - the knowable Parabrahma ; समासतः - (is) briefly ; उक्तम् - set forth. ; विज्ञाय - Knowing ; एतत् - this, ; मत्-भक्तः - My devotee ; उपपद्यते - attains ; मत्-भावाय - My form.

Thus, the field, knowledge, and the knowable Parabrahma is briefly set forth. Knowing this, My devotee attains My form.

Intent - This way, the field is in the form of the body (verses BG 13.5 - BG 13.6), knowledge (verses BG 13.7 - BG 13. 11), and knowable Parabrahma (verses BG 13.12 - BG 13.17) are described. My devotee endowed with the means described in the verses (BG 13.7 - BG 13.11) with true direct intuitive knowledge attains My form. Elaborating, "The entire adjunct-form phenomenal world is the field. It is insentient, transformable, and insignificant and has no power. The field-knower is in the form of Real-Conscious-Bliss. It does not transform by the transformations of the field, and though in all transformations its power is existent, it is dissociated from all of them." With true direct intuitive knowledge, "I am the power in all fields, and dissociated from all, that field-knower Ātmā, I alone am" My devotee attains My form; that is, has union with oneness in Me.

(The knowledge of the field and the field-knower that is described previously, the same is described in the form of Prakṛti and the Puruṣa -)

प्रकृतिं पुरुषं चैव विद्ध्यनादी उभावपि |
विकारांश्च गुणांश्चैव विद्धि प्रकृतिसम्भवान् || BG 13.19 ||

विद्धि - Know ; उभौ - both ; प्रकृतिम् - Prakṛti ; च - and ; पुरुषम् - the Puruṣa ; एव - to be ; अनादी - beginningless. ; च - And, ; अपि - also ; विद्धि - know ; विकारान् - the transformations ; च - and ; गुणान् - the constituents ; प्रकृति-सम्भवान् - are born of Prakṛti ; एव - only.

Know both Prakṛti and the Puruṣa to be beginningless. Also, know the transformations and the constituents are born of Prakṛti.

Intent - The term beginningless (अनादि, Anādi) means not created, that which is without creation and so unborn and thus beginningless. Among the two, the Puruṣa being ever, unborn, and imperishable is beginningless, and Prakṛti, a perception in the Puruṣa, is beginningless like a snake in the rope. In the Puruṣa, this Prakṛti is not born by some initiation and result, it is a perception burst, so it is delusional only, unreal, and insentient. That is how both Prakṛti and the Puruṣa are depicted as beginningless. Contrary to the above, if both are believed to be beginningless from being ever, unborn and imperishable, then it is impossible. Two things of equal beingness and, thus, power are bound by space, time, and material. Therefore, both are perishable and so cannot be beginningless. The Puruṣa is existent, immovable, and immutable, and all constituents and transformations are only the results of Prakṛti. The entire world results from Prakṛti and the Vivarta of the conscious Puruṣa. **It should be kept in mind that with the imagined relationship with Prakṛti, the "conscious (Cetana)" is named the "Puruṣa."** Through knowledge, upon the determination of the absence of this imagined relationship, it is only the pure conscious element.

(Creation of the world occurs through the mutual relationship of Prakṛti and the Puruṣa. Regarding that, to whatever degree both are causal, is next described -)

कार्यकरणकर्तृत्वे हेतुः प्रकृतिरुच्यते |
पुरुषः सुखदुःखानां भोक्तृत्वे हेतुरुच्यते || BG 13.20 ||

प्रकृति - Prakṛti ; उच्यते - is said to be ; हेतुः - the cause of ; कार्य - actions, ; करण - instruments (in the form of the body, senses, and others), ; कर्तृत्वे - (and) doership. ; पुरुषः - The Puruṣa (bound with Prakṛti) ; उच्यते - is said to be ; हेतुः - the cause ; भोक्तृत्वे - of the experience ; सुखदुःखानाम् - of pleasure and pain.

Prakṛti is the cause of actions, instruments, and doership. The Puruṣa is said to be the cause of the experience of pleasure and pain.

Intent - The great elements (earth, water, fire, wind, and space) and produced from them the gross body, the phenomenal world, and the five objects of senses (smell, taste, form, touch, and sound) are the work (Kārya). The ten senses, mind, intellect, and ego are the instruments (Karaṇa). Prakṛti is the doer, the material cause of actions and instruments. It is the cause of actions, instruments, and doership. Without Prakṛti, the materialization of actions and instruments is impossible. That is why Prakṛti is described as the cause of actions and instruments. At the same time, the Puruṣa is the cause of experiencing pleasure and pain. Without the Puruṣa, it is impossible to experience pleasure and pain, so the Puruṣa is described as the cause of pleasure and pain.

Just as the staff of a king produces for his enjoyment - palaces, gardens, and other enjoyment locations, delicious cuisines and sweets and other enjoyment substances, and knives, forks, spoons, plates, and other instruments for enjoyment; in the same way, Prakṛti instantaneously creates enjoyment location, enjoyable and instrumental phenomenal world for the enjoyment of the Puruṣa. In this, there is not an iota of doership of the Puruṣa. The Puruṣa is causal, only to the extent of experiencing pleasure and pain through the Prakṛti-created substances. Just as a person enjoys milk or tea with a cup, the Puruṣa enjoys the entire phenomenal world through the body, senses, mind, and intellect. The body, senses, mind, and intellect being the instruments of enjoyment are Karaṇa. The phenomenal world of activities with smell, taste, form, touch, and sound in the five sense objects is to be enjoyed. The gross body is the enjoyment location. Prakṛti is the creator of all actions and instruments, and the only purpose for the creation is for this Puruṣa to taste the fruits of his sown seeds of Karma in the form of pleasure and pain. Thus, the purpose of the Puruṣa is only to taste the fruits.

In the earlier verse, it is stated that the entire effort of Prakṛti is for the experience of the Puruṣa only. **The terms Puruṣa, Jīva, Jīvātmā, and field-knower are synonymous. In essence, they mean doer-experiencer with the sense of I-ness in the body (देहाभिमानी कर्ता-भोक्ता, Dehābhimānī Kartā-Bhoktā). In the absence of the doer-experiencer notion, meaning eliminating the imagined relationship with Prakṛti, the Puruṣa is the pure "conscious," the supreme imperishable Reality, the supreme Self, the supreme Brahman, the Parabrahma.**

(Now, a doubt arises, why does the Puruṣa experience pleasure and pain and suffer transmigration? The doubt is resolved next -)

पुरुष: प्रकृतिस्थो हि भुङ्क्ते प्रकृतिजान्गुणान् |
कारणं गुणसङ्गोऽस्य सदसद्योनिजन्मसु || BG 13.21 ||

पुरुष: - The Puruṣa ; प्रकृतिस्थ: - seated in Prakṛti ; भुङ्क्ते - experiences ; गुणान् - the constituents ; प्रकृतिजान् - born of Prakṛti. ; गुणसङ्ग: - Attachment to the constituents ; हि - is only ; कारणम् - the cause ; अस्य - of his ; जन्मसु - birth ; सदसद्योनि - in superior and inferior wombs.

The Puruṣa seated in Prakṛti experiences the constituents born of Prakṛti. Attachment to the constituents is only the cause of his birth in superior and inferior wombs.

Intent - The Puruṣa being beginningless, unborn, and imperishable by his nature, is ever-unchanged (नित्य-निर्विकार, Nitya-Nirvikāra). In such a state, the relationship of a transient thing, like Prakṛti, with an ever-unchanged thing, and the bondage of experiencing pleasure and pain of that ever-unchanged due to the relationship with that transient thing, is not due to any supreme objective but is imaginary and born of ignorance. Only because of the ignorance of his true nature, the Puruṣa seated in Prakṛti, assuming a sense of oneness with Prakṛti and imagining the attributes and effects of Prakṛti in himself, has acquired bondage with Prakṛti and thus has become just like Prakṛti. In essence, it has mistakenly taken Prakṛti as himself. Pleasure and pain, attachment, and aversion are all the works of the constituents of Prakṛti. However, assuming them in himself, he experiences, "I am happy, I am unhappy, I am confused, I am wise, and so on." The doership of actions are in the body, mind, and intellect (which are the effects of the constituents of Prakṛti); however, mistakenly assuming the entire doership of the body, mind, and intellect in himself, has started to see, "I am awake, I am asleep, I am eating, I am drinking, I am listening, I am seeing, I am resolving" and other such forms in itself. The cause for birth in superior and inferior wombs is ignorance - the association and attachment of doership and enjoyership with the constituents of Prakṛti. Just as a wealthy person in a dream state sees himself as a pauper and suffers the consequences born from there, in the same way, the Puruṣa, in the drunken stupor of ignorance, has become bonded to Prakṛti. The Puruṣa assuming doership of the body and senses in himself, tied to the rules of Prakṛti, through good and bad deeds, roams around in superior and inferior wombs and thus experiences pleasure and pain.

(However, in reality, through knowledge, with the removal of ignorance -)

उपद्रष्टानुमन्ता च भर्ता भोक्ता महेश्वरः |
परमात्मेति चाप्युक्तो देहेऽस्मिन्पुरुषः परः || BG 13.22 ||

पुरुषः - The Puruṣa ; अस्मिन् - (seated in) this ; देहे - body ; अपि - (is) indeed ; परः - unassociated (with Prakṛti) ; च - and ; इति - as such ; उक्तः- is said to be ; उपद्रष्टा - the Close Observer, ; अनुमन्ता - the Sanctioner, ; भर्ता - the Sustainer, ; भोक्ता - the Experiencer, ; महेश्वरः - the Maheśvara, ; च - and ; परमात्मा - the Paramātmā.

Puruṣa seated in the body is unassociated with Prakṛti and is said to be the Close Observer, the Sanctioner, the Sustainer, the Experiencer, the Maheśvara, and the Paramātmā.

Intent - In the previous verse, it is shown that the association with Prakṛti and the bondage to experiences for the Puruṣa are only ignorance born, not always but only transitory, and not real but only imaginary. If this association is deemed true, then the bondage of experience for the Puruṣa has to remain forever. If the bondage is forever, then liberation is impossible. Liberation instruments such as preceptors and scriptures will be without any purpose, and the effort towards liberation will be unfruitful. However, in reality, it is not so. He gets into delusional bondage of birth and death because of the ignorance of his true nature and assuming doership and enjoyership of Prakṛti in himself. Just as an illusory snake in a rope does not make the rope venomous, the water of a desert mirage does not wet the desert; imagined association with an imagined Prakṛti, the Puruṣa, is not bound to the supreme objective. With knowledge, upon the removal of ignorance, the Puruṣa is neither a doer nor an enjoyer. However, staying extremely close to the activities of Prakṛti - meaning the body, senses, mind, and intellect, which are the instruments for actions and enjoyments, and sitting dissociated in them, himself not doing anything, just being an observer, the Puruṣa is said to be the Close Observer (उपद्रष्टा, Upadraṣṭā), just as someone proficient in oblation science (Yajña-Vidyā) not performing oblations himself, just observes merits and faults neutrally in the activities of oblations performed by family priests and institutors of oblations. Without being active in Prakṛti, meaning not being active in the activities of the conscience and the senses, and seen as agreeable, that is, being a witness of the activities of the conscience and not ever preventing it, thereby providing real sanction, the Puruṣa is said to be the Sanctioner (अनुमन्ता, Anumantā), just as in his dance performance a lead actor provides beats to an actress giving his approval.

With his own power, holding and sustaining the body and senses, the Puruṣa is said to be the Sustainer (भर्ता, Bhartā). Sense objects related dispositions in the form of pleasure and pain of the conscience seem to be grasped through the perception of the Puruṣa. Instincts in the form of "I am happy, I am unhappy" happen only because of the proximity of the Puruṣa and so the term Bhartā, Sustainer. With some thought, one can see that the terms Observer, Sanctioner, Sustainer, and Experiencer are applied to the activities of Prakṛti because of the proximity of the witnessing Puruṣa. In reality, the Puruṣa being the master of Brahmā and others, is called the Great Supreme Lord (महेश्वर, Maheśvara, Lord Śiva) and is the Ātmā of all movable and immovable beings and thus with own pure Saccidānanda form is called the supreme Self (परमात्मा, Paramātmā). Just as with the adjuncts of the pot, there is no distinction and limitation of the space. In the same manner with the adjunct of bodies, there cannot be any distinction and limitation of the Puruṣa. It is ever and devoid of distinctions and limitations in its true nature.

{Enunciating fruit of this discernment, Bhagavāna concludes this subject -}

य एवं वेत्ति पुरुषं प्रकृतिं च गुणैः सह |
सर्वथा वर्तमानोऽपि न स भूयोऽभिजायते || BG 13.23 ||

सः - One ; यः - who ; एवम् - thus ; वेत्ति - knows ; पुरुषम् - the Puruṣa ; च - and ; प्रकृतिम् - Prakṛti ; गुणैः सह - with its constituents, ; अपि - (because of the power of this knowledge) though ; वर्तमानः - engaged in activity ; सर्वथा - in all ways ; न - is not ; अभिजायते - born ; भूयः - again.

One who thus knows the Puruṣa and Prakṛti with its constituents, though engaged in activity in all ways, is not born again.

Intent - One who truly knows, "The entire phenomenal world of activities and the instruments such as the body, senses, mind, and intellect are only the work of Prakṛti, and by the imagined relationship with Prakṛti, the constituents, actions, birth, and others of Prakṛti are delusionally perceived in the Puruṣa; in reality, the Puruṣa is untouched by them. Just as in a mirror, notwithstanding the perception of faces, the mirror itself is not touched by the dirt in the form of the faces; in the same fashion, the Puruṣa is untainted by the constituents and activities of Prakṛti. That witnessing Puruṣa (Ātmā) I am." Separate from Prakṛti, one who directly knows his true witnessing form, such a person engaged in activities in all ways is free and is not born again. The above verse states that those who have truly known the true nature of Prakṛti and the Puruṣa, such knowers of the Truth, no matter how they conduct themselves, are not reborn and bound by any scriptural injunctions.

(How does such a knower of the Truth (Tattva-Vettā) behave? That is articulated next -)

ध्यानेनात्मनि पश्यन्ति केचिदात्मानमात्मना |
अन्ये साङ् ख्येन योगेन कर्मयोगेन चापरे || BG 13.24 ||

केचित् - Some ; पश्यन्ति - perceive ; आत्मानम् - the Self ; आत्मनि - seated in the heart ; आत्मना - by pure and subtle intellect ; ध्यानेन - with meditation, ; अन्ये - others ; साङ्ख्येन - with Sāṅkhya- ; योगेन - Yoga, ; च - and ; अपरे - others ; कर्म-योगेन - with Karma-Yoga

Some perceive the Self seated in the heart by pure and subtle intellect with meditation, others with Sāṅkhya-Yoga, and others with Karma-Yoga.

Intent - Following the above manner, those knowers with direct experience have transcendentally dissociated the constituents and effects of Prakṛti from their Ātmā; they are not subject to scriptural injunctions and are free even while alive. As long as they are alive and have not left the body, they remain engaged in activities consistent with their physical and mental nature, though not by any duty. Among them, some with the potency of Sattvaguṇa, free from all activities, like Śrī Śukadeva, are absorbed in meditation and Samādhī (समाधी, oneness with the Ātmā) and melting all inner-dispositions nourish only inner-disposition of oneness in the Ātmā (Ātmākāra-Vṛtti). Meditation means one-pointed thought after withdrawing the mind and the sense-organs (like the ears from sound) and fixing the mind on the inner-self with a constant thought in an unbroken stream to perceive the Ātmā. Some, like Sage Yājñavalkya, abandoning activities remain absorbed in renunciation and, through Sāṅkhya-Yoga in the form of analytic thought, perceive the Ātmā through the pure, subtle intellect. Others like King Janaka, engaging their body and senses in all worldly dealings without any duty or doership through Karma-Yoga, see all those activities only as miracles of their own witnessing Ātmā. Though commensurate with Prārabdha (प्रारब्ध),[117]the behavior of all these realized persons is distinct. Yet by resolving these ever-free do not see any duty in their own Ātmā, and their activities remain free from grasping and relinquishing intellect like a child, just as a playtime.

From the above, one ought to not deem that for a seeker, meditation, Sāṅkhya, and Karma-Yoga are articulated as three independent paths or means for Self-Realization (आत्म-साक्षात्कार, Ātma-Sākṣātkāra, attaining union with oneness in the Supreme Being). That is so because Self-Realization is only possible through the inner disposition of oneness in the Ātmā, and such disposition can only happen through analytical thinking. Through Karma or meditation, it is impossible for the inner disposition to become one with the true nature of the Ātmā, so these three cannot be independent paths for Self-Realization. This verse is not meant for a seeker but is only for observing the varied behavior of the realized (Jñānī). Karma-Yoga, by its nature,

[117] Prārabdha (प्रारब्ध) means that portion of accumulated past actions now ready to materialize or to be experienced.

cannot be an independent path for Self-Realization. Meditation can be done only of something different from oneself; one cannot be an object of meditation. That is why, Ātmā being its true nature, cannot be something to be meditated on (Dhyeya), but as the story of the "Daśama Puruṣa" depicted in the footnote of the Intent of BG 2.29, can only be the one that ought to be known (Jñeya).

(Those who have not known as provided in the previous verse and are seekers, their description is provided next -)

अन्ये त्वेवमजानन्त: श्रुत्वान्येभ्य उपासते |
तेऽपि चातितरन्त्येव मृत्युं श्रुतिपरायणा: || BG 13.25 ||

तु - However, ; अजानन्तः - not knowing ; एवम् - thus, ; अन्ये - others ; उपासते - worship ; श्रुत्वा - hearing ; अन्येभ्यः - from others (about the Self). ; च - And ; श्रुति-परायणाः - absorbed in hearing, ; ते - they ; अपि - also (on their time) ; अतितरन्ति - overcome ; मृत्युम् - death ; एव - indeed.

However, not knowing thus, others worship hearing from others about the Self. Absorbed in hearing, they also overcome death.

Intent - Other seekers, not knowing that the Ātmā is dissociated from the entire family of body and others of Prakṛti, and as such hearing from other knowers of the Truth and scriptures, with their instructed means and tactics, become ready for the search for the Ātmā. With faith and readiness, they who are endowed with means, becoming absorbed in listening and truly realizing their Ātmā as dissociated and as a witness-observer, at some point in time, will cross over the mortal ocean of the phenomenal world.

(Now, until the end of the chapter, the Truth above is again stated -)

यावत्सञ्जायते किञ्चित्सत्वं स्थावरजङ्गमम् |
क्षेत्रक्षेत्रज्ञसंयोगात्तद्विद्धि भरतर्षभ || BG 13.26 ||

भरतर्षभ - Hey Bharatarṣabha (Arjuna)! ; यावत् किञ्चित् - Whatever ; सत्त्वम् - being ; सञ्जायते - is born, ; स्थावर-जङ्गमम् - (either) stationary or moving, ; विद्धि - know ; तत् - it ; संयोगात् - to be due to the union of ; क्षेत्र - the field and ; क्षेत्रज्ञ - the field-knower.

Hey Arjuna! Whatever being is born, either stationary or moving, know it to be due to the union of the field and the field-knower.

Intent - Only through the union of the field and the field-knower, movable and immovable beings are created. However, a union can happen only between two substances of equal Reality. The union of dissimilar substances cannot ever happen. Just as the fire of a dream cannot even touch the conscious body, the union of dissimilar substances such as the field (Prakṛti) and the field-knower (Puruṣa) is impossible. The field is a substance of ordinary or phenomenal Reality, but the field-knower has transcendental Reality beyond time and space. Here, the intention is that just as in support of a rope, an imagined snake is perceived, in the same way, in support of the conscious field-knower, the insentient, and thus imagined field and its transformations are perceived. The field-knower, immovably existent as the underlying support, provides a perception of all superimposed effects. Their union is not transcendental but imaginary. Due to the lack of discriminative knowledge of the field and the field-knower, the union in question is an instance of superimposition of the two and their constituents, and both are essentially different. Such union produces all movable and immovable beings of the phenomenal world.

समं सर्वेषु भूतेषु तिष्ठन्तं परमेश्वरम् |
विनश्यत्स्वविनश्यन्तं य: पश्यति स पश्यति || BG 13.27 ||

सः - He, ; यः - who ; पश्यति - sees ; अविनश्यन्तम् - the unperishable ; परमेश्वरम् - Supreme Lord ; समम् - equally ; तिष्ठन्तम् - existent ; सर्वेषु - in all ; विनश्यत्सु - perishable ; भूतेषु - beings, ; पश्यति - sees (truly).

He, who sees the unperishable Supreme Lord equally existent in all perishable beings, sees truly.

Intent - All beings, having the attribute of birth and death, are dissimilar by their nature. In all transformations of these dissimilar beings, one who sees the unperishable Supreme Lord as one unmodifiable, unmovable, and immutable he truly sees. Despite it being existent in all transformations, it is dissociated from its underlying support form, and one who knows the existent-conscious separate from the body as his own Ātmā is a true knower; he is a true seer.

समं पश्यन्हि सर्वत्र समवस्थितमीश्वरम् |
न हिनस्त्यात्मनात्मानं ततो याति परां गतिम् || BG 13.28 ||

हि - Indeed, ; पश्यन् - beholding ; समं - the same ; ईश्वरम् - Lord ; समवस्थितम् - equally existent ; सर्वत्र - everywhere, ; न - (one does) not ; हिनस्ति - injure ; आत्मानम् - the Self ; आत्मना - by the self ; ततः - and thus ; याति - attains ; पराम् - the supreme ; गतिम् - goal.

Indeed, beholding the Lord equally existent everywhere, one does not injure the Self by the self and thus attains the supreme goal.

Intent - Such a person sees the Lord, devoid of all dissimilarities, existent equally everywhere, like the space. With this true perspective, he does not injure his Ātmā, so he attains the highest goal. Grasping it otherwise, that is deeming the pure conscious Ātmā devoid of all distinctions and limitations, as his body is the root of all sins and the origin of the creation of all pain and suffering in the form of birth and death. One who has not known his Ātmā; is the injurer of his Ātmā. However, that knower of the truth who has the direct intuitive transcendental realization of the Ātmā perceives in the phenomenal world of dissimilar bodies the Lord exists equally everywhere as his true nature. Thus, he attains the supreme goal - liberation with this true perspective.

प्रकृत्यैव च कर्माणि क्रियमाणानि सर्वशः |
यः पश्यति तथात्मानमकर्तारं स पश्यति || BG 13.29 ||

च - Additionally, ; सः - He ; यः - who ; पश्यति - sees ; कर्माणि - actions ; सर्वशः - on all sides ; एव - are solely ; क्रियमाणानि - done ; प्रकृत्या - by Prakṛti, ; तथा - and ; आत्मानम् - the Self, ; अकर्तारम् - as a non-doer, ; पश्यति - sees (the Truth).

He who sees actions on all sides are solely done by Prakṛti, and the Self, as a non-doer, sees the Truth.

Intent - In reality, the effects or transformations of Prakṛti, that is, the Mahat,[118]ego, mind, and sense-organs are the ones engaged in action, but due to ignorance, the Puruṣa with the sense of oneness with Prakṛti assumes her dealings in himself and deems "I am a doer." He finds himself in the bondage of such pains as birth and death with such actual perspective. In contrast, a person with his analytic vision leaving the dealings and actions of Prakṛti on herself and getting rid of doership-sentiment remains situated as a witness; such a person becomes free from the pains of birth and death. Liberation is dependent on this true perspective. That is why such a seer-knower is indeed a true seer, and he is free. Prakṛti, Māyā, Avidyā, Ajñāna are synonymous.

यदा भूतपृथग्भावमेकस्थमनुपश्यति |
तत एव च विस्तारं ब्रह्म सम्पद्यते तदा || BG 13.30 ||

यदा - When (one) ; अनुपश्यति - perceives ; भूत-पृथक्-भावम् - a diverse variety of beings ; एकस्थम् - existent in one (supreme Self) ; च - and ; ततः - from Whom ; एव - alone ; विस्तारम् - (plurality) is spreading, ; तदा - then ; सम्पद्यते - he becomes ; ब्रह्म - the Brahman.

---

[118] Mahat (महत्) means the great element intellect. Vedānta refers it to be the first "great element" evolved out of the union of Prakṛti and the Puruṣa.

When one perceives a diverse variety of beings existent in one supreme Self and from Whom plurality is spreading, he becomes the Brahman.

Intent - Just as varied gold ornaments are existent in gold, and the creation and destruction of those ornaments, it is only gold, only in the middle, they are with name-form distinctions such as gold-ring or gold-necklace. However, in their true nature, they are nothing but gold. In the same way, the five great elements and the entire phenomenal world created by the great elements (which is the transformation of Prakṛti), though holding varied name forms like pot, cloth, hut, and so forth, but in all of their beginning and end only one Asti-Bhāti-Priya Being is seated. In the middle, though they hold varied name forms, yet in the root of all, devoid of all distinctions, the one existent-conscious is playing the game. They are all proceeding from the one Supreme Being, and in all of them, there is only one Supreme Being. In all these varied effects, he does not see various causes. He knows only one Supreme Being in all of these diverse effects and causes. Such a person knows his Ātmā truly, and having achieved the Brahman-form, he becomes the Brahman.

(Deeming one Ātmā in all bodies, there may be a doubt that it may have a relationship with the faults of all, Bhagavāna states -)

अनादित्वान्निर्गुणत्वात्परमात्मायमव्ययः |
शरीरस्थोऽपि कौन्तेय न करोति न लिप्यते || BG 13.31 ||

कौन्तेय - Hey Kaunteya (Arjuna)! ; अपि - Though ; शरीरस्थः - existent in the body, अयम् - this ; अनादित्वात् - beginningless, ; निर्गुणत्वात् - attributeless, ; अव्ययः - (and) imperishable ; परमात्मा - supreme Self ; न - neither ; करोति - acts ; न - nor ; लिप्यते - is stained.

Hey Arjuna! Though existent in the body, the beginningless, attributeless, and imperishable supreme Self neither acts nor is stained.

Intent - In the stainlessness of the Supreme Being, two causes are articulated, one beginningless and the other attributeless. One that has a cause and is created or born is said to have a beginning (सादि, Sādi). Such substances with a beginning are bound by space, time, and material, and such bounded substances are always with attributes. In contrast, the Supreme Being, being eternal and unborn, does not have any cause and is "सर्व परिच्छेद विनिर्मुक्त गुणातीत, devoid of all limitations, beyond the reach of the constituents" and thus unborn and imperishable. That is why, even though it exists in all bodies, it neither acts nor is stained. To act and to be stained is only in substances that are "सादि सगुण एवम् परिच्छिन्न, having a beginning, with the constituents and thus limited." In substances that are "अनादि निर्गुण व अपरिच्छिन्न, beginningless attributeless and unlimited," there is neither any effect nor any stain.

(On this subject, Bhagavāna provides an example -)

यथा सर्वगतं सौक्ष्म्यादाकाशं नोपलिप्यते |
सर्वत्रावस्थितो देहे तथात्मा नोपलिप्यते || BG 13.32 ||

यथा - Just as ; सर्वगतम् - the all-pervading ; आकाशम् - space ; न - is not ; उपलिप्यते - stained ; सौक्ष्म्यात् - due to its subtlety (by anyone), ; तथा - so is ; आत्मा - the Self, ; अवस्थितः - present ; सर्वत्र - everywhere ; देहे - in the body, ; न - not ; उपलिप्यते - stained.

Just as the all-pervading space is not stained due to its subtlety, so is the Self, present everywhere in the body, not stained.

Intent - Just as the space is ubiquitous and subtle, on its dependence, the entire phenomenal world of pots and pans is created. Without the subtle space, the creation of the phenomenal world is impossible. Again, the destruction of the phenomenal world also happens on the dependence on space. However, with the creation and the destruction of the phenomenal world, there is no creation and destruction of space.

The space is unstained in that creation and destruction. In the same manner, pervading everywhere in all bodies, the Ātmā is unstained by the changes of the body, notwithstanding the fruition of all those changes happens on the dependence of the Ātmā.

यथा प्रकाशयत्येक: कृत्स्नं लोकमिमं रवि: |
क्षेत्रं क्षेत्री तथा कृत्स्नं प्रकाशयति भारत || BG 13.33 ||

भारत - Hey Bhārata (Arjuna)! ; यथा - Just as ; एकः - the one ; रविः - sun ; प्रकाशयति - illuminates ; इमम् - this ; कृत्स्नम् - entire ; लोकम् - world, ; तथा - so does ; क्षेत्री - the field's Owner (the Self) ; प्रकाशयति - illuminate ; कृत्स्नम् - the entire ; क्षेत्रम् - field (bodies).

Hey Arjuna! Just as the one sun illuminates this entire world, so does the field's Owner illuminate the entire field.

Intent - Just as the sun illuminates the entire world of good and bad materials and their merits and demerits, and yet it does not get stained, in the same manner, the Ātmā in the form of the field-knower, with its light, illuminates the great elements, ego, and others (as stated in the verses BG 12.5 and 12.6) to the smaller of the smallest, the entire field and its transformations. Still, it remains unstained "is as is."

(The entire essence of the chapter is provided in the last verse -)

क्षेत्रक्षेत्रज्ञयोरेवमन्तरं ज्ञानचक्षुषा |
भूतप्रकृतिमोक्षं च ये विदुर्यान्ति ते परम् || BG 13.34 ||

एवम् - Thus, ; ते - those ; ये - who ; विदुः - perceive, ; ज्ञान-चक्षुषा - with the eye of knowledge, ; अन्तरम् - the difference between ; क्षेत्र-क्षेत्रज्ञयोः - the field and the field-knower ; च - and ; भूत-प्रकृति-मोक्षम् - the way of release from Prakṛti (the cause of materiality), ; यान्ति - attain ; परम् - the supreme (Status).

Those who perceive, with the eye of knowledge, the difference between the field and the field-knower and the way of release from Prakṛti, the cause of materiality, attain the supreme Status.

Intent - Through the spiritual guidance of a preceptor and scriptures described above, a person who directly experiences the difference between the field and the field-knower that the perceptible field is without its existence and like a snake in a rope is illusorily perceived on the dependence of the field-knower. With the wisdom that provides a complete and clear distinction between real and unreal, good and bad, they who, in essence, can discriminate own Ātmā from the material cause Prakṛti, and knowing Prakṛti as worthless forsake it like a swan forsaking water from a mixture of milk and water, they are only the ones who attain the supreme Status, the Brahman.

From verse BG 12.26 to the end of the chapter, the terms Kṣetrajña, Parameśvara, Īśvara, Ātmā, Brahma, and Kṣetrī are used. However, there is no difference in the intended meaning with the difference in words. The meaning of all the words is only one "निर्विकार सर्वविशेष-विनिर्मुक्त सामन्य-चेतन, the unmodifiable, attributeless common-conscious."

ॐ तत्सदिति श्रीमद्भगवद्गीतासूपनिषत्सु ब्रह्मविध्यायां योगशास्त्रे

श्रीकृष्णार्जुनसम्वादे क्षेत्रक्षेत्रज्ञविभागयोगो नाम

त्रयोदशोऽध्यायः || BG 13 ||

Oṃ Tat Sat

In the Śrīmad Bhagavad Gītā Upaniṣad

The Yoga Science of the Knowledge of Self-Realization

The Discourse of Lord Śrī Kṛṣṇa and Arjuna

This Thirteenth Chapter

Yoga Named - The Yoga of the Field and the knower of the Field

Clarification

In the twelfth chapter, Bhagavāna described the process, sequence, the constituents, and results of His manifest-form worship, through which entry into the unmanifest-form is possible. In this chapter, Bhagavāna describes His unmanifest form beyond the reach of words and the mind; no one can describe it through words and speech, which is why the assignment of an adjunct with a discriminative attribute is made to describe it. Holding an adjunct of the body as the field (Kṣetra) and placed within the field is the witnessing attributeless Ātmā as the field-knower (Kṣetrajña). Just as grain is obtained only with husk, not without husk, however, the husk is abandoned once grain is procured; in the same way, one ought to search in the adjunct field (phenomenal world of the body), the grain in the form of field-knower, and then grasping the essence field-knower, ought to abandon the worthless field.

In verses BG 12.5 and 12.6, Bhagavāna briefly described the field of twenty-four elements and transformations such as desire, antipathy, et al. In it, one ought to search for the field-knower. That is, by whose power this field and its transformations are born, sustained, and annihilated, should be known as the field-knower. It is apparent that the fruition of all efforts and dealings always happens in some form of light; in darkness, no activity is possible. "अस्मिन्महामोहमये कटाहे भूतानि कालः पचति, in this cauldron of the greatly enchanted phenomenal world, in whose light, time devours beings," that should be known as the field-knower. Even in the absence of the insentient light of the sun, one who remains illuminated, and both darkness and light are illuminated by whom, such unlost existent common in all is self-illuminated, that is, known as the field-knower. The insentient light of the sun does not illuminate the true nature of a substance; all it does is oppose the darkness that shrouds the substance. However, the existent light illuminating the substance, remaining behind in the material space, illuminates both the existence and non-existence of the substance, which is knowable in the form of the field-knower.

The field-knower is the Ātmā of all beings. It is not attained by action (Kriyā-Sādhya). It is only attained by knowledge (Jñāna-Sādhya). Action achieved goal can be the only one that is separate from one; however, that field-knower is its own Ātmā and is the underlying support of the paltry ego. Without completely removing this sheath-form ego from its root, attainment of that field-knower is impossible. Removal of ego is not possible by actions such as blows of truncheon or sticks. Only through knowledge of the underlying support field-knower is its removal possible, just as removing an illusory snake is only possible with the direct knowledge of the rope. Though the complete removal of this paltry ego is only through knowledge of the underlying support (the field-knower-knowledge), as long as it is in a developed state and not controlled, it will not allow its opponent, the knowledge, to grow. Like enemies and disease, they cannot perish right at the root as long as they are robust. First, its control is necessary, and then only it can be uprooted.

The ego must be controlled first. That is why Bhagavāna articulated those means (Sādhana) through which it can be controlled, and thus knowledge can take hold. Being helpful in knowledge, the means provided in the verses (BG 13.7 - BG 13.11) are defined as knowledge. Nourishing this ego-form snake are conceit, hypocrisy, and violence, which, while eating, are delicious but are indeed poisonous. Forsaking conceit, hypocrisy, and violence and replacing them with humility, unostentatiousness, and non-violence, a pungent meal is served so that accumulated poison can melt away. At the same time, it is necessary to be able to forgive those who have offended us. We ought to have mental and verbal simplicity and an absence of crookedness in conduct, such as eating, drinking, clothing and recreation. Service with the body, mind, and wealth of the preceptor, not only his body but also his words, ought to be worshipped. That is necessary for developing faith, and indeed faith is a supreme means of achieving knowledge. Cleanliness both within and outside, and through control of the mind, restraint of the senses to keep the mind and the senses under check, so that, unlike an uncontrolled horse, it would not drop the living being in the worldly ditch. Aversion to the sense objects, perceiving evil and reflecting on the loss of the attributes of life (such as loss of mobility, the decline in intellectual power, enfeeblement of energy, and many other pains of old age), and perceiving evil and reflecting on pain of the various diseases in the body. Lack of excessive love towards wife, children, or abode and abandonment of excessive attachment and mineness in desired objects and remaining even-minded in acquiring desired and undesired. Undivided-unwavering devotion to the manifest form (Bhagavāna Vāsudeva), residing in solitary places like forests, riverbanks, and temples that are naturally pure or are made pure by cleaning and are free from snakes, tigers, and other animals and insects. The constant pursuit of spiritual knowledge, perception of the aim of true knowledge - all these eighteen means being the cause of knowledge are said to be knowledge. What is other than that is ignorance. Through discernment (Viveka), dispassion (Vairāgya), the sixfold virtues (Ṣaṭ-Sampatti) such as control of the mind and restraint of the senses, controlling the ego, Bhagavāna commended to move the flow of the mind towards seeking the Ātmā.

In addition, in the verses (BG 13.12 - BG 13.18), Bhagavāna described the knowable field-knower supreme Self (the Parabrahma) to be attained through the narrated means and analytic thinking. Moreover, He explained that the Parabrahma being beyond the range of words and the mind could neither be called existent nor non-existent. The ambrosiac liberation can only be attained by knowing it. Not being able to be reached by words such as existent or non-existent, it should not be assumed that the Parabrahma is null; that it is not there at all. However, it has hands, feet, eyes, heads, mouths, and ears from all sides. In all of them, it is pervaded. This does not mean that the Parabrahma has adjuncts of hands, feet, eyes, heads, mouth, and ears. That is not so. Indeed, it is the one to illuminate them with its brilliance. It is beyond the reach of the senses and the constituents. The knowable field-knower is omnipresent, unassociated with all, free from time, space, and material limitations, the Real-Conscious-Bliss. Describing the field, the field-knower, and the true nature of knowledge, Bhagavāna said, "My devotee knowing it, becomes one with Me."

After that, knowledge is articulated in terms of Prakṛti and the Puruṣa from verses (BG 13.19 - BG 13.23). It is shown that whatever is perceived in the phenomenal world in terms of the constituents (Guṇa) and transformations (Vikāra) are all works of Prakṛti. Actions (Kārya), instruments (Karaṇa), and in the form of the doer (Kartā), whatever is grasped, in all of them, the cause is Prakṛti. However, with an ignorance-born sense of oneness with Prakṛti, the Puruṣa experiences Prakṛti-born constituents. Only because of the association with these constituents acquires births in superior and inferior wombs. In reality, all this is the morass of ignorance. Through knowledge, with the removal of ignorance, the Puruṣa in witness-form is the Close Observer (Upadraṣṭā), the Sanctioner (Anumantā), with its power is the Sustainer (Bhartā) of the entire world, existent in the body is dissociated from it, and being the Lord of the deities is the Great Supreme Lord (Maheśvara). Bhagavāna articulating the fruit of that knowledge, said that one who, through analytic thinking, truly knows himself separate from Prakṛti, even while engaging in activities in all ways, is not reborn.

Describing the glory of knowledge and varied activities of the knower of the Truth (Tattva-Vettā Jñānī), Bhagavāna said that some perceive the Ātmā through meditation, some through Sāṅkhya Yoga - the path of renunciation, and others through Karma-Yoga - the path of activity. In other words, for those Self-Realized persons, all their efforts and activities become just a miracle of their Ātmā. However, other persons not knowing so, listening to knowers, endowed with means, engage themselves in the search for the Ātmā, such persons absorbed in hearing also, in due time with Self-Realization, cross over the ocean of death (BG 13.24 - BG 13.25).

In the end, concluding the chapter Bhagavāna said that whatever movable and immovable beings are born, know them due to the union of the field (Prakṛti) and the field-knower (Puruṣa). A true seer sees the imperishable Supreme Lord equally existent in all perishable beings dissociated and fully pervaded. That person only sees his Ātmā situated equally everywhere and so does not injure his Ātmā by himself. He does not grasp otherwise his Ātmā, and so attains the highest Status (BG 13.26 - BG 13.34).

In this chapter, to provide knowledge of the attributeless Supreme Being, Bhagavāna formulated the field (Prakṛti), the field-knower (Puruṣa), and instrumental knowledge and described His profound form, holding which one can attain oneness in that form. It is made clear that the Puruṣa experiences births in superior and inferior wombs only because of his association with the Prakṛti-born constituents and their transformations, and those associations with the constituents of Prakṛti are born of ignorance (BG 13.21). In reality, the Puruṣa is dissociated from the body and senses - all dealings of Prakṛti as a Close Observer and is the Lord of all deities (BG 13.22). In the next chapter, the constituents of Prakṛti are described, with whose association there is bondage or freedom of the Puruṣa.

CHAPTER 14

THE YOGA OF THE THREEFOLD CONSTITUENTS

{In this chapter, to articulate how the ever-free (नित्य-मुक्त, Nitya-Mukta) is bound or free, based on its relationship with the constituents of Prakṛti -}

श्रीभगवानुवाच |
परं भूय: प्रवक्ष्यामि ज्ञानानां ज्ञानमुत्तमम् |
यज्ज्ञात्वा मुनय: सर्वे परां सिद्धिमितो गता: || BG 14.1 ||
श्रीभगवान् उवाच - Śrī Bhagavān said -

भूयः - Again, ; प्रवक्ष्यामि - I shall state ; परम् - the highest ; उत्तमम् - (and) best ; ज्ञानम् - knowledge ; ज्ञानानाम् - among all forms of knowledge, ; ज्ञात्वा - mastering ; यत् - which ; सर्वे - all ; मुनयः - sages ; गताः - have attained ; पराम् - supreme ; सिद्धिम् - perfection ; इतः - after leaving the body.

Śrī Bhagavān said -

Again, I shall state the highest and the best knowledge among all forms of knowledge, mastering which all sages have attained supreme perfection after leaving the body.

Intent - The term "भूयः, again" indicates that this knowledge is described in previous chapters, and I am going to elucidate once again the highest and the best knowledge beyond which there is nothing. That being the goal of this knowledge, it is called the highest or supreme knowledge. Being endowed with the unbeatable results is called the best knowledge. On the dependence on the ever-free Ātmā, Prakṛti creates the entire phenomenal world of the bodies and the senses through transformations of the constituents. However, none of this stains the Ātmā. To truly know so is the unbeatableness compared to all worldly sacrifices and austerities. A living being can be free from the bondage of the world only with this knowledge, not by any other means. Only with this transcendental knowledge have all sages attained perfection of liberation.

(The fruit of this knowledge is described next -)

इदं ज्ञानमुपाश्रित्य मम साधर्म्यमागता: |
सर्गेऽपि नोपजायन्ते प्रलये न व्यथन्ति च || BG 14.2 ||

उपाश्रित्य - Resorting to ; इदम् - this ; ज्ञानम् - knowledge, ; आगताः - (those who) have attained ; मम - My ; साधर्म्यम् - own nature ; अपि - indeed ; न - are not ; उपजायन्ते - born ; सर्गे - at the time of the manifestation (of the world) ; च - and ; न - are not ; व्यथन्ति - distressed ; प्रलये - at the time of its dissolution.

Resorting to this knowledge, those who have attained My own nature are not born at the time of the manifestation of the world and are not distressed at the time of its dissolution.

Intent - With the power of this knowledge, released from the mortal world of birth and death, they attain union with oneness in the Supreme Being and become ever free. Even at the time of the manifestation of the world, they are not born, nor at the time of its dissolution. Even when Lord Brahmā perishes, they are not distressed and do not lapse from the state of release.

मम योनिर्महद् ब्रह्म तस्मिन्गर्भं दधाम्यहम् |
सम्भवः सर्वभूतानां ततो भवति भारत || BG 14.3 ||

भारत - Hey Bhārata (Arjuna)! ; मम - My ; योनिः - womb ; महत् ब्रह्म - is the Mahat-Brahma. ; अहम् - I ; दधामि - place ; गर्भम् - (My conscious) seed ; तस्मिन् - in it. ; ततः - Thence, (with the union of the sentient and the insentient), ; सम्भवः - the creation ; सर्व-भूतानाम् - of all beings ; भवति - materializes.

Hey Arjuna! My womb is the Mahat-Brahma. I place My conscious seed in it. Thence, the creation of all beings materializes.

Intent - Whatever transformations are perceived, all are the effects of Prakṛti, the Māyā of the Supreme Being, consisting of the three constituents. The "महत् ब्रह्म, Mahat-Brahma," the great Brahman, due to its vastness with all its effects and because it is their cause and the controller, is described as the womb (Yoni), the source of the origin of all beings. Bhagavāna states that in this great Brahman, I place My conscious seed for the birth of Hiraṇyagarbha (हिरण्यगर्भ), from whence everything emanates. Without the conscious power in the insentient Prakṛti, there cannot be any transformation. That is why the Lord's power is described in the form of a seed. With the union of the sentient and the insentient, the creation of living beings is narrated.

सर्वयोनिषु कौन्तेय मूर्तयः सम्भवन्ति याः |
तासां ब्रह्म महद्योनिरहं बीजप्रदः पिता || BG 14.4 ||

कौन्तेय - Hey Kaunteya (Arjuna)! ; याः - Whatever ; मूर्तयः - forms (lives) ; सम्भवन्ति - arise ; सर्व-योनिषु - from all kinds of wombs, ; तासाम् - their ; योनिः - womb ; महत्-ब्रह्म - is the great Brahman. ; अहम् - I am ; पिता - the father, ; बीज-प्रदः - provider of the seed.

Hey Arjuna! Whatever lives arise from all kinds of wombs, their womb is the great Brahman. I am the father, provider of the seed.

Intent - Deities, ancestors, humans, animals, birds or insects, whatever varied lives are born, the womb of all those lives is the great Brahman, the Māyā consisting of the three constituents, and I am the provider of the conscious seed. Just as a pregnant woman holding a fetus takes care of all activities until the birth of the child, the father, after impregnating, is dissociated with all those activities, in the same way, holding the seed of the power of the conscious Supreme Being, all kinds of beings are born of Prakṛti (Māyā). However, the conscious (Cetana) remains detached and a witness in all those dealings. Through the transformations of the constituents, Prakṛti creates all forms.

(So, what are those constituents? How do they bind one?)

सत्त्वं रजस्तम इति गुणाः प्रकृतिसम्भवाः |
निबध्नन्ति महाबाहो देहे देहिनमव्ययम् || BG 14.5 ||

महा-बाहो - Hey Mahābāho (Arjuna)! ; प्रकृति-सम्भवाः - Prakṛti-born ; गुणाः - constituents ; सत्त्वम् - Sattva, ; रजः - Rajas, ; तमः - (and) Tamas, ; इति - as such ; निबध्नन्ति - bind ; अव्ययम् - the imperishable ; देहिनम् - Self ; देहे - in the body.

Hey Arjuna! Prakṛti-born constituents Sattva, Rajas, and Tamas bind the imperishable Self in the body.

Intent - The constituents (गुण, Guṇa) of Prakṛti are named Sattva (सत्त्व, the cause of purity), Rajas (रजस्, the cause of activity), and Tamas (तमस्, the cause of sixfold mutations). The meaning of the term Guṇa (गुण) is technical in that it does not denote characteristics like color inherent in substances. Neither are there explicit distinctions between the constituents and what they constitute. They are externally dependent, being related to the field-knower. All of these three constituents are present in everyone and everything. It is the proportion that is different. The interplay of these constituents defines the character of an individual or a thing. In the existence of ignorance, all three constituents, based on their proportional attributes, bind the imperishable Jīvātmā.

तत्र सत्त्वं निर्मलत्वात्प्रकाशकमनामयम् |
सुखसङ्गेन बध्नाति ज्ञानसङ्गेन चानघ || BG 14.6 ||

अनघ - Hey Anagha (Arjuna)! ; तत्र - There ; सत्त्वम् - Sattvaguṇa ; निर्मलत्वात् - being the purest, ; प्रकाशकम् - is illumining (and) ; अनामयम् - healing. ; बध्नाति - It binds ; सुख-सङ्गेन - with attachment to pleasure ; च - and ; ज्ञान-सङ्गेन - knowledge.

Hey Arjuna! There Sattvaguṇa being the purest, is illumining and healing. It binds with attachment to pleasure and knowledge.

रजो रागात्मकं विद्धि तृष्णासङ्गसमुद्भवम् |
तन्निबध्नाति कौन्तेय कर्मसङ्गेन देहिनम् || BG 14.7 ||

कौन्तेय - Hey Kaunteya (Arjuna)! ; विद्धि - Know ; रजः - Rajoguṇa ; राग-आत्मकम् - in the form of deep desire ; तृष्णा-सङ्ग-समुद्भवम् - that creates thirst and attachment. ; तत् - It ; निबध्नाति - binds ; देहिनम् - the Jīvātmā ; कर्म-सङ्गेन - with attachment to action.

Hey Arjuna! Know Rajoguṇa in the form of deep desire that creates thirst and attachment. It binds the Jīvātmā with attachment to action.

तमस्त्वज्ञानजं विद्धि मोहनं सर्वदेहिनाम् |
प्रमादालस्यनिद्राभिस्तन्निबध्नाति भारत || BG 14.8 |

तु - Again, ; भारत - hey, Bhārata (Arjuna)! ; विद्धि - know ; तमः - Tamoguṇa ; अज्ञानजम् - as born of ignorance. ; तत् - It ; मोहनम् - deludes ; सर्व-देहिनाम् - all beings (and) ; निबध्नाति - binds them ; प्रमाद-आलस्य-निद्राभिः - with negligence, indolence, and sleep.

Again, hey, Arjuna! Know Tamoguṇa as born of ignorance. It deludes all beings and binds them with negligence, indolence, and sleep.

The intent of verses (BG 14.6 - BG 14.8) - Though all three constituents are born of ignorance, because of deep ignorance (गाढ-तमोगुण, Gāḍha-Tamoguṇa), Tamoguṇa is called as born of ignorance. In the existence of ignorance, they bind the imperishable Jīvātmā by their attributes. It is in the following manner -

Sattvaguṇa is the purest and is illuminating. In a dirt-free mirror, just as one can perceive one's face, in the same way, in the pure Sattvaguṇa, one can perceive the bliss-form and knowledge-form Ātmā. Whatever pleasure-yielding inclinations are born, they are all the effects of Sattvaguṇa, and the awakening of all worldly pleasures happens in Sattvaguṇa only. Whatever desires are in the heart, being the effect of Rajoguṇa, keeps the heart fickle. When sought-after things are acquired, then with Rajoguṇa satisfied, Sattvaguṇa awakens. In the Sattvaguṇa endowed inclinations, with the clue of the Ātmā, pleasure-yielding inclinations awake. All worldly pleasures thus are fruitful only because of Sattvaguṇa. Because of its relationship, Sattvaguṇa binds the Jīvātmā with an attachment that such pleasure continues to be acquired constantly. However, looking through the lens of the Truth, the Ātmā is all bliss-form and all knowledge-form. That is why for bliss-form achieving happiness is impossible. Yet, due to ignorance about facing from there, in its existence, Sattvaguṇa binds the imperishable Ātmā with the attachment to worldly pleasure and knowledge.

Rajoguṇa is in the form of deep desire and vacillations. With its association, it produces thirst and attachment in the immutable Jīvātmā. To satisfy attachment flow, it unites the inactive Jīvātmā in Karma. With Rajoguṇa, whatever causes produce vacillations, their satisfaction can only be by Karma.

Tamoguṇa is in the form of darkness and inanimateness. In its existence, due to deep insentience, it deludes the knowledge-form Jīvātmā with ignorance and binds it with negligence, indolence, and sleep.

(This way, the bondage of the three constituents was described. Then, again Bhagavāna narrates the dealings of the three constituents briefly -)

सत्त्वं सुखे सञ्जयति रज: कर्मणि भारत |
ज्ञानमावृत्य तु तम: प्रमादे सञ्जयत्युत || BG 14.9 ||

भारत - Hey Bhārata (Arjuna)! ; सत्त्वम् - Sattvaguṇa ; सञ्जयति - unites ; सुखे - in pleasure, ; रजः - Rajoguṇa ; कर्मणि - in action ; तु - and again ; आवृत्य - shrouding ; ज्ञानम् - knowledge, ; तमः - Tamoguṇa ; उत - also ; सञ्जयति - unites ; प्रमादे - in negligence.

Hey Arjuna! Sattvaguṇa unites in pleasure, Rajoguṇa in action and shrouding knowledge, Tamoguṇa unites in negligence.

Intent - Tamoguṇa, with its shrouding nature, covers discerning knowledge. It drives one to negligence, so the performance of one's proper duty is not successful. The term Pramāda (प्रमाद) here means not performing acquired duty.

(When do the constituents operate in the aforementioned manner? -)

रजस्तमश्चाभिभूय सत्त्वं भवति भारत |
रज: सत्त्वं तमश्चैव तम: सत्त्वं रजस्तथा || BG 14.10 ||

भारत - Hey Bhārata (Arjuna)! ; सत्त्वम् - Sattvaguṇa ; भवति - awakens ; अभिभूय - by suppressing ; रजः - Rajoguṇa ; च - and ; तमः - Tamoguṇa. ; रजः - (Suppressing) Rajoguṇa ; च - and ; सत्त्वम् - Sattvaguṇa, ; तमः - Tamoguṇa (awakens). ; तथा एव - Likewise, ; तमः - (suppressing) Tamoguṇa ; सत्त्वम् - (and) Sattvaguṇa, ; रजः - Rajoguṇa (awakens).

Hey Arjuna! Sattvaguṇa awakens by suppressing Rajoguṇa and Tamoguṇa. Suppressing Rajoguṇa and Sattvaguṇa, Tamoguṇa awakens. Likewise, suppressing Tamoguṇa and Sattvaguṇa, Rajoguṇa awakens.

Intent - In all beings, the three constituents are existent. They do not perish. Sometimes one constituent is dominant, while at other times, some other constituent. When one constituent is dominant, the other two remain suppressed but do not perish. When a constituent is dominant in a thing, that thing is known as with that constituent. For instance, when Sattvaguṇa is dominant in a thing, it is known as Sattvaguṇī (सत्त्वगुणी, endowed with Sattvaguṇa) and produces as effect pleasure and knowledge. Likewise, when Rajoguṇa is dominant, it affects activity and thirst. When Tamoguṇa is dominant, effects such as shrouding of knowledge and negligence are produced.

(What are the signs of the domination of each of the constituents? -)

सर्वद्वारेषु देहेऽस्मिन्प्रकाश उपजायते |
ज्ञानं यदा तदा विद्याद्विवृद्धं सत्त्वमित्युत || BG 14.11 ||

यदा - When ; प्रकाशः - the light ; ज्ञानम् - of knowledge ; उपजायते - is born ; सर्व-द्वारेषु - in every entrance ; अस्मिन् - of this ; देहे - body, ; तदा - then ; उत - indeed ; विद्यात् - (it should) be known ; सत्त्वम् - (that) Sattvaguṇa ; विवृद्धम् - is dominant, ; इति - as such.

When the light of knowledge is born in each body entrance, then it should be known that Sattvaguṇa is dominant.

Intent - The term Sarva-Dvāreṣu (सर्व-द्वारेषु) refers to all the entrances of cognition such as the ears, eyes, mind of the body. The light of knowledge here refers to awareness (चेतना, Cetanā), and thus the power of apprehension (बोध-शक्ति, Bodha-Śakti) form of knowledge.

लोभ: प्रवृत्तिरारम्भ: कर्मणामशम: स्पृहा |
रजस्येतानि जायन्ते विवृद्धे भरतर्षभ || BG 14.12 ||

भरतर्षभ - Hey Bharatarṣabha (Arjuna)! ; लोभः - Greed, ; प्रवृत्तिः - activity, ; आरम्भः - the commencement ; कर्मणाम् - of actions, ; अशमः - disquiet, ; स्पृहा - (and) desire, ; एतानि - these ; जायन्ते - appear ; विवृद्धे - upon the dominance ; रजसि - of the Rajoguṇa.

Hey Arjuna! Greed, activity, the commencement of actions, disquiet, and desire appear upon the dominance of the Rajoguṇa.

अप्रकाशोऽप्रवृत्तिश्च प्रमादो मोह एव च |
तमस्येतानि जायन्ते विवृद्धे कुरुनन्दन || BG 14.13 ||

कुरु-नन्दन - Hey Kurunandana (Arjuna)! ; अप्रकाशः - Absence of discernment, ; च - and ; अप्रवृत्तिः - absence of activity (in actions), ; प्रमादः - negligence, ; च - and ; मोहः - delusion, ; एव - indeed ; एतानि - these ; जायन्ते - arise ; विवृद्धे - upon the dominance ; तमसि - of Tamoguṇa.

Hey Arjuna! Absence of discernment, absence of activity, negligence, and delusion arise upon the dominance of Tamoguṇa.

(At the time of death, whatever constituent is dominant, based on its relationship, destinations, where one goes are described next -)

यदा सत्त्वे प्रवृद्धे तु प्रलयं याति देहभृत् |
तदोत्तमविदां लोकानमलान्प्रतिपद्यते || BG 14.14 ||

प्रलयम् याति - Passing away ; यदा - when ; सत्त्वे - Sattvaguṇa ; प्रवृद्धे - is predominant, ; तदा - then ; तु - indeed ; देह-भृत् - the embodied Self ; प्रतिपद्यते - is born in ; अमलान् - the pure ; लोकान् - worlds of ; उत्तम-विदाम् - the best discerners.

Passing away when Sattvaguṇa is predominant, the embodied Self is born in the pure worlds of the best discerners.

रजसि प्रलयं गत्वा कर्मसङ्गिषु जायते |
तथा प्रलीनस्तमसि मूढयोनिषु जायते || BG 14.15 ||

गत्वा - Gone to ; प्रलयम् - death ; रजसि - with dominant Rajoguṇa, ; जायते - one is born ; कर्म-सङ्गिषु - amongst those driven by action. ; तथा - Moreover, ; प्रलीनः - having attained death ; तमसि - with the dominant Tamoguṇa, ; जायते - one is born ; मूढ-योनिषु - amongst the deluded.

Gone to death with dominant Rajoguṇa, one is born amongst those driven by action. Moreover, having attained death with the dominant Tamoguṇa, one is born amongst the deluded.

(Fruits of action are commensurate with their constituents -)

कर्मण: सुकृतस्याहु: सात्त्विकं निर्मलं फलम् |
रजसस्तु फलं दु:खमज्ञानं तमस: फलम् || BG 14.16 ||

आहुः - It is said that ; सुकृतस्य - for laudable ; कर्मणः - acts, ; फलम् - the fruit ; निर्मलम् - is pure ; सात्त्विकम् - Sāttvika; ; रजसः - for Rajas (acts), ; फलम् - the fruit ; दुःखम् - is pain; ; तु - and ; तमसः - for Tamas (acts), ; फलम् - the fruit ; अज्ञानम् - is ignorance.

It is said that for laudable acts, the fruit is pure Sāttvika; for Rajas acts, the fruit is pain; and for Tamas acts, the fruit is ignorance.

Intent - The fruits of laudable acts (सुकृत-कर्म, Sukṛta-Karma), that is, desireless actions (Niṣkāma-Karma), are said to be pure and Sāttvika. The fruits are pleasure, knowledge, and dispassion. The fruits of Rajas are said to be pain and sorrow, and that of Tamas is said to be ignorance and delusion.

(What else emanates from these constituents? -)

सत्त्वात्सञ्जायते ज्ञानं रजसो लोभ एव च |
प्रमादमोहौ तमसो भवतोऽज्ञानमेव च || BG 14.17 ||

सत्त्वात् - With Sattvaguṇa, ; ज्ञानम् - knowledge ; सञ्जायते - is born, ; लोभः - Greed ; एव - only (arises), ; रजसः - with Rajoguṇa, ; च - and ; प्रमादमोहौ - negligence, delusion, ; च - and ; एव - also ; अज्ञानम् - ignorance ; भवतः - arise ; तमसः - (with) Tamoguṇa ;

With Sattvaguṇa, knowledge is born. Greed arises with Rajoguṇa, and negligence, delusion, and ignorance arise with Tamoguṇa.

(Destinations are articulated based on the constituents -)

ऊर्ध्वं गच्छन्ति सत्त्वस्था मध्ये तिष्ठन्ति राजसाः |
जघन्यगुणवृत्तिस्था अधो गच्छन्ति तामसाः || BG 14.18 ||

सत्त्वस्थाः - Those situated in Sattva ; गच्छन्ति - go ; ऊर्ध्वम् - up, ; राजसाः - located in Rajas ; तिष्ठन्ति - remain in ; मध्ये - the middle, (and) ; तामसाः - Tamogunī (persons) ; जघन्य-गुण-वृत्तिस्थाः - located in the lowest constituents ; गच्छन्ति - go ; अधः - down.

Those situated in Sattva go up, Rajas remain in the middle, and Tamogunī persons in the lowest constituents go down.

Intent - Those situated in Sattvaguṇa go up, that is, higher abodes such as the world of deities. Rājasika persons remain in the middle (the human world). Situated in sleep, indolence, negligence, and delusion (the effect of Tamoguṇa) go downwards. That is, end up in inferior forms of existence such as animals.

(Up to here, as is briefly described in verse BG 13.21, how with the imagined association of Prakṛti with the Puruṣa, the Puruṣa acquires superior and inferior species is narrated at length).

(Now, how can a person go beyond the reach of the constituents, that knowledge is articulated -)

नान्यं गुणेभ्यः कर्तारं यदा द्रष्टानुपश्यति |
गुणेभ्यश्च परं वेत्ति मद्भावं सोऽधिगच्छति || BG 14.19 ||

यदा - When ; द्रष्टा - the percipient ; अनुपश्यति - sees ; न - no ; कर्तारम् - doer ; अन्यम् - other ; गुणेभ्यः - than the constituents ; च - and ; वेत्ति - knows (Me) ; परम् - beyond ; गुणेभ्यः - the constituents, ; सः - he ; अधिगच्छति - attains ; मत्-भावम् - My form.

When the percipient sees no doer other than the constituents and knows Me beyond the constituents, he attains My form.

Intent - "There is no other doer than the constituents. The acts, instruments, and doer are the effects of the constituents" - when the enlightened person sees and knows that the doer is only the constituents that have transformed themselves into the body, organs, and objects of perception and know his Ātmā to be beyond the range of the constituents, knows his Ātmā dissociated from the dealings of the constituents just as an observer-witness, such a realized person attains My Saccidānanda-form.

(This way -)

गुणानेतानतीत्य त्रीन्देही देहसमुद्भवान् |
जन्ममृत्युजरादु:खैर्विमुक्तोऽमृतमश्नुते || BG 14.20 ||

देही - The embodied Self ; विमुक्तः - is liberated from ; जन्म-मृत्यु-जरा-दुःखैः - birth, death, old age, and pains ; अश्नुते - (and) attains ; अमृतम् - immortality ; अतीत्य - by transcending ; एतान् - these ; त्रीन् - three ; गुणान् - constituents ; देह-समुद्भवान् - from where the body has come from.

The embodied Self is liberated from birth, death, old age, and pains and attains immortality by transcending the three constituents from where the body has come from.

Intent - In reality, the Jīvātmā has no relationship with the three constituents. Their transformations (the body, senses, mind, and intellect) and the pains in the form of birth, old age, and death are due to their relationship with the body. However, it is only through ignorance that an imaginary relationship is formed. That is similar to the fault of sleep, where a dreamer has an unreal, imaginary relationship with the body of the dream world. An unreal, imaginary relationship with the body of the dream world and not a real one. Upon removal of the sleep fault, the relationship with the body of the dream world disappears upon awakening. In the same manner, the Jīvātmā, based on the knowledge above, freed from the ignorance-sleep having won over the three constituents, their effects in the form of the body, senses, mind, and intellect, and with their relationship to the pains of birth, old age, and death, while alive, experiences the ambrosiac Ātmā, attains union with oneness in the Paramātmā.

(Hearing the profound words of Bhagavāna, Arjuna posed a question -)

अर्जुन उवाच |
कैर्लिङ्गैस्त्रीन्गुणानेतानतीतो भवति प्रभो |
किमाचार: कथं चैतांस्त्रीन्गुणानतिवर्तते || BG 14.21 ||
अर्जुन उवाच - Arjuna said -

प्रभो - Hey Lord! ; कैः - What ; भवति - are ; लिङ्गैः - the characteristics of ; अतीतः - (those) who have transcended ; एतान् - these ; त्रीन् गुणान् - three constituents? ; किम्-आचारः - How do they behave? ; च - And, ; कथम् - how ; अतिवर्तते - do they go beyond ; एतान् - these ; त्रीन् गुणान् - three constituents?

Arjuna said -

Hey Lord! What are the characteristics of those who have transcended the three constituents? How do they behave? How do they go beyond the three constituents?

{In this manner, Arjuna asked about the characteristics, behavior, and approach of a Guṇātīta who is free from or beyond the constituents of Prakṛti}

(In response -)

श्रीभगवानुवाच |
प्रकाशं च प्रवृत्तिं च मोहमेव च पाण्डव |
न द्वेष्टि सम्प्रवृत्तानि न निवृत्तानि काङ्क्षति || BG 14.22 ||

उदासीनवदासीनो गुणैर्यो न विचाल्यते |
गुणा वर्तन्त इत्येवं योऽवतिष्ठति नेङ्गते || BG 14.23 ||
श्रीभगवान् उवाच - Śrī Bhagavān said -

पाण्डव - Hey Pāṇḍava (Arjuna)! ; प्रकाशम् - Light (with Sattvaguṇa), ; च - and ; प्रवृत्तिम् - activity (with Rajoguṇa), ; च - and ; मोहम् - delusion (are produced with Tamoguṇa). ; न - (One who is beyond the constituents) does not ; द्वेष्टि - hate ; सम्प्रवृत्तानि - (the constituents) that are active ; च - and ; एव - also ; न - does not ; काङ्क्षति - desire ; निवृत्तानि - (the constituents) that are absent.

आसीनः - Seated ; उदासीनवत् - indifferent, ; यः - one ; न - is not ; विचाल्यते - disturbed ; गुणैः - by the constituents. ; अवतिष्ठति - Situated ; इति - this way, ; यः - one ; न - does not ; इङ्गते - waver, ; गुणाः - (knowing) the constituents ; एव - are only ; वर्तन्ते - active.

Śrī Bhagavān said -

Hey Arjuna! Light with Sattvaguṇa, activity with Rajoguṇa, and delusion are produced with Tamoguṇa. One who is beyond the constituents does not hate the constituents that are active and does not desire the constituents that are absent. Seated indifferent, one is not disturbed by the constituents. Situated this way, one does not waver, knowing the constituents are only active.

The intent of verses (BG 14.22 - BG 1.23) - Sitting indifferent, one is not disturbed by the constituents. This way, one does not waver, knowing the constituents are only active. Those beyond the constituents do not hate non-agreeable constituents rising in activities and do not desire agreeable constituents absent in activities. "Activities that are the effect of Rajoguṇa and delusion and negligence that are the effect of Tamoguṇa are not dear to my heart. Why have they arisen in me? The effect of Sattvaguṇa is knowledge and pleasure. They are dear to my heart. Why have they disappeared? They ought to arise in my heart," - in this manner, one who does not hate active constituents and does not desire absent constituents, in such true knowers' perspective, with the power of being situated in the Ātmā, all constituents and activities are unreal like the performance of an illusionist. Even if an illusionist produces our archenemy in his performance, perceiving him as unreal, we would not even desire to harm that enemy. Even if pleasure and pain-form of goodies were placed in our front, again perceived as unreal, we would not desire to eat them. This perspective provides a direct experience of unreality (अपरोक्ष मिथ्यात्व दृष्टि, Aparokṣa Mithyātva Dṛṣṭi) of one who is situated indifferent to the activity and the non-activity of the constituents, like in the fight between two people, a third person seeing the fight remains in witness-form just an observer. Further, "In me, there is no stain of these constituents and activities" - with such a firm resolve, one who does not waver and remains immovable is known as Guṇātīta (गुणातीत), a transcendent sage.

(Ought to know self-experienced characteristics of a transcendent sage were narrated. Their conduct is next described -)

समदुःखसुखः स्वस्थः समलोष्टाश्मकाञ्चनः |
तुल्यप्रियाप्रियो धीरस्तुल्यनिन्दात्मसंस्तुतिः || BG 14.24 ||
मानापमानयोस्तुल्यस्तुल्यो मित्रारिपक्षयोः |
सर्वारम्भपरित्यागी गुणातीतः स उच्यते || BG 14.25 ||

स्वस्थः - Situated in own Self, ; धीरः - one who is beyond the constituents is ; समदुःखसुखः - alike in pleasure and pain, ; तुल्यप्रियाप्रियः - alike in pleasant and unpleasant, ; समलोष्टाश्मकाञ्चनः - treats equally clod, stone, and gold, ; तुल्यनिन्दात्मसंस्तुतिः - (and) has equanimity in censure and praise.

सः - One who ; तुल्यः - is the same ; मानापमानयोः - in honor and disgrace, ; तुल्यः - equal ; मित्रारिपक्षयोः - towards friends and foes, ; सर्वारम्भपरित्यागी - (and) does not initiate any actions ; उच्यते - is called ; गुणातीतः - Guṇātīta.

Situated in own Self, one who is beyond the constituents is alike in pleasure and pain, pleasant and unpleasant, treats equally clod, stone, and gold, and has equanimity in censure and praise. One who is the same in honor and disgrace, equal towards friends and foes, and does not initiate any actions is called Guṇātīta.

The intent of verses (BG 14.24 - BG 14.24) - Here, "does not initiate any actions" refers to activities undertaken to promote purposes, seen or unseen. As a doer, he renounces all Karma, except for those that are necessary for bodily sustenance. Such a sage, knowing the dissimilarities viz. pleasure and pain, honor and disgrace as the attributes of the conscience, is situated separately from them "is as is" in his witness-conscious Ātmā. With a firm resolve, "Whether it is the conscience, or whether they are pleasure or pain characteristics of the conscience, they are all illusory waves of my own Ātmā, and are the effects of the constituents, with whose rising or setting, there is no mutation in my Ātmā" - does not see any stain from them in his Ātmā. In the rising and setting of these opposing characteristics, he remains immovable. In contrast, in his conscience, a person actively balancing the opposing characteristics and suppressing those opposing characteristics may appear as if he is in equanimity but is really without equanimity. As in his perspective, the beingness of the mutually opposing characteristics is present. He has not directly experienced them unreal like the performance of an illusionist. That is why he fears his opposing characteristics, and he is not equanimous in the existence of opposing characteristics. However, with the power of his analytic perspective, one who has realized the Truth is dissociated from all constituents and their mutually opposing effects and is only their spectator is indeed a transcendent sage.

(How does one transcend the three constituents? -)

मां च योऽव्यभिचारेण भक्तियोगेन सेवते |
स गुणान्समतीत्यैतान्ब्रह्मभूयाय कल्पते || BG 14.26 ||

च - Moreover, ; सः - one ; यः – who, ; अव्यभिचारेण - with unwavering ; भक्ति-योगेन - devotional Yoga, ; सेवते - worships ; माम् - Me, ; समतीत्य - transcending ; एतान् - these ; गुणान् - constituents, ; कल्पते - becomes fit ; ब्रह्म-भूयाय - to be like the Brahman.

One who, with unwavering devotional Yoga, worships Me, transcending the constituents, becomes fit to be like the Brahman.

Intent - A devotion where the mind is sometimes in the Lord and at other times in the phenomenal world is called wavering (व्यभिचारी, Vyabhicārī) worship. Without it, that is offering the body, mind, and wealth at the feet of the Lord, and free from all desires, one whose aim in life is only the attainment of the Lord and who continuously remains in the contemplation of the Lord is called unwavering (अव्यभिचारिणी, Avyabhicāriṇī) worship. With this devotional Yoga, those who worship the Lord transcending the constituents become fit to attain liberation. As was discussed at the end of Chapter 11 - Clarification, only in the undivided devotion of the Lord is there the ability to accept the sacrifice of ego. When the paltry ego is offered to the Lord, naturally, the bondage of the constituents becomes loose as only the ego has a relationship with the constituents.

ब्रह्मणो हि प्रतिष्ठाहममृतस्याव्ययस्य च |
शाश्वतस्य च धर्मस्य सुखस्यैकान्तिकस्य च || BG 174.27 ||

हि - Indeed, ; अहम् - I am ; प्रतिष्ठा - the substrate ; ब्रह्मणः - of the Brahman, ; अमृतस्य - the Immortal, ; च - and ; अव्ययस्य - the Imperishable, ; च - and ; शाश्वतस्य - the eternal ; धर्मस्य - Righteousness, ; च - and ; एकान्तिकस्य - the pure ; सुखस्य - Bliss.

Indeed, I am the substrate of the Brahman, the Immortal, the Imperishable, the eternal Righteousness, and the pure Bliss.

Intent - The form of Brahman attained by a transcendent sage is narrated. The Brahman is imperishable and immortal. Up to the sphere of Brahmā (ब्रह्मलोक, Brahmaloka), whatever appears as immortal is neither imperishable nor unsurpassed (निरतिशय, Niratiśaya), but is perishable and with the fault of the attribute of more or less. However, the Brahman is imperishable ambrosia and is free from the faults of decay and the attribute of more or less. It is the limit of everlasting righteousness (शाश्वत-धर्म, Śāśvata-Dharma).

Worldly righteousness is not everlasting. Righteousness that may be righteous may be unrighteous for someone else, and what may be righteous at one time may be unrighteous at some other time. Therefore, worldly righteousness is not eternal, but the Brahman, the righteousness of all righteousness, is eternal. The Brahman holds all righteousness, and the result of all righteousness is the attainment of the Brahman. Upon its attainment, all righteousness terminates. That is why it is the eternal Dharma. The Brahman is the limit of the ultimate (एकान्तिक, Ekāntika) bliss. The worldly pleasures being mixed with pain and being perishable are not final. The Brahman, free of union with anyone, "एकमेवाद्वितीयम्, (Ātmā is unique,) only one without a second,"[119]is nothing but bliss. With real knowledge, forsaking the adjuncts, the inner Being is determined in Brahman's form.

ॐ तत्सदिति श्रीमद्भगवद्गीतासूपनिषत्सु ब्रह्मविध्यायां योगशास्त्रे

श्रीकृष्णार्जुनसम्वादे गुणत्रयविभागयोगो नाम

चतुर्दशोऽध्यायः || BG 14 ||

Oṃ Tat Sat

In the Śrīmad Bhagavad Gītā Upaniṣad

The Yoga Science of the Knowledge of Self-Realization

The Discourse of Lord Śrī Kṛṣṇa and Arjuna

This Fourteenth Chapter

Yoga Named - The Yoga of the Threefold Constituents

Clarification

In the thirteenth chapter, to attain union with oneness in His true nature, Bhagavāna articulated His attributeless form. It is shown that in reality, the Puruṣa (field-knower, Jīvātmā) is ever continuous, dissociated, and unstained from Prakṛti. Only because of the imagined association with the ignorance born constituents of Prakṛti, imagining illusory bondage, he roams around in inferior and superior worlds. In reality, perceiving thoughtfully, he is the Close Observer and the Sanctioner of all dealings of Prakṛti. Directly experiencing this true Reality, all bondage and liberation imaginations become unreal. In this chapter, the effects of bondage and liberation due to the association with the constituents of Prakṛti are formulated so that the burden of doership and enjoyership can be on the head of the constituents, and one can experience own Ātmā dissociated and ever-free.

In the first verse, that knowledge was lauded, with whose direct experience all sages after leaving the body have attained supreme perfection in the form of liberation. The root of all bondages is the ignorance-born sense of oneness with Prakṛti. Except for this knowledge, there is no other approach for liberation from the bondage of Prakṛti, nor will there be. Whenever and whoever is liberated from the bondage of Prakṛti is liberated only on the dependence of this knowledge. Activities such as sacrifices, charities, or austerities cannot liberate one from the bondage of Prakṛti, nor will they be. That is why this knowledge is called the highest (परम, Parama) knowledge, and its great fruit described is that with the power of this knowledge, one is not born at the time of the manifestation of the world and is not distressed at the time of its dissolution (BG 14.2). Then, Bhagavāna stated that My womb is the Mahat-Brahma. In it, I place My conscious seed. With the union of the sentient and insentient, the creation of all beings materializes. The essence is that in the production of varied fruits, though the earth is the cause, without seeds, even the earth is not capable of providing fruits. Likewise, though Prakṛti transforms into the form of all beings, without the power of the Lord, it cannot dance to show her performance and remains only null. In the four kinds (sweat-born,

[119] Chāndogya Upaniṣad (छान्दोग्य उपनिषद्) 6.2.1

germination-born, egg-born, and placenta-born) and the four tones (चतुर-वाणी, Catura-Vāṇī),[120]whatever forms are created as the effect, in them, Prakṛti is the mother-womb, and the conscious Puruṣa is the father providing the conscious seed with his power. The entire phenomenal world is the transformation of Prakṛti and is the Vivarta of the conscious Puruṣa (BG 14.3).

In addition, Bhagavāna described the three constituents Sattva, Rajas, and Tamas of Prakṛti, who, with their association, put the dissociated-imperishable Ātmā in the bondage of the body and create distinctions in the one without distinctions. Then, Bhagavāna described types of bondages associated with the constituents, those which bind the bliss-form Ātmā with the attachment of pleasure, those which bind the satiated with the attachment of thirst, and those which bind the ever awake to the attachment of indolence and sleep (BG 14.4 - BG 14.8). After that, Bhagavāna described varied fruits or effects of the three constituents and narrated how one constituent becomes dominant by suppressing the other two (BG 14.9 - BG 14.10). Moreover, when a constituent is dominant, how its characteristics manifest is also described (BG 14.11 - BG 14.13). Furthermore, under the dominance of a particular constituent, when the embodied Ātmā leaves the body, the kinds of destinations the unborn immortal attains are described. Based on the distinctions of the constituents, three types of Karma and thus their fruits are described. The attributeless embodied Ātmā with the dominance of Sattvaguṇa goes to higher worlds such as those of the deities, with the dominance of Rajoguṇa remains in the middle human world, and with the dominance of Tamoguṇa roams around in the inferior worlds such as those of animals and does not get peace anywhere (BG 14.14 - BG 14.18).

After that, Bhagavāna narrated the analytic perspective that, in reality, the Puruṣa (field-knower) is all-pervading and thus dissociated and therefore does not have either a higher destination or lower destination. Only due to an ignorance-born sense of oneness with Prakṛti, deeming the constituents and their transformations in itself, the embodied Ātmā imagines the higher and lower, good and bad, and even though eternally united in Me harbors sentiment of separation. However, in reality, by its nature, it is not moved. It "is as is" in its nature. Just as adjuncts such as pots and pans cannot divide the pervasive space, transformations of the Prakṛti (the body, mind, and senses) can never separate the impartite Ātmā. Just as a snake cannot bite the space, wind cannot shake the space, the constituents and their effects of the Prakṛti cannot move the immovable immutable Ātmā. Just as waves cannot wet the ocean, the constituents and their effects being the miracles of the Ātmā, cannot influence the Ātmā. Accordingly, with an analytic perspective, when the Puruṣa firmly resolves as being dissociated from the constituents and their effects and knows directly, "Constituents are only the doers of Karma, there is no one else other than the constituents in the form of a doer, I, the witness is in every way dissociated from them" - then he acquires My true nature and unites with oneness in Me. Liberated from all three constituents, with the strength of this knowledge, becomes free from the pains of birth, old age, or disease and enjoys ambrosiac liberation (BG 14.19 - BG 14.20).

In reality, old age, disease, or death were never before in the Puruṣa. Only in the ignorance sleep with oneness in Prakṛti does he imagine so. However, with the awakening of knowledge, imagined pains of old age, disease, and death are automatically liberated. Had old age, disease, and death been real, Bhagavāna would have commanded sacrifices and austerities for their liberation. Knowledge could not have released them because the fruit of knowledge is only the removal of ignorance. With knowledge, no substance can perish. Bhagavāna never commanded so. In reality, birth, disease, or death are not real. Therefore, with the awakening of knowledge, the imagined birth, disease, or death in the Ātmā remains imaginary only. Just as with the rope knowledge, liberation of the illusory snake in the rope remains illusory.

---

[120] Catura-Vāṇī (चतुर-वाणी) means the four types of tones used in the chanting of Vedic hymns ; 1) Vaikharī (वैखरी, Mantra chanting with high tone), 2) Madhyamā (मध्यमा, Mantra chanting without lips moving so that it is inaudible to anyone), 3) Paśyantī (पश्यन्ती, Mantra chanting heartily without the tongue moving and the mind engrossed in the meaning of the chant), and 4) Parā (परा, Mantra chanting with inner-disposition steady in the meaning of the chant providing bliss and the intellect becoming steadfast in the Self).

On this, Arjuna asked about the characteristics of those who have transcended the three constituents, how they behave, and how one can go beyond the three constituents (BG 14.21). In response, Bhagavāna described the characteristics and behavior of a transcendent sage (Guṇātīta) who is free from or beyond the constituents of Prakṛti in the verses (BG 14. 22 - BG 14. 25) and said that a person who is situated in own witnessing Ātmā and has transcended the constituents, such a person, upon the enlightening of the characteristics and activity of the constituents becoming active, knowing them essenceless neither hates them nor upon their being inactive, knowing them insignificant, desires them; just as one who knows the true nature of a rope and an oyster shell, unlike an ignorant person, neither is afraid of the perceived snake nor desires the perceived silver. Accordingly, one who is seated indifferent to the activity and non-activity of the constituents is called a Guṇātīta (transcendent sage). "Constituents are only active in the kingdom of Prakṛti; they do not stain me, the substrate Ātmā" - with such a firm resolve, he stays unmoved in his own witnessing Ātmā. Maturing such perspective, he remains equal in dualities such as pleasure and pain, honor and dishonor. Those dualities exist only in Prakṛti, and their being and not-being remain in the conscience. Only due to the influence of ignorance, the Puruṣa becoming conscience-form, despite being devoid of dualities, imagines them in himself.

However, with the strength of knowledge, when he knows his Ātmā separate as a witness of the conscience, even though the dualities remain in the conscience, he does not see them in his Ātmā. In this way, a transcendent sage's self-experienced characteristics and behavior were narrated. In acquiring this state, the approach recommended was unwavering worship of the Lord. The intent is that the influence of the constituents is only in discriminating-vision. With a discriminating vision, when there is a sentiment of superiority and inferiority and good and bad, then, in such a state, the constituents rule. Liberation of discriminating vision is possible only by unwavering worship of the Lord. That is why freeing one from the constituents, the cause of the attainment of the Brahman, is only unwavering worship. When means are active unwavering worship is sentiment-predominant and is thus achieved by action. However, it is automatically achieved in the state of maturity of knowledge. Seeing the I-you world in the form of the worshipped by melting the worshipper and the worshipped sentiment is called the maturity of this devotion. In the end, narrating the form of the Brahman, the Brahman that the unwavering worship can attain, the chapter is ended(BG 14.26 - BG 14.27).

In this chapter, the sequence of the bondage of the Puruṣa with Prakṛti is narrated. An approach towards liberation from the constituents to attain union in the Ātmā, as well as the characteristics of the liberated, are described.

CHAPTER 15

THE YOGA OF THE SUPREME PERSONALITY

(In the fourteenth chapter, the way the Ātmā is bound by the constituents and how liberation from the association with the constituents is achieved with knowledge was formulated. In this chapter, Bhagavāna describes the Truth on whose dependence fruition of liberation and bondage is successful.)

श्रीभगवानुवाच |
ऊर्ध्वमूलमध:शाखमश्वत्थं प्राहुरव्ययम् |
छन्दांसि यस्य पर्णानि यस्तं वेद स वेदवित् || BG 15.1 ||
श्रीभगवान् उवाच - Śrī Bhagavān said -

प्राहुः - They speak ; अव्ययम् - of the imperishable ; अश्वत्थम् - fig tree ; ऊर्ध्व-मूलम् - whose roots are upwards ; अधः-शाखम् - (and) whose branches are downwards. ; यस्य - Its ; पर्णानि - leaves ; छन्दांसि - are the Vedic hymns. ; सः - He, ; यः - who ; वेद - knows ; तम् - it, ; वेदवित् - knows the Vedas.

Śrī Bhagavān said -

They speak of the imperishable fig tree whose roots are upwards and whose branches are downwards. Its leaves are the Vedic hymns. He, who knows it, knows the Vedas.

Intent - It is only because of the power of the Māyā of the Supreme Being (Paramātmā) that there is a manifestation of the Saṃsāra, the world of transmigrating lives. The Paramātmā is the root of the Saṃsāra-tree, the base of the Saṃsāra, and is subtler than the subtle (Sūkṣmāti-Sūkṣma) and omnipresent (Sarva-Vyāpī) and thus beyond the best (Parātpara). The Paramātmā being subtler than the subtle, is said to be above, and so the fig tree in the form of the Saṃsāra is called Ūrdhva-Mūla (ऊर्ध्व-मूल), whose roots are upwards. Adhaḥ-Śākham (अधः-शाखम्) means its branches are spread down. The essence is that due to ignorance, when a Jīva falls down from its nature as the Paramātmā, then it is dropped in the Saṃsāra that has many branches (wombs, types of life), and so this Saṃsāra is called Adhaḥ-Śākham. In the second verse, the meaning of the term Śākhā (शाखा, branch) is also Yoni (womb, types of life). Alternatively, the roots of a tree are always down, and the branches are up. A tree can't have its roots up and branches down. Ūrdhva-Mūla and Adhaḥ-Śākham are impossible; hence in the existent Paramātmā, the existence of the non-existent Saṃsāra is like the darkness of the sun, always impossible. Thus, from an impossibility perspective, the fig tree in the form of the Saṃsāra is called "ऊर्ध्वमूल अधः-शाखम्, whose roots are up and branches down."

Knowledge of the Lord is named Vedas. Just as there are innumerable leaves of a fig tree, knowledge of the Lord is infinite. There is no beauty in a fig tree's trunks, branches, and twigs except for the leaves.

The beauty of the fig tree is only because of the leaves, and humans can enjoy peace and happiness under the shade and greenery of the leaves. Similarly, in the Saṃsāra, Jīva has no joy related to its relationship with the Saṃsāra. Only in support of greenery and shade of renunciation and knowledge filled Vedas, Jīva afflicted by the threefold afflictions (त्रिताप, Tritāpa)[121]can acquire peace and happiness. The real essence of the essenceless Saṃsāra is to take refuge in the renunciation and knowledge-filled Vedas. "न श्वः अपि स्थाता इति अश्वत्थः, what does not remain (in the same form) even (till) tomorrow." That is why the Saṃsāra-tree is called Aśvattha (fig tree) because it does not remain steady.

In satire, Bhagavāna said - "अश्वत्थम् अव्ययम् प्राहुः, they (ignorant people) call the unsteady Aśvattha tree (Saṃsāra) imperishable." The intention is that, in reality, the Saṃsāra is not there. There is a groundless perception of the Saṃsāra only because of the ignorance of the true nature of the Paramātmā. That is similar to how in the ignorance of a rope, a snake is perceived in it without any grounds, and fear ensues. In reality, the snake does not come from anywhere; the snake is always in the form of a rope. Likewise, in the ignorance of the true nature of own self as the Paramātmā, the I-you Saṃsāra is perceived in the Paramātmā and is the cause of the pains of birth, old age, and so on. In reality, though, the Saṃsāra is only the Brahman, the underlying ground. That is the drumbeat of the Vedas. Accordingly, one who knows the Saṃsāra as the substrate Brahman is a true knower of the Vedas.

अधश्चोर्ध्वं प्रसृतास्तस्य शाखा गुणप्रवृद्धा विषयप्रवालाः |
अधश्च मूलान्यनुसन्ततानि कर्मानुबन्धीनि मनुष्यलोके || BG 15.2 ||

गुण-प्रवृद्धाः - Flourishing because of the constituents, ; तस्य - its ; शाखाः - branches, ; विषय-प्रवालाः - (and) sense-object twigs ; प्रसृताः - have spread ; अधः - below ; च - and ; ऊर्ध्वम् - above. ; च - And, अधः - below ; मनुष्य-लोके - in the human world, ; मूलानि - (its) roots ; अनुसन्ततानि - have spread ; कर्म-अनुबन्धीनि - that bind one with actions.

Flourishing because of the constituents, its branches, and sense-object twigs have spread below and above. Below in the human world, its roots have spread that bind one with actions.

Intent - In the seven upper worlds and the seven lower worlds, infinite branches of the Saṃsāra-tree in the form of types of life such as deities, humans, and Tiryaga (तिर्यग, birds, animals, and insects) have spread up and down all over. In the Saṃsāra-tree up to Brahmā, the abode of the Yoni of the deities is part of the up branches, and the abode of the animal Yoni is part of the down branches. These branches in the form of Yonis are nourished by the three constituents Sattva, Rajas, and Tamas. In the branches, there are twigs in the form of the five objects of senses, viz. sound, touch, form, taste, and smell. With the association of the three constituents and the five sense objects, Jīva roams around up and down in infinite Yonis. In the flourishing of the varied branches (Yonis), these constituents and sense objects are the cause. For a Jīva, the association with the constituents is internal, and the association with the sense objects is external. Just as how much a Jīva is endowed with the constituents, commensurate is his fondness and activity in external objects; and commensurate with his fondness and activity, Jīva acquires Yoni. This way, the constituents flourish the branches (Yonis), and the external objects, through their attachment, make these branches mature.

The infinite roots of the infinite branches are nothing but the impressions (Vāsanā) such as attachment and aversion. Only because of these impressions does Jīva acquire Yonis, and that is why the roots (in the form of impressions) of the branches (Yonis) are spreading below. Based on individual Karma, those impressions bind a Jīva. Based on how Jīva performs actions, so are the resultant impressions left in his heart. Just as

[121] Tritāpa (त्रिताप) means the threefold afflictions. They are 1) Daihika-Tāpa (दैहिक-ताप, bodily and mental afflictions. Diseases like fever, cancer are body related sufferings. Anger, greed, passion are mental afflictions), 2) Daivika-Tāpa (दैविक-ताप, natural afflictions such as storms, floods or droughts), and 3) Bhautika-Tāpa (भौतिक-ताप, material sufferings such as those caused by humans, animals or insects).

impressions are, so is the Yoni acquired. Therefore, based on Karma, impressions are said to be the roots of the branches (Yonis).

In human life-form, impressions formed based on done deeds are described as roots. In other life forms, actions are not the cause of impressions. The intention is that Yonis, other than humans, are not regions of action (कर्मभूमि, Karmabhūmi) but regions of enjoyment (भोगभूमि, Bhogabhūmi). Only in the human Yoni actions are in the seed-form, and for the enjoyment, they create impressions. Other than humans, in lower life forms, the five sheaths that cover the Ātmā are not fully developed; in some life forms, only one, in some two, in some three, and some four sheaths are developed. With the incompleteness of the five sheaths, doership-intellect is not awakened in those life forms. As a result, actions cannot produce impressions and dynamic impressions (Saṃskāras) in those life forms. Accordingly, only in the human life form, actions being the cause of impressions and dynamic impressions, Yonis are depicted as roots; based on those impressions and dynamic impressions, acquisition of up or down Yonis is stated.

In the human world, impressions based on Karma are the roots of the up or down life forms, which in the heart of a Jīva is becoming healthier below, and the three constituents are nourishing the branches (Yonis). Such was the description of the extent of the Saṃsāra-tree.

(From analytic perspective the Saṃsāra-tree is described -)

न रूपमस्येह तथोपलभ्यते नान्तो न चादिर्न च सम्प्रतिष्ठा |
अश्वत्थमेनं सुविरूढमूल मसङ्गशस्त्रेण दृढेन छित्त्वा || BG 15.3 ||
ततः पदं तत्परिमार्गितव्यं यस्मिन्गता न निवर्तन्ति भूयः |
तमेव चाद्यं पुरुषं प्रपद्ये यतः प्रवृत्तिः प्रसृता पुराणी || BG 15.4 ||

तथा - As such ; इह - here ; अस्य - its ; रूपम् - form ; न - is not ; उपलभ्यते - perceived. ; न - (It has) no ; आदिः - beginning, ; च - and ; न - no ; अन्तः - end, ; च - and ; न - no ; सम्प्रतिष्ठा - substrate. ; छित्त्वा - Cutting ; एनम् - this ; सुविरूढ-मूलम् - deep-rooted ; अश्वत्थम् - fig tree ; दृढेन - with a strong ; असङ्ग-शस्त्रेण - weapon of detachment,

ततः - then ; तत् - that ; पदम् - "Status" ; परिमार्गितव्यं - ought to be sought, ; गताः - having gone ; यस्मिन् - from where ; न - there is no ; निवर्तन्ति - return ; भूयः - again, ; च - with (a sentiment,) ; प्रपद्ये - "I take refuge in ; तम् - that ; आद्यम् - primeval ; पुरुषम् - Supreme Personality ; एव - alone, ; यतः - whence ; पुराणी - this eternal ; प्रवृत्तिः - activity ; प्रसृता - has emanated."

Here its form is not perceived. It has no beginning, no end, and no substrate. Cutting the deep-rooted fig tree with a strong weapon of detachment, then that "Status" ought to be sought, having gone from where there is no return, with a sentiment, "I take refuge in that primeval Supreme Personality alone, whence this eternal activity has emanated."

Intent - The way the Saṃsāra-tree was described earlier, in reality, it has not sprung up from some initiation transformation. It has sprung up dreamlike serendipitously and is the morass of delusionary ignorance. It is like a dream, like the water of a desert mirage. Because the root of the Saṃsāra is the Paramātmā, there is no transformation of the Saṃsāra in the form of beginning, sustentation, and dissolution in it. However, in all three states of the Saṃsāra - creation, sustentation, and dissolution, the substrate Parabrahma "is as is." Only on its dependence is the perception of such creation, sustentation, and dissolution of the Saṃsāra. Just as there is a perception of a face in a mirror, even though the face does not touch the mirror - the creation, sustentation, and dissolution of the face in the mirror is merely the thought process of the perceiver. Alternatively, just as there is a perception of the creation, sustentation, and destruction of name-form gold ornaments on the dependence on gold, no state of the name-form gold ornaments can touch gold. Had there been any touch of the modifications of the always-transforming Saṃsāra with the root Paramātmā, then the Paramātmā would have been modifiable. If the Paramātmā were modifiable, then it would have been perishable. That is so because, by rule, all modifiable things are perishable, and they never stay steady.

If the Parabrahma were perishable, then it could not have been the root of the Saṃsāra because a perishable thing can't exist in support of a perishable thing. Just as the existence of zero (0) in support of zero (0) is impossible, but in support of one (1), the existence of zero is possible.

Accordingly, with tactic, example, and measure, no taint of the well-spread Saṃsāra-tree is ever found in the existent Paramātmā. That is why, on the dependence of that existent Paramātmā, the not there Saṃsāra is only a perception, similar to how there is an illusory perception in support of an existent rope unreal snake. The way in support of a real rope, an unreal snake in the delusion time is perceived as real, in the same way, during the time of ignorance with the power of the existent Paramātmā, the unreal Saṃsāra appears real, and even not being there appears as if it were there. Accordingly, when the unreal Saṃsāra cannot ever stain its cause, the Paramātmā, then how can its creation be alleged? How can its sustentation be alleged? How can its dissolution be alleged? If in the rope - creation, sustentation, and dissolution of an illusory snake can be said, then in the Paramātmā - creation, sustentation, and dissolution of the Saṃsāra can be alleged. How can creation be when there is no resultant effect in the real existent cause? How can there be sustentation and dissolution if there is no creation?

"इह अस्य रूपम् न उपलभ्यते, here its form is not perceived." From an analytic perspective, the Saṃsāra-tree, as described, is not found because it has no creation, sustentation, or dissolution. The association of I-ness and mineness has made the roots of the non-existent Saṃsāra-tree stout. Indeed, I-ness and mineness are its stout roots, which can only be cut by a strong weapon in the form of renunciation of all attachments (सर्व-सङ्ग-परित्याग, Sarva-Saṅga-Parityāga). As long as a Jīva is bound by the association of I-ness and mineness, the roots of the Saṃsāra-tree cannot be cut. However, it can spread furthermore, as the Saṃsāra-tree is standing on the support of I-ness and mineness association. Even if the association of I-ness and mineness, the support of the Saṃsāra-tree, is cut by renunciation of all attachments, that may not be enough. It is necessary to search for the substrate supreme Status (परम-पद, Parama-Pada) in which both the underlying I-ness and mineness association and the supported Saṃsāra-tree are imaginary. Without entering into the supreme Status substrate, freedom from the coming and going (आवागमन, Āvāgamana) from the Saṃsāra is impossible. Entry into the supreme Status establishes absence in the past, present, and future of the Saṃsāra, just as with the knowledge of the real rope, there is complete non-existence of an illusory snake and born thereof fear. That is why one ought to seek refuge in the primeval Supreme Personality in whom this eternal activity of the world of transmigrating lives is perceived.

Renunciation of all attachments and the search for the supreme Status are the two approaches narrated for the uprooting of the Saṃsāra-tree.

(Next, the means for the search are stated -)

निर्मानमोहा जितसङ्गदोषा अध्यात्मनित्या विनिवृत्तकामाः |
द्वन्द्वैर्विमुक्ताः सुखदुःखसंज्ञै गच्छन्त्यमूढाः पदमव्ययं तत् || BG 15.5 ||

निर्मान-मोहाः - Free from vanity and delusion, ; जितसङ्गदोषाः - having overcome the flaws of attachment, ; अध्यात्म-नित्याः - ever involved in the search for the Self, ; विनिवृत्त-कामाः - free from lust, ; विमुक्ताः - liberated from ; द्वन्द्वैः - dualities ; सुख-दुःख-संज्ञैः - like pleasure and pain, ; अमूढाः - such undeluded (sages) ; गच्छन्ति - attain ; तत् - that ; अव्ययं - imperishable ; पदम् - "Status."

Free from vanity and delusion, having overcome the flaws of attachment, ever involved in the search for the Self, free from lust, liberated from dualities like pleasure and pain, such undeluded sages attain the imperishable "Status."

Intent - Vanity, delusion, attachment, material desires, and dualities such as pleasure and pain - all these are stated to be left instruments (हेय-साधन, Heya-Sādhana). That much was said about strong weapons of detachment (असङ्ग-शस्त्र, Asaṅga-Śastra). Then, in the search for the supreme Status, only moving towards the Supreme Being was stated as an accepted (Upādeya) means of activity. Vanity, attachment, desires, and dualities - are impediments to moving towards the Supreme Being. That is why, with the liberation of the faults, those without vanity (निर्मान, Nirmāna), without attachment (निर्मोह, Nirmoha) help move towards the Supreme Being. Association with the knowers of the Reality and with contemplation on the scriptures that provide the Truth, to be ready for analytic thinking on the true nature of the Paramātmā, is called moving towards the Supreme Being (अध्यात्म-परायणता, Adhyātma-Parāyaṇatā).

If it was deemed acceptable by Bhagavāna, as some have unequivocally suggested, that desireless actions are an independent means to attain the supreme Status, then at this location, there should have been some indication of it. If desireless actions as means were directly agreeable, then such a statement could have been made, but that is not the case. In reality, from the perspective of the Bhagavāna, as stated in verse BG 15.3, when the Saṃsāra-tree is not created, how can Karma be included in the toolbox of the instruments? From the Bhagavāna's perspective, the Saṃsāra-tree is born only due to ignorance and is made stout by the attachments of I-ness and mineness. That is why, to shear this I-ness and mineness attachments, the application of a strong weapon of detachment is articulated; and for the liberation of ignorance in the form of moving towards the Supreme Being, knowledge is communicated. Only knowledge is the opposer of ignorance; action is not the opposer of ignorance. Karma is indeed the effect of ignorance; how can it be mentioned here? Light can only remove darkness; actions such as truncheon blows can never remove darkness.

(Next, the very nature of the supreme Status is further distinguished -)

न तद्भासयते सूर्यो न शशाङ्को न पावक: |
यद्गत्वा न निवर्तन्ते तद्धाम परमं मम || BG 15.6 ||

सूर्य: - The sun ; न - (does) not ; भासयते - illuminate ; तत् - it, ; न - neither ; शशाङ्क: - (does) the moon ; न - nor ; पावक: - fire, ; गत्वा - gone ; यत् - where ; न - (one does) not ; निवर्तन्ते - return, ; तत् - that is ; मम - My ; परमम् - supreme ; धाम - abode.

The sun does not illuminate it, neither does the moon nor fire, gone where one does not return, that is My supreme abode.

Intent - The supreme Status is so omnipresent and undiminishing self-effulgence that all space, time, material, attributes, actions, substances, and intuitive knowledge are illuminated. However, it is not illuminated by anything else. The supreme Status cannot be illuminated by the sun, and neither the moon nor fire; its brilliance illuminates them. With some thought, one can see that the perishable light from the sun and the intuitive knowledge of the conscience cannot illuminate anything, but on the support of that thing can only oppose darkness or oppose the shroud. In the actual illumination of a thing, one cannot find any purpose; their only purpose is to oppose darkness showing its disdain towards it. In reality, only the supreme Status illuminates everything, be it stationary, be it mobile, be it sentient, be it insentient, be it darkness, or be it light - it is the common light of all things. Only by its authoritative common light are all things illuminated even though they are unreal (Asat) yet perceived as real (Sat).

Such supreme luminaire Status is My supreme abode, attaining which there is no return (Punarāvṛtti, rebirth). There is nowhere to go or come again once such Status is reached, and then all the comings and goings remain only illusory. The coming and going are always in the attribute of limitation. However, My supreme Status is without limitations. When it is unlimited, then how can there be rebirth after attaining that Status? It ought to be remembered that the attainment of the supreme Status and the supreme abode is not possible by any kind of dealings in the form of Karma. Entry in Me is possible only through analytic thinking (Tattva-Jñāna). Through the glory of Tattva-Jñāna, a knower of the Truth has the direct experience that there was never any separation from My supreme Status. There was always union with oneness in Me. In the always attained (Nitya-Prāpta) Me, there was the delusion of separation, which is liberated by analytic thinking.

ममैवांशो जीवलोके जीवभूत: सनातन: |
मन:षष्ठानीन्द्रियाणि प्रकृतिस्थानि कर्षति || BG 15.7 ||

मम - My ; सनातनः - eternal ; अंशः - "part" ; एव - alone, ; जीव-भूतः - becoming a Jīvātmā ; जीव-लोके - in the Saṃsāra, ; कर्षति - attracts ; इन्द्रियाणि - the senses ; मनः-षष्ठानि - with the mind as the sixth ; प्रकृति-स्थानि - situated in Prakṛti.

My eternal "part" alone, becoming a Jīvātmā in the Saṃsāra, attracts the senses with the mind as the sixth situated in Prakṛti.

Intent - The supreme Status that Bhagavāna described in the previous verse, its closest location is provided in this verse as follows. In the body, there are five cognitive senses: skin, tongue, eyes, nose, and ears, and correspondent five sense-objects touch, taste, form, smell, and sound. With whatever sense the mental disposition (मनो-वृत्ति, Mano-Vṛtti) is united, only those corresponding sense objects are grasped. Even though they all have their individual dealings, there is no conjunction of the dealings of one with the dealings of the other. However, the one grasping the dealings of all with one sentiment, "I am hearing, I am seeing, I am touching," and the one united in the mind and senses unites the mind with one sense and separates it from other senses. Like a telephone exchange connecting and disconnecting telephone lines, the one situated in the body-form exchange connects and disconnects the mind with the senses. With whose existence, and thus power, there is the fruition of all these dealings, that Jīvātmā is indeed My eternal part, and it is My supreme Status in witness-form. Although superimposition (Adhyāsa) of doership and enjoyership is perceived in a Jīvātmā, in reality, Jīvātmā in its true nature is a non-doer and non-enjoyer. Only due to ignorance, in oneness with ego, it is perceived as a doer-enjoyer, yet in reality, it is only the light in the witness-form observer of the dealings of the ego, and thus the mind and senses.

"My eternal part (अंश, Aṃśa) alone becoming a Jīvātmā" - here, the meaning of the term Aṃśa is not a separate fragment, like a piece of stone that is a separate fragment of a large rock. Here the meaning of the term Aṃśa is its true nature. For instance, when there is something extremely dear, people often use the term Aṃśa in the sense of nature or form - when one says, "My son is my Aṃśa," it means "My son is like me." It does not mean the son is a physical component of the person. If the term Aṃśa is understood as a separate part, then one should be mindful that Bhagavāna calls a Jīvātmā His eternal Aṃśa. If a Jīvātmā is deemed as a separate eternal part of Bhagavāna, then the oneness of a Jīvātmā and the Paramātmā is not possible, and then efforts for the sake of liberation would be in vain. However, it is not so. The intention is that a Jīvātmā is My eternal form, only because of the limiting adjunct of Avidyā, even though in reality it is one with Me, yet it is perceived as separate from Me. Just as with the limiting adjunct of a pot, the impartite space appears as a separate pot-space. The separation ceases to exist once the limiting adjunct is removed. The idea is already formulated in Chapter 13, where the part is articulated as imagined due to limitations imposed by nescience.

(A Jīvātmā attracts the six senses, so how does it attract?)

शरीरं यदवाप्नोति यच्चाप्युत्क्रामतीश्वर: |
गृहीत्वैतानि संयाति वायुर्गन्धानिवाशयात् || BG 15.8 ||

ईश्वरः - (When) a Jīvātmā ; उत्क्रामति - leaves ; यत् - that ; शरीरम् - (first) body, ; च - and ; अपि - again ; अवाप्नोति - acquires ; यत् - that (second body), ; गृहीत्वा - grasping ; एतानि - these (six senses) ; संयाति - takes them (to the new body), ; इव - like ; गन्धान् - fragrance ; वायुः - by wind ; आशयात् - from flowers.

When a Jīvātmā leaves the body and acquires a second body, grasping the six senses takes them to the new body, like fragrance by the wind from flowers.

Intent - A Jīvātmā, the embodied Ātmā, has no permanent relationship with the body. There is only an occasional relationship for enjoyment, not real but imaginary. When the cause of enjoyment is exhausted, the Jīvātmā attracting the instruments of enjoyment (the mind and the senses) leaves just as the wind takes away fragrance from flowers. Though perceived as taking or leaving the body, it neither takes the body nor leaves the body. It is dissociated from taking or leaving, and indeed the light with which it appears taking or leaving is the same Jīvātmā, My supreme Status. With the limiting adjunct of a pot, with the being and not-being of the pot, the pot-enclosed space is imagined as being and not-being. However, the pot-enclosed space does not become or not-become. With the coming and going of the subtle and causal body, coming and going is imagined in the witness-form Jīvātmā. In reality, the witness-form Jīvātmā being itself immovable is existent before it comes and goes where it has to go. That witness-form is My supreme Status, going where this Saṃsāra-tree is uprooted.

(What are those six senses with the mind? -)

श्रोत्रं चक्षुः स्पर्शनं च रसनं घ्राणमेव च |
अधिष्ठाय मनश्चायं विषयानुपसेवते || BG 15.9 ||

अयम् - This (Jīvātmā) ; उपसेवते - experiences ; विषयान् - objects (resorting to) ; श्रोत्रम् - the ears, ; चक्षुः - eyes, ; च - and ; स्पर्शनम् - skin, ; च - and ; रसनम् - tongue, ; च - and ; घ्राणम् - nose, ; एव - only ; अधिष्ठाय - with the support of ; मनः - the mind.

The Jīvātmā experiences objects resorting to the ears, eyes, skin, tongue, and nose with the support of the mind.

Intent - The five senses on their own cannot experience their objects. However, with whatever sense the mind is united, that sense can experience its object, just as employees are active under their manager. That is why the mind is called the presider (Adhiṣṭhātā) over the senses. In reality, the Jīvātmā being unmodifiable is not the experiencer of objects. However, due to oneness with the mind, mind-created (मनस्कृत, Manaskṛta) experiences are attributed to the witness-form Jīvātmā. The Jīvātmā, in its true nature, is just the spectator of the experiences. Though the Jīvātmā, depending on the mind, is perceived as experiencing objects through the senses, in reality, it is dissociated from them all.

(Despite that -)

उत्क्रामन्तं स्थितं वापि भुञ्जानं वा गुणान्वितम् |
विमूढा नानुपश्यन्ति पश्यन्ति ज्ञानचक्षुषः || BG 15.10 ||

विमूढाः - The deluded ; न - do not ; अनुपश्यन्ति - see (the Jīvātmā) ; उत्क्रामन्तम् - leaving, ; वा - or ; स्थितम् - staying, ; वा - or ; भुञ्जानम् - experiencing ; गुण-अन्वितम् - through the association with the constituents. ; अपि - Only ; ज्ञान-चक्षुषः - the one with the eyes of wisdom ; पश्यन्ति - perceives.

The deluded do not see the Jīvātmā leaving, staying, or experiencing through the association with the constituents. Only the one with the eyes of wisdom perceives.

Intent - Departure from one body, stay in another body, and enjoy objects and transformations of the constituents in the form of pleasure and pain - in all acts of the constituents, the Ātmā is present ever-continuous. Only with its existence is there the fruition of all acts of the constituents. Knowing the Ātmā analytically, liberation in the form of attainment of the supreme Status and the supreme abode is successful. Ignorant humans do not know that the Ātmā has effulgence brighter than the sun, and indeed not knowing it, they flow away into the Saṃsāra ocean. In reality, in the Jīvātmā, there is no departing in the form of leaving the body, no staying, and no experiencing of enjoyment objects nor association with the constituents. First, perceived as departing from the body, in reality, there is no departing in it; and second, appearing as situated in the body, there is no behavior in the form of staying. Perceived as associated with the constituents and thus experiencing enjoyment objects, it neither is stained by the constituents nor becomes an experiencer. Indeed, it is present in all departures, all staying, harmony of all constituents, and enjoyment. However, it does not do anything; it is a non-doer and is only in witness form, an observer. All departing, staying, and enjoyment are fruitful only on its existence and thus power, yet it is dissociated from them. In reality, all these departing and staying, and constituents and enjoyment are in the kingdom of Prakṛti. Due to the limiting adjunct of nescience, they are imagined in the witness-form Jīvātmā. That is why, in the witness-form Jīvātmā, there is no stain from those modifications. Just as in the space, the name pot-enclosed space or the activity of bringing water are all imagined from the perspective of the limiting adjunct of the pot; without the adjunct of the pot, there is neither any name pot-enclosed space in the pervasive space nor is there any activity of bringing water. Though the fruition of these names and acts happens in support of the space, the space in itself "is as is" dissociated. In the same way, in the pervasive-conscious, the names Jīvātmā and thus Sākṣī (witness) and the acts of departing, staying, and enjoying are imagined from the perspective of limiting adjunct of nescience. Though all these names, forms, and acts happen in its support, without its existence, all these dealings are impossible, and even then, it "is as is" as it was.

From the above perspective, it is a doer of everything (Sarva-Kartā) yet is a non-doer (Akartā); it is an experiencer of everything (Sarva-Bhoktā) yet is a non-experiencer (Abhoktā). Accordingly, one who is present in all transformations of the constituents and experiences, the supreme Status is not seen by the deluded. However, whose eyes of wisdom have opened up, such discerning sages directly perceive the supreme Status in themselves, becoming liberated while alive.

यतन्तो योगिनश्चैनं पश्यन्त्यात्मन्यवस्थितम् |
यतन्तोऽप्यकृतात्मानो नैनं पश्यन्त्यचेतसः || BG 15.11 ||

यतन्तः - Persevering ; योगिनः - Yogīs ; पश्यन्ति - see ; एनम् - this (supreme Status) ; अवस्थितम् - situated ; आत्मनि - only within the heart, ; च - but ; अचेतसः - those undiscerning ; अकृत-आत्मानः - with an impure conscience ; न - do not ; पश्यन्ति - see ; एनम् - it, ; अपि - even ; यतन्तः - striving.

Persevering Yogīs see the supreme Status situated only within the heart, but those undiscerning with an impure conscience do not see it, even striving.

Intent - Striving Yogīs who have their minds in union directly see the witness-form supreme Status in the heart, "That I am." However, those whose conscience has not become pure from the impurities of worldly attachments, such ignorant humans, even after trying, cannot see that bliss-form supreme Status, even though it is incredibly close. With the fault of sleep, it is like a mother who cannot see her child clinging to her chest and "My child is lost! My child is lost!" screams in her dream. The intention is that effort of every living being is in the search for that supreme bliss. They run for that supreme Status, whether it is a discerning sage or an ignorant human. However, even striving and having heard from preceptors and scriptures, those ignorant humans cannot see that supreme-bliss sitting right in their hearts, and all their efforts remain worthless. Just as one cannot see one's face even though one is extremely close to a mirror covered with impurities, the conscience of the ignorant, covered by the dirt of worldly attachments and not mopped by the broom of dispassion, does not perceive own true Ātmā even though it is extremely contiguous, and instead of seeing own true Ātmā only sees the world of the bodies and senses.

In verse BG 15.4, the supreme Status that Bhagavāna commanded to search, and upon whose acquisition the final exemption from transmigration (Apunarāvṛtti) was promised, that extremely close location of the supreme Status with whose attainment the entire Saṃsāra-tree would be uprooted was narrated. In the following four verses, Bhagavāna provides the omnipresence and beingness of the Ātmā of all beings and articulates that in the Saṃsāra, whatever name, form, and actions manifest, they all materialize because of the power of that supreme Status; they are all its miracles, and that supreme Status is My true nature.

यदादित्यगतं तेजो जगद्भासयतेऽखिलम् |
यच्चन्द्रमसि यच्चाग्नौ तत्तेजो विद्धि मामकम् || BG 15.12 ||

तेजः - The luminosity ; आदित्य-गतं - in the sun ; यत् - that ; भासयते - illuminates ; अखिलम् - the entire ; जगत् - world, ; तेजः - the brilliance ; यत् - which ; चन्द्रमसि - is in the moon ; च - and ; यत् - which ; अग्नौ - is in the fire, ; विद्धि - know ; तत् - them ; मामकम् - to be Mine alone.

The luminosity in the sun that illuminates the entire world, the brilliance in the moon and fire, know them to be Mine alone.

Intent - The brilliance in the sun, moon, and fire is not their own. They have acquired their brilliance by borrowing from the supreme Status. "My luminosity is not like the qualitative brilliance in the sun. Devoid of all attributes, it remains the same, all-pervading and common luminosity." In the sun and moon, the attribute of their brilliance is based on the special purity of their limiting adjuncts. For instance, because of the impurity of the adjunct, one in front of clay and wood cannot perceive one's image; however, in water and mirror, as the adjuncts become purer, commensurately, the image becomes clearer. In the same way, "My common luminosity even though is always same and all-pervading, based on the purity of the adjuncts of the sun and the moon, in them, there is corresponding brilliance."

गामाविश्य च भूतानि धारयाम्यहमोजसा |
पुष्णामि चौषधी: सर्वा: सोमो भूत्वा रसात्मक: || BG 15.13 ||

च - And ; आविश्य - entering ; गाम् - into the earth, ; अहम् - I ; धारयामि - sustain ; भूतानि - all beings ; ओजसा - with My power, ; च - and ; भूत्वा - becoming ; सोमः - the moon ; पुष्णामि - I nourish ; सर्वाः - all ; ओषधीः - medicinal herbs and plants ; रसात्मकः - with (My) sapidity.

Entering into the earth, I sustain all beings with My power. Becoming the moon, I nourish all medicinal herbs and plants with My sapidity.

Intent - The might with which the earth is sustaining all beings, and with the massive load it does not collapse and splinter, that might is not hers, but only with the power of My supreme Status, she becomes mighty to sustain all. That is, My divine form present in the earth sustains all. Similarly, the sapidity with which the moon has become sapid nourishes all plants, crops, and medicinal herbs and fills them with flavor; that sapidity is not of the moon. Indeed, My sapidity with which the moon has become sapid and is distributing the sap to the herbs, just as a king's treasurer takes food from the king's food repository and distributes it to the hungry, satisfying their hunger.

अहं वैश्वानरो भूत्वा प्राणिनां देहमाश्रित: |
प्राणापानसमायुक्त: पचाम्यन्नं चतुर्विधम् || BG 15.14 ||

भूत्वा - Becoming ; वैश्वानरः - the fire of digestion ; आश्रितः - (and) residing ; देहम् - in the body ; प्राणिनाम् - of the living beings, ; प्राण-अपान-समायुक्तः - together with inhalation and exhalation, ; अहम् - I ; पचामि - digest ; चतुः-विधम् - fourfold ; अन्नम् - foods.

Becoming the fire of digestion and residing in the body of the living beings, together with inhalation and exhalation, I digest fourfold foods.

Intent - The fire of digestion (वैश्वानर, Vaiśvānara) situated in all living beings with the bellows of in-breath (Prāṇa-Vāyu) and out-breath (Apāna-Vayu) digests four kinds of foods: 1) masticable (भक्ष्य, Bhakṣya), 2) swallowable (भोज्य, Bhojya), 3) lickable (लेह्य, Lehya), and 4) suckable (चोष्य, Coṣya). That bellows action, meaning the inhalation and exhalation and the digestive power is not of the Vaiśvānara fire; however, it becomes powerful to engage in its activities only with My power. That is similar to how the fire-deity devoid of power was able to burn the Khāṇḍava forest by the power of Bhagavāna (Ādi-Parva - Mahābhārata).

सर्वस्य चाहं हृदि सन्निविष्टो मत्त: स्मृतिर्ज्ञानमपोहनं च |
वेदैश्च सर्वैरहमेव वेद्यो वेदान्तकृद्वेदविदेव चाहम् || BG 15.15 ||

अहम् - I ; सन्निविष्टः - am situated ; हृदि - in the heart ; सर्वस्य - of all ; च - and ; मत्तः - through Me (emanates) ; स्मृतिः - memory, ; ज्ञानम् - knowledge ; च - and ; अपोहनम् - forgetfulness. ; सर्वैः - Through all ; वेदैः - the Vedas, ; अहम् - I ; एव - alone am ; वेद्यः - to be known. ; च - And ; अहम् - I am ; वेद-वित् - the knower of the Vedas ; च - and ; एव - also ; वेदान्त-कृत् - the cause of the Vedānta.

I am situated in the heart of all and through Me emanates memory, knowledge and forgetfulness. Through all the Vedas, I alone am to be known. I am the knower of the Vedas and the cause of the Vedānta.

Intent - The light situated in the hearts of all beings and in which light the memory (स्मृति-वृत्ति, Smṛti-Vṛtti), the current knowledge (अनुभव-वृत्ति, Anubhava-Vṛtti) and their absence shine, that light is Mine only. That is how a lamp flame with its light lights up the existence and non-existence of all things in a house. That thing ought to be known by the Vedas, that I am. Here I am the cause of the Vedānta, and there I am the knower of the Vedas. That is, the knower, the knowledge, and the ought to be known threesome are existent only through Me, and I am in all of them.

(In this manner, from verse BG 15.12 up to here, both far and near, Bhagavāna described his pervasiveness and being the Ātmā of all.)

(Now, separate from the adjuncts of perishable and imperishable, the adjunctless-form of the Paramātmā is articulated in the following verses -)

द्वाविमौ पुरुषौ लोके क्षरश्चाक्षर एव च |
क्षर: सर्वाणि भूतानि कूटस्थोऽक्षर उच्यते || BG 15.16 ||

इमौ - (There are) these ; द्वौ - two ; पुरुषौ - persons (groups of adjuncts) ; लोके - in the world, ; क्षरः - the perishable ; च - and ; अक्षरः - the imperishable. ; सर्वाणि - All ; भूतानि - beings ; उच्यते - are said to be ; क्षरः - perishable, ; च - and ; अक्षरः - the imperishable ; एव - is indeed ; कूटस्थः - the Māyā.

There are two persons (groups of adjuncts) in the world, the perishable and the imperishable. All beings are said to be perishable, and the imperishable is the Māyā.

Intent - The term Puruṣa (पुरुष) normally means a person. Here, in verse, it is intended to represent a group of adjuncts. The term Kṣara (क्षर) means perishable. Whatever there are consists of the five great elements: earth, water, fire, wind, and space (पञ्च-भूतात्मक, Pañca-Bhūtātmaka) and consists of the five objects of senses: touch, taste, form, smell, and sound (पञ्च-विषयात्मक, Pañca-Viṣayātmaka), from Mahat-Tattva to the perceptible world, being transformations and subject to creation and destruction is said to be Kṣara-Puruṣa (क्षर-पुरुष, perishable person). The term Kūṭastha here means Māyā, the seed of creating the perishable group of adjuncts (Kṣara-Puruṣa). The entire perishable group of adjuncts is the transformation of Māyā. Māyā, which is the refuge of all desires and dynamic impressions (Saṃskāras) of all beings, is called Akṣara-Puruṣa (अक्षर-पुरुष, imperishable person) - meaning the imperishable group of adjuncts. Again, to clarify, the term Puruṣa is in the sense of division. Whatever there is in the world can be divided into two divisions. One is the act or effect of Māyā, which is the Kṣara-Puruṣa. The other being Māyā itself as the effect is Akṣara-Puruṣa. The term Kūṭa (कूट) means one who is deceptively situated. That is, in reality, it is not in its true nature. The way it is perceived is only due to ignorance. It is the one that deludes the Jīva. That is why Māyā here is said to be Kūṭastha. During the period of ignorance, even with the dissolution of the Saṃsāra, it does not perish and remains in seed-form during the dissolution. That is why it is called imperishable. Other than the perishable and imperishable, untouched by the taints of these two groups of adjuncts, is the Supreme Personality.

उत्तम: पुरुषस्त्वन्य: परमात्मेत्युदाहृत: |
यो लोकत्रयमाविश्य बिभर्त्यव्यय ईश्वर: || BG 15.17 ||

तु - However, ; अन्यः - distinct from these ; उत्तमः - is the supreme ; पुरुषः - Personality, ; उदाहृतः - said to be ; परम्-आत्मा - the Paramātmā ; इति - as such. ; आविश्य - Entering ; लोक-त्रयम् - the three worlds, ; यः अव्ययः - the imperishable ; ईश्वरः - Lord ; बिभर्ति - sustains all.

Distinct from these is the Supreme Personality, said to be the Paramātmā. Entering the three worlds, the imperishable Lord sustains all.

Intent - The One that is distinct from the perishable (Kṣara) and imperishable (Akṣara), that is, on Whose dependence fruition of both happen, in Whom there is the absence in the past, present, and future. One Who is neither perishable nor imperishable, such Supreme Personality, Who is the underlying support of both, is called the Paramātmā. The imperishable Lord enters the three worlds, the earth, the heavens, and the space, and with His power holds the three yet is dissociated from them. The Uttama (उत्तम, supreme) Puruṣa (पुरुष, Personality) is best known as Puruṣottama, the Supreme Personality, the celebrated name of the Lord.

(Etymologizing the name Puruṣottama to articulate its denotive power, Bhagavāna presents Himself as the unsurpassed -)

यस्मात्क्षरमतीतोऽहमक्षरादपि चोत्तमः |
अतोऽस्मि लोके वेदे च प्रथितः पुरुषोत्तमः || BG 15.18 ||

यस्मात् - Since ; अहम् - I ; अतीतः - surpass ; क्षरम् - the perishable ; च - and ; अपि - also ; उत्तमः - (am) exalted above ; अक्षरात् - the imperishable, ; अतः - that is why ; लोके - (both) in the world (in common speech) ; च - and ; वेदे - in the Vedas, ; अस्मि - I am ; प्रथितः - celebrated ; पुरुषोत्तमः - as the Puruṣottama.

Since I surpass the perishable and am exalted above the imperishable, both in common speech and in the Vedas, I am celebrated as the Puruṣottama.

Intent - I am beyond the perishable scene and the transforming world. Though the origination, sustentation, and dissolution of the perishable world are on My dependence, I am immutably existent "as I am." I am exalted above the imperishable Māyā. That is because the imperishable Māyā is only perceived during the period of ignorance when it shows her true colors. However, upon awakening knowledge, its absence in the past, present, and future materializes, yet My non-existence does not happen. I am ever existent. Accordingly, being exalted above the perishable and imperishable personalities both in the world (in everyday speech) and in the Vedas, I am celebrated as the Puruṣottama - the Supreme Personality.

(The fruit of knowing the Supreme Personality is narrated -)

यो मामेवमसम्मूढो जानाति पुरुषोत्तमम् |
स सर्वविद्भजति मां सर्वभावेन भारत || BG 15.19 ||

भारत - Hey Bhārata (Arjuna)! ; असम्मूढः - The undeluded ; यः - who ; जानाति - knows ; माम् - Me ; पुरुषोत्तमम् - the "Puruṣottama" ; एवम् - thus, ; सः - he ; सर्व-वित् - the all-knowing ; भजति - adores ; माम् - Me ; सर्व-भावेन - in all sentiments.

Hey Arjuna! The undeluded who knows Me the Puruṣottama thus, he the all-knowing adores Me in all sentiments.

Intent - Just as in the ocean, water perceived as waves or eddies is nothing but the form of water. Similarly, the Saṃsāra with attributes perceived in the one that is the existent common in all is indeed in the form of the existent common in all. In the underlying support (the Brahman), the imagined Saṃsāra is in the form of the Brahman. A knower of the Truth directly experiences Me the Puruṣottama that "I am That." Such an all-knowing, who knows the Ātmā of all as his Ātmā, with all his sentiments adores Me. In all his mental dispositions, he only sees Me and dwells in Me.

(Elucidating the knowledge of the Truth of the Lord, it is extolled -)

इति गुह्यतमं शास्त्रमिदमुक्तं मयानघ |
एतद्बुद्ध्वा बुद्धिमान्स्यात्कृतकृत्यश्च भारत || BG 15.20 ||

अनघ - Hey Anagha (Arjuna)! ; इति - Thus, ; इदम् - this ; गुह्यतमम् - most profound ; शास्त्रम् - Śāstra ; उक्तम् - is spoken ; मया - by Me. ; भारत - Hey, Bhārata (Arjuna, the descendent of Bharata)! ; बुद्ध्वा - Knowing ; एतत् - it, ; स्यात् - one becomes ; बुद्धिमान् - wise ; च - and ; कृतकृत्यः - contented.

Hey Arjuna! Thus, this most profound Śāstra is spoken by Me. Hey, descendent of Bharata! Knowing it, one becomes wise and contented.

Intent - "In all the scriptures, this scripture is the most profound" - this way, the fifteenth chapter was extolled as scripture because the Truth embedded in all scriptures and Śrīmad Bhagavad Gītā is articulated here. Knowing this Truth, humans can become wise and contented. Knowing this Truth, there is nothing else to know, and in the Saṃsāra, whatever is proper to be done, that is accomplished by them, and there is nothing else left to be accomplished. Except for that, there is no end to duty by any approach. The liberation in the form of contentment is dependent directly on experiencing this knowledge. Without it, only through actions, attainment of contentment is impossible and is like a flower in the sky.

ॐ तत्सदिति श्रीमद्भगवद्गीतासूपनिषत्सु ब्रह्मविध्यायां योगशास्त्रे

श्रीकृष्णार्जुनसम्वादे पुरुषोत्तमयोगो नाम

पंचदशोऽध्यायः || BG 15 ||

Oṃ Tat Sat

In the Śrīmad Bhagavad Gītā Upaniṣad

The Yoga Science of the Knowledge of Self-Realization

The Discourse of Lord Śrī Kṛṣṇa and Arjuna

This Fifteenth Chapter

Yoga Named - The Yoga of the Supreme Personality

Clarification

In the fourteenth chapter, Bhagavāna described the three constituents of Prakṛti, association with whom liberation and bondage materialize in the Ātmā. To attain union in one's true nature, in this chapter Bhagavāna articulates the true nature of the Ātmā, the trueness of the substrate (Adhiṣṭhāna) Paramātmā, and the illusory nature of the Saṃsāra that is superimposed (Adhyasta) on the Paramātmā.

In the first verse, the impossibility of the Saṃsāra was narrated. Giving it a metaphor for a tree, it is shown to have roots upwards (Ūrdhva-Mūla) and branches spread down (Adhaḥ-Śākham). The root of the Saṃsāra can only be the existent Paramātmā. Besides that, nothing can be held as the root. That is so because, separate from it, whatever there is, it is all unreal (Mithyā), not there, just delusional born of ignorance and is merely a transformation or effect. The creation of a delusional thing is impossible from something delusional. A delusional thing absent before and after, only perceived in the middle time, is by itself nothing (null-form), and nothing cannot be the cause of something.

Moreover, that which is an action or effect is caused (Janya), being in the form of creation and destruction (Utpatti-Nāśa) is delusional or unreal (Mithyā). Anything in the form of action (Kārya) cannot be the cause of the unreal Saṃsāra. Therefore, the Paramātmā is the only one that can be held as the root of the Saṃsāra. No mutations of the Saṃsāra can touch it. In it, without any initiation and transformation, the Saṃsāra materialized serendipitously, just as a dream world emerges in sleep, which is never steady. Accordingly, from an impossibility perspective, the Saṃsāra is with branches that are spread down, and surprisingly Bhagavāna said, "The deluded call the Saṃsāra imperishable. However, those who know it really are the real knowers of the Vedas."

In the second verse, the extent of the spread of the Saṃsāra-tree was narrated and said that only actions of human life flourish it. The third verse stated that just as the extent of the Saṃsāra-tree is perceived from a physical perspective, it is not found so from an analytic perspective. Because in the existent Paramātmā, neither creation nor sustentation or dissolution of the Mithyā Saṃsāra-tree can be seen. Only due to nescience with the association of I-ness and mineness, the unreal Saṃsāra-tree is made stout by imagination, just as a child becomes fearful of seeing his shadow, imagining it as a non-existent ghost. That is why Bhagavāna commanded to shear the Saṃsāra-tree with a strong weapon of detachment. The fourth verse stated that one ought to search for the underlying support - the supreme Status - in which the imagined Saṃsāra is perceived. Accordingly, a strong weapon in the form of renunciation of all attachments (Sarva-Saṅga-Parityāga) and the search for the supreme Status are the only two approaches depicted to uproot the Saṃsāra-tree. In the fifth verse, instruments necessary to renounce attachments to be accumulated were articulated. Then from the sixth verse up to the end of the chapter, the location of that supreme Status that is nearer than the nearest and farther than the farthest was articulated. Attaining such Status absence of the Saṃsāra-tree is determined in the past, present, and future, as follows -

The Status that even the sun, moon, and fire cannot illuminate, and once gone there, there is no return to the world of transmigrating lives. That is My supreme Status. In this world, the one called Jīva, the Jīvātmā, the individual self, the soul - in their pure form is My eternal form. That is, the Jīvātmā, before ignorance, was My form, and upon liberation from ignorance, is also My form. Only in the time of nescience, due to its influence, a delusional perception of separation from Me sets in, though in reality, even in that time, there is no separation, just as a billionaire sees himself in his dream as a pauper, does not make him a pauper. Just as a person enjoys his meals with the help of spoons and forks, in the same way, bound by ignorance, a Jīvātmā experiences objects of the senses and mind. When it exhausts its enjoyments, then taking with it the instruments of enjoyments, viz. the mind and senses, enters another body and enjoys its accumulated assets, just as a mountaineer moves from one camp to the next and there utilizes his backpacked food and gear. Though supreme Status exists in departing, staying, and leaving, it is doing everything but is "not doing anything" and is dissociated from all, yet the deluded do not see. Only the ones with the eyes of wisdom see and attain union with oneness in Me - the supreme Status. The luminosity in the sun, which illuminates the entire world, the brilliance in the moon and the fire are all Mine alone. Just as a flag furling full mast on the palace indicates the king's presence, in the same way, the brilliance in the sun and the moon is indicative of the presence of My effulgence. Entering into the earth, I sustain all beings with My power. Becoming the moon, I nourish all plants and herbs with My sapidity. Becoming the fire of digestion (Vaiśvānara) and residing in the body of living beings, together with inhalation and exhalation, I digest fourfold foods. Residing in the hearts of all with My light, I illuminate all kinds of knowledge - memories, current knowledge, and forgetfulness (BG 15.6 - BG 15.15).

Accordingly, whatever light exists - be it in knowledge, substances, attributes, or acts - the location of its existence was provided. In summarizing, Bhagavāna stated that in the Saṃsāra, there are two kinds of persons (groups of adjuncts). One is the group of manifest entities in the form of creation and destruction called Kṣara-Puruṣa (perishable person). The other, unmanifest Māyā, which does not perish even upon the destruction of living beings, is called the Akṣara-Puruṣa (imperishable person). However, distinct from these two is the Uttama (best) Puruṣa (person) known as the Puruṣottama, the Supreme Personality, Lord Viṣṇu - Who enters the three worlds of the perishable and imperishable and sustains them all. Though the creation and destruction act of the perishable materialize near Me, I am unborn and eternal; that is why I am beyond and dissociated from the perishable.

Additionally, the performance of the imperishable and transformable Māyā materializes only under My illumination. That Māyā cannot make Me dance. That is why I am the best. I am celebrated as the Puruṣottama in the Vedas and the world. Whether it is the transformable Saṃsāra (perishable person) or the transformable Māyā (imperishable person), both are without their existence and thus power; only because of My power are they perceived as if they had power. Further, they are perceived as such only in the time of their delusionary knowledge, just as how in a rope a snake is perceived in the time of delusionary knowledge. In reality, the snake is only in the form of a rope.

In the same way, both the modifiable world and the modifiable Māyā are nothing but My form. One who truly knows Me as such the Puruṣottama, that all-knowing undeluded person who sees everything as the

Brahman adores Me in all sentiments. That is, "यत्र यत्र मनो याति तत्र तत्र समाधाय:, wherever that person's mind goes he only experiences his true Ātmā."

This way, Bhagavāna articulated how upon finding the supreme Status, the Saṃsāra-tree is uprooted. In the end, Bhagavāna said - "Hey Arjuna! I have spoken this most profound Śāstra. Knowing it, one becomes wise and contented." The intent being liberation in the form of contentment (कृतकृत्यता, Kṛtakṛtyatā) is dependent only on knowledge.

Chapter 16

The Yoga of the Attributes - Divine and Demonic

{In the fifteenth chapter, to search for the supreme Status, Bhagavāna provided knowledge of His true nature. Accumulation of helpful divine attributes (दैवी-सम्पत्ति, Daivī-Sampatti) and abandonment of detrimental demonic attributes (आसुरी-सम्पत्ति, Āsurī-Sampatti) is articulated in the attainment of that knowledge. Among them, first, the divine attributes are narrated -}

श्रीभगवानुवाच |
अभयं सत्त्वसंशुद्धिर्ज्ञानयोगव्यवस्थितिः |
दानं दमश्च यज्ञश्च स्वाध्यायस्तप आर्जवम् || BG 16.1 ||
अहिंसा सत्यमक्रोधस्त्यागः शान्तिरपैशुनम् |
दया भूतेष्वलोलुप्त्वं मार्दवं ह्रीरचापलम् || BG 16.2 ||
तेजः क्षमा धृतिः शौचमद्रोहोनातिमानिता |
भवन्ति सम्पदं दैवीमभिजातस्य भारत || BG 16.3 ||
श्रीभगवान् उवाच - Śrī Bhagavān said -

अभयम् - Fearlessness, ; सत्त्व-संशुद्धिः - mental purity, ; ज्ञान-योग-व्यवस्थितिः - uniquely situated in knowledge and Yoga, ; दानम् - charity, ; दमः - restraint of the senses, ; यज्ञः - the performance of sacrifices, ; स्वाध्यायः - self-study (of the scriptures), ; च - and ; तपः - austerity, ; च - and ; आर्जवम् - simplicity,

अहिंसा - non-violence, ; सत्यम् - truthfulness, ; अक्रोधः - the absence of anger, ; त्यागः - renunciation, ; शान्तिः - tranquility, ; अपैशुनम् - the absence of fault-finding, ; दया - kindness towards ; भूतेषु - living beings, ; अलोलुप्त्वम् - uncovetousness, ; मार्दवम् - gentleness, ; ह्रीः - shyness, ; अचापलम् - steadiness,

तेजः - splendor, ; क्षमा - forgiveness, ; धृतिः - fortitude, ; शौचम् - cleanliness, ; अद्रोहः - benevolence, ; न अति-मानिता - (and) humility, ; भारत - hey, Bhārata (Arjuna)! ; भवन्ति - these are ; अभिजातस्य - those born ; दैवीम् - with divine ; सम्पदम् - attributes.

Śrī Bhagavān said -

Fearlessness, mental purity, uniquely situated in knowledge and Yoga, charity, restraint of the senses, the performance of sacrifices, self-study of the scriptures, austerity, simplicity, non-violence, truthfulness, the absence of anger, renunciation, tranquility, the absence of fault-finding, kindness towards living beings, uncovetousness, gentleness, shyness, steadiness, splendor, forgiveness, fortitude, cleanliness, benevolence, and humility, hey, Arjuna! These are those born with divine attributes.

The intent of verses (BG 16.1 - BG 16.3) - Fear is a natural, powerful and primitive emotion in the conscience involving a universal biochemical response and a high emotional response. Its absence is called fearlessness

(अभय, Abhaya). Pure conduct without guile in dealings with others and the purging of attachments from the heart is called mental purity (सत्त्व-संशुद्धि, Sattva-Saṃśuddhi). Knowing elements such as the Ātmā through preceptors and scriptures is called knowledge (ज्ञान, Jñāna) and experiencing the known through control of the senses and concentration (एकाग्रता, Ekāgratā) is called Yoga (योग, union). To be absorbed (तन्मय, Tanmaya) in both of them is to uniquely situate (व्यवस्थिति, Vyavasthiti). These are the predominant divine attributes. Ability-based donation of food and other substances is called charity (दान, Dāna). Restraint of the senses is called Dama (दम), and sacrifices such as Agnihotra (अग्निहोत्र) and worship of the deities are called Yajña (यज्ञ). Thoughtfully studying the scriptures related to the Lord is called self-study (स्वाध्याय, Svādhyāya). Austerity (तप, Tapa) is covered in Chapter 17. Additionally, straightforwardness and absence of crookedness in mental and vocal conduct related to eating, drinking, and clothing are called simplicity (आर्जव, Ārjava). Non-violence (अहिंसा, Ahiṃsā) means not injuring or hurting anyone through the body, mind, or speech. Truthfulness (सत्य, Satya) means pleasant but true words of speech. Subduing anger upon facing anger-producing occasions, absence of anger is called (अक्रोध, Akrodha). Relinquishment (त्याग, Tyāga) means giving up the body-related worldly personal interests. The steadiness of the conscience is called tranquility (शान्ति, Śānti). To disclose faults of others to third parties is called Paiśunya (पैशुन्य, fault finding); its absence is called Apaiśunya (अपैशुन्य). Kindness towards the suffering is called Dayā (दया). The absence of attachment to sense-objects, uncovetousness is called Aloluptva (अलोलुप्त्व). Mārdava (मार्दव) means gentleness, Hrī (ह्री) means shyness, and absence of worthless efforts, steadiness is called Acāpalya (अचापल्य). The influence of truth in the heart, face, and words that others are bound to follow the path of truth is splendor (तेज, Teja). Not desiring retaliation on those who have offended is called forgiveness (क्षमा, Kṣamā). Dhṛti (धृति) means fortitude. Cleanliness (शौच, Śauca) is of two kinds. One is external cleanliness, such as cleaning the body with water and soap or soil and the surroundings clean. The other internal cleanliness is the mental purity from attachment and aversion. Benevolence (अद्रोह, Adroha) is the absence of despite towards anyone, and "न अति-मानिता" means humility or the absence of excessive pride. Hey Arjuna! These are the attributes of a person born with divine attributes. These are the attributes in a person who is fit to become a divinity and, in the future, whose good is definite.

(Next, the attributes of a person born with demonic attributes are narrated -)

दम्भो दर्पोऽभिमानश्च क्रोधः पारुष्यमेव च |
अज्ञानं चाभिजातस्य पार्थ सम्पदमासुरीम् || BG 16.4 ||

पार्थ - Hey Pārtha (Arjuna)! ; दम्भः - Hypocrisy, ; दर्पः - arrogance, ; अभिमानः - excessive vanity, ; च - and ; क्रोधः - anger, ; च - and ; पारुष्यम् - harshness, ; च - and ; एव - also ; अज्ञानम् - ignorance ; अभिजातस्य - (are the attributes of a person) born with ; आसुरीम् - demonic ; सम्पदम् - attributes.

Hey Arjuna! Hypocrisy, arrogance, excessive vanity, anger, harshness, and ignorance are the attributes of a person born with demonic attributes.

Intent - Hypocrisy (दम्भ, Dambha) means ostentatious religiosity. Arrogance (दर्प, Darpa) means haughtiness due to knowledge, wealth, or family. Abhimāna (अभिमान) means excessive vanity. Anger (क्रोध, Krodha) means agitation in the conscience. Harshness (पारुष्य, Pāruṣya) refers to blunt speech such as calling a one-eyed person "a man with bright eyes" and so forth. Ignorance (अज्ञान, Ajñāna) means non-discernment, non-discriminative cognition, or erroneous notions regarding duties and other actions. These are the attributes of a person born with "demonic attributes."

दैवी सम्पद्विमोक्षाय निबन्धायासुरी मता |
मा शुचः सम्पदं दैवीमभिजातोऽसि पाण्डव || BG 16.5 ||

दैवी सम्पत् - Divine attributes ; मता - are deemed ; विमोक्षाय - for liberation (Mokṣa) ; आसुरी - (and) demonic (attributes are deemed) ; निबन्धाय - for bondage. ; पाण्डव - (Therefore,) hey, Pāṇḍava (Arjuna)! ; मा - Do not ; शुचः - grieve. ; असि - You are ; अभिजातः - born with ; दैवीम् - divine ; सम्पदम् - attributes.

Divine attributes are deemed for liberation and demonic attributes for bondage. Therefore, hey, Arjuna! Do not grieve. You are born with divine attributes.

Intent - With the relationship of I-ness, mineness, self-interest, desires, and attachments, there is bondage with the Saṃsāra, and freedom from them is liberation (मुक्ति, Mukti). The more this relationship of I-ness and mineness is firm the more firmly the bondage of the Saṃsāra binds humans. Conversely, the slacker this relationship is, the looser the bondage will be. Demonic attributes with their relationship make I-ness and mineness firm, similar to how extreme cold makes water freeze. That is why it is deemed detrimental. However, divine attributes make I-ness and mineness subtle, similar to how water turns into a vapor by the heat of the fire. It is then that a human becomes fit and qualified for the search for the supreme Status, and so it is said to be the cause for liberation. Seeing Arjuna perplexed, perhaps wondering - "Are my attributes divine or demonic?" - Bhagavāna said - "Hey Arjuna! Do not grieve. You are born with divine attributes." In the future, your good is definite.

द्वौ भूतसर्गौ लोकेऽस्मिन्दैव आसुर एव च |
दैवो विस्तरश: प्रोक्त आसुरं पार्थ मे शृणु || BG 16.6 ||

दैवः - Divine ; च - and ; आसुरः - demonic ; एव - are ; द्वौ - the two orders of ; भूत-सर्गौ - human creations ; अस्मिन् - in this ; लोके - world. ; पार्थ - Hey Pārtha (Arjuna)! ; दैवः - Divine ; प्रोक्तः - is spoken ; विस्तरशः - extensively. ; शृणु - Hear ; मे - from Me - ; आसुरम् - the demonic.

Divine and demonic are the two orders of human creations in this world. Hey Arjuna! Divine is spoken extensively. Hear from Me - the demonic.

Intent - At the beginning of the creation, two sets of progenies of Prajāpati - the deities (Sura, Deva) and the demons (Asura, Dānava, Daitya) are narrated in the Śruti. Just as wars between the deities and the demons are described in the scriptures, there is always a battle between good and bad in the heart of every human being. So, in the hearts of humans, both of them must reside. With the dominance of divine attributes in the hearts of some, demonic attributes are suppressed; and in some, demonic attributes are dominant, and divine attributes are suppressed, though both are there. In every being, at different times, one can see the strength or weakness of both. In some periods, one can see divine attributes and, at other times, demonic attributes.

(Now, up to the end of the chapter, demonic attributes are described. That is so because only with the knowledge of their true nature one can abandon them -)

प्रवृत्तिं च निवृत्तिं च जना न विदुरासुरा: |
न शौचं नापि चाचारो न सत्यं तेषु विद्यते || BG 16.7 ||

आसुराः - Demonic ; जनाः - humans ; न - do not ; विदुः - discern ; प्रवृत्तिम् - (between) action ; च - and ; निवृत्तिम् - inaction. ; न - Neither ; शौचम् - cleanliness ; च - nor ; आचारः - pure conduct, ; च - and ; अपि - also ; न - no ; सत्यम् - truthfulness ; विद्यते - exist ; तेषु - in them.

Demonic humans do not discern between action and inaction. Neither cleanliness nor pure conduct or truthfulness exist in them.

Intent - Humans with demonic nature do not know what is proper for them to do or what is not proper for them to do. What they should accumulate and abandon - to secure happiness in this and the next world. However, believers of the body as the Ātmā decide every duty and non-duty, holding body-perspective and self-interest at the forefront. Hence, they gain neither happiness in this world nor the next world. There is a doctrine in the kingdom of Prakṛti that the firmer the body-related selfishness is, commensurately the fully armed Saṃsāra will stand up against it, and as a result, attachment, hate, envy, and anger will be waiting to greet it. The demonic natured neither know nor practice cleanliness, pure conduct, and truthfulness - the first limbs of righteousness. Instead, they are active in a behavior filled with dirtiness, impure conduct, and untruthfulness.

असत्यमप्रतिष्ठं ते जगदाहुरनीश्वरम् |
अपरस्परसम्भूतं किमन्यत्कामहैतुकम् || BG 16.8 ||

ते - They ; आहुः - declare that ; जगत् - the world ; असत्यम् - is untrue, ; अप्रतिष्ठम् - ungrounded, ; अनीश्वरम् - without a Supreme Being, ; अपरस्पर-सम्भूतं - created by mutual conjugation ; काम-हैतुकम् - for sexual gratification. ; किम् - (Other than that,) what ; अन्यत् - else is its cause?

They declare that the world is untrue, ungrounded, without a Supreme Being, created by mutual conjugation for sexual gratification. Other than that, what else is its cause?

Intent - Those with demonic attributes say that this world is not true. Just as we are, for the most part, full of lies, so is the world. It is groundless. It does not have any support in the form of righteousness or unrighteousness. It is without the Supreme Being. There is no one to maintain order from the perspective of righteousness and unrighteousness, piety, and sin. Besides, the world is born of conjugal relations between males and females, just for sexual gratification. Other than that, what else is its cause? There is no transcendent cause like righteousness and unrighteousness. The materialistic thinking of lust alone is the origin of living beings.

एतां दृष्टिमवष्टभ्य नष्टात्मानोऽल्पबुद्धयः |
प्रभवन्त्युग्रकर्माणः क्षयाय जगतोऽहिताः || BG 16.9 ||

अवष्टभ्य - Holding ; एताम् - such ; दृष्टिम् - views, ; नष्ट-आत्मानः - (these) lost souls ; अल्प-बुद्धयः - with weak minds ; उग्र-कर्माणः - (and) cruel actions ; प्रभवन्ति - are born ; अहिताः - as enemies ; जगतः - of the world ; क्षयाय - for its destruction.

Holding such views, these lost souls with weak minds and cruel actions are born as enemies of the world for its destruction.

Intent - "There is no righteousness or unrighteousness, no piety or sin. There is no Supreme Being to provide fruits of Karma, but this world is just for enjoyment" - holding such perspective, the feeble-minded stray from the path of the higher good. Only keeping a vision towards enjoyment and breaking the norms of the society and the Vedas, they behave fiercely violent toward the destruction of the world.

(This way, those persons -)

काममाश्रित्य दुष्पूरं दम्भमानमदान्विताः |
मोहाद्गृहीत्वासद्ग्राहान्प्रवर्तन्तेऽशुचिव्रताः || BG 16.10 ||

दम्भ-मान-मद-अन्विताः - Endowed with hypocrisy, vanity, and arrogance, ; आश्रित्य - resorting to ; दुष्पूरम् - insatiable ; कामम् - desires ; मोहात् - (and) ignorance ; गृहीत्वा - holding ; अशुचि-व्रताः - impure resolve, ; प्रवर्तन्ते - they conduct themselves ; असत्-ग्राहान् - with vile behavior.

Endowed with hypocrisy, vanity, and arrogance, resorting to insatiable desires and ignorance holding impure resolve, they conduct themselves with vile behavior.

चिन्तामपरिमेयां च प्रलयान्तामुपाश्रिताः |
कामोपभोगपरमा एतावदिति निश्चिताः || 16.11 ||

उपाश्रिताः - Bound by ; अपरिमेयाम् - endless ; चिन्ताम् - anxieties ; प्रलयान्ताम् - until death ; च - and ; काम-उपभोग-परमाः - intent on the gratification of the objects of desire, ; निश्चिताः - (they) believe ; इति - that ; एतावत् - (there is nothing beyond) "this much."

Bound by endless anxieties until death and intent on the gratification of the objects of desire, they believe there is nothing beyond "this much."

आशापाशशतैर्बद्धा: कामक्रोधपरायणा: |
ईहन्ते कामभोगार्थमन्यायेनार्थसञ्चयान् || BG 16.12 ||

बद्धाः - Bound by ; आशा-पाश-शतैः - hundreds of desire nooses ; काम-क्रोध-परायणाः - (and) absorbed in desire and anger, ; ईहन्ते - (they) seek ; अर्थ-सञ्चयान् - accumulation of wealth ; अन्यायेन - by unjust means ; काम-भोगार्थम् - for the gratification of the sense objects.

Bound by hundreds of desire nooses and absorbed in desire and anger, they seek accumulation of wealth by unjust means for the gratification of the sense objects.

Intent - When a human being forgets his true nature, an absence of discrimination ensues. From the absence of discrimination, delusion takes hold, and from delusion is born desire. With the strengthening of desire - expectations, anxiety, and anger make themselves known, similar to how his entourage of ministers and assistants arrive upon the arrival of a king. With desire, there is an expectation that happiness will be acquired upon satisfaction of the desire. However, when there is a sentiment of failure in the expectation, then anxiety burns the heart. With obstacles in the fulfillment of desire, a flame of anger sets ablaze just as when oil is poured on the fire. Expectations, anxiety, and anger are the roots of pain, which incinerates living beings like the fire of hell. As desires become stronger, commensurately discrimination perishes, and delusion flourishes. There is the nourishment of delusion from desires, and vice-a-versa with delusion, there is the nourishment of desires. Each of them mutually gains strength from the other. Then as desires and delusion become stronger, the ego becomes solidly insentient, and expectations, anxiety, and anger become stronger. Such is the bizarre puzzle of Prakṛti. Were desires bound by righteousness, the limits of humanity, and the Vedas, then upon a due time, becoming weak, they can reduce ego and delusion, and in proportionality, reduce expectations, anxiety, and anger. However, these masters of demonic attributes have said goodbye to all the limits and have firmly embraced only desires and gratification. In their hearts, breaking the limits of the banks, the flow of the merging three - expectations, anxiety, and anger is definite. As a result, it becomes easy for needles and pins of pain and affliction to engage. With some thought, it is seen that at the root of desires, the objective is only happiness, but look at the profundity of ignorance; instead of happiness, unhappiness is bought.

(How are their ideas? -)

इदमद्य मया लब्धमिमं प्राप्स्ये मनोरथम् |
इदमस्तीदमपि मे भविष्यति पुनर्धनम् || BG 16.13 ||

अद्य - Today, ; मया - I have ; लब्धम् - gained ; इदम् - this; ; प्राप्स्ये - I shall fulfill ; इमम् - these ; मनोरथम् - desires. ; मे - I ; अस्ति - have ; इदम् - this ; धनम् - wealth; ; पुनः - again, (I) ; अपि - will also ; भविष्यति - have ; इदम् - that much.

Today, I have gained this; I shall fulfill these desires. I have this wealth; again, I will have that much.

Intent - As of now, I have accumulated so much wealth, and I will acquire more. I have so much wealth, but I need more to become famous and well known for my riches.

असौ मया हत: शत्रुर्हनिष्ये चापरानपि |
ईश्वरोऽहमहं भोगी सिद्धोऽहं बलवान्सुखी || BG 16.14 ||

असौ - That ; शत्रुः - enemy ; हतः - is slain ; मया - by me, ; च - and ; हनिष्ये - I shall kill ; अपरान् - others ; अपि - too. ; अहं - I am ; ईश्वरः - the Lord. ; अहम् - I am ; भोगी - the enjoyer. ; अहम् - I am ; सिद्धः - perfect, ; बलवान् - strong (and) ; सुखी - happy.

That enemy is slain by me, and I shall kill others too. I am the Lord. I am the enjoyer. I am perfect, strong, and happy.

आढ्योऽभिजनवानस्मि कोऽन्योऽस्ति सदृशो मया |
यक्ष्ये दास्यामि मोदिष्य इत्यज्ञानविमोहिताः || BG 16.15 ||

अस्मि - I am ; आढ्यः - wealthy ; अभिजनवान् - (and) high-born. ; कः - Who ; अन्यः - else ; अस्ति - is ; सदृशः - like ; मया - me? ; यक्ष्ये - I will perform sacrifices, ; दास्यामि - donate, ; मोदिष्ये - (and) rejoice. ; इति - Thus, ; अज्ञान-विमोहिताः - (he) remains ignorantly deluded.

I am wealthy and high-born. Who else is like me? I will perform sacrifices, donate, and rejoice. Thus, he remains ignorantly deluded.

Intent - Being born with a silver spoon in a family of noted Vedic scholars, "I am wealthy and of high birth. There is no one equal to me. Besides, by sacrifices, I shall surpass others. I shall give donations, and I shall rejoice to my heart's content." Thus, with demonic attributes, they are ignorantly deluded, having lost their power of discrimination.

(How is the nature of such persons? -)

अनेकचित्तविभ्रान्ता मोहजालसमावृताः |
प्रसक्ताः कामभोगेषु पतन्ति नरकेऽशुचौ || BG 16.16 ||

अनेक-चित्त-विभ्रान्ताः - Mentally confused in many ways, ; मोह-जाल-समावृताः - caught in a net of delusion, ; प्रसक्ताः - (and) with unending attachment ; काम-भोगेषु - to lustful enjoyments, ; पतन्ति - (they) fall into ; अशुचौ - the unclean ; नरके - hell.

Mentally confused in many ways, caught in a net of delusion, and with unending attachment to lustful enjoyments, they fall into the unclean hell.

आत्मसम्भाविताः स्तब्धा धनमानमदान्विताः |
यजन्ते नामयज्ञैस्ते दम्भेनाविधिपूर्वकम् || BG 16.17 ||

आत्म-सम्भाविताः - Self-exalted, ; स्तब्धाः - stubborn, ; धन-मान-मद-अन्विताः - with excessive pride in wealth and fame, ; ते - they ; दम्भेन - hypocritically ; यजन्ते - worship ; नाम-यज्ञैः - through nominal sacrifices ; अविधि-पूर्वकम् - devoid of scriptural injunctions.

Self-exalted, stubborn, with excessive pride in wealth and fame, they hypocritically worship through nominal sacrifices devoid of scriptural injunctions.

Intent - They exalt themselves believing themselves to be the repository of all excellence, devoid of politeness, with excessive pride of wealth and fame, hypocritically worship through sacrifices only in name and without following injunctions of the scriptures.

अहङ्कारं बलं दर्पं कामं क्रोधं च संश्रिताः |
मामात्मपरदेहेषु प्रद्विषन्तोऽभ्यसूयकाः || BG 16.18 ||

संश्रिताः - Subdued by ; अहङ्कारम् - egoism, ; बलम् - power, ; दर्पम् - arrogance, ; कामम् - lust, ; क्रोधम् - anger, ; च - and ; अभ्यसूयकाः - envy, ; प्रद्विषन्तः - (they) are hateful ; माम् - towards Me (the Lord) ; आत्म-पर-देहेषु - existent in theirs and bodies of others.

Subdued by egoism, power, arrogance, lust, anger, and envy, they are hateful towards Me existent in theirs and bodies of others.

Intent - Absorbed in egoism, power (to suppress others with desires and attachments), arrogance, lust, anger, and jealousy, those who bad-mouth others are hateful to the Lord - dwelling in them and others. They do not know that only one Lord is sitting in themselves and their opponents. Thus, by strengthening the distinction of unreal body-form adjuncts, the venom of antipathy spewed will touch that Reality and, in the end, will return to inflict themselves.

(What is the end of those with such demonic attributes? -)

तानहं द्विषत: क्रूरान्संसारेषु नराधमान् |
क्षिपाम्यजस्रमशुभानासुरीष्वेव योनिषु || BG 16.19 ||

अहम् - I ; अजस्रम् - repeatedly ; क्षिपामि - cast down ; तान् - those ; द्विषतः - hateful, ; क्रूरान् - cruel, ; अशुभान् - impious, ; नराधमान् - (and) vile humans ; संसारेषु - in the Saṃsāra ; आसुरीषु - in demonic ; योनिषु - wombs ; एव - only.

I repeatedly cast down those hateful, cruel, impious, and vile humans in the Saṃsāra in demonic wombs only.

Intent - The demonic wombs mean violent species like tigers and lions.

आसुरीं योनिमापन्ना मूढा जन्मनि जन्मनि |
मामप्राप्यैव कौन्तेय ततो यान्त्यधमां गतिम् || BG 16.20 ||

कौन्तेय - Hey Kaunteya (Arjuna)! ; मूढाः - The deluded, ; आपन्नाः - having acquired ; आसुरीम् - demonic ; योनिम् - wombs ; जन्मनि जन्मनि - birth after birth, ; अप्राप्य - not attaining ; माम् - Me, ; यान्ति - go ; ततः - (to lower than) that ; अधमाम् - lowest ; गतिम् - state ; एव - indeed.

Hey Arjuna! The deluded, having acquired demonic wombs birth after birth, not attaining Me, go to lower than that lowest state indeed.

Intent - Those lacking discrimination, the deluded born in demonic wombs, birth after birth, plunge further down by not attaining Me.

(Next, all conceivable demonic attributes are summarized as the three, whose absence perishes the entire group of demonic attributes -)

त्रिविधं नरकस्येदं द्वारं नाशनमात्मन: |
काम: क्रोधस्तथा लोभस्तस्मादेतत्त्रयं त्यजेत् || BG 16.21 ||

नाशनम् - Destroyers of ; आत्मनः - oneself ; इदम् - (are) these ; त्रिविधम् - threefold ; द्वारम् - gates ; नरकस्य - of hell - ; कामः - lust, ; क्रोधः - anger, ; तथा - and ; लोभः - greed. ; तस्मात् - Therefore, ; एतत् - these ; त्रयम् - three ; त्यजेत् - should be abandoned.

Destroyers of oneself are these threefold gates of hell - lust, anger, and greed. Therefore, these three should be abandoned.

Intent - The gateway leading to hell is three kinds; each is destructive to the Ātma. Those who desire their good and desire to stay away from hell ought to abandon all three. They are the ones to take the Ātma to the lowest depths and are the roots of all evil and thus the cause of hell. What are they? 1) Lust (काम, Kāma), 2) anger (क्रोध, Krodha), and 3) greed (लोभ, Lobha).

(What can one achieve by abandoning them? -)

एतैर्विमुक्त: कौन्तेय तमोद्वारैस्त्रिभिर्नर: |
आचरत्यात्मन: श्रेयस्ततो याति परां गतिम् || BG 16.22 ||

कौन्तेय - Hey Kaunteya (Arjuna)! ; विमुक्तः - Released from ; एतैः - these ; त्रिभिः - three ; तमो-द्वारैः - doors of darkness, ; नरः - a person (who) ; आचरति - conducts ; आत्मनः - for his own ; श्रेयः - good ; ततः - then ; याति - attains ; पराम् - the supreme ; गतिम् - goal.

Hey Arjuna! Released from these three doors of darkness, a person who conducts for his good attains the supreme goal.

Intent - Bhagavāna provides the best means for a person with demonic attributes to attain the supreme goal by articulating forceful abandonment of the roots of all evil - lust, anger, and greed. The three doors of darkness to hell. Knowing them as gentle serpents, feeding milk will not be uplifting. Slaying the three and engaging in conduct in one's good, acquiring divine attributes, then slowly, with effort through the realization of the Truth, one can attain the supreme goal of liberation, not by any other means.

यः शास्त्रविधिमुत्सृज्य वर्तते कामकारतः |
न स सिद्धिमवाप्नोति न सुखं न परां गतिम् || BG 16.23 ||

उत्सृज्य - Discarding ; शास्त्र-विधिम् - scriptural injunctions ; यः - who ; वर्तते - behaves ; काम-कारतः - in his arbitrary licentious way, ; सः - he ; अवाप्नोति - attains ; न - neither ; सिद्धिम् - perfection ; न - nor ; सुखम् - happiness ; न - or ; पराम् - the supreme ; गतिम् - goal.

Discarding scriptural injunctions who behaves in his arbitrary licentious way, he attains neither perfection nor happiness or the supreme goal.

Intent - Here, scriptural injunctions referred to are the Vedas. The authority of the Vedas is the cause that brings about the rejection of demonic attributes and promotes action leading to the good. Those who behave arbitrarily by abandoning the above injunctions cannot achieve perfection; they can neither be happy in this world nor attain the supreme goal in the next world. That is, they fall from both worlds. In summary, the effort of every being is for the happiness of this or the next world; alternatively, the fitness of the effort is definitely at least for one of the three. However, with such conduct, he cannot acquire all three.

तस्माच्छास्त्रं प्रमाणं ते कार्याकार्यव्यवस्थितौ |
ज्ञात्वा शास्त्रविधानोक्तं कर्म कर्तुमिहार्हसि || BG 16.24 ||

तस्मात् - Therefore, ; शास्त्रम् - Śāstra ; ते - shall be your ; प्रमाणम् - guide ; कार्य-अकार्य-व्यवस्थितौ - regarding what should or should not be done. ; ज्ञात्वा - Knowing ; शास्त्र-विधान-उक्तम् - said injunctions of Śāstra ; अर्हसि - you ought to ; कर्तुम् - perform ; कर्म - actions ; इह - here.

Therefore, Śāstra shall be your guide regarding what should or should not be done. Knowing said injunctions of Śāstra, you ought to perform it here.

Intent - In "कर्म कर्तुम् इह अर्हसि, you ought to perform Karma here," the term इह is understood as here, on the land where one has authority. Where there is a doubt about "Whether one ought to do or ought not to do," then at that location, it is proper to act following Śāstra.

ॐ तत्सदिति श्रीमद्भगवद्गीतासूपनिषत्सु ब्रह्मविध्यायां योगशास्त्रे

श्रीकृष्णार्जुनसम्वादे दैवासुरसंपद्विभागयोगो नाम

षोडशोऽध्यायः || BG 16 ||

Oṃ Tat Sat

In the Śrīmad Bhagavad Gītā Upaniṣad

The Yoga Science of the Knowledge of Self-Realization

The Discourse of Lord Śrī Kṛṣṇa and Arjuna

This Sixteenth Chapter

Yoga Named - The Yoga of the Attributes - Divine and Demonic

Clarification

In the fifteenth chapter, to search for the supreme Status, Bhagavāna provides knowledge of His true nature. Accumulation of helpful divine attributes (Daivī-Sampatti) and abandonment of detrimental demonic attributes (Āsurī-Sampatti) are articulated in attaining that knowledge. First, a description of divine attributes was provided in the verses (BG 16.1 - BG 16.3). The heart can become pure from the worldly attachments, desires, and dissimilarities of attachment and aversion and can become fit for analytic thinking. There is a doctrine that just as a substance is, so should be the vessel. If fresh butter is stored in a clean earthen pot, it would be tasty, nourish the body, and be likable.

In contrast, if butter is put in a container used to store kerosene, it would not be tasty. Instead of nourishing the body, it would produce poison and would be the cause of hate. Through analytic thinking, the valueless Saṃsāra is perceived as worthless like a burnt rope without any ability for bondage, and by whose influence the pain-yielding Saṃsāra turns into supreme-bliss. That is why, making analytic thinking pure from the impurities of desire, fear, anger, violence, fault finding, covetousness, unsteadiness, attachment, aversion, vanity, delusion, and despite and placing it in a vessel cleansed by the control of the mind, restraint of the senses, charity, self-study of the scriptures related to the Lord, simplicity, truthfulness, kindness, gentleness, splendor, forgiveness, fortitude and cleanliness, then this analytic thought-form butter comes out exquisitely tasty so that even the taste garnered from the entire world appears drab and tasteless. Then it nourishes the mind so that he is asleep from the world with its influence even while awake. Even at the time of dissolution, agitation does not move him.

Contrary to the above, if the butter is put in a vessel laced with hypocrisy, arrogance, excessive vanity, harshness, and ignorance, then whether it is for self or the rest of the world, it will be nothing but the cause of dread. Through it, like Virocana (विरोचन, son of Prahlāda), only the Dehātmavāda (देहात्मवाद, belief that the body is the Ātmā) will be nourished, and both in this and the next world undecaying restlessness and afflictions will continue. That is why the divine attributes for liberation and the demonic attributes for bondage are articulated in the verses (BG 16.4 - BG 16.6). Accordingly, the world is divided between the deities and the demons.

After that, demonic attributes were narrated in the verses (BG 16.7 - BG 16.12), wherein it is shown that the demons do not know what duty is and what is not, what they ought to do and ought not to do. Indeed, they hold contrary views and break the four limbs - devout austerity, cleanliness, kindness, and truthfulness. In their place, liven up unrighteousness with the drumbeat of lust, dirtiness, harshness, and untruthfulness, in whose influence neither faith nor theism (आस्तिकता, Āstikatā) can be found anywhere. Discarding the measures of words, they are only the followers of visible proof and display their misconception by believing that there is nothing like the power of the doer-holder, the controller of the world - the supreme Self. To such an extent that removing the Ātma from the heart-form throne in its place has installed a paltry animalistic ego as the all-doer-holder. Accordingly, in their desire-filled lives, sense gratification is their only goal, and indeed with their conduct, they have left even Virocana far behind. As a result, infinite anxieties, wishes, and anger reside in their hearts up to the end time, and like leeches, enjoy blood from their hearts.

In addition, evil resolves to arise in the demons are narrated in the verses (BG 16.13 - BG 16.15), and their ordinary nature is narrated in the verses (BG 16.16 - BG 16.18). Then, in the verses (BG 16.19 - BG 16.20), Bhagavāna described their end and said. "I repeatedly cast them down in the Saṃsāra in demonic wombs. The deluded having acquired demonic wombs birth after birth, not attaining Me indeed go to lower than that lowest state." After that, all conceivable demonic attributes are summarized by lust, anger, and greed as the three gates of hell. It is shown that by abandoning the three doors of darkness, a person who conducts for his good attains the supreme goal. To know what one ought to do and what one ought not to do, Bhagavāna stated Śāstra as the guide to be followed and commanded to act only by Śāstra (BG 16.21 - BG 16.24).

CHAPTER 17

THE YOGA OF THE THREEFOLD FAITH

(At the end of the sixteenth chapter, regarding a doubt, "what one ought to do or ought to not do," at that location, Bhagavāna provided Śāstra as the guide to be followed and commanded to act only by Śāstra. Upon this -)

अर्जुन उवाच |
ये शास्त्रविधिमुत्सृज्य यजन्ते श्रद्धयान्विता: |
तेषां निष्ठा तु का कृष्ण सत्त्वमाहो रजस्तम: || BG 17.1 ||
अर्जुन उवाच - Arjuna said -

कृष्ण - Hey Śrī Kṛṣṇa! ; उत्सृज्य - Abandoning ; शास्त्र-विधिम् - scriptural injunctions ; ये - those who ; यजन्ते - worship (only) ; अन्विताः - with ; श्रद्धया - faith; ; तु - again ; का - what ; तेषाम् - is their ; निष्ठा - status - ; सत्त्वम् - Sāttvika, ; रजः - Rājasika, ; आहो - or ; तमः - Tāmasika?

Arjuna said -

Hey Śrī Kṛṣṇa! Abandoning scriptural injunctions those who worship only with faith; what is their status - Sāttvika, Rājasika, or Tāmasika?

Intent - Knowing scriptural injunctions and abandoning them, such worship is neither with faith nor can it be called with faith. However, this question is for those persons who have not known those injunctions and, without knowing, they are ready for worship. What is their status (निष्ठा, Niṣṭhā)? Are they Sāttvika, Rājasika or Tāmasika? Not knowing the injunctions means no scriptural injunctions are present there. What is there is only the conscience with a sentiment of faith. It is not meant for those who know scriptural injunctions and yet ignore them and worship in their way.

श्रीभगवानुवाच |
त्रिविधा भवति श्रद्धा देहिनां सा स्वभावजा |
सात्त्विकी राजसी चैव तामसी चेति तां शृणु || BG 17.2 ||
श्रीभगवान् उवाच - Śrī Bhagavān said -

एव - Indeed, ; त्रिविधा - threefold ; भवति - is ; सा - that ; श्रद्धा - faith ; देहिनाम् - of embodied beings ; स्वभावजा - according to past impressions - ; सात्त्विकी - Sāttvika, ; च - and ; राजसी - Rājasika, ; च - and ; तामसी - Tāmasika ; इति - as such. ; शृणु - (Now,) listen to ; ताम् - those (classifications).

Śrī Bhagavān said -

Indeed, threefold is the faith of embodied beings according to past impressions - Sāttvika, Rājasika, and Tāmasika. Listen to those classifications.

Intent - Faith is of three kinds inherent in human beings. Svabhāva (स्वभाव) means own nature, disposition, or impressions, which are the resultants of acts of previous lives. Faith is what is born of these resultants.

सत्त्वानुरूपा सर्वस्य श्रद्धा भवति भारत |
श्रद्धामयोऽयं पुरुषो यो यच्छ्रद्धः स एव सः || BG 17.3 ||

भारत - Hey Bhārata (Arjuna)! ; श्रद्धा - The faith ; सर्वस्य - of all (humans) ; सत्त्व-अनुरूपा भवति- conforms to their conscience. ; अयम् - (All of) these ; पुरुषः - humans ; श्रद्धामयः - possess faith. ; एव - Also, ; सः - he ; यः - who ; यत्-श्रद्धः - is with whatever faith, ; सः - (so is) he.

Hey Arjuna! The faith of all humans conforms to their conscience. All humans possess faith. He who is with whatever faith, so is he.

Intent - Faith is an attribute of the conscience (Antaḥkaraṇa) dependent on good and bad impressions of previous lives. To whatever extent the conscience is endowed with impressions, in accordance with that extent, the person is endowed with faith, and thus his natural sentiments. Further, in accordance with that faith and sentiments, he acquires body, class, and family. The transmigratory life is largely dependent on the faith of an individual. All humans are endowed with some form of faith, and they are as their faith is; their nature is like their faith. One can thus infer their faith based on the manner of their worship.

यजन्ते सात्त्विका देवान्यक्षरक्षांसि राजसाः |
प्रेतान्भूतगणांश्चान्ये यजन्ते तामसा जनाः || BG 17.4 ||

सात्त्विकाः - (Persons with) Sāttvika (faith worship) ; देवान् - deities, ; राजसाः - (those with) Rājasika (faith) ; यजन्ते - worship ; यक्ष-रक्षांसि - semi-deities and evil demons, ; च - and ; अन्ये - other ; जनाः - persons with ; तामसाः - Tāmasika (faith) ; यजन्ते - worship ; प्रेतान् - evil spirits ; भूतगणान् - (and) hosts of ghosts

Persons with Sāttvika faith worship deities, those with Rājasika faith worship semi-deities and evil demons, and persons with Tāmasika faith worship evil spirits and hosts of ghosts.

Intent - Not knowing scriptural injunctions, even if injunctions are abandoned, those with the Sāttvika faith by their nature worship deities. Their classification is Sāttvika. Their temperament is goodness, purity, and virtuosity. Those with the Rājasika faith naturally worship Yakṣa (यक्ष, a class of semi-deities) and Rākṣasa (राक्षस, evil demons), and their classification is Rājasika. Their temperament is passion, the cause of activity. Those with the Tāmasika faith worship Preta (प्रेत, evil spirits) and Bhūtagaṇa (भूतगण, hosts of ghosts), and their classification is Tāmasika. Their temperament is laced with ignorance, the cause of sixfold mutations (lust, anger, greed, delusion, excessive pride, and envy).

Accordingly, in response to the query of Arjuna, threefold faith and categories are described. Among them, the Sāttvika category is commanded to be accumulated, whereas Rājasika and Tāmasika are stated to be abandoned.

(The nature of demonic persons is described in the following two verses -)

अशास्त्रविहितं घोरं तप्यन्ते ये तपो जनाः |
दम्भाहङ्कारसंयुक्ताः कामरागबलान्विताः || BG 17.5 ||
कर्षयन्तः शरीरस्थं भूतग्राममचेतसः |
मां चैवान्तःशरीरस्थं तान्विद्ध्यासुरनिश्चयान् || BG 17.6 ||

ये - Those ; जनाः - persons ; तप्यन्ते - who perform ; घोरम् - stern ; तपः - austerities ; अशास्त्र-विहितम् - not ordained by the scriptures ; दम्भ-अहङ्कार-संयुक्ताः - but with hypocrisy and egotism, ; काम-राग-बल-अन्विताः - (and who) by the force of lust and attachment

कर्षयन्तः - torture ; भूत-ग्रामम् - the organs ; शरीरस्थम् - of the body ; च - and ; माम् - Me ; अन्तः-शरीरस्थम् - situated in the conscience, ; एव - indeed ; विद्धि - know ; तान् - those ; अचेतसः - ignorant (persons) ; आसुर-निश्चयान् - to be of demonic resolve.

Those who perform stern austerities not ordained by the scriptures but with hypocrisy and egotism, and who by the force of lust and attachment torture the organs of the body and Me situated in the conscience, know those ignorant persons to be of demonic resolve.

Intent - On the one hand, ignoring scriptural injunctions, stern austerities are performed, and on the other hand, hypocrisy, egotism, lust, and attachment have taken over control. The body's sense organs are tortured, and in vain, Me, the existent Lord in the heart, is debilitated. Those worthless efforts of the undiscerning are neither in the present nor in their end for happiness but are the ones to ruin this and the other world. They should be known as demons only and should be kept distant.

(Based on the distinctions in the threefold faith and resolve, a description of the food, sacrifice, charity, and austerity is in order. Because without knowing the true nature and the merits and demerits of a thing, accumulation or abandonment cannot be effectuated. That is why Bhagavāna vows to provide such threefold distinctions -)

आहारस्त्वपि सर्वस्य त्रिविधो भवति प्रियः |
यज्ञस्तपस्तथा दानं तेषां भेदमिमं शृणु || BG 17.7 ||

तु - Indeed ; आहारः - food ; प्रियः - dear ; सर्वस्य - to all ; भवति - is ; त्रिविधः - of three kinds, ; तथा - and ; अपि - so is ; यज्ञः - sacrifice, ; तपः - austerity, ; दानम् - (and) charity. ; शृणु - Listen ; इमम् - this ; तेषाम् - to their ; भेदम् - distinctions.

Food dear to all is of three kinds, and so is sacrifice, austerity, and charity. Listen to their distinctions.

Intent - For those with Sāttvika faith and resolve, for those with Rājasika faith and resolve, and for those with Tāmasika faith and resolve - their dear food, sacrifice, austerity, and charity are Sāttvika, Rājasika, and Tāmasika, respectively. Can there be any doubt about that? That is because, for all living beings, all dealings are based on the constituents of their nature. From these foods, sacrifice, austerity, and charity, one can perceive the person's faith and resolve. There, Sāttvika food and sacrifice are acceptable (Upādeya), and their accumulation is a human duty. However, Rājasika and Tāmasika are to be left (Heya), so it is the human duty to abandon them.

(First, threefold foods are described -)

आयुःसत्त्वबलारोग्यसुखप्रीतिविवर्धनाः |
रस्याः स्निग्धाः स्थिरा हृद्या आहाराः सात्त्विकप्रियाः || BG 17.8 ||

आहाराः - Foods ; विवर्धनाः - that promote ; आयुः - longevity, ; सत्त्व - purity, ; बल - power, ; आरोग्य - health, ; सुख - happiness, ; प्रीति - and satisfaction; ; रस्याः - (and) are savory, ; स्निग्धाः - greasy, ; स्थिराः - stable, ; हृद्याः - (and) pleasing to the heart ; सात्त्विक-प्रियाः - are dear to persons of Sāttvika temperament.

Foods that promote longevity, purity, power, health, happiness, and satisfaction; and are savory, greasy, stable, and pleasing to the heart are dear to persons of Sāttvika temperament.

कट्वम्ललवणात्युष्णतीक्ष्णरूक्षविदाहिनः |
आहारा राजसस्येष्टा दुःखशोकामयप्रदाः || BG 17.9 ||

आहाराः - Foods ; इष्टाः - dear ; राजसस्य - to a Rājasika (temperament are) ; कटु - pungent, ; अम्ल - sour, ; लवण - salty, ; अति-उष्ण - excessively warm, ; तीक्ष्ण - piquant, ; रूक्ष - dry, ; विदाहिनः - (and) burning. ; प्रदाः - (They) produce ; दुःख - pain, ; शोक - suffering ; आमय - (and) sickness.

Foods dear to a Rājasika temperament are pungent, sour, salty, excessively warm, piquant, dry, and burning. They produce pain, suffering, and sickness.

यातयामं गतरसं पूति पर्युषितं च यत् |
उच्छिष्टमपि चामेध्यं भोजनं तामसप्रियम् || BG 17.10 ||

भोजनम् - Foods ; प्रियम् - dear to ; तामस - a Tāmasika (temperament) ; यातयामम् - are ill-cooked, ; गत-रसम् - tasteless, ; पूति - putrid, ; पर्युषितम् - stale, ; च - and ; यत् - whatever is ; उच्छिष्टम् - waste, ; च - and ; अपि - also ; अमेध्यम् - unfit for sacrifice.

Foods dear to a Tāmasika temperament are ill-cooked, tasteless, putrid, stale, waste, and unfit for sacrifice.

Intent - Food cooked and kept throughout the night that is left over after eating is called waste (उच्छिष्ट, Ucchiṣṭa). Food that is unfit for sacrifice is called impure (अमेध्य, Amedhya).

(Now, threefold sacrifices are narrated -)

अफलाकाङ्क्षिभिर्यज्ञो विधिदृष्टो य इज्यते |
यष्टव्यमेवेति मन: समाधाय स सात्त्विक: || BG 17.11 ||

सात्त्विकः- Sāttvika ; यज्ञः - sacrifice ; सः - is that ; यः - which ; इज्यते - is done ; विधि-दृष्टः - following scriptural injunctions ; अफल-आकाङ्क्षिभिः - without the expectation of fruits ; समाधाय - (and) with a resolute ; मनः - thought ; इति - that - ; यष्टव्यम् - "Performing sacrifice is our duty ; एव - indeed."

Sāttvika sacrifice is done following scriptural injunctions without the expectation of fruits and with a resolute thought that - "Performing sacrifice is indeed our duty."

अभिसन्धाय तु फलं दम्भार्थमपि चैव यत् |
इज्यते भरतश्रेष्ठ तं यज्ञं विद्धि राजसम् || BG 17.12 ||

भरत-श्रेष्ठ - Hey Bharata-Śresṭha (Arjuna, the best of the descendants of Bharata)! ; तु - However, ; विद्धि - know ; यत् - that ; यज्ञम् - sacrifice ; राजसम् - Rājasika, ; तम् - which is ; इज्यते - performed ; दम्भार्थम् - hypocritically ; च - and ; अपि - also ; अभिसन्धाय - with the desire for ; फलम् - its fruit ; एव - only.

Hey Arjuna! Know that sacrifice Rājasika, which is performed hypocritically and with the desire for its fruit.

विधिहीनमसृष्टान्नं मन्त्रहीनमदक्षिणम् |
श्रद्धाविरहितं यज्ञं तामसं परिचक्षते || BG 17.13 ||

यज्ञम् - The sacrifice ; विधि-हीनम् - that is not scripturally enjoined, ; श्रद्धा-विरहितम् - (performed) without faith, ; असृष्ट-अन्नम् - without an offering of food, ; मन्त्र-हीनम् - without (sacred) chants (of the Vedic hymns), ; अदक्षिणम् - (and) without remunerations (to the priests) ; परिचक्षते - is called ; तामसम् - Tāmasika.

The sacrifice that is not scripturally enjoined, performed without faith, without an offering of food, without sacred chants, and without remunerations is called Tāmasika.

(Next, threefold austerities are described -)

देवद्विजगुरुप्राज्ञपूजनं शौचमार्जवम् |
ब्रह्मचर्यमहिंसा च शारीरं तप उच्यते || BG 17.14 ||

पूजनम् - Reverence ; देव - towards the deities, ; द्विज - the twice-born, ; गुरु - the preceptors ; प्राज्ञ - (and) the wise scholars; ; शौचम् - cleanliness, ; आर्जवम् - simplicity, ; ब्रह्मचर्यम् - celibacy, ; च - and ; अहिंसा - non-violence ; उच्यते - are said to be ; शारीरम् - bodily ; तपः - austerities.

Reverence towards the deities, the twice-born, the preceptors, and the wise scholars; cleanliness, simplicity, celibacy, and non-violence are bodily austerities.

Intent - Twice-born (द्विज, Dvija) in this verse means a Brāhmaṇa. Who are twice-born? Generally, animals born from eggs are believed to be born twice, when the egg is produced and the second time when the eggs are out, like birds. Yajñopavīta Saṃskāra is considered a second birth; hence, a person such as a Brāhmaṇa wearing Yajñopavīta is called a Dvija.

अनुद्वेगकरं वाक्यं सत्यं प्रियहितं च यत् |
स्वाध्यायाभ्यसनं चैव वाङ्मयं तप उच्यते || BG 17.15 ||

वाक्यम् - Words ; यत् - that are ; अनुद्वेगकरम् - unoffending, ; सत्यम् - truthful, ; च - and ; प्रिय-हितम् - pleasant, and beneficial, ; च - and ; एव - also ; स्वाध्याय-अभ्यसनम् - self-study of the scriptures ; उच्यते - is said to be ; वाङ्मयम् - verbal ; तपः - austerity.

Words that are unoffending, truthful, pleasant, beneficial, and self-study of the scriptures are said to be verbal austerity.

Intent - Words that do not hurt anyone's feelings, without fawning over but truthful, and not harsh but pleasant, and beneficial for this and the next world - endowed with the four attributes are verbal austerity. Of the four, even if one is missing, it cannot be said to be verbal austerity. In verbal austerity, all four are necessary.

मनः प्रसादः सौम्यत्वं मौनमात्मविनिग्रहः |
भावसंशुद्धिरित्येतत्तपो मानसमुच्यते || BG 17.16 ||

मनः-प्रसादः - Mental calmness, ; सौम्यत्वम् - gentleness, ; मौनम् - silence, ; आत्म-विनिग्रहः - self-control, ; भाव-संशुद्धिः - (and) extreme emotional purity ; इति - as such - ; एतत् - these ; उच्यते - are said to be ; मानसम् - mental ; तपः - austerities.

Mental calmness, gentleness, silence, self-control, and extreme emotional purity - are said to be mental austerities.

Intent - Mental calmness entails profound mental tranquility devoid of anxiety. Silence (मौन, Mauna) requires restraint of speech through mental restraint. Self-control is control of the mind in general instead of silence, where control of the mind is only regarding speech. Extreme emotional purity (भाव-संशुद्धि, Bhāva-Saṃśuddhi) consists in pure conduct with others without deceit and done with sincerity.

(This way, three kinds of austerities, bodily, verbal, and mental, are enunciated.)

श्रद्धया परया तप्तं तपस्तत्त्रिविधं नरैः |
अफलाकाङ्क्षिभिर्युक्तैः सात्त्विकं परिचक्षते || BG 17.17 ||

तत् - Those ; त्रिविधम् - threefold ; तपः - austerities ; तप्तम् - performed ; युक्तैः - by mentally united ; नरैः - persons ; परया - with supreme ; श्रद्धया - faith ; अफल-आकाङ्क्षिभिः - without expectation of rewards ; परिचक्षते - are said to be ; सात्त्विकम् - Sāttvika.

The threefold austerities performed by mentally united persons with supreme faith without expectation of rewards are said to be Sāttvika.

Intent - The threefold austerities, viz. bodily, verbal, and mental - when performed with complete faith by united persons and without desire for any rewards, is said to be Sāttvika.

सत्कारमानपूजार्थं तपो दम्भेन चैव यत् |
क्रियते तदिह प्रोक्तं राजसं चलमध्रुवम् || BG 17.18 ||

तपः - The austerity ; यत् - that ; एव - is indeed ; क्रियते - performed ; दम्भेन - hypocritically ; च - and ; सत्कार-मान-पूजार्थम् - to garner respect, honor, and reverence ; तत् - that ; इह - is here (in this world) ; प्रोक्तम् - said to be ; अध्रुवम् - temporary, ; चलम् - perishable, (and) ; राजसम् - Rājasika.

The austerity performed hypocritically and to garner respect, honor, and reverence is temporary, perishable, and Rājasika.

Intent - Satkāra (सत्कार) means respect, felicitation expressed such as "this is a holy person, a devout ascetic." Māna (मान) means honor, such as actively getting up and receiving and paying homage. Pūjā (पूजा) means reverence, such as acts of offering flowers, feeding, or washing feet. Some perform austerities disingenuously to win respect, honor, or reverence. That is "here (इह, Iha)" in this world called Rājasika. The fruits of such austerities are temporary and perishable.

मूढग्राहेणात्मनो यत्पीडया क्रियते तपः ।
परस्योत्सादनार्थं वा तत्तामसमुदाहृतम् ॥ BG 17.19 ॥

तपः - The austerity ; यत् - that is ; क्रियते - performed ; मूढ-ग्राहेण - obstinately ; पीडया - torturing ; आत्मनः - oneself ; वा - or ; उत्सादनार्थम् - harming ; परस्य - others ; तत् - that ; उदाहृतम् - is said to be ; तामसम् - Tāmasika.

The austerity performed obstinately torturing oneself or harming others is Tāmasika.

Intent - The term Mūḍha-Grāheṇa (मूढ-ग्राहेण) means delusional force or obstinacy due to lack of discrimination. Torturing oneself refers to torturing the body, mind, and speech.

दातव्यमिति यद्दानं दीयतेऽनुपकारिणे ।
देशे काले च पात्रे च तद्दानं सात्त्विकं स्मृतम् ॥ BG 17.20 ॥

दानम् - Charity ; यत् - that ; दीयते - is given ; अनुपकारिणे - without expecting in return ; तत् - (with a sentiment) that ; दातव्यम् इति - "donating is our duty" ; च - and ; पात्रे - to a worthy (person) ; काले - at the (right) time ; च - and ; देशे - place ; स्मृतम् - is deemed to be ; सात्त्विकम् - Sāttvika ; दानम् - charity.

Charity given without expecting in return with a sentiment that "donating is our duty" to a worthy person at the right time and place is Sāttvika.

Intent - A charity that makes up for the deficiency in an eligible place, time, and the recipient is said to be the right charity in place, time, and recipient. Like the right place, such as the holy land of Kurukṣetra, or the right time such as the transmigration of the sun from one constellation of the zodiac to the next, or the right recipient - the knower of the six limbs of the Vedas Brāhmaṇa are said to be the right place, time and recipient. The right charities are like water in summer, warm clothes in winter, wells in a barren land, food for monks, or medicine for the ill, based on a recipient, place, and time.

यत्तु प्रत्युपकारार्थं फलमुद्दिश्य वा पुनः ।
दीयते च परिक्लिष्टं तद्दानं राजसं स्मृतम् ॥ BG 17.21 ॥

तु - However, ; दानम् - a charity ; यत् - that ; दीयते - is given ; प्रति-उपकारार्थम् - with an expectation for something in return ; च - and ; उद्दिश्य - an eye ; फलम् - towards reward ; वा - or ; परिक्लिष्टम् - given reluctantly ; तत् - that ; पुनः - is again ; स्मृतम् - said to be ; राजसम् - Rājasika.

A charity given with an expectation for something in return and an eye towards reward or given reluctantly is Rājasika.

Intent - Rājasika charity is given with an expectation for something in return, hoping that the recipient will return a favor in due course or expect that giving will produce something beneficial. In today's environment, donations are more like the expectation of return; they may provide substantial tax benefits or name and fame for some. Where donations are made for name and fame or with a hope of acquiring happiness of spouse, children, or that of the next world - are done with an eye towards a reward.

अदेशकाले यद्दानमपात्रेभ्यश्च दीयते |
असत्कृतमवज्ञातं तत्तामसमुदाहृतम् || BG 17.22 ||

तत् - That ; दानम् - charity ; यत् - which ; दीयते - is given ; असत्कृतम् - disrespectfully ; च - and ; अवज्ञातम् - contemptuously ; अपात्रेभ्यः - to undeserving recipients ; अदेश-काले - at the wrong place and time ; उदाहृतम् - is said to be ; तामसम् - Tāmasika.

Charity given disrespectfully and contemptuously to undeserving recipients at the wrong place and time is Tāmasika.

Intent - Wrong place is an unrighteous location where barbarous and unclean persons reside. The wrong time is a period unfavorable for accumulating religious merits, such as the sun's transition from month to month. Undeserving recipients are thieves and charlatans. There was a discussion on place and time in Sāttvika charity. Contrary to that, in places and times when those consuming prohibited foods and involved in evil acts of thievery and deception are given charities, they ought to be known as wrong places, times, and recipients and are considered Tāmasika. Even when the charities are done at the right time and place but if accompanied by unpleasant speech, without obeisance, and given unwillingly, they are considered Tāmasika.

(This way, based on their nature, attributes related to whatever food, sacrifice, charity, and austerity that are dear to individuals of threefold Sāttvika, Rājasika, and Tāmasika resolves, and faith is described. Helping attain the supreme Status, Sāttvika foods, sacrifice, charity, and austerity are acceptable, and Rājasika and Tāmasika being detrimental are not acceptable. Now, to enrich sacrifice, charity, and austerity endowed with excellence, based on scriptural injunctions following spiritual guidance is provided -)

ॐ तत्सदिति निर्देशो ब्रह्मणस्त्रिविधः स्मृतः |
ब्राह्मणास्तेन वेदाश्च यज्ञाश्च विहिताः पुरा || BG 17.23 ||

ओम् - "Oṃ (ॐ) ; तत् - Tat ; सत् - Sat" ; स्मृतः - is deemed ; इति - to constitute ; त्रिविधः - the threefold (syllable) ; निर्देशः - designation ; ब्रह्मणः - of the Brahman. ; पुरा - In the beginning, ; तेन - from this (triple syllable designation) ; ब्राह्मणाः - Brāhmaṇa, ; च - and ; वेदाः - Vedas, ; च - and ; यज्ञाः - sacrifices ; विहिताः - were set up.

"Oṃ(ॐ) Tat Sat" is deemed to constitute the threefold syllable designation of the Brahman. In the beginning, from this triple syllable designation - Brāhmaṇa, Vedas, and sacrifices were set up.

Intent - By which a thing is pointed out is called Nirdeśa (निर्देश). The Brahman is pointed out or designated by the three syllables "Oṃ Tat Sat, ॐ तत् सत्" in Vedānta. The Brahman, though pointed out by the three syllables, in reality, is devoid of name-form attributes. In this threefold manner, at the beginning of the creation, Brāhmaṇa (priests), Vedas, and sacrifices were set up. The term Pura (पुरा, in the beginning) is meant to extol the designations.

तस्माद् ॐ इत्युदाहृत्य यज्ञदानतपःक्रियाः |
प्रवर्तन्ते विधानोक्ताः सततं ब्रह्मवादिनाम् || BG 17.24 ||

तस्मात् - Therefore, ; ब्रह्म-वादिनाम् - Brāhmaṇa, who recites the Vedas, ; सततम् - always ; प्रवर्तन्ते - commences ; विधान-उक्ताः - ordained ; यज्ञ-दान-तपः-क्रियाः - rites of sacrifice, charity, and austerity ; उदाहृत्य - with the utterance of ; ओम् - "Oṃ (ॐ)" ; इति - as such.

Therefore, Brāhmaṇa, who recites the Vedas, always commences ordained rites of sacrifice, charity, and austerity with the utterance of "Oṃ (ॐ)."

Intent - Only after the utterance of Oṃ (ॐ), the designation of the Brahman, all scripturally ordained rites of sacrifice, charity, or austerity are commenced. Ordained rituals are deemed to possess good attributes (सद्गुण, Sadguṇa) because they have been offered to the Brahman with faith.

तदित्यनभिसन्धाय फलं यज्ञतप:क्रिया: |
दानक्रियाश्च विविधा: क्रियन्ते मोक्षकाङ्क्षिभि: || BG 17.25 ||

विविधाः - Various ; यज्ञ-तपः-क्रियाः - rites of sacrifices, austerities, ; च - and ; दान-क्रियाः - charities ; क्रियन्ते - are commenced ; मोक्ष-काङ्क्षिभिः - by seekers of liberation, ; अनभिसन्धाय - not desiring ; फलम् - reward, ; तत् - (only after the utterance of the syllable) "Tat," ; इति - as such.

Various rites of sacrifices, austerities, and charities are commenced by seekers of liberation, not desiring reward, only after the utterance of the syllable "Tat."

सद्भावे साधुभावे च सदित्येतत्प्रयुज्यते |
प्रशस्ते कर्मणि तथा सच्छब्द: पार्थ युज्यते || BG 17.26 ||

पार्थ - Hey Pārtha (Arjuna)! ; शब्दः - The word ; सत् - "Sat" ; इति - as such ; प्रयुज्यते - is used to denote ; सत्-भावे - existence ; च - and ; साधु-भावे - righteousness. ; तथा - Additionally, ; एतत् - this ; सत् - "Sat" ; युज्यते - is used ; प्रशस्ते - in a noble ; कर्मणि - deed.

Hey Arjuna! The word "Sat" is used to denote existence and righteousness. Additionally, "Sat" is used in a noble deed.

Intent - For the existence of something that is not yet existent, the term "Sat" is used, like the birth of a son who is not yet born or the righteousness of a person who is wicked in the past. In addition, in any noble deed like sacrifice or charity, the term "Sat" - Satkarma (सत्कर्म, noble deed) is used.

यज्ञे तपसि दाने च स्थिति: सदिति चोच्यते |
कर्म चैव तदर्थीयं सदित्येवाभिधीयते || BG 17.27 ||

सत् - "Sat" ; इति - as such ; एव - is also ; उच्यते - used to denote ; स्थितिः - a steadfast state ; यज्ञे - of sacrifice, ; च - and ; तपसि - austerity, ; च - and ; दाने - charity. ; च - Additionally, ; कर्म - acts ; तत्-अर्थीयम् - dedicated to the Lord ; एव - are also ; अभिधीयते - called ; सत् - "Sat" ; इति - as such.

Sat" is used to denote a steadfast state of sacrifice, austerity, and charity. Additionally, acts dedicated to the Lord are also called "Sat."

Intent - Thus, the three syllables denoting the Brahman are described. With their faithful application and the power of their Sāttvika faith, even the non-Sāttvika or non-meritorious acts turn into Sāttvika - such was the glory of faith narrated.

(Next, criticizing the absence of faith, the chapter is ended -)

अश्रद्धया हुतं दत्तं तपस्तप्तं कृतं च यत् |
असदित्युच्यते पार्थ न च तत्प्रेत्य नो इह || BG 17.28 ||

पार्थ - Hey Pārtha (Arjuna)! ; अश्रद्धया - Without faith, ; यत् - whatever is ; हुतम् - sacrificed, ; दत्तम् - given as charity, ; तप्तम् - endured ; तपः - as austerity ; च - and ; कृतम् - other acts performed, ; तत् - they ; उच्यते - are said to be ; असत् - "Asat" ; इति - as such. ; न - (They are effective) neither ; इह - here ; च नो - nor ; प्रेत्य - hereafter.

Hey Arjuna! Without faith, whatever is sacrificed, given as charity, endured as austerity, and other acts performed, they are said to be "Asat." They are effective neither here nor hereafter.

Intent - Even if sacrifice, charity, and austerity are Sāttvika by nature, without Sāttvika faith, they remain non-Sāttvika. Neither they are beneficial in this world nor helpful in attaining the supreme Status. That is why faith is primary.

ॐ तत्सदिति श्रीमद्भगवद्गीतासूपनिषत्सु ब्रह्मविद्यायां योगशास्त्रे

श्रीकृष्णार्जुनसम्वादे श्रद्धात्रयविभागयोगो नाम

सप्तदशोऽध्यायः || BG 17 ||

Oṃ Tat Sat

In the Śrīmad Bhagavad Gītā Upaniṣad

The Yoga Science of the Knowledge of Self-Realization

The Discourse of Lord Śrī Kṛṣṇa and Arjuna

This Seventeenth Chapter

Yoga Named - The Yoga of the Threefold Faith

Clarification

At the end of the sixteenth chapter, regarding a doubt, "what one ought to do or ought to not do," at that location, Bhagavāna provided Śāstra as the guide to be followed and commanded to act only in accordance with Śāstra. Hearing so, at the beginning of this chapter, Arjuna posed a question, "Abandoning scriptural injunctions those who worship only with faith, what is their status - Sāttvika, Rājasika, or Tāmasika? " (BG 17.1). In response, Bhagavāna indicated that there are threefold distinct faiths in humans - Sāttvika, Rājasika, and Tāmasika that are naturally caused by the impressions of good and bad actions of previous lives. In the conscience of individuals, as the impressions (Saṃskāras) of good and bad Karma become stronger, commensurate faith is produced naturally with their influence. Further, a person acquires body, family, conduct, and wisdom under that faith. That is why this transmigratory life is largely dependent on an individual's faith. All humans are endowed with some faith, and they are as their faith is. Their nature is like their faith. Under this doctrine, not knowing scriptural injunctions, even if injunctions are abandoned, those with Sāttvika faith by their own nature worship deities, and their classification is Sāttvika. Their temperament is goodness, purity, and virtuosity. Those with Rājasika faith naturally worship semi-deities (Yakṣa), and evil demons (Rākṣasa), and their classification is Rājasika. Their temperament is passion, the cause of activity. Those with the Tāmasika faith worship evil spirits (Preta) and hosts of ghosts (Bhūtagaṇa), and their classification is Tāmasika. Their temperament is laced with ignorance, the cause of sixfold mutations - lust, anger, greed, delusion, excessive pride, and envy (BG 17.2 - BG 17.4).

After that, for individuals with demonic faith, their conduct is described to encourage abandonment of such behavior. Consistent with individual nature, based on threefold faiths, distinct attributes of food, sacrifice, charity, and austerity that are dear to them were articulated. The Sāttvika food, sacrifice, charity, and austerity being helpful in the attainment of the supreme Status are acceptable, and their accumulation is a human duty. However, Rājasika and Tāmasika are detrimental and so are to be left. Therefore, it is a human duty to abandon them (BG 17.5 - BG 17.7). There the attributes of threefold foods (Sāttvika, Rājasika, and Tāmasika) are described in the verses (BG 17.8 - BG 17.10), and the attributes of threefold sacrifices are described in the verses (BG 17.11 - BG 17.13). After that, dividing the austerities into three by bodily, verbal, and mental distinctions, threefold attributes are described based on the threefold constituents in the verses (BG 17.14 - BG 17.19). Threefold charities are provided in the verses (BG 17.20 - BG 17.22).

Accordingly, in the word faith, what is meant is Sāttvika faith. That is acceptable, that is permissible. However, contrary to it, Rājasika and Tāmasika faiths being Heya (to be left) cannot be included in the meaning of the word faith but can be only called without faith (अश्रद्धा, Aśraddhā) or disbelief. In the end, only Sāttvika faith was the one that was lauded, by whose influence non-Sāttvika sacrifices, charities, and austerities become Sāttvika. After that, the Brahman was designated by the three syllables Oṃ Tat Sat (ॐ तत् सत्) by whose application Sāttvika faith is established in sacrifices, charities, and austerities, and with that Sāttvika faith even acts not enjoined by the scriptures become endowed with scriptural injunctions. That is because the life force of scriptural injunctions is only Sāttvika faith, and indeed scriptural injunctions aim to awaken Sāttvika faith by whatever means possible. Where there is Sāttvika faith, scriptural injunctions are automatically fulfilled. In the end, sacrifices, charities, and austerities without faith are declared as Asat, not noble, and shown ineffective in this world and the next world. Accordingly, describing scriptural injunctions and threefold faiths, the chapter is ended.

Chapter 18

The Yoga of Liberation and Renunciation

{The entire science of Śrīmad Bhagavad Gītā is articulated in this chapter, and so it is indeed an epilogue. Listening to the discussion on renunciation (संन्यास, Saṃnyāsa) and relinquishment (त्याग, Tyāga) at various locations in previous chapters and knowing renunciation and relinquishment as the core subject, Arjuna asked Bhagavāna the last question -}

अर्जुन उवाच |
सन्न्यासस्य महाबाहो तत्त्वमिच्छामि वेदितुम् |
त्यागस्य च हृषीकेश पृथक्केशिनिषूदन || BG 18.1 ||
अर्जुन उवाच - Arjuna Said

महाबाहो - Hey Mahābāho (Śrī Kṛṣṇa), ; हृषीकेश - Hṛṣīkeśa (the Lord of the senses), ; केशिनिषूदन - Keśiniṣūdana (the slayer of demon Keśi)! ; इच्छामि - I would like ; वेदितुम् - to know ; तत्त्वम् - the distinction ; संन्यासस्य - between renunciation ; च - and ; त्यागस्य - relinquishment ; पृथक् - separately.

Arjuna Said

Hey Śrī Kṛṣṇa, the Lord of the senses, the slayer of demon Keśi! I would like to know the distinction between renunciation and relinquishment separately.

Intent - Even though Arjuna asked to know the distinction between renunciation and relinquishment separately, the meaning of the word Saṃnyāsa (renunciation) and the word Tyāga (relinquishment) is not separate like a pot and a cloth, but their meaning is identical. That is why, grasping them both in the same sense, Bhagavāna responds first by providing four prevalent opinions connected with renunciation and relinquishment.

श्रीभगवानुवाच |
काम्यानां कर्मणां न्यासं सन्न्यासं कवयो विदु: |
सर्वकर्मफलत्यागं प्राहुस्त्यागं विचक्षणा: || BG 18.2 ||
श्रीभगवान् उवाच - Śrī Bhagavān said -

कवयः - The wise ; विदुः - know ; न्यासम् - abandonment of ; कर्मणाम् - actions ; काम्यानाम् - prompted by desire ; संन्यासम् - as "renunciation." ; विचक्षणाः - The thoughtfully competent ; प्राहुः - declare ; सर्व-कर्म-फल-त्यागम् - forsaking all fruits of actions ; त्यागम् - as "relinquishment."

Śrī Bhagavān said -

The wise know abandonment of actions prompted by desire as "renunciation." The thoughtfully competent declare forsaking all fruits of actions as "relinquishment."

Intent - Karma in the form of sacrifices, charities, and penances done to acquire wealth, children, wife, honor or respect and to get rid of enemies, illness, or obstacles are said to be activities prompted by desire (काम्य-कर्म, Kāmya-Karma). Many wise men deem, "By its nature, abandonment of activities prompted by desire is renunciation (Saṃnyāsa). That is because desire makes them the cause for bondage. Other daily obligatory and occasional duties and rituals (नित्य-नैमित्तिक-कर्म, Nitya-Naimittika-Karma) are not the cause for bondage." Other intellectually competent persons believe, "Sacrifices, charities, and penances - all activities related to stages of life (Varṇāśrama) as well as provision of what is not possessed and preservation what is possessed (bodily Yoga-Kṣema) and all other obligatory activities should be performed without desire for this world and the next - and that is the relinquishment, and that is renunciation. Relinquishment of mere Karma is not Tyāga because Karma on its own is not the cause for bondage. Only the desires for reward are."

त्याज्यं दोषवदित्येके कर्म प्राहुर्मनीषिण: |
यज्ञदानतप:कर्म न त्याज्यमिति चापरे || BG 18.3 ||

एके - Some ; मनीषिणः - intellectuals ; प्राहुः - declare ; कर्म - actions (by their nature) ; दोषवत् - are with fault. ; इति - Thus ; त्याज्यम् - (they) ought to be relinquished. ; च - And ; अपरे - others (declare) ; यज्ञ-दान-तपः-कर्म - acts of sacrifice, charity, and austerity ; न - should not ; त्याज्यम् - be relinquished ; इति - as such.

Some intellectuals declare actions are with fault. They ought to be relinquished. Others declare acts of sacrifice, charity, and austerity should not be relinquished.

Intent - Some intellectuals say, "Actions by their nature are with a fault; there is no action in the world that is beneficial to any degree or for all. That is why all actions are mixed with piety and sin. Additionally, even when actions are pious, they put a doer in the bondage of birth and death to enjoy rewards. Thus, being the cause of bondage, actions by their nature are relinquishable, and the relinquishment of all actions is named Saṃnyāsa (renunciation)." However, others say, "First, it is impossible to relinquish all actions naturally. Second, the world deteriorates by relinquishing sacrifice, charity, and austerity. That is why performing sacrifice, charity, austerity, and relinquishing other actions is indeed renunciation."

निश्चयं शृणु मे तत्र त्यागे भरतसत्तम |
त्यागो हि पुरुषव्याघ्र त्रिविध: सम्प्रकीर्तित: || BG 18.4 ||

भरतसत्तम - Hey Bharatasattama (Arjuna), ; पुरुष-व्याघ्र - Puruṣa-Vyāghra (Arjuna, the tiger among men)! ; शृणु - Hear ; मे - My ; निश्चयम् - opinion ; तत्र - there ; त्यागे - on the subject of relinquishment. ; त्यागः - Relinquishment ; हि - certainly ; सम्प्रकीर्तितः - is declared ; त्रिविधः - to be of three kinds.

Hey Arjuna, the tiger among men! Hear My opinion on the subject of relinquishment. Relinquishment is of three kinds.

{The meanings of the words "Tyāga (relinquishment)" and "Saṃnyāsa (renunciation)" are identical, that is why the response is given using only the term Tyāga (relinquishment).}

यज्ञदानतप:कर्म न त्याज्यं कार्यमेव तत् |
यज्ञो दानं तपश्चैव पावनानि मनीषिणाम् || BG 18.5 ||

यज्ञ-दान-तपः-कर्म - Acts of sacrifice, charity, and austerity ; न - should not be ; त्याज्यम् - relinquished; ; तत् - they ; एव - should certainly ; कार्यम् - be performed. ; यज्ञः - Sacrifice, ; दानम् - charity, ; च - and ; तपः - austerity ; एव - indeed ; पावनानि - purify ; मनीषिणाम् - wise men.

Acts of sacrifice, charity, and austerity should not be relinquished; they should certainly be performed. Sacrifice, charity, and austerity indeed purify wise men.

एतान्यपि तु कर्माणि सङ्गं त्यक्त्वा फलानि च |
कर्तव्यानीति मे पार्थ निश्चितं मतमुत्तमम् || BG 18.6 ||

तु - However, ; अपि - even ; एतानि - these ; कर्माणि - activities ; कर्तव्यानि - should be performed ; त्यक्त्वा - without ; सङ्गम् - attachment ; च - and ; फलानि - (expectation of) rewards. ; पार्थ - Hey Pārtha (Arjuna)! ; इति - That is ; मे - My ; निश्चितम् - firm and ; उत्तमम् - most valid ; मतम् - opinion.

However, even these activities should be performed without attachment and expectation of rewards. Hey Arjuna! That is My firm and most valid opinion.

Intent - If activities of sacrifice, charity, and austerity are performed with attachment and desire for rewards, they cause bondage. As is said in verse BG 18.5, they cannot purify anyone. The above activities have been called "purifiers" only for the wise men who have relinquished attachment and desires and have not been called purifiers for those desire-ridden (Sakāmī). This verse clearly states that the activities of sacrifice, charity, and austerity ought to be done by relinquishing both attachment and desire. Sacrifice, charity, and austerity performed with attachment and desire ought not to be considered a duty; that is My firm and most valid opinion.

नियतस्य तु सन्न्यास: कर्मणो नोपपद्यते |
मोहात्तस्य परित्यागस्तामस: परिकीर्तित: || BG 18.7 ||

तु - Because, ; संन्यासः - to renounce ; नियतस्य - obligatory ; कर्मणः - acts ; न - is not ; उपपद्यते - proper. ; तस्य - Their ; परित्यागः - renunciation ; मोहात् - due to ignorance ; परिकीर्तितः - is said to be ; तामसः - Tāmasika.

To renounce obligatory acts is not proper. Their renunciation due to ignorance is said to be Tāmasika.

Intent - Under Varṇāśrama, in every stage of life of individuals of all functional classes of society, one should perform without any desire whatever obligatory duties that are ordained so that faults of impurities and vacillations resident in the heart are removed. Suppose one renounces obligatory duties due to ignorance with a view that, for me, there is no duty to perform before the removal of these faults. In that case, it is like applying little soap to dirty clothes and taking it away before the clothes are clean, rendering them unfit to be dyed. Similarly, delusionally renouncing obligatory acts does not remain the cause of any fruit. It is indeed Tāmasika renunciation.

दु:खमित्येव यत्कर्म कायक्लेशभयात्यजेत् |
स कृत्वा राजसं त्यागं नैव त्यागफलं लभेत् || BG 18.8 ||

काय-क्लेश-भयात् - Due to fear of bodily distress, ; कर्म - (if) actions ; त्यजेत् - are relinquished ; इति - as ; एव - indeed ; दुःखम् - painful, ; सः - such ; त्यागम् - relinquishment ; राजसम् - is Rājasika. ; एव - Indeed, ; त्याग-फलम् - a reward for the relinquishment ; न - does not ; लभेत् - accrue ; कृत्वा - by performing ; यत् - such (relinquishment).

Due to fear of bodily distress, if actions are relinquished as painful, such relinquishment is Rājasika. A reward does not accrue by performing such relinquishment.

Intent - When actions are relinquished before purging impurities from the conscience, relinquishment does not remain a cause for any fruit. Nevertheless, relinquishment done without a delusional sentiment that actions are without meaning is not Tāmasika. Yet knowing actions have consequences and relinquishing them is just like continuing to suffer from headaches despite knowing the benefit of sandalwood for headaches but abandoning the idea because of the trouble involved in massaging the forehead.

(Compared to the above two relinquishments -)

कार्यमित्येव यत्कर्म नियतं क्रियतेऽर्जुन |
सङ्गं त्यक्त्वा फलं चैव स त्यागः सात्त्विको मतः || BG 18.9 ||

अर्जुन - Hey Arjuna! ; यत् - That ; नियतम् - ordained ; कर्म - action ; क्रियते - performed ; इति - as ; कार्यम् एव - "ought to be done" ; त्यक्त्वा - giving up ; सङ्गम् - attachment ; च - and ; फलम् - fruit, ; सः - such ; त्यागः - relinquishment ; मतः - is deemed ; सात्त्विकः - Sāttvika ; एव - indeed.

Hey Arjuna! Ordained action performed as "ought to be done," giving up attachment and fruit, such relinquishment is deemed Sāttvika.

Intent - "Certain actions should be performed this way and not any other way" - such resolve in the heart is called attachment (Āsakti). Giving up this attachment and desire for reward, performing acts ordained by scriptural injunctions based on individual fitness for fulfilling one's duty, and with a sentiment of offering to the Lord, is deemed Sāttvika. The conscience is purged of impurities through such emotional actions, and relinquishment becomes fruitful. Actions by their nature are not the cause of bondage; however, they are helpful in the liberation of Rajoguṇī mental vacillations. The cause of bondage is attachment and desire for reward only, so their relinquishment is deemed Sāttvika. Accordingly, giving up emotional attachment and reward, the pure conscience becomes fit to contemplate the Ātmā.

(Next is shown how, being purified through the performance of obligatory duties and oriented towards the knowledge of the Ātmā, the conscience gradually becomes devoted to the knowledge of the Ātmā-)

न द्वेष्ट्यकुशलं कर्म कुशले नानुषज्जते |
त्यागी सत्त्वसमाविष्टो मेधावी छिन्नसंशयः || BG 18.10 ||

त्यागी - A renouncer ; सत्त्व-समाविष्टः - endowed with pure Sattva, ; मेधावी - intelligent ; छिन्न-संशयः - (and) whose doubts have gone ; न - neither ; द्वेष्टि - hates ; अकुशलम् - unmeritorious ; कर्म - acts ; न - nor ; अनुषज्जते - attaches ; कुशले - to meritorious acts.

A renouncer endowed with pure Sattva, intelligent and whose doubts have gone, neither hates unmeritorious acts nor attaches to meritorious acts.

Intent - When a renouncer, whose doubts about doership and enjoyership have gone, is pervaded by Sattva, discrimination between the Ātmā and the non-Ātmā (Anātmā) is generated. The cause of the discriminating knowledge of the Ātmā and the non-Ātmā is pure Sattvaguṇa. One, who is detached from the body, senses, mind, and intellect and is established in his distinctionless (Nirviśeṣa) Ātmā, and whose ego "I am a doer-enjoyer" of the activities of body, senses, mind, and intellect is uprooted, is, in reality, a true renouncer of everything and is indeed a non-doer even though he is doing everything. Such a renouncer neither hates desire-filled acts that they will be the cause of my bondage nor is active in any desireless acts with an attachment that by this act I will acquire purity. Through the realization of the Reality, moving out of the body, senses, mind, and intellect, he has attained union with oneness in the Ātmā. In his view, the superimposed existence of the body, senses, mind, and intellect has disappeared, just as water does not perceive any existence of waves or eddies but sees them all in the form of water alone. His vision is out of all dissimilar sentiments such as meritorious and non-meritorious, desire-filled and desireless, and good and evil. Now he is no longer a doer of the activities of body, senses, mind, and intellect, but only as a witness of their activities - just their observer and does not see any taint from them in himself.

(Relinquishment of a knower of the Truth is spoken. Now, that of one with ego in the body is articulated -)

न हि देहभृता शक्यं त्यक्तुं कर्माण्यशेषतः |
यस्तु कर्मफलत्यागी स त्यागीत्यभिधीयते || BG 18.11 ||

हि - Because ; अशेषतः - completely ; त्यक्तुम् - relinquishing ; कर्माणि - all actions ; देह-भृता - by embodied beings ; न - is not ; शक्यम् - possible. ; तु - However, ; सः - one ; यः - who ; कर्म-फल-त्यागी - relinquishes rewards of actions ; इति - as such ; अभिधीयते - is said to be ; त्यागी - a relinquisher.

Completely relinquishing all actions by embodied beings is impossible. However, one who relinquishes rewards of actions is said to be a relinquisher.

Intent - One who has ego in the body may be praised as a relinquisher (त्यागी, Tyāgi), but the term relinquisher (Tyāgi) cannot be applied truly. Because what ought to be relinquished is the ego in the body, by whose relinquishment, relinquishment of everything (Sarva-Tyāga) is established and that he has not yet relinquished.

(Next, the threefold rewards of Karma and for whom they are, are narrated -)

अनिष्टमिष्टं मिश्रं च त्रिविधं कर्मणः फलम् |
भवत्यत्यागिनां प्रेत्य न तु सन्न्यासिनां क्वचित् || BG 18.12 ||

फलम् - The fruit ; कर्मणः - of action ; त्रिविधम् - is threefold - ; अनिष्टम् - bad, ; इष्टम् - good, ; च - and ; मिश्रम् - mixed. ; भवति - (It) accrues ; अत्यागिनाम् - to non-relinquishers ; प्रेत्य - after death ; तु - but ; न क्वचित् - never ; संन्यासिनाम् - to renouncers.

The fruit of action is threefold - bad, good, and mixed. It accrues to non-relinquishers after death but never to renouncers.

Intent - Bad fruit of Karma is hell and the acquisition of birth in the wombs of animals, birds, or insects. The good fruit of Karma is the acquisition of birth in the wombs of deities. Fruit of mixed Karma is birth in the human womb. Commensurate with individual Karma, there are distinct fruits for those who have not relinquished everything under BG 18.10. However, there is no fruit for those renouncers (knowers of the Truth who have relinquished everything). They do not have self-conceit in any of the five causes of action. For the embodied beings with conceit in the body, who have relinquished fruits of actions, under BG 18.9, the relinquishment is Sāttvika. Yet, due to I-ness in the body and the conceit of fruit relinquishment, they are bound to receive good fruits while they do not receive bad fruits.

पञ्चैतानि महाबाहो कारणानि निबोध मे |
साङ्ख्ये कृतान्ते प्रोक्तानि सिद्धये सर्वकर्मणाम् || BG 18.13 ||

महाबाहो - Hey Mahābāho (Arjuna)! ; निबोध - Know ; मे - from Me ; एतानि - these ; पञ्च - five ; कारणानि - causes ; प्रोक्तानि - set forth ; साङ्ख्ये - in Sāṅkhya ; कृत-अन्ते - doctrine ; सिद्धये - for accomplishing ; सर्व-कर्मणाम् - all actions.

Hey Arjuna! Know from Me the five causes set forth in Sāṅkhya doctrine for accomplishing all actions.

अधिष्ठानं तथा कर्ता करणं च पृथग्विधम् |
विविधाश्च पृथक्चेष्टा दैवं चैवात्र पञ्चमम् || BG 18.14 ||

अधिष्ठानम् - The ground (the body in which activities manifest), ; च - and ; कर्ता - the doer (the delimited Self with I-ness in the body), ; च - and ; पृथक्-विधम् - various kinds of ; करणम् - instruments (the senses), ; च - and ; विविधाः - manifold ; पृथक् - distinct ; चेष्टाः - efforts, ; तथा - and ; एव - also ; अत्र - here ; पञ्चमम् - the fifth ; दैवम् - is Daiva.

The ground, the doer, various kinds of instruments, manifold distinct efforts, and the fifth is Daiva.

Intent - The five causes are:

1. Adhiṣṭhāna (अधिष्ठान, ground) - The body that is the support for the appearance of desire, knowledge, and actions.
2. Kartā (कर्ता, doer) - The delimited Ātmā who is the doer-enjoyer with an I-ness sense in the body. The delimited Ātmā, Jīva, Jīvātmā, and Soul are synonymous.
3. Karaṇa (करण, instrument) - Various kinds of instruments through which actions are performed, such as A) the five cognitive senses (पञ्च-ज्ञानेन्द्रिय, Pañca-Jñānendriya): 1) skin (त्वक, Tvaka), 2) tongue (रसना, Rasanā), 3) eyes (चक्षु, Cakṣu), 4) nose (घ्राण, Ghrāṇa) and 5) ears (श्रोत्र, Śrotra), B) the five action-organs (पञ्च-कर्मेन्द्रिय, Pañca-Karmendriya): 1) mouth (वाक, Vāka) with the faculty of voice, 2) hands (पाणि, Pāṇi) with the faculty of grasping (Grahaṇa) and holding (Dhāraṇa), 3) feet (पाद, Pāda) with the faculty of locomotion (Gamana), 4) anus (पायु, Pāyu) with the faculty of excretion and 5) genitals (उपस्थ, Upastha) with the faculty of reproduction, C) the mind and D) the intellect.
4. Ceṣṭā (चेष्टा, effort) - The manifold distinct efforts of the vital breaths of air (प्राण, Prāṇa) such as the in-breath, the out-breath through which activities in the senses, mind, and intellect happen.
5. Daiva (दैव, the presiding deity) - Various presiding deities that control the mind and senses. The Adhideva (अधिदेव) of eyes is the sun-deity, the Adhideva of ears is the directions, and so on. The power of these presiding deities is known as Adhidaiva-Śakti (अधिदैव-शक्ति). The intention is that senses grasp their objects with the grace of these deities.

शरीरवाङ्मनोभिर्यत्कर्म प्रारभते नर: |
न्याय्यं वा विपरीतं वा पञ्चैते तस्य हेतव: || BG 18.15 ||

एते - These ; पञ्च - are the five ; हेतवः - causes ; तस्य - of ; यत् - whatever ; कर्म - activity ; नरः - a human ; प्रारभते - initiates ; शरीर-वाक्-मनोभिः - with the body, speech or mind, ; वा - whether ; न्याय्यम् - (it is) right ; वा - or ; विपरीतं - wrong.

These are the five causes of whatever activity a human initiates with the body, speech, or mind, whether right or wrong.

Intent - Whatever activities are performed by a human being, they can be divided into three parts - bodily, verbal, and mental; there cannot be any activity separate from them. Accordingly, whether the threefold activities are in accordance with or opposed to the scriptures, righteous or unrighteous, merit or demerit, the above five are the causes. Without the five, there cannot be a success of any activity.

तत्रैवं सति कर्तारमात्मानं केवलं तु य: |
पश्यत्यकृतबुद्धित्वान्न स पश्यति दुर्मति: || BG 18.16 ||

तु - However, ; तत्र - there, ; सति - despite ; एवम् - being so, ; अकृत-बुद्धित्वात् - due to impure intelligence, ; यः - one who ; पश्यति - sees ; आत्मानम् - own pure Self ; केवलम् - alone ; कर्तारम् - as a doer, ; सः - that ; दुर्मतिः - ill-disposed ; न - does not ; पश्यति - see truly.

Despite being so, due to impure intelligence, one who sees own pure Self alone as a doer, that ill-disposed does not see truly.

Intent - Based on those above, despite the five causes, due to impure intelligence, a person sees his non-doer pure Ātmā as a doer. Doer of activities is only these five causes. Still, because of his mental ill-disposition not seeing causality in them, one who holds doership conceit in own pure non-doer Ātmā is a contrary-viewer. Because of his contrary vision, he is hung by the chokehold of birth and death. The root of all bondages is this ignorance.

(Who has true vision? On this Bhagavāna says -)

यस्य नाहङ्‌ कृतो भावो बुद्धिर्यस्य न लिप्यते |
हत्वाऽपि स इमाँल्लोकान्न हन्ति न निबध्यते || BG 18.17 ||

सः - He ; यस्य - whose ; भावः - sentiment, ; अहङ्कृतः - "I am a doer," ; न - does not exist ; यस्य - and whose ; बुद्धिः - intellect ; न - is not ; लिप्यते - tainted, ; अपि - even ; हत्वा - slaying ; इमान् - all these ; लोकान् - living beings, ; न - neither ; हन्ति - slays ; न - nor ; निबध्यते - is bound.

Whose sentiment, "I am a doer," does not exist and whose intellect is not tainted, even slaying all living beings, neither slays nor is bound.

Intent - Through transcendental knowledge of the Ātmā, whose ignorance-based superimposition of the body and the five causes articulated in verse BG 18.14 on the Ātmā is destroyed. Such a person does not grasp any of the five causes as the Ātmā but has realized the Ātmā as detached from the five causes and does not see any taint of the five in the Ātmā. He sees the five as doers of all activities and not "I." "I" am only the witness-observer of their operations. Accordingly, being situated in the Ātmā, his intellect is not tainted by the activities. Even slaying all living beings with the five causes of actions, such a person, because of his persistent detachment, neither becomes a doer of the slaying operation nor is bound by sin in their result. Because of his right understanding, his I-ness in the body not remaining, all natural nescience born Karma are renounced by him. He is free from the threefold fruits of Karma - bad, good, and mixed. That is the true renunciation (Saṃnyāsa), that is the true relinquishment (Tyāga) - that is where there is even relinquishment of relinquishment.

At the beginning of the chapter, Arjuna posed a question to know the truth about renunciation (Saṃnyāsa) and relinquishment (Tyāga). Up to here, the subject is discussed. That is indeed the epilogue of the meaning of the science of Gītā, and it is the true Karma-Saṃnyāsa. Scholars with penetrating discrimination should ponder the essence of Vedic wisdom. Liberation or cessation of the birth-death transmigratory life is dependent only on the success of this thought and resolve.

(This way, providing the epilogue of the scripture, Bhagavāna now provides factors that impel actions -)

ज्ञानं ज्ञेयं परिज्ञाता त्रिविधा कर्मचोदना |
करणं कर्म कर्तेति त्रिविधः कर्मसंग्रहः || BG 18.18 ||

ज्ञानम् - Knowledge, ; ज्ञेयम् - the object of knowledge, ; परिज्ञाता - and the knower ; त्रिविधा - are the three constituents ; कर्म-चोदना - that impel action. ; करणम् - Instruments, ; कर्म - action, ; कर्ता - and doer ; इति - as such ; त्रिविधः - are the threefold ; कर्म-सङ्ग्रहः - collective constituents of action.

Knowledge, the object of knowledge, and the knower are the three constituents that impel action. Instruments, action, and doer are the threefold collective constituents of action.

Intent - In this verse, ignoring distinctions among specific cognitions, knowledge, in general, is intended. That by which something is enlightened, known, and understood is called knowledge (Jñāna). The object of knowledge is called knowable, to be known (Jñeya). The one who knows the object is called the knower (Jñātā). Action is induced only when knowledge, knowable, and knower converge. For instance, through the threesome (knower, to be known and knowledge), when good or bad awareness of substance, attribute, and act occurs, the activity commences for either acquisition or rejection. That is why the three are impellers of action. The fruition of the operation of action is only upon the convergence of doer, instruments, and acts. The five causes discussed in verse BG 18.14 are included within the three. Entrusting ears, eyes et al. their functions, the adjunct Jīva is called a doer. Through which action is performed is called an instrument (करण, Karaṇa). The ten senses are the external instruments, whereas the four - mind, intellect, Citta, and ego are the internal instruments. Moreover, acts through which something is effectuated are called Karma.

(Next is set forth the threefold distinctions among knowledge, action, and doer based on Sattva, Rajas, and Tamas, the threefold constituents of Prakṛti -)

ज्ञानं कर्म च कर्ता च त्रिधैव गुणभेदत: |
प्रोच्यते गुणसङ् ख्याने यथावच्छृणु तान्यपि || BG 18.19 ||

गुण-सङ्ख्याने - In Sāṅkhya philosophy - ; ज्ञानम् - knowledge, ; च - and ; कर्म - action, ; च - and ; कर्ता - doer ; प्रोच्यते - are said to be ; एव - just ; त्रिधा - of three kinds ; गुण-भेदतः - based on the three constituents (of Prakṛti), ; अपि - Also, ; शृणु - listen ; तानि - to them ; यथावत् - as they are.

In Sāṅkhya philosophy - knowledge, action, and doer are said to be of three kinds based on the three constituents. Listen to them as they are.

(First, three-fold knowledge is described -)

सर्वभूतेषु येनैकं भावमव्ययमीक्षते |
अविभक्तं विभक्तेषु तज्ज्ञानं विद्धि सात्त्विकम् || BG 18.20 ||

विद्धि - Know ; तत् - that ; ज्ञानम् - knowledge ; सात्त्विकम् - to be Sāttvika ; येन - by which ; ईक्षते - one sees ; एकम् - one ; अविभक्तम् - undivided ; अव्ययम् - immutable ; भावम् - existent ; विभक्तेषु सर्व-भूतेषु - in all separate living beings.

Know that knowledge to be Sāttvika by which one sees one undivided immutable existent in all separate living beings.

Intent - Just as earrings or necklaces made from gold are only gold, the terms earrings and necklace are just name forms. There is not an iota of those name forms in gold. Though they are viewed as various forms by a goldsmith, a gold dealer sees them only as gold and remunerates only on the value of gold. From unmanifest to stationary and movable, there is only one undivided existent in all beings - the Supreme Reality. This Supreme Reality does not mutate by itself or through the mutation of its attributes. It is one and the only cause of all beings. That knowledge by which all the beings are perceived in the form of the Existent-Conscious-Bliss, the cause of all, such oneness knowledge ought to be known as Sāttvika.

पृथक्त्वेन तु यज्ज्ञानं नानाभावान्पृथग्विधान् |
वेत्ति सर्वेषु भूतेषु तज्ज्ञानं विद्धि राजसम् || BG 18.21 ||

तु - However, ; विद्धि - know ; तत् - that ; ज्ञानम् - knowledge ; राजसम् - as Rājasika ; यत् - by which ; ज्ञानम् - knowledge ; वेत्ति - one knows ; सर्वेषु - all ; भूतेषु - beings ; पृथक्त्वेन - as separate ; पृथक्-विधान् - manifold ; नाना-भावान् - existences.

However, know that knowledge as Rājasika by which one knows all beings as separate manifold existences.

Intent - Rājasika knowledge is where one knows varied beings as different in different bodies. Where causal perspective is absent and in various objects of gross vision such as pots and pans, perception of action becomes resolute. Such knowledge is known as Rājasika.

यत्तु कृत्स्नवदेकस्मिन्कार्ये सक्तमहैतुकम् |
अतत्त्वार्थवदल्पं च तत्तामसमुदाहृतम् || BG 18.22 ||

तु - But, ; तत् - that (knowledge) ; उदाहृतम् - is said to be ; तामसम् - Tāmasika, ; यत् - which ; अहैतुकम् - unreasonably ; सक्तम् - attaches ; एकस्मिन् - to a single ; कार्ये - act ; कृत्स्नवत् - as if "this is everything." ; अतत्त्वार्थवत् - (It) is unveracious ; च - and ; अल्पम् - insignificant.

That knowledge is said to be Tāmasika, which unreasonably attaches to a single act as if "this is everything." It is unveracious and insignificant.

Intent - Single act as if "this is everything," the attachment to a single object as if it were the whole, with such knowledge, humans grasp the perishable body as the Ātmā and get attached as if "this is everything." That which is unveridical and paltry is said to be Tāmasika.

(Next, threefold actions are described -)

नियतं सङ्गरहितमरागद्वेषत: कृतम् |
अफलप्रेप्सुना कर्म यतत्सात्त्विकमुच्यते || BG 18.23 ||

कर्म - An act ; यत् - that is ; नियतम् - obligatory, ; तत् - that ; कृतम् - is done ; अफल-प्रेप्सुना - by one without desire for fruit, ; सङ्ग-रहितम् - attachment, ; अराग-द्वेषतः - passion, or aversion ; उच्यते - is said to be ; सात्त्विकम् - Sāttvika.

An obligatory act done without desire for fruit, attachment, passion, or aversion is said to be Sāttvika.

Intent - Obligatory means scripturally prescribed.

यत्तुकामेप्सुना कर्म साहङ्कारेण वा पुन: |
क्रियते बहुलायासं तद्राजसमुदाहृतम् || BG 18.24 ||

तु - But, ; कर्म - an act ; यत् - that is ; क्रियते - done ; बहुल-आयासम् - laboriously ; काम-ईप्सुना - by one with a desire for fruit ; वा - or ; साहङ्कारेण - with egoism ; पुनः - again ; तत् - that ; उदाहृतम् - is called ; राजसम् - Rājasika.

An act done laboriously by one with a desire for fruit or egoism is called Rājasika.

अनुबन्धं क्षयं हिंसामनपेक्ष्य च पौरुषम् |
मोहादारभ्यते कर्म यतत्तामसमुच्यते || BG 18.25 ||

यत् - That ; कर्म - act ; आरभ्यते - undertaken ; मोहात् - due to delusion ; अनपेक्ष्य - without regard to ; अनुबन्धम् - consequence, ; क्षयम् - loss, ; हिंसाम् - violence, ; च - and ; पौरुषम् - competence ; तत् - that ; उच्यते - is called ; तामसम् - Tāmasika.

Act undertaken due to delusion without regard to consequence, loss, violence, and competence is called Tāmasika.

Intent - When one engages in activities disregarding result, loss of wealth, power, ability, injury to self and others with violence in the mode of delusion, ignorance, or lack of discrimination - they are due to Tamoguṇa. The acts are Tāmasika.

(Next, different kinds of doers are set forth -)

मुक्तसङ्गोऽनहंवादी धृत्युत्साहसमन्वित: |
सिद्ध्यसिद्ध्योर्निर्विकार: कर्ता सात्त्विक उच्यते || BG 18.26 ||

कर्ता - A doer ; उच्यते - is said to be ; सात्त्विकः - Sāttvika ; अनहं-वादी - (who is) unegoistic, ; मुक्त-सङ्गः - devoid of attachment, ; धृति-उत्साह-समन्वितः - endowed with resolve and zeal, ; निर्विकारः - (and) unchanged ; सिद्धि-असिद्ध्योः - in success and failure.

A doer is said to be Sāttvika who is unegoistic, devoid of attachment, endowed with resolve and zeal, and unchanged in success and failure.

Intent - A Sāttvika person with attributes set forth above is impelled by the mandates of scriptures and not driven by greed for the fruits of Karma.

रागी कर्मफलप्रेप्सुर्लुब्धो हिंसात्मकोऽशुचि: |
हर्षशोकान्वित: कर्ता राजस: परिकीर्तित: || BG 18.27 ||

कर्ता - A doer ; परिकीर्तितः - is called ; राजसः - Rājaṣika, ; रागी - who is attached, ; कर्म-फल-प्रेप्सुः - seeks fruits of action, ; लुब्धः - is greedy, ; हिंसात्मकः - violent, ; अशुचिः - unclean, ; हर्ष-शोक-अन्वितः - (and) with joy and sorrow.

A doer is called Rājasika, who is attached, seeks fruits of action, is greedy, violent, unclean, and with joy and sorrow.

अयुक्त: प्राकृत: स्तब्ध: शठो नैष्कृतिकोऽलस: |
विषादी दीर्घसूत्री च कर्ता तामस उच्यते || BG 18.28 ||

कर्ता - A doer (who is) ; अयुक्तः - unfocused, ; प्राकृतः - uncultured, ; स्तब्धः - stiff, ; शठः - swindler, ; नैष्कृतिकः - malicious, ; अलसः - indolent, ; विषादी - downcast, ; च - and ; दीर्घ-सूत्री - procrastinator ; उच्यते - is called ; तामसः - Tāmasika.

A doer who is unfocused, uncultured, stiff, swindler, malicious, indolent, downcast, and procrastinator is called Tāmasika.

Intent - Unfocused is one whose mind is vacillating. Stiff like a cane who, with his excessive vanity, does not bend. Malicious undermines others or ruins their livelihood. Indolent to the extent of not even performing his own duty. A downcast is the one who is ever despondent, always with a pessimistic outlook. The procrastinator is ever tardy and even delays taking up urgent work.

बुद्धेर्भेदं धृतेश्चैव गुणतस्त्रिविधं शृणु |
प्रोच्यमानमशेषेण पृथक्त्वेन धनञ्जय || BG 18.29 ||

धनञ्जय - Hey Dhanañjaya (Arjuna)! ; एव - Also ; शृणु - listen to ; अशेषेण - without remainder (the fully) ; प्रोच्यमानम् - spoken ; त्रिविधम् - threefold ; भेदम् - distinctions ; बुद्धेः - of intellect ; च - and ; धृतेः - resolve ; गुणतः - by the constituents ; पृथक्त्वेन - separately.

Hey Arjuna! Listen to the fully spoken threefold distinctions of intellect and resolve by the constituents separately.

(Next, three kinds of intellect are set forth -)

प्रवृत्तिंच निवृत्तिं च कार्याकार्ये भयाभये |
बन्धं मोक्षं च या वेत्तिबुद्धि: सा पार्थ सात्त्विकी || BG 18.30 ||

या - That ; बुद्धिः - intellect ; सात्त्विकी - is Sāttvika, ; पार्थ - hey Pārtha (Arjuna)! ; सा - That ; वेत्ति - knows ; प्रवृत्तिम् - activity ; च - and ; निवृत्तिम् - inactivity, ; कार्य-अकार्ये - duty and nonduty, ; भय-अभये - fear and fearlessness, ; च - and ; बन्धम् - bondage ; च - and ; मोक्षम् - liberation.

That intellect is Sāttvika, hey Arjuna! That knows activity and inactivity, duty and nonduty, fear and fearlessness, bondage and liberation.

Intent - Activity or actions lead to bondage, whereas its opposite, inactivity or inaction, leads to liberation. The words occur in the same sentence with bondage and liberation and thus, are understood as the path of action (Karma-Mārga) and the path of renunciation (Saṃnyāsa-Mārga). The intellect that throws light on the objects of the verse and enjoins in renunciation, duty, injunctions, fearlessness, and the path of liberation, freeing one from activity, nonduty, prohibitions, fear, and bondage; that intellect is called Sāttvika.

यया धर्ममधर्मं च कार्यं चाकार्यमेव च |
अयथावत्प्रजानाति बुद्धि: सा पार्थ राजसी || BG 18.31 ||

सा - That ; बुद्धिः - intellect ; एव - is indeed ; राजसी - Rājasika, ; पार्थ - hey Pārtha (Arjuna)! ; यया - By which ; अयथावत् - (one does) not truly ; प्रजानाति - understand ; धर्मम् - righteousness ; च - and ; अधर्मम् - unrighteousness, ; च - and ; कार्यम् - duty ; च - and ; अकार्यम् - non-duty.

That intellect is Rājasika, hey Arjuna! By which one does not truly understand righteousness and unrighteousness, duty and non-duty.

अधर्मं धर्ममिति या मन्यते तमसावृता |
सर्वार्थान्विपरीतांश्च बुद्धि: सा पार्थ तामसी || BG 18.32 ||

सा - That ; बुद्धिः - intellect ; तामसी - is Tāmasika, ; पार्थ - hey Pārtha (Arjuna)! ; या - Which ; आवृता - shrouded ; तमसा - in Tamas ; मन्यते - deems ; अधर्मम् - unrighteousness ; इति - as ; धर्मम् - righteousness ; च - and ; सर्व-अर्थान् - all kinds of things ; विपरीतान् - contrarily.

That intellect is Tāmasika, hey Arjuna! Shrouded in Tamas deems unrighteousness as righteousness and all kinds of things contrarily.

(Next, Bhagavāna provides three kinds of resolves -)

धृत्या यया धारयते मन:प्राणेन्द्रियक्रिया: |
योगेनाव्यभिचारिण्या धृति: सा पार्थ सात्त्विकी || BG 18.33 ||

सा - That ; अव्यभिचारिण्या - unfaltering ; धृतिः - resolve ; सात्त्विकी - is Sāttvika, ; पार्थ - hey Pārtha (Arjuna)! ; यया - By which ; धृत्या - through concentration ; योगेन - Yoga ; धारयते - (one) can be sustain ; मनः-प्राण-इन्द्रिय-क्रियाः - the functions of the mind, the vital breaths of air and the senses.

That unfaltering resolve is Sāttvika, hey Arjuna! Through concentration, one can sustain the functions of the mind, the vital breaths of air, and the senses.

Intent - Resolve ought to be unfaltering. Unwavering so that the functions of the mind, the vital breaths of air, and the senses are stopped from taking a path contrary to the scriptures. It is done by meditation (Dhyāna-Yoga) through concentration (Dhāraṇā), introspective focus, and one-pointedness of the mind. The term unfaltering refers to unbroken concentration.

यया तु धर्मकामार्थान्धृत्या धारयतेऽर्जुन |
प्रसङ्गेन फलाकाङ् क्षी धृति: सा पार्थ राजसी || BG 18.34 ||

तु - But, ; सा - that ; धृतिः - resolve ; राजसी - is Rājasika, ; अर्जुन - hey Arjuna, ; पार्थ - Pārtha (the son of Pṛthā)! ; यया - By which ; धृत्या - resolve, ; प्रसङ्गेन - (while) occasionally ; फल-आकाङ्क्षी - desiring fruits (of action), ; धारयते - (one) upholds ; धर्म-काम-अर्थान् - righteousness, lust, and wealth,

That resolve is Rājasika, hey Arjuna! By which resolve, while occasionally desiring fruits of action, one upholds righteousness, lust, and wealth.

यया स्वप्नं भयं शोकं विषादं मदमेव च |
न विमुञ्चति दुर्मेधा धृति: सा पार्थ तामसी || BG 18.35 ||

सा - That ; धृतिः - resolve is ; तामसी - Tāmasika, ; पार्थ - hey Pārtha (Arjuna)! ; यया - By which ; दुर्मेधाः - an evil-minded ; एव - also ; न - does not ; विमुञ्चति - give up ; स्वप्नम् - sleep, ; भयम् - fear, ; शोकम् - sorrow, ; विषादम् - despair, ; च - and ; मदम् - indulgence.

That resolve is Tāmasika, hey Arjuna! By which an evil-minded does not give up sleep, fear, sorrow, despair, and indulgence.

(Threefold actions and their accessories based on the constituents of Prakṛti were set forth. Next is described threefold pleasures -)

सुखं त्विदानीं त्रिविधं शृणु मे भरतर्षभ |
अभ्यासाद्रमते यत्र दु:खान्तं च निगच्छति || BG 18.36 ||

तु - Again, ; भरतर्षभ - hey Bharatarṣabha (Arjuna)! ; इदानीम् - Now ; शृणु - listen ; मे - from Me ; त्रिविधम् - the threefold ; सुखम् -pleasures, ; यत्र - wherein ; रमते - one rejoices ; अभ्यासात् - through practice ; च - and ; निगच्छति - achieves ; दुःखान्तम् - the end of pain.

Again, hey, Arjuna! Now listen from Me the threefold pleasures, wherein one rejoices through practice and achieves the end of pain.

Intent - Experience of pleasure wherein one rejoices and even reaches the end of pain through practice or repeated efforts. That pleasure is the subject.

यत्तदग्रे विषमिव परिणामेऽमृतोपमम् |
तत्सुखं सात्त्विकं प्रोक्तमात्मबुद्धिप्रसादजम् || BG 18.37 ||

तत् - That ; यत् - which ; इव - seems like ; विषम् - poison ; अग्रे - in the beginning ; परिणामे - but in the end ; अमृत-उपमम् - is like ambrosia; ; तत् - that ; सुखम् - pleasure ; आत्म-बुद्धि-प्रसादजम् - born of the pure intellect situated in the self-knowledge ; प्रोक्तम् - is called ; सात्त्विकम् - Sāttvika.

That which seems like poison in the beginning but in the end is like ambrosia; that pleasure born of the pure intellect situated in the self-knowledge is called Sāttvika.

Intent - Sāttvika pleasure, in the beginning, is like poison. At the start of concentration, meditation, dispassion, and Samādhī, the efforts are painful or difficult; however, it is ambrosiac with the maturity of knowledge. It emanates from the clarity of the mind developed with the knowledge of the Ātmā.

विषयेन्द्रियसंयोगाद्यत्तदग्रेऽमृतोपमम् |
परिणामे विषमिव तत्सुखं राजसं स्मृतम् || BG 18.38 ||

तत् - That ; सुखम् - pleasure ; स्मृतम् - is said to be ; राजसम् - Rājasika, ; यत् - which ; अग्रे - in the beginning, ; विषय-इन्द्रिय-संयोगात् - due to contact between objects and senses, ; अमृत-उपमम् - is ambrosiac (but) ; तत् - that ; इव - is like ; विषम् - poison ; परिणामे - in the end.

That pleasure is said to be Rājasika, which in the beginning, due to contact between objects and senses, is ambrosiac but is like poison in the end.

Intent - Pleasures born of contact between the senses and their objects at first provide lots of happiness. However, they are like poison after experiencing them, leading to a decline in power, vigor, beauty, intelligence, understanding, wealth, and zeal. They are the destroyers of this and the next world.

यदग्रे चानुबन्धे च सुखं मोहनमात्मनः |
निद्रालस्यप्रमादोत्थं तत्तामसमुदाहृतम् || BG 18.39 ||

तत् - That ; सुखम् - pleasure ; निद्रा-आलस्य-प्रमाद-उत्थम् - born of sleep, indolence, and negligence ; उदाहृतम् - is called ; तामसम् - Tāmasika, ; यत् - which ; मोहनम् - deludes ; आत्मनः - oneself ; अग्रे - at the beginning ; च - and ; च - also ; अनुबन्धे - the end.

That pleasure born of sleep, indolence, and negligence is called Tāmasika, which deludes oneself at the beginning and the end.

(Now, the theme of the threefold constituents is concluded -)

न तदस्ति पृथिव्यां वा दिवि देवेषु वा पुनः |
सत्त्वं प्रकृतिजैर्मुक्तं यदेभिः स्यात्त्रिभिर्गुणैः || BG 18.40 ||

तत् - That ; पृथिव्याम् - in this world ; वा - or ; दिवि - heaven ; वा - or ; पुनः - again ; देवेषु - among the deities, ; न - no ; सत्त्वम् - (sentient or insentient) being ; अस्ति - exists ; यत् - who ; स्यात् - is ; मुक्तम् - free ; एभिः - from these ; त्रिभिः - three ; गुणैः - constituents ; प्रकृतिजैः - born of Prakṛti.

In this world, heaven or among the deities, no being exists who is free from these three constituents born of Prakṛti.

Intent - There is no being, sentient or insentient, on this earth, heaven, or among the deities devoid of the Sāttvika, Rājasika, and Tāmasika constituents born of Prakṛti. Whatever movable and immobile transformations of Prakṛti exist, they are all endowed with those constituents. Accordingly, the entire Saṃsāra being the transformation of the three constituents is Triguṇātmaka consisting of the three constituents of Prakṛti.

{Now, in the epilogue of Gītā, the essence of the approach for liberation from the Triguṇātmaka Saṃsāra is stated. In this context, it is necessary to know the activities of the four functional classes of the society (चतुर-वर्ण, Catura-Varṇa). They are provided next -}

ब्राह्मणक्षत्रियविशां शूद्राणां च परन्तप |
कर्माणि प्रविभक्तानि स्वभावप्रभवैर्गुणैः || BG 18.41 ||

परन्तप - Hey Parantapa (Arjuna)! ; कर्माणि - The activities of ; ब्राह्मण-क्षत्रिय-विशाम् - Brāhmaṇa, Kṣatriya, Vaiśya, ; च - and ; शूद्राणाम् - Śūdra ; प्रविभक्तानि - are distributed ; गुणैः - according to the constituents ; स्वभाव-प्रभवैः - of their nature.

Hey Arjuna! The activities of Brāhmaṇa, Kṣatriya, Vaiśya, and Śūdra are distributed according to the constituents of their nature.

Intent - Brāhmaṇa, Kṣatriya, and Vaiśya being fit for Upanayana,[122]sacrifice, and learning of the Vedas are grouped. Not being fit, the Śūdra is held in a separate classification. The above classes are based on the functional classification of the society in terms of the various stages of life, generally known as the Varṇāśrama (वर्णाश्रम) system. The term Varṇāśrama is a compound of the term Varṇa (वर्ण) and the term Āśrama (आश्रम).

The term Varṇa (वर्ण) generally means color, complexion, and also many had used as caste anglicized from Portuguese "casta" when they came to India in the late fifteenth century. From the Vedantic perspective personality or nature of individuals are varied based on the extent of goodness, purity, virtuosity (Sāttvika), passion (Rājasika), and sixfold mutations viz. lust, anger, greed, delusion, excessive pride, and envy (Tāmasika) constituents present in their personality, and thus their suitability for distinct professional duties and activities. The system of Varṇāśrama naturally evolved to maintain the sustainability of the society. It is not an artificial system but refers to natural classifications that appear to various degrees in all humanities. Individuals have different innate tendencies for work and exhibit a variety of personal attributes. There are also natural phases in life when performing certain activities is easier and more rewarding. Axiomatically individuals best realize their potential by considering such natural arrangements and that society should be structured and organized accordingly. Lord Śrī Kṛṣṇa provides the classification in terms of the four major functions necessary for the sustainability of humanity: 1) education, entrusted to Brāhmaṇa, 2) security, entrusted to Kṣatriya, 3) commerce, entrusted to Vaiśya and 4) labor, entrusted to Śūdra. The innate attributes of a Brāhmaṇa are provided in BG 18.42 Brahma-Prakṛti (ब्रह्म-प्रकृति), a Kṣatriya in BG 18.43 Kṣātra-Prakṛti (क्षात्र-प्रकृति), a Vaiśya and a Śūdra in BG 18.44 Vaiśya-Prakṛti (वैश्य-प्रकृति) and Śūdra-Prakṛti (शूद्र-प्रकृति) respectively.

The term Āśrama (आश्रम) signifies the four stages of life: 1) Bachelor student stage (ब्रह्मचर्य-आश्रम, Brahmacarya-Āśrama), 2) Householder stage (गृहस्थ-आश्रम, Gṛhastha-Āśrama), 3) Retired stage (वानप्रस्थ-आश्रम, Vānaprastha-Āśrama) and 4) Renunciation stage (संन्यास-आश्रम, Saṃnyāsa-Āśrama):

1. Brahmacarya-Āśrama means the first bachelor student stage of life from childhood to around 25. This stage focuses on education and includes the practice of celibacy. In Vedic times, students went and lived in a Gurukula (house of a preceptor), acquiring knowledge of science, philosophy,

---

[122] Upanayana-Saṃskāra (उपनयन-संस्कार). It is a rite of passage in which a preceptor accepts and draws a child towards knowledge and initiates the second birth. The ritual includes the acceptance of a three- layered cotton thread popularly known as Yajñopavīta. After accepting and wearing this Yajñopavīta, a person is known as Dvija - born second time.

scriptures, and logic, practicing self-discipline, working to earn remuneration (दक्षिणा, Dakṣiṇā) to be paid to the preceptor, and learning to live a life of Dharma (righteousness, morals, duties).

2. Gṛhastha-Āśrama means the second stage of an individual's married life, from the age of 25 to the age of 50, with the duties of maintaining a household, raising a family, educating own children, and leading a family-centered and virtuous social life. Gṛhastha stage is considered the most important of all stages in a sociological context, as human beings in this stage not only pursue a moral life, they produce food and wealth that sustain people in other stages of life and the continuation of progeny. The stage also represents where the most intense physical, sexual, emotional, occupational, social, and material attachments exist in a human being's life.
3. Vānaprastha-Āśrama means one who gives up worldly life or literally retires to the forest. In this third stage of life, from the age of 50 to 75, a person hands over household responsibilities to the next generation, takes an advisory role, and gradually withdraws from the world. It is a transition phase from a householder's life with a greater emphasis on wealth, pleasure, and desires to one with a greater focus on spiritual liberation.
4. Saṃnyāsa-Āśrama means the last stage of life marked by the renunciation of material desires and prejudices, represented by a state of disinterest and detachment from material life, generally without any meaningful property or home, and focused on liberation, peace, and simple spiritual life. Anyone could enter this stage after completing the Brahmacarya stage of life.

It should be kept in mind that the functional classifications were not intended to represent the superiority of one over the other. The distribution of activities was based on one's nature, that is, the intrinsic attributes rather than birth in those functional classifications. The classes were not considered higher or lower amongst themselves. Each class and Āśrama had its own specified function. What may be desirable for one section of society may be degrading for another. For example, absolute non-violence, which includes refraining from animal sacrifice, is essential for the priestly class but considered wholly unworthy of a Kṣatriya. Generating wealth and producing children are essential for householders, but intimate contact with money and women is spiritually suicidal for the renouncer. Underlying all these apparent differences was the common goal of advancing in spiritual life based on eternal righteousness (Sanātana-Dharma). Since the center of society was the Supreme Being, everyone worked according to their intrinsic attributes to sustain themselves and the society, and make their life a success by progressing towards the realization of the supreme imperishable Reality, the Brahman. Thus, in the system, there was unity in diversity. Diversity is inherent in nature and can never be removed. We have various limbs in our body, and they all perform different functions. Expecting all limbs to perform the same functions is futile. Seeing them all as different is not a sign of ignorance but factual knowledge of their utilities. Similarly, the variety among human beings cannot be ignored. Party leaders formulate ideologies even in communist countries where equality is the foremost principle. The military wields guns and protects the nation; farmers cultivate the land, and industrial workers do mechanical jobs. The four classes of occupations exist there, despite all attempts to equalize. The Varṇāśrama system recognized the diversity in human nature and scientifically prescribed duties and occupations matching people's nature.

शमो दमस्तप: शौचं क्षान्तिरार्जवमेव च |
ज्ञानं विज्ञानमास्तिक्यं ब्रह्मकर्म स्वभावजम् || BG 18.42 ||

एव - Also, ; शम: - control of the mind, ; दम: - restraint of the senses, ; तप: - austerity (as per BG 17), ; शौचम् - purity, ; क्षान्ति: - forgiveness, ; आर्जवम् - simplicity, ; आस्तिक्यम् - faith in preceptors and scriptures, ; ज्ञानम् - knowledge of the scriptures, ; च - and ; विज्ञानम् - realized knowledge ; स्वभावजम् - are natural ; ब्रह्म-कर्म - activities of a Brāhmaṇa.

Control of the mind, restraint of the senses, austerity, purity, forgiveness, simplicity, faith in preceptors and scriptures, knowledge of the scriptures, and realized knowledge are natural activities of a Brāhmaṇa.

शौर्यं तेजो धृतिर्दाक्ष्यं युद्धे चाप्यपलायनम् |
दानमीश्वरभावश्च क्षात्रं कर्म स्वभावजम् || BG 18.43 ||

शौर्यम् - Valor, ; तेजः - splendor, ; धृतिः - fortitude, ; दाक्ष्यम् - skill, ; दानम् - charity, ; च - and ; ईश्वर-भावः - leadership attribute, ; च - and ; अपि - also ; अपलायनम् - not fleeing ; युद्धे - in war ; स्वभावजम् - are natural ; कर्म - activities ; क्षात्रम् - of a Kṣatriya.

Valor, splendor, fortitude, skill, charity, leadership attribute, and not fleeing in war are natural activities of a Kṣatriya.

Intent - Here, Īśvara-Bhāva (ईश्वर-भाव, leadership attribute) refers to the lordliness of ruling over subjects.

कृषिगौरक्ष्यवाणिज्यं वैश्यकर्म स्वभावजम् |
परिचर्यात्मकं कर्म शूद्रस्यापि स्वभावजम् || BG 18.44 ||

स्वभावजम् - Natural ; वैश्य-कर्म - activities of a Vaiśya are ; कृषि - agriculture, ; गौरक्ष्य - protection of cows, ; वाणिज्यम् - (and) commerce. ; अपि - Also, ; परिचर्यात्मकम् - serving through labor ; स्वभावजम् - is a natural ; कर्म - activity ; शूद्रस्य - of a Śūdra.

Natural activities of a Vaiśya are agriculture, protection of cows, and commerce. Serving through labor is a natural activity of a Śūdra.

(If selfish worldly interests are relinquished, and activities distributed by functional classes are put into practice with a righteousness perspective, then the fruit of such activities is the attainment of higher worlds, as narrated in Śruti and Purāṇa. However, if those respective activities are performed to attain the Lord with a transcendental perspective, then -)

स्वे स्वे कर्मण्यभिरतः संसिद्धिं लभते नरः |
स्वकर्मनिरतः सिद्धिं यथा विन्दति तच्छृणु || BG 18.45 ||

नरः - A person ; लभते - acquires ; संसिद्धिम् - perfection ; अभिरतः - through devotion ; स्वे स्वे - to own ; कर्मणि - (natural) activity. ; शृणु - Listen to ; तत् - that ; यथा - how ; सिद्धिम् - perfection ; विन्दति - is acquired ; स्वकर्म-निरतः - through (devotion to) one's natural activity.

A person acquires perfection through devotion to own natural activity. Listen to how perfection is acquired through devotion to one's natural activity.

Intent - If one's allotted natural activities, with attributes mentioned previously, are truly conducted with righteousness, their fruits are the acquisition of the superior worlds, and upon depletion of accumulated piety, they are thrust back to this world "क्षीणे पुण्ये मर्त्यलोकं विशन्ति." They never achieve fitness of perfection to attain the Lord. However, if functional class activities are performed to attain the Lord, then as their fruit, with the destruction of impurities, through purity of the conscience, they acquire perfection of fitness for the discipline of knowledge. Upon the success of the fitness for the discipline of knowledge, perfection to attain the Lord is acquired.

(Now, the way that perfection is acquired, you listen to that -)

यतः प्रवृत्तिर्भूतानां येन सर्वमिदं ततम् |
स्वकर्मणा तमभ्यर्च्य सिद्धिं विन्दति मानवः || BG 18.46 ||

स्वकर्मणा - Through the performance of natural activities (as worship), ; मानवः - a human ; विन्दति - attains ; सिद्धिम् - perfection - ; अभ्यर्च्य - worshipping (not by just lighting a lamp) ; तम् - That (Paramātmā) ; यतः - from Whom ; भूतानाम् - all beings ; प्रवृत्तिः - have proceeded (and) ; येन - by Whom ; सर्वम् - all ; इदम् - this ; ततम् - is pervaded.

Through the performance of natural activities as worship, a human attains perfection - worshipping That from Whom all beings have proceeded and by Whom all this is pervaded.

Intent - When all limbs and organs of the body properly work according to their functions, then it remains healthy. However, even if the smallest of the limbs or organs do not function properly, the entire body is inflicted with pain and sickness. In the same way, the world as a whole is the body of the Cosmic-Form Lord, the four functional classes and the four stages of life, and every being is the limb and organ of the Cosmic Body. Therefore, when all functional classes in their stages of life are zealously devoted to their respective natural activities, and all humans are cautiously engaged in activities according to their innate attributes, the entire Cosmic Body can remain healthy. However, if individuals of functional classes abandon their natural activities or allotted duties, then the Cosmic Body bearing the shock would become disorderly. That is why it is incumbent upon all individuals, irrespective of their functional class or the stage of their lives, to be helpful through their innate activities in moving the cycle of the Saṃsāra. So is ordained by the Lord. Knowing as a duty ordained by the Lord to engage in own natural activities with desireless sentiment is worshipping the Lord. As its fruit, purity of the conscience is achieved. That is the perfection of fitness for the discipline of knowledge, which in the pure conscience can awaken knowledge. It is not that only a Brāhmaṇa is eligible for knowledge; however, all four functional classes (Brāhmaṇa, Kṣatriya, Vaiśya, and Śūdra) with desireless sentiment through their actions worshipping the Lord can acquire purity of the conscience without any obstacle by the grace of the Lord, and thereby become eligible for knowledge.

श्रेयान्स्वधर्मो विगुण: परधर्मात्स्वनुष्ठितात् |
स्वभावनियतं कर्म कुर्वन्नाप्नोति किल्बिषम् || BG 18.47 ||

स्वनुष्ठितात् - Compared to properly performed ; पर-धर्मात् - duty of others ; स्वधर्म: - own duty ; विगुण: - (even if) defective ; श्रेयान् - is better. ; कुर्वन् - (Because) by engaging in ; कर्म - actions ; स्वभाव-नियतम् - based on own intrinsic nature ; न - (one does) not ; आप्नोति - incur ; किल्बिषम् - sin.

Compared to properly performed duty of others, own duty even if defective is better. Because by engaging in actions based on own intrinsic nature, one does not incur sin.

Intent - Just as feces-urine discharging action-organs of the body performing qualityless menial work are not seen as flawed, but indeed their daily activities are seen as helpful in maintaining the health of the body. Accordingly, in the world, own duty (Svadharma), actions befitting own individual intrinsic attributes, even if they are defective, are better than those of others that are their best. Here, the duties and attendant actions being natural are easy. They provide protection from the shock that may be imposed on the Cosmic-Body should they be relinquished. There, based on the above perspective, own actions by helping to move the cycle of the Saṃsāra and actions worshipping the Lord are beneficial. As a result, sin is far removed, and the perfection of fitness for the discipline of knowledge is acquired. That is the true nature of Karma. In the kingdom of Prakṛti, constituents and faults are dependent. For instance, compared to the activities of a Brāhmaṇa, the activities of a Śūdra are inferior. Compared to Śūdra activities, Brāhmaṇa activities are superior.

Nevertheless, if Śūdra relinquishes his natural activities and conducts the activities of a Brāhmaṇa, it would be beneficial neither for him nor for society. For instance, what would happen if an illiterate person who cannot even read or write is appointed as a professor at a university? Would it be good for him? Would it be helpful to the students and society? In the present, when someone is born in a class and family and not anywhere else without cause, the past impressions of past lives determine his present birth in the class and family. If that is so, then his current duties and thus actions ought to be accordant with his intrinsic nature. For humans, intrinsic actions become beneficial, and actions contrary to the intrinsic nature become detrimental, just as for a child in the first grade, step-wise order of class studies is responsible for taking him from the first grade to the twelfth grade of the high school. However, if the step-wise, orderly studies are ignored, he is unlikely to reach and be in the twelfth grade. Accordingly, activities accordant with intrinsic nature are easy and beneficial, as clarified by Bhagavāna in the verses (BG 18.45 - BG 18.47), "If actions accordant with own class are performed properly then as its fruit one acquires the opulence of the heavens, and with leftover Karma-Saṃskāras (remaining accumulated impressions of past actions), based on fruits of action, birth is acquired endowed with best region, class, family, religion, longevity, education, conduct, wealth, happiness and intelligence. And, if the intrinsic activities are conducted with the desireless sentiment, it provides fitness for the discipline of knowledge." Therefore, from all perspectives, for humans performing actions befitting their intrinsic nature is beneficial and does not by working against one's nature.

सहजं कर्म कौन्तेय सदोषमपि न त्यजेत् |
सर्वारम्भा हि दोषेण धूमेनाग्निरिवावृता: || BG 18.48 ||

कौन्तेय - Hey Kaunteya (Arjuna)! ; कर्म - Actions ; सहजम् - determined by nature, ; सदोषम् - (even if) defective, ; न - should not ; त्यजेत् - be abandoned. ; हि - For, ; सर्वारम्भाः - all activities ; अपि - are indeed ; आवृताः - shrouded ; दोषेण - by flaws ; इव - as ; अग्निः - fire ; धूमेन - is by smoke.

Hey Arjuna! Actions determined by nature, even if defective, should not be abandoned. For, all activities are shrouded by flaws as fire is by smoke.

Intent - Karma is in the kingdom of Māyā and is the work of ignorance. That is why it can't be without flaws in nature. Just as fire is veiled by smoke in the beginning, in the same manner, Karma is veiled by flaws to some degree. Just as how fire produced with smoke cooks food and becomes smokeless, in the same way, natural Karma, even with flaws, with the influence of desireless sentiment, purifies the conscience and becomes devoid of flaws. That is why, as long as individuals are bound by ignorance and are only fit for Karma, until then, they should not relinquish their natural activities even if they are flawed.

{Through actions, the perfection in the fitness for the discipline of knowledge is described. Now, as its fruit - Naiṣkarmya-Siddhi (नैष्कर्म्य-सिद्धि, actionlessness perfection) is provided -}

असक्तबुद्धि: सर्वत्र जितात्मा विगतस्पृह: |
नैष्कर्म्यसिद्धिं परमां सन्न्यासेनाधिगच्छति || BG 18.49 ||

असक्त-बुद्धिः - (One whose) intellect is unattached ; सर्वत्र - everywhere, ; विगत-स्पृहः - free from desires ; जित-आत्मा - (and) self-disciplined, ; अधिगच्छति - attains ; परमाम् - the supreme ; नैष्कर्म्य-सिद्धिम् - perfection of actionlessness ; संन्यासेन - by renunciation.

One whose intellect is unattached everywhere, free from desires and self-disciplined, attains the supreme perfection of actionlessness by renunciation.

Intent - One whose mind is unattached to objects like children, wife, or wealth that are the seats of attachment, whose inner-self or the conscience is disciplined, who has conquered his mind and senses by subduing attachment, aversion, desire, and anger, whose desires for bodily enjoyments have departed and is content in whatever is easily received for the sustenance of the body, such a person through renunciation with true direct knowledge of the oneness of the Ātmā and the Brahman attains the supreme perfection of Naiṣkarmya. Becoming detached from the body and senses, he attains oneness of his Ātmā with the actionless Brahman, that is, Tātvika-Saṃnyāsa (तात्विक-संन्यास, true total renunciation). At that time, the body and senses are engaged in their respective activities, but he neither sees those activities in his Ātmā nor is a doer of those activities, but only as a witness - their observer. Through the right knowledge, he acquires the supreme perfection of Naiṣkarmya in the form of total renunciation of all actions (Sarva-Karma-Saṃnyāsa).

(Bhagavāna provides the sequence of steps to attain the supreme perfection of Naiṣkarmya for a person of pure conscience with a sentiment of devotion to the Lord through actions determined by own intrinsic nature -)

सिद्धिं प्राप्तो यथा ब्रह्म तथाप्नोति निबोध मे |
समासेनैव कौन्तेय निष्ठा ज्ञानस्य या परा || BG 18.50 ||

कौन्तेय - Hey Kaunteya (Arjuna)! ; निबोध - Know ; मे - from Me ; समासेन - briefly, ; प्राप्तः - having acquired ; सिद्धिम् - fitness (for the disciple of knowledge), ; यथा - how ; आप्नोति - (one) attains ; ब्रह्म - Brahman, ; तथा - and ; या - which ; एव - (is) indeed ; परा - the supreme ; निष्ठा - consummation ; ज्ञानस्य - of knowledge..

Hey Arjuna, Know from Me briefly, having acquired fitness, how one attains Brahman, the supreme consummation of knowledge.

Intent - The fitness referred to herein is related to the initial fitness of the body and senses for the discipline of knowledge born of the grace of the Lord by devotion through actions and not for the ultimate attainment.

बुद्ध्या विशुद्धया युक्तो धृत्यात्मानं नियम्य च |
शब्दादीन्विषयांस्त्यक्त्वा रागद्वेषौ व्युदस्य च || BG 18.51 ||
विविक्तसेवी लघ्वाशी यतवाक्कायमानस: |
ध्यानयोगपरो नित्यं वैराग्यं समुपाश्रित: || BG 18.52 ||
अहङ्कारं बलं दर्पं कामं क्रोधं परिग्रहम् |
विमुच्य निर्मम: शान्तो ब्रह्मभूयाय कल्पते || BG 18.53 ||

युक्तः - United with ; विशुद्धया - a dispassionately pure ; बुद्ध्या - intellect, ; च - and ; नियम्य - controlling ; आत्मानम् - the mind ; धृत्या - with (Sāttvika) resolve, ; त्यक्त्वा - abandoning ; शब्दादीन् - sound and other ; विषयान् - objects, ; च - and ; व्युदस्य - destroying ; राग-द्वेषौ - attachment and aversion,

विविक्त-सेवी - dwells lonely, ; लघु-आशी - eats lightly, ; यत-वाक्-काय-मानसः - controls the body, mind, and speech, ; नित्यम् - ever ; ध्यान-योग-परः - engaged in meditation-Yoga, ; समुपाश्रितः - resorts ; वैराग्यम् - to dispassion,

विमुच्य - relinquishing ; अहङ्कारम् - egoism, ; बलम् - force, ; दर्पम् - arrogance, ; कामम् - lust, ; क्रोधम् - anger, ; परिग्रहम् - (and) accumulation of possessions - ; शान्तः - (such) a tranquil person ; निर्ममः - (and) without mineness ; कल्पते - is fit ; ब्रह्म-भूयाय - for the status of the Brahman.

United with a dispassionately pure intellect, controlling the mind with resolve, abandoning sound and other objects, destroying attachment and aversion, dwells lonely, eats lightly, controls the body, mind, and speech, ever engaged in meditation-Yoga, resorts to dispassion, relinquishing egoism, force, arrogance, lust, anger, and accumulation of possessions - such a tranquil person without mineness is fit for the status of the Brahman.

Intent - Endowed with dispassionate intellect, without deceit, with resolve, controlling the senses, abandoning all sense-objects except for those necessary for sustenance and even those without fondness, getting rid of likes and dislikes, residing in solitary places like forests, riverbanks, caves, eating lightly that helps in winning over the fault of sleep, keeping the body, mind, and speech under control as one would a horse, engaging in meditation contemplating on the Ātmā through concentration and one whose attachment to enjoyments of this and the next world have evaporated, such dispassionate person relinquishing egoism, the force of lust and fondness, excessive vanity, lust, anger and accumulation of personal things, with a tranquil mind and without mineness, becomes fit to attain the status of the Brahman.

(Based on the above sequence -)

ब्रह्मभूत: प्रसन्नात्मा न शोचति न काङ्‌क्षति |
सम: सर्वेषु भूतेषु मद्भक्तिं लभते पराम् || BG 18.54 ||

ब्रह्म-भूतः - Becoming the Brahman, ; प्रसन्न-आत्मा - a tranquil-minded (person) ; न - neither ; शोचति - grieves ; न - nor ; काङ्क्षति - desires. ; समः - With equanimity ; सर्वेषु - towards all ; भूतेषु - beings, ; लभते - (he) gains ; पराम् - supreme ; मत्-भक्तिम् - devotion unto Me.

Becoming the Brahman, a tranquil-minded person neither grieves nor desires. With equanimity towards all beings, he gains supreme devotion unto Me.

Intent - Based on the sequence depicted in the verses (BG 18.51 - BG 18.53), a person endowed with the accessories, having the benefit of the knowledge of the Ātmā, removing I-ness sense from the body (that is, removing ignorance born superimposition of the body from the Ātmā), and situating with oneness in own (free from all distinctions and free from limitations) Ātmā, neither grieves nor desires for anything. It is due to the conceit in the body that with discriminating and limiting vision, grief and desires are stuck as thorns in the heart and are hurting. Upon removing the thorns, he is free from all these ordinary pains and, like water in the waves, situated in all beings with I-ness, attains My knowledge endowed supreme devotion.

भक्त्या मामभिजानाति यावान्यश्चास्मि तत्त्वत: |
ततो मां तत्त्वतो ज्ञात्वा विशते तदनन्तरम् || BG 18.55 ||

भक्त्या - By that devotion, ; अभिजानाति - he comprehends ; माम् - Me ; तत्त्वतः - in the truth ; यावान् - about My extent ; च - and ; यः - Who ; अस्मि - I am. ; ततः - Then ; ज्ञात्वा - knowing ; माम् - Me ; तत्त्वतः - in reality, ; तत्-अनन्तरम् - (he) immediately ; विशते - enters (into Me.)

By that devotion, he comprehends Me in the truth about My extent and Who I am. Then knowing Me in reality, he immediately enters into Me.

Intent - Employing that devotion, that person knows Me, what My extent is and Who I am in truth. Because of the adjunct of ignorance, even though perceived as consisting of the phenomenal world of the five great elements, in reality, I am detached from the world, and there is no taint from it in Me. Though this world is nothing without Me, there is nothing of it in Me. Though this world is perceived with attributes on the dependence of Me, the one that is existent common in all (Sattā-Sāmānya), it cannot touch Me. By My being existent, I shine the being and non-being of all those entities, yet I am "as I am." Common gold remains the same "is as is" as gold, though there is a perception of gold earrings and gold necklaces. Without the common gold, the gold earrings and gold necklaces have no existence, and the name forms are nothing in the gold. Though the common gold illuminates the being and non-being of those gold ornaments, it does not suffer being and non-beingness with their being and non-being. This Tattva-Sākṣātkāra, realization of the true knowledge is named knowledge endowed supreme devotion. With this supreme devotion, the devotee knowing Me in truth, losing his limited ego in Me, immediately enters Me and attains Tātvika-Yoga (true union with oneness in Me).

सर्वकर्माण्यपि सदा कुर्वाणो मद्व्यपाश्रय: |
मत्प्रसादादवाप्नोति शाश्वतं पदमव्ययम् || BG 18.56 ||

अपि - Though ; सदा - always ; कुर्वाणः - performing ; सर्व-कर्माणि - all actions, ; मत्-व्यपाश्रयः - (being) in My refuge, ; अवाप्नोति - (he) attains ; शाश्वतम् - eternal ; अव्ययम् - immutable ; पदम् - Status ; मत्-प्रसादात् - by My grace.

Though always performing all actions, being in My refuge, he attains eternal immutable Status by My grace.

Intent - In whose view there is nothing except Me the witness-observer, being in My refuge (मत्-व्यपाश्रय), oriented towards Me with the sentiment that I am the all-round support, such devotee, even though is involved in all kinds of activities, by My grace, attains the eternal immutable Status. Like a lotus leaf, constantly engaged in actions, is not tainted by any actions and is not bound by them.

(That being the case -)

चेतसा सर्वकर्माणि मयि सन्न्यस्य मत्परः |
बुद्धियोगमुपाश्रित्य मच्चित्तः सततं भव || BG 18.57 ||

उपाश्रित्य - Taking support of ; बुद्धि-योगम् - Jñāna-Yoga, ; चेतसा - mentally ; संन्यस्य - surrendering ; सर्व-कर्माणि - all actions ; मयि - to Me, ; मत्-परः - having oriented towards Me, ; सततम् - always ; भव - be one ; मत्-चित्तः - with your mind on Me.

Taking support of Jñāna-Yoga, mentally surrendering all actions to Me, having oriented towards Me, always be one with your mind on Me.

Intent - Buddhi-Yoga or Jñāna-Yoga was heretofore described earlier in Chapter 2. It is that realization of the Truth, "Neither am I doing anything nor there is any duty on me to do anything, but I am the witnessing non-disappearing light, in whose illumination the body, senses, mind, and intellect are engaged in their duties, and yet they do not touch me." It is only through this intellect that there is a Tātvika-Yoga (a true union) in the Lord, not by any other way, and it is only with this intellect there is total renunciation of all actions. "Hey Arjuna! With the support of this intellect, mentally surrendering all actions to Me, having oriented towards Me, always have your mind concentrated on Me." That is, become detached from all duties and actions of the body, senses, mind, and intellect, doing everything through them, remain a non-doer, and in all actions see Me as the witnessing non-action. This way, the spiritual guidance given in Chapter 2 of Buddhi-Yoga is presented as the epilogue of the entire Gītā.

मच्चित्तः सर्वदुर्गाणि मत्प्रसादात्तरिष्यसि |
अथ चेत्वमहङ्कारान्न श्रोष्यसि विनङ्क्ष्यसि || BG 18.58 ||

मत्-चित्तः - (With your) mind fixed on Me, ; तरिष्यसि - you will overcome ; सर्व-दुर्गाणि - all obstacles ; मत्-प्रसादात् - by My grace. ; अथ - But, ; चेत् - if ; त्वम् - you ; न - do not ; श्रोष्यसि - listen (to My words) ; अहङ्कारात् - due to ego, ; विनङ्क्ष्यसि - you will perish.

With your mind fixed on Me, you will overcome all obstacles by My grace. But, if you do not listen to My words due to ego, you will perish.

Intent - Hey, Arjuna! With your mind fixed on Me, you will by My grace overcome all obstacles such as "I, Arjuna, slayer of all these relatives, by their deaths family lineage will be destroyed, by which righteousness of community and family will be destroyed, women of the family will become immoral, children of mixed functional classes will be born, and as a result, there will be the downfall of the ancestors." That is, when you hand over the flute, in the form of your body, removing the "I am a doer" ego and doership-intellect, to Me - the all-witness Ātmā of all, then I, Myself will produce the most melodious notes that will be the cause for supreme-bliss instead of your grief. In reality, even though these obstacles do not touch your pure Ātmā, only the ignorance born doership-ego and doership-intellect are becoming the cause of these obstacles. With your mind fixed on Me, free from the ignorance born doership-ego and doership-intellect, you will easily overcome the challenges. However, if you do not heed My advice, that is, do not accept and act on it, you will perish.

यदहङ्कारमाश्रित्य न योत्स्य इति मन्यसे |
मिथ्यैष व्यवसायस्ते प्रकृतिस्त्वां नियोक्ष्यति || BG 18.59 ||

आश्रित्य - Resorting ; अहङ्कारम् - to ego ; यत् - if (you) ; मन्यसे - think, ; न योत्स्ये - "I will not fight," ; इति - as such ; ते - your ; एषः - this ; व्यवसायः - decision ; मिथ्या - is erroneous. ; प्रकृतिः - Your nature ; त्वाम् - (will force) you ; नियोक्ष्यति - to engage (in the war).

Resorting to ego if you think, “I will not fight,” your decision is erroneous. Your nature will force you to engage.

Intent - Without renouncing doership-ego and doership-intellect, resorting to egoism if you think that “I will not fight,” then that resolve of yours is erroneous because, under scriptural injunctions, it is your obligatory duty. In delusion, if you hope to abandon it, according to verse BG 18.7, relinquishment will be Tāmasika. Additionally, it would be against your Kṣatriya nature, forcing you to engage in the war.

स्वभावजेन कौन्तेय निबद्धः स्वेन कर्मणा |
कर्तुं नेच्छसि यन्मोहात्करिष्यस्यवशोऽपि तत् || BG 18.60 ||

कौन्तेय - Hey Kaunteya (Arjuna)! ; अपि - (You will) also ; अवशः - helplessly ; करिष्यसि - do ; तत् - that ; यत् - what ; न - you do not ; इच्छसि - desire ; कर्तुम् - to do ; मोहात् - by delusion ; निबद्धः - bound by ; स्वेन - your own (heroic and other) ; स्वभावजेन - natural ; कर्मणा - activities.

Hey Arjuna! You will also helplessly do what you do not desire to do by delusion bound by your natural activities.

Intent - Your desire not to fight due to delusion (non-discrimination), you will do unavoidably. Your innate nature of heroism will compel you.

ईश्वरः सर्वभूतानां हृद्देशेऽर्जुन तिष्ठति |
भ्रामयन्सर्वभूतानि यन्त्रारूढानि मायया || BG 18.61 ||

अर्जुन - Hey Arjuna! ; ईश्वरः - The Lord ; तिष्ठति - is seated ; हृत्-देशे - in the heart ; सर्व-भूतानाम् - of all beings ; भ्रामयन् - moving around ; सर्व-भूतानि - all beings ; मायया - with Māyā ; यन्त्र-आरूढानि - (as though) mounted on a machine (like puppets).

Hey Arjuna! The Lord is seated in the heart of all beings moving around all beings with Māyā as though mounted on a machine.

Intent - Just as puppets mounted on a machine are not independent, if they resolve not to perform due to ego, then that ego is erroneous. Because when the puppeteer starts moving the strings to which the puppets are tied, they will have to dance helplessly, proving their ego false. In the same manner, Īśvara (ईश्वर, the Lord),[123]sustainer of all, seated in the hearts of all beings and mounted on the machine-like Prakṛti, is moving around all beings with strings of their individual Karma. Through His existent power, all beings are made to dance around by Māyā of the immovable Lord. Now you, Arjuna, mounted on the machine (Prakṛti), have a false ego against Prakṛti that “I will not fight with the body,” that resolve of yours is false. Because when that puppeteer sitting in your heart moves the strings based on your intrinsic nature, you will have to dance to His tune, and your ego of abandonment will stay far away. The body and senses are the transformations of Prakṛti and are mounted on the Prakṛti-like moving disc. When that disc moves, how can those mounted on it stay stationary?

(That is why it is only beneficial that -)

तमेव शरणं गच्छ सर्वभावेन भारत |
तत्प्रसादात्परां शान्तिं स्थानं प्राप्स्यसि शाश्वतम् || BG 18.62 ||

भारत - Hey Bhārata (Arjuna)! ; सर्व-भावेन - With all sentiments, ; गच्छ - surrender ; तम् - unto His ; शरणम् - refuge ; एव - alone. ; तत्-प्रसादात् - By His grace, ; प्राप्स्यसि - you will attain ; पराम् - supreme ; शान्तिम् - peace ; शाश्वतम् - and eternal ; स्थानम् - Status.

---

[123] Superimposition of the adjunct of Māyā on the “conscious” is named “Īśvara”, and by the elimination or Bādha (बाध, the determination of absence) of the adjunct Māyā, it is the witness and pure Brahman.

Hey Arjuna! With all sentiments, surrender unto His refuge alone. By His grace, you will attain supreme peace and eternal Status.

Intent - Do not become a doer of all activities happening through the body, senses, mind, and intellect. Dump all the weight of doership on Him, the one resident inside them, Who is the doer-holder. You just become a performer through the body, senses, mind, and intellect like a puppet based on indications provided by Him. Abandoning your doership-ego, attain oneness with Him and take refuge in Him through your sentiments. Through analytic thinking, removing the superimposition of the body from the Ātmā, situate in the pure witnessing Ātmā. With the attainment of the oneness grace of that Antaryāmi (the Lord residing within), you will attain supreme peace and eternal Status. In this form, your efforts will be successful. Contrary to this, if you hold a false ego of abandoning your prescribed duty, then that being Asat (not true), your efforts will fail.

इति ते ज्ञानमाख्यातं गुह्याद्गुह्यतरं मया |
विमृश्यैतदशेषेण यथेच्छसि तथा कुरु || BG 18.63 ||

इति - This way, ; गुह्यतरं - the most profound ; गुह्यात् - of profound ; ज्ञानम् - knowledge ; आख्यातम् - is articulated ; मया - by Me ; ते - to you. ; विमृश्य - Contemplate ; एतत् - this (knowledge) ; अशेषेण - thoroughly, ; कुरु - (and) do ; तथा - so ; यथा - as ; इच्छसि - you wish.

This way, the most profound of profound knowledge is articulated by Me to you. Contemplate this knowledge thoroughly, and do as you wish.

(Now, Bhagavāna briefly provides the essence of the entire science of Gītā -)

सर्वगुह्यतमं भूयः शृणु मे परमं वचः |
इष्टोऽसि मे दृढमिति ततो वक्ष्यामि ते हितम् || BG 18.64 ||

भूयः - Again, ; शृणु - listen ; मे - to My ; सर्व-गुह्यतमम् - extremely profound ; परमम् - supreme ; वचः - words. ; इति - Because you ; असि - are ; दृढम् - very ; इष्टः - dear ; मे - to Me, ; ततः - so ; वक्ष्यामि - I will say ; हितम् - what is good ; ते - for you.

Again, listen to My extremely profound supreme words. Because you are very dear to Me, I will say what is good for you.

(What are those profound words? -)

मन्मना भव मद्भक्तो मद्याजी मां नमस्कुरु |
मामेवैष्यसि सत्यं ते प्रतिजाने प्रियोऽसि मे || BG 18.65 ||

मत्-मनाः - With (your) mind fixed on Me, ; भव - be ; मत्-भक्तः - My devotee, ; मत्-याजी - My worshipper ; नमस्कुरु - (and) offer obeisance ; माम् - to Me. ; असि - (Doing so,) being ; प्रियः - dear ; मे - to Me, ; सत्यम् - (I) truly ; प्रतिजाने - promise (that) ; ते - you ; एव - indeed ; एष्यसि - will attain ; माम् - Me.

With your mind fixed on Me, be My devotee, My worshipper and offer obeisance to Me. Doing so, being dear to Me, I truly promise that you will attain Me.

Intent - Your mind that has formed its existence separate from the all-witness Me, and establishing a separate house in the three and a half hand island cooking own meals, uproot such mind from there and plant it in Me so that it loses its existence and becomes My form. Thereby, as its fruit, the three and a half hand kingdom is destroyed, and the rule over the entire world is attained. Hey Arjuna! Become My devotee instead of being a devotee of worldly relatives, orient towards Me and through all your efforts worship Me. Through all your efforts, with your eye on Me, you offer obeisance to Me. Doing so, you will attain Me. That is My true promise to you as you are dear to Me.

(Thus, concluding His supreme profound guidance, reminding Arjuna of those attributes that he had displayed as the cause of his grief in Chapter 1, Bhagavāna says -)

सर्वधर्मान्परित्यज्य मामेकं शरणं व्रज |
अहं त्वां सर्वपापेभ्यो मोक्षयिष्यामि मा शुच: || BG 18.66 ||

परित्यज्य - Giving up ; सर्व-धर्मान् - all duties, ; व्रज - seek ; शरणम् - refuge ; माम् - in Me ; एकम् - alone. ; शुचः - Grieve ; मा – not. ; अहम् - I ; मोक्षयिष्यामि - shall free ; त्वाम् - you ; सर्व-पापेभ्यः - from all sins.

Giving up all duties, seek refuge in Me alone. Grieve not. I shall free you from all sins.

Intent - All duties such as family, functional class, region, and those of sacrifices, austerities, and whatever other duties there are, surrendering them all, come to My refuge alone. In the term duty (Dharma), non-duty (Adharma) is implicit. What is sought is freedom from Karma. Just as rivers flowing through varied paths are there to enter the ocean, in the same way, all duties (righteous acts) through their performance directly or through succession are there only for attaining oneness in Me, the Ātmā of all. All these acts remain righteous as long as they are helpful and not obstacles in attaining Me. However, whenever they become obstacles, as their performance is not righteous, it is only one's duty to abandon them. Savory food is only good if it does not upset the stomach and helps nourish the body. However, when it upsets the stomach, not consuming it is helpful in not harming the body. Accordingly, make all of your acts focused on attaining Me. I will free you with the abandonment of detrimental acts where you can incur sin. That is because attaining Me, all acts automatically succeed, just as watering a plant, its branches and twigs become profuse. Abandoning all distinctions of I-you and limited-vision and merging in the pure Brahman-vision (the underlying support of the entire perceptible world) is the attainment of the exclusive refuge of the Lord. That supreme Status is the goal of all acts of righteousness, and reaching there, one attains freedom from all sins and the transmigratory life of birth and death, not by any other means.

(Having concluded the science of Gītā and reiterated it, Bhagavāna explains the traditions of Śāstra -)

इदं ते नातपस्काय नाभक्ताय कदाचन |
न चाशुश्रूषवे वाच्यं न च मां योऽभ्यसूयति || BG 18.67 ||

न - Do not ; वाच्यम् - impart ; इदम् - this (Śāstra) ; ते - (spoken) to you ; कदाचन - at any time ; अतपस्काय - to a non-ascetic (one without control over the senses), ; न - nor ; अभक्ताय - to a non-devotee, ; च - and ; न - nor ; अशुश्रूषवे - to one who does not seek ; च - and ; न - nor ; यः - to one who ; अभ्यसूयति - reviles ; माम् - Me.

Do not impart this to a non-ascetic, a non-devotee, or one who does not seek or reviles Me.

Intent - This Śāstra, imparted to you for your good, should not be heard by those who are non-ascetics, whose mind and senses are unrestrained. Even if one is an ascetic but is not devoted to a deity or a preceptor should not hear it. Further, even if one is an ascetic and a devotee but does not seek to hear, he should not hear it. Moreover, one perceiving Me Vāsudeva as an ordinary human being and accusing Me of boastfulness and assigning Me self-praised faults, such persons who criticize Me should also not hear it. However, those who are ascetics, devotees, seekers, and faultless are the ones who ought to hear it.

(Next, the rewards accruing to those who follow traditions are narrated -)

य इदं परमं गुह्यं मद्भक्तेष्वभिधास्यति |
भक्तिं मयि परां कृत्वा मामेवैष्यत्यसंशय: || BG 18.68 ||

कृत्वा - Carrying out ; मयि - My ; पराम् - utmost ; भक्तिम् - worship, ; यः - one who ; अभिधास्यति - imparts ; इमम् - this ; परमम् - most ; गुह्यम् - profound knowledge ; मत्-भक्तेषु - to My devotees ; असंशयः - undoubtedly ; एष्यति - attains ; माम् - Me ; एव - indeed.

Carrying out My utmost worship, one who imparts this most profound knowledge to My devotees undoubtedly attains Me.

Intent - One who imparts this profound knowledge to the aforementioned eligible devotees, such a person with desireless sentiment contemplating on it with My utmost worship, shall indeed attain Me. In it, there is no doubt. With desireless sentiment, one who will impart this knowledge to eligible devotees will acquire that fruit which is the fruit of My utmost worship.

न च तस्मान्मनुष्येषु कश्चिन्मे प्रियकृत्तमः |
भविता न च मे तस्मादन्यः प्रियतरो भुवि || BG 18.69 ||

च - Moreover, ; मनुष्येषु - among humans, ; न - no ; कश्चित् - one ; तस्मात् - (other) than he ; प्रिय-कृत्तमः - does deeds extremely dear ; मे - to Me. ; च - Additionally, ; अन्यः - other ; तस्मात् - than him, ; भविता - there is ; न - none ; भुवि - on the earth ; प्रियतरः - dearer ; मे - to Me.

Among humans, no one other than he does deeds extremely dear to Me. Other than him, there is none on the earth dearer to Me.

Intent - In the present, there is no one to perform acts extremely dear to Me other than him, and in the future, there will be no one dearer to Me other than him.

(That was said about the ones who impart knowledge.)

(In the following two verses, Bhagavāna talks about seekers and listeners -)

अध्येष्यते च य इमं धर्म्यं संवादमावयोः |
ज्ञानयज्ञेन तेनाहमिष्टः स्यामिति मे मतिः || BG 18.70 ||

च - Moreover, ; यः - whoever ; अध्येष्यते - shall study ; इमम् - this ; धर्म्यम् - righteous ; संवादम् - dialogue ; आवयोः - of ours, ; अहम् - I ; स्याम् - shall be ; इष्टः - worshipped ; ज्ञान-यज्ञेन - by the sacrifice of knowledge ; तेन - through them. ; इति - That ; मे - is My ; मतिः - opinion.

Whoever shall study this righteous dialogue of ours, I shall be worshiped by the sacrifice of knowledge through them. That is My opinion.

Intent - Those who study this dialogue of ours shall have offered Me a sacrifice in the form of knowledge. Among various forms of sacrifices such as rituals, chanting aloud, chanting in a low tone, or chanting mentally, the study of Gītā is exalted as equal to a mental sacrifice. To study Gītā is to sacrifice unto Me most excellently.

श्रद्धावाननसूयश्च शृणुयादपि यो नरः |
सोऽपि मुक्तः शुभाँल्लोकान्प्राप्नुयात्पुण्यकर्मणाम् || BG 18.71 ||

श्रद्धावान् - Endowed with faith ; च - and ; अनसूयः - without envy ; सः - one ; यः - who ; शृणुयात् अपि - listens also (to the Gītā), ; अपि - even ; नरः - (such) a person ; मुक्तः - freed (from sins), ; प्राप्नुयात् - acquires ; शुभान् - auspicious ; लोकान् - abodes ; पुण्य-कर्मणाम् - of pious doers.

Endowed with faith and without envy, one who listens to the Gītā, even such a person freed from sins, acquires auspicious abodes of pious doers.

Intent - Faithful and without envy, whoso at least listens to the Gītā will be liberated from sins and secure the abodes of the performers of rites like Agnihotra. Api (अपि, even) indicates what excellent fruits await him who understands its sense.

(Whether Arjuna grasped the knowledge of Śāstra, Bhagavāna asks -)

कच्चिदेतच्छ्रुतं पार्थ त्वयैकाग्रेण चेतसा |
कच्चिदज्ञानसम्मोहः प्रनष्टस्ते धनञ्जय || BG 18.72 ||

पार्थ - Hey Pārtha (Arjuna), ; धनञ्जय - Hey Dhanañjaya (Arjuna, the conqueror of wealth)! ; कच्चित् त्वया - Have you ; श्रुतम् - heard ; एतत् - this (Gītā Śāstra) ; एकाग्रेण - with a concentrated ; चेतसा - mind? ; कच्चित् - Has ; ते - your ; अज्ञान-सम्मोहः - confusion born of ignorance (that I am a doer) ; प्रनष्टः - been destroyed?

Hey Arjuna, the conqueror of wealth! Have you heard this with a concentrated mind? Has your confusion born of ignorance been destroyed?

Intent - Have you grasped what I have told you with a concentrated mind? Has your non-discernment born of nescience perished? For this, you made an effort to listen to My spiritual guidance.

अर्जुन उवाच |
नष्टो मोहः स्मृतिर्लब्धा त्वत्प्रसादान्मयाच्युत |
स्थितोऽस्मि गतसन्देहः करिष्ये वचनं तव || BG 18.73 ||
अर्जुन उवाच - Arjuna said -

अच्युत - Hey (Śrī Kṛṣṇa,) the infallible one! ; त्वत् - With Your ; प्रसादात् - grace, ; मोहः - (my) confusion ; नष्टः - is dispelled, (and) ; मया - I have ; लब्धा - regained ; स्मृतिः - memory (of the Truth). ; स्थितः - Being ; गत-सन्देहः - free from doubts, ; अस्मि - I ; करिष्ये - shall obey ; तव - Your ; वचनम् - command.

Arjuna said -

Hey Śrī Kṛṣṇa, the infallible one! With Your grace, my confusion is dispelled, and I have regained memory. Being free from doubts, I shall obey Your command.

Intent - With Your grace now, I have regained memory regarding the Truth. The knowledge of the Ātmā, the Self, by which the sentient-insentient knot of the heart has melted. "I am a slayer of these relatives, and they are going to die" such ignorance born confusion based on an intellect that superimposed the body, senses, and others on the pure Ātmā, and which was the cause of the travesties in the form of the Saṃsāra - the world of transmigratory lives, a veritable ocean hard to cross, is now dispelled. "I am bound by some duty, performing or not performing, I will be tainted by piety or sin" doubts regarding duty and its rewards have evaporated. Now, free from duty and without any doubt, I am ready to obey Your command (आज्ञा, Ājñā).

सञ्जय उवाच |
इत्यहं वासुदेवस्य पार्थस्य च महात्मनः |
संवादमिममश्रौषमद्भुतं रोमहर्षणम् || BG 18.74 ||
सञ्जय उवाच - Sañjaya said -

इति - Thus, ; अहम् - I ; अश्रौषम् - heard ; इमम् - this ; अद्भुतम् - amazing ; रोम-हर्षणम् - hair-raising ; संवादम् - dialogue ; वासुदेवस्य - between Śrī Vāsudeva ; च - and ; महात्मनः - the great being ; पार्थस्य - Arjuna.

Sañjaya said -

Thus, I heard this amazing hair-raising dialogue between Śrī Vāsudeva and the great being Arjuna.

व्यासप्रसादाच्छ्रुतवानेतद्गुह्यमहं परम् |
योगं योगेश्वरात्कृष्णात्साक्षात्कथयतः स्वयम् || BG 18.75 ||

व्यास-प्रसादात् - By the grace of Śrī Vyāsa (having acquired divine sight), ; अहम् - I ; श्रुतवान् - heard ; एतत् - this ; परम् - most ; गुह्यम् - profound ; योगम् - Yoga ; साक्षात् - directly ; कथयतः - spoken by ; योगेश्वरात् - Yogeśvara ; कृष्णात् - Śrī Kṛṣṇa ; स्वयम् - Himself.

By the grace of Śrī Vyāsa, I heard this most profound Yoga directly from Yogeśvara Śrī Kṛṣṇa Himself.

Intent - Śrī Vyāsa had granted a divine vision to Sañjaya so he could observe the war and narrate its account to King Dhṛtarāṣṭra. Sañjaya says I heard the most profound knowledge of attaining union with oneness in the Ātmā directly from the divine mouth of Lord Śrī Kṛṣṇa.

राजन्संस्मृत्य संस्मृत्य संवादमिममद्भुतम् |
केशवार्जुनयोः पुण्यं हृष्यामि च मुहुर्मुहुः || BG 18.76 ||

राजन् - Hey Rājan (King Dhṛtarāṣṭra)! ; संस्मृत्य संस्मृत्य - Recalling repeatedly ; इमम् - this ; अद्भुतम् - amazing ; च - and ; पुण्यम् - holy ; संवादम् - dialogue ; केशव-अर्जुनयोः - between Keśava (Śrī Kṛṣṇa) and Arjuna, ; हृष्यामि - I am rejoicing ; मुहुः मुहुः - again and again .

Hey King Dhṛtarāṣṭra! Recalling repeatedly this amazing and holy dialogue between Śrī Kṛṣṇa and Arjuna, I am rejoicing again and again.

तच्च संस्मृत्य संस्मृत्य रूपमत्यद्भुतं हरेः |
विस्मयो मे महानराजन्हृष्यामि च पुनः पुनः || BG 18.77 ||

राजन् - Hey Rājan (King Dhṛtarāṣṭra)! ; च - Also, ; संस्मृत्य संस्मृत्य - repeatedly recalling ; तत् - that ; अति - most ; अद्भुतम् - amazing ; रूपम् - form ; हरेः - of Hari (Lord Śrī Kṛṣṇa), ; मे - I am ; महान् - greatly ; विस्मयः - amazed, ; च - and ; हृष्यामि - I rejoice ; पुनः पुनः - over and over again.

Hey King Dhṛtarāṣṭra! Repeatedly recalling the most amazing form of Lord Śrī Kṛṣṇa, I am greatly amazed, and I rejoice over and over again.

यत्र योगेश्वरः कृष्णो यत्र पार्थो धनुर्धरः |
तत्र श्रीर्विजयो भूतिर्ध्रुवा नीतिर्मतिर्मम || BG 18.78 ||

यत्र - Where ; योगेश्वरः - Yogeśvara ; कृष्णः - Śrī Kṛṣṇa is (seated, and) ; यत्र - where ; धनुर्धरः - the (great) archer ; पार्थः - Arjuna is, ; तत्र - there ; मम - in my ; मतिः - opinion, (resides) ; श्रीः - auspiciousness, ; विजयः - victory, ; भूतिः - prosperity, ; ध्रुवा - (and) immovable ; नीतिः - order.

Where Yogeśvara Śrī Kṛṣṇa is, where the great archer Arjuna is, there, in my opinion, reside auspiciousness, victory, prosperity, and immovable order.

Intent - On the side where the Lord of Yoga (of whom all Yoga are born) Śrī Kṛṣṇa is, and Arjuna, the bearer of the great bow Gāṇḍīva is, definitely dwells auspiciousness, victory, prosperity, and stable order. That is my opinion.

ॐ तत्सदिति श्रीमद्भगवद्गीतासूपनिषत्सु ब्रह्मविध्यायां योगशास्त्रे

श्रीकृष्णार्जुनसम्वादे मोक्षसंन्यासयोगो नाम

अष्टादशोऽध्यायः || BG 18 ||

Oṃ Tat Sat

In the Śrīmad Bhagavad Gītā Upaniṣad

The Yoga Science of the Knowledge of Self-Realization

The Discourse of Lord Śrī Kṛṣṇa and Arjuna

This Eighteenth Chapter

Yoga Named - The Yoga of Liberation and Renunciation

Clarification

This chapter is the epilogue of the entire Gītā Śāstra. Listening to the discussion on renunciation (Saṃnyāsa) and relinquishment (Tyāga) at various locations in previous chapters and knowing renunciation and relinquishment as the core subject, Arjuna asked Bhagavāna the last question - "Hey Śrī Kṛṣṇa! I would like to know the distinction between renunciation and relinquishment separately (BG 18.1). Even though Arjuna asked to know the difference between renunciation and relinquishment individually, the meaning of the word Saṃnyāsa (renunciation) and the word Tyāga (relinquishment) is not separate like a pot and a cloth, but their meaning is identical. That is why, grasping them both in the same sense, Bhagavāna responds first by providing four prevalent opinions connected with renunciation and relinquishment.

1. In the opinion of the first group, relinquishment of actions prompted by desire (काम्य-कर्म, Kāmya-Karma) is Saṃnyāsa (संन्यास, renunciation).
2. In the opinion of the second group, relinquishing fruits of action rather than actions is Saṃnyāsa.
3. In the opinion of the third group, actions by their nature are at fault and so are proper to be relinquished.
4. In the opinion of the fourth group, acts in the form of sacrifice (Yajña), charity (Dāna), and austerity (Tapa) ought not to be relinquished, but relinquishing all acts other than them is Saṃnyāsa (BG 18.2 - BG 18.3).

In providing His opinion on the subject, Bhagavāna showed relinquishment to be of three types and said that sacrifice, charity, and austerity ought not to be relinquished. These acts purify individuals, and as a duty, they ought to be done without attachment and relinquishing the fruits. Contrary to this, relinquishment of desire-ridden acts is not Saṃnyāsa because leaving aside desired-ridden acts; even other acts bind humans. Second, it is impossible to relinquish all actions by their nature, so those acts cannot be Saṃnyāsa either. Third, relinquishment of all fruits of action (Sarva-Karma-Phala-Tyāga) cannot be Saṃnyāsa because without offering those acts to the Lord, even when there is no desire for the fruits of action, yet per BG 3.9, those acts, not being for the sake of the Lord (Bhagavad-Artha), are not in the form of sacrifice offered to the Lord. They are not the cause for real fruits. It is not enough to just relinquish fruits of action, but those acts have to be done as a sacrifice to the Lord. Fourth, sacrifice, charity, and austerity devoid of attachment and giving up fruits of action are not relinquishment either. Because sacrifice, charity, and austerity done with attachment and fruits are the cause of piety, whose fruit is at the most acquisition of the higher worlds. In reality, relinquishment and renunciation are the ones that provide liberation from the bondage of actions directly or by succession. Thus, acts done for the sake of the Lord, traditionally helpful in securing freedom from the bondage of actions, come within the meaning of Saṃnyāsa. In addition, separate from the above four views, Bhagavāna articulated His view and said that one ought not to relinquish obligatory acts (Niyata-Karma) because, with the obligation to perform those duties, their abandonment due to ignorance is Tāmasika. Additionally, holding those acts as a duty but relinquishing them due to fear of distress to the body does not become the cause for any fruit and is Rājasika. Sāttvika relinquishment is where ordained duties are performed with the sentiment that they "ought to be done," giving up attachment and fruits (BG 18.4 - BG 18.6).

Further, Bhagavāna talking about true relinquishment, said that one who has realized the Truth neither hates desire-ridden Karma nor is attached to desireless acts. He is detached from the body, senses, mind, and intellect and is situated in his distinctionless (Nirviśeṣa) Ātmā and his ego that "I am a doer-enjoyer" of the activities of the body, senses, mind, and intellect is uprooted. Having attained the vision of perceiving only one Ātmā in all, rejoicing in the Paramānanda (supreme-bliss), all distinctions and doership senses evaporate. In his view, the distinction between desired and desireless wishes and attachment and aversion do not remain. All his acts become non-acts. He is indeed a true renouncer of everything and is a real non-doer even doing everything. In contrast, for one who has ego in the body, such complete relinquishment of actions is impossible for him. For such persons giving up fruits of action offered to the Lord can be said to be relinquishment (Tyāga). Thereafter, threefold fruits of Karma - bad, good, and mixed are described for those who are not seated in the Ātmā, have not relinquished everything, and whose acts have not become non-action (Akarma).

In the success of any Karma, the following five causes are described:

1. Adhiṣṭhāna (अधिष्ठान, ground) - The body that is the support for the appearance of desire, knowledge, and actions.
2. Kartā (कर्ता, doer) - The delimited Ātmā who is the doer-enjoyer with an I-ness sense in the body. The delimited Ātmā, Jīva, Jīvātmā, and Soul are synonymous.
3. Karaṇa (करण, instrument) - Various kinds of instruments through which actions are performed, such as A) the five cognitive senses: skin, tongue, eyes, nose, and ears, B) the five action faculties: mouth, hands, feet, anus and genitals, C) the mind and D) the intellect.
4. Ceṣṭā (चेष्टा, effort) - The manifold distinct efforts of the vital breaths of air (प्राण, Prāṇa) such as the in-breath, the out-breath through which activities in the senses, mind, and intellect happen.
5. Daiva (दैव, the presiding deity) - Various presiding deities that control the mind, senses, et al. The Adhideva (अधिदेव) of eyes is the sun-deity, Adhideva of ears is the directions. The power of these presiding deities is known as Adhidaiva-Śakti (अधिदैव-शक्ति). The intention is that the senses grasp their objects with the grace of these deities.

Accordingly, whether bodily, verbal, and mental activities are in accordance with or opposed to scriptures, whatever righteous or unrighteous, meritorious or unmeritorious acts are performed, their fruition is only due to the above five causes; without the five, there cannot be a success of any activity. Despite that, due to ignorance, one who does not know them as the doers but holds doership-ego in own Ātmā, such an ill-disposed person does not know anything and only because of this ignorance falls in the bondage of the world of birth and death. However, in contrast, a knower of the Truth who does not have self-conceit does not have a doership I-ness sense in the Ātmā but knows the above five causes as the real doers and own Ātmā as the witness-observer of their activities. Such a person even slaying the entire world does not slay. With the influence of this knowledge, he is not in the bondage of piety and sin and thus birth and death. That is real relinquishment (Tātvika-Tyāga). That is the total renunciation of all actions (Sarva-Karma-Saṃnyāsa). Making this knowledge directly realized (Aparokṣa), one is freely liberated from all bondages of piety and sin, thus birth and death. This knowledge and this renunciation are indeed the real intent of Gītā (BG 18.1-BG 18.17).

The truth of relinquishment and renunciation is thus narrated. Then, knower (Jñātā), knowledge (Jñāna), and to be known (Jñeya), the threefold impellers of actions, and doer (Kartā), acts (Kriyā), and instruments (Karaṇa), the threefold accessories for Karma are narrated, upon whose convergence activities happen. After that, knowledge, action, and doer distinctions are provided (BG 18.18 - BG 18.19). There, from the distinctions of Sattva, Rajas, and Tamas in the verses (BG 18.20 - BG 18.22), three kinds of knowledge in the verses (BG 18.23 - BG 18.25), three kinds of Karma and in the verses (BG 18.26 - BG 18.28) three kinds of doers are narrated. Based on the threefold constituents three types of intellect in the verses (BG 18.29 - BG 18.32) and three types of resolves in the verses (BG 18.33 - BG 18.35) are narrated. Subsequently, the pleasure which is the fruit of all these activities is described in the verses (BG 18.36 - BG 18.40) based on the distinctions of the threefold constituents - Sāttvika, Rājasika, and Tāmasika. It is made amply clear that there is no substance on the earth, heavens, or the deities devoid of the threefold constituents of Prakṛti.

In addition, in the epilogue of Gītā, with the desire to provide the essence of the approach for liberation from the world of transmigrating lives, natural distinctions of activities and duties of the four functional classes viz. Brāhmaṇa, Kṣatriya, Vaiśya, and Śūdra are narrated in the verses (BG 18.41 - BG 18.44). It is shown that relinquishing selfishness and desires related to this world if only from a righteousness perspective individuals perform their functional class activities based on their intrinsic nature, then opulence of the heaven is acquired as a fruit. However, if activities are performed based on functional class responsibilities with a vision of the highest good to attain the Lord, then as its fruit, with the destruction of sins through purity of the conscience, perfection in the form of fitness for the discipline of knowledge is acquired. Upon the success of the fitness for the discipline of knowledge, one attains the supreme Status - the Lord. On this subject, Bhagavāna showed the simplest approach. With desireless sentiment, based on innate attributes by actions, in the form of worship of the Supreme Lord through Whom all activities of the world are happening and one Who is pervading everything, one can purify one's conscience and acquire the grace of the Lord, by which perfection in the form of fitness for the discipline of knowledge is acquired. Here, one ought not to think that the grace of the Lord can be acquired by a Brāhmaṇa only. Not so, the smallest of one's acts, irrespective of the functional class, done in accordance with own nature even if it is defective, is better than performing the best of others. It can indeed become the cause for the grace of the Lord. When a lowest grade state employee discharges his responsibilities, keeping the state's interest in the forefront, he deserves as much credit for his unselfish work as the head of the agency he works for. The state cannot function without the head of the agency. In the same way, the state employee is a limb of the agency, and without him, the agency cannot function. In the same manner, individuals performing their ordained duties, devoid of desires, by their innate attributes, do not incur sin; and can acquire the grace of the Lord. That is why defective as they may be, one ought not to abandon actions and duties that are based on one's own intrinsic nature, as Karma by their nature are with fault just as fire by nature is always with smoke. Indeed, with the influence of desireless sentiments, they can become faultless, and with the purity of the conscience, they can liberate one from their bondage (BG 18.45 - BG 18.48). The perfection in the fitness for the discipline of knowledge is described through actions. Then to achieve actionlessness perfection (Naiṣkarmya-Siddhi), Bhagavāna enumerated a number of accessories to be pursued, such as: being endowed with intellect without deceit and with resolve, controlling the senses, abandoning all sense-objects, getting rid of likes and dislikes, residing in solitary places like forests, riverbanks, caves, eating lightly, winning over the fault of sleep, keeping the body, the mind and speech under control, engaging in meditation and relinquishing egoism, the force of lust and fondness, excessive vanity, lust, anger and accumulation of personal things. It is shown that a person endowed with such attributes through the force of practice attains the status of the Brahman, and situated in all beings in the form of the Ātmā attains My knowledge endowed supreme devotion. With that supreme devotion, he comprehends Me in Truth as to what My extent is and who I am. Then knowing Me in Truth, he immediately enters into Me and attains Tātvika-Yoga, from where he does not leave. Doing everything, by My grace, attains eternal immutable Status (BG 18.49 - BG 18.56). That is why - "Hey Arjuna! Taking support of Buddhi-Yoga, mentally surrendering all actions to Me, having oriented towards Me, always be one with your mind on Me." That is, become detached from all duties and actions of the body and senses. Doing everything through them, remain a non-doer, and in all actions, see Me as the witnessing non-action. You will easily overcome all bodily, verbal, and mental obstacles by doing so. If, due to ego, you do not listen to My words, then you will perish. Buddhi-Yoga or Jñāna-Yoga was heretofore described earlier in Chapter 2. It is that realization of the Truth, "Neither am I doing anything nor there is any duty on me to do anything, but I am the all-witness non-disappearing light, in whose illumination the body, senses, mind, and intellect are engaged in their duties, and yet they do not touch me." It is only through this intellect that there is Tātvika-Yoga (a true union) in the Lord, not by any other way, and it is only with this intellect there is total renunciation of all actions (Sarva-Karma-Saṃnyāsa) (BG 18. 57 - BG 18.58). Without renouncing doership-ego and doership-intellect, resorting to egoism if you think that "I will not fight," then that resolve is erroneous because, under scriptural injunctions, it is your obligatory duty (Niyata-Karma). In delusion, if you hope to abandon it, according to verse BG 18.7, that relinquishment will be Tāmasika. Additionally, it would be against your Kṣatriya nature, forcing you to engage in the war. Īśvara (the Lord), sustainer of all, seated in the hearts of all beings and mounted on the machine-like Prakṛti, is moving around all beings with strings of their individual Karma. Through His existent power, all beings are made to dance around by Māyā of the immovable Lord. You, Arjuna mounted on the machine (Prakṛti), have a false ego against Prakṛti that "I will not fight with the body." Your resolve is false. Because when that puppeteer situated in your heart based on your nature moves the strings, you will have to dance to His tune, and your ego of abandonment will stay far away. Do not become the doer of all activities happening through the body, senses, mind, and intellect. However, the one resident inside them, Who is the doer-holder, dump all the weight of the doership on Him. You just become a performer through the body like a puppet based on indications provided by Him. Abandoning your doership-ego, attain oneness with Him and take refuge in Him through your sentiments. Through analytic thinking, removing the superimposition of the body from the Ātmā, situate in the pure all-witness Ātmā. With the oneness grace of that Lord residing within, you will attain supreme peace and eternal Status. In this form, your efforts will be successful. Contrary to this, if you hold an erroneous ego of abandoning your prescribed duty, then that being Asat (not true), your efforts will fail (BG 18.59 - BG 18.62). In the end, Bhagavāna said to Arjuna - "Contemplate over this knowledge completely, and do as you wish." Then, Bhagavāna concluded his guidance, providing extremely profound supreme words to His dear devotee - "Giving up all duties seek refuge in Me alone. Grieve not, I shall free you from all sins" (BG 18.63 - BG 18.66).

After that, having concluded the science of Gītā and reiterated it, the traditions of Śāstra are explained. Bhagavāna described the fitness of those who are fit to hear this Śāstra and expressed his gratitude towards those who impart this knowledge, and the fruits accruing to those who study and hear are narrated (BG 18.67 - BG 18.71). Then, Bhagavāna asked Arjuna - "Have you heard this with a concentrated mind? Has your confusion, born of ignorance, been destroyed?" In response, Arjuna said - "Hey, Śrī Kṛṣṇa! With Your grace, my confusion is dispelled, and I have regained memory. Being free from doubts, I shall obey Your command." In the end, Sañjaya told King Dhṛtarāṣṭra that - "where there is Lord Śrī Kṛṣṇa, there is auspiciousness (श्री, Śrī) and victory (विजय, Vijay) (BG 18.72 - BG 18.78)."

ॐ श्री परमात्मने नमः

Oṃ! May my obeisance be to the supreme imperishable Reality

Śrīmad Bhagavad Gītā Dhyāna

ॐ पार्थाय प्रतिबोधितां भगवता नारायणेन स्वयं व्यासेन
ग्रथितां पुराणमुनिना मध्ये महाभारतम् ।
अद्वैतामृतवर्षिणीं भगवतीम्- अष्टादशाध्यायिनीम् अम्ब
त्वामनुसन्दधामि भगवद्-गीते भवद्वेषिणीम् ॥ 1॥

Oṃ! Śrīmad Bhagavad Gītā spoken by Lord Nārāyaṇa Himself to Pārtha, enlightening him, composed in the middle of the Mahābhārata by the divine Sage Vyāsa.

O, Divine Mother! The showerer of the ambrosia of Advaita. O, mother of eighteen chapters! I meditate on thee. O, Bhagavad Gītā! Destroyer of the delusion of the manifestation (Saṃsāra).

नमोऽस्तु ते व्यास विशालबुद्धे फुल्लारविन्दायतपत्रनेत्र ।
येन त्वया भारततैलपूर्णः प्रज्वालितो ज्ञानमयः प्रदीपः ॥ 2॥

Salutations unto thee, O, Vyāsa! Of great intellect, with eyes like the petals of a fully blossomed lotus, by whom the lamp of knowledge, filled with the oil of the Mahābhārata, is lit.

प्रपन्नपारिजाताय तोत्रवेत्रैकपाणये ।
ज्ञानमुद्राय कृष्णाय गीतामृतदुहे नमः ॥ 3॥

Salutations O, Lord Kṛṣṇa! Bestower of all desires like the Pārijāta tree, the holder of a cane in one hand to drive His cows, the holder of the symbol of divine knowledge, and the milker of the divine ambrosia of Śrīmad Bhagavad Gītā.

सर्वोपनिषदो गावो दोग्धा गोपाल नन्दनः ।
पार्थो वत्सः सुधीर्भोक्ता दुग्धं गीतामृतं महत् ॥ 4॥

All the Upaniṣads are cows. Śrī Kṛṣṇa is a milker. Arjuna is a calf. Wise and pure men drink the milk, the supreme immortal ambrosia of the Bhagavad Gītā.

वसुदेवसुतं देवं कंसचाणूरमर्दनम् ।
देवकीपरमानन्दं कृष्णं वन्दे जगद्गुरुम् ॥ 5॥

O, son of Vasudeva! O, Lord who destroyed Kaṃsa and Cāṇūra! O, Joy of mother Devakī! Salutations O, Śrī Kṛṣṇa! Teacher of the world!

भीष्मद्रोणतटा जयद्रथजला गान्धारनीलोत्पला शल्यग्राहवती
कृपेण वहनी कर्णेन वेलाकुला ।
अश्वत्थामविकर्णघोरमकरा दुर्योधनावर्तिनी सोत्तीर्णा खलु पाण्डवै
रणनदी कैवर्तकः केशवः ॥ 6॥

Bhīṣma and Droṇa were the two banks, Jayadratha was the water, King of Gāndhāra Śakuni was the blue lotus, Śalya was the crocodile, Kṛpācārya was current, and Karṇa was the mighty wave.

Aśvatthāmā and Vikarṇa were the dangerous alligators, Duryodhana was the whirlpool, and Pāṇḍavas crossed the river of the battle of Mahābhārata with Kṛṣṇa as their helmsman.

पाराशर्यवचः सरोजममलं गीतार्थगन्धोत्कटं नानाख्यानककेसरं
हरिकथा-सम्बोधनाबोधितम् ।
लोके सज्जनषट्पदैरहरहः पेपीयमानं मुदा भूयाद्भारतपङ्कजं
कलिमल-प्रध्वंसिनः श्रेयसे ॥ 7॥

May, the lotus of the Mahābhārata, born in the lake of the words of the son of Parāśara (Vyāsa), sweet with the fragrance of the import of the Bhagavad Gītā, with many stories as its stamens, fully opened by the discourse of Śrī Hari, the destroyer of the sins of Kali-Yuga, and drunk joyously by the bees of good men.

मूकं करोति वाचालं पङ्गुं लङ्घयते गिरिम् ।
यत्कृपा तमहं वन्दे परमानन्दमाधवम् ॥ 8॥

I salute Mādhava! The source of supreme bliss, whose grace makes the dumb eloquent and the cripple cross mountains.

यं ब्रह्मा वरुणेन्द्ररुद्रमरुतः स्तुन्वन्ति दिव्यैः स्तवैः वेदैः
साङ्गपदक्रमोपनिषदैः गायन्ति यं सामगाः ।
ध्यानावस्थिततद्गतेन मनसा पश्यन्ति यं योगिनः यस्यान्तं न विदुः सुरासुरगणाः
देवाय तस्मै नमः ॥ 9॥

Salutation to Him! Whom Brahmā, Varuṇa, Indra, Rudra, and Maruta worship with divine hymns, Who is pleased by Sāma-Veda choruses singing the Vedas and Upaniṣads following the word sequence, Who is beheld by Yogīs absorbed in Him through meditation and whose end is not known even by hosts of Deva and Asura.

Antecedent

The epic Mahābhārata (महाभारत), scribed by Śrī Kṛṣṇadvaipāyana Vedavyāsa (श्री कृष्णद्वैपायन वेदव्यास) over five thousand years ago, is a tale of the Kaurava (कौरव) dynasty, the descendants of the great King Bharata (भरत) ruler of the Empire Bhārata (भारत). It begins with the son of King Pratīpa (प्रतीप), the mighty King Śāntanu (शान्तनु), who begot through Jāhnavī-Gaṅgā (जाह्नवी-गङ्गा) a son named Devavrata (देवव्रत), an extremely bright, truthful, and total devotee of his father. One day King Śāntanu strolling along the banks of river Yamunā (यमुना) sensing a unique fragrance, embarked on to search for it. Following the scent, he came upon beautiful Satyavatī (सत्यवती), the adopted daughter of a local angler named Dhīvara (धीवर). Śāntanu was so smitten with the beauty of Satyavatī that he fell in love with her and desired to marry her. Upon asking for his consent, her father agreed to the marriage on the condition that Satyavatī's son would inherit the throne of Hastināpura (हस्तिनापुर). King Śāntanu was unable to give his word on accession as his eldest son Devavrata was the rightful heir to the throne and returned to his palace dejected. Being exceedingly enamored with Satyavatī, unable to marry her, he remained forlorn and grief-stricken. When Devavrata came to know the cause of his father's dejection, his deep love and devotion towards his father impelled him to find Satyavatī's father. He promised Dhīvara that he would renounce all his claims to the throne of Hastināpura in favor of Satyavatī's children. Upon this, skeptical Dhīvara said, "Though you are an embodiment of veracity and bound by your words, what is the guarantee that one of your descendants does not break this promise?"

Holding his father's happiness paramount, in the presence of assembled Kṣatriyas, Devavrata responded, "I promise lifelong celibacy to ease your fear, and I will fulfill your wish. With this vow, there will be no prospective progeny of mine who could challenge the right to the throne." Upon hearing this vow, Dhīvara gladly agreed to the marriage of Satyavatī and Śāntanu. Devavrata brought Satyavatī to Śāntanu, purging whose grief Devavrata became Kṛtārtha (कृतार्थ). Being ecstatically pleased, King Śāntanu gave a boon to Devavrata of "Svecchā Mṛtyu (स्वेच्छामृत्यु)," complete control over his own death. When Devavrata sacrificed all of his worldly happiness with a deep devotion to his father, then the deities of the heavens showered flowers on him with divine utterance (Ākāśavāṇī, आकाशवाणी) "भीष्मोऽयं, this is Bhīṣma (भीष्म, stern)." Devavrata came to be prominently known as Bhīṣma.

King Śāntanu had two sons through Satyavatī, Citrāngada (चित्रान्गद), and Vicitravīrya (विचित्रवीर्य). After some time, upon the death of King Śāntanu, Citrāngada acquired the throne of Hastināpura. Soon after that, in a battle with a Gandharva (गन्धर्व), he was killed, and Vicitravīrya gained the throne. Vicitravīrya married Aṃbikā (अंबिका) and Aṃbālikā (अंबालिका), the two daughters of the King of Kāśī (काशी). However, after enjoying worldly enjoyments for some seven years, Vicitravīrya died without any progeny. Mother Satyavatī, being distressed with the calamity, came to Bhīṣma and, with his acquiescence, invoked her son

Vedavyāsa, who was born with Ṛṣi Parāśara's (ऋषि पराशर) seed when she was in her adolescence. Way earlier, leaving his mother, Vedavyāsa had told her that all she had to do was recall him whenever she faced any difficulty. Vedavyāsa immediately manifested himself and listened to her anxiety upon her invocation. With Vedavyāsa's grace, Aṃbikā gave birth to Dhṛtarāṣṭra, Aṃbālikā gave birth to Pāṇḍu, and one Dāsī (दासी, a female in servitude) gave birth to the righteous wise statesman Vidūra (विदुर). Beholding the frightful form of Vedavyāsa, Aṃbikā had closed her eyes with fear, and so Dhṛtarāṣṭra (धृतराष्ट्र) was born blind. Aṃbālikā seeing the same shape, had become pale, and so the second son being of pale (पाण्डु, Pāṇḍu) anemic color was recognized as Pāṇḍu. Bhīṣma raised all three children as his sons and made them skillful in righteousness (Dharma), public policy (Nīti), and the science of archery (धनुर्विद्या, Dhanurvidyā). Upon reaching mature ages, being a fit and competent younger brother, Pāṇḍu was declared king of Hastināpura as the older brother Dhṛtarāṣṭra was blind. Vidūra being the son of a Dāsī, did not have the right to be the king. Dhṛtarāṣṭra was married to princess Gāndhārī (गांधारी) of the kingdom of Gāndhāra (गान्धार). Before her marriage, when Gāndhārī heard that she was to wed a blind prince, she immediately put a blindfold over her eyes and vowed not to see anyone all her life. Pāṇḍu married two times, one with Pṛthā (पृथा), also known as Kuntī (कुन्ती), the daughter of King Śūrasena (शूरसेन) of the Yadu (यदु) dynasty, and the second Mādrī (माद्री), the princess of Madradeśa (मद्रदेश). Vidūra married princess Pāraśavī (पारशवी), daughter of King Devaka (देवक).

In adolescence, Kuntī had the good fortune of serving the great seer Durvāsā (दुर्वासा), who, upon being pleased, imparted to Kuntī a Mahāmantra (महामन्त्र). The fruit of the Mantra was that remembering whichever deity with the utterance of the Mantra - the deity would instantaneously appear and grace her with a son. Innocently, to test the Mantra, she uttered it, remembering Sūryadeva (सूर्यदेव), by which a son endowed with Kavaca (कवच) and Kuṇḍala (कुण्डल) was born. Being unmarried and adolescent upon acquiring a son, fearing outrage and backlash from society, she abandoned the newly born adrift in a basket on the Gaṅgā in the hope that someone would find and raise him. The child was rescued and brought up by Adhiratha (अधिरथ), a charioteer (सारथी, Sārathī) of King Dhṛtarāṣṭra. The child later on prominently came to be known as Karṇa (कर्ण). Once when King Pāṇḍu, on his hunting venture in a forest by mistake, wounded a sage son perceiving him like a deer, he incurred the wrath of the sage. As a result of the curse, Pāṇḍu was unable to enjoy a sexual relationship with his queens. Anguished by this pain, Pāṇḍu left for the forest with both of his wives for penance and austerity, leaving the kingdom in the hands of Dhṛtarāṣṭra. In the forest, Kuntī, with the command of Pāṇḍu, utters the Mantra three times, invoking Dharmarāja (धर्मराज), Vāyu (वायु), and Indra (इन्द्र) sequentially, gave birth to Yudhiṣṭhira (युधिष्ठर), Bhīma (भीम), and Arjuna (अर्जुन). Again, Kuntī had Mādrī utter the Mantra two times, invoking twin Aśvanī Kumāras (अश्वनी कुमार) giving birth to Nakula (नकुल) and Sahadeva (सहदेव). Thus, the five Pāṇḍavas were born. Upon the death of Pāṇḍu, Mādrī became Satī (सती) on the same funeral pyre as Pāṇḍu, and Kuntī returned to Hastināpura with the five Pāṇḍavas. When Pāṇḍu was residing in the forest, one day, Vedavyāsa, distressed with hunger and thirst, came to Dhṛtarāṣṭra. At that time, Gāndhārī served the sage with utmost devotion and exceptionally well. Pleased with the dedicated service, Vedavyāsa granted Gāndhārī a boon of one hundred sons, by which Duryodhana (दुर्योधन), Duḥśāsana (दुःशासन), Vikarṇa (विकर्ण), and other ninety-seven sons were born who later on became prominent as Kauravas. In their childhood, both Pāṇḍavas and Kauravas spent time together playfully. Compared to the Kauravas, the Pāṇḍavas were more powerful, particularly Bhīma, who being very naughty, harassed the Kauravas all the time. Sometimes he would dunk them in the river, sometimes drag them in muck, or when they were climbing trees, make them fall on the ground by violently shaking the trees. Seeing and experiencing the strength of the Pāṇḍavas, the Kauravas harbored intense envy against the Pāṇḍavas. Especially Duryodhana was worried and thought that physically it was impossible to defeat the Pāṇḍavas. They should be slain by deceit. With this objective, one day in the gardens, a joint family dinner was planned, and all enjoyed delicious meals. However, in the food of Bhīma, the Halāhala (हलाहल) poison was deceptively spread. Upon eating, Bhīma became unconscious and fell to the ground, unknown to others. After dinner, all left for their abodes. However, Duryodhana remained behind and sought the right opportunity, tied Bhīma, and threw him in the river. In the meantime, not seeing Bhīma return home, mother Kuntī and brothers were distressed. Here, Bhīma, submerged and lying at the bottom of the river, was repeatedly bit by poisonous snakes. "Poison being the medicine of poison," his poison from the body came out. Becoming conscious and happy, he returned home and paid obeisance at the feet of all elders. Mother Kuntī and all brothers who were distressed earlier were glad to see Bhīma safe and sound. Bhīma disclosed the entire event to Yudhiṣṭhira, who advised him to keep it a secret.

Coming out of their childhood to acquire knowledge of sciences and especially archery, the Pāṇḍavas and Kauravas were entrusted first to Kṛpācārya (कृपाचार्य) and then Droṇācārya (द्रोणाचार्य) because of his fame and proficiency in archery and supernatural weapons. Karṇa also became a disciple of Droṇācārya. In addition, Aśvatthāmā (अश्वत्थामा) and princes of other kingdoms far and foreign came to the Gurukula (गुरुकुल) of Droṇācārya to learn. In the field of archery, Arjuna excelled. Bhīma and Duryodhana excelled in swinging Gadā (गदा); Yudhiṣṭhira became a master in using spears and handling war chariots. Nakula and Sahadeva became proficient in swordsmanship. To exhibit the skills of his pupils, upon completion of their education, Droṇācārya invited Bhīṣma and other preceptors to a specially prepared stadium outside Hastināpura. All showed their abilities and skills.

Between Bhīma and Duryodhana, a great Gadā battle ensued and continued for a long time, each showing wholehearted prowess. That is when Droṇācārya put his son Aśvatthāmā in between and stopped the fight. Upon entry of Arjuna on the field, spectators in the stadium became exuberant, hailed him, and upon witnessing his unsurpassed skill and talent, they could not stop praising him with claps and loud cheers. That filled the hearts of Duryodhana and the Kauravas with extreme jealousy. Then, amidst stepped Karṇa and roared, "What is so great? What Arjuna demonstrated, I can also do the same." Then Karṇa demonstrated the same skills Arjuna had displayed earlier, which made Duryodhana very happy. On this, Arjuna and Karṇa's arguments ensued, and a duel between the two was agreed upon. However, preceptor Kṛpācārya said, "One who is himself not a king and whose Jāti (जाति, class) and lineage is unknown, his duel with a prince is forbidden (निषिद्ध, Niṣiddha)." At that very instant, Duryodhana granting the kingdom of Aṅga to Karṇa said, "By just being born in a high family, one does not become fit to be a king." The gesture of Duryodhana so touched Karṇa that he vowed lifelong loyalty to Duryodhana no matter what. As the duel was about to happen, Adhiratha, the foster-father of Karṇa, jumped into the field and stopped the contest as the sun was about to set. After that, as a Guru-Dakṣiṇā, Droṇācārya asked all his pupils to capture Drupada (द्रुपद), the King of Pañcāla (पञ्चाल), who had earlier insulted him. Kauravas could not accomplish the task. Pāṇḍavas won over Drupada, seized him, and brought him to Droṇācārya, who took half of the kingdom and set Drupada free. Feeling extremely powerless, Drupada made a mental resolve to slay Droṇācārya and, to accomplish that initiated a sacrifice (Yajña) to acquire a son who would fulfill his resolution. As a fruit of the sacrifice, a son Dhṛṣṭadyumna (धृष्टद्युम्न) and a daughter Kṛṣṇā (कृष्णा), also known as Draupadī (द्रौपदी), were born.

Recognizing the excellent fitness of Pāṇḍavas in archery, Dhṛtarāṣṭra began to harbor a doubt that it was now impossible for his sons to be crowned king of Hastināpura. Duryodhana and his brothers were also very jealous. That is why, to kill the Pāṇḍavas, with everyone's consent, they built a sizable beautiful palace made from wax (लाक्षागृह, Lākṣāgṛha) in the town of Vāraṇāvata (वारणावत). Dhṛtarāṣṭra convinced the Pāṇḍavas to live there peacefully with their mother, Kuntī. Yudhiṣṭhira honoring the command of the elder Dhṛtarāṣṭra, accepting his duty, agreed to move into the new palace, despite having a clue that there was something wrong. Even Vidūra had expressed his concern and told the Pāṇḍavas to be cautious. Immediately after moving into the palace, the Pāṇḍavas secretly got a tunnel built with an exit far in the forest, and when the palace was set ablaze, they safely escaped to the forest. However, a woman of the Kevaṭa (केवट) class with her five sons sleeping in the palace unfortunately perished. The next day, finding six corpses, people surmised that the five Pāṇḍavas with their mother had burnt to death, and Dhṛtarāṣṭra performed their final rites. In the meantime, the Pāṇḍavas moved deep into the forest, changing their attire to remain incognito.

Distressed with pain in the woods, at the command of Vedavyāsa, they moved to the town of Cakrānagarī (चक्रानगरी) and resided in the home of a Brāhmaṇa (ब्राह्मण). In the guise of being Brāhmaṇa, they lived on alms (भिक्षा, Bhikṣā). One day on their way to collect Bhikṣā, they heard about an arrangement of a Svayaṃvara (स्वयंवर) of princess Draupadī by King Drupada. On the news, they all went as Brāhmaṇa to the event.

In the Svayaṃvara, aspirants had to hit a fish's eye with an arrow using the reflection of a fish placed on a rotating wheel over a pan filled with liquid. None of the eligible suitors were able to hit the mark. Arjuna seeing what was happening, impulsively without realizing he was in the guise of a Brāhmaṇa, with his Kṣatriya nature, got up and hit the eye of the fish, looking down at the reflection of the fish. Immediately Draupadī got up and placed a garland around Arjuna's neck, expressing her acceptance. In the evening, the Pāṇḍavas came home with Draupadī and, before entering the house, said, "Mother, today in Bhikṣā, we got a wonderful thing." Without looking, as she would usually say from inside the house said, "Whatever you got, five of you enjoy together." Accepting such command, the duty-bound five Pāṇḍavas married Draupadī. After that, they all lived near Kind Drupada.

Here, Duryodhana, hearing about the marriage of the Pāṇḍavas with Draupadī, was grief-stricken. Now, how can the Pāṇḍavas be destroyed? On this, Karṇa agreed with Duryodhana to attack the kingdom of Pañcāla unannounced. However, not receiving acquiescence from Pitāmaha Bhīṣma, Droṇācārya, and statesman Vidūra, Dhṛtarāṣṭra disallowed such aggression. After that, on behalf of the Kauravas, Vidūra went to King Drupada and brought the Pāṇḍavas back to Hastināpura. To foster harmony and reduce the fire of envy that was burning in the hearts of the Kauravas, Dhṛtarāṣṭra split the kingdom between the Pāṇḍavas and Kauravas. The capital of the Pāṇḍava kingdom was Indraprastha (इन्द्रप्रस्थ), and that of the Kauravas remained Hastināpura.

After the wedding with Draupadī, the brothers decided that when one brother was with Draupadī, none of the remaining four should be in that location. Moreover, a specific time was provided for each Pāṇḍava to be with Draupadī, and all agreed to a twelve-year punishment of exile in a forest should there be a violation of the agreement. Draupadī bore five sons, one from each Pāṇḍava. Upon expiration of his time, when one day Arjuna left the residence of Draupadī and Yudhiṣṭhira entered the residence, at that time Arjuna heard screams of a Brāhmaṇa whose cows were stolen. Bound by his Kṣatriya duty, Arjuna immediately went to fetch his bow and arrow that he had forgotten in the residence of Draupadī and retrieved the cows from the thieves. Arjuna spent twelve years in the forest away from the family as a penalty for violating the agreed-upon rules. He visited various holy places to behold and pay obeisance. During his pilgrimage, he married Śrī Kṛṣṇa's sister Subhadrā (सुभद्रा), through whom he begot a son named Abhimanyu (अभिमन्यु).

At one time, when Śrī Kṛṣṇa and Arjuna were sitting on the banks of river Yamunā, Agni (fire-deity) manifested in human form and expressed the desire to burn the Khāṇḍava (खाण्डव) forest and thus oblate all insects, animals, Dānavas (दानव), Rākṣasas (राक्षस) and other entities. He devotionally requested that they guard the forest with weapons so no one could escape. Additionally, he asked for help to stop Indra, who protected the forest with his rain. At that time, Arjuna did not possess weapons such as bows and arrows, nor did he have any chariot to assist Agnideva (अग्निदेव, fire-deity). So, Agni, through Varuṇadeva (वरुणदेव, water-deity), gifted Arjuna the great bow Gāṇḍīva (गाण्डीव), a quiver with the power to constantly remain full of arrows and an excellent monkey bannered (कपि-ध्वज, Kapi-Dhvaja) chariot yoked by best horses. Arjuna then assisted Agni in burning the Khāṇḍava forest. In that fierce fire, except for Mayadānava (मयदानव) and the four sons of sage Mandapāla (मन्दपाल), all insects, animals, Dānava, and Rākṣasa perished. On the command of Śrī Kṛṣṇa, Mayadānava built a unique magical Assembly Hall for Yudhiṣṭhira, who, upon the Upadeśa of divine sage Nārada, resolved to perform Rājasūya (राजसूय) Yajña. Śrī Kṛṣṇa was entirely in agreement with the Yajña. With the assistance of Śrī Kṛṣṇa, killing Jarāsandha (जरासन्ध), the King of Magadha (मगध), all Kings in captivity were freed, all of whom accepted subordination under and sovereignty of Yudhiṣṭhira. Marching in all four directions, the four brothers became victorious. That is when the Rājasūya Yajña commenced, in which Vedavyāsa himself took the form of Brahmā. Kings and Brāhmaṇa from all over assembled; even the Kauravas came. King Yudhiṣṭhira assigned duties to his brothers, Kauravas, and others, and Śrī Kṛṣṇa took on the service of washing the feet of the invitees. In the Yajña, the first worship (Pūjā) was done of Śrī Kṛṣṇa. On this, Śiśupāla (शिशुपाल) got very angry and determined to ruin the Yajña. However, Śrī Kṛṣṇa slew Śiśupāla and the Yajña was completed. All guests departed, except for Duryodhana and his maternal uncle Śakuni (शकुनि) remained to see the Assembly Hall.

While he was beholding the magical Assembly Hall, sensing the floor of quartz as the water, he started to stroll, lifting his clothes. Where he thought the floor was of quartz, he got wet in the water. Where sensing open doors of quartz, he banged his head on the wall. Seeing the plight of Duryodhana, Pāṇḍavas, and especially Draupadī could not hold laughing. With this disrespect and seeing the luxury of the Pāṇḍavas, the heart of Duryodhana was set ablaze with envy. Smitten by jealousy, he told his uncle Śakuni that he would commit suicide if he did not get all that wealth and luxury. Śakuni told Duryodhana that the Pāṇḍavas could not be defeated on the battlefield or by virtuous means. The only way to defeat them was to exploit the weakness of Yudhiṣṭhira, his fondness for gambling. Being an expert cheat in the dice game, Śakuni prodded Duryodhana to invite Yudhiṣṭhira to Hastināpura. Reaching Hastināpura with the approval from Dhṛtarāṣṭra, he invited Yudhiṣṭhira to Hastināpura. To tempt and defeat Yudhiṣṭhira, Śakuni provoked Yudhiṣṭhira for the game of dice, but Yudhiṣṭhira showed reluctance to gamble. Upon mocking by Śakuni, finally, Yudhishthira accepted the provocation and, in the process, bet his kingdom, his brothers, himself, and eventually his wife in the 20th round of the game of dice. Śakuni won everything. Draupadī, who was in her period and only a single Śāṭikā (शाटिका, commonly known as Sari), was dragged by Duḥśāsana on the floor by her hair, screaming, "Dāsī, Dāsī." She was brought to the Assembly Hall, and Duḥśāsana started to disrobe her to make her nude. However, as she was stripped, she prayed, seeking refuge from Lord Śrī Kṛṣṇa, who came to her support by adding material as Duḥśāsana was removing. Duḥśāsana continued to pull the Śāṭikā; however, there was no end to her Śāṭikā. Finally, he was tired and dropped to the floor. After that, Duryodhana exposed his thighs and commanded Draupadī to sit on them. Draupadī's extreme humiliation and abject treatment would have made any person tremble with pity. Even while such shame was happening, Yudhiṣṭhira, the Dharmavīra (धर्मवीर), sat with a bowed head. Only Bhīma made a firm vow in front of all assembled, "In battle, if I do not slash Duḥśāsana's chest and drink his blood, and if I do not smash this Duryodhana's thighs to pieces, then I take an oath not to attain the same great end as my ancestors." In the end, Dhṛtarāṣṭra became fearful, and to please Draupadī, he told her that he would grant any wish she had. Draupadī said, "Free my husbands from servitude (दासत्व, Dāsatva)." Dhṛtarāṣṭra granted her wish. Upon being free, Bhīma told Yudhiṣṭhira, "If you give me permission, I want to kill all these enemies at this very instant." However, calming Bhīma, Yudhiṣṭhira, with palms folded, prayed before Dhṛtarāṣṭra, "You are our revered elder. We will do as you command." On this, Dhṛtarāṣṭra returned everything that the Pāṇḍavas had lost in the dice game.

Kauravas started to worry that letting the Pāṇḍavas free was like feeding snakes milk. Once again, they invited Pāṇḍavas to gamble. Pitāmaha Bhīṣma, Droṇācārya, and Vidūra expressed their displeasure and advised not to sow seeds that would destroy the family lineage. However, blinded by his love for his sons, Dhṛtarāṣṭra did not heed their words. Again, the game of dice commenced. This time the condition was that whoever lost the game would have to stay in exile for twelve years, and in the thirteenth year, they would have to be incognito. Should they be recognized, they would have to spend another twelve years in the forest. Again, the Pāṇḍavas lost, removing their royal garments and putting on bark and deerskin, leaving for the woods with Draupadī and Dhaumya Purohita. In front walked Yudhiṣṭhira with his face covered and bowed. Behind him walked Arjuna, spraying sand in the wind. Nakula had his body covered in wet mud, and Sahadeva had covered his head with ashes. With her hair untied, hiding her face, Draupadī was sobbing, and Dhaumya Purohita was uttering fit for the last rites Sāma-Veda Mantra. Vidūra told the intention of all these to Dhṛtarāṣṭra as "With the power of the influence of piety of Dharmarāja Yudhiṣṭhira, this entire sinful kingdom will perish." Listening to such profound words, Dhṛtarāṣṭra, with face covered, sat with head drooped. "Those who have committed abject insult of Draupadī, when will these arms get the opportunity to settle the score?" with such a sentiment, Bhīma was walking behind, looking at his arms. "With innumerable arrows like the many particles of sand, I will riddle the bodies of enemies," strewing sand indicated Arjuna's resolve. "On the road, beholding my handsome body, no woman may be enamored," Nakula had covered his body with wet mud. To hide, Sahadeva had applied ashes on his face. "Just as my hair is untied and spread, and I am crying, in the same way, women of the Kauravas will cry," so was the sentiment expressed by Draupadī's conduct. "With the slaying of the Kauravas, in the funeral rites, such hymns will be intoned," so was the behavior of Dhaumya Purohita expressed. Listening to such words of Vidūra, Dhṛtarāṣṭra began to take heavy long breaths.

With many Brāhmaṇa accompanying the Pāṇḍavas, Yudhiṣṭhira was concerned about providing food. With the guidance of Dhaumya Purohita, Yudhiṣṭhira began to worship Sūryadeva. Pleased with the worship, Sūryadeva graced Yudhiṣṭhira with an inexhaustible food vessel (अक्षयपात्र, Akṣayapātra); until Draupadī finished her meals the utensil would continue to provide food unending. Even in the forest, the evil Kauravas did not let the Pāṇḍavas live peacefully. Once, to show off their luxury, when the Kauravas went to the woods under the pretense of hunting, there was a battle with Citrasena (चित्रसेन) Gandharva, who defeated the Kauravas and captured them with their wives. At that time, the Pāṇḍavas, with their might, freed the Kauravas, by which Duryodhana was extremely shamed. After that, Duryodhana, pleasing Ṛṣi Durvāsā, prodded him to go to the forest with the intent of dishonoring the Pāṇḍavas. However, with the grace of Śrī Kṛṣṇa, Ṛṣi Durvāsā ran away fearful. Again, at one time, when the Pāṇḍavas were not in their Āśrama, Jayadratha (जयद्रथ, son-in-law of Duryodhana) attempted to molest Draupadī. However, just as the attempt was made, the Pāṇḍavas returned, defeated, and captured Jayadratha. Only upon Yudhiṣṭhira's request did the Pāṇḍavas not slay Jayadratha and allow him to live.

Enduring many obstacles, twelve years of forest life passed, and the year of incognito living commenced. Changing their attire, including Draupadī, they separately approached King Virāṭa (विराट), seeking employment. Yudhiṣṭhira was appointed minister in the court and prominently came to be known as Brāhmaṇa Kaṅka (कङ्क). Bhīma, displaying his cooking and wrestling skills, was appointed head chef. Draupadī showing her talent in Śṛṅgāra (शृङ्गार, adornments), was appointed to serve queen Sudeśanā (सुदेशना) and came to be known as Sairandhrī (सैरन्ध्री). In female attire, pretending to be a eunuch, Arjuna was appointed to teach dance and music and became known as Bṛhannalā (बृहन्नला). Nakula was appointed head of the horse stable by presenting himself as an expert in training horses and became known as Granthika (ग्रन्थिक). Sahadeva was appointed head of the cattle ranch by displaying his skill in tending cows and became known as Tantripāla (तन्त्रिपाल). This way, engrossed in service, they all displayed their skill. Here, because of his evil intention to molest Sairandhrī (Draupadī), Kīcaka (कीचक), brother of Sudeśanā, was slain by Bhīma. When the incognito year was just about to end, the Kaurava army attacked the capital of Virāṭa from one flank, and on the other flank, Suśarmā (सुशर्मा), the King of Matsya (मत्स्य) kingdom, attacked.

First, after an intense battle, Suśarmā captured King Virāṭa, at which point Bhīma entered the war and defeating Suśarmā freed King Virāṭa. On the other flank, Arjuna went sent as the Sārathī of Virāṭa's son, where Arjuna defeated Droṇācārya, Aśvatthāmā, and Pitāmaha Bhīṣma and made them retreat. On the third day of the battle, with the completion of the incognito period, the Pāṇḍavas disclosed their real identities to King Virāṭa. Hearing so, King Virāṭa was utterly astonished. He married his daughter Uttarā (उत्तरा) to Abhimanyu, son of Arjuna. After the wedding, Pāṇḍavas conferred with Śrī Kṛṣṇa, Drupada, and Kāśīrāja (काशीराज), who had come to the wedding to regain their kingdom. All agreed, "Ridden with their evil and deceptive nature from childhood, it is not likely that the Kauravas would easily hand over Indraprastha. Therefore, an emissary will be sent, and then only war will be considered." With this decision, an emissary was sent to Kauravas. Additionally, emissaries were sent to several kings seeking assistance should there be a war.

When Duryodhana heard about this, he also sent emissaries to seek assistance from other kings. Both Arjuna and Duryodhana personally went to Dvārakā (द्वारका) to seek help from Śrī Kṛṣṇa. Both went concomitantly.

At that time, Śrī Kṛṣṇa was in bed resting. Duryodhana, due to his ego, sat near the head, and Arjuna, with humility and servitude, sat by the lotus feet of Śrī Kṛṣṇa. Upon awaking, Śrī Kṛṣṇa saw Arjuna and, when he lifted his head, saw Duryodhana. After exchanging well wishes, upon query on their visit, both requested assistance from Śrī Kṛṣṇa. Śrī Kṛṣṇa said, "We will assist both sides. On one side will be My Nārāyaṇī-Senā (नारायणी-सेना), and on the other side, I will be alone; however, I will not lift any weapon. Since I saw Arjuna first and is also younger, he will have the first choice to name either of the options." On this, Arjuna happily accepted the unarmed Śrī Kṛṣṇa, and Duryodhana, extremely pleased that Arjuna had not chosen the supreme Nārāyaṇī Senā, returned home smiling. At Arjuna's request, Śrī Kṛṣṇa accepted to be his Sārathī. Kaurava side assembled eleven Akṣauhiṇī[124] (अक्षौहिणी) armies, whereas the Pāṇḍava side assembled seven Akṣauhiṇī troops.

While both sides were preparing for war, on behalf of the Pāṇḍavas, the Purohita of King Drupada went to Hastināpura and, appearing before Dhṛtarāṣṭra, Bhīṣma, and Vidūra, seeking a peaceful settlement, said, "You are all familiar with your royal duties. At this critical juncture, it is imperative to recall those responsibilities. There is a grave fear of bloody rivers flowing should they be broken. Being the progeny of the same father, both Kauravas and Pāṇḍavas have equal rights over the kingdom passed on by succession. How can Kauravas kick Pāṇḍavas out and exclusively rule over the kingdom? From childhood, all the misdeeds Kauravas have inflicted on the Pāṇḍavas by deceit through gambling, snatching their kingdom, abjectly insulting Draupadī, and binding them in duty the obstacles and hardship they have endured during exile in the forest, they are all in front you. Despite all the atrocities, the Pāṇḍavas are willing to forget the past and desirous to settle. Kindly return Indraprastha from Duryodhana to the Pāṇḍavas. There is still time to settle."

Listening to the statesmanlike proposition of the Brāhmaṇa, Bhīṣma praised him, and Dhṛtarāṣṭra agreeing with the praise of the Brāhmaṇa, sent Sañjaya to the Pāṇḍavas to about-face from the war. Upon listening to Sañjaya, Yudhiṣṭhira said, "We have never expressed any view that would indicate that we are bent on war. We are ready to forget all those atrocities, the deceit in the dice game, the abject insult of Draupadī, and the endurance of obstacles and hardships during exile in the forest. All we want is our kingdom back." Yudhiṣṭhira sent a message to Duryodhana that abandon unrighteousness and greed, hand over Indraprastha to us, or be ready for war. With it, a respectful message was sent to Pitāmaha Bhīṣma, "Lord! Just as you had once saved the Kuru Dynasty from ruination in the past, in the same way, protect us all from the fire of the war." Likewise, Yudhiṣṭhira also sent separate messages through Sañjaya to Dhṛtarāṣṭra and Vidūra and, in the end, after lots of thought, told Sañjaya, "What you are telling is correct. Humans cannot forsake attachment to wealth and power. On this matter, higher responsibility is on us. Listen to our last words. We are willing to forget everything. We five brothers will be content with only five towns and are prepared to forsake the rest of the kingdom."

Returning to Hastināpura, Sañjaya conveyed the message from the Pāṇḍavas to Pitāmaha Bhīṣma and the rest. Both Bhīṣma and Droṇācārya tried to convince the Kauravas that the Pāṇḍavas were on the side of righteousness and they should accept their proposal and settle. Even Dhṛtarāṣṭra, in the presence of the elders and the preceptors, said, "Son! Just as the Pāṇḍavas have amassed means for the war, it would be stupidity to fight them. With war, I do not see any good for Kauravas. Honor the words of Pitāmaha Bhīṣma and Droṇācārya and accept the moral proposition of the Pāṇḍavas and avoid the terrible bloody war." However, Duryodhana could not stand such advice and angrily said, "Father! Why are you grieving unnecessarily? In what way are we powerless? The direct evidence of our power is that the Pāṇḍavas have now dropped their demand to only five towns." Even Karṇa acquiesced with Duryodhana and said, "I am

---

[124] Akṣauhiṇī (अक्षौहिणी) is a battle formation consisting of 21,870 chariots; 21,870 elephants; 65,610 horses and 109,350 infantry. Thus, Akṣauhiṇī consists of 218,700 warriors (not including the charioteers). The ratio is 1 chariot : 1 elephant : 3 cavalry : 5 infantry soldiers.

powerful. I will take responsibility to slay the Pāṇḍavas." Bhīṣma could not stand the self-praise from the mouth of Karṇa and, in extreme anger, said, "Time has snatched your intellect; that is why you are saying so. You do not have even sixteenth of the power of the Pāṇḍavas. When Arjuna badly defeated your side in the war with Virāṭa, where were you sleeping? When Arjuna made all Kauravas unconscious and took off their clothes, were you not there? When the Gandharva made a spectacle of the Kauravas and their spouses, why did the Pāṇḍavas have to come and save all in your presence? Aren't you ashamed talking about your pride? Relying on the assistance from an unrighteous human like you, Kauravas will be devoured by time." Karṇa became agitated with anger and left for his residence murmuring. After Karṇa left, everyone tried to convince Duryodhana, but he did not listen to anyone.

Hearing the news, Yudhiṣṭhira consulted with Śrī Kṛṣṇa and said, "Lord! You have seen how we have endured all the atrocities inflicted on us by the Kauravas, yet we have let them go with equanimity. Losing our righteous authority over our kingdom, how long do I have to see my brothers endure pain? You are a well-wisher of both sides. The matter is serious. I am desirous to hear Your advice." In response, Śrī Kṛṣṇa said, "Before commencement of the war, I will personally go to Hastināpura and attempt to make one last effort in the interest of both sides." Saying so, with Sātyaki (सात्यकि), he came to Hastināpura, and in front of all assembled, he told Dhṛtarāṣṭra, "Hey, Chief of the descendants of the great King Bharata! In My view, by forging a treaty between the Pāṇḍavas and Kauravas, you ought to stop the flow of the river of blood of the brave. I am here with one last effort to avoid war with prayer. You are the head of the Kuru lineage. It is indeed distressful that your sons display unrighteous conduct despite your presence. Only because of them will grave calamity befall the Kuru family. If you do not cool this fire, there is a danger of destroying the entire Kuru family from the root. Establishing peace is in your and our hands. You control the Kauravas, and I will calm the Pāṇḍavas. Hey King Dhṛtarāṣṭra! One more time, whatever atrocities the Kauravas have inflicted on the Pāṇḍavas, ponder over them with a calm mind. It is your highest duty that for righteousness (Dharma) and truth (Satya) and nothing but for your interest, give half of the kingdom to the Pāṇḍavas and establish peace. Rest, do what you believe is right." Listening to the righteous words of Śrī Kṛṣṇa, all mentally praised Him, but no one dared to openly express their sentiments. At the same time, many sages who were present also tried to explain the path of righteousness with all kinds of divine narrations. However, there was no impact on Duryodhana. Instead, with anger, he said, "Whatever intellect Parameśvara has given us, we will act accordingly. Whatever future is destined for us, we will acquire it. Why are you all worried? Do not trouble yourself unnecessarily." Listening to the defiant words of his son, Dhṛtarāṣṭra said to Śrī Kṛṣṇa, "Hey Keśava! Your words are proper, happiness-yielding, and righteous. There is no doubt about it. By whatever means, kindly make him calm and understand the gravity of the situation. I would be greatly indebted to You. I am not independent. He does not listen to me."

Upon the plea of Dhṛtarāṣṭra, Śrī Kṛṣṇa said to Duryodhana, "Brother! With this conduct of yours, grave calamity is about to happen. Resolving it, do good to your brothers, family, and friends. All your elders and preceptors agree to establish a treaty with the Pāṇḍavas. You ought to heed their advice. You hope to defeat the Pāṇḍavas, relying on them who cannot match the power of the Pāṇḍavas. If you think that you can defeat Arjuna, I suggest you pick the most powerful person of your choice from your side to fight with Arjuna. Whatever is the duel's outcome, victory or defeat will depend on it. What is the benefit of the loss of innumerable lives? If you cannot take this risk, give the Pāṇḍavas their kingdom and free yourself and your friends from fear." Bhīṣma, consenting with the words of Śrī Kṛṣṇa, also tried to make Duryodhana understand, but to no avail. Then Vidūra said, "Duryodhana! We do not grieve for you. We are distressed for your elderly parents, who, with your evil conduct and the prospect of the destruction of the Kaurava family, will become lonely orphans like birds with torn wings. We are distressed over such thoughts." Again, Dhṛtarāṣṭra tried to make Duryodhana understand, "Son! The words of Śrī Kṛṣṇa are, from all perspectives, good for everyone. There will be no reduction in the luxury you enjoy by accepting and giving away half the kingdom. With the grace and help of the Lord, you will be able to expand your kingdom far beyond. Disrespecting the Lord's advice, your defeat is inevitable." In the end, Droṇācārya said, "Duryodhana! Arjuna has not put on his battle outfit, nor has he twanged his Gāṇḍīva. There is still time to correct your error. It would be nice if you gave the Pāṇḍavas their Indraprastha. They will embrace you, and all the assembled kings seeing you are getting together, will depart to their kingdoms with tears of happiness."

Duryodhana did not respond to anyone. Turning towards Śrī Kṛṣṇa, he said harshly, "Vāsudeva! You should have talked to us thoughtfully. What bravery have You seen of the Pāṇḍavas that You have become their devotee? You and Pitāmaha Bhīṣma are all bent on criticizing us. We do not see what our fault is? With the gambling addiction, the Pāṇḍavas lost their kingdom, which we returned. However, those addicts even betted exile to the forest and lost. What is our fault there? Knowing us as enemies, they have started to assemble armies to scare us. Do you think we are scared of them? In front of the enemies, instead of bowing our heads, we prefer to lay on the bed of arrows on the battlefield. In our youth, our father had given them half of the kingdom. However, now we will not give any land, not even the size of a needlepoint, even if everything perishes." When Śrī Kṛṣṇa saw that Duryodhana would not listen to anyone, He sternly said, "Duryodhana! The thought you have of brave hearts laying on the bed of arrows will happen in due time. What family infamy! You gave poison to Bhīma, attempted to burn the Pāṇḍavas in the Lākṣāgṛha, you ghastly insulted Draupadī in the full assembly, and with deceit in gambling, you snatched their kingdom. Now, after fulfilling their promise when they have a right to get back their kingdom, you are telling them that you won't give even a needlepoint land. You have insulted the elders and preceptors, yet you claim innocence. On the battlefield, when you are wounded and in agony, then you will regret what you have said."

When Śrī Kṛṣṇa spoke those words, Duryodhana did not say a word; he got up and left. Then Śrī Kṛṣṇa told Bhīṣma, Droṇācārya, and others assembled, "Hey, great beings! Elderly Kauravas, not controlling this Duryodhana right from childhood, have fed milk to the snake. Now listen to what I have to say. The destruction of the family can be saved by only one approach. When My evil uncle Kaṃsa (कंस) tortured his father and committed innumerable atrocities against his subjects, all his relatives left him. He was slain by Me, restoring peace, and now we all Yādavas (यादव) are living in happiness. If you all abandon this evil Duryodhana, the Kaurava family will be saved." Upon such words of Bhagavāna, Dhṛtarāṣṭra became fearful and summoned Gāndhārī to the Assembly Hall and requested her to make Duryodhana understand. Gāndhārī said, "Lord! The cause of all this is your weakness. You have known his sinful conduct, yet you have condoned and permitted such behavior. Now it is beyond your and my power." She called Duryodhana to the Assembly and said, "Son! Engulfed with lust and anger, you have lost your mind and are not listening to the beneficial words of the elders and preceptors. How can you hope to win the kingdom when you cannot win over your unrighteous intellect? Whatever atrocities you have committed against the Pāṇḍavas, it would be proper for you to atone by returning Pāṇḍavas to their rightful kingdom. They are righteous souls and have a right over their kingdom, so settling the dispute protects all. In our old age, do not inflict pain and suffering." Even on this, the evil soul did not answer. He got up and left to plan with Śakuni, Karṇa, and Duḥśāsana how to capture and imprison Śrī Kṛṣṇa. Sātyaki came to know this plan and went to the Assembly and told Śrī Kṛṣṇa in his ears. Śrī Kṛṣṇa said to Dhṛtarāṣṭra, "Are you listening? Duryodhana wants to imprison Me. Well, whatever happens, do not fear. I am here as an emissary, and abandoning My emissary duties, I will not punish him." Again, Duryodhana was called to the Assembly, and Vidūra said," By inappropriate conduct with Śrī Kṛṣṇa, do not invite your death." At which, Bhagavāna started to laugh loudly, and the entire Assembly lighted up with divine brightness. All were in awe, beholding such a fantastic scene. Śrī Kṛṣṇa left the Assembly and mounted His chariot. Dhṛtarāṣṭra walked out and expressed his inability, at which time Bhagavāna addressed all and said, "I came here to forge a treaty. Here, Dhṛtarāṣṭra is not independent, and Duryodhana does not want to settle. There is no other path except war." Saying so, He asked Karṇa to go with Him out of Hastināpura, where He tried to convince Karṇa to join the side of the Pāṇḍavas. However, Karṇa refused, "Doing so would be ingratitude." Knowing that he was indeed the son of Kuntī and brother of the Pāṇḍavas, he did atone for all the atrocities committed against his brothers. When he did not move from his determination, then Bhagavāna told him to let all know that the month was appropriate for the war, and from that day on the seventh day, the battle will commence.

Not being successful in the last-ditch effort to establish peace, Bhagavāna Śrī Kṛṣṇa came back to Upaplavya (उपप्लव्य) city and narrating what happened advised the Pāṇḍavas to be ready for the war. King Drupada, Virāṭa, Dhṛṣṭadyumna, Śikhaṇḍī (शिखण्डी), Sātyaki, Cekitāna (चेकितान), and Bhīma, the seven great warriors (Mahārathī), were appointed as Commanders (सेनापति, Senāpati) of the seven Akṣauhiṇī armies. There, the eleven Akṣauhiṇī army of the Kauravas was put in command of Kṛpācārya, Droṇācārya, Śalya (शल्य), Jayadratha, Sudakṣiṇa (सुदक्षिण), Kṛtavarmā (कृतवर्मा), Aśvatthāmā, Karṇa, Bhūriśravā (भूरिश्रवा), Śakuni and Vālhika (वाल्हिक). Pitāmaha Bhīṣma was appointed as the Chief Commander. The veracious truth-loving Pitāmaha Bhīṣma, even though he desired a Pāṇḍava victory, yet being bound by his vow to the throne of Hastināpura, considered proper to die on the side of the Kauravas. His being the Chief Commander of the Kaurava army, Bhīṣma had placed a condition not to slay the Pāṇḍavas with his own hands and told Duryodhana that only to please him, he will not retreat slaying hundreds of warriors. Similarly, having eaten the salt of the Kauravas, Droṇācārya and Kṛpācārya also did not separate themselves from them.

This way, being ready, armies of Pāṇḍavas and Kauravas assembled on the bloodthirsty battlefield of Kurukṣetra (कुरुक्षेत्र). The battlefield had a circular area of at least seventy-five kilometers. Pāṇḍava army faced the east, and the Kaurava army faced the west. The entire Kurukṣetra reverberated with trumpeting of elephants, the neighing of horses, ululation of warriors, twanging of bowstrings, clanging of swords, and tumultuous blaring of conches, drums, small drums, large kettledrums, and blow horns. Before the commencement of the war, Yudhiṣṭhira dropped his weapons, and so did his brothers. They marched straight to the Kaurava army and, falling at the feet of Pitāmaha Bhīṣma, offered their obeisance with Sāṣṭāṅga Daṇḍavat Praṇāma. Yudhiṣṭhira sought permission from the elder Pitāmaha for the war, which Bhīṣma Pitāmaha gave with blessings for their victory. Similarly, permission was sought from preceptors Droṇācārya and Kṛpācārya and also from Śalya.

GLOSSARY

A (अ) is a negating prefix that means "not" when compounded with nouns. It may be translated with "non" or "un."

Aṃśa (अंश) means part or degree.

Aka (अक) is a suffix meaning relating.

Akartavya (अकर्तव्य) means misdeed or a duty that is not permissible.

Akartā (अकर्ता) means a non-doer.

Akarma (अकर्म) means non-action or actionless.

Akarmī (अकर्मी) means a non-doer.

Akalyāṇakārī (अकल्याणकारी) means detrimental.

Akāṭya (अकाट्य) means uncuttable or irrefutable.

Akīrti (अकीर्ति) means infamy.

Akuśala (अकुशल) means unmeritorious.

Akṛtābhyāgama-Doṣa (अकृताभ्यागम-दोष) means a fault incurred when one acquires fruits without the performance of Karma. In other words, to be in the bondage of fruits without performing Karma is considered contrary to the rules.

Akṛtrima (अकृत्रिम) means natural or not artificial.

Akṛtsnavit (अकृत्स्नवित्) means one with limited knowledge. It means one who has incomplete knowledge.

Akrodha (अक्रोध) means free from anger or absence of agitation in mind.

Akledya (अक्लेद्य) means unwettable.

Akṣaya (अक्षय) means undecaying, imperishable, undying, unfailing, or inexhaustible.

Akṣayapātra (अक्षय-पात्र) means an inexhaustible vessel, a vessel whose contents are always full.

Akṣara (अक्षर) means imperishable.

Akhaṇḍa (अखण्ड) means intact or one that does not get divided.

Akhila (अखिल) means complete, whole, or without a gap.

Agocara (अगोचर) means imperceptible by the senses or beyond the reach or cognizance of the senses.

Agni (अग्नि) means fire.

Agniṣṭoma-Yajña (अग्निष्टोम-यज्ञ) means a five-day sixteen-priest sacrifice offered to Indra to attain the world of Indra (Svarga, heaven)

Agnihotra (अग्निहोत्र) means a ceremony consisting of making oblations to a consecrated fire.

Agrasara (अग्रसर) means to advance or forward.

Aṅga (अङ्ग) means limb or part.

Aṅgīkāra (अङ्गीकार) means embracement or adoption. It can also mean to acknowledge or accept.

Acara (अचर) means stationary.

Acala (अचल) means immovable.

Acalatā (अचलता) means immovability.

Acāpalya (अचापल्य) means steadiness or the absence of worthless efforts.

Acitta (अचित्त) means destitute of reason.

Acintya (अचिन्त्य) means imponderable, unthinkable, or beyond thought.

Acireṇa (अचिरेण) means not long, very soon, or immediately.

Aceta (अचेत) means unaware, not conscious of, or asleep.

Acchedya (अच्छेद्य) means unslashable.

Acyuta (अच्युत) means infallible or one who does not fall.

Aja (अज) means unborn or existing from eternity.

Ajanmā (अजन्मा) means unborn.

Ajara (अजर) means not subject to old age or ever young.

Ajeya (अजेय) means invincible or unconquerable.

Ajña (अज्ञ) means ignorant or unwise.

Ajñāta (अज्ञात) means unknown.

Ajñāna (अज्ञान) means ignorance, spiritual ignorance, or false knowledge.

Ajñāna-Kāla (अज्ञान-काल) means period of ignorance.

Ajñāna-Janya (अज्ञान-जन्य) means that which is born of ignorance. Ajñāna (अज्ञान) means ignorance, spiritual ignorance, or false knowledge. Janya (जन्य) means born of, arising from, or produced from.

Añjalī (अञ्जली) means a divine offering.

Aṭala (अटल) means consistent, firm, steady, or solid.

Aṇḍa-Jā (अण्ड-जा) means egg-born.

Ataḥ (अतः) means hence or thus.

Atattva (अतत्त्व) means untruth or unreality.

Ati (अति) means excessive, over, or beyond. It can also mean most or extremely.

Ativyāpti (अतिव्याप्ति) means exceeding pervasion.

Ativyāpti-Doṣa (अतिव्याप्ति-दोष) means a fault wherein characteristics not only spread in the target but also in the non-target. For instance, describing the characteristics of a cow as cows have horns becomes an Ativyāpti-Doṣa, because then characteristics also apply to female cows.

Atiśaya (अतिशय) means abundant.

Atiśayatā-Doṣa (अतिशयता-दोष) means a fault arising out of an attribute of more or less (न्यूनाधिकता, Nyūnādhikatā) in enjoyments. In the world, enjoyment of one may be greater than the second, and enjoyment of the second may be lesser than the third resulting in a mutual attribute of more or less enjoyment. There may be a pain in looking at one with greater enjoyment. While in looking at one with equal enjoyment, there may be jealousy. In contrast, there may be excessive pride in looking at one with lesser enjoyment. This way, these enjoyments are with Atiśayatā-Doṣa.

Atīta (अतीत) means beyond. It can also mean gone by or past.

Atītya (अतीत्य) means transcending or crossing over.

Atyanta (अत्यन्त) means complete, absolute, or highest.

Atyantābhāva (अत्यन्ताभाव) means absolute non-existence.

Athavā (अथवा) means or, alternatively, or rather.

Adaṇḍya (अदण्ड्य) means not punishable.

Adambha (अदम्भ) means unostentatiousness or absence of hypocrisy.

Adāhya (अदाह्य) means unburnable.

Adṛśya (अदृश्य) means invisible. It can also mean latent or not fit to be seen.

Adṛśyatā (अदृश्यता) means invisibility.

Adbhuta (अद्भुत) means amazing, astonishing, or surprising.

Adroha (अद्रोह) means the absence of hate or despite.

Adhaḥ (अधः) means lower or inferior.

Adhaḥpatana (अधःपतन) means down fall or ruination.

Adhama (अधम) means lowest, vilest, or worst. It can also mean a paramour.

Adharma (अधर्म) means unrighteousness, that which is contrary to righteousness.

Adharmī (अधर्मी) means one who is non-righteous.

Adhika (अधिक) means more, abundant.

Adhikaraṇa (अधिकरण) means support.

Adhikāra (अधिकार) means authority or power. It can also mean fitness.

Adhikārī (अधिकारी) means one who is endowed with the fourfold means (साधन-चतुष्टय, Sādhana-Catuṣṭaya) who is competent and eligible for knowledge. In general, it means one who is fit. It expresses the eligibility and competence to undertake a discipline.

Adhigacchati (अधिगच्छति) means attains, realizes, or goes to.

Adhibhūta (अधिभूत) means perishable matter.

Adhibhautika (अधिभौतिक) means material or that which is perishable.

Adhiṣṭhātā (अधिष्ठाता) means a presider.

Adhiṣṭhāna (अधिष्ठान) means ground, underlying truth, substratum, resting upon, basis. A true thing on whose dependence delusion exists is the Adhiṣṭhāna of that delusion. In a snake delusion in a rope, the rope is the Adhiṣṭhāna.

Adhiṣṭhānatā (अधिष्ठानता) means underlying truthiness or essence.

Adhīna (अधीन) means subordinate or dependent.

Adhogati (अधोगति) means bad end, lowest depths of degradation, or descending into an inferior form of existence. It can also represent falling, going downwards, or degradation.

Adhyasta (अध्यस्त) means falsely cognized thing placed upon or wrongly ascribed. A delusional thing is Adhyasta, like the snake is Adhyasta in a rope.

Adhyātma (अध्यात्म) means transcendent knowledge of the Self, the supreme imperishable Reality. It can also mean spiritual knowledge in general.

Adhyāropa (अध्यारोप) means superimposition of the unreal on the real, like a false perception of a snake in a rope that is not a snake. To discuss a minor subject while keeping a significant objective in the forefront to prove is also called Adhyāropa. For instance, someone needs buttermilk, and keeping that in mind asking his friend - Do you have cows? Do they give milk? Do you convert milk to yogurt? Do your extract butter? Such words are called Adhyāropa.

Adhyāsa (अध्यास) means superimposition, false attribution, or a sense of mistaken ascription of essential nature to something which does not belong to it. Delusion is known as Adhyāsa. There are two types of Adhyāsa: 1) Arthādhyāsa (अर्थाध्यास): Delusional thing is known as Arthādhyāsa, like the delusional snake in a rope, and 2) Jñānādhyāsa (ज्ञानाध्यास): Delusional knowledge is known as Jñānādhyāsa, like the knowledge of the snake.

Adhyāhāra (अध्याहार) means superficial connection. It can also mean reasoning or inferring.

Adhruva (अध्रुव) means not fixed, not permanent, uncertain, or transient.

Anadhikāra (अनधिकार) means the absence of authority. It can also mean unworthy or unqualified.

Ananta (अनन्त) means infinite.

Ananya (अनन्य) means undivided, exclusive, only one, no other, or unique.

Ananya-Bhakti (अनन्य-भक्ति) means undivided devotion, exclusive devotion, or worship of only one and no other.

Anabhiṣvaṅga (अनभिष्वङ्ग) means lack of excessive love.

Anargala (अनर्गल) means free, unrestrained, or without bars or checks.

Anartha (अनर्थ) means travesty or disaster. It can also mean evil or worthless.

Anasūya (अनसूय) means without envy, without spite, or without a vision of seeing faults.

Anātma (अनात्म) means non-Ātmā like.

Anātmā (अनात्मा) means that which is not the Ātmā.

Anādara (अनादर) means disregard, disrespect, or contemptuous neglect.

Anādi (अनादि) means without origin or having no beginning.

Anāditā (अनादिता) means the state of having no beginning.

Anāmaya (अनामय) means free from disease, not pernicious, or ambrosiac.

Anāyāsa (अनायास) means with ease or absence of exertion.

Anārya (अनार्य) means ignoble, not respectable, not honorable, or unworthy.

Anāśinaḥ (अनाशिनः) means imperishable.

Anāsakta (अनासक्त) means unattached.

Aniketa (अनिकेत) means homeless.

Anitya (अनित्य) means transient or not everlasting.

Aniyata (अनियत) means not prescribed, unregulated, uncontrolled, not fixed, or indefinite.

Anirdeśya (अनिर्देश्य) means ineffable or indescribable.

Anivārya (अनिवार्य) means unavoidable.

Anivāryatā (अनिवार्यता) means unavoidability.

Aniścayātmaka (अनिश्चयात्मक) means irresolute.

Aniścita (अनिश्चित) means undetermined or undecided.

Aniṣṭa (अनिष्ट) means malefic.

Anīti (अनीति) means contrary to the rules.

Anukampā (अनुकम्पा) means compassion or pity.

Anukūla (अनुकूल) means agreeable, favorable, or likable.

Anukūla-Buddhi (अनुकूल-बुद्धि) means favorable intelligence, friendly intelligence, or intellect that likes some things.

Anukūla-Vṛtti (अनुकूल-वृत्ति) means agreeable mental state.

Anugata (अनुगत) means behind.

Anugrah (अनुग्रह्) means to favor, to oblige. It can also mean grace, compassion, kindness, or mercy.

Anudbuddharupa (अनुद्बुद्धरुप) means in ignorance.

Anudvegakara (अनुद्वेगकर) means one that does not cause distress or anxiety.

Anupalabdhi (अनुपलब्धि) means non-perception or negative cognitive proof.

Anubhavagamya (अनुभवगम्य) means a posteriori.

Anubhava-Vṛtti (अनुभव-वृत्ति) means current knowledge.

Anumantā (अनुमन्ता) means sanctioner.

Anumāna (अनुमान) means inference.

Anumeya (अनुमेय) means inferable. It can also mean to be inferred, proved, or conjectured.

Anumodana (अनुमोदन) means to sanction or approve.

Anurāga (अनुराग) means to be enamored or to be in intense love.

Anurupa (अनुरुप) means in accordance with or commensurate with.

Anurodha (अनुरोध) means request, plea, or appeal.

Anuṣṭhāna (अनुष्ठान) means undertaking, carrying out, or doing.

Anusaṃdhāna (अनुसंधान) means inquiry, investigation, or close inspection.

Anusaṃdhānātmaka (अनुसंधानात्मक) means probing.

Anusāra (अनुसार) means in accordance with.

Anta (अन्त) means end.

Antaḥ (अन्तः) means internal.

Antaḥkaraṇa (अन्तःकरण) means the conscience, inner cause, or internal instrument in the subtle body (सूक्ष्म-शरीर, Sūkṣma-Śarīra) consisting of four components: 1) the mind (मनस्, Manas), 2) the intellect (बुद्धि, Buddhi), 3) the subconscious mind (चित्त, Citta) and 4) the ego (अहंकार, Ahaṃkāra).

Antataḥ (अन्ततः) means finally.

Antara (अन्तर) means inner.

Antaraṅga (अन्तरङ्ग) means internal. It can also mean being closely connected to the Ātmā.

Antarātmā (अन्तरात्मा) means the conscience.

Antarāya (अन्तराय) means obstacle, intervention, hindrance, or impediment.

Antargata (अन्तर्गत) means within.

Antarbhāva (अन्तर्भाव) means internal disposition or nature.

Antarmukha (अन्तर्मुख) means turned inwards.

Antaryāmi (अन्तर्यामि) means the in-dwelling witness-observer Supreme Lord.

Antima (अन्तिम) means final, last, or ultimate.

Andhakāra (अन्धकार) means darkness.

Anna (अन्न) means food.

Annamaya-Kośa (अन्नमय-कोश) means the Sheath of Food. It is the outermost grossest sheath of the physical self-nourished by food. It is the gross physical body and includes a) Pañca-Jñānendriya (पञ्च-ज्ञानेन्द्रिय)) or the five sense faculties: 1) skin (त्वक, Tvaka) with the sense of touch, 2) tongue (रसना, Rasanā) with the sense of taste, 3) eyes (चक्षु, Cakṣu) with the sense of sight, 4) nose (घ्राण, Ghrāṇa) with the sense of smell, 5) ears (श्रोत्र, Śrotra) with the sense of hearing; and b) Pañca-Karmendriya (पञ्च-कर्मेन्द्रिय) or the five action faculties: 1) mouth (वाक, Vāka) with the sense of voice, 2) hands (पाणि, Pāṇi) with the sense of grasping, receiving, gathering, collecting (Grahaṇa) and holding (Dhāraṇa), 3) feet (पाद, Pāda) with the sense of walking, moving, locomotion (Gamana), 4) anus (पायु, Pāyu) with the sense of excretion, 5) genitals (उपस्थ, Upastha) with the sense of reproduction. Birth and death are the attributes of the Annamaya-Kośa. The personality of an individual, physique, and traits depends on the condition of Annamaya-Kośa, the formation of which continues life afterlife.

Anyaḥ (अन्यः) means other.

Anyathā (अन्यथा) means otherwise or or.

Anyathā-Grahaṇa (अन्यथा-ग्रहण) means to know something as different from what it is.

Anyāya (अन्याय) means injustice.

Anyonyādhyāsa (अन्योन्याध्यास) means delusion of one in the second and delusion of the second in the first.

Anvaya (अन्वय) means concordance, agreement. For instance, in logic, an agreement exists between two things, such as between a string and roses, to form a garland. The fact that, without the string that holds together the roses, there is no garland of roses is Anvaya.

Anvaya-Vyatireka (अन्वय-व्यतिरेक) means an analytic process of separation and connection to indicate inference in which reason is co-present or is co-absent with the significant term, as the pair of positive and negative instantiations representing both inductive and deductive reasoning. For instance, in the example of roses strung to form a garland, without the string which holds together the roses, there is no garland of roses; it is Anvaya. The string is separate from the roses is Vyatireka.

Anveṣaṇa (अन्वेषण) means inquiry or search.

Apamāna (अपमान) means disrespect, insult, or dishonor.

Aparādha (अपराध) means offense, crime, or fault.

Aparicchinna (अपरिच्छिन्न) means undivided, unlimited, or continuous.

Aparihārya (अपरिहार्य) means unavoidable.

Aparokṣa (अपरोक्ष) means direct experience.

Aparokṣa-Jñāna (अपरोक्ष-ज्ञान) means transcendental knowledge, knowledge of the Ātmā attained through the process of reason and discrimination between the real and the unreal.

Apalāyana (अपलायन) means not fleeing

Apavitra (अपवित्र) means impure.

Apahṛta (अपहृत) means taken away, carried off, or stolen.

Apādāna (अपादान) means taking away, removal, or ablation. It can also mean from where the action is performed.

Apāra (अपार) means not having an opposite shore, boundless, or unbounded.

Api (अपि) means even, and, also, moreover, besides, assuredly. or surely.

Apunarāvṛtti (अपुनरावृत्ति) means a status from where one does not return, final exemption from the transmigratory life of birth and death.

Apekṣā (अपेक्षा) means compared to, regard to, consideration of, hope, or need.

Apekṣākṛta (अपेक्षाकृत) means comparatively or relatively.

Apekṣita (अपेक्षित) means expected, wished, considered, or referred to.

Apaiśunya (अपैशुन्य) means the absence of fault-finding.

Aprakaṭa (अप्रकट) means unmanifest.

Apratima (अप्रतिम) means matchless or unsurpassed.

Apratīkāra (अप्रतीकार) means unretaliating.

Apratyakṣa (अप्रत्यक्ष) means indirect, not visible, or not evident.

Aprameya (अप्रमेय) means indeterminable or one that is not the subject of validation by the senses.

Aprāpta (अप्राप्त) means unattained or unacquired.

Apriya (अप्रिय) means unpleasant, disliked, or disagreeable.

Abādhya (अबाध्य) means unrestricted.

Abhaya (अभय) means fearlessness.

Abhāva (अभाव) means absence, not-being, not existing, or not occurring.

Abhāvarupa (अभावरुप) means the form of not-being.

Abhi (अभि) is a prefix meaning to or towards.

Abhijana (अभिजन) means family or lineage. It can also indicate noble descent.

Abhinna (अभिन्न) means united or not divided.

Abhiprāya (अभिप्राय) means aim, purpose, or intention.

Abhipreta (अभिप्रेत) means accepted, approved, intended, or implied.

Abhimāna (अभिमान) means pride, self-conceit, insidiousness, or excessive vanity. It can mean "I-ness," belief, or conception (especially an erroneous one regarding oneself). It can also mean superimposition.

Abhimānātmaka (अभिमानात्मक) means egoistic.

Abhimānī (अभिमानी) means owner, conceiver, or one who has self-conceit or self-importance. It can also indicate I-ness in.

Abhilāṣā (अभिलाषा) means aspiration or desire.

Abhilāṣī (अभिलाषी) means desirer.

Abhiṣvaṅga (अभिष्वङ्ग) means excessive love, excessive affection, or excessive attachment.

Abhisaṃdhāna (अभिसंधान) means attachment or interest in any object. It can also mean speech or deliberate declaration.

Abhihita (अभिहित) means named, called, declared, or held forth.

Abhīpsita (अभीप्सित) means desired or acceptable.

Abheda (अभेद) means oneness or nondifference.

Abhedarupa (अभेदरुप) means in oneness.

Abhyanunādayan (अभ्यनुनादयन्) means resounding or reverberating.

Abhyāsa (अभ्यास) means practice, repeated efforts, or continued application to master. The flow of homogeneous inclinations (Sajātīya-Vṛtti) is named Abhyāsa. It can also mean withdrawing the mind from all sides and repeatedly fixing on one support.

Abhyudaya (अभ्युदय) means rising, elevation, or prosperity.

Amantavya (अमन्तव्य) means unsanctioned, not approved, or not regarded.

Amara (अमर) means undying, immortal, or imperishable.

Amarṣa (अमर्ष) means jealous anger.

Amāna (अमान) means humility, humbleness, or without conceit.

Amānitva (अमानित्व) means humility.

Amūḍhatā (अमूढता) means the absence of confusion, lack of delusion, or clarity of thought.

Amṛta (अमृत) means ambrosia or nectar. It can also mean immortal.

Amṛtamaya (अमृतमय) means ambrosiac

Amedhya (अमेध्य) means unfit for sacrifice or impure.

Amla (अम्ल) means sour. Lemon, lime, grapefruit, tamarind, and tomato have a sour taste. It is primarily the result of citric acid, lactic acid, malic acid, oxalic acid, and ascorbic acid.

Ayana (अयन) means going. It can also mean battlefront, an entrance to an array of troops.

Ayukta (अयुक्त) means not united. It can also mean improper or unsuitable.

Ari (अरि) means foe or enemy.

Arisūdana (अरिसूदन) means killer of the enemy.

Aruci (अरुचि) means aversion or dislike.

Arcana (अर्चन) means to worship.

Artha (अर्थ) means wealth, material or worldly possessions. In a broader context, it means the instruments for the sustenance of life and incorporates wealth, career, and activity to make a living, financial security, and economic prosperity. It can also mean purpose or aim.

Artha-Kāma (अर्थ-काम) means material and sensual.

Arthavāda (अर्थवाद) means empty praise.

Arthāt (अर्थात्) means that is to say.

Arthādhyāsa (अर्थाध्यास) means a thing of delusion, like the delusional snake in a rope.

Arthāpatti (अर्थापत्ति) means postulation or derivation from circumstances.

Arthārthi (अर्थार्थी) means seeker of material gain, seeker of wealth, or worldly possessions.

Arpaṇa (अर्पण) means offering.

Alaṃ-Buddhi (अलं-बुद्धि) means satiety, satisfaction, or feeling of contentment.

Alīka (अलीक) means impossible.

Alupta (अलुप्त) means not lost, undiminished, or not cut off.

Alaukika (अलौकिक) means not belonging to this world, uncommon or divine.

Alpa (अल्प) means puny or small.

Alpa-Buddhi (अल्प-बुद्धि) means weak-minded, feeble-minded, or unwise.

Alpajña (अल्पज्ञ) means with limited knowledge.

Ava (अव) is a prefix meaning down or under. It is used to provide negativity in the meaning of the word. For example, अवमान means dishonor, disgrace, which is the opposite of मान, meaning honor, grace.

Avakāśa (अवकाश) means free time. It can also mean opportunity.

Avacchinna (अवच्छिन्न) means separation or detachment.

Avajñāta (अवज्ञात) means to despise, disrespect, or contempt.

Avatāra (अवतार) means incarnation.

Avatīrṇa (अवतीर्ण) means alighted or descended. It can also mean incarnated.

Avadhi (अवधि) means a limit or boundary. It can also mean a period or a time.

Avalaṃbana (अवलंबन) means dependency.

Avalaṃbita (अवलंबित) means supported.

Avaśaḥ (अवशः) means helplessly.

Avaśya (अवश्य) means certainly or inevitably.

Avaśyambhāvī (अवश्यम्भावी) means inevitable.

Avasara (अवसर) means opportunity.

Avasthā (अवस्था) means state or condition.

Avasthātīta (अवस्थातीत) means one who is beyond states or conditions.

Avahelanā (अवहेलना) means to disregard or disdain.

Avāṅmanasagocara (अवाङ्मनसगोचर) means which is beyond the reach of speech and mind.

Avāpta (अवाप्त) means to obtain or get.

Avāstavika (अवास्तविक) means not real.

Avikārī (अविकारी) means immutable, unmodifiable, or unchangeable.

Avicāra (अविचार) means without reflection or thought.

Avicāravaśa (अविचारवश) means that which does not have the power to think.

Avidyā (अविद्या) means ignorance, nescience. An elusive power (Śakti) in the Brahman is sometimes regarded as one with Māyā and sometimes as different from it. It forms the condition of an individual Jīva and is otherwise called ignorance or impure-Māyā. It forms the causal body of a Jīva. It is an impure element.

Avidyā-Viśiṣṭa-Cetana (अविद्या-विशिष्ट-चेतन) means the conscious element endowed especially with nescience (ignorance), where the cause of transformations - the intellect, mind, and senses all dissolve in their cause Avidyā.

Avidhyamāna (अविध्यमान) means not seen.

Avidhyamānatā (अविध्यमानता) means absence or non-existence.

Avināśī (अविनाशी) means imperishable or indestructible.

Avibhakta (अविभक्त) means undivided.

Aviveka (अविवेक) means the absence of judgment or discrimination.

Avivekī (अविवेकी) means undiscerning or ignorant.

Avyakta (अव्यक्त) means unmanifest, imperceptible, or invisible. It is the unevolved state of Prakṛti that is devoid of transformations. It is also known as Māyā (माया) or Śakti (शक्ति, power) of the Supreme Lord.

Avyaktatā (अव्यक्तता) means imperceptibility or invisibility.

Avyabhicāriṇī (अव्यभिचारिणी) means unwavering, resolute, steadfast, or not having any tendency to deviate.

Avyabhicārī (अव्यभिचारी) means unwavering or unfaltering.

Avyaya (अव्यय) means imperishable or immutable.

Avyavahita (अव्यवहित) means contiguous or adjoining.

Avyāpti (अव्याप्ति) means insufficient pervasion or inadequate pervasion.

Avyāpti-Doṣa (अव्याप्ति-दोष) means a fault of insufficient pervasion. It is wherein characteristics do not spread entirely or in every target part. For instance, describing the characteristics of a cow as cows are brown becomes Avyāpti-Doṣa, because the brown characteristics do not spread in the entire class of cows.

Aśakta (अशक्त) means incapable or weak.

Aśāṃti (अशांति) means restlessness, unrest, or disturbance.

Aśāstrīya (अशास्त्रीय) means unscriptural or not conforming to scriptures.

Aśuddhi (अशुद्धि) means impurity.

Aśubha (अशुभ) means bad or evil.

Aśoṣya (अशोष्य) means undryable.

Aśma (अश्म) means a stone.

Aśvattha (अश्वत्थ) means the holy fig tree.

Aśvinī-Mudrā (अश्विनी-मुद्रा) involves rhythmically contracting the anal sphincter to direct Prāṇa upward along the spine. To practice Aśvinī-Mudrā from a seated Āsana, inhale and hold the breath, then contracts the sphincter muscles for a second or two, doing four or five contractions before dropping the chin and exhaling.

Aṣṭāṅga-Yoga (अष्टाङ्ग-योग) means the Yoga consisting of eight limbs: 1) moral codes (यम, Yama), 2) observances (नियम, Niyama), 3) postures (आसन, Āsana), 4) breath-control (प्राणायाम, Prāṇāyāma), 5) sense-control (प्रत्याहार, Pratyāhāra), 6) concentration (धारणा, Dhāraṇā), 7) meditation (ध्यान, Dhyāna) and 8) absorption into the Reality (समाधि, Samādhī).

Asaṃgata (असंगत) means inappropriate.

Asaṃgatā (असंगता) means disassociation or unattachment.

Asaṃgati (असंगति) means incompatibility.

Asaṃbandhatā (असंबन्धता) means irrelevance.

Asaṃbhāvanā (असंभावना) means the impossibility of comprehending, want of congruity, or absence of compatibility.

Asaṃskṛta (असंस्कृत) means imperfect.

Asakta (असक्त) means unattached or detached.

Asakti (असक्ति) means lack of affection, lack of love, or lack of attachment.

Asaṅga (असङ्ग) means disassociated, unassociated, or unattached.

Asat (असत्) means unreal or untrue. That which has no being or is non-existent.

Asatya (असत्य) means not true or falsehood.

Asapatnam (असपत्नम्) means without rival.

Asamāhita (असमाहित) means not united or not joined.

Asamīcīnatā (असमीचीनता) means inexpediency or injudiciousness.

Asammūḍha (असम्मूढ) means undeluded.

Asamyagadarśī (असम्यगदर्शी) means one with an improper perspective.

Asāra (असार) means without essence, without value, or meaningless.

Asāratā (असारता) means vacuity, worthlessness, or futility.

Asiddhi (असिद्धि) means failure or imperfect accomplishment.

Asīma (असीम) means unlimited or endless.

Asura (असुर) means a demon. They are the descendants of Diti (दिति) and Danu (दनु) {daughters of Prajāpati Dakṣa, प्रजापति दक्ष} and Saptarṣi Kaśyapa. Descendants of Diti are Daitya and of Danu are Dānava. They are demons of the first order in perpetual hostility with the deities (Sura).

Asūyā (असूया) means faultfinding or malice.

Asau (असौ) means that or he.

Asta (अस्त) means set or end.

Astitva (अस्तित्व) means existence, being, or reality.

Asti-Bhāti-Priya (अस्ति-भाति-प्रिय) means the Existent Conscious Bliss. Asti (अस्ति) means the sense of perpetual existence, the sense of Astitva (अस्तित्व, existence, of being), the sense of Sat (सत्, real). Bhāti (भाति) means the sense of knowledge, illumination, wisdom, the sense of consciousness (भातित्व, Bhātitva). Priya (प्रिय) means the sense of happiness or Ānanda (आनन्द, bliss). Asti-Bhāti-Priya is synonymous with Saccidānanda (सच्चिदानन्द, Real Conscious Bliss), a compound word from Sat (सत्), meaning that which is the real, existent, or true essence, Cit (चित्), meaning the conscious element, and Ānanda (आनन्द) meaning bliss. All three are considered inseparable from the nature of the supreme imperishable Reality or the Brahman

Asthira (अस्थिर) means unsteady, unstable, or not firm.

Asmi (अस्मि) means I am.

Aham-Kartā-Buddhi (अहं-कर्ता-बुद्धि) means "I am a doer" intellect. The embodiment of "I am a doer" in the intellect.

Ahaṃkāra (अहंकार) means ego. It provides conceit or conception of individuality, the sense of self. It is the inner disposition of I-ness (अभिमानात्मक-वृत्ति, Abhimānātmaka-Vṛtti) which identifies the Ātmā (Self) with the body as "I," the "I-ness" sense in the body, sense-organs, mind, and intellect.

Ahaṃgraha-Dhyāna (अहंग्रह-ध्यान) means a meditation in which the meditator identifies himself with the pure Ātmā, the Brahman or the Supreme Personality, and meditates to become one with that source.

Ahaṃtā (अहंता) means I-ness or egoism.

Ahaṃtā-Mamatā (अहंता-ममता) means I-ness and mineness, where Ahaṃtā (अहंता) means I-ness and Mamatā (ममता) means mineness or meum.

Aham (अहम्) means I.

Aham-Abhimāna (अहम्-अभिमान) means I-ness conceit.

Aham-Buddhi (अहम्-बुद्धि) means I-ness intellect.

Aham-Bhāva (अहम्-भाव) means I-ness sentiment.

Ahamrupa (अहम्रुप) means I-form.

Aharana (अहरन) means instruments of a goldsmith, such as an anvil or a stake.

Aharāgame (अहरागमे) means at the beginning of Brahmā's day.

Ahiṃsā (अहिंसा) means non-violence or not injuring anyone through body, mind, or speech.

Ā (आ) means to, at.

Ākāra (आकार) means shape or form.

Ākāśa (आकाश) means space.

Ākāśavata (आकाशवत) means like space.

Ākāśavāṇī (आकाशवाणी) means divine utterances, voices from the sky, or voices from the heavens.

Ākula (आकुल) means confounded, confused, or perplexed.

Ākṛti (आकृति) means form or shape.

Āgamana (आगमन) means coming.

Āgraha (आग्रह) means request. It can also mean obstinacy or whim.

Ācaraṇa (आचरण) means conduct, demeanor, or behavior.

Ācarya (आचार्य) means a preceptor, a guru, or a teacher.

Ācarya-Upāsanā (आचार्य-उपासना) means service of a preceptor with body, mind, and wealth, and with faith and devotion to procure his grace.

Ājñā (आज्ञा) means command or order.

Ājñā-Cakra (आज्ञा-चक्र) is located in the center of the forehead between the eyebrows. It is not a part of the physical body but is considered a part of the Pranic System. The Ājñā-Cakra is correspondent with the pineal gland.

Ātatāyī (आततायी) means a heinous crime committer. It is used on an armed person who kills an unarmed person or one who uses poison to kill.

Ātma (आत्म) means own.

Ātma-Abhimāna (आत्म-अभिमान) means self-conceit. It can also mean superimposition on the Ātmā.

Ātma-Kalyāṇa (आत्म-कल्याण) means own well-being, own good.

Ātma-Nivedana (आत्म-निवेदन) means self-surrender (to the divine).

Ātma-Parāyaṇa (आत्म-परायण) means to move towards the Ātmā, to be devoted or absorbed in the Ātmā.

Ātma-Parāyaṇatā (आत्म-परायणता) means moving towards the Ātmā through association with knowers of the Truth (Tattva-Vettā), with contemplation of scriptures that provide the Truth (सच्छास्त्र, Sacchāstra) and to be ready for analytic thinking on the true nature of the Paramātmā.

Ātma-Buddhi (आत्म-बुद्धि) means self-knowledge, own wisdom, own sense, or own intellect. It can also mean I-ness sense.

Ātma-Rati (आत्म-रति) means to rejoice or delight in the Ātmā.

Ātmavān (आत्मवान्) means focused on the Ātmā.

Ātma-Vinigraha (आत्म-विनिग्रह) means self-control, the imposing of discipline on the body, mind, and senses when they function against our genuine interest and confining activities in the righteous path.

Ātma-Sākṣātkāra (आत्म-साक्षात्कार) means Self-Realization. It is the transcendental experience of attaining union with oneness in the Ātmā.

Ātma-Sukha (आत्म-सुख) means own happiness

Ātma-Svarupa (आत्म-स्वरुप) means true nature of own Ātmā.

Ātmā (आत्मा) in ordinary terms means the Soul, inner Self. The pure Ātmā is referred to as the pure Self, meaning the supreme imperishable Reality, whence all existence arises, by which everything is sustained and into which everything ultimately dissolves. The delimited Ātmā is the pure Ātmā (pure Self) on whom I-ness ego of the body, senses, mind, and intellect are superimposed due to nescience.

Ātmākāra (आत्माकार) means in the true nature of the Ātmā.

Ātmākāra-Vṛtti (आत्माकार-वृत्ति) means the inner disposition of oneness in the Ātmā.

Ātmānusandhāna (आत्मानुसन्धान) means Self-query, contemplation to attain union in the Ātmā.

Ātmonnati (आत्मोन्नति) means exaltation of the Ātmā.

Ātyantika (आत्यन्तिक) means complete or absolute.

Ādatta (आदत्त) means to take, receive, accept, or assume.

Ādara (आदर) means respect.

Ādi (आदि) means et al., and others. It can also mean beginning.

Āditya (आदित्य) are the twelve sons of Aditi (the daughter of Prajāpati Dakṣa) enumerated as: 1. Dhātā (धाता), 2. Mitra (मित्र), 3. Aryamā (अर्यमा), 4. Śukra (शुक्र), 5. Varuṇa (वरुण), 6. Aṃśa (अंश), 7. Bhaga (भग), 8. Vivasvān (विवस्वान्), 9. Pushā (पूषा), 10. Savitā (सविता), 11. Tvaṣṭā (त्वष्टा), and 12. Vāmana (वामन).

Ādhāra (आधार) means support or substratum.

Ādhārabhūta (आधारभूत) means underlying or substrate.

Ādheya (आधेय) means a thing to be placed or supported. It can also mean attribute or predicate.

Ādheyabhūta (आधेयभूत) means that which is placed or supported.

Ānaka (आनक) means a sizeable military drum.

Ānandamaya-Kośa (आनन्दमय-कोश) means the Sheath of Supreme Bliss. It is the innermost subtlest sheath of the Pañca-Kośa (पञ्च-कोश, the five sheaths that cover the Ātmā as described in Taittirīya Upaniṣad 2.1-5). When the mind and senses cease functioning in a deep sleep, it still stands between the finite world and the Ātmā. The sheath typically has its most total play during deep sleep, while it has only a partial manifestation in the dream and wakeful states. The Ānandamaya-Kośa is a reflection of the Ātmā as the Real-Conscious-Bliss (सच्चिदानन्द, Saccidānanda).

Ānayana (आनयन) means bringing or leading nearby.

Āpa (आप) means water.

Ābrahmstambha (आब्रह्मस्तम्ब) means to or at the Infinite Pillar of Origin of the world that has no beginning or end and is beyond time and space.

Ābhāsa (आभास) means inkling, perception, or a sense of the presence of something. A thing that does not have actual existence but is perceived as real in someone else's reality is known as Ābhāsa. A person's shadow is a person's Ābhāsa.

Ābhāsa-Mātra (आभास-मात्र) means inkling only, perception only, or illusory only.

Āmaya (आमय) means sickness

Āmarṣa (आमर्ष) means jealousy. It can also mean intolerance, anger, or impatience.

Āraṃbha (आरंभ) means to initiate or to begin.

Āratī (आरती) means an offering ceremony in which lights with wicks soaked in Ghī are lit and songs are sung praising the deity.

Ārādhya (आराध्य) means one to be worshipped or propitiated.

Āruḍha (आरुढ) means mounted, seated, ascended, risen, or stepped up.

Āropa (आरोप) means attribution or assignment.

Āropaṇa (आरोपण) means attribution.

Ārjava (आर्जव) means simplicity. It is straightforwardness and absence of crookedness in mental and vocal conduct related to eating, drinking, and clothing.

Ārta (आर्त) means sick, suffering, injured, oppressed, or unhappy.

Ārthika (आर्थिक) means materially. It can also mean financially or monetarily.

Ārya (आर्य) means noble.

Ālaṃbana (आलंबन) means support, dependence, or mounting.

Ālaya (आलय) means abode or dwelling.

Ālasya (आलस्य) means laziness, idleness, or indolence.

Āvaraṇa (आवरण) means covering, especially veil of ignorance.

Āvaśyaka (आवश्यक) means necessary.

Āvaha (आवह) means to bring, produce, lead, or tend.

Āvāgamana (आवागमन) means coming and going, especially in the senses of birth and death.

Āvāhana (आवाहन) means to invoke.

Āviṣṭa (आविष्ट) means possessed or filled.

Āvṛta(आवृत) means covered.

Āvṛtti (आवृत्ति) means repetition.

Āveśa (आवेश) means frenzy, possession, anger, or wrath.

Āśaya (आशय) means intention or point.

Āśā (आशा) means expectation or hope.

Āścarya (आश्चर्य) means astonishment, marvel, or wonder.

Āścaryamaya (आश्चर्यमय) means marvelous, wonderful, or miraculous.

Āśraya (आश्रय) means dependence, support, or shelter.

Āśrayī (आश्रयी) means dependent.

Āśrita (आश्रित) means dependent, seeking refuge, or resorting to asylum.

Āśvāsana (आश्वासन) means to provide assurance or comfort.

Āsakta (आसक्त) means attached.

Āsakti (आसक्ति) means excessive attachment, excessive fondness, or excessive love.

Āsana (आसन) means seat or a place.

Āsupterāmṛte (आसुप्तेरामृते) means from a conscious or awake state to sleep and from birth to death.

Āsura (आसुर) means belonging to demons (Asura).

Āsurī (आसुरी) means demonic.

Āsurī-Sampatti (आसुरी-सम्पत्ति) means demonic attributes.

Āstikatā (आस्तिकता) means theism or faith in preceptors and scriptures. It can also mean beingness or existence.

Āhuti (आहुति) means sacrifice.

Aiśvarya (ऐश्वर्य) means lordliness, power, supremacy, or opulence.

Auṣadha (औषध) means medicinal herbs and plants.

Bandhana (बन्धन) means bondage.

Bandhāyamāna (बन्धायमान) means boundable.

Bandhu (बन्धु) means a relative or anyone connected or associated with another.

Bala (बल) means power, might, vigor, or strength.

Balavāna (बलवान) means one with might, vigor, or strength.

Bahirmukha (बहिर्मुख) means outward-facing.

Bām̐surī (बाँसुरी) means a flute.

Bādhaka (बाधक) means opposing, hindering, oppressing, or detrimental.

Bādhita (बाधित) means opposed or oppressed.

Bāndhava (बान्धव) means a relative.

Bāla-Buddhi (बाल-बुद्धि) means intellect of a child.

Bāhya (बाह्य) means outside or external.

Bīja (बीज) means seed.

Buddhi (बुद्धि) means the intellect. It is characterized by inner-disposition of decision-making (निश्चयात्मक-वृत्ति, Niścayātmaka-Vṛtti). It is derived from the root Budh (बुध्), which means to be awake, to observe, to know. Discriminative in nature, intellect is that which can discern real (सत्, Sat) from unreal (असत्, Asat), right from wrong, good from bad, piety from sin, and thereby provide a selection of a wise choice.

Buddhimāna (बुद्धिमान) means wise or intelligent. It means a person endowed with the ability of true reasoning and discernment or who can decide, judge, and make cognitive discrimination and differentiation.

Bodha (बोध) means knowing or understanding. It can also mean awakening or arousing.

Bodhana (बोधन) means enlightening or teaching.

Bodha-Śakti (बोध-शक्ति) means the power of apprehension.

Bauddhika (बौद्धिक) means an intellectual.

Brahma (ब्रह्म) derived from Brah (ब्रह्) "the pervasive," means the supreme imperishable Reality, the Ātmā, the Self or Paramātmā, whence all existence arises, by which everything is sustained and into which everything ultimately dissolves.

Brahmacarya (ब्रह्मचर्य) means a state of chastity, the practice of celibacy. It can also mean the state of an unmarried religious student.

Brahmacarya-Āśrama (ब्रह्मचर्य-आश्रम) means the first bachelor student stage of life from childhood to around the age of 25. This stage focuses on education and includes the practice of celibacy. In Vedic times, the student went and lived in a house of a preceptor (Gurukula, गुरुकुल), acquiring knowledge of science, philosophy, scriptures, and logic, practicing self-discipline, working to earn remuneration (दक्षिणा, Dakṣiṇā) to be paid to the preceptor, and learning to live a life of righteousness, morals, and duties.

Brahmacārī (ब्रह्मचारी) means a celibate student.

Brahma-Jñāna (ब्रह्म-ज्ञान) means realization of the Brahman.

Brahma-Dṛṣṭi (ब्रह्म-दृष्टि) means seeing everything as the Brahman. Terms Sama-Dṛṣṭi (सम-दृष्टि) meaning seeing everything equally, and Ekatva-Dṛṣṭi (एकत्व-दृष्टि) meaning seeing everything in oneness are also used to express the same intent of seeing everything as the Brahman only.

Brahman (ब्रह्मन्) derived from Brah (ब्रह्) "pervasive," means the supreme imperishable Reality, the pure Self, the pure Ātma or the Paramātmā (परमात्मा). The Brahman is formless and without attributes (निर्गुण, Nirguṇa), without distinctions (निर्विशेष, Nirviśeṣa), self-existent, absolute, and immutable, whence all existence arises, by which everything is sustained and into which everything ultimately dissolves. The Brahman is, by definition, super-sensuous. It is beyond comprehension or cognition. It cannot even be understood inferentially, for every inferential dynamic depends upon a repeatedly perceived concomitance between that which is to be proved and its characteristics (e.g., between fire and smoke). The Brahman associated with its potency, Māyā (शक्ति, Śakti), appears as the Lord (Īśvara, Bhagavāna), the qualified Brahman, the creator, preserver, and destroyer of the world. The Brahman is outside time, space, and causality. The empirical world is completely dependent on Brahman. It is dependent and changing, but it is not non-existent in the physical plane of nescience. Changes in empirical order do not affect the integrity of the Brahman. The Brahman is real, and the world perceived as real is apparent, imagined, and unreal. Any change, duality, or plurality is an illusion. The empirical world is just a misapprehension of the real Brahman.

Brahma-Prakṛti (ब्रह्म-प्रकृति) means the innate attributes of a Brāhmaṇa (ब्राह्मण). The attributes enumerated in BG 18.42 are 1) control of the mind (शम, Śama), 2) restraint of the senses (दम, Dama), 3) austerity (तप, Tapa) as per BG 17, 4) purity (शौच, Śauca), cleanliness within and outside, 5) forgiveness (क्षान्ति, Kṣānti), 6) simplicity (आर्जव, Ārjava), 7) faith in the preceptors and the scriptures (आस्तिक्य, Āstikya), 8) knowledge of the scriptures (ज्ञान, Jñāna) and 9) realized knowledge (विज्ञान, Vijñāna), transcendental experience of the understood knowledge of the scriptures.

Brahma-Stamba (ब्रह्म-स्तम्ब) means the Infinite Pillar of Origin of the world that has no beginning or end and is beyond time and space.

Brahma-Svarupa (ब्रह्म-स्वरुप) means in the true nature of the supreme imperishable Reality or the Brahman.

Brahmā (ब्रह्मा) is the creator part of the supreme Tri-Murti - Śiva, Viṣṇu, and Brahmā. According to Śiva Purāṇa 2.1.7, Brahmā was created by Lord Śiva (शिव) with Pārvatī (पार्वती) from his right limb through the umbilical lotus (पङ्कज) called Hiraṇmaya (हिरण्मय) that sprang from the lake of the navel of the Supreme Personality Lord Viṣṇu while sleeping.

Brahmāṇḍa (ब्रह्माण्ड) means the creation, the world.

Brahmātmaikya (ब्रह्मात्मैक्य) means oneness of the Brahman and the Ātmā.

Brahmārpaṇa (ब्रह्मार्पण) means offering to the Brahman.

Bhakta (भक्त) means a devotee.

Bhakti (भक्ति) means devotion or worship.

Bhakṣya (भक्ष्य) means masticable or to be broken by teeth and eaten.

Bhagavat-Prāpti (भगवत्-प्राप्ति) means attainment of the Lord.

Bhagavāna (भगवान) means the Supreme Lord Viṣṇu. The term Bhagavāna is a compound word from two disyllables Bhaga (भग) and Vāna (वान). The disyllable Vāna (वान) means possessor. Viṣṇu Purāṇa 6.5.74 denotes the six Bhaga (भग) or attributes - Total (समग्र), lordliness (ऐश्वर्य), power (वीर्य), renown (यशसः), splendor (श्रियः), knowledge (ज्ञान) and dispassion (वैराग्य).

Bhaya (भय) means fear or danger.

Bhayānaka (भयानक) means fearful, terrible, dreadful, or formidable.

Bhartā (भर्ता) means sustainer.

Bhava (भव) means the Saṃsāra or the world.

Bhavitavya (भवितव्य) means about to happen.

Bhastrikā (भस्त्रिका) means a bellows and in Prāṇāyāma involves a rapid and forceful process of inhalation and exhalation powered by the movement of the diaphragm. The movement of air is accompanied by an audible sound.

Bhasma (भस्म) means ashes.

Bhāva (भाव) means emotion, sentiment. Any subjective process of arousing mental states or emotional waves originating in the mind in the form of a thought or resolve is called Bhāva. It can also mean becoming, being, or existing. It can also mean nature or status.

Bhāvagata (भावगत) means mental.

Bhāvanā (भावना) means sentiment, feeling, notion, or inner resolve.

Bhāva-Pradhāna (भाव-प्रधान) means sentiment predominant.

Bhāvamaya (भावमय) means emotional or having a feeling.

Bhāvarupa (भावरुप) means existing or actual.

Bhāva-Śūnya (भाव-शून्य) means the absence of being. It can also mean without sentiments.

Bhāva-Saṃśuddhi (भाव-संशुद्धि) means extreme emotional purity.

Bhāvātmaka (भावात्मक) means with sentiments or with emotions.

Bhāvābhāva (भावाभाव) means being and not-being, presence and absence, or taking birth and dying.

Bhāvuka (भावुक) means a devotee. It can also mean being or becoming.

Bhāvotpādaka (भावोत्पादक) means that which produces sentiments.

Bhāvodgāra (भावोद्गार) means emanation of sentiments.

Bhāsa (भास) means awareness. It can also mean radiance.

Bhikṣā (भिक्षा) means an act of alms or asking.

Bhinna (भिन्न) means that which is separate.

Bhīṣma (भीष्म) means stern. It is a prominent epithet for the veracious prince Devavrata (देवव्रत), son of King Śāntanu (शान्तनु) of the Kaurava (कौरव) dynasty and Jāhnavī-Gaṅgā (जाह्नवी-गङ्गा). He took a stern vow of celibacy and renounced the right to the throne of Hastināpura (हस्तिनापुर) so that his father could marry Satyavatī (सत्यवती).

Bhūta (भूत) means spirit or ghost. It can also mean living being. As an adjective, it can mean been, become, or past.

Bhūtagaṇa (भूतगण) means hosts of ghosts. It can also mean numerous beings or manifestations.

Bhūtagrāmam (भूतग्रामं) means a multitude of beings or a mass of beings.

Bhūta-Dṛṣṭi (भूत-दृष्टि) means the vision of seeing living beings.

Bhūtaprāṇī (भूतप्राणी) means living beings

Bhūta-Bhautika (भूत-भौतिक) means animate and inanimate or living and non-living.

Bhūtasamudāya (भूतसमुदाय) means the body and the senses that are the work (result) of the Pañcabhūta (पञ्चभूत).

Bhūmi (भूमि) means a place or land.

Bhūmikā (भूमिका) can mean preface, ground. It can also mean a story.

Bhṛgulatā (भृगुलता) means the footprint of Saptarṣi Bhṛgu (भृगु).

Bheda (भेद) means distinction, discrimination, or differentiation. It can also mean disunion or separation.

Bheda-Dṛṣṭi (भेद-दृष्टि) means discriminating-vision.

Bhoktā (भोक्ता) means experiencer or an enjoyer of the fruits.

Bhoktrutva (भोक्त्रुत्व) means enjoyership.

Bhoga (भोग) means to conclude, experience, or enjoy. It can also mean fruits that can be enjoyed or enjoyment objects.

Bhogabhūmi (भोगभूमि) means the region of enjoyment.

Bhogāyatana (भोगायतन) means the one who partakes in enjoyments. The gross body is the Bhogāyatana of an individual Jīva. Just as a householder lives in a house, a Jīva lives in the gross body.

Bhogārtha (भोगार्थ) means for the purpose of enjoyment.

Bhogya (भोग्य) means to be enjoyed or enjoyable.

Bhogya-Padārtha (भोग्य-पदार्थ) means to be enjoyed matter or an enjoyable matter.

Bhojana (भोजन) means food. It can also mean to eat.

Bhojya (भोज्य) means swallowable. It can also mean to be eaten or enjoyed.

Bhautika (भौतिक) means anything elemental or material.

Bhautika-Tāpa (भौतिक-ताप) means material sufferings such as those caused by humans, animals, or insects.

Bhrama (भ्रम) means delusion.

Bhrama-Jñāna (भ्रम-ज्ञान) means delusional knowledge.

Bhramamātra (भ्रममात्र) means delusional only.

Bhraṣṭa (भ्रष्ट) means fallen or ruined.

Bhrānti (भ्रान्ति) means delusion.

Cakra (चक्र) means wheel, circle, or discus.

Cakṣu (चक्षु) means eyes with the sense of sight.

Cañcala (चञ्चल) means unsteady, fickle, or moving back and forth.

Cañcalatā (चञ्चलता) means unsteadiness or fickleness.

Catura (चतुर) means astute, deft, or skillful.

Catura-Āśrama (चतुर-आश्रम) means the four stages of life: 1) bachelor student stage (ब्रह्मचर्य-आश्रम, Brahmacarya-Āśrama), 2) householder stage (गृहस्थ-आश्रम, Gṛhastha-Āśrama), 3) retired stage (वानप्रस्थ-आश्रम, Vānaprastha-Āśrama) and 4) renunciation stage (संन्यास-आश्रम, Saṃnyāsa-Āśrama).

Catura-Khāni (चतुर-खानि) means the four mines or kinds: 1) sweat-born (स्वेद-जा, Sveda-Jā), 2) germination-born (उद्भिज-जा, Udbhija-Jā), 3) egg-born (अण्ड-जा, Aṇḍa-Jā), and 4) placenta-born (जरायु-जा, Jarāyu-Jā).

Catura-Varṇa (चतुर-वर्ण) means the fourfold functional class system of the society. Śrīmad Bhagavad Gītā provides the classification in terms of four primary functions necessary for the sustainability of the humanity: 1) education, entrusted to the Brāhmaṇa, 2) security, entrusted to the Kṣatriya, 3) commerce, entrusted to the Vaiśya and 4) labor, entrusted to the Śūdra. The innate attributes of a Brāhmaṇa (ब्रह्म-प्रकृति, Brahma-Prakṛti) are provided in BG 18.42; a Kṣatriya (क्षात्र-प्रकृति, Kṣātra-Prakṛti) are in BG 18.43, a Vaiśya (वैश्य-प्रकृति, Vaiśya-Prakṛti) and a Śūdra (शूद्र-प्रकृति, Śūdra-Prakṛti) are in BG 18.44.

Catura-Vāṇī (चतुर-वाणी) means the four types of tones used in the chanting of Vedic hymns 1) Vaikharī (वैखरी, Mantra chanting with high tone), 2) Madhyamā (मध्यमा, Mantra chanting without lips moving so that it is inaudible to anyone), 3) Paśyantī (पश्यन्ती, Mantra chanting heartily without the tongue moving and the mind engrossed in the meaning of the chant), and 4) Parā (परा, Mantra chanting with inner disposition steady in the meaning of the chant providing bliss and the intellect becoming steadfast in the Self).

Caturvidha-Anna (चतुर्विध-अन्न) means the fourfold foods: 1) masticable (भक्ष्य, Bhakṣya), 2) swallowable (भोज्य, Bhojya), 3) lickable (लेह्य, Lehya) and 4) suckable (चोष्य, Coṣya).

Catuṣṭaya (चतुष्टय) means fourfold.

Camatkāra (चमत्कार) means miracle.

Camūm (चमूम्) means army or military force.

Cara (चर) means moving.

Caraṇa-kamala (चरण-कमल) means lotus-feet.

Caraṇa-Pūjā (चरण-पूजा) means to pay homage to a person by touching their feet or performing other prescribed rituals at their feet.

Carācara (चराचर) means moving and stationary.

Cala (चल) means movable.

Calāyamāna (चलायमान) means movable, unsteady, wavering, or unstable.

Cāṇḍāla (चाण्डाल) means an outcast, a person of the lowest and most despised of a mixed functional class born from a Śūdra father and a Brāhmaṇa mother. It is also used to describe dog eaters.

Cijjaḍa-Granthi (चिज्जड-ग्रन्थि) means a knot that is sentient (Cetana) in some part and insentient (Jaḍa) in some part.

Citta (चित्त) means the subconscious mind, characterized by an inner disposition of probing (अनुसंधानात्मक-वृत्ति, Anusaṃdhānātmaka-Vṛtti) within the mind and the intellect. Active even in the state of deep sleep (सुषुप्ति-अवस्था, Suṣupti-Avasthā), it is the substratum where dynamic impressions (संस्कार, Saṃskāra) of actions (कर्म, Karma) are embedded. It is the recorder and holder of past impressions, reactions, and desires, whether remembered consciously or not.

Cintana (चिन्तन) means thinking or reflecting.

Cintā (चिन्ता) means anxiety or worry.

Cintāmaṇi (चिन्तामणि) means a wish-fulfilling jewel.

Cuṭaki (चुटकि) means the thumb and the middle finger snap.

Cetana (चेतन) means the conscious element.

Cetanatattva (चेतनतत्त्व) means the conscious principle, the conscious element.

Cetanamātra (चेतनमात्र) means only the conscious.

Cetanasattā (चेतनसत्ता) means the conscious Reality.

Cetanā (चेतना) means consciousness, awareness, or apprehension.

Ceṣṭā (चेष्टा) means effort.

Caitanya (चैतन्य) means consciousness related to the Ātmā. It can also mean intelligence.

Coṣya (चोष्य) means suckable

Cyuta (च्युत) means moved or shaken.

Chala (छल) means deception.

Chāyā (छाया) means shadow.

Chāyāvāna (छायावान) means one with shadow.

Chinna-Bhinna (छिन्न-भिन्न) means to shatter, disband, or annihilate.

Dakṣiṇā (दक्षिणा) means offering or donation after the performance of rituals.

Dakṣiṇāyana (दक्षिणायन) means movement of the sun towards the south. It is a compound word from Dakṣiṇa (दक्षिण) meaning south and Ayanam (अयनम्) meaning movement, path. This movement begins a day after the summer solstice around June 21 and continues for six months to the winter solstice around December 21.

Dagdha (दग्ध) means to burn or to incinerate.

Daṇḍa (दण्ड) means punishment. It can also mean a stick.

Daṇḍavat-Praṇāma (दण्डवत्-प्रणाम) is a process of paying respectful obeisance and total surrender by lying fully prostrate on the ground like a stick.

Daṇḍita (दण्डित) means punished.

Dama (दम) means restraint of the senses.

Damana (दमन) means restraining, taming, subduing, or overpowering. It can also mean self-restraint or self-control.

Dambha (दम्भ) means hypocrisy.

Dambhī (दम्भी) means a hypocrite.

Dayā (दया) means kindness, mercy, or compassion.

Daridra (दरिद्र) means indigent, poor, or needy.

Darpa (दर्प) means arrogance, haughtiness, or insolence.

Darśana (दर्शन) means vision, seeing, or ocular perception. It can also mean divine experience.

Darśī (दर्शी) means one that sees or knows.

Dākṣya (दाक्ष्य) means skill, cleverness, or dexterity.

Dāna (दान) means the act of giving, donation, or charity.

Dānava (दानव) are a class of Asura or demons held to be implacable enemies of the deities or Sura. They are the descendants of Danu (daughter of Prajāpati Dakṣa) and Saptarṣi Kaśyapa

Dārśanika (दार्शनिक) means acquainted or connected with philosophical systems.

Dāsatva (दासत्व) means servitude.

Dāsī (दासी) means a female in servitude.

Dāsya (दास्य) means serving in general. It can also mean serving the divine.

Digdarśana (दिग्दर्शन) means to show direction or to point out a general mode or manner.

Divi (दिवि) means the sky or the space.

Divya (दिव्य) means divine.

Diśā (दिशा) means direction.

Dīna (दीन) means miserable, wretched, or afflicted.

Dīpa-Śikhā (दीप-शिखा) means lamp flame.

Duḥkha (दुःख) means grief, sorrow, or suffering.

Duḥkhadāyī (दुःखदायी) means painful or agonizing.

Duḥkharupa (दुःखरुप) means grievous.

Dundubhi (दुन्दुभि) means a large kettledrum.

Duratyayā (दुरत्यया) means insurmountable or difficult to overcome

Durāgraha (दुराग्रह) means foolish obstinacy, headstrongness, or pertinacity.

Durācārī (दुराचारी) means one with evil conduct or who is vicious.

Durgati (दुर्गति) means a bad destination, lousy end, hell, misfortune, or degradation.

Durgamya (दुर्गम्य) means difficult to enter, difficult to traverse, or difficult to crossover.

Durgamyatā (दुर्गम्यता) means difficulty to crossover.

Durjaya (दुर्जय) means invincible or challenging to be conquered.

Durbuddhi (दुर्बुद्धि) means evil-minded or with bad intellect.

Durmati (दुर्मति) means blockhead, weak-minded, or foolish.

Durlabha (दुर्लभ) means difficult to be obtained, hard, scarce, or rare.

Durvāsanā (दुर्वासना) means malevolence, malicious impressions, or bad inclinations.

Durviejñeya (दुर्विज्ञेय) means difficult to understand or abstruse.

Duṣkṛta (दुष्कृत) means bad deed.

Duṣṭa (दुष्ट) means evil or bad.

Dūṣita (दूषित) means defiled.

Dṛḍha (दृढ) means unyielding, assertive, or firm.

Dṛḍhatā (दृढता) means assertiveness or determination.

Dṛḍhavratī (दृढव्रती) means a steadfast devotee. It can also mean persistent.

Dṛśya (दृश्य) means visible or conspicuous. It can also mean visible objects.

Dṛṣṭā (दृष्टा) means observer.

Dṛṣṭānta (दृष्टान्त) means an example or a paragon.

Dṛṣṭi (दृष्टि) means perspective, view, or sight.

Deva (देव) means deity. They are the descendants of Aditi (daughter of Prajāpati Dakṣa) and Saptarṣi Kaśyapa. The terms Deva (देव), Devatā (देवता), or Sura (सुर) are interchangeable terms and mean deity.

Devagaṇa (देवगण) means mass of deities.

Devarṣi (देवर्षि) means divine sage, generally meaning Nārada Muni.

Deśa (देश) means space, region, or place.

Deśa-Kāla (देश-काल) means space and time.

Deśa-Kāla-Vastu (देश-काल-वस्तु) means space-time-material

Deśa-Pariccheda (देश-परिच्छेद) means space bounded. That which exists in one place or region but not in others is Deśa Pariccheda.

Deśa-Paricchedya (देश-परिच्छेद्य) means one that is bounded by space, that which is in one space and not in another.

Deha (देह) means body.

Dehadhārī (देहधारी) means embodied.

Deha-Sambandha (देह-सम्बन्ध) means connection with the body.

Deha-Sākṣī (देह-साक्षी) means the witness in the body.

Dehātīta (देहातीत) means one who has transcended the body.

Dehātmavāda (देहात्मवाद) means a belief that the body is the Ātmā.

Dehātmavādī (देहात्मवादी) means those who believe the body is the Ātmā.

Dehādhyāsa (देहाध्यास) means delusional superimposition of the body on the Ātmā.

Dehābhimāna (देहाभिमान) means I-ness sense in the body or considering the body as the Ātmā.

Dehābhimānī (देहाभिमानी) means one who has an I-ness sense in the body or one who considers his body as his Ātmā.

Dehendriya (देहेन्द्रिय) means the body and senses.

Daitya (दैत्य) are a class of Asura or demons held to be implacable enemies of the deities or Sura. They are the descendants of Diti (daughter of Prajāpati Dakṣa) and Saptarṣi Kaśyapa.

Daiva (दैव) means the presiding deity. There are various presiding deities that control the mind, senses, and others. The Adhideva (अधिदेव) of eyes is the sun-deity, Adhideva of ears is the directions. The power of these presiding deities is known as Adhidaiva-Śakti (अधिदैव-शक्ति).

Daivika-Tāpa (दैविक-ताप) means natural afflictions such as storms, floods, or droughts.

Daivī (दैवी) means divine.

Daivī-Sampatti (दैवी-सम्पत्ति) means divine attributes or assets.

Daivī-Sampadā (दैवी-सम्पदा) means divine attributes.

Daihika-Tāpa (दैहिक-ताप) means bodily and mental afflictions. Diseases like fever and cancer are body-related sufferings. Anger, greed, and passion are mental afflictions.

Doṣa (दोष) means fault, flaw, or defect.

Doṣa-Dṛṣṭi (दोष-दृष्टि) means one who sees faults or one whose perspective is spiteful or with malice.

Doṣavat (दोषवत्) means with a fault or with a flaw.

Dravībhūta (द्रवीभूत) means sentimental. It can also mean melting or liquefying.

Dravya (द्रव्य) means substance.

Dravya-Guṇa-Karma (द्रव्य-गुण-कर्म) means substance-attribute-act.

Droha (द्रोह) means hostility, injury, treachery, or offense.

Dvandva (द्वन्द्व) means duality, pair, or couple.

Dvāra (द्वार) means gate, door, or entrance.

Dvija (द्विज) means one who is born twice. Animals born from eggs are believed to be born twice, when the egg is produced and the second time when the eggs are out, like birds. Yajñopavīta Saṃskāra (one of the sixteen rites of passage in a person's life) is considered a second birth; hence, a person such as a Brāhmaṇa wearing Yajñopavīta (यज्ञोपवीत, sacred thread) is called a Dvija.

Dveṣa (द्वेष) means antipathy, hate, spite, or despite.

Dveṣī (द्वेषी) means antagonist, hateful, spiteful, or despiteful.

Dvaita (द्वैत) means duality.

Dhanurvidyā (धनुर्विद्या) means the science of archery.

Dhartā (धर्ता) means holder.

Dharma (धर्म) means righteousness, virtue, or morality. It can also mean duty. It can also mean attributes, characteristics, or nature. The word 'Dharma' (धर्म) is derived from the root Dhṛ (धृ), meaning 'to hold,' 'to bear,' 'to carry' or 'to support.' धारणात् धर्मः - that which holds together or supports is Dharma. In this sense, Dharma encompasses all ethical, moral, social, and other values or principles, codes of conduct, and behavior that contribute to the well-being, sustenance, and harmonious functioning of individuals, societies, and nations and prevent their disintegration. The term Dharma also means religion.

Dharmamaya (धर्ममय) means righteous, virtuous, or moral.

Dharmayuddha (धर्मयुद्ध) means righteous war.

Dharmātmā (धर्मात्मा) means one who is virtuous or moral.

Dharmī (धर्मी) means one whose constituent nature

Dhātā (धाता) means sustainer or supporter.

Dhānya (धान्य) means grain.

Dhāraṇa (धारण) means to hold or to maintain.

Dhāraṇa-Kartā (धारण-कर्ता) means one who holds or who maintains.

Dhāraṇā (धारणा) means concentration, introspective focus, or one-pointedness of the mind. The root of the word is Dhṛ (धृ), meaning «to hold, maintain, or keep.»

Dhīra (धीर) means a person with fortitude, steadfastness, or resoluteness. It can also mean a wise person.

Dhūrta (धूर्त) means a swindler or a cheat. It can also mean cunning, crafty, or fraudulent.

Dhṛti (धृति) means sustentation, holding, or supporting. It can also mean resolve, fortitude, endurance, patience, or steadiness.

Dhairya (धैर्य) means patience or calmness.

Dhyāna (ध्यान) means meditation, contemplation, or reflection. Meditation means one-pointed thought after withdrawing the mind and the sense organs, like the ears, from sound and fixing the mind on the inner self with a constant thought in an unbroken stream to perceive the Self.

Dhyeya (ध्येय) means to be meditated on.

Dhruva (ध्रुव) means unwavering.

Dhvaṃsa (ध्वंस) means destruction.

Ekatā (एकता) means harmony, unison, or oneness.

Ekatva (एकत्व) means oneness or unity.

Ekatva-Dṛṣṭi (एकत्व-दृष्टि) means seeing everything in oneness or seeing everything as only the Brahman.

Eka-Deśī (एक-देशी) means belonging to only one region.

Eka-Deśīya (एक-देशीय) means limited to only one region.

Ekamātra (एक-मात्र) means only one.

Ekarasa (एकरस) means who always remains the same, always the same, or that never changes.

Ekākī (एकाकी) means alone.

Ekāgra (एकाग्र) means fixed on one object or point, concentrated, or focused.

Ekāgratā (एकाग्रता) means concentration or focus.

Ekānta (एकान्त) means in a lonely or solitary place.

Ekāntika (एकान्तिक) means final or ultimate.

Eti (एति) means arrival or approach. It can also mean to receive or to get.

Eva (एव) means too, indeed, or certainly.

Evam (एवम्) means thus, and thus, and then, in this way, in such a manner, such, or so.

Gaṇa (गण) means hosts of entities, groups, or classes of entities. It can also mean class (of animate and inanimate beings).

Gaṇanā (गणना) means reckoning or considering. It can also mean counting.

Gata (गत) means gone or free.

Gata-Sandeha (गत-सन्देह) means free of doubts.

Gati (गति) means destination or abode. It can also mean movement, motion, or flow.

Gadā (गदा) means a spherical-end mace, a weapon with a spherical head mounted on a shaft. It is the weapon of Śrī Hanumāna (हनुमान), Bhīma (भीम), and others.

Gandha (गन्ध) means odor or fragrance.

Gandharva (गन्धर्व) are generally known as minstrels with superb musical skills and are married to Apsarā (अप्सरा) in the world of deities. They act as messengers between the deities and the humans. In Vedic times, marriages contracted by mutual consent and without formal rituals were known as "Gandharva Vivāha."

Gamana (गमन) means going.

Gamanāgamana (गमनागमन) means going and coming.

Gambhīra (गम्भीर) means solemn, deep, or serious.

Garbha (गर्भ) means embryo.

Galita (गलित) means melted, lost, perished, decayed, dropped, or loosened.

Gahana (गहन) means deep, impenetrable, inexplicable, or hard to be understood.

Gāḍha (गाढ) means deep or strong.

Gāndhāra (गान्धार) was an ancient region in the Kabul, Peshawar, Swat, and Taxila areas of what is now northwestern Pakistan and eastern Afghanistan.

Guḍākā (गुडाका) means sleep.

Guḍākeśa (गुडाकेश) means one who has a sleep (darkness, ignorance) under control, generally referred to as Arjuna (अर्जुन).

Guṇa (गुण) in general means attributes, qualities, or characteristics. In Vedantic terms, it means the constituents of Prakṛti or constituents of all material substances. There are three constituents, viz. Sattva (सत्त्व) or Sattvaguṇa (सत्त्वगुण), Rajas (रजस्) or Rajoguṇa (रजोगुण) and Tamas (तमस्) or Tamoguṇa (तमोगुण).

Guṇa-Karma-Vibhāga (गुण-कर्म-विभाग) means the distinction between the constituents and actions of Prakṛti.

Guṇa-Doṣa (गुण-दोष) means the fault of virtues and vices, merits and demerits.

Guṇa-Pariṇāma (गुण-परिणाम) means the transformations of the constituents.

Guṇa-Vibhāga (गुण-विभाग) means work or products of the constituents of Prakṛti. Collectively it includes the following: The five great elements (पञ्चभूत, Pañcabhūta): 1) earth (पृथ्वी, Pṛthvī), 2) water (आप, Āpa), 3) fire (अग्नि, Agni), 4) wind (वायु, Vāyu) and 5) space (आकाश, Ākāśa); 6) mind (मनस्, Manas); 7) intellect (बुद्धि, Buddhi); 8) ego (अहंकार, Ahaṃkāra); the five cognition organs (पञ्च-ज्ञानेन्द्रिय, Pañca-Jñānendriya): 9) skin (त्वक, Tvaka) with the sense of touch, 10) tongue (रसना, Rasanā) with the sense of taste, 11) eyes (चक्षु, Cakṣu) with the sense of sight, 12) nose (घ्राण, Ghrāṇa) with the sense of smell, 13) ears (श्रोत्र, Śrotra) with the sense of hearing; the five action organs (पञ्च-कर्मेन्द्रिय, Pañca-Karmendriya): 14) mouth (वाक, Vāka) with the organ of voice, 15) hands (पाणि, Pāṇi) with the organ to receive, gather, collect (ग्रहण, Grahaṇa) and hold (धारण, Dhāraṇa), 16) feet (पाद, Pāda) with the organ to walk, move, locomotion (गमन, Gamana), 17) anus (पायु, Pāyu) with the organ of excretion, 18) genitals (उपस्थ, Upastha) with the organ of reproduction; the five vital breaths of air (पञ्च-प्राण, Pañca-Prāṇa): 19) Prāṇa-Vāyu (प्राण-वायु), 20) Apāna-Vāyu (अपान-वायु), 21) Samāna-Vāyu (समान-वायु), 22) Udāna-Vāyu (उदान-वायु), 23) Vyāna-Vāyu (व्यान-वायु) ; and the five objects of senses (पञ्च-विषय, Pañca-Viṣaya): 24) sound (शब्द, Śabda), 25) touch (स्पर्श, Sparśa), 26) form (रूप, Rupa), 27) taste (रस, Rasa), and 28) smell (गन्ध, Gandha).

Guṇātīta (गुणातीत) means free from or beyond the constituents of Prakṛti, a transcendent sage.

Guru (गुरु) means a preceptor or a spiritual master. In general terms, it means a teacher or a guide.

Gurukula (गुरुकुल) means ancient education system wherein disciples lived with the preceptor in his home.

Guru-Dakṣiṇā (गुरु-दक्षिणा) means a traditional gesture of acknowledgment, respect, and thanks to a preceptor, which may be monetary, but may also be a special task a preceptor wants the disciple to accomplish.

Guhya (गुह्य) means profound, secret, private, or confidential.

Guhyatama (गुह्यतम) means most profound.

Gṛhastha-Āśrama (गृहस्थ-आश्रम) means the second stage of an individual's married life from the age of 25 to the age of 50, with the duties of maintaining a household, raising a family, educating own children, and leading a family-centered and virtuous social life. Gṛhastha stage is the most important of all stages in a sociological context, as human beings in this stage not only pursue a moral life, they produce food and wealth that sustain people in other stages of life, as well as the continuation of progeny. The stage also represents where the most intense physical, sexual, emotional, occupational, social, and material attachments exist in a human being's life.

Gopanīya (गोपनीय) means secret, private, or confidential.

Gomukha (गोमुख) means a musical horn.

Govinda (गोविन्द) means one who tends cows, an epithet of Śrī Kṛṣṇa.

Gauṇa (गौण) means minor, secondary, or subordinate.

Gaurakṣya (गौरक्ष्य) means protection of the cows.

Ghaniṣṭa (घनिष्ट) means close.

Grantha (ग्रन्थ) means a scripture.

Grasta (ग्रस्त) means stricken.

Grahaṇa (ग्रहण) means to grasp, take, or seize. It can also mean to hold.

Grahaṇa-Tyāga (ग्रहण-त्याग) means grasping-rejecting, taking-leaving, or holding-abandoning.

Grāsa (ग्रास) means a bitten morsel or a mouthful. It can also mean eclipse.

Grāhaka (ग्राहक) means one who grasps or seizes.

Grāhya (ग्राह्य) means can be grasped, held, seized, or taken.

Grīvā (ग्रीवा) means neck, back part of neck, or nape.

Glāni (ग्लानि) means debility, decline, or decay.

Ghaṭa (घट) means a pot.

Ghaṭākāśa (घटाकाश) means a pot enclosed space.

Ghaṭī (घटी) means time consisting of 24 minutes. There are 2.5 Ghaṭī in an hour.

Ghaṭī-Yantra (घटी-यन्त्र) means a clock, any contrivance for measuring time, or an hourglass.

Ghṛta (घृत) means Ghī (clarified butter).

Ghora (घोर) means fearful, severe, or grave.

Ghrāṇa (घ्राण) means nose with the sense of smell.

Haṃsa-Vṛtti (हंस-वृत्ति) means best welfare attitude towards all. Haṃsa (हंस) means a swan. It is said that a swan can drink milk from a mixture of milk and water by separating milk and discarding water. It is changing a bad attitude to a good attitude, even after hearing or seeing bad things about anyone.

Haṭha (हठ) means by force or obstinacy.

Hanana (हनन) means to slay, kill, or destroy.

Han (हन्) means to kill or hurt.

Harṣa (हर्ष) means joy or happiness.

Harṣa-Śoka (हर्ष-शोक) means joy-sorrow or happiness-lamentation.

Halāhala (हलाहल) means the poison produced during the Samudra-Manthana (समुद्र-मन्थन) when the ocean of milk (Kṣīra-Sāgara, क्षीर-सागर) was churned by the Devatā (deities) and the Asura (demons) to procure Ambrosia (Amṛta).

Havana (हवन) means a votive ritual wherein offerings are poured into the consecrated fire. It is commonly known as Homa (होम) or Yajña (यज्ञ), and the term is derived from the root Hu (हु), meaning to pour into the fire, to offer or sacrifice. Sacrificers pour offerings and libations into the consecrated fire with hymns sung to the sounds of Svāhā (स्वाहा). The oblations and offerings typically consist of Ghī, milk, curd, sugar, saffron, grains, coconut, scented water, incense, seeds, petals, and herbs.

Havi (हवि) means anything offered as an oblation in the consecrated fire, such as Ghī, milk, curd, sugar, saffron, grains, coconut, scented water, incense, seeds, petals, and herbs.

Hasta (हस्त) means "is there." It can also mean a hand.

Hastī (हस्ती) means an elephant.

Hi (हि) means undoubtedly, indeed, surely, certainly because, of course, also, or even.

Hiṃsā (हिंसा) means injury or harm. It is said to be of three kinds: 1) mental as bearing malice; 2) verbal, as abusive language and 3) personal, as acts of violence.

Hī (ही) means too or also.

Hīnatā (हीनता) means inferiority or deficiency.

Hutam (हुतम्) means oblations offered. It can also mean an act of votive ritual of offering oblations.

Hṛta (हृत) means taken, seized, or lost.

Hṛdayadeśa (हृदयदेश) means the bright space in the heart for contemplation and immediate perception of the Brahman.

Hṛdayastha (हृदयस्थ) means resting or residing in the heart.

Hṛdayākāśa (हृदयाकाश) means the bright space in the heart for contemplation and immediate perception of the Brahman.

Hṛdya (हृद्य) means dear to the heart. It can also mean in the heart, internal, or inward.

Hṛṣī (हृषी) means pleasing.

Hṛṣīka (हृषीक) means a body faculty or the senses.

Hṛṣīkeśa (हृषीकेश) means the Lord of the senses, one who is a master over his senses or has control over the senses. An epithet of Śrī Kṛṣṇa.

Hetu (हेतु) means cause.

Heya (हेय) means to be left or to abandon.

Heyatā (हेयता) means abandonability.

Homa (होम) means a votive ritual wherein offerings are poured into the consecrated fire. It is commonly known as Havana or Yajña, and the term is derived from the root Hu (हु), meaning to pour into the fire, to offer or sacrifice. Sacrificers pour offerings and libations into the consecrated fire with Vedic hymns sung to the sounds of Svāhā. The oblations and offerings typically consist of Ghī, milk, curd, sugar, saffron, grains, coconut, scented water, incense, seeds, petals, and herbs.

Hrī (ह्री) means modesty or shyness from immoral conduct.

Icchā (इच्छा) means desire or wish.

Icchita (इच्छित) means desired, wished for, or yearned for.

Iḍā (इडा) means the lunar Nāḍī that begins and ends on the left side of the Suṣumnā Nāḍī. It is cool and nurturing by nature and is said to control all mental processes and the more feminine aspects of our personality. Whitish color like that of the full moon is used to represent the subtle vibrational attribute of Iḍā.

Iti (इति) means thus, in this manner, or like that.

Iti Śrī (इति श्री) means the end.

Idaṃ (इदं) means this.

Idaṃtā (इदंता) means this-ness.

Idaṃrupa (इदंरूप) means this form.

Indriya (इन्द्रिय) means the sense organs. The five sense organs are the eyes, tongue, nose, skin, and ear to sense: form (रुप, Rupa), taste (रस, Rasa), smell (गन्ध, Gandha), touch (स्पर्श, Sparśa) and sound (शब्द, Śabda) respectively.

Indriya-Grāmaṃ (इन्द्रिय-ग्रामम्) means the entire group of the senses.

Indriya-Nirapekṣa (इन्द्रिय-निरपेक्ष) means independent of the senses.

Indriya-Sāpekṣa (इन्द्रिय-सापेक्ष) means sense dependent.

Indriyātīta (इन्द्रियातीत) means beyond the senses.

Indriyārāmī (इन्द्रियारामी) means one who is engrossed in the delight of the sense-objects.

Indhana (इन्धन) means firewood.

Iṣṭa (इष्ट) means coveted, sought after, desired, or revered.

Iha (इह) means here.

Ihalaukika (इहलौकिक) means related to this world.

Īrṣyā (ईर्ष्या) means jealousy or envy.

Īś (ईश्) means one who commands.

Īśvara (ईश्वर) means the Lord. Īśvara is the Saguṇa-Brahman, the Brahman with attributes.

Īśvara-Arpaṇa (ईश्वर-अर्पण) means offering to the Lord.

Īśvarīya (ईश्वरीय) means Lordly.

Jagata (जगत) means the world.

Jaṅgama (जङ्गम) means movable.

Jaṭharāgni (जठराग्नि) means the digestive stomach fire or gastric juice.

Jaḍa (जड) means insentient, inanimate, or lifeless.

Jaḍa-Svarupa (जड-स्वरुप) means inanimate or lifeless form.

Jana (जन) means a person.

Janārdana (जनार्दन) means the one who inflicts pain on evil persons, an epithet of Śrī Kṛṣṇa.

Janita (जनित) means born, produced, or begotten.

Janma (जन्म) means birth.

Janma-Janmāṃtara (जन्म-जन्मांतर) means birth and rebirth

Janmāṃtara (जन्मांतर) means another state of existence or another birth.

Janya (जन्य) means caused by or caused by someone.

Japa (जप) means repetitive chanting of Vedic hymns, Mantra, or names of divine manifestations.

Jaya (जय) means victory.

Jarā (जरा) means old age.

Jarāyu-Jā (जरायु-जा) means placenta born.

Jala (जल) means water.

Jalāśaya (जलाशय) means a reservoir or basin.

Jāgṛti (जागृति) means awakening.

Jāgrata (जाग्रत) means awake or conscious.

Jāti (जाति) means class or community.

Jāti-Dharma (जाति-धर्म) means traditions and duties of a class in which one is born.

Jālandhara-Bandha (जालन्धर-बन्ध). जालन्धर is a compound word from Jāla (जाल) meaning web or net and Dhara (धर) meaning holding. The term Bandha (बन्ध) means locking or contracting. It is performed by extending the neck and elevating the sternum (breastbone) before dropping the head so that the chin may rest on the chest. Meanwhile, the tongue pushes up against the palate in the mouth

Jijñāsā (जिज्ञासा) means desire to know.

Jijñāsu (जिज्ञासु) means a seeker, one who is keen on knowing, desirous of knowing, or inquisitive.

Jitātmā (जितात्मा) means one who is self-controlled, one who has subdued his Ātmā in the form of the conglomerate of the body, senses, mind, and intellect.

Jitendriya (जितेन्द्रिय) means one who has subdued his senses. The five sense organs are the eyes, tongue, nose, skin, and ear to sense form (रुप, Rupa), taste (रस, Rasa), smell (गन्ध, Gandha), touch (स्पर्श, Sparśa) and sound (शब्द, Śabda) respectively.

Jitendriyatā (जितेन्द्रियता) means subduedness of senses.

Jīva (जीव) means the conscious element in the body, which is the doer-enjoyer. It is the embodied Ātmā, the delimited Ātmā. It is the pure Ātmā on whom I-ness sense of the body, senses, mind, and intellect are superimposed due to nescience. It is referred to as Jīvātmā (जीवात्मा), Dehī (देही), Śarīrī (शरीरी), Jīva-Sākṣī (जीव-साक्षी), Soul, or Spirit. Just as there is no distinction between space enclosed in a pot and the pervasive space, upon the destruction of the pot is only the pervasive space. Likewise, there is no distinction between the pure Jīvātmā and the Paramātmā (the Supreme Being).

Jīvana (जीवन) means life.

Jīvanmukta (जीवन्मुक्त) means one who has realized knowledge of the supreme imperishable Reality and is free from the bondage of the world of birth and death.

Jīvātmā (जीवात्मा) means the conscious element in the body, which is the doer-enjoyer. It is the embodied Ātmā, the delimited Ātmā. It is the pure Ātmā on whom I-ness sense of the body, senses, mind, and intellect are superimposed due to nescience. It is referred to as Jīva (जीव), Dehī (देही), Śarīrī (शरीरी), Jīva-Sākṣī (जीव-साक्षी), Soul, or Spirit. Just as there is no distinction between space enclosed in a pot and the pervasive space, upon the destruction of the pot is only the pervasive space. Likewise, there is no distinction between the pure Jīvātmā and the Paramātmā (the Supreme Being)

Jñāta (ज्ञात) means known.

Jñātā (ज्ञाता) means the knower.

Jñāna (ज्ञान) means knowledge in general.

Jñāna-Cakṣu (ज्ञान-चक्षु) means the eyes of wisdom.

Jñānaniṣṭha (ज्ञाननिष्ठ) means engaged in cultivating true knowledge

Jñānaniṣṭha-Citta (ज्ञाननिष्ठ-चित्त) means mind in transcendent knowledge.

Jñāna-Niṣṭhā (ज्ञान-निष्ठा) means the discipline of knowledge.

Jñānavāna (ज्ञानवान) means knowledgeable or undeluded.

Jñāna-Vijñāna (ज्ञान-विज्ञान): Through preceptors and scriptures, knowing the Ātmā and the Anātmā is called knowledge (Jñāna), and to experience it uniquely is called realized knowledge (Vijñāna). In other words, understanding the substance spoken in the scriptures is called Jñāna, and experiencing intuitively (Aparokṣa) the understood subject of the scriptures is called Vijñāna.

Jñāna-Sādhya (ज्ञान-साध्य) means achieved by knowledge.

Jñānāgni (ज्ञानाग्नि) means the fire of knowledge.

Jñānādhyāsa (ज्ञानाध्यास) means delusional knowledge, like the knowledge of a snake in a rope.

Jñānāvasthita (ज्ञानावस्थित) means in the state of knowledge, occupied by wisdom or engaged in cultivating wisdom.

Jñānī (ज्ञानी) means a knower, one who is undeluded, wise, or learned. It can also mean one who has realized knowledge of the Brahman.

Jñānījana (ज्ञानीजन) means undeluded, wise, or learned persons.

Jñeya (ज्ञेय) means to be known or ought to be known.

Jyoti (ज्योति) means light.

Jyotirmaya (ज्योतिर्मय) means consisting of light or brilliance.

Kaṭibaddha (कटिबद्ध) means ready or prepared.

Kaṭu (कटु) means pungent. Onions, ginger, and chili pepper have a pungent taste. It is created by the presence of volatile aromatic oils, resins, and mustard.

Kaṭhora (कठोर) means harsh, hard, or severe.

Kaṇamātra (कणमात्र) means an iota or infinitesimal component.

Kathā (कथा) means devotional narrations.

Kathana (कथन) means narration or discourse.

Kadācit (कदाचित्) means at some time, at any time, perhaps, possibly, maybe, or never.

Kadācitka (कदाचित्क) means probable.

Kapaṭa (कपट) means fraud.

Kapi-Dhvaja (कपि-ध्वज) means a monkey-banner or a monkey imprinted flag.

Kapilā (कपिला) means brown.

Kapha (कफ) means phlegm, one of the body's three humors.

Kamalapatrākṣa (कमलपत्राक्ष) means lotus-eyed or the one with lotus leaf eyes

Kampāyamāna (कम्पायमान) means trembling or vibrating.

Karaṇa (करण) means an instrument, means. Various kinds of instruments through which actions materialize are enumerated as A) the five cognitive senses (पञ्च-ज्ञानेन्द्रिय, Pañca-Jñānendriya): 1) skin (त्वक, Tvaka) with the sense of touch, 2) tongue (रसना, Rasanā) with the sense of taste, 3) eyes (चक्षु, Cakṣu) with the sense of sight, 4) nose (घ्राण, Ghrāṇa) with the sense of smell and 5) ears (श्रोत्र, Śrotra) with the sense of hearing, B) the five action faculties (पञ्च-कर्मेन्द्रिय, Pañca-Karmendriya): 1) mouth (वाक, Vāka) with the faculty of voice, 2) hands (पाणि, Pāṇi) with the sense of grasping (Grahaṇa) and holding (Dhāraṇa), 3) feet (पाद, Pāda) with the sense of locomotion (Gamana), 4) anus (पायु, Pāyu) with the sense of excretion and 5) genitals (उपस्थ, Upastha) with the sense of reproduction, C) the mind and D) the intellect.

Karāmalakavata (करामलकवत) means just like a walnut within one's grip. It is a compound word from Kara (कर) meaning hand or grip, Amalaka (अमलक) meaning walnut, and Vata (वत) meaning like.

Karuṇā (करुणा) means compassion or pity.

Karuṇāmaya (करुणामय) means compassionate.

Kartavya (कर्तव्य) means duty.

Kartavyatā (कर्तव्यता) means necessity, obligation, or the state of being necessary to be done.

Kartavya-Buddhi (कर्तव्य-बुद्धि) means duty-bound intellect.

Kartā (कर्ता) means doer.

Kartāpana (कर्तापन) means doership.

Kartā-Buddhi (कर्ता-बुद्धि) means doer-intellect or doer sense.

Kartā-Bhoktā (कर्ता-भोक्ता) means doer-experiencer.

Karttṛtva (कर्त्तृत्व) means doership.

Karttṛtva-Ahaṃkāra (कर्त्तृत्व-अहंकार) means doership-ego.

Karttṛtva-Buddhi (कर्त्तृत्व-बुद्धि) means doership-intellect.

Karttṛtvādhyāsa (कर्त्तृत्वाध्यास) means doership delusion.

Karttṛtvābhimāna (कर्त्तृत्वाभिमान) means doership I-ness or doership-ego.

Karma (कर्म) means action, act, or deed in general. From a Vedantic perspective, a good or bad activity that produces emotion (Bhāva, भाव) in humans is called Karma.

Karmakāṇḍa (कर्म-काण्ड) means that part of Śruti (श्रुति) or the Vedas, which relates to ceremonial acts and sacrificial rites directed towards material benefits or liberation.

Karma-Tyāga (कर्म-त्याग) means relinquishment of action.

Karma-Phala (कर्म-फल) means fruits of action.

Karmabhūmi (कर्मभूमि) means a region of action.

Karma-Racita (कर्म-रचित) means created by Karma.

Karma-Vibhāga (कर्म-विभाग) means mutual interaction among the products (गुण-विभाग, Guṇa-Vibhāga) of the constituents of Prakṛti.

Karma-Saṃskāra (कर्म-संस्कार) means a dynamic impression of righteous or unrighteous action. Collectively they are dynamic psychological imprints left in the subconscious by actions, whether conscious or unconscious, internal or external, desirable or undesirable. They influence a person's nature, response, and state of mind. These imprints are not merely passive vestiges of actions and intentions but dynamic forces constantly pushing a Jīva. These impressions wait to return to the conscious level of the mind, influencing the future in the form of expectations, sense of self-worth, habits, innate dispositions, and emotions, propelling one's life and generating future actions. They are referred to as behavioral traits either as default from birth or perfected over time through conscious shaping of the conscience.

Karma-Hīnatā (कर्म-हीनता) means deficient action or inferior action.

Karmādhikārī (कर्माधिकारी) means one who has fitness in Karma or is qualified to engage in Karma.

Karmī (कर्मी) means a doer. It can also mean one who acts by the Śāstra.

Karmendriya (कर्मेन्द्रिय) means the five action organs: 1) mouth (वाक, Vāka) with the organ of voice, 2) hands (पाणि, Pāṇi) with the organ to grasp, receive, gather, collect (ग्रहण, Grahaṇa) and hold (धारण, Dhāraṇa), 3) feet (पाद, Pāda) with the organ to walk, move or for locomotion (गमन, Gamana), 4) anus (पायु, Pāyu) with the organ of excretion and 5) genitals (उपस्थ, Upastha) with the organ of reproduction.

Kalpa (कल्प) means a day of Brahmā or 4.32 billion years.

Kalpanā (कल्पना) means imagination or creating in the mind.

Kalpavṛkṣa (कल्पवृक्ष) means a wish-fulfilling divine tree.

Kalpita (कल्पित) means imagined, made up, fabricated, or fallacious.

Kalyāṇa (कल्याण) means good or benefit.

Kalyāṇakārī (कल्याणकारी) means beneficial.

Kavaca (कवच) means chest armor.

Kaścit (कश्चित्) means someone.

Kaṣāya (कषाय) means astringent. Pomegranates, chickpeas, and parsley have an astringent taste. It is a flavor of dryness produced by tannins in the bark, leaves, and outer rinds of fruits. It can also mean contamination or attachment to worldly objects.

Kaṣṭa (कष्ट) means difficult, grievous, or painful.

Kaṣṭatara (कष्टतर) or more difficult.

Kastūrī-Mṛga (कस्तूरी-मृग) means a musk deer. The musk gland is found only in adult males and lies in a sac between the genitals and the umbilicus.

Kā (का) means what (is the purpose of).

Kāñcana (काञ्चन) means gold.

Kāṇḍa (काण्ड) means a component or section.

Kāntimāna (कान्तिमान) means radiant or shining.

Kāma (काम) means desire, wish, passion, lust, the pleasure of the senses, the aesthetic enjoyment of life, affection, or love.

Kāmadhenu (कामधेनु) means the divine cow of Indra, the king of the deities. To the one in possession, Kāmadhenu is said to provide all coveted objects of desire.

Kāmanā (कामना) means desire, intense craving, pleasure-seeking, longing, or yearning.

Kāmya (काम्य) means desirable or amiable.

Kāyaratā (कायरता) means cowardice.

Kāra (कार) suffix is an agentive suffix. It converts a noun to a related noun that describes the subject. For example, कला (art) + कार = कलाकार (artist), संगीत (music) + कार = संगीतकार (composer)

Kāraka (कारक) means instruments that bring about action.

Kāraṇa (कारण) means a cause, reason. That which produces an act (कार्य, Kārya) is known as Kāraṇa. There are two types of Kāraṇa: 1) Upādāna-Kāraṇa (उपादान-कारण): Material cause. That which enters the work and without which work cannot sustain is known as Upādāna-Kāraṇa. Like clay is the Upādāna-Kāraṇa of a pot, and 2) Nimitta-Kāraṇa (निमित्त-कारण)): Instrumental cause. That exists neutral before the work and whose destruction does not destroy the work. Like the potter wheel, or a stick is Nimitta-Kāraṇa of a pot.

Kāraṇatā (कारणता) means causality or causation.

Kāraṇa-Śarīra (कारण-शरीर) means the causal body.

Kārya (कार्य) means work, action, what is done, or the effect of a cause.

Kāryarupa (कार्यरूप) means functional form.

Kāla (काल) means time.

Kālakūṭa (कालकूट) means a black mass, the poison produced during the Samudra Manthana when the ocean of milk (Kṣīra-Sāgara) was churned by the deities and the demons to procure Ambrosia (Amṛta).

Kāla-Pariccheda (काल-परिच्छेद) means time differentiated. That which exists in one time but not in others is Kāla-Pariccheda.

Kāla-Paricchedya (काल-परिच्छेद्य) means one that is bound by time, that which is in one time and not in another.

Kālātīta (कालातीत) means beyond the reach of time.

Kālāvacchinna (कालावच्छिन्न) means a position in time series.

Kāliya-Nāga (कालिय-नाग) is a dreaded multi-fanged serpent in the river Yamunā. His story is provided in the 16th Chapter of the 10th Canto of Śrīmad Bhāgavata Purāṇa.

Kālpanika (काल्पनिक) means imaginary, existing only in fancy, or fictitious.

Kiñcita (किञ्चित) means anything. It can also mean a little bit.

Kilbiṣa (किल्बिष) means sin.

Kīrtana (कीर्तन) means musical recitations of religious hymns, Mantra and praise of the Lord.

Kīrti (कीर्ति) means fame, honor, or glory.

Kuṇṭhita (कुण्ठित) means blunted or dulled.

Kuṇḍala (कुण्डल) means an earring.

Kupathya (कुपथ्य) means improper or unsuitable.

Kumbhaka (कुम्भक) means the retention of breath.

Kuru-Pravīra (कुरु-प्रवीर) means heroic among the Kurus.

Kurusattama (कुरुसत्तम) means the best of the descendants of the Kurus.

Kula (कुल) means family, lineage, or ancestry.

Kulaghātī (कुलघाती) means destroyer of family or lineage.

Kuladharma (कुलधर्म) means family traditions and duties.

Kulāla (कुलाल) means a potter.

Kuśala (कुशल) means meritorious. It can mean clever, competent, or skillful. It can also mean well, healthy, or in good condition.

Kuśalatā (कुशलता) means competency, skill, or dexterity.

Kuśā (कुशा) means sacred grass with long pointed stalks.

Kūṭastha (कूटस्थ) means immutable, changeless, or firmly fixed. Kūṭa (कूट) is referred to as externally attractive but internally defective, often having false form, false evidence, and so on. Another meaning of the term Kūṭa (कूट) is Anvil, a firm base on which a blacksmith forges hot iron, and so the term Kūṭastha can mean something that is fixed, changeless as an Anvil. In Vedānta, what is variously known as Māyā (माया), Avyakta (अव्यक्त), and what has, within it, numerous seeds of empirical life like nescience are also said to be Kūṭa. Thus, Kūṭa is Māyā, by whose existence (Sattā), the real (सत्, Sat) is cognized. In that Kūṭa Māyā, the Imperishable is situated as a witness (साक्षी, Sākṣī) and the underlying support (अधिष्ठाता, Adhiṣṭhātā) and so it is called Kūṭastha or the Immutable.

Kṛta (कृत) means made, done, or performed.

Kṛtakṛtya (कृतकृत्य) means contented or one who has attained his objective.

Kṛtakṛtyatā (कृतकृत्यता) means contentment.

Kṛtaghnatā (कृतघ्नता) means ingratitude.

Kṛtajñatā (कृतज्ञता) means gratitude or thankfulness.

Kṛtanāśa-Doṣa (कृतनाश-दोष) means a fault incurred when done deeds become fruitless without the enjoyment of their fruits.

Kṛtārtha (कृतार्थ) means one who has attained an objective or has accomplished a purpose.

Kṛtopāsaka (कृतोपासक) means whose devotion has attained its objective.

Kṛtopāsti (कृतोपास्ति) means the performance of propitiation.

Kṛtrima (कृत्रिम) means artificial.

Kṛtsna (कृत्स्न) means entire (Truth).

Kṛtsnavit (कृत्स्नवित्) means Sarvajña or all-knowing. It means one who knows the entire Satya (Truth). There is nothing left to be known.

Kṛpaṇa (कृपण) means miserable, wretched, or lowly.

Kṛpā (कृपा) means grace.

Kṛśa (कृश) means lean or emaciated.

Kṛṣi (कृषि) means agriculture.

Kena (केन) means how, whence, why, or by what?

Kevala (केवल) means mere, only.

Keśa (केश) means hair.

Komala (कोमल) means gentle, soft, tender, or delicate.

Kośa (कोश) means sheath or covering. It can also mean repository.

Kautuka (कौतुक) means curiosity.

Kauśalatā (कौशलता) means competency, skill, or dexterity.

Kauśalam (कौशलम्) means skill or dexterity.

Kaustubha-Maṇi (कौस्तुभ-मणि) means the fourth jewel that came out from the churning of the ocean (Samudra-Manthana).

Krama (क्रम) means order or sequence.

Krama-Mukti (क्रम-मुक्ति) means sequential liberation.

Krama-Samuccaya (क्रम-समुच्चय) is a view that first, with desireless actions (Niṣkāma-Karma), purity of the conscience (Antaḥkaraṇa) is achieved, and after that liberation is attained with knowledge.

Kriyamāṇa (क्रियमाण) means current, being done, or that which is happening currently.

Kriyā (क्रिया) means an act or an action.

Kriyāvāna (क्रियावान) means one that performs various duties and acts.

Kriyā-Sādhya (क्रिया-साध्य) means achieved by action.

Krūra (क्रूर) means cruel.

Krodha (क्रोध) means anger.

Kleśa (क्लेश) means pain, distress, suffering, or anguish.

Klaibya (क्लैब्य) means impotence or unmanliness.

Kvacit (क्वचित्) means at any time.

Kṣaṇa (क्षण) means moment or flash.

Kṣaṇa-Bhaṅgura (क्षण-भङ्गुर) means ephemeral or transient.

Kṣaṇika (क्षणिक) means momentary or transient.

Kṣati (क्षति) means the damage, injury, or harm.

Kṣamā (क्षमा) means forgiveness, forbearance, or to remain undisturbed towards even offenders. It can also mean patience.

Kṣaya (क्षय) means depletion, reduction, or decay. It can also mean destruction.

Kṣaya-Doṣa (क्षय-दोष) means a fault of perishability.

Kṣara (क्षर) means perishable.

Kṣātra-Prakṛti (क्षात्र-प्रकृति) means the innate attributes of a Kṣatriya (क्षत्रिय). Attributes enumerated in BG 18.43 are: 1) valor (Śaurya, शौर्य), 2) splendor (तेज, Teja), 3) fortitude (धृति, Dhṛti), 4) skill (Dākṣya, दाक्ष्य), 5) charity (दान, Dāna), 6) leadership attribute (Īśvara-Bhāva, ईश्वर-भाव) and 7) not fleeing in war (Apalāyana Yuddhe, अपलायन-युद्धे).

Kṣīṇa (क्षीण) means diminish, expend, or purge.

Kṣīra (क्षीर) means milk.

Kṣīra-Nīra-Viveka (क्षीर-नीर-विवेक) means wisdom that provides a complete and clear distinction between real and unreal, good and bad. It is said that a swan is endowed with such a wisdom. He can drink Kṣīra (क्षीर, milk) from a mixture of milk and water (नीर, water), leaving behind water.

Kṣudhā (क्षुधा) means hunger.

Kṣubdha (क्षुब्ध) means agitated or disturbed.

Kṣetra (क्षेत्र) means a field. It can also mean the body.

Kṣetrajña (क्षेत्रज्ञ) means knower of the field (Kṣetra) or the body. It is also referred to as Dehī (देही) or Śarīrī (शरीरी).

Kṣematara (क्षेमतर) means more auspicious or greater happiness.

Kṣobha (क्षोभ) means agitation, disturbance.

Kṣobhita (क्षोभित) means agitated or disturbed.

Kha (ख) means empty space.

Khaṇḍana (खण्डन) means refutation.

Khaṇḍita (खण्डित) means broken in pieces, torn, damaged, or destroyed.

Khapuṣpa (खपुष्प) means a flower in the sky or an imaginary flower.

Lakṣaṇa (लक्षण) means characteristics, attribute, designation, or accurate description.

Lakṣmī (लक्ष्मी) means wealth or riches. It is also the name of the goddess of wealth, fortune, love, beauty, joy, and prosperity. She is associated with Māyā and represents Rajoguṇa and the Power of Desire. Along with Pārvatī and Sarasvati, she forms the trinity of goddesses - the Tridevī (त्रिदेवी). Goddess Lakṣmī is also referred to as Śrī (श्री).

Lakṣya (लक्ष्य) means aim, the object aimed at.

Lakṣyārtha (लक्ष्यार्थ) means implied sense. Where the meaning of the word is not ascertained by Śakti-Vṛtti (naming process) but by Lakṣaṇa-Vṛtti (characteristic process). The knowledge of Nirviśeṣa-Brahma is through Lakṣaṇa, and so it is called Lakṣyārtha.

Labhate (लभते) means acquires.

Laya (लय) means dissolution, disappearance, or absorption in.

Lavaṇa (लवण) means salty or saline.

Lākṣāgṛha (लाक्षागृह) means a house of wax.

Lābha (लाभ) means a benefit, gain, or profit.

Līna (लीन) means to merge in.

Līlā (लीला) means divine play.

Līlā-Vigraha (लीला-विग्रह) means divine play forms.

Lupta (लुप्त) means to disappear.

Lepa (लेप) means taint, stain, coating, or covering.

Lepāyamāna (लेपायमान) means coatable or taintable.

Lehya (लेह्य) means lickable.

Loka (लोक) means the world.

Lokasaṃgraha (लोकसंग्रह) means public well-being. Setting one's behavior as an example for people to emulate is called Lokasaṃgraha.

Lopa (लोप) means absence or disappearance.

Lobha (लोभ) means greed, avarice, or covetousness.

Loṣṭa (लोष्ट) means a clod or a lump of soil.

Laukika (लौकिक) means worldly, or belonging to or occurring in ordinary life.

Mata (मत) means opinion, doctrine, or view.

Mat-Citta (मत्-चित्त) means with the subconscious mind in Me the witness-form Paramātmā.

Matparaḥ (मत्परः) means devoted to Me or moving towards Me.

Matsara (मत्सर) means envy or jealousy.

Mada (मद) means excessive pride, hubris, excessive self-confidence, or arrogance.

Madbhāva (मद्भाव) means My status.

Madhura (मधुर) means sweet, pleasant, or delightful.

Madhusūdana (मधुसूदन) means the slayer of the demon Madhu, an epithet of Śrī Kṛṣṇa.

Manana (मनन) means to contemplate, to think critically by sitting in a secluded place on heard or read subject.

Mananaśīla (मननशील) means contemplative or pensive.

Manamohinī (मनमोहिनी) means an enticer of the mind or the heart. It can also mean one who pleases the mind.

Manas (मनस्) means the mind, characterized by the inner disposition of developing thought and its variant (संकल्पविकल्पात्मक-वृत्ति, Saṃkalpavikalpātmaka-Vṛtti). It is an inner instrument that receives information from the external world with the help of the sense organs and presents them to the intellect for decision-making.

Manuṣya (मनुष्य) means human.

Manogata (मनोगत) means mental or existing or passing in the mind.

Manomaya-Kośa (मनोमय-कोश) means "The Sheath of the Mind," or the mental faculty that receives all sensory inputs, interprets, and desires. It includes (पञ्च-ज्ञानेन्द्रिय, Pañca-Jñānendriya) or the five sense faculties: 1) skin (त्वक, Tvaka) with the sense of touch, 2) tongue (रसना, Rasanā) with the sense of taste, 3) eyes (चक्षु, Cakṣu) with the sense of sight, 4) nose (घ्राण, Ghrāṇa) with the sense of smell and 5) ears (श्रोत्र, Śrotra) with the sense of hearing. It is the cause of diversity, "I" and "mine."

Manoratha (मनोरथ) means desire or mental creation.

Mano-Vṛtti (मनो-वृत्ति) means mental disposition.

Mantavya (मन्तव्य) means to be approved or sanctioned, to be regarded or considered. It can also mean opinion.

Mantra (मन्त्र) means Vedic hymn or sacred syllable used in chants.

Manthana (मन्थन) means churning.

Manda (मन्द) means faint.

Manyate (मन्यते) means to think, deem, regard, or consider.

Mama (मम) means for or by me. It can also mean mine.

Mamatā (ममता) means mineness or meum.

Maya (मय) is a suffix meaning composed of or consisting of.

Mayadānava (मयदानव) means a demon named Maya.

Mayī (मयी) is a suffix meaning empowered with

Maraṇa (मरण) means death.

Maruta (मरुत) are the forty-nine wind-deities enumerated as: Sattvajyoti (सत्त्वज्योति), Āditya (आदित्य), Satyajyoti (सत्यज्योति), Tiryagjyoti (तिर्यग्ज्योति), Sajyoti (सज्योति), Jyotiṣmān (ज्योतिष्मान्), Harita (हरित), Ṛtajit (ऋतजित्), Satyajit (सत्यजित्), Suṣeṇa (सुषेण), Senajit (सेनजित्), Satyamitra (सत्यमित्र), Abhimitra (अभिमित्र), Harimitra (हरिमित्र), Kṛta (कृत), Satya (सत्य), Dhruva (ध्रुव), Dhartā (धर्ता), Vidhartā (विधर्ता), Vidhāraya (विधारय), Dhvānta (ध्वान्त), Dhuni (धुनि), Ugra (उग्र), Bhīma (भीम), Abhiyu (अभियु), Sākṣipa (साक्षिप), Īdṛk (ईदृक्), Anyādṛk (अन्यादृक्), Yādṛk (यादृक्), Pratikṛt (प्रतिकृत्), Ṛk (ऋक्), Samiti (समिति), Saṃrambha (संरम्भ), Idṛksa (ईदृक्ष), Puruṣa (पुरुष), Anyādṛkṣa (अन्यादृक्ष), Cetasa (चेतस), Samitā (समिता), Samidṛkṣa (समिदृक्ष), Pratidṛkṣa (प्रतिदृक्ष), Maruti (मरुति), Sarata (सरत), Deva (देव), Dish (दिश), Yajuḥ (यजुः), Anudṛk (अनुदृक्), Sāma (साम), Mānuṣa (मानुष) and Viś (विश्).

Marma (मर्म) means a core, vital component, or essence.

Maryādā (मर्यादा) means bounds or limits of morality and propriety.

Mala (मल) means impurity or dirt.

Mala-Doṣa (मल-दोष) means a fault of impurity. It is formed as a malicious disposition (Durvāsanā) in the conscience. It can be removed by desireless deeds (Niṣkāma-Karma).

Malina (मलिन) means dirty.

Mahatīm (महतीम्) means large.

Mahat (महत्) means the great element of intellect. Vedānta refers to it as the first great element that evolved out of the union of Prakṛti and the Puruṣa. It can also mean great from the term Mahā (महा).

Mahat-Brahma (महत्-ब्रह्म) means Prakṛti of the three constituents, the primal matter with three different innate attributes.

Maharṣi (महर्षि) means a great seer or a great sage.

Mahākāśa (महाकाश) means the pervasive space.

Mahāna (महान) means great.

Mahānubhāva (महानुभाव) means whose conduct is worth emulating.

Mahā-Bandha (महा-बन्ध) means the great lock. The Mahā-Bandha is the combination of all three internal locks (Bandha) gradually assumed and held, in the following order: Jālandhara-Bandha, Uḍḍiyāna-Bandha, and finally Mūla-Bandha. Releasing of the locks goes in the same order

Mahābhūta (महाभूत), known as the great elements, are five in number: 1) earth (पृथ्वी, Pṛthvī), 2) water (आप, Āpa), 3) fire (अग्नि, Agni), 4) wind (वायु, Vāyu) and 5) space (आकाश, Ākāśa). Because they pervade all transformations of Prakṛti, they are called great (महान, Mahāna), and being the cause of the Pañcīkṛta of the Pañcabhūta, they are subtle. Pañcīkṛta (पञ्चीकृत) means done by Pañcīkaraṇa (पञ्चीकरण), which is an action by which anything is constituted of the five elements (1/2 of one and 1/8 of the other four elements). Mahābhūta is also known as Pañca-Mahābhūta (पञ्च-महाभूत) or Pañcabhūta (पञ्चभूत).

Mahā-Yuga (महा-युग) consists of 4,320,000 years of humans, comprised of Sat-Yuga (सत्-युग) 1,728,000 years, Tretā-Yuga (त्रेता-युग) 1,296,000 years, Dvāpara-Yuga (द्वापर-युग) 864,000 years and Kali-Yuga (कलि-युग) 432,000 years. In one Mahā-Yuga, there are 12,000 years of Devatā. A day of Brahmā, also known as Kalpa, consists of 1000 Mahā-Yuga or 4.32 billion years of humans and 12 million years of Devatā

Mahārathī (महारथी) means a great warrior who has mastery over all forms of weapons, battle formations, and combat skills. Such a warrior is said to have the ability to match the strength of ten thousand ordinary warriors single-handedly.

Mahimā (महिमा) means glory, greatness, or majesty.

Mahiṣī (महिषी) means a female cow.

Maheśvara (महेश्वर) means the Great Supreme Lord, Lord Śiva.

Mātrā (मात्रा) means size, quantity, duration, number, or degree.

Mādradeśa (माद्रदेश) was an ancient region in the modern Sialkot in the Punjab province of Pakistan.

Māna (मान) means honor, respect, praise, or compliment. It can also mean pride or esteem.

Māna-Apamāna (मान-अपमान) means honor-dishonor or respect-disrespect.

Mānasika (मानसिक) means mental.

Māndya (मान्द्य) means slowness or weakness.

Mānya (मान्य) means deemed or acceptable.

Māyā (माया) is the delusive power (शक्ति, Śakti), the power of being, of the supreme imperishable Reality by which the supreme imperishable Reality appears in the space-time as the world that is neither immutable nor non-existent in the physical plane of nescience. It is the object of three kinds of knowledge: 1) according to revealed knowledge, it is unreal; 2) according to reasoning, it is indescribable; and 3) according to the perceptions of the empirical person, it is real. In common usage, it is used to express delusion or unreality.

Māyāmayī (मायामयी) means empowered with Māyā.

Māyāmātra (मायामात्र) means only unreal or illusionary.

Māyārupa (मायारुप) means delusional, apparent, or unreal.

Māyā-Viśiṣṭa-Cetana (माया-विशिष्ट-चेतन) means the conscious element with Māyā.

Māhātmā (माहात्मा) means great being.

Māhātmya (माहात्म्य) means magnanimity or greatness.

Mitāhārī (मिताहारी) means one who eats light and less.

Mitra (मित्र) means friend.

Mithyā (मिथ्या) means not in reality, delusional, untruthful, fraudulent, or deceitful.

Mithyā-Kārya (मिथ्या-कार्य) means delusional action.

Mithyācāritva (मिथ्याचारित्व) means untruthful or fraudulent behavior.

Mithyācārī (मिथ्याचारी) means one whose behavior is untruthful or fraudulent.

Mithyātva (मिथ्यात्व) means unreality, falsity, or illusion.

Mithyātva-Niścaya (मिथ्यात्व-निश्चय) means determination of unreality.

Mithyā-Buddhi (मिथ्या-बुद्धि) means untrueness sense.

Miśra (मिश्र) means mixed.

Mukta (मुक्त) means free.

Mukti (मुक्ति) means liberation or to be free from.

Muktiprada (मुक्तिप्रद) means giver of freedom. It can also mean redemptory.

Mukhya (मुख्य) means main or principal. It can also mean coming from the mouth or the face.

Mukhyatā (मुख्यता) means pre-eminence.

Muni (मुनि) means a sage.

Mumukṣu (मुमुक्षु) means a desirer for liberation.

Mūḍha (मूढ) means deluded, confused, bewildered, or adrift.

Mūḍhabhāva (मूढभाव) means mental clouding, blurring of judgment, confusion, or bewilderment.

Mūrkha (मूर्ख) means stupid, foolish.

Mūrtimāna (मूर्तिमान) means personification.

Mūla (मूल) means root or base.

Mūla-Bandha (मूल-बन्ध) where Mūla (मूल) means root, base and in Yoga refers to root or base of spine and Bandha (बन्ध) means catching hold of. In Yoga, it is a posture where the body from the anus to the navel is contracted and lifted up and towards the spine. That is qualified in that the actual muscle contracted is not the sphincter muscle nor the muscle which creates urination, but the muscle equidistant between the two.

Mūlādhāra (मूलाधार) means root and basis of existence. It is a compound word from Mūla (मूल), meaning root, and Ādhāra (आधार), meaning basis. Mūlādhāra-Cakra is located near the coccygeal plexus beneath the sacrum, and its superficial activation point is located between the perineum and the coccyx or the pelvic bone. Because of its location and connection with the act of excretion, it is associated with the anus. Mūlādhāra is said to be the base from which the three main psychic channels (Nāḍī) emerge: the Iḍā, Piṅgalā, and Suṣumnā.

Mṛtyu (मृत्यु) means death.

Medhā (मेधा) means intelligence.

Medhāvī (मेधावी) means intelligent.

Mokṣa (मोक्ष) means liberation. Attainment of eternal (नित्य, Nitya) and immovable (अचल, Acala) happiness (सुख, Sukha) and complete (अत्यन्त, Atyanta) removal (निव्रुत्ति, Nivrutti) of pain and suffering (दुःख, Duḥkha) is Mokṣa. Alternatively, attainment of the Brahman and freedom from the bondage of the Saṃsāra is Mokṣa, meaning liberation from the Saṃsāra of transmigrating lives and attainment of the supreme-bliss (Paramānanda).

Mokṣa-Parāyaṇa (मोक्ष-परायण) means one who continuously strives for the supreme goal of liberation.

Mokṣārthī (मोक्षार्थी) means one who has an intense desire for liberation.

Modaka (मोदक) means sweet dessert.

Moha (मोह) means delusion, perplexity, or bewilderment. It can mean infatuation, fondness, or endearment. It can also mean ignorance.

Mohita (मोहित) means confused, stupefied, deluded, or bewildered.

Mauna (मौन) means silence.

Napuṃsaka (नपुंसक) means impotent or unmanly.

Namaskāra (नमस्कार) means obeisance, salutation, or exclamatory adoration and worship.

Namra (नम्र) means humble or reverential.

Namra-Bhāva (नम्र-भाव) means humility.

Naraka (नरक) means hell.

Navadhā-Bhakti (नवधा-भक्ति) means the nine-fold devotion consisting of: (1) listening to the holy scriptures (श्रवण, Śravaṇa), (2) chanting (कीर्तन, Kīrtana), (3) remembering teachings of the holy scriptures (स्मरण, Smaraṇa), (4) serving at the lotus-feet of the Lord (पाद-सेवन, Pāda-Sevana), (5) worshipping (अर्चन, Arcana), (6) bowing to the Lord (वन्दन, Vandana), (7) serving the Lord (दास्य, Dāsya), (8) friendship with the Lord (सख्य, Sakhya), and (9) surrender to the Lord (आत्म-निवेदन, Ātma-Nivedana).

Naśvaratā (नश्वरता) means mortality or transiency.

Naṣṭa (नष्ट) means lost, disappeared, perished, or disappeared.

Nāḍī (नाडी) means the channels through which the Prāṇa of the physical body, the subtle body, and the causal body are said to flow.

Nāḍī-Śodhana (नाडी-शोधन) is a Yoga practice that purifies the energy channels in the subtle body through alternate nostril breathing.

Nānātva (नानात्व) means manifoldness or plurality.

Nāma (नाम) means name.

Nāma-Nirdeśa (नाम-निर्देश) means pointing out the name or name-indication.

Nāyaka (नायक) means a leader or a chief.

Nārāyaṇī-Senā (नारायणी-सेना) means the supreme army of all times of Lord Śrī Kṛṣṇa, King of Dvārakā (द्वारका).

Nāśa (नाश) means destruction.

Nāśaka (नाशक) means destroyer, remover, or annihilator.

Nāśavāna (नाशवान) means perishable or destroyable.

Nāstika (नास्तिक) means an atheist or unbeliever.

Niḥśvāsa (निःश्वास) means from the breath.

Nikṛṣṭa (निकृष्ट) means inferior, low, despised, vile, or outcast.

Nikṛṣṭatā (निकृष्टता) means lowness or vileness.

Nigraha (निग्रह) means restraint, repression, keeping down, or keeping back.

Nijātma (निजात्म) means own self.

Nijātma-Svarupa (निजात्म-स्वरुप) means own true nature.

Nitya (नित्य) means eternal, ever, or always.

Nitya-Karma (नित्य-कर्म) means daily obligatory duties or rituals.

Nitya-Nirantara (नित्य-निरन्तर) means ever continuous.

Nitya-Nirvikāra (नित्य-निर्विकार) means ever unchanged.

Nitya-Nivrutta (नित्य-निवृत्त) means always inactive.

Nitya-Nūtana (नित्य-नूतन) means always present.

Nitya-Prāk-Siddhatva (नित्य-प्राक्-सिद्धत्व) means eternal pre-existence.

Nitya-Prāpta (नित्य-प्राप्त) means always attained.

Nitya-Mukta (नित्य-मुक्त) means ever free.

Nitya-Yukta (नित्य-युक्त) means ever established.

Nididhyāsana (निदिध्यासन) means profound and repeated meditation.

Nidrā (निद्रा) means sleep.

Nidrāvasthā (निद्रावस्था) means the state of sleep.

Nindā (निन्दा) means criticism or denouncement.

Nindā-Stuti (निन्दा-स्तुति) means criticism and praise.

Nindita (निन्दित) means denounced, censured, or criticized.

Nimitta (निमित्त) means instrumental. It can also mean cause.

Nimitta-Kāraṇa (निमित्त-कारण) means instrumental cause. That exists neutral before the work and whose destruction does not destroy work. A potter, wheel, or a stick are Nimitta-Kāraṇa of a pot.

Nimna (निम्न) means low or inferior.

Niyata (नियत) means obligatory, prescribed, controlled, or fixed.

Niyata-Karma (नियत-कर्म) means obligatory acts.

Niyati (नियति) means the fixed order of things, destiny, or fate.

Niyama (नियम) means rites, observances, or positive duties.

Niyamita (नियमित) means guided, regulated, restrained, or prudent.

Niyojita (नियोजित) means enjoined or impelled. It can also mean appointed or authorized.

Niratiśaya (निरतिशय) means unsurpassed or supreme.

Nirantara (निरन्तर) means continuous.

Nirapekṣa (निरपेक्ष) means independent of or indifferent to.

Nirahaṃkāra (निरहंकार) means free from egotism or without ego.

Nirākaraṇa (निराकरण) means resolution.

Nirākāra (निराकार) means formless or without shape.

Nirālaṃba (निरालंब) means without support.

Nirālasya (निरालस्य) means freedom from laziness. It can also mean alertness or diligence.

Nirāśa (निराश) means without hope.

Nirāśī (निराशी) means one who has no desire whatsoever.

Nirāśrayī (निराश्रयी) means not dependent.

Niruddha (निरुद्ध) means held back, stopped, or shut. It can also mean covered or veiled.

Nirupādhika (निरुपाधिक) means adjunctless, without attributes, or absolute.

Nirūpaṇa (निरूपण) means formulation or articulation.

Niroga (निरोग) means without disease or healthy.

Nirodha (निरोध) means cessation or stoppage. It can also mean confinement or enclosing.

Nir (निर्) is a prefix meaning not or without.

Nirguṇa (निर्गुण) means devoid of material attributes, without attributes, or properties.

Nirdiṣṭa (निर्दिष्ट) means enunciated, prescribed, or given.

Nirdeśa (निर्देश) means to point out or indicate.

Nirdvandva (निर्द्वन्द्व) means without duality.

Nirbhayatā (निर्भयता) means fearlessness.

Nirmama (निर्मम) means without mineness, unselfish, disinterested, or free from all worldly connections.

Nirmala (निर्मल) means pure.

Nirmalatā (निर्मलता) means purity.

Nirmāna (निर्मान) means without vanity.

Nirmāyika (निर्मायिक) means free from Māyā, not illusory, or not deceptive.

Nirlepa (निर्लेप) means unsmeared or stainless.

Nirlepatā (निर्लेपता) means untaintedness or stainlessness.

Nirvāṇa (निर्वाण) means liberation from material existence, Mokṣa, Parama-Gati, or Parama-Śānti.

Nirvāṇa-Brahma (निर्वाण-ब्रह्म) means oneness in the Brahman with liberation from the worldly cycle of birth and death.

Nirvāta (निर्वात) means wind-free or calm.

Nirvāsanika (निर्वासनिक) means without impressions or inner dispositions.

Nirvāha (निर्वाह) means sufficiency, accomplishing, performing, or carrying on.

Nirvikalpa (निर्विकल्प) means without variant thought. It is a compound word from Nis (निस्), meaning without, and Vikalpa (विकल्प), meaning alternative or variant thought.

Nirvikalpa-Samādhī (निर्विकल्प-समाधि) means absorption without self-consciousness. It is a mergence of the mental activity in the Ātmā to such a degree that the distinctions (Vikalpa) of the knower, the act of knowing, and the known object become dissolved as waves vanish in water.

Nirvikāra (निर्विकार) means unchanged, without transformation, or unmodified.

Nirviśeṣa (निर्विशेष) means without distinction, indiscriminateness, absence of difference, or without categories.

Nirviṣayaka (निर्विषयक) means objectless.

Nivartaka (निवर्तक) means remover or expeller.

Nivedana (निवेदन) means offering. It can also mean announcing or proclaiming.

Niveśa (निवेश) means to absorb, enter, deposit, or deliver. It can also mean habitation.

Nivrutti (निव्रुत्ति) means retirement, liberation, or removal. It can also mean inaction.

Niścaya (निश्चय) means to resolve. It can also mean determination.

Niścayātmaka (निश्चयात्मक) means resolute.

Niścayātmaka-Vṛtti (निश्चयात्मक-वृत्ति) means deciding instinct.

Niścala (निश्चल) means motionless, steady, or unflinching.

Niścita (निश्चित) means determined, decided, or ascertained.

Niśceṣṭa (निश्चेष्ट) means motionless.

Niśceṣṭā (निश्चेष्टा) means an attribute of being motionless.

Niśreyasa (निश्रेयस) means liberation or Mokṣa.

Niṣiddha (निषिद्ध) means forbidden or prohibited.

Niṣiddha-Karma (निषिद्ध-कर्म) means forbidden acts.

Niṣiddha-Sakāmī (निषिद्ध-सकामी) means one who covets forbidden desire-ridden acts or who covets prohibited acts.

Niṣedha (निषेध) means prohibitive regulative principles or prohibition.

Niṣkaṇṭaka (निष्कण्टक) means secure or free from thorns or enemies.

Niṣkapaṭa (निष्कपट) means guileless or free from deceit or fraud.

Niṣkarṣa (निष्कर्ष) means the extract or essence.

Niṣkāma-Karma (निष्काम-कर्म) means desireless actions.

Niṣkāma-Karmī (निष्काम-कर्मी) means one who performs desireless actions.

Niṣkāma-Bhakta (निष्काम-भक्त) means desireless devotee.

Niṣkāma-Bhāva (निष्काम-भाव) means desireless sentiment.

Niṣkāmī (निष्कामी) means whose actions are desireless or one who has no desire or attachment.

Niṣkriya (निष्क्रिय) means actionless or inactive.

Niṣṭhā (निष्ठा) means discipline, faith, status, position, dedication, steadfastness, or persistence in what is undertaken. From the Vedantic perspective firm resolve of the Citta is called Niṣṭhā.

Niṣprapañca (निष्प्रपञ्च) means pure, entirely transcendental to material existence, subject to no expansion or manifoldness, or free from secular proceedings.

Niṣphala (निष्फल) means bearing no fruits, without fruits, or fruitless.

Nis (निस्) means out, forth. As a verb prefix, it implies separation (away from, outside of), certainty, completeness, or fullness.

Nistāra (निस्तार) means deliverance, rescue, or liberation.

Nistraiguṇya (निस्त्रैगुण्य) means free of the three constituents.

Nissaṅga (निस्सङ्ग) means alone or not with anyone.

Nissāra (निस्सार) means without essence or pointless.

Nihita (निहित) means placed, laid, deposited, fixed, or kept in.

Nīti (नीति) means order, rule, generally for dealings and conduct, moral philosophy, ethics, guidance, or wisdom.

Nītinipuṇa (नीतिनिपुण) means a statesman, an expert in diplomacy, or an expert in the laws.

Nīra (नीर) means water.

Nūtana (नूतन) means new, fresh, or belonging to the present.

Nṛpa (नृप) means a king, protector of men. It can also mean in music a kind of measure.

Netra (नेत्र) means eye.

Nesta (नेस्त) means not there.

Naimittika-Karma (नैमित्तिक-कर्म) means occasional duties or rituals. Generally, it is performed for a specific reason, at a specific time, on a specific day, or on a similar day.

Naiṣkarmya (नैष्कर्म्य) means actionlessness, freedom from reaction, or that which does not produce the experience of the resultant action or exemption from acts and their consequences. It is not to come in the bondage of actions even after performing actions and scorching the seeds of actions in the fire of knowledge and making it actionless and without fruits.

Naiṣkarmya-Siddhi (नैष्कर्म्य-सिद्धि) means perfection of actionlessness, a state acquired through knowledge wherein even after doing everything one is a non-doer (Akartā, अकर्ता) or indeed not doing anything and one does not come into the bondage of actions (कर्म, Karma).

Naiṣkṛtika (नैष्कृतिक) means taker of livelihood of others.

Naiṣṭhika (नैष्ठिक) means highest, final, steady, or immovable.

Naiṣṭhika-Śānti (नैष्ठिक-शान्ति) means steady peace.

Naulī (नौली) is one of the actions (Kriyā) of cleaning the abdominal region - digestive faculties, small intestine - and is based on a massage of the internal belly faculties by a circular movement of the abdominal muscles. It is performed standing with the feet apart, and the knees bent. There are four steps, which are learned one after another: 1) Uḍḍiyāna-Bandha: the abdominal lock in which the lungs are emptied, and the abdomen is pulled inwards and upwards under the lower edge of the ribcage, 2) Madhyāna-Naulī: only the central muscles of the abdomen are contracted, 3) Vama-Naulī: only the left muscles of the abdomen are contracted and 4) Dakṣiṇā-Naulī: only the right muscles of the abdomen are contracted.

Nyāsa (न्यास) means to abandon, put away, or leave.

Nyūna (न्यून) means less, diminished, low, or vile.

Nyūnatā (न्यूनता) means deficiency or want. It can also mean inferiority.

Nyūnādhikatā (न्यूनाधिकता) means the attribute of more or less.

Oja (ओज) means splendor, vitality, or luster.

Ota-Prota (ओत-प्रोत) means pervaded, woven, threaded, or entwined. The term Ota (ओत) means woven, and the term Prota (प्रोत) means sewed or stitched.

Oṣadhī (ओषधी) means herbs.

Pakṣapāta (पक्षपात) means partisanship, favoritism, or bias.

Pakṣī (पक्षी) means a bird.

Paṅkaja (पङ्कज) means born in mud or lotus.

Pañca-Karmendriya (पञ्च-कर्मेन्द्रिय) means the five action organs: 1) mouth (वाक, Vāka) for voice, 2) hands (पाणि, Pāṇi) for grasping, receiving, gathering, collecting (Grahaṇa) and holding (Dhāraṇa), 3) feet (पाद, Pāda) for walking, moving, locomotion (Gamana), 4) anus (पायु, Pāyu) for excretion and 5) genitals (उपस्थ, Upastha) for reproduction.

Pañca-Kośa (पञ्च-कोश) means the five sheaths that cover the Ātmā as described in Taittirīya Upaniṣad (2.1-5), from gross to fine are: 1) the Sheath of Food (अन्नमय-कोश, Annamaya-Kośa), 2) the Sheath of the Vital Breaths of Air

(प्राणमय-कोश, Prāṇamaya-Kośa) consisting of the five action faculties viz. mouth, hands, feet, anus and the genitals and five vital breaths of air, viz. Prāṇa, Apāna, Samāna, Udāna, and Vyāna, 3) the Sheath of the Mind (मनोमय-कोश, Manomaya-Kośa) consisting of the five cognitive senses viz. skin, tongue, eyes, nose and ears, and mind, 4) the Sheath of Discernment (विज्ञानमय-कोश, Vijñānamaya-Kośa) consisting of the five cognitive senses and the intellect and 5) the Sheath of the Supreme Bliss (आनन्दमय-कोश, Ānandamaya-Kośa).

Pañca-Jñānendriya (पञ्च-ज्ञानेन्द्रिय) means the five cognitive sense organs: 1) skin (त्वक, Tvaka), 2) tongue (रसना, Rasanā), 3) eyes (चक्षु, Cakṣu), 4) nose (घ्राण, Ghrāṇa) and 5) ears (श्रोत्र, Śrotra).

Pañca-Tanmātra (पञ्च-तन्मात्र) means the five rudimentary or subtle elements: 1) sound (शब्द, Śabda), 2) touch (स्पर्श, Sparśa), 3) taste (रस, Rasa), 4) form (रुप, Rupa) and 5) smell (गन्ध, Gandha).

Pañca-Prāṇa (पञ्च-प्राण) means the five vital breaths of air: 1) Prāṇa-Vāyu (प्राण-वायु), 2) Apāna-Vāyu (अपान-वायु), 3) Samāna-Vāyu (समान-वायु), 4) Udāna-Vāyu (उदान-वायु), 5) Vyāna-Vāyu (व्यान-वायु).

Pañca-Bhūtātmaka (पञ्च-भूतात्मक) means consisting of the five great elements or the Pañcabhūta, where Pañcabhūta (पञ्चभूत) means the five subtle components of the Prakṛti: 1) earth (पृथ्वी, Pṛthvī), 2) water (आप, Āpa), 3) fire (अग्नि, Agni), 4) wind (वायु, Vāyu) and 5) space (आकाश, Ākāśa).

Pañca-Mahāyajña (पञ्च-महायज्ञ) means the five great sacrifices: 1) worship of the divine entities (देव-यज्ञ, Deva-Yajña), 2) worship of knowledge (ब्रह्म-यज्ञ, Brahma-Yajña), 3) worship of the ancestors (पितृ-यज्ञ, Pitṛ-Yajña), 4) worship of all living entities (भूत-यज्ञ, Bhūta-Yajña) and 5) worship of the guests (अतिथि-यज्ञ, Atithi-Yajña).

Pañca-Viṣaya (पञ्च-विषय) means the five objects of senses: 1) touch (स्पर्श, Sparśa), 2) taste (रस, Rasa), 3) form (रूप, Rupa), 4) smell (गन्ध, Gandha) and 5) sound (शब्द, Śabda).

Pañcāmṛta (पञ्चामृत) means a mixture of cow milk, curd, honey, sugar, and Ghī used as an offering at a worship ritual (Pūjā) and distributed to the devotees as Prasāda.

Pañcīkaraṇa (पञ्चीकरण) means an action by which anything is constituted of the five elements (1/2 of one and 1/8 of the other four elements).

Paḍāva (पडाव) means a camp or a rest area.

Paṇava (पणव) means a small drum.

Paṇḍita (पण्डित) means a man of discrimination, one with wisdom. It is derived from Paṇḍ (पण्ड्), meaning knowledge of the Ātmā or Self, and so a Paṇḍita is one who knows the Ātmā or the Self.

Pāṇḍu (पाण्डु) means pale, anemic. The term also refers to Pāṇḍu, the King of Hastināpura (हस्तिनापुर), younger brother of Dhṛtarāṣṭra (धृतराष्ट्र) and father of the Pāṇḍavas

Pativratā (पतिव्रता) means a devoted and virtuous wife.

Pathya (पथ्य) means suitable or proper. It can also mean dietary regime and physical activity

Pada (पद) means status, position.

Padaccheda (पदच्छेद) means disaggregation of compound words, the action of separating each term according to the rules of grammar.

Padadalita (पददलित) means trampled by feet or downtrodden.

Padārtha (पदार्थ) means matter, substance, or elements.

Padārthagata (पदार्थगत) means material or elemental.

Padcyuta (पद्च्युत) means dismissal, firing, or removal from office.

Padma (पद्म) means a lotus.

Payas (पयस्) means milk or any fluid or juice.

Para (पर) means distant, beyond, ancient, or past.

Paraṃparā (परंपरा) means regular succession, tradition, or heritage.

Paratantra (परतन्त्र) means not independent.

Paratā (परता) means the highest degree, of absoluteness.

Parabrahma (परब्रह्म) means the attributeless Brahman.

Parama (परम) means highest.

Parama-Gati (परम-गति) means the supreme destination or final exemption from transmigrating life.

Parama-Nirvāṇa (परम-निर्वाण) means the ultimate liberation. Attainment of eternal and immovable happiness and complete removal of pain and suffering is liberation. Alternatively, attainment of the Brahman and freedom from the bondage of Saṃsāra is liberation. That is liberation from the Saṃsāra of transmigrating lives and attaining the supreme-bliss (Paramānanda).

Parama-Pada (परम-पद) means the supreme Status.

Parama-Śraddhā (परम-श्रद्धा) means absolute faith.

Paramāṇu (परमाणु) means the smallest subtle particle. A compound word from Parama (परम) meaning ultimate and Aṇu (अणु) meaning particle, atom.

Paramātma-Darśana (परमात्म-दर्शन) means seeing the Supreme Being or having a divine experience.

Paramātmā (परमात्मा) means the Supreme Being, the Brahman.

Paramānanda (परमानन्द) means supreme-bliss.

Paramārtha (परमार्थ) means the highest and most excellent good. The highest good is attaining the supreme imperishable Reality or the Brahman.

Paramārtha-Tattva (परमार्थ-तत्व) means the supreme Truth, the supreme imperishable Reality.

Parameśvara (परमेश्वर) means the Supreme Lord.

Paraloka (परलोक) means another world or heaven.

Paravaśa (परवश) means helpless, subdued, subject to another's will, or subservient.

Parasaṃvedhya (परसंवेध्य) means not realized by the experience of someone else.

Paraspara (परस्पर) means mutual.

Parākrama (पराक्रम) means to show courage or to excel.

Parākramī (पराक्रमी) means gallant or valiant.

Parātpara (परात्पर) means beyond the best or farther than beyond.

Parāmarśa (परामर्श) means advice or counsel.

Parāyaṇa (परायण) means devoted, absorbed. It can also mean being oriented towards, going towards, or continuously striving for.

Parāyaṇatā (परायणता) means absorption, the sense of moving towards.

Parigraha (परिग्रह) means possessions, belongings, or accumulations. It can also mean seizing, holding, or taking.

Paricaryātmaka (परिचर्यात्मक) means consists of servicing or providing labor.

Paricintan (परिचिन्तन्) means contemplation.

Paricchinna (परिच्छिन्न) means limited or circumscribed. It can also mean cut-off or divided.

Paricchinna-Ahaṃkāra (परिच्छिन्न-अहंकार) means limited I-ness sense.

Paricchinnatā (परिच्छिन्नता) means the attribute of limitation.

Paricchinna-Dṛṣṭi (परिच्छिन्न-दृष्टि) means limited vision.

Pariccheda (परिच्छेद) means limit, extent, or boundary.

Pariccheda-Vinirmukta (परिच्छेद-विनिर्मुक्त) means free from limitations.

Paricchedya (परिच्छेद्य) means one that can be limited or bounded.

Pariṇāma (परिणाम) means transformation, result, or effect. That work produced by the mutation (विकार, Vikāra) of the material cause is known as the Pariṇāma. Like yogurt is the Pariṇāma of milk.

Pariṇāmī (परिणामी) means resulting.

Pariṇāmī-Upādāna (परिणामी-उपादान) means a transforming cause. It is a cause that changes in the process of work. Like milk is the Pariṇāmī-Upādāna of yogurt.

Parityāga (परित्याग) means renunciation or abandonment.

Paritrāṇa (परित्राण) means deliverance, preservation, or protection.

Paridevanā (परिदेवना) means lamentation.

Paripūrṇa (परिपूर्ण) means full, complete.

Parimāṇa (परिमाण) means measure.

Pariśrama (परिश्रम) means to toil, hard work, or great pain.

Paristhiti (परिस्थिति) means situation, circumstances.

Parihāra (परिहार) means avoidance.

Parihārya (परिहार्य) means avoidable.

Pare (परे) means subsequently, later, or in the future. It can also mean being beyond.

Parokṣa (परोक्ष) means indirect, imperceptible. Parokṣa (परोक्ष) is a compound word from Parā (परा) meaning beyond and Akṣa (अक्ष) meaning eye, and so Parokṣa means beyond the eye, beyond the range of sight.

Paropakāra (परोपकार) means benevolence, charity, or assisting others.

Parṇa (पर्ण) means a leaf, pinion, or feather.

Paryanta (पर्यन्त) means edge or limit.

Paryavasāna (पर्यवसान) means the end, termination.

Paryāpta (पर्याप्त) means sufficient or adequate. It can also mean obtained or gained.

Paryāya (पर्याय) means synonym.

Paryuṣita (पर्युषित) means stale or not fresh.

Parvata (पर्वत) means a mountain.

Pala (पल) means time consisting of 24 seconds. There is 2.5 Pala in a minute.

Pavitra (पवित्र) means purified, holy, or sanctified.

Paśu (पशु) means an animal.

Pākhaṇḍa (पाखण्ड) means hypocrisy.

Pāṭha (पाठ) means recitation, recital, or reading.

Pāṇi (पाणि) means hands, the organ to grasp, receive, gather, or hold.

Pāṇḍava (पाण्डव) means the son of Pāṇḍu

Pātra (पात्र) means a vessel or a pot. It can also mean a fit or worthy person.

Pātheya (पाथेय) means food and necessities for travel.

Pāda (पाद) means feet, the organ to walk, move or for locomotion.

Pāda-Sevana (पाद-सेवन) means serving at the lotus-feet of the divine.

Pāpa (पाप) means sin.

Pāpī (पापी) means a sinner or an unrighteous person.

Pāmara (पामर) means iniquitous, one who bows down before the scriptures and public morality but gets involved in arbitrary and unrestrained enjoyment of objects of pleasure and tramples the interests of others for own self-interest.

Pāyu (पायु) means anus, with the organ of excretion.

Pāyu (पायु) means anus.

Pāramārthika (पारमार्थिक) means relating to the objective of the Supreme Reality or relating to the spiritual or transcendental realm.

Pāramārthika-Dṛṣṭi (पारमार्थिक-दृष्टि) means spiritual or transcendental perspective.

Pāramārthika-Sattā (पारमार्थिक-सत्ता) means transcendental Reality. It is beyond time and space. It exists at all times - past, present, and future. The Brahman has transcendental Reality.

Pāralaukika (पारलौकिक) means relating to the next world.

Pāruṣya (पारुष्य) means harshness or roughness.

Pāṣāṇa (पाषाण) means a stone.

Piṅgalā (पिङ्गला) means the solar Nāḍī that begins and ends to the right of the Suṣumnā Nāḍī. It is warm and stimulating by nature, controls all vital somatic processes, and oversees the more masculine aspects of our personality. The vibrational attribute of Piṅgalā is represented by reddish-orange color.

Piṇḍa (पिण्ड) means a round mass or a round lump of morsel.

Piṇḍodaka-Kriyā (पिण्डोदक-क्रिया) means the performance (क्रिया, Kriyā) of the offering of a round mass generally of rice (पिण्ड, Piṇḍa) and water (उदक, Udaka) in a ritual to pay homage to the departed ancestors.

Pitāmaha (पितामह) means grandfather.

Pitṛ (पितृ) means father, forefather, or ancestor.

Pitta (पित्त) means bile, the bilious humor (one of the three humors secreted between the stomach and bowels and flowing through the liver and permeating the spleen, heart, eyes, and skin). Its chief attribute is heating.

Pipāsā (पिपासा) means thirst.

Pipāsu (पिपासु) means thirsty.

Piśāca (पिशाच) means a male in the Piśāca Yoni. It refers to an unliberated soul of a dead man who often performs painful and unfavorable acts.

Piśācinī (पिशाचिनी) means a female in the Piśāca Yoni. It refers to an unliberated soul of a dead woman who often performs painful and unfavorable acts.

Pujārī (पुजारी) means a priest.

Puṇya (पुण्य) means piety, pious, saintly, pure, virtuous, or righteous.

Puṇya-Phala (पुण्य-फल) means fruits of piety.

Puṇya-Racita (पुण्य-रचित) means created by piety.

Puṇyātmā (पुण्यात्मा) means a pious being.

Putra (पुत्र) means son.

Punaḥ (पुनः) means anew or again.

Punarāvṛtti (पुनरावृत्ति) means a return to the mortal world of birth and death or repeated births.

Punarjanma (पुनर्जन्म) means rebirth.

Purāṇa (पुराण) means ancient. It can also mean always present.

Purātana (पुरातन) means ancient or belonging to the past.

Puruṣa (पुरुष) means a person or a human.

Puruṣa-Ṛṣabha (पुरुष-ऋषभ) means a person with the might of a bull, the excellent one.

Puruṣārtha (पुरुषार्थ) means object of human pursuit. It is a compound word from Puruṣa (पुरुष, a person, a human) and Artha (अर्थ, objective). Thus, Puruṣārtha is the object of human pursuit, the subject of the desire of all living beings. It can also mean effort.

Puruṣottama (पुरुषोत्तम) means the Supreme Personality. It is a compound word from Uttama (उत्तम), meaning best, highest, or supreme, and Puruṣa (पुरुष), meaning Personality.

Purohita (पुरोहित) means a Vedic family priest.

Puṣṭi (पुष्टि) means nourishment or prosperity.

Pūjā (पूजा) means a worship ritual performed to offer devotional homage and prayer to a deity. It can also mean showing reverence.

Pūjya (पूज्य) means worthy of worship.

Pūti (पूति) means putrid or foul-smelling.

Pūraka (पूरक) means prolonged inhalation.

Pūrṇa (पूर्ण) means complete.

Pūrṇatā (पूर्णता) means completeness or fullness.

Pūrṇāhuti (पूर्णाहुति) means completion of an oblation.

Pūrti (पूर्ति) means fulfillment, completion, satiety, or satisfaction.

Pūrvakṛta (पूर्वकृत) means done in a prior existence, done earlier, or done before.

Pūrvakṛta-Karma (पूर्वकृत-कर्म) means actions performed earlier or performed in a prior existence.

Pūrvāṅga (पूर्वाङ्ग) means constituent part of the preceding or former body.

Pṛthaka (पृथक) means separate, apart, or distinct.

Pṛthaktva (पृथक्त्व) means separateness.

Pṛthvī (पृथ्वी) means the earth.

Paiśunya (पैशुन्य) means faultfinding.

Pauruṣa (पौरुष) means humanness, competence, ability, or virility.

Paulkasa (पौल्कस) means a person born from a Śūdra father and a Kṣatriya mother.

Prakaṭa (प्रकट) means manifest. It can also mean to appear.

Prakāra (प्रकार) means way, mode, manner, or kind.

Prakāśa (प्रकाश) means light or illumination.

Prakṛti (प्रकृति) means nature. It is the primal matter with three different constituents known as Guṇa (गुण), the Sattva सत्त्व or Sattvaguṇa (सत्त्वगुण), the Rajas (रजस्) or Rajoguṇa (रजोगुण) and Tamas (तमस्) or Tamoguṇa (तमोगुण), whose equilibrium is the basis of all observed empirical reality.

Pracaṇḍa (प्रचण्ड) means intense or severe.

Prajā (प्रजा) means progeny, children, procreation, or people.

Prajāpālana (प्रजापालन) means protection of subjects or people.

Prajñā (प्रज्ञा) means wisdom, intelligence, knowledge, or judgment. It can also mean to know or understand.

Prajvalita (प्रज्वलित) means ablaze.

Praṇāma (प्रणाम) means obeisance, prostration, or greetings.

Pratāpa (प्रताप) means majesty, splendor, or glory.

Prati (प्रति) is a prefix meaning towards.

Pratikāra (प्रतिकार) means opposition or retaliation.

Pratikūla (प्रतिकूल) means antagonistic or unfavorable.

Pratikūla-Buddhi (प्रतिकूल-बुद्धि) means antagonistic intelligence, unfavorable intelligence, unfriendly intelligence, or intellect that disfavors or dislikes some things.

Pratikūla-Vṛtti (प्रतिकूल-वृत्ति) means antagonistic mental state.

Pratipādana (प्रतिपादन) means to bestow, grant, or give. It can also mean stating or setting forth.

Pratipādita (प्रतिपादित) means set forth or stated.

Pratipādhya (प्रतिपाध्य) means predicable or propounded.

Pratibandhaka (प्रतिबन्धक) means impediment, obstructing, preventing, or resisting.

Pratibimba (प्रतिबिम्ब) means a reflection, reflected image, or mirrored form.

Pratiyogitā (प्रतियोगिता) means correlation.

Pratiṣṭhā (प्रतिष्ठा) means base, foundation, or ground.

Pratīta (प्रतीत) means to perceive, cognize, be aware of, or appear.

Pratīti (प्रतीति) means perception, cognition, awareness, appearance, or knowledge.

Pratīti-Kāla (प्रतीति-काल) means at the time of cognition.

Pratīyamāna (प्रतीयमान) means one that seems to appear.

Pratyakṣa (प्रत्यक्ष) means visible, evident, perceptible, direct, or cognizable by any faculty of sense. It can also mean perception.

Pratyaya (प्रत्यय) means intelligence, understanding, or consciousness. It can also mean belief, faith, form conviction, or certainty.

Pratyavāya (प्रत्यवाय) means fault that provides a contrary result.

Prathita (प्रथित) means known or celebrated.

Pradāna (प्रदान) means to bestow or to grant.

Pradviṣ (प्रद्विष्) means to hate or to dislike.

Pradhāna (प्रधान) means predominant, primary, or an essential part of anything.

Pradhvaṃsa (प्रध्वंस) means to annihilate or destroy.

Prapañca (प्रपञ्च), also known as Jagata (जगत) or Saṃsāra (संसार), means the phenomenal world. It is the aggregation of the five great elements of Prakṛti, viz. earth, water, fire, wind, and space.

Prabala (प्रबल) means potent or powerful.

Prabalatā (प्रबलता) means potency or power.

Prabuddha (प्रबुद्ध) means awakened or enlightened.

Prabodha (प्रबोध) means awake. It can also mean wakefulness, understanding, or becoming conscious.

Prabhavati (प्रभवति) means are manifest.

Prabhavanti (प्रभवन्ति) means it emanates.

Prabhā (प्रभा) means light, splendor, luster, effulgence, or radiance.

Prabhāva (प्रभाव) means might, power, majesty, dignity, strength, or efficacy. It can also mean influence.

Pramāṇa (प्रमाण) means a measure, standard, or guide.

Pramāṇita (प्रमाणित) means clearly shown, demonstrated, or proved.

Pramātha (प्रमाथ) means tormenting, torturing, or excessive paining.

Pramāthi (प्रमाथि) means agitating or turbulent.

Pramāda (प्रमाद) means negligence, indulgence, or error. It means indulgence in objective pleasures like one intoxicated. It can also mean requiring oversight.

Pramādī (प्रमादी) means negligent or insane.

Prayatnaśīla (प्रयत्नशील) means attempter or striver.

Prayojana (प्रयोजन) means purpose or motive.

Pralaya (प्रलय) is an eonic term for dissolution of the material world specified for different periods. In the dissolution, the material world merges into the unmanifest Prakṛti.

Pralāpa (प्रलाप) means to lament or mourn

Pravartita (प्रवर्तित) means to move or to operate.

Pravāha (प्रवाह) means a flow or stream. It can also mean a continuous train of thought or a course of action.

Praviṣṭa (प्रविष्ट) means entered into.

Pravīra (प्रवीर) means most excellent, distinguished, or heroic.

Pravṛtta (प्रवृत्त) means active.

Pravṛtti (प्रवृत्ति) means activity.

Pravṛddha (प्रवृद्ध) means fully grown, augmented, or increased.

Praveśa (प्रवेश) means entrance.

Praśaṃsā (प्रशंसा) means to praise or commendation.

Praśānta (प्रशान्त) means serene, peaceful, or quiescent.

Prasanna (प्रसन्न) means to be pleased.

Prasannatā (प्रसन्नता) means grace, serenity, clearness, or purity.

Prasāda (प्रसाद) means grace, benediction, or favor. It can also mean a propitiatory offering or a consecrated food offered to a deity, which after the ritual is shared and eaten by the devotees.

Prasiddha (प्रसिद्ध) means known, established in existence, or celebrated.

Prasthāna-Trayī (प्रस्थान-त्रयी) means the three canonical texts of Vedānta having epistemic authority. It consists of 1) the Upaniṣads, known as Upadeśa-Prasthāna (injunctive texts) and the Śruti-Prasthāna (the starting point or axiom of revelation), especially the principal Upaniṣads, 2) the Brahma-Sūtra, known as Sūtra-Prasthāna or Nyāya-Prasthāna or Yukti-Prasthāna (logical text or axiom of logic), and 3) the Bhagavad Gītā, known as Sādhanā-Prasthāna (practical text), and the Smṛti-Prasthāna (the starting point or axiom of remembered tradition)

Prākṛtarupa (प्राकृतरुप) means natural or innate form.

Prākṛtika (प्राकृतिक) means natural or derived from nature.

Prāk (प्राक्) means pre, before, or previously.

Prāk-Siddhatva (प्राक्-सिद्धत्व) means pre-existence.

Prāṇa (प्राण) means vital breaths of air.

Prāṇamaya-Kośa (प्राणमय-कोश) means the Sheath of Prāṇa that vitalizes and holds together the body and mind. It permeates the entire body and is manifested as breath. Life continues as long as this vital force exists in entities.

Prāṇa-Vāyu (प्राण-वायु) means in-breath, forward-moving air, and its flow is inwards and upward. It nourishes the brain and the eyes and governs the reception of all things: food, air, senses, and thoughts and is the fundamental energy in the body and directs and feeds into the four other winds (Vāyus). Its action is crystallization, its expression is cyclical, and its associated Cakra and element are Anāhata and air.

Prātibhāsika (प्रातिभासिक) means virtual, apparent, or illusory.

Prātibhāsika-Sattā (प्रातिभासिक-सत्ता) means apparent or illusory Reality. It is one where the determination of absence in the past, present, and future (त्रिकालाभाव-निश्चय, Trikālābhāva-Niścaya) can be made without Self-Realization. Dreamworld (स्वप्न-प्रपन्च, Svapna-Prapanca), an illusory snake has an apparent Reality because, upon removal of the defect (दोष, Doṣa) without Self-Realization, the snake can be realized as unreal.

Prādurbhāva (प्रादुर्भाव) means manifestation, come into existence, or arise.

Prāptavya (प्राप्तव्य) means to be obtained or got.

Prāptavyatā (प्राप्तव्यता) means attainableness or receivableness.

Prāpti (प्राप्ति) means attainment or receipt.

Prāyaḥ (प्रायः) means mostly or in all probability.

Prāyaścitta (प्रायश्चित्त) means penance, expiation, or atonement.

Prārabdha (प्रारब्ध) means that portion of accumulated past actions that are now ready to materialize or to be experienced.

Prārabdha-Kośa (प्रारब्ध-कोश) means a repository of past actions ready for fruition.

Priya (प्रिय) means pleasant or agreeable. It can mean beloved. It can also mean the sense of happiness or bliss.

Priya-Apriya (प्रिय-अप्रिय) means pleasant-unpleasant, liked-disliked, or desirable-undesirable.

Prīti (प्रीति) means affection or love. It can also mean satisfaction, happiness, or benefit.

Preta (प्रेत) means evil spirit.

Prema (प्रेम) means love.

Prema-Bhakti (प्रेम-भक्ति) means devotion with pure love. It is the perfected stage of devotion characterized by pure love.

Premī (प्रेमी) means lover.

Preya (प्रेय) means dear or more agreeable.

Preraka (प्रेरक) means setting in motion or impelling.

Preraṇā (प्रेरणा) means inspiration.

Prerita (प्रेरित) means impelled, induced, urged, or prompted.

Prauḍhatā (प्रौढता) means maturity or ripeness

Phala (फल) means fruit or result.

Phaladāyaka (फलदायक) means giver of fruits.

Phalaprada (फलप्रद) means bringing reward.

Phalapradātā (फलप्रदाता) means giver of fruits.

Phalabhoga (फलभोग) means enjoyment of fruits.

Phala-Vyāpti (फल-व्याप्ति) means the cognition of knowing some substance in a separate form from one's own through measures such as the senses.

Phalāśā (फलाशा) means desire or hope for fruits.

Phalāśī (फलाशी) means an enjoyer of the fruits.

Phalonmukha (फलोन्मुख) means facing fruits or ready for fruition. It is a compound word from Phala (फल) meaning fruit and Unmukha (उन्मुख) meaning facing, oriented.

Ṛta (ऋत) means order or rule. It is the principle of the natural order, which regulates and coordinates the operation of the world and everything within it.

Ṛṣi (ऋषि) means a seer or a sage.

Ṝṇa (ॠण) means obligation or debt.

Racanā (रचना) means composition.

Racita (रचित) means created.

Rajata (रजत) means silver or silver-colored.

Rajas (रजस्) means the second of the three constituents of Prakṛti or constituent attributes of all material substances {the other two being Sattva (सत्त्व) and Tamas (तमस्)}. It is also referred to as Rajoguṇa (रजोगुण) and predominates in humans. It is the attribute of passion and is the cause of activity. It produces fickleness (Cañcalatā) and agitation (Kṣobha).

Rajoguṇa (रजोगुण) means the second of the three constituents of Prakṛti or constituent attributes of all material substances. It predominates in humans and is the cause of activity. It produces fickleness (Cañcalatā) and agitation (Kṣobha).

Rajoguṇī (रजोगुणी) means endowed with Rajoguṇa.

Rati (रति) means to delight in, fondness for, rejoice, repose, or rest in.

Rattī (रत्ती) means iota.

Ramaṇīya (रमणीय) means elegant or beautiful.

Ramaṇīyatā (रमणीयता) means elegance or beauty.

Rasa (रस) means sapidity or taste. It can also mean sentiment or an internal instinct. The term Rasa primarily denotes taste or flavor. However, in literature, it has the connotation of emotional experience.

Rasanā (रसना) means tongue with the sense of taste.

Rasa-Saṃyukta (रस-संयुक्त) means with sentiments.

Rasātmaka (रसात्मक) means like ambrosiac.

Rasya (रस्य) means savory, tasty, palatable, or juicy.

Rahasya (रहस्य) means secret, mysterious, mystic, deep, or subtle.

Rahita (रहित) means without or devoid.

Rākṣasa (राक्षस) means a demon in general or an evil demon. They are regarded as produced from the feet of Brahmā and are powerful beings who embody sensual enjoyment, revenge, and wrath.

Rāga (राग) means attachment, passion, fondness, or deep love.

Rāga-Dveṣa (राग-द्वेष) means passion-dispassion, attachment-aversion, attraction-repulsion, like-dislike, or love-hatred.

Rājarṣi (राजर्षि) means Royal sages.

Rājasika (राजसिक) means endowed with the attribute of passion, or endowed with that which is the cause of activity. It produces fickleness and agitation.

Rājasī (राजसी) means possessing the attribute of Rajoguṇa or that which causes activity. It can also mean royal or noble.

Rājya (राज्य) means a kingdom or a state.

Rāśi (राशि) means a division (of living beings).

Rāhitya (राहित्य) means destituteness, free from, or without.

Rīti (रीति) means way, custom, practice, method, or manner.

Ruci (रुचि) means fondness, liking, or taste.

Rudra (रुद्र) are eleven in number: 1. Hara (हर), 2. Bahurūpa (बहुरूप), 3. Trayambaka (त्रयम्बक), 4. Aparājita (अपराजित), 5. Vṛṣākapi (वृषाकपि), 6. Śambhu (शम्भु), 7. Kapardī (कपर्दी), 8. Raivata (रैवत), 9. Mṛgavyādha (मृगव्याध), 10. Śarva (शर्व) and 11. Kapālī (कपाली).

Rupa (रुप) means form or nature.

Rūkṣa (रूक्ष) means dry.

Recaka (रेचक) means exhalation.

Roga (रोग) means disease or sickness.

Romāncakārī (रोमान्चकारी) means hair raising.

Śaṃkha (शंख) means a conch.

Śakti (शक्ति) means power or energy.

Ṣaṭ-Koṭi (शत-कोटि) means billion. A compound word where Ṣaṭ (शत) means 100 and Koṭi (कोटि) means 10 million.

Śatru (शत्रु) means enemy or foe.

Śabda (शब्द) means sound.

Śama (शम) means control of the mind.

Śaraṇa (शरण) means refuge.

Śaraṇāgata (शरणागत) means one who has surrendered or one who has gone for refuge.

Śarīra (शरीर) means body.

Śarīradhāri (शरीरधारि) means incarnate, corporeal, or bodied.

Śalya (शल्य) means a dart, spear, or arrow. It can also mean anything tormenting or causing pain.

Śastra (शस्त्र) means a weapon.

Śastra-Vidyā (शस्त्र-विद्या) means knowledge of weaponry.

Śāna (शान) means pride.

Śānta (शान्त) means calm, tranquil, appeased, or purified.

Śānti (शान्ति) means peace or tranquility.

Śāligrāma (शालिग्राम) is a black fossilized shell worshipped in the form of Lord Viṣṇu.

Śāśvata (शाश्वत) means everlasting or permanent.

Śāśvata-Dharma (शाश्वत-धर्म) means everlasting righteousness.

Śāstra (शास्त्र) means any instrument of teaching, especially any religious treatise, a sacred book, or composition of divine authority.

Śāstra-Vihita (शास्त्र-विहित) means based on Śāstra, in conformance with Śāstra, in agreement with Śāstra, or supported by Śāstra.

Śikhā-Sūtra (शिखा-सूत्र) means the lock of hair on the crown and the Yajñopavīta or sacred thread.

Śithila (शिथिल) means slack, loose, lax, weak, or feeble.

Śithilatā (शिथिलता) means laxity.

Śukti (शुक्ति) means oyster shell.

Śuca (शुच) means to grieve, lament, or mourn.

Śucīna (शुचीन) means pure, pious, or clean.

Śuddha (शुद्ध) means pure.

Śuddha-Svarupa (शुद्ध-स्वरुप) means own pure, true nature, where Śuddha (शुद्ध) means pure and Svarupa (स्वरुप) is a compound word from Sva (स्व) meaning self, own and Rupa (रुप) meaning form, so Svarupa means one's form, true nature, or essence.

Śuddhātmā (शुद्धात्मा) means the pure Ātmā.

Śuddhi (शुद्धि) means purity.

Śubha (शुभ) means auspicious or good.

Śubha-Ācaraṇa (शुभ-आचरण) means virtuous conduct.

Śubha-Sakāmī (शुभ-सकामी) means one who covets virtuous desire-ridden acts.

Śubhāśubha (शुभाशुभ) means good-bad. It is a compound word from Śubha (शुभ), meaning auspicious or good and Aśubha (अशुभ), meaning bad or evil.

Śuṣka (शुष्क) means dried, dried up, or shrunk. It can also mean useless or fruitless.

Śūdra-Prakṛti (शूद्र-प्रकृति) means the innate attributes of a Śūdra. The attributes enumerated in BG 18.44 consist of servicing or providing labor (Paricaryātmaka, परिचर्यात्मक).

Śūnya (शून्य) means null or zero.

Śūnyatā (शून्यता) means nullness or emptiness.

Śūra (शूर) means valor.

Śṛgāla (शृगाल) means jackal.

Śṛṅgāra (शृङ्गार) means adornments or beautifications.

Śeṣa (शेष) means remainder or that which remains or is left.

Śoka (शोक) means sorrow or lamentation.

Śocati (शोचति) means laments or grieves.

Śoṣaṇa (शोषण) means drying up.

Śauca (शौच) means purity or cleanliness. It includes both external and internal cleanliness. Nourishing oneself with a pure diet from pure materials rightfully procured and cleaning the defilements of the body through water and soil are all exterior cleanliness. Purity from attachment and aversion is called internal cleanliness.

Śaurya (शौर्य) means valor or heroism.

Śmaśāna (श्मशान) means cremation grounds.

Śraddhā (श्रद्धा) means faith, trust, or confidence. It can also mean respect or reverence. In Vedānta, it means faith in the words of preceptors and scriptures.

Śraddhāmaya (श्रद्धामय) means full of faith.

Śraddhāvāna (श्रद्धावान) means one with steady faith. One who has immovable trust in the words of Guru-Śāstra.

Śraddheya (श्रद्धेय) means one in whom there is faith. It can also mean to be trusted, trustworthy

Śramaṇa (श्रमण) means one who performs acts of austerity, an ascetic, monk, devotee, or a religious mendicant.

Śravaṇa (श्रवण) means listening to holy scriptures.

Śrī (श्री) means prosperity, auspiciousness, welfare, wealth, or treasure.

Śrīmatām (श्रीमताम्) means prosperous householders.

Śrīmat (श्रीमत्) means endowed with opulence, wealth, or prosperity. It can also mean endowed with radiance or brilliance.

Śrīmāna (श्रीमान) means prosperous.

Śrīvatsa (श्रीवत्स) means the abode of Śrī Lakṣmī

Śreṇi (श्रेणि) means level. It can also mean a line, series, or row.

Śreya (श्रेय) means beneficial, conducive to welfare, benevolent, or auspicious. It can also mean superior or the highest good.

Śreyaskara (श्रेयस्कर) means more efficacious for securing happiness.

Śreṣṭha (श्रेष्ठ) means great, excellent, superior, or most splendid.

Śrotra (श्रोत्र) means ears with the sense of hearing.

Śrauta (श्रौत) means observances ordained by the Vedas.

Ślokabaddha (श्लोकबद्ध) means composed in the verses.

Ṣaṭ-Kāraka (षट-कारक) means sixfold instruments of action: (1) doer (कर्ता, Kartā) of the act; (2) action (कर्म, Karma) meaning the activity of the act; (3) instruments (करण, Karaṇa) by which act is performed; (4) for whom the act is performed (संप्रदान, Saṃpradāna); (5) from where the act is performed (अपादान, Apādāna); and (6) in which act is performed (अधिकरण, Adhikaraṇa). A Kāraka relation means a relationship between a noun and the verbal activity with which it is connected.

Ṣaṭ-Pramāṇa (षट्-प्रमाण) means the six measures that provide correct knowledge and the truth: 1) perception (प्रत्यक्ष, Pratyakṣa), 2) inference (अनुमान, Anumāna), 3) comparison and analogy (उपमान, Upamāna), 4) postulation, derivation from circumstances (अर्थापत्ति, Arthāpatti), 5) non-perception, negative cognitive proof (अनुपलब्धि, Anupalabdhi) and 6) word, a testimony of past or present reliable experts (शब्द, Śabda)

Ṣaṭ-Rasa (षट्-रस) means six tastes: 1) sweet (मधुर, Madhura), 2) salty (लवण, Lavaṇa), 3) bitter (तिक्त, Tikta), 4) sour (अम्ल, Amla), 5) pungent (कटु, Kaṭu) and 6) astringent (कषाय, Kaṣāya)

Ṣaṭ-Sampatti (षट्-सम्पत्ति) means the sixfold virtues enumerated as a) control of the mind (शम, Śama), b) restraint over the senses (दम, Dama), c) faith in the words of the preceptors and the scriptures (श्रद्धा, Śraddhā) d) absence of mental vacillations (समाधान, Samādhāna), e) desistance from the relinquishment of actions (Karma-Tyāga) and vile objects (उपराम, Uparāma), f) tolerance to bear dualities such as heat and cold, pleasure and pain, hunger and thirst (तितिक्षा, Titikṣā).

Ṣaḍ-Bhāva-Vikāra (षड्-भाव-विकार) means the sixfold transformations of the material world: 1) to be born (जायते, Jāyate), 2) to remain (अस्ति, Asti), 3) to result into (विपरिणमते, Vipariṇamate), 4) to grow (वर्धते, Vardhate), 5) to decay (अपक्षीयते, Apakṣīyate) and 6) to die (विनश्यति, Vinaśyati).

Ṣaḍvikāra (षड्विकार): The six sixfold mutations: 1) lust (काम, Kāma), 2) anger (क्रोध, Krodha), 3) greed (लोभ, Lobha), 4) delusion (मोह, Moha), 5) excessive pride (मद, Mada) and 6) envy (मत्सर, Matsara).

Ṣaḍvikāravāna (षड्विकारवान) means one with sixfold mutations.

Ṣoḍaśa-Saṃskāra (षोडश-संस्कार) means the sixteen rites of passage in a human being's life as described in Vedantic scriptures: 1) Garbhādhāna-Saṃskāra (गर्भाधान-संस्कार), 2) Puṃsavana-Saṃskāra (पुंसवन-संस्कार), 3) Sīmaṃtonnayana-Saṃskāra (सीमंतोन्नयन-संस्कार, 4) Jātakarma-Saṃskāra (जातकर्म-संस्कार), 5) Nāmakaraṇa- Saṃskāra (नामकरण-संस्कार), 6) Niṣkramaṇa-Saṃskāra (निष्क्रमण-संस्कार), 7) Annaprāśana-Saṃskāra (अन्नप्राशन-संस्कार), 8) Cūḍākaraṇa-Saṃskāra (चूडाकरण-संस्कार), 9) Karṇavedha-Saṃskāra (कर्णवेध-संस्कार), 10) Vidyāraṃbha-Saṃskāra (विद्यारंभ-संस्कार), 11) Upanayana-Saṃskāra (उपनयन-संस्कार), 12) Vedāraṃbha-Saṃskāra (वेदारंभ-संस्कार), 13 Keśāṃta-Saṃskāra (केशांत-संस्कार), 14) Samāvartana-Saṃskāra (समावर्तन-संस्कार), 15) Vivāha-Saṃskāra (विवाह-संस्कार) and 16) Antyeṣṭi-Saṃskāra (अन्त्येष्टि-संस्कार)

Sa (स) as a prefix when compounded with nouns forms adjectives and adverbs. It may be translated by with, together, or along with, accompanied by, added to, having, possessing, or containing.

Saṃkalpa (संकल्प) means a thought, resolve, or determination.

Saṃkalpa-Vikalpa (संकल्प-विकल्प) means thought, and its alternative, where Saṃkalpa (संकल्प) means thought, resolve, or determination and Vikalpa (विकल्प) means alternative or variant thought.

Saṃkalpavikalpātmaka (संकल्पविकल्पात्मक) means the ability to develop thought and its variant or alternative.

Saṃkīrṇa (संकीर्ण) means adulterated or mingled.

Saṃketa (संकेत) means hint or signal.

Saṃkoca (संकोच) means contraction or collapse. It can also mean hesitance.

Saṃkṣepa (संक्षेप) means brief.

Saṃkucita (संकुचित) means contracted or shrunk.

Saṃkhyā (संख्या) means number or sum. It can also mean calculation or measurement.

Saṃgati (संगति) means harmonious connection, congruity, or coming together.

Saṃgrāma (संग्राम) means battle, war, fight, combat, or conflict.

Saṃgha (संघ) means group.

Saṃjñake (संज्ञके) means which is called.

Saṃjñā (संज्ञा) means title or name.

Saṃjñārtha (संज्ञार्थ) means for a sign or an indication.

Saṃtapta (संतप्त) means afflicted or tormented.

Saṃtāpa (संताप) means affliction. It can also mean burning heat

Saṃtoṣa-Prada (संतोष-प्रद) means satisfactory or one that gives satisfaction.

Saṃnyāsa (संन्यास) means renunciation.

Saṃnyāsa-Āśrama (संन्यास-आश्रम) means the last stage of life marked by the renunciation of material desires and prejudices, represented by a state of disinterest and detachment from material life, generally without any meaningful property or home, and focused on liberation, peace, and simple spiritual life. Anyone could enter this stage after completing the Brahmacarya stage of life.

Saṃpādana (संपादन) means to acquire or to accomplish.

Saṃpradāna (संप्रदान) means bestowal, gift, or donation. It can also mean for whom the act is performed.

Saṃbhāvita (संभावित) means one who is held in high esteem or who is highly regarded.

Saṃyata (संयत) means restrained, curbed, or subdued.

Saṃyatātmā (संयतात्मा) means restrained or controlled.

Saṃyatendriya (संयतेन्द्रिय) means one who has senses or passions under control.

Saṃyama (संयम) means self-control.

Saṃyamī (संयमी) means self-controlled.

Saṃyukta (संयुक्त) means conjoined or combined.

Saṃyoga (संयोग) means conjunction, connection, or union.

Saṃlagna (संलग्न) means attached or united.

Saṃlagnatā (संलग्नता) means engagement.

Saṃvigna (संविग्न) means distressed or agitated

Saṃvedya (संवेद्य) means to be known, understood, or experienced

Saṃsarga (संसर्ग) means conjunction or sensual attachment. It can also mean acquaintance or close contact.

Saṃsargī (संसर्गी) means an acquaintance or a close contact.

Saṃsāra (संसार) means the world of transmigrating lives. Saṃsāra is that which does Saṃsaraṇa (संसरण, that which passes through a succession of states, birth-rebirth of living beings). The terms Saṃsāra, Jagata, Prapañca, or world, are synonymous.

Saṃsāra-Cakra (संसार-चक्र) means the worldly cycle of birth and death.

Saṃsārī (संसारी) means worldly.

Saṃsiddhi (संसिद्धि) means complete perfection or purity of the conscience. It can also mean completion, accomplishment, or attainment.

Saṃskāra (संस्कार) means a dynamic impression. Collectively they are dynamic psychological imprints left in the subconscious by actions, whether conscious or unconscious, internal or external, desirable or undesirable. They influence a person's nature, response, and state of mind. These imprints are not merely passive vestiges of actions and intentions but dynamic forces constantly pushing a Jīva. These impressions wait to return to the conscious level of the mind, influencing the future in the form of expectations, sense of self-worth, habits, innate dispositions, and emotions, propelling one's life and generating future actions. They are referred to as behavioral traits either as default from birth or perfected over time through conscious shaping of the conscience.

Saṃskṛta (संस्कृत) means refined or perfected. It can also mean well done or completely formed.

Saṃsmṛti (संस्मृति) means remembrance or recollection.

Sakāma (सकाम) means with desires.

Sakāmatā (सकामता) means desirousness, desire-ridden, or lasciviousness.

Sakāmī (सकामी) means desire-ridden. It can also mean lascivious or one who lusts.

Sakāśa (सकाश) means near or present.

Sakti (सक्ति) means affection, love, or attachment.

Sakhā (सखा) means friend.

Sakhya (सख्य) means friendship.

Saguṇa (सगुण) means having attributes or qualities.

Saguṇarupa (सगुणरुप) means the form having attributes.

Saṅga (सङ्ग) means meeting, union, coming together, or union. It can also mean association or attraction of the mind.

Saṅgraha (सङ्ग्रह) means collection.

Saṅghāta (सङ्घात) means aggregation.

Sacakṣu (सचक्षु) means with eyes.

Sacitta (सचित्त) means endowed with reason.

Saceta (सचेत) means conscious.

Saccidānanda (सच्चिदानन्द) means the Real Conscious Bliss. It is a compound word from Sat (सत्), meaning that which is the real, existent, or true essence, Cit (चित्), meaning conscious, and Ānanda (आनन्द) meaning bliss. All three are considered inseparable from the nature of the supreme imperishable Reality or the Brahman. The terms Ultimate Reality, Absolute Truth, Absolute Principle, Supreme Reality, and Supreme Self are synonyms.

Sacchāstra (सच्छास्त्र) means Śāstra that provides the Truth. It is a compound word from Sat (सत्) true and Śāstra (शास्त्र), meaning an instrument of teaching, especially any religious treatise, a sacred book, or composition of divine authority

Sajātīya (सजातीय) means homogeneous or similar.

Sajātīya-Bheda (सजातीय-भेद) means homogeneous distinction.

Sajīva (सजीव) means alive.

Sañcālaka (सञ्चालक) means controller.

Sañcita (सञ्चित) means accumulated.

Sañcita-Karma (सञ्चित-कर्म) means accumulated actions. The sum of past actions - all actions, good and bad.

Sañcita-Kośa (सञ्चित-कोश) means a repository of accumulated past actions.

Sañjanayan (सञ्जनयन्) means to arouse or to excite.

Satata (सतत) means constantly, always, ever, perpetual, or continual.

Satata-Yukta (सतत-युक्त) means ever united.

Satoguṇī (सतोगुणी) means having pure or virtuous attributes.

Sat (सत्) means real or true. From the Vedantic perspective, it is used to denote the existent Self or the pure Ātmā. It is also used for righteousness and noble deeds.

Satkarma (सत्कर्म) means noble deed.

Satkāra (सत्कार) means respect or reverence.

Sattā (सत्ता) means Reality, beingness, presence, or existence. Authority or power is implied with presence or existence.

Sattāmātra (सत्तामात्र) means the supreme imperishable Reality or the primeval Reality from which knowledge arises as light from a flame.

Sattā-Śūnya (सत्ता-शून्य) means without the presence or existence.

Sattā-Sāmānya (सत्ता-सामान्य) means the one that is the existent common in all.

Sattā-Sphūrti (सत्ता-स्फूर्ति) means power.

Sattva (सत्त्व) means pure or virtuous. It is the first of the three constituents of Prakṛti or constituent attributes of all material substances {the other two being Rajas (रजस्) and Tamas (तमस्)}. It is also referred to as Sattvaguṇa (सत्त्वगुण) and predominates in the deities (देव, Deva). It is the cause of goodness, purity, and virtuosity.

Sattvaguṇa (सत्त्वगुण) means the first of the three constituents of Prakṛti or constituent attributes of all material substances. It predominates in the deities (देव, Deva). It is the cause of goodness, purity, and virtuosity.

Sattvaguṇamaya (सत्त्वगुणमय) means consisting of Sattvaguṇa.

Sattvaguṇātmaka (सत्त्वगुणात्मक) means with Sattvaguṇa.

Sattvaguṇī (सत्त्वगुणी) means endowed with Sattvaguṇa.

Satya (सत्य) means true or real.

Satyakāma (सत्यकाम) means truth loving.

Satyatā (सत्यता) means reality, truth, or trueness.

Satyatva (सत्यत्व) means reality, truth, or veracity.

Satya-Vastu (सत्य-वस्तु) means true thing.

Satyasaṃkalpa (सत्यसंकल्प) means whose resolve becomes fact.

Satya-Svarupa (सत्य-स्वरुप) means own true nature, where Satya (सत्य) means true, and Svarupa (स्वरुप) means one's form, true nature, or essence. It can also mean the true nature of the supreme imperishable Reality.

Satsaṅga (सत्सङ्ग) means spiritual discourse or sitting and listening to enlightened knowers. It can also mean association with genuine people or being with righteous companions.

Sat-Svarupa (सत्-स्वरुप) means true nature, whose nature is in the form of Sat (सत्, true, real, or existent).

Sadācāra (सदाचार) means virtuous conduct, good manners, or practice of good men.

Sadupayoga (सदुपयोग) means good use.

Sadguṇa (सद्गुण) means good attributes or virtues.

Sadguru (सद्गुरु) means a true preceptor. It is a compound word from Sat (सत्), meaning true and Guru (गुरु), meaning a preceptor.

Sadbuddhi (सद्बुद्धि) means righteous or virtuous intellect. It can also mean proper or correct thinking.

Sadbhāva (सद्भाव) means true sentiment. It can also mean true beingness.

Sadrūpa (सद्रूप) means true nature.

Sadhyo-Mukti (सध्यो-मुक्ति) means immediate liberation.

Sanātana (सनातन) means everlasting, always present, or eternal. It can also mean ancient.

Sankhiyā (सन्खिया) refers to a medicine of Ayurveda. A very deadly poison, in its natural state, is white, red, yellow, and black colors. White is used for medicine.

Santa (सन्त) means righteous, saintly, or holy.

Santuṣṭa (सन्तुष्ट) means fully satisfied or pleased.

Sandeha (सन्देह) means doubt.

Sannidhi (सन्निधि) means nearness or closeness.

Saptarṣi (सप्तर्षि) collectively refers to the seven great seers (Maharṣi) of each Manvantara. Currently, we are in the Vaivasvata Manvantara with the following seven Maharṣis: Maharṣi Kaśyapa (कश्यप), Maharṣi Atri (अत्रि), Maharṣi Vasīṣṭha (वसीष्ठ), Maharṣi Viśvāmitra (विश्वामित्र), Maharṣi Gautama (गौतम), Maharṣi Jamadagni (जमदग्नि) and Maharṣi Bhāradvāja (भारद्वाज) as cited in Bṛhadāraṇyaka Upaniṣad (बृहदारण्यक उपनिषद्) 2.2.6.

Saphala (सफल) means bearing fruits or fruitful.

Sama (सम) means identical, similar, or like.

Samatā (समता) means equilibrium.

Samatva (समत्व) means equanimity.

Samadarśī (समदर्शी) means one who sees all with equanimity or equi-sighted.

Sama-Dṛṣṭi (सम-दृष्टि) means seeing everything equally or with equanimity

Samanvaya (समन्वय) means mutual connection, connected sequence or consequence, or regular succession or order.

Samanvita (समन्वित) means connected or associated with.

Samabuddhi (समबुद्धि) means equanimity of the mind or the sameness of judgment or intellect. It can also mean complete understanding.

Samarupa (समरुप) means similar form.

Samarpaṇa (समर्पण) means total dedication.

Samaṣṭi (समष्टि) means aggregate or collective.

Samaṣṭi-Dṛṣṭi (समष्टि-दृष्टि) means aggregate view or collective view.

Sama-Samuccaya (सम-समुच्चय) is a view that desireless actions (Niṣkāma-Karma) and knowledge are two independent and equal strength paths in the attainment of liberation, one not dependent on the other

Samādhāna (समाधान) means reconciliation, justification of a statement, or proof. It can also mean the absence of vacillations.

Samādhī (समाधी) means oneness with the Self or Paramātmā.

Samāna (समान) means alike or similar.

Samālocanā (समालोचना) means criticism.

Samāsa (समास) means an aggregation of words to form compound words or a euphonic combination.

Samāhita (समाहित) means united or joined.

Samāhita-Citta (समाहित-चित्त) means mind in union.

Samīcīna (समीचीन) means judicious, proper, correct, or just. It can also mean being or remaining together, connected, united, complete, or whole.

Samuccaya (समुच्चय) means collection. It can also mean the conjugation of words.

Samudāya (समुदाय) means multitude, mass, or group.

Samudra (समुद्र) means sea.

Samūla (समूल) means with the root.

Samṛddha (समृद्ध) means prosperous.

Sampatti (सम्पत्ति) means wealth or opulence. It can also mean attribute.

Sampadā (सम्पदा) means attributes. It can also mean assets or treasures.

Sampradāya (सम्प्रदाय) means tradition or spiritual lineage.

Sambandha (सम्बन्ध) means relation or connection.

Sambandhi (सम्बन्धि) means relative.

Sambandhita (सम्बन्धित) means connected.

Sambhūta (सम्भूत) means arisen or born.

Sammati (सम्मति) means consent or permission.

Sammukha (सम्मुख) means in front.

Sammoha (सम्मोह) means confusion, bewilderment, mental clouding, blurring of judgment, an illusion of the mind, or delusion.

Samyaka (सम्यक) means correct or proper.

Samyagadarśī (सम्यगदर्शी) means one with a proper perspective.

Sarala (सरल) means simple, sincere, or candid.

Sarga (सर्ग) means creation.

Sarva (सर्व) means total, all, entire, whole, or every.

Sarva-Kartā (सर्व-कर्ता) means a doer of everything.

Sarva-Karma-Phala-Tyāga (सर्व-कर्म-फल-त्याग) means relinquishment of the rewards of all actions.

Sarva-Karma-Saṃnyāsa (सर्व-कर्म-संन्यास) means total renunciation of doership and thus all actions.

Sarvagata (सर्वगत) means ubiquitous or all-pervading.

Sarvajña (सर्वज्ञ) means omniscient.

Sarvataḥ (सर्वतः) means from all sides, in every direction, everywhere, or all around.

Sarva-Tyāga (सर्व-त्याग) means relinquishment of everything.

Sarvatra (सर्वत्र) means everywhere.

Sarvathā (सर्वथा) means by all ways or by all means.

Sarva-Bhūta (सर्व-भूत) means all living beings.

Sarva-Bheda-Vinirmukta (सर्व-भेद-विनिर्मुक्त) means free from all distinctions.

Sarvarupa (सर्वरुप) means the form of all-forms.

Sarvarupatā (सर्वरुपता) means the attribute of being in all diverse forms.

Sarva-Vyāpī (सर्व-व्यापी) means omnipresent.

Sarvaśaḥ (सर्वशः) means in all possible ways, in all respects, wholly, completely, or everywhere.

Sarva-Saṅga (सर्व-सङ्ग) means union with all or attachment to all.

Sarva-Saṅga-Parityāga (सर्व-सङ्ग-परित्याग) means relinquishment of all attachments. It means the absence of desire for children, wealth, renown, and fame.

Sarva-Saṅga-Vinirmukta (सर्व-सङ्ग-विनिर्मुक्त) means free from attachment to all.

Sarva-Sākṣī (सर्व-साक्षी) means that who witnesses or beholds all.

Sarvātmatā (सर्वात्मता) means the beingness of the Ātmā of all beings.

Sarvātma-Dṛṣṭi (सर्वात्म-द्रष्टि) means seeing one Ātmā in all beings.

Sarvātmā (सर्वात्मा) means the Ātmā of all beings.

Sarvātmaikya (सर्वात्मैक्य) means the existence of one Ātmā in all beings.

Sarvātmaikya-Dṛṣṭi (सर्वात्मैक्य-द्रष्टि) means the vision of beholding one Ātmā in all beings.

Sarvotkṛṣṭa (सर्वोत्कृष्ट) means unbeatable.

Sarvotkṛṣṭatā (सर्वोत्कृष्टता) means unbeatableness.

Sarvottama (सर्वोत्तम) means the best.

Savikalpa (सविकल्प) means with an alternative or with variant thought.

Savyasācin (सव्यसाचिन्) means a skillful bowman or one who can ambidextrously shoot arrows.

Sahaja (सहज) means innate or natural.

Sahāyaka (सहायक) means aiding, rendering assistance, or helpful.

Sahiṣṇutā (सहिष्णुता) means tolerance.

Sā (सा) means that is.

Sāṃpradāyika (सांप्रदायिक) means sectarian or communal.

Sākṣāt (साक्षात्) means in the presence of, before the very eyes, visibly, or direct.

Sākṣātkāra (साक्षात्कार) means direct or intuitive perception. It can also mean experiencing, proving, or verifying.

Sākṣī (साक्षी) means witness.

Sākṣī-Dṛṣṭā (साक्षी द्रष्टा) means the witness-observer. The immovable (अचल, Acala) and immutable (कूटस्थ, Kūṭastha) pure conscious element in the body that passively observes and illuminates the actions and mutations of the body is known as Sākṣī-Dṛṣṭā. The words Sākṣī and Dṛṣṭā are synonymous.

Sākṣī-Cetana (साक्षी-चेतन) means the witness-conscious.

Sākṣya (साक्ष्य) means visible to. It can also mean testimony or evidence.

Sāṅkhya (साङ्ख्य) means the science of Vedānta wherein are enumerated the principles to be known.

Sāttvika (सात्त्विक) means the attribute of goodness, purity, and virtuosity

Sāttvikī (सात्त्विकी) means possessing attribute of Sattvaguṇa or that which causes purity and virtuosity.

Sādi (सादि) means having a beginning.

Sādhaka (साधक) means a seeker, religious practitioner, one who follows a particular Sādhanā, or one who has gone through a specific initiation. It can also mean instrumental.

Sādhaka-Bādhaka (साधक-बाधक) means instrumental-detrimental, helper-oppose.

Sādhana (साधन) means accessories, means, or instruments.

Sādhana-Kāla (साधन-काल) means when means are active.

Sādhana-Catuṣṭaya (साधन-चतुष्टय) means the fourfold means: 1) discernment (विवेक, Viveka). The ability to discern between the real and the unreal, between the permanent and the impermanent, between the Ātmā and the non-Ātmā; 2) dispassion (वैराग्य, Vairāgya) for pleasures of this world and of heavens; 3) the sixfold virtues (षट्-सम्पत्ति, Ṣaṭ-Sampatti): a) control of the mind (शम, Śama), b) restraint over the senses (दम, Dama), c) faith in the words of preceptors and scriptures (श्रद्धा, Śraddhā), d) absence of mental vacillations (समाधान, Samādhāna), e) desistance from the relinquishment of actions (कर्म-त्याग, Karma-Tyāga) and vile objects (उपराम, Uparāma), f) tolerance (तितिक्षा, Titikṣā) to bear dualities such as heat and cold, pleasure and pain, hunger and thirst and 4) intense desire for liberation (मुमुक्षुत्व, Mumukṣutva).

Sādhana-Sampanna (साधन-सम्पन्न) means possessing means.

Sādhana-Sādhya (साधन-साध्य) means instrument and goal

Sādhanā (साधना) means performance, propitiation.

Sādhu (साधु) means pious, righteous, or virtuous.

Sādhya (साध्य) means goal, to be attained, or fulfilled.

Sādhyā (साध्या) are a group of twelve deities, the sons of Sādhyā (the daughter of Prajāpati Dakṣa) and Dharma and enumerated as 1. Manas (मनस्), 2. Anumantā (अनुमन्ता), 3. Prāṇa (प्राण), 4. Nara (नर), 5. Apāna (अपान), 6. Vīryavān (वीर्यवान्), 7. Naya (नय), 8. Haya (हय), 9. Haṃsa (हंस), 10. Nārāyaṇa (नारायण), 11. Vibhu (विभु) and 12. Prabhu (प्रभु).

Sāna (सान) means a grindstone.

Sānta (सान्त) means with an end.

Sāpekṣa (सापेक्ष) means dependent on.

Sāpekṣatā (सापेक्षता) means dependence.

Sāmagrī (सामग्री) means accessories, substance, or material.

Sāmānya (सामन्य) means common, general, or usual.

Sāmarthya (सामर्थ्य) means ability or capacity.

Sāmīpya-Mukti (सामीप्य-मुक्ति) means liberation where the devotee becomes a personal associate close to the Supreme Personality.

Sāmyatā (साम्यता) means equality, sameness, or evenness.

Sāmyāvasthā (साम्यावस्था) means equilibrium or the state of equipoise.

Sāyujya (सायुज्य) means oneness (Ekatva).

Sāyujya-Mukti (सायुज्य-मुक्ति) means oneness or merger (Ekatva) with the attributeless and formless Brahman through knowledge.

Sāra (सार) means essence or gist.

Sāra-Asāra Viveka (सार-असार विवेक) means the ability to discern between real and unreal, right and wrong.

Sārathī (सारथि) means a charioteer or one who controls a horse-drawn chariot.

Sārupya-Mukti (सारुप्य-मुक्ति) means liberation where the devotee acquires the form of the Supreme Personality, including Śaṃkha(conch), Sudarśana-Cakra (spinning disk-like weapon meaning "disk of auspicious vision"), Gadā (sphere ended mace) and Padma (lotus) except for Śrīvatsa (abode of Śrī Lakṣmī), Bhṛgulatā (footprint of Saptarṣi Bhṛgu) and Kaustubha-Maṇi (the fourth jewel that came out from Samudra-Manthana), located on the chest of the Supreme Personality.

Sārthaka (सार्थक) means meaningful.

Sārthakatā (सार्थकता) means meaningfulness, significance, or importance.

Sārvabhauma (सार्वभौम) means the whole earth. It can also mean humankind's salvation nature.

Sārṣṭi-Mukti (सार्ष्टि-मुक्ति) means liberation where the devotee receives the same opulence as the Supreme Personality.

Sālokya-Mukti (सालोक्य-मुक्ति) means liberation where the devotee attains the abode of the Supreme Personality, that is, goes to live in the same sphere or world (Loka) of the Supreme Personality.

Sāṣṭāṅga-Daṇḍavat-Praṇāma (साष्टांग-दण्डवत्-प्रणाम) means eight-limb long prostration, where two toes, two knees, chest, forehead, and two palms joined and stretched above the head touch the ground in the process of paying respectful obeisance and total surrender.

Sāhitya (साहित्य) means association, with.

Siddha (सिद्ध) means proven. It can also mean to accomplish or to establish. It can also mean a person who is accomplished, who has fulfilled his objectives, or a perfected sage. Right from birth, a person who has attained abundant righteousness (Atiśaya-Dharma), knowledge (Jñāna), dispassion (Vairāgya), and lordliness (Aiśvarya) is called a Siddha.

Siddhatva (सिद्धत्व) means validation or establishment. It can also mean perfection or a perfect state.

Siddhānta (सिद्धान्त) means a tenet, a theory, or a principle.

Siddhi (सिद्धि) means fruition, accomplishment, fulfillment, or success. It can also mean perfection or pre-eminence.

Siddhi-Asiddhi (सिद्धि-असिद्धि) means success-failure.

Sukṛta (सुकृत) means good deed.

Sukha (सुख) means happiness or pleasure.

Sukha-Buddhi (सुख-बुद्धि) means pleasure-driven intellect.

Sukha-Svarupa (सुख-स्वरुप) means bliss-form or whose nature is only bliss.

Sugama (सुगम) means easy.

Sudarśana-Cakra (सुदर्शन-चक्र) means a spinning discus with "auspicious vision," the weapon of Lord Viṣṇu.

Sudṛḍha (सुदृढ) means very tenacious, very firm, or very assertive.

Sundara (सुन्दर) means beautiful.

Subuddhi (सुबुद्धि) means good intellect, wise, or intelligent.

Surakṣita (सुरक्षित) means well protected or carefully guarded.

Sura-Gaṇa (सुर-गण) means a mass of deities.

Sulakṣaṇa (सुलक्षण) means good or auspicious characteristics.

Sulabha (सुलभ) means easily obtained or attained.

Suvarṇa (सुवर्ण) means gold.

Suṣupti (सुषुप्ति) means deep sleep.

Suṣupti-Avasthā (सुषुप्ति-अवस्था) means deep-sleep state.

Suṣumnā (सुषुम्ना) is the primary central channel interpenetrating the cerebrospinal axis. It runs from the base of the spine to the crown of the head, passing through each of the seven Cakra in its course. It is the channel through which Kuṇḍalinī-Śakti rises up from its origin at the Mūlādhāra-Cakra to the Sahasrāra-Cakra at the crown of the head. In subtle body terms, Suṣumnā Nāḍī is the path to enlightenment.

Suhṛda (सुहृद) means good-hearted. It can also mean a friend or a well-wisher.

Suhṛdatā (सुहृदता) means good-heartedness.

Suhṛdatā-Parāyaṇa (सुहृदता-परायण) means taking one to pure heartedness.

Sūkṣma (सूक्ष्म) means subtle.

Sūkṣma-Śarīra (सूक्ष्म-शरीर) means the subtle body. It is an aggregation of the following nineteen subtle elements: the five subtle action faculties (mouth, hands, feet, anus, and genitals), the five subtle cognitive sense faculties (skin, tongue, eyes, nose, and ears), the five vital breaths of air (Prāṇa-Vāyu, Apāna-Vāyu, Samāna-Vāyu, Udāna-Vāyu, and Vyāna-Vāyu), the mind, intellect, Citta, and ego.

Sūkṣmāti-Sūkṣma (सूक्ष्माति-सूक्ष्म) means subtler than the subtle or smaller than the smallest.

Sūtra (सूत्र) means that which runs through like a thread or holds together everything.

Sūdana (सूदन) means one who kills.

Sūd (सूद्) means to kill or slay.

Sṛṣṭi (सृष्टि) means anything created, creation, Brahmāṇḍa, or the world.

Senāpati (सेनापति) means army commander or an army general.

Sevaka (सेवक) means servant or one who serves.

Sevā (सेवा) means service, homage, reverence, or devotion.

Sevī (सेवी) means the server or worshipper. It can also mean dweller or inhabitor.

Sopādhika (सोपाधिक) means with an adjunct (Upādhi).

Sopāna (सोपान) means stairs, steps, or ladder.

Sopāna-Krama (सोपान-क्रम) means stepwise or hierarchal.

Saumya (सौम्य) means gentle, calm, serene, mild, or "resembling the moon."

Stabdha (स्तब्ध) means crooked or obstinate. It can also mean firm, stiff, or immovable.

Stuti (स्तुति) means invocation. It can also mean to praise, glorify, or laud.

Strī (स्त्री) means a female or woman.

Stha (स्थ) means that resides in, stays in, or rests in.

Sthala (स्थल) means location.

Sthāṇu (स्थाणु) means standing firmly or stationary.

Sthānīya (स्थानीय) means having its place in, or being in.

Sthāvara (स्थावर) means immovable.

Sthita (स्थित) means to stand, positioned, placed, or situated.

Sthitadhī (स्थितधी) means one with stable wisdom.

Sthitaprajña (स्थितप्रज्ञ) means a sage of stable wisdom.

Sthiti (स्थिति) means staying, standing, or remaining.

Sthira (स्थिर) means steady, stable, fixed, or firm.

Sthiratā (स्थिरता) means steadiness or stability.

Sthūla (स्थूल) means gross or tangible.

Sthūla-Śarīra (स्थूल-शरीर) means the gross body.

Sthairya (स्थैर्य) means steadfastness.

Snigdha (स्निग्ध) means sticky.

Sneha (स्नेह) means affection or fondness.

Sparśa (स्पर्श) means the sense of touch.

Spaṣṭa (स्पष्ट) means clearly perceived, distinctly visible, distinct, clear, or evident.

Spṛhā (स्पृहा) means longing or yearning.

Sphaṭika-Maṇi (स्फटिक-मणि) means quartz gem.

Sphuraṇa (स्फुरण) means pulsation, vibration, or activity.

Sphuraṇarupa (स्फुरणरुप) means pulsating.

Sphūrti (स्फूर्ति) means vitality or vigor. It can also mean sudden appearance or manifestation.

Smaraṇa (स्मरण) means to remember or to recollect. It can also mean remembering the teachings of holy scriptures.

Smārta (स्मार्त) means an act or rite enjoined by Smṛti.

Smṛti (स्मृति) means memory.

Smṛti-Vṛtti (स्मृति-वृत्ति) means past knowledge or memory.

Sruva (स्रुव) means a small wooden ladle.

Srota (स्रोत) means a fountainhead.

Svagata (स्वगत) means intrinsic.

Svagata-Bheda (स्वगत-भेद) means intrinsic distinction. That by which one part of a substance is discriminated against another. Parts like hands, feet, and eyes in one's body have intrinsic distinctions.

Svajana (स्वजन) means relatives, own people, or kinsmen.

Svataḥ (स्वतः) means of own self or of own accord.

Svataḥ-Siddha (स्वतः-सिद्ध) means Ipso Facto or by that very fact or act.

Svatantra (स्वतन्त्र) means independent or free.

Svadharma (स्वधर्म) means the law of one's own life or one's duty.

Svadhā (स्वधा) means the ancestral oblation or the food given in the cause of ancestors.

Svapna (स्वप्न) means dream.

Svapnavata (स्वप्नवत) means dreamlike.

Svabhāva (स्वभाव) means one's nature or disposition.

Svayaṃ (स्वयं) means by one›s self.

Svayaṃvara (स्वयंवर) means an ancient practice in which a girl of marriageable age chose a husband from a group of suitors.

Svarupa (स्वरुप) is a compound word from Sva (स्व) meaning self, own and Rupa (रुप) meaning form, so Svarupa means one's real form, true nature, or essence.

Svarga (स्वर्ग) means divinity world or heaven.

Svargavāsī (स्वर्गवासी) means one who resides in Svarga (heaven).

Svasaṃvedhya (स्वसंवेध्य) means to be self-experienced

Svasattā (स्वसत्ता) means own presence or own existence. With presence or existence, authority or power is implied.

Svasattā-Śūnya (स्वसत्ता-शून्य) means without its existence.

Svāṅga (स्वाङ्ग) means guise or farce.

Svādhīna (स्वाधीन) means self-dependent or independent.

Svādhīnatā (स्वाधीनता) means self-dependency or independence.

Svādhyāya (स्वाध्याय) means self-study of scriptures.

Svābhāvika (स्वाभाविक) means arising from one's nature, natural or inherent.

Svāmī (स्वामी) means master. It can also mean husband or owner.

Svārtha (स्वार्थ) means self-interest.

Svārtha-Parāyaṇa (स्वार्थ-परायण) means self-interested or intent on own advantage.

Svecchā (स्वेच्छा) means one›s own wish or free will.

Svecchā-Mṛtyu (स्वेच्छा-मृत्यु) means complete control over own death or having the power to die at own will.

Sveda-Jā (स्वेद-जा) means sweat born.

Taṭastha (तटस्थ) means indifferent or neutral.

Tat (तत्) means that.

Tattva (तत्त्व) means the true principle, the Reality, the Truth in Vedānta. The Tat (तत्) in Tattva is the name of all, and the all is Brahman. However, Tattva also means the general nature of a substance, the primary principles, elements, states or categories of existence, and the building blocks of the world. According to Sāṅkhya Philosophy there are 25 Tattva; 1) Avyakta (अव्यक्त, imperceptible Prakṛti, Māyā); 2) Manas (मनस्, mind); 3) Buddhi (बुद्धि, intellect); 4) Ahaṃkāra (अहंकार, ego); Pañcabhūta (पञ्च-भूत) or the five gross components of Prakṛti: 5) Pṛthvī (पृथ्वी, earth), 6) Āpa (आप, water), 7) Agni (अग्नि, fire), 8) Vāyu (वायु, wind) and 9) Ākāśa (आकाश, space); Pañca-Tanmātra or the five rudimentary or subtle elements: 10) Śabda (शब्द, sound), 11) Sparśa (स्पर्श, touch), 12) Rasa (रस, taste), 13) Rupa (रुप, form), 14) Gandha (गन्ध, odor); Pañca-Jñānendriya (पञ्च-ज्ञानेंद्रिय) or five sense faculties: 15) Tvaka (त्वक) means skin with sense of touch, 16) Rasanā (रसना) means tongue with the sense of taste, 17) Cakṣu (चक्षु) means eyes with the sense of sight, 18) Ghrāṇa (घ्राण) means nose with the sense of smell, 19) Śrotra (श्रोत्र) means ears with the sense of hearing; Pañca-Karmendriya (पञ्च-कर्मेन्द्रिय) or five action faculties: 20) Vāka (वाक) means mouth with the sense of voice, 21) Pāṇi (पाणि) means hands with the sense of Grahaṇa (receive, gather, collect) and Dhāraṇa (hold), 22) Pāda (पाद) means feet with the sense of Gamana (walk, move, locomotion), 23) Pāyu (पायु) means anus with the sense of excretion, 24) Upastha (उपस्थ) means genitals with the sense of reproduction; and 25) Puruṣa (पुरुष, Jīvātmā).

Tattva-Cintana (तत्त्व-चिन्तन) means analytic thinking - about the Reality.

Tattvajña (तत्त्वज्ञ) means a knower of the Truth.

Tattva-Jñāna (तत्त्व-ज्ञान) means analytic knowledge of the Truth.

Tattva-Jñāna-Artha (तत्त्व-ज्ञान-अर्थ) means the content of knowledge of the Truth.

Tattvataḥ (तत्त्वतः) means essentially.

Tattva-Darśī (तत्त्व-दर्शी) means seers of Reality.

Tattva-Dṛṣṭi (तत्त्व-दृष्टि) means analytic perspective.

Tattva-Vicāra (तत्त्व-विचार) means analytic thought.

Tattva-Vettā (तत्त्व-वेत्ता) means a knower of the Truth.

Tatpara (तत्पर) means ready or ready with means. It can also mean being very devoted or eagerly engaged.

Tatparatā (तत्परता) means readiness. It can also mean total devotion.

Tatparāyaṇa (तत्परायण) means one who is continuously striving to attain the Paramātmā.

Tatra (तत्र) means there or in that subject or place.

Tathā (तथा) means and, also, or like that.

Tathāpi (तथापि) means but still, and yet, or however.

Tathya (तथ्य) means truth.

Tadākāra (तदाकार) means having that appearance.

Tadbuddhi (तद्बुद्धि) means one whose intellect is directed towards the Paramātmā.

Tana-Mana (तन-मन) means the body and the mind. Where Tana (तन) means the body and Mana {as} (मन) means the mind.

Tandrā (तन्द्रा) means sleep.

Tanniṣṭha (तन्निष्ठ) means one who is established with firm faith in Paramātmā-Svarupa.

Tanmaya (तन्मय) means absorbed in or become one with.

Tanmātra (तन्मात्र) means rudimentary or subtle elements that are the primordial causes of the five great elements of physical manifestation known as the Pañcabhūta. The five Tanmātra are: 1) smell (गन्ध, Gandha) corresponding to earth (पृथ्वी, Pṛthvī), 2) taste (रस, Rasa) corresponding to water (आप, Āpa), 3) form (रुप, Rupa) corresponding to fire (अग्नि, Agni), 4) touch (स्पर्श, Sparśa) corresponding to the wind (वायु, Vāyu) and 5) sound (शब्द, Śabda) corresponding to space (आकाश, Ākāśa).

Tapa (तप) means austerity or restraint of the body, senses, and mind.

Tapasyā (तपस्या) means austerity or penance.

Tapasvi (तपस्वि) means an ascetic or a person with austerity.

Tapta (तप्त) means having endured, suffered, or undergone.

Tamas (तमस्) means the last of the three constituents of Prakṛti or constituent attributes of all material substances {the other two being Sattva (सत्त्व) and Rajas (रजस्)}. It is also referred to as Tamoguṇa (तमोगुण) and predominates in demons (असुर, Asura). It is the cause of the sixfold mutations (षड्विकार, Ṣaḍvikāra): 1) lust (काम, Kāma), 2) anger (क्रोध, Krodha), 3) greed (लोभ, Lobha), 4) delusion (मोह, Moha), 5) excessive pride (मद, Mada) and 6) envy (मत्सर, Matsara).

Tamoguṇa (तमोगुण) means the last of the three constituents of Prakṛti or constituent attributes of all material substances. It predominates in demons (असुर, Asura). It is the cause of the sixfold mutations (षड्विकार, Ṣaḍvikāra): 1) lust (काम, Kāma), 2) anger (क्रोध, Krodha), 3) greed (लोभ, Lobha), 4) delusion (मोह, Moha), 5) excessive pride (मद, Mada) and 6) envy (मत्सर, Matsara).

Taraṃga (तरंग) means a wave.

Taraṃgāyamāna (तरंगायमान) means one with waves or wavy.

Tarpaṇa (तर्पण) means offering made to entities such as Pitṛ (fathers), Devarṣi, or divinities.

Tā (ता) suffix generally converts an adjective to a noun. For example, the adjective सुन्दर (Sundara, beautiful) to noun सुन्दरता (Sundaratā, beauty).

Tātparya (तात्पर्य) means intent or purport.

Tātvika (तात्विक) means true or real.

Tādātmya (तादात्म्य) means the sense of oneness or qualitative equality. An example of something that has attained Tādātmya is an iron rod heated by fire to such a degree that it acts as fire and burns other objects. The iron is said to have obtained oneness or Tādātmya with fire.

Tādātmya-Sambandha (तादात्म्य-सम्बन्ध) means mutual (Paraspara, परस्पर) nondifference (Abheda, अभेद).

Tādātmyādhyāsa (तादात्म्याध्यास) means oneness delusion. That is, knowing oneness when in reality there is no oneness.

Tāni (तानि) means them.

Tāpa (ताप) means affliction, suffering, pain, or sorrow. It can also mean heat or glow.

Tāmasika (तामसिक) means endowed with ignorance, the cause of sixfold mutations viz. lust, anger, greed, delusion, excessive pride, and envy.

Tāmasī (तामसी) means possessing attribute of Tamoguṇa or that, which causes the sixfold mutations (षड्विकार, Ṣaḍvikāra): 1) lust (काम, Kāma), 2) anger (क्रोध, Krodha), 3) greed (लोभ, Lobha), 4) delusion (मोह, Moha), 5) excessive pride (मद, Mada) and 6) envy (मत्सर, Matsara).

Tikta (तिक्त) means bitter. Bitter gourd, kale, eggplant, turmeric, dandelion, and coffee have a bitter taste.

Titikṣā (तितिक्षा) means endurance, forbearance, or patience.

Tiraskāra (तिरस्कार) means disdain or contempt.

Tiryaga (तिर्यग) means the species of birds, animals, and insects.

Tilānjali (तिलान्जलि) means to sacrifice or forsake. In terms of a ritual, it is an oblation with a handful of water and sesame seeds to the deceased.

Tīkṣṇa (तीक्ष्ण) means incisive, penetrating, or sharp. It can also mean piquant or acrid.

Tīvra (तीव्र) means intense.

Tu (तु) means certainly, indeed, or but.

Tuccha (तुच्छ) means paltry, trivial, meager, or miserable.

Tumula (तुमुल) means tumultuous or thunderous.

Tulya (तुल्य) means equal, of the same kind.

Tuṣṭi (तुष्टि) means contentment or satisfaction in whatever is obtained.

Tṛṇa (तृण) means a blade of grass or straw (often a symbol of minuteness and worthlessness).

Tṛpta (तृप्त) means satiated, satisfied with, or content.

Tṛṣṇā (तृष्णा) means thirst. It can also mean desire.

Te (ते) means they.

Teja (तेज) means brilliance or splendor.

Tyāga (त्याग) means relinquishment, leaving, abandoning, or forsaking.

Tyājya (त्याज्य) to be left or abandoned

Trikāṇḍa (त्रिकाण्ड) means the three components of the Vedas: 1) Karmakāṇḍa (कर्मकाण्ड), Upāsanākāṇḍa (उपासनाकाण्ड) and 3) Jñānakāṇḍa (ज्ञानकाण्ड).

Trikāṇḍātmaka (त्रिकाण्डात्मक) means consisting of three components (Kāṇḍa).

Trikāla (त्रिकाल) means the past, present, and future time.

Trikālabādhya (त्रिकालबाध्य) means one whose determination of unreality (मिथ्यात्व-निश्चय, Mithyātva-Niścaya) cannot be made in the past, present, and future.

Trikālābhāva (त्रिकालाभाव) means absent in the past, present, and future.

Triguṇa (त्रिगुण) means the three constituents of the Prakṛti

Triguṇamayī (त्रिगुणमयी) means having three constituents.

Triguṇātīta (त्रिगुणातीत) means free from or beyond the three constituents of Prakṛti.

Triguṇātmaka (त्रिगुणात्मक) means consisting of the three constituents of Prakṛti.

Tritāpa (त्रिताप) means the threefold afflictions. They are 1) Daihika-Tāpa (दैहिक-ताप, bodily and mental afflictions. Diseases like fever or cancer are body-related sufferings. Anger, greed, or passion are mental afflictions), 2) Daivika-Tāpa (दैविक-ताप, natural afflictions such as storms, floods, or droughts), and 3) Bhautika-Tāpa (भौतिक-ताप, material sufferings such as those caused by humans, animals or insects).

Triloka (त्रिलोक) means the three worlds: 1) Brahmaloka (Devaloka) - the realms of the Deva (deities), 2) Bhūloka (Pṛthvīloka) - the realms of the humans, animals and plants and 3) Pātālaloka (the world below) - the realms of the Asura, hellish beings, or the infernal.

Trividha (त्रिविध) means threefold or three kinds.

Tryambaka (त्र्यम्बक) means the three-eyed Lord Śiva.

Tvaka (त्वक) means skin with a sense of touch.

Tvam (त्वम्) means you.

Uṝṇa (उऋृण) means debt-free.

Ukta (उक्त) means said or proclaimed.

Ukti (उक्ति) means proclamation.

Ugra (उग्र) means frightful, fierce, or ferocious.

Ucita (उचित) means befitting or proper.

Ucca (उच्च) means high, elevated, superior, or exalted.

Uccāraṇa (उच्चारण) means utterance or pronunciation.

Ucchiṣṭa (उच्छिष्ट) means waste, rejected, leftover, or spit out of the mouth.

Ucchedana (उच्छेदन) means cutting off, destroying, or extirpating.

Ujjavala (उज्जवल) means brighter.

Ujjāyī (उज्जायी) Prāṇāyāma is a diaphragmatic breath, which first fills the lower belly (said to activate the first and second Cakra), rises to the lower rib cage (said to correspond to the third and fourth Cakra), and finally moves into the upper chest and throat. Inhalation and exhalation are both done through the nose. The ocean sound is created by moving the glottis as air passes in and out. As the throat passage is narrowed, so is the airway, the passage of air through which creates a rushing sound. The length and speed of the breath are controlled by the diaphragm, the strengthening of which is, in part, the purpose of Ujjāyī. The inhalations and exhalations are equal in duration and are controlled in a manner that causes no distress.

Uta (उत) means woven. It can also mean and, also, even, or.

Utkaṭa (उत्कट) means fervent.

Utkarṣa (उत्कर्ष) means to uplift or progress.

Utkṛṣṭa (उत्कृष्ट) means excellent.

Uttama (उत्तम) means most elevated or excellent.

Uttara-Kāla (उत्तर-काल) means future time.

Uttarāyana (उत्तरायन) means the movement of the sun towards the north. It is a compound word from Uttara (उत्तर) meaning north and Ayanam (अयनम्) meaning movement, path. This movement occurs a day after the winter solstice around December 21 and continues for six months until the summer solstice around June 21.

Uttarottara (उत्तरोत्तर) means gradual.

Uttejita (उत्तेजित) means to excite, arouse or incite.

Utthāna (उत्थान) means rising or appearing.

Utpatti (उत्पत्ति) means creation.

Utpatti-Sthiti-Laya (उत्पत्ति-स्थिति-लय) means creation, sustentation and dissolution.

Utpanna (उत्पन्न) means to arise or to be born.

Utsāha (उत्साह) means enthusiasm, zeal, or effort. It can also mean joy.

Udaka (उदक) means water offered in a ceremony to pay homage to the departed fathers or ancestors.

Udapāna (उदपान) means a reservoir, pond, or a well.

Udaya (उदय) means to rise.

Udara (उदर) means belly or stomach.

Udāna-Vāyu (उदान-वायु) means the ascending air. It is the Prāṇa-Vāyu that directs Prāṇa from lower to upper levels of consciousness, and its action is metabolization, its expression is verbal, and its associated Cakra and elements are Viśuddha and Ājñā and ether.

Udāra (उदार) means generous, exalted, or noble.

Udāratā (उदारता) means generosity.

Udāsīna (उदासीन) means neutral or indifferent.

Udgāra (उद्गार) means pouring out or emitting.

Uddiṣṭa (उद्दिष्ट) means desired or mentioned.

Uddeśya (उद्देश्य) means objective, purpose, or aim.

Uddhata (उद्धत) means aggressive, excited, or stirred up.

Uddhāra (उद्धार) means elevating, lifting up, or the act of raising. It can also mean deliverance.

Udbuddha (उद्बुद्ध) means awakened or aroused.

Udbodha (उद्बोध) means awakening or arousing.

Udbhija-Jā (उद्भिज-जा) means germination born.

Udvega (उद्वेग) means distress, anxiety, or apprehension.

Unnati (उन्नति) means exaltation or advancement.

Unmatta (उन्मत्त) means insane or delirious.

Unmukha (उन्मुख) means facing or oriented.

Upakāra (उपकार) means a benefit, service, or help.

Upadeśa (उपदेश) means pointing out, spiritual guidance, preaching, or counsel.

Upadraṣṭā (उपद्रष्टा) means close observer.

Upamā (उपमा) means liken or to compare. It can also mean resemblance or similarity.

Upamāna (उपमान) means comparison and analogy.

Upayoga (उपयोग) means use or application

Uparata (उपरत) means to desist from, to go away, or to run away.

Uparāma (उपराम) means desist, cease, or stop. It can mean complete cessation or being satiated. It can also mean an aversion to forsaking action and poisonous objects despite possessing means.

Uparāmatā (उपरामता) means desistance, cessation.

Upaśama (उपशम) means cessation, abatement, or control. It can also mean becoming quiet.

Upasaṃhāra (उपसंहार) means epilogue, end, or conclusion

Upastha (उपस्थ) means the genitals, the organ of reproduction.

Upahata (उपहृत) means affected or distressed

Upahita (उपहित) means placed within. A thing that is separated by an adjunct with discriminative attributes is known as Upahita, like the space within the pot is Upahita in the pot.

Upādāna-Kāraṇa (उपादान-कारण) means material cause. That which enters the work and without which the work cannot sustain is known as Upādāna-Kārana. Like the clay is the Upādāna-Kāraṇa of a pot.

Upādeya (उपादेय) means to be accepted, chosen, or taken.

Upādeyatā (उपादेयता) means acceptability.

Upādhi (उपाधि) means an adjunct with discriminative attributes. From the Vedantic perspective, Upādhi refers to what separates some substance but does not enter or manifest in the separated substance. Like a pot that separates pot-enclosed space from the pervasive space but does not enter into the true nature of the space. The pot is the Upādhi of the intrinsic space. It can also mean designation, limitation, or condition related to time and space.

Upāya (उपाय) means approach.

Upārjana (उपार्जन) means the act of gaining, acquiring, or procuring.

Upāsaka (उपासक) means follower, worshipper, or one who waits upon.

Upāsanā (उपासना) means to worship or method of worship.

Upāsti (उपास्ति) means propitiation, worship, or service.

Upekṣā (उपेक्षा) means to let go. It can also mean even-mindedness.

Ubhaya (उभय) means both.

Ubhaya-Bhraṣṭa (उभय-भ्रष्ट) means both ruinous.

Ullaṅghana (उल्लङ्घन) means to rise above, pass over, or transcend. It can also mean transgression.

Ūrṇanābhi (ऊर्णनाभि) means a spider.

Ūrdhva (ऊर्ध्व) means higher, superior, rising, or trending upwards.

Ūrdhvagati (ऊर्ध्वगति) means higher destination.

Ūrdhva-Mūla (ऊर्ध्व-मूल) means whose roots are upwards.

Va (व) means and

Vaṃśa (वंश) means dynasty.

Vacana (वचन) means word, sentence, or statement.

Vañcaka (वञ्चक) means a swindler.

Vañcita (वञ्चित) means deprived.

Vatsala (वत्सल) means kind, loving, tender, fond of, or devoted to.

Vadha (वध) means to kill or slaughter.

Vana (वन) means forest

Vandana (वन्दन) means bowing to the divine.

Varadāna (वरदान) means a grant of a boon or request.

Varavaśa (वरवश) means naturally.

Varjita (वर्जित) means excluded or devoid.

Varṇa (वर्ण) means principal classes of the society. Lord Śrī Kṛṣṇa provides classification in terms of the four primary functions necessary for the sustainability of the humanity: 1) education, entrusted to Brāhmaṇa, 2) security, entrusted to Kṣatriya, 3) commerce, entrusted to Vaiśya and 4) labor, entrusted to Śūdra. The innate attributes of a Brāhmaṇa (ब्रह्म-प्रकृति, Brahma-Prakṛti) are in BG 18.4; a Kṣatriya (क्षात्र-प्रकृति, Kṣātra-Prakṛti) are in BG 18.43, a Vaiśya (वैश्य-प्रकृति, Vaiśya-Prakṛti) and a Śūdra (शूद्र-प्रकृति, Śūdra-Prakṛti) are in BG 18.44.

Varṇasaṃkara (वर्णसंकर) means mixed functional class.

Varṇasaṃkaratā (वर्णसंकरता) means the attribute of mixed functional classes.

Varṇāśrama (वर्णाश्रम) means stages of life, based on the functional classification of the society.

Vartamāna (वर्तमान) means current or present.

Vartma (वर्त्म) means path.

Varṣā (वर्षा) means rain.

Vaśa (वश) means to subdue, control, or dominate.

Vaśāt (वशात्) means subdued or under obligation.

Vaśībhūta (वशीभूत) means become controlled, subjugated, or subdued.

Vasu (वसु) are the eight children of Aditi (daughter of Prajāpati Dakṣa) and Saptarṣi Kaśyapa enumerated as 1. Dhara (धर), 2. Dhruva (ध्रुव), 3. Soma (सोम), 4. Ahaḥ (अहः), 5. Anila (अनिल), 6. Anala (अनल), 7. Pratyūṣa (प्रत्यूष) and 8. Prabhāsa (प्रभास).

Vastī (वस्ती) means habitation.

Vastu (वस्तु) means thing.

Vastugata (वस्तुगत) means material or objective.

Vastutaḥ (वस्तुतः) means in fact, in reality, actually, or verily.

Vastu-Pariccheda (वस्तु-परिच्छेद) means material distinction. That in which difference between class (जाति, Jāti) and individual (व्यक्ति, Vyakti) exists is Vastu Pariccheda.

Vastu-Paricchedya (वस्तु-परिच्छेद्य) means one where the distinction between things or materials exists. Just as a pot is distinguished from a cloth and vice versa, both the pot and cloth being distinguishable are Vastu-Paricchedya.

Vahida (वहिद) means oneness status or oneness Bhāva, non-duality, or Advaita.

Vāka (वाक) means mouth, the organ of voice.

Vācārambhaṇa (वाचारम्भण) is the use of name-form to explain the material cause of the name-form. For instance, the name-form gold chain provides knowledge of gold as the material cause.

Vācika (वाचिक) means verbal.

Vācyārtha (वाच्यार्थ) means directly expressed meaning. The meaning of a word is known based on the naming process (Śakti-Vṛtti) of the word. For instance, in the sentence "Bring Book," both words carry their original meaning.

Vāñchita (वाञ्छित) means desired or requisite.

Vāṇijya (वाणिज्य) means commerce.

Vāṇī (वाणी) means voice or speech. It can also mean utterance or verbal expressions.

Vāta (वात) means wind (one of the three humors of the body).

Vādinaḥ (वादिनः) means orator.

Vāna (वान) means possessor.

Vānaprastha-Āśrama (वानप्रस्थ-आश्रम) means one who gives up worldly life or retires to the forest. In this third stage of life, from the age of 50 to 75, a person hands over household responsibilities to the next generation, takes an advisory role, and gradually withdraws from the world. It is a transition phase from a householder's life with a greater emphasis on wealth, pleasure, and desires to one with a greater focus on spiritual liberation.

Vāyu (वायु) means wind or air.

Vārṣṇeya {वार्ष्णेय) means descendent of Vṛṣṇi (वृष्णि), Śrī Kṛṣṇa.

Vāsanā (वासना) means impressions. They are inherent latencies and tendencies resulting from previous actions. They are assimilated with predispositions, tendencies, or propensities of the mind in the present due to past experiences. With continuous ongoing desires, subliminal traces or subtle fingerprints remain in the mind. Thereby a state of constant agitation remains - always planning the future and thinking about the past, preventing one from living in a state of clarity that arises in the awareness of the eternal present moment. It can also mean desire.

Vāsanārupa (वासनारुप) means in the form of desire or impression.

Vāstava (वास्तव) means per se or in reality.

Vāstavika (वास्तविक) means real.

Vikampa (विकम्प) means to waver, to tremble, or to be disturbed.

Vikarāla (विकराल) means ghastly, horrible, or terrible.

Vikarma (विकर्म) means forbidden action.

Vikalpa (विकल्प) means alternative or variant thought.

Vikasita (विकसित) means opened, expanded, or dominant.

Vikāra (विकार) means mutation, modification, transformation, or change.

Vikārī (विकारी) means modifiable or changeable.

Vikāsa (विकास) means development.

Vikṛta (विकृत) means deformed or distorted.

Vikṛti (विकृति) means modification or change.

Vikṣipta (विक्षिप्त) means agitated, distorted, or bewildered.

Vikṣepa (विक्षेप) means vacillations or the tossing of the mind which obstructs concentration.

Vikṣepa-Doṣa (विक्षेप-दोष) means the fault of vacillations. When it is incurred, the mind cannot remain steady and immovable. It can only be removed by devotion (Upāsanā).

Vigatarāga (विगतराग) means devoid of passion or affection.

Viguṇa (विगुण) means imperfect or void of attributes.

Vigraha (विग्रह) means form or idol. It can also mean regarding a conflict.

Vighna (विघ्न) means obstacle or hindrance.

Vicakṣaṇa (विचक्षण) means clear-sighted or thoughtfully competent.

Vicalita (विचलित) means bewildered, blinded, obscured, or deviated from.

Vicāra (विचार) means thought, reflection, pondering, deliberation, or consideration.

Vicitratā (विचित्रता) means variegation or variety.

Vijātīya (विजातीय) means heterogeneous.

Vijñāna (विज्ञान) means realized knowledge, the direct experience of understood knowledge of the scriptures. It can also mean science, doctrine, or proficiency.

Vijñānamaya-Kośa (विज्ञानमय-कोश) means the Sheath of Discernment or the faculty of the intellect characterized by decision making disposition (Niścayātmaka-Vṛtti). Discriminative in nature, it can discern real from unreal, piety from sin, right from wrong, good from bad, and thereby select a wise choice.

Vitta (वित्त) means wealth or anything found.

Vidāhina (विदाहिन) means burning.

Vidūra (विदूर) means wise or skillful. Vidūra, a righteous, wise statesman, the half-brother of Dhṛtarāṣṭra and Pāṇḍu, was born of a maid with the seed of Vedavyāsa.

Videha (विदेह) means bodyless or incorporeal.

Videha-Mokṣa (विदेह-मोक्ष) means liberation after death or liberation from the body.

Vidyā (विद्या) means knowledge, learning, or science.

Vidvān (विद्वान्) means a wise or a learned person.

Vidhāna (विधान) means to enumerate. It can also mean a statement of particulars, performance, or execution.

Vidhi (विधि) means scriptural injunctions or regulative injunctive principles. It can also mean procedure.

Vidhi-Niṣedha (विधि-निषेध) means regulative injunctions and prohibitions.

Vidheya (विधेय) means to be done or performed.

Vidhyamāna (विध्यमान) means being in existence or present.

Vidhyamānatā (विध्यमानता) means presence or existence.

Vinaya (विनय) means politeness.

Vinigraha (विनिग्रह) means restraint or control.

Vinirmukta (विनिर्मुक्त) means liberated, free, or exempt from.

Vinodamātra (विनोदमात्र) means only for pastime, playing, or amusing oneself.

Vinda (विन्द) means to find, get, or gain.

Vinyāsa (विन्यास) is a smooth transition between postures in Yoga characterized by stringing postures together so that one moves from one posture to another seamlessly, using breath, such as Sūrya-Namaskāra. It is also known as flow Yoga.

Viparīta (विपरीत) means contrary, opposite, reversed, or contrary to rule.

Viparītatā (विपरीतता) means opposition or a contradiction.

Vipaścita (विपश्चित) means one who is discerning.

Vipra (विप्र) means wise or learned. It can also mean a Brāhmaṇa.

Viphala (विफल) means fruitless, useless, or vain.

Vibhakta (विभक्त) means divided.

Vibhāga (विभाग) means division, difference, distinction, separation, distribution, or apportionment.

Vibhinna (विभिन्न) means divided, separated, manifold, or various.

Vibhu (विभु) means all-pervading or omnipresent.

Vibhūti (विभूति) means divine manifestations. It can also mean glory, opulence, or splendor.

Vibhrānta (विभ्रान्त) means confused or bewildered.

Vimukta (विमुक्त) means completely free or liberated.

Vimukha (विमुख) means turning away or backward. It can also mean adverse or averse.

Vimūḍha (विमूढ) means confounded or bewildered. It can also mean foolish.

Viyukta (वियुक्त) means separated, disjoined, detached, or disunited.

Viyoga (वियोग) means disjunction or separation.

Virājamāna (विराजमान) means enthroned or sitting.

Virodha (विरोध) means opposition.

Virodhī (विरोधी) means averse.

Vilakṣaṇatā (विलक्षणता) means singularity or peculiarity.

Vilāpa (विलाप) means lament or moan.

Vilīna (विलीन) means to dissolve, melt, or disappear.

Vivaraṇa (विवरण) means explanation, description, account, or exegesis.

Vivarta (विवर्त) means an apparent or an imagined thing. An apparent imagined (मिथ्या, Mithyā) thing that is perceived in and without mutating its real material cause (Upādāna) is the Vivarta of its material cause. Like a delusional snake in a rope is the Vivarta of the actual rope. A thing in the form of a Vivarta has neither reality nor the ability to produce mutation in its underlying substrate (Adhiṣṭhāna).

Vivartopādāna (विवर्तोपादान) means a cause in which delusion is perceived. It is a compound word from Vivarta (विवर्त) and Upādāna (उपादान). It is a cause where real work is not created but is merely perceived. An actual rope is said to be the Vivartopādāna of a delusional snake because, in reality, the snake is not born though there is a perception that there is a snake.

Vivāda (विवाद) means contention or dispute.

Vivikta (विविक्त) means solitary, isolated, or alone.

Viveka (विवेक) means discernment. What is the essence (Sāra), and what is without essence (Asāra)? Such a truly correct thought is known as Viveka. It is the discrimination between the real and the unreal, the permanent and the impermanent, the Self and the non-Self.

Vivekī (विवेकी) means discerning, judicious, prudent, or wise.

Viśiṣṭa (विशिष्ट) means pre-eminent, distinguished, or chief.

Viśuddha (विशुद्ध) means completely purified or virtuous.

Viśuddhātmā (विशुद्धात्मा) means pure conscience.

Viśeṣa (विशेष) means unique, special, or specific. It can also mean excellence.

Viśeṣṭatā (विशेष्टता) means uniqueness or excellence.

Viśrāma (विश्राम) means to rest or repose.

Viśvāsa (विश्वास) means faith.

Viśvedeva (विश्वेदेव) are a group of ten deities known as the protectors of humans and guardians of the world. They are the sons of Viśvā (विश्वा, the daughter of Prajāpati Dakṣa) and Dharma, enumerated as 1. Vasu (वसु), 2. Satya (सत्य), 3. Kratu (क्रतु), 4. Dakṣa (दक्ष), 5. Kāla (काल), 6. Kāma (काम), 7. Dhṛti (धृति), 8. Kuru (कुरु), 9. Purūravas (पुरूरवस्,), 10. Mādravasa (माद्रवस).

Viś (विष) means poison.

Viṣama (विषम) means unequal, dissimilar, or different.

Viṣamatā (विषमता) means inequality, imbalance, dissimilarity, or difference.

Viṣaya (विषय) means subject. It can also mean objects.

Viṣayaka (विषयक) means relating to an object.

Viṣaya-Padārtha (विषय-पदार्थ) means object matter.

Viṣaya-Bhoga (विषय-भोग) means enjoyment or experience of worldly objects.

Viṣayī (विषयी) means materialistic.

Viṣavat (विषवत्) means poisonous.

Viṣāda (विषाद) means sad, despondent, or depressed.

Viṣūcikā (विषूचिका) means a disease where indigestion is accompanied by evacuation in both directions. It is known as cholera.

Visarga (विसर्ग) means creation or production.

Vistāra (विस्तार) means enormity, vastness, expansion, or spreading.

Vistṛta (विस्तृत) means expanded, broad, spread, or extensive.

Vismaraṇa (विस्मरण) means amnesia or forgetting.

Vismita (विस्मित) means taken back or stunned.

Vismṛti (विस्मृति) means loss of memory or forgetfulness.

Vihita (विहित) means prescribed or enjoined.

Vīrya (वीर्य) means courage or strength.

Vīryavān (वीर्यवान्) means heroic, brave, or courageous.

Vṛka (वृक) means a wolf.

Vṛka-Udara (वृक-उदर) means one who has a belly of a wolf.

Vṛkṣa (वृक्ष) means a tree.

Vṛtti (वृत्ति) means the mental state, instinct, inner disposition, tendency, or inclination.

Vṛtti-Jñāna (वृत्ति-ज्ञान) means instinctive knowledge.

Vṛtti-Vyāpti (वृत्ति-व्याप्ति) means knowledge wherein the inner disposition does not become an object shaped like a pot. The only motive of the inner disposition is to disrupt the conduct of the one in support of the object, and the object becomes self-luminous by its illumination.

Vṛthā (वृथा) means in vain or to no purpose.

Vṛddhi (वृद्धि) means growth or increase.

Vega (वेग) means current or flow. It can also mean speed or velocity.

Vettā (वेत्ता) means knower or cognizant.

Vedanā (वेदना) means agony, pain, or torture.

Veda-Pāṭha (वेद-पाठ) means reading or recital of the Vedas.

Vedānta (वेदान्त) means the end of the Vedas and reflects ideas espoused in the Upaniṣads, specifically, knowledge and liberation.

Vepathu (वेपथु) means quivering or trembling.

Vaimanasya (वैमनस्य) means friction, discord, grudge, or ill will.

Vairāgya (वैराग्य) means dispassion, renunciation, freedom from all worldly desires, distaste for, loathing of, or indifference to. Vairāgya means becoming devoid of passion (Vigatarāga) in visible and invisible objects through the repeated vision of seeing faults (Doṣa-Dṛṣṭi).

Vairāgyavāna (वैराग्यवान) means possessing the attribute dispassion or renunciation.

Vaiśya-Prakṛti (वैश्य-प्रकृति) means the innate attributes of a Vaiśya. The attributes enumerated in BG 18.44 are agriculture (कृषि, Kṛṣi), protection of cows (गौरक्ष्य, Gaurakṣya), and commerce (वाणिज्य, Vāṇijya).

Vaiśvānara (वैश्वानर) means common to all humankind. It is an epithet of Agni. It can also mean the fire of digestion.

Vyaktayaḥ (व्यक्तयः) means manifested (Saṃsāra).

Vyakti (व्यक्ति) means individual.

Vyaktidhārī (व्यक्तिधारी) means holding limited individuality or human form.

Vyaktirupa (व्यक्तिरुप) means embodied form.

Vyaktiviśeṣa (व्यक्तिविशेष) means a special person.

Vyatireka (व्यतिरेक) means discordance, difference, distinction, or separation. For instance, in logic, discord exists between two things, such as between a string and roses to form a garland. The fact that the string is separate from the roses is Vyatireka.

Vyatīta (व्यतीत) passed, gone, or elapsed.

Vyathā (व्यथा) means anguish, anxiety, or pain.

Vyathita (व्यथित) means distressed, afflicted, frantic, or anxious.

Vyabhicārī (व्यभिचारी) means faltering or wavering. It can also mean adulterous.

Vyaya (व्यय) means perishable or decaying.

Vyavacchedakatā (व्यवच्छेदकता) means discrimination.

Vyavasāyātmika (व्यवसायात्मिक) means resolute.

Vyavasthā (व्यवस्था) means set-up, order, system, or arrangement.

Vyavasthiti (व्यवस्थिति) means to situate uniquely.

Vyavahāra (व्यवहार) means dealings.

Vyavahārika (व्यवहारिक) means practical, customary, ordinary, or worldly.

Vyavahārika-Sattā (व्यवहारिक-सत्ता) means ordinary or practical Reality. It is one where the determination of absence in the past, present, and future (त्रिकालाभाव-निश्चय) cannot be made without Self-Realization (ब्रह्म-ज्ञान, Brahma-Jñāna). The conscious world (जाग्रत-प्रपन्च) has ordinary Reality because, without Self-Realization, it cannot be realized as unreal.

Vyaṣṭi (व्यष्टि) means an individual.

Vyaṣṭi-Dṛṣṭi (व्यष्टि-दृष्टि) means individual view.

Vyākula (व्याकुल) means consternated, anxious, perplexed, or distressed.

Vyākulatā (व्याकुलता) means distress, anxiousness, or perplexity.

Vyādhi (व्याधि) means disease.

Vyāpaka (व्यापक) means pervasive.

Vyāpāra (व्यापार) means operations, avocation, or business.

Vyāpī (व्यापी) means pervasive.

Vyāpti (व्याप्ति) means pervasion.

Vyāvṛta (व्यावृत) means to uncover or open

Vrata (व्रत) means a religious vow or practice.

Yakṣa (यक्ष) are a broad class of semi-deities, usually benevolent and inoffensive disposition, but sometimes mischievous or capricious, connected with water, fertility, trees, the forest, treasure, and wilderness. They are described as attendants of Kubera (कुबेर), the deity of wealth, and employed to guard his gardens and treasures.

Yajana (यजन) means to worship.

Yajamāna (यजमान) means an Institutor of oblations.

Yajña (यज्ञ) means a sacrifice, an oblation, an observance, or an act in general for the propitiation of a deity.

Yajña-Vidyā (यज्ञ-विद्या) means oblation science.

Yajñopavīta (यज्ञोपवीत) means sacred thread.

Yatī (यती) means an ascetic who has completely restrained his passions.

Yat (यत्) means who, what, or which. It can also mean since or wherefore.

Yatna (यत्न) means endeavor or effort.

Yathā (यथा) means just as.

Yathārtha (यथार्थ) means truly, accordant with reality, conformable to truth, or the true meaning.

Yathāvata (यथावत) means as it is, precisely, or truly.

Yathokta (यथोक्त) means as truly spoken.

Yadi (यदि) means if, lest, perchance, or if perhaps.

Yadyapi (यद्यपि) means although.

Yantra (यन्त्र) means a machine or gadget.

Yama (यम) means to rein or to restrain.

Yaśa (यश) means honor, fame, or glory.

Yasyāṃ (यस्यां) means in which.

Yā (या) means that.

Yācanā (याचना) means beseech or plead.

Yātayāma (यातयाम) means ill cooked, raw, or half-ripe.

Yānti (यान्ति) means to go, approach, attain, or merge.

Yāvata (यावत) means all that, as much, or as long as.

Yukta (युक्त) means established, steady, united, joined or yoked.

Yukta-Ātmā (युक्त-आत्मा) means with a steadfast mind.

Yukti (युक्ति) means tactic.

Yukti-Yukta (युक्ति-युक्त) means convincing, reasonable, or sound.

Yuga (युग) means the age of the world.

Yuddha (युद्ध) means war. It can also mean fighting.

Ye (ये) means these.

Yoga-Kṣema (योग-क्षेम) means the gain and preservation. It is the provision of what is not and preserving what is possessed.

Yoga-Bhraṣṭa (योग-भ्रष्ट) means one who is fallen from Yoga. It means unsuccessful from both the Path of Karma and the Path of Knowledge, unsupported and deluded.

Yoga-Yukta (योग-युक्त) means established in Yoga. It is where one is established with oneness in the Ātmā, free from I-ness conceit in the body and the mind.

Yogāruḍha (योगारुढ) means ascended in Yoga.

Yogin (योगिन्) means Yogī, the Lord of Yoga. It is an epithet of Śrī Kṛṣṇa.

Yogeśvara (योगेश्वर) means the Lord of Yoga or Master of Yoga, an epithet of Śrī Kṛṣṇa.

Yogya (योग्य) means apropos, apt, right, proper, appropriate, or suitable.

Yoni (योनि) means womb, types of life, or forms of existence, viz. human, animal, etc. It can also mean source of birth, origin, or birthplace.

Pronunciation Guide

Devanagari	IAST	Pronunciation	Description
अ	a	like the "**u**" in b**u**t	Short guttural vowel
आ	ā	like the "**a**" in f**a**r	Long "a" vowel
इ	i	like the "**i**" in p**i**n	Short palatal vowel
ई	ī	like the "**ee**" in b**ee**t	Long "i" vowel
उ	u	like the "**u**" in f**u**ll	Short labial vowel
ऊ	ū	like the "**oo**" in r**oo**t	Long "u" vowel
ऋ	ṛ	like the "**ri**" in **ri**m, slightly rolled "r"	Short retroflex vowel
ॠ	ṝ	like the "**ree**" in **ree**f, rolled "r"	Long "ṛ" vowel
ऌ	ḷ	like the "**lry**" in jewe**lry**	Short retroflex-dental vowel
ए	e	like the "**a**" in m**a**te	Long guttural-palatal vowel
ऐ	ai	like the "**ai**" in **ai**sle	Long guttural-palatal diphthong
ओ	o	like the "**o**" in b**o**at	Long guttural-labial diphthong
औ	au	like the "**ou**" in l**ou**d	Long guttural-labial diphthong
ं	ṃ	like the "**n**" in the French word bo**n**	Nasal "m", ½ length of short vowel
ः	ḥ	like **aha**	½ length of short vowel

Devanagari		IAST		Pronunciation	Description
क्	क	k	ka	like the "**k**" in **k**ite	Hard guttural consonant
ख्	ख	kh	kha	like the "**kh**" in Ec**kh**art	Hard guttural-aspirate consonant
ग्	ग	g	ga	like "**g**" in **g**ive	Soft guttural consonant
घ्	घ	gh	gha	like the "**gh**" in do**gh**ouse	Soft guttural-aspirate consonant
ङ्	ङ	ṅ	ṅa	like the "**ng**" in si**ng**	Soft guttural-nasal consonant
च्	च	c	ca	like the "**ch**" in **ch**ose	Hard guttural-palatal consonant
छ्	छ	ch	cha	like the "**ch-h**" in cat**ch-h**er	Hard palatal-aspirate consonant
ज्	ज	j	ja	like the "**j**" in **j**ust	Soft palatal consonant
झ्	झ	jh	jha	like the "**dgeh**" in he**dgeh**og	Soft palatal-aspirate consonant
ञ्	ञ	ñ	ña	like the "**ny**" in ca**ny**on	Soft palatal-nasal consonant
ट्	ट	ṭ	ṭa	like the "**t**" in **t**ub	Hard retroflex consonant
ठ्	ठ	ṭh	ṭha	like the "**th**" in po**th**ole	Hard retroflex-aspirate consonant
ड्	ड	ḍ	ḍa	like the "**d**" in **d**ot	Soft retroflex consonant
ढ्	ढ	ḍh	ḍha	like the "**dh**" in go**dh**ead	Soft retroflex-aspirate consonant
ण्	ण	ṇ	ṇa	like the "**n**" in tur**n**	Soft retroflex-nasal consonant
त्	त	t	ta	like the "**t**" in **t**ub	Hard dental consonant
थ्	थ	th	tha	like the "**th**" in but**th**ead	Hard dental-aspirate consonant

Devanagari		IAST		Pronunciation	Description
द्	द	d	da	like the “**d**” in **d**ove	Soft dental consonant
ध्	ध	dh	dha	like the “**dh**” in re**dh**ot	Soft dental-aspirate consonant
न्	न	n	na	like the “**n**” in **n**ut	Soft dental-nasal consonant
प्	प	p	pa	like the “**p**” in **p**unk	Hard labial consonant
फ्	फ	ph	pha	like the “**ph**” in u**ph**ill	Hard labial-aspirate consonant
ब्	ब	b	ba	like the “**b**” in **b**ird	Soft labial consonant
भ्	भ	bh	bha	like the “**bh**” in a**bh**or	Soft labial-aspirate consonant
म्	म	m	ma	like the “**m**” in **m**other	Soft labial-nasal consonant
य्	य	y	ya	like the “**y**” in **y**es	Soft palatal semivowel
र्	र	r	ra	like the “**r**” in **r**un	Soft retroflex semivowel
ल्	ल	l	la	like the “**l**” in **l**unge	Soft dental semivowel
व्	व	v	va	like the “**w**” in **w**on	Soft labial semivowel
श्	श	ś	śa	like the “**sh**” in ca**sh**	Hard palatal sibilant
ष्	ष	ṣ	ṣa	like “**sh**” in **sh**ine	Hard retroflex sibilant
स्	स	s	sa	like the “**s**” in **s**urf	Hard dental sibilant
ह्	ह	h	ha	like the “**h**” in **h**um	Soft guttural sonant aspirate

सर्वधर्मान्परित्यज्य मामेकं शरणं व्रज |
अहं त्वां सर्वपापेभ्यो मोक्षयिष्यामि मा शुच: || BG 18.66 ||

Giving up all duties, seek refuge in Me alone.
Grieve not. I shall free you from all sins.

Universal Prayer

Oṃ(ॐ) Tat Sat

O, Lord! With undivided supreme faith and without expectation, I beseech thee for Your grace to endow me with wisdom and power not to hurt anyone mentally, verbally, or bodily by my thoughts, words, and deeds.

O, Lord! With undivided supreme faith and without expectation, I beseech Thee for Your grace to endow me with a tongue that utters only unoffending, truthful, pleasant, and beneficial words.

O, Lord! With undivided supreme faith and without expectation, I beseech Thee for Your grace to endow me with a resolve to abandon lust, anger, and greed.

O, Lord! With undivided supreme faith and without expectation, I beseech Thee for Your grace to endow me with a resolve to partake only foods that promote longevity, purity, power, health, happiness, satisfaction and are savory, stable, and pleasing to the heart.

O, Lord! With undivided supreme faith and without expectation, I beseech Thee for Your grace to endow me with the sixfold virtues, 1) control of the mind, 2) restraint over the senses, 3) faith in the words of the preceptors and the scriptures, 4) absence of mental vacillations, 5) desistance from the relinquishment of actions and vile objects, and 6) tolerance to bear dualities such as heat and cold, pleasure and pain, hunger and thirst. O, Lord! Grant me a resolve to remain in Your knowledge and Your undivided devotion.

Lightning Source UK Ltd.
Milton Keynes UK
UKHW020929100223
416696UK00003B/234

9 781636 407036